ART HISTORY

Volume II   Fifth Edition

ART HISTORY

MARILYN STOKSTAD

Judith Harris Murphy Distinguished Professor of Art History Emerita
The University of Kansas

MICHAEL W. COTHREN

Scheuer Family Professor of Humanities
Department of Art, Swarthmore College

PEARSON

Boston   Columbus   Indianapolis   New York   San Francisco   Upper Saddle River
Amsterdam   Cape Town   Dubai   London   Madrid   Milan   Munich   Paris   Montréal   Toronto
Delhi   Mexico City   São Paulo   Sydney   Hong Kong   Seoul   Singapore   Taipei   Tokyo

Editorial Director: Craig Campanella
Editor in Chief: Sarah Touborg
Senior Sponsoring Editor: Helen Ronan
Editorial Assistant: Victoria Engros
Vice-President, Director of Marketing: Brandy Dawson
Executive Marketing Manager: Kate Mitchell
Marketing Assistant: Paige Patunas
Managing Editor: Melissa Feimer
Project Managers: Barbara Cappuccio and Marlene Gassler
Senior Operations Supervisor: Mary Fischer
Operations Specialist: Diane Peirano
Media Director: Brian Hyland
Senior Media Editor: David Alick
Media Project Manager: Rich Barnes
Pearson Imaging Center: Corin Skidds
Printer/Binder: Courier / Kendallville
Cover Printer: Lehigh-Phoenix Color / Hagerstown

This book was designed by
Laurence King Publishing Ltd, London
www.laurenceking.com

Editorial Manager: Kara Hattersley-Smith
Senior Editor: Clare Double
Production Manager: Simon Walsh
Page Design: Nick Newton
Cover Design: Jo Fernandes
Picture Researcher: Evi Peroulaki
Copy Editor: Jennifer Speake
Indexer: Vicki Robinson

Cover image: Faith Ringgold, *Tar Beach* (Part I from the Women on a Bridge series), 1988. Acrylic on canvas, bordered with printed, painted, quilted, and pieced cloth, 74⅜″ × 68½″ (190.5 × 174 cm). Photo: Solomon R. Guggenheim Museum, New York/© Faith Ringgold 1988.

Credits and acknowledgments borrowed from other sources and reproduced, with permission, in this textbook appear on the appropriate page within text or on the credit pages in the back of this book.

Library of Congress Cataloging-in-Publication Data
Stokstad, Marilyn
  Art history / Marilyn Stokstad, Judith Harris Murphy Distinguished
Professor of Art History Emerita, The University of Kansas, Michael W.
Cothren, Scheuer Family Professor of Humanities, Department of Art,
Swarthmore College. -- Fifth edition.
    pages cm
  Includes bibliographical references and index.
  ISBN-13: 978-0-205-87347-0 (hardcover)
  ISBN-10: 0-205-87347-2 (hardcover)
  1. Art--History--Textbooks. I. Cothren, Michael Watt. II. Title.
  N5300.S923 2013
  709--dc23

                    2012027450

10 9 8 7 6 5 4 3 2

Prentice Hall
is an imprint of

PEARSON

www.pearsonhighered.com

ISBN 10:   0-205-87757-5
ISBN 13: 978-0-205-87757-7

Books à la carte
ISBN 10:   0-205-93844-2
ISBN 13: 978-0-205-93844-5

Brief Contents

Contents

30 Eighteenth- and Early Nineteenth-Century Art in Europe and North America 904

31 Mid- to Late Nineteenth-Century Art in Europe and the United States 962

Letter from the Author

Dear Colleagues

Energized by an enthusiasm that was fueled by conviction, I taught my first introductory art history survey course in the late 1970s, soon after the dawn of a period of crisis and creativity in the discipline of art history that challenged the fundamental assumptions behind the survey and questioned the canon of works that had long served as its foundation. Some professors and programs abandoned the survey altogether; others made it more expansive and inclusive. We all rethought what we were doing, and the soul searching this required made many of us better teachers—more honest and relevant, more passionate and convincing. It was for the subsequent generation of students and teachers, ready to reap the benefits of this refined notion of art history, that Marilyn Stokstad conceived and created her new survey textbook during the 1990s, tailored for students whose lives would unfold in the twenty-first century. It is a humbling honor to have become part of this historic project.

Reconsidering and refining what we do as professors and students of art history, however, did not cease at the turn of the century. The process continues. Like art, our teaching and learning changes as we and our culture change, responding to new expectations and new understandings. Opportunities for growth sometimes emerge in unexpected situations. Recently, while I was inching through sluggish suburban traffic with my daughter Emma—a gifted fifth-grade teacher—I confessed my disappointment in my survey students' dismal performance on the identification portion of their recent exam, lamenting their seeming inability to master basic information about the set of works I expected them to know. "Why," I asked rhetorically, "was it so difficult for them to learn these facts?" Emma's unexpected answer, rooted in her exploration of Grant Wiggins and Jay McTigue's *Understanding by Design* during a graduate course on curriculum development, shifted the question and reframed the discussion. "Dad," she said, "you are focusing on the wrong aspect of your teaching. What are you trying to accomplish by asking your students to learn those facts for identification on the exam? Question and explore your objectives first, then determine whether your assessment is actually the best way to encourage its accomplishment."

Emma's question, posed while I was planning this fifth edition of *Art History*, inspired me to pause and reflect more broadly on what it is that we seek to accomplish in art history survey courses. I initiated a series of conversations with professors across the country to take me beyond my own experience and into a national classroom. Many of you provided illuminating feedback, sharing goals and strategies, searching with me for a way of characterizing a shared set of learning outcomes that underlie the survey courses we teach as a way of introducing our students in the present to the study of art from the past. Talking with you helped me formulate language for the essential ideas we want our students to grasp, and characterize succinctly the kinds of knowledge and skills that are required to master them. From these conversations and your feedback, I developed a set of four fundamental outcomes envisioned for the book as a whole, outcomes that would be reflected within each chapter in four coordinated learning objectives at the beginning, and four assessment questions at the end. These overall learning outcomes aim to encompass the goals we share as we introduce the history of art to beginners. Thinking about them has already helped me refocus on what it is I am trying to accomplish in my own classroom. It certainly has alleviated the frustration I shared with Emma about my students' performance on slide IDs. I am now working on new ways to assess their engagement in relation to two fundamental goals—the "big ideas" that are embodied in these learning outcomes: building a knowledge base to anchor cultural understanding, and encouraging the extended examination of works of art, what I call "slow looking."

I hope these ideas, goals, and outcomes resonate as much with you as they have with me, that they will invite you to continue to think with me about the reasons why we believe the study of art history is meaningful and important for our students. After all, our discipline originated in dialogue, and it is rooted in the desire—maybe even the need—to talk with each other about why works of art matter and why they affect us so deeply. I would love to hear from you—mcothre1@swarthmore.edu.

Warm regards,

Michael Cothren

What's New

WHY USE THIS NEW EDITION?

Art history—what a wonderful, fascinating, and fluid discipline that evolves as the latest research becomes available for debate and consideration. The fifth edition of *Art History* has been revised to reflect these new discoveries, recent research and fresh interpretive perspectives, and also to address the changing needs of the audience—both students and educators. With these goals in mind, and by incorporating feedback from our many users and reviewers, we have sought to make this fifth edition an improvement over its earlier incarnations in sensitivity, readability, and accessibility without losing anything in comprehensiveness, in scholarly precision, or in its ability to engage readers.

To facilitate student learning and understanding of art history, the fifth edition is centered on four key Learning Outcomes. These overarching outcomes helped steer and shape this revision with their emphasis on the fundamental reasons we teach art history to undergraduates:

LEARNING OUTCOMES FOR *ART HISTORY*

Explore and understand the developing traditions and cultural exchanges represented by major monuments of world art by

1. Identifying the hallmarks of regional and period styles in relation to their technical, formal, and expressive character;
2. Understanding the principal themes, subjects, and symbols in the art of a variety of cultures, periods, and locations;
3. Probing the relationship of works of art to human history by exploring their cultural, economic, political, social, spiritual, moral, and intellectual contexts, and
4. Recognizing and applying the critical thinking, creative inquiry, and disciplined reasoning that stand behind art-historical interpretation, as well as the vocabulary and concepts used to describe and characterize works of art with clarity and power.

Each chapter opens with **Learn About It** objectives to help students focus on the upcoming chapter material and ends with corresponding **Think About It** assessment questions. These tools are rooted in the four learning outcomes stated above and help students think through, apply the chapter material, and synthesize their own viewpoints.

OTHER HIGHLIGHTS OF THE NEW EDITION INCLUDE THE FOLLOWING:

- The chapters are coordinated with significantly expanded MyArtsLab resources that enrich and reinforce student learning (see p. xvi).
- Crosscurrent Questions at the end of each chapter encourage students to compare works from different chapters and probe the relationship of recurrent themes across cultures, times, and places.
- Enriched **Recovering the Past** boxes document the discovery, re-evaluation, restoration, or conservation of works of art, such as the bronze She-Wolf that was once considered Etruscan and has recently been interpreted as medieval.
- **Closer Look** features appear in each chapter, guiding students in their exploration of details within a single work of art and helping students to understand issues of usage, iconography, and style. Each Closer Look is expanded and narrated within MyArtsLab to explore technique, style, subject matter, and cultural context.
- **Broader Look** boxes in each chapter offer an in-depth contextual treatment of a single work of art.
- **Global coverage has been deepened** with the addition of new works of art and revised discussions that incorporate new scholarship, especially in the area of South and Southeast Asia, whose chapters have been expanded.
- Throughout, **images have been updated** whenever new and improved images were available or works of art have been cleaned or restored.
- **New works have been added** to the discussion in many chapters to enhance and enrich what is said in the text. For example, the Disk of Enheduanna, Sphinx of Taharqo, garden mural from Livia's villa at Primaporta, and monastery of St. Catherine's on Mount Sinai. In addition, the following artists are now discussed through new, and more representative, works: Bihzad, Giovanni Pisano, Duccio, Verrocchio, Giambologna, Bronzino, Gentileschi, Hals, Steen, Rubens, Sharaku, Turner, Friedrich, Monet, Degas, Gauguin, Cézanne, and Warhol.
- **New artists have been added**, notably, Sultan Muhammad, Joan Mitchell, Diane Arbus, and Ed Ruscha.
- The **language used to characterize works of art**—especially those that attempt to capture the lifelike appearance of the natural world—has been **refined and clarified** to bring greater precision and nuance.
- In response to readers' requests, **discussion of many major monuments** has been revised and expanded.
- **Byzantine art** has been separated from the treatment of Jewish and Early Christian art for expanded treatment in a new chapter (8) of its own.

MyArtsLab lets your students experience and interact with art

This program will provide a better teaching and learning experience for you and your students. Here's how:

The new MyArtsLab delivers proven results in helping individual students succeed. Its automatically graded assessments, personalized study plan, and interactive eText provide engaging experiences that personalize, stimulate, and measure learning for each student.

▶ The Pearson eText lets students access their textbook anytime, anywhere, and any way they want—including downloading to an iPad or listening to chapter audio read by Michael Cothren and Brian Seymour. Includes a unique scale feature showing students the size of a work in relation to the human figure.

● Personalized study plan for each student promotes critical-thinking skills. Assessment tied to videos, applications, and chapters enables both instructors and students to track progress and get immediate feedback.

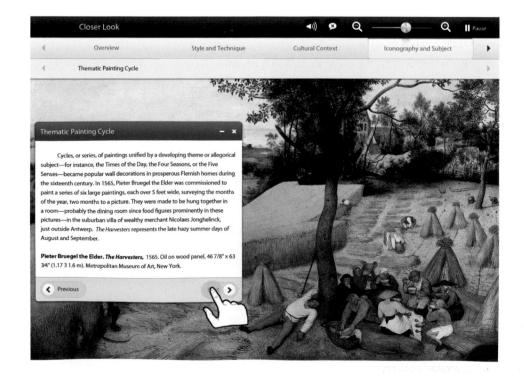

Cycles, or series, of paintings unified by a developing theme or allegorical subject—for instance, the Times of the Day, the Four Seasons, or the Five Senses—became popular wall decorations in prosperous Flemish homes during the sixteenth century. In 1565, Pieter Bruegel the Elder was commissioned to paint a series of six large paintings, each over 5 feet wide, surveying the months of the year, two months to a picture. They were made to be hung together in a room—probably the dining room since food figures prominently in these pictures—in the suburban villa of wealthy merchant Nicolaes Jonghelinck, just outside Antwerp. *The Harvesters* represents the late hazy summer days of August and September.

Pieter Bruegel the Elder. *The Harvesters,* 1565. Oil on wood panel, 46 7/8" x 63 3/4" (1.17 3 1.6 m). Metropolitan Museum of Art, New York.

● **New:** Henry Sayre's *Writing About Art* 6th edition is now available online in its entirety as an eText within MyArtsLab.

◀ **New and expanded:** Closer Look tours—interactive walkthroughs featuring expert audio—offer in-depth looks at key works of art. *Now optimized for mobile.*

● **New and expanded:** Over 75 in total, 360-degree architectural panoramas and simulations of major monuments help students understand buildings—inside and out. *Now optimized for mobile.*

► **New:** Students on Site videos—over 75 in total, produced and edited by students for students, these 2–3 minute videos provide "you are there" impressions of major monuments, reviewed and approved by art historians. To learn more about how your students can participate, please visit **www.pearsonfreeagent.com**

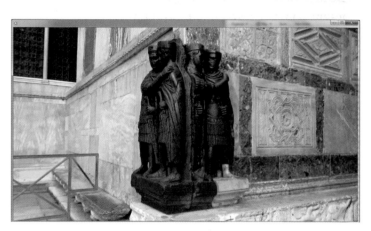

BREAK THROUGH TO A NEW WORLD OF LEARNING

MyArtsLab consistently and positively impacts the quality of learning in the classroom. When educators require and integrate MyArtsLab in their course, students and instructors experience success. Join our ever-growing community of 50,000 users across the country giving their students access to the high quality rich media and assessment on MyArtsLab.

"Students who use MyArtsLab perform better on their exams than students who do not."
—*Cynthia Kristan-Graham, Auburn University*

"MyArtsLab also makes students more active learners. They are more engaged with the material."
—*Maya Jiménez, Kingsborough Community College*

"MyArtsLab keeps students connected in another way to the course material. A student could be immersed for hours!"
—*Cindy B. Damschroder, University of Cincinnati*

"I really enjoy using MyArtsLab. At the end of the quarter, I ask students to write a paragraph about their experience with MyArtsLab and 97% of them are positive."
—*Rebecca Trittel, Savannah College of Art and Design*

Join the conversation!
www.facebook.com/stokstadcothren

Give Your Students Choices

ORDERING OPTIONS

Pearson arts titles are available in the following formats to give you and your students more choices—and more ways to save.

MyArtsLab with eText: the Pearson eText lets students access their textbook anytime, anywhere, and any way they want, including listening online or downloading to an iPad.

MyArtsLab with eText Combined: 0-205-88736-8
MyArtsLab with eText Volume I: 0-205-94839-1
MyArtsLab with eText Volume II: 0-205-94846-4

Build your own Pearson Custom e-course material. Pearson offers the first eBook-building platform that empowers educators with the freedom to search, choose, and seamlessly integrate multimedia. *Contact your Pearson representative to get started.*

The **Books à la Carte edition** offers a convenient, three-hole-punched, loose-leaf version of the traditional text at a discounted price—allowing students to take only what they need to class. Books à la Carte editions are available both with and without access to MyArtsLab.

Books à la Carte edition Volume I: 0-205-93840-X
Books à la Carte edition Volume I plus MyArtsLab: 0-205-93847-7
Books à la Carte edition Volume II: 0-205-93844-2
Books à la Carte edition Volume II plus MyArtsLab: 0-205-93846-9

The **CourseSmart eTextbook** offers the same content as the printed text in a convenient online format—with highlighting, online search, and printing capabilities. **www.coursesmart.com**

Art History **Portable edition** has all of the same content as the comprehensive text in six slim volumes. If your survey course is Western, the Portable Edition is available in value-package combinations to suit Western-focused courses (Books 1, 2, 4, and 6). Portable Edition volumes are also available individually for period or region specific courses.

Book 1 – Ancient Art (Chapters 1–6): 978-0-205-87376-0
Book 2 – Medieval Art (Chapters 7–9, 15–18):
    978-0-205-87377-7
Book 3 – A View of the World, Part One (Chapters 9–14):
    978-0-205-87378-4
Book 4 – Fourteenth to Seventeenth Century Art (Chapters 18–23):
    978-0-205-87379-1
Book 5 – A View of the World, Part Two (Chapters 24–29):
    978-0-205-87380-7
Book 6 – Eighteenth to Twenty-first Century Art (Chapters 30–33):
    978-0-205-87756-0

INSTRUCTOR RESOURCES

All of our instructor resources are found on MyArtsLab and are available to faculty who adopt *Art History*. These resources include:

PowerPoints featuring nearly every image in the book, with captions and without captions.

Teaching with MyArtsLab PowerPoints help instructors make their lectures come alive. These slides allow instructors to display the very best rich media from MyArtsLab in the classroom—quickly and easily.

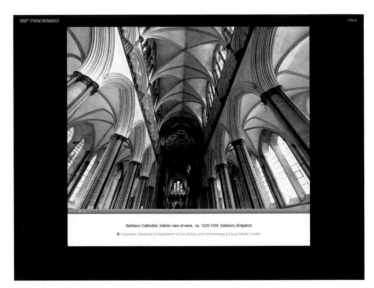

Instructor's Manual and Test Item File
This is an invaluable professional resource and reference for new and experienced faculty.

The Class Preparation Tool collects these and other presentation resources in one convenient online destination.

Acknowledgments and Gratitude

Art History, which was first published in 1995 by Harry N. Abrams, Inc. and Prentice Hall, Inc., continues to rely, each time it is revised, on the work of many colleagues and friends who contributed to the original texts and subsequent editions. Their work is reflected here, and we extend to them our enduring gratitude.

In preparing this fifth edition, we worked closely with two gifted and dedicated editors at Pearson/Prentice Hall, Sarah Touborg and Helen Ronan, whose almost daily support in so many ways was at the center of our work and created the foundation of what we have done. We are continually bolstered by the warm and dedicated support of Yolanda de Rooy, Pearson's President of the Social Sciences and the Arts, and Craig Campanella, Editorial Director. Also at Pearson, Barbara Cappuccio, Marlene Gassler, Melissa Feimer, Cory Skidds, Brian Mackey, David Nitti, and Carla Worner supported us in our work. At Laurence King Publishing, Clare Double, Kara Hattersley-Smith, Julia Ruxton, and Simon Walsh oversaw the production of this new edition. For layout design we thank Nick Newton and for photo research we thank Evi Peroulaki. Much appreciation also goes to Brandy Dawson, Director of Marketing, and Kate Stewart Mitchell, Marketing Manager extraordinaire, as well as the entire Social Sciences and Arts team at Pearson.

FROM MARILYN STOKSTAD: The fifth edition of *Art History* represents the cumulative efforts of a distinguished group of scholars and educators. Over four editions, the work done in the 1990s by Stephen Addiss, Chutsing Li, Marylin M. Rhie, and Christopher D. Roy for the original book has been updated and expanded by David Binkley and Patricia Darish (Africa); Claudia Brown and Robert Mowry (China and Korea); Patricia Graham (Japan); Rick Asher (South and Southeast Asia); D. Fairchild Ruggles (Islamic); Claudia Brittenham (Americas); Sara Orel and Carol Ivory (Pacific Cultures); and Bradford R. Collins, David Cateforis, Patrick Frank, and Joy Sperling (Modern). For this fifth edition, Robert DeCaroli reworked the chapters on South and Southeast Asia.

In addition, I want to thank University of Kansas colleagues Sally Cornelison, Susan Craig, Susan Earle, Charles Eldredge, Kris Ercums, Sherry Fowler, Stephen Goddard, Saralyn Reece Hardy, Marsha Haufler, Marni Kessler, Amy McNair, John Pulz, Linda Stone Ferrier, and John Younger for their help and advice. My thanks also to my friends Katherine Giele and Katherine Stannard, William Crowe, David Bergeron, and Geraldo de Sousa for their sympathy and encouragement. Of course, my very special thanks go to my sister, Karen Leider, and my niece, Anna Leider.

FROM MICHAEL COTHREN: Words are barely adequate to express my gratitude to Marilyn Stokstad for welcoming me with such trust, enthusiasm, and warmth into the collaborative adventure of revising this historic textbook, conceived and written for students in a new century. Working alongside her—and our extraordinary editors Sarah Touborg and Helen Ronan—has been delightful and rewarding, enriching, and challenging. I look forward to continuing the partnership.

My work was greatly facilitated by the research assistance and creative ideas of Moses Hanson-Harding, and I continued to draw on the work of Fletcher Coleman and Andrew Finegold, who helped with research on the previous edition. I also have been supported by a host of colleagues at Swarthmore College. Generations of students challenged me to hone my pedagogical skills and steady my focus on what is at stake in telling the history of art. My colleagues in the Art Department—especially Stacy Bomento, June Cianfrana, Randall Exon, Laura Holzman, Constance Cain Hungerford, Patricia Reilly, and Tomoko Sakomura—have answered all sorts of questions, shared innumerable insights on works in their areas of expertise, and offered unending encouragement and support. I am so lucky to work with them.

Many art historians have provided assistance, often at a moment's notice, and I am especially grateful to Betina Bergman, Claudia Brown, Elizabeth A.R. Brown, Brigitte Buettner, David Cateforis, Madeline Harrison Caviness, Sarah Costello, Cynthia Kristan-Graham, Joyce de Vries, Cheri Falkenstien-Doyle, Sharon Gerstel, Kevin Glowaki, Ed Gyllenhaal, Julie Hochstrasser, Vida J. Hull, Penny Jolly, Barbara Kellum, Alison Kettering, Benton Kidd, Ann Kuttner, Anne Leader, Steven A. LeBlanc, Cary Liu, Elizabeth Marlowe, Thomas Morton, Kathleen Nolan, David Shapiro, Mary Shepard, Larry Silver, David Simon, Donna Sadler, Jeffrey Chipps Smith, and Mark Tucker.

I was fortunate to have the support of many friends. John Brendler, David Eldridge, Stephen Lehmann, Mary Marissen, Denis Ott, and Bruce and Carolyn Stephens, patiently listened and truly relished my enjoyment of this work.

My preparation for this work runs deep. My parents, Mildred and Wat Cothren, believed in me from the day I was born and made significant sacrifices to support my education from pre-school through graduate school. From an early age, Sara Shymanski, my elementary school librarian, gave me courage through her example and loving encouragement to pursue unexpected passions for history, art, and the search to make them meaningful in both past and present. Françoise Celly, my painting professor during a semester abroad in Provence, by sending me to study the Romanesque sculpture of Autun, began my journey toward art history. At Vanderbilt, Ljubica Popovich fostered this new interest by teaching me about Byzantine art. My extraordinary daughters Emma and Nora remain a constant inspiration. I am so grateful for their delight in my passion for art's history, and for their dedication to keeping me from taking myself too seriously. My deepest gratitude is reserved for Susan Lowry, my wife and soul-mate, who brings joy to every facet of my life. She is not only patient and supportive during the long distractions of my work on this book; she has provided help in so very many ways. The greatest accomplishment of my life in art history occurred on the day I met her at Columbia in 1973.

If the arts are ultimately an expression of human faith and integrity as well as human thought and creativity, then writing and producing books that introduce new viewers to the wonders of art's history, and to the courage and visions of the artists and art historians that stand behind it—remains a noble undertaking. We feel honored to be a part of such a worthy project.

Marilyn Stokstad   *Michael W. Cothren*
Lawrence, KS   *Swarthmore, PA*
Spring 2012

IN GRATITUDE: As its predecessors did, this fifth edition of *Art History* benefited from the reflections and assessments of a distinguished team of scholars and educators. The authors and Pearson are grateful to the following academic reviewers for their numerous insights and suggestions for improvement: Kirk Ambrose, University of Colorado, Boulder; Lisa Aronson, Skidmore College; Mary Brantl, St. Edward's University; Denise Budd, Bergen Community College; Anne Chapin, Brevard College; Sheila Dillon, Duke University; William Ganis, Wells College; Sharon Gerstel, University of California, Los Angeles; Kevin Glowacki, Texas A&M University; Amy Golahny, Lycoming College; Steve Goldberg, Hamilton College; Bertha Gutman, Delaware County Community College; Deborah Haynes, University of Colorado, Boulder; Eva Hoffman, Tufts University; Mary Jo Watson, University of Oklahoma; Kimberly Jones, University of Texas, Austin; Barbara Kellum, Smith College; Sarah Kielt Costello, University of Houston; Cynthia Kristan-Graham, Auburn University; Paul Lavy, University of Hawaii at Manoa; Henry Luttikhuizen, Calvin College; Elizabeth Mansfield, New York University; Michelle Moseley Christian, Virginia Tech; Eleanor Moseman, Colorado State University; Sheila Muller, University of Utah; Elizabeth Olton, University of Texas at San Antonio; David Parrish, Purdue University; Tomoko Sakomura, Swarthmore College; Erika Schneider, Framingham State University; David Shapiro; Richard Sundt, University of Oregon; Tilottama Tharoor, New York University; Sarah Thompson, Rochester Institute of Technology; Rebecca Turner, Savannah College of Art and Design; Linda Woodward, LSC Montgomery.

This edition has continued to benefit from the assistance and advice of scores of other teachers and scholars who generously answered questions, gave recommendations on organization and priorities, and provided specialized critiques during the course of work on previous editions.

We are grateful for the detailed critiques from the following readers across the country who were of invaluable assistance during work on the third and fourth editions: Craig Adcock, University of Iowa; Charles M. Adelman, University of Northern Iowa; Fred C. Albertson, University of Memphis; Kimberly Allen-Kattus, Northern Kentucky University; Frances Altvater, College of William and Mary; Michael Amy, Rochester Institute of Technology; Susan Jane Baker, University of Houston; Jennifer L. Ball, Brooklyn College, CUNY; Samantha Baskind, Cleveland State University; Tracey Boswell, Johnson County Community College; Jane H. Brown, University of Arkansas at Little Rock; Stephen Caffey, Texas A&M University; Charlotte Lowry Collins, Southeastern Louisiana University; Roger J. Crum, University of Dayton; Brian A. Curran, Penn State University; Cindy B. Damschroder, University of Cincinnati; Michael T. Davis, Mount Holyoke College; Juilee Decker, Georgetown College; Laurinda Dixon, Syracuse University; Rachael Z. DeLue, Princeton University; Anne Derbes, Hood College; Caroline Downing, State University of New York at Potsdam; Laura Dufresne, Winthrop University; Suzanne Eberle, Kendall College of Art & Design of Ferris State University; April Eisman, Iowa State University; Dan Ewing, Barry University; Allen Farber, State University of New York at Oneonta; Arne Flaten, Coastal Carolina University; John Garton, Cleveland Institute of Art; Richard Gay, University of North Carolina, Pembroke; Regina Gee, Montana State University; Rosi Gilday, University of Wisconsin, Oshkosh; Mimi Hellman, Skidmore College; Julie Hochstrasser, University of Iowa; Eunice D. Howe,

University of Southern California; Phillip Jacks, George Washington University; Evelyn Kain, Ripon College; Nancy Kelker, Middle Tennessee State University; Patricia Kennedy, Ocean County College; Jennie Klein, Ohio University; Katie Kresser, Seattle Pacific University; Cynthia Kristan-Graham, Auburn University; Barbara Platten Lash, Northern Virginia Community College; William R. Levin, Centre College; Susan Libby, Rollins College; Henry Luttikhuizen, Calvin College; Lynn Mackenzie, College of DuPage; Elisa C. Mandell, California State University, Fullerton; Pamela Margerm, Kean University; Elizabeth Marlowe, Colgate University; Marguerite Mayhall, Kean University; Katherine A. McIver, University of Alabama at Birmingham; Dennis McNamara, Triton College; Gustav Medicus, Kent State University; Lynn Metcalf, St. Cloud State University; Janine Mileaf, Swarthmore College; Jo-Ann Morgan, Coastal Carolina University; Johanna D. Movassat, San Jose State University; Beth A. Mulvaney, Meredith College; Dorothy Munger, Delaware Community College; Jacqueline Marie Musacchio, Wellesley College; Bonnie Noble, University of North Carolina at Charlotte; Leisha O'Quinn, Oklahoma State University; Lynn Ostling, Santa Rosa Junior College; Willow Partington, Hudson Valley Community College; Martin Patrick, Illinois State University; Ariel Plotek, Clemson University; Patricia V. Podzorski, University of Memphis; Albert Reischuck, Kent State University; Margaret Richardson, George Mason University; James Rubin, Stony Brook University; Jeffrey Ruda, University of California, Davis; Donna Sandrock, Santa Ana College; Michael Schwartz, Augusta State University; Diane Scillia, Kent State University; Joshua A. Shannon, University of Maryland; Karen Shelby, Baruch College; Susan Sidlauskas, Rutgers University; Jeffrey Chipps Smith, University of Texas, Austin; Royce W. Smith, Wichita State University; Stephanie Smith, Youngstown State University; Stephen Smithers, Indiana State University; Janet Snyder, West Virginia University; Laurie Sylwester, Columbia College (Sonora); Carolyn Tate, Texas Tech University; Rita Tekippe, University of West Georgia; James Terry, Stephens College; Michael Tinkler, Hobart and William Smith Colleges; Amelia Trevelyan, University of North Carolina at Pembroke; Julie Tysver, Greenville Technical College; Jeryln Woodard, University of Houston; Reid Wood, Lorain County Community College. Our thanks also to additional expert readers including: Susan Cahan, Yale University; David Craven, University of New Mexico; Marian Feldman, University of California, Berkeley; Dorothy Johnson, University of Iowa; Genevra Kornbluth, University of Maryland; Patricia Mainardi, City University of New York; Clemente Marconi, Columbia University; Tod Marder, Rutgers University; Mary Miller, Yale University; Elizabeth Penton, Durham Technical Community College; Catherine B. Scallen, Case Western University; Kim Shelton, University of California, Berkeley.

Many people reviewed the original edition of *Art History* and have continued to assist with its revision. Every chapter was read by one or more specialists. For work on the original book and assistance with subsequent editions thanks goes to: Barbara Abou-el-Haj, SUNY Binghamton; Roger Aiken, Creighton University; Molly Aitken; Anthony Alofsin, University of Texas, Austin; Christiane Andersson, Bucknell University; Kathryn Arnold; Julie Aronson, Cincinnati Art Museum; Michael Auerbach, Vanderbilt University; Larry Beck; Evelyn Bell, San Jose State University; Janetta Rebold Benton, Pace University; Janet Berlo, University of Rochester; Sarah Blick, Kenyon College; Jonathan Bloom, Boston College; Suzaan Boettger; Judith Bookbinder, Boston College; Marta Braun, Ryerson University; Elizabeth

Broun, Smithsonian American Art Museum; Glen R. Brown, Kansas State University; Maria Elena Buszek, Kansas City Art Institute; Robert G. Calkins; Annmarie Weyl Carr; April Clagget, Keene State College; William W. Clark, Queens College, CUNY; John Clarke, University of Texas, Austin; Jaqueline Clipsham; Ralph T. Coe; Robert Cohon, The Nelson-Atkins Museum of Art; Alessandra Comini; James D'Emilio, University of South Florida; Walter Denny, University of Massachusetts, Amherst; Jerrilyn Dodds, City College, CUNY; Lois Drewer, Index of Christian Art; Joseph Dye, Virginia Museum of Art; James Farmer, Virginia Commonwealth University; Grace Flam, Salt Lake City Community College; Mary D. Garrard; Paula Gerson, Florida State University; Walter S. Gibson; Dorothy Glass; Oleg Grabar; Randall Griffey, Amherst College; Cynthia Hahn, Florida State University; Sharon Hill, Virginia Commonwealth University; John Hoopes, University of Kansas; Reinhild Janzen, Washburn University; Wendy Kindred, University of Maine at Fort Kent; Alan T. Kohl, Minneapolis College of Art; Ruth Kolarik, Colorado College; Carol H. Krinsky, New York University; Aileen Laing, Sweet Briar College; Janet LeBlanc, Clemson University; Charles Little, The Metropolitan Museum of Art; Laureen Reu Liu, McHenry County College; Loretta Lorance; Brian Madigan, Wayne State University; Janice Mann, Bucknell University; Judith Mann, St. Louis Art Museum; Richard Mann, San Francisco State University; James Martin; beth Parker McLachlan; Tamara Mikailova, St. Petersburg, Russia, and Macalester College; Anta Montet-White; Anne E. Morganstern, Ohio State University; Winslow Myers, Bancroft School; Lawrence Nees, University of Delaware; Amy Ogata, Cleveland Institute of Art; Judith Oliver, Colgate University; Edward Olszewski, Case Western Reserve University; Sara Jane Pearman; John G. Pedley, University of Michigan; Michael Plante, Tulane University; Eloise Quiñones-Keber, Baruch College and the Graduate Center, CUNY; Virginia Raguin, College of the Holy Cross; Nancy H. Ramage, Ithaca College; Ann M. Roberts, Lake Forest College; Lisa Robertson, The Cleveland Museum of Art; Barry Rubin; Charles Sack, Parsons, Kansas; Jan Schall, The Nelson-Atkins Museum of Art; Tom Shaw, Kean College; Pamela Sheingorn, Baruch College, CUNY; Raechell Smith, Kansas City Art Institute; Lauren Soth; Anne R. Stanton, University of Missouri, Columbia; Michael Stoughton; Thomas Sullivan, OSB, Benedictine College (Conception Abbey); Pamela Trimpe, University of Iowa; Richard Turnbull, Fashion Institute of Technology; Elizabeth Valdez del Alamo, Montclair State College; Lisa Vergara; Monica Visoná, University of Kentucky; Roger Ward, Norton Museum of Art; Mark Weil, St. Louis; David Wilkins; Marcilene Wittmer, University of Miami.

Use Notes

The various features of this book reinforce each other, helping the reader to become comfortable with terminology and concepts that are specific to art history.

Starter Kit and Introduction   The Starter Kit is a highly concise primer of basic concepts and tools. The Introduction explores the way they are used to come to an understanding of the history of art.

Captions   There are two kinds of captions in this book: short and long. Short captions identify information specific to the work of art or architecture illustrated:

> artist (when known)
> title or descriptive name of work
> date
> original location (if moved to a museum or other site)
> material or materials a work is made of
> size (height before width) in feet and inches, with meters and
>   centimeters in parentheses
> present location

The order of these elements varies, depending on the type of work illustrated. Dimensions are not given for architecture, for most wall paintings, or for most architectural sculpture. Some captions have one or more lines of small print below the identification section of the caption that gives museum or collection information. This is rarely required reading; its inclusion is often a requirement for gaining permission to reproduce the work.

Longer, discursive captions contain information that complements the narrative of the main text.

Definitions of Terms   You will encounter the basic terms of art history in three places:

> **In the Text,** where words appearing in boldface type are defined, or glossed, at their first use.
>
> **In Boxed Features,** on technique and other subjects, where labeled drawings and diagrams visually reinforce the use of terms.
>
> **In the Glossary,** at the end of the volume (p. 1138), which contains all the words in boldface type in the text and boxes.

Maps   At the beginning of each chapter you will find a map with all the places mentioned in the chapter.

Boxes   Special material that complements, enhances, explains, or extends the narrative text is set off in six types of tinted boxes.

Art and Its Contexts and A Broader Look boxes expand on selected works or issues related to the text. A Closer Look boxes use leader-line captions to focus attention on specific aspects of important works. Elements of Architecture boxes clarify specifically architectural features, often explaining engineering principles or building technology. Technique boxes outline the techniques and processes by which certain types of art are created. Recovering the Past boxes highlight the work of archaeologists who uncover and conservators who assure the preservation and clear presentation of art.

Bibliography   The bibliography at the end of this book beginning on page 1147 contains books in English, organized by general works and by chapter, that are basic to the study of art history today, as well as works cited in the text.

Learn About It   Placed at the beginning of each chapter, this feature captures in bulleted form the key learning objectives, or outcomes, of the chapter. They point to what will have been accomplished upon its completion.

Think About It   These critical thinking questions appear at the end of each chapter and help students assess their mastery of the learning objectives (Learn About It) by asking them to think through and apply what they have learned.

MyArtsLab prompts   These notations are found throughout the chapter and are keyed to MyArtsLab resources that enrich and reinforce student learning.

Dates, Abbreviations, and Other Conventions   This book uses the designations BCE and CE, abbreviations for "Before the Common Era" and "Common Era," instead of BC ("Before Christ") and AD ("Anno Domini," "the year of our Lord"). The first century BCE is the period from 99 BCE to 1 BCE; the first century CE is from the year 1 CE to 99 CE. Similarly, the second century CE is the period from 199 BCE to 100 BCE; the second century CE extends from 100 CE to 199 CE.

Circa ("about") is used with approximate dates, spelled out in the text and abbreviated to "c." in the captions. This indicates that an exact date is not yet verified.

An illustration is called a "figure," or "fig." Thus, figure 6–7 is the seventh numbered illustration in Chapter 6, and fig. Intro-3 is the third figure in the Introduction. There are two types of figures: photographs of artworks or of models, and line drawings. Drawings are used when a work cannot be photographed or when a diagram or simple drawing is the clearest way to illustrate an object or a place.

When introducing artists, we use the words *active* and *documented* with dates, in addition to "b." (for "born") and "d." (for "died"). "Active" means that an artist worked during the years given. "Documented" means that documents link the person to that date.

Accents are used for words in French, German, Italian, and Spanish only. With few exceptions, names of cultural institutions in Western European countries are given in the form used in that country.

Titles of Works of Art   It was only over the last 500 years that paintings and works of sculpture created in Europe and North America were given formal titles, either by the artist or by critics and art historians. Such formal titles are printed in italics. In other traditions and cultures, a single title is not important or even recognized.

In this book we use formal descriptive titles of artworks where titles are not established. If a work is best known by its non-English title, such as Manet's *Le Déjeuner sur l'Herbe (The Luncheon on the Grass)*, the original language precedes the translation.

Starter Kit

Art history focuses on the visual arts—painting, drawing, sculpture, prints, photography, ceramics, metalwork, architecture, and more. This Starter Kit contains basic information and addresses concepts that underlie and support the study of art history. It provides a quick reference guide to the vocabulary used to classify and describe art objects. Understanding these terms is indispensable because you will encounter them again and again in reading, talking, and writing about art.

Let us begin with the basic properties of art. A work of art is a material object having both form and content. It is often described and categorized according to its *style* and *medium*.

FORM

Referring to purely visual aspects of art and architecture, the term *form* encompasses qualities of *line*, *shape*, *color*, *light*, *texture*, *space*, *mass*, *volume*, and *composition*. These qualities are known as *formal elements*. When art historians use the term *formal*, they mean "relating to form."

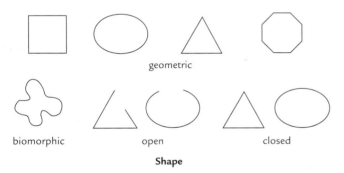

geometric

biomorphic   open   closed

Shape

Line and **shape** are attributes of form. Line is an element—usually drawn or painted—the length of which is so much greater than the width that we perceive it as having only length. Line can be actual, as when the line is visible, or it can be implied, as when the movement of the viewer's eyes over the surface of a work follows a path determined by the artist. Shape, on the other hand, is the two-dimensional, or flat, area defined by the borders of an enclosing *outline* or *contour*. Shape can be *geometric*, *biomorphic* (suggesting living things; sometimes called *organic*), *closed*, or *open*. The *outline* or *contour* of a three-dimensional object can also be perceived as line.

Color has several attributes. These include *hue*, *value*, and *saturation*.

Hue is what we think of when we hear the word *color*, and the terms are interchangeable. We perceive hues as the result of differing wavelengths of electromagnetic energy. The visible spectrum, which can be seen in a rainbow, runs from red through violet. When the ends of the spectrum are connected through the hue red-violet, the result may be diagrammed as a color wheel. The primary hues (numbered 1) are red, yellow, and blue. They are known as primaries because all other colors are made by combining these hues. Orange, green, and violet result from the mixture of two primaries and are known as secondary hues (numbered 2). Intermediate hues, or tertiaries (numbered 3), result from the mixture of a primary and a secondary. Complementary colors are the two colors directly opposite one

another on the color wheel, such as red and green. Red, orange, and yellow are regarded as warm colors and appear to advance toward us. Blue, green, and violet, which seem to recede, are called cool colors. Black and white are not considered colors but neutrals; in terms of light, black is understood as the absence of color and white as the mixture of all colors.

Value is the relative degree of lightness or darkness of a given color and is created by the amount of light reflected from an object's surface. A dark green has a deeper value than a light green, for example. In black-and-white reproductions of colored objects, you see only value, and some artworks—for example, a drawing made with black ink—possess only value, not hue or saturation.

Value scale from white to black.

+ WHITE   PURE HUE   + BLACK

Value variation in red.

Saturation, also sometimes referred to as *intensity*, is a color's quality of brightness or dullness. A color described as highly saturated looks vivid and pure; a hue of low saturation may look a little muddy or grayed.

PURE HUE   DULLED   PURE HUE

Intensity scale from bright to dull.

Texture, another attribute of form, is the tactile (or touch-perceived) quality of a surface. It is described by words such as *smooth, polished, rough, prickly, grainy,* or *oily.* Texture takes two forms: the texture of the actual surface of the work of art and the implied (illusionistically described) surface of objects represented in the work of art.

Space is what contains forms. It may be actual and three-dimensional, as it is with sculpture and architecture, or it may be fictional, represented illusionistically in two dimensions, as when artists represent recession into the distance on a flat surface—such as a wall or a canvas—by using various systems of perspective.

Mass and volume are properties of three-dimensional things. Mass is solid matter—whether sculpture or architecture—that takes up space. Volume is enclosed or defined space, and may be either solid or hollow. Like space, mass and volume may be illusionistically represented on a two-dimensional surface, such as in a painting or a photograph.

Composition is the organization, or arrangement, of forms in a work of art. Shapes and colors may be repeated or varied, balanced symmetrically or asymmetrically; they may be stable or dynamic. The possibilities are nearly endless and artistic choice depends both on the time and place where the work was created as well as the objectives of individual artists. Pictorial depth (spatial recession) is a specialized aspect of composition in which the three-dimensional world is represented on a flat surface, or *picture plane.* The area "behind" the picture plane is called the *picture space* and conventionally contains three "zones": *foreground, middle ground,* and *background.*

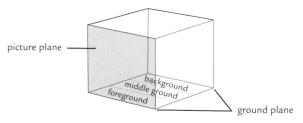

Various techniques for conveying a sense of pictorial depth have been devised by artists in different cultures and at different times. A number of them are diagrammed here. In some European art, the use of various systems of *perspective* has sought to create highly convincing illusions of recession into space. At other times and in other cultures, indications of recession are actually suppressed or avoided to emphasize surface rather than space.

TECHNIQUE | Pictorial Devices for Depicting Recession in Space

overlapping

In overlapping, partially covered elements are meant to be seen as located behind those covering them.

diminution

In diminution of scale, successively smaller elements are perceived as being progressively farther away than the largest ones.

vertical perspective

Vertical perspective stacks elements, with the higher ones intended to be perceived as deeper in space.

atmospheric perspective

Through atmospheric perspective, objects in the far distance (often in bluish-gray hues) have less clarity than nearer objects. The sky becomes paler as it approaches the horizon.

divergent perspective   **intuitive perspective**

In divergent or reverse perspective, forms widen slightly and imaginary lines called orthogonals diverge as they recede in space.

Intuitive perspective takes the opposite approach from divergent perspective. Forms become narrower and orthogonals converge the farther they are from the viewer, approximating the optical experience of spatial recession.

linear perspective

Linear perspective (also called scientific, mathematical, one-point and Renaissance perspective) is a rationalization or standardization of intuitive perspective that was developed in fifteenth-century Italy. It uses mathematical formulas to construct images in which all elements are shaped by, or arranged along, orthogonals that converge in one or more vanishing points on a horizon line.

CONTENT

Content includes *subject matter*, but not all works of art have subject matter. Many buildings, paintings, sculptures, and other art objects include no recognizable references to things in nature nor to any story or historical situation, focusing instead on lines, colors, masses, volumes, and other formal elements. However, all works of art—even those without recognizable subject matter—have content, or meaning, insofar as they seek to communicate ideas, convey feelings, or affirm the beliefs and values of their makers, their patrons, and usually the people who originally viewed or used them.

Content may derive from the social, political, religious, and economic *contexts* in which a work was created, the *intention* of the artist, and the *reception* of the work by beholders (the audience). Art historians, applying different methods of *interpretation*, often arrive at different conclusions regarding the content of a work of art, and single works of art can contain more than one meaning because they are occasionally directed at more than one audience.

The study of subject matter is called *iconography* (literally, "the writing of images") and includes the identification of *symbols* —images that take on meaning through association, resemblance, or convention.

STYLE

Expressed very broadly, *style* is the combination of form and composition that makes a work distinctive. *Stylistic analysis* is one of art history's most developed practices, because it is how art historians recognize the work of an individual artist or the characteristic manner of groups of artists working in a particular time or place. Some of the most commonly used terms to discuss *artistic styles* include *period style*, *regional style*, *representational style*, *abstract style*, *linear style*, and *painterly style*.

Period style refers to the common traits detectable in works of art and architecture from a particular historical era. It is good practice not to use the words "style" and "period" interchangeably. Style is the sum of many influences and characteristics, including the period of its creation. An example of proper usage is "an American house from the Colonial period built in the Georgian style."

Regional style refers to stylistic traits that persist in a geographic region. An art historian whose specialty is medieval art can recognize Spanish style through many successive medieval periods and can distinguish individual objects created in medieval Spain from other medieval objects that were created in, for example, Italy.

Representational styles are those that describe the appearance of recognizable subject matter in ways that make it seem lifelike.

> **Realism** and **Naturalism** are terms that some people used interchangeably to characterize artists' attempts to represent the observable world in a manner that appears to describe its visual appearance accurately. When capitalized, Realism refers to a specific period style discussed in Chapter 31.

> **Idealization** strives to create images of physical perfection according to the prevailing values or tastes of a culture. The artist may work in a representational style and idealize it to capture an underlying value or expressive effect.

> **Illusionism** refers to a highly detailed style that seeks to create a convincing illusion of physical reality by describing its visual appearance meticulously.

Abstract styles depart from mimicking lifelike appearance to capture the essence of a form. An abstract artist may work from nature or from a memory image of nature's forms and colors, which are simplified, stylized, perfected, distorted, elaborated, or otherwise transformed to achieve a desired expressive effect.

> **Nonrepresentational (or Nonobjective) Art** is a term often used for works of art that do not aim to produce recognizable natural imagery.

> **Expressionism** refers to styles in which the artist exaggerates aspects of form to draw out the beholder's subjective response or to project the artist's own subjective feelings.

Linear describes both styles and techniques. In linear styles artists use line as the primary means of definition. But linear paintings can also incorporate *modeling*—creating an illusion of three-dimensional substance through shading, usually executed so that brushstrokes nearly disappear.

Painterly describes a style of representation in which vigorous, evident brushstrokes dominate, and outlines, shadows, and highlights are brushed in freely.

MEDIUM AND TECHNIQUE

Medium (plural, *media*) refers to the material or materials from which a work of art is made. Today, literally anything can be used to make a work of art, including not only traditional materials like paint, ink, and stone, but also rubbish, food, and the earth itself.

Technique is the process that transforms media into a work of art. Various techniques are explained throughout this book in Technique boxes. Two-dimensional media and techniques include painting, drawing, prints, and photography. Three-dimensional media and techniques are sculpture (for example, using stone, wood, clay or cast metal), architecture, and many small-scale arts (such as jewelry, containers, or vessels) in media such as ceramics, metal, or wood.

Painting includes wall painting and fresco, illumination (the decoration of books with paintings), panel painting (painting on wood panels), painting on canvas, and handscroll and hanging scroll painting. The paint in these examples is pigment mixed with a liquid vehicle, or binder. Some art historians also consider pictorial media such as mosaic and stained glass—where the pigment is arranged in solid form—as a type of painting.

Graphic arts are those that involve the application of lines and strokes to a two-dimensional surface or support, most often paper. Drawing is a graphic art, as are the various forms of printmaking. Drawings may be sketches (quick visual notes, often made in preparation for larger drawings or paintings); studies (more carefully drawn analyses of details or entire compositions); cartoons (full-scale drawings made in preparation for work in another medium, such as fresco, stained glass, or tapestry); or complete artworks in themselves. Drawings can be made with ink, charcoal, crayon, or pencil. Prints, unlike drawings, are made in multiple copies. The various forms of printmaking include woodcut, the intaglio processes (engraving, etching, drypoint), and lithography.

Photography (literally, "light writing") is a medium that involves the rendering of optical images on light-sensitive surfaces. Photographic images are typically recorded by a camera.

Sculpture is three-dimensional art that is *carved*, *modeled*, *cast*, or *assembled*. Carved sculpture is subtractive in the sense that the image is created by taking away material. Wood, stone, and ivory are common materials used to create carved sculptures. Modeled sculpture is considered additive, meaning that the object is built up from a material, such as clay, that is soft enough to be molded and shaped. Metal sculpture is usually cast or is assembled by welding or a similar means of permanent joining.

Sculpture is either free-standing (that is, surrounded by space) or in pictorial relief. Relief sculpture projects from the background surface of the same piece of material. High-relief sculpture projects far from its background; low-relief sculpture is only slightly raised; and sunken relief, found mainly in ancient Egyptian art, is carved into the surface, with the highest part of the relief being the flat surface.

Ephemeral arts include processions, ceremonies, or ritual dances (often with décor, costumes, or masks); performance art; earthworks; cinema and video art; and some forms of digital or computer art. All impose a temporal limitation—the artwork is viewable for a finite period of time and then disappears forever, is in a constant state of change, or must be replayed to be experienced again.

Architecture creates enclosures for human activity or habitation. It is three-dimensional, highly spatial, functional, and closely bound with developments in technology and materials. Since it is difficult to capture in a photograph, several types of schematic drawings are commonly used to enable the visualization of a building:

> **Plans** depict a structure's masses and voids, presenting a view from above of the building's footprint or as if it had been sliced horizontally at about waist height.

Plan: Philadelphia, Vanna Venturi House

Sections reveal the interior of a building as if it had been cut vertically from top to bottom.

Section: Rome, Sta. Costanza

Isometric drawings show buildings from oblique angles either seen from above ("bird's-eye view") to reveal their basic three-dimensional forms (often cut away so we can peek inside) or from below ("worm's-eye view") to represent the arrangement of interior spaces and the upward projection of structural elements.

Isometric cutaway from above: Ravenna, San Vitale

Isometric projection from below: Istanbul, Hagia Sophia

Introduction

Intro-1 • Mark Rothko MAGENTA, BLACK, GREEN, ON ORANGE (NO. 3/NO. 13)
1949. Oil on canvas, 7'1⅜" × 5'5" (2.165 × 1.648 m). Museum of Modern Art, New York.

The title of this book seems clear. It defines a field of academic study and scholarly research that has achieved a secure place in college and university curricula across North America. But *Art History* couples two words—even two worlds—that are less well focused when separated. What is art? In what sense does it have a history? Students of art and its history should pause and engage, even if briefly, with these large questions before beginning the journey surveyed in the following chapters.

WHAT IS ART?

Artists, critics, art historians, and the general public all grapple with this thorny question. The *Random House Dictionary* defines "art" as "the quality, production, expression, or realm of what is beautiful, or of more than ordinary significance." Others have characterized "art" as something human-made that combines creative imagination and technical skill, and satisfies an innate desire for order and harmony—perhaps a human hunger for the beautiful. This seems

---

LEARN ABOUT IT

I.1 Explore the methods and objectives of visual analysis.

I.2 Assess the way art historians identify conventional subject matter and symbols in the process called iconography.

I.3 Survey the methods used by art historians to analyze works of art and interpret their meaning within their original cultural contexts.

I.4 Trace the process of art-historical interpretation in a case study.

((•— **Listen** to the chapter audio on myartslab.com

relatively straightforward until we start to look at modern and contemporary art, where there has been a heated and extended debate concerning "What is Art?" The focus is often far from questions of transcendent beauty, ordered design, or technical skill, and centers instead on the conceptual meaning of a work for an elite target audience or the attempt to pose challenging questions or unsettle deep-seated cultural ideas.

The works of art discussed in this book represent a privileged subset of artifacts produced by past and present cultures. They were usually meant to be preserved, and they are currently considered worthy of conservation and display. The determination of which artifacts are exceptional—which are works of art—evolves through the actions, opinions, and selections of artists, patrons, governments, collectors, archaeologists, museums, art historians, and others. Labeling objects as art is usually meant to signal that they transcended or now transcend in some profound way their practical function, often embodying cherished cultural ideas or asserting foundational values. Sometimes it can also mean they are considered beautiful, well designed, and made with loving care, but this is not always the case. We will discover that at various times and places, the complex notion of what is art has little to do with standards of skill or beauty. Some critics and historians argue broadly that works of art are tendentious embodiments of power and privilege, hardly sublime expressions of beauty or truth. After all, art can be unsettling as well as soothing, challenging as well as reassuring, whether made in the present or surviving from the past.

Increasingly, we are realizing that our judgments about what constitutes art—as well as what constitutes beauty—are conditioned by our own education and experience. Whether acquired at home, in classrooms, in museums, at the movies, or on the Internet, our responses to art are learned behaviors, influenced by class, gender, race, geography, and economic status as well as education. Even art historians find that their definitions of what constitutes art—and what constitutes artistic quality—evolve with additional research and understanding. Exploring works by twentieth-century painter Mark Rothko and nineteenth-century quilt-makers Martha Knowles and Henrietta Thomas demonstrates how definitions of art and artistic value are subject to change over time.

Rothko's painting, **MAGENTA, BLACK, GREEN, ON ORANGE (NO. 3/NO. 13)** (**FIG. Intro–1**), is a well-known example of the sort of abstract painting that was considered the epitome of artistic sophistication by the mid-twentieth-century New York art establishment. It was created by an artist who meant it to be a work of art. It was acquired by the Museum of Modern Art in New York, and its position on the walls of that museum is a sure sign of its acceptance as art by a powerful cultural institution. However, beyond the context of the American artists, dealers, critics, and collectors who made up Rothko's art world, such paintings were often received with skepticism. They were seen by many as incomprehensible—lacking both technical skill and recognizable subject matter, two criteria that were part of the general public's

definition of art at the time. Abstract paintings soon inspired a popular retort: "That's not art; my child could do it!" Interestingly enough, Rothko saw in the childlike character of his own paintings one of the qualities that made them works of art. Children, he said, "put forms, figures, and views into pictorial arrangements, employing out of necessity most of the rules of optical **perspective** and geometry but without the knowledge that they are employing them." He characterized his own art as childlike, as "an attempt to recapture the freshness and naiveté of childish vision." In part because they are carefully crafted by an established artist who provided these kinds of intellectual justifications for their character and appearance, Rothko's abstract paintings are broadly considered works of art and are treasured possessions of major museums across the globe.

Works of art, however, do not always have to be created by individuals who perceive themselves as artists. Nor are all works produced for an art market surrounded by critics and collectors ready to explain, exhibit, and disperse them, ideally to prestigious museums. Such is the case with this quilt (**FIG. Intro–2**), made by Martha Knowles and Henrietta Thomas a century before Rothko's painting. Their work is similarly composed of blocks of color, and like Rothko, they produced their visual effect by arranging these flat chromatic shapes carefully and regularly on a rectangular field. But this quilt was not meant to hang on the wall of an art museum. It is the social product of a friendship, intended as an intimate gift, presented to a loved one for use in her home. An inscription on the quilt itself makes this clear—"From M.A. Knowles to her

Intro–2 • Martha Knowles and Henrietta Thomas
MY SWEET SISTER EMMA
1843. Cotton quilt, 8'11" × 9'1" (2.72 × 2.77 m). International Quilt Studies Center, University of Nebraska, Lincoln, Nebraska.

This book contains much more than paintings and textiles. Within these pages you will also encounter sculpture, vessels, books, jewelry, tombs, chairs, photographs, architecture, and more. But as with Rothko's *Magenta, Black, Green, on Orange (No. 3/No. 13)* (see FIG. Intro–1) and Knowles and Thomas's *My Sweet Sister Emma* (see FIG. Intro–2), criteria have been used to determine which works are selected for inclusion in a book titled *Art History*. Architecture presents an interesting case.

Buildings meet functional human needs by enclosing human habitation or activity. Many works of architecture, however, are considered "exceptional" because they transcend functional demands by manifesting distinguished architectural design or because they embody in important ways the values and goals of the culture that built them. Such buildings are usually produced by architects influenced, like painters, by great works and traditions from the past. In some cases they harmonize with, or react to, their natural or urban surroundings. For such reasons, they are discussed in books on the history of art.

Typical of such buildings is the church of Nôtre-Dame-du-Haut in Ronchamp, France, designed and constructed between 1950 and 1955 by Swiss architect Charles-Edouard Jeanneret, better known by his pseudonym, Le Corbusier. This building is the product of a significant historical moment, rich in international cultural meaning. A pilgrimage church on this site had been destroyed during World War II, and the creation here of a new church symbolized the end of a devastating war, embodying hopes for a brighter global future. Le Corbusier's design—drawing on sources that ranged from Algerian mosques to imperial Roman villas, from crab shells to airplane wings—is sculptural as well as architectural. It soars at the crest of a hill toward the sky but at the same time seems solidly anchored in the earth. And its coordination with the curves of the natural landscape complement the creation of an outdoor setting for religious ceremonies (to the right in the figure) to supplement the church interior that Le Corbusier characterized as a "container for intense concentration." In fact, this building is so renowned today as a monument of modern architecture, that the bus-loads of pilgrims who arrive at the site are mainly architects and devotees of architectural history.

Intro–3 • Le Corbusier
NÔTRE-DAME-DU-HAUT
Ronchamp, France. 1950–1955.

Sweet Sister Emma, 1843." Thousands of such friendship quilts were made by women during the middle years of the nineteenth century for use on beds, either to provide warmth or as a covering spread. Whereas quilts were sometimes displayed to a broad and enthusiastic audience of producers and admirers at competitions held at state and county fairs, they were not collected by art museums or revered by artists until relatively recently.

In 1971, at the Whitney Museum in New York—an establishment bastion of the art world in which Rothko moved and worked—art historians Jonathan Holstein and Gail van der Hoof mounted an exhibition entitled "Abstract Design in American Quilts," demonstrating the artistic affinity we have already noted in comparing the way Knowles and Thomas, like Rothko, create abstract patterns with fields of color. Quilts were later accepted—or perhaps "**appropriated**"—as works of art and hung on the walls of a New York art museum because of their visual similarities with the avant-garde, abstract works of art created by establishment, New York artists.

Art historian Patricia Mainardi took the case for quilts one significant step further in a pioneering article of 1973 published in *The Feminist Art Journal*. Entitled, "Quilts: The Great American Art," her argument was rooted not only in the aesthetic affinity of quilts with the esteemed work of contemporary abstract painters, but also in a political conviction that the definition of art had to be broadened. What was at stake here was historical veracity. Mainardi began, "Women have always made art. But for most women, the arts highest valued by male society have been closed to them for just that reason. They have put their creativity instead into the needlework arts, which exist in fantastic variety wherever there are women, and which in fact are a universal female art, transcending race, class, and national borders." She argued for the inclusion of quilts within the history of art to give deserved attention to the work of women artists who had been excluded from discussion because they created textiles and because they worked outside the male-dominated professional structures of the art world—because they were women. Quilts now hang as works of art on the walls of museums and appear with regularity in books that survey the history of art.

As these two examples demonstrate, definitions of art are rooted in cultural systems of value that are subject to change. And as they change, the list of works considered by art historians is periodically revised. Determining what to study is a persistent part of the art historian's task.

WHAT IS ART HISTORY?

There are many ways to study or appreciate works of art. Art history represents one specific approach, with its own goals and its own methods of assessment and interpretation. Simply put, art historians seek to understand the meaning of art from the past within its original cultural contexts, both from the point of view of its producers—artists, architects, and patrons—as well as from the point of view of its consumers—those who formed its original audience. Coming to an understanding of the cultural meaning of a work of art requires detailed and patient investigation on many levels, especially with art that was produced long ago and in societies distinct from our own. This is a scholarly rather than an intuitive exercise. In art history, the work of art is seen as an embodiment of the values, goals, and aspirations of its time and place of origin. It is a part of culture.

Art historians use a variety of theoretical perspectives and a host of interpretive strategies to come to an understanding of works of art within their cultural contexts. But as a place to begin, the work of art historians can be divided into four types of investigation:

1. assessment of physical properties,
2. analysis of visual or formal structure,
3. identification of subject matter or conventional symbolism, and
4. integration within cultural context.

ASSESSING PHYSICAL PROPERTIES

Of the methods used by art historians to study works of art, this is the most objective, but it requires close access to the work itself. Physical properties include shape, size, materials, and technique. For instance, many pictures are rectangular (e.g., see FIG. Intro–1), but some are round (see page xxxiii, FIG. C). Paintings as large as Rothko's require us to stand back if we want to take in the whole image, whereas some paintings (see page xxxii, FIG. A) are so small that we are drawn up close to examine their detail. Rothko's painting and Knowles and Thomas's quilt are both rectangles of similar size, but they are distinguished by the materials from which they are made—oil paint on canvas versus cotton fabric joined by stitching. In art history books, most physical properties can only be understood from descriptions in captions, but when we are in the presence of the work of art itself, size and shape may be the first thing we notice. To fully understand **medium** and technique, however, it may be necessary to employ methods of scientific analysis or documentary research to elucidate the practices of artists at the time when and place where the work was created.

ANALYZING FORMAL STRUCTURE

Art historians explore the visual character that artists bring to their works—using the materials and the techniques chosen to create them—in a process called **formal analysis**. On the most basic level, it is divided into two parts:

- assessing the individual visual elements or formal vocabulary that constitute pictorial or sculptural communication, and
- discovering the overall arrangement, organization, or structure of an image, a design system that art historians often refer to as **composition**.

THE ELEMENTS OF VISUAL EXPRESSION Artists control and vary the visual character of works of art to give their subjects and ideas meaning and expression, vibrancy and persuasion, challenge or delight (see "A Closer Look," page xxxii). For example, the motifs, objects, figures, and environments within paintings can be sharply defined by line (see FIGS. Intro–2, Intro–4), or they can be suggested by a sketchier definition (see FIGS. Intro–1, Intro–5). Painters can simulate the appearance of three-dimensional form through **modeling** or shading (see FIG. Intro–4 and page xxxiii, FIG. C), that is, by describing the way light from a single source will highlight one side of a solid while leaving the other side in shadow. Alternatively, artists can avoid any strong sense of three-dimensionality by emphasizing patterns on a surface rather than forms in space (see FIG. Intro–1 and page xxxii, FIG. A). In addition to revealing the solid substance of forms through modeling, dramatic lighting can also guide viewers to specific areas of a picture (see page xxxii, FIG. B), or it can be lavished on every aspect of a picture to reveal all its detail and highlight the vibrancy of its color (see page xxxiii, FIG. D). Color itself can be muted or intensified, depending on the mood artists want to create or the tastes and expectations of their audiences.

LINE

A. Carpet Page from the Lindisfarne Gospels
From Lindisfarne, England.
c. 715–720. Ink and tempera
on vellum, 13⅜″ × 9⁷⁄₁₆″ (34 ×
24 cm). British Library, London.
Cotton MS Nero D.IV fol. 26v

Every element in this complicated painting is sharply outlined by abrupt barriers between light and dark or between one color and another; there are no gradual or shaded transitions. Since the picture was created in part with pen and ink, the linearity is a logical extension of medium and technique. And although line itself is a "flattening" or two-dimensionalizing element in pictures, a complex and consistent system of overlapping gives the linear animal forms a sense of shallow but carefully worked-out three-dimensional relationships to one another.

LIGHT

B. Georges de la Tour *The Education of the Virgin*
c. 1650. Oil on canvas, 33″ × 39½″ (83.8 × 100.4 cm). The Frick Collection, New York.

The source of illumination is a candle depicted within the painting. The young girl's upraised right hand shields its flame, allowing the artist to demonstrate his virtuosity in painting the translucency of human flesh.

Since the candle's flame is partially concealed, its luminous intensity is not allowed to distract from those aspects of the painting most brilliantly illuminated by it—the face of the girl and the book she is reading.

 View the Closer Look for visual elements of pictorial expression: line, light, form, and color on myartslab.com

FORM

C. Michelangelo
The Holy Family (Doni Tondo)

c. 1503. Oil and tempera on panel, diameter 3′11¼″ (1.2 m). Galleria degli Uffizi, Florence.

The complex overlapping of their highly three-dimensionalized bodies conveys the somewhat contorted spatial positioning and relationship of these three figures.

Through the use of modeling or shading—a gradual transition from lights to darks—Michelangelo imitates the way solid forms are illuminated from a single light source—the side closest to the light source is bright while the other side is cast in shadow—and gives a sense of three-dimensional form to his figures.

In a technique called **foreshortening**, the carefully calculated angle of the Virgin's elbow makes it seem to project out toward the viewer.

The actual three-dimensional projection of the sculpted heads in medallions around the frame—designed for this painting by Michelangelo himself—heightens the effect of fictive three-dimensionality in the figures painted on its flat surface.

Junayd chose to flood every aspect of his painting with light, as if everything in it were illuminated from all sides at once. As a result, the emphasis here is on jewel-like color. The vibrant tonalities and dazzling detail of the dreamy landscape are not only more important than the simulation of three-dimensional forms distributed within a consistently described space; they actually upstage the human drama taking place against a patterned, tipped-up ground in the lower third of the picture.

COLOR

D. Junayd *Humay and Humayun*, from a manuscript of the *Divan* of Kwaju Kirmani

Made in Baghdad, Iraq. 1396. Color, ink, and gold on paper, 12⅝″ × 9⁷⁄₁₆″ (32 × 24 cm). British Library, London. MS Add. 18113, fol. 31r

Thus, artists communicate with their viewers by making choices in the way they use and emphasize the elements of visual expression, and art-historical analysis seeks to reveal how artists' decisions bring meaning to a work of art. For example, in two paintings of women with children (see FIGS. Intro-4, Intro-5), Raphael and Renoir work with the same visual elements of line, form, light, and color in the creation of their images, but they employ these shared elements to differing expressive ends. Raphael concentrates on line to clearly differentiate each element of his picture as a separate form. Careful modeling describes these outlined forms as substantial solids surrounded by space. This gives his subjects a sense of clarity, stability, and grandeur. Renoir, on the other hand, foregrounds the flickering of light and the play of color as he downplays the sense of three-dimensionality in individual forms. This gives his image a more ephemeral, casual sense. Art historians pay close attention to such variations in the use of visual elements—the building blocks of artistic expression—and use visual analysis to characterize the expressive effect of a particular work, a particular artist, or a general period defined by place and date.

COMPOSITION When art historians analyze composition, they focus not on the individual elements of visual expression but on the overall arrangement and organizing design or structure of a work of art. In Raphael's **MADONNA OF THE GOLDFINCH** (FIG. Intro-4), for example, the group of figures has been arranged in a triangular shape and placed at the center of the picture. Raphael emphasized this central weighting by opening the clouds to reveal a

patch of blue in the middle of the sky, and by flanking the figural group with lacelike trees. Since the Madonna is at the center and since the two boys are divided between the two sides of the triangular shape, roughly—though not precisely—equidistant from the center of the painting, this is a bilaterally symmetrical composition: on either side of an implied vertical line at the center of the picture, there are equivalent forms on left and right, matched and balanced in a mirrored correspondence. Art historians refer to such an implied line—around which the elements of a picture are organized—as an **axis**. Raphael's painting has not only a vertical, but also a horizontal axis, indicated by a line of demarcation between light and dark—as well as between degrees of color saturation—in the terrain of the landscape. The belt of the Madonna's dress is aligned with this horizontal axis, and this correspondence, taken with the coordination of her head with the blue patch in the sky, relates her harmoniously to the natural world in which

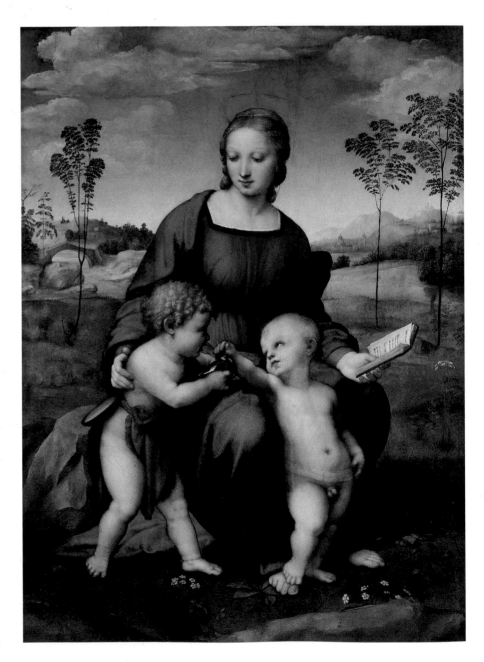

Intro-4 • Raphael MADONNA OF THE GOLDFINCH (MADONNA DEL CARDELLINO)
1506. Oil on panel, 42″ × 29½″ (106.7 × 74.9 cm). Galleria degli Uffizi, Florence.

The vibrant colors of this important work were revealed in the course of a careful, ten-year restoration, completed only in 2008.

Intro-5 • Auguste Renoir **MME. CHARPENTIER AND HER CHILDREN** 1878. Oil on canvas, 60½″ × 74⅞″ (153.7 × 190.2 cm). Metropolitan Museum of Art, New York.

she sits, lending a sense of stability, order, and balance to the picture as a whole.

The main axis in Renoir's painting of **MME. CHARPENTIER AND HER CHILDREN** (**FIG. Intro-5**) is neither vertical, nor horizontal, but diagonal, running from the upper right to the lower left corner of the painting. All major elements of the composition are aligned along this axis—dog, children, mother, and the table and chair that represent the most complex and detailed aspect of the setting. The upper left and lower right corners of the painting balance each other on either side of the diagonal axis as relatively simple fields of neutral tone, setting off and framing the main subjects between them. The resulting arrangement is not bilaterally symmetrical, but blatantly asymmetrical, with the large figural mass pushed into the left side of the picture. And unlike Raphael's composition, where the spatial relationship of the figures and their environment is mapped by the measured placement of elements that become increasingly smaller in scale and fuzzier in definition as they recede into the background, the relationship of Renoir's figures to their spatial environment is less clearly defined as they recede into the background along the dramatic diagonal axis. Nothing distracts us from the bold informality of this family gathering.

Both Raphael and Renoir arrange their figures carefully and purposefully, but they follow distinctive compositional systems that communicate different notions of the way these figures interact with each other and the world around them. Art historians pay special attention to how pictures are arranged because composition is one of the principal ways artists charge their paintings with expressive meaning.

IDENTIFYING SUBJECT MATTER

Art historians have traditionally sought subject matter and meaning in works of art with a system of analysis that was outlined by Erwin Panofsky (1892–1968), an influential German scholar who was expelled from his academic position by the Nazis in 1933 and spent the rest of his career of research and teaching in the United States. Panofsky proposed that when we seek to understand the subject of a work of art, we derive meaning initially in two ways:

- First we perceive what he called "natural subject matter" by recognizing forms and situations that we know from our own experience.
- Then we use what he called "**iconography**" to identify the conventional meanings associated with forms and figures as bearers of narrative or symbolic content, often specific to a particular time and place.

Some paintings, like Rothko's abstractions and Knowles and Thomas's quilt, do not contain subjects drawn from the world around us, from stories, or from conventional symbolism, but Panofsky's scheme remains a standard method of investigating

A CLOSER LOOK | Iconography

The study and identification of conventional themes, motifs, and symbols to elucidate the subject matter of works of art.

These grapes sit on an imported, Italian silver *tazza*, a luxury object that may commemorate northern European prosperity and trade. This particular object recurs in several of Peeters's other still lifes.

An image of the artist herself appears on the reflective surface of this pewter tankard, one of the ways that she signed her paintings and promoted her career.

Luscious fruits and flowers celebrate the abundance of nature, but because these fruits of the earth will eventually fade, even rot, they could be moralizing references to the transience of earthly existence.

These coins, including one minted in 1608–1609, help focus the dating of this painting. The highlighting of money within a still life could reference the wealth of the owner—or it could subtly allude to the value the artist has crafted here in paint.

Detailed renderings of insects showcased Peeters's virtuosity as a painter, but they also may have symbolized the vulnerability of the worldly beauty of flowers and fruit to destruction and decay.

This knife—which appears in several of Peeters's still lifes—is of a type that is associated with wedding gifts.

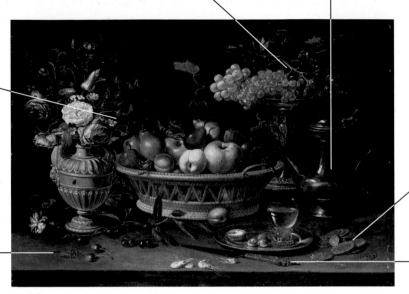

A. Clara Peeters *Still Life with Fruit and Flowers*
c. 1612. Oil on copper, 25⅕″ × 35″ (64 × 89 cm). Ashmolean Museum, Oxford.

Quince is an unusual subject in Chinese painting, but the fruit seems to have carried personal significance for Zhu Da. One of his friends was known as the Daoist of Quince Mountain, a site in Hunan Province that was also the subject of a work by one of his favorite authors, Tang poet Li Bai.

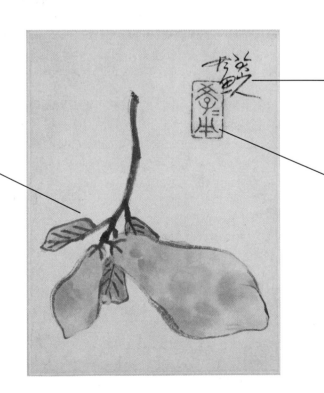

The artist's signature reads "Bada Shanren painted this," using a familiar pseudonym in a formula and calligraphic style that the artist ceased using in 1695.

This red block is a seal with an inscription drawn from a Confucian text: "Teaching is half of learning." This was imprinted on the work by the artist as an aspect of his signature, a symbol of his identity within the picture, just as the reflection and inscribed knife identify Clara Peeters as the painter of her still life.

B. Zhu Da (Bada Shanren) *Quince (Mugua)*
1690. Album leaf mounted as a hanging scroll; ink and colors on paper, 7⅞″ × 5¾″ (20 × 14.6 cm). Princeton University Art Museum.

View the Closer Look for iconography on myartslab.com

meaning in works of art that present narrative subjects, portray specific people or places, or embody cultural values with iconic imagery or allegory.

NATURAL SUBJECT MATTER We recognize some things in works of visual art simply by virtue of living in a world similar to that represented by the artist. For example, in the two paintings by Raphael and Renoir just examined (see FIGS. Intro–4, Intro–5), we immediately recognize the principal human figures in both as a woman and two children, boys in the case of Raphael's painting, girls in Renoir's. We can also make a general identification of the animals: a bird in the hand of Raphael's boys, and a pet dog under one of Renoir's girls. And natural subject matter can extend from an identification of figures to an understanding of the expressive significance of their postures and facial features. We might see in the boy who snuggles between the knees of the woman in Raphael's painting, placing his own foot on top of hers, an anxious child seeking the security of physical contact with a trusted caretaker—perhaps his mother—in response to fear of the bird he reaches out to touch. Many of us have seen insecure children take this very pose in response to potentially unsettling encounters.

The closer the work of art is in both time and place to our own situation temporally and geographically, the easier it sometimes is to identify what is represented. But although Renoir painted his picture over 125 years ago in France, the furniture in the background still looks familiar, as does the book in the hand of Raphael's Madonna, painted five centuries before our time. But the object hanging from the belt of the scantily clad boy at the left in this painting will require identification for most of us. Iconographic investigation is necessary to understand the function of this form.

ICONOGRAPHY Some subjects are associated with conventional meanings established at a specific time or place; some of the human figures portrayed in works of art have specific identities; and some of the objects or forms have symbolic or allegorical meanings in addition to their natural subject matter. Discovering these conventional meanings of art's subject matter is called iconography. (See "A Closer Look," opposite.)

For example, the woman accompanied in the outdoors by two boys in Raphael's *Madonna of the Goldfinch* (see FIG. Intro–4) would have been immediately recognized by members of its intended early sixteenth-century Florentine audience as the Virgin Mary. Viewers would have identified the naked boy standing between her knees as her son Jesus, and the boy holding the bird as Jesus' cousin John the Baptist, sheathed in the animal skin garment that he would wear in the wilderness and equipped with a shallow cup attached to his belt, ready to be used in baptisms. Such attributes of clothing and equipment are often critical in making iconographic identifications. The goldfinch in the Baptist's hand was at this time and place a symbol of Christ's death on the cross, an allegorical implication that makes the Christ Child's retreat

into secure contact with his mother—already noted on the level of natural subject matter—understandable in relation to a specific story. The comprehension of conventional meanings in this painting would have been almost automatic among those for whom it was painted, but for us, separated by time and place, some research is necessary to recover associations that are no longer part of our everyday world.

Although it may not initially seem as unfamiliar, the subject matter of Renoir's 1878 portrait of *Mme. Charpentier and her Children* (see FIG. Intro–5) is in fact even more obscure. There are those in twenty-first-century American culture for whom the figures and symbols in Raphael's painting are still recognizable and meaningful, but Marguérite-Louise Charpentier died in 1904, and no one living today would be able to identify her based on the likeness Renoir presumably gave to her face in this family portrait commissioned by her husband, the wealthy and influential publisher Georges Charpentier. We need the painting's title to make that identification. And Mme. Charpentier is outfitted here in a gown created by English designer Charles Frederick Worth, the dominant figure in late nineteenth-century Parisian high fashion. Her clothing was a clear attribute of her wealth for those who recognized its source; most of us need to investigate to uncover its meaning. But a greater surprise awaits the student who pursues further research on her children. Although they clearly seem to our eyes to represent two daughters, the child closest to Mme. Charpentier is actually her son Paul, who at age 3, following standard Parisian bourgeois practice, has not yet had his first haircut and still wears clothing comparable to that of his older sister Georgette, perched on the family dog. It is not unusual in art history to encounter situations where our initial conclusions on the level of natural subject matter will need to be revised after some iconographic research.

INTEGRATION WITHIN CULTURAL CONTEXT
Natural subject matter and iconography were only two of three steps proposed by Panofsky for coming to an understanding of the meaning of works of art. The third step he labeled "**iconology**," and its aim is to interpret the work of art as an embodiment of its cultural situation, to place it within broad social, political, religious, and intellectual contexts. Such integration into history requires more than identifying subject matter or conventional symbols; it requires a deep understanding of the beliefs and principles or goals and values that underlie a work of art's cultural situation as well as the position of an artist and patron within it.

In "A Closer Look" (opposite), the subject matter of two **still life** paintings (pictures of inanimate objects and fruits or flowers taken out of their natural contexts) is identified and elucidated, but to truly understand these two works as bearers of cultural meaning, more knowledge of the broader context and specific goals of artists and audiences is required. For example, the fact that Zhu Da (1626–1705) became a painter was rooted more in the political than the artistic history of China at the middle of the seventeenth century. As a member of the imperial family of the Ming dynasty, his life of privilege was disrupted when the Ming were overthrown during the Manchu conquest of China in 1644. Fleeing for his life, he sought refuge in a Buddhist monastery, where he wrote poetry and painted. Almost 40 years later, in the aftermath of a nervous breakdown (that could have been staged to avoid retribution for his family background), Zhu Da abandoned his monastic life and developed a career as a professional painter, adopting a series of descriptive pseudonyms—most notably Bada Shanren ("mountain man of eight greatnesses") by which he is most often known today. His paintings are at times saturated with veiled political commentary; at times they seek to accommodate the expectations of collectors to assure their marketability; and in paintings like the one illustrated here (see page xxxvi, FIG. B), the artist seems to hark back to the contemplative, abstract, and spontaneous paintings associated with great Zen masters such as Muqi (c. 1201–after 1269), whose calligraphic pictures of isolated fruits seem almost like acts of devotion or detached contemplations on natural forms, rather than the works of a professional painter.

Clara Peeters's still life (see page xxxvi, FIG. A), on the other hand, fits into a developing Northern European painting tradition within which she was an established and successful professional, specializing in portrayals of food and flowers, fruit and reflective objects. Still-life paintings in this tradition could be jubilant celebrations of the abundance of the natural world and the wealth of luxury objects available in the prosperous mercantile society of the Netherlands. Or they could be moralizing "**vanitas**" paintings, warning of the ephemeral meaning of those worldly possessions, even of life itself. But this painting has also been interpreted in a more personal way. Because the type of knife that sits in the foreground near the edge of the table was a popular wedding gift, and since it is inscribed with the artist's own name, some have suggested that this still life could have celebrated Peeters's marriage. Or this could simply be a witty way to sign her picture. It certainly could be personal and at the same time participate in the broader cultural meaning of still-life paintings. Mixtures of private and public meanings have been proposed for Zhu Da's paintings as well. Some have seen the picture of quince illustrated here (see page xxxvi, FIG. B) as part of a series of allegorical "self-portraits" that extend across his career as a painter. Art historians frequently reveal multiple meanings when interpreting single works. Art often represents complex cultural and personal situations.

A CASE STUDY: ROGIER VAN DER WEYDEN'S PHILADELPHIA *CRUCIFIXION*

The basic, four-part method of art historical investigation and interpretation just outlined and explored may become clearer when its extended use is traced in relation to one specific work of art. A particularly revealing subject for such a case study is a seminal and somewhat perplexing painting now in the Philadelphia Museum of Art—the **CRUCIFIXION WITH THE VIRGIN AND ST. JOHN THE EVANGELIST** (FIG. Intro-6) by Rogier van der Weyden (c. 1400–1464), a Flemish artist who will be featured in Chapter 19. Each of the four levels of art-historical inquiry reveals important information about this painting, information that has been used by art historians to reconstruct its relationship to its artist, its audience, and its broader cultural setting. The resulting interpretation is rich, but also complex. An investigation this extensive will not be possible for all the works of art in the following chapters, where the text will focus only on one or two facets of more expansive research. Because of the amount and complexity of information involved in a thorough art-historical interpretation, it is sometimes only in a second reading that we can follow the subtleties of its argument, after the first reading has provided a basic familiarity with the work of art, its conventional subjects, and its general context.

PHYSICAL PROPERTIES

Perhaps the most striking aspect of this painting's physical appearance is its division into two separate tall rectangular panels, joined by a frame to form a coherent, almost square composition. These are oak panels, prepared with chalk to form a smooth surface on which to paint with mineral pigments suspended in oil. A technical investigation of the painting in 1981 used infrared reflectography to reveal a very sketchy under-drawing beneath the surface of the paint, proving to the investigators that this painting is almost entirely the work of Rogier van der Weyden himself. Famous and prosperous artists of this time and place employed many assistants to work in large production workshops, and they would make detailed under-drawings to ensure that assistants replicated the **style** of the master. But in cases where the masters themselves intended to execute the work, only summary compositional outlines were needed. Modern technical investigation of Rogier's painting also used **dendrochronology** (the dating of wood based on the patterns of the growth rings) to date the oak panels and consequently the painting itself, now securely situated near the end of the artist's career, c. 1460.

The most recent restoration of the painting—during the early 1990s by Mark Tucker, Senior Conservator at the Philadelphia Museum of Art—returned it, as close as possible, to current views of its original fifteenth-century appearance (see "De-restoring and Restoring Rogier van der Weyden's *Crucifixion*," page xl). This project included extensive technical analysis of almost every aspect of the picture, during which a critical clue emerged, one that may lead to a sharper understanding of its original use. X-rays revealed dowel holes and plugs running in a horizontal line about one-fourth of the way up from the bottom across the entire expanse of the two-panel painting. Tucker's convincing research suggests that the dowels would have attached these two panels to the backs of wooden boxes that contained sculptures in a complex work of art that hung over the altar in a fifteenth-century church.

Intro–6 • Rogier van der Weyden CRUCIFIXION WITH THE VIRGIN AND ST. JOHN THE EVANGELIST
c. 1460. Oil on oak panels, 71″ × 73″ (1.8 × 1.85 m). John G. Johnson Collection, Philadelphia Museum of Art.

FORMAL STRUCTURE

The visual organization of this two-part painting emphasizes both connection and separation. It is at the same time one painting and two. Continuing across both panels is the strip of midnight blue sky and the stone wall that constricts space within the picture to a shallow corridor, pushing the figures into the foreground and close to the viewer. The shallow strip of mossy ground under the two-figure group in the left panel continues its sloping descent into the right panel, as does the hem of the Virgin's ice-blue garment. We look into this scene as if through a window with a mullion down the middle and assume that the world on the left continues behind this central strip of frame into the right side.

On the other hand, strong visual forces isolate the figures within their respective panels, setting up a system of "compare and contrast" that seems to be at the heart of the painting's design. The striking red cloths that hang over the wall are centered directly behind the figures on each side, forming internal frames that highlight them as separate groups and focus our attention back and forth between them rather than on the pictorial elements that unite their environments. As we begin to compare the two sides,

Ever since Rogier van der Weyden's strikingly asymmetrical, two-panel rendering of the *Crucifixion* (see FIG. Intro–6) was purchased by Philadelphia lawyer John G. Johnson in 1906 for his spectacular collection of European paintings, it has been recognized not only as one of the greatest works by this master of fifteenth-century Flemish painting, but as one of the most important European paintings in North America. Soon after the Johnson Collection became part of the Philadelphia Museum of Art in 1933, however, this painting's visual character was significantly transformed. In 1941, the museum employed freelance restorer David Rosen to work on the painting. Deciding that Rogier's work was seriously marred by later overpainting and disfigured by the discoloration of old varnish, he subjected the painting to a thorough cleaning. He also removed the strip of dark blue paint forming the sky above the wall at the top—identifying it as an eighteenth-century restoration—and replaced it with gold leaf to conform with remnants of gold in this area that he assessed as surviving fragments of the original background. Rosen's restoration of Rogier's painting was uncritically accepted for almost half a century, and the gold background became a major factor in the interpretations of art historians as distinguished as Erwin Panofsky and Meyer Schapiro.

In 1990, in preparation for a new installation of the work, Rogier's painting received a thorough technical analysis by Mark Tucker, the museum's Senior Conservator. There were two startling discoveries:

- The dark blue strip that had run across the top of the picture before Rosen's intervention was actually original to the painting. Remnants of paint left behind in 1941 proved to be the same azurite blue that also appears in the clothing of the Virgin, and in no instance did the traces of gold discovered in 1941 run under aspects of the original paint surface. Rosen had removed Rogier's original midnight blue sky.

- What Rosen had interpreted as disfiguring varnish streaking the wall and darkening the brilliant cloths of honor hanging over it were actually Rogier's careful painting of lichens and water stains on the stone and his overpainting on the fabric that had originally transformed a vermillion undercoat into deep crimson cloth.

In meticulous work during 1992–1993, Tucker cautiously restored the painting based on the evidence he had uncovered. Neither the lost lichens and water stains nor the toning crimson overpainting of the hangings were replaced, but a coat of blue-black paint was laid over Rosen's gold leaf at the top of the panels, taking care to apply the new layer in such a way that should a later generation decide to return to the gold leaf sky, the midnight tonalities could be easily removed. That seems an unlikely prospect. The painting as exhibited today comes as close as possible to the original appearance of Rogier's *Crucifixion*. At least we think so.

---

it becomes increasingly clear that the relationship between figures and environment is quite distinct on each side of the divide.

The dead figure of Christ on the cross, elevated to the very top of the picture, is strictly centered within his panel, as well as against the cloth that hangs directly behind him. The grid of masonry blocks and creases in the cloth emphasizes his rectilinear integration into a system of balanced, rigid regularity. His head is aligned with the cap of the wall, his flesh largely contained within the area defined by the cloth. His elbows mark the juncture of the wall with the edge of the hanging, and his feet extend just to the end of the cloth, where his toes substitute for the border of fringe they overlap. The environment is almost as balanced. The strip of dark sky at the top is equivalent in size to the strip of mossy earth at the bottom of the picture, and both are visually bisected by centered horizontals—the cross bar at the top and the alignment of bone and skull at the bottom. A few disruptions to this stable, rectilinear, symmetrical order draw the viewers' attention to the panel at the left: the downward fall of the head of Christ, the visual weight of the skull, the downturn of the fluttering loin cloth, and the tip of the Virgin's gown that transgresses over the barrier to move in from the other side.

John and Mary merge on the left into a single figural mass that could be inscribed into a half-circle. Although set against a rectilinear grid background comparable to that behind Jesus, they contrast with, rather than conform to, the regular sense of order. Their curving outlines offer unsettling unsteadiness, as if they are toppling to the ground, jutting into the other side of the frame. This instability is reinforced by their postures. The projection of Mary's knee in relation to the angle of her torso reveals that she is collapsing into a curve, and the crumpled mass of drapery circling underneath her only underlines her lack of support. John reaches out to catch her, but he has not yet made contact with her body. He strikes a stance of strident instability without even touching the ground, and he looks blankly out into space with an unfocused expression, distracted from, rather than concentrating on, the task at hand. Perhaps he will come to his senses and grab her. But will he be able to catch her in time, and even then support her, given his unstable posture? The moment is tense; the outcome is unclear. But we are moving into the realm of natural subject matter. The poignancy of this concentrated portrayal seems to demand it.

ICONOGRAPHY

The subject of this painting is among the most familiar themes in the history of European art. The dead Jesus has been crucified on the cross, and two of his closest associates—his mother and John, one of his disciples—mourn his loss. Although easily recognizable, the austere and asymmetrical presentation is unexpected. More usual is an earlier painting of this subject by the same artist, **CRUCIFIXION TRIPTYCH WITH DONORS AND SAINTS** (**FIG. Intro–7**), where he situates the crucified Christ at the center

Intro-7 • Rogier van der Weyden **CRUCIFIXION TRIPTYCH WITH DONORS AND SAINTS**
c. 1440. Oil on wooden panels, 39¾" × 55" (101 × 140 cm). Kunsthistorisches Museum, Vienna.

of a symmetrical arrangement, the undisputed axial focus of the composition. The scene unfolds here within an expansive landscape, populated with a wider cast of participants, each of whom takes a place with symmetrical decorum on either side of the cross. Because most crucifixions follow some variation on this pattern, Rogier's two-panel portrayal (see FIG. Intro-6) in which the cross is asymmetrically displaced to one side, with a spare cast of attendants relegated to a separately framed space, severely restricted by a stark stone wall, requires some explanation. As does the mysterious dark world beyond the wall, and the artificial backdrop of the textile hangings.

This scene is not only austere and subdued; it is sharply focused, and the focus relates it to the specific moment in the story that Rogier decided to represent. The Christian Bible contains four accounts of Jesus' crucifixion, one in each of the four Gospels. Rogier took two verses in John's account as his painting's text (John 19:26–27), cited here in the Douai-Reims literal English translation (1582, 1609) of the Latin Vulgate Bible that was used by Western European Christians during the fifteenth century:

> When Jesus therefore had seen his mother and the disciple standing whom he loved, he saith to his mother: Woman, behold thy son. After that, he saith to the disciple: Behold thy mother. And from that hour, the disciple took her to his own.

Even the textual source uses conventions that need explanation, specifically the way the disciple John is consistently referred to in this Gospel as "the disciple whom Jesus loved." Rogier's painting, therefore, seems to focus on Jesus' call for a newly expanded relationship between his mother and a beloved follower. More specifically, he has projected us slightly forward in time to the moment when John needs to respond to that call—Jesus has died; John is now in charge.

There are, however, other conventional iconographic associations with the crucifixion that Rogier has folded into this spare portrayal. Fifteenth-century viewers would have understood the skull and femur that lie on the mound at the base of the cross as the bones of Adam—the first man in the Hebrew Bible account of creation—on whose grave Jesus' crucifixion was believed to have taken place. This juxtaposition embodied the Christian belief that Christ's sacrifice on the cross redeemed believers from the death that Adam's original sin had brought to human existence.

Mary's swoon and presumed loss of consciousness would have evoked another theological idea, the *co-passio*, in which Mary's anguish while witnessing Jesus' suffering and death was seen as a parallel passion of mother with son, both critical for human salvation. Their connection in this painting is underlined visually by the similar bending of their knees, inclination of their heads, and closing of their eyes. They even seem to resemble each other in facial likeness, especially when compared to John.

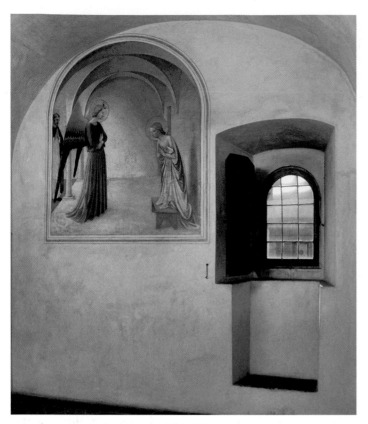

Intro-8 • VIEW OF A MONK'S CELL IN THE MONASTERY OF SAN MARCO, FLORENCE
Including Fra Angelico's fresco of the *Annunciation*. c. 1438–1445.

CULTURAL CONTEXT

In 1981 art historian Penny Howell Jolly published an interpretation of Rogier's Philadelphia *Crucifixion* as the product of a broad personal and cultural context. In addition to building on the work of earlier art historians, she pursued two productive lines of investigation to explain the rationale for this unusually austere presentation:

- the prospect that Rogier was influenced by the work of another artist, and
- the possibility that the painting was produced for an institutional context that called for a special mode of visual presentation and a particular iconographic focus.

FRA ANGELICO AT SAN MARCO We know very little about the life of Rogier van der Weyden, but we do know that in 1450, when he was already established as one of the principal painters in northern Europe, he made a pilgrimage to Rome. Either on his way to Rome, or during his return journey home, he stopped off in Florence and saw the **altarpiece**, and presumably also the frescos, that Fra Angelico (c. 1400–1455) and his workshop had painted during the 1440s at the monastery of San Marco. The evidence of Rogier's contact with Fra Angelico's work is found in a work Rogier painted after he returned home, based on a panel of the San Marco altarpiece. For the Philadelphia *Crucifixion*,

however, it was Fra Angelico's devotional frescos on the walls of the monks' individual rooms (or cells) that seem to have had the greatest impact (**FIG. Intro-8**). Jolly compared the Philadelphia *Crucifixion* with a scene of the Mocking of Christ at San Marco to demonstrate the connection (**FIG. Intro-9**). Fra Angelico presented the sacred figures with a quiet austerity that recalls Rogier's unusual composition. More specific parallels are the use of an expansive stone wall to restrict narrative space to a shallow foreground corridor, the description of the world beyond that wall as a dark sky that contrasts with the brilliantly illuminated foreground, and the use of a draped cloth of honor to draw attention to a narrative vignette from the life of Jesus, to separate it out as an object of devotion.

THE CARTHUSIANS Having established a possible connection between Rogier's unusual late painting of the crucifixion and frescos by Fra Angelico that he likely saw during his pilgrimage to Rome in 1450, Jolly reconstructed a specific context of patronage and meaning within Rogier's own world in Flanders that could explain why the paintings of Fra Angelico would have had such an impact on him at this particular moment in his career.

During the years around 1450, Rogier developed a personal and professional relationship with the monastic order of

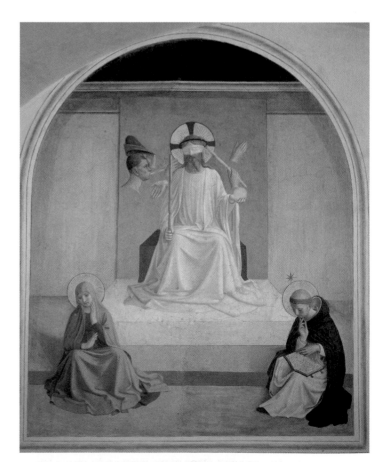

Intro-9 • Fra Angelico MOCKING OF CHRIST WITH THE VIRGIN MARY AND ST. DOMINIC
Monastery of San Marco, Florence. c. 1441–1445.

Intro–10 • DETAIL OF FIG. Intro-6 SHOWING PART OF THE LEFT WING

individual dormitory rooms of Carthusian monks. The reference in this painting to the *co-passio* of the Virgin provides supporting evidence since this theological idea was central to Carthusian thought and devotion. The *co-passio* was even reflected in the monks' own initiation rites, during which they re-enacted and sought identification with both Christ's sacrifice on the cross and the Virgin's parallel suffering.

In Jolly's interpretation, the religious framework of a Carthusian setting for the painting emerges as a personal framework for the artist himself, since this *Crucifixion* seems to be associated with important moments in his own life—his religious pilgrimage to Rome in 1450 and the initiation of his oldest son as a Carthusian monk at about the same time. Is it possible that the sense of loss and separation that Rogier evoked in his portrayal of a poignant moment in the life of St. John (**FIG. Intro-10**) could have been especially meaningful to the artist himself at the time this work was painted?

A CONTINUING PROJECT The final word has not been spoken in the interpretation of this painting. Mark Tucker's recent work on the physical evidence revealed by x-ray analysis points toward seeing these two panels as part of a large sculptured altarpiece. Even if this did preclude the prospect that it is the **panel painting** Rogier donated to the chapel of St. Catherine at Hérrines, it does not negate the relationship Jolly drew with Fra Angelico, nor the Carthusian context she outlined for the work's original situation. It simply reminds us that our historical understanding of works such as this will evolve when new evidence about them emerges.

As the history of art unfolds in the ensuing chapters of this book, it will be important to keep two things in mind as you read the characterizations of individual works of art and the larger story of their integration into the broader cultural contexts of those who made them and those for whom they were initially made. Art-historical interpretations are built on extended research comparable to that we have just summarily surveyed for Rogier van der Weyden's Philadelphia *Crucifixion*. But the work of interpretation is never complete. Art history is a continuing project, a work perpetually in progress.

the Carthusians, and especially with the Belgian Charterhouse (or Carthusian monastery) of Hérrines, where his oldest son was invested as a monk in 1450. Rogier gave money to Hérrines, and texts document his donation of a painting to its chapel of St. Catherine. Jolly suggested that the Philadelphia *Crucifixion* could be that painting. Its subdued colors and narrative austerity are consistent with Carthusian aesthetic attitudes, and the walled setting of the scene recalls the enclosed gardens that were attached to the

THINK ABOUT IT

I.1 Analyze the composition of one painting illustrated in this Introduction.

I.2 Characterize the difference between natural subject matter and iconography, focusing your discussion on a specific work of art.

I.3 What are the four separate steps proposed here for characterizing the methods used by art historians to interpret works of art? Characterize the cultural analysis in step four by showing

the way it expands our understanding of one of the still lifes in the Closer Look.

I.4 What aspect of the case study of Rogier van der Weyden's Philadelphia *Crucifixion* was especially interesting to you? Why? How did it broaden your understanding of what you will learn in this course?

✓—**Study** and review on myartslab.com

18–1 • Ambrogio Lorenzetti FRESCOS OF THE SALA DEI NOVE (OR SALA DELLA PACE)
Palazzo Pubblico, Siena, Italy. 1338–1339. Length of long wall about 46′ (14 m).

Fourteenth-Century Art in Europe

In 1338, the Nine—a council of merchants and bankers that governed Siena as an oligarchy—commissioned frescos from renowned Sienese painter Ambrogio Lorenzetti (c. 1295– c. 1348) for three walls in the chamber within the Palazzo Pubblico where they met to conduct city business. This commission came at the moment of greatest prosperity and security since the establishment of their government in 1287.

Lorenzetti's frescos combine allegory with panoramic landscapes and cityscapes to visualize and justify the beneficial effects of the Sienese form of government. The moral foundation of the rule of the Nine is outlined in a complicated allegory in which seated personifications (far left in **FIG. 18–1**) of Concord, Justice, Peace, Strength, Prudence, Temperance, and Magnanimity, not only diagram good governance but actually reference the Last Judgment in a bold assertion of the relationship between secular rule and divine authority. This tableau contrasts with a similar presentation of bad government, where Tyranny is flanked by the personified forces that keep tyrants in power—Cruelty, Treason, Fraud, Fury, Division, and War. A group of scholars would have devised this complex program of symbols and meanings; it is unlikely that Lorenzetti would have known the philosophical works that underlie them. Lorenzetti's fame, however, and the wall paintings' secure position among the most remarkable surviving mural programs of the period, rests on the other part of this ensemble—the effects of good and bad government in city and country life (see **FIG. 18–15**).

Unlike the tableau showing the perils of life under tyrannical rule, the panoramic view of life under good government—which in this work of propaganda means life under the rule of the Nine—is well preserved. A vista of fourteenth-century Siena—identifiable by the cathedral dome and tower peeking over the rooftops in the background—showcases carefree life within shops, schools, taverns, and worksites, as the city streets bustle with human activity. Outside, an expansive landscape highlights agricultural productivity.

Unfortunately, within a decade of the frescos' completion, life in Siena was no longer as stable and carefree. The devastating bubonic plague visited in 1348—Ambrogio Lorenzetti himself was probably one of the victims—and the rule of the Nine collapsed in 1355. But this glorious vision of joyful prosperity preserves the dreams and aspirations of a stable government, using some of the most progressive and creative ideas in fourteenth-century Italian art, ideas we will see developed at the very beginning of the century, and whose history we will trace over the next two centuries through the Renaissance.

LEARN ABOUT IT

18.1 Compare and contrast the Florentine and Sienese styles of narrative painting as exemplified by Giotto and Duccio.

18.2 Investigate the Bible stories that were the subject of fourteenth-century sacred art, as well as the personal and political themes highlighted in secular art.

18.3 Assess the close connections between works of art and their patrons in fourteenth-century Europe.

18.4 Explore the production of small-scale works, often made of precious materials and highlighting extraordinary technical virtuosity, that continues from the earlier Gothic period.

((•— **Listen** to the chapter audio on myartslab.com

MAP 18-1 • EUROPE IN THE FOURTEENTH CENTURY

Following its outbreak in the Mediterranean in 1347, the Black Death swept across the European mainland over the next four years.

The Spread of
the Black Death
- 1347
- mid–1348
- early 1349
- late 1349
- 1350
- 1351
- after 1351
- minor outbreak

FOURTEENTH-CENTURY EUROPE

Literary luminaries Dante, Petrarch, Boccaccio, Chaucer, and Christine de Pizan (see "A New Spirit in Fourteenth-Century Literature," opposite) and the visionary painters Giotto, Duccio, Jean Pucelle, and Master Theodoric participated in a cultural explosion that swept through fourteenth-century Europe, and especially Italy. The poet Petrarch (1304–1374) was a towering figure in this change, writing his love lyrics in Italian, the language of everyday life, rather than Latin, the language of ceremony and high art. Similarly, the deeply moving murals of Florentine painter Giotto di Bondone (c. 1277–1337) were rooted in his observation of the people around him, giving the participants in sacred narratives both great dignity and striking humanity, thus making them familiar, yet new, to the audiences that originally experienced them. Even in Paris—still the artistic center of Europe as far as refined taste and technical sophistication were concerned—the painter Jean Pucelle began to show an interest in experimenting with established conventions.

For Petrarch and his contemporaries, the essential qualifications for a writer were an appreciation of Greek and Roman authors and an ability to observe the people living around them. Although fluent in Latin, they chose to write in the language of their own time and place—Italian, English, French. Leading the way was Dante Alighieri (1265–1321), who wrote *The Divine Comedy*, his great summation of human virtue and vice, and ultimately human destiny, in Italian, establishing his daily vernacular as worthy to express great literary themes.

Francesco Petrarca, called simply Petrarch (1304–1374), raised the status of secular literature with his sonnets to his unattainable beloved, Laura, his histories and biographies, and his writings on the joys of country life in the Roman manner. Petrarch's imaginative updating of Classical themes in a work called *The Triumphs*—which examines the themes of Chastity triumphant over Love, Death over Chastity, Fame over Death, Time over Fame, and Eternity over Time—provided later Renaissance poets and painters with a wealth of allegorical subject matter.

More earthy, Giovanni Boccaccio (1313–1375) perfected the art of the short story in *The Decameron*, a collection of amusing and moralizing tales told by a group of young Florentines who moved to the countryside to escape the Black Death. With wit and sympathy, Boccaccio presents the full spectrum of daily life in Italy. Such secular literature, written in Italian as it was then spoken in Tuscany, provided a foundation for fifteenth-century Renaissance writers.

In England, Geoffrey Chaucer (c. 1342–1400) was inspired by Boccaccio to write his own series of stories, *The Canterbury Tales*, told by pilgrims traveling to the shrine of St. Thomas à Becket (1118?–1170) in Canterbury. Observant and witty, Chaucer depicted the pretensions and foibles, as well as the virtues, of humanity.

Christine de Pizan (1364–c. 1431), born in Venice but living and writing at the French court, became an author out of necessity when she was left a widow with three young children and an aged mother to support. Among her many works are a poem in praise of Joan of Arc and a history of famous women—including artists—from antiquity to her own time. In *The Book of the City of Ladies*, she defended women's abilities and argued for women's rights and status.

These writers, as surely as Giotto, Duccio, Peter Parler, and Master Theodoric, led the way into a new era.

Changes in the way that society was organized were also under way, and an expanding class of wealthy merchants supported the arts as patrons. Artisan guilds—organized by occupation—exerted quality control among members and supervised education through an apprenticeship system. Admission to the guild came after examination and the creation of a "masterpiece"—literally, a piece fine enough to achieve master status. The major guilds included cloth finishers, wool merchants, and silk manufacturers, as well as pharmacists and doctors. Painters belonged to the pharmacy guild, perhaps because they used mortars and pestles to grind their colors. Their patron saint, Luke, who was believed to have painted the first image of the Virgin Mary, was also a physician—or so they thought. Sculptors who worked in wood and stone had their own guild, while those who worked in metals belonged to another. Guilds provided social services for their members, including care of the sick and funerals for the deceased. Each guild had its patron saint, maintained a chapel, and participated in religious and civic festivals.

Despite the cultural flourishing and economic growth of the early decades, by the middle of the fourteenth century much of Europe was in crisis. Prosperity had fostered population growth, which began to exceed food production. A series of bad harvests compounded this problem with famine. To make matters worse, a prolonged conflict known as the Hundred Years' War (1337–1453) erupted between France and England. Then, in mid century, a lethal plague known as the Black Death swept across Europe (MAP 18–1), wiping out as much as 40 percent of the population. In spite of these catastrophic events, however, the strong current of cultural change still managed to persist through to the end of the century and beyond.

ITALY

As great wealth promoted patronage of art in fourteenth-century Italy, artists began to emerge as individuals, in the modern sense, both in their own eyes and in the eyes of patrons. Although their methods and working conditions remained largely unchanged from the Middle Ages, artists in Italy contracted freely with wealthy townspeople and nobles as well as with civic and religious bodies. Perhaps it was their economic and social freedom that encouraged ambition and self-confidence, individuality and innovation.

FLORENTINE ARCHITECTURE AND METALWORK

The typical medieval Italian city was a walled citadel on a hilltop. Houses clustered around the church and an open city square. Powerful families added towers to their houses, both for defense and as expressions of family pride. In Florence, by contrast, the ancient Roman city—with its axial rectangular plan and open city squares—formed the basis for civic layout. The cathedral stood northeast of the ancient forum and a street following the Roman plan connected it with the Piazza della Signoria, the seat of the government.

THE PALAZZO DELLA SIGNORIA The Signoria (ruling body, from *signore*, meaning "Lord") that governed Florence met

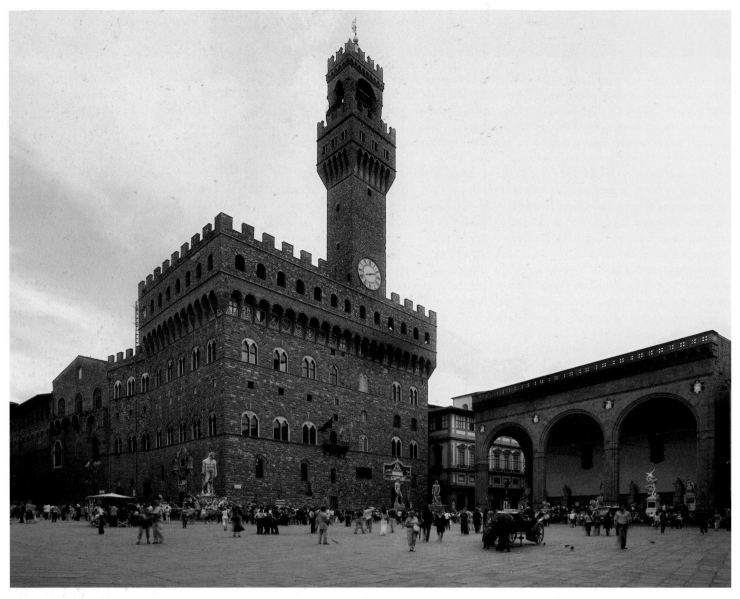

18-2 • PIAZZA DELLA SIGNORIA WITH PALAZZO DELLA SIGNORIA (TOWN HALL) 1299–1310,
AND LOGGIA DEI LANZI (LOGGIA OF THE LANCERS), 1376–1382
Florence.

in the **PALAZZO DELLA SIGNORIA**, a massive fortified build-ing with a bell tower 300 feet tall (**FIG. 18-2**). The building faces a large square, or piazza, which became the true center of Flor-ence. The town houses around the piazza often had benches along their walls to provide convenient public seating. Between 1376 and 1382, master builders Benci di Cione and Simone Talenti constructed a huge **loggia** or covered open-air corridor at one side—now known as the Loggia dei Lanzi (Loggia of the Lanc-ers)—to provide a sheltered locale for ceremonies and speeches.

THE BAPTISTERY DOORS In 1330, Andrea Pisano (c. 1290–1348) was awarded the prestigious commission for a pair of gilded bronze doors for Florence's Baptistery of San Giovanni, situated directly in front of the cathedral. (Andrea's "last" name means "from Pisa," and he was not related to Nicola and Giovanni

Pisano.) The doors were completed within six years and display 20 scenes from the **LIFE OF ST. JOHN THE BAPTIST** (the San Giovanni to whom the baptistery is dedicated) set above eight personifications of the Virtues (**FIG. 18-3**). The overall effect is two-dimensional and decorative: a grid of 28 rectangles with repeated quatrefoils filled by the graceful, patterned poses of delicate human figures. Within the quatrefoil frames, however, the figural compositions create the illusion of three-dimensional forms mov-ing within the described spaces of natural and architectural worlds.

The scene of John baptizing a multitude (**FIG. 18-4**) takes place on a shelflike stage created by a forward extension of the rocky natural setting, which also expands back behind the figures into a corner of the quatrefoil frame. Composed as a rectangular group, the gilded figures present an independent mass of mod-eled forms. The illusion of three-dimensionality is enhanced by the

18–3 • Andrea Pisano LIFE OF ST. JOHN THE BAPTIST
South doors, baptistery of San Giovanni, Florence. 1330–1336. Gilded bronze, each panel 19¼″ × 17″ (48 × 43 cm). Frame, Ghiberti workshop, mid 15th century.

The bronze vine scrolls filled with flowers, fruits, and birds on the lintel and jambs framing the door were added in the mid fifteenth century.

way the curving folds of their clothing wrap around their bodies. At the same time, their graceful gestures and the elegant fall of their drapery reflect the soft curves and courtly postures of French Gothic art.

FLORENTINE PAINTING

Florence and Siena, rivals in so many ways, each supported a flourishing school of painting in the fourteenth century. Both grew out of local thirteenth-century painting traditions and engendered individual artists who became famous in their own time. The Byzantine influence—the *maniera greca* ("Greek style")—continued to provide models of dramatic pathos and narrative iconography, as well as stylized features including the use of gold for drapery folds and striking contrasts of highlights and shadows in the modeling of individual forms. By the end of the fourteenth century, the painter and commentator Cennino Cennini (see "Cennino

Cennini on Panel Painting," page 546) would be struck by the accessibility and modernity of Giotto's art, which, though it retained traces of the *maniera greca*, was moving toward the depiction of a lifelike, contemporary world anchored in solid, three-dimensional forms.

CIMABUE In Florence, this stylistic transformation began a little earlier than in Siena. About 1280, a painter named Cenni di Pepi (active c. 1272–1302), better known by his nickname "Cimabue," painted a panel portraying the **VIRGIN AND CHILD ENTHRONED** (FIG. 18-5), perhaps for the main altar of the church of Santa Trinità in Florence. At over 12 feet tall, this enormous painting set a new precedent for monumental altarpieces. Cimabue surrounds the Virgin and Child with angels and places a row of Hebrew Bible prophets beneath them. The hierarchically scaled figure of Mary holds the infant Jesus in her lap. Looking out at the viewer while gesturing toward her son as the path to salvation, she adopts a formula popular in Byzantine iconography since at least the sixth century (see FIG. 8–14).

Mary's huge throne, painted to resemble gilded bronze with inset enamels and gems, provides an architectural framework for the figures. Cimabue creates highlights on the drapery of Mary, Jesus, and the angels with thin lines of gold, as if to capture their divine radiance. The viewer seems suspended in space in front of the image, simultaneously looking down on the projecting elements of the throne and Mary's lap, while looking straight ahead

at the prophets at the base of the throne and the angels at each side. These spatial ambiguities, the subtle asymmetries within the centralized composition, the Virgin's engaging gaze, and the individually conceived faces of the old men give the picture a sense of life and the figures a sense of presence. Cimabue's ambitious attention to spatial volumes, his use of delicate modeling in light and shade to simulate three-dimensional form, and his efforts to give naturalistic warmth to human figures had an impact on the future development of Florentine painting.

18–5 • Cimabue VIRGIN AND CHILD ENTHRONED
Most likely painted for the high altar of the church of Santa Trinità, Florence. c. 1280. Tempera and gold on wood panel, 12′7″ × 7′4″ (3.53 × 2.2 m). Galleria degli Uffizi, Florence.

 Watch a video about the egg tempera process on myartslab.com

GIOTTO DI BONDONE According to the sixteenth-century chronicler Giorgio Vasari, Cimabue discovered a talented shepherd boy, Giotto di Bondone (active c. 1300–1337), and taught him to paint; "not only did the young boy equal the style of his master, but he became such an excellent imitator of nature that he completely banished that crude Greek [i.e., Byzantine] style and revived the modern and excellent art of painting, introducing good drawing from live natural models, something which had not been done for more than two hundred years" (Vasari, translated by Bondanella and Bondanella, p. 16). After his training, Giotto may have collaborated on murals at the prestigious church of St. Francis in Assisi. We know he worked for the Franciscans in Florence and absorbed facets of their teaching. St. Francis's message of simple, humble devotion, direct experience of God, and love for all creatures was gaining followers throughout western Europe, and it had a powerful impact on thirteenth- and fourteenth-century Italian literature and art.

Compared to Cimabue's *Virgin and Child Enthroned*, Giotto's altarpiece of the same subject (**FIG. 18-6**), painted about 30 years later for the church of the Ognissanti (All Saints) in Florence,

18-6 • Giotto di Bondone VIRGIN AND CHILD ENTHRONED
Most likely painted for the high altar of the church of the Ognissanti (All Saints), Florence. 1305–1310. Tempera and gold on wood panel, 10'8" × 6'8¼" (3.53 × 2.05 m). Galleria degli Uffizi, Florence.

The two techniques used in mural painting are *buon* ("true") *fresco* ("fresh"), in which water-based paint is applied on wet plaster, and *fresco secco* ("dry"), in which paint is applied to a dry plastered wall. The two methods can be used on the same wall painting.

The advantage of *buon fresco* is its durability. A chemical reaction occurs as the painted plaster dries, which bonds the pigments into the wall surface. In *fresco secco*, by contrast, the color does not become part of the wall and tends to flake off over time. The chief disadvantage of *buon fresco* is that it must be done quickly without mistakes. The painter plasters and paints only as much as can be completed in a day, which explains the Italian term for each of these sections: **giornata**, or a day's work. The size of a *giornata* varies according to the complexity of the painting within it. A face, for instance, might take an entire day, whereas large areas of sky can be painted quite rapidly. In Giotto's Scrovegni Chapel, scholars have identified 852 separate *giornate*, some worked on concurrently within a single day by assistants in Giotto's workshop.

In medieval and Renaissance Italy, a wall to be frescoed was first prepared with a rough, thick undercoat of plaster known as the *arriccio*. When this was dry, assistants copied the master painter's composition onto it with reddish-brown pigment or charcoal. The artist made any necessary adjustments. These underdrawings, known as **sinopia**, have an immediacy and freshness that are lost in the finished painting. Work proceeded in irregularly shaped *giornate* conforming to the contours of major figures and objects. Assistants covered one section at a time with a fresh, thin coat of very fine plaster—the *intonaco*—over

the *sinopia*, and when this was "set" but not dry, the artist worked with pigments mixed with water, painting from the top down so that drips fell on unfinished portions. Some areas requiring pigments such as ultramarine blue (which was unstable in *buon fresco*), as well as areas requiring gilding, would be added after the wall was dry using the *fresco secco* technique.

arriccio

wall

sinopia drawing

water-based paint on damp *intonaco*

intonaco layer

buon fresco

exhibits greater spatial consistency and sculptural solidity while retaining some of Cimabue's conventions. The position of the figures within a symmetrical composition reflects Cimabue's influence. Gone, however, are Mary's modestly inclined head and the delicate gold folds in her drapery. Instead, light and shadow play gently across her stocky form, and her action—holding her child's leg instead of pointing him out to us—seems less contrived. This colossal Mary overwhelms her slender Gothic tabernacle of a throne, where figures peer through openings and haloes overlap faces. In spite of the hierarchic scale and the formal, enthroned image and flat, gold background, Giotto has created the sense that these are fully three-dimensional beings, whose plainly draped, bulky bodies inhabit real space. The Virgin's solid torso is revealed by her thin tunic, and Giotto's angels are substantial solids whose foreshortened postures project from the foreground toward us, unlike those of Cimabue, which stay on the surface along lateral strips composed of overlapping screens of color.

Although he was trained in the Florentine tradition, many of Giotto's principal works were produced elsewhere. After a sojourn in Rome during the last years of the thirteenth century, he was called to Padua in northern Italy soon after 1300 to paint frescos (see "Buon Fresco," above) for a new chapel being constructed at the site of an ancient Roman arena—explaining why it is usually

referred to as the Arena Chapel. The chapel was commissioned by Enrico Scrovegni, whose family fortune was made through the practice of usury—which at this time meant charging interest when loaning money, a sin so grave that it resulted in exclusion from the Christian sacraments. Enrico's father, Regibaldo, was a particularly egregious case (he appears in Dante's *Inferno* as the prototypical usurer), but evidence suggests that Enrico followed in his father's footsteps, and the building of the Arena Chapel next to his new palatial residence seems to have been conceived at least in part as a penitential act, part of Enrico's campaign not only to atone for his father's sins, but also to seek absolution for his own. He was pardoned by Pope Benedict XI (pontificate 1303–1304).

That Scrovegni called two of the most famous artists of the time—Giotto and Giovanni Pisano (see FIG. 17-36)—to decorate his chapel indicates that his goals were to express his power, sophistication, and prestige, as well as to atone for his sins. The building itself has little architectural distinction. It is a simple, barrel-vaulted room that provides broad walls, a boxlike space to showcase Giotto's paintings (FIG. 18-7). Giotto covered the entrance wall with the *Last Judgment* (not visible here), and the sanctuary wall with three highlighted scenes from the life of Christ. The Annunciation spreads over the two painted architectural frameworks on either side of the high arched opening into the sanctuary itself.

18-7 • Giotto di Bondone **SCROVEGNI (ARENA) CHAPEL, VIEW TOWARD EAST WALL**
Padua. 1305–1306. Frescos.

 View the Closer Look for the Scrovegni Chapel on myartslab.com

Below this are, to the left, the scene of Judas receiving payment for betraying Jesus, and, to the right, the scene of the Visitation, where the Virgin, pregnant with God incarnate, embraces her cousin Elizabeth, pregnant with John the Baptist. The compositions and color arrangement of these two scenes create a symmetrical pairing that encourages viewers to relate them, comparing the ill-gotten financial gains of Judas (a rather clear reference to Scrovegni usury) to the miraculous pregnancy that brought the promise of salvation.

Giotto subdivided the side walls of the chapel into framed pictures. A dado of faux-marble and allegorical **grisaille** (monochrome paintings in shades of gray) paintings of the Virtues and Vices support vertical bands painted to resemble marble inlay into which are inserted painted imitations of carved medallions. The central band of medallions spans the vault, crossing a brilliant, lapis-blue, star-spangled sky in which large portrait disks float like glowing moons. Set into this framework are three horizontal bands of rectangular narrative scenes from the life of the Virgin and her parents at the top, and Jesus along the middle and lower registers,

constituting together the primary religious program of the chapel.

Both the individual scenes and the overall program display Giotto's genius for distilling complex stories into a series of compelling moments. He concentrates on the human dimensions of the unfolding drama—from touches of anecdotal humor to expressions of profound anguish—rather than on its symbolic or theological weight. His prodigious narrative skills are apparent in a set of scenes from Christ's life on the north wall (**FIG. 18-8**). At top left Jesus performs his first miracle, changing water into wine at the wedding feast at Cana. The wine steward—looking very much like the jars of new wine himself—sips the results. To the right is the Raising of Lazarus, where boldly modeled and individualized figures twist in space. Through their postures and gestures they react to the human drama by pleading for Jesus' help, or by expressing either astonishment at the miracle or revulsion at the smell of death. Jesus is separated from the crowd. His transforming gesture is highlighted against the dark blue of the background, his profile face locked in communication with the similarly isolated

18-8 • Giotto di Bondone MARRIAGE AT CANA, RAISING OF LAZARUS, LAMENTATION, AND RESURRECTION/NOLI ME TANGERE
North wall of Scrovegni (Arena) Chapel, Padua. 1305–1306. Fresco, each scene approx. 6'5″ × 6' (2 × 1.85 m).

Lazarus, whose eyes—still fixed in death—let us know that the miracle is just about to happen.

On the lower register, where Jesus' grief-stricken followers lament over his dead body, Giotto conveys palpable human suffering, drawing viewers into a circle of personal grief. The stricken Virgin pulls close to her dead son, communing with mute intensity, while John the Evangelist flings his arms back in convulsive despair and others hunch over the corpse. Giotto has linked this somber scene—much as he linked the scene of Judas' pact and the Visitation across the sanctuary arch—to the mourning of Lazarus on the register above through the seemingly continuous diagonal implied by the sharply angled hillside behind both scenes and by the rhyming repetition of mourners in each scene—facing in opposite directions—who throw back their arms to express their emotional state. Viewers would know that the mourning in both

scenes is resolved by resurrection, portrayed in the last picture in this set.

Following traditional medieval practice, the fresco program is full of scenes and symbols like these that are intended to be contemplated as coordinated or contrasting juxtapositions. What is new here is the way Giotto draws us into the experience of these events. This direct emotional appeal not only allows viewers to imagine these scenes in relation to their own life experiences; it also embodies the new Franciscan emphasis on personal devotion rooted in empathetic responses to sacred stories.

One of the most gripping paintings in the chapel is Giotto's portrayal of the **KISS OF JUDAS**, the moment of betrayal that represents the first step on Jesus' road to the Crucifixion (**FIG. 18-9**). Savior and traitor are slightly off-center in the near foreground. The expansive sweep of Judas' strident yellow cloak—the same outfit he wore at the scene of his payment for the betrayal on the strip of wall to the left of the sanctuary arch—almost completely swallows Christ's body. Surrounding them, faces glare from all directions. A bristling array of weapons radiating from the confrontation draws attention to the encounter between Christ and Judas and documents the militarism of the arresting battalion. Jesus stands solid, a model of calm resolve that recalls his visual characterization in the Resurrection of Lazarus, and forms a striking foil to the noisy and chaotic aggression that engulfs him. Judas, in simian profile, purses his lips for the treacherous kiss that will betray Jesus to his captors, setting up a mythic confrontation of good and evil. In a subplot to the left, Peter lunges forward to sever the ear of a member of the arresting retinue. They are behind another broad sweep of fabric, this one extended by an ominous figure seen from behind and completely concealed except for the clenched hand that pulls at Peter's mantle. Indeed, a broad expanse of cloth and lateral gestures creates a barrier along the picture plane—as if to protect viewers from the compressed chaos of the scene itself. Rarely has this poignant event been visualized with such riveting power.

SIENESE PAINTING

Like their Florentine rivals, Sienese painters were rooted in thirteenth-century pictorial traditions, especially those of Byzantine art. Sienese painting emphasized the decorative potential of narrative painting, with brilliant, jewel-like colors and elegantly posed figures. For this reason, some art historians consider Sienese art more conservative than Florentine art, but we will see that it has its own charm, and its own narrative strategies.

DUCCIO DI BUONINSEGNA Siena's foremost painter was Duccio di Buoninsegna (active 1278–1318), whose creative synthesis of Byzantine and French Gothic sources transformed the tradition in which he worked. Between 1308 and 1311, Duccio and his workshop painted a huge altarpiece commissioned for Siena Cathedral and known as the **MAESTÀ** ("Majesty") (**FIG. 18-10**). Creating this altarpiece—assembled from many wood panels bonded together before painting—was an arduous undertaking. The work was not only large—the central panel alone was 7 by 13 feet—but it had to be painted on both sides since it could

18-10 • Duccio di Buoninsegna
CONJECTURAL RECONSTRUCTION OF THE FRONT (A) AND BACK (B) OF THE MAESTÀ ALTARPIECE
Made for Siena Cathedral. 1308–1311. Tempera and gold on wood, main front panel 7′ × 13′ (2.13 × 4.12 m).

Read the document related to Duccio's *Maestà* on myartslab.com

18–11 • Duccio di Buoninsegna
RAISING OF LAZARUS
From the predella of the back of the
Maestà altarpiece (lower right corner of
FIG. 18–10B), made for Siena Cathedral.
1308–1311. Tempera and gold on
wood, 17⅛″ × 18¼″ (43.5 × 46.4 cm).
Kimbell Art Museum, Fort Worth, Texas.

be seen from all directions when installed on the main altar at the center of the sanctuary.

Because the *Maestà* was dismantled in 1771, its power and beauty can only be imagined from scattered parts, some still in Siena but others elsewhere. FIGURE 18–10A is a reconstruction of how the front of the original altarpiece might have looked. It is dominated by a large representation of the Virgin and Child in Majesty (thus its title of *Maestà*), flanked by 20 angels and ten saints, including the four patron saints of Siena kneeling in the foreground. Above and below this lateral tableau were small narrative scenes from the last days of the life of the Virgin (above) and the infancy of Christ (spread across the predella). An inscription running around the base of Mary's majestic throne places the artist's signature within an optimistic framework: "Holy Mother of God, be thou the cause of peace for Siena and life to Duccio because he painted thee thus." This was not Duccio's first work for the cathedral. In 1288, he had designed a stunning stained-glass window portraying the Death, Assumption, and Coronation of the Virgin for the huge circular opening in the east wall of the sanctuary. It would have hovered over the installed *Maestà* when it was placed on the altar in 1311.

On the back of the *Maestà* (FIG. 18–10B) were episodes from the life of Christ, focusing on his Passion. Sacred narrative unfolds in elegant episodes enacted by graceful figures who seem to dance their way through these stories while still conveying emotional content. Characteristic of Duccio's narrative style is the scene of the **RAISING OF LAZARUS** (FIG. 18–11). Lyrical figures enact the event with graceful decorum, but their highly charged glances and expressive gestures—especially the bold reach of Christ—convey a strong sense of dramatic urgency that contrasts with the tense stillness that we saw in Giotto's rendering of this same moment of confrontation (see FIG. 18–8). Duccio's shading of drapery, like his modeling of faces, faithfully describes the figures' three-dimensionality, but the crisp outlines of the jewel-colored shapes created by their clothing, as well as the sinuous continuity of folds and gestures, generate rhythmic patterns crisscrossing the surface. Experimentation with the portrayal of space extends from the receding rocks of the mountainous landscape to carefully studied interiors, here the tomb of Lazarus whose heavy door was removed by the straining hug of a bystander to reveal the shrouded figure of Jesus' resurrected friend, propped up against the door jamb.

Duccio's rendering of the **BETRAYAL OF JESUS** (FIG. 18–12) is more expansive, both pictorially and temporally, occupying one of the broadest panels in the altarpiece (see FIG. 18–10B, lower center) and encompassing within this one composition several moments in the sequential narrative of its subject matter. The tableau is centered and stabilized by the frontal figure of Jesus, whose dark mantle with its sinuous gold trim stands out from the densely packed, colorful crowd of figures surrounding him. Judas approaches from the left to identify Jesus; although the heads of betrayer and betrayed touch in this moment, Duccio avoids the psychological power of Giotto's face-to-face confrontation in the Scrovegni chapel (see FIG. 18–9). Flanking Duccio's stable, packed central scene of betrayal, are two subsequent moments in the story, each pulling our attention away from the center and toward the sides. To the left, with a forceful stride and dynamic gesture, the apostle Peter lunges to sever the ear of a member of the arresting party, while on the other side of the composition a group of fearful apostles rushes gracefully but with united resolve to escape the central scene, abandoning Jesus to his fate. Within the complexity of this broad, multi-figure, continuous narrative, Duccio manages to express—through the postures and facial expressions of his figures—the emotional charge of these pivotal moments in the narrative of Christ's Passion. At the same time, he creates a dazzling picture, as rich in color and linear elegance as it is faithful to the human dimensions of the situations it portrays.

The enthusiasm with which citizens greeted a great painting or altarpiece like the *Maestà* demonstrates the power of images as well as the association of such magnificent works with the glory of the city itself. According to a contemporary account, on December 20, 1311, the day that Duccio's altarpiece was carried from his workshop to the cathedral, all the shops were shut, and everyone in the city participated in the procession, with "bells ringing joyously, out of reverence for so noble a picture as is this" (Holt, p. 69).

SIMONE MARTINI The generation of painters who followed Duccio continued to paint in the elegant style he established, combining the evocation of three-dimensional form with a graceful continuity of linear pattern. One of Duccio's most successful and innovative followers was Simone Martini (c. 1284–1344), whose paintings were in high demand throughout Italy, including in Assisi where he covered the walls of the St. Martin Chapel with frescos between 1312 and 1319. His most famous work, however, was commissioned in 1333 for the cathedral of his native Siena, an altarpiece of the **ANNUNCIATION** flanked by two saints (**FIG. 18-13**) that he painted in collaboration with his brother-in-law, Lippo Memmi.

18-12 • Duccio di Buoninsegna BETRAYAL OF JESUS
From the back of the *Maestà* altarpiece (lower center of FIG. 18–10B), made for Siena Cathedral. 1308–1311.
Tempera and gold on wood, 22½″ × 40″ (57.2 × 101.6 cm). Museo dell'Opera del Duomo, Siena.

Il Libro dell' Arte (*The Book of Art*) of Cennino Cennini (c. 1370–1440) is a compendium of Florentine painting techniques from about 1400 that includes step-by-step instructions for making panel paintings, a process also used in Sienese paintings of the same period.

The wood for the panels, he explains, should be fine-grained, free of blemishes, and thoroughly seasoned by slow drying. The first step in preparing such a panel for painting was to cover its surface with clean white linen strips soaked in a **gesso** made from gypsum, a task, he tells us, best done on a dry, windy day. Gesso provided a ground, or surface, on which to paint, and Cennini specified that at least nine layers should be applied. The gessoed surface should then be burnished until it resembles ivory. Only then could the artist sketch the composition of the work with charcoal made from burned willow twigs. At this point, advised Cennini, "When you have finished drawing your figure, especially if it is in a very valuable [altarpiece], so that you are counting on profit and reputation from it, leave it alone for a few days, going back to it now and then to look it over and improve it wherever it still needs something. When it seems to you about right (and bear in mind that you may copy and examine things done by other good masters; that it is no shame to you) when the figure is satisfactory, take the feather and rub it over the drawing very lightly, until the drawing is practically effaced" (Cennini, trans. Thompson, p. 75). At this point, the final design would be inked in with a fine squirrel-hair brush. Gold leaf, he advises, should be affixed on a humid day, the tissue-thin sheets carefully glued down with a mixture of fine powdered clay and egg white on the reddish clay ground called bole. Then the gold is burnished with a gemstone or the tooth of a carnivorous animal. Punched and incised patterning should be added to the gold leaf later.

Fourteenth- and fifteenth-century Italian painters worked principally in tempera paint, powdered pigments mixed with egg yolk, a little water, and an occasional touch of glue. Apprentices were kept busy grinding pigments and mixing paints, setting them out for more senior painters in wooden bowls or shell dishes.

Cennini outlined a detailed and highly formulaic painting process. Faces, for example, were always to be done last, with flesh tones applied over two coats of a light greenish pigment and highlighted with touches of red and white. The finished painting was to be given a layer of varnish to protect it and intensify its colors.

Read the document related to Cennino Cennini on myartslab.com

18–13 • Simone Martini and Lippo Memmi ANNUNCIATION Made for Siena Cathedral. 1333. Tempera and gold on wood, 10′ × 8′9″ (3 × 2.67 m). Galleria degli Uffizi, Florence.

18-14 • AERIAL VIEW OF THE CAMPO IN SIENA WITH THE PALAZZO PUBBLICO (CITY HALL INCLUDING ITS TOWER) FACING ITS STRAIGHT SIDE
Siena. Palazzo Pubblico 1297–c. 1315; tower 1320s–1340s.

The smartly dressed figure of Gabriel—the extended flourish of his drapery behind him suggesting he has just arrived, and with some speed—raises his hand to address the Virgin. The words of his message are actually incised into the gold-leafed gesso of the background, running from his opened mouth toward the Virgin's ear: *Ave gratia plena dominus tecum* (Luke 1:28: "Hail, full of grace, the Lord is with thee"). Seemingly frightened—at the very least startled—by this forceful and unexpected celestial messenger, Mary recoils into her lavish throne, her thumb inserted into the book she had been reading to safeguard her place, while her other hand pulls at her clothing in an elegant gesture of nobility ultimately deriving from the courtly art of thirteenth-century Paris (see Solomon, second lancet from the right in FIGURE 17–11).

AMBROGIO LORENZETTI The most important civic structure in Siena was the **PALAZZO PUBBLICO (FIG. 18-14)**, the town hall which served as the seat of government, just as the Palazzo della Signoria did in rival Florence (see FIG. 18-2). There are similarities between these two buildings. Both are designed as strong, fortified structures sitting on the edge of a public piazza; both have a tall tower, making them visible signs of the city from a considerable distance. The Palazzo Pubblico was constructed from 1297 to c. 1315, but the tower was not completed until 1348, when the bronze bell, which rang to signal meetings of the ruling council, was installed.

The interior of the Palazzo Pubblico was the site of important commissions by some of Siena's most famous artists. In c. 1315, Simone Martini painted a large mural of the Virgin in Majesty surrounded by saints—clearly based on Duccio's recently installed *Maestà*. Then, in 1338, the Siena city council commissioned Ambrogio Lorenzetti to paint frescos for the council room of the Palazzo known as the Sala dei Nove (Chamber of the Nine) or Sala della Pace (Chamber of Peace) on the theme of the contrast between good and bad government (see FIG. 18–1).

Ambrogio painted the results of both good and bad government on the two long walls. For the expansive scene of **THE EFFECTS OF GOOD GOVERNMENT IN THE CITY AND IN THE COUNTRY**, and in tribute to his patrons, Ambrogio created an idealized but recognizable portrait of the city of Siena and its immediate environs (**FIG. 18-15**). The cathedral dome and the distinctive striped campanile are visible in the upper left-hand corner; the streets are filled with the bustling activity of productive citizens who also have time for leisurely diversions. Ambrogio shows the city from shifting viewpoints so we can see as much as possible, and renders its inhabitants larger in scale than the buildings around them so as to highlight their activity. Featured in the foreground is a circle of dancers—probably a professional troupe of male entertainers masquerading as women as part of a spring festival—and above them, at the top of the painting, a band of masons stand on exterior scaffolding constructing the wall of a new building.

The Porta Romana, Siena's gateway leading to Rome, divides the thriving city from its surrounding countryside. In this panoramic landscape painting, Ambrogio describes a natural world marked by agricultural productivity, showing activities of all seasons simultaneously—sowing, hoeing, and harvesting. Hovering above the gate that separates city life and country life is a woman clad in a wisp of transparent drapery, a scroll in one hand and a miniature gallows complete with a hanged man in the other. She represents Security, and her scroll bids those coming to the city to enter without fear because she has taken away the power of the guilty who would harm them.

The world of the Italian city-states—which had seemed so full of promise in Ambrogio Lorenzetti's *Good Government* fresco—was transformed as the middle of the century approached into uncertainty and desolation by a series of natural and societal disasters. In 1333, a flood devastated Florence, followed by banking failures in the 1340s, famine in 1346–1347, and epidemics of the bubonic plague, especially virulent in the summer of 1348, just a few years after Ambrogio's frescos were completed. Some art historians have traced the influence of these calamities on the visual arts at the middle of the fourteenth century (see "The Black Death," page 550). Yet as dark as those days must have seemed to the men and women living through them, the strong currents of cultural and artistic change initiated earlier in the century would persist. In a relatively short span of time, the European Middle Ages gave way in Florence to a new movement that would blossom in the Italian Renaissance.

FRANCE

At the beginning of the fourteenth century, the royal court in Paris was still the arbiter of taste in western Europe, as it had been in the days of King Louis IX (St. Louis). During the Hundred Years' War, however, the French countryside was ravaged by armed struggles and civil strife. The power of the nobility, weakened significantly by warfare, was challenged by townsmen, who took advantage of new economic opportunities that opened up in the wake of the conflict. As centers of art and architecture, the duchy of Burgundy, England, and, for a brief golden moment, the court of Prague began to rival Paris.

French sculptors found lucrative new outlets for their work—not only in stone, but in wood, ivory, and precious metals, often decorated with enamel and gemstones—in the growing demand among wealthy patrons for religious art intended for homes as well as churches. Manuscript painters likewise created lavishly illustrated books for the personal devotions of the wealthy and powerful. And

18-15 • Ambrogio Lorenzetti THE EFFECTS OF GOOD GOVERNMENT IN THE CITY AND IN THE COUNTRY
Sala dei Nove (also known as Sala della Pace), Palazzo Pubblico, Siena, Italy. 1338–1339. Fresco, total length about 46′ (14 m).

architectural commissions focused on exquisitely detailed chapels or small churches, often under private patronage, rather than on the building of grand cathedrals funded by Church institutions.

MANUSCRIPT ILLUMINATION

By the late thirteenth century, private prayer books became popular among wealthy patrons. Because they contained special prayers to be recited at the eight canonical devotional "hours" between morning and night, an individual copy of one of these books came to be called a **Book of Hours**. Such a book included everything the lay person needed for pious practice—psalms, prayers and offices of the Virgin and other saints (such as the owners' patron or the patron of their home church), a calendar of feast days, and sometimes prayers for the dead. During the fourteenth century, a richly decorated Book of Hours was worn or carried like jewelry, counting among a noble person's most important portable possessions.

THE BOOK OF HOURS OF JEANNE D'ÉVREUX Perhaps at their marriage in 1324, King Charles IV gave his 14-year-old queen, Jeanne d'Évreux, a tiny Book of Hours—it fits easily when open within one hand—illuminated by Parisian painter Jean Pucelle (see "A Closer Look," page 551). This book was so precious to the queen that she mentioned it and its illuminator specifically in her will, leaving this royal treasure to King Charles V. Pucelle painted the book's pictures in *grisaille*—monochromatic painting in shades of gray with only delicate touches of color. His style clearly derives from the courtly mode established in Paris at the time of St. Louis, with its softly modeled, voluminous draperies gathered loosely and falling in projecting diagonal folds around tall, elegantly posed figures with carefully coiffed curly hair, broad foreheads, and delicate features. But his conception of space, with figures placed within coherent, discrete architectural settings, suggests a firsthand knowledge of contemporary Sienese art.

Jeanne appears in the initial *D* below the Annunciation, kneeling in prayer before a lectern, perhaps using this Book of Hours to guide her meditations, beginning with the words written on this page: *Domine labia mea aperies* (Psalm 51:15: "O Lord, open thou my lips"). The juxtaposition of the praying Jeanne's portrait with a scene from the life of the Virgin Mary suggests that the sacred scene is actually a vision inspired by Jeanne's meditations. The young queen might have identified with and sought to feel within herself Mary's joy at Gabriel's message. Given what we know of Jeanne's own life story and her royal husband's predicament, it might also have directed the queen's prayers toward the fulfillment of his wish for a male heir.

In the Annunciation, Mary is shown receiving the archangel Gabriel in a Gothic building that seems to project outward from the page toward the viewer, while rejoicing angels look on from windows under the eaves. The group of romping youths at the bottom of the page at first glance seems to echo the angelic jubilation. Folklorists have suggested, however, that the children are playing "froggy in the middle" or "hot cockles," games in which one child was tagged by the others. To the medieval viewer, if the game symbolized the mocking of Christ or the betrayal of Judas, who "tags" his friend, it would have evoked a darker mood by referring to the picture on the other page of this opening, foreshadowing Jesus' imminent death even as his life is beginning.

📖— **Read** the document related to *The Effects of Good Government in the City and in the Country* on myartslab.com

A deadly outbreak of the bubonic plague, known as the Black Death after the dark sores that developed on the bodies of its victims, spread to Europe from Asia, both by land and by sea, in the middle of the fourteenth century. At least half the urban population of Florence and Siena—some estimate 80 percent—died during the summer of 1348, probably including the artists Andrea Pisano and Ambrogio Lorenzetti. Death was so quick and widespread that basic social structures crumbled in the resulting chaos; people did not know where the disease came from, what caused it, or how long the pandemic would last.

Mid-twentieth-century art historian Millard Meiss proposed that the Black Death had a significant impact on the development of Italian art in the middle of the fourteenth century. Pointing to what he saw as a reactionary return to hieratic linearity in religious art, Meiss theorized that artists had retreated from the rounded forms that had characterized the work of Giotto to old-fashioned styles, and that this artistic change reflected a growing reliance on traditional religious values in the wake of a disaster that some interpreted as God's punishment of a world in moral decline.

An altarpiece painted in 1354–1357 by Andrea di Cione, nicknamed Orcagna ("Archangel"), under the patronage of Tommaso Strozzi—the so-called Strozzi Altarpiece (**FIG. 18–16**)—is an example of the sort of paintings that led Meiss to his interpretation. This painting's otherworldly vision is dominated by a central figure of Christ, presumably enthroned, but without any hint of an actual seat, evoking the image of the judge at the Last Judgment, outside time and space. The silhouetted outlines of the standing and kneeling saints emphasize surface over depth; the gold expanse of floor beneath them does not offer any reassuring sense of spatial recession to contain them and their activity. Throughout, line and color are more prominent than form.

Recent art historians have stepped back from Meiss's contextual explanation of stylistic change. Some have pointed out logical relationships between style and subject in the works Meiss cites; others have seen in them a mannered outgrowth of current style rather than a reversion to an earlier style; still others have discounted the underlying notion that stylistic change is connected with social situations. But there is a clear relationship of works such as the Strozzi Altarpiece with death and judgment, sanctity and the promise of salvation—themes also suggested in the narrative scenes on the **predella** (the lower zone of the altarpiece): Thomas Aquinas's ecstasy during Mass, Christ's miraculous walk on water to rescue Peter, and the salvation of Emperor Henry II because of a pious donation. While these are not uncommon scenes in sacred art, it is easy to see a relationship between their choice as subject matter here and the specter cast by the Black Death over a world that had just imagined its prosperity in pathbreaking works of visual art firmly rooted in references to everyday life (see FIG. 18–15).

18–16 • Andrea di Cione (nicknamed Orcagna) ENTHRONED CHRIST WITH SAINTS, FROM THE STROZZI ALTARPIECE
Strozzi Chapel, Santa Maria Novella, Florence. 1354–1357. Tempera and gold on wood, 9′ × 9′8″ (2.74 × 2.95 m).

Read the document related to the Black Death on myartslab.com

A CLOSER LOOK | The Hours of Jeanne d'Évreux

by Jean Pucelle, Two-Page Opening with the Kiss of Judas and the Annunciation.
Paris. c. 1324–1328. *Grisaille* and color on vellum, each page 3⅝″ × 2⁷⁄₁₆″ (9.2 × 6.2 cm).
Metropolitan Museum of Art, New York. The Cloisters Collection (54.1.2), fols. 15v–16r

In this opening Pucelle juxtaposes complementary scenes drawn from the Infancy and Passion of Christ, placed on opposing pages, in a scheme known as the Joys and Sorrows of the Virgin. The "joy" of the Annunciation on the right is paired with the "sorrow" of the betrayal and arrest of Christ on the left.

Christ sways back gracefully as Judas betrays him with a kiss. The S-curve of his body mirrors the Virgin's pose on the opposite page, as both accept their fate with courtly decorum.

The prominent lamp held aloft by a member of the arresting battalion informs the viewer that this scene takes place at night, in the dark.

The angel who holds up the boxlike enclosure where the Annunciation takes place is an allusion to the legend of the miraculous transportation of this building from Nazareth to Loreto in 1294.

Christ reaches casually down to heal Malchus, the assistant of the high priest whose ear Peter had just cut off in angry retaliation for his participation in the arrest of Jesus.

Scenes of secular amusements from everyday life, visual puns, and off-color jokes appear at the bottom of many pages of this book. Sometimes they relate to the themes of the sacred scenes above them. These comic knights riding goats may be a commentary on the lack of valor shown by the soldiers assaulting Jesus, especially if this wine barrel conjured up for Jeanne an association with the Eucharist.

The candle held by the cleric who guards the "door" to Jeanne's devotional retreat, as well as the rabbit emerging from its burrow in the marginal scene, are sexually charged symbols of fertility that seem directly related to the focused prayers of a child bride required to produce a male heir.

 View the Closer Look for the Hours of Jeanne d'Évreux on myartslab.com

Fourteenth-century Paris was renowned for more than its goldsmiths (see FIG. 18–20). Among the most sumptuous and sought-after Parisian luxury products were small chests assembled from carved ivory plaques that were used by wealthy women to store jewelry or other personal treasures. The entirely secular subject matter of these chests explored romantic love. Indeed, they seem to have been courtship gifts from smitten men to desired women, or wedding presents offered by grooms to their brides.

A chest from around 1330–1350, now in the Walters Museum (FIGS. 18–17, 18–18, 18–19), is one of seven that have survived intact; there are fragments of a dozen more. It is a delightful and typical example. Figural relief covers five exterior sides of the box: around the perimeter and on the hinged top. The assembled panels were joined by metal hardware—strips, brackets, hinges, handles, and locks—originally

wrought in silver. Although some chests tell a single romantic story in sequential episodes, most, like this one, anthologize scenes drawn from a group of stories, combining courtly romance, secular allegory, and ancient fables.

On the lid of the Walters casket (see FIG. 18–18), jousting is the theme. Spread over the central two panels, a single scene catches two charging knights in the heat of a tournament, while trumpeting heralds call the attention of spectators, lined up above in a gallery to observe this public display of virility. The panel at right mocks the very ritual showcased in the middle panels by pitting a woman against a knight, battling not with lances but with a long-stemmed rose (symbolizing sexual surrender) and an oak bough (symbolizing fertility). Instead of observing these silly goings-on, however, the spectators tucked into the upper architecture pursue their own amorous flirtations. Finally, in the scene on the left,

knights use crossbows and a catapult to hurl roses at the Castle of Love, while Cupid returns fire with his seductive arrows.

On the front of the chest (see FIG. 18–17), generalized romantic allegory gives way to vignettes from a specific story. At left, the long-bearded Aristotle teaches the young Alexander the Great, using exaggerated gestures and an authoritative text to emphasize his point. Today's lesson is a stern warning not to allow the seductive power of women to distract the young prince from his studies. The subsequent scene, however, pokes fun at his eminent teacher, who has become so smitten by the wiles of a young beauty named Phyllis that he lets her ride him around like a horse, while his student observes this farce, peering out of the castle in the background. The two scenes at right relate to an eastern legend of the fountain of youth, popular in medieval Europe. A line of bearded elders approaches the fountain

18-17 • SMALL IVORY CHEST WITH SCENES FROM COURTLY ROMANCES
Made in Paris. c. 1330–1350. Elephant ivory with modern iron mounts, height 4½″ (11.5 cm), width 9¹¹⁄₁₆″ (24.6 cm), depth 4⅞″ (12.4 cm). The Walters Art Museum, Baltimore.

from the left, steadied by their canes. But after having partaken of its transforming effects, two newly rejuvenated couples, now nude, bathe and flirt within the fountain's basin. The man first in line for treatment, stepping up to climb into the fountain, looks suspiciously like the figure of the aging Aristotle, forming a link between the two stories on the casket front.

Unlike royal marriages of the time, which were essentially business contracts based on political or financial exigencies, the romantic love of the aristocratic wealthy involved passionate devotion. Images of gallant knights and their coy paramours, who could bring intoxicating bliss or cruelly withhold their love on a whim, captured the popular Gothic imagination. They formed the principal subject matter on personal luxury objects, not only chests like this, but mirror backs, combs, writing tablets, even ceremonial saddles. And these stories evoke themes that still captivate us since they reflect notions of desire and betrayal, cruel rejection and blissful folly, at play in our own romantic conquests and relationships to this day. In this way they allow us some access to the lives of the people who commissioned and owned these precious objects, even if we ourselves are unable to afford them.

18–18 • ATTACK ON THE CASTLE OF LOVE
Top of the chest in FIG. 18–17.

18-19 • TRISTAN AND ISEULT AT THE FOUNTAIN; CAPTURE OF THE UNICORN
Left short side of the chest in FIG. 18–17.

Two other well-known medieval themes are juxtaposed on this plaque from the short side of the ivory chest. At left, Tristan and Iseult have met secretly for an illicit romantic tryst, while Iseult's husband, King Mark, tipped off by an informant, observes them from a tree. But when they see his reflection in a fountain between them, they alter their behavior accordingly, and the king believes them innocent of the adultery he had (rightly) suspected. The medieval bestiary ("book of beasts") claimed that only a virgin could capture the mythical unicorn, which at right lays his head, with its aggressively phallic horn, into the lap of just such a pure maiden so that the hunter can take advantage of her alluring powers over the animal to kill it with his phallic counterpart of its horn, a large spear.

METALWORK AND IVORY

Fourteenth-century French sculpture is intimate in character. Religious subjects became more emotionally expressive; objects became smaller and demanded closer scrutiny from the viewer. In the secular realm, tales of love and valor were carved on luxury items to delight the rich (see "An Ivory Chest with Scenes of Romance," page 552). Precious materials—gold, silver, and ivory—were preferred.

THE VIRGIN AND CHILD FROM SAINT-DENIS
A silver-gilt image of a standing **VIRGIN AND CHILD** (**FIG. 18-20**) is a rare survivor that verifies the acclaim that was accorded fourteenth-century Parisian goldsmiths. An inscription on the base documents the statue's donation to the abbey church of Saint-Denis in 1339 and the donor's name, the same Queen Jeanne d'Évreux whose Book of Hours we have just examined. In a style that recalls the work of artist Jean Pucelle in that Book of Hours, the Virgin holds Jesus in her left arm with her weight on her left leg, standing in a graceful, characteristically Gothic S-curve pose. Mary originally wore a crown, and she still holds a large enameled and jeweled *fleur-de-lis*—the heraldic symbol of royal France—which served as a reliquary container for strands of Mary's hair. The Christ Child, reaching out tenderly to caress his mother's face, is babylike in both form and posture. On the base, minuscule statues of prophets stand on projecting piers to separate 14 enameled scenes from Christ's Infancy and Passion, reminding us of the suffering to come. The apple in the baby's hand carries the theme further with its reference to Christ's role as the new Adam, whose sacrifice on the cross—medieval Christians believed—redeemed humanity from the first couple's fall into sin when Eve bit into the forbidden fruit.

ENGLAND

Fourteenth-century England prospered in spite of the ravages of the Black Death and the Hundred Years' War with France. English life at this time is described in the brilliant social commentary of Geoffrey Chaucer in the *Canterbury Tales* (see "A New Spirit in Fourteenth-Century Literature," page 533). The royal family, especially Edward I (r. 1272–1307)—the castle builder—and many of the nobles and bishops were generous patrons of the arts.

EMBROIDERY: OPUS ANGLICANUM
Since the thirteenth century, the English had been renowned for pictorial needlework, using colored silk and gold threads to create images as detailed as contemporary painters produced in manuscripts. Popular throughout

18-20 • VIRGIN AND CHILD
c. 1324–1339. Silver gilt and enamel, height 27⅛" (69 cm).
Musée du Louvre, Paris.

Europe, the art came to be called *opus anglicanum* ("English work"). The popes had more than 100 pieces in the Vatican treasury. The names of several prominent embroiderers are known, but in the thirteenth century no one surpassed Mabel of Bury St. Edmunds, who created both religious and secular articles for King Henry III (r. 1216–1272).

THE CHICHESTER-CONSTABLE CHASUBLE This *opus anglicanum* liturgical vestment worn by a priest during Mass (**FIG. 18-21**) was embroidered c. 1330–1350 with images formed by subtle gradations of colored silk. Where gold threads were laid and couched (tacked down with colored silk), the effect resembles the burnished gold-leaf backgrounds of manuscript illuminations.

The Annunciation, the Adoration of the Magi, and the Coronation of the Virgin are set in cusped, crocketed ogee (S-shape) arches, supported on animal-head corbels and twisting branches sprouting oak leaves with seed-pearl acorns. Because the star and crescent moon in the Coronation of the Virgin scene are heraldic emblems of Edward III (r. 1327–1377), perhaps he or a family member commissioned this luxurious vestment.

During the celebration of the Mass, especially as the priest moved, *opus anglicanum* would have glinted in the candlelight amid treasures on the altar. Court dress was just as rich and colorful, and at court such embroidered garments proclaimed the rank and status of the wearer. So heavy did such gold and bejeweled garments become that their wearers often needed help to move.

18-21 • LIFE OF THE VIRGIN, BACK OF THE CHICHESTER-CONSTABLE CHASUBLE
From a set of vestments embroidered in *opus anglicanum* from southern England. c. 1330–1350. Red velvet with silk and metallic thread and seed pearls, length 4′3″ (129.5 cm), width 30″ (76 cm). Metropolitan Museum of Art, New York. Fletcher Fund, 1927 (27 162.1)

ARCHITECTURE

In the later years of the thirteenth century and early years of the fourteenth, a distinctive and influential Gothic architectural style, popularly known as the "Decorated style," developed in England. This change in taste has been credited to Henry III's ambition to surpass St. Louis, who was his brother-in-law, as a royal patron of the arts.

THE DECORATED STYLE AT EXETER One of the most complete Decorated-style buildings is **EXETER CATHEDRAL**. Thomas of Witney began construction in 1313 and remained master mason from 1316 to 1342. He supervised construction of the nave and redesigned upper parts of the choir. He left the towers of the original Norman cathedral but turned the interior into a dazzling stone forest of colonnettes, moldings, and vault ribs (**FIG. 18-22**). From piers formed by a cluster of colonnettes rise multiple moldings that make the arcade seem to ripple. Bundled colonnettes spring from sculptured foliate corbels (brackets that project from a wall) between the arches and rise up the wall to support conical clusters of 13 ribs that meet at the summit of the vault, a modest 69 feet above the floor. The basic structure here is the four-part vault with intersecting cross-ribs, but the designer added additional ribs, called tiercerons, to create a richer linear pattern. Elaborately carved **bosses** (decorative knoblike elements) signal the point where ribs meet along the ridge of the vault. Large bar-tracery clerestory windows illuminate the 300-foot-long nave. Unpolished gray marble shafts, yellow sandstone arches, and a white French stone, shipped from Caen, add subtle gradations of color to the upper wall.

Detailed records survive for the building of Exeter Cathedral, documenting work over the period from 1279 to 1514, with only two short breaks. They record where masons and carpenters were housed (in a hostel near the cathedral) and how they were paid (some by the day with extra for drinks, some by the week, some for each finished piece); how materials were acquired and transported (payments for horseshoes and fodder for the horses); and, of course, payments for the building materials (not only stone and wood but rope for measuring and parchment on which to draw forms for the masons). The bishops contributed generously to the building funds. This was not a labor only of love.

Thomas of Witney also designed the intricate, 57-foot-high bishop's throne (at right in FIGURE 18-22), constructed by Richard de Galmeton and Walter of Memburg, who led a team of a dozen carpenters. The

18-22 • INTERIOR, EXETER CATHEDRAL
Devon, England. Thomas of Witney, choir, 14th century and bishop's throne, 1313–1317; Robert Lesyngham, east window, 1389–1390.

canopy resembles embroidery translated into wood, with its maze of pinnacles, bursting with leafy crockets and tiny carved animals and heads. To finish the throne in splendor, Master Nicolas painted and gilded the wood. When the bishop was seated on his throne wearing embroidered vestments like the Chichester-Constable Chasuble (see FIG. 18–21), he must have resembled a golden image in a shrine—more a symbol of the power and authority of the Church than a specific human being.

THE PERPENDICULAR STYLE AT EXETER During years following the Black Death, work at Exeter Cathedral came to a standstill. The nave had been roofed but not vaulted, and the windows had no glass. When work could be resumed, tastes had changed. The exuberance of the Decorated style gave way to an austere style in which rectilinear patterns and sharp angular shapes replaced intricate curves, and luxuriant foliage gave way to simple stripped-down patterns. This phase is known as the Perpendicular style.

In 1389–1390, well-paid master mason Robert Lesyngham rebuilt the great east window (see FIG. 18–22, far wall), designing its tracery in the new Perpendicular style. The window fills the east wall of the choir like a glowing altarpiece. A single figure in each light stands under a tall painted canopy that flows into and blends with the stone tracery. The Virgin with the Christ Child stands in the center over the high altar, with four female saints at the left and four male saints on the right, including St. Peter, to whom the church is dedicated. At a distance, the colorful figures silhouetted against the silver *grisaille* glass become a band of color, conforming to and thus reinforcing the rectangular pattern of the mullions and transoms. The combination of *grisaille*, silver-oxide stain (staining clear glass with shades of yellow or gold), and colored glass produces a glowing wall and casts a cool, silvery light over the nearby stonework.

Perpendicular architecture heralds the Renaissance style in its regularity, its balanced horizontal and vertical lines, and its plain wall or window surfaces. When Tudor monarchs introduced Renaissance art into the British Isles, builders were not forced to rethink the form and structure of their buildings; they simply changed the ornament from the pointed cusps and crocketed arches of the Gothic style to the round arches and columns and capitals of Roman Classicism. The Perpendicular style itself became an English architectural vernacular. It has even been popular in the United States, especially for churches and college buildings.

THE HOLY ROMAN EMPIRE

By the fourteenth century, the Holy Roman Empire existed more as an ideal fiction than a fact. The Italian territories had established their independence, and in contrast to England and France, Germany had become further divided into multiple states with powerful regional associations and princes. The Holy Roman emperors, now elected by Germans, concentrated on securing the fortunes of their families. They continued to be patrons of the arts, promoting local styles.

MYSTICISM AND SUFFERING

The by-now-familiar ordeals of the fourteenth century—famines, wars, and plagues—helped inspire a mystical religiosity in Germany that emphasized both ecstatic joy and extreme suffering. Devotional images, known as *Andachtsbilder* in German, inspired worshipers to contemplate Jesus' first and last hours, especially during evening prayers, or vespers, giving rise to the term *Vesperbild* for the image of Mary mourning her son. Through such religious exercises, worshipers hoped to achieve understanding of the divine and union with God.

VESPERBILD In this well-known example (**FIG. 18–23**), blood gushes from the hideous rosettes that form the wounds of an emaciated and lifeless Jesus who teeters improbably on the lap of his

18-23 • VESPERBILD (PIETÀ)
From the Middle Rhine region, Germany. c. 1330. Wood and polychromy, height 34½″ (88.4 cm). Landesmuseum, Bonn.

hunched-over mother. The Virgin's face conveys the intensity of her ordeal, mingling horror, shock, pity, and grief. Such images took on greater poignancy since they would have been compared, in the worshiper's mind, to the familiar, almost ubiquitous images of the young Virgin mother holding her innocent and loving baby Jesus.

THE HEDWIG CODEX The extreme physicality and emotionalism of the *Vesperbild* finds parallels in the actual lives of some medieval saints in northern Europe. St. Hedwig (1174–1243), married at age 12 to Duke Henry I of Silesia and mother of his seven children, entered the Cistercian convent of Trebniz (in modern Poland) on her husband's death in 1238. She devoted the rest of her life to caring for the poor and seeking to emulate the suffering of Christ by walking barefoot in the snow. As described in her *vita* (biography), she had a particular affection for a small ivory statue of the Virgin and Child, which she carried with her at all times, and which "she often took up in her hands to envelop it in love, so that out of passion she could see it more often and through the seeing could prove herself more devout, inciting her to even greater love of the glorious Virgin. When she once blessed the sick with this image they were cured immediately" (translation from Schleif, p. 22). Hedwig was buried clutching the statue, and when her tomb was opened after her canonization in 1267, it was said that although most of her body had deteriorated, the fingers that still gripped the beloved object had miraculously not decayed.

A picture of Hedwig serves as the frontispiece (**FIG. 18-24**) of a manuscript of her *vita* known as the Hedwig Codex, commissioned

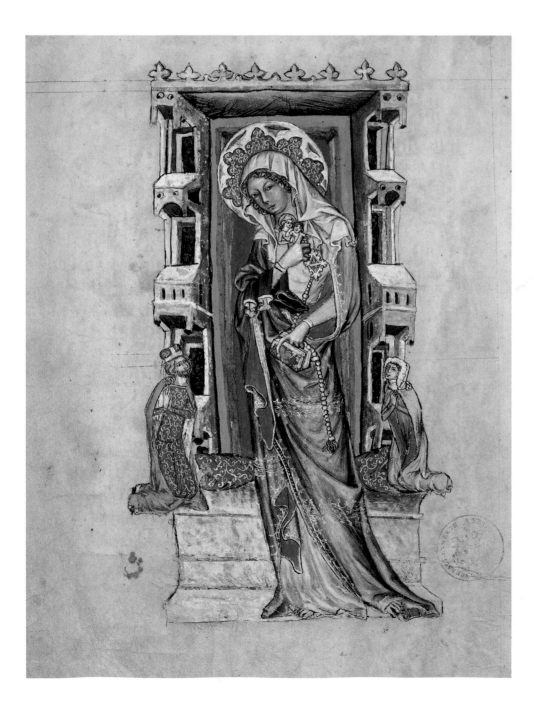

18-24 • ST. HEDWIG OF SILESIA WITH DUKE LUDWIG I OF LIEGNITZ-BRIEG AND DUCHESS AGNES
Dedication page of the Hedwig Codex. 1353. Ink and paint on parchment, 13⁷⁄₁₆″ × 9¾″ (34 × 25 cm). The J. Paul Getty Museum, Los Angeles. MS. Ludwig XI 7, fol. 12v

in 1353 by one her descendants, Ludwig I of Liegnitz-Brieg. Duke Ludwig and his wife, Agnes, are shown here kneeling on either side of St. Hedwig, dwarfed by the saint's architectural throne and her own imposing scale. With her prominent, spidery hands, she clutches the famous ivory statue, as well as a rosary and a prayer book, inserting her fingers within it to maintain her place as if our arrival had interrupted her devotions. She has draped her leather boots over her right wrist in a reference to her practice of removing them to walk in the snow. Hedwig's highly volumetric figure stands in a swaying pose of courtly elegance derived from French Gothic, but the fierce intensity of her gaze and posture are far removed from the mannered graciousness of the smiling angel of Reims (see statue at far left in FIG. 17-14), whose similar gesture

and extended finger are employed simply to grasp his drapery and assure its elegant display.

THE SUPREMACY OF PRAGUE

Charles IV of Bohemia (r. 1346–1378) was raised in France, and his admiration for the French king Charles IV was such that he changed his own name from Wenceslas to Charles. He was officially crowned king of Bohemia in 1347 and Holy Roman Emperor in 1355. He established his capital in Prague, which, in the view of his contemporaries, replaced Constantinople as the "New Rome." Prague had a great university, a castle, and a cathedral overlooking a town that spread on both sides of a river joined by a stone bridge, a remarkable structure itself.

choir

nave

18-25 • Heinrich and Peter Parler PLAN AND INTERIOR OF THE CHURCH OF THE HOLY CROSS, SCHWÄBISCH GMÜND
Germany. Begun in 1317 by Heinrich Parler; choir by Peter Parler begun in 1351; vaulting completed 16th century.

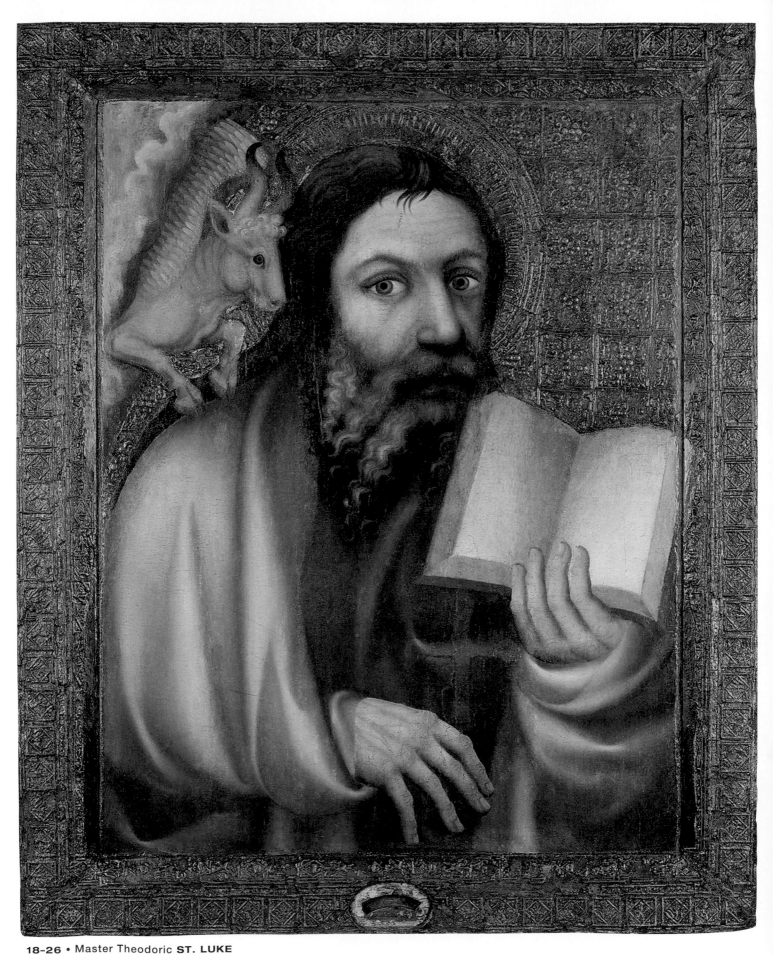

18-26 • Master Theodoric ST. LUKE
Holy Cross Chapel, Karlstejn Castle, near Prague. 1360–1364. Paint and gold on panel, 45¼" × 37" (115 × 94 cm).

When Pope Clement VI made Prague an archbishopric in 1344, construction began on a new cathedral in the Gothic style—to be named for St. Vitus. It would also serve as the coronation church and royal pantheon. But the choir was not finished for Charles's first coronation, so he brought Peter Parler from Swabia to complete it.

THE PARLER FAMILY In 1317, Heinrich Parler, a former master of works on Cologne Cathedral, designed and began building the church of the Holy Cross in Schwäbisch Gmünd, in southwest Germany. In 1351, his son Peter (c. 1330–1399), the most brilliant architect of this talented family, joined the workshop. Peter designed the choir (**FIG. 18-25**) in the manner of a hall church whose triple-aisled form was enlarged by a ring of deep chapels between the buttresses. The contrast between Heinrich's nave and Peter's choir (seen clearly in the plan of FIGURE 18-25) illustrates the increasing complexity of rib patterns covering the vaults, which emphasizes the unity of interior space rather than its division into bays.

Called by Charles IV to Prague in 1353, Peter turned the unfinished St. Vitus Cathedral into a "glass house," adding a vast clerestory and glazed triforium supported by double flying buttresses, all covered by net vaults that created a continuous canopy over the space. Because of the success of projects such as this, Peter and his family became the most successful architects in the Holy Roman Empire. Their concept of space, luxurious decoration, and intricate vaulting dominated central European architecture for three generations.

MASTER THEODORIC At Karlstejn Castle, a day's ride from Prague, Charles IV built another chapel, covering the walls with gold and precious stones as well as with paintings. There were 130 paintings of the saints serving as reliquaries, with relics inserted into their frames. Master Theodoric, the court painter, provided drawings on the wood panels, and he painted about 30 images himself. Figures are crowded into—even extend over—their frames, emphasizing their size and power. Master Theodoric was head of the Brotherhood of St. Luke, and the way that his painting of **ST. LUKE** (**FIG. 18-26**), patron saint of painters, looks out at the viewer has suggested to scholars that this may be a self-portrait. His personal style combined a preference for substantial bodies, oversized heads and hands, dour and haunted faces, and soft, deeply modeled drapery, with a touch of grace derived from the French Gothic style. The chapel, consecrated in 1365, so pleased the emperor that in 1367 he gave the artist a farm in appreciation of his work.

Prague and the Holy Roman Empire under Charles IV had become a multicultural empire where people of different religions (Christians and Jews) and ethnic heritages (German and Slav) lived side by side. Charles died in 1378, and without his strong central government, political and religious dissent overtook the empire. Jan Hus, dean of the philosophy faculty at Prague University and a powerful reforming preacher, denounced the immorality he saw in the Church. He was burned at the stake, becoming a martyr and Czech national hero. The Hussite Revolution in the fifteenth century ended Prague's—and Bohemia's—leadership in the arts.

THINK ABOUT IT

18.1 Compare and contrast Giotto's and Duccio's renderings of the biblical story of Christ's Raising of Lazarus (FIGS. 18–8, 18–11).

18.2 Discuss Ambrogio Lorenzetti's engagement with secular subject matter in his frescos for Siena's Palazzo Pubblico (FIG. 18–15). How did these paintings relate to their sociopolitical context?

18.3 Discuss the circumstances surrounding the construction and decoration of the Scrovegni (Arena) Chapel, with special attention to its relationship to the life and aspirations of its patron.

18.4 Choose one small work of art in this chapter that is crafted from precious materials with exceptional technical skill. Explain how it was made and how it was used. How does the work of art relate to its cultural and social context?

CROSSCURRENTS

FIG. 16–26

FIG. 18–20

Depictions of the Virgin Mary holding the infant Jesus represent a continuing theme in the history of European Christian art, developed early on, and continuing to this day. Describe the relationship between the mother and child in these two examples. Characterize the difference in artistic style. How does the choice of medium contribute to the distinction between them? How were they used?

 Study and review on myartslab.com

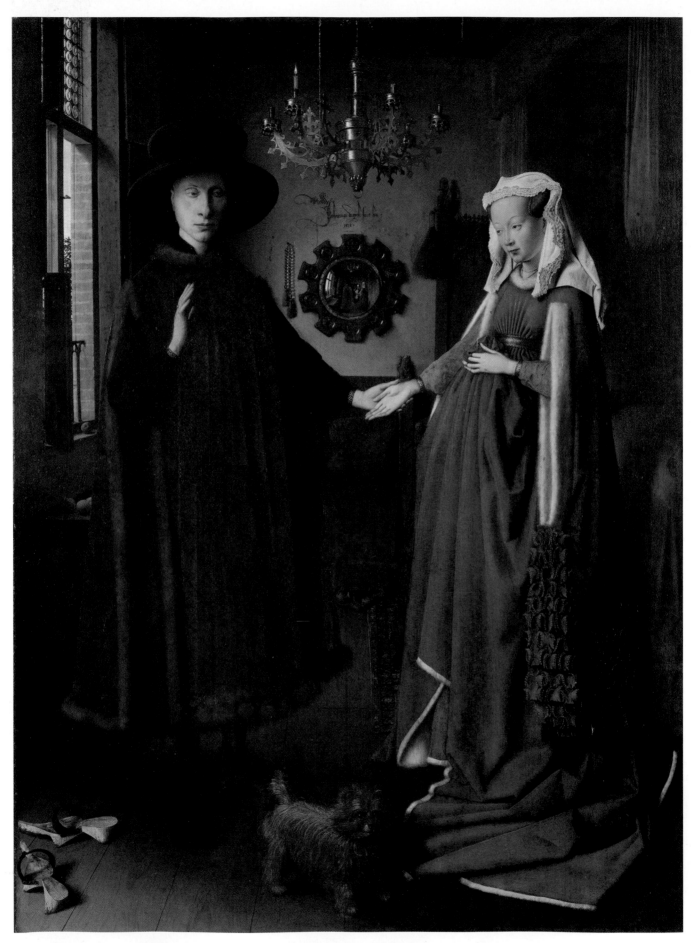

19–1 • Jan van Eyck DOUBLE PORTRAIT OF GIOVANNI ARNOLFINI AND HIS WIFE
1434. Oil on wood panel, 33″ × 22½″ (83.8 × 57.2 cm). The National Gallery, London.

Fifteenth-Century Art in Northern Europe

Fifteenth-century Europe saw the emergence of wealthy merchants whose rise to power was fueled by individual accomplishment, rather than hereditary succession within noble families. Certainly Giovanni Arnolfini—the pasty gentleman with the extravagant hat in this double portrait (**FIG. 19–1**)—earned, rather than inherited, the right to have himself and his wife recorded by renowned artist Jan van Eyck. It was the wealth and connections he made as an Italian cloth merchant providing luxury fabrics to the Burgundian court that put him in the position to commission such a precious picture, in which both patron and painter are identified with conspicuous clarity. Giovanni's face looks more like a personal likeness than anything we have seen since ancient Rome, and not only did Jan van Eyck inscribe his name above the convex mirror ("Jan van Eyck was here, 1434") but his personal painting style also carries the stamp of authorship. The doll-like face of the woman standing next to Giovanni is less individualized. Has she lifted her skirt over her belly so she can follow Giovanni, who has taken her by the hand? Or are most modern observers correct in assuming that she is pregnant? This painting is full of mysteries.

The precise identity of the couple is still open to scholarly debate. And is this a wedding, a betrothal, or perhaps security for a shady financial deal? Recently it has been interpreted as a memorial to a beloved wife lost to death, perhaps in childbirth. Only the wealth of the couple is beyond dispute. They are surrounded by luxury objects: lavish bed hangings, sumptuous chandelier, precious oriental carpet, rare oranges, not to mention their extravagant clothing. The man wears a fur-lined, silk velvet *heuque* (sleeveless overgarment). The woman's gown not only employs more costly wool fabric than necessary to cover her slight body; the elaborate cutwork decoration and white fur lining of her sleeves is an ostentatious indicator of cost. In fact, the painting itself—probably hung in the couple's home—was an object of considerable value.

Even within its secular setting, however, the picture resonated with sacred meaning. The Church still provided spiritual grounding for men and women of the Renaissance. The crystal prayer beads hanging next to the convex mirror imply the couple's piety, and the mirror itself—a symbol of the all-seeing eye of God—is framed with a circular cycle of scenes from Christ's Passion. A figure of St. Margaret—protector of women in childbirth—is carved at the top of a post in the highbacked chair beside the bed, and the perky *Affenpinscher* in the foreground may be more than a pet. Dogs served as symbols of fidelity and also have funerary associations, but choosing a rare, ornamental breed for inclusion here may have been yet another opportunity to express wealth.

LEARN ABOUT IT

19.1 Analyze how Flemish painters gave scrupulous attention to describing the textures and luminosity of objects in the natural world and in domestic interiors, as well as having an extraordinary interest in evoking human likeness in portraits.

19.2 Uncover the complex symbolic meanings that saturated both settings and subjects of northern European paintings.

19.3 Explore the ways in which northern European paintings of the fifteenth century captured in concrete form the spiritual visions of their meditating donors.

19.4 Investigate the emergence of printing as a major pictorial medium.

((•— **Listen** to the chapter audio on myartslab.com

THE NORTHERN RENAISSANCE

Revitalized civic life and economic growth in the late fourteenth century gave rise to a prosperous middle class that supported scholarship, literature, and the arts. Their patronage resulted in the explosion of learning and creativity that we call the Renaissance (French for "rebirth")—a term that was assigned to this period by later historians.

A major manifestation of the Renaissance in northern Europe was a growing and newly intense interest in the natural world manifested in the close observation and detailed recording of nature. Artists depicted birds, plants, and animals with breathtaking descriptive accuracy. They applied the same scrutiny to people and objects, modeling forms with light and shadow to give them the semblance of three-dimensionality. These carefully described subjects were situated into spatial settings, applying an intuitive perspective system by diminishing their scale as they receded into the distance. In the portrayal of landscapes—which became a northern specialty—artists used atmospheric perspective in which distant elements appear increasingly indistinct and less colorful as they approach the background. The sky, for instance, becomes paler near the horizon and the distant landscape turns bluish-gray.

One aspect of the desire for accurate visual depictions of the natural world was a new interest in individual personalities. Fifteenth-century portraits have an astonishingly lifelike quality, combining careful—sometimes seemingly unflattering—surface description with an uncanny sense of vitality. Indeed, the individual becomes important in every sphere. More names of artists survive from the fifteenth century, for example, than in the entire span from the beginning of the Common Era to the year 1400, and some artists begin regularly to sign their work.

The new power of cities in Flanders and the greater Netherlands (present-day Belgium, Luxembourg, and the Netherlands) (MAP 19–1) provided a critical tension and balance with the traditional powers of royalty and the Church. Increasingly, the urban lay public sought to express personal and civic pride by sponsoring secular architecture, sculptured monuments, or paintings directed toward the community. The commonsense values of the merchants formed a solid underpinning for the Northern Renaissance, but their influence remained intertwined with the continuing power of the Church and the royal and noble courts. Giovanni Arnolfini's success at commerce and negotiation provided the funding for his extraordinary double portrait (see FIG. 19–1), but he was able to secure the services of Jan van Eyck only with the cooperation of the duke of Burgundy.

ART FOR THE FRENCH DUCAL COURTS

The dukes of Burgundy (controlling present-day east-central France, Belgium, Luxembourg, and the Netherlands) were the most powerful rulers in northern Europe for most of the fifteenth century. Their domain encompassed not only Burgundy itself but also the Flemish and Netherlandish centers of finance and trade, including the thriving cities of Ghent, Bruges, Tournai, and Brussels. The major seaport, Bruges, was the commercial center of northern Europe, rivaling the Italian city-states of Florence, Milan, and Venice as an economic hub. In the late fourteenth century, Burgundian Duke Philip the Bold (r. 1363–1404) had acquired territory in the Netherlands—including the politically desirable region of Flanders—by marrying the daughter of the Flemish count. Though dukes Philip the Bold of Burgundy, Jean of Berry, and Louis of Anjou were brothers of King Charles V of France, their interests rarely coincided. Even the threat of a common enemy, England, during the Hundred Years' War was not a strong unifying factor, since Burgundy and England were often allied because of common financial interests in Flanders.

While the French king held court in Paris, the dukes held even more splendid courts in their own cities. The dukes of Burgundy and Berry (central France), not the king in Paris, were the real arbiters of taste. Especially influential was Jean, duke of Berry, who commissioned many works from Flemish and Netherlandish painters in the fashionable International Gothic style.

This new, composite style emerged in the late fourteenth century from the multicultural papal court in Avignon in southern France, where artists from Italy, France, and Flanders worked side by side. The International Gothic style became the prevailing manner of late fourteenth-century Europe. It is characterized by slender, gracefully posed figures whose delicate features are framed by masses of curling hair and extraordinarily complex headdresses. Noble men and women wear rich brocaded and embroidered fabrics and elaborate jewelry. Landscape and architectural settings are miniaturized; however, details of nature—leaves, flowers, insects, birds—are rendered in nearly microscopic detail. Spatial recession is represented by rising tiled floors in rooms that are open to view like stage sets, by fanciful mountains and meadows with high horizon lines, and by progressive diminution in the size of receding objects and by atmospheric perspective. Artists and patrons preferred light, bright colors and a liberal use of gold in manuscript and panel paintings, tapestries, and polychromed sculpture. International Gothic was so appealing that it endured well into the fifteenth century.

PAINTING AND SCULPTURE FOR THE CHARTREUSE DE CHAMPMOL

One of Philip the Bold's most lavish projects was the Carthusian monastery, or *chartreuse* ("charterhouse"), at Champmol, outside Dijon, his Burgundian capital city. Land was acquired in 1377 and 1383, and construction began in 1385. The monastic church was intended to house the family's tombs, and the monks were expected to pray continuously for the souls of Philip and his family. Carthusian monasteries were particularly expensive to maintain because Carthusian monks did not provide for themselves by farming or other physical work but were dedicated exclusively to prayer and solitary meditation.

MAP 19-1 •
FIFTEENTH-
CENTURY
NORTHERN
EUROPE

The dukes of Burgundy—whose territory included much of present-day Belgium and Luxembourg, the Netherlands, and eastern France—became the cultural and political leaders of western Europe. Their major cities of Bruges (Belgium) and Dijon (France) were centers of art and industry as well as politics.

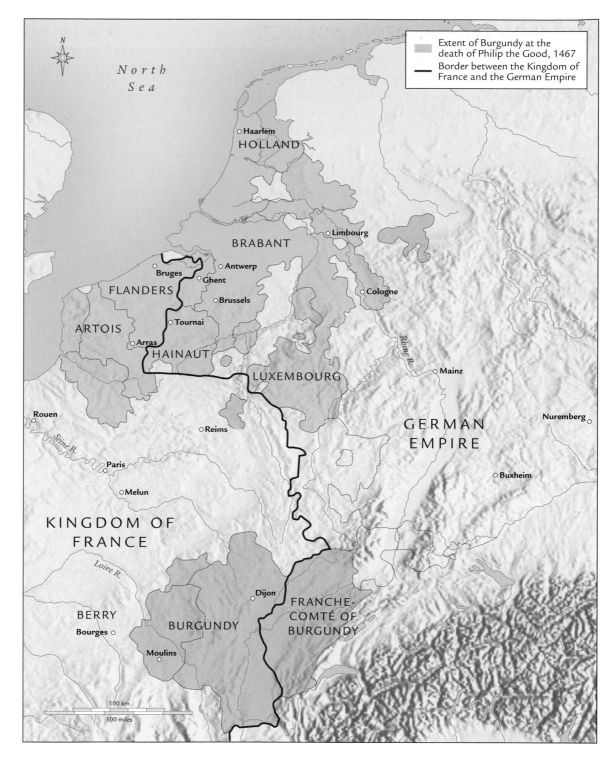

Extent of Burgundy at the death of Philip the Good, 1467

Border between the Kingdom of France and the German Empire

MELCHIOR BROEDERLAM The duke ordered a magnificent carved and painted altarpiece (see "Altars and Altarpieces," page 566) for the Chartreuse de Champmol. The interior of the altarpiece, carved and gilded by Jacques de Baerze, depicts scenes of the Crucifixion flanked by the Adoration of the Magi and the Entombment. The exteriors of the protective shutters of this triptych were covered not by carvings but by two paintings by Melchior Broederlam (active 1381–1410) showing scenes from the life of the Virgin and the infancy of Christ (**FIG. 19-2**).

Broederlam situates his closely observed, International-Style figures within fanciful miniature architectural and landscape settings. His lavish use of brilliantly seductive colors foregrounds one of the features that made International Gothic so popular.

The archangel Gabriel greets Mary while she is at prayer. She sits in a Gothic room with a back door leading into the dark interior of a Romanesque rotunda that symbolizes the Temple of Jerusalem as a repository of the Old Law. According to legend, Mary was an attendant in the Temple prior to her marriage to

The altar in a Christian church symbolizes both the table of Jesus' Last Supper and the tombs of Christ and the saints. As a table, the altar is the site where priests celebrate Mass. And as a tomb, it traditionally contained a relic before the Reformation, placed in a reliquary on the altar, beneath the floor on which the altar rests, or even enclosed within the altar itself.

Altarpieces are painted or carved constructions placed at the back of or behind the altar so that altar and altarpiece appear visually to be joined. By the fifteenth century, important altarpieces had evolved into large and elaborate architectural structures filled with images and protected by movable wings that function like shutters. An altarpiece can sit on a base, called a predella. A winged altarpiece can be a diptych, in which two panels are hinged together; a **triptych**, in which two wings fold over a center section, forming a diptych when closed; or a **polyptych**, consisting of many panels.

diptych   **triptych**   **altar and polyptych altarpiece**

Joseph. The tiny enclosed garden and conspicuous pot of lilies are symbols of Mary's virginity. In International Gothic fashion, both the interior and exterior of the building are shown, and the floors are tilted up at the back to give clear views of the action. Next, in the Visitation, just outside the temple walls, the now-pregnant Mary greets her older cousin Elizabeth, who will soon give birth to John the Baptist.

On the right shutter is the Presentation in the Temple. Mary and Joseph have brought the newborn Jesus to the Temple for his redemption as a first-born son and for Mary's purification, where Simeon takes the baby in his arms to bless him (Luke 2:25–32). At the far right, the Holy Family flees to Egypt to escape King Herod's order that all Jewish male infants be killed. The family travels along treacherous terrain similar to that in the Visitation scene, where a path leads the viewers' eyes up from the foreground and into the distance along a rising ground plane. Broederlam has created a sense of light and air around his solid figures. Anecdotal details drawn from the real world are scattered throughout the pictures—a hawk flies through the golden sky, the presented baby looks anxiously back at his mother, and Joseph drinks from a flask and carries the family belongings in a satchel over his shoulder on the journey to Egypt. The statue of a pagan god, visible at the upper right, breaks and tumbles from its pedestal as the Christ Child approaches. A new era dawns and a new religion replaces the old, among both Jews and gentiles.

CLAUS SLUTER Flemish sculptor Jean de Marville (active 1366–1389) initially directed the decoration of the Chartreuse, and when he died in 1389, he was succeeded by his talented assistant Claus Sluter (c. 1360–1406), from Haarlem, in Holland. Sluter's distinctive work survives in a monumental **WELL OF MOSES** carved for the main cloister (**FIG. 19-3**), begun in 1395 and left unfinished at Sluter's death.

The design of this work was complex. A pier rose from the water to support a large free-standing figure of Christ on the cross, mourned by the Virgin Mary, Mary Magdalen, and John the Evangelist. Forming a pedestal for this Crucifixion group at the viewers' eye level are life-size stone figures from the Hebrew Bible who Christians believe foretold the coming of Christ: Moses, David, and the prophets Jeremiah, Zachariah, Daniel, and Isaiah. This concept may have been inspired by contemporary mystery plays, in which prophets foretell and explain events of Christ's Passion. Sluter's patriarchs and prophets are distinct individuals, physically and psychologically. Moses' sad old eyes blaze out from a memorable face entirely covered with a fine web of wrinkles. Even his horns are wrinkled. (These horns are traditional attributes based on a mistranslation of Exodus 34:29–35 in the Latin Vulgate Bible, where the rays of light radiating from Moses' face become horns.) A mane of curling hair and beard cascades over his heavy shoulders and chest, and an enormous cloak envelops his body. Beside him stands David, in the voluminous robes of a medieval king, the very personification of nobility.

19-2 • Melchior Broederlam ANNUNCIATION, VISITATION, PRESENTATION IN THE TEMPLE, AND FLIGHT INTO EGYPT

Exterior of the wings of the altarpiece of the Chartreuse de Champmol. 1393–1399. Oil on wood panel, 5′5¾″ × 4′1¼″ (1.67 × 1.25 m). Musée des Beaux-Arts, Dijon.

Sluter looked at human figures in new ways—as a weighty mass defined by voluminous drapery that lies in deep folds and falls in horizontal arcs and cascading lines—both concealing and revealing the body, creating strong highlights and shadows. With the vigorous, imposing, and highly individualized figures of the Well of Moses, Sluter abandoned the idealized faces, elongated figures, and vertical drapery of International Gothic for particularized description and the broad horizontal movement of forms. He retained, however, the detailed naturalism and rich colors (now almost lost but revealed in recent cleaning) and surfaces still preferred by his patrons.

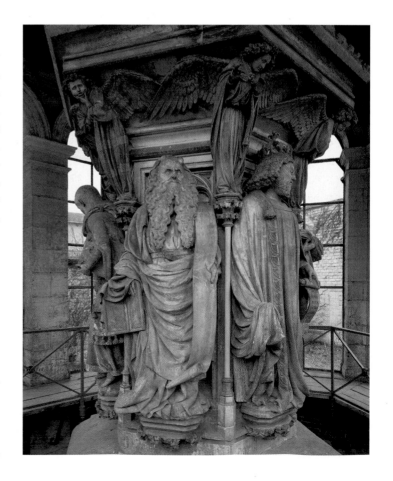

19-3 • Claus Sluter WELL OF MOSES, DETAIL OF MOSES AND DAVID

The Chartreuse de Champmol, Dijon, France. 1395–1406. Limestone with traces of paint, height of figures about 5′8″ (1.69 m).

The sculpture's original details included metal used for buckles and even eyeglasses. It was also painted: Moses wore a gold mantle with a blue lining over a red tunic; David's gold mantle had a painted lining of ermine, and his blue tunic was covered with gold stars and wide bands of ornament.

Since most formal apprenticeships were not open to them, medieval and Renaissance women artists typically learned to paint from their husbands and fathers. Noblewomen, who were often educated in convents, also learned to draw, paint, and embroider. One of the earliest examples of a signed work by a woman is in a tenth-century Spanish manuscript of the Apocalypse illustrated by an artist named Ende (see FIG. 15–11), who describes herself as "painter and servant of God." In the twelfth century, a German nun named Guda not only signed her work but also included a self-portrait (see FIG. 16–34).

Examples proliferate during the later Middle Ages. In the fourteenth century, Jeanne de Montbaston and her husband, Richart, worked together as book illuminators under the auspices of the University of Paris. After Richart's death, Jeanne maintained the workshop and, following the custom of the time, was sworn in as a *libraire* (publisher) by the university in 1353. Bourgot, the daughter of the miniaturist Jean le Noir, illuminated books for King Charles V of France and Duke Jean of Berry. In the fifteenth century, women could be admitted to guilds in the Flemish towns of Ghent, Bruges, and Antwerp.

In a French edition of a book by the Italian author Boccaccio entitled *Concerning Famous Women*, there is a picture of Thamyris, an artist of antiquity, at work in her studio (FIG. 19–4). She appears in fifteenth-century dress, painting an image of the Virgin and Child. At the right, an assistant grinds and mixes her colors. In the foreground, her brushes and paints are laid out neatly and conveniently on a table.

19-4 • PAGE WITH THAMYRIS
From Giovanni Boccaccio's *De Claris Mulieribus* (*Concerning Famous Women*). 1402. Ink and tempera on vellum, 14″ × 9½″ (35.5 × 24 cm). Bibliothèque Nationale, Paris.

MANUSCRIPT ILLUMINATION

Besides religious texts, wealthy patrons treasured richly illuminated secular writings such as herbals (encyclopedias of plants), health manuals, and works of history and literature. A typical manuscript page (see FIG. 19-4) might have leafy tendrils framing the text, decorated opening initials, and perhaps a small inset picture. Only the most lavish books would have full-page miniature paintings, set off with frames. The pictures in these books are conceived as windows looking into rooms or out onto landscapes with distant horizons.

THE LIMBOURG BROTHERS Among the finest Netherlandish painters at the beginning of the century were three brothers—Paul, Herman, and Jean Limbourg—their "last" name referring to their home region. At this time people generally did not have family names in the modern sense, but were known instead by their first names, often followed by a reference to their place of origin, parentage, or occupation.

About 1404, the Limbourg brothers entered the service of avid bibliophile Duke Jean of Berry (1340–1416), for whom they produced their most impressive surviving work, the so-called **TRÈS RICHES HEURES** (Very Sumptuous Book of Hours), between 1411 and 1416 (FIGS. 19-5, 19-6). A Book of Hours, in addition to containing prayers and readings used in daily devotion, also included a calendar of holy days. The Limbourgs created full-page illustrations for the calendar in the *Très Riches Heures*, with subjects including both peasant labors and aristocratic pleasures of each month in a framed lower field, while elaborate calendar devices, with the chariot of the sun and the zodiac symbols, fill a

19-5 • Paul, Herman, and Jean Limbourg FEBRUARY: LIFE IN THE COUNTRY, TRÈS RICHES HEURES
1411–1416. Colors and ink on parchment, 11⅜″ × 8¼″ (29 × 21 cm). Musée Condé, Chantilly, France.

 View the Closer Look for *February: Life in the Country* on myartslab.com

19-6 • Paul, Herman, and Jean Limbourg JANUARY: THE DUKE OF BERRY AT TABLE, TRÈS RICHES HEURES
1411–1416. Colors and ink on parchment, 11⅜″ × 8¼″ (29 × 21 cm). Musée Condé, Chantilly, France.

semicircular area on the upper part of the page. Like most European artists of the time, the Limbourgs showed the laboring classes in a light acceptable to aristocrats—that is, happily working for the nobles' benefit or displaying an uncouth lifestyle for aristocratic amusement. At times, however, the peasants seem to be enjoying the pleasures of their leisure moments.

In the February page (see FIG. 19-5), farm folks relax cozily before a blazing fire. Although many country people at this time lived in hovels, this farm looks comfortable and well maintained, with timber-framed buildings, a row of beehives, a sheepfold, and tidy woven wattle fences. In the distance are a village and church. Within this scene, although all are much lower in social standing than the duke himself, there is a hierarchy of class. Largest in scale and most elegantly dressed is the woman closest to us, perhaps the owner of the farm, who carefully lifts her overgarment, balancing it daintily with both hands as she warms herself. She shares her

fire with a couple, smaller because farther in the background, who wear more modest clothing and are considerably less well behaved, especially the uncouth man, who exposes himself as he lifts his clothing to take advantage of the fire's warmth.

One of the most remarkable aspects of this painting is the way it conveys the feeling of cold winter weather: the leaden sky and bare trees, the soft snow and huddled sheep, the steamy breath of the bundled-up worker blowing on his hands, and the comforting smoke curling from the farmhouse chimney. The artists employ several International Gothic conventions: the high placement of the **horizon line**, the small size of trees and buildings in relation to people, and the cutaway view of the house showing both interior and exterior. The muted palette is sparked with touches of yellowish-orange, blue, and patches of bright red, including the man's turban at the lower left. Scale relationships seem consistent with our experience in the natural world since as the landscape recedes, the size of figures and buildings diminishes progressively in stages from foreground to middle ground to background.

19-7 • Mary of Burgundy Painter MARY AT HER DEVOTIONS, HOURS OF MARY OF BURGUNDY
Before 1482. Colors and ink on parchment, size of image 7½″ × 5¼″ (19.1 × 13.3 cm). Österreichische Nationalbibliothek, Vienna.

by 5¼ inches, earthly reality and a religious vision have been rendered equally tangible (**FIG. 19-7**). The painter conjures up a complex pictorial space. We look not only through the "window" of the illustration's frame but through another window in the wall of the room depicted in the foreground of the painting. The artist shows real virtuosity in representing these worlds. Spatial recession leads the viewer into the far reaches of the church interior, past the Virgin and the gilded altarpiece in the sanctuary to two people conversing in the far distance. The filmy veil covering Mary of Burgundy's steeple headdress is exquisitely described, as is the transparency of the glass vase, and the distinctive bull's eye glass (circular panes whose center "lump" was formed by the glassblower's pontil) filling the foreshortened, open window.

Mary of Burgundy appears twice. She is seated in the foreground by a window, reading from, or contemplating a picture within, her Book of Hours, held carefully and protected by a lush green cloth, perhaps from the diminutive dog cuddled into her lap. She appears again in the background, within the representation of the personal vision inspired by her private meditations. A glorious Gothic church may form the setting for her vision, but it results not from attendance at Mass nor from the direction of a priestly advisor. She experiences it in private, a reward for her personal faith. Christians were encouraged in this period to imagine themselves participating in biblical stories and sacred events so as to feel within bodies and souls the experiences of the protagonists. Secluded in her private space, and surrounded by devotional aids on the window ledge—book, rosary, and symbolic flowers (carnations symbolized the nails of the Crucifixion, the irises Mary's sorrow)—it seems that Mary of Burgundy is doing just that. In her vision, she kneels with attendants and angels in front of a gracefully human Virgin and Child.

TEXTILES

In the fifteenth and sixteenth centuries, the best European tapestries came from Flanders. Major weaving centers at Brussels, Tournai, and Arras produced intricately woven wall hangings for royal and aristocratic patrons across Europe, important church officials including the pope, and even town councils. Among the most common subjects were foliage and flower patterns, scenes from the lives of the saints, and themes from Classical mythology and history, such as the Battle of Troy seen hanging on the walls of Duke Jean of Berry's reception room (see **FIG. 19-6**). Tapestries provided both insulation and luxurious decoration for the stone walls of castle halls, churches, and municipal buildings, and because they were much more expensive than wall or panel paintings, they also showed off the owners' wealth. Since they were portable, many were included in aristocratic baggage as courts moved from residence to residence.

The price of a tapestry depended on the artists involved, the work required, and the materials used. Rarely was a fine, commissioned series woven only with wool; instead, tapestry producers enhanced the weaving with silk, and with silver and gold threads

In contrast, the illustration for the other winter month—January—depicts an aristocratic household (see **FIG. 19-6**). The duke of Berry himself sits behind a table laden with food and rich tableware, presiding over his New Year's feast and surrounded by servants and allies. His chamberlain invites smartly dressed courtiers to greet the duke (the words written overhead say "approach"), who is himself singled out visually by the red cloth of honor with his heraldic arms—swans and the lilies of France—hanging over him and by a large fire screen that circles his head like a secular halo. Tapestries with battle scenes cover the walls. Such luxury objects attest to the wealth and lavish lifestyle of this great patron of the arts, a striking contrast to the farm life that will be revealed in February when turning to the next page in the book.

THE MARY OF BURGUNDY PAINTER One of the finest painters of Books of Hours later in the century was an artist known as the Mary of Burgundy Painter—so called because he painted a Book of Hours for Mary of Burgundy (1457–1482), only child of Charles the Bold. Within a full-page miniature in a book only 7½

19-8 • UNICORN IS FOUND AT THE FOUNTAIN
From the Hunt of the Unicorn tapestry series. c. 1495–1505. Wool, silk, and silver- and gilt-wrapped thread
(13–21 warp threads per inch), 12′1″ × 12′5″ (3.68 × 3.78 m). Metropolitan Museum of Art, New York.
Gift of John D. Rockefeller Jr., The Cloisters Collection, 1937 (37.80.2)

that must have glittered on the walls of princely residences, especially at night, illuminated by flickering lamps or candles. Because silver and gold threads were made of silk wrapped with real silver and gold, people later burned many tapestries to retrieve the precious materials. As a result, few royal tapestries in France survived the French Revolution. If a greater percentage had survived, these luxurious and monumental textile wall paintings would surely figure more prominently in the history of art.

THE UNICORN TAPESTRY Tapestries were often produced in series. One of the best known is the Hunt of the Unicorn series from c. 1500. Four of the seven surviving hangings present scenes of people and animals set against a dense field of trees and flowers, with a distant view of a castle, as in the **UNICORN IS FOUND AT THE FOUNTAIN** (FIG. 19–8). The unusually fine condition of the tapestry allows us to appreciate its rich colors and the subtlety in modeling the faces, the tonal variations in the animals' fur, and even the depiction of reflections in the water. The technical skill of its weavers is astonishing.

In tapestry, designs are woven directly into the fabric. The Unicorn tapestries seem to have been woven on huge, horizontal looms, where weavers interwove fine weft yarn of wool and silk—dyed in a multitude of colors from the creative combination of three vegetal dyes—onto the parallel strands of the coarser wool warp. Weavers worked from behind what would be the front surface of the finished tapestry, following the design on a full-scale cartoon laid on the floor under the loom. They could only see the actual effect of their work by checking the front with mirrors. Making a tapestry panel this large was a collaborative effort that required the organizational skills of a talented production manager and five or six weavers working side by side on a single loom. What is so extraordinary about their work is the skillful way they created curving lines—since the tapestry process is based on a rectilinear network of threads, curves have be simulated—and the lighting effects of shading and reflections, which require using yarn in the same hue with a multitude of values.

The subject of this series concerns the unicorn, a mythical horselike animal with a single long twisted horn and said to be supernaturally swift; it could only be captured by a virgin, to whom it came willingly. Thus, the unicorn became both a symbol of the Incarnation (Christ is the unicorn captured by the Virgin Mary) and also a metaphor for romantic love (see FIG. 18-19). The capture and killing of the unicorn was also equated with Christ's death on the cross to save humanity.

The natural world represented so splendidly in this tapestry also has potential symbolic meaning. For instance, lions represented valor, faith, courage, and mercy, and even—because they were thought to breathe life into their cubs—the Resurrection of Christ. The stag is another Resurrection symbol (it sheds and grows its antlers) and a protector against poisonous serpents and evil in general. Even today we see rabbits as symbols of fertility, and dogs of fidelity. Many of the easily identifiable flowers and trees also carry both religious and secular meaning. There is a strong theme of marriage: the strawberry is a common symbol of sexual love; the pansy means remembrance; and the periwinkle, a cure for spiteful feelings and jealousy. The trees include oak for fidelity, beech for nobility, holly for protection against evil, hawthorn for the power of love, and pomegranate and orange for fertility.

COPE OF THE ORDER OF THE GOLDEN FLEECE Surviving vestments of the Order of the Golden Fleece are remarkable examples of Flemish textiles. The Order of the Golden Fleece was an honorary fraternity founded by Duke Philip the Good of Burgundy in 1430 with 23 knights chosen for their moral character and bravery. Religious services were an integral part of the order's meetings, and opulent liturgical and clerical objects were created for the purpose.

The surface of the sumptuous cope (cloak) in **FIGURE 19-9** is divided into compartments filled with the standing figures of saints. At the top of the neck edge, as if presiding over the company, is an enthroned figure of Christ, flanked along the front edge by

19-9 • COPE OF THE ORDER OF THE GOLDEN FLEECE
Flemish. Mid 15th century. Cloth with gold and colored silk embroidery, 5'4 9/16" × 10'9 5/16" (1.64 × 3.3 m). Imperial Treasury, Vienna.

Whereas Italian artists favored tempera, using it almost exclusively for panel painting until the end of the fifteenth century (see "Cennino Cennini on Panel Painting," page 546), Flemish artists preferred oil paints, in which powdered pigments are suspended in linseed—and occasionally walnut—oil. They exploited the potential of this medium during the fifteenth century with a virtuosity that has never been surpassed.

Tempera had to be applied in a very precise manner because it dried almost as quickly as it was laid down. Shading was restricted to careful overlying strokes in graded tones ranging from white and gray to dark brown and black. Because tempera is opaque—light striking its surface does not penetrate to lower layers of color and reflect back—the resulting surface is **matte**, or dull, taking on a sheen only with burnishing or an overlay of varnish.

On the other hand, oil paint is a viscous medium which takes much longer to dry, and while it is still wet changes can be made easily. Once applied, the paint has time to smooth out during the drying process, erasing traces of individual brushstrokes on the surface of the finished panel. Perhaps even more importantly, oil paint is translucent when applied in very thin layers, called glazes. Light striking a surface built up of glazes penetrates to the lower layers and is reflected back, creating the appearance of an interior glow. These luminous effects enabled artists to capture jewel-like colors and the varying effects of light on changing textures, enhancing the illusion that viewers are looking at real objects rather than their painted imitation.

So brilliant was Jan van Eyck's use of oil paint that he was credited by Giorgio Vasari with inventing the medium. Actually, it had been in use since at least the twelfth century, when it is described in Theophilus Presbyter's *De diversis artibus* (see "Stained-Glass Windows," page 501).

Watch a video about the processes of oil painting and grinding oil paint on myartslab.com

---

scholar-saints in their studies. The embroiderers worked with great precision to match the illusionistic effects of contemporary Flemish painting. The particular stitch used here is known as couching. Gold threads are tacked down using unevenly spaced colored silk threads to create images and an iridescent effect.

PAINTING IN FLANDERS

A strong economy based on the textile industry and international trade provided stability and money for a Flemish efflorescence in the arts. Civic groups, town councils, and wealthy merchants were important patrons in the Netherlands, where the cities were self-governing and largely independent of landed nobility. Guilds oversaw nearly every aspect of their members' lives, and high-ranking guild members served on town councils and helped run city governments. Even experienced artists who moved from one city to another usually had to work as assistants in a local workshop until they met the requirements for guild membership.

Throughout most of the fifteenth century, Flemish art and artists were greatly admired across Europe. Artists from abroad studied Flemish works, and their influence spread even to Italy. Only at the end of the fifteenth century did a pervasive preference for Netherlandish painting give way to a taste for the new styles of art and architecture developing in Italy.

THE FOUNDERS OF THE FLEMISH SCHOOL

Flemish panel painters preferred using an oil medium rather than the tempera paint that was standard in the works of Italian artists. Since it was slow to dry, oil paint provided flexibility, and it had a luminous quality (see "Oil Painting," above). Like manuscript illuminations, Flemish panel paintings provided a window onto a scene rendered with keen attention to describing individual features—people, objects, or aspects of the natural world—with consummate skill.

THE MASTER OF FLÉMALLE Some of the earliest and most outstanding exponents of the new Flemish style were painters in the workshop of an artist known as the Master of Flémalle, identified by some art historians as Robert Campin (active 1406–1444). About 1425–1430, these artists painted the triptych now known as the **MÉRODE ALTARPIECE**, after its later owners (**FIG. 19–10**). Its relatively small size—slightly over 2 feet tall and about 4 feet wide with the wings open—suggests that it was probably made for a small private chapel.

The Annunciation of the central panel is set in a Flemish home and incorporates common household objects, many invested with symbolic religious meaning. The lilies in the **majolica** (glazed earthenware) pitcher on the table, for example, often appear in Annunciations to symbolize Mary's virginity. The hanging water pot in the background niche refers to Mary's purity and her role as the vessel for the Incarnation of God. What seems at first to be a towel hung over the prominent, hinged rack next to the niche may be a tallis (Jewish prayer shawl). Some art historians have referred to these as "hidden" or "disguised" symbols because they are treated as a normal part of the setting, but their routine religious meanings would have been obvious to the intended audience.

Some have interpreted the narrative episode captured in the central panel as the moment immediately following Mary's acceptance of her destiny. A rush of wind riffles the book pages and snuffs the candle (the flame, symbolic of God's divinity, extinguished at the moment he takes human form) as a tiny figure of Christ carrying a cross descends on a ray of light. Having accepted the miracle of the Incarnation (God assuming human form), Mary reads her Bible while sitting humbly on the footrest of the long bench. Her

19–10 • Workshop of the Master of Flémalle MÉRODE ALTARPIECE (TRIPTYCH OF THE ANNUNCIATION) (OPEN)

c. 1425–1430s. Oil on wood panel, center 25¼″ × 24⅞″ (64.1 × 63.2 cm); each wing approx. 25⅜″ × 10¾″ (64.5 × 27.6 cm). Metropolitan Museum of Art, New York. The Cloisters Collection, 1956 (56.70)

In the late nineteenth century, this triptych was associated with a group of stylistically related works and assigned to an artist called the Master of Flémalle, who was subsequently identified by some art historians as a documented artist named Robert Campin. Recently, however, experts have questioned this association and proposed that the triptych we now see was the work of several artists working within the workshop that created the stylistic cluster. Current opinion holds that the *Annunciation* was initially created as an independent panel, and shortly afterward expanded into a triptych with the addition of the side panels under the patronage of the donor in the foreground at left. Finally, some time later in the 1430s, the figure of his wife was added behind him, presumably on the occasion of his marriage.

 View the Closer Look for the Mérode Altarpiece on myartslab.com

position becomes a symbol of her submission to God's will. Other art historians have proposed that the scene represents the moment just prior to the Annunciation. In this view, Mary is not yet aware of Gabriel's presence, and the rushing wind is the result of the angel's rapid entry into the room, where he appears before her, half kneeling and raising his hand in salutation.

In the left wing of the triptych, the donors—presumably a married couple—kneel in an enclosed garden, another symbol of Mary's virginity, before the open door of the house where the Annunciation is taking place, implying that the scene is a vision engendered by their faithful meditations, comparable to the vision we have already seen in the Hours of Mary of Burgundy (see FIG. 19–7). Such presentations, very popular with Flemish patrons, allowed those who commissioned a religious work to appear in the same space and time, and often on the same scale, as religious figures. The donors' eyes, which seem oddly unfocused, are directed not outward but inward, intent on the spiritual exercise of imagining their own presence within this sacred narrative.

On the right wing, Joseph is working in his carpentry workshop. A prosperous Flemish city is exquisitely detailed in the view through

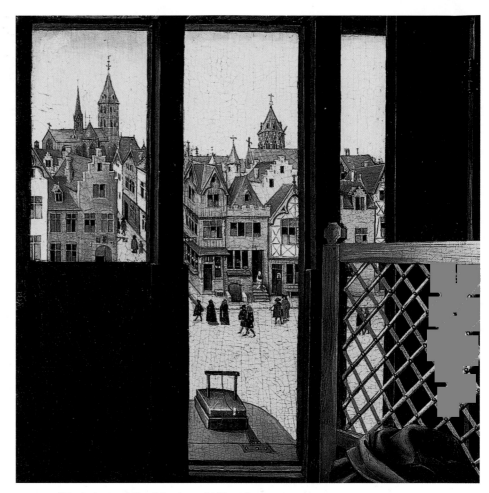

19–11 • Workshop of the Master of Flémalle A FLEMISH CITY
Detail of the right wing of the Mérode Altarpiece (FIG. 19–10).

the shop window, with people going about their daily business (**FIG. 19-11**). Even here there is religious symbolism. On the windowsill of Joseph's shop is a mousetrap (another sits on the workbench next to him), which fifteenth-century viewers would understand as a reference to Christ as the bait in a trap set by God to catch Satan. Joseph is drilling holes in a small board used as a drainboard for making wine, calling to mind the Eucharist and Christ's Passion.

The complex and consistent treatment of light in the Mérode Altarpiece represents a major preoccupation of Flemish painters. The strongest illumination comes from an unseen source at the upper left in front of the **picture plane** (the picture's front surface) as if sunlight were entering through the opened front of the room. More light comes from the rear windows, and a few painted, linear rays come from the round window at left, a symbolic vehicle for the Christ Child's descent. Jesus seems to slide down the rays of light linking God with Mary, carrying the cross of human salvation over his shoulder. The light falling on the Virgin's lap emphasizes this connection, and the transmission of the symbolic light through a transparent panel of glass (which remains intact) recalls the virginal nature of Jesus' conception.

JAN VAN EYCK In 1425, Jan van Eyck (active 1420s–1441) became court painter to Duke Philip the Good of Burgundy (r. 1419–1467), who was the uncle of the king of France and one of the most sophisticated men in Europe. Philip made Jan one of his confidential employees and even sent him on a diplomatic mission to Portugal, charged with painting a portrait of a prospective bride for himself. The duke alluded to Jan's remarkable technical skills in a letter of 1434–1435, saying that he could find no other painter equal to his taste or so excellent in art and science. So brilliant was Jan's use of oil glazes that he was mistakenly credited with the invention of **oil painting** (see "Oil Painting," page 573).

Jan's 1433 portrait of a **MAN IN A RED TURBAN** (**FIG. 19-12**) projects a particularly strong sense of personality, and the signed and dated frame also bears Jan's personal motto—"As I can, [but not as I would]"—in Greek letters at the top. Since these letters also form an anagram of his own name, most scholars see this painting as a self-portrait in which physical appearance seems recorded in a magnifying mirror. We see the stubble of a day's growth of beard on his chin and cheeks, and every carefully described wrinkle around the artist's eyes, reddened from the strain of his work,

19-12 • Jan van Eyck MAN IN A RED TURBAN
1433. Oil on wood panel, 13⅛″ × 10¼″ (33.3 × 25.8 cm). National Gallery, London.

and reflecting light that seems to emanate from our own space. That same light source gives the inscriptions the *trompe l'oeil* sense of having been engraved into the frame, heightening the illusionistic wizardry of Jan's painting. Is Jan looking out directly at us, or are we seeing his reflection in a mirror?

In his lifetime, one of the most famous works of Jan van Eyck was a huge polyptych with a very complicated and learned theological program that he (perhaps in collaboration with his brother Hubert) painted for a chapel in what is now the Cathedral of St. Bavo in Ghent (see "The Ghent Altarpiece," page 578). The three-dimensional mass of the figures, the voluminous draperies as well as their remarkable surface realism, and the scrupulous attention to the luminous details of textures as variable as jewels and human flesh, are magnificent examples of Jan's artistic wizardry. He has carefully controlled the lighting within this multi-panel ensemble to make it appear that the objects represented are illuminated by

sunlight coming through the window of the very chapel where it was meant to be installed. Jan's painting is firmly grounded in the terrestrial world even when he is rendering a visionary subject.

The Ghent altarpiece may have been Jan's most famous painting during his lifetime, but his best-known painting today is a distinctive double portrait of a couple identified as a Giovanni Arnolfini and his wife (see FIG. 19-1). Early interpreters saw this fascinating work as a wedding or betrothal. Above the mirror on the back wall (FIG. 19-13), the artist inscribed the words: *Johannes de eyck fuit hic 1434* ("Jan van Eyck was here 1434"). More normal as a signature would have been, "Jan van Eyck made this," so the words "was here" might suggest that Jan served as a witness to a matrimonial episode portrayed in the painting. Jan is not the only witness recorded in the painting. The convex mirror between the figures reflects not only the back of the couple but a front view of two visitors standing in the doorway, entering the room. Perhaps one of them is the artist himself.

New research has complicated the developing interpretation of this painting by revealing that the Giovanni Arnolfini traditionally identified as the man in this painting married his wife Giovanna Cenami only in 1447, long after the date on the wall and Jan van Eyck's own death. One scholar has proposed that the picture is actually a prospective portrait of Giovanni and Giovanna's marriage in the future, painted in 1434 to secure the early transfer of the dowry from her father to her future husband. Others have more recently suggested the man portrayed here is a different Giovanni Arnolfini, accompanied either by his putative second wife or a memorial portrait of his first wife, Costanza Trenta, who died the year before this picture was painted, perhaps in childbirth. The true meaning of this fascinating masterpiece may remain a mystery, but it is doubtful that scholars will stop trying to solve it.

ROGIER VAN DER WEYDEN Little as we know about Jan van Eyck, we know even less about the life of Rogier van der Weyden (c. 1400–1464). Not a single existing work of art bears his name. He may have studied under the Master of Flémalle, but the relationship is not altogether clear. Having first established himself in 1432 as an independent master in Tournai, Rogier maintained at the peak of his career a large workshop in Brussels, where he was the official city painter, attracting apprentices and shop assistants from as far away as Italy. To establish the stylistic characteristics of Rogier's art, scholars have turned to a painting of the **DEPOSITION** (FIG. 19-16), an altarpiece commissioned by

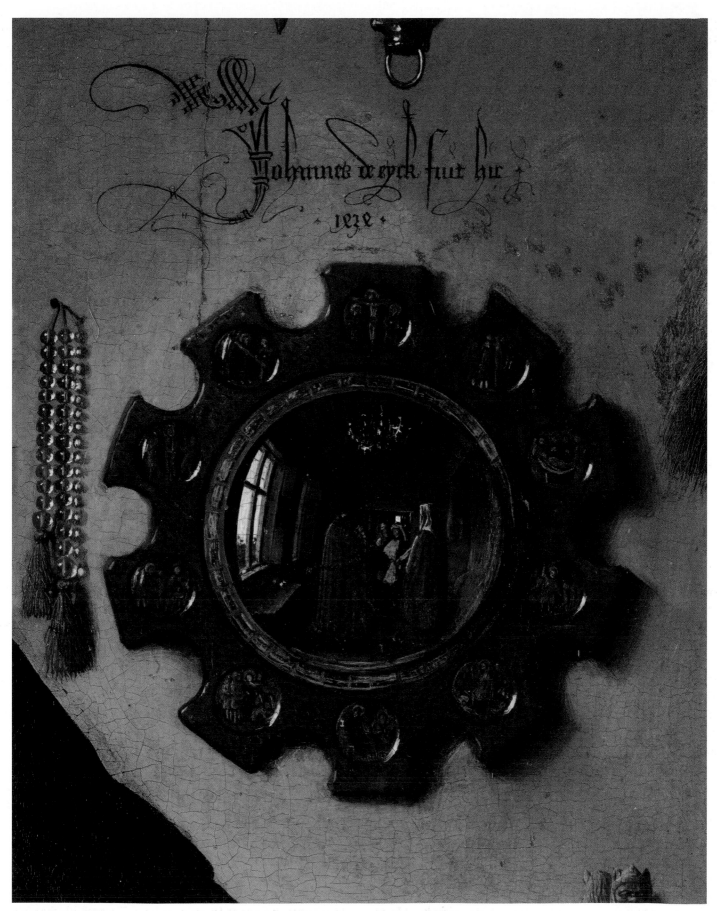

19–13 • Jan van Eyck **DETAIL OF MIRROR AND SIGNATURE IN A DOUBLE PORTRAIT OF GIOVANNI ARNOLFINI AND HIS WIFE** (FIG. 19–1)
1434. Oil on wood panel. The National Gallery, London.

An inscription on the frame of the Ghent Altarpiece seems to identify both Jan and Hubert van Eyck as its artists: "The painter Hubert van Eyck, greater than whom no one was found, began [this work]; and Jan, his brother, second in art, having carried through the task at the expense of Jodocus Vyd, invites you by this verse, on the sixth of May [1432], to look at what has been done."

Many art historians believe Hubert began this altarpiece, and after his death in 1426, Jan completed it, when free of ducal responsibilities in 1430–1432. Others believe the entire painting was produced by Jan and his workshop, Hubert perhaps being responsible for the frame. At least commission and situation are clear. Jodocus Vijd, who appears with his wife Isabella Borluut on the outside of the polyptych's two shutters—both visible only when the altarpiece is closed—commanded the work. One of a wealthy family of financiers, Jodocus was a city official in Ghent—holding an office comparable to mayor in 1433–1434—and the altarpiece was part of a renovation he funded in the family chapel at the parish church of St. John (now the Cathedral of St. Bavo). He also endowed daily Masses in the chapel for the couple's salvation, and that of their ancestors.

When the altarpiece was closed (FIG. 19-14), the exterior of the shutters displayed the striking likenesses of the donor couple kneeling to face painted statues of SS. John the Baptist (patron of Ghent) and John the Evangelist (patron of this church) that recall those on Sluter's *Well of Moses* (see FIG. 19-3). Above this row is an expansive rendering of the Annunciation—whose somber color scheme coordinates with the *grisaille* statues painted below—situated in an upstairs room that looks out over a panoramic cityscape. As in Simone Martini's Annunciation altarpiece (see FIG. 18-13), the words that issue from Gabriel's mouth ("Hail, full of grace, the Lord is with

thee") appear on the painting's surface, and here there is Mary's response as well ("Behold the handmaid of the Lord"), only it is painted upside down since it is directed to God, who hovers above her head as the dove of the Holy Spirit. Prophets and sibyls perch in the irregular compartments at the top, unfurling scrolls recording their predictions of Christ's coming.

When the shutters were opened (FIG. 19-15) on Sundays and feast days, the mood changed. The effect is no longer muted,

but rich in both color and implied sound. Dominating the altarpiece by size, central location, and brilliant color is the enthroned, red-robed figure of God, wearing the triple papal crown, with an earthly crown at his feet, and flanked by the Virgin Mary and John the Baptist, each holding an open book. To either side are first angel musicians and then Adam and Eve, represented as lifelike nudes. Adam seems to have been painted from a model, from whom Jan reproduced even the "farmer's

19-14 • Jan and Hubert (?) van Eyck GHENT ALTARPIECE (CLOSED), ANNUNCIATION WITH DONORS
Completed 1432. Oil on panel, height 11′5″ (3.48 m). Cathedral of St. Bavo, Ghent.

tan" of his hands and face. Eve displays clear features of the female anatomy; the pigmented line running downward from her navel appears frequently during pregnancy. Each of the three themes of the upper register—God with Mary and John, musical angels, and Adam and Eve—is set in a distinct space: the holy trio in a golden shrine, angels against a blue sky, Adam and Eve in shallow stone niches.

The five lower panels present a unified field. A vast landscape with meadows, woods, and distant cities is set against a continuous horizon. A diverse array of saints—apostles, martyrs, confessors, virgins, hermits, pilgrims, warriors, judges—assembles to adore the Lamb of God as described in the book of Revelation. The Lamb stands on an altar, blood flowing into a chalice, ultimately leading to the fountain of life.

The Ghent altarpiece became a famous work of art almost as soon as it was completed. To celebrate Duke Philip the Good's visit to the city in 1458, citizens of Ghent welcomed him with *tableaux vivants* (living pictures) of its scenes. German artist Albrecht Dürer traveled to Ghent to see the altarpiece in 1521. During the French occupation of Flanders in 1794 it was transferred to Paris (returned in 1815), and during World War II it was confiscated by the Nazis. It is now displayed within a secure glass case in the baptismal chapel of the church for which it was made.

19-15 • Jan and Hubert (?) van Eyck GHENT ALTARPIECE (OPEN), ADORATION OF THE MYSTIC LAMB
Completed 1432. Oil on panel, 11'5¾" × 15'1½" (3.5 × 4.6 m). Cathedral of St. Bavo, Ghent.

Read the document related to Jan van Eyck and the Ghent Altarpiece on myartslab.com

19–16 • Rogier van der Weyden DEPOSITION
From an altarpiece commissioned by the crossbowmen's guild, Louvain, Belgium. Before 1443, possibly c. 1435–1438.
Oil on wood panel, 7'2⅝" × 8'7⅛" (2.2 × 2.62 m). Museo del Prado, Madrid.

🔍 **View** the Closer Look for the *Deposition* on myartslab.com

the Louvain crossbowmen's guild (crossbows can be seen in the tracery painted in the upper corners) sometime before 1443, the date of the earliest known copy of it by another artist.

The Deposition was a popular theme in the fifteenth century because of its potential for dramatic, personally engaging portrayal. Rogier sets the act of removing Jesus' body from the cross on the shallow stage of a gilt wooden box, just like the case of a carved and painted altarpiece. The ten solid, three-dimensional figures, however, are not simulations of polychromed wood carving, but near life-size renderings of actual human figures who seem to press forward into the viewers' space, allowing them no escape from the forceful expressions of heartrending grief. Jesus' friends seem palpably real, with their portraitlike faces and scrupulously described contemporary dress, as they tenderly and sorrowfully remove his body from the cross for burial. Jesus' corpse dominates the center of the composition, drooping in a languid curve, framed

by jarringly thin, angular arms. His pose is echoed by the rhyming form of the swooning Virgin. It is as if mother and son share in the redemptive passion of his death on the cross, encouraging viewers to identify with them both, or to join their assembled companions in mourning their fate. Although united by sorrow, the mourning figures react in personal ways, from the intensity of Mary Magdalen at far right, wringing her hands in anguish, to John the Evangelist's blank stare at left, lost in grief as he reaches to support the collapsing Virgin. The anguish of the woman behind him, mopping her tear-soaked eyes with the edge of her veil, is almost unbearably poignant.

Rogier's choice of color and pattern balances and enhances his composition. The complexity of the gold brocade worn by Joseph of Arimathea, who offered his new tomb for the burial, and the contorted pose and vivid dress of Mary Magdalen increase the visual impact of the right side of the panel to counter the pictorial weight of the larger number of figures at the left. The palette contrasts subtle, slightly muted colors with brilliant expanses of blue and red, while white accents focus the viewers' attention on the main subjects. The whites of the winding cloth and the tunic of the youth on the ladder set off Jesus' pale body, as the white turban and shawl emphasize the ashen face of Mary.

Another work by Rogier, painted at about the same time as the Deposition, is both quieter and more personal. It represents the evangelist St. Luke executing a preparatory drawing in silverpoint for a painting of the Virgin and Child who seem to have materialized to pose for him (**FIG. 19-17**). The painting is based on a legend with origins in sixth-century Byzantium of a miraculous appearance of the Virgin and Child to Luke so he could record their appearance and pass on his authentic witness to his Christian followers. Rogier's version takes place in a carefully defined interior space that opens onto a garden, and from there into a distant vista of urban life before dissolving into the countryside through which a winding river guides our exploration all the way to the horizon. The Virgin is preoccupied with a routine maternal activity. Her baby has pulled away from her breast, producing a smile and flexing his hand—familiar gestures of actual babies during nursing. The good mother and happy baby are observed by Luke, who, half-kneeling, captures the

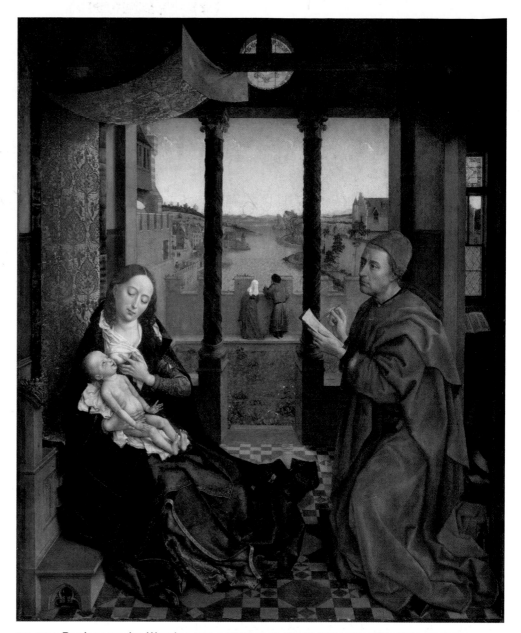

19-17 • Rogier van der Weyden **ST. LUKE DRAWING THE VIRGIN AND CHILD**
c. 1435–1440. Oil and tempera on wood panel, 54¼″ × 43⅝″ (137.7 × 110.8 cm).
Museum of Fine Arts, Boston.

scene in a silverpoint sketch, a common preliminary step used by fifteenth-century Flemish painters in the planning of their paintings, especially portraits. And the portraitlike quality of Luke's face here has led scholars to propose that this image of a saint is a self-portrait of its artist.

Art historians have traditionally interpreted this painting in two ways. Some see it—especially if it is a self-portrait—as a document of Rogier's sense of his own profession. They see him distancing himself and his fifteenth-century Flemish colleagues from identification with the laboring artisans of the Middle Ages, and staking a claim for his special role as an inspired creator who recorded sacred visions in valuable, individualistic works of art. The notion of Rogier's own identification with Luke in this painting is supported by the fact that later artists emulated his composition

in creating their own self-portraits as the century progressed. But other art historians, proposing that this painting was created for the chapel of the guildhall of the painters in Brussels (the evidence is suggestive but unclear), have interpreted it as a claim for the importance of the painters' profession because it is rooted in saintly legend. Perhaps this extraordinary picture was both self-fashioning and professional propaganda. But it was also a devotional image. Luke's tenuous, half-kneeling posture, and his dreamy, introspective gaze certainly remind us that one of the tasks of painters in this period was to create inspiring pictures of religious visions that are also materialized by meticulous references to the real world. This most certainly is that. (For another painting by Rogier van der Weyden, see FIG. Intro-6, and its discussion in the Introduction.)

PAINTING AT MID CENTURY: THE SECOND GENERATION

The extraordinary accomplishments of the Master of Flémalle, Jan van Eyck, and Rogier van der Weyden attracted many followers in Flanders. The work of this second generation of Flemish painters may have been simpler, more direct, often easier to understand than that of their predecessors, but they produced extraordinary works of great emotional power. They were in large part responsible for the rapid spread of the Flemish style throughout Europe.

PETRUS CHRISTUS Among the most interesting of these painters was Petrus Christus (active 1444–c. 1475/1476), who became a citizen of Bruges in 1444 and signed and dated six paintings in a career that extended over three decades.

In 1449, Christus painted a portrait of a goldsmith, serving two well-dressed customers in his shop (see "A Closer Look," opposite). A halo around the head of the seated figure—not originally a part of the painting—was removed by restorers in 1993. This coincided with a reevaluation of the subject matter of the work, now seen as a vocational portrait of an actual goldsmith, rather than an image of St. Eloi, patron saint of goldsmiths, set in the present. Both finished products and raw materials of the jeweler's trade sit on the shelves behind the goldsmith: containers, rings, brooches, a belt buckle, a string of beads, pearls, gemstones, coral, and crystal cylinders. A betrothal belt curls across the counter. Such a combination of objects suggests that the painting expresses the hope for health and well-being for the couple who may be in the process of procuring rings for their upcoming marriage.

As in Jan van Eyck's double portrait, a convex mirror extends the viewer's field of vision, in this instance to the street outside, where two men appear. One is stylishly dressed in red and black, and the other holds a falcon, another indication of high status. Whether or not the reflected image has symbolic meaning, the mirror would have had practical value in a goldsmith's shop, allowing him to observe the approach of potential customers to the counter outside his shop window.

DIERIC BOUTS Dieric Bouts (active c. 1444–1475) is best known among Flemish painters as a storyteller, and he exercised those skills in a series of large altarpieces, with narrative scenes drawn from the life of Christ and the lives of the saints. But he also created more intimate pictures, such as this tender rendering of the **VIRGIN AND CHILD**, just 8½ inches tall (**FIG. 19-18**). Even it evokes a story. Mary holds her baby securely, using both of her plain, strong hands to surround completely the lower part of his body. The baby reaches across his mother's chest and around her neck, pulling himself closer to press his face next to hers, cheek to cheek, nose to nose, mouth to mouth, eyes locked together, forming a symmetrical system that links them in pattern and almost melds them into a single mirrored form. It is as if a fifteenth-century St. Luke had captured a private moment

19-18 • Dieric Bouts VIRGIN AND CHILD
c. 1455–1460. Oil on wood panel, 8½″ × 6½″ (21.6 × 16.5 cm). Metropolitan Museum of Art, New York.

between the Virgin and Child—a dimpled mother and baby looking very much like the actual people in the artist's world—during their miraculous appearance to sit as his model (compare FIG. 19-17). The concept is actually not so far-fetched. Bouts's painting is modeled after a fourteenth-century Italian image in the cathedral of Cambrai that in the fifteenth century was believed to have been painted by St. Luke himself.

HUGO VAN DER GOES Hugo van der Goes (c. 1440–1482), dean of the painters' guild in Ghent (1468–1475), united the intellectual prowess of Jan van Eyck with the emotional sensitivity of Rogier van der Weyden to create an entirely new personal style. Hugo's major work was an exceptionally large altarpiece, more than 8 feet tall, of the Nativity (**FIG. 19-19**), commissioned by Tommaso Portinari, head of the Medici bank in Bruges. Painted probably between 1474 and 1476, the triptych was sent to Florence and installed in 1483 in the Portinari family chapel, where it had a noticeable impact on Florentine painters.

Tommaso, his wife Maria Baroncelli, and their three oldest children are portrayed kneeling in prayer on the side panels of the

A CLOSER LOOK | *A Goldsmith in his Shop*

by Petrus Christus. 1449. Oil on oak panel, 38⅝″ × 33½″ (98 × 85 cm).
Metropolitan Museum of Art, New York. Robert Lehman Collection, 1975. 1975.1.110

The coat of arms of the dukes of Guelders hangs from a chain around this man's neck, leading some to speculate that the woman, who is the more active of the pair, is Mary of Guelders, niece of Duke Philip the Good, who married King James II of the Scots the same year this picture was painted.

Goldsmiths were expected to perform all their transactions, including the weighing of gold, in public view to safeguard against dishonesty. Here the scales tip toward the couple, perhaps an allusion to the scales of the Last Judgment, which always tip to the side of the righteous.

Three types of coins rest on the shop counter: "florins" from Mainz, "angels" from English King Henry VI's French territories, and "riders" minted under Philip the Good. Such diversity of currency could show the goldsmith's cosmopolitanism, or they could indicate his participation in money changing, since members of that profession belonged to the same guild as goldsmiths.

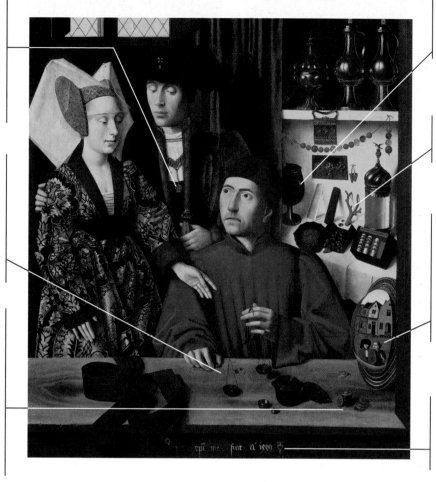

This coconut cup was supposed to neutralize poison. The slabs of porphyry and rock crystal were "touchstones," used to test gold and precious stones.

The red coral and serpents' tongues (actually fossilized sharks' teeth) were intended to ward off the evil eye.

Two men, one with a falcon on his arm, are reflected in the obliquely placed mirror as they stand in front of the shop. The edges of the reflection catch the red sleeve of the goldsmith and the door frame, uniting the interior and exterior spaces and drawing the viewer into the painting.

The artist signed and dated his work in a bold inscription that appears just under the tabletop at the bottom of the painting: "Master Petrus Christus made me in the year 1449."

View the Closer Look for *A Goldsmith in his Shop* on myartslab.com

---

wing interiors. On the left wing, looming larger than life behind Tommaso and his son Antonio, are their name saints—SS. Thomas and Anthony of Egypt. Since the younger son, Pigello, born in 1474, was apparently added after the original composition was set, his saintly counterpart is lacking. On the right wing, Maria and her daughter Margherita are presented by SS. Mary Magdalen and Margaret.

The theme of the altarpiece is the Nativity as told by Luke (2:10–19). The central panel represents the Adoration of the newborn Christ Child by Mary and Joseph, a host of angels, and the shepherds who have rushed in from the fields. In the middle ground of the wings are additional scenes. Winding their way through the winter landscape are two groups headed for Bethlehem. On the left wing, Mary and Joseph travel there to take part in a census. Near term in her pregnancy, Mary has dismounted from her donkey and staggers, supported by Joseph. On the right wing,

a servant of the three Magi, who are coming to honor the awaited Savior, asks directions from a peasant.

Hugo paints meadows and woods meticulously, and he used atmospheric perspective to approximate distance in the landscape. He shifts figure size hierarchically for emphasis: The huge figures of Joseph, Mary, and the shepherds are the same size as the patron saints on the wings, in contrast to the much smaller Portinari family and still smaller angels. Hugo also uses light, as well as the gestures and gazes of the figures, to focus our eyes on the center panel where the mystery of the Incarnation takes place. Instead of lying swaddled in a manger or in his mother's arms, Jesus rests naked and vulnerable on the barren ground. Rays of light emanate from his body. This image was based on the visionary writing of the medieval Swedish mystic St. Bridget (who composed her work c. 1360–1370), which describes Mary kneeling to adore the Christ Child immediately after giving birth.

19-19 • Hugo van der Goes PORTINARI ALTARPIECE (OPEN)
c. 1474–1476. Tempera and oil on wood panel; center 8′3½″ × 10′ (2.53 × 3.01 m), wings each 8′3½″ × 4′7½″ (2.53 × 1.41 m). Galleria degli Uffizi, Florence.

As in the work of Jan van Eyck, aspects of the setting of this painting are infused with symbolic meaning. In the foreground, the wheatsheaf refers both to the location of the event at Bethlehem, which in Hebrew means "house of bread," and to the Eucharistic Host, which represents the body of Christ. The majolica albarello is decorated with vines and grapes, alluding to the Eucharistic wine, which represents the blood of Christ. It holds a red lily for Christ's blood and three irises—white for purity and purple for Christ's royal ancestry. The seven blue columbines in the glass vessel remind the viewer of the Virgin's future sorrows, and scattered on the ground are violets, symbolizing humility. But Hugo's artistic vision transcends such formal religious symbolism. For example, the shepherds, who stand in unaffected awe before the miraculous event, are among the most sympathetically rendered images of common people to be found in the art of any period, and the portraits of the Portinari children are unusually sensitive renderings of the delicate features of youthful faces.

HANS MEMLING The artist who seems to summarize and epitomize painting in Flanders during the second half of the fifteenth century is German-born Hans Memling (c. 1435–1494). Memling combines the intellectual depth and virtuoso rendering of his predecessors with a delicacy of feeling and exquisite grace, a "prettiness" that made his work exceptionally popular. Memling may have worked in Rogier van der Weyden's Brussels workshop in the 1460s, but soon after Rogier's death in 1464, Memling moved to Bruges, where he developed an international clientele that supported a thriving workshop. He also worked for local patrons.

In 1487, the 24-year-old Maarten van Nieuwenhove (1463–1500), member of a powerful political family in Bruges (he would himself become mayor of Bruges in 1497), commissioned from Memling a diptych that combined a meticulously detailed portrait with a visionary apparition of the Virgin and Child, presented as a powerful fiction of their physical encounter in Maarten's own home (**FIG. 19-20**). This type of devotional diptych was a specialty of Rogier van der Weyden, but Memling transforms the type into something more intimate by placing it in a domestic setting. An expensively outfitted figure of Maarten appears in the right wing of the diptych, seen from an oblique angle, hands folded in prayer. He seems caught in a moment of introspection inspired by personal devotions—his Book of Hours lies still open on the table in front of him. The window just over his shoulder holds a stained-glass rendering of his name saint, Martin, in the top pane, while a recognizable landmark in Bruges can be seen through the opening below. The Virgin and Child on the adjacent panel are presented frontally, and the strong sense of specific likeness characterizing Maarten's portrait has given way to an idealized delicacy and grace in the visage of the Virgin that complements the extravagance of her clothing. Although she does not seem to be focusing on him, a completely nude Jesus stretches out on the silk pillow in front of her; she stabilizes him with one hand and offers him an apple with the other. This seems a clear reference to their roles as the new Adam and Eve, ready to redeem the sin brought into the world by the first couple. The stained glass behind them is filled with heraldry, devices, and a motto associated with Maarten's family.

Memling's construction of a coherent interior space for these figures is both impressive and meaningful. We are looking through two windows into a rectangular room containing this devotional group. The pillow under the Christ Child casts a shadow, painted on the lower frame of the left panel, to intensify the illusion, and the Virgin's scarlet mantle extends under the division between the two wings of the diptych to reappear on Maarten's side of the painting underneath his Book of Hours. This mantle not only connects the two sides of the painting spatially but also relates Maarten's devotional exercise and the apparition of the Virgin and Child. This relationship is also documented with a device already familiar to us in paintings by Jan van Eyck (see FIG. 19–13) and Petrus Christus (see "A Closer Look," page 583). On the shadowy back wall, over the Virgin's right shoulder and set against the closed shutters of

a window, is a convex mirror that reflects the backs of both Maarten and Mary, bearing visual witness to their presence together within his domestic space and undoing the division between them that is endemic to the diptych format. Maarten's introspective gaze signals that for him the encounter is internal and spiritual, but Memling transforms Maarten's private devotion into a concrete public statement that promotes an image of his piety and freezes him in perpetual prayer. We bear witness to his vision as an actual event.

EUROPE BEYOND FLANDERS

Flemish art—its complex symbolism and visionary meaning, its coherent configurations of atmospheric space, its luminous colors and sensuous surface textures—delighted wealthy patrons and well-educated courtiers both inside and outside Flanders. At first, Flemish artists worked in foreign courts or their works were commissioned and exported abroad. Flemish manuscripts, tapestries, altarpieces, and portraits appeared in palaces and chapels throughout Europe. Soon regional artists traveled to Flanders to learn oil-painting techniques and practice emulating the Flemish style. By

19–20 • Hans Memling DIPTYCH OF MAARTEN VAN NIEUWENHOVE
1487. Oil on wood panel, each panel (including frames) 20½″ × 16¼″ (52 × 41.5 cm). Hans Memling Museum, Musea Brugge, Sint-Jans Hospital, Bruges.

the end of the fifteenth century, distinctive regional variations of Flemish art could be found throughout Europe, from the Atlantic Ocean to the Danube.

FRANCE

The centuries-long struggle for power and territory between France and England continued well into the fifteenth century. When King Charles VI of France died in 1422, England claimed the throne for the king's 9-month-old grandson, Henry VI of England. The plight of Charles VII, the late French king's son, inspired Joan of Arc to raise an army to return him to the throne. Thanks to Joan's efforts, Charles was crowned at Reims in 1429. Although Joan was burned at the stake in 1431, the revitalized French forces drove the English from French lands. In 1461, Louis XI succeeded his father, Charles VII, as king of France. Under his rule the French royal court again became a major source of patronage for the arts.

JEAN FOUQUET The leading court artist of fifteenth-century France, Jean Fouquet (c. 1425–1481), was born in Tours and may have trained in Paris as an illuminator and in Bourges in the workshop of Jacob de Littemont, Flemish court painter to Charles VII. He was part of a French delegation to Rome in 1446–1448, but by mid century he had established a workshop in Tours and was a renowned painter. Fouquet drew from contemporary Italian Classicism, especially in rendering architecture, and he was also strongly influenced by Flemish illusionism. He painted pictures of Charles VII, the royal family, and courtiers; he also illustrated manuscripts and designed tombs.

Among the court officials who commissioned paintings from Fouquet was Étienne Chevalier, treasurer of France under Charles VII. Fouquet painted a diptych for him that was installed over the tomb of Chevalier's wife Catherine Budé (d. 1452) in the church of Notre-Dame in Melun (**FIG. 19-21**). Chevalier appears in the left panel, kneeling in prayer with clasped hands and an introspective, meditative gaze within an Italianate palace, accompanied by his name saint Stephen (Étienne in French). Fouquet describes the courtier's ruddy features with a mirrorlike precision that is reminiscent of Flemish art. He is expensively dressed in a heavy red wool garment lined with fur, and his "bowl cut" represents the latest fashion in Parisian coiffure. St. Stephen's features convey a comparable sense of likeness and sophistication. A deacon in the Early Christian church in Jerusalem, Stephen was the first Christian martyr, stoned to death for defending his beliefs. Here he wears the fifteenth-century liturgical vestments of a deacon and carries a large stone on a closed Gospel book as evidence of his martyrdom. A trickle of blood can be seen on his tonsured head (male members of religious orders shaved the tops of their heads as a sign of humility). Placing his arm around Étienne Chevalier's back, the saint seems to be introducing the treasurer to the Virgin and Child in the adjacent panel.

19-21 • Jean Fouquet ÉTIENNE CHEVALIER AND ST. STEPHEN, VIRGIN AND CHILD
The Melun Diptych. c. 1452–1455. Oil on oak panel. Left wing: 36½″ × 33½″ (92.7 × 85.5 cm), Staatliche Museen zu Berlin, Preussischer Kulturbesitz, Gemäldegalerie; right wing: 37¼″ × 33½″ (94.5 × 85.5 cm), Koninklijk Museum voor Schone Kunsten, Antwerp, Belgium.

The Virgin and Child, however, exist in another world. A supernatural vision unfolds here as the queen of heaven is enthroned surrounded by red and blue seraphim and cherubim, who form a tapestrylike background. Even the Virgin seems a celestial being, conceived by Fouquet as a hybrid of careful description and powerful abstraction. Her fashionable, tightly waisted bodice has been unlaced so she can present her spherical breast to a substantial, seated baby, who points across the juncture between the two wings of the diptych to acknowledge Chevalier. According to tradition, Fouquet gave this image of the Virgin the features of the king's much loved and respected mistress, Agnès Sorel, who died in 1450. The original frame that united these two panels—now divided between two museums—into a diptych is lost, but among the fragments that remain is a stunning medallion self-portrait that served as the artist's signature.

JEAN HEY, THE MASTER OF MOULINS Perhaps the greatest French follower of Jean Fouquet is an artist who for many years was known as the Master of Moulins after a large triptych he painted at the end of the fifteenth century under the patronage of Duke Jean II of Bourbon, for the Burgundian Cathedral of Moulins. This triptych combines the exuberance of Flemish attention to brilliant color and the differentiation of surface texture with a characteristically French air of reserved detachment. Recently the work of this artist has been associated with the name Jean Hey, a painter of Flemish origin, who seems to have been trained in the workshop of Hugo van der Goes, but who pursued his career at the French court.

This charming portrait (**FIG. 19–22**)—which may have been one half of a devotional diptych comparable to that painted by Memling for Maarten van Nieuwenhove (see **FIG.** 19–20)—portrays Margaret of Austria (1480–1530), daughter of Emperor Maximilian I, who had been betrothed to the future French king Charles VIII (r. 1483–1498) at age 2 or 3 and was being brought up at the French court. She would return home to her father in 1493 after Charles decided to pursue another, more politically expedient marriage (after two political marriages of her own, the widowed Margaret would eventually become governor of the Habsburg Netherlands), but Hey captures her at a tender moment a few years before those troubled times. She kneels in front of a strip of wall between two windows that open onto a lush country landscape, fingering the pearl beads of her rosary. Details of her lavish velvet and ermine outfit not only proclaim her wealth but provide the clues to her identity—the *Cs* and *Ms* embroidered on her collar signal her betrothal to Charles and the ostentatious *fleur-de-lis* pendant set with large rubies and pearls proclaims her affiliation with the French court. But it is the delicacy and sweet vulnerability of this 10-year-old girl that are most arresting. They recall Hugo van der Goes's sensitivity to the childlike qualities of the young members of donor families (see **FIG.** 19–19) and provide one strong piece of evidence for ascribing Hey's training to the workshop of this Flemish master.

19–22 • Jean Hey (The Master of Moulins) **PORTRAIT OF MARGARET OF AUSTRIA**
c. 1490. Oil on wood panel, 12⅞″ × 9⅛″ (32.7 × 23 cm).
Metropolitan Museum of Art, New York. Robert Lehman Collection

FLAMBOYANT ARCHITECTURE The great age of cathedral building that had begun in the second half of the twelfth century was essentially over by the end of the fourteenth century, but growing urban populations needed houses, city halls, guildhalls, and more parish churches. It was in buildings such as these that late Gothic architecture took form in a style we call "Flamboyant" because of its repeated, twisted, flamelike tracery patterns. Late Gothic masons covered their buildings with increasingly elaborate, complex, and at times playful architectural decoration. Like painters, sculptors also turned to describing the specific nature of the world around them, and they covered capitals and moldings with ivy, hawthorn leaves, and other vegetation, not just the conventional acanthus motifs inherited from the Classical world.

The **CHURCH OF SAINT-MACLOU** in Rouen, which was begun after a fund-raising campaign in 1432 and dedicated in 1521, is an outstanding and well-preserved example of Flamboyant Gothic (**FIG. 19–23**) probably designed by the Paris architect Pierre Robin. A projecting porch bends to enfold the façade of the church in a screen of tracery. Sunlight on the flame-shape openings casts ever-changing shadows across the intentionally complex surface. **Crockets**—small, knobby leaflike ornaments that line the

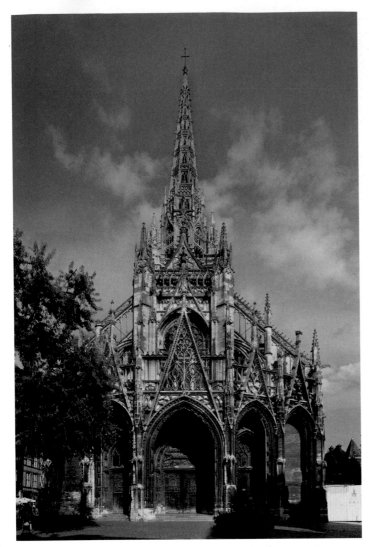

19-23 • Pierre Robin (?) CHURCH OF SAINT-MACLOU, ROUEN
Normandy, France. West façade, 1432–1521; façade c. 1500–1514.

GERMANY AND SWITZERLAND

Present-day Germany and Switzerland were situated within the Holy Roman Empire, a loose confederation of primarily German-speaking states. Artisan guilds grew powerful and trade flourished under the auspices of the Hanseatic League, an association of cities and trading outposts, stimulating a strengthening of the merchant

courtyard

19-24 • PLAN (A) AND INTERIOR COURTYARD (B) OF JACQUES COEUR HOUSE
Bourges, France. 1443–1451.

steep gables and slender buttresses—break every defining line. In the Flamboyant style, decoration sometimes disguises structural elements with an overlay of tracery and ornament in geometric and natural shapes, all to dizzying effect.

The house of Jacques Coeur, a fabulously wealthy merchant in Bourges, reflects the popularity of the Flamboyant style for secular architecture (**FIG. 19-24**). Built at great expense between 1443 and 1451, it survives almost intact, although it has been stripped of its rich furnishings. The rambling, palatial house is built around an irregular open courtyard, with spiral stairs in octagonal towers giving access to the upper-floor rooms. Tympana over doors indicate the function of the rooms within; for example, over the door to the kitchen a cook stirs the contents of a large bowl. Among the carved decorations are puns on the patron's surname, Coeur (meaning "heart" in French). The house was also Jacques Coeur's place of business, so it had large storerooms for goods and a strong-room for treasure.

19-25 • Konrad Witz MIRACULOUS DRAFT OF FISHES
From an altarpiece for the Cathedral of St. Peter, Geneva, Switzerland. 1444. Oil on wood panel,
4′3″ × 5′1″ (1.29 × 1.55 m). Musée d'Art et d'Histoire, Geneva.

class. The Fugger family, for example, began their spectacular rise from simple textile workers and linen merchants to bankers for the Habsburgs and the popes.

KONRAD WITZ Germanic fifteenth-century artists worked in two very different styles. Some, clustered around Cologne, continued the International Gothic style with increased prettiness, softness, and sweetness of expression. Other artists began an intense investigation and detailed description of the physical world. The major exponent of the latter style was Konrad Witz (active 1434–1446). A native of Swabia in southern Germany, Witz moved to Basel (in present-day Switzerland), where he found a rich source of patronage in the Church.

Witz's last large commission before his early death in 1446 was an altarpiece dedicated to St. Peter for the cathedral of Geneva, signed and dated to 1444. In one of its scenes—the **MIRACU-LOUS DRAFT OF FISHES** (**FIG. 19-25**)—Jesus appears posthumously to his disciples as they fish on the Sea of Galilee and Peter

leaps from the boat to greet him. But Witz sets the scene on the Lake of Geneva, with the distinctive dark mountain (the Mole) rising on the north shore and the snow-covered Alps shining in the distance. Witz records every nuance of light and water—the rippling surface, the reflections of boats, figures, and buildings, even the lake bottom. Peter's body and legs, visible through the water, are distorted by the refraction. It is one of the earliest times in European art that an artist captures both the appearance and the spirit of nature.

MICHAEL PACHER In Germanic lands, patrons preferred altarpieces that featured polychromed wood carvings rather than the large ensembles of panel paintings that we saw in Flanders (for example, "The Ghent Altarpiece," page 578). One of the greatest artists working in this tradition was painter and sculptor Michael Pacher (1435–1498), based in Bruneck, now in the Italian Alps. In 1471, Benedict Eck, abbot of Mondsee, commissioned from Pacher for the pilgrimage church of St. Wolfgang a grand high

19-26 • Michael Pacher
**ST. WOLFGANG
ALTARPIECE**
Church of St. Wolfgang,
Austria. 1471–1481. Carved,
painted, and gilt wood; wings
are oil on wood panel.

altarpiece that is still installed in its original church setting (**FIG. 19-26**). The surviving contract specifies materials and subject matter and even documents the cost—1,200 Hungarian florins— but sets no time limit for its completion. Pacher and his shop worked on it for ten years.

When it is open (as in FIG. 19-26), a dizzyingly complicated sculptural ensemble aligns up the middle, flanked by four large panel paintings portraying scenes from the life of the Virgin on the opened shutters. Both the design and execution were supervised by Pacher, but many other artists collaborated with him on the actual carving and painting. In the main scene, the wood carvings create a vision in Paradise where Christ crowns his mother as the queen of heaven, flanked by imposing images of local saints. The use of soft wood facilitated deep undercutting and amazing detail in the rendering of these figures, and the elaborate polychromy and gold leaf sheathed them in a shimmering finish that glitters in the changing patterns of natural light or the flickering glow of candles. It must have been an otherworldly sight.

19-27 • THE BUXHEIM ST. CHRISTOPHER
Mid 15th century. Hand-colored woodcut, 11⅜″ × 8⅛″ (28.85 × 20.7 cm).
Courtesy of the Director and Librarian, the John Rylands University Library, the University of Manchester, England.

The Latin text reads, "Whenever you look at the face of St. Christopher, you will not die a terrible death that day."

the block and the quality of the printing are very high. Lines vary in width to strengthen major forms. Delicate lines are used for inner modeling (facial features) and short parallel lines to indicate shadows (the inner side of draperies). The date 1423, which is cut into the block, was once thought to identify this print as among the earliest to survive. Recent studies have determined that the date refers to some event, and the print is now dated at mid century.

MARTIN SCHONGAUER Engraving may have originated with goldsmiths and armorers, who recorded their work by rubbing lampblack into the engraved lines and pressing paper over the plate. German artist Martin Schongauer (c. 1435–1491), who learned engraving from his goldsmith father, was an immensely skillful printmaker who excelled both in drawing and in the difficult technique of shading from deep blacks to faintest grays using only line. In **THE TEMPTATIONS OF ST. ANTHONY**, probably engraved during the 1470s (**FIG. 19-28**), Schongauer illustrated the original biblical meaning of temptation as a physical assault

THE GRAPHIC ARTS

Printmaking emerged in Europe at the end of the fourteenth century with the development of printing presses and the increased local manufacture and wider availability of paper. The techniques used by printmakers during the fifteenth century were woodcut and engraving (see "Woodcuts and Engravings on Metal," page 592). **Woodblocks** cut in relief had long been used to print designs on cloth, but only in the fifteenth century did the printing of images and texts on paper and the production of books in multiple copies of a single edition, or version, begin to replace the copying of each book by hand. Both hand-written and printed books were often illustrated, and printed images were sometimes hand-colored.

SINGLE SHEETS

Large quantities of single-sheet prints were made using woodcut and engraving techniques in the early decades of the fifteenth century. Often artists drew the images for professional woodworkers to cut from the block.

THE BUXHEIM ST. CHRISTOPHER Devotional images were sold as souvenirs to pilgrims at holy sites. **THE BUXHEIM ST. CHRISTOPHER** was found in the Carthusian monastery of Buxheim, in southern Germany, glued to the inside of the back cover of a manuscript (**FIG. 19-27**). St. Christopher, patron saint of travelers and protector from the plague, carries the Christ Child across the river. His efforts are witnessed by a monk holding out a light to guide him to the monastery door, but ignored by the hardworking millers on the opposite bank. Both the cutting of

19-28 • Martin Schongauer THE TEMPTATIONS OF ST. ANTHONY
c. 1470–1480. Engraving, 12¼″ × 9″ (31.1 × 22.9 cm).
Metropolitan Museum of Art, New York. Rogers Fund, 1920 (20.5.2)

Woodcuts are made by drawing on the smooth surface of a block of fine-grained wood, then cutting away all the areas around the lines with a sharp tool called a gouge, leaving the lines in high relief. When the block's surface is inked and a piece of paper pressed down hard on it, the ink on the relief areas transfers to the paper to create a reverse image. The effects can be varied by making thicker and thinner lines, and shading can be achieved by placing the lines closer or farther apart. Sometimes the resulting black-and-white images were then painted by hand.

Engraving on metal requires a technique called **intaglio**, in which the lines are cut into the plate with tools called gravers or **burins**. The engraver then carefully burnishes the plate to ensure a clean, sharp image. Ink is applied over the whole plate and forced down into the lines, then the plate's surface is carefully wiped clean of the excess ink. When paper and plate are held tightly together by a press, the ink in the recessed lines transfers to the paper.

Woodblocks and metal plates could be used repeatedly to make nearly identical images. If the lines of the block or plate wore down, the artists could repair them. Printing large numbers of identical prints of a single version, called an edition, was usually a team effort in a busy workshop. One artist would make the drawing. Sometimes it was drawn directly on the block or plate with ink, in reverse of its printed direction, sometimes on paper to be transferred in reverse onto the plate or block by another person, who then cut the lines. Others would ink and print the images.

In the illustration of books, the plates or blocks would be reused to print later editions and even adapted for use in other books. A set of blocks or plates for illustrations was a valuable commodity and might be sold by one workshop to another. Early in publishing, there were no copyright laws, and many entrepreneurs simply had their workers copy book illustrations onto woodblocks and cut them for their own publications.

Watch a video about the process of woodcut on myartslab.com

---

rather than a subtle inducement. Wildly acrobatic, slithery, spiky demons lift Anthony up off the ground to torment and terrify him in midair. The engraver intensified the horror of the moment by condensing the action into a swirling vortex of figures beating, scratching, poking, tugging, and no doubt shrieking at the stoical saint, who remains impervious to all, perhaps because of his power to focus inwardly on his private meditations.

PRINTED BOOKS

The explosion of learning in Europe in the fifteenth century encouraged experiments in faster and cheaper ways of producing books than by hand-copying them. The earliest printed books were block books, for which each page of text, with or without illustrations, was cut in relief on a single block of wood. Movable-type printing, in which individual letters could be arranged and locked together, inked, and then printed onto paper, was first achieved in Europe in the workshop of Johann Gutenberg in Mainz, Germany. More than 40 copies of Gutenberg's Bible, printed around 1455, still exist. As early as 1465, two German printers were working in Italy, and by the 1470s there were presses in France, Flanders, Holland, and Spain. With the invention of this fast way to make a number of identical books, the intellectual and spiritual life of Europe—and with it the arts—changed forever.

THE NUREMBERG CHRONICLE The publication of the *Nuremberg Chronicle* by prosperous Nuremberg printer Anton Koburger was the culmination of his complicated collaboration with scholars, artists, and investors, in an early capitalist enterprise that is a landmark in the history of printed books. The text of this history of the world was compiled by physician and scholar Hartmann Schedel, drawing from the work of colleagues and the extensive holdings of his private library. When Koburger set out to publish Schedel's compilation, he sought financial support from Sebald Schregel and his brother-in-law Sebastian Kammermaister, who had a proven record of patronage in book publishing. He also contracted in the 1480s with artists Michael Wolgemut and Wilhelm Pleydenwurff to produce the woodcut illustrations and in 1491 to work on the layout.

The *Nuremberg Chronicle* was published in 1493 in an edition of 2,500. Woodcut illustrations—1,809 in total—were dispersed throughout the book, spreading across the width of whole pages or tucked into the text along either margin. Those interested in purchasing the book could obtain it in Latin or German, on parchment or on paper, bound or unbound, as it came from the press or tinted with color. It seems fitting that the only instance of a double-page picture—filling the entire expanse of an opening with text restricted to headings and labels—is a

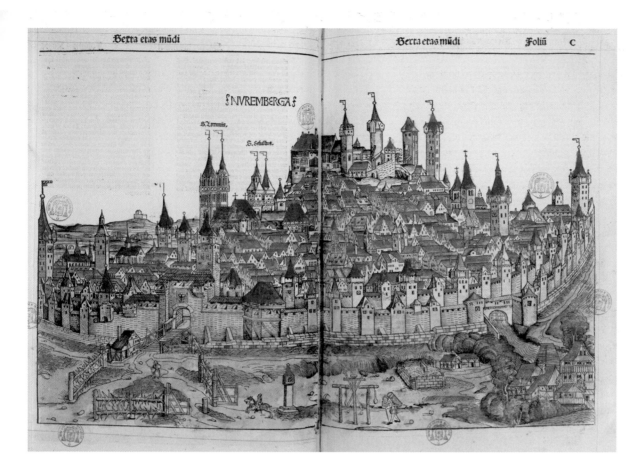

Getta etas mūdi   Getta etas mūdi   Foliū   C

§NVREMBERGA§

S. Laurentis,

S. Sebaldus,

19–29 • Michael Wolgemut, Wilhelm Pleydenwurff, and workshop **THE CITY OF NUREMBERG** *Nuremberg Chronicle*, published by Anton Koberger in 1493. Woodcut within a printed book, hand-colored after printing, each page 18½″ × 12¾″ (47 × 32.4 cm). Bibliothèque Mazarine, Paris.

panoramic view of the city of Nuremberg where this collaborative enterprise was centered (**FIG. 19–29**). Illustrated here is a view of this expansive cityscape in a copy of the book that was originally owned by a bibliophile who could afford to have the woodcuts hand-painted with color to enhance the appearance of this proud Renaissance city's portrait. As we will see, Nuremberg was the site of significant artistic developments in the sixteenth century as well.

THINK ABOUT IT

19.1 Explain how oil-painting technique allowed fifteenth-century Flemish painters to achieve unprecedented descriptive effects in their work. Support your answer by discussing one specific work in this chapter.

19.2 Discuss the symbolic meanings that fifteenth-century viewers would have comprehended in the objects contained in the domestic environment of either the Mérode Altarpiece (FIG. 19–10) or the Arnolfini double portrait (FIG. 19–1).

19.3 How have fifteenth-century northern paintings been characterized as devotional visions of the patrons who are portrayed within them? Use a specific work discussed in this chapter as the focus of your answer.

19.4 Why did printmaking become a major pictorial medium in northern Europe during the fifteenth century? Choose a work discussed in this chapter and explain how it supports your answer.

CROSSCURRENTS

FIG. 18–13

FIG. 19–10

These two paintings portray the same subject. Both were used as altarpieces. But they were painted by artists working in different places and trained in different traditions. Characterize the differences in style and narrative presentation. How are these features related to the cultural context of each?

✔—**Study** and review on myartslab.com

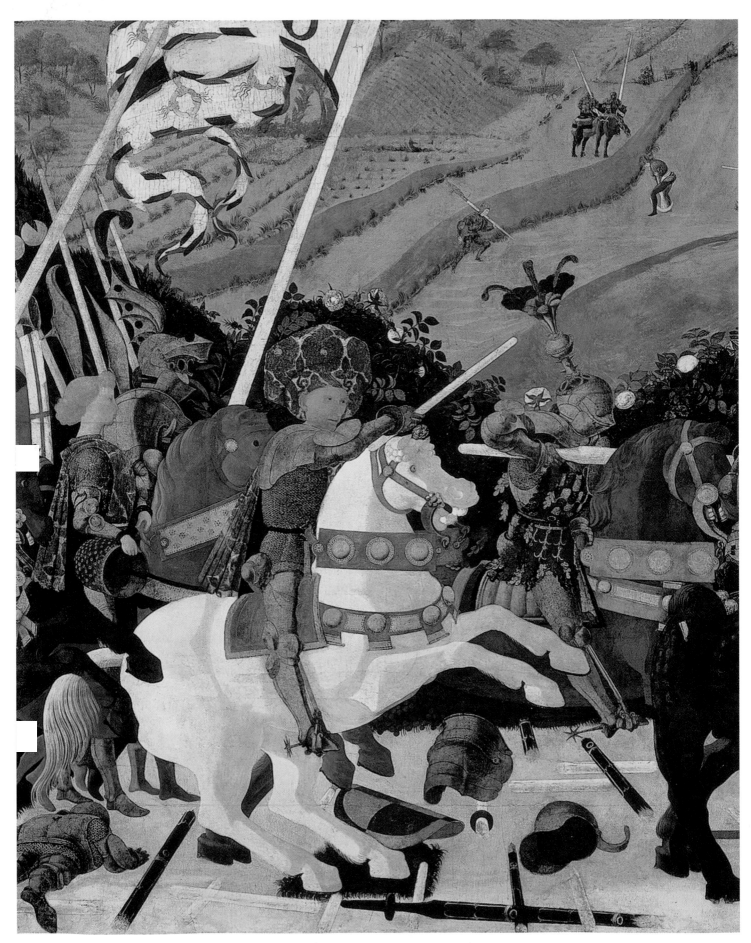

20-1 • Paolo Uccello **NICCOLÒ DA TOLENTINO LEADING THE CHARGE**

Detail from *The Battle of San Romano* (FIG. 20–24), 1438–1440. Tempera on wood panel. National Gallery, London.

Renaissance Art in Fifteenth-Century Italy

This ferocious but bloodless battle seems to take place in a dream, but it depicts a historical event (**FIG. 20–1**). Under an elegantly fluttering banner, the Florentine general Niccolò da Tolentino leads his men against the Sienese at the Battle of San Romano, which took place on June 1, 1432. The battle rages across a shallow stage defined by the debris of warfare arranged in a neat pattern on a pink ground and backed by blooming hedges. In the center foreground, Niccolò holds aloft a baton of command, the sign of his authority. His bold gesture—together with his white horse and outlandish, though quite fashionable, crimson and gold damask hat—ensures that he dominates the scene. His knights charge into the fray, and when they fall, like the soldier at the lower left, they join the many broken lances on the ground—all arranged in conformity with the new mathematical depiction of receding space called **linear perspective**, posed to align with the implied lines that would converge at a single point on the horizon.

An eccentric Florentine painter nicknamed Paolo Uccello ("Paul Bird") created the panel painting (see FIG. 20–24) from which the detail in FIGURE 20–1 is taken. It is one of three related panels—now separated, hanging in major museums in Florence, London, and Paris—commissioned by Lionardo Bartolini Salimbeni (1404–1479), who led the Florentine governing Council of Ten during the war against Lucca and Siena. Uccello's remarkable accuracy when depicting armor from the 1430s, heraldic banners, and even fashionable fabrics and crests surely would have appealed to Lionardo's civic pride. The hedges of oranges, roses, and pomegranates—all ancient fertility symbols—suggest that Lionardo might have commissioned the paintings at the time of his wedding in 1438. Lionardo and his wife, Maddalena, had six sons, two of whom inherited the paintings.

According to a complaint brought by Damiano, one of the heirs, Lorenzo de' Medici, the powerful *de facto* ruler of Florence, "forcibly removed" the paintings from Damiano's house. They were never returned, and Uccello's masterpieces are recorded in a 1492 inventory as hanging in the Medici palace. Perhaps Lorenzo, who was called "the Magnificent," saw Uccello's heroic pageant as a trophy more worthy of a Medici merchant prince. We will certainly discover that princely patronage was a major factor in the genesis of the Italian Renaissance as it developed in Florence during the early years of the fifteenth century.

LEARN ABOUT IT

20.1 Examine how sculptors were instrumental in the early development of the Italian Renaissance by increasing the lifelike qualities of human figures and drawing inspiration from ancient Roman sculpture.

20.2 Explore how an interest in scientific investigation blossomed into the development and use of linear perspective throughout fifteenth-century Italian painting.

20.3 Assess the role of wealthy merchants and *condottieri* in driving the development of Renaissance art and architecture.

20.4 Consider how the new focus on artistic competition and individual achievement created a climate for innovative and ambitious works.

((•—[Listen to the chapter audio on myartslab.com

HUMANISM AND THE ITALIAN RENAISSANCE

By the end of the Middle Ages, the most important Italian cultural centers lay north of Rome in the cities of Florence, Milan, and Venice, and in the smaller duchies of Mantua, Ferrara, and Urbino. Both political power and artistic patronage were dominated by wealthy families: the Medici in Florence, the Montefeltro in Urbino, the Gonzaga in Mantua, the Visconti and Sforza in Milan, and the Este in Ferrara (MAP 20–1). Cities grew in wealth and independence as people migrated from the countryside in unprecedented numbers. As in northern Europe, commerce became increasingly important. Money conferred status, and a shrewd business or political leader could become very powerful. The period saw the rise of mercenary armies led by entrepreneurial (and sometimes brilliant) military commanders called *condottieri*, who owed allegiance only to those who paid them well; their employer might be a city-state, a lord, or even the pope. Some *condottieri*, like Niccolò da Tolentino (see FIG. 20–1), became rich and famous. Others, like Federico da Montefeltro (see FIG. 20–31), were lords or dukes themselves, with territories of their own in need of protection. Patronage of the arts was an important public activity with political overtones. As one Florentine merchant, Giovanni Rucellai, succinctly noted, he supported the arts "because they serve the glory of God, the honour of the city, and the commemoration of myself" (cited in Baxandall, p. 2).

The term Renaissance (French for "rebirth") was only applied to this period by later historians. However, its origins lie in the thought of Petrarch and other fourteenth-century Italian writers, who emphasized the power and potential of human beings for great individual accomplishment. These Italian humanists also looked back at the thousand years extending from the disintegration of the Western Roman Empire to their own day and determined that the achievements of the Classical world were followed by what they perceived as a period of decline—a "middle" or "dark" age. They proudly saw their own era as a third age characterized by a revival or rebirth ("renaissance"), when humanity began to emerge from what they erroneously saw as intellectual and cultural stagnation to appreciate once more the achievement of the ancients and the value of rational, scientific investigation. They looked to the accomplishments of the Classical past for inspiration and instruction, and in Italy this centered on the heritage of ancient Rome. They sought the physical and literary records of the ancient world—assembling libraries, collecting sculpture and fragments of architecture, and beginning archaeological investigations. Their aim was to live a rich, noble, and productive life—usually within the framework of Christianity, but always adhering to a school of philosophy as a moral basis.

Artists, like the humanists, turned to Classical antiquity for inspiration, emulating what they saw in ancient Roman sculpture and architecture, even as they continued to fulfill commissions for predominantly Christian subjects and buildings. But from the secular world a number of home furnishings such as birth trays and marriage chests have survived, richly painted with allegorical and mythological themes (see "The Morelli–Nerli Wedding Chests," page 616). Patrons began to collect art for their personal enjoyment.

Like Flemish artists, Italian painters and sculptors increasingly focused their attention on rendering the illusion of physical reality. They did so in a more analytical way than the northerners. Rather than seeking to describe the detailed visual appearance of nature through luminosity and textural differentiation, Italian artists aimed at achieving lifelike but idealized weighty figures set within a rationally configured space organized through strict adherence to a mathematical system called linear perspective, which achieved the illusion of a measured and continuously receding space (see "Renaissance Perspective," page 610).

FLORENCE

In seizing Uccello's battle painting (see FIG. 20–1), Lorenzo de' Medici was asserting the role his family had come to expect to play in the history of Florence. The fifteenth century witnessed the rise of the Medici from among the most successful of a newly rich middle class (primarily merchants and bankers) to become the city's virtual rulers. Unlike the hereditary aristocracy, the Medici emerged from obscure roots to make their fortune in banking; from their money came their power.

The competitive Florentine atmosphere that had fostered mercantile success and civic pride also cultivated competition in the arts and encouraged an interest in ancient literary texts. This has led many to consider Florence the cradle of the Italian Renaissance. Under Cosimo the Elder (1389–1464), the Medici became leaders in intellectual and artistic patronage. They sponsored philosophers and other scholars who wanted to study the Classics, especially the works of Plato and his followers, the Neoplatonists. Neoplatonism distinguished between the spiritual (the ideal or Idea) and the physical (Matter) and encouraged artists to represent ideal figures. But it was writers, philosophers, and musicians—and not artists—who dominated the Medici Neoplatonic circle. Architects, sculptors, and painters learned their craft in apprenticeships and were therefore considered manual laborers. Nevertheless, interest in the ancient world rapidly spread from the Medici circle to visual artists, who gradually began to see themselves as more than laborers. Florentine society soon recognized their best works as achievements of a very high order.

Although the Medici were the *de facto* rulers, Florence was considered a republic. The Council of Ten (headed for a time by Salimbeni, who commissioned Uccello's *Battle of San Romano*) was a kind of constitutional oligarchy where wealthy men formed the government. At the same time, the various guilds wielded tremendous power; guild membership was a prerequisite for holding government office. Consequently, artists could look to the Church and the state—the city government and the guilds—as well as private individuals for patronage, and these patrons expected the

MAP 20–1 • FIFTEENTH-CENTURY ITALY

Powerful families divided the Italian peninsula into city-states: the Medici in Florence, the Visconti and Sforza in Milan, the Montefeltro in Urbino, the Gonzaga in Mantua, and the Este in Ferrara. After 1420, the popes ruled Rome, while in the south Naples and Sicily were French and then Spanish (Aragonese) territories. Venice maintained its independence as a republic.

artists to reaffirm and glorify their achievements with works that were not only beautiful but intellectually powerful.

ARCHITECTURE

The defining civic project of the early years of the fifteenth century was the completion of Florence Cathedral with a magnificent dome over the high altar. The construction of the cathedral had begun in the late thirteenth century and had continued intermittently during the fourteenth century. As early as 1367, builders had envisioned a very tall dome to span the huge interior space of the crossing, but they lacked the engineering know-how to construct it. When interest in completing the cathedral revived, around 1407, the technical solution was proposed by a young sculptor-turned-architect, Filippo Brunelleschi.

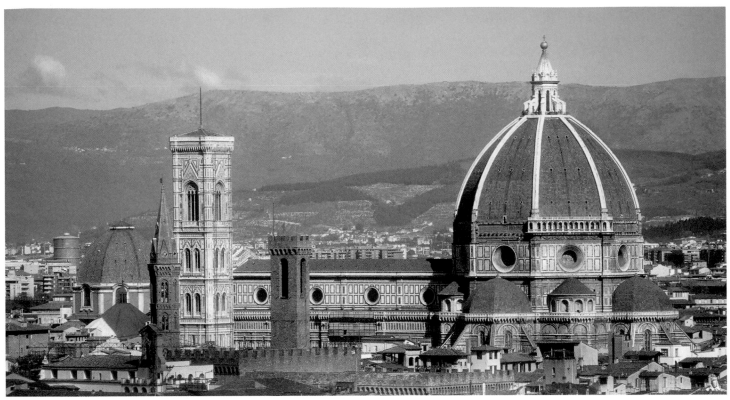

20-2 • Filippo Brunelleschi DOME OF FLORENCE CATHEDRAL (SANTA MARIA DEL FIORE)
1420–1436; lantern completed 1471.

👁 **Watch** an architectural simulation about Brunelleschi's dome on myartslab.com

20-3 • SCHEMATIC DRAWING OF FLORENCE CATHEDRAL
The separate, central-plan building in front of the façade is the baptistery. Adjacent to the façade is a tall tower designed by Giotto in 1334.

FILIPPO BRUNELLESCHI Filippo Brunelleschi (1377–1446) achieved what many considered impossible: He solved the problem of the dome of Florence Cathedral. Brunelleschi had originally trained as a goldsmith (see "The Competition Reliefs," page 603). To further his education, he traveled to Rome to study ancient Roman sculpture and architecture, and it was on his return to Florence that he tackled the dome. After the completion of a tall octagonal drum in 1412, Brunelleschi designed the dome itself in 1417, and it was built between 1420 and 1436 (**FIGS. 20-2, 20-3**). A revolutionary feat of engineering, the dome is a double shell of masonry 138 feet across. The octagonal outer shell is supported on eight large and 16 lighter ribs. Instead of using a costly and even dangerous scaffold and centering, Brunelleschi devised a system in which temporary wooden supports were cantilevered out from the drum. He moved these supports up as building progressed. As the dome was built up course by course, each portion of the structure reinforced the next one. Vertical marble ribs interlocked with horizontal sandstone rings, connected and reinforced with iron rods and oak beams. The inner and outer shells were linked internally by a system of arches. When completed, this self-buttressed unit required no external support to keep it standing.

An oculus (round opening) in the center of the dome was surmounted by a lantern designed in 1436. After Brunelleschi's death, this crowning structure, made up of Roman architectural forms, was completed by another Florentine architect, Michelozzo di Bartolomeo (1396–1472). The final touch—a gilt-bronze ball by Andrea del Verrocchio—was added in 1468–1471 (but replaced in 1602 with a smaller one).

Other commissions came quickly after the cathedral dome project established Brunelleschi's fame. From about 1418 until his death in 1446, Brunelleschi was involved in a series of influential projects. In 1419, he designed a foundling hospital for the city (see "The Foundling Hospital," page 600). Between 1419 and 1423, he built the elegant Capponi Chapel in the church of Santa Felicità (see **FIG. 21-29**). For the Medicis' parish church of San Lorenzo, he designed and built a centrally planned sacristy (a room where ritual attire and vessels are kept), from 1421 to 1428, and also conceived plans for a new church.

Brunelleschi's **SAN LORENZO** has a basilican plan with a long nave flanked by side aisles that open into shallow lateral chapels (**FIG. 20-4**). A short transept and square crossing lead to a square sanctuary flanked by additional chapels opening off the transept. Brunelleschi based his mathematically regular plan on a square module—a basic unit of measure that could be multiplied or

0 _____ 40m

20-4 • Filippo Brunelleschi (continued by Michelozzo di Bartolomeo) INTERIOR (A) AND PLAN (B) OF CHURCH OF SAN LORENZO, FLORENCE
c. 1421–1428; nave (designed 1434?) 1442–1470.

In 1419, the guild of silk manufacturers and goldsmiths (Arte della Seta) in Florence undertook a significant public service: It established a large public orphanage and commissioned the brilliant young architect Filippo Brunelleschi to build it near the church of the Santissima Annunziata (Most Holy Annunciation), which housed a miracle-working painting of the Annunciation, making it a popular pilgrimage site. Completed in 1444, the Foundling Hospital—**OSPEDALE DEGLI INNOCENTI**—was unprecedented in terms of scale and design (**FIG. 20-5**).

Brunelleschi created a building that paid homage to traditional forms while introducing features that we associate with the Italian Renaissance style. Traditionally, a charitable foundation's building had a portico open to the street to provide shelter, and Brunelleschi built an arcade of striking lightness and elegance,

using smooth round columns and richly carved capitals—his own interpretation of the Classical Corinthian order. Although we might initially assume that the sources for this arcade lay in the Roman architecture of Classical antiquity, columns were not actually used in antiquity to support free-standing arcades, only to support straight architraves. In fact, it was local Romanesque architecture that was the source for Brunelleschi's graceful design. It is the details of capitals and moldings that bring an air of the antique to this influential building.

The underlying mathematical basis for Brunelleschi's design—traced to the same Pythagorean proportional systems that were believed to create musical harmony—creates a distinct sense of harmony in this graceful arcade. Each bay encloses a cube of space defined by the 10-*braccia* (20-foot) height of the columns and the diameter of the arches.

Domical vaults, half again as high as the columns, cover the cubes. The bays at the end of the arcade are slightly larger than the rest, creating a subtle frame for the composition. Brunelleschi defined the perfect squares and semicircles of his building with dark gray stone (*pietra serena*) against plain white walls. His training as a goldsmith and sculptor (see "The Competition Reliefs," page 603) served him well as he led his artisans to carve crisp, elegantly detailed capitals and moldings for the covered gallery.

A later addition to the building seems eminently suitable: About 1487, Andrea della Robbia, who had inherited the family ceramics firm and its secret **glazing** formulas from his uncle Luca, created for the spandrels between the arches glazed terra-cotta medallions (**FIG. 20-6**) that signified the building's function. Molds were used in the ceramic workshop to facilitate the production of the series of similar babies in swaddling clothes that float at the center of each medallion. The molded terra-cotta forms were covered with a tin glaze to make the sculptures both weatherproof and decorative, and the baby-blue ceramic backgrounds—a signature color for the della Robbia family workshop—makes them seem to float as celestial apparitions. This is not altogether inappropriate. Although they clearly refer to the foundlings (*innocenti*) cared for in the hospital, they are also meant to evoke the "innocent" baby boys martyred by King Herod in his attempt to rid his realm of the potential rival the Magi had journeyed to venerate (Matthew 2:16).

Andrea della Robbia's adorable ceramic babies—which remain among the most beloved images of the city of Florence—seem to lay claim to the human side of Renaissance humanism, reminding viewers that the city's wealthiest guild cared for the most helpless members of society. Perhaps the Foundling Hospital spoke to fifteenth-century Florentines of an increased sense of social responsibility. Or perhaps, by so publicly demonstrating social concerns, the wealthy guild that sponsored it solicited the approval and support of the lower classes in the cut-throat power politics of the day.

20-6 • Andrea della Robbia **INFANT IN SWADDLING CLOTHES (ONE OF THE HOLY INNOCENTS MASSACRED BY HEROD)**
Ospedale degli Innocenti (Foundling Hospital), Florence. 1487. Glazed terra cotta.

20-5 • Filippo Brunelleschi **OSPEDALE DEGLI INNOCENTI (FOUNDLING HOSPITAL), FLORENCE**
Designed 1419; begun under Brunelleschi's direct supervision 1421–1427; construction continued into the 1440s.

20-7 • Attributed to Michelozzo di Bartolomeo FAÇADE, PALAZZO MEDICI-RICCARDI, FLORENCE
Begun 1446 (the view shown here includes a two-bay extension constructed during the 18th century).

For the palace site, Cosimo de' Medici the Elder chose the Via de' Gori at the corner of the Via Larga, the widest city street at that time. Despite his practical reasons for constructing a large residence and the fact that he chose simplicity and austerity over grandeur in the exterior design, his detractors commented and gossiped. As one exaggerated, "[Cosimo] has begun a palace which throws even the Colosseum at Rome into the shade."

THE MEDICI PALACE Brunelleschi may have been involved in designing the nearby Medici Palace (now known as the Palazzo Medici-Riccardi) in 1446. According to Giorgio Vasari, the sixteenth-century artist and theorist who wrote the first modern history of art, Cosimo de' Medici the Elder rejected Brunelleschi's model for the **palazzo** as too grand (any large house was called a *palazzo*—"palace"). Many now attribute the design of the building to Michelozzo. The austere exterior (**FIG. 20-7**) was in keeping with the Florentine political climate and concurrent religious attitudes, imbued with the Franciscan ideals of poverty and charity. Like many other European cities, Florence had sumptuary laws, which forbade ostentatious displays of wealth—but they were often ignored. For example, private homes were supposed to be limited to a dozen rooms, but Cosimo acquired and demolished 20 small houses to provide the site for his new residence. His house was more than a dwelling place; it was his place of business, his company headquarters. The palazzo symbolized the family and established its proper place in the Florentine social hierarchy.

Huge in scale—each story is more than 20 feet high—the building is marked by harmonious proportions and elegant, Classically inspired details. On one side, the ground floor originally opened through large, round arches onto the street, creating in effect a loggia that provided space for the family business. These arches were walled up in the sixteenth century and given windows designed by Michelangelo. The large, **rusticated** stone blocks—that is, blocks with their outer faces left rough—facing the lower story clearly set it off from the upper two levels. In fact, all three stories are distinguished by stone surfaces that vary from sculptural at the ground level to almost smooth dressed stone on the third floor.

The builders followed the time-honored tradition of placing rooms around a central courtyard. Unlike the plan of the house of Jacques Coeur (see FIG. 19-24), however, the **PALAZZO MEDICI-RICCARDI COURTYARD** is square in plan with rooms arranged symmetrically (**FIG. 20-8**). Round arches on slender columns form a continuous arcade under an enclosed second story. Disks

divided and applied to every element of the design, creating a series of clear, harmonious spaces. Architectural details, all in a Classical style, were carved in **pietra serena**, a gray Tuscan sandstone that became synonymous with Brunelleschi's interiors. Below the plain clerestory with its unobtrusive openings, the arches of the nave arcade are carried on tall, slender Corinthian columns made even taller by the insertion of an impost block between the column capital and the springing of the round arches—one of Brunelleschi's favorite details. Flattened architectural moldings in *pietra serena* repeat the arcade in the outer walls of the side aisles, and each bay is covered by its own shallow domical vault. Brunelleschi's rational approach, clear sense of order, and innovative incorporation of Classical motifs inspired later Renaissance architects, many of whom learned from his work firsthand by completing his unfinished projects.

20-8 • COURTYARD WITH SGRAFFITO DECORATION, PALAZZO MEDICI-RICCARDI, FLORENCE
Begun 1446.

In 1401, the building supervisors of the baptistery of Florence Cathedral decided to commission a new pair of bronze doors, funded by the powerful wool merchants' guild. Instead of choosing a well-established sculptor with a strong reputation, a competition was announced for the commission. This prestigious project would be awarded to the artist who demonstrated the greatest talent and skill in executing a trial piece: a bronze relief representing Abraham's sacrifice of Isaac (Genesis 22:1–13) composed within the same Gothic quatrefoil framework used in Andrea Pisano's first set of bronze doors for the baptistery, made in the 1330s (see FIG. 18–3). The narrative subject was full of dramatic potential. Abraham, commanded by God to slay his beloved son Isaac as a burnt offering, has traveled to the mountains for the sacrifice. Just as he is about to slaughter Isaac, an angel appears, commanding him to save his son and substitute a ram tangled in the bushes behind him.

Two competition panels have survived, those submitted by the presumed finalists—Filippo Brunelleschi and Lorenzo Ghiberti, both young artists in their early twenties. Brunelleschi's composition (FIG. 20–9) is rugged and explosive, marked by raw dramatic intensity. At the right, Abraham lunges forward, grabbing his son by the neck, while the angel swoops energetically to stay his hand just as the knife is about to strike. Isaac's awkward pose embodies his fear and struggle. Ghiberti's version (FIG. 20–10) is quite different, suave and graceful rather than powerful and dramatic. Poses are controlled and choreographed; the harmonious pairing of son and father contrasts sharply with the wrenching struggle in Brunelleschi's rendering. And Ghiberti's Isaac is not a stretched, scrawny youth, but a fully idealized Classical figure exuding calm composure.

Brunelleschi's biographer, Antonio di Tuccio Manetti, claimed that the competition ended in a tie, and that when the committee decided to split the commission between the two young artists, Brunelleschi withdrew. It is possible, however, that the cloth merchants actually chose Ghiberti to make the doors. They might have preferred the suave elegance of his figural composition. Perhaps they liked the prominence of elegantly disposed swags of cloth, reminders of the source of their patronage and prosperity. But they also could have been swayed by the technical superiority of Ghiberti's relief. Unlike Brunelleschi, Ghiberti cast background and figures mostly as a single piece, making his bronze stronger, lighter, and less expensive to produce. The finished doors—installed in the baptistery in 1424—were so successful that Ghiberti was commissioned to create another set (see FIG. 20–16), his most famous work, hailed by Michelangelo as the "Gates of Paradise." Brunelleschi would refocus his career on buildings rather than bronzes, becoming one of the most important architects of the Italian Renaissance (see FIGS. 20–2, 20–3, 20–4, 20–5).

20–9 • Filippo Brunelleschi SACRIFICE OF ISAAC
1401–1402. Bronze with gilding, 21″ × 17½″ (53 × 44 cm) inside molding. Museo Nazionale del Bargello, Florence.

20–10 • Lorenzo Ghiberti SACRIFICE OF ISAAC
1401–1402. Bronze with gilding, 21″ × 17½″ (53 × 44 cm) inside molding. Museo Nazionale del Bargello, Florence.

bearing the Medici arms surmount each arch in a frieze decorated with swags in **sgraffito** work (decoration produced by scratching through a darker layer of plaster or glaze). Such classicizing elements, inspired by the study of Roman ruins, gave the great house an aura of dignity and stability that enhanced the status of its owners. The Medici Palace inaugurated a new fashion for monumentality and regularity in residential Florentine architecture. Wealthy Florentine families soon emulated it in their own houses.

SCULPTURE

The new architectural language inspired by ancient Classical forms was accompanied by a similar impetus in sculpture. By 1400, Florence had enjoyed internal stability and economic prosperity for

over two decades. However, until 1428, the city and its independence were challenged by two great anti-republican powers: the duchy of Milan and the kingdom of Naples. In an atmosphere of wealth and civic patriotism, Florentines turned to commissions that would express their self-esteem and magnify the importance of their city. A new attitude toward realism, space, and the Classical past set the stage for more than a century of creativity. Sculptors led the way.

ORSANMICHELE In 1339, 14 of Florence's most powerful guilds had been commissioned to fill the ground-floor niches that decorated the exterior of **ORSANMICHELE**—a newly completed loggia that served as a grain market—with sculpted images of their patron saints (**FIG. 20-11**). By 1400, only three had fulfilled this assignment. In the new climate of republicanism and civic pride, the government pressured the guilds to furnish their niches with statuary. In the wake of this directive, Florence witnessed a dazzling display of sculpture produced by the most impressive local practitioners, including Nanni di Banco, Lorenzo Ghiberti, and Donatello, each of whom took responsibility for filling three niches.

In about 1409, Nanni di Banco (c. 1385–1421), son of a sculptor in the Florence Cathedral workshop, was commissioned by the stonecarvers' and woodworkers' guild (to which he himself belonged) to produce **THE FOUR CROWNED MARTYRS** (**FIG. 20-12**). According to tradition, these third- or fourth-century Christian martyrs were sculptors, executed for refusing to make an image of a pagan Roman god for Emperor Diocletian. Although the architectural setting is Gothic in style, Nanni's figures—with their solid bodies, heavy, form-revealing togas, noble hair and beards, and portraitlike features—reveal his interest in ancient Roman sculpture, particularly portraiture (see **FIG. 6-22**). They stand as a testimony to this sculptor's role in the Florentine revival of interest in antiquity.

The saints convey a new spatial relationship to the building and to the viewer. They stand in a semicircle, with feet and drapery protruding beyond the floor of the niche and into the viewer's space. The saints appear to be four

20-11 • EXTERIOR VIEW OF ORSANMICHELE SHOWING SCULPTURE IN NICHES
Florence. Begun 1337.

At street level, Orsanmichele was constructed originally as an open loggia (similar to the Loggia dei Lanzi in FIG. 18–2); in 1380 the spaces under the arches were filled in. In this view of the southeast corner, appearing on the receding wall to the left is first (in the foreground on the corner pier) Donatello's *St. George*, then, Nanni di Banco's *Four Crowned Martyrs*. However, the sculptures seen in this photograph are modern replicas; the originals have been removed to museums for safekeeping.

individuals interacting within their own world, but a world that opens to engage with passing pedestrians (see FIG. 20-11). The relief panel below the niche shows the four sculptors at work, embodied with a similar solid vigor. Nanni deeply undercut both figures and objects to cast shadows that enhance the illusion of three-dimensionality.

Donatello (Donato di Niccolò di Betto Bardi, c. 1386/1387–1466) also received three commissions for the niches at Orsanmichele during the first quarter of the century. Like Nanni, a member of the guild of stonecarvers and woodworkers, he worked

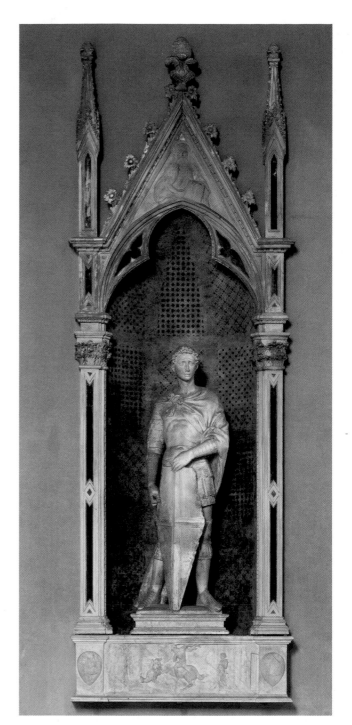

20-13 • Donatello ST. GEORGE
Formerly in Orsanmichele, Florence. 1417–1420. Marble, height 6′5″ (1.95 m). Museo Nazionale del Bargello, Florence.

20-12 • Nanni di Banco THE FOUR CROWNED MARTYRS
c. 1409–1417. Marble, height of figures 6′ (1.83 m). Photographed *in situ* before removal of the figures to the Museo di Orsanmichele, Florence.

in both media, as well as in bronze. During a long and productive career, he developed into one of the most influential and distinguished figures in the history of Italian sculpture, approaching each commission as if it were the opportunity for a new experiment. One of Florence's lesser guilds—the armorers and swordmakers—called on Donatello to carve a majestic and self-assured **ST. GEORGE** for their niche (FIG. 20-13). As originally conceived, the saint would have been a standing advertisement for their trade,

20-14 • Donatello DAVID
c. 1446–1460(?). Bronze, height 5′2¼″ (1.58 m). Museo Nazionale del Bargello, Florence.

This sculpture is first recorded as being in the courtyard of the Medici Palace in 1469, where it stood on a base inscribed with these lines:
  The victor is whoever defends the fatherland.
  All-powerful God crushes the angry enemy.
  Behold, a boy overcomes the great tyrant.
  Conquer, O citizens!

👁 **Watch** a video about the process of lost-wax casting on myartslab.com

carrying a metal sword in his right hand and probably wearing a metal helmet and sporting a scabbard, all now lost. The figure has remarkable presence, even without his accessories. St. George stands in solid contrapposto, legs braced to support his armor-heavy torso, the embodiment of alertness and courage. He seems to stare out into our world, perhaps surveying his most famous adversary—a dragon that was holding a princess captive—lurking unsettlingly in the space behind us. With his wrinkled brow and determined expression, he is tense, alert, focused, if perhaps also slightly worried. Donatello's complex psychological characterization of this warrior-saint particularly impressed Donatello's contemporaries, not least among them his potential patrons.

For the base of the niche, Donatello carved a remarkable shallow relief showing St. George slaying the dragon and saving the princess, a well-known part of his story. The contours of the foreground figures are slightly undercut to emphasize their mass, while the landscape and architecture are in progressively lower relief until they are barely incised rather than carved, an ingenious emulation of the painters' technique of atmospheric perspective. This is also a pioneering example of linear perspective (see "Renaissance Perspective," page 610), in which the orthogonals converge on the figure of the saint himself, using this burgeoning representational system not only to simulate spatial recession but also to provide narrative focus.

DONATELLO Donatello's long career as a sculptor in a broad variety of media established him as one of the most successful and admired sculptors of the Italian Renaissance. He excelled in part because of his attentive exploration of human emotions and expression, as well as his ability to solve the technical problems posed by various media—from lost-wax casting in bronze and carved marble to polychromed wood. In a bronze **DAVID**, he produced the first life-size, free-standing nude since antiquity (**FIG. 20-14**), and in his portrait of the soldier Erasmo da Narni, one of the first life-size bronze equestrian portraits of the Renaissance (see **FIG. 20-15**).

Since nothing is known about the circumstances of its creation, the *David* has been the subject of continuing inquiry and speculation. Although the statue clearly draws on the Classical tradition of heroic nudity, the meaning of this sensuous, pre-pubescent boy in a jaunty laurel-trimmed shepherd's hat and boots has long piqued interest. Some art historians have stressed an overt homoeroticism, especially in the openly effeminate conception of David and the way a wing from the helmet on Goliath's severed head caresses the young hero's inner thigh. Others have seen in David's angular pose and boyish torso a sense that he is poised between childish interests and adult responsibility, an image of improbable heroism. David was a potent political image in Florence, a symbol of the citizens' resolve to oppose tyrants regardless of their superior power, since virtue brings divine support and preternatural strength, and we will see other Florentine Renaissance renderings of this biblical hero. Indeed, an inscription engraved into the base where the sculpture once stood suggests that it could have celebrated the Florentine triumph over the Milanese in 1425, a victory that brought resolution to a quarter-century struggle with despots and helped give Florence a vision of itself as a strong, virtuous republic.

In 1443, Donatello was probably called to Padua to execute an **EQUESTRIAN STATUE** (**FIG. 20-15**) to commemorate the Paduan general of the Venetian army, Erasmo da Narni, nicknamed "Gattamelata" (meaning "Honeyed Cat"—a reference to his mother, Melania Gattelli). If any image could be said to characterize the self-made men of the Italian Renaissance, surely it would be those of the *condottieri*—the brilliant generals such as Gattamelata and Niccolò da Tolentino (see **FIG. 20-1**) who organized the armies and fought for any city-state willing to pay for their services. As guardians for hire, they were tough, opportunistic mercenaries. But they also subscribed to an ideal of military and civic virtue.

Horsemanship was more than a necessary skill for the *condottieri*. The horse, a beast of enormous brute strength, symbolized animal passions, and skilled horsemanship demonstrated physical and intellectual control—self-control, as well as control of the animal—the triumph of the intellect, of "mind over matter."

Donatello's sources for this statue were surviving Roman bronze equestrian portraits, notably the famous image of Marcus Aurelius (see **FIG. 6-57**), which the sculptor certainly knew from his stay in Rome, as well as the famous set of Roman bronze horses installed on the façade of St. Mark's Cathedral in Venice. Viewed from a distance, Donatello's man–animal juggernaut, installed on a high marble base in front of the church of Sant'Antonio in Padua, seems capable of thrusting forward at the first threat. Seen up close, however, the man's sunken cheeks, sagging jaw, ropy neck, and stern but sad expression suggest a warrior grown old and tired from the constant need for military vigilance and rapid response.

THE GATES OF PARADISE The bronze doors that Lorenzo Ghiberti (1381?–1455) produced for the Florentine Baptistery after winning his famous competition with Brunelleschi in 1401 (see "The Competition Reliefs," page 603) were such a success that in 1425 he was awarded the commission for yet another set of bronze doors for the east side of the Baptistery, facing the doors of the cathedral; his first set of doors was moved to the north side. The new door panels, funded by the wool manufacturers' guild, were a significant conceptual leap from the older schemes of 28 small scenes employed for Ghiberti's earlier doors and those of Andrea Pisano in the fourteenth century (see **FIG. 18-3**). Ghiberti departed entirely from the old arrangement, producing a set of ten scenes from the Hebrew Bible—from the Creation

20-15 • Donatello EQUESTRIAN STATUE OF ERASMO DA NARNI (GATTAMELATA)
Piazza del Santo, Padua. 1443–1453. Bronze, height approx. 12′2″ (3.71 m).

to the reign of Solomon—composed in rectangular fields, like a set of framed paintings. Michelangelo reportedly said that the results, installed in 1452, were worthy of the **"GATES OF PARADISE"**—the name by which they are now commonly known (**FIG. 20-16**).

Ghiberti organized the space in the ten square reliefs either by a system of linear perspective with obvious orthogonal lines (see "Renaissance Perspective," page 610) or more intuitively by a series of arches or rocks or trees charting the path into the distance. Foreground figures are grouped in the lower third of each panel, while the other figures decrease gradually in size to map their positioning in deep space. The use of a system of perspective, with clearly differentiated background and foreground, also helped Ghiberti combine a series of related events, separated by narrative time, within a single pictorial frame.

The story of **JACOB AND ESAU** (Genesis 25 and 27) fills the center panel of the left door. Ghiberti creates a coherent and measurable space peopled by graceful, idealized figures (**FIG. 20-17**). He pays careful attention to one-point perspective in laying out the architectural setting. Squares in the pavement establish the receding lines of the orthogonals that seem to converge on a central vanishing point under the loggia, while towering arches overlap and gradually diminish in size from foreground to background to define the receding space above the figures. The story unfolds in a series of individual episodes and begins in the background. On the rooftop (upper right) Rebecca stands, listening as God warns of her unborn sons' future conflict; under the left-hand arch she gives birth to the twins. The adult Esau sells his rights as oldest son to his brother Jacob, and when he goes hunting (center right), Rebecca and Jacob plot against him. Finally, in the right foreground, Jacob receives Isaac's blessing, while in the center, Esau faces his father. Ghiberti's portrayal of the scene relates more closely to developments in painting than to contemporary sculpture. Ghiberti not only signed his work, but also included his self-portrait in the medallion beside the lower right-hand corner of this panel.

20-17 • Lorenzo Ghiberti JACOB AND ESAU, PANEL OF THE "GATES OF PARADISE" (EAST BAPTISTERY DOORS)
Formerly on the Baptistery of San Giovanni, Florence. c. 1435. Gilded bronze, 31¼" (79 cm) square. Museo dell'Opera del Duomo, Florence.

PAINTING

Wealthy patrons commissioned murals and large altarpieces for their local churches and smaller panel paintings for their houses and private chapels. Artists experienced in fresco were in great demand and traveled widely to execute wall and ceiling decorations. At first the Italians showed little interest in oil painting, for the most part using tempera even for their largest works. But, in the last decades of the century, oil painting became popular in Venice.

MASACCIO Even though his brief career lasted less than a decade, Tommaso di Ser Giovanni di Mone Cassai (1401–1428/1429?), nicknamed "Masaccio" (meaning "Big Tom"), established a new direction in Florentine painting, much as Giotto had a century earlier. He did this by integrating monumental and consistently scaled figures into rational architectural and natural settings using linear perspective. The chronology of Massaccio's works is uncertain, but his fresco of the **TRINITY** in the church of Santa Maria Novella in Florence must have been painted around 1426, the date on the Lenzi family tombstone that once stood in front of it (**FIGS. 20-19, 20-20**).

Masaccio's fresco was meant to give the illusion of a stone funerary monument and altar table set below a deep **aedicula** (framed niche) in the wall. The effect of looking up into a barrel-vaulted niche was made plausible through precisely rendered linear perspective. The eye level of an adult male viewer standing within

20-16 • Lorenzo Ghiberti "GATES OF PARADISE" (EAST BAPTISTERY DOORS)
Formerly on the Baptistery of San Giovanni, Florence. 1425–1452. Gilt bronze, height 15' (4.57 m). Museo dell'Opera del Duomo, Florence.

The door panels, commissioned by the wool manufacturers' guild, depict ten scenes from the Hebrew Bible beginning with the Creation in the upper left panel. The murder of Abel by his brother, Cain, follows in the upper right panel, succeeded in the same left–right paired order by the Flood and the drunkenness of Noah, Abraham sacrificing Isaac, the story of Jacob and Esau, Joseph sold into slavery by his brothers, Moses receiving the Tablets of the Law, Joshua and the fall of Jericho, David and Goliath, and finally Solomon and the queen of Sheba. Ghiberti placed his own portrait as a signature in the frame at the lower right corner of the Jacob and Esau panel. He wrote in his *Commentaries* (c. 1450–1455): "I strove to imitate nature as clearly as I could, and with all the perspective I could produce, to have excellent compositions with many figures."

TECHNIQUE | Renaissance Perspective

Fifteenth-century Italian artists developed a system known as linear, or mathematical perspective that enabled them to represent three dimensions on a two-dimensional surface, simulating the recession of space in the visible world pictorially in a way they found convincing. The sculptor and architect Filippo Brunelleschi first demonstrated the system about 1420, and the theorist and architect Leon Battista Alberti codified it in 1436 in his treatise *Della Pittura* (*On Painting*).

For Alberti, in one-point linear perspective a picture's surface was conceived as a flat plane that intersected the viewer's field of vision at right angles. This highly artificial concept presumed a viewer standing dead center at a prescribed distance from a work of art. From this single fixed vantage point, everything would appear to recede into the distance at the same rate, following imaginary lines called orthogonals that met at a single **vanishing point** on the horizon. By using orthogonals in concert with controlled diminution of scale as forms move back toward the vanishing point, artists could replicate the optical illusion that things appear to grow smaller, rise higher, and come closer together as they get farther away from us. Linear perspective makes pictorial spaces seem almost like extensions of the viewer's real space, creating a compelling, even exaggerated sense of depth (**FIG. 20–18**).

Linear perspective is not the only way to simulate spatial recession in two-dimensional painting (See "Pictorial Devices for Depicting Recession in Space," page xxiii). In atmospheric perspective, for example, variations in color and clarity convey the feeling of distance when objects and landscape are portrayed less clearly, and colors become grayer, in the background, imitating the natural effects of a loss of clarity and color when viewing things in the distance through an atmospheric haze.

20–18 • Perugino CHRIST GIVING THE KEYS TO ST. PETER, WITH A SCHEMATIC DRAWING SHOWING THE ORTHOGONALS AND VANISHING POINT

Fresco on the right wall of the Sistine Chapel (see FIG. 20–33), Vatican, Rome. 1481. 11′5½″ × 18′8½″ (3.48 × 5.70 m).

Christ Giving the Keys to St. Peter is a remarkable study in linear perspective. The clear demarcation of the paving stones of the piazza provides a network of orthogonal and horizontal lines for the measured placement of the figures. People and buildings become increasingly, and logically, smaller as the space recedes. Horizontally, the composition is divided between the foreground frieze of figures and the widely spaced background buildings, vertically by the open space at the center between Christ and Peter and by the symmetrical architectural forms on either side of this central axis. Perugino's painting is, among other things, a representation of Alberti's ideal city, described in *De re aedificatoria* as having a "temple" (that is, a church) at the very center of a great open space raised on a dais and separate from any other buildings that might obstruct it.

the church determined the horizon line on which the vanishing point was centered, just below the kneeling figures above the altar. And the painting demonstrates not only Masaccio's intimate knowledge of Brunelleschi's perspective experiments (see "Renaissance Perspective," above), but also his architectural style (see FIG. 20–4). The painted architecture is an unusual combination of Classical orders. On the wall surface, Corinthian pilasters support a plain architrave below a cornice, while inside the niche Renaissance variations on Ionic columns support framing arches at the front and rear of the barrel vault. The "source" of the consistent illumination of the architecture lies in front of the picture, casting reflections on the coffers, or sunken panels, of the ceiling.

The figures are organized in a measured progression through space. At the near end of the recessed, barrel-vaulted space is the Trinity—Jesus on the cross, the dove of the Holy Spirit poised in downward flight above his tilted halo, and God the Father, who stands behind to support the cross from his elevated perch on a high platform. As in many scenes of the Crucifixion, Jesus is flanked by the Virgin Mary and John the Evangelist, who contemplate the scene on either side of the cross. Mary gazes calmly out at us, her raised hand drawing our attention to the Trinity. Members of the Lenzi family kneel in front of the pilasters—thus closer to us than the Crucifixion; the red robes of the male donor signify that he was a member of the governing council of Florence. Below these donors, in an open sarcophagus, is a skeleton, a grim reminder of the Christian belief that since death awaits us all, our only hope is redemption and the promise of life in the hereafter, rooted in Christ's sacrifice on the cross. The inscription above the skeleton reads: "I was once that which you are, and what I am you also will be."

20-20 • SECTION DIAGRAM OF THE ILLUSIONISTIC SPATIAL WORLD PORTRAYED IN MASACCIO'S TRINITY
After Gene Brucker, *Florence: The Golden Age*, Berkeley, 1998.

horizon

picture plane

viewing point

20-21 • Masaccio THE EXPULSION OF ADAM AND EVE FROM PARADISE
Brancacci Chapel, church of Santa Maria del Carmine, Florence.
c. 1427. Fresco, 7′ × 2′11″ (214 × 90 cm).

Cleaning and restoration of the Brancacci Chapel paintings revealed the remarkable speed and skill with which Masaccio worked. He painted Adam and Eve in four *giornate* (each *giornata* of fresh plaster representing a day's work). Working from the top down and left to right, he painted the angel on the first day; on the second day, the portal; Adam on the third day; and Eve on the fourth.

THE BRANCACCI CHAPEL Masaccio's brief career culminated in the frescos he painted on the walls of the Brancacci Chapel in the church of Santa Maria del Carmine in Florence. Reproduced here are two of the best-known scenes: **THE EXPULSION OF ADAM AND EVE FROM PARADISE** (FIG. 20-21) and **THE TRIBUTE MONEY** (FIG. 20-22). In *The Expulsion*, he presented Adam and Eve as monumental nude figures, combining his studies of the human figure with an intimate knowledge of ancient Roman sculpture. In contrast to Flemish painters, who sought to record every visible detail of a figure's surface (compare Adam and Eve from FIG. 19–15), Masaccio focused on the mass of the bodies formed by the underlying bone and muscle structure, and a single light source emphasizes their tangibility with modeled forms and cast shadows. Departing from earlier interpretations of the event that emphasized wrongdoing and the fall from grace, Masaccio concerns himself with the psychological impact of shame on these first humans, who have been cast out of paradise mourning and protesting, thrown naked into the world.

In *The Tribute Money* (see FIG. 20-22), Masaccio portrays an incident from the life of Jesus that highlights St. Peter (Matthew 17:24–27), to whom this chapel was dedicated. In the central scene a tax collector (dressed in a short red tunic and seen from behind) asks Peter (in the left foreground with the short gray beard) if Jesus pays the Jewish temple tax (the "tribute money" of the title). Set against the stable backdrop of a semicircular block of apostolic observers, a masterful series of dynamic diagonals in the postures and gestures of the three main figures interlocks them in a compositional system that imbues their interaction with a sense of tension calling out for resolution. Jesus instructs Peter to "go to the sea, drop in a hook, and take the first fish that comes up," which Peter does at the far left. In the fish's mouth is a coin, which Peter gives to the tax collector at the far right. The tribute story was especially significant for Florentines because in 1427, to raise money for defense against military aggression, the city enacted a graduated tax, based on the value of people's personal property.

The Tribute Money is particularly remarkable for its early use of both linear and atmospheric perspective to integrate figures, architecture, and landscape into a consistent whole. Jesus, and the apostles surrounding him, form a clear central focus, from which the landscape seems to recede naturally into the far distance. To foster this illusion, Masaccio used linear perspective in the depiction of the house, and then reinforced it by diminishing the sizes of the distant barren trees and reducing the size of the crouching Peter at far left. The central vanishing point established by the orthogonals of the house corresponds with the head of Jesus.

The cleaning of the painting in the 1980s revealed that it was painted in 32 *giornate* (a *giornata* is a section of fresh plaster that could be prepared and painted in a single day; see "*Buon Fresco*," page 539). The cleaning also uncovered Masaccio's subtle use of color to create atmospheric perspective in the distant landscape, where mountains fade from grayish-green to grayish-white and the houses and trees on their slopes are loosely sketched to simulate

20-22 • Masaccio THE TRIBUTE MONEY
Brancacci Chapel, church of Santa Maria del Carmine, Florence. c. 1427. Fresco, 8'1" × 19'7" (2.46 × 6 m).

🔍 **View** the Closer Look for *The Tribute Money* on myartslab.com

the lack of clear definition when viewing things in the distance through a haze. Green leaves were painted on the branches *al secco* (meaning "on the dry plastered wall").

As in *The Expulsion*, Masaccio modeled the foreground figures here with bold highlights and long shadows on the ground toward the left, giving a strong sense of volumetric solidity and implying a light source at the far right, as if the scene were lit by the actual window in the rear wall of the Brancacci Chapel. Not only does the lighting give the forms sculptural definition; the colors vary in tone according to the strength of the illumination. Masaccio used a wide range of hues—pale pink, mauve, gold, blue-green, seafoam-green, apple-green, peach—and a sophisticated shading technique using contrasting colors, as in Andrew's green robe which is shaded with red instead of darker green. The figures of Jesus and the apostles originally had gold-leaf haloes, several of which have flaked off. Rather than silhouette the heads against consistently flat gold circles (e.g. see FIG. 18–12), however, Masaccio conceived of haloes as gold disks hovering in space above each head that moved with the heads as they moved, and he foreshortened them depending on the angle from which each head is seen.

Some stylistic innovations take time to be fully accepted, and Masaccio's innovative depictions of volumetric solidity, consistent lighting, and spatial integration—though they clearly had an impact on his immediate successors—were perhaps best appreciated by a later generation of painters. Many important sixteenth-century Italian artists, including Michelangelo, studied and sketched Masaccio's Brancacci Chapel frescos, as they did Giotto's work in

the Scrovegni Chapel. In the meantime, painting in Florence after Masaccio's death developed along somewhat different lines.

PAINTING IN FLORENCE AFTER MASACCIO

The tradition of covering walls with frescos continued uninterrupted through the fifteenth century. Between 1438 and 1445, Fra Angelico's decoration of the Dominican monastery of San Marco in Florence was one of the most extensive projects.

FRA ANGELICO Guido di Piero da Mugello (c. 1395/1400–1455), earned his nickname "Fra Angelico" ("Angelic Brother") through his piety as well as his painting: in 1984, he was beatified, the first step toward sainthood. Fra Angelico is first documented painting in Florence in 1417–1418, and he remained an active painter after taking vows as a Dominican monk in nearby Fiesole between 1418 and 1421.

Between 1438 and 1445, in the monastery of San Marco, Fra Angelico and his assistants—probably working under the patronage of Cosimo de' Medici—created paintings to inspire meditation in each monk's cell (44 in all; see FIGS. Intro–8, Intro–9), in the chapter house (meeting room), and even in the corridors (hallways). At the top of the stairs in the north corridor, where the monks passed frequently on their way to their individual cells, Fra Angelico painted a serene picture of the **ANNUNCIATION** (FIG. 20–23). To describe the quiet, measured space where the demure archangel greets the unassuming, youthful Mary, Fra Angelico used linear perspective with striking sensitivity, extending the monks'

20-23 • Fra Angelico
ANNUNCIATION
North dormitory corridor, monastery of San Marco, Florence. c. 1438–1445. Fresco, 7'1" × 10'6" (2.2 × 3.2 m).

The shadowed vault of the portico is supported by a wall on one side and by slender Ionic and Corinthian columns on the other, a new building technique used by Brunelleschi (see FIG. 20-5).

stairway and corridor outward into an imagined portico and garden beside the Virgin's home. The slender, graceful figures wear quietly flowing draperies and assume modest poses. Natural light falling from the left models their forms gently, casting an almost supernatural radiance over their faces and hands. This is a sacred vision rendered in a contemporary setting, welcoming the monks to the most intimate areas of the monastery and preparing them for their private meditations. The line of Latin text running along the bottom of the picture directs the monks, "As you revere this figure of the intact Virgin while passing before it, beware lest you omit to say a Hail Mary."

UCCELLO At mid century, when Fra Angelico was still painting his radiant visions of Mary and Jesus in the monastery of San Marco, other artists explored different directions. Thoroughly conversant with the theories of Brunelleschi and Alberti, they had mastered the techniques (and tricks) of depicting figures in a constructed architectural space. Paolo Uccello devoted himself with

20-24 • Paolo Uccello **THE BATTLE OF SAN ROMANO**
1438–1440. Tempera on wood panel, approx. 6' × 10'6" (1.82 × 3.2 m). National Gallery, London.

20-25 • Andrea del Castagno THE LAST SUPPER
Refectory, convent of Sant'Apollonia, Florence. 1447. Fresco, width approx. 16' × 32' (4.6 × 9.8 m).

Castagno worked quickly, completing this huge mural in at most 32 days.

special fervor to the study of linear perspective (**FIG. 20-24**; see also FIG. 20-1). In his biographies of Italian artists, Vasari described Uccello as a man so obsessed with the science of perspective that he neglected his painting, his family, and even his pet birds (his *uccelli*). According to Vasari, Uccello's wife complained that he sat up drawing all night and when she called to him to come to bed he would say, "Oh, what a sweet thing this perspective is!" (Vasari, trans. Bondanella and Bondanella, p. 83).

CASTAGNO Andrea del Castagno (c. 1417/19–1457) is best known for a fresco of **THE LAST SUPPER** painted for a convent of Benedictine nuns in 1447 (**FIG. 20-25**). The subject was often painted in monastic refectories (dining halls) to remind the monks or nuns of Christ's Last Supper with his first followers and encourage them to see their daily gatherings for meals almost as a sacramental act rooted in this biblical tradition. Here Castagno has not portrayed the scene in the biblical setting of an "upper room." Rather, the humble house of the original account has become a great palace with sumptuous marble revetment. The most brilliantly colored and wildly patterned marble panel frames the off-center heads of Christ and Judas to focus viewers on the most important part of the picture. Judas takes his traditional position on the viewer's side of the table, separated from the other apostles. Equally conventional is the seemingly sleeping figure of St. John, head collapsed onto the tabletop (John 13:23). The lines of floor tiles, ceiling rafters, and paneled walls draw viewers into the scene, notably the nuns who would have seen the painting as an extension of their own dining hall. At first, the lines

of the orthogonals seem perfectly logical, but close examination reveals that only the lines of the ceiling converge to a single point. Two windows light the painting's room from the direction of the actual refectory windows, further unifying the two spaces.

FRA FILIPPO LIPPI During the middle of the fifteenth century, portraiture comes into its own as a major artistic form in Italy, and among the most extraordinary—if enigmatic—examples is this **PORTRAIT OF A WOMAN AND MAN** (**FIG. 20-27**), an early work of Fra Filippo Lippi (c. 1406–1469). This painting is also the earliest surviving double portrait of the Italian Renaissance. Lippi grew up as an orphan in the Carmelite church where Masaccio had painted frescos in the Brancacci Chapel, and art historians have stressed the impact this work had on Lippi's development as an artist. But although he may have absorbed Masaccio's predilection for softly rounded forms situated in carefully mapped spaces, in Lippi's hands these artistic tools became the basis for pictures that often ask more questions than they answer, by stressing outline at the same time as form, and by creating complex and often confusing spatial systems.

The emphasis in this double portrait is squarely on the woman. She is spotlighted in the foreground, sharply profiled against a window that serves as an unsettling internal frame, not big enough to contain her. This window opens onto a vista, clearly a fragment of a larger world, but one that highlights an orthogonal to emphasize a spatial recession only partially revealed. The woman blocks most of this vista with her shining visage and sumptuous costume—notably its embroidered velvet, fur lining, and luminous

The palazzos of wealthy Florentine families housed not only panels painted with portraits or Madonnas; they were also appointed with massive pieces of elaborate furniture. Constructed of richly carved wood that was gilded and often covered with paintings, these household objects were not a minor sideline, but a central feature of the fifteenth-century Florentine art world. Some of the most impressive surviving examples of Renaissance furniture are great chests—called **cassoni**—that were used to store clothing and other precious personal objects in a couple's bedroom. They were frequently commissioned in pairs on the occasion of a wedding.

Marriages between members of wealthy Florentine families were not the result of romantic connections between two young people. They were political alliances and economic transactions that involved the transfer of capital and the exchange of gifts as displays of wealth. In preparation for such high-class marriages, husbands refurbished their living quarters in the family palazzo where they would bring a bride into the household. We have a detailed accounting of the extent of work, as well as the required expenditure, when 30-year-old Lorenzo di Matteo Morelli prepared his apartments for the arrival of his young bride, Vaggia di Tanai Nerli, after their marriage in 1472. His commissioning of a pair of *cassoni*—one for him and one for Vaggia—represented almost two-thirds of the entire cost of redecoration. Fortunately, the two chests still survive (**FIG. 20–26**). They are among the most important and best-preserved Renaissance *cassoni* that have come down to us, especially since they still maintain the original backboard—called a *spalliera*—that was produced concurrent with and hung on the wall directly behind the chests when they were placed in Lorenzo's bedroom. The lion's feet on which the chests now stand are modern additions, and the *spalliera* was originally hung as one continuous painting above both *cassoni*, not two separate panels mounted behind each lid as in the current configuration. Otherwise these chests give a strong sense of their original appearance.

Like most Renaissance *cassoni*, Lorenzo's chest is painted with pictures drawn from stories that extol moral virtues, and reflect some of their values and glories on Lorenzo himself. The long painted scene on the front tells the story of ancient Roman hero Marcus Furius Camillus' defeat of the Gauls as he

chases them out of Rome. On the *spalliera*, *trompe l'oeil* curtains part to reveal the scene of another Roman hero defending a bridge against insurmountable odds. Presumably Lorenzo wanted to be seen as a heroic descendant of such illustrious Romans—strong, brave, and triumphant. The scenes portrayed on Vaggia's chest (like Lorenzo's, identified by her coat of arms) challenge her to care for the children she is expected to produce and practice the virtues of temperance, prudence, and patience that were valued in Florentine patrician brides.

The Morelli–Nerli *cassoni* passed from Lorenzo to his son, and they remained in the Morelli family at least until 1680, maybe into the nineteenth century, when they first appeared together in the art market. Elaborate Renaissance furniture became coveted items in the homes of wealthy art collectors in late nineteenth-century Europe and America, where the new owners doubtless saw themselves as worthy successors to the wealthy and powerful merchants who had commissioned them at the height of the Italian Renaissance.

20–26 • Jacopo del Sellaio, Biagio d'Antonio (painters), and Zanobi di Domenico (woodworker) CASSONE MADE FOR THE MARRIAGE OF LORENZO DI MATTEO MORELLI AND VAGGIA DI TANAI NERLI (ONE OF A SET OF TWO)

1472. Tempera and gold on wood, chest 83½″ × 75″ × 30″ (212 × 193 × 76.2 cm). The Samuel Courtauld Trust, The Courtauld Gallery, London. (F.1947.LF.4)

20-27 • Fra Filippo Lippi PORTRAIT OF A WOMAN AND MAN (ANGIOLA DI BERNARDO SAPITI AND LORENZO DI RANIERI SCOLARI?)
c. 1435–1445. Tempera on wood panel, 25¼″ × 16½″ (64.1 × 41.9 cm). Metropolitan Museum of Art, New York.

Some art historians have seen in the sumptuousness of this woman's costume an indication that she is a newlywed, outfitted in the extravagant clothing and jewelry presented to her by her husband at the time of their marriage, especially since the pearls sewn with gold threads into the embroidery on her sleeve spell out the word *lealtà*, meaning "loyalty." Florentine law prevented a woman from wearing such ostentatious expressions of wealth—especially the jewelry—more than three years after her marriage.

pearls. There is no engagement with the viewer and little sense of likeness. And it is not at all clear where or to what she directs her attention, especially since the gaze of the man in the background does not meet hers. He is even more of a mystery. We see only a masklike sliver of his profile—capped by the red *berretta* that signals his high status—although the substantiality of his face is reinforced by the strong shadow it casts against the window casement through which he looks. Unlike the woman, who clasps her inert hands in front of her as if to highlight her rings, this man fidgets with his

fingers, perhaps to draw our attention to the heraldic device below him that may identify him as a member of the Scolari family. This could be a double portrait of Lorenzo di Ranieri Scolari and Angiola di Bernardo Sapiti, who married in 1436 and welcomed a son in 1444. But what does the painting say about them? Does it commemorate their marriage, celebrate the birth of their child, or memorialize one of their deaths? All have been proposed by art historians as an explanation for this innovative double portrait, but it remains a puzzle to be pondered. Could that pondering be the point of the picture?

ITALIAN ART IN THE SECOND HALF OF THE FIFTEENTH CENTURY

In the second half of the fifteenth century, the ideas and ideals of artists like Brunelleschi, Donatello, and Masaccio began to spread from Florence to the rest of Italy, as artists who had trained or worked in Florence traveled to other cities to work, carrying the style with them. Northern Italy embraced the new Classical ideas swiftly, especially in the ducal courts at Urbino and Mantua. Venice and Rome also emerged as innovative art centers in the last quarter of the century.

URBINO

Under Federico da Montefeltro, Urbino developed into a thriving artistic center. A new palace was under construction, and prominent architects and artists were brought into the court to make the new princely residence a showcase of ducal splendor.

THE PALACE AT URBINO Construction of the palace had been under way for about 20 years in 1468 when Federico hired Luciano Laurana (c. 1420/1425–1479) to direct the work. Among Laurana's major contributions to the palace were closing the courtyard with a fourth wing and redesigning the courtyard façades (**FIG. 20-28**). The result is a superbly rational solution to the problems created in courtyard design by the awkward juncture of the arcades at the four corners. The ground-level portico on each side has arches supported by columns, but piers embellished with pilasters bridge the corner angles. This arrangement avoided the awkward visual effect of two arches springing from a single column (see **FIG. 20-8**) and gave the corner a greater sense of stability. A variation of the composite capital (a Corinthian capital with added Ionic volutes) was used, perhaps for the first time, on the ground level. Corinthian pilasters flank the windows in the story above, forming divisions that repeat the bays of the portico. (The two low upper stories were added later.) The plain architrave was engraved with inscriptions lauding Federico's many virtues, added when the count became duke of Urbino in 1476.

The interior of the Urbino palace likewise reflected its patron's embrace of new Renaissance ideas and interest in Classical antiquity, seen in carved marble fireplaces and window and door surrounds. In creating luxurious home furnishings and interior decorations for sophisticated clients such as Federico, Italian artists found freedom to experiment with new subjects, treatments, and techniques. Among these was the creation of remarkable **trompe l'oeil** ("fool-the-eye") effects using scrupulously applied linear perspective and foreshortening in **intarsia** (wood inlay) decoration. An extraordinary example is on the walls of Federico da Montefeltro's **STUDIOLO**, or study, a room for private conversation and the owner's collection of fine books and art objects (**FIG. 20-29**). The work, probably done by the architect and woodworker Giuliano da Maiano (1432–1490), carries the date 1476.

20-29 • Giuliano da Maiano (?) **STUDIOLO OF FEDERICO DA MONTEFELTRO**
Ducal palace, Urbino. 1476. Intarsia, height 7'3" (2.21 m).

The elaborate scenes in the small room are created entirely of wood inlaid on flat surfaces. Each detail is rendered with convincing illusionism: pilasters, carved cupboards with latticed doors, niches with statues, paintings, and built-in tables. Prominent in the decorative scheme is the prudent and industrious squirrel, a Renaissance symbol of the ideal ruler: in other words, of Federico da Montefeltro. A large "window" looks out onto an elegant marble loggia with a distant view of the countryside through its arches; and the shelves, cupboards, and tables are filled with all manner of fascinating things—scientific instruments, books, even the duke's armor hanging like a suit in a closet.

PIERO DELLA FRANCESCA Federico brought the artist Piero della Francesca (c. 1415–1492) to Urbino. Piero had worked in Florence in the 1430s before settling in his native Borgo San Sepolcro, a Tuscan hill town under papal control. He knew current art theory and art practice—including Brunelleschi's system of spatial illusion and linear perspective, Masaccio's powerful modeling of forms and atmospheric perspective, and Alberti's theoretical treatises. Piero was one of the few practicing artists who also wrote his own books of theory. Not surprisingly, in his treatise on perspective he emphasized the geometry and the volumetric construction of forms and spaces that were so apparent in his own work.

These characteristic features of Piero's painting are marvelously apparent in a serene image of the **BAPTISM OF CHRIST** that has become one of Piero's signature works (**FIG. 20-30**). It was commissioned by the Graziani family, probably during the 1450s, for the priory of San Giovanni Battista in Borgo San Sepolchro. The central figure of Christ dominates the painting, standing in a shallow stream of glassy water under a tree of manicured regularity. Christ's legs and the sleek tree trunk set up a series of emphatically upright forms, one of many formal relationships that reverberate both across the picture's surface and into its carefully measured space. Feet and ankles rotate across the lower quarter of the painting, providing a clear and well-distributed sense of grounding for the figural composition, while the radically foreshortened dove (Holy Spirit), John's baptismal dish, and the clouds create a rhythmic line of horizontals that adds stability above and creates a staccato rhythm that merges foreground and background on the painting's surface. The mirrored profiles and gestures of the outside angel and the baptizing John provide an internal frame for the central action. Such carefully crafted formal

20-30 • Piero della Francesca BAPTISM OF CHRIST
c. 1450. Tempera on wood panel, 66″ × 45¾″ (1.67 × 1.16 m). National Gallery, London.

The three angels standing in a cluster at left, partially overlapped by the foreground tree, have been interpreted as an emblem of concord—representing the rapprochement reached between the Roman and Byzantine Christian churches in 1439 at the Council of Florence. Another reference to this council has been seen in the exotic costumes of the figures in the far background. Since the accord reached at the council was very short-lived, this interpretation would move the date of the painting into the early 1440s rather than the 1450s.

20–31 • Piero della Francesca BATTISTA SFORZA AND FEDERICO DA MONTEFELTRO
c. 1474. Oil on wood panel, each 18½″ × 13″ (47 × 33 cm). Galleria degli Uffizi, Florence.

Battista Sforza died in 1472 at age 26, shortly after the birth of her ninth child, a son who would one day be duke. We are told that Federico was disconsolate. Some arranged aristocratic marriage alliances blossomed into loving partnerships, and it seems that one such was memorialized in this double portrait.

correspondences infuse this picture with an air of beatific calm and peaceful stasis—a stillness suggesting that nothing will ever change, no one will ever move in this frozen moment within a story that, for Christian believers, actually changed everything.

Piero traveled widely—to Rome, to the Este court in Ferrara, and especially to Urbino. In about 1474, he painted the portraits of **FEDERICO DA MONTEFELTRO** and his recently deceased wife, **BATTISTA SFORZA** (**FIG. 20-31**). The small panels resemble Flemish painting in their detail and luminosity, their record of surfaces and textures, and their vast landscapes. But in traditional Italian fashion, figures are portrayed in strict profile, disengaged psychologically from the viewer. The profile format also allowed for an accurate recording of Federico's likeness without emphasizing two disfiguring scars—the loss of his right eye from a lance blow and his broken nose. His good left eye is shown, and the angular profile of his nose might easily be merely a distinctive family trait. Typically, Piero emphasized the underlying geometry of

the forms. Dressed in the most elegant fashion (Federico wears his red ducal robe and Battista's jewels are meticulously recorded), they are silhouetted against a panoramic landscape. These are the hills around Urbino, seemingly dissolving into infinity through an atmospheric perspective as subtle and luminous as in any Flemish panel painting. Piero used another northern European device in the harbor view just in front of Federico, where the water narrows into a river that leads us into the distant landscape (see **FIG. 19-17**). He would have had contact in Urbino with the Flemings who were also working there.

MANTUA

Ludovico Gonzaga, the marquis of Mantua, ruled a territory that lies on the north Italian plain between Venice and Milan. Like Federico, he made his fortune as a *condottiere*. Ludovico was schooled by humanist teachers and created a court where humanist ideas flourished in art as well as in literature.

20-32 • Andrea Mantegna **TWO VIEWS OF THE CAMERA PICTA, DUCAL PALACE, MANTUA**
1465–1474. Fresco, diameter of false oculus 8′9″ (2.7 m); room 26′6″ square (8 m square).

MANTEGNA Working at Ludovico's court was Andrea Mantegna (1431–1506), a painter trained in Padua and profoundly influenced by the sculptor Donatello, who arrived in Padua in 1443 and worked there for a decade. Mantegna learned the Florentine system of linear perspective and pushed to their limits experiments in radically foreshortened forms and dramatic spatial recessions. He went to work for Ludovico Gonzaga in 1460, and he continued to work for the Gonzaga family for the rest of his life.

Perhaps his finest works are the frescos of the **CAMERA PICTA** ("Painted Room"), a tower chamber in Ludovico's palace, which Mantegna decorated between 1465 and 1474 (**FIG. 20-32**). Around the walls the family—each member seemingly identified by a portrait likeness—receives in landscapes and in loggias the return of Ludovico's son, Cardinal Francesco Gonzaga. On the domed ceiling, the artist painted a *tour de force* of radical perspective in a technique called *di sotto in sù* ("from below upwards"). The room appears to be open to a cloud-filled sky through a large oculus in a simulated marble- and mosaic-covered vault. On each side of a precariously balanced planter, four young women—one an African, outfitted in an exotic turban—peer over a marble balustrade into the room below, while a fourth looks dreamily upward. Joined by a large peacock, several putti play around the balustrade, three standing on the interior ledge of a cornice, unprotected by

the balustrade, toes projecting into space but seemingly oblivious to the danger of their perch. This ceiling began a long tradition of illusionistic ceiling painting that culminated in the extravagant and explosive ceilings of Baroque churches (see Chapter 23).

ROME

Rome's development into a Renaissance center of the arts was greatly enhanced when Pope Sixtus IV called to the city in the early 1480s a group of young Florentine and Umbrian artists to decorate the walls of his newly built chapel (1479–1481), now named the **SISTINE CHAPEL** after him (**FIG. 20-33**). Botticelli and Ghirlandaio were among the most famous artists summoned to the chapel to paint, but many art historians believe that Perugino was the supervising artist in charge of the project.

PERUGINO Pietro Vannucci, called "Perugino" (c. 1445–1523), was originally from near the town of Perugia in Umbria (thus the nickname), and he worked for a while in Florence, but by 1479 he was in Rome. Two years later, he was working on the Sistine murals. One of his contributions, *Christ Giving the Keys to St. Peter* (foreground painting at lower right in FIG. 20-33; also FIG. 20-18), portrayed the event that provided biblical support for the supremacy of papal authority (Matthew 16:19). In a light-filled piazza in which banded paving stones provide a geometric

20-33 • VIEW OF
THE SISTINE CHAPEL
SHOWING PAINTINGS
COMMISSIONED FOR
THE SIDE WALLS BY
POPE SIXTUS IV
Vatican, Rome. At lower right, Perugino's *Christ Giving the Keys to St. Peter*, c. 1480–1482. 11′5½″ × 18′8½″ (3.48 × 5.70 m).

grid for perspectival recession, the figures stand like chess pieces on the squares, scaled to size according to their distance from the picture plane and modeled by a consistent light source from the upper left. Triumphal arches inspired by ancient Rome frame the church and focus attention on the center of the composition, where the vital key is being transferred. The carefully calibrated scene is softened by the subdued colors, the distant idealized landscape and cloudy skies, and the variety of the figures' positions.

FLORENCE

Florence remained a thriving artistic center throughout the fifteenth century. Sculptors continued to explore Classical themes and experiment with the representation of the human form. Florentine painting pursued a love of material opulence, an interest in describing the natural world, and a poetic, mystical spirit, motivated by the patronage of citizens who sought to advertise their wealth and prestige as well as by the religious fervor that arose at the very end of the century.

20-34 • Andrea del Verrocchio DAVID
Commissioned by Lorenzo de' Medici for the Medici Palace. c. 1470–1475. Bronze with gilded details, height 49⅝" (1.26 m). Museo Nazionale del Bargello, Florence.

VERROCCHIO One of the most prestigious and active workshops in Florence was that of Andrea di Michele Cioni (1435–1488), nicknamed "Verrocchio" ("true eye"). Trained as a goldsmith, but best known for his works as a painter and bronze sculptor, Verrocchio was also a gifted teacher, counting among his pupils Perugino and Leonardo da Vinci. Around 1470, Lorenzo de' Medici commissioned from Verrocchio a bronze statue of David for the Palazzo Medici, the location where Donatello's sculpture of the same subject (see FIG. 20-14) was then displayed. Verrocchio's work (FIG. 20-34) seems to have been conceived as a response to the demure, sleek, but awkwardly boyish nude of his famous predecessor. Verrocchio's triumphant biblical hero is a poised and proud adolescent, modestly clothed and confidently looking out to meet the gaze of the viewer. Although slight, he is equipped with the developing musculature required for the

daunting task—whose accomplishment is signaled by the severed head of his foe, displayed like a trophy between his feet. The careful attention to the textural details of hair and clothing reveal Verrocchio's training as a goldsmith.

POLLAIUOLO Florentine sculptors not only created large-scale figures, but also small works designed to inspire the mind and delight the eye of its private owner. The ambitious and multi-talented Antonio del Pollaiuolo (c. 1431–1498)—goldsmith, embroidery designer, printmaker, sculptor, and painter—who came to work for the Medici family in Florence about 1460, created mostly small bronze sculptures. His **HERCULES AND ANTAEUS** of about 1475 is one of the largest (FIG. 20-35). This study of complex interlocking figures has an explosive energy that can best be appreciated by viewing it from every angle.

20-35 • Antonio del Pollaiuolo HERCULES AND ANTAEUS
c. 1475. Bronze, height with base 18" (45.7 cm). Museo Nazionale del Bargello, Florence.

20-36 • Antonio del Pollaiuolo
THE BATTLE OF THE NUDES
c. 1465–1470. Engraving, 15⅛″ × 23¼″
(38.3 × 59 cm). Cincinnati Art Museum,
Ohio. Bequest of Herbert Greer French.
1943.118

Statuettes of religious subjects were still popular, but humanist patrons were beginning to collect bronzes of Classical subjects. Many sculptors, especially those trained as goldsmiths, started to cast small copies after well-known ancient works. Some artists also executed original designs *all'antica* ("in the antique style") to appeal to a cultivated humanist taste. Hercules was always a popular figure; as a patron of Florence, he was on the city seal. Among the many courageous acts by which Hercules gained immortality was the slaying of the evil Antaeus in a wrestling match by lifting him off the earth, the source of the giant's great physical power.

An engraving by Pollaiuolo, **THE BATTLE OF THE NUDES** (**FIG. 20-36**), reflects two interests of Renaissance scholars—the study of Classical sculpture and anatomical research. Pollaiuolo may have intended this, his only known—but highly influential—print, as a study in composition involving the human figure in action. The naked men, fighting each other ferociously against a tapestrylike background of foliage, seem to have been drawn from a single model in a variety of poses, many of which were taken from Classical sources. Like the artist's *Hercules and Antaeus*, much of the engraving's fascination lies in its depiction of the muscles of the male body reacting under tension, more impressive than accurate—anatomical accuracy was clearly not the point.

20-37 • Domenico Ghirlandaio **SCENES FROM THE LIFE OF ST. FRANCIS; ALTARPIECE WITH NATIVITY AND ADORATION OF THE SHEPHERDS**
Sassetti Chapel, church of Santa Trinità, Florence. 1483–1486. Fresco, chapel 12′2″ deep × 17′2″ wide (3.7 × 5.25 m).

20-38 • Domenico Ghirlandaio CONFIRMATION OF THE FRANCISCAN RULE BY POPE HONORIUS III
Sassetti Chapel, church of Santa Trinità, Florence. 1483–1486. Fresco, width at base 17'2" (5.25 m).

GHIRLANDAIO The most prolific later fifteenth-century Florentine painting workshop was that of Domenico di Tommaso Bigordi (1449–1494), known as "Ghirlandaio" ("Garland-Maker"), a nickname first adopted by his father, who was a goldsmith noted for his floral wreaths. A skilled storyteller, the younger Ghirlandaio reinterpreted the art of earlier fifteenth-century painters into a visual language of descriptive immediacy and structural clarity.

Among Ghirlandaio's most impressive narrative programs was the fresco cycle of the **LIFE OF ST. FRANCIS**, commissioned by the wealthy manager of the Medici bank, Francesco Sassetti, and painted between 1483 and 1486 on the walls of the Sassetti family burial chapel in the Florentine church of Santa Trinità (**FIG. 20-37**). In the uppermost tier of the paintings (**FIG. 20-38**), Pope Honorius gives a confirmation of the Franciscan order to the kneeling figure of St. Francis, with the Loggia dei Lanzi and the Palazzo della Signoria (see **FIG. 18-2**) in the background. The foreground figures—arranged in a composition that parallels the sacred scene behind them—are portrait likenesses of well-known Florentines. At far right are (from left to right) poet Antonio Pucci, Lorenzo de' Medici, the patron Francesco Sassetti, and his son Federigo, all

of whom seem to be receiving the approaching retinue coming up the stairs at the lower center of the fresco—humanist poet Poliziano leading his pupils, the sons of Lorenzo de' Medici. Just below this scene, in the middle register (see **FIG. 20-37**), a small boy who has fallen from an upper window is resurrected by St. Francis. This miracle is likewise witnessed by contemporary Florentines, including other members of the Sassetti family and Ghirlandaio himself, and the scene takes place in the piazza outside the actual church of Santa Trinità. Ghirlandaio has thus transferred both events from thirteenth-century Rome to contemporary Florence, painting recognizable views of the city and portraits of living Florentines, delighting in local color and anecdotal detail. Perhaps Renaissance painters, like Gothic painters, represented sacred narratives in contemporary settings to emphasize their current relevance, or perhaps they and their patrons simply enjoyed seeing themselves dressed in their finery, witnessing these dramas within the cities of which they were justifiably proud.

The altarpiece Ghirlandaio painted for the Sassetti Chapel portrays the **NATIVITY AND ADORATION OF THE SHEP-HERDS** (**FIG. 20-39**). It is still in its original frame, still in the

IPSVM QVEM GENVIT ADORAVIT MARIA

20–39 • Domenico Ghirlandaio NATIVITY AND ADORATION OF THE SHEPHERDS
Altarpiece in the Sassetti Chapel, church of Santa Trinità, Florence. 1485. Panel, 65¾″ square (1.67 m square).

place for which it was painted (see FIG. 20-37). The influence of Hugo van der Goes's Portinari Altarpiece (see FIG. 19–19), which had been placed on the high altar of the church of Sant'Egidio two years earlier, in 1483, is strong. Ghirlandaio's Christ Child also lies on the ground, adored by the Virgin while rugged shepherds kneel at the right. Ghirlandaio even copies some of Hugo's flowers—although here the iris, a symbol of the Passion, springs not from a vase, but from the earth in the lower right corner. But Ghirlandaio highlights references to Classical Rome. First to catch the eye are the two Classical pilasters with Corinthian capitals, one of which is dated by inscription to 1485. The manger is an ancient sarcophagus with an inscription that promises resurrection (as in the fresco directly above the altarpiece where St. Francis is reviving a child); and in the distance a Classical arch inscribed with a reference to the

Roman general Pompey the Great frames the road along which the Magi travel. Weighty, restrained actors replace the psychologically intense figures of Hugo's painting. Ghirlandaio joins a clear foreground, middle ground, and background in part by the road and in part by **aerial perspective**, which creates a seamless transition of color, from the sharp details and primary hues of the Adoration to the soft gray mountains in the distance.

BOTTICELLI Like most artists in the second half of the fifteenth century, Alessandro di Mariano di Vanni Filipepi (1445–1510), called "Botticelli" ("the little barrel," a nickname borrowed from his older brother), painted sculptural figures that were modeled by light from a consistent source and placed in a setting rendered illusionistic by linear perspective. An outstanding portraitist, he, like

20-40 • Sandro Botticelli BIRTH OF VENUS

c. 1484–1486. Tempera and gold on canvas, 5′8⅞″ × 9′1⅞″ (1.8 × 2.8 m). Galleria degli Uffizi, Florence.

Ghirlandaio, often included recognizable contemporary figures among the saints and angels in religious paintings. He worked in Florence, often for the Medici, then was called to Rome in 1481 by Pope Sixtus IV to help decorate the new Sistine Chapel along with Ghirlandaio, Perugino, and other artists.

Botticelli returned to Florence that same year and entered a new phase of his career. Like other artists working for patrons steeped in Classical scholarship and humanistic thought, he was exposed to philosophical speculations on beauty—as well as to the examples of ancient art in his employers' collections. For the Medici, Botticelli produced secular paintings of mythological subjects inspired by ancient works and by contemporary Neoplatonic thought. Art historian Michael Baxandall has shown that these works were also patterned on the slow movements of fifteenth-century Florentine dance, in which figures acted out their relationships to one another in public performances that would have influenced the thinking and viewing habits of both painters and their audience.

The overall appearance of Botticelli's *Primavera*, or *Spring* (see "A Closer Look," page 628), recalls Flemish tapestries (see FIG. 19–8), which were very popular in Italy at the time. And its subject—like the subjects of many tapestries—is a highly complex **allegory** (a symbolic illustration of a concept or principle), interweaving Neoplatonic ideas with esoteric references to Classical sources. In simple terms, Neoplatonic philosophers and poets conceived Venus, the goddess of love, as having two natures. The first ruled over earthly, human love and the second over universal, divine love. In this way the philosophers could argue that Venus was a Classical equivalent of the Virgin Mary. *Primavera* was painted at the time of the wedding of Lorenzo di Pierfrancesco de' Medici and Semiramide d'Appiano in 1482. The theme suggests love and fertility in marriage, and the painting can be read as a lyrical wish for a similar fecundity in the union of Lorenzo and Semiramide—a sort of highly refined fertility dance.

Several years later, some of the same mythological figures reappeared in Botticelli's **BIRTH OF VENUS** (FIG. 20-40), in which the central image represents the Neoplatonic idea of divine love in the form of a nude Venus based on an antique statue type known as the "modest Venus" that ultimately derives from Praxiteles' *Aphrodite of Knidos* (see FIG. 5-53). Botticelli's Classical goddess of love and beauty, born of sea foam, averts her eyes from our gaze as she floats ashore on a scallop shell, carefully arranging her hands and hair to hide—but actually drawing attention to—her sexuality. Indeed, she is an arrestingly alluring figure, set within a graceful composition organized by Botticelli's characteristically decorative, almost calligraphic use of line. Blown by the wind—Zephyr (with his love, the nymph Chloris)—Venus arrives at her earthly home. She is welcomed by a devotee who offers her a garment embroidered with flowers. The circumstances of this commission are uncertain. It is painted on canvas, which suggests that it may have been a banner or a painted tapestrylike wall hanging.

Botticelli's later career was apparently affected by a profound spiritual crisis. While the artist was creating his mythologies for the Medici, a Dominican monk, Fra Girolamo Savonarola (active in Florence 1490–1498), was preaching impassioned sermons denouncing the worldliness of Florence. Many Florentines reacted with orgies of self-recrimination, and processions of weeping penitents wound through the streets. Botticelli, too, may have fallen into a state of religious fervor. In a dramatic gesture of repentance, he burned many of his earlier paintings and began to produce highly emotional pictures pervaded by an intense religiosity.

A CLOSER LOOK | *Primavera*

by Sandro Botticelli, c. 1482. Tempera on wood panel.
6'8" × 10'4" (2.03 × 3.15 m). Galleria degli Uffizi, Florence.

Mercury, the sign for the month of May, disperses the winter clouds with his caduceus. This staff, wound about with serpents, became a symbol for the medical profession. The name Medici means "doctors."

Venus, clothed in contemporary costume and crowned with a marriage wreath, appears in her role as the goddess of wedded love. The presence of both Venus and Mercury may be an astrological reference; prominent Neoplatonist Marsilio Ficino told Lorenzo de Pierfrancesco de' Medici that these planets were aligned in his horoscope.

The setting of the painting is a grove of orange trees. These hold a double meaning—both suggestive of Venus' Garden of the Hesperides, with its golden fruit, and perhaps an allusion to the Medici, whose coat of arms featured golden orbs.

This three-figure grouping tells a story. Zephyrus, the west wind, is accosting the virgin nymph Chloris, identifiable from the roses pouring out of her mouth. Once Zephyrus makes her his bride, Chloris is transformed into the goddess Flora, the elaborately dressed personification of spring at the front of the group.

The gold flames decorating Mercury's garment are also an attribute of St. Lawrence, the namesake of Lorenzo di Pierfrancesco de' Medici, for whom this painting was made. The laurel tree (*laurus* in Latin) behind Zephyrus also alludes to Lorenzo's name.

The Three Graces symbolize ideal female virtues—Chastity, Beauty, Love. Venus' son Cupid—the embodiment of romantic desire—playfully aims his arrow at them.

So accurate is their representation, 138 of the 190 flowering plants depicted in the painting have been identified. Almost all grow in the neighborhood of Florence between the months of March and April, and most carry symbolic associations with love and marriage.

Flora scatters flowers held in a fold of her dress at the level of her womb, equating the fecundity brought about by changing seasons with female procreative fertility.

 View the Closer Look for *Primavera* on myartslab.com

VENICE

In the last quarter of the fifteenth century, Venice emerged as a major Renaissance art center. Ruled as an oligarchy (government by a select few) with an elected duke (*doge* in the Venetian dialect), the city government was founded at the end of the Roman Empire and survived until the Napoleonic era. In building their city, the Venetians had turned marshes into a commercial seaport, and they saw the sea as a resource, not a threat. They depended on naval power and on the natural defense of their lagoons rather than city walls. Venice turned toward the east, especially after the crusaders' conquest of Constantinople in 1204, designing the church of St. Mark as a great Byzantine building sheathed in mosaics (see FIG. 8-24A). In addition to its long history of painting and sculpture, Venice excelled in the arts of textiles and jewelry, gold and enamel, glass and mosaic, fine printing and bookbinding.

VENETIAN PALACES Venice was a city of waterways with few large public spaces. Even palaces had only small interior courtyards and tiny gardens, and were separated by narrow alleys. Their façades overlooked the canals, permitting owners to project on these major thoroughfares the large portals, windows, and loggias that proclaimed their importance through the lavishness of their residences—a sharp contrast to the fortresslike character of most Florentine town houses (see FIG. 20-7). But, as with the Florentine great houses, Venetian owners combined in these structures a place of business with a dwelling.

The **CA D'ORO** (House of Gold), home of the wealthy nobleman Marino Contarini, has a splendid front with three superimposed loggias facing the Grand Canal (**FIG. 20-41**). The house was constructed between 1421 and 1437, and its asymmetrical elevation is based on a traditional Byzantine plan. A wide central hall ran from front to back all the way through the building to a small inner courtyard with a well and garden. An outside stair led to the main floor on the second level. The entrance on the canal permitted goods to be delivered directly into the warehouse that constituted the ground floor. The principal floor, on the second level, had a salon and reception room opening on the richly decorated loggia. It was filled with light from large windows, and more light reflected off the polished terrazzo floor. Private family rooms filled the upper stories. Contarini's instructions to his contractors and workers specified that the façade was to be painted with white enamel and ultramarine blue and that the red stones in the patterned wall should be oiled to make them even brighter. Details of carving, such as coats of arms and balls on the crest at the roofline, were to be gilded. Beautiful as the palace is today, in the fifteenth and sixteenth centuries it must have been truly spectacular.

THE BELLINI BROTHERS The domes of the church of St. Mark dominated the city center, and the rich colors of its glowing mosaics captured painters' imaginations. Perhaps it was their love of color that encouraged the Venetian painters to embrace the oil medium for both panel and canvas painting.

The most important Venetian artists of this period were two brothers: Gentile (c. 1429–1507) and Giovanni (c. 1430–1516) Bellini, whose father, Jacopo (c. 1400–1470), had also been a central figure in Venetian art. Andrea Mantegna became part of this circle when he married Jacopo's daughter in 1453.

Gentile Bellini celebrated the daily life of the city in large, lively narratives, such as the **PROCESSION OF THE RELIC OF THE TRUE CROSS BEFORE THE CHURCH OF ST. MARK** (**FIG. 20-42**). Every year on the feast of St. Mark (April 25), the Confraternity of St. John the Evangelist carried the miracle-working relic of the True Cross in a procession through the square in front of the church. Bellini's painting of 1496 depicts an event that had occurred in 1444: the miraculous recovery of a sick child whose father (the man in red kneeling to the right of the relic) prayed for help as the relic passed by. Gentile has rendered the cityscape with great attention to detail. The mosaic-encrusted Byzantine

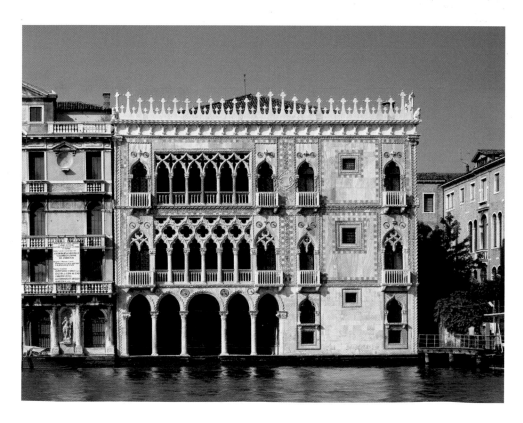

20-41 • CA D'ORO (CONTARINI PALACE), VENICE
1421–1437.

20-42 • Gentile Bellini
PROCESSION OF THE RELIC OF THE TRUE CROSS BEFORE THE CHURCH OF ST. MARK
1496. Oil on canvas, 12′ × 24′5″ (3.67 × 7.45 m). Galleria dell'Accademia, Venice.

Cathedral of St. Mark (see FIG. 8–24A) forms a backdrop for the procession, and the doge's palace and base of the bell tower can be seen at the right. The gold reliquary is carried under a canopy, surrounded by marchers with giant candles, led by a choir and followed at the far right by the doge and other officials. Gentile's procession serves as a reminder that fifteenth-century piazzas and buildings were sites of ritual ceremony, and it was in moments such as this that they were brought to life.

Gentile's brother Giovanni amazed and attracted patrons with his artistic virtuosity for almost 60 years. The **VIRGIN AND CHILD ENTHRONED WITH SS. FRANCIS, JOHN THE BAPTIST, JOB, DOMINIC, SEBASTIAN, AND LOUIS OF TOULOUSE** (FIG. 20–43), painted about 1478 for the chapel of the Hospital of San Giobbe (St. Job), exhibits a dramatic perspectival view up into a tunnel vault that leads to an apse. Giovanni may have known his brother-in-law Mantegna's early experiments in radical foreshortening and in the use of a low vanishing point. Here Giovanni positions the vanishing point for the rapidly converging lines of the architecture at bottom center, just above the

20-43 • Giovanni Bellini **VIRGIN AND CHILD ENTHRONED WITH SS. FRANCIS, JOHN THE BAPTIST, JOB, DOMINIC, SEBASTIAN, AND LOUIS OF TOULOUSE**
(Computer reconstruction.) Originally commissioned for the chapel of the Hospital of San Giobbe, Venice. c. 1478. Oil on wood panel, 15′4″ × 8′4″ (4.67 × 2.54 m). Galleria dell'Accademia, Venice. The original frame is in the church of San Giobbe, Venice.

Art historians have given the special name **sacra conversazione** ("holy conversation") to this type of composition that shows saints, angels, and sometimes even the painting's donors in the same pictorial space with the enthroned Virgin and Child. Despite the name, no "conversation" or spoken interaction takes place in a literal sense. Instead, the individuals portrayed are joined in a mystical and eternal communion that occurs outside human time and space.

20-44 • Giovanni Bellini
ST. FRANCIS IN ECSTASY
c. 1470s. Oil and tempera on wood
panel, 49″ × 55⅞″ (125 × 142 cm).
The Frick Collection, New York.

Giovanni Bellini's painting of **ST. FRANCIS IN ECSTASY** (FIG. 20-44), also from the 1470s, recalls Flemish painting in the fine detail with which he rendered the natural world. The saint stands bathed in early morning sunlight, his outspread hands displaying his stigmata. Francis had moved to a cave in the barren wilderness in his search for communion with God, but in the world Giovanni creates for him, the fields blossom and flocks of animals graze. The grape arbor over his desk adds to the atmosphere of sylvan delight. Like most of the fifteenth-century religious art we have seen, however, Bellini presents viewers with a natural world saturated in symbolism. Here a relationship between St. Francis

floor. His figures stand in a Classical architectural interior with a coffered barrel vault reminiscent of Masaccio's *Trinity* (see FIG. 20-19). The gold mosaic, with its identifying inscription and stylized seraphim (angels of the highest rank), recalls Byzantine art and the long tradition of Byzantine-inspired painting and mosaics produced in Venice.

and Moses is outlined. The tree symbolizes the burning bush; the stream, the miraculous spring brought forth by Moses. The crane and donkey represent the monastic virtue of patience. The detailed description, luminous palette, and symbolic surroundings suggest Flemish art, but the golden light suffusing the painting is unmistakably Venetian.

THINK ABOUT IT

20.1 Explain how one Florentine sculptor discussed in this chapter helped establish the increasing naturalism and growing emulation of Classical models that would be central to the early Italian Renaissance.

20.2 Discuss Masaccio's use of linear perspective in either *The Tribute Money* or *Trinity with the Virgin, St. John the Evangelist, and Donors*. How does he use this technique? Illustrate your points with a comparative reference to a work discussed earlier in this chapter or in a previous chapter.

20.3 Choose a wealthy merchant or *condottiere* and discuss how his patronage fostered the emergence of the Renaissance in fifteenth-century Italy. Make reference to specific works in forming your answer.

20.4 Discuss the 1401 competition to choose an artist to create the bronze doors of the Florence Baptistery. How did the competition affect the careers of the two finalists, Ghiberti and Brunelleschi?

CROSSCURRENTS

FIG. 19–15   FIG. 20–21

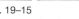

Compare the representation of the human nude in these two examples of Renaissance art, one from Flanders and one from Florence. How do these works relate to the character of art in these two parts of Europe in the early fifteenth century? How do they embody the cultural expectations of their time and place?

✔—⎡**Study** and review on myartslab.com

21-1 • Raphael STANZA DELLA SEGNATURA

Vatican, Rome. Fresco in the left lunette, *Parnassus*; in the right lunette, *The School of Athens*. 1510–1511.

Sixteenth-Century Art in Italy

Two young artists—Raphael and Michelangelo—although rivals in almost every sense, were linked in service to Pope Julius II (pontificate 1503–1513) in the early years of the sixteenth century. Raphael was painting the pope's private library (1509–1511) while, nearby, Michelangelo painted the ceiling of his Sistine Chapel (1508–1512). The pope demanded an art that reflected his imperial vision of a new, worldwide Church based on humanistic ideas, which he would lead as a new St. Peter, founding a second great age of papal dominion. In fulfilling this proud demand, Raphael and Michelangelo, following the lead of Leonardo da Vinci, united Renaissance principles of harmony and balance with a new monumentality based on Classical ideals, and they knit these elements into a dynamic and synthetic whole, rich in color and controlled by cohesive design. Working alongside Leonardo and the architect Donato Bramante, they created a style we call the High Renaissance.

Julius II intended the **STANZA DELLA SEGNATURA**, or Room of the Signature, to be his personal study (**FIG. 21–1**). Raphael sought to create an ideal setting for papal activities, with murals proclaiming that all human knowledge exists under the power of divine wisdom. He organized the mural program itself like a library, separated into divisions of theology, philosophy, poetry, and law. He created pictorial allegories to illustrate each theme. On one wall, churchmen discussing the sacraments represent theology, while across the room ancient philosophers led by Plato and Aristotle debate in the School of Athens. Plato holds his book *Timaeus*, in which creation is seen in terms of geometry, and in which humanity encompasses and explains the universe. Aristotle holds his *Nicomachean Ethics*, a decidedly human-centered book concerned with relations among people. Ancient representatives of the academic curriculum—Grammar, Rhetoric, Dialectic, Arithmetic, Music, Geometry, and Astronomy—surround them. On a window wall, Justice, holding a sword and scales, assigns each his due. Across the room, Poetry and the Arts are represented by Apollo and the Muses, and the poet Sappho reclines against the fictive frame of an actual window. Raphael included his own portrait among the onlookers on the extreme lower right in the *School of Athens* fresco and signed the painting with his initials—a signal that both artists and patrons were becoming increasingly aware of their individual significance.

Raphael achieved a lofty style in keeping with papal ambition—using ideals of Classical grandeur, professing faith in human rationality and perfectibility, and celebrating the power of the pope as God's earthly administrator. But when Raphael died at age 37 on April 6, 1520, the grand moment was already passing: Luther and the Protestant Reformation were challenging papal authority, and the world would never be the same again.

LEARN ABOUT IT

21.1 Compare the emphasis on drawing and clearly structured compositions in the work of Roman and Florentine painters with their Venetian counterparts' exploration of the expressive potential of color and dynamic figural arrangements.

21.2 Examine the architectural creativity lavished on the design of both grand churches and pleasurable retreats to embody themes of wealth and power in sixteenth-century Italy.

21.3 Trace the shift in the artistic center of Italy from Florence to Rome, and recognize the efforts of Pope Julius II to create a new "golden age."

21.4 Explore the intentional subversion of Classical style and decorum in the work of Mannerist artists.

((•—[**Listen** to the chapter audio on myartslab.com

EUROPE IN THE SIXTEENTH CENTURY

The sixteenth century was an age of social, intellectual, and religious ferment that transformed European culture. It was marked by continual warfare triggered by the expansionist ambitions of warring rulers. The humanism of the fourteenth and fifteenth centuries, with its medieval roots and its often uncritical acceptance of the authority of Classical texts, slowly developed into a critical exploration of new ideas, the natural world, and distant lands. Cartographers began to acknowledge the Earth's curvature and the degrees of distance, giving Europeans a more accurate understanding of their place within the world. The printing press sparked an explosion in book production, spreading new ideas through the translation and publication of ancient and contemporary texts, broadening the horizons of educated Europeans and encouraging the development of literacy. Since travel was growing more common, artists and their work became mobile, and the world of art was transformed into a more international community.

At the start of the sixteenth century, England, France, and Portugal were nation-states under strong monarchs. German-speaking central Europe was divided into dozens of principalities, counties, free cities, and small territories. But even states as powerful as Saxony and Bavaria acknowledged the supremacy of the Habsburg Holy Roman Empire—in theory the greatest power in Europe. Charles V, elected emperor in 1519, also inherited Spain, the Netherlands, and vast territories in the Americas. Italy, which was divided into numerous small states, was a diplomatic and military battlefield where, for much of the century, the Italian city-states, Habsburg Spain, France, and the papacy fought each other in shifting alliances. Popes behaved like secular princes, using diplomacy and military force to regain control over central Italy and in some cases to establish family members as hereditary rulers.

The popes' incessant demands for money, to finance the rebuilding of St. Peter's as well as their self-aggrandizing art projects and luxurious lifestyles, aggravated the religious dissent that had long been developing, especially north of the Alps. Early in the century, religious reformers within the established Church challenged beliefs and practices, especially Julius II's sale of indulgences promising forgiveness of sins and assurance of salvation in exchange for a financial contribution to the Church. Because they protested, these northern European reformers came to be called Protestants; their demand for reform gave rise to a movement called the Reformation.

The political maneuvering of Pope Clement VII (pontificate 1523–1534) led to a direct clash with Holy Roman Emperor Charles V. In May 1527, Charles's troops attacked Rome, beginning a six-month orgy of killing, looting, and burning. The Sack of Rome, as it is called, shook the sense of stability and humanistic confidence that until then had characterized the Renaissance, and it sent many artists fleeing from the ruined city. Nevertheless, Charles saw himself as the leader of the Catholic forces—and he was the sole Catholic ally Clement had at the time. In 1530, Clement VII crowned Charles emperor in Bologna.

Sixteenth-century patrons valued artists highly and rewarded them well, not only with generous commissions but sometimes even with high social status. Charles V, for example, knighted the painter Titian. Some painters and sculptors became entrepreneurs and celebrities, selling prints of their works on the side and creating international reputations for themselves. Many artists recorded their activities—professional and private—in diaries, notebooks, and letters that have come down to us. In addition, contemporary writers began to report on the lives of artists, documenting their physical appearance and assessing their individual reputations. In 1550, Giorgio Vasari wrote the first survey of Italian art history (revised and expanded in 1568)—*Lives of the Most Excellent Architects, Painters, and Sculptors*—organized as a series of critical biographies but at its core a work of critical judgment. Vasari also commented on the role of patrons, and argued that art had become more realistic and more beautiful over time, reaching its apex of perfection in his own age. From his characterization developed our notion of this period as the High Renaissance—that is, as a high point in art since the early experiments of Cimabue and Giotto, marked by a balanced synthesis of Classical ideals and a lifelike rendering of the natural world.

During this period, the fifteenth-century humanists' notion of painting, sculpture, and architecture not as manual arts but as liberal (intellectual) arts, requiring education in the Classics and mathematics as well as in the techniques of the craft, became a topic of intense interest. And from these discussions arose the Renaissance formulation—still with us today—of artists as divinely inspired creative geniuses, a step above most of us in their gifts of hand and mind. This idea weaves its way through Vasari's work like an organizing principle. And this newly elevated status to which artists aspired favored men. Although few artists of either sex had access to the humanist education required by the sophisticated, often esoteric, subject matter used in paintings (usually devised by someone other than the artist), women were denied even the studio practice necessary to study and draw from nude models. Furthermore, it was almost impossible for an artist to achieve international status without traveling extensively and frequently relocating to follow commissions—something most women could not do. Still, some European women managed to follow their gifts and establish careers as artists during this period despite the obstacles that blocked their entrance into the profession.

ITALY IN THE EARLY SIXTEENTH CENTURY: THE HIGH RENAISSANCE

Italian art between the mid-1480s and the 1520s has been called the "High Renaissance." As we have already seen with the "High Classical" period in ancient Athens, the term "High Renaissance"

MAP 21–1 • RENAISSANCE AND EARLIER MONUMENTS IN ROME

In addition to situating the principal works of the Roman Renaissance that emerged from Julius II's campaign to revitalize the papal city, this map also locates the surviving works of Roman antiquity that would have been available to the Renaissance artists and architects who masterminded the Classical revival.

encapsulates an art-historical judgment, claiming that what happened in Rome at this time represents a pinnacle of achievement within a longer artistic movement, and that it set standards for the future (**MAP 21–1**). High Renaissance art is characterized by a sense of gravity and decorum, a complex but ordered relationship of individual parts to the whole, and an emulation of the principles artists saw in ancient Classical art. Art historian Sydney Freedberg has stressed the way High Renaissance art fuses the real and the ideal, characterizing Leonardo's *Mona Lisa*, for example, as "a rare perfection between art and reality; an image in which a breathing instant and a composure for all time are held in suspension" (Freedberg, p. 28).

Two important practical developments at the turn of the sixteenth century affected the arts in Italy. Technically, the use of tempera had almost completely given way to the more flexible oil

painting medium; and economically, with increasing commissions from private sources, artists no longer depended so heavily on the patronage of the Church, the court, or civic associations.

THREE GREAT ARTISTS OF THE EARLY SIXTEENTH CENTURY

Florence's renowned artistic tradition attracted a stream of young artists to that city, traveling there to study its many artistic treasures, not least of which were Masaccio's solid, monumental figures, with their eloquent facial features, poses, and gestures, in the Brancacci Chapel paintings. The young Michelangelo's sketches of the chapel frescos document the importance of Masaccio to his developing style. In fact, Leonardo, Michelangelo, and Raphael—the three leading artists of the High Renaissance—all worked early in their careers in Florence, although they soon moved to other centers of patronage and their influence spread well beyond that city, even beyond Italy.

LEONARDO DA VINCI Leonardo da Vinci (1452–1519) was 12 or 13 when his family moved to Florence from the Tuscan village of Vinci. After an apprenticeship in the shop of the Florentine painter and sculptor Andrea del Verrocchio, and a few years on his own, Leonardo traveled to Milan in 1481 or 1482 to work for the ruling Sforza family.

Leonardo spent much of his time in Milan on military and civil engineering projects, including both urban-renewal and fortification plans for the city, but he also created a few key monuments of Renaissance painting. In April 1483, Leonardo contracted with the Confraternity of the Immaculate Conception to paint an altarpiece for their chapel in the church of San Francesco Grande in Milan, a painting now known as **THE VIRGIN OF THE ROCKS** (FIG. 21-2). The contract stipulates a painting of the Virgin and Child with angels, but Leonardo added a figure of the young John the Baptist, who balances the composition at the left, pulled into dialogue with his younger cousin Jesus by the long, protective arm of the Virgin. She draws attention to her child by extending her other hand over his head, while the enigmatic figure of the angel—who looks out without actually making eye contact with the viewer—points to the center of interaction. The stable, balanced, pyramidal figural group—a compositional formula that will become a standard feature of High Renaissance Classicism—is set against an exquisitely detailed landscape that dissolves mysteriously into the misty distance.

To assure their dominance in the picture, Leonardo picks out the four figures with spotlights, creating a strong **chiaroscuro** (from the Italian words *chiaro*, meaning "light," and *oscuro*, meaning "dark") that enhances their modeling as three-dimensional forms. This painting is an excellent early example of a specific variant of this technique, called **sfumato** ("smoky"), in which there are subtle, almost imperceptible, transitions between light and dark in shading. *Sfumato* becomes a hallmark of Leonardo's style, although the effect is artificially enhanced in this painting by the yellowing of its thick varnish, which masks the original vibrancy of its color.

At Duke Ludovico Sforza's request, Leonardo painted **THE LAST SUPPER** (FIGS. 21-3, 21-4) in the refectory, or dining hall, of the monastery of Santa Maria delle Grazie in Milan between 1495 and 1498. In fictive space defined by a coffered ceiling and four pairs of tapestries that seem to extend the refectory itself into another room, Jesus and his disciples are seated at a long table placed parallel to the picture plane and to the monastic diners who would have been seated in the hall below. In a sense, Jesus' meal with his disciples prefigures the daily gathering of

21-2 • Leonardo da Vinci THE VIRGIN OF THE ROCKS
c. 1485. Oil on wood panel (now transferred to canvas), 6′6″ × 4′ (1.9 × 1.2 m). Musée du Louvre, Paris.

21-3 • Leonardo da Vinci THE LAST SUPPER
Refectory of the monastery of Santa Maria delle Grazie, Milan, Italy. 1495–1498. Tempera and oil on plaster, 15'2" × 28'10" (4.6 × 8.8 m).

👁—**Watch** a video about Leonardo da Vinci's *The Last Supper* on myartslab.com

21-4 • REFECTORY OF THE MONASTERY OF SANTA MARIA DELLE GRAZIE, SHOWING LEONARDO'S LAST SUPPER
Milan, Italy.

Instead of painting in fresco, Leonardo devised an experimental technique for this mural. Hoping to achieve the freedom and flexibility of painting on wood panel, he worked directly on dry *intonaco*—a thin layer of smooth plaster—with an oil-and-tempera paint for which the formula is unknown. The result was disastrous. Within a short time, the painting began to deteriorate, and by the middle of the sixteenth century its figures could be seen only with difficulty. In the seventeenth century, the monks saw no harm in cutting a doorway through the lower center of the composition. The work has barely survived the intervening period, despite many attempts to halt its deterioration and restore its original appearance. It narrowly escaped complete destruction in World War II, when the refectory was bombed to rubble. The coats of arms at the top are those of patron Ludovico Sforza, duke of Milan (r. 1494–1499), and his wife, Beatrice.

21-5 • Leonardo da Vinci MONA LISA
c. 1503–1506. Oil on wood panel, 30¼″ × 21″ (77 × 53 cm). Musée du
Louvre, Paris. (INV. 779)

Read the document related to Leonardo da Vinci on
myartslab.com

young John the Evangelist and the elderly Peter, rather than iso-
lating Judas on the opposite side of the table. Judas, Peter, and
John were each to play an essential role in Jesus' mission: Judas
set in motion the events leading to Jesus' sacrifice; Peter led the
Church after Jesus' death; and John, the visionary, foretold the Second Coming and the Last Judgment in the book of Revelation.

The painting's careful geometry, the convergence of its perspective lines, the stability of its pyramidal forms, and Jesus' calm
demeanor at the mathematical center of all the commotion, work
together to reinforce the sense of gravity, balance, and order.
The clarity and stability of this painting epitomize High Renaissance style.

Leonardo returned to Florence in 1500, after the French, who
had invaded Italy in 1494, claimed Milan by defeating Leonardo's
Milanese patron, Ludovico Sforza. Perhaps the most famous of his
Florentine works is the portrait he painted between about 1503
and 1506 known as the **MONA LISA** (FIG. 21-5). The subject may
have been 24-year-old Lisa Gherardini del Giocondo, the wife of
a prominent Florentine merchant. Leonardo never delivered the
painting and kept it with him for the rest of his life. In a departure
from tradition, the young woman is portrayed without jewelry,
not even a ring. The solid pyramidal form of her halflength figure—another departure from traditional portraiture, which was
limited to the upper torso—is silhouetted against distant hazy
mountains, giving the painting a sense of mystery reminiscent of
The Virgin of the Rocks (see FIG. 21-2). Mona Lisa's facial expression
has been called "enigmatic" because her gentle smile—typical of
Leonardo's women and angels (see FIG. 21-2)—is not accompanied
by the warmth one would expect to see in her eyes, which have
boldly shifted to the side to look straight out at the viewer. It is
this expressive complexity, and the sense of psychological presence
it gives the human face—especially in the context of the masklike
detachment that was more characteristic of Renaissance portraiture (compare FIG. 20-31, or even FIG. 21-8)—that makes the innovative *Mona Lisa* so arresting and haunting, even today.

A fiercely debated topic in Renaissance Italy was the question
of the relative merits of painting and sculpture. Leonardo insisted
on the supremacy of painting as the best and most complete means
of creating an illusion of the natural world, while Michelangelo
argued for sculpture. Yet in creating a painted illusion, Leonardo
considered color to be secondary to the depiction of sculptural
volume, which he achieved through his virtuosity in *sfumato*.
He also unified his compositions by covering them with a thin,
lightly tinted varnish, which enhanced the overall smoky haze.
Because early evening light tends to produce a similar effect naturally, Leonardo considered dusk the finest time of day and recom-
mended that painters set up their studios in a courtyard with black
walls and a linen sheet stretched overhead to reproduce twilight.

Leonardo's fame as an artist is based on only a few works,
for his many interests took him away from painting. Unlike his
humanist contemporaries, he was not particularly interested
in Classical literature or archaeology. Instead, his passions were

this local monastic community at mealtimes. The stagelike space
recedes from the table to three windows on the back wall, where
the vanishing point of the one-point linear perspective lies behind
Jesus' head. A stable, pyramidal Jesus at the center is flanked by his
12 disciples, grouped in four interlocking sets of three.

On one level, Leonardo has painted a scene from a story—
one that captures the individual reactions of the apostles to Jesus'
announcement that one of them will betray him. Leonardo was
an acute observer of human behavior, and his art captures human
emotions with compelling immediacy. On another level, *The Last
Supper* is a symbolic evocation of Jesus' coming sacrifice for the
salvation of humankind, the foundation of the institution of the
Mass. Breaking with traditional representations of the subject (see
FIG. 20-25) to create compositional clarity, balance, and cohesion,
Leonardo placed the traitor Judas—clutching his money bags in
the shadows—within the first triad to Jesus' right, along with the

Artists throughout history have turned to geometric shapes and mathematical proportions to seek the ideal representation of the human form. Leonardo, following the first-century BCE Roman architect and engineer Vitruvius, equated the ideal man with both circle and square. Ancient Egyptian artists had laid out square grids as aids to design (see "Egyptian Pictorial Relief," page 64). Medieval artists adapted a variety of figures, from triangles to pentagrams (see "Villard de Honnecourt," page 511).

Vitruvius, in his ten-volume *De architectura* (*On Architecture*), wrote: "For if a man be placed flat on his back, with his hands and feet extended, and a pair of compasses centered at his navel, the fingers

and toes of his two hands and feet will touch the circumference of a circle described therefrom. And just as the human body yields a circular outline, so too a square figure may be found from it. For if we measure the distance from the soles of the feet to the top of the head, and then apply that measure to the outstretched arms, the breadth will be found to be the same as the height" (Book III, Chapter 1, Section 3). Vitruvius determined that the ideal body should be eight heads high. Leonardo added his own observations in the reversed writing he always used in his notebooks when he created his well-known diagram for the ideal male figure, called the **VITRUVIAN MAN** (FIG. 21–6).

21–6 • Leonardo da Vinci VITRUVIAN MAN
c. 1490. Ink, 13½″ × 9⅝″ (34.3 × 24.5 cm). Galleria dell'Accademia, Venice.

21-7 • Raphael THE SMALL COWPER MADONNA
c. 1505. Oil on wood panel, 23⅜″ × 17⅜″ (59.5 × 44.1 cm). National
Gallery of Art, Washington, DC. Widener Collection (1942.9.57)

In the distance on a hilltop, Raphael has painted a scene he knew well
from his childhood, the domed church of San Bernardino, two miles
outside Urbino. The church contains the tombs of dukes of Urbino,
Federico and Guidobaldo da Montefeltro, and their wives (see FIG.
20–31). Donato Bramante, whose architecture was key in establishing
the High Renaissance style, may have designed the church.

Leonardo returned to Milan in 1508 and lived there until
1513. He also lived for a time in the Vatican at the invitation of
Pope Leo X, but there is no evidence that he produced any works
of art during his stay. In 1516, he accepted the French king Francis
I's invitation to relocate to France as an advisor on architecture,
taking the *Mona Lisa*, as well as other important works, with him.
He remained at Francis's court until his death in 1519.

RAPHAEL About 1505—while Leonardo was working on the
Mona Lisa—Raphael (Raffaello Santi or Sanzio, 1483–1520)
arrived in Florence from his native Urbino after studying in Perugia with the city's leading artist, Perugino (see FIG. 20-18). Raphael
quickly became successful in Florence, especially with small, polished paintings of the Virgin and Child, such as **THE SMALL
COWPER MADONNA** (named for a modern owner) of about
1505 (FIG. 21-7). Already a superb painter technically, the youthful Raphael shows his indebtedness to his teacher in the delicate
tilt of the figures' heads, the brilliant tonalities, and the pervasive
sense of serenity. But Leonardo's impact is also evident here in
the simple grandeur of these monumental shapes, the pyramidal
composition activated by the spiraling movement of the child,
and the draperies that cling to the Virgin's substantial form. In
other Madonnas from this period, Raphael included the young
John the Baptist (see FIG. Intro-4), experimenting with the multiple
figure interactions pioneered by Leonardo in *The Virgin of the
Rocks* (see FIG. 21-2).

At the same time as he was producing engaging images of
elegant Madonnas, Raphael was also painting flawlessly executed
portraits of prosperous Florentine patrons. To commemorate the
marriage in 1504 of 30-year-old cloth merchant Agnelo Doni to
Maddalena Strozzi, the 15-year-old daughter of a powerful banking family, Doni commissioned from Raphael **pendant** portraits of
the newlyweds (FIG. 21-8). Like Piero della Francesca in his portraits of Battista Sforza and Federico da Montefeltro (see FIG. 20-31),
Raphael silhouettes Maddalena and Agnelo against a meticulously
described panoramic landscape. But unlike their predecessors, they
turn to address the viewer. Agnelo is commanding but casual,
leaning his arm on a balustrade to add three-dimensionality to his
posture. Maddalena's pose imitates Leonardo's innovative presentation of his subject in the *Mona Lisa* (see FIG. 21-5), which Raphael
had obviously seen in progress, but with Maddalena there is no
sense of mystery, indeed little psychological presence, and Raphael
follows tradition in emphasizing the sumptuousness of her clothing and making ostentatious display of her jewelry. The wisps of
hair that escape from her sculpted coiffure are the only hint of
human vulnerability.

Raphael left Florence about 1508 for Rome, where Pope
Julius II put him to work almost immediately decorating rooms
(*stanze*, singular *stanza*) in the papal apartments. In the Stanza
della Segnatura (see FIG. 21-1)—the pope's private library—Raphael painted the four branches of knowledge as conceived in the
sixteenth century: Religion (the *Disputà*, depicting discussions

mathematics, engineering, and the natural world. He compiled
volumes of detailed drawings and notes on anatomy, botany, geol-
ogy, meteorology, architectural design, and mechanics. In his
drawings of human figures, he sought not only the precise details
of anatomy but also the geometric basis of perfect proportions (see
"The Vitruvian Man," page 639). Leonardo's searching mind is
evident in his drawings, not only of natural objects and human
beings, but also of machines, so clearly and completely worked
out that modern engineers have used them to construct working models. He designed flying machines, a kind of automobile, a
parachute, and all sorts of military equipment, including a mobile
fortress. His imagination outran his means to bring his creations
into being. For one thing, he lacked a source of power other than
men and horses. For another, he may have lacked focus and follow-
through. His contemporaries complained that he never finished
anything and that his inventions distracted him from his painting.

21-8 • Raphael AGNELO DONI AND MADDALENA STROZZI
c. 1506. Oil on wood panel, each 24½″ × 17¼″ (63 × 45 cm). Palazzo Pitti, Florence.

These portraits were not the only paintings commissioned by Agnelo Doni to commemorate his upwardly mobile marriage alliance with Maddalena Strozzi. He ordered a tondo portraying the Holy Family from rival artist Michelangelo (see Introduction, "A Closer Look," page xxxi FIG. C). Vasari reports that although the original price for that painting was set at 70 ducats, Doni only sent Michelangelo 40. In order to obtain his painting, the patron eventually had to pay the artist double the original price—140 ducats.

concerning the true presence of Christ in the Eucharistic Host), Philosophy (*The School of Athens*), Poetry (*Parnassus*, home of the Muses), and Law (the Cardinal Virtues under *Justice*).

Raphael's most influential achievement in the papal rooms was *The School of Athens*, painted about 1510–1511 (see "A Closer Look," page 642). Here, the painter seems to summarize the ideals of the Renaissance papacy in a grand conception of harmoniously arranged forms in a rational space, as well as in the calm dignity of the figures that occupy it. If the learned Julius II did not actually devise the subjects, he certainly must have approved them. Greek philosophers Plato and Aristotle take center stage—placed to the right and left of the vanishing point—silhouetted against the sky and framed under three successive barrel vaults. Surrounding Plato and Aristotle are mathematicians, naturalists, astronomers, geographers, and other philosophers, debating and demonstrating their theories with and to onlookers and each other. The scene takes

place in an immense barrel-vaulted interior, flooded with a clear, even light from a single source, and seemingly inspired by the new design for St. Peter's, under construction at the time. The grandeur of the building is matched by the monumental dignity of the philosophers themselves, each of whom has a distinct physical and intellectual presence. The sweeping arcs of the composition are activated by the variety and energy of their poses and gestures, creating a dynamic unity that is a prime characteristic of High Renaissance art.

In 1515, Raphael was commissioned by Pope Leo X (pontificate 1513–1521) to provide designs on themes from the Acts of the Apostles to be woven into tapestries for the strip of blank wall below the fifteenth-century wall paintings of the Sistine Chapel (a surface now decorated with painted simulations of hanging drapery: see FIG. 20-33). For the production of the tapestries, woven in Brussels, Raphael and his large workshop of assistants made

A CLOSER LOOK | *The School of Athens*

by Raphael, fresco in the Stanza della Segnatura, Vatican, Rome.
c. 1510–1511. 19′ × 27′ (5.79 × 8.24 m).

Looking down from niches in the walls are sculptures of Apollo (the god of sunlight, rationality, poetry, music, and the fine arts) and Minerva (the goddess of wisdom and the mechanical arts).

Plato points upward to the realm of ideas and pure forms that were at the center of his philosophy. His pupil Aristotle gestures toward his surroundings, signifying the empirical world that for him served as the basis for understanding.

The figure bent over a slate with a compass is Euclid, the father of geometry. Vasari claimed that Raphael gave this mathematician the portrait likeness of Bramante, the architect whose redesigned St. Peter's was under construction not far from this room and who was also a distant relative of Raphael.

Raphael placed his own portrait in a group that includes the geographer Ptolemy, who holds a terrestrial globe, and the astronomer Zoroaster, who holds a celestial globe.

The brooding figure of Heraclitus, a late addition to the composition, is a portrait of Michelangelo, who was working next door on the ceiling of the Sistine Chapel, and whose monumental figural style is here appropriated (or is it mimicked?) by Raphael. The stonecutter's boots on his feet refer to Michelangelo's self-identification—or Raphael's insistence that he be seen—as a sculptor rather than a painter.

This figure is usually identified as Diogenes the Cynic following Vasari's account of the painting. It is more likely that he is Socrates, however. The cup next to him could refer to his deadly draught of hemlock, and his recumbent position recalls his teaching from his prison bed.

The group of figures gathered around Euclid illustrate the various stages of understanding: literal learning, dawning comprehension, anticipation of the outcome, and assisting the teacher. Raphael received acclaim for his ability to communicate so clearly through the poses and expressions of his figures.

 View the Closer Look for *The School of Athens* on myartslab.com full-scale charcoal drawings, then painted over them with color for the weavers to match (see "Raphael's Cartoons for Tapestries in the Sistine Chapel," page 648). Pictorial weaving was the most prestigious and expensive kind of wall decoration. With murals by the leading painters of the fifteenth century above and Michelangelo's work circling over all, Raphael must have felt both honored and challenged. The pope had given him the place of honor among the artists in the papal chapel.

MICHELANGELO'S EARLY WORK Michelangelo Buonarroti (1475–1564) was born in the Tuscan town of Caprese into an impoverished Florentine family that laid a claim to nobility—a claim the artist carefully advanced throughout his life. He grew up in Florence, where at age 13 he was apprenticed to Ghirlandaio (see FIG. 20-37), in whose workshop he learned the technique of fresco painting and studied drawings of Classical monuments. Soon the talented youth joined the household of Lorenzo the Magnificent, head of the ruling Medici family, where he came into contact with Neoplatonic philosophy and the family's distinguished sculpture collection. After Lorenzo died in 1492, Michelangelo traveled to Venice and Bologna, then returned to Florence.

Michelangelo's major early work at the turn of the century was a marble sculpture of the **PIETÀ**, commissioned by a French cardinal and installed as a tomb monument in Old St. Peter's (**FIG. 21-9**). The theme of the *pietà* (in which the Virgin supports and mourns the dead Jesus in her lap), long popular in northern Europe (see FIG. 18-23), was an unusual theme in Italy at the time. Michelangelo traveled to the marble quarries at Carrara in central Italy

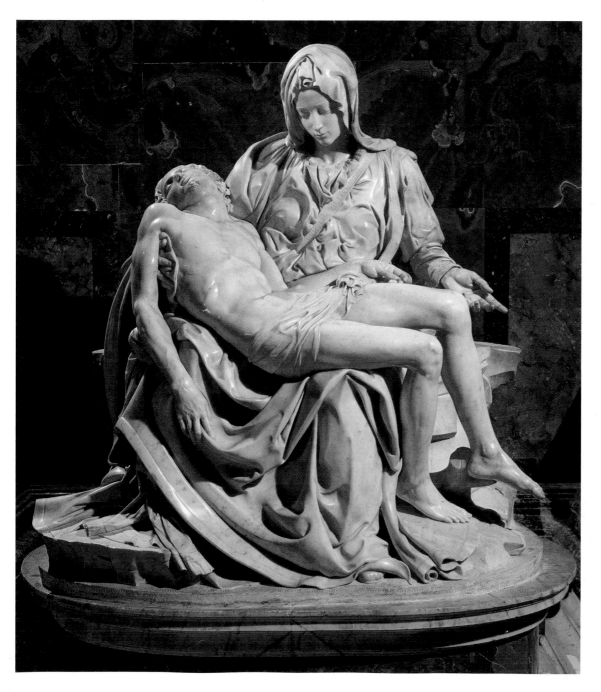

21-9 • Michelangelo
PIETÀ
c. 1500. Marble, height 5′8½″ (1.74 m). St. Peter's, Vatican, Rome.

📖 **Read** the document related to Michelangelo on myartslab.com to select the block from which to make this large work, a practice he was to continue for nearly all his sculpture. The choice of stone was important to him because he envisioned his sculpture as already existing within the marble, needing only his tools to set it free. Michelangelo was a poet as well as an artist, and later wrote in his Sonnet 15: "The greatest artist has no conception which a single block of marble does not potentially contain within its mass, but only a hand obedient to the mind can penetrate to this image."

Michelangelo's Virgin is a young woman of heroic stature holding the unnaturally smaller, lifeless body of her grown son. Inconsistencies of scale and age are forgotten, however, when contemplating the sweetness of expression, technical virtuosity of the carving, and smooth modeling of the luscious forms. Michelangelo's compelling vision of beauty was meant to be seen up close so that the viewer can look directly into Jesus' face. The 25-year-old artist is said to have slipped into the church at night to sign the statue on a strap across the Virgin's breast after it was finished, answering directly questions that had come up about the identity of its creator.

In 1501, Michelangelo accepted a Florentine commission for a statue of the biblical hero **DAVID** (**FIG. 21-10**), to be placed high atop a buttress of the cathedral. But when it was finished in 1504, the *David* was so admired that the city council instead placed it in the principal city square, next to the Palazzo della Signoria (see FIG. 18-2), the seat of Florence's government. There it stood as a reminder of Florence's republican status, which was briefly reinstated after the expulsion of the powerful Medici oligarchy in 1494. Although in its muscular nudity Michelangelo's *David* embodies the antique ideal of the athletic male nude, the emotional power of its expression and its concentrated gaze are entirely new. Unlike Donatello's bronze *David* (see FIG. 20-14), this is not a triumphant hero with the trophy head of the giant Goliath already under his feet. Slingshot over his shoulder and a rock in his right hand, Michelangelo's *David* knits his brow and stares into space, seemingly preparing himself psychologically for the danger ahead, a mere youth confronting a gigantic experienced warrior. No match for his opponent in experience, weaponry, or physical strength, Michelangelo's powerful *David* stands for the supremacy

21-10 • Michelangelo DAVID
1501–1504. Marble, height 17′ (5.18 m) without pedestal. Galleria dell'Accademia, Florence.

Michelangelo's most famous sculpture was cut from an 18-foot-tall marble block. The sculptor began with a small model in wax, then sketched the contours of the figure as they would appear from the front on one face of the marble. According to his friend and biographer Vasari, Michelangelo then chiseled in from the drawn-on surface, as if making a figure in very high relief. The completed statue took four days to move on tree-trunk rollers down the narrow streets of Florence from the cathedral workshop to its location outside the Palazzo della Signoria (see FIG. 18–2). In 1504, the Florentines gilded the tree stump and added a gilded wreath to the head and a belt of 28 gilt-bronze leaves, since removed. In 1873, the statue was replaced by a copy, and the original was moved into the museum of the Florence Academy.

21–11 • INTERIOR, SISTINE CHAPEL
Vatican, Rome. Built 1475–1481; ceiling painted 1508–1512; end wall, 1536–1541. The ceiling measures 45′ × 128′ (13.75 × 39 m).

of right over might—a perfect emblem for the Florentines, who had recently fought the forces of Milan, Siena, and Pisa, and still faced political and military pressure.

THE SISTINE CHAPEL Despite Michelangelo's contractual commitment to Florence Cathedral for additional statues, in 1505, Pope Julius II, who saw Michelangelo as an ideal collabora-

tor in the artistic aggrandizement of the papacy, arranged for him to come to Rome to work on the spectacular tomb Julius planned for himself. Michelangelo began the tomb project, but two years later the pope ordered him to begin painting the ceiling of the **SISTINE CHAPEL** instead (**FIG. 21–11**).

Michelangelo considered himself a sculptor, but the strong-minded pope wanted paintings; work began in 1508. Michelangelo

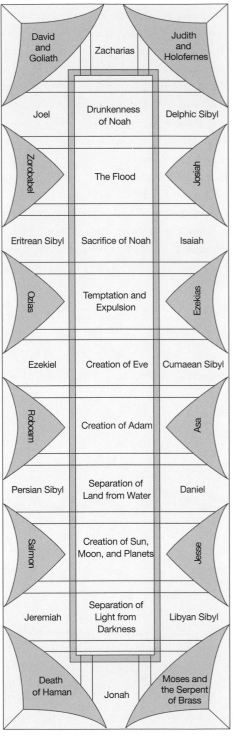

David and Goliath	Zacharias	Judith and Holofernes
Joel	Drunkenness of Noah	Delphic Sibyl
Zorobabel	The Flood	Josiah
Eritrean Sibyl	Sacrifice of Noah	Isaiah
Ozias	Temptation and Expulsion	Ezekias
Ezekiel	Creation of Eve	Cumaean Sibyl
Roboam	Creation of Adam	Asa
Persian Sibyl	Separation of Land from Water	Daniel
Salmon	Creation of Sun, Moon, and Planets	Jesse
Jeremiah	Separation of Light from Darkness	Libyan Sibyl
Death of Haman	Jonah	Moses and the Serpent of Brass

ALTAR

21–12 • Michelangelo SISTINE CHAPEL CEILING WITH DIAGRAM IDENTIFYING SCENES
1508–1512. Fresco.

complained bitterly in a sonnet to a friend: "This miserable job has given me a goiter….The force of it has jammed my belly up beneath my chin. Beard to the sky….Brush splatterings make a pavement of my face…. I'm not a painter." Despite his physical misery as he stood on a scaffold, painting the ceiling just above him, the results were extraordinary, and Michelangelo established a new and remarkably powerful style in Renaissance painting.

Julius's initial order for the ceiling was simple: *trompe l'oeil* coffers to replace the original star-spangled blue decoration. Later he wanted the 12 apostles seated on thrones on the triangular spandrels between the lunettes framing the windows. According to Michelangelo, when he objected to the limitations of Julius's plan, the pope told him to paint whatever he liked. This Michelangelo presumably did, although he was certainly guided by a theological advisor and his plan no doubt required the pope's approval.

In Michelangelo's design, an illusionistic marble architecture establishes a framework for the figures and narrative scenes on the vault of the chapel (**FIG. 21-12**). Running completely around the ceiling is a painted cornice with projections supported by pilasters decorated with "sculptured" *putti*. Between the pilasters are figures of prophets and sibyls (female seers from the Classical world) who were believed to have foretold Jesus' birth. Seated on the fictive cornice are heroic figures of nude young men called *ignudi* (singular, *ignudo*), holding sashes attached to large gold medallions. Rising behind the *ignudi*, shallow bands of fictive stone span the center of the ceiling and divide it into nine compartments containing successive scenes from Genesis—recounting the Creation, the Fall, and the Flood—beginning over the altar and ending near the chapel entrance. God's earliest acts of creation are therefore closest to the altar, the Creation of Eve at the center of the ceiling, followed by the imperfect actions of humanity: Temptation, Fall, Expulsion from Paradise, and God's eventual destruction of all people except Noah and his family by the Flood. The eight triangular spandrels over the windows, as well as the lunettes crowning them, contain paintings of the ancestors of Jesus.

Perhaps the most familiar scene on the ceiling is the **CREATION OF ADAM** (**FIG. 21-13**), where Michelangelo captures the moment when God charges the languorous Adam—in a pose adapted from the Roman river-god type—with the spark of life. As if to echo the biblical text, Adam's heroic body, outstretched arm, and profile almost mirror those of God, in whose image he has been created. Emerging under God's other arm, and looking across

21-13 • Michelangelo **CREATION OF ADAM, SISTINE CHAPEL CEILING**
1511–1512. Fresco, 9′2″ × 18′8″ (2.8 × 5.7 m).

The Sistine Chapel was a major focus of papal patronage throughout the Renaissance. The building was constructed in 1475–1481 by Sixtus IV, who also began its painted embellishment by calling a constellation of illustrious artists to Rome in the early 1480s to create a band of framed frescos recounting the life of Moses on one wall and the life of Christ on the other (see FIG. 20–33). Between 1508 and 1512, Michelangelo painted the chapel's ceiling at the behest of Julius II. And soon after he became pope in 1513, Leo X commissioned Raphael to produce ten cartoons (full-size preparatory designs for a work of art executed in another medium) for a lavish set of tapestries portraying scenes from the lives of SS. Peter and Paul that would complete the decorative program on the chapel's lower level. At the time, these would have been considered its most prestigious and expensive works of art. The tapestry program cost Leo X more than five times what Julius II had paid Michelangelo to paint the ceiling. For designing the program and producing the cartoons, however, Raphael only received a sixteenth of the total cost of the tapestries; the expense here involved production more than design.

The cartoons were created in Raphael's workshop between 1515 and 1516. Raphael was clearly the intellect behind the compositions, and he participated in the actual preparation and execution. This was a prestigious commission that would reflect directly on the reputation of the master. But he could not have accomplished this imposing task in a little over a year without the collaboration of numerous assistants working in his thriving workshop. The completed cartoons—first drawn with charcoal on paper (160–170 separate sheets were glued together to form the expanse of a single tapestry) and then overpainted with color—were sent to Brussels, where they were woven into tapestries in the workshop of Pieter van Aelst. The first was complete in 1517, seven were hanging in the chapel for Christmas 1519, and the entire cycle was installed by Leo X's death in 1521.

The process of creation, from design through production, can be charted by examining the tapestry portraying *Christ's Charge to Peter* (John 21:15–17; Matthew 16:17–19) at three stages in its development. We have Raphael's preliminary drawing (FIG. 21–14), where models—it is tempting to see these as Raphael's assistants, stripped to their underwear to help the master work out his composition—are posed to enact the moment when Jesus addresses his apostles. This is a preliminary idea for the pose of Christ. In the final cartoon (FIG. 21–15), Raphael changes Christ's gesture so that he addresses the kneeling Peter specifically rather than the whole apostolic group; for the patron, this would be an important detail since papal power rested in the belief that Christ had transferred authority to Peter, who was considered the first pope, with subsequent popes inheriting this authority in unbroken succession. Comparison of drawing and cartoon also reveals an important aspect of the design process. The cartoon reverses the figural arrangement of the drawing because in the production process the tapestry would be woven from the back, and if the weavers followed the reversed version of the composition on the cartoon, the resulting tapestry (FIG. 21–16) would show the scene in its intended orientation. Comparison of cartoon and tapestry also indicates that the weavers were not required to follow their models slavishly. They have embellished the costume of Christ, perhaps in an attempt to assure that the viewers' attention will be immediately directed to this most important figure in the scene.

After they had been used to create the tapestries hung in the Sistine Chapel, Raphael's cartoons remained in Brussels, where several additional sets of tapestries were made from them—one for Henry VIII of England, another for Francis I of France—before seven surviving cartoons were acquired in 1623 by the future Charles I of England. They remain in the British Royal Collection. The tapestries themselves, although still in the Vatican, are displayed in the museum rather than on the walls of the chapel for which they were originally conceived, as one of the most prestigious artistic projects from the peak of the Roman High Renaissance.

21–14 • Raphael **STUDY FOR CHRIST'S CHARGE TO PETER**
c. 1515. Red chalk. Royal Library, Windsor Castle.

21–15 • Raphael and assistants **CARTOON FOR TAPESTRY PORTRAYING CHRIST'S CHARGE TO PETER**
c. 1515–1516. Distemper on paper (now transferred to canvas), 11'1" × 17'4" (3.4 × 5.3 m). Lent by Her Majesty the Queen to the Victoria & Albert Museum, London.

21–16 • Shop of Pieter van Aelst, Brussels, after cartoons by Raphael and assistants **CHRIST'S CHARGE TO PETER**
Woven 1517, installed 1519 in the Sistine Chapel. Wool and silk with silver-gilt wrapped threads. Musei Vaticani, Pinacoteca, Rome.

him in the direction of her future mate, is the robust and energetic figure of Eve before her creation.

MICHELANGELO AT SAN LORENZO After the Medici regained power in Florence in 1512, and Leo X (Giovanni de' Medici) succeeded Julius in 1513, Michelangelo became chief architect for Medici family projects at the church of San Lorenzo in Florence—including a new chapel for the tombs of Lorenzo the Magnificent, his brother Giuliano, and two younger dukes, also named Lorenzo and Giuliano, ordered in 1519 for the so-called New Sacristy (see FIG. 20-4). The older men's tombs were never built to Michelangelo's designs, but the unfinished tombs for the younger relatives were placed on opposite side walls (FIG. 21-17).

Each of the two monuments consists of an idealized portrait of the deceased, who turns to face the family's unfinished ancestral tomb. The men are dressed in a sixteenth-century interpretation of Classical armor and seated in wall niches above pseudo-Classical sarcophagi. Balanced precariously atop the sarcophagi are male and female figures representing the times of day. Their positions would not seem so unsettling had reclining figures of river gods been installed below them, as originally planned, but even so there is a conspicuous tension here between the substantiality of the figures and the limitations imposed on them by their architectural surrounds. In the tomb illustrated here, Michelangelo represents Giuliano as the Active Life, and his sarcophagus figures are allegories of Night and Day. Night at left is accompanied by her symbols: a star and crescent moon on her tiara; poppies, which induce sleep; and an owl under the arch of her leg. The huge mask at her back may allude to Death, since Sleep and Death were said to be the children of Night. Some have seen in this mask that glares out at viewers in the chapel a self-portrait of the artist, serving both as signature and as a way of proclaiming his right to be here because of his long relationship with the family. On the other tomb, Lorenzo, representing the Contemplative Life, is supported by Dawn and Evening.

Concurrent with work on the Medici tombs was the construction of a new library at San Lorenzo. The idea for the library belongs to Cardinal Giulio de' Medici and dates to 1519, but it was only after he was elected Pope Clement VII in 1523 that the money became available to realize it. Michelangelo was commissioned to design and also supervise construction of the new **VESTIBULE** (FIG. 21-18) and reading room and to spare

21-17 • Michelangelo TOMB OF GIULIANO DE' MEDICI WITH ALLEGORICAL FIGURES OF NIGHT AND DAY
New Sacristy (Medici Chapel), church of San Lorenzo, Florence. 1519–1534. Marble, height of seated figure approx. 5'10" (1.8 m).

✳ **Explore** the architectural panoramas of the New Sacristy in the church of San Lorenzo on myartslab.com no expense in making them both grand and ambitious. The pope paid keen attention to the library's progress—not, he said, to verify the quality of the design, but because the project had a special interest for him.

Michelangelo coordinated his work within a decorative tradition established at San Lorenzo when Brunelleschi designed the church itself a century earlier (see FIG. 20–4), using stylized architectural elements carved in dark gray *pietra serena*, set against and within a contrasting white wall. However, Michelangelo plays with the Classical architectural etiquette that Brunelleschi had used to create such clarity, harmony, and balance in the nave.

In Michelangelo's vestibule, chunky columns are recessed into rectangular wall niches that can barely contain them. They are crowded and overlapped by the aggressive lateral extension of the pediment over the door. The door itself is broken into parts, sides jutting forward as fluted pilasters that are then partially obscured by the frame around the opening. The three flights of stairs leading up to the reading room almost fill the vestibule, and the central stairs cascade forward forcefully toward visitors, hardly encouraging them to go against the flow and step up. Through their playfulness, these creative combinations of architectural forms draw attention to themselves and their design rather than the function of the building itself or the comfortable accommodation of its users, prime characteristics of the Mannerist architecture then coming into fashion.

Fearing for his life when ongoing political struggles flared up in Florence, Michelango returned to Rome in 1534 and settled permanently. He had left both the Medici Chapel and the library unfinished. In 1557, he sent a plaster model of the library staircase to Florence to assure that its completion conformed to his design. In 1545, his students had assembled the tomb sculptures, including unfinished figures of the times of day, into the composition we see today.

The figures of the dukes are finely finished, but the times of day are notable for their contrasting areas of rough unfinished and polished marble. These are the only unfinished sculptures Michelangelo apparently permitted to be put in place, and we do not know what his reasons were. Specialists in Renaissance art history characterize these works with the word *nonfinito* ("unfinished"), proposing that Michelangelo had begun to view his artistic

21–18 • Michelangelo VESTIBULE OF THE LAURENTIAN LIBRARY
Church of San Lorenzo, Florence. Begun 1524; stairway designed 1550s.

creations as symbols of human imperfection. Indeed, Michelangelo's poetry often expressed his belief that humans could achieve perfection only in death.

ARCHITECTURE IN ROME AND THE VATICAN

The election of Julius II as pope in 1503 crystallized a resurgence of papal power, but France, Spain, and the Holy Roman Empire all had designs on Italy. During his ten-year papacy, Julius fought wars and formed alliances to consolidate his power. He also enlisted Bramante, Raphael, and Michelangelo to carry out his vision of a revitalized Rome as the center of a new Christian architecture, inspired by the achievements of their fifteenth-century predecessors as well as the monuments of antiquity. Although most commissions were for churches, opportunities also arose to create urban palaces and country villas.

BRAMANTE Donato Bramante (1444–1514) was born near Urbino and trained as a painter, but turned to architectural design early in his career. About 1481, he became attached to the Sforza court in Milan, where he would have known Leonardo da Vinci. In 1499, Bramante settled in Rome, but work came slowly. The architect was nearing 60 when Julius II asked him to redesign St. Peter's (see "St. Peter's Basilica," opposite) and the Spanish rulers Queen Isabella and King Ferdinand commissioned a small shrine over the spot in Rome where the apostle Peter was believed to have been crucified (**FIG. 21-19**). In this tiny building, known as Il Tempietto ("Little Temple"), Bramante combined his interpretation of the principles of Vitruvius and Alberti from the stepped base, to the Tuscan columns and Doric frieze (Vitruvius had advised that the Doric order be used for temples to gods of particularly forceful character), to the elegant balustrade. The centralized plan and the tall drum supporting a hemispheric dome recall Early Christian shrines built over martyrs' relics, as well as ancient Roman circular temples. Especially notable is the sculptural effect of the building's exterior, with its deep wall niches and sharp contrasts of light and shadow. Bramante's design called for a circular cloister around the church, but the cloister was never built.

ARCHITECTURE, PAINTING, AND SCULPTURE IN NORTHERN ITALY

While Rome was Italy's preeminent arts center at the beginning of the sixteenth century, wealthy and powerful families elsewhere also patronized the arts and letters just as the Montefeltro and Gonzaga had in Urbino and Mantua during the fifteenth century. The architects and painters working for these sixteenth-century patrons created fanciful structures and developed a new colorful, illusionistic painting style. The result was witty, elegant, and finely executed art designed to appeal to the jaded taste of the intellectual elite in cities such as Mantua, Parma, Bologna, and Venice.

21-19 • Donato Bramante
IL TEMPIETTO, CHURCH OF SAN PIETRO IN MONTORIO
Rome. 1502–1510; dome and lantern were restored in the 17th century.

The history of St. Peter's in Rome is a case study of the effects of individual and institutional demands on the design, construction, and remodeling of a major religious building. The original church—now called Old St. Peter's—was built in the fourth century by Constantine, the first Christian Roman emperor, to mark the grave of the apostle Peter, the first bishop of Rome and therefore considered the first pope. Because the site was so holy, Constantine's architect had to build a structure large enough to hold the crowds of pilgrims who came to visit St. Peter's tomb. To provide a platform for the church, a huge terrace was cut into the side of the Vatican Hill, across the Tiber River from the city. Here Constantine's architect erected a basilica with a new feature, a transept, to allow large numbers of visitors to approach the shrine at the front of the apse. The rest of the church was, in effect, a covered cemetery, carpeted with the tombs of believers who wanted to be buried near the apostle's grave. When it was built, Constantine's basilica, as befitted an imperial commission, was one of the largest buildings in the Roman world (interior length 368 feet, width 190 feet). For more than a thousand years it was the most important pilgrimage site in Europe.

In 1506, Pope Julius II made the astonishing decision to demolish the Constantinian basilica, which had fallen into disrepair, and to replace it with a new building. That anyone, even a pope, should have had the nerve to pull down such a venerated building is an indication of the extraordinary self-assurance of the Renaissance—and of Julius himself. To design and build the new church, the pope appointed Donato Bramante, who envisioned the new St. Peter's as a central-plan building, in the shape of a cross with four arms of equal length, crowned by an enormous dome. This design was intended to emulate the Early Christian tradition of constructing domed and round buildings over the tombs of martyrs, itself derived from the Roman practice of building centrally planned tombs (see "Longitudinal-Plan and Central-Plan Churches," page 225). In Renaissance thinking, the central plan and dome symbolized the perfection of God.

The deaths of pope and architect in 1513 and 1514 put a temporary halt to the project. Successive plans by Raphael, Antonio da Sangallo, and others extended one arm of the cross to provide the church with an extended nave. However, when Michelangelo was appointed architect in 1546, he returned to the centralized plan and simplified Bramante's design to create a single, unified space covered with a hemispherical dome. The dome was finally completed some years after Michelangelo's death by Giacomo della Porta, who retained Michelangelo's basic design but gave the dome a taller profile (see FIG. 21–39).

During the Counter-Reformation, the Catholic Church emphasized congregational worship; as a result, more space was needed to house the congregation and allow for processions. To expand the church— and to make it more closely resemble Old St. Peter's—Pope Paul V in 1606 commissioned the architect Carlo Maderno to change Michelangelo's central plan back once again into a longitudinal plan. Maderno extended the nave to its final length of slightly more than 636 feet and added a new façade, thus completing St. Peter's as we see it is today. Later in the seventeenth century, the sculptor and architect Gianlorenzo Bernini created an elaborate approach to the basilica by surrounding the space in front of it with a great colonnade, like a huge set of arms extended to embrace the faithful as they approach the principal church of Western Christendom.

Old St. Peter's
4th century

Bramante, plan for New St. Peter's
1506

Michelangelo, plan for New St. Peter's
1546–1564

Maderno, plan of St. Peter's Basilica
1607–1612

👁—|**Watch** an architectural simulation about St. Peter's Basilica on myartslab.com

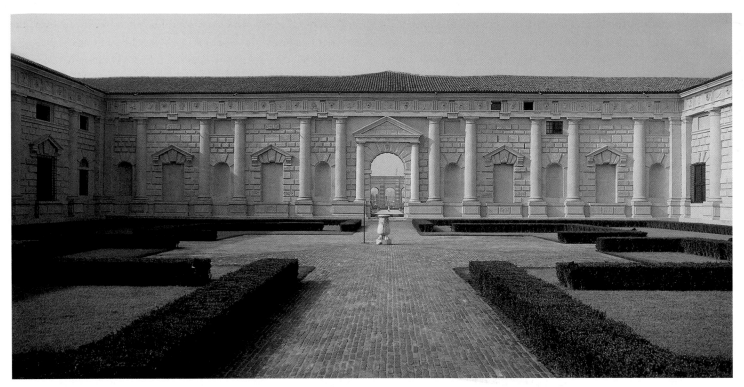

21-20 • Giulio Romano **COURTYARD FAÇADE, PALAZZO DEL TÈ, MANTUA**
1527–1534.

GIULIO ROMANO In Mantua, Federigo II Gonzaga (r. 1519–1540) continued the family tradition of patronage when, in 1524, he lured a Roman follower of Raphael, Giulio Romano (c. 1499–1546), to build him a pleasure palace. Indeed, the Palazzo del Tè (**FIG. 21-20**) devoted more space to gardens, pools, and stables than to rooms for residential living. Since Federigo and his erudite friends would have known Classical orders and proportions, they could appreciate the playfulness with which they are used here. The building is full of visual jokes, such as lintels masquerading as arches and triglyphs that slip sloppily out of place. Like the similar, if more sober, subversions of Classical architectural decorum in Michelangelo's contemporary Laurentian Library (see **FIG. 21-18**), its sophisticated humor and exquisite craft have been seen as a precursor to Mannerism or as a manifestation of Mannerism itself.

Giulio Romano continued his witty play in the decoration of the two principal rooms. One, dedicated to the loves of the gods, depicted the marriage of Cupid and Psyche. The other room is a remarkable feat of *trompe l'oeil* painting in which the entire building seems to be collapsing around the viewer as the gods defeat

21-21 • Giulio Romano **FALL OF THE GIANTS**
Sala dei Giganti, Palazzo del Tè. 1530–1532. Fresco.

the giants (**FIG. 21-21**). Here, Giulio Romano accepted the challenge Andrea Mantegna had laid down in the Camera Picta of the Gonzaga Palace (see **FIG. 20-32**), painted for Federigo's grandfather: to dissolve architectural barriers and fantasize a world of playful delight beyond the walls and ceilings. But the Palazzo del Tè was not just fun and games. The unifying themes were love and politics, the former focused on the separate apartments built to house Federigo's mistress, Isabella Boschetti. The palace was constructed in part as a place where they could meet beyond the watchful gaze of her husband. But the decoration also seems to reflect Federigo's dicey alliance with Charles V, who stayed in the palace in 1530 and again in 1532, when the scaffolding was removed from the Sala dei Giganti so the emperor could see the paintings in progress. He must have been impressed with his host's lavish new residence, and doubtless he saw a connection between these reeling paintings and his own military successes.

CORREGGIO At about the same time that Giulio Romano was building and decorating the Palazzo del Tè, in nearby Parma an equally skillful master, Correggio (Antonio Allegri da Correggio, c. 1489–1534), was creating similarly theatrical effects with dramatic foreshortening in Parma Cathedral. Correggio's great work,

21-22 • Correggio ASSUMPTION OF THE VIRGIN
Main dome, interior, Parma Cathedral, Italy. c. 1526–1530. Fresco, diameter of base of dome approx. 36′ (11 m).

21–23 • Properzia de' Rossi **JOSEPH AND POTIPHAR'S WIFE**
Cathedral of San Petronio, Bologna. 1525–1526. Marble, 1'9" × 1'11" (54 × 58 cm). Museo de San Petronio, Bologna.

securing additional commissions. This particular relief, according to Vasari, was inspired by her own love for a young man, which she got over by carving this panel. Joseph escapes, running, as the partially clad seductress snatches at his cloak. Properzia is the only woman Vasari included in the 1550 edition of *Lives of the Artists*.

VENICE AND THE VENETO

In the sixteenth century the Venetians did not see themselves as rivals of Florence and Rome, but rather as their superiors. Their city was the greatest commercial sea power in the Mediterranean; they had challenged Byzantium and now they confronted the Muslim Turks. Favored by their unique geographical situation—protected by water and controlling sea routes in the Adriatic Sea and the eastern Mediterranean—the Venetians became wealthy and secure patrons of the arts. Their Byzantine heritage, preserved by their conservative tendencies, encouraged an art of rich patterned surfaces emphasizing light and color.

The idealized style and oil-painting technique initiated by the Bellini family in the late fifteenth century (see Chapter 20) were developed further by sixteenth-century Venetian painters. Venetians were the first in Italy to use oils for painting on both wood panel and canvas. Possibly because they were a seafaring people accustomed to working with large sheets of canvas, and possibly because humidity made their walls crack and mildew, the Venetians were also the first to cover walls with large canvas paintings instead of frescos. Because oils dried slowly, errors could be corrected and changes made easily during the work. The flexibility of the canvas support, coupled with the radiance and depth of oil-suspended pigments, eventually made oil on canvas the preferred medium, especially since it was particularly well suited to the rich color and lighting effects favored by Giorgione and Titian, two of the city's major painters of the sixteenth century.

GIORGIONE The career of Giorgione (Giorgio da Castelfranco, c. 1475–1510) was brief—he died from the plague—and most scholars accept fewer than ten paintings as entirely by his hand. But his importance to Venetian painting is critical. He introduced new, enigmatic pastoral themes, known as **poesie** (or "painted poems"), that were inspired by the contemporary literary revival

the **ASSUMPTION OF THE VIRGIN** (**FIG. 21-22**), a fresco painted between about 1526 and 1530 in the cathedral's dome, distantly recalls the illusionism of Mantegna's ceiling in the Gonzaga palace, but Correggio has also assimilated Leonardo da Vinci's use of *sfumato* and Raphael's idealism into his own style. Correggio's *Assumption* is a dazzling illusion—the architecture of the dome seems to dissolve and the forms seem to explode through the building, drawing viewers into the swirling vortex of saints and angels who rush upward amid billowing clouds to accompany the Virgin as she soars into heaven. Correggio's sensual rendering of the figures' flesh and clinging draperies contrasts with the spirituality of the theme (the miraculous transporting of the Virgin to heaven at the moment of her death). The viewer's strongest impression is of a powerful, upward-spiraling motion of alternating cool clouds and warm, alluring figures.

PROPERZIA DE' ROSSI Very few women had the opportunity or inclination to become sculptors. Properzia de' Rossi (c. 1490–1529/30), who lived in Bologna, was an exception. She mastered many arts, including engraving, and was famous for her miniature sculptures, including an entire *Last Supper* carved on a peach pit! She carved several pieces in marble—two sibyls, two angels, and this relief of **JOSEPH AND POTIPHAR'S WIFE**—for the Cathedral of San Petronio in Bologna (**FIG. 21-23**). Vasari wrote that a rival male sculptor prevented her from being paid fairly and from of ancient pastoral verse but defy specific narrative or symbolic interpretation. He is significant above all for his appreciation of nature in landscape painting. His early life and training are undocumented, but his work suggests that he studied with Giovanni Bellini. Perhaps Leonardo da Vinci's subtle lighting system and mysterious, intensely observed landscapes also inspired him.

One of Giorgione's most compelling works, called today **THE TEMPEST** (FIG. 21-24), was painted shortly before his death, potentially in response to personal, private impulses—as with

many modern artists—rather than to fulfill the dictates of an external commission. Simply trying to understand what is happening in this enigmatic picture piques our interest. At the right, a woman is seated on the ground, nude except for the end of a long white cloth thrown over her shoulders. Her nudity seems maternal, her sensuality generative rather than erotic, as she nurses the baby, protectively and lovingly embraced at her side. Across the dark, rocky edge of her elevated perch stands a mysterious man, variously interpreted as a German mercenary soldier and as an urban

21-24 • Giorgione THE TEMPEST
c. 1506. Oil on canvas, 32″ × 28¾″ (82 × 73 cm). Galleria dell'Accademia, Venice.

🔍 **View** the Closer Look for *The Tempest* on myartslab.com

21–25 • Giorgione or Titian THE PASTORAL CONCERT OR ALLEGORY ON THE INVENTION OF PASTORAL POETRY
c. 1510. Oil on canvas, 41¼″ × 54¾″ (105 × 136.5 cm). Musée du Louvre, Paris.

dandy wandering in the country. His shadowed head turns in the direction of the woman, but he only appears to have paused for a moment before turning back toward the viewer or resuming his journey along the path. X-rays of the painting show that Giorgione altered the composition while he was still working on the paint-ing—the man replaces a second nude woman, in this case bathing. Between the figures, a spring gushes to feed a lake surrounded by substantial houses, and in the far distance a bolt of lightning splits the darkening sky. Indeed, the artist's attention seems focused as much on the landscape and the unruly elements of nature than on the figures posed within it. Some interpreters have seen in the lake, the verdant ground, the billowing clouds, and the lightning bolt, references to the Classical elements of water, earth, air, and fire.

For a few years before Giorgione's untimely death in 1510, he was associated with Tiziano Vecellio, a painter better known today as Titian (c. 1488–1576). The painting known as **THE PASTORAL**

CONCERT (**FIG. 21-25**) has been attributed to both of them, although scholarly opinion today favors Titian. As in Giorgione's *The Tempest*, the idyllic, fertile landscape, here bathed in golden, hazy late-afternoon sunlight, seems to be one of the main subjects of the painting. In this mythic world, two men—an aristocratic musician in rich red silks and a barefoot, singing peasant in home-spun cloth—turn toward each other, seemingly unaware of the two naked women in front of them. One woman plays a pipe and the other pours water into a well; their swaths of white dra-pery sliding to the ground enhance rather than hide their nudity. Are they the musicians' muses? Behind the figures, the sunlight illuminates another shepherd and his animals near lush woodland. The painting evokes a golden age of love and innocence recalled in ancient Roman and Italian Renaissance pastoral poetry. In fact, the painting is now interpreted as an allegory on the invention of poetry. Both artists were renowned for painting sensuous female nudes whose bodies seem to glow with an incandescent light, inspired by flesh and blood beauty as much as any source from poetry or art.

TITIAN Titian's early life is obscure. He supposedly began an apprenticeship as a mosaicist, then studied painting under Gentile and Giovanni Bellini, perhaps working later with Giorgione. He certainly absorbed Giorgione's style, and completed at least one of Giorgione's unfinished paintings.

In 1519, Jacopo Pesaro, commander of the papal fleet that had defeated the Turks in 1502, commissioned Titian to commemorate the victory in a votive altarpiece for a side-aisle chapel in the Franciscan church of Santa Maria Gloriosa dei Frari in Venice. Titian worked on the painting for seven years and changed the

21-26 • Titian PESARO MADONNA
1519–1526. Oil on canvas, 16′ × 8′10″ (4.9 × 2.7 m). Side-aisle altarpiece, Santa Maria Gloriosa dei Frari, Venice.

In the sixteenth century, many wealthy women, from both the aristocracy and the merchant class, were enthusiastic patrons of the arts. The Habsburg princesses Margaret of Austria and Mary of Hungary presided over brilliant humanist courts. The marchesa of Mantua, **ISABELLA D'ESTE** (1474–1539; **FIG. 21-27**), became a patron of painters, musicians, composers, writers, and literary scholars. Married to Francesco II Gonzaga at age 15, she had great wealth, and a brilliant mind that made her a successful diplomat and administrator. A true Renaissance woman, her motto was the epitome of rational thinking— "Neither through Hope nor Fear." An avid collector of manuscripts and books, she sponsored the publication of an edition of Virgil while still in her twenties. She also collected ancient art and objects, as well as works by contemporary Italian artists such as Mantegna, Leonardo, Perugino, Correggio, and Titian. Her study in her Mantuan palace was a veritable museum. The walls above the storage and display cabinets were painted in fresco by Mantegna, and the carved wood ceiling was covered with mottoes and visual references to Isabella's impressive literary interests.

21-27 • Titian ISABELLA D'ESTE
1534–1536. Oil on canvas, 40⅛″ × 25⁹⁄₁₆″ (102 × 64.1 cm).
Kunsthistorisches Museum, Vienna.

concept three times before he finally came up with a revolutionary composition—one that complemented the viewer's approach from the left. He created an asymmetrical setting of huge columns on high bases soaring right out of the frame (**FIG. 21-26**). Into this architectural setting, he placed the Virgin and Child on a high throne at one side and arranged saints and the Pesaro family below on a diagonal axis, crossing at the central figure of St. Peter (a reminder of Jacopo's role as head of the papal forces in 1502). The red of Francesco Pesaro's brocade garment and of the banner diagonally across sets up a contrast of primary colors against St. Peter's blue tunic and yellow mantle and the red and blue draperies of the Virgin. St. Maurice (behind the kneeling Jacopo at the left) holds the banner with the papal arms, and a cowering Turkish captive reminds the viewer of the Christian victory. The arresting image of the youth who turns to meet our gaze at lower right guarantees our engagement, and light floods in from above, illuminating not only this and other faces, but also the great columns, where *putti* in the clouds carry a cross. Titian was famous for his mastery of light and color even in his own day, but this altarpiece demonstrates that he also could draw and model as solidly as any Florentine. The perfectly balanced

composition, built on color, and on diagonals instead of a vertical and horizontal grid, looks forward to the art of the seventeenth century.

In 1529, Titian, who was well known outside Venice, began a long professional relationship with Emperor Charles V, who vowed to let no one else paint his portrait and ennobled Titian in 1533. The next year Titian was commissioned to paint a portrait of Isabella d'Este (see "Women Patrons of the Arts," above). Isabella was past 60 when Titian portrayed her in 1534–1536, but she asked to appear as she had in her twenties. Titian was able to satisfy her wish by referring to an early portrait by another artist, but he also conveyed the mature Isabella's strength, self-confidence, and energy.

No photograph can convey the vibrancy of Titian's paint surfaces, which he built up in layers of pure colors, chiefly red, white, yellow, and black. A recent scientific study of Titian's paintings revealed that he ground his pigments much finer than had earlier wood-panel painters. The complicated process by which he produced many of his works began with a charcoal drawing on the prime coat of lead white that was used to seal the pores and smooth the surface of the rather coarse Venetian canvas. The artist then

21-28 • Titian "VENUS" OF URBINO
c. 1538. Oil on canvas, 3'11" × 5'5" (1.19 × 1.65 m). Galleria degli Uffizi, Florence.

built up the forms with fine glazes of different colors, sometimes in as many as 10 to 15 layers. Titian had the advantage of working in Venice, the first place to have professional retail "color sellers." These merchants produced a wide range of specially prepared pigments, even mixing their oil paints with ground glass to increase their glowing transparency. Not until the second half of the sixteenth century did color sellers open their shops in other cities.

Paintings of nude reclining women became especially popular in sophisticated court circles, where male patrons could enjoy and appreciate the "Venuses" under the cloak of respectable Classical mythology. Seemingly typical of such paintings is the **"VENUS"** Titian delivered to Guidobaldo della Rovere, duke of Urbino, in spring 1538 (**FIG. 21-28**). Here, we seem to see a beautiful Venetian courtesan, with deliberately provocative gestures, stretching languidly on her couch in a spacious palace, her glowing flesh and golden hair set off by white sheets and pillows. But for its original audience, art historian Rona Goffen has argued, the painting was more about marriage than mythology or seductiveness. The multiple matrimonial references in this work include the pair of *cassoni* (see FIG. 20-26) where servants are removing or storing

the woman's clothing in the background, the bridal symbolism of the myrtle and roses she holds in her hand, and even the spaniel snoozing at her feet—a traditional symbol of fidelity and domesticity, especially when sleeping so peacefully. Titian's picture might be associated with Duke Guidobaldo's marriage in 1534 to the 10-year-old Giulia Verano. Four years later, when this painting arrived, she would have been considered an adult rather than a child bride. It seems to represent not a Roman goddess nor a Venetian courtesan, but a physically and emotionally mature bride welcoming her husband into their lavish bedroom.

MANNERISM

A new style developed in Florence and Rome in the 1520s that some art historians have associated with the death of Raphael and labeled "Mannerism," a word deriving from the Italian *maniera* (meaning "style"). Mannerism developed into an anti-Classical movement in which artificiality, grace, and elegance took priority over the ordered balance and lifelike references that were hallmarks of High Renaissance art. Patrons favored esoteric subjects, displays of extraordinary technical virtuosity, and the pursuit of beauty for its own sake. Painters and sculptors quoted from ancient and modern works of art in the same self-conscious manner that contemporary poets and authors were quoting from ancient and modern literary classics. Architects working in the Mannerist style designed buildings that defied uniformity and balance and used Classical orders in unconventional, even playful, ways.

PAINTING

Painters working in the Mannerist style fearlessly manipulated and distorted accepted formal conventions, creating contrived compositions and irrational spatial environments. Figures take on elongated proportions, complicated artificial poses, enigmatic gestures, and dreamy expressions. The pictures are full of quoted references to the works of illustrious predecessors.

PONTORMO The frescos and altarpiece painted between 1525 and 1528 by Jacopo Carucci da Pontormo (1494–1557) for the 100-year-old **CAPPONI CHAPEL** in the church of Santa Felicità in Florence (**FIG. 21-29**) bear the hallmarks of early Mannerist painting. Open on two sides, Brunelleschi's chapel forms an interior loggia in which frescos on the right-hand wall depict the Annunciation and tondi (circular paintings) on the pendentives under the cupola represent the four evangelists. In the *Annunciation* the Virgin accepts the angel's message but also seems moved by the adjacent vision of her future sorrow, as she turns to see her son's body lowered from the cross in the **DEPOSITION**, portrayed in the altarpiece on the adjoining wall (**FIG. 21-30**).

Pontormo's ambiguous composition in the *Deposition* enhances the visionary quality of the altarpiece. Shadowy ground and cloudy sky give no sense of a specific location, and little sense

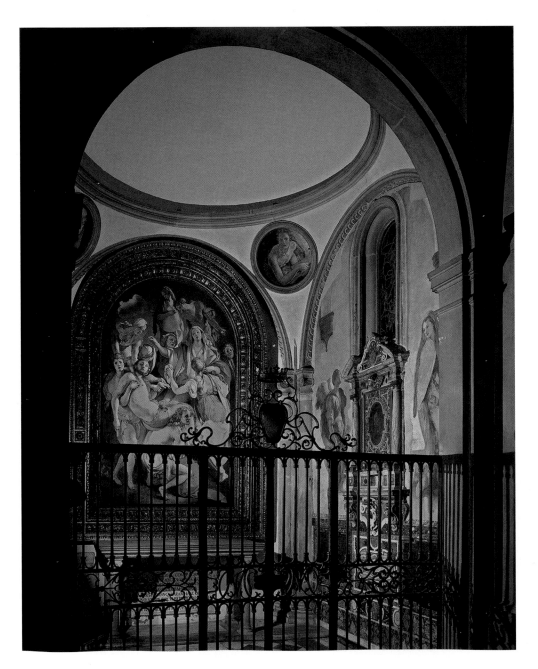

21-29 • CAPPONI CHAPEL, CHURCH OF SANTA FELICITÀ, FLORENCE
Chapel by Filippo Brunelleschi for the Barbadori family, 1419–1423; acquired by the Capponi family, who ordered paintings by Pontormo, 1525–1528.

21-30 • Pontormo DEPOSITION

Altarpiece in Capponi Chapel, church of Santa Felicità, Florence. 1525–1528. Oil and tempera on wood panel, 10′3″ × 6′4″ (3.1 × 1.9 m).

The dreamy-eyed male figure in the background shadows at upper right is a self-portrait of the artist.

of grounding for the figures. Some press forward into the viewer's space, while others seem to levitate or stand precariously on tiptoe. Pontormo chose a moment just after Jesus' removal from the cross, when the youths who have lowered him pause to regain their hold on the corpse, which recalls Michelangelo's Vatican *Pietà* (see FIG. 21–9). Odd poses and drastic shifts in scale charge the scene emotionally, but perhaps most striking is the use of weird colors in odd juxtapositions—baby blue and pink with accents of olive-green, yellow, and scarlet. The overall tone of the picture is set by the unstable youth crouching in the foreground, whose skintight

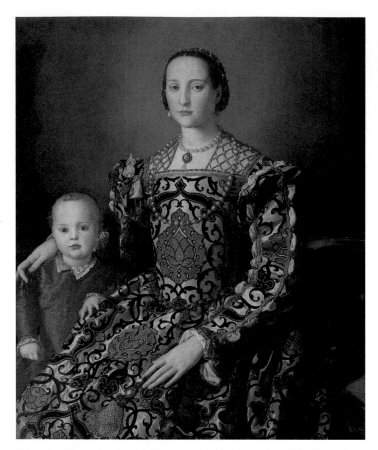

21-32 • Bronzino **PORTRAIT OF ELEONORA OF TOLEDO AND HER SON GIOVANNI DE' MEDICI**
1545. Oil on wood panel, 45¼″ × 37¾″ (115 × 96 cm). Galleria degli Uffizi, Florence.

21-31 • Parmigianino **MADONNA OF THE LONG NECK**
1534–1540. Oil on wood panel, 7′1″ × 4′4″ (2.16 × 1.32 m). Galleria degli Uffizi, Florence.

Art historian Elizabeth Cropper has noted the visual relationship between the shape of the swelling, tapering-necked, ovoid vessel held by the figure at far left and the form of the figure of the Virgin herself and has proposed that this visual analogy references a sixteenth-century literary conceit that related ideal beauty in women to the slender necks and swelling shapes of antique vessels.

bright pink shirt is shaded in iridescent, pale gray-blue, and whose anxious expression is projected out of the painting, directly at the viewer.

PARMIGIANINO When Parmigianino (Francesco Mazzola, 1503–1540) left his native Parma in 1524 for Rome, the strongest influence on his work was Correggio (see FIG. 21–22). In Rome, however, Parmigianino met Giulio Romano; he also studied the work of Raphael and Michelangelo. What he assimilated developed into a distinctive Mannerist style, calm but strangely unsettling. After the Sack of Rome in 1527, he moved to Bologna and then back to Parma.

Left unfinished at the time of his early death is a disconcerting painting known as the **MADONNA OF THE LONG NECK** (FIG. 21–31). The unnaturally proportioned figure of Mary, whose massive legs and lower torso contrast with her narrow shoulders and long neck and fingers, is presumably seated on a throne, but there is no seat in sight. The languid expanse of the sleeping child recalls the pose of the ashen Christ in a *pietà*; indeed, there is more than a passing resemblance here to Michelangelo's famous sculpture in the Vatican, even to the inclusion of a diagonal band across the Virgin's chest (see FIG. 21–9). The plunge into a deep background to the right reveals a startlingly small St. Jerome, who unrolls a scroll in front of huge white columns from what was to be a temple in the unfinished background, whereas at the left a crowded mass of blushing boys blocks any view into the background. Like Pontormo, Parmigianino presents a well-known image in a challenging manner calculated to intrigue viewers.

BRONZINO About 1522, Agnolo di Cosimo di Mariano Tori (1503–1572), whose nickname of "Bronzino" means "copper-colored" (just as we might call someone "Red"), became Pontormo's pupil and assistant, probably helping with the tondi on the pendentives of the Capponi Chapel (see FIG. 21-29). In 1530, he established his own workshop, though he continued to work with Pontormo on occasional large projects. By 1540, he was court painter to the Medici. Although he produced altarpieces, fresco decorations, and tapestry designs over his long career, he is best known today for his elegant portraits, the focus of his work for Duke Cosimo I de' Medici (r. 1537–1574). Bronzino's virtuosity in rendering costumes and settings, juxtaposed with the masklike quality given to the vacant faces of his subjects, results in cold and formal portraits, but the self-contained demeanor of his subjects admirably conveys their haughtiness and reflects the absolutism of Cosimo's rule.

Typical is an elegantly restrained state portrait of 1545 portraying Cosimo's wife, **ELEONORA OF TOLEDO** (1522–1562) and their second son, Giovanni de' Medici (FIG. 21-32). Bronzino characteristically portrayals this mother and son as aloof and self-assured, their class and connection much more prominent than any sense of individual likeness or personality. In a real sense, this double portrait is an iconic embodiment of dynastic power and an assurance of Medici succession. Giovanni, however, did not succeed his father as duke—that path was taken by his elder brother Francesco. Instead he pursued a fast-tracked career in the Church. Already archbishop of Pisa, in 1560, at age 17, he became a cardinal, only two years before both he and his mother died of malaria.

Bronzino's **ALLEGORY WITH VENUS AND CUPID** is one of the strangest paintings of the sixteenth century (FIG. 21-33). It contains all the formal, iconographical, and psychological characteristics of Mannerist art and could almost stand alone as a summary of the movement. Seven figures, three masks, and a dove interweave in an intricate, claustrophobic formal composition pressed breathlessly into the foreground plane. Taken as individual images, they display the exaggerated poses, graceful forms, polished surfaces, and delicate colors that characterize Mannerist art. But a closer look into this composition uncovers disturbing erotic attachments and bizarre irregularities. The painting's complex allegory and relentless ambiguity probably delighted mid-sixteenth-century courtiers who enjoyed equally sophisticated wordplay and esoteric Classical references, but for us it defies easy explanation. Nothing is quite what it seems.

Venus and her son Cupid engage in an unsettlingly lascivious dalliance, encouraged by a *putto* sauntering in from the right—representing Folly, Jest, or Playfulness—who is about to throw pink roses at them while stepping on a thorny branch that draws blood from his foot. Cupid gently kisses his mother and pinches her erect nipple while Venus snatches an arrow from his quiver, leading some scholars to suggest that the painting's title should be *Venus Disarming Cupid*. Venus holds the golden apple of discord given to her by Paris; her dove conforms to the shape of Cupid's foot without actually touching it, while a pair of masks lying at her feet reiterate the theme of duplicity. An old man, Time or Chronos, assisted by an outraged Truth or Night, pulls back a curtain to expose the couple. Lurking just behind Venus a monstrous serpent—which has the upper body and head of a beautiful young girl and the legs and claws of a lion—crosses her hands to hold a honeycomb and the stinger at the end of her tail. This strange hybrid has been interpreted both as Fraud and Pleasure.

21-33 • Bronzino ALLEGORY WITH VENUS AND CUPID
Mid 1540s. Oil on panel, 57½" × 46" (1.46 × 1.16 m). National Gallery, London.
Reproduced by courtesy of the Trustees of the National Gallery, London

View the Closer Look for *Allegory with Venus and Cupid* on myartslab.com

In the shadows to the left, a pale and screaming man tearing at his hair has recently been identified as a victim of syphilis, which raged as an epidemic during this period. The painting could, therefore, be a warning of the dangers of this disease, believed in the sixteenth century to be spread principally by coitus, kissing, and breast feeding, all of which are alluded to in the intertwined Cupid and Venus. But the complexity of the painting makes room for multiple meanings, and deciphering them would be typical of the sorts of games enjoyed by sixteenth-century intellectuals. Perhaps the allegory tells of the impossibility of constant love and the folly of lovers, which becomes apparent across time. Or perhaps it is an allegorical warning of the dangers of illicit sexual liaisons, including the pain, hair loss, and disfiguration of venereal disease. It could be both, and even more. Duke Cosimo commissioned the painting himself and presented it as a diplomatic gift to French King Francis I, who would doubtless have relished its overt eroticism and flawless execution.

SOFONISBA ANGUISSOLA Northern Italy, more than any other part of the peninsula, produced a number of gifted women artists. In the latter half of the sixteenth century, Bologna, for example, boasted some two dozen women painters and sculptors, as well as a number of learned women who lectured at the university. Sofonisba Anguissola (c. 1532–1625), born into a noble

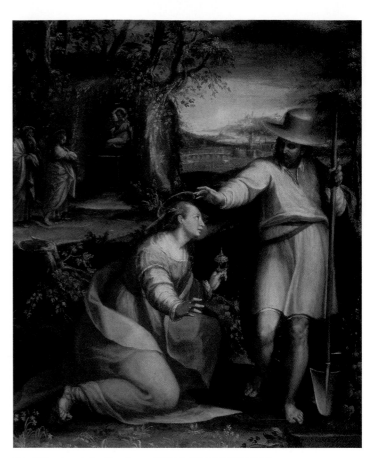

21-35 • Lavinia Fontana **NOLI ME TANGERE**
1581. Oil on canvas, 47⅜″ × 36⅝″ (120.3 × 93 cm). Galleria degli Uffizi, Florence.

family in Cremona (between Bologna and Milan), was unusual in that she was not the daughter of an artist. Her father gave all his children a humanistic education and encouraged them to pursue careers in literature, music, and especially painting. He consulted Michelangelo about Sofonisba Anguissola's artistic talents in 1557, asking for a drawing that she might copy and return to be critiqued. Michelangelo evidently obliged, because her father wrote an enthusiastic letter of thanks.

Anguissola was a gifted portrait painter who also created miniatures, an important aspect of portraiture in the sixteenth century, when people had few means of recording the features of a lover, friend, or family member. Anguissola painted a miniature **SELF-PORTRAIT** holding a medallion, the border of which spells out her name and home town, Cremona (**FIG. 21-34**). The interlaced letters at the center of the medallion pose a riddle; they seem to form a monogram with the first letters of her sisters' names: Minerva, Europa, Elena. Such names are further evidence of the Anguissola family's enthusiasm for the Classics.

In 1560, Anguissola accepted the invitation of the queen of Spain to become a lady-in-waiting and court painter, a post she held for 20 years. Unfortunately, most of her Spanish works were lost in a seventeenth-century palace fire, but a 1582 Spanish inventory described her as "an excellent painter of portraits above all

21-34 • Sofonisba Anguissola **SELF-PORTRAIT**
c. 1552. Oil on parchment on cardboard, 3¼″ × 2½″ (8.3 × 6.4 cm). Museum of Fine Arts, Boston. Emma F. Munroe Fund 60.155

the painters of this time"—extraordinary praise in a court that patronized Titian. After her years at court, she retired to Spanish-controlled Sicily, where she died in her nineties. Anthony Van Dyck met her in Palermo in 1624, where he sketched her and claimed that she was then 96 years old. He wrote that she advised him on positioning the light for her portrait, asking that it not be placed too high because the strong shadows would bring out her wrinkles.

LAVINIA FONTANA Bolognese artist Lavinia Fontana (1552–1614) learned to paint from her father. By the 1570s, her success was so well rewarded that her husband, the painter Gian Paolo Zappi, gave up his own painting career to care for their large family and help his wife with the technical aspects of her work, such as framing. In 1603, Fontana moved to Rome as an official painter to the papal court. She also soon came to the attention of the Habsburgs, who became major patrons.

While still in her twenties, Fontana painted a **NOLI ME TANGERE (FIG. 21-35)**, where Christ reveals himself for the first time to Mary Magdalen following his Resurrection, warning her not to touch him (John 20:17). Christ's broad-brimmed hat and spade refer to the passage in John's Gospel claiming that Mary Magdalen at first thought Christ was the gardener. In the middle distance Fontana portrays a second version of the Resurrection, where women followers of Christ discover an angel in his empty tomb. This secondary scene's dizzying diagonal plunge into depth is a typical feature of late Mannerist painting in Italy, as are the affected pose of the foreground Christ and the elongated proportions of the Magdalen.

SCULPTURE

Mannerist sculpture—often small in size and made from precious metals—stylizes body forms and foregrounds displays of technical skill in ways that are reminiscent of Mannerist painting.

CELLINI The Florentine goldsmith and sculptor Benvenuto Cellini (1500–1571), who wrote a dramatic—and scandalous—autobiography and a practical handbook for artists, worked in the French court at Fontainebleau. There he made the famous **SALT-CELLAR OF KING FRANCIS I (FIG. 21-36)**,

a table accessory transformed into an elegant sculptural ornament by fanciful imagery and superb execution. In gold and enamel, the Roman sea god Neptune, representing the source of salt, sits next to a tiny boat-shaped container for the seasoning, while a personification of Earth guards the plant-derived pepper, contained in the triumphal arch to her right. Representations of the seasons and the times of day on the base refer to both daily meal schedules and festive seasonal celebrations. The two main figures lean away from each other at impossible angles yet are connected and visually balanced by glance, gestures, and coordinated poses—mirroring each other with one bent and one straight leg. Their supple, elongated bodies and small heads reflect the Mannerist conventions of artists like Parmigianino (see FIG. 21-31). Cellini wrote, "I represented the Sea and the Land, both seated, with their legs intertwined just as some branches of the sea run into the land and the land juts into the sea…" (Cellini, *Autobiography*, translated by G. Bull, p. 291).

GIAMBOLOGNA In the second half of the sixteenth century, probably the most influential sculptor in Italy was Jean Boulogne, better known by his Italian names, Giovanni Bologna or Giambologna (1529–1608). Born in Flanders, he settled during the 1550s in Florence, where he worked at the court of Duke Cosimo I de' Medici. He not only influenced and trained a later generation of Italian sculptors; he also spread the Mannerist style to the north through artists who came to study his work.

Although Giambologna's prodigious artistic output included elaborate fountains and many works in bronze—both imposing

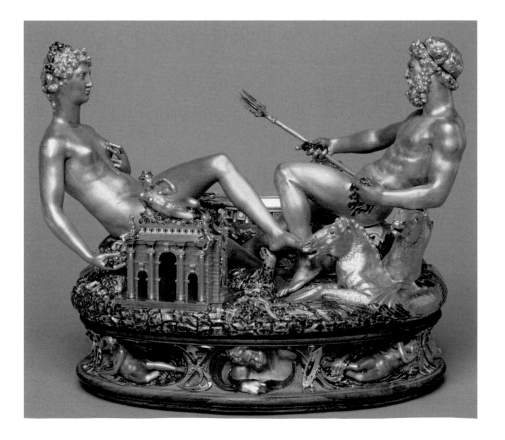

21-36 • Benvenuto Cellini SALTCELLAR OF KING FRANCIS I OF FRANCE
1540–1543. Gold and enamel, 10½″ × 13⅛″ (26.67 × 33.34 cm). Kunsthistorisches Museum, Vienna.

Read the document related to Benvenuto Cellini on myartslab.com public monuments and exquisitely rendered statuettes—his most famous sculpture is a monumental marble carving now known as **THE CAPTURE OF A SABINE WOMAN** (FIG. 21–37), a title given to it by a member of the Florentine Academy of Design only after it was finished. Giambologna himself conceived of this composition of three nude figures—spiraling upward in energetic, intertwined torsion—not in relation to any particular subject or story, but as a formal exercise in figural representation and technical virtuosity. In spite of the deep undercutting and projecting gestures, this cohesive column of figures was carved from a single block of marble. Because of the spiraling composition—created by twisting figural cohesion and the projection of dramatic gestures—viewers must walk around the sculpture to explore it; it cannot be fully grasped from any single viewpoint. Grand Duke Francesco I de' Medici installed Giambologna's masterpiece in a place of honor at the front of the Loggia dei Lanzi, where it remains today (see FIG. 18–2).

21-37 • Giambologna THE CAPTURE OF A SABINE WOMAN
1581–1582. Marble, height 13′6″ (4.1 m). Loggia dei Lanzi, Florence.

ART AND THE COUNTER-REFORMATION

Pope Clement VII, whose miscalculations had spurred Emperor Charles V to attack and destroy Rome in 1527, also misjudged the threat to the Church and to papal authority posed by the Protestant Reformation. His failure to address the issues raised by the reformers enabled the movement to spread. His successor, Paul III (pontificate 1534–1549), the rich and worldly Roman noble Alessandro Farnese, was the first pope to pursue Church reform in response to the rise of Protestantism. In 1536, he appointed a commission to investigate charges of Church corruption and later convened the Council of Trent (1545–1563) to define Catholic dogma, initiate disciplinary reforms, and regulate the training of clerics.

Pope Paul III also addressed Protestantism through repression and censorship. In 1542, he instituted the Inquisition, a papal office that sought out heretics for interrogation, trial, and sentencing. The enforcement of religious unity extended to the arts. Traditional images of Christ and the saints were sanctioned, but art was scrutinized for traces of heresy and profanity. Guidelines issued by the Council of Trent limited what could be represented in Christian art and led to the destruction of some works. At the same time, art became a powerful weapon of propaganda, especially in the hands of members of the Society of Jesus, a new religious order founded by the Spanish nobleman Ignatius of Loyola (1491–1556) and confirmed by Paul III in 1540. Dedicated to piety, education, and missionary work, the Jesuits, as they are known, spread worldwide and became important leaders of the Counter-Reformation movement and the revival of the Catholic Church.

ART AND ARCHITECTURE IN ROME AND THE VATICAN

To restore the heart of the city of Rome, Paul III began rebuilding the Capitoline Hill as well as continuing work on St. Peter's. His commissions include some of the finest art and architecture of the late Italian Renaissance. His first major commission brought Michelangelo, after a quarter of a century, back to the Sistine Chapel.

MICHELANGELO'S LATE WORK In his early sixties, Michelangelo complained bitterly of feeling old, but he nonetheless undertook the important and demanding task of painting the **LAST JUDGMENT** on the 48-foot-high end wall above the Sistine Chapel altar between 1536 and 1541 (FIG. 21–38).

21–38 • Michelangelo LAST JUDGMENT, SISTINE CHAPEL
1536–1541. Fresco, 48′ × 44′ (14.6 × 13.4 m).

Dark, rectangular patches intentionally left by recent restorers (visible, for example, in the upper left and right corners) contrast with the vibrant colors of the chapel's frescos. These dark areas show just how dirty the walls had become over the centuries before their recent cleaning.

Read the document related to Michelangelo's poetry on myartslab.com

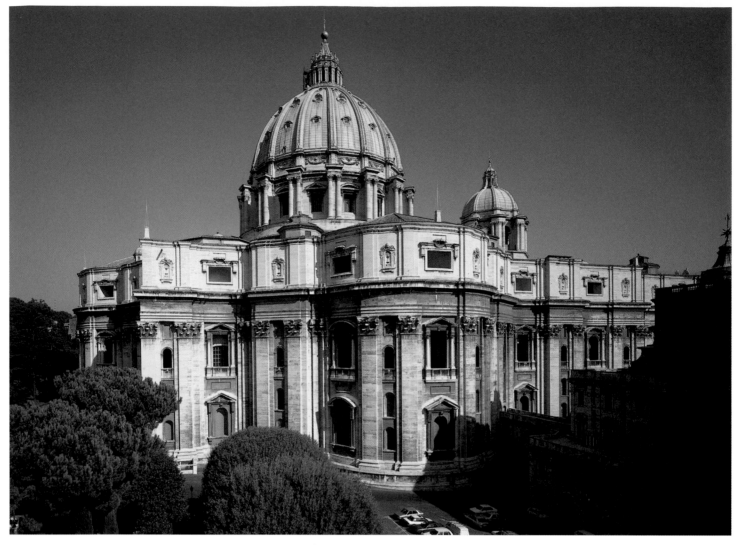

21-39 • Michelangelo ST. PETER'S BASILICA, VATICAN
c. 1546–1564; dome completed 1590 by Giacomo della Porta; lantern 1590–1593. View from the west.

Abandoning the clearly organized medieval conception of the Last Judgment, in which the saved are neatly separated from the damned, Michelangelo painted a writhing swarm of resurrected humanity. At left (on Christ's right side), the dead are dragged from their graves and pushed up into a vortex of figures around Christ, who wields his arm like a sword of justice. The shrinking Virgin under Christ's raised right arm represents a change from Gothic tradition, where she had sat enthroned beside, and equal in size to, her son. To the right of Christ's feet is St. Bartholomew, who in legend was martyred by being skinned alive. He holds his flayed skin, and Michelangelo seems to have painted his own distorted features on the skin's face. Despite the efforts of several saints to save them at the last minute, the damned are plunged toward hell on the right, leaving the elect and still-unjudged in a dazed, almost uncomprehending state. On the lowest level of the mural, right above the altar, is the gaping, fiery entrance to hell, toward which Charon, the ferryman of the dead to the underworld, propels his craft. The painting was long interpreted as a grim and constant reminder to celebrants of the Mass—the pope and his

cardinals—that ultimately they too would face stern judgment at the end of time. Conservative clergy criticized the painting for its frank nudity, and after Michelangelo's death they ordered bits of drapery to be added by artist Daniele da Volterra to conceal the offending areas, earning Daniele the unfortunate nickname *Il Braghettone* ("breeches painter").

Another of Paul III's ambitions was to complete the new St. Peter's, a project that had been under way for 40 years (see "St. Peter's Basilica," page 653). Michelangelo was well aware of the work done by his predecessors—from Bramante to Raphael to Antonio da Sangallo the Younger. The 71-year-old sculptor, confident of his architectural expertise, demanded the right to deal directly with the pope, rather than through a committee of construction deputies. Michelangelo further shocked the deputies—but not the pope—by undoing parts of Sangallo's design, then simplifying and strengthening Bramante's central plan, long associated with shrines of Christian martyrs. Although seventeenth-century additions and renovations dramatically changed the original plan of the church and the appearance of its interior, Michelangelo's

21-40 • Vignola and Giacomo della Porta
PLAN AND FAÇADE OF THE CHURCH OF IL GESÙ, ROME
c. 1573–1584.

ST. PETER'S (FIG. 21-39) still can be seen in the contrasting forms of the flat and angled exterior walls and the three surviving hemicycles (semicircular structures). Colossal pilasters, blind windows (frames without openings), and niches surround the sanctuary of the church. The current dome, erected by Giacomo della Porta in 1588–1590, retains Michelangelo's basic design: segmented with regularly spaced ribs, seated on a high drum with pedimented windows between paired columns, and surmounted by a tall lantern.

The aging Michelangelo—often described by his contemporaries as difficult, even arrogant—alternated between periods of depression and frenzied activity. Yet he was devoted to his friends and helpful to young artists. He believed that his art was divinely inspired and became increasingly devoted to religious works—many left unfinished—that subverted Renaissance ideals of human perfectibility and denied the idealism of youth. In the process he pioneered new stylistic directions that would inspire succeeding generations of artists.

VIGNOLA A young artist who worked to meet the need for new Roman churches was Giacomo Barozzi (1507–1573), known as Vignola after his native town. He worked in Rome during the late 1530s, surveying ancient Roman monuments and providing illustrations for an edition of Vitruvius. From 1541 to 1543, he was in France with Francesco Primaticcio at the château of Fontainebleau. After returning to Rome, he secured the patronage of the Farnese family and profited from the Counter-Reformation church-building inititatives.

Catholicism's new emphasis on individual, emotional participation brought a focus on sermons and music, requiring churches with wide naves and unobstructed views of the altar, instead of the complex interiors of medieval and earlier Renaissance churches. Ignatius of Loyola was determined to build **IL GESÙ**, the Jesuit headquarters church in Rome, according to these precepts, although he did not live to see it finished (FIG. 21-40). The cornerstone was laid in 1540, but construction of Il Gesù did not begin until 1568, after a period of fund-raising. Cardinal Alessandro Farnese (Paul III's namesake and grandson) donated to the project in 1561 and selected Vignola as architect. After Vignola died in 1573, Giacomo della Porta finished the dome and façade to his own designs.

Il Gesù was admirably suited for congregational worship. Vignola designed a wide, barrel-vaulted nave with shallow connected side chapels; there are no aisles and only truncated transepts contained within the line of the outer walls—enabling all worshipers to gather in the central space. A single huge apse and dome over the crossing directed attention to the altar. The design also allows the building to fit compactly into a city block—a requirement that now often overrode the desire to orient a church along an east–west axis. The symmetrical façade, in Vignola's original design as well as della Porta's variation on it, emphasized the central portal with Classical pilasters, engaged columns and pediments, and volutes scrolling out laterally to hide the buttresses of the central vault and to link the tall central section with the lower sides.

As finally built by Giacomo della Porta, the façade design would have significant influence well into the next century. The early Renaissance grid of Classical pilasters and entablatures is abandoned for a two-story design that coordinates paired columns or pilasters, aligned vertically to tie together the two stories of the central block which corresponds with the nave elevation. The main entrance, with its central portal aligned with a tall upper-story window, became the focus of the composition. Centrally aligned pediments break into the level above, leading the eye upward to the cartouches with coats of arms—here of both Cardinal Farnese, the patron, and the Jesuits (whose arms display the initials IHS, the monogram of Christ).

LATER SIXTEENTH-CENTURY ART IN VENICE AND THE VENETO

By the second half of the sixteenth century, Venice ruled supreme as "queen of the Adriatic." Her power was not, however, unchallenged, and the Turks were a constant threat. In 1571, allied with Spain and the pope, the Christian fleet with Venetian ships defeated the Turkish fleet at the Battle of Lepanto, establishing Christian preeminence for future generations. Victorious and wealthy, Venetians built palaces and villas to contain their lavish lifestyle, filling them with lush oil paintings.

OIL PAINTING

Rather than the cool, formal, technical perfection sought by Mannerist painters, Venetian artists expanded upon the manner initiated by Giorgione and Titian, concerning themselves above all with color, light, and expressively loose brushwork.

VERONESE Paolo Caliari (1528–1588) took his nickname "Veronese" from his hometown, Verona, but he worked mainly in Venice. His paintings are nearly synonymous today with the popular image of Venice as a splendid city of pleasure and pageantry sustained by a nominally republican government and great mercantile wealth. Veronese's elaborate architectural settings and costumes, still lifes, anecdotal vignettes, and other everyday details—often unconnected with the main subject—proved immensely appealing to Venetian patrons.

One of Veronese's most famous works is a *Last Supper* that he renamed *Feast in the House of Levi* (see "Veronese is Called before the Inquisition," opposite), painted in 1573 for the Dominican monastery of SS. Giovanni e Paolo. At first glance, the subject of the painting seems to be primarily its architectural setting and only secondarily Christ seated at the table. Symmetrically disposed balustraded stairways lead to an enormous loggia framed by colossal arches, beyond which sits an imaginary city of white marble. Within this grand setting, lifelike figures in lavish costumes strike theatrical poses, surrounded by the sort of anecdotal details loved by the Venetians—like parrots and monkeys—but detested by the Church's inquisitors, who saw them as profane distractions in a representation of the Last Supper.

TINTORETTO Jacopo Robusti (1518–1594), called Tintoretto ("Little Dyer," because his father was a dyer), carried Venetian painting in another direction. Tintoretto's goal, declared on a sign in his studio, was to combine Titian's coloring with the drawing of Michelangelo. His large painting of **THE LAST SUPPER** (**FIG. 21-42**) for the choir of Palladio's church of San Giorgio Maggiore (see **FIG. 21-44**) is quite different from Leonardo da Vinci's painting of the same subject almost a century earlier (see **FIG. 21-3**). Instead of Leonardo's frontal view of a closed and logical space with massive figures reacting in individual ways to Jesus' statement, Tintoretto views the scene from a corner, with the vanishing point on a high horizon line at far right. The table, coffered ceiling, and inlaid floor all seem to plunge dramatically into the distance. The figures, although still large bodies modeled by flowing draperies, turn and move in a continuous serpentine line that unites apostles, servants, and angels. Tintoretto used two internal light sources: one real, the other supernatural. Over the near end of the table, light streams from the oil lamp flaring exuberantly, with angels swirling out from the flame and smoke. A second light emanates from Jesus himself and is repeated in the glow of the apostles' haloes. The intensely spiritual, otherworldly mood is enhanced by deep colors flashed with dazzling highlights on elongated figures, consistent with Mannerist tendencies. The still lifes on the tables and homey details like the cat that peers in the foreground basket connect with viewers' own experiences. And the narrative emphasis has shifted from Leonardo's more worldly study of personal betrayal to Tintoretto's reference to the institution of the Eucharist. Jesus offers bread and wine to a disciple in the manner of a priest administering the sacrament at the altar next to the painting.

The speed with which Tintoretto drew and painted was the subject of comment in his own time, and the brilliance and immediacy so admired in his work today—his slashing brushwork was much appreciated by twentieth-century gestural painters—were occasionally derided as evidence of carelessness in his own time. Rapid production may have been a byproduct of his working methods. Tintoretto had a large workshop of assistants and he usually provided only the original conception, the beginning

According to the New Testament, Jesus revealed his impending death to his disciples during a seder, a meal celebrating the Jewish festival of Passover. This occasion, known to Christians as the Last Supper, and situated in the Gospels on the evening before the Crucifixion, was a popular theme in sixteenth-century European art. But in 1573, when the painter Veronese delivered an enormous canvas of this subject to fulfill a commission (FIG. 21–41), the patrons were shocked. Some were offended by the grandiose pageantry of the scene. Others protested the impiety of surrounding Jesus with a man picking his teeth, scruffy dogs, and foreign soldiers. As a result of the furor, Veronese was called before the Inquisition to explain his painting. There he justified himself first by asserting that the picture actually depicted not the Last Supper, but rather the feast in the house of Simon, a small dinner held shortly before Jesus' final entry into Jerusalem. He also noted that artists customarily invent details in their pictures and that he had received a commission to paint the piece "as I saw fit." His argument fell on unsympathetic ears, and he was ordered to change the painting. Later he sidestepped the issue by changing its title to that of another banquet, one given by the tax collector Levi, whom Jesus had called to follow him (Luke 5:27–32). Perhaps with this change of subject, Veronese took a modest revenge on the Inquisitors: When Jesus himself was criticized for associating with such unsavory people at this meal, he replied, "I have not come to call the righteous to repentance but sinners" (Luke 5:32).

21–41 • Veronese FEAST IN THE HOUSE OF LEVI
From the refectory of the monastery of SS. Giovanni e Paolo, Venice. 1573. Oil on canvas, 18'3" × 42' (5.56 × 12.8 m). Galleria dell'Accademia, Venice.

Read the document related to Paolo Veronese on myartslab.com

drawings, and the final brilliant touches on the finished paintings. Tintoretto's workshop included members of his family—of his eight children, four became artists. His oldest daughter, Marietta Robusti, worked with him as a portrait painter, and two or perhaps three of his sons also joined the shop. So skillfully did Marietta capture her father's style and technique that today art historians cannot identify her work in the shop.

ARCHITECTURE: PALLADIO

Just as Veronese and Tintoretto expanded upon the rich Venetian tradition of oil painting initiated by Giorgione and Titian, Andrea Palladio dominated architecture during the second half of the century by expanding upon the principles of Alberti and ancient Roman architecture. His buildings—whether villas, palaces, or churches—were characterized by harmonious symmetry and controlled ornamentation. Born Andrea di Pietro della Gondola (1508–1580), probably in Padua, Palladio began his career as a stonecutter. After moving to Vicenza, he was hired by the nobleman, humanist scholar, and amateur architect Giangiorgio Trissino, who gave him the nickname "Palladio" for the Greek goddess of wisdom, Pallas Athena, and the fourth-century Roman writer Palladius. Palladio learned

21-42 • Tintoretto THE LAST SUPPER
Church of San Giorgio Maggiore, Venice. 1592–1594. Oil on canvas, 12′ × 18′8″ (3.7 × 5.7 m).

Tintoretto, who had a large workshop, often developed a composition by creating a small-scale model like a miniature stage set, which he populated with wax figures. He then adjusted the positions of the figures and the lighting until he was satisfied with the entire scene. Using a grid of horizontal and vertical threads placed in front of this model, he could easily sketch the composition onto squared paper for his assistants to copy onto a large canvas. His assistants also primed the canvas, blocking in the areas of dark and light, before the artist himself, free to concentrate on the most difficult passages, finished the painting. This efficient working method allowed Tintoretto to produce a large number of paintings in all sizes.

Latin at Trissino's small academy and accompanied his benefactor on three trips to Rome, where he made drawings of Roman monuments.

Over the years, Palladio became involved in several publishing ventures, including a guide to Roman antiquities and an illustrated edition of Vitruvius. He also published his own books on architecture—including ideal plans for country estates, using proportions derived from ancient Roman buildings—that for centuries would be valuable resources for architectural design. Despite their theoretical bent, his writings were often more practical than earlier treatises. Perhaps his early experience as a stonemason provided him with the knowledge and self-confidence to approach technical problems and discuss them as clearly as he did theories of ideal proportion and uses of the Classical orders. By the eighteenth

century, Palladio's *Four Books of Architecture* had been included in the libraries of most educated people. Thomas Jefferson had one of the first copies in America.

SAN GIORGIO MAGGIORE By 1559, when he settled in Venice, Palladio was one of the foremost architects in Italy. In 1565, he undertook a major architectural commission: the monastery **CHURCH OF SAN GIORGIO MAGGIORE** (**FIG. 21-43**). His variation on the traditional Renaissance façade for a basilica—a wide lower level fronting the nave and side aisles, surmounted by a narrower front for the nave clerestory—creates the illusion of two temple fronts of different heights and widths, one set inside the other. At the center, colossal columns on high pedestals support an entablature and pediment; these columns correspond

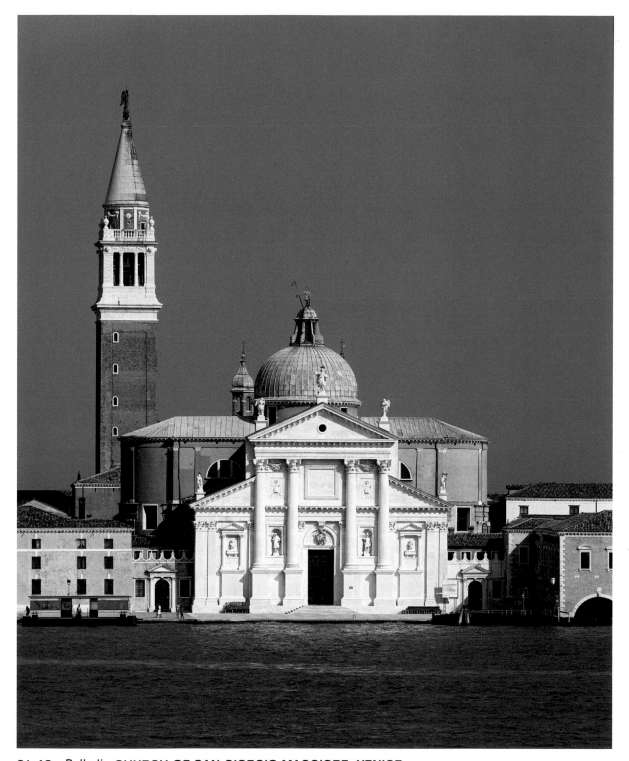

21-43 • Palladio CHURCH OF SAN GIORGIO MAGGIORE, VENICE
Plan 1565; construction 1565–1580; façade 1597–1610; campanile 1791. Finished by Vincenzo Scamozzi following Palladio's design.

to the width of the nave within. Behind the taller temple front, a second front consists of pilasters supporting another entablature and pediment; this wider front spans the entire width of the church, including the triple aisle. Although the façade was not built until after the architect's death, his original design was followed.

The interior of **SAN GIORGIO** (**FIG. 21–44**) is a fine example of Palladio's harmoniously balanced geometry, expressed here in strong verticals and powerfully opened arches. The tall engaged columns and shorter pilasters of the nave arcade piers echo the two levels of orders on the façade, thus helping to unify the building's exterior and interior.

21-44 • NAVE, CHURCH OF SAN GIORGIO MAGGIORE, VENICE
Begun 1566. Tintoretto's *Last Supper* (not visible) hangs to the left of the altar.

THE VILLA ROTONDA Palladio's versatility was already apparent in numerous villas built early in his career. In the 1560s, he started his most famous and influential villa just outside Vicenza (**FIGS. 21-45, 21-46**). Although villas were working farms, Palladio designed this one in part as a retreat, literally a party house. To maximize vistas of the countryside, he placed a porch elevated at the top of a wide staircase on each face of the building. The main living quarters are on this second level, and the lower level is reserved for the kitchen, storage, and other utility rooms. Upon its completion in 1569, the building was dubbed the **VILLA ROTONDA** because it had been inspired by another round building, the Roman Pantheon. The plan shows the geometric clarity of Palladio's conception: a circle inscribed in a small square inside a larger square, with symmetrical rectangular compartments and identical rectangular projections from each of its faces. The use of a central dome on a domestic building was a daring innovation that effectively secularized the dome and initiated what was to become a long tradition of domed country houses, particularly in England and the United States.

21-45 • Palladio PLAN OF VILLA ROTONDA, VICENZA
Italy. Begun 1560s.

21-46 • Palladio EXTERIOR VIEW OF VILLA ROTONDA
Italy. Begun 1560s.

After its purchase in 1591 by the Capra family, the Villa Rotonda became known as the Villa Capra.

Read the document related to Andrea Palladio on myartslab.com

THINK ABOUT IT

21.1 Some art historians have claimed that whereas Rome and Florence were oriented toward drawing, Venice was oriented toward color. Evaluate this claim, discussing specific works from each tradition in forming your answer.

21.2 Analyze either the Palazzo del Tè (FIG. 21-20) or the Villa Rotonda (FIG. 21-46). Explain how the design of the building differs from the design of grand churches during this same period, even though architects clearly used Classical motifs in both sacred and secular contexts.

21.3 Discuss Julius II's efforts to aggrandize the city of Rome and create a new golden age of papal art. Focus your answer on at least two specific works—one in painting and the other architectural—that he commissioned.

21.4 Select either Pontormo's *Deposition* (FIG. 21-30) or Parmigianino's *Madonna of the Long Neck* (FIG. 21-31), and explain why the painting characterizes Mannerist style. How does your chosen work depart from the Classical norms of the High Renaissance? How would you characterize their relationship to Michelangelo's *Last Judgment* (FIG. 21-38)?

CROSSCURRENTS

Ch. 20
Closer Look,
page 628

FIG. 21-33

These two paintings, each commissioned by a powerful political figure, combine Classical and allegorical themes in unusual ways. Each addresses a select audience. Compare the nature of the message each painting presents and evaluate how the style of presentation relates to the traditions and objectives of Florentine art during the period when it was painted.

Study and review on myartslab.com

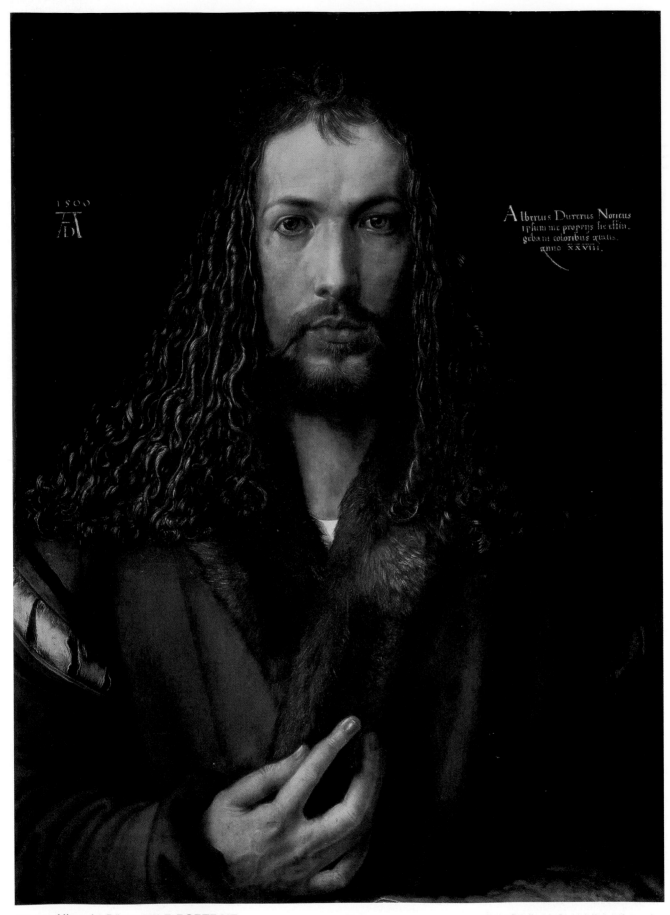

22–1 • Albrecht Dürer **SELF-PORTRAIT**
1500. Signed "Albrecht Dürer of Nuremberg…age 28." Oil on wood panel, 26¼″ × 19¼″ (66.3 × 49 cm). Alte Pinakothek, Munich.

Sixteenth-Century Art in Northern Europe and the Iberian Peninsula

This striking image (**FIG. 22–1**), dated 1500, seems to depict a blessing Christ, meant to rivet our attention and focus our devotion. But an inscription to the right of the iconic visage identifies this as a **SELF-PORTRAIT** of Albrecht Dürer, painted when he was 28 years old. We are already familiar with the practice of artists painting their own image. Self-portraits appear with some frequency during the Middle Ages (see FIGS. 16–34, 17–23); they truly blossom during the Renaissance (see FIGS. 19–12, 21–34). But this image is still peculiar, marked by an artistic hubris that may embarrass us. The picture becomes less puzzling, however, seen in context.

Dürer strikes an odd pose for a self-portrait—frontal and hieratic, intentionally recalling iconic images of Christ as *Salvator Mundi* (Savior of the World) that were very popular in northern Europe. Dürer even alters the natural color of his own hair to align the image more closely with contemporary notions of Christ's physical appearance. But there is no reason to see this as blasphemous. Since a principal component of contemporary Christian devotion was the attempt to imitate Christ in the believer's own life, Dürer could be visualizing a popular spiritual practice. He could also be literalizing the biblical statement that humans are created in the image of God. But he is also claiming that artists are learned and creative geniuses—perhaps God-like—not laboring craftsmakers. He wrote, "The more we know, the more we resemble the likeness of Christ who truly knows all things" (Snyder, p. 314).

Dürer had traveled to Italy in 1494–1495, where he encountered a new conception of artists as noble intellectuals, participants in humanistic discourse, purveyors of ideas as well as pictures. In 1498, back in Nuremberg, he published a woodcut series on the Apocalypse (see FIG. 22–7) that brought him a kind of international notice that was new to the German art world. He certainly had reason to feel pride. This stable, triangular composition—so consistent with High Renaissance norms of harmony and balance—could reflect Dürer's Italian adventure. But at its core, this picture fits into a long-standing northern European interest in the meticulous description of surface texture—the soft sheen of human flesh, the reflective wetness of eyes, the matte softness of cloth, and the tactile quality of hair, emphasized here by the way Dürer's hand fingers the fur collar of his outfit, encouraging viewers also to feel it as they see it. Ultimately what is showcased here are Dürer's awesome artistic gifts of hand as much as his intellectual gifts of mind, two aspects perhaps emblemized by the brightly illuminated body parts that align on a vertical axis to dominate this arresting self-portrait.

LEARN ABOUT IT

22.1 Recognize characteristic aspects of earlier Northern Renaissance style that continue into the work of sixteenth-century artists and evaluate the impact of new ideas coming from Italy.

22.2 Assess the relationship between the religious conflicts in northern Europe and the growing interest in new secular subjects in works of art as well as the focus on new themes in sacred art.

22.3 Investigate the broadening of regional interaction in the art of European courts as artists traveled across Europe to work for wealthy patrons and study with acclaimed masters.

22.4 Explore the continuing interest among northern European artists and patrons in the virtuosity of works in media such as wood and gold.

((•—Listen to the chapter audio on myartslab.com

MAP 22–1 • WESTERN EUROPE DURING THE REFORMATION, C. 1560

Sixteenth-century Europe remained largely Roman Catholic, except in Switzerland and the far north, where the impact of the Protestant Reformation was strongest.

Legend:
- Roman Catholic
- Lutheran
- Orthodox
- Anglican
- Calvinist
- Roman Catholic minorities
- Calvinist minorities
- Anabaptist minorities
- Islamic minorities
- Scattered Jewish minorities

THE REFORMATION AND THE ARTS

In spite of the dissident movements and heresies that had challenged the Roman Catholic Church through the centuries, its authority and that of the pope always prevailed—until the sixteenth century (**MAP 22-1**). Then, against a backdrop of broad dissatisfaction with financial abuses and decadent lifestyles among the clergy, religious reformers from within the Church itself challenged first its practices and then its beliefs.

Two of the most important reformers in the early sixteenth century were themselves Catholic priests and trained theologians: Desiderius Erasmus (1466?–1536) of Rotterdam in Holland, who worked to reform the Roman Catholic Church from within, and Martin Luther (1483–1546) in Germany, who eventually broke with it. Indeed, many locate the beginning of the Reformation in 1517, when Luther issued his "95 Theses" calling for Church

reform. Among Luther's concerns were the practice of selling indulgences (guarantees of relief from the punishment required after death for forgiven sins) and the excessive veneration of saints and their relics, which he considered superstitious. Luther and others emphasized individual faith and regarded the Bible as the ultimate religious authority. As they challenged the pope's supremacy, it became clear that the Protestants had to break away from Rome. The Roman Catholic Church condemned Luther in 1521.

Increased literacy and the widespread use of the printing press aided the reformers and allowed scholars throughout Europe to enter the religious debate. In Germany, the wide circulation of Luther's writings—especially his German translation of the Bible and his works maintaining that salvation comes through faith alone—eventually led to the establishment of the Protestant (Lutheran) Church there. In Switzerland, John Calvin (1509–1564) led an even more austere Protestant revolt; and in England, King Henry VIII (r. 1509–1547) broke with Rome in 1534, for reasons of his own. By the end of the sixteenth century, Protestantism in some form prevailed throughout northern Europe.

Leading the Catholic cause was Holy Roman Emperor Charles V. Europe was racked by religious war from 1546 to 1555 as Charles battled Protestant forces in Germany, until a meeting of the provincial legislature of Augsburg in 1555 determined that the emperor must accommodate the Protestant Reformation in his lands. By the terms of the peace, local rulers could select the religion of their subjects—Catholic or Protestant. Tired of the strain of government and prematurely aged, Charles abdicated in 1556 and retired to a monastery in Spain, where he died in 1558. His son Philip II inherited Habsburg Spain and the Spanish colonies, while his brother Ferdinand led the Austrian branch of the dynasty.

The years of political and religious strife had a grave impact on artists and art. Some artists found their careers at an end because of their reformist religious sympathies. Then, as Protestantism gained ascendancy, it was Catholic artists who had to leave their homes to seek patronage abroad. There was also widespread destruction of religious art. In some places, Protestant zealots smashed sculpture and stained-glass windows and destroyed or whitewashed religious paintings to rid churches of what they considered idols—though Luther himself never directly supported iconoclasm (the smashing of religious images). With the sudden loss of patronage for religious art in the newly Protestant lands, many artists turned to portraiture and other secular subjects, including moralizing depictions of human folly and weaknesses, still lifes (paintings of inanimate objects), and landscapes. The popularity of these themes stimulated the burgeoning of a free art market, centered in Antwerp.

GERMANY

In German-speaking regions, the arts flourished until religious upheavals and iconoclastic purges took their toll at mid century. German cities had strong business and trade interests, and their merchants and bankers accumulated self-made, rather than inherited, wealth. They ordered portraits of themselves and fine furnishings for their large, comfortable houses. Entrepreneurial artists, like Albrecht Dürer, became major commercial successes.

SCULPTURE

Although, like the Italians, German Renaissance sculptors worked in stone and bronze, they produced their most original work in wood, especially fine-grained limewood. Most of these wooden images were gilded and painted, continuing an interest in heightening naturalism, until Tilman Riemenschneider began to favor natural wood finishes.

TILMAN RIEMENSCHNEIDER Tilman Riemenschneider (c. 1460–1531) became a master in 1485 and soon had the largest workshop in Würzburg, including specialists in both wood and stone sculpture. Riemenschneider attracted patrons from other cities, and in 1501 he signed a contract with the church of St.

James in Rothenburg, where a relic said to be a drop of Jesus' blood was preserved. The **ALTARPIECE OF THE HOLY BLOOD** (**FIG. 22-2**) is a spectacular limewood construction standing nearly 30 feet high. Erhart Harschner, a specialist in architectural shrines,

22-2 • Tilman Riemenschneider ALTARPIECE OF THE HOLY BLOOD (WINGS OPEN)
Sankt Jakobskirche (church of St. James), Rothenburg ob der Tauber, Germany. Center, *Last Supper*. c. 1499–1505. Limewood, glass, height of tallest figure 39″ (99.1 cm), height of altar 29′6″ (9 m).

In Nuremberg, a city known for its master metalworkers, Hans Krug (d. 1519) and his sons Hans the Younger and Ludwig were among the finest. They created marvelous display pieces for the wealthy, such as this silver-gilt **APPLE CUP** (FIG. 22-3). Made about 1510, a gleaming apple, in which the stem forms the handle of the lid, balances on a leafy branch that serves as its base.

The Krug family was responsible for the highly refined casting and finishing of the final product, but several artists worked together to produce such pieces—one drawing designs, another making the models, and others creating the final piece in metal. A drawing by Dürer may have been the basis for the apple cup. Though we know of no piece of goldwork by the artist himself, Dürer was a major catalyst in the growth of Nuremberg as a key center of German goldsmithing. He accomplished this by producing designs for metalwork throughout his career. Designers played an essential role in the metalwork process. With design in hand, the modelmaker created a wooden form for the goldsmith to follow. The result of this artistic collaboration was a technical *tour de force*, an intellectual conceit, and an exquisite object.

22-3 • Workshop of Hans Krug (?) APPLE CUP
c. 1510–1515. Gilt silver, height 8½″ (21.5 cm). Germanisches Nationalmuseum, Nuremberg.

had begun work on the elaborate Gothic frame in 1499, and was paid 50 florins for his work. Riemenschneider was commissioned to provide the figures and scenes to be placed within this frame. He was paid 60 florins for the sculpture, giving us a sense of the relative value patrons placed on their contributions.

The main panel of the altarpiece portrays the moment at the Last Supper when Christ revealed that one of his followers would betray him. Unlike Leonardo da Vinci, who chose the same moment (see FIG. 21-3), Riemenschneider puts Judas at center stage and Jesus off-center at the left. The disciples sit around the table. As the event is described in the Gospel of John (13:21–30), Jesus extends a morsel of food to Judas, signifying that he will be the traitor who sets in motion the events leading to the Crucifixion. One apostle points down, a strange gesture until we realize that he is pointing to the crucifix in the predella, to the relic of Christ's blood, and to the altar table, the symbolic representation of the table of the Last Supper and the tomb of Christ.

Rather than creating individual portraits of the apostles, Riemenschneider repeated an established set of facial types. His figures have large heads, prominent features, sharp cheekbones, sagging jowls, baggy eyes, and elaborate hair with thick wavy locks and deeply drilled curls. The muscles, tendons, and raised veins of hands and feet are also especially lifelike. His assistants and apprentices copied these faces and figures, either from drawings or from three-dimensional models made by the master. In the altarpiece, deeply hollowed folds create active patterns in the voluminous draperies whose strong highlights and dark shadows harmonize the figural composition with the intricate carving of the framework. The Last Supper is set in a "real" room containing actual benches for the figures. Windows in the back wall are glazed with bull's-eye glass so that natural light shines in from two directions to illuminate the scene, producing changing effects depending on the time of day and the weather. Although earlier sculpture had been painted and gilded, Riemenschneider introduced the use of a natural wood finish toned with varnish. This meant that details of both figures and environment had to be carved into the wood itself, not added later with paint. Since this required more skillful carvers and more time for them to carve, this new look was a matter of aesthetics, not cost-saving.

In addition to producing an enormous number of religious images for churches, Riemenschneider was politically active in Würzburg, serving as mayor in 1520. His career ended during the Peasants' War (1524–1526), an early manifestation of the Protestant movement. His support for the peasants led to a fine and imprisonment in 1525, and although he survived, Riemenschneider produced no more sculpture and died in 1531.

22-4 • Nikolaus Hagenauer (central panels and predella) and Matthias Grünewald (wings) **ISENHEIM ALTARPIECE (OPEN)**

From the Community of St. Anthony, Isenheim, Alsace, France. Center panels and predella: *St. Anthony Enthroned between SS. Augustine and Jerome, Christ and the Apostles*, c. 1500. Painted and gilt limewood, center panel 9′9½″ × 10′9″ (2.97 × 3.28 m), predella 2′5½″ × 11′2″ (0.75 × 3.4 m). Wings: *SS. Anthony and Paul the Hermit* (left); *The Temptation of St. Anthony* (right). 1510–1515. Oil on wood panel, 8′2½″ × 3′½″ (2.49 × 0.93 m). Musée d'Unterlinden, Colmar, France.

NIKOLAUS HAGENAUER Prayer was the principal source of solace and relief to the ill before the advent of modern medicine. About 1505, the Strasbourg sculptor Nikolaus Hagenauer (active 1493–1530s) carved an altarpiece for the abbey of St. Anthony in Isenheim near Colmar (**FIG. 22-4**) where a hospital specialized in the care of patients with skin diseases, including the plague, leprosy, and St. Anthony's Fire (caused by eating rye and other grains infected with the ergot fungus). The shrine includes images of SS. Anthony, Jerome, and Augustine. Three tiny men—their size befitting their subordinate status—kneel at the feet of the saints: the donor, Jean d'Orliac, and two men offering a rooster and a piglet.

In the predella below, Jesus and the apostles bless the altar, Host, and assembled patients in the hospital. The flesh of the sculpted figures was painted in lifelike colors, but most of the altarpiece was gilded to enhance its resemblance to a metalwork reliquary. A decade later, Matthias Grünewald painted wooden shutters to cover the shrine (see **FIGS. 22-5, 22-6**).

PAINTING

The work of two very different German artists has come down to us from the first decades of the sixteenth century. Matthias Grünewald continued currents of medieval mysticism and emotional spirituality to create extraordinarily moving paintings. Albrecht Dürer, on the other hand, used intense observation of the world to render lifelike representations of nature, mathematical perspective to create convincing illusions of space, and a reasoned canon of proportions to standardize depictions of the human figure.

MATTHIAS GRÜNEWALD As a court artist to the archbishop of Mainz, Matthias Grünewald (Matthias Gothart Neithart, c. 1470/1475–1528) was a man of many talents, who worked as an architect and hydraulic engineer as well as a painter. He is best known today for paintings on the shutters or wings attached to Nikolaus Hagenauer's carved Isenheim Altarpiece (see **FIG. 22-4**). The completed altarpiece is impressive in size and complexity.

22-5 • Matthias Grünewald ISENHEIM ALTARPIECE (CLOSED)
From the Community of St. Anthony, Isenheim, Alsace, France. Center panels: *Crucifixion*; predella: *Lamentation*; side panels: *SS. Sebastian* (left) and *Anthony Abbot* (right). c. 1510–1515. Date 1515 on ointment jar. Oil on wood panel, center panels 9′9½″ × 10′9″ (2.97 × 3.28 m) overall, each wing 8′2½″ × 3′½″ (2.49 × 0.93 m), predella 2′5½″ × 11′2″ (0.75 × 3.4 m). Musée d'Unterlinden, Colmar, France.

22-6 • Matthias Grünewald ISENHEIM ALTARPIECE (FIRST OPENING)
Left to right: *Annunciation, Virgin and Child with Angels, Resurrection*. c. 1510–1515. Oil on wood panel, center panel 9′9½″ × 10′9″ (2.97 × 3.28 m), each wing 8′2½″ × 3′½″ (2.49 × 0.93 m). Musée d'Unterlinden, Colmar, France.

Grünewald painted one set of fixed wings and two sets of movable ones, plus one set of panels to cover the predella. The altarpiece could be exhibited in different configurations depending upon the church calendar. The wings and carved wooden shrine complemented one another, the inner sculpture seeming to bring the surrounding paintings to life, and the painted wings protecting the precious carvings.

On weekdays, when the altarpiece was closed, viewers saw a grisly image of the Crucifixion in a darkened landscape, a *Lamentation* below it on the predella, and life-size figures of SS. Sebastian and Anthony Abbot—both associated with the plague—standing on *trompe l'oeil* pedestals on the fixed wings (**FIG. 22-5**). The intensity of feeling here has suggested that Grünewald may have been inspired by the visions of St. Bridget of Sweden, a fourteenth-century mystic whose works—including morbidly detailed descriptions of the Crucifixion—were published in Germany beginning in 1492. Grünewald has scrupulously described the horrific character of the tortured body of Jesus, covered with gashes from his beating and pierced by the thorns used to form a crown for his head. His ashen body, clotted blood, open mouth, and blue lips signal his death. In fact, he appears already to be decaying, an effect enhanced by the palette of putrescent green, yellow, and purplish-red—all described by St. Bridget. She wrote, "The color of death spread through his flesh...." An immaculately garbed Virgin Mary has collapsed in the arms of a ghostlike John the Evangelist, and Mary Magdalen has fallen in anguish to her knees; her clasped hands with outstretched fingers seem to echo Jesus' fingers, cramped in rigor mortis. At the right, John the Baptist points to Jesus and repeats his prophecy, "He shall increase." The Baptist and the lamb, holding a cross and bleeding from its breast into a golden chalice, allude to baptism, the Eucharist, and to Christ as the sacrificial Lamb of God. In the predella below, Jesus' bereaved mother and friends prepare his racked body for burial—an activity that must have been a common sight in the abbey's hospital.

In contrast to these grim scenes, the first opening displays events of great joy—the Annunciation, the Nativity, and the Resurrection—appropriate for Sundays and feast days (**FIG. 22-6**). Praying in front of these pictures, the patients must have hoped for miraculous recovery and taken comfort in these visions of divine rapture and orgiastic color. Unlike the awful darkness of the Crucifixion, the inner scenes are brilliantly illuminated, in part by phosphorescent auras and haloes; stars glitter in the night sky of the Resurrection. The technical virtuosity of Grünewald's painting alone is enough to inspire euphoria.

The central panels show the heavenly and earthly realms joined in one space. In a variation on the northern European visionary tradition, the new mother adores her miraculous Christ Child while envisioning her own future as queen of heaven amid angels and cherubims. Grünewald portrayed three distinct types of angels in the foreground—young, mature, and a feathered hybrid with a birdlike crest on its human head. The range of ethnic types

in the heavenly realm may have emphasized the global dominion of the Church, whose missionary efforts were expanding as a result of European exploration. St. Bridget describes the jubilation of the angels as "the glowing flame of love."

The second opening of the altarpiece (see **FIG. 22-4**) reveals Hagenauer's sculpture and was reserved for the special festivals of St. Anthony. The wings in this second opening show to the left the meeting of St. Anthony with the hermit St. Paul, and to the right St. Anthony attacked by horrible demons, perhaps inspired by the horrors of the diseased patients, but also modeled in part on Schongauer's well-known print of the same subject (see **FIG. 19-28**). The meeting of the two hermits in the desert glorifies the monastic life, and in the wilderness Grünewald depicts medicinal plants used in the hospital's therapy. Grünewald painted the face of St. Paul with his own self-portrait, while St. Anthony is a portrait of the donor and administrator of the hospital, the Italian Guido Guersi, whose coat of arms Grünewald painted on the rock next to him.

As with Riemenschneider, Grünewald's involvement with the Peasants' War may have damaged his artistic career. He left Mainz and spent his last years in Halle, whose ruler was the chief protector of Martin Luther and a long-time patron of Grünewald's contemporary Albrecht Dürer.

ALBRECHT DÜRER Studious, analytical, observant, and meticulous—and as self-confident as Michelangelo—Albrecht Dürer (1471–1528) was the foremost artist of the German Renaissance. He made his home in Nuremberg, where he became a prominent citizen. Nuremberg was a center of culture as well as of business, with an active group of humanists and internationally renowned artists. It was also a leading publishing center. Dürer's father was a goldsmith and must have expected his son to follow in his trade (see "German Metalwork: A Collaborative Venture," page 682). Dürer did complete an apprenticeship in gold working, as well as in stained-glass design, painting, and the making of woodcuts—which he learned from Michael Wolgemut, illustrator of the *Nuremberg Chronicle* (see **FIG. 19-29**). It was as a painter and graphic artist, however, that he built his artistic fame.

In 1490, Dürer began traveling to extend his education. He went to Basel, Switzerland, hoping to meet Martin Schongauer, but arrived after the master's death. By 1494, Dürer had moved from Basel to Strasbourg. His first trip to Italy (1494–1495) introduced him to Italian Renaissance ideas and attitudes and, as we considered at the beginning of this chapter, to the concept of the artist as an independent creative genius. In his self-portrait of 1500 (see **FIG. 22-1**), Dürer represents himself as an idealized, Christ-like figure in a severely frontal pose, staring self-confidently at the viewer.

On his return to Nuremberg, Dürer began to publish his own prints to bolster his income, and ultimately it was prints, not paintings, that made his fortune. His first major publication, *The Apocalypse*, appeared simultaneously in German and Latin editions in 1497–1498. It consisted of a woodcut title page and 14 full-page

22-7 • Albrecht Dürer THE FOUR HORSEMEN OF THE APOCALYPSE
From *The Apocalypse*. 1497–1498. Woodcut, 15½″ × 11⅛″ (39.4 × 28.3 cm). Metropolitan Museum of Art, New York. Gift of Junius S. Morgan, 1919 (19.73.209)

his late fifteenth-century predecessors, he fills the foreground with large, active figures.

Perhaps as early as the summer of 1494, Dürer began to experiment with engravings, cutting the metal plates himself with an artistry rivaling Schongauer's. His growing interest in Italian art and his theoretical investigations are reflected in his 1504 engraving **ADAM AND EVE** (FIG. 22-8), which represents his first documented use of ideal human proportions based on Roman copies of ancient Greek sculpture. He may have seen figures of Apollo and Venus in Italy, and he would have known ancient sculpture from contemporary prints and drawings. But around these idealized human figures he represents plants and animals with typically northern attention to descriptive detail.

Dürer filled the landscape with symbolic content reflecting the medieval theory that after Adam and Eve disobeyed God, they and their descendants became vulnerable to imbalances in the body fluids that controlled human temperament. An excess of black bile from the liver would produce melancholy, despair, and greed; yellow bile caused anger, pride, and impatience; phlegm in the lungs resulted in lethargy and apathy; and an excess of blood made a person unusually optimistic but also compulsively interested in the pleasures of the flesh. These four human temperaments, or

22-8 • Albrecht Dürer ADAM AND EVE
1504. Engraving, 9⅞″ × 7⅝″ (25.1 × 19.4 cm). Philadelphia Museum of Art. Purchased: Lisa Nora Elkins Fund

illustrations with the text printed on the back of each. Perhaps best known is **THE FOUR HORSEMEN OF THE APOCALYPSE** (FIG. 22-7), based on figures described in Revelation 6:1–8: a crowned rider, armed with a bow, on a white horse (Conquest); a rider with a sword, on a red horse (War); a rider with a set of scales, on a black horse (Plague and Famine); and a rider on a sickly pale horse (Death). Earlier artists had simply lined up the horsemen in the landscape, but Dürer created a compact, overlapping group of wild riders charging across the world and trampling its cowering inhabitants, men and women, clerical and lay.

Dürer probably did not cut his own woodblocks but employed a skilled carver who followed his drawings faithfully. Dürer's dynamic figures show affinities with Schongauer's *Temptation of St. Anthony* (see FIG. 19-28). He adapted Schongauer's metal-engraving technique to the woodcut medium, using a complex pattern of lines to model the forms. Dürer's early training as a goldsmith is evident in his meticulous attention to detail, and in his decorative cloud and drapery patterns. Following the tradition established by

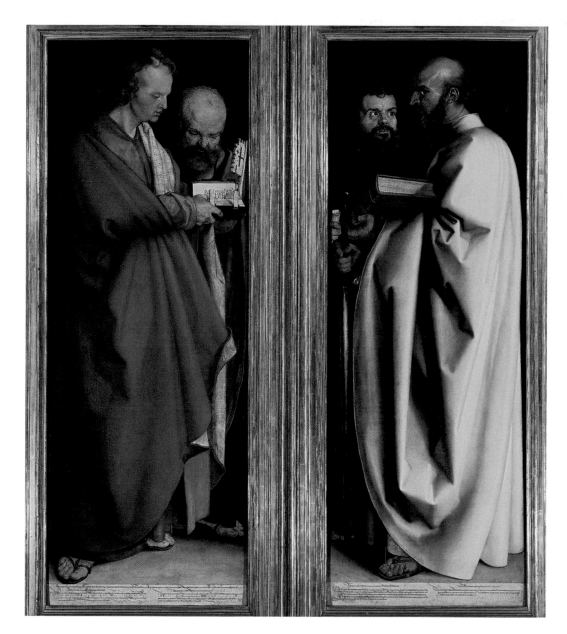

22–9 • Albrecht Dürer
FOUR APOSTLES
1526. Oil on wood panel, each panel 7'1½" × 2'6" (2.15 × 0.76 m). Alte Pinakothek, Munich.

Dürer presented these panels to the city of Nuremberg, which had already adopted Lutheranism as its official religion. Dürer wrote, "For a Christian would no more be led to superstition by a picture or effigy than an honest man to commit murder because he carries a weapon by his side. He must indeed be an unthinking man who would worship picture, wood, or stone. A picture therefore brings more good than harm, when it is honourably, artistically, and well made" (Snyder, p. 333).

personalities, are symbolized here by the melancholy elk, the choleric cat, the phlegmatic ox, and the sanguine (or sensual) rabbit. The mouse is a symbol of Satan (see the mousetrap in FIG. 19–11), whose earthly power, already manifest in the Garden of Eden, was capable of bringing human beings to a life of woe through their own bad choices. Adam seems to be releasing the mouse into the world of his paradise as he contemplates eating the forbidden fruit that Eve receives from the snake. Dürer placed his signature prominently on a placard hung on a tree branch in Adam's grasp and on which perches a parrot—possibly symbolizing false wisdom, since it can only repeat mindlessly what it hears.

Dürer's familiarity with Italian art was greatly enhanced by a second, leisurely trip over the Alps in 1505–1506. Thereafter, he seems to have resolved to reform the art of his own country by publishing theoretical writings and manuals that discussed Italian Renaissance problems of perspective, ideal human proportions, and the techniques of painting.

Dürer admired Martin Luther, but they never met. In 1526, the artist openly professed his Lutheranism in a pair of inscribed panels, the **FOUR APOSTLES** (FIG. 22–9). On the left panel, the elderly Peter, who normally has a central position as the first pope, has been displaced with his keys to the background by Luther's favorite evangelist, John, who holds an open Gospel that reads "In the beginning was the Word," reinforcing the Protestant emphasis on the Bible. On the right panel, Mark stands behind Paul, whose epistles were particularly admired by the Protestants. A long inscription on the frame warns the viewer not to be led astray by "false prophets" but to heed the words of the New Testament as recorded by these "four excellent men." Below each figure are excerpts from their letters and from the Gospel of Mark—drawn from Luther's German translation of the New Testament—warning against those who do not understand the true Word of God. These paintings were surely meant to chart the possibility of a Protestant visual art.

FONTIS NYMPHA SACRI SOM-
NVM NE RVMPE QVIESCO ·

22–10 • Lucas Cranach the Elder NYMPH OF THE SPRING
c. 1537. Oil on panel, 19″ × 28½″ (48.5 × 72.9 cm). National Gallery of Art, Washington, DC.

LUCAS CRANACH THE ELDER Martin Luther's favorite painter, Lucas Cranach the Elder (1472–1553), moved his work-shop to Wittenberg in 1504, after a number of years in Vienna. In addition to the humanist milieu of its university and library, Wittenberg offered the patronage of the Saxon court. Appointed court painter to Elector Frederick the Wise, Cranach created woodcuts, altarpieces, and many portraits.

Just how far German artists' style and conception of the fig-ure could differ from Italian Renaissance idealism is easily seen in Cranach's **NYMPH OF THE SPRING** (**FIG. 22–10**), especially when compared with Titian's *"Venus" of Urbino* (see FIG. 21–28). The sleeping nymph was a Renaissance theme, not an ancient one. Cranach was inspired by a fifteenth-century inscription on a fountain beside the Danube, cited in the upper left corner of the painting: "I am the nymph of the sacred font. Do not inter-rupt my sleep for I am at peace." Cranach records the Danube landscape with characteristic northern attention to detail and turns his nymph into a rather provocative young woman, who glances slyly out at the viewer through half-closed eyes. She has cast aside a fashionable red velvet gown, but still wears her jewelry, which together with her transparent veil enhances rather than conceals

her nudity—especially those coral beads that fall between her breasts, mapping their contours. Unlike other artists working for Protestant patrons, many of whom looked on earthly beauty as a sinful vanity, Cranach seems delighted by earthly things—the lush foliage that provides the nymph's couch, the pair of partridges (symbols of Venus and married love), and Cupid's bow and quiver of arrows hanging on the tree. Could this nymph be a living beauty from the Wittenberg court? She is certainly not an embodiment of an idealized, Classical Venus.

HANS BALDUNG GRIEN Cranach's slightly younger con-temporary Hans Baldung (1484/1485–1545)—his nickname tag "Grien" ("green," apparently a favorite color) dates from his apprenticeship days and was used to distinguish him from the numerous other apprentices named Hans—is known for very different visualizations of women. Born into an affluent and well-educated family, Baldung was working in Strasbourg by 1500, before moving to Nuremberg in 1503 and eventually joining Dürer's workshop in 1505–1507. Over the course of his long career, he also worked in Halle and Freiburg, but his principal artistic home was Strasbourg, where he lived out a

22-11 • Hans Baldung Grien DEATH AND THE MATRON

c. 1520–1525. Oil on wood panel, 12⅜″ × 7⅜″ (31.3 × 18.7 cm). Öffentliche Kunstsammlung, Basel.

Although more erotically charged and certainly more dramatic than Dürer's Eve in FIG. 22–8, Baldung's woman is based in certain ways on this famous image, which was engraved while he was assisting in Dürer's workshop. In many respects, the similarities in pose (especially the feet) and form (wide hips with narrowing waist and torso) only point up the differences in expressive content.

prosperous professional life as a painter, printmaker, and stained-glass designer.

During the first half of his career, Baldung created a series of paintings on the theme of **DEATH AND THE MATRON** that juxtapose sensuality with mortality, voluptuousness with decay, attraction with repulsion. The example in **FIG. 22-11** (painted in about 1520–1525 for a private collector in Basel) uses brilliant illumination and expansive posture to draw our attention first to the voluptuous nude, fleshier and considerably more sensual than Cranach's nymph (see FIG. 22-10) or Dürer's Eve (see FIG. 22-8). But this focus is soon overtaken by a sense of surprise that mirrors her own, as she turns her head to discover that the figure stroking

her hair and clutching at her breast is not her lover but Death himself. The putrid decay of his yellowing flesh contrasts sharply with her soft contours, and his bony molting head is the antithesis of her full pink cheeks, flowing tresses, and soft traces of body hair. That the encounter takes place in a cemetery, on top of a tombstone, serves to underline the warning against the transitory pleasures of the flesh, but Baldung also seems to depend on the viewers' own erotic engagement to make the message not only moral but personal.

ALBRECHT ALTDORFER Landscape, with or without figures, became a popular theme in the sixteenth century. In the fifteenth

22–12 • Albrecht Altdorfer
DANUBE LANDSCAPE
c. 1525. Oil on vellum on
wood panel, 12″ × 8½″ (30.5
× 22.2 cm). Alte Pinakothek,
Munich.

century, northern artists had examined and recorded nature with
the care and enthusiasm of biologists, but painted landscapes were
reserved for the backgrounds of figural compositions, usually
sacred subjects. In the 1520s, however, religious art found little
favor among Protestants. Landscape painting, on the other hand,
had no overt religious content, although it could be seen as a
reflection or even glorification of God's works on Earth. The

most accomplished German landscape painter of the period was
Albrecht Altdorfer (c. 1480–1538).

Altdorfer probably received his early training in Bavaria from
his father, but he became a citizen of Regensburg in 1505 and
remained there painting the Danube River Valley for the rest of
his life. **DANUBE LANDSCAPE** of about 1525 (**FIG. 22-12**) is
an early example of pure landscape painting, without a narrative

subject, human figures, or overt religious significance. A small work on vellum laid down on a wood panel, it shows a landscape that seems to be a minutely detailed reproduction of the natural terrain, but the forest seems far more poetic and mysterious than Dürer's or Cranach's carefully observed views of nature. The low mountains, gigantic lacy pines, neatly contoured shrubberies, and fairyland castle with red-roofed towers at the end of a winding path announce a new sensibility. The eerily glowing yellow–white horizon below moving gray and blue clouds in a sky that takes up more than half the composition prefigures the Romanticism of German landscape painting in later centuries.

FRANCE

Renaissance France followed a different path from that taken in Germany. In 1519, Pope Leo X came to an agreement with French King Francis I (r. 1515–1547) that spared the country the turmoil suffered in Germany. Furthermore, whereas Martin Luther had devoted followers in France, French reformer John Calvin (1509–1564) fled to Switzerland in 1534, where he led a theocratic state in Geneva.

During the second half of the century, however, warring political factions favoring either Catholics or Huguenots (Protestants) competed to exert power over the French crown, with devastating consequences. In 1560, the devoutly Catholic Catherine de' Medici, widow of Henry II (r. 1547–1559), became regent for her young son, Charles IX, and tried, but failed, to balance the warring factions. Her machinations ended in religious polarization and a bloody conflict that began in 1562. When her third son, Henry III (r. 1574–1589), was murdered by a fanatical Dominican friar, a Protestant cousin, Henry, king of Navarre, the first Bourbon king, inherited the throne. Henry converted to Catholicism and ruled as Henry IV. Backed by a country sick of bloodshed, he quickly settled the religious question by proclaiming tolerance of Protestants in the Edict of Nantes in 1598.

A FRENCH RENAISSANCE UNDER FRANCIS I

Immediately after his ascent to the throne, Francis I sought to "modernize" the French court by acquiring the versatile talents of Leonardo da Vinci, who moved to France in 1516. Officially, Leonardo was there to advise the king on royal architectural projects and, the king said, for the pleasure of his conversation. Francis supported an Italian-inspired Renaissance in French art and architecture throughout his long reign.

JEAN CLOUET Not all the artists working at the court of Francis I, however, were Italian. Flemish artist Jean Clouet (c. 1485–c. 1540) found great favor at the royal court, especially as a portrait painter. About the same time that he became principal court painter in 1527, he produced an official portrait of the king (**FIG. 22-13**). Clouet created a flattering image of Francis by modulating the king's distinctive features with soft shading and highlighting the nervous activity of his fingers. At the same time he conceived an image of pure power. Elaborate, puffy sleeves broaden the king's shoulders to fill the entire width of the panel, much as Renaissance parade armor turned scrawny men into giants. The detailed rendering of the delicately worked costume of silk, satin, velvet,

22-13 • Jean Clouet FRANCIS I
1525–1530. Oil and tempera on wood panel, 37¾″ × 29⅛″ (95.9 × 74 cm). Musée du Louvre, Paris.

Women played an important role in the patronage of the arts during the Renaissance. Nowhere is their influence stronger than in the châteaux of the Loire River Valley. At Chenonceau (**FIG. 22–14**), built beside and literally over the River Cher, a tributary of the Loire, women built, saved, and restored the château. Catherine Briconnet and her husband, Thomas Bohier, originally acquired the property, including a fortified mill, on which they built their country residence. Catherine supervised the construction, which included such modern conveniences as a straight staircase (an Italian and Spanish feature) instead of traditional medieval spiral stairs, and a kitchen inside the château instead of in a distant outbuilding. After Thomas died in 1524 and Catherine in 1526, their son gave Chenonceau to King Francis I.

King Henry II, Francis's son, gave Chenonceau to his mistress Diane de Poitiers in 1547. She managed the estate astutely, increased its revenue, developed the vineyards, added intricately planted gardens in the Italian style, and built a bridge across the Cher. When Henry died in a tournament, his queen, Catherine de' Medici (1519–1589), appropriated the château for herself.

Catherine, like so many in her family a great patron of the arts, added the two-story gallery to the bridge at Chenonceau, as well as outbuildings and additional formal gardens. Her parties were famous: mock naval battles on the river, fireworks, banquets, dances, and on one occasion two choruses of young women dressed as mermaids in the moat and nymphs in the shrubbery—who were then chased about by young men costumed as satyrs!

When Catherine's third son became king as Henry III in 1574, she gave the château to his wife, Louise of Lorraine, who lived in mourning at Chenonceau after Henry III was assassinated in 1589. She wore only white and covered the walls, windows, and furniture in her room with black velvet and damask. She left Chenonceau to her niece when she died.

In the eighteenth and nineteenth centuries, women continued to determine the fate of Chenonceau. During the French Revolution (1789–1793), the owner, Madame Dupin, was so beloved by the villagers that they protected her and saved her home. Then, in 1864, Madame Pelouze bought Chenonceau and restored it by removing Catherine de' Medici's Italian "improvements."

Chenonceau continued to play a role in the twentieth century. During World War I, it was used as a hospital. During the German occupation in World War II (1940–1942), when the River Cher formed the border with Vichy "Free" France, the gallery bridge at Chenonceau became an escape route.

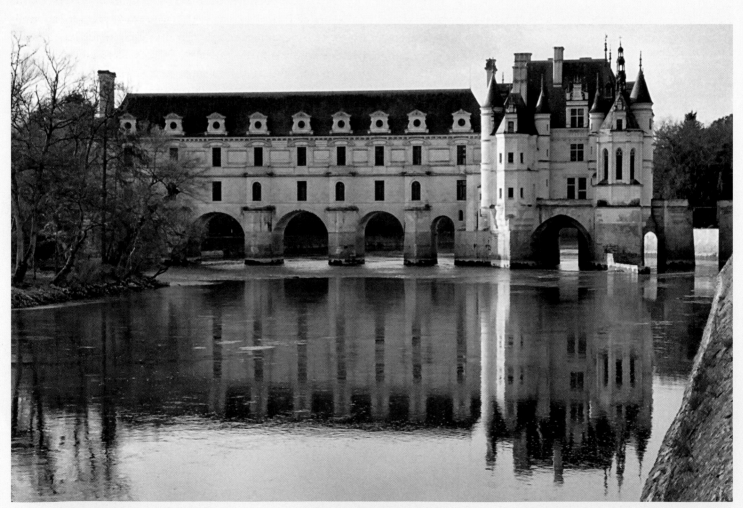

22-14 • CHÂTEAU OF CHENONCEAU
Touraine, France. Original building (at right) 1513–1521; gallery on bridge at left by Philibert de l'Orme, finished c. 1581.

jewels, and gold embroidery could be painted separately from the portrait itself. Royal clothing was often loaned to the artist or modeled by a servant to spare the "sitter" the boredom of posing. In creating such official portraits, the artist sketched the subject, then painted a prototype that, upon approval, became the model for numerous replicas made for diplomatic and family purposes.

THE CHÂTEAU OF CHENONCEAU With the enthusiasm of Francis for things Italian and the widening distribution of Italian books on architecture, the Italian Renaissance style soon infiltrated French architecture. Builders of elegant rural palaces, called **châteaux**, were quick to introduce Italianate decoration to otherwise Gothic buildings, but French architects soon adapted Classical principles of building design as well.

One of the most beautiful châteaux was not built as a royal residence, although it soon became one. In 1512, Thomas Bohier, a royal tax collector, bought the castle of Chenonceau on the River Cher, a tributary of the Loire (see "The Castle of the Ladies," opposite). He demolished the old castle, leaving only a tower. Using the piers of a water mill on the river bank as part of the foundations, he and his wife erected a new Renaissance home. The plan reflects the Classical principles of geometric regularity and symmetry—a rectangular building with rooms arranged on each side of a wide central hall. Only the library and chapel, which are corbelled out over the water, break the line of the walls. In the upper story, the builders used traditional features of medieval castles—battlements, corner turrets, steep roofs, and dormer windows. The owners died soon after the château was finished

in 1521, and their son gave it to Francis I, who turned it into a hunting lodge.

Later, Roman-trained French Renaissance architect Philibert de l'Orme (d. 1570) designed a gallery on a bridge across the river for Catherine de' Medici, completed about 1581 and incorporating contemporary Italianate window treatments, wall molding, and cornices that harmonized almost perfectly with the forms of the original turreted building.

FONTAINEBLEAU Having chosen as his primary residence the medieval hunting lodge at Fontainebleau, Francis I began transforming it into a grand country palace. In 1530, he imported a Florentine artist, the Mannerist painter Rosso Fiorentino (1495–1540), to direct the project. After Rosso died, he was succeeded by his Italian colleague Francesco Primaticcio (1504–1570), who had earlier worked with Giulio Romano in Mantua (see FIG. 21-20), before joining Rosso in 1532, and would spend the rest of his career working on the decoration of Fontainebleau. During that time, he also commissioned and imported a large number of copies and casts of original Roman sculpture, from the newly discovered Laocoön (see FIG. 5-64) to the relief decoration on the Column of Trajan (see FIG. 6-48). These works provided an invaluable visual resource of figures and techniques for the northern European artists employed on the Fontainebleau project.

Among Primaticcio's first projects at Fontainebleau was the redecoration, in the 1540s, of the rooms of the king's official mistress, Anne, duchess of Étampes (**FIG. 22-15**). The artist combined woodwork, stucco relief, and fresco painting in his complex but

22-15 • Primaticcio STUCCO AND WALL PAINTING, CHAMBER OF THE DUCHESS OF ÉTAMPES, CHÂTEAU OF FONTAINEBLEAU
France. 1540s.

22-16 • Pierre Lescot and Jean Goujon **WEST WING OF THE COUR CARRÉE, PALAIS DU LOUVRE, PARIS**
Begun 1546.

whimsical and graceful interior design. The lithe figures of stucco nymphs, with their elongated bodies and small heads, recall Parmigianino's paintings (see FIG. 21-31). Their spiraling postures and teasing bits of clinging drapery are playfully erotic. Garlands, mythological figures, and Roman architectural ornament almost overwhelm the walls with visual enrichment, yet the whole remains ordered and lighthearted. The first School of Fontainebleau, as this Italian phase of the palace decoration is called, established an Italianate tradition of Mannerism in painting and interior design that spread to other centers in France and into the Netherlands.

THE LOUVRE Before the defeat of Francis I at Pavia by Holy Roman Emperor Charles V, and the king's subsequent imprisonment in Spain in 1525, the French court had been a mobile unit, and the locus of French art resided outside Paris in the Loire Valley. After his release in 1526, Francis made Paris his bureaucratic seat, and the Île-de-France—Paris and its region—took the artistic lead. The move to the capital gave birth to a style of French Classicism when Francis I and Henry II decided to modernize the medieval castle of the Louvre. Work began in 1546, with the replacement of the west wing of the square court, or **COUR CARRÉE (FIG. 22-16)**, by architect Pierre Lescot (c. 1510–1578) working with sculptor Jean Goujon (1510–1568). They designed

a building that incorporated Renaissance ideals of balance and regularity with Classical architectural details and rich sculptural decoration. The irregular rooflines seen in a château such as the one at Chenonceau (see FIG. 22-14, right part of the building) gave way to discreetly rounded arches and horizontal balustrades. Classical pilasters and entablatures replaced Gothic buttresses and stringcourses. A round-arched arcade on the ground floor suggests an Italian loggia. On the other hand, the sumptuousness of the decoration recalls the French Flamboyant style (see Chapter 19), only with Classical pilasters and acanthus replacing Gothic colonnettes and cusps.

SPAIN AND PORTUGAL

The sixteenth century saw the peak of Spanish political power. The country had been united in the fifteenth century by the marriage of Isabella of Castile and Ferdinand of Aragon. Only Navarre (in the Pyrenees) and Portugal remained outside the union of the crowns. (See "Sculpture for the Knights of Christ at Tomar," opposite.) When Isabella and Ferdinand's grandson Charles V abdicated in 1556, his son Philip II (r. 1556–1598) became the king of Spain, the Netherlands, and the Americas, as well as ruler of Milan, Burgundy, and Naples, but Spain was Philip's permanent residence.

One of the most beautiful, if also one of the strangest, sixteenth-century sculptures in Portugal seems to float over the cloisters of the convent of Christ in Tomar. Unexpectedly, in the heart of the castle-monastery complex, one comes face to face with the Old Man of the Sea. He supports on his powerful shoulders an extraordinary growth—part roots and trunk of a gnarled tree; part tangled mass of seaweed, algae, ropes, and anchor chains. Barnacle- and coral-encrusted piers lead the eye upward, revealing a large lattice-covered window, the great **WEST WINDOW** of the church of the Knights of Christ (**FIG. 22–17**).

When, in 1314, Pope Clement V disbanded the Templars (a monastic order of knights founded in Jerusalem after the First Crusade), King Dinis of Portugal offered them a renewed existence as the Knights of Christ. As a result, in 1356, they made the former Templar castle and monastery in Tomar their headquarters. When Prince Henry the Navigator (1394–1460) became the grand master of the order, he invested their funds in the exploration of the African coast and the Atlantic Ocean. The Templar insignia, the squared cross, became the emblem used on the sails of Portuguese ships.

King Manuel I of Portugal (r. 1495–1521) commissioned the present church, with its amazing sculpture by Diogo de Arruda, in 1510. So distinctive is the style developed under King Manuel by artists like the Arruda brothers, Diogo (active 1508–1531) and Francisco (active 1510–1547), that Renaissance art in Portugal is called "Manueline." In the window of Tomar, every surface is carved with architectural and natural detail associated with the sea. Twisted ropes form the corners of the window; the coral pillars support great swathes of seaweed. Chains and cables drop through the watery depths to the place where the head of a man—could this Old Man of the Sea be a self-portrait of Diogo de Arruda? —emerges from the roots of a tree. Above the window, more ropes, cables, and seaweed support the emblems of the patron—armillary spheres at the upper outside corners (topped by pinnacles) and at dead center, the coat of arms of Manuel I with its Portuguese castles framing the five wounds of Christ. Topping the composition is the square cross of the Order of Christ—clearly delineated against the wall of the chapel.

The armillary sphere became a symbol of the era. This complex form of a celestial globe, with the sun at the center surrounded by rings marking the paths of the planets, was a teaching device that acknowledged the new scientific theory that the sun, not the Earth, is the center of the solar system. (Copernicus only published his theories in 1531 and 1543.) King Manuel's use of the armillary sphere as his emblem signals his determination to make Portugal the leader in the exploration of the sea. Indeed, in Manuel's reign the Portuguese reached India and Brazil.

22-17 • Diogo de Arruda **WEST WINDOW, CHURCH IN THE CONVENT OF CHRIST, TOMAR**
Portugal. c. 1510. Commissioned by King Manuel I of Portugal.

For more than half a century, he supported artists in Spain, Italy, and the Netherlands. His navy, the famous Spanish Armada, halted the advance of Islam in the Mediterranean and secured control of most of the Americas. Despite enormous effort, however, Philip could not suppress the revolt of the northern provinces of the Netherlands, nor could he prevail in his war against the English, who destroyed his navy in 1588. He was able to gain control of the entire Iberian peninsula, however, by claiming Portugal in 1580, and it remained part of Spain until 1640.

ARCHITECTURE

Philip built **THE ESCORIAL** (**FIG. 22-18**), the great monastery-palace complex outside Madrid, partly to comply with his father's direction to construct a "pantheon" in which all Spanish kings might be buried and partly to house his court and government. In 1559, Philip summoned from Italy Juan Bautista de Toledo (d. 1567), who had been Michelangelo's supervisor of work at St. Peter's from 1546 to 1548. Juan Bautista's design for the monastery-palace reflected his indoctrination in Bramante's Classical principles in

Rome, but the king himself dictated the severity and size of the structure. The Escorial's grandeur comes from its overwhelming size, fine proportions, and excellent masonry. The complex includes not only the royal residence but also the Royal Monastery of San Lorenzo, a school, a library, and a church, its crypt serving as the royal burial chamber. The plan was said to resemble a gridiron, the instrument of martyrdom of its patron saint, Lawrence, who was roasted alive.

In 1572, Juan Bautista's assistant, Juan de Herrera, was appointed architect, and he immediately changed the design, adding second stories on all wings and breaking the horizontality of the main façade with a central frontispiece that resembled the superimposed temple fronts that were fashionable on Italian churches at this time (see FIGS. 21–40, 21–43). Before beginning the church in the center of the complex, Philip solicited the advice of Italian architects—including Vignola and Palladio. The final design combined ideas that Philip approved and Herrera carried out, and it embodies Italian Classicism in its geometric clarity, symmetry, and superimposed temple-front façade. In its austerity, it embodies the deep religiosity of Philip II.

PAINTING

The most famous painter working in Spain during the last quarter of the sixteenth century was Domenikos Theotokopoulos (1541–1614), who arrived in Spain in 1577 after working for ten years in Italy. "El Greco" ("The Greek"), as he is called, was trained as an icon painter in the Byzantine manner in his native Crete, then under Venetian rule. In about 1566, he entered Titian's studio in Venice, where he also studied the paintings of Tintoretto and Veronese. From about 1570 to 1577, he worked in Rome, living for a time in the Farnese Palace. Probably encouraged by Spanish church officials whom he met in Rome, El Greco eventually settled in Toledo, seat of the Spanish archbishop. He had hoped for a court appointment, but Philip II—a great patron of the Venetian painter Titian and a collector of Netherlandish artists such as Bosch—disliked the painting he had commissioned from El Greco for the Escorial and never again gave him work.

In Toledo, El Greco joined the circle of humanist scholars. He wrote that the artist's goal should be to copy nature, that Raphael relied too heavily on the ancients, and that the Italians' use of mathematics to achieve ideal proportions hindered their painting of nature. At this same time an intense religious revival was under way in Spain, expressed in the impassioned preaching of Ignatius of Loyola, as well as in the poetry of two great Spanish mystics: St. Teresa of Ávila (1515–1582) and her follower St. John of the Cross (1542–1591). El Greco's style—rooted in Byzantine icon painting and strongly reflecting the rich colors and loose brushwork of Venetian painting—was well equipped to express the intense spirituality of these mystics.

In 1586, the Orgaz family commissioned El Greco to paint a large altarpiece honoring an illustrious fourteenth-century ancestor. Count Orgaz had been a great benefactor of the Church, and at his funeral in 1323, SS. Augustine and Stephen were said to have appeared to lower his body into his tomb as his soul was seen ascending to heaven. El Greco's painting the **BURIAL OF COUNT ORGAZ** (FIG. 22-19) captures these miracles in a Mannerist composition that recalls Pontormo (see FIG. 21-30), packing the pictorial field with figures and eliminating specific reference to the spatial setting. An angel lifts Orgaz's ghostly soul along the central axis of the painting toward the enthroned Christ at the apex of the

22-18 • Juan Bautista de Toledo and Juan de Herrera **THE ESCORIAL**
Madrid. 1563–1584. Detail from an anonymous 18th-century painting.

22-19 • El Greco BURIAL OF COUNT ORGAZ
Church of Santo Tomé, Toledo, Spain. 1586. Oil on canvas, 16′ × 11′10″ (4.88 × 3.61 m).

View the Closer Look for *Burial of Count Orgaz* on myartslab.com

canvas. The otherworldly luminescence emanating from Christ in this heavenly vision is quite unlike the natural light below, where El Greco surrounded the burial scene with portraits of the local aristocracy and religious notables. He placed his own 8-year-old son at the lower left next to St. Stephen and signed the painting on the boy's white kerchief. El Greco may also have put his own features on the man just above the saint's head, the only other figure who, like the child, looks straight out at the viewer.

THE NETHERLANDS

In the Netherlands, the sixteenth century was an age of bitter religious and political conflict. Despite the opposition of the Spanish Habsburg rulers, the Protestant Reformation took hold in the northern provinces. Seeds of unrest were sown still deeper over the course of the century by continued religious persecution, economic hardship, and inept governors. Widespread iconoclasm characterized 1566–1567, and a long battle for independence began with a revolt in 1568 that lasted until Spain relinquished all claims to the region 80 years later. As early as 1579, when the seven northern Protestant provinces declared themselves the United Provinces, the discord split the Netherlands, eventually dividing it along religious lines into the United Provinces (the present-day Netherlands) and Catholic Flanders (present-day Belgium).

Despite such turmoil, Antwerp and other cities developed into thriving art centers. The Reformation led artists to seek patrons outside the Church. While courtiers and burghers alike continued to commission portraits, the demand arose for small paintings with interesting secular subjects appropriate for homes. For example, some artists became specialists known for their landscapes or satires. In addition to painting, textiles, ceramics, printmaking, and sculpture in wood and metal flourished in the Netherlands. Flemish tapestries were sought after and highly prized across Europe, as they had been in the fifteenth century, and leading Italian artists made cartoons to be woven into tapestries in Flemish workshops (see "Raphael's Cartoons for Tapestries in the Sistine Chapel," page 648). The **graphic arts** emerged as an important medium, providing many artists with another source of income. Pieter Bruegel the Elder, for instance, began his career drawing amusing and moralizing images to be printed and published by At the Four Winds, an Antwerp publishing house.

Like Vasari in Italy, Carel van Mander (1548–1606) recorded the lives of his Netherlandish contemporaries in engaging biographies that mix fact and gossip. He, too, intended his 1604 book *Het Schilder-boeck* (*The Painter's Book*) to be a survey of the history of art, and he included material from the ancient Roman writers Pliny and Vitruvius as well as from Vasari's revised and expanded *Lives*, published in 1568.

ART FOR ARISTOCRATIC AND NOBLE PATRONS

Artistic taste among the wealthy bourgeoisie and noble classes in the early sixteenth-century Netherlands was characterized by a striking diversity, encompassing the imaginative and difficult visions of Hieronymus Bosch, as well as the more Italianate compositions of Jan Gossaert. In the later years of his life, Bosch's membership in a local but prestigious confraternity called the Brotherhood of Our Lady seems to have opened doors to noble patrons such as Count Hendrick III of Nassau and Duke Philip the Fair. His younger contemporary Gossaert left the city of Antwerp as a young man to spend the majority of his active years as the court painter for the natural son of Duke Philip the Good. His art also attracted members of the Habsburg family, including Charles V, who were seduced by Gossaert's combination of northern European and Italian styles.

HIERONYMUS BOSCH Among the most fascinating Netherlandish painters to modern viewers is Hieronymus Bosch (1450–

22-20 • Hieronymus Bosch GARDEN OF EARTHLY DELIGHTS (OPEN)
c. 1505–1515. Oil on wood panel, center panel 7′2½″ × 6′4¾″
(2.20 × 1.95 m), each wing 7′2½″ × 3′2″ (2.20 × 0.97 m).
Museo del Prado, Madrid.

Despite—or perhaps because of—its bizarre subject matter, this triptych was woven in 1566 into tapestries, and at least one painted copy was made as well. Bosch's original triptych was sold at the onset of the Netherlands Revolt and sent in 1568 to Spain, where it entered the collection of Philip II.

Read the document related to Hieronymus Bosch on myartslab.com

1516), who depicted the sort of imaginative fantasies more often associated with medieval than Renaissance art. A superb colorist and virtuoso technician, Bosch spent his career in the town whose name he adopted, 's-Hertogenbosch. Bosch's religious devotion is certain, and his range of subjects shows that he was well educated. Challenging and unsettling paintings such as his **GARDEN OF EARTHLY DELIGHTS** (**FIG. 22-20**) have led modern scholars to label Bosch both a mystic and a social critic. The subject of the triptych seems to be founded on Christian belief in the natural state of human sinfulness, but it was not painted for a church.

In the left wing, God introduces doll-like figures of Adam and Eve, under the watchful eye of the owl of perverted wisdom. The owl symbolizes both wisdom and folly. Folly had become an important concept to the northern European humanists, who believed in the power of education. They believed that people would choose to follow the right way once they knew it. Here the owl peers out from an opening in the spherical base of a fantastic pink fountain in a lake from which vicious creatures creep out into the world.

In the central panel, the Earth teems with such monsters, but also with vivacious human revelers and luscious huge fruits, symbolic of fertility and sexual abandon. In hell, at the right, sensual pleasures—eating, drinking, music, and dancing—become instruments of torture in a dark world of fire and ice. The emphasis in the right wing on the torments of hell, with no hint of the rewards of heaven, seems to caution that damnation is the natural outcome of a life lived in ignorance and folly, that humans ensure their damnation through their self-centered pursuit of pleasures of the flesh—the sins of gluttony, lust, greed, and sloth—outlined with such fantastic and graphic abandon in the central panel.

One scholar has proposed that the central panel is a parable on human salvation in which the practice of alchemy—the process that sought to turn common metals into gold—parallels Christ's power to convert human dross into spiritual gold. In this theory, the bizarre fountain at the center of the lake in the middle distance can be seen as an alchemical "marrying chamber," complete with the glass vessels for collecting the vapors of distillation. Others see the theme known as "the power of women." In this interpretation, the central pool is the setting for a display of seductive women and sex-obsessed men. Women frolic alluringly in the pool while men dance and ride in a mad circle trying to attract them. In this strange garden, men are slaves to their own lust. An early seventeenth-century critic focused on the fruit, writing that the triptych was known as *The Strawberry Plant* because it represented the "vanity and glory and the passing taste of strawberries or the strawberry plant and its pleasant odor that is hardly remembered once it has passed." Luscious fruits of obvious sexual symbolism—strawberries, cherries, grapes, and pomegranates—appear everywhere in the garden, serving as food, as shelter, and even as a boat. Is human life as fleeting and insubstantial as the taste of a strawberry? Yet another modern reading sees the central tableau imagining the course of life in paradise, assuming that Adam and Even had not consigned humanity to sin by eating the forbidden fruit.

Conforming to a long tradition of triptych altarpieces made for churches, Bosch painted a more sober, *grisaille* picture on the reverse of the side wings. When the triptych is closed, a less enigmatic, but equally fascinating, scene is displayed (**FIG. 22-21**). A transparent, illusionistic rendering of a receding sphere floating within a void encloses the flat circular shelf of Earth on its third day of creation. Fragments of the fantastic fruit that will appear fully formed in the interior pictures float here in the primordial sea, while ominous dark clouds promise the rain that will nurture them into their full seductive ripeness. A tiny crowned figure of God the Creator hovers in a bubble within dark clouds at upper left, displaying a book, perhaps a Bible opened to the words from Psalm 33:9 that are inscribed across the top: "For he spoke, and it came to be; he commanded, and it stood firm."

The *Garden of Earthly Delights* was commissioned by an aristocrat (probably Count Hendrick III of Nassau) for his Brussels town house, and the artist's choice of a triptych format, which suggests an altarpiece, may have been an understated irony. In a private home the painting surely inspired lively discussion, even ribald commentary, much as it does today in the Prado Museum. Perhaps that, rather than a single meaning or interpretation, is the true intention behind this dazzling display of artistic imagination.

JAN GOSSAERT In contrast to the private visions of Bosch, Jan Gossaert (c. 1478–c. 1533) maintained traditional subject matter and embraced the new Classical art of Italy. Gossaert (who later called himself Mabuse after his native city Maubeuge) entered the service of Philip, the illegitimate son of the duke of Burgundy, accompanying him to Italy in 1508, and remaining in his service after Philip became archbishop of Utrecht in 1517.

Gossaert's "Romanizing" style—inspired by Italian Mannerist paintings and decorative details drawn from ancient Roman art—is evident in his painting of **ST. LUKE DRAWING THE VIRGIN MARY** (**FIG. 22-22**), a traditional subject we already know from a painting by Rogier van der Weyden (see FIG. 19-17). In Gossaert's version, the artist's studio is an extraordinary structure of Classical piers and arches, carved with a dense ornament of foliage and medallions. Mary and the Christ Child appear in a blaze of golden light and clouds before the saint, who kneels at a desk, his hand guided by an angel as he records the vision in a drawing. Luke's crumpled red robe replicates fifteenth-century drapery conventions in a seeming reference to Rogier's famous picture. Seated above and behind Luke on a round, columnar structure, Moses holds the Tablets of the Law, referencing his own visions of God on Mount Sinai. Just as Moses had removed his shoes in God's presence, so has Luke in the presence of his vision. Gossaert, like Dürer before him, seems to be staking a claim for the divine inspiration of the artist.

22-22 • Jan Gossaert ST. LUKE DRAWING THE VIRGIN MARY
1520. Oil on panel, 43⅜″ × 32¼″ (110.2 × 81.9 cm). Kunsthistorisches Museum, Vienna.

ANTWERP

During the sixteenth century, Antwerp was the commercial and artistic center of the southern Netherlands. Its deep port made it an international center of trade (it was one of the European centers for trade in spices), and it was the financial center of Europe. Painting, printmaking, and book production flourished in this environment, attracting artists and craftsmakers from all over Europe. The demand for luxury goods fostered the birth of the art market, in which art was transformed into a commodity for both local and international consumption. In responding to this market system, many artists became specialists in one area, such as portraiture or landscape, working with art dealers, who emerged as middlemen, further shaping the commodification of art, its production, and its producers.

QUENTIN MASSYS Early accounts of the prosperous Antwerp artist Quentin Massys (1466–1530) claim that he began working in his native Louvain as a blacksmith (his father's profession) but changed to painting to compete with a rival for the affections of a young woman; Carel van Mander claims he was a self-trained

22-23 • Quentin Massys MONEY CHANGER AND HIS WIFE
1514. Oil on panel, 28″ × 26¾″ (71.2 × 68 cm). Kunsthistorisches Museum, Vienna.

artist. We know he entered the Antwerp painters' guild in 1491, and at his death in 1530 he was among its most prosperous and renowned members, supervising a large workshop to meet the market in this burgeoning art center.

One of his most fascinating paintings—**MONEY CHANGER AND HIS WIFE** (FIG. 22-23)—recalls, like Gossaert's *St. Luke*, a famous fifteenth-century work, in this case the picture of a goldsmith painted for the Antwerp goldsmiths' guild by Petrus Christus (see "A Closer Look," page 583). Here, however, a couple is in charge of business, and they present us with two different profiles of engagement. The soberly dressed proprietor himself focuses intently on weighing coins in a suspended balance. His brightly outfitted wife—dressed in an archaic fifteenth-century costume that harks back to a golden age of Flemish painting—looks to the side, distracted by her husband's activity from the attention she was giving to the meticulously described Book of Hours spread out on the table in front of her. It would be easy to jump to the conclusion that this is a moral fable, warning of the danger of losing "sight" of religious obligations because of a preoccupation with affairs of business. But the painting is not that simple. An inscription that ran around the original frame quoted Leviticus 19:36—"You shall have honest balances and honest weights"—claiming just business practices as a form of righteous living. Is it possible the moral here juxtaposes not worldliness and spirituality, but attentive and distracted devotional practice? The sidetracked wife seems to have been idly flipping through her prayer book before turning to observe what her husband is doing, whereas a man in a red turban reflected in the convex mirror next to her Book of Hours is caught in rapt attention to the book in front of him, and the nature of his reading is suggested by the church steeple through the window behind him. The sermon here concerns the challenge of godly living in a worldly society, but wealth itself is not necessarily the root of the problem.

CATERINA VAN HEMESSEN Antwerp painter Caterina van Hemessen (1528–1587) developed an illustrious reputation as a portraitist. She had learned to paint from her father, the Flemish Mannerist Jan Sanders van Hemessen, who was dean of the Antwerp painters' guild in 1548, but the quiet realism and skilled rendering of her subjects is distinctively her own. To maintain focus on her foreground subjects, van Hemessen painted

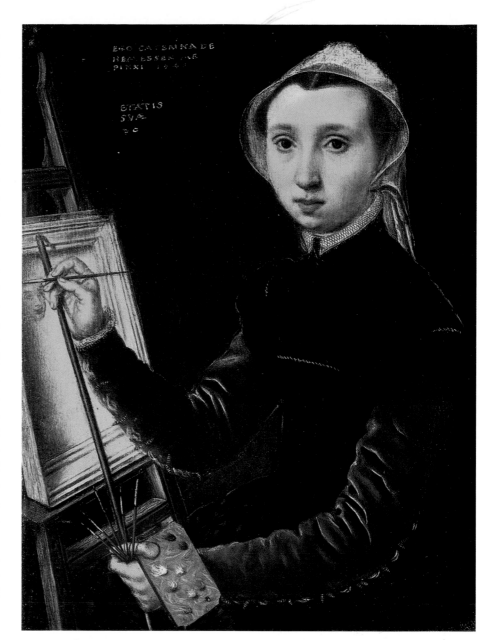

22-24 • Caterina van Hemessen SELF-PORTRAIT
1548. Oil on wood panel, 12¼″ × 9¼″ (31.1 × 23.5 cm). Öffentliche Kunstsammlung, Basel.

them against even, dark-colored backgrounds, on which she identified the sitter by name and age, signing and dating each work. The inscription in her **SELF-PORTRAIT** (FIG. 22-24) reads: "I Caterina van Hemessen painted myself in 1548. Her age 20." In delineating her own features, van Hemessen presented a serious young person who looks up to acknowledge us, interrupting her work on a portrait of a woman client. Between the date of this self-portrait and 1552, she painted ten signed and dated portraits of women, which seems to have been a specialty. She became a favored court artist to Mary of Hungary, sister of Emperor Charles V and regent of the Netherlands, for whom she painted not only portraits but also religious works, and whom she followed back to Spain when Mary ceased to be regent in 1556.

Cycles, or series, of paintings unified by a developing theme or allegorical subject—for instance, the Times of the Day, the Four Seasons, or the Five Senses—became popular wall decorations in prosperous Flemish homes during the sixteenth century. In 1565, Pieter Bruegel the Elder was commissioned to paint a series of six large paintings, each over 5 feet wide, surveying the months of the year, two months to a picture. They were made to be hung together in a room—probably the dining room since food figures prominently in these pictures—in the suburban villa of wealthy merchant Nicolaes Jonghelinck, just outside Antwerp.

RETURN OF THE HUNTERS (FIG. 22-25) represents December and January. The bleak landscape is gripped by winter as hunters return home at dusk with meager results: a single rabbit slung over the largest man's shoulder. But the landscape, rather than the figures, seems to be the principal subject here. A row of trees forms a receding set, consistently diminishing in scale, to draw our attention into the space of the painting along the orthogonal descent on the hillside of houses on the left. Like the calendar illustrations of medieval Books of Hours, the landscape is filled with behavior emblematic of the time of year: the singeing of the pig outside the farmhouse at left, the playful movement of ice skaters across frozen fields. We see it all from an omnipotent elevated viewpoint, like one of the birds that perch in the trees or glide across the snow-covered fantasy of an alpine background.

The mood is very different in the painting representing the hazy late summer days of August and September (**FIG. 22-26**). Birds still perch and glide, and a silhouetted tree still dominates the foreground—as if Bruegel wanted to set up obvious relationships between the scenes so that viewers would assess them comparatively—but the setting here is more rural than residential. Architecture keeps its distance or is screened by foliage. Agricultural workers trudge through their labor, harvesting grain, and gathering stalks into tidy sheaves, ready for transport. The figural focus, however, is in the foreground, on a shift of workers on their lunch break—serving themselves from baskets, gnawing on hard pieces of bread, spooning milk from bowls, or gulping from an uplifted jug. One man takes the

22-25 • Pieter Bruegel the Elder RETURN OF THE HUNTERS
1565. Oil on wood panel, 3'10½" × 5'3¾" (1.18 × 1.61 m). Kunsthistorisches Museum, Vienna.

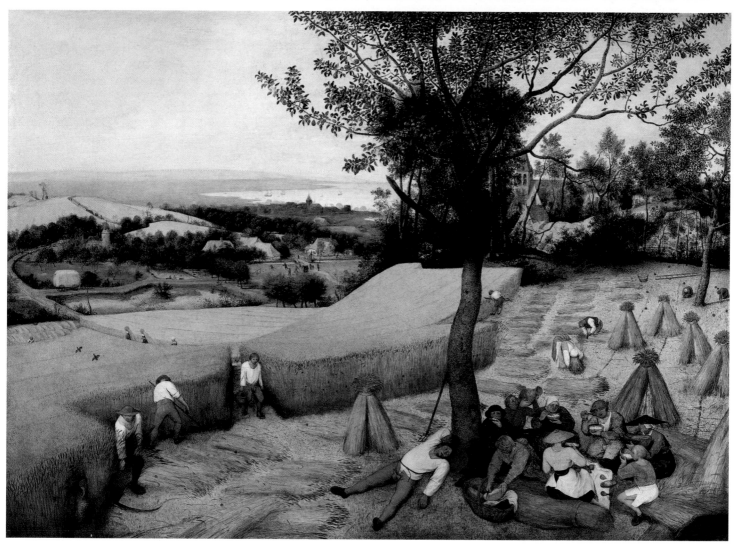

22-26 • Pieter Bruegel the Elder THE HARVESTERS
1565. Oil on wood panel, 46⅞″ × 63¾″ (1.17 × 1.6 m). Metropolitan Museum of Art, New York. Rogers Fund, 1919. (19.164)

opportunity of this break for a quick nap. Some have seen in this lounging figure an emblem of sloth, or a wanton display of uncouth behavior, reminiscent of the embarrassing exposure of the peasant couple invited in to warm themselves before the fire in the farmhouse of the February page of Duke Jean de Berry's *Très Riches Heures* (see FIG. 19–5), painted by the Netherlandish Limbourg brothers a century and a half earlier.

Indeed, Bruegel's series of the months invites comparison with this venerable tradition—dating to the early Middle Ages—of showing peasant activity within the calendar cycles of prayer books made for wealthy patrons. Were they amused by peasant behavior? Did they enjoy representations of the productivity of their land and the availability of willing laborers to work it? Or do these vignettes embody their own longings for a

simpler life, idealized for them as a harmony between the natural world and the people who live on it, and off it? But the peasants enjoying the good life in this sunny scene of harvesting are only on a lunch break. Another shift is already hard at work in the fields, and the wealth of the patrons who supported the growth of an art market was dependent on the labor of countless folks like them.

Read the document related to Pieter Bruegel on myartslab.com

A CLOSER LOOK | *The French Ambassadors*

by Hans Holbein the Younger. 1533. Oil on wood panel.
81⅛″ × 82⅝″ (2.07 × 2.1 m). National Gallery, London.

Embossing on the sheath of the dagger tells us that de Dinteville is 28, while an inscription on the edge of the book (Bible?) under de Selve's arm records that he is 24.

This globe has Polisy, the de Dinteville family estate, marked at the center. It was here that this painting was hung when the ambassador returned to France at the end of 1533.

These objects on the top shelf were used to observe natural heavenly phenomena and chart the passage of time. The items displayed on the lower shelf relate more to terrestrial concerns.

Music is a common symbol of harmony in this period, and the broken string on this lute has been understood as an allusion to the discord created by the sweep of Protestant reform across Europe.

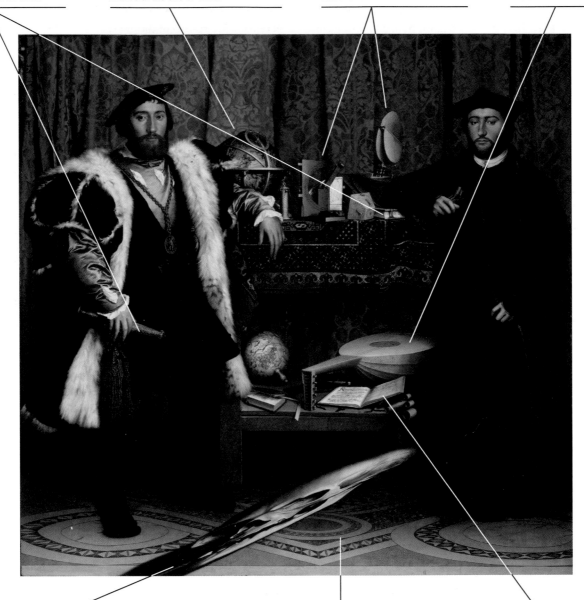

This bizarre, but prominently placed skull—as well as the skull badge that appears on de Dinteville's cap—reminded viewers of their own mortality. The foreground skull is distorted by anamorphosis, in which images are stretched horizontally with the use of a trapezoidal grid so that they must be viewed from the side to appear correctly proportioned.

This pavement—known as "Cosmati work" after the thirteenth-century Italian family that specialized in it—is copied from the floor in Westminster Abbey and may proclaim the ambassadors' involvement in a holy enterprise of reconciliation. The artist signed the painting on the left edge of the floor: "Johannes Holbein pingebat, 1533."

This is a Lutheran hymnal published in 1527, open at one of Luther's best-known compositions: "Come, Holy Ghost, our souls inspire." Neither man was a Protestant, but some of de Selve's contemporaries saw him as sympathetic to the cause of the reformers.

 View the Closer Look for *The French Ambassadors* on myartslab.com

PIETER BRUEGEL THE ELDER So popular did the works of Hieronymus Bosch remain that, nearly half a century after his death, Pieter Bruegel (c. 1525–1569) began his career by imitating them. Like Bosch, he often painted large narrative works crowded with figures, and he chose moralizing or satirical subject matter. He traveled throughout Italy, but, unlike many Renaissance artists, he did not record the ruins of ancient Rome or the wonders of the Italian cities. Instead, he seems to have been fascinated by the landscape, particularly the formidable jagged rocks and sweeping panoramic views of Alpine valleys, which he recorded in detailed drawings. Back home in his studio, he made an impressive leap of the imagination as he painted the flat and rolling lands of Flanders as broad panoramas, even adding imaginary mountains on the horizon. He also visited country fairs to sketch the farmers and townspeople who became the focus of his paintings, presenting humans not as unique individuals but as well-observed types, whose universality makes them familiar even today.

Bruegel depicted nature in all seasons and in all moods. *Return of the Hunters* (see "Bruegel's Cycle of the Months," page 704) captures the bleak atmosphere of early nightfall during a damp, cold winter, with a freshness that recalls the much earlier paintings of his compatriots the Limbourgs (see FIG. 19-5). The hunters are foregrounded before a sharp plunge into space; the juxtaposition of near and far without middle ground is a typically sixteenth-century device. But this is clearly not an accidental image; it is a slice of everyday life faithfully reproduced within a carefully calculated composition. The same can be said of Bruegel's portrayal of late summer harvest (see FIG. 22-26), where the light is warmer, the landscape lush and verdant, the human activity rooted in agricultural labor or a momentary respite from it. As a depiction of Netherlandish life, these peasant scenes focusing on landscape represent a relative calm before the storm. Three years after they were painted, the anguished struggle of the northern provinces for independence from Spain began.

ENGLAND

Tudor England, in spite of the disruption caused by the Reformation, was economically and politically stable enough to provide sustained support for the arts, as Henry VIII strived to compete with the wealthy, sophisticated court of Francis I. Music, literature, and architecture flourished, but painting was principally left to foreigners.

As a young man, Henry VIII (r. 1509–1547) was loyal to the Church, defending it against Luther's attacks. He was rewarded by the pope in 1521 by being granted the title "Defender of the Faith." But when the pope refused to annul his marriage to Catherine of Aragon, Henry broke with Rome. By action of Parliament in 1534 he became the "Supreme Head on Earth of the Church and Clergy of England." He mandated an English translation of the Bible in every church, and in 1536 and 1539, he dissolved the monasteries, confiscating their great wealth and rewarding his followers with monastic lands and buildings. Shrines and altars were stripped of their jewels and precious metals to bolster the royal purse, and in 1548, during the reign of Henry's son, Edward VI, religious images were officially prohibited.

During the brief reign of Mary (r. 1553–1558), England officially returned to Catholicism, but the accession of Elizabeth in 1558 confirmed England as a Protestant country. So effective was Elizabeth, who ruled until 1603, that the last decades of the sixteenth century in England are called the Elizabethan Age.

ARTISTS IN THE TUDOR COURT

A remarkable record of the appearance of Tudor notables survives in portraiture. Since the Tudors had long favored Netherlandish and German artists, it is hardly surprising that it was a German-born painter, Hans Holbein the Younger (c. 1497–1543), who shaped the taste of the English court and upper classes.

HANS HOLBEIN Holbein first visited London from 1526 to 1528 and was introduced by the Dutch scholar Erasmus to the humanist circle around the English statesman Thomas More. He returned to England in 1532 and was appointed court painter to Henry VIII about four years later. During the 1530s, he created a spectacular series of portraits of nobles and diplomats associated with the Tudor court. The court's climate of international interaction is captured in a double portrait that Holbein painted in 1533 (see "A Closer Look," opposite)—a German painter's rendering in England of two French diplomats, one of them representing the court of Francis I in the Vatican. *The French Ambassadors* foregrounds Holbein's virtuosity as a painter and constructs a rich characterization of Jean de Dinteville, French ambassador to England, and his friend Georges de Selve, bishop of Lavaur and ambassador to the Holy See. With a loving detail that recalls the work of Jan van Eyck, the artist describes the surface textures and luminosity of the many objects placed in the painting to reflect the intellectual gifts and symbolize the political accomplishments of these two men. References in these objects to the conflicts between European states, and within the Catholic Church itself, imply that these bright and confident young ambassadors will apply their considerable diplomatic skills to finding a resolution.

PORTRAITS OF ELIZABETH Queen Elizabeth I carefully controlled the way artists represented her in official portraits and was known to have imprisoned artists whose unofficial images did not meet with her approval. A stark and hieratic regal image by Flemish artist Marcus Gheeraerts typifies the look she was after (FIG. 22-27). Called the Ditchley Portrait because it seems to have been commissioned for Ditchley, the estate of her courtier Sir Henry Lee, to commemorate the Queen's visit in 1592, the full-length figure of Elizabeth—more costume than body—stands supreme on a map of her realm with her feet in Oxfordshire, near Ditchley. The stark whiteness of her elaborate dress and the pale abstraction of her severe face assert the virginal purity that she cultivated as a part of her image. A storm passes out of the picture

22-28 • Nicholas Hilliard **GEORGE CLIFFORD, THIRD EARL OF CUMBERLAND**
c. 1595. Watercolor on vellum on card, oval 2¾″ × 2³⁄₁₆″
(7.1 × 5.8 cm). The Nelson-Atkins Museum of Art, Kansas
City, Missouri. Gift of Mr. and Mrs. John W. Starr through the
Starr Foundation. F58-60/188

on the right while the sun breaks through on the left. It is as if the queen is in control not only of England but of nature itself.

NICHOLAS HILLIARD In 1570, Nicholas Hilliard (1547–1619) arrived in London from southwest England to pursue a career as a jeweler, goldsmith, and painter of miniatures. Hilliard never received a court appointment, but he created miniature portraits of the queen and court notables, including **GEORGE CLIFFORD** (1558–1605), third earl of Cumberland (**FIG. 22-28**). Cumberland was a regular participant in the annual tilts and festivals celebrating the anniversary of Elizabeth's ascent to the throne. In Hilliard's miniature, Cumberland, a man of about 30, wears a richly engraved and gold-inlaid suit of armor, forged for his first appearance in 1583 (see "Armor for Royal Games," opposite). Hilliard gives him a marked air of courtly jauntiness, with a stylish beard, mustache, and curled hair, but Cumberland is also humanized by his direct gaze and receding

The medieval tradition of holding tilting, or jousting, competitions at English festivals and public celebrations continued during Renaissance times. Perhaps most famous were the Accession Day Tilts, held annually to celebrate the anniversary of Elizabeth I's coming to the throne. The gentlemen of the court, dressed in armor made especially for the occasion, held mock battles in the queen's honor. They rode their horses from opposite directions, trying to strike each other with long lances during six passes, as judges rated their performances.

The elegant armor worn by George Clifford, third Earl of Cumberland, at the Accession Day Tilts has been preserved in the collection of the Metropolitan Museum of Art in New York (FIG. 22–29). Tudor roses and back-to-back capital *E*s in honor of the queen decorate the armor's surface. As the queen's champion, beginning in 1590, Clifford also wore her jeweled glove attached to his helmet as he met all comers in the tiltyard of Whitehall Palace in London.

Made by Jacob Halder in the royal armories at Greenwich, the 60-pound suit of armor is recorded in the sixteenth-century Almain Armourers' Album along with its "exchange pieces." These allowed the owner to vary his appearance by changing mitts, side pieces, or leg protectors, and also provided backup pieces if one were damaged.

22-29 • Jacob Halder ARMOR OF GEORGE CLIFFORD, THIRD EARL OF CUMBERLAND
Made in the royal workshop at Greenwich, England. c. 1580–1585. Steel and gold, height 5′9½″ (1.77 m). Metropolitan Museum of Art, New York. Munsey Fund, 1932 (32.130.6)

hairline. Cumberland's motto—"I bear lightning and water"—is inscribed on a stormy sky, with a lightning bolt in the form of a caduceus, one of his emblems. After all, he was that remarkable Elizabethan type—a naval commander and a gentleman pirate.

ARCHITECTURE

To increase support for the Tudor dynasty, Henry and his successors granted titles to rich landowners. To display their wealth and status, many of these newly created aristocrats embarked on extensive building projects, constructing lavish country residences, which sometimes surpassed the French châteaux in size and grandeur. Rooted in the Perpendicular Gothic style (see FIG. 18–22), Elizabethan architecture's severe walls and broad expanses of glass were modernized by replacing medieval ornament with Classical motifs copied from architectural handbooks and pattern books. The first architectural manual in English, published in 1563, was written by John Shute, one of the few builders who had spent time in Italy. Most influential were the treatises on architectural design by the Italian architect Sebastiano Serlio.

HARDWICK HALL One of the grandest of all the Elizabethan houses was Hardwick Hall, the home of Elizabeth, countess of Shrewsbury, known as "Bess of Hardwick" (FIG. 22–30). When she was in her seventies, the redoubtable countess—who inherited riches from all four of her deceased husbands—employed Robert Smythson (c. 1535–1614), England's first Renaissance architect, to build Hardwick Hall (1591–1597).

The medieval great hall was transformed into a two-story entrance hall, with rooms arranged symmetrically around it—a nod to Classical balance. A sequence of rooms leads to a grand stair up to the long gallery and **HIGH GREAT CHAMBER** on the second floor that featured an ornately carved fireplace (FIG. 22–31). It was here the countess received guests, entertained, and sometimes dined. Illuminated by enormous windows, the room seems designed to showcase a precious set of six Brussels tapestries featuring the story of Ulysses. They serve as yet another reminder of the international character of the lavish decoration of residences created for wealthy Renaissance patrons throughout Europe during the sixteenth century.

22-30 • Robert Smythson HARDWICK HALL
Derbyshire, England. 1591–1597.

22-31 • Robert Smythson HIGH GREAT CHAMBER, HARDWICK HALL
Derbyshire, England. 1591–1597. Brussels tapestries 1550s; painted plaster sculpture by Abraham Smith.

THINK ABOUT IT

22.1 Explore the impact of Italian art and ideas on the work and persona of German artist Albrecht Dürer. Choose one of his works from the chapter, and discuss its Italianate features and the ways in which it departs from and draws on earlier northern European traditions.

22.2 Discuss the impact of the Protestant Reformation on the visual arts in northern Europe, focusing your discussion on types of subject matter that patrons sought.

22.3 Choose one European court that employed artists working in a "foreign" tradition from another part of Europe and assess how this internationalism fostered the breaking down of regional and national boundaries in European art. Be sure to ground your discussion in the work of specific artists.

22.4 Choose a work of art discussed in this chapter that displays extraordinary technical skill in more than one medium. How was its virtuosity achieved, and how is it highlighted as an important factor in the work's significance?

CROSSCURRENTS

FIG. 19–17

FIG. 22–22

Gossaert's painting of St. Luke drawing the Virgin Mary suggests that he knew Rogier van der Weyden's famous earlier painting of the same subject. Compare these two works, separated in date by almost a century, discussing Gossaert's references to Rogier's painting but also characterizing the way each of these two artists embodied the style that characterizes their particular moment in the history of art. What did these paintings mean for their original audience?

✓—⌈**Study** and review on myartslab.com

23–1 • Gianlorenzo Bernini ST. TERESA OF ÁVILA IN ECSTASY
Cornaro Chapel, church of Santa Maria della Vittoria, Rome. 1645–1652. Marble, height of the group 11′6″ (3.5 m).

Seventeenth-Century Art in Europe

In the church of Santa Maria della Vittoria in Rome, the sixteenth-century Spanish mystic **ST. TERESA OF ÁVILA** (1515–1582, canonized 1622) swoons in ecstasy on a bank of billowing marble clouds (**FIG. 23–1**). A puckish angel tugs open her robe, aiming a gilded arrow at her breast. Gilded bronze rays of supernatural light descend, even as actual light illuminates the figures from a hidden window above. This dramatic scene, created by Gianlorenzo Bernini (1598–1680) between 1645 and 1652, represents a famous vision described with startling physical clarity by Teresa, in which an angel pierced her body repeatedly with an arrow, transporting her to a state of ecstatic oneness with God, charged with erotic associations.

The sculpture is an exquisite example of the emotional, theatrical style perfected by Bernini in response to the religious and political climate in Rome during the period of spiritual renewal known as the Counter-Reformation. Many had seen the Protestant Reformation of the previous century as an outgrowth of Renaissance Humanism with its emphasis on rationality and independent thinking. In response, the Catholic Church took a reactionary, authoritarian position, supported by the new Society of Jesus founded by Ignatius of Loyola (d. 1556, canonized 1622). In the "spiritual exercises" (1522–1523) initiated by St. Ignatius, Christians were enjoined to use all their senses to transport themselves emotionally as they imagined the events on which they were meditating. They were to feel the burning fires of hell or the bliss of heaven, the lashing of the whips and the flesh-piercing crown of thorns. Art became an instrument of propaganda and also a means of leading the spectator to a reinvigorated Christian practice and belief.

Of course, the arts had long been used to convince or inspire, but nowhere more effectively than by the Catholic Church in the seventeenth century. To serve the educational and evangelical mission of the revitalized and conservative Church, paintings and sculpture had to depict events and people accurately and clearly, following guidelines established by religious leaders. Throughout Catholic Europe, painters such as Rubens and Caravaggio created brilliant religious art under official Church sponsorship. And although today some viewers find this sculpture of St. Teresa uncomfortably charged with sexuality, the Church approved of the depictions of such sensational and supernatural mystical visions. They helped worshipers achieve the emotional state of religious ecstasy that was a goal of the Counter-Reformation.

LEARN ABOUT IT

23.1 Explore how the work of Bernini and Caravaggio established a new dramatic intensity, technical virtuosity, and unvarnished naturalism that blossomed into a style we call Baroque that spread across Europe during the seventeenth century.

23.2 Examine the development of portraiture, still life, landscape, and genre scenes as major subjects for painting, especially within the prosperous art market of the Netherlands.

23.3 Analyze the way that seventeenth-century artists created works that embodied the power and prestige of the monarchy as well as works that furthered the Counter-Reformation agenda of the Roman Catholic Church.

23.4 Assess the resurgence of Classicism, especially in the work of seventeenth-century French artists and architects.

((•— Listen to the chapter audio on myartslab.com

"BAROQUE"

The intellectual and political forces set in motion by the Renaissance and Reformation of the fifteenth and sixteenth centuries intensified during the seventeenth century. Religious wars continued, although gradually the Protestant forces gained control in the north, where Spain recognized the independence of the Dutch Republic in 1648. Catholicism maintained its primacy in southern Europe, the Holy Roman Empire, and France through the efforts of an energized papacy, aided by the new Society of Jesus, also known as the Jesuit Order (**MAP 23-1**). At the same time, scientific advances compelled people to question their worldview. Of great importance was the growing understanding that the Earth was not the center of the universe, but a planet revolving around the sun. As rulers' economic strength began to slip away, artists found patrons in the Church and the secular state, as well as in the newly confident and prosperous urban middle class. What evolved was a style that art historians have called "Baroque." The label may be related to the Italian word *barocco*, a jeweler's term for an irregularly shaped pearl—something beautiful, fascinating, and strange.

Baroque art deliberately evokes intense emotional responses from viewers. Dramatically lit, theatrical compositions often combine several media within a single work as artists highlight their technical virtuosity. But the seventeenth century also saw its own version of Classicism, a more moving and dramatic variant of Renaissance ideals and principles featuring idealization based on observation of the material world; balanced (though often asymmetrical) compositions; diagonal movement in space; rich, harmonious colors; and the inclusion of visual references to ancient Greece and Rome. Many seventeenth-century artists sought lifelike depiction of their world in portraiture, **genre paintings** (scenes from everyday life), still life (paintings of inanimate objects such as food, fruit, or flowers), and religious scenes enacted by ordinary people in ordinary settings. Intense emotional involvement, lifelike renderings, and Classical references may exist in the same work, and are all part of the stylistic complexion of the seventeenth century.

The role of viewers also changed. Italian Renaissance painters and patrons had been fascinated with the visual possibilities of perspective and treasured idealism of form and subject which kept viewers at a distance, reflecting intellectually on what they were seeing. Seventeenth-century masters, on the other hand, sought to engage viewers as participants in the work of art, and often reached out to incorporate or activate the world beyond the frame into the nature and meaning of the work itself. In Catholic countries, representations of horrifying scenes of martyrdom or the passionate spiritual life of mystics in religious ecstasy sought to inspire viewers to a reinvigorated faith by making them feel what was going on, not simply by causing them to think about it. In Protestant countries, images of communal parades and city views sought to inspire pride in civic accomplishments. Viewers participated in works of art like audiences in a theater—vicariously but completely—as the work of art drew them visually and emotionally into its orbit. The

seventeenth-century French critic Roger de Piles (1635–1709) described this exchange when he wrote: "True painting ... calls to us; and has so powerful an effect, that we cannot help coming near it, as if it had something to tell us" (Puttfarken, p. 55).

ITALY

Seventeenth-century Italy remained a divided land in spite of a common history, language, and geography. The Kingdom of Naples and Sicily was Spanish; the Papal States crossed the center; Venice maintained its independence as a republic; and the north remained divided among small principalities. Churchmen and their families remained powerful patrons of the arts, especially as they sought to use art in revitalizing the Roman Catholic Church. The Council of Trent (concluded 1563) had set guidelines for Church art that went against the arcane, worldly, and often lascivious trends exploited by Mannerism. The clergy's call for clarity, simplicity, chaste subject matter, and the ability to rouse a very Catholic piety in the face of Protestant revolt found a response in the fresh approaches to subject matter and style offered by a new generation of artists.

ARCHITECTURE AND SCULPTURE IN ROME

A major goal of the Counter-Reformation was the proper embellishment of churches and their settings. Pope Sixtus V (pontificate 1585–1590) had begun the renewal in Rome by cutting long, straight avenues through the city to link the major pilgrimage churches with one another and with the main gates of Rome. Sixtus also ordered open spaces—piazzas—to be cleared in front of major churches, marking each site with an Egyptian obelisk. In a practical vein, he also reopened one of the ancient aqueducts to stabilize the city's water supply. Unchallengeable power and vast financial resources were required to carry out such an extensive plan of urban renewal and to refashion Rome—parts of which had been the victim of rapacity and neglect since the Middle Ages—once more into the center of spiritual and worldly power.

The Counter-Reformation popes had great wealth, although they eventually nearly bankrupted the Church with their building programs. Sixtus began to renovate the Vatican and its library; he completed the dome of St. Peter's and built splendid palaces. The Renaissance ideal of the central-plan church continued to be used for the shrines of saints, but Counter-Reformation thinking called for churches with long, wide naves to accommodate large congregations assembled to hear inspiring sermons as well as to participate in the Mass. In the sixteenth century, the decoration of new churches had been relatively austere, but seventeenth- and eighteenth-century Catholic taste favored opulent and spectacular visual effects to heighten the emotional involvement of worshipers.

ST. PETER'S BASILICA IN THE VATICAN Half a century after Michelangelo had returned St. Peter's Basilica to Bramante's original vision of a central-plan building, Pope Paul V Borghese

MAP 23-1 • SEVENTEENTH-CENTURY EUROPE

Protestantism still dominated northern Europe, while in the south Roman Catholicism remained strong after the Counter-Reformation. The Habsburg empire was now divided into two parts, under separate rulers.

(pontificate 1605–21) commissioned Carlo Maderno (1556–1629) to provide the church with a longitudinal nave and a new façade (**FIG. 23-2**). Construction began in 1607, and everything but the façade bell towers was completed by 1615 (see "St. Peter's Basilica," page 653). Rooted in the design of of Il Gesù's façade (see FIG. 21-40), Maderno's façade for St. Peter's steps forward in three progressively projecting planes: from the corners to the doorways flanking the central entrance area, then the entrance area, then the central doorway itself. Similarly, the colossal orders connecting the first and second stories are flat pilasters at the corners but fully round columns where they flank the doorways. These columns support a continuous entablature that also steps out—following the columns—as it moves toward the central door.

When Maderno died in 1629, Gianlorenzo Bernini (1598–1680), his collaborator of five years, succeeded him as Vatican architect. Bernini was taught by his father, and part of his training involved sketching the Vatican collection of ancient sculpture, such as *Laocoön and His Sons* (see FIG. 5-64), as well as the many examples of Renaissance painting in the papal palace. Throughout his life, Bernini admired antique art and, like other artists of this period, considered himself a Classicist. Today, we not only appreciate his strong debt to the Renaissance tradition but also acknowledge the way he broke through that tradition to develop a new, Baroque style.

When Urban VIII was elected pope in 1623, he unhesitatingly gave the young Bernini the daunting task of designing an enormous bronze baldachin, or canopy, over the high altar of St. Peter's. The church was so large that a dramatic focus on the altar was essential. The resulting **BALDACCHINO** (**FIG. 23-3**), completed in 1633, stands almost 100 feet high and exemplifies the

23-2 • Carlo Maderno and Gianlorenzo Bernini ST. PETER'S BASILICA AND PIAZZA, VATICAN, ROME
Maderno, façade, 1607–1626; Bernini, piazza design, c. 1656–1657.

Perhaps only a Baroque artist of Bernini's talents could have unified the many artistic periods and styles that come together in St. Peter's Basilica (starting with Bramante's original design for the building in the sixteenth century). The basilica in no way suggests a piecing together of parts made by different builders at different times but rather presents itself as a triumphal unity of all the parts in one coherent whole.

Baroque objective to create multimedia works, combining architecture and sculpture—and sometimes painting as well—that defy simple categorization. The gigantic corner columns symbolize the union of Christianity and its Jewish tradition—the vine of the Eucharist climbing the twisted columns associated with the Temple of Solomon. They support an entablature with a crowning element topped with an orb (a sphere representing the universe) and a cross (symbolizing the reign of Christ). Figures of angels and *putti* decorate the entablature, which is hung with tasseled panels in imitation of a cloth canopy. This imposing work not only marks the site of the tomb of St. Peter, but also serves as a tribute to Urban VIII and his family, the Barberini, whose emblems— honeybees and suns on the tasseled panels, and laurel leaves on the climbing vines—are prominently displayed.

Between 1627 and 1641, Bernini and several other sculptors, again in multimedia extravaganzas, rebuilt Bramante's crossing piers as giant reliquaries. Statues of SS. Helena, Veronica, Andrew, and Longinus stand in niches below alcoves containing

their relics, to the left and right of the *baldacchino*. Visible through the *baldacchino*'s columns in the apse of the church is another reliquary: the gilded-stone, bronze, and stucco shrine made by Bernini between 1657 and 1666 for the ancient wooden throne thought to have belonged to St. Peter as the first bishop of Rome. The Chair of Peter symbolized the direct descent of Christian authority from Peter to the current pope, a belief rejected by Protestants and therefore deliberately emphasized in Counter-Reformation Catholicism. Above the shrine, a brilliant stained-glass window portrays the Holy Spirit as a dove surrounded by an oval of golden rays. Adoring gilded angels and gilt-bronze rays fan out around the window and seem to extend the penetration of the natural light— and the Holy Spirit—into the apse of the church. The gilding also reflects the light back to the window, creating a dazzling, ethereal effect that the seventeenth century, with its interest in mystics and visions, would equate with the activation of divinity.

At approximately the same time that he was at work on the Chair of Peter, Bernini designed and supervised the building of a

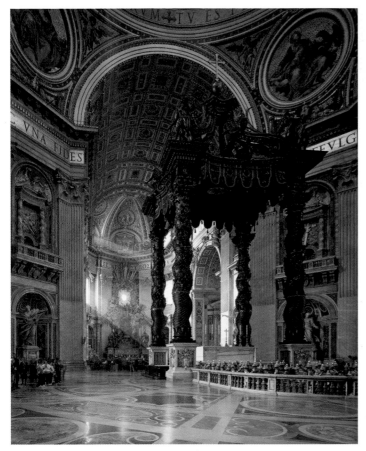

23-3 • Gianlorenzo Bernini BALDACCHINO
St. Peter's Basilica, Vatican, Rome. 1624–1633. Gilt bronze, height approx. 100′ (30.48 m). Chair of Peter shrine, 1657–1666; gilt bronze, marble, stucco, and glass. Pier decorations, 1627–1641; gilt bronze and marble.

BERNINI AS SCULPTOR Even after Bernini's appointment as Vatican architect in 1629, he was still able to accept outside commissions by virtue of his large workshop. In fact, he first became famous as a sculptor, and he continued to create sculpture throughout his career, for both the papacy and private clients. A man of many talents, he was also a painter and even a playwright—an interest that dovetailed with his genius for theatrical and dramatic presentation.

Bernini's **DAVID** (**FIG. 23-4**), made for a nephew of Pope Paul V in 1623, introduced a new type of three-dimensional composition that intrudes forcefully into the viewer's space. The young hero bends at the waist and twists far to one side, ready to launch the lethal rock at Goliath. Unlike Donatello's sassy boy (see **FIG. 20-14**) and Verrocchio's poised and proud adolescent (see **FIG. 20-34**)—both already victorious—or Michelangelo's pensive young man contemplating the task ahead (see **FIG. 21-10**), Bernini's more mature David, with his lean, sinewy body, tightly clenched mouth, and straining muscles, is all tension, action, and determination. By creating a twisting figure caught in movement, Bernini

23-4 • Gianlorenzo Bernini DAVID
1623. Marble, height 5′7″ (1.7 m). Galleria Borghese, Rome.

colonnade to form a huge double piazza in front of the entrance to St. Peter's (see **FIG. 23-2**). The open space that he had to work with was irregular, and an Egyptian obelisk and a fountain previously installed by Sixtus V had to be incorporated into the overall plan. Bernini's remarkable design frames the oval piazza with two enormous curved porticos, or covered walkways, supported by Tuscan columns. These curved porticos are connected to two straight porticos, which lead up a slight incline to the two ends of the church façade. Bernini characterized his design as the "motherly arms of the Church" reaching out to the world. He had intended to build a third section of the colonnade closing the side of the piazza facing the church so that only after pilgrims had crossed the Tiber River bridge and made their way through narrow streets, would they encounter the enormous open space before the imposing church. This element of surprise would have made the basilica and its setting an even more awe-inspiring vision. The approach today—along the grand avenue of the Via della Conciliazione running from the Tiber to the Basilica—was conceived by Mussolini in 1936 as part of his masterplan to transform Rome into a grand fascist capital.

23-5 • Gianlorenzo Bernini **CORNARO CHAPEL, CHURCH OF SANTA MARIA DELLA VITTORIA, ROME**
1642–1652.

📖—**Read** the document related to Gianlorenzo Bernini on myartslab.com

👁—**Watch** an architectural simulation about the Cornaro Chapel on myartslab.com

In the center of the chapel and framed by columns in the huge oval niche above the altar, Bernini's marble group *St. Teresa of Ávila in Ecstasy* (see FIG. 23-1) represents a vision described by the Spanish mystic in which an angel pierced her body repeatedly with an arrow, transporting her to a state of indescribable pain, religious ecstasy, and a sense of oneness with God. St. Teresa and the angel, who seem to float upward on clouds, are cut from a heavy mass of solid marble supported on a seemingly drifting pedestal that was fastened by hidden metal bars to the chapel wall. Bernini's skill at capturing the movements and emotions of these figures is matched by his virtuosity in simulating different textures and colors in the pure white medium of marble; the angel's gauzy, clinging draperies seem silken in contrast with Teresa's heavy woolen monastic robe. Bernini effectively used the configuration of the garment's folds to convey the saint's swooning, sensuous body beneath, even though only Teresa's face, hands, and bare feet are actually visible.

Kneeling against what appear to be balconies on both sides of the chapel are marble portrait sculptures of Federigo, his deceased father (a Venetian doge), and six cardinals of the Cornaro family. The figures are informally posed and naturalistically portrayed. Two read from their prayer books, others exclaim at the miracle taking place in the light-infused realm above the altar, and one leans out from his seat, apparently to look at someone entering the chapel—perhaps the viewer, whose space these figures share. Bernini's intent was not to produce a spectacle for its own sake,

incorporates the surrounding space within his composition, implying the presence of an unseen adversary somewhere behind the viewer. Thus, the viewer becomes part of the action, rather than its displaced and dispassionate observer.

From 1642 until 1652, Bernini worked on the decoration of the funerary chapel of Venetian cardinal Federigo Cornaro (FIG. 23-5) in the Roman church of Santa Maria della Vittoria, designed by Carlo Maderno earlier in the century. The Cornaro family chapel was dedicated to the Spanish saint Teresa of Ávila, canonized only 20 years earlier. Bernini designed it as a rich and theatrical setting for the portrayal of a central event in Teresa's life. He covered the walls with multicolored marble panels and crowned them with a projecting cornice supported by marble pilasters.

but to capture a critical, dramatic moment at its emotional and sensual height, and by doing so guide viewers to identify totally with the event—and perhaps be transformed in the process.

BORROMINI'S CHURCH OF SAN CARLO The intersection of two of the wide, straight avenues created by Pope Sixtus V inspired city planners to add a special emphasis, with fountains marking each of the four corners of the crossing. In 1634, Trinitarian monks decided to build a new church at the site and awarded the commission for San Carlo alle Quattro Fontane (St. Charles at the Four Fountains) to Francesco Borromini (1599–1667). Borromini, a nephew of architect Carlo Maderno, had arrived in Rome in 1619 from northern Italy to enter his uncle's

workshop. Later, he worked under Bernini's supervision on the decoration of St. Peter's, and some details of the *Baldacchino*, as well as its structural engineering, are now attributed to him, but San Carlo was his first independent commission. Unfinished at Borromini's death, the church was nevertheless completed according to his design.

SAN CARLO ALLE QUATTRO FONTANE stands on a narrow piece of land, with one corner cut off to accommodate one of the fountains that give the church its name (**FIG. 23-6**). To fit the irregular site, Borromini created an elongated central-plan interior space with undulating walls. Robust pairs of columns support a massive entablature, over which an oval dome, supported on pendentives, seems to float (**FIG. 23-7**). The coffers (inset panels in geometric shapes) filling the interior of the oval-shaped dome form an eccentric honeycomb of crosses, elongated hexagons, and octagons. These coffers decrease sharply in size as they approach the apex, or highest point, where the dove of the Holy Spirit hovers in a climax that brings together the geometry used in the chapel: oval, octagon, circle, and—very important—a triangle, symbol of the Trinity as well as of the church's patrons. The dome appears to be shimmering and inflating—almost floating up and away—thanks to light sources placed in the lower coffers and the lantern.

It is difficult today to appreciate how audacious Borromini's design for this small church was. He abandoned the modular, additive system of planning taken for granted by every architect since Brunelleschi. He worked instead from an overriding geometrical scheme, as a Gothic architect might, subdividing modular units to

23-6 • Francesco Borromini **FAÇADE (A) AND PLAN (B) OF THE CHURCH OF SAN CARLO ALLE QUATTRO FONTANE**
Rome. 1638–1667.

23-7 • Francesco Borromini VIEW INTO THE DOME OF THE CHURCH OF SAN CARLO ALLE QUATTRO FONTANE Rome. 1638–1667.

undulating, sculpture-filled screen punctuated with large columns and deep concave and convex niches that create dramatic effects of light and shadow. Borromini also gave his façade a strong vertical thrust in the center by placing over the tall doorway a statue-filled niche, then a windowed niche covered with a canopy, then a giant, forward-leaning cartouche held up by angels carved in such high relief that they appear to hover in front of the wall. The entire composition is crowned with a balustrade broken by the sharply pointed frame of the cartouche. As with the design of the building itself, Borromini's façade was enthusiastically imitated in northern Italy and especially in northern and eastern Europe.

PAINTING

Painting in seventeenth-century Italy followed one of two principal paths: the ordered Classicism of the Carracci or the dramatic naturalism of Caravaggio. Although the leading exponents of these paths were northern Italians—the Carracci family was from Bologna, and Caravaggio was born in or near Milan—they were all eventually drawn to Rome, the center of power and patronage. The Carracci family, like Caravaggio, were schooled in northern Italian Renaissance traditions, with its emphasis on *chiaroscuro*, as well as in Venetian color and *sfumato*. The Carracci quite consciously rejected the artifice of the Mannerist style and fused their northern roots with the central Italian High Renaissance insistence on line (*disegno*), compositional structure, and figural solidity. They looked to Raphael, Michelangelo, and antique Classical sculpture for their ideal figural types and their expressive but decorous compositions. Caravaggio, on the other hand, satisfied the Baroque demand for drama and clarity by developing realism in a powerful new direction. He painted people he saw in the world around him—even the lowlife of Rome—and worked directly from models without elaborate drawings and compositional notes. Unlike the Carracci, he claimed to ignore the influence of the great masters so as to focus steadfastly on a sense of immediacy and invention.

obtain more complex, rational shapes. For example, the elongated, octagonal plan of San Carlo is composed of two triangles set base to base along the short axis of the plan (see FIG. 23-6B). This diamond shape is then subdivided into secondary triangular units made by calculating the distances between what will become the concave centers of the four major and five minor niches. Yet Borromini's conception of the whole is not medieval. The chapel is dominated horizontally by a Classical entablature that breaks any surge upward toward the dome. Borromini's treatment of the architectural elements as if they were malleable was also unprecedented. His contemporaries understood immediately what an extraordinary innovation the church represented; the Trinitarian monks who had commissioned it received requests for plans from visitors from all over Europe. Although Borromini's innovative work had little impact on the architecture of Classically minded Rome, it was widely imitated in northern Italy and beyond the Alps.

Borromini's design for San Carlo's façade (see FIG. 23-6A), executed more than two decades later, was as innovative as his planning of the interior. He turned the building's front into an

THE CARRACCI The brothers Agostino (1557–1602) and Annibale Carracci (1560–1609) and their cousin Ludovico (1555–1619) shared a studio in Bologna. As their re-evaluation of the High Renaissance masters attracted interest among their peers, they opened their doors to friends and students and then, in 1582, founded an art academy, where students drew from live models and studied art theory, Renaissance painting, and antique Classical sculpture. The Carracci placed a high value on accurate drawing, complex figure compositions, complicated narratives, and technical expertise in both oil and fresco painting. During its short life, the academy had an impact on the development of the arts—and art education—through its insistence on both life drawing (to achieve naturalism) and aesthetic theory (to achieve artistic harmony).

In 1595, Annibale was hired by Cardinal Odoardo Farnese to decorate the principal rooms of his family's immense Roman palace. In the long *galleria* (gallery), to celebrate the wedding of Duke Ranuccio Farnese of Parma to the niece of the pope, the artist was requested to paint scenes of love based on Ovid's *Metamorphoses* (**FIG. 23-8**). Undoubtedly, Annibale and Agostino, who assisted him, felt both inspiration and competition from the important

Farnese collection of antique sculpture exhibited throughout the palace.

The primary image, set in the center of the vault, is *The Triumph of Bacchus and Ariadne*, a joyous procession celebrating the wine god Bacchus's love for Ariadne, whom he rescued after her lover, Theseus, abandoned her on the island of Naxos. Annibale combines the great northern Italian tradition of ceiling

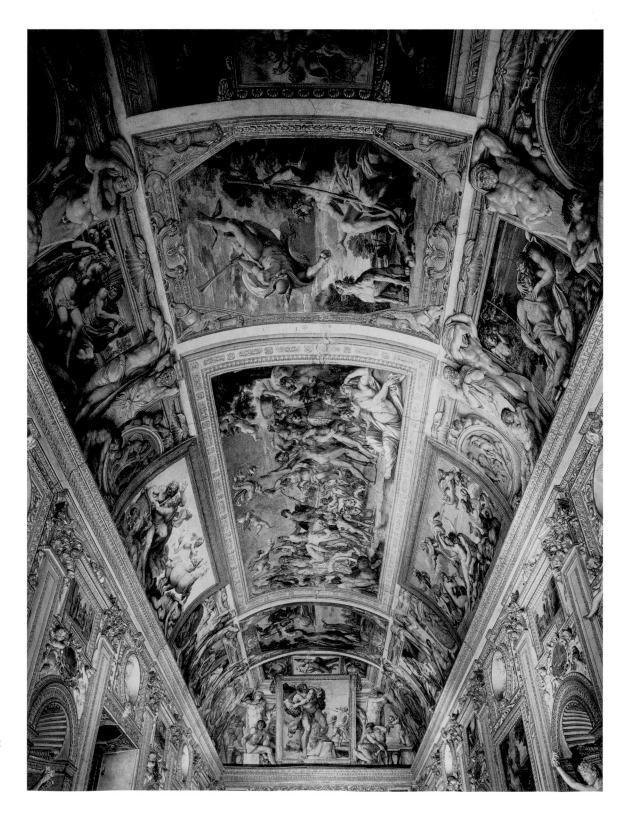

23-8 • Annibale Carracci **CEILING OF GALLERY, PALAZZO FARNESE**
Rome. 1597–1601. Fresco, approx. 68′ × 21′ (20.7 × 6.4 m).

23-9 • Caravaggio BACCHUS
1595–1596. Oil on canvas, 37″ × 33½″ (94 × 85.1 cm). Galleria degli Uffizi, Florence.

painting—seen in the work of Mantegna and Correggio (see FIGS. 20-32, 21-22)—with his study of central Italian Renaissance painters and the Classical heritage of Rome. Annibale organized his complex theme by using illusionistic devices to create multiple levels of reality. Painted imitations of gold-framed easel paintings called *quadri riportati* ("transported paintings") appear to "rest" on the actual cornice of the vault and overlap "bronze" medallions that are flanked, in turn, by realistically colored *ignudi*, dramatically lit from below. The viewer is invited to compare the warm flesh tones of these youths, and their lifelike poses, with the more idealized "painted" bodies in the framed scenes next to them. Above, paintings of stucco-colored sculptures of herms (plain shafts topped by human torsos) twist and turn as they support the painted framework of the vault, exposing a variety of feelings with their expressions and seemingly communicating with one another. Many of Annibale's ideas are inspired by motifs in Michelangelo's Sistine Chapel ceiling (see FIG. 21-12). The figure types, true to their source, are heroic, muscular, and drawn with precise anatomical accuracy.

But instead of Michelangelo's cool illumination and intellectual detachment, the Carracci ceiling glows with a warm light that recalls the work of the Venetian painters Titian and Veronese, and seems buoyant with optimism and lively engagement.

The ceiling was highly admired, famous from the moment it was finished. The proud Farnese family generously allowed young artists to sketch the figures there, so that Carracci's masterpiece influenced Italian art well into the following century.

CARAVAGGIO Michelangelo Merisi (1571–1610), known as "Caravaggio" after his family's home town in Lombardy, introduced a powerfully frank realism and dramatic, theatrical lighting and gesture to Italian Baroque art. The young painter brought an interest, perhaps a specialization, in still-life painting with him when he arrived in Rome from Milan late in 1592 and found studio work as a specialist painter of fruit and vegetables. When he began to work on his own, he continued to paint still lifes but also began to include half-length figures with them. By this time, his reputation had grown to the extent that an agent offered to market his pictures.

Caravaggio painted for a small, sophisticated circle associated with the household of art patron Cardinal del Monte, where the artist was invited to reside. His subjects from this early period of the 1590s include not only still lifes but also genre scenes featuring fortune-tellers, cardsharps, and glamorous young men dressed as musicians or mythological figures. The **BACCHUS** of 1595–1596 (**FIG. 23-9**) is among the most polished of these early works. Caravaggio seems to have painted exactly what he saw, reproducing the "farmer's tan" of those parts of this partially dressed youth's skin—hand and face—that have been exposed to the sun, as well as the dirt under his fingernails. The figure himself is strikingly androgynous. Made up with painted lips and smoothly arching eyebrows, he seems to offer the viewer the gorgeous goblet of wine held delicately in his left hand, while fingering the black bow that holds his loose clothing together at the waist. Is this a provocative invitation to an erotic encounter or a young actor outfitted for the role of Bacchus, god of wine? Does the juxtaposition of the youth's invitation with a still life of rotting fruit transform this into an image about the transitory nature of sensual pleasure, either admonishing viewers to avoid sins of the flesh or encouraging them to enjoy life's pleasures while they can? The ambiguity seems to make the painting even more provocative.

Most of Caravaggio's commissions after 1600 were religious, and reactions to them were mixed. On occasion, patrons rejected his powerful, sometimes brutal, naturalism as unsuitable to the subject's dignity. Critics differed as well. An early critic, the Spaniard Vincente Carducho, wrote in his *Dialogue on Painting* (Madrid, 1633) that Caravaggio was an "omen of the ruin and demise of painting" because he painted "with nothing but nature before him, which he simply copied in his amazing way" (Enggass and Brown, pp. 173–174). Others recognized him as a great innovator who reintroduced realism into art and developed new, dramatic lighting effects. Seventeenth-century art historian Giovanni Bellori described Caravaggio's painting as

> … reinforced throughout with bold shadows and a great deal of black to give relief to the forms. He went so far in this manner of working that he never brought his figures out into the daylight, but placed them in the dark brown atmosphere of a closed room, using a high light that descended vertically over the principal parts of the bodies while leaving the remainder in shadow in order to give force through a strong contrast of light and dark.…
> (Bellori, *Lives of the Painters*, Rome, 1672, in Enggass and Brown, p. 79)

Caravaggio's approach has been likened to the preaching of Filippo Neri (1515–1595), the Counter-Reformation priest and mystic who founded a Roman religious group called the Congregation of the Oratory. Neri, called the Apostle of Rome and later canonized, focused his missionary efforts on ordinary people for whom he strove to make Christian history and doctrine understandable and meaningful. Caravaggio, too, interpreted his religious subjects directly and dramatically, combining intensely observed figures, poses, and expressions with strongly contrasting effects of light and color. His knowledge of Lombard painting, where the influence of Leonardo was strong, must have facilitated his development of the technique now known as **tenebrism**, in which forms emerge from a dark background into a strong light that often falls from a single source outside the painting. The effect is that of a theatrical spotlight.

One of Caravaggio's first religious commissions—paintings for the Contarelli Chapel in the French community's church of St. Louis (San Luigi dei Francesi)—included *The Calling of St. Matthew*, painted about 1599–1600 (see "Caravaggio in the Contarelli Chapel," page 724). The subject is conversion, a common Counter-Reformation theme. Jesus calls Levi, the tax collector, to join his apostles (Matthew 9:9; Mark 2:14). Levi—who will become St. Matthew—sits at a table, counting or collecting money, surrounded by elegant young men in plumed hats, velvet doublets, and satin shirts. Nearly hidden behind the back of a beckoning apostle—probably St. Peter—at the right, the gaunt-faced Jesus points dramatically at Levi with a gesture that is repeated in the presumed (other than Jesus, identities are not certain here) tax collector's own surprised response of pointing to himself, as if to say, "Who, me?" An intense raking light enters the painting from upper right, as if it were coming from the chapel's actual window above the altar to spotlight the important features of this darkened scene. Viewers encountering the painting obliquely across the empty space of the chapel interior seem to be witnessing the scene as it is occurring, elevated on a recessed stage opening through the wall before them.

The emotional power of Caravaggio's theatrical approach to sacred narrative is nowhere more evident than in his rendering of **THE CONVERSION OF ST. PAUL** for the Cerasi Chapel in Santa Maria del Popolo (**FIG. 23-12**). This is one of two paintings commissioned for this chapel in 1600; the other portrayed the Crucifixion of St. Peter. The first pair was rejected when Caravaggio delivered them, and they were acquired by a private collector (see also "Caravaggio in the Contarelli Chapel," page 724). This second version of Paul's conversion is direct and simple. Caravaggio focuses on Paul's internal involvement with a pivotal moment, not its external cause. There is no indication of a heavenly apparition, only Paul's response to it. There is no clear physical setting, only mysterious darkness. And Paul's experience is personal. Whereas he has been flung from his horse and threatens to tumble into the viewers' own space—arms outstretched and legs akimbo, bathed in a strong spotlight—the horse and groom behind him seem oblivious to Paul's experience. The horse actually takes up more space in the painting than the saint, and the unsettling position of its lifted foreleg, precariously poised over the sprawled body of Paul, adds further tension to an already charged presentation.

As soon as he had established himself as an up-and-coming artist during the 1590s, Caravaggio turned to a series of important commissions for religious paintings in the chapels of Roman churches. Unlike in the Renaissance, where frescos were applied directly to the walls, Caravaggio produced large oil paintings on canvas in his studio, only later installing them within the chapels to form coordinated ensembles. Several such installations survive, giving us the precious opportunity to experience the paintings as Caravaggio and his patrons intended. One of these intact programs, in the **CONTARELLI CHAPEL** of San Luigi dei Francesi (**FIG. 23–10**), was Caravaggio's earliest religious commission in Rome, perhaps obtained through the efforts of Cardinal del Monte, who had supported the artist through the 1590s.

This church served the French community in Rome, and the building itself was constructed between 1518 and 1589, its completion made possible by the patronage of Catherine de' Medici, queen of France. The chapel Caravaggio decorated was founded in 1565 by Mathieu Cointrel—Matteo Contarelli—a French noble at the papal court who would serve as a financial administrator under Gregory XIII (pontificate 1572–1585). Although earlier artists had been called on to provide paintings for the chapel, it was only after Contarelli's death in 1585 that the executors of his will brought the decoration to completion, hiring Giuseppe Cesare in 1591

to paint the ceiling frescos, and Caravaggio in 1599 to provide paintings of scenes from the life of the patron's patron saint: **THE CALLING OF ST. MATTHEW** on the left wall (**FIG. 23–11**) and *The Martyrdom of St. Matthew* on the right (not visible in FIG. 23–10), both installed in July 1600.

The commissioning document was explicit, requiring the artist to show, in *The Calling of St. Matthew*, the saint rising from his seat to follow Christ in ministry. But Caravaggio was never very good at following the rules. Among the group of smartly dressed Romans who form Matthew's circle of cohorts seated at the left, no one rises to leave. Art historians have

not even been able to agree on which figure is Matthew. Most identify him with a bearded man in the center, interpreting his pointing gesture as a self-referential, questioning response to Jesus' call. But some see Matthew in the figure hunched over the scattered coins at far left, seemingly unmoved by Jesus' presence. In this case, the bearded figure's pointing would question whether this bent-over colleague was the one Jesus sought. The painting is marked by mystery, not by the clarity sought by Counter-Reformation guidelines.

In February 1602, Caravaggio received a second commission for the Contarelli Chapel, this time for a painting over the altar

23–10 • CONTARELLI CHAPEL, SAN LUIGI DEI FRANCESI
Rome. Paintings by Caravaggio 1599–1602.

showing St. Matthew, accompanied by his angelic symbol and writing his Gospel. It was to be completed within three months, but Caravaggio did not receive payment for the picture until September of that year, and the painting he delivered was rejected. The clergy considered Caravaggio's rendering of the saint unacceptably crude and common, his cross-legged pose uncouth and unnecessarily revealing. The fleshiness of the angel, who sidles cozily up to Matthew, was judged inappropriately risqué. In short, the painting was inconsistent with guidelines for saintly decorum set for artists by the Council of Trent. Caravaggio had to paint a second, more decorous altarpiece for the chapel (seen in FIG. 23–10), with a nobler Matthew and a more distant angel. The rejected version was snapped up by Roman collector Vincenzo Giustiniani, who actually paid for the replacement in order to acquire the more sensational original. Unfortunately, this first painting was destroyed in the 1945 bombing of Berlin during World War II.

23-11 • Caravaggio THE CALLING OF ST. MATTHEW
Contarelli Chapel, church of San Luigi dei Francesi, Rome. 1599–1600. Oil on canvas, 10′7½″ × 11′2″ (3.24 × 3.4 m).

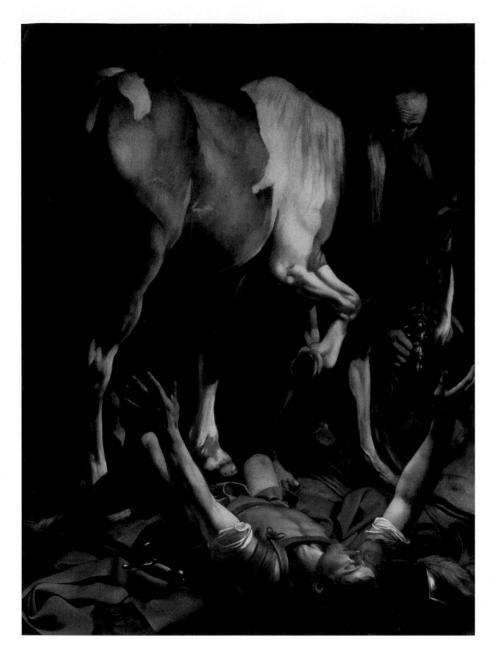

23-12 • Caravaggio THE CONVERSION OF ST. PAUL
Cerasi Chapel, Santa Maria del Popolo, Rome.
c. 1601. Oil on canvas, 7'6" × 5'8" (2.3 × 1.75 m).

Read the document related to Caravaggio on myartslab.com

ARTEMISIA GENTILESCHI One of Caravaggio's most brilliant Italian followers was Artemisia Gentileschi (1593–c. 1652/1653), whose international reputation helped spread the Caravaggesque style beyond Rome. Artemisia first studied and worked under her father, Orazio, one of the earliest followers of Caravaggio. In 1616, she moved from Rome to Florence, where she worked for Grand Duke Cosimo II de' Medici and was elected, at the age of 23, to the Florentine Academy of Design.

One of her most famous paintings, and a clear example of her debt to Caravaggio's tenebrism and naturalism, is the painting **JUDITH BEHEADING HOLOFERNES** (**FIG. 23-13**), which she gave to Cosimo II shortly before she left Florence to return to Rome in 1620. The subject is drawn from the biblical book of Judith, which recounts the story of the destructive invasion of Judah by the Assyrian general Holofernes, when the brave and beautiful Jewish widow Judith risked her life to save her people. Using her charm to gain Holofernes' trust, Judith enters his tent with her maidservant while he is drunk and beheads him with his own sword. Gentileschi emphasizes the grisly facts of this heroic act, as the women struggle to subdue the terrified Holofernes while blood spurts wildly from the severing of his jugular. The artist's dramatic spotlighting and a convergence of compositional diagonals rivet our attention on the most sensational aspects of the scene pushed toward us in the foreground. Throughout her life, Gentileschi painted many such images of heroic biblical women, which art historians have interpreted in relation to her own struggle to claim her rightful place in an art world dominated by overpowering men.

Despite the great esteem in which Caravaggio was held by some, especially the younger generation of artists, his violent temper repeatedly got him into trouble. During the last decade of his life, he was frequently arrested, initially for minor offenses such as carrying arms illegally or street brawling. But in May of 1606 he killed a man in a duel fought over a disputed tennis match and had to flee Rome as a fugitive under a death sentence. He supported himself while on the run by painting in Naples, Malta, and Sicily. The Knights of Malta awarded him the cross of their religious and military order in July 1608, but in October he was imprisoned for insulting one of their number, and again he escaped and fled. Caravaggio died on July 18, 1610, just short of his 39th birthday, of a fever contracted during a journey back to Rome where he expected to be pardoned of his capital offense. Caravaggio's unvarnished realism and tenebrism influenced nearly every important European artist of the seventeenth century.

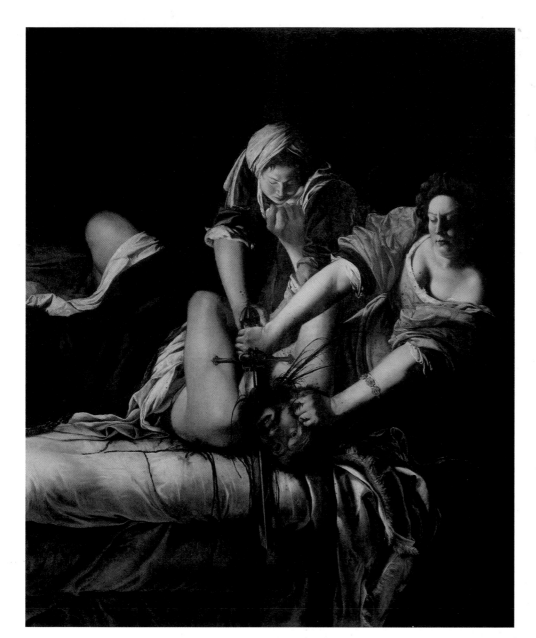

BAROQUE CEILINGS: CORTONA AND GAULLI Theatricality, intricacy, and the opening of space reached an apogee in Baroque ceiling decoration—complex constructions combining architecture, painting, and stucco sculpture. These grand illusionistic projects were carried out on the domes and vaults of churches, civic buildings, palaces, and villas, and went far beyond even Michelangelo's Sistine Chapel ceiling (see FIG. 21-11) or Correggio's dome at Parma (see FIG. 21-22). Baroque ceiling painters sought the drama of an immeasurable heaven that extended into vertiginous zones far beyond the limits of High Renaissance taste. To achieve this, they employed the system of *quadratura* (literally, "squaring" or "gridwork"): an architectural setting painted in meticulous perspective and usually requiring that it be viewed from a specific spot to achieve the desired effect of soaring space. The resulting viewpoint is called *di sotto in sù* ("from below to above"), which we first saw, in a limited fashion, in Mantegna's ceiling in Mantua (see FIG. 20-32).

Because it required such careful calculation, figure painters usually had specialists in *quadratura* paint the architectural frame for them.

Pietro Berrettini (1596–1669), called "Pietro da Cortona" after his hometown, carried the development of the Baroque ceiling away from Classicism into a more strongly unified and illusionistic direction. Trained in Florence and inspired by Veronese's ceiling in the Doge's Palace, which he saw on a trip to Venice in 1637, the artist was commissioned in the early 1630s by the Barberini family of Pope Urban VIII to decorate the ceiling of the audience hall of their Roman palace.

Pietro da Cortona's great fresco **THE GLORIFICATION OF THE PAPACY OF URBAN VIII** became a model for a succession of Baroque illusionistic palace ceilings throughout Europe (FIG. 23-14). He structured his mythological scenes around a vault-like skeleton of architecture, painted in *quadratura*, that appears to be attached to the actual cornice of the room. But in contrast

Divine Providence (in gold against an open sky) gestures toward three giant bees surrounded by a huge laurel wreath (both Barberini emblems) carried by Faith, Hope, and Charity. Immortality offers a crown of stars, while other figures present the crossed keys and the triple-tiered crown of the papacy. Around these figures are scenes of Roman gods and goddesses, who demonstrate the pope's wisdom and virtue by triumphing over the vices. So complex was the imagery that a guide gave visitors an explanation, and one member of the household published a pamphlet, still in use today, explaining the painting.

The most spectacular of all illusionistic Baroque ceilings is Giovanni Battista Gaulli's **THE TRIUMPH OF THE NAME OF JESUS AND FALL OF THE DAMNED** (FIG. 23-15), which fills the vault of the Jesuit church Il Gesù (see FIG. 21-40). In the 1560s, Giacomo da Vignola had designed an austere interior for Il Gesù, but when the Jesuits renovated their church a century later, they commissioned a religious allegory to cover the nave's plain ceiling. Gaulli (1639–1709) designed and executed the spectacular illusion between 1672 and 1685, fusing sculpture and painting to eliminate any appearance of architectural division. It is difficult to sort carved three-dimensional figures from the painted imitations, and some paintings are on real panels that extend over the actual architectural frame. Gaulli, who arrived in Rome from Genoa in 1657, had worked in his youth for Bernini, from whom he absorbed a taste for drama and multimedia effects. The elderly Bernini, who worshiped daily at Il Gesù, may well have offered his personal advice to his former assistant, and Gaulli was certainly familiar with other illusionistic paintings in Rome as well, including Pietro da Cortona's Barberini ceiling (see FIG. 23-14).

to Annibale Carracci's neat separations and careful *quadro riportato* framing (see FIG. 23-8), Pietro's figures weave in and out of their setting in active and complex profusion; some rest on the actual cornice, while others float weightlessly against the sky. Instead of Annibale's warm, nearly even light, Pietro's dramatic illumination, with its bursts of brilliance alternating with deep shadows, fuses the ceiling into a dense but unified whole.

The subject is an elaborate allegory of the virtues of the pope. Just below the center of the vault, seated at the top of a pyramid of clouds and figures personifying Time and the Fates,

23-15 • Giovanni Battista Gaulli THE TRIUMPH OF THE NAME OF JESUS AND FALL OF THE DAMNED
Vault of the church of Il Gesù, Rome. 1672–1685. Fresco with stucco figures.

Gaulli's astonishing creation went beyond anything that had preceded it in unifying architecture, sculpture, and painting. Every element is dedicated to creating the illusion that clouds and angels have descended through an opening in the top of the church into the upper reaches of the nave. The extremely foreshortened figures are projected as if seen from below, and the whole composition is focused off-center on the golden aura around the letters IHS, the monogram of Jesus and the insignia of the Jesuits. The subject is, in fact, the Last Judgment, with the elect rising joyfully toward the name of God and the damned plummeting through the ceiling toward the nave floor. The sweeping extension of the work into the nave space, the powerful appeal to the viewer's emotions, and the near-total unity of the multimedia visual effect—all hallmarks of Italian Baroque—were never surpassed.

SPAIN

When the Holy Roman Emperor Charles V abdicated in 1556, he left Spain and its American colonies, as well as the Netherlands, Burgundy, Milan, and the Kingdom of Naples and Sicily to his son Philip II and the Holy Roman Empire (Germany and Austria) to his brother Ferdinand. Ferdinand and the Habsburg emperors who succeeded him ruled their territories from Vienna in Austria, but much of German-speaking Europe remained divided into small units in which local rulers decided on the religion of their territory. Catholicism prevailed in southern and western Germany and in Austria, while the north was Lutheran.

The Spanish Habsburg kings Philip III (r. 1598–1621), Philip IV (r. 1621–1665), and Charles II (r. 1665–1700) reigned over a weakening empire. After repeated local rebellions, Portugal reestablished its independence in 1640. The Kingdom of Naples remained in a constant state of unrest. After 80 years of war, the Protestant northern Netherlands—which had formed the United Provinces—gained independence in 1648. Amsterdam grew into one of the wealthiest cities in Europe, and the Dutch Republic became an increasingly serious threat to Spanish trade and colonial possessions. The Catholic southern Netherlands (Flanders) remained under Spanish and then Austrian Habsburg rule.

What had seemed an endless flow of gold and silver from the Americas to Spain diminished, as precious-metal production in Bolivia and Mexico lessened. Agriculture, industry, and trade at home also suffered. As they tried to defend the Roman Catholic Church and their empire on all fronts, the Spanish kings squandered their resources and finally went bankrupt in 1692. Nevertheless, despite the decline of the Habsburgs' Spanish empire, seventeenth-century writers and artists produced some of the greatest Spanish literature and art, and the century is often called the Spanish Golden Age.

PAINTING IN SPAIN'S GOLDEN AGE

The primary influence on Spanish painting in the fifteenth century had been the art of Flanders; in the sixteenth, it had been the art of Florence and Rome. Seventeenth-century Spanish painting, profoundly influenced by Caravaggio's powerfully dramatic art, was characterized by an ecstatic religiosity combined with realistic surface detail that emerges from the deep shadows of tenebrism.

JUAN SÁNCHEZ COTÁN Late in the sixteenth century, Spanish artists developed a significant interest in paintings of artfully arranged objects rendered with intense attention to detail. Juan Sánchez Cotán (1561–1627) was one of the earliest painters of these pure still lifes in Spain. In **STILL LIFE WITH QUINCE, CABBAGE, MELON, AND CUCUMBER** (**FIG. 23-16**), of about 1602, he contrasts the irregular, curved shapes of the fruits and vegetables with the angular geometry of their setting. His precisely ordered subjects—two of which are suspended from strings—form a long, sagging arc from the upper left to the lower right. The fruits and vegetables appear within a *cantarero* (primitive larder), but it is unclear why they have been arranged in this way. Set in a strong light against impenetrable darkness, this highly artificial arrangement of strikingly lifelike forms suggests not only a fascination with spatial ambiguity, but also a contemplative sensibility and interest in the qualities of objects that look forward to the work of Zurbarán and Velázquez.

JUSEPE DE RIBERA Jusepe (or José) de Ribera (c. 1591–1652) was born in Seville but studied in Rome and settled in Spanish-ruled Naples; in Italy, he was known as "Lo Spagnoletto" ("the Little Spaniard"). He combined the Classical and Caravaggesque styles he had learned in Rome to create a new Neapolitan—and eventually Spanish—style. Ribera became the link extending

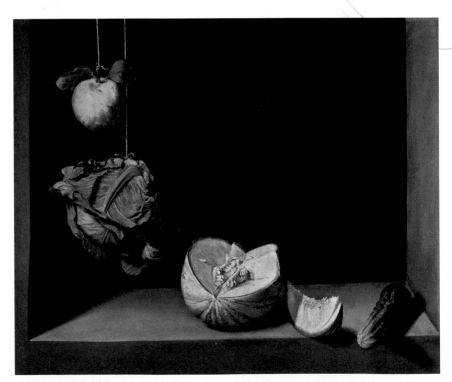

23-16 • Juan Sánchez Cotán **STILL LIFE WITH QUINCE, CABBAGE, MELON, AND CUCUMBER**
c. 1602. Oil on canvas, 27⅛″ × 33¼″ (68.8 × 84.4 cm). San Diego Museum of Art. Gift of Anne R. and Amy Putnam

compression of the figures into the foreground space heightens our sense of being witness to this scene (see FIG. 23–12).

FRANCISCO DE ZURBARÁN Francisco de Zurbarán (1598–1664) represents another martyrdom, in this case already accomplished, in his 1628 painting of **ST. SERAPION** (**FIG. 23–18**). Little is known of his early years before 1625, but Zurbarán came under the influence of the Caravaggesque taste prevalent in Seville, the major city in southwestern Spain, while his interest in abstract design has been traced to the heritage of Islamic art in Spain.

Zurbarán primarily worked for the monastic orders. In this painting, he portrays the martyrdom of Serapion, member of the thirteenth-century Mercedarians, a Spanish order founded to rescue the Christian prisoners of the Moors. Following the vows of his order, Serapion sacrificed himself in exchange for Christian captives. The dead man's pallor, his rough hands, and the coarse ropes contrast with the off-white of his creased Mercedarian habit, its folds carefully arranged in a pattern of highlights and varying depths of shadow. The only colors are the red and gold of the insignia. This timelessly immobile composition is like a tragic still life, a study of fabric and flesh become inanimate, silent, and at rest.

23–17 • Jusepe de Ribera MARTYRDOM OF ST. BARTHOLOMEW
1634. Oil on canvas, 41¼″ × 44⅞″ (1.05 × 1.14 m). National Gallery of Art, Washington, DC. Rosenwald Collection (1950.14.744)

from Caravaggio in Italy to the Spanish masters Zurbarán and Velázquez.

During this period, the Church—aiming to draw people back to Catholicism—commissioned portrayals of heroic martyrs who had endured shocking torments as witness to their faith. Ribera's painting of the **MARTYRDOM OF ST. BARTHOLOMEW**, the apostle who was martyred by being skinned alive, captures the horror of the violence to come while emphasizing the saint's spirituality and acceptance (**FIG. 23–17**). The bound Bartholomew looks heavenward as his executioner tests the sharpness of the knife that he will soon use on his living victim. Ribera has learned the lessons of Caravaggio well, as he highlights the intensely realistic faces with the dramatic light of tenebrism and describes the aging wrinkled flesh in great detail. The

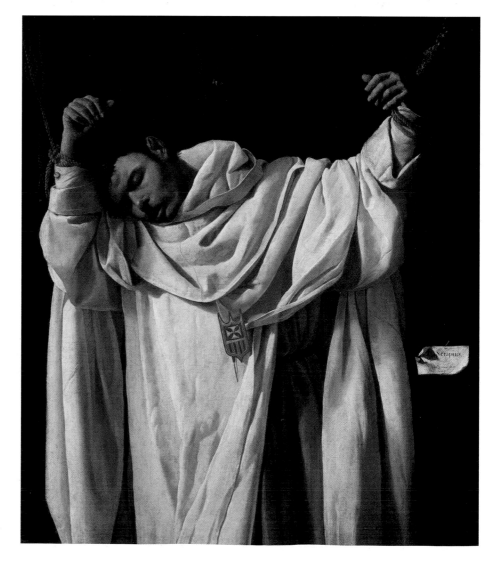

23–18 • Francisco de Zurbarán ST. SERAPION
1628. Oil on canvas, 47½″ × 40¾″ (120.7 × 103.5 cm). Wadsworth Atheneum, Hartford, Connecticut. Ella Gallup Sumner and Mary Catlin Sumner Collection Fund

DIEGO VELÁZQUEZ Diego Rodríguez de Silva y Velázquez (1599–1660), the greatest painter to emerge from the Caravaggesque school of Seville, shared Zurbarán's fascination with objects. He entered Seville's painters' guild in 1617. Like Ribera, he began his career as a tenebrist and naturalist. During his early years, he painted scenes set in taverns, markets, and kitchens, and emphasized still lifes of various foods and kitchen utensils. His early **WATER CARRIER OF SEVILLE** (**FIG. 23-19**) is a study of surfaces and textures of the splendid ceramic pots that characterized folk art through the centuries. Velázquez was devoted to studying and sketching from life: The man in the painting was a well-known Sevillian waterseller. Like Sánchez Cotán, Velázquez arranged the elements of his paintings with almost mathematical rigor. The objects and figures allow the artist to exhibit his virtuosity in rendering sculptural volumes and describing contrasting textures illuminated by dramatic natural light. Light reflects in different ways off the glazed waterpot at the left and the coarser clay jug in the foreground; it is absorbed by the rough wool and dense velvet of the costumes; it is refracted as it passes through the clear glass held by the man and the waterdrops on the jug's surface.

In 1623, Velázquez moved to Madrid, where he became court painter to the young King Philip IV, a prestigious position that he held until his death in 1660. The opportunity to study paintings in the royal collection, as well as to travel, enabled the development of his distinctive personal style. The Flemish painter Peter Paul Rubens, during a 1628–1629 diplomatic visit to the Spanish court, convinced the king that Velázquez should visit Italy. Velázquez made two trips, the first in 1629–1631 and the second in 1649–1651. He was profoundly influenced by contemporary Italian painting, and on the first trip seems to have taken a special interest in narrative paintings with complex figure compositions.

Velázquez's Italian studies and his growing skill in composition are apparent in both figure and landscape paintings. In **THE SURRENDER AT BREDA** (**FIG. 23-20**), painted in 1634–1635, Velázquez treats the theme of triumph and conquest in an entirely new way—far removed from traditional gloating military propaganda. Years earlier, in 1625, Ambrosio Spinola, the duke of Alba and the Spanish governor, had defeated the Dutch at Breda. As Velázquez imagined the scene of surrender, the opposing armies stand on a hilltop overlooking a vast valley where the city of Breda burns and soldiers are still deployed. The Dutch commander, Justin of Nassau, hands over the keys of Breda to the victorious Spanish commander. The entire exchange seems extraordinarily gracious, an emblem of a courtly ideal of gentlemanly conduct. The victors stand at attention, holding their densely packed lances upright in a vertical pattern—giving the painting its popular name, "The Lances"—while the defeated Dutch, a motley group, stand out of order, with pikes and banners drooping. In fact, according to reports, no keys were involved and the Dutch were more presentable in appearance than the Spaniards. Velázquez has taken liberties with historical fact to create for his Spanish patron a work of art that rendered the meaning of the surrender, rather than its actual appearance.

Velázquez displays here his compositional virtuosity and his extraordinary gifts as a visual storyteller. A strong diagonal, starting in the sword of the Dutch soldier in the lower left foreground and ending in the checked banner on the

23-19 • Diego Velázquez WATER CARRIER OF SEVILLE
c. 1619. Oil on canvas, 41½″ × 31½″ (105.3 × 80 cm). Victoria & Albert Museum, London.

23-20 • Diego Velázquez THE SURRENDER AT BREDA (THE LANCES)
1634–1635. Oil on canvas, 10'7⁄8″ × 12'1⁄2″ (3.07 × 3.67 m). Museo del Prado, Madrid.

upper right, unites the composition and moves the viewer from the defeated to the victorious soldiers in the direction of the surrender itself. Portraitlike faces, meaningful gestures, and controlled color and texture convince us of the reality of the scene. Across the upper half of the huge canvas, the landscape background is startling. Velázquez painted an entirely imaginary Netherlands in greens and blues worked with flowing, liquid brushstrokes. Luminosity is achieved by laying down a thick layer of lead white and then flowing the layers of color over it. The silvery light forms a background for dramatically silhouetted figures and weapons. Velázquez revealed a breadth and intensity unsurpassed in his century, and became an inspiration to modern artists such as Manet and Picasso.

Perhaps Velázquez's most striking, certainly his most enigmatic work is the enormous multiple portrait, nearly 10½ feet tall and over 9 feet wide, known as **LAS MENINAS (THE MAIDS OF HONOR)** (FIG. 23-21), painted in 1656, near the end of his life. This painting continues to challenge viewers and stimulate debate

among art historians. Velázquez draws viewers directly into the scene. In one interpretation, the viewer stands in the very space occupied by King Philip and his queen, whose reflections can be seen in the large mirror on the back wall, perhaps a clever reference to Jan van Eyck's *Double Portrait of Giovanni Arnolfini and his Wife* (see FIG. 19-1), which was a part of the Spanish royal collection at this time. Echoing pictorially the claim made in Jan's signature, Velázquez himself is also present, brushes in hand, beside a huge canvas. The central focus, however, is neither the artist nor the royal couple but their brilliantly illuminated 5-year-old daughter, the Infanta (princess) Margarita, who is surrounded by her attendants, most of whom are identifiable portraits.

No consensus exists today on the meaning of this monumental painting. It is a royal portrait; it is also a self-portrait of Velázquez standing at his easel. But fundamentally, *Las Meninas* is a personal statement. Throughout his life, Velázquez had sought respect and acclaim for himself and for the art of painting. Here, dressed as a courtier, the Order of Santiago on his chest (added later) and the

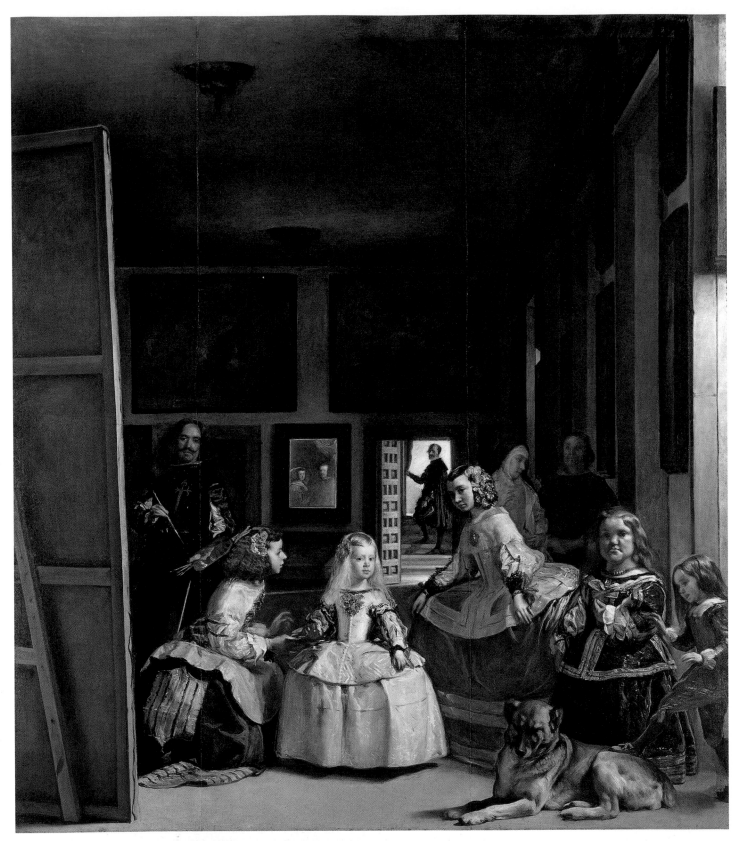

23–21 • Diego Velázquez LAS MENINAS (THE MAIDS OF HONOR)
1656. Oil on canvas, 10′5″ × 9′1½″ (3.18 × 2.76 m). Museo del Prado, Madrid.

The cleaning of *Las Meninas* in 1984 revealed much about Velázquez's methods. He used a minimum of underdrawing, building up his forms with layers of loosely applied paint and finishing off the surfaces with dashing highlights in white, lemon yellow, and pale orange. Rather than using light to model volumes in the time-honored manner, Velázquez tried to depict the optical properties of light reflecting from surfaces. On close inspection his forms dissolve into a maze of individual strokes of paint.

View the Closer Look for *Las Meninas (The Maids of Honor)* on myartslab.com keys of the palace tucked into in his sash, Velázquez proclaims the dignity and importance of painting itself.

BARTOLOMÉ ESTEBAN MURILLO The Madrid of Velázquez was the center of Spanish art. Seville declined after an outbreak of plague in 1649, but it remained a center for trade with the Spanish colonies, where the work of Bartolomé Esteban Murillo (1617–1682) had a profound influence on art and religious iconography. Many patrons wanted images of the Virgin Mary and especially of the Immaculate Conception, the controversial idea that Mary was born free from original sin. Although the Immaculate Conception became Catholic dogma only in 1854, the con-

cept, as well as devotion to Mary, grew during the seventeenth and eighteenth centuries.

Counter-Reformation authorities had provided specific instructions for artists painting the Virgin of the Immaculate Conception: Mary was to be dressed in blue and white, her hands folded in prayer, as she is carried upward by angels, sometimes in large flocks. She may be surrounded by an unearthly light ("clothed in the sun") and may stand on a crescent moon in reference to the woman of the Apocalypse (see FIG. 15-10). Angels often carry palms and symbols of the Virgin, such as a mirror, a fountain, roses, and lilies, and they may vanquish the serpent, Satan. The Church exported to the New World many paintings faithful to these orthodox guidelines by Murillo, Zurbarán, and others. When the indigenous population began to visualize the Christian story (see FIG. 30-46), paintings such as Murillo's **THE IMMACULATE CONCEPTION** (FIG. 23-22) provided prompts for their imaginings.

ARCHITECTURE IN SPAIN

Turning away from the severity displayed in the sixteenth-century El Escorial monastery-palace (see FIG. 22-18), seventeenth-century Spanish architects again embraced the lavish decoration that had characterized their art since the fourteenth century. Profusions of ornament swept back into fashion, first in huge *retablos* (altarpieces), then in portals (main doors often embellished with sculpture), and finally in entire buildings.

THE CATHEDRAL OF SANTIAGO DE COMPOSTELA In the seventeenth century, the role of St. James as patron saint of Spain was challenged by the supporters of St. Teresa of Ávila and then by supporters of St. Michael, St. Joseph, and other popular saints. It became important to the archbishop and other leaders in Santiago de Compostela, where the cathedral of St. James was located, to re-establish their primacy. They reinforced their efforts to revitalize the regular flow of pilgrims to the city, undertaken by Spaniards since the ninth century, and used architecture as part of their campaign.

Renewed interest in pilgrimages to the shrines of saints in the seventeenth century brought an influx of pilgrims, and consequently financial security, to the city and the Church. The cathedral chapter ordered an elaborate façade to be added to the twelfth-century pilgrimage church (FIG. 23-23). A

23-22 • Bartolomé Esteban Murillo **THE IMMACULATE CONCEPTION** c. 1660–1665. Oil on canvas, 81⅛″ × 56⅝″ (2.06 × 1.44 m). Museo del Prado, Madrid.

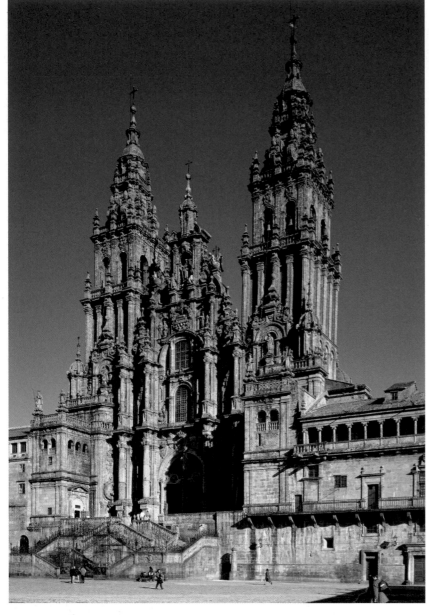

23-23 • WEST FAÇADE, CATHEDRAL OF ST. JAMES, SANTIAGO DE COMPOSTELA, SPAIN
South tower 1667–1680; north tower and central block finished mid 18th century by Fernando de Casas y Nóvoas.

FLANDERS AND THE NETHERLANDS

Led by the nobleman Prince William of Orange, the Netherlands' Protestant northern provinces (present-day Holland) rebelled against Spain in 1568. The seven provinces joined together as the United Provinces in 1579 and began the long struggle for independence, achieved only in the seventeenth century. The king of Spain considered the Dutch heretical rebels, but finally the Dutch prevailed. In 1648, the United Provinces joined emissaries from Spain, the Vatican, the Holy Roman Empire, and France on equal footing in peace negotiations. The resulting Peace of Westphalia recognized the independence of the northern Netherlands.

FLANDERS

After a period of relative autonomy from 1598 to 1621 under Habsburg regents, Flanders, the southern—and predominantly Catholic—part of the Netherlands, returned to direct Spanish rule. Catholic churches were restored and important commissions focused on sacred art. As Antwerp, the capital city and major arts center of the southern Netherlands, gradually recovered from the turmoil of the religious wars, artists of great talent flourished there. Painters like Peter Paul Rubens and Anthony van Dyck established international reputations that brought them important commissions from foreign as well as local patrons.

RUBENS Peter Paul Rubens (1577–1640), whose painting has become synonymous with Flemish Baroque art, was born in Germany, where his father, a Protestant, had fled from his native Antwerp to escape religious persecution. In 1587, after her husband's death, Rubens's mother and her children returned to Antwerp and to Catholicism. Rubens decided in his late teens to become an artist and at age 21 was accepted into the Antwerp painters' guild, a testament to his energy, intelligence, and skill. Shortly thereafter, in 1600, he left for Italy. In Venice, his work came to the attention of the duke of Mantua, who offered him a court post. His activities on behalf of the duke over the next eight years did much to prepare him for the rest of his long and successful career. The duke had him copy famous paintings in collections all over Italy to add to the ducal collection.

Rubens visited every major Italian city, went to Madrid as the duke's emissary, and spent two extended periods in Rome, where he studied the great works of Roman antiquity and the Italian Renaissance. While in Italy, Rubens studied the paintings of two contemporaries, Caravaggio and Annibale Carracci. By 1607

south tower was built in 1667–1680 and then later copied as the north tower.

The last man to serve as architect and director of works at the cathedral, Fernando de Casas y Nóvoas (active 1711–1749), tied the disparate elements together at the west end—towers, portal, stairs—in a grand design focused on a veritable wall of glass, popularly called "The Mirror." His design culminates in a free-standing gable soaring above the roof, visually linking the towers, and framing a statue of St. James. The extreme simplicity of the cloister walls and the archbishop's palace at each side of the portal heightens the dazzling effect of this enormous expanse of glass windows, glittering, jewel-like, in their intricately carved granite frame.

23-24 • Peter Paul Rubens
SELF-PORTRAIT WITH ISABELLA BRANDT
1609–1610. Oil on canvas, 5'9" × 4'5" (1.78 × 1.36 m). Alte Pinakothek, Munich.

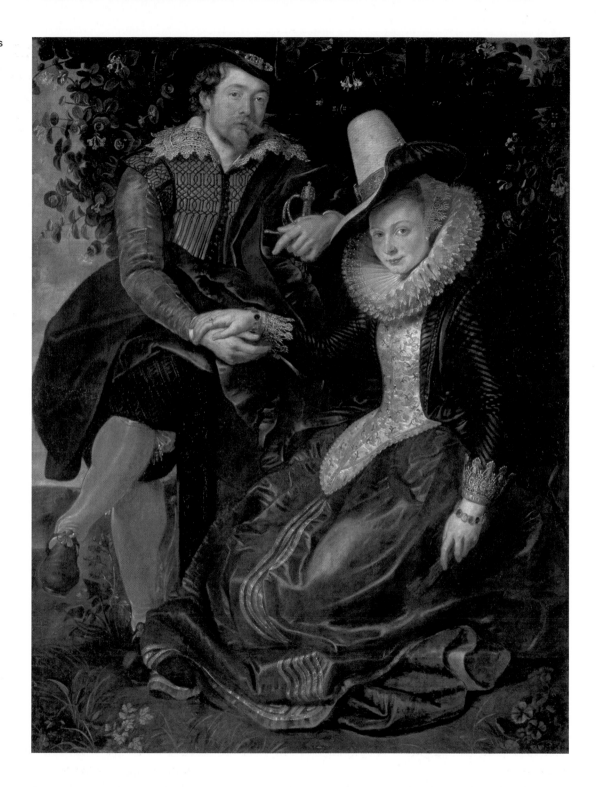

Rubens had persuaded the duke of Mantua to buy the former's *Death of the Virgin* (c. 1601–1602), which had been rejected by Caravaggio's patrons because of its shocking realism.

In 1608, Rubens returned to Antwerp, where in 1609 he accepted a position as court painter to the Habsburg regents of Flanders, Archduke Albert and Princess Isabella Clara Eugenia, the daughter of Philip II. Ten days after that appointment, he married the 18-year-old Isabella Brandt (1596–1626), an alliance that was financially beneficial to the artist, then almost twice the age of his bride. He commemorated the marriage with a spectacular double portrait of himself and his bride seated together in front of a honeysuckle bower that evokes a state of marital bliss (**FIG. 23-24**). The self-confident couple look out to engage viewers directly, and the rich detail of their lavish costumes is described with meticulous precision, foregrounding both the artist's virtuosity and the couple's wealth and sophistication. They join right hands in a traditional gesture of marriage, and the artist slips his foot into the folds of Isabella's flowing red skirt, suggesting a more intimate connection between them. They would have three children before Isabella's untimely death in 1626.

23-25 • Peter Paul Rubens RUBENS'S HOUSE
Italianate addition built 1610–1615. Looking toward the garden:
house at left, studio at right; house restored and opened as a
museum in 1946. From an engraving of 1684. Museum Mayer
van den Bergh.

In 1611, Rubens purchased a residence in Antwerp. The
original house was large and typically Flemish, but Rubens
added a studio in the Italian manner across a courtyard, joining
the two buildings by a second-floor gallery over the entrance
portal (**FIG. 23-25**). Beyond the courtyard lay the large formal
garden, laid out in symmetrical beds. The living room permitted access to a gallery overlooking Rubens's huge studio, a
room designed to accommodate large paintings and to house
what became virtually a painting factory. The tall, arched windows provided ample light for the single, two-story room, and

23-26 • Peter Paul Rubens THE RAISING OF THE CROSS
Made for the Church of St. Walpurga, Antwerp, Belgium. 1610–1611. Oil on panel, center panel 15′1⅞″ × 11′1½″
(4.62 × 3.39 m), each wing 15′1⅞″ × 4′11″ (4.62 × 1.52 m). Now in Cathedral of Our Lady, Antwerp.

23-27 • Peter Paul Rubens HENRY IV RECEIVING THE PORTRAIT OF MARIE DE' MEDICI

1621–1625. Oil on canvas, 12'11⅛" × 9'8⅛" (3.94 × 2.95 m). Musée du Louvre, Paris.

📖— **Read** the document related to Peter Paul Rubens on myartslab.com

a large door permitted the assistants to move finished paintings out to their designated owners. Through the gates at one side of the courtyard, one can see the architectural features of the garden.

Rubens's first major commission in Antwerp was a large canvas triptych for the main altar of the church of St. Walpurga, **THE RAISING OF THE CROSS** (FIG. 23-26), painted in 1610–1611. He extended the central action and the landscape through all three panels. At the center, Herculean figures strain to haul upright the wooden cross with Jesus already stretched upon it. At the left, the followers of Jesus join in mourning, and at the right, soldiers supervise the execution. The drama and intense emotion of Caravaggio is merged here with the virtuoso technique of Annibale Carracci, but transformed and reinterpreted according to Rubens's own unique ideal of thematic and formal unity. The heroic nude figures, dramatic lighting effects, dynamic diagonal composition, and intense emotions show his debt to Italian art, but the rich colors and careful description of surface textures reflect his native Flemish tradition.

Rubens's expressive visual language was deemed as appropriate for representing secular rulers as it was for dramatic religious subjects. Moreover, his intelligence, courtly manners, and personal charm made him a valuable and trusted courtier to his royal patrons, who included Philip IV of Spain, Queen Marie de' Medici of France, and Charles I of England. In 1621, Marie de' Medici, who had been regent for her son Louis XIII, asked Rubens to paint the story of her life, to glorify her role in ruling France, and also to commemorate the founding of the new Bourbon royal dynasty. In 24 paintings, Rubens portrayed Marie's life and political career as one continuous triumph overseen by the ancient gods of Greece and Rome.

In the painting depicting the royal engagement (FIG. 23-27), Henry IV immediately falls in love with Marie as he gazes at her

A CLOSER LOOK | *Prometheus Bound*

by Peter Paul Rubens and Frans Snyders.
c. 1611–1618. Oil on canvas, 95½″ × 82½″ (2.43 × 2.1 m). Philadelphia Museum of Art.

The struggle between Prometheus and the eagle was interpreted allegorically during the seventeenth century, sometimes as the struggle involved in artistic creativity, or as the heroism involved in enduring suffering of body or soul. Some saw in Prometheus a prototype of the Christ of the Crucifixion, an association furthered here by the placement of the gash on Prometheus' side.

The eagle in this picture was painted by Frans Snyders, a specialist in painting animals and flowers whom Rubens brought in to render the detailed feathers and powerful posture of this bird of prey.

The eagle has pierced Prometheus' side to devour his liver, an action that identifies the subject here. This hero of Greek myth was chained to Mount Caucasus and sentenced to this sensational punishment because, in direct defiance of Zeus' command, he stole fire from Mount Olympus and sneaked it to earth so humankind would no longer be confined to cold and darkness. And since Prometheus' liver regenerated over each night, his fate was to have it plucked out again and again, day after day.

The talons of the eagle are poised to dig into the sensitive areas of the groin and face of the struggling hero to underline for viewers the excruciating nature of his pain.

After the main composition was complete, Rubens added this 17½ inch strip of canvas to the left side of the painting to provide a more expansive space for the dramatic action, allow the inclusion at lower left of the fire that got Prometheus into trouble, and provide the bright light on the horizon that some have interpreted as a touch of optimism to counteract the enduring punishment enacted in the foreground.

These small chains that confine Prometheus to the rock seem hardly adequate to confine the powerfully muscular hero, as Rubens conceives him, leading some to speculate that the artist wanted his incarceration to seem more psychological than physical.

 View the Closer Look for *Prometheus Bound* on myartslab.com

---

portrait, shown to him—at the exact center of the composition—by Cupid and Hymen, the god of marriage. The supreme Roman god Jupiter and his wife Juno look down approvingly from the clouds. A personification of France encourages Henry, outfitted with steel breastplate and silhouetted against a landscape in which the smoke of a battle lingers in the distance, to abandon war for love, as *putti* play below with the rest of his armor. The ripe colors, lavish textures, and dramatic diagonals give sustained visual excitement to these enormous canvases, making them not only important works of art but also political propaganda of the highest order.

To satisfy his clients all over Europe, Rubens employed dozens of assistants, many of whom were, or became, important painters in their own right. Using workshop assistants was standard practice for a major artist, but Rubens was particularly methodical, training or hiring specialists in costumes, still lifes, landscapes, portraiture, and animal painting who together could complete works from his detailed sketches. Some of his most spectacular paintings were collaborations. Frans Snyders (1579–1657), a specialist in painting animals and flowers, was brought in by Rubens to paint the enormous eagle who devours the liver of the mythical hero in **PROMETHEUS BOUND** (see "A Closer Look," above), begun in 1611–12 and perhaps worked on as late as 1618. The dramatic lighting, dynamic composition, and loose, energetic brushwork of this painting—which the artist kept for a while in his own personal collection—was clearly Rubens's own, while the tight and detailed technique of Snyders sets up within the painting a telling representational contrast between the massive predator and its writhing, muscular victim. Among Rubens's other collaborators were his friend and neighbor Jan Brueghel the Elder (1568–1625, son of Pieter Bruegel the Elder, see "Bruegel's Cycle of the Months," page 704) and Anthony van Dyck.

PORTRAITS AND STILL LIFES In addition to collaborating with Rubens, Anthony van Dyck (1599–1641), had an illustrious independent career as a portraitist. Son of an Antwerp silk merchant, he was listed as a pupil of the dean of Antwerp's Guild of St. Luke at age 10. He had his own studio and roster of pupils at age 16 but was not made a member of the guild until 1618, the year after he began his association with Rubens as a specialist in painting heads. The need to blend his work seamlessly with that of Rubens enhanced Van Dyck's technical skill. After a trip to the English court of James I (r. 1603–1625) in 1620, Van Dyck traveled to Italy and worked as a portrait painter for seven years before returning to Antwerp. In 1632, he returned to England as the court painter to Charles I (r. 1625–1649), by whom he was knighted and given a studio, a summer home, and a large salary.

Van Dyck's many portraits of the royal family provide a sympathetic record of their features and demeanor. In **CHARLES I AT THE HUNT** (FIG. 23-28), of 1635, Van Dyck was able, by clever manipulation of the setting, to portray the king truthfully and still present him as an imposing figure. Dressed casually for the hunt and standing on a bluff overlooking a distant view (a device used by Rubens to enhance the stature of Henry IV; see FIG. 23-27), Charles, who was in fact very short, appears here taller than his pages and even than his horse, since its head is down and its heavy body is partly off the canvas. The viewer's gaze is diverted from the king's delicate and rather short frame to his pleasant features, framed by his jauntily cocked cavalier's hat and the graceful cascade of his hair. As if in decorous homage, the tree branches bow gracefully toward him, echoing the curving lines of the hat.

Our term, "still life," for paintings of artfully arranged objects on a table, comes from the Dutch *stilleven*, a word coined about 1650. The Antwerp artist Clara Peeters (1594–c. 1657) specialized

23-28 • Anthony van Dyck
CHARLES I AT THE HUNT
1635. Oil on canvas, 8'11" × 6'11" (2.75 × 2.14 m). Musée du Louvre, Paris.

23-29 • Clara Peeters STILL LIFE WITH FLOWERS, GOBLET, DRIED FRUIT, AND PRETZELS
1611. Oil on panel, 20½″ × 28¾″ (52 × 73 cm). Museo del Prado, Madrid.

Like many "breakfast pieces," this painting features a pile of pretzels among the elegant tableware. The salty, twisted bread was called *pretzel* (from the Latin *pretiola*, meaning "small reward") because it was invented by German monks to reward children who had learned their prayers. The twisted shapes represented the crossed arms of a child praying.

in still-life tabletop arrangements (see Introduction, "A Closer Look," page xxxiv, FIG. A). She was a precocious young woman whose career seems to have begun before she was 14. Of some 50 paintings now attributed to her (of which more than 30 are signed), many are of the type called "breakfast pieces," showing a table set for a meal of bread and fruit. Peeters was one of the first artists to combine flowers and food in a single painting, as in her **STILL LIFE WITH FLOWERS, GOBLET, DRIED FRUIT, AND PRETZELS (FIG. 23-29)**, of 1611. Peeters arranged rich tableware and food against neutral, almost black backgrounds, the better to emphasize the fall of light over the contrasting surface textures. In a display of precious objects that must have appealed to her clients, the luxurious goblet and bowl contrast with simple stoneware and pewter, as do the delicate flowers with the homey pretzels. The pretzels, piled on the pewter tray, are a particularly interesting Baroque element, with their complex multiple curves.

THE DUTCH REPUBLIC

The House of Orange was not notable for its patronage of the arts, but patronage improved significantly under Prince Frederick Henry (r. 1625–1647), and Dutch artists found many other eager patrons among the prosperous middle class in Amsterdam, Leiden, Haarlem, Delft, and Utrecht. The Hague was the capital city and the preferred residence of the House of Orange, but Amsterdam was the true center of power, because of its sea trade and the enterprise of its merchants, who made the city an international commercial center. The Dutch delighted in depictions of themselves and their country—the landscape, cities, and domestic life—not to mention beautiful and interesting objects to be seen in still-life paintings and interior scenes. A well-educated people, the Dutch were also fascinated by history, mythology, the Bible, new scientific discoveries, commercial expansion abroad, and colonial exploration.

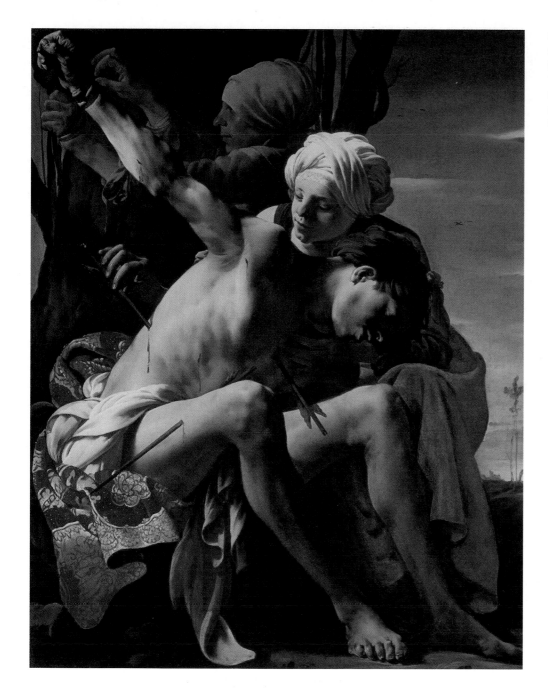

23–30 • Hendrick ter Brugghen
ST. SEBASTIAN TENDED BY ST. IRENE
1625. Oil on canvas, 58¹⁵⁄₁₆″ × 47½″
(149.6 × 120 cm). Allen Memorial
Art Museum, Oberlin College, Ohio.
R.T. Miller Jr. Fund (1953.256)

Visitors to the Netherlands in the seventeenth century noted the popularity of art among merchants and working people. This taste for art stimulated a free market for paintings that functioned like other commodity markets. Artists had to compete to capture the interest of the public by painting on speculation. Specialists in particularly popular types of images were most likely to be financially successful, and what most Dutch patrons wanted were paintings of themselves, their country, their homes, their possessions, and the life around them—characterized by active trade, bustling mercantilism, Protestant religiosity, and jarring class distinctions. The demand for art also gave rise to an active market for the graphic arts, both for original compositions and for copies of paintings, since one copperplate could produce hundreds of impressions, and worn-out plates could be reworked and used again.

THE INFLUENCE OF ITALY Hendrick ter Brugghen (1588–1629) had spent time in Rome, perhaps between 1608 and 1614, where he must have seen Caravaggio's works and became an enthusiastic follower. On his return home, in 1616, Ter Brugghen entered the Utrecht painters' guild, introducing Caravaggio's style into the Netherlands in paintings such as **ST. SEBASTIAN TENDED BY ST. IRENE** (**FIG. 23–30**), and becoming the best known of the Utrecht "Caravaggisti." The sickly gray-green flesh of the nearly dead St. Sebastian, painted in an almost monochromatic palette, contrasts with the brilliant red and gold brocade of what seems to be his crumpled garment. Actually this is the cope of the bishop of Utrecht, which had survived destruction by Protestants and become a symbol of Catholicism in Utrecht. The saint is cast as a heroic figure, his strong, youthful body still bound to the tree. But St. Irene (the patron saint of nurses) delicately removes one of the arrows that pierce him, and her maid reaches to untie his wrists. In a typically Baroque manner, the powerful diagonal created by St. Sebastian's left arm dislodges him from the triangular stability of the group. The immediacy and emotional engagement of the work are enhanced by crowding all the figures into the foreground plane, an effect strengthened by the low horizon line, another aspect of this painting that recalls the work of Caravaggio. The tenebrism and dramatic lighting effects are likewise Caravaggesque, as is the frank realism of the women's faces, with reddened noses and rosy cheeks. Rembrandt, Vermeer, and Rubens all admired Ter Brugghen's painting.

FRANS HALS Frans Hals (c. 1581/1585–1666), the leading painter of Haarlem, developed a style grounded in the Netherlandish love of description and inspired by the Caravaggesque style introduced by artists such as Ter Brugghen. Like Velázquez, he tried to recreate the optical effects of light on the shapes and textures of objects. He painted boldly, with slashing strokes and angular patches of paint. Only when seen at a distance do the colors merge into solid forms over which a flickering light seems to move. In Hals's hands, this seemingly effortless, loose technique suggests the spontaneity of an infectious joy in life. He was known primarily as a portraitist.

Seventeenth-century Dutch portraiture took many forms, ranging from single figures in sparsely furnished settings to allegorical depictions of groups in elaborate costumes surrounded by symbols and attributes. Although the faithful description of facial features and costumes was the most important gauge of a portrait's

success, some painters, like Hals, went beyond likeness to convey a sense of mood or emotion in the sitter. Fundamentally, portraits functioned as social statements of the sitters' status coupled with a clear sense of identity rooted in recognizable faces.

Group portraiture documenting the membership of corporate organizations was a Dutch specialty, and Hals painted some of the greatest examples. These large canvases, filled with many individuals who shared the cost of the commission, challenged painters to present a coherent, interesting composition that nevertheless gave equal attention to each individual portrait. Most artists arranged their sitters in neat rows to depict every face clearly, but in **OFFICERS OF THE HAARLEM MILITIA COMPANY OF ST. ADRIAN** (**FIG. 23-31**) of about 1627, Hals transforms the group portrait into a lively social event. The company, made up of several guard units, was charged with the military protection of Haarlem. Officers came from the upper middle class and held their commissions for three years, whereas the ordinary guards were tradespeople and craftsmakers. Each company was organized like a guild, traditionally under the patronage of a saint, and functioned mainly as a fraternal order, holding archery competitions and taking part in city processions. Hals's composition is based on a strong underlying geometry of diagonal lines—gestures, banners, and sashes—balanced by the stabilizing perpendiculars of table, window, and tall glass. The black suits and hats make the white ruffs and sashes of rose, white, and baby blue even more brilliant.

Although Hals focused his career on portraits of wealthy members of Haarlem's merchant class, he also painted images of eccentric local figures that, although they follow the format of portraiture, functioned as genre paintings by commenting on the

**23-31 • Frans Hals
OFFICERS OF THE
HAARLEM MILITIA
COMPANY OF
ST. ADRIAN**
c. 1627. Oil on canvas,
6′ × 8′8″ (1.83 × 2.67 m).
Frans Halsmuseum, Haarlem.

23-32 • Frans Hals MALLE BABBE
c. 1630–1633. Oil on canvas, 30⅞″ × 26″ (78.5 × 66.2 cm).
Staatliche Museen, Berlin.

to the same workhouse for the mentally impaired as Hals's own son Pieter, raising the question of whether this lively vignette of pub life was meant as a celebration of local color or as a bracing social commentary.

JUDITH LEYSTER A painting that had long been praised as one of Hals's finest works is actually by Judith Leyster (c. 1609–1660), Hals's contemporary. A cleaning uncovered her distinctive signature, the monogram "JL" with a star, which refers to her surname, meaning "pole star." Leyster's work shows clear echoes of her exposure to the Utrecht painters who had enthusiastically adopted the principal features of Caravaggio's style. Since Leyster signed in 1631 as a witness at the baptism in Haarlem of one of Hals's children, it is assumed they were close; she may also have worked in his shop. She entered Haarlem's Guild of St. Luke in 1633, which allowed her to take pupils into her studio, and her competitive relationship with Frans Hals around that time is made clear by the complaint she lodged against him in 1635 for luring away one of her apprentices.

Leyster is known primarily for informal scenes of daily life, which often carry an underlying moralistic theme. In her lively **SELF-PORTRAIT** of 1635 (**FIG. 23-33**), the artist has interrupted her work to lean back and look at viewers, as if they had just entered the room. Her elegant dress and the fine chair in which

nature of modern life. Among the most striking of these is a painting of the 1630s, portraying a laughing—presumably inebriated—older woman with a large beer tankard in her right hand and a shadowy owl perched on her shoulder, known as **MALLE BABBE** (**FIG. 23-32**). The figure is based on a real individual, a well-known Haarlem barmaid who was eventually confined to a charitable mental institution; the word "Malle" means loony or mad, and the owl was a popular symbol of folly. Hals's painting technique in this character study is looser and more energetic than in most of his formal portraits, where he often restrained his stylistic exuberance to conform to the expectations of his wealthy sitters. Here he felt freer in a painting that may have had personal significance. The historical Malle Babbe was confined

23-33 • Judith Leyster SELF-PORTRAIT
1635. Oil on canvas, 29⅜″ × 25⅝″ (74.6 × 65.1 cm).
National Gallery of Art, Washington, DC.
Gift of Mr. and Mrs. Robert Woods Bliss (1949.6.4)

she sits are symbols of her success as an artist whose popularity was based on the very type of painting in progress on her easel. One critic has suggested that her subject—a man playing a violin—may be a visual pun on the painter with palette and brush. Leyster's understanding of light and texture is truly remarkable. The brushwork she used to depict her own flesh and delicate ruff is more controlled than Hals's loose technique, and forms an interesting contrast to the broad strokes of thick paint she used to create her full, stiff skirt. She further emphasized the difference between her portrait and her painting by executing the image on her easel in lighter tones and softer, looser brushwork. The narrow range of colors sensitively dispersed in the composition and the warm spotlighting are typical of Leyster's mature style.

REMBRANDT VAN RIJN The most important painter working in Amsterdam in the seventeenth century was Rembrandt van Rijn (1606–1669). One of nine children born in Leiden to a miller and his wife, Rembrandt studied under Pieter Lastman (1583–1633), the principal painter in Amsterdam at the time. From Lastman, a history painter who had worked in Rome, Rembrandt absorbed an interest in the naturalism, drama, and tenebrism championed by Caravaggio. By the 1630s, Rembrandt was established in Amsterdam primarily as a portrait painter, although he also painted a wide range of narrative themes and landscapes.

In his first group portrait, **THE ANATOMY LESSON OF DR. NICOLAES TULP** (**FIG. 23-34**) of 1632, Rembrandt combined his scientific and humanistic interests. Frans Hals had activated the group portrait rather than conceiving it as a simple reproduction of posed figures and faces; Rembrandt transformed it into a charged moment from a life story. Dr. Tulp, head of the surgeons' guild from 1628 to 1653, sits right of center, while a group of fellow physicians gathers around to observe the cadaver and learn from the famed anatomist. Rembrandt built his composition on a sharp diagonal that pierces space from right to left, uniting

23-34 • Rembrandt van Rijn **THE ANATOMY LESSON OF DR. NICOLAES TULP**
1632. Oil on canvas, 5′3¾″ × 7′1¼″ (1.6 × 2.1 m). Mauritshuis, The Hague.

View the Closer Look for *The Anatomy Lesson of Dr. Nicolaes Tulp* on myartslab.com

23-35 • Rembrandt van Rijn THE COMPANY OF CAPTAIN FRANS BANNING COCQ (THE NIGHT WATCH)
1642. Oil on canvas, 11′11″ × 14′4″ (3.63 × 4.37 m) (cut down from the original size). Rijksmuseum, Amsterdam.

the cadaver on the table, the calculated arrangement of speaker and listeners, and the open book into a dramatic narrative event. Rembrandt makes effective use of Caravaggio's tenebrist technique, as the figures emerge from a dark and undefined ambience, their attentive faces framed by brilliant white ruffs. Radiant light streams down to spotlight the ghostly flesh of the cadaver, drawing our attention to the extended arms of Dr. Tulp, who flexes his own left hand to demonstrate the action of the cadaver's arm muscles that he lifts up with silver forceps. Unseen by the viewers are the illustrations of the huge book, presumably an edition of Andreas Vesalius's study of human anatomy, published in Basel in 1543, which was the first attempt at accurate anatomical illustrations in print. Rembrandt's painting has been seen as an homage to Vesalius and to science, as well as a portrait of the members of the Amsterdam surgeons' guild.

Prolific and popular with his Amsterdam clientele, Rembrandt ran a busy studio, producing works that sold for high prices. The prodigious output of his large workshop and of the many followers who imitated his manner has made it difficult for scholars to define his body of work, and many paintings formerly attributed to Rembrandt have recently been assigned to other artists. Rembrandt's mature work reflected his cosmopolitan city environment, his study of science and nature, and the broadening of his artistic vocabulary by the study of Italian Renaissance art, chiefly from engravings and paintings imported by the busy Amsterdam art market.

In 1642, Rembrandt was one of several artists commissioned by a wealthy civic-guard company to create large group portraits of its members for its new meeting hall. The result, **THE COMPANY OF CAPTAIN FRANS BANNING COCQ** (FIG. 23-35), carries the idea of a group portrait as a dramatic event even farther. Because

Rembrandt was the first artist to popularize **etching** as a major form of artistic expression. Etching is an intaglio technique, meaning that the design is carved out of the surface of the printing plate. First the metal plate is coated on both sides with an acid-resistant resin that dries hard without being brittle. Then, instead of laboriously cutting the lines of the desired image directly into the plate as in an engraving (see "Woodcuts and Engravings on Metal," page 592) the artist scratches delicately through the resin with a sharp needle to expose the metal. The plate is then immersed in acid, which eats into the metal exposed by the drawn lines. By controlling the time the acid stays on different parts of the plate, the artist can make shallow, fine lines or deep, heavy ones. After the resin coating is removed from the surface of the plate, an impression is taken. If changes need to be made, lines can be "erased" with a sharp metal scraper. Not surprisingly, a complex image with a wide range of tones requires many steps.

Another intaglio technique for registering images with incised lines on a metal plate is called **drypoint**, in which a sharp needle is used to scratch lines directly into the metal. In drypoint, however, the burr (metal pushed up by the drypoint needle) is left in place. Unlike engraving, in which the burr is scraped off, here both the burr and the groove hold the ink. This creates a printed line with a rich black appearance that is impossible to achieve with engraving or etching alone. Unfortunately, drypoint burr is fragile, and no more than a dozen prints can be made before it flattens and loses its character. Rembrandt's earliest prints were entirely etched, but later he added drypoint to develop tonal richness.

👁—|**Watch** a video about the process of intaglio on myartslab.com

a dense layer of grime had darkened and obscured its colors, this painting was once thought to be a nocturnal scene and was therefore called *The Night Watch*. After cleaning and restoration in 1975–1976, it now exhibits a natural golden light that sets afire the palette of rich colors—browns, blues, olive-green, orange, and red—around a central core of lemon yellow in the costume of a lieutenant. To the dramatic group composition, showing a company forming for a parade in an Amsterdam street, Rembrandt added several colorful but seemingly unnecessary figures. While the officers stride purposefully forward, the rest of the men and several mischievous children mill about. The radiant young girl in the left middle ground, carrying a chicken with prominent claws (*klauw* in Dutch), may be a pun on the kind of guns (*klower*) that gave the name (the *Kloveniers*) to the company. Chicken legs with claws also are part of its coat of arms. The complex interactions of the figures and the vivid, individualized likenesses of the militiamen make this one of the greatest group portraits in the Dutch tradition.

In his enthusiasm for printmaking as an important art form with its own aesthetic qualities, Rembrandt was remarkably like Albrecht Dürer (see FIGS. 22-7, 22-8). Beginning in 1627, he focused on etching, which uses acid to inscribe a design on metal

23-36 • Rembrandt van Rijn THREE CROSSES (FIRST STATE)
1653. Drypoint, 15⅛″ × 17¾″ (38.5 × 45 cm). Rijksmuseum, Amsterdam.

23-37 • Rembrandt van Rijn THREE CROSSES (FOURTH STATE)
1653. Drypoint, 15⅛″ × 17¾″ (38.5 × 45 cm). Metropolitan Museum of Art, New York.

plates. About a decade later, he began to experiment with making additions to his compositions in the drypoint technique, in which the artist uses a sharp needle to scratch shallow lines in a plate. Because etching and drypoint allow the artist to work directly on the plate, the style of the finished print can have the relatively free and spontaneous character of a drawing (see "Etching and Drypoint," opposite). In these works Rembrandt alone took charge of the creative process, from the preparation of the plate to its inking and printing, and he constantly experimented with the technique, with methods of inking, and with papers for printing. Rembrandt's prints were sought after, widely collected, and attracted high prices, even in his lifetime.

Rembrandt's deep speculations on the meaning of the life of Christ evolve in a series of prints of the **THREE CROSSES**, that comes down to us in five states, or stages, of the creative and printing process, in this case created exclusively using the drypoint technique. (Only the first and fourth states are reproduced here.) Rembrandt sought to capture the moment described in the Gospels when, during the Crucifixion, darkness covered the Earth and Jesus cried out, "Father, into thy hands I commend my spirit." In the first state (**FIG. 23-36**), the centurion kneels in front of the cross while other terrified people run from the scene. The Virgin Mary and St. John share the light flooding down from heaven. By the fourth state (**FIG. 23-37**), Rembrandt has completely reworked and reinterpreted the theme. As in the first state, the shattered hill of Golgotha dominates the foreground, but now the scene is considerably darker, and some of the people in the first state, including even Mary and Jesus' friends, have almost disappeared. The horseman holding the lance now faces Jesus. The composition has become more compact, the individual elements are simplified, and the emotions are intensified. An oval of light below the base of the cross draws viewers' attention to the figure of Jesus, and the people around him are trapped in mute confrontation. The first state is a detailed rendering of a narrative moment, bustling with detail; the fourth state reduces the event to its mysterious essence. The eternal battles of dark and light, doom and salvation, evil and good—all seem to be waged anew.

As he aged, Rembrandt painted ever more brilliantly, varying textures and paint from the thinnest glazes to thick **impasto** (heavily applied pigments), creating a rich, luminous *chiaroscuro*, ranging from deepest shadow to brilliant highlights in a dazzling display of gold, red, and chestnut-brown. His sensitivity to the human

condition is perhaps nowhere more powerfully expressed than in his late self-portraits, which became more searching as he aged. Distilling a lifetime of study and contemplation, he expressed an internalized spirituality new in the history of art. In his **SELF-PORTRAIT** of 1658 (**FIG. 23-38**), the artist assumes a regal pose, at ease, with arms and legs spread, holding a staff as if it were a baton of command. Yet we know that fortune no longer smiled on him; he had declared bankruptcy in 1656, and over the two-year period between that moment and this self-portrait he had sold his private art collection and even his house to cover his debts. It is possible to relate the stress of this situation to the way he represents himself here. A few well-placed brushstrokes suggest the physical tension in the fingers and the weariness of the deep-set eyes. Mercilessly analytical, the portrait depicts the furrowed brow, sagging flesh, and aging face of one who has suffered pitfalls but managed to survive, retaining his dignity.

23-38 • Rembrandt van Rijn **SELF-PORTRAIT**
1658. Oil on canvas, 52⅝″ × 40⅞″ (133.6 × 103.8 cm). The Frick Collection, New York.

JOHANNES VERMEER One of the most intriguing Dutch artists of this period is Johannes Vermeer (1632–1675), who was also an innkeeper and art dealer. He entered the Delft artists' guild in 1653 and painted only for local patrons. Meticulous in his technique, with a unique and highly structured compositional approach and soft, liquid painting style, Vermeer produced fewer than 40 canvases that can be securely attributed to him. The more these paintings are studied, the more questions arise about the artist's life and his methods. Vermeer's **VIEW OF DELFT** (**FIG. 23-39**), for example, is no simple cityscape. Although the artist convinces the viewer of its authenticity, he does not paint a photographic reproduction of the scene; Vermeer moves buildings around to create an ideal composition. He endows the city with a timeless stability by a stress on horizontal lines, the careful placement of buildings, the quiet atmosphere, and the clear, even light that seems to emerge from beneath low-lying clouds. Vermeer may have experimented with the mechanical device known as the **camera obscura** (see Chapter 31, page 968), not as a method of reproducing the image but as another tool in the visual analysis of the composition. The camera obscura would have enhanced optical distortions that led to the "beading" of highlights (seen here on the harbored ships and dark gray architecture), which creates the illusion of brilliant light but does not dissolve the underlying form.

Most of Vermeer's paintings portray enigmatic scenes of women in their homes, alone or with a servant, occupied with some refined activity, such as writing, reading letters, or playing a musical instrument. These are quiet and still interior scenes, gentle in color, asymmetrical but strongly geometric in organization. By creating a contained and consistent architectonic world in which each object adds to the clarity and balance of the composition, Vermeer transports everyday scenes to a level of unearthly perfection. An even, pearly light from a window often gives solidity to the figures and objects in a room. All emotion is subdued, evoking a mood of quiet meditation. Vermeer's brushwork is so controlled that it becomes invisible, except when he paints his characteristic pools of reflected light as tiny, pearl-like droplets of color.

In **WOMAN HOLDING A BALANCE** (**FIG. 23-40**), studied equilibrium creates a monumental composition and a moment of supreme stillness. The woman contemplates the balance in her right hand, drawing our attention to the act of weighing and judging. Her hand and the scale are central, but directly behind her head, on the wall of the room, is a painting of the Last Judgment, highlighting the figure of Christ the Judge in a gold aureole above her head. The juxtaposition seems to turn Vermeer's genre scene into a metaphor for eternal judgment, a sobering religious reference that may reflect the artist's own position as a Catholic living in a Protestant country. The woman's moment of quiet introspection in front of the gold and pearls displayed on the table before her, shimmering with reflected light from the window, also evokes the *vanitas* theme of the transience of earthly life, allowing the painter to comment on the ephemeral quality of material things.

GENRE SCENES Continuing a long Netherlandish tradition, seventeenth-century genre paintings—generally made for private patrons and depicting scenes of contemporary daily life—were often laden with symbolic references, although their meaning is not always clear to us now. A clean house might indicate a virtuous housewife and mother, while a messy household suggested laziness and the sin of sloth. Ladies dressing in front of mirrors certainly could be succumbing to vanity, and drinking parties led to overindulgence and lust.

Gerard ter Borch (1617–1681) was one of the most refined of the genre painters. In his painting traditionally known as **THE SUITOR'S VISIT** (**FIG. 23–41**), from about 1658, a well-dressed man bows gracefully to an elegant woman arrayed in white satin, who stands in a sumptuously furnished room in which another woman plays a lute. Another man, in front of a fireplace, turns to observe the newcomer. The painting appears to represent a prosperous gentleman paying a call on a lady of equal social status,

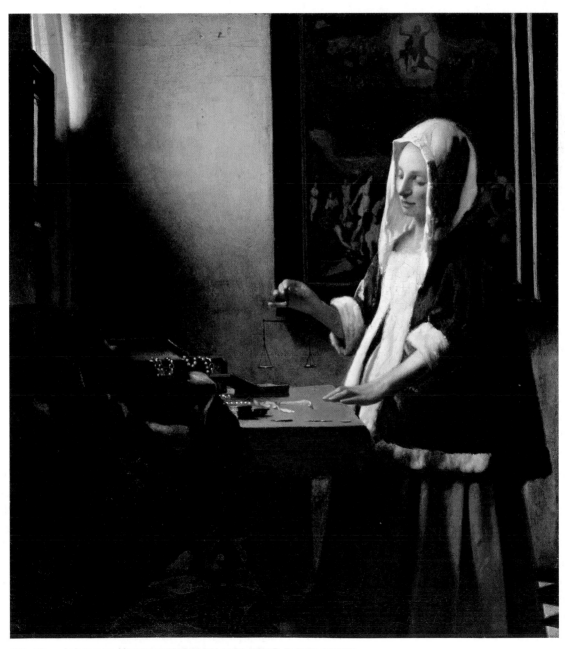

23-40 • Johannes Vermeer WOMAN HOLDING A BALANCE
c. 1664. Oil on canvas, 15⅝″ × 14″ (39.7 × 35.5 cm). National Gallery of Art, Washington, DC. Widener Collection (1942.9.97)

Watch a video about Vermeer's *Woman Holding a Balance* on myartslab.com

23-41 • Gerard ter Borch **THE SUITOR'S VISIT**
c. 1658. Oil on canvas, 32½″ × 29⅝″ (82.6 × 75.3 cm). National Gallery of Art, Washington, DC. Andrew W. Mellon Collection

possibly a courtship scene. The spaniel and the musician seem to be simply part of the scene, but we are already familiar with the dog as a symbol of fidelity, and stringed instruments were said to symbolize, through their tuning, the harmony of souls and thus, possibly, a loving relationship. On the other hand, music making was also associated with sensory pleasure evoked by touch. Ter Borch's exquisite rendering highlights the lace, velvet, and especially the satin of these opulent outfits, potentially symbols of personal excess. If there is a moral lesson, it is presented discreetly and ambiguously.

Another important genre painter is Jan Steen (1626–1679), whose larger brushstrokes contrast with the meticulous treatment of Ter Borch and reveal an artistic affinity with Frans Hals. Steen painted over 800 works but never achieved financial success. Most of his scenes used everyday life to portray moral tales, illustrate proverbs and folk sayings, or make puns to amuse the spectator. Since Steen traveled throughout the Netherlands all his life, and since during the 1670s he was a tavern owner in Leiden, he had many sources of inspiration for the lively human dramas highlighted in his paintings.

Jan Steen's paintings of children are especially remarkable, for he captured not only their childish physiques but also their fleeting moods and expressions with rapid and fluid brushstrokes. A characteristic example is his painting **THE FEAST OF ST. NICHOLAS** (FIG. 23-42), from the 1660s. Steen's household setting holds none of the intimate order and quiet stillness favored by Vermeer, nor the elegant decorum and guarded interaction portrayed by Ter Borch. This is a scene of noisy commotion within a joyous family get-together, where children react in various ways—disappointment, delight, possessiveness—to the pre-Christmas gifts St. Nicholas has left for them in their shoes. Steen renders the objects scattered in the disordered foreground with meticulous attention to the details of surface texture, but the focus here is the festive atmosphere of a boisterous holiday morning and the folksy figures who delight in the celebration.

Emanuel de Witte (1617–1692) of Rotterdam specialized in architectural interiors, first in Delft in 1640 and then in Amsterdam after settling there permanently in 1652. Although many of his interiors were composites of features from several locations combined in one idealized architectural view, De Witte also painted faithful "portraits" of actual buildings. One of these is his **PORTUGUESE SYNAGOGUE, AMSTERDAM** (FIG. 23-43) of 1680. The synagogue shown here, which still stands in Amsterdam, is a rectangular hall divided into one wide central aisle with narrow

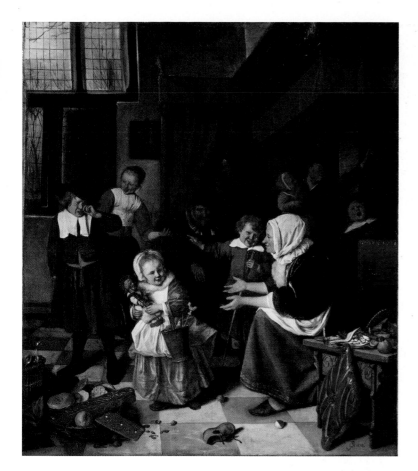

23-42 • Jan Steen **THE FEAST OF ST. NICHOLAS**
c. 1660–1665. Oil on canvas, 32¼″ × 27¾″ (82 × 70.5 cm).
Rijksmuseum, Amsterdam.

were well-to-do merchants. Fund-raising for a new synagogue began in 1670, and in 1671 Elias Bouman and Daniel Stalpaert began work on the building. With its classical architecture, Brazilian jacaranda-wood furniture, and 26 brass chandeliers, this synagogue was considered one of the most impressive buildings in Amsterdam.

LANDSCAPE The Dutch loved the landscapes and vast skies of their own country, but landscape painters worked in their studios rather than in nature, and they were never afraid to rearrange, add to, or subtract from a scene in order to give their compositions formal organization or a desired mood. Starting in the 1620s, landscape painters generally adhered to a convention in which little color was used beyond browns, grays, and beiges. After 1650, they tended toward more individualistic styles, but nearly all brought a broader range of colors into play. One continuing motif was the emphasis on

side aisles, each covered with a wooden barrel vault resting on lintels supported by columns. De Witte's shift of the viewpoint slightly to one side has created an intriguing spatial composition, and strong contrasts of light and shade add dramatic movement to the simple interior. The elegant couple and the dogs in the foreground provide both a sense of scale for the architecture and some human interest for viewers.

Today, this painting is interesting not only as a work of art, but also as a record of seventeenth-century synagogue architecture, documenting Dutch religious tolerance in an age when European Jews were often persecuted. Expelled from Spain and Portugal from the late fifteenth century on, many Jews had settled in Amsterdam, and their community numbered about 2,300 people, most of whom

23-43 • Emanuel de Witte **PORTUGUESE SYNAGOGUE, AMSTERDAM**
1680. Oil on canvas, 43½″ × 39″ (110.5 × 99.1 cm).
Rijksmuseum, Amsterdam.

Architects Daniel Stalpaert and Elias Bouman built the synagogue in 1671–1675.

23-44 • Jacob van Ruisdael VIEW OF HAARLEM FROM THE DUNES AT OVERVEEN
c. 1670. Oil on canvas, 22″ × 24¼″ (55.8 × 62.8 cm). Royal Picture Gallery, Mauritshuis, The Hague.

cloud-filled expanses of sky dominating a relatively narrow horizontal band of earth below.

The Haarlem landscape specialist Jacob van Ruisdael (1628/29–1682), whose popularity drew many pupils to his workshop, was especially adept at both the invention of dramatic compositions and the projection of moods. His **VIEW OF HAARLEM FROM THE DUNES AT OVERVEEN** (FIG. 23-44), painted about 1670, celebrates the flatlands outside Haarlem that had been reclaimed from the sea as part of a massive landfill project that the Dutch compared with God's restoration of the Earth after Noah's Flood. Such a religious interpretation may be referenced here in the prominent Gothic church of St. Bavo, looming on the horizon.

There may be other messages as well. While almost three-quarters of this painting is devoted to a rendering of the powerfully cloudy sky, tiny humans can be seen laboring below, caught in the process of spreading white linen across the broad fields to bleach in the sun. This glorification of the industriousness of citizens engaged in one of Haarlem's principal industries must have made the painting particularly appealing to the patriotic local market.

STILL LIFES AND FLOWER PIECES The Dutch were so proud of their still-life painting tradition that they presented a flower painting by Rachel Ruysch to the French queen Marie de' Medici during her state visit to Amsterdam. Like genre paintings,

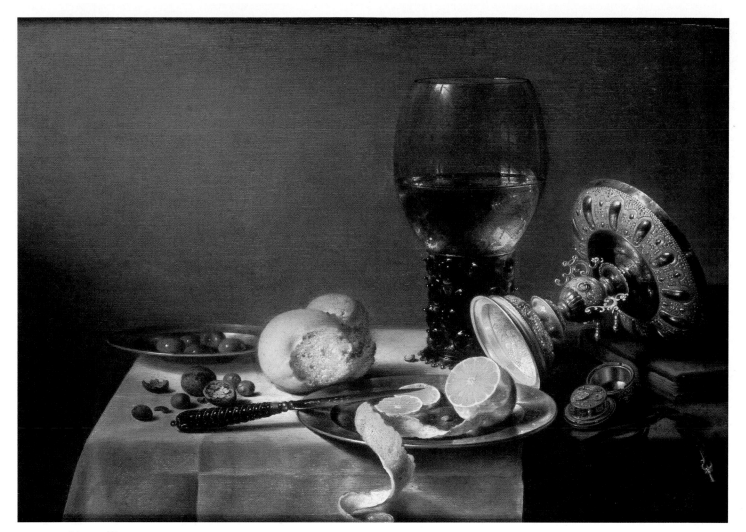

23-45 • Pieter Claesz STILL LIFE WITH TAZZA
1636. Oil on panel, 17⅜″ × 24″ (44 × 61 cm). Royal Cabinet of Paintings Mauritshuis, The Hague.

The heavy round glass is a Roemer, a relatively inexpensive, everyday item, as are the pewter plates. The silver cup (*tazza*) was a typical ornamental piece. Painters owned and shared such valuable props, and this and other showpieces appear in many paintings.

a still-life painting might carry moralizing connotations and commonly had a *vanitas* theme, reminding viewers of the transience of life and material possessions, even art. Yet it can also document and showcase the wealth of its owner.

One of the first Dutch still-life painters was Pieter Claesz (1596/97–1660) of Haarlem, who, like Antwerp artist Clara Peeters (see FIG. 23-29), painted "breakfast pieces," that is, meals of bread, fruits, and nuts. In subtle, nearly monochromatic paintings, such as **STILL LIFE WITH TAZZA** (FIG. 23-45), Claesz seems to give life to inanimate objects. He organizes dishes in diagonal positions to give a strong sense of space—here reinforced by the spiraling strip of lemon peel, foreshortened with the plate into the foreground and reaching toward the viewer's own space—and he renders the maximum contrast of textures within a subtle palette of yellows, browns, greens, and silvery whites. The tilted silver *tazza* contrasts with the half-filled glass, which becomes a towering monumental presence and permits Claesz to display his skill at transparencies

and reflections. Such paintings suggest the prosperity of Claesz's patrons. The food might be simple, but the silver ornamental cup graced the tables of only the wealthy. The meticulously painted timepiece could suggest deeper meanings—it alludes to human technological achievement, but also to the inexorable passage of time and the fleeting nature of human life, thoughts also prompted by the interrupted breakfast, casually placed knife, and toppled tableware.

Still-life paintings in which cut-flower arrangements predominate were referred to simply as "flower pieces." Significant advances were made in botany during the seventeenth century through the application of orderly scientific methods and objective observation (see "Science and the Changing Worldview," page 756). Then, as now, the Dutch were major growers and exporters of flowers, especially the tulips that appear in nearly every flower piece in dozens of exquisite variations. The Dutch tradition of flower painting peaked in the long career of Rachel Ruysch (1664–1750)

From the mid-sixteenth through the seventeenth centuries, new discoveries about the natural world brought a sense of both the grand scale and the microscopic detail of the universe. To publish their theories and research, early scientists learned to draw or depended on artists to draw what they discovered in the world around them. This practice would continue until the invention of photography in the nineteenth century.

Artist and scientist were seldom the same person, but Anna Maria Sibylla Merian (1647–1717) contributed to botany and entomology both as a researcher and as an artist. German by birth and Dutch by training, Merian was once described by a Dutch contemporary as a painter of worms, flies, mosquitoes, spiders, "and other filth." In 1699, the city of Amsterdam subsidized Merian's research on plants and insects in the Dutch colony of Surinam in South America, where she spent two years exploring the jungle and recording insects. On her return to the Dutch Republic, she published the results of her research as **THE METAMORPHOSIS OF THE INSECTS OF SURINAM**, illustrated with 72 large plates engraved after her watercolors (**FIG. 23–46**). For all her meticulous scientific accuracy, Merian carefully arranged her depictions of exotic insects and elegant fruits and flowers into skillful and harmonious compositions.

But interest in scientific exploration was not limited to the Netherlands. The writings of philosophers Francis Bacon (1561–1626) in England and René Descartes (1596–1650) in France helped establish a new scientific method of studying the world by insisting on scrupulous objectivity and logical reasoning. Bacon argued that the facts be established from observation and tested by controlled experiments. Descartes, who was also a mathematician, argued for the deductive method of reasoning, in which conclusions were arrived at logically from basic premises.

In 1543, the Polish scholar Nicolaus Copernicus (1473–1543) published *On the Revolutions of the Heavenly Spheres*, which contradicted the long-held view that the Earth is the center of the universe (the Ptolemaic theory) by arguing instead that it and the other planets revolve around the sun. The Church put Copernicus's work on its *Index of Prohibited Books* in 1616, but Johannes Kepler (1571–1630) continued demonstrating that the planets revolve around the sun in elliptical orbits. Galileo Galilei (1564–1642), an astronomer, mathematician, and physicist, developed the telescope as a tool for observing the heavens and provided further confirmation of Copernican theory but since the Church prohibited its teaching, Galileo was tried for heresy by the Inquisition and forced to recant his views.

The new seventeenth-century science turned to the study of the very small as well as to the vast reaches of space. This included the development of the microscope by the Dutch lens-maker and amateur scientist Anton van Leeuwenhoek (1632–1723). Leeuwenhoek perfected grinding techniques and increased the power of his lenses far beyond what was required for a simple magnifying glass. Ultimately, he was able to study the inner workings of plants and animals and even see micro-organisms.

23-46 • Anna Maria Sibylla Merian **PLATE 9 FROM THE METAMORPHOSIS OF THE INSECTS OF SURINAM**
1719. Hand-colored engraving, 18⅞″ × 13″ (47.9 × 33 cm). National Museum of Women in the Arts, Washington, DC. Gift of Wallace and Wilhelmina Holladay Collection, funds contributed by Mr. and Mrs. George G. Anderman and an anonymous donor (1976.56)

of Amsterdam. Her flower pieces were highly prized for their sensitive, free-form arrangements and their unusual and beautiful color harmonies. During her 70-year career, she became one of the most sought-after and highest-paid still-life painters in Europe—her paintings brought in twice what Rembrandt's did.

In her **FLOWER STILL LIFE** (**FIG. 23-47**), painted shortly after the end of the century, Ruysch placed the container at the center of the canvas's width, then created an asymmetrical floral arrangement of pale oranges, pinks, and yellows rising from lower left to top right of the picture, offset by the strong diagonal of the tabletop. To further balance the painting, she placed highlighted blossoms and leaves on the dark left half of the canvas and silhouetted them against the light wall area on the right. Ruysch often emphasized the beauty of curving flower stems and enlivened her

23-47 • Rachel Ruysch FLOWER STILL LIFE

After 1700. Oil on canvas, 30″ × 24″ (76.2 × 61 cm). The Toledo Museum of Art, Ohio. Purchased with funds from the Libbey Endowment. Gift of Edward Drummond Libbey (1956.57)

(regency 1610–1617; see FIG. 23-27), as regent for her 9-year-old son, Louis XIII (r. 1610–1643). When Louis came of age, the brilliant and unscrupulous Cardinal Richelieu became chief minister and set about increasing the power of the crown at the expense of the French nobility. The death of Louis XIII again left France with a child king, the 5-year-old Louis XIV (r. 1643–1715). His mother, Anne of Austria, became regent, with the assistance of another powerful minister, Cardinal Mazarin. At Mazarin's death in 1661, Louis XIV began his long personal reign, assisted by yet another able minister, Jean-Baptiste Colbert.

compositions with interesting additions, such as casually placed pieces of fruit or insects, in this case a large gray moth (lower left) and two snail shells.

Flower painting was almost never a straightforward depiction of actual fresh flowers. Instead, artists made color sketches of fresh examples of each type of flower and studied scientifically accurate color illustrations in botanical publications. In the studio, using their sketches and notebooks, they would compose bouquets of perfect specimens of a variety of flowers that could never be found blooming at the same time. The short life of flowers was a poignant reminder of the fleeting nature of beauty and of human life.

FRANCE

Early seventeenth-century France was marked by almost continuous foreign and civil wars. The assassination of King Henry IV in 1610 left France in the hands of the queen, Marie de' Medici

An absolute monarch whose reign was the longest in European history, Louis XIV made the French court the envy of every ruler in Europe. He became known as *le Roi Soleil* ("the Sun King") and was sometimes glorified in art through identification with the Classical sun god, Apollo. In a 1701 portrait by court painter Hyacinthe Rigaud (1659–1743), the richly costumed **LOUIS XIV** is framed by a lavish, billowing curtain (**FIG. 23-48**). Proudly showing off his elegant legs, the 63-year-old monarch poses in a blue robe of state, trimmed with gold *fleurs-de-lis* and lined with white ermine. He wears the high-heeled shoes he devised to compensate for his shortness. Despite his pompous pose and magnificent surroundings, the directness of the king's gaze and the frankness of his aging face make him appear surprisingly human.

The arts, like everything else, came under royal control. In 1635, Cardinal Richelieu had founded the French Royal Academy, directing the members to compile a definitive dictionary and grammar of the French language. In 1648, the Royal Academy

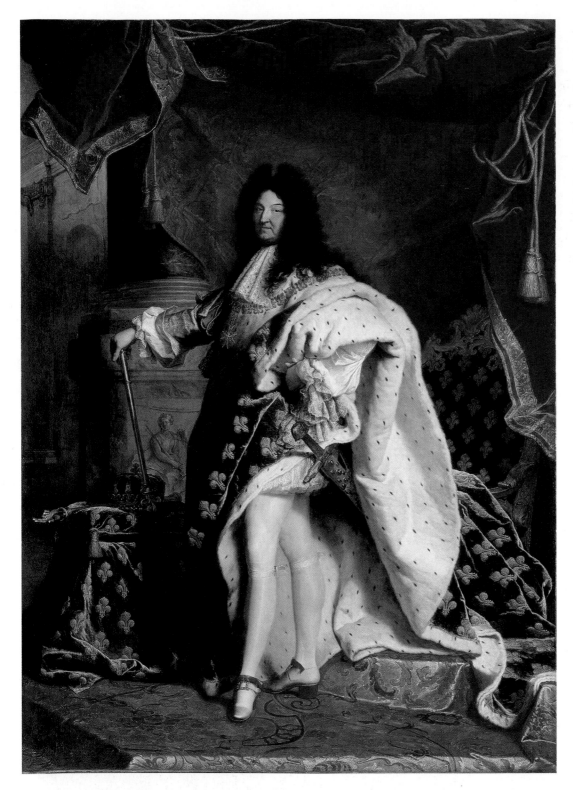

23-48 • Hyacinthe Rigaud
LOUIS XIV
1701. Oil on canvas, 9′2″ × 7′10¾″ (2.19 × 2.4 m). Musée du Louvre, Paris.

Louis XIV had ordered this portrait as a gift for his grandson, the future Philip V of Spain (r. 1700–1746), but when Rigaud finished the painting, Louis liked it too much to give it away and only three years later ordered a copy from Rigaud to give to his grandson. The request for copies of royal portraits was not unusual since the aristocratic families of Europe were linked through marriage. Paintings made appropriate gifts and at the same time memorialized important political alliances by recording them in visual form.

 View the Closer Look for *Louis XIV* on myartslab.com

of Painting and Sculpture was founded, which, as reorganized by Colbert in 1663, maintained strict control over the arts (see "Grading the Old Masters," page 763). Although it was not the first European arts academy, none before it had exerted such dictatorial authority—an authority that lasted in France until the late nineteenth century. Membership of the academy assured an artist of royal and civic commissions and financial success, but many talented artists did well outside it.

ARCHITECTURE AND ITS DECORATION AT VERSAILLES

French architecture developed along Classical lines in the second half of the seventeenth century under the influence of François Mansart (1598–1666) and Louis Le Vau (1612–1670). When the Royal Academy of Architecture was founded in 1671, its members developed guidelines for architectural design based on the belief that mathematics was the true basis of beauty. Their chief sources for ideal models were the books of Vitruvius and Palladio.

In 1668, Louis XIV began to enlarge the small château built by Louis XIII at Versailles, not far from Paris. Louis moved to the palace in 1682 and eventually required his court to live in Versailles; 5,000 aristocrats lived in the palace itself, together with 14,000 servants and military staff members. The town had another 30,000 residents, most of whom were royal employees. The designers of the palace and park complex at Versailles were Le Vau, Charles Le Brun (1619–1690), who oversaw the interior decoration, and André Le Nôtre (1613–1700), who planned the gardens (see "Garden Design," page 761). For both political and sentimental reasons, the old château was left standing, and the new building went up around it. This project consisted of two phases: the first additions by Le Vau, begun in 1668; and an enlargement completed after Le Vau's death by his successor, Jules Hardouin-Mansart (1646–1708), from 1670 to 1685.

Hardouin-Mansart was responsible for the addition of the long lateral wings and the renovation of Le Vau's central block on the garden side to match these wings (**FIG. 23-49**). The three-story façade has a lightly rusticated ground floor, a main floor lined with enormous arched windows separated by Ionic columns or pilasters, an attic level whose rectangular windows are also flanked by

pilasters, and a flat, terraced roof. The overall design is a sensitive balance of horizontals and verticals relieved by a restrained overlay of regularly spaced projecting blocks with open, colonnaded porches.

In his renovation of Le Vau's center-block façade, Hardouin-Mansart enclosed the previously open gallery on the main level, creating the famed **HALL OF MIRRORS** (**FIG. 23-50**), which is about 240 feet (73 meters) long and 47 feet (13 meters) high. He achieved architectural symmetry and a sense of both splendor and expansiveness by lining the interior wall with Venetian glass mirrors, matching in size and shape the arched windows in the opposing wall. Mirrors were small and extremely expensive in the seventeenth century, and these huge walls of reflective glass were created by fitting 18-inch panels together. They reflect the natural light from the windows and give the impression of an even larger space; at night, the reflections of flickering candles must have turned the mirrored gallery into a shimmering tableau in which the king and courtiers saw themselves as they promenaded.

Inspired by Carracci's Farnese ceiling (see **FIG. 23-8**), Le Brun decorated the vaulted ceiling with paintings on canvas (more stable in the damp northern climate) glorifying the reign and military triumphs of Louis XIV, accompanied by Classical gods. In 1642, Le Brun had studied in Italy, where he came under the influence

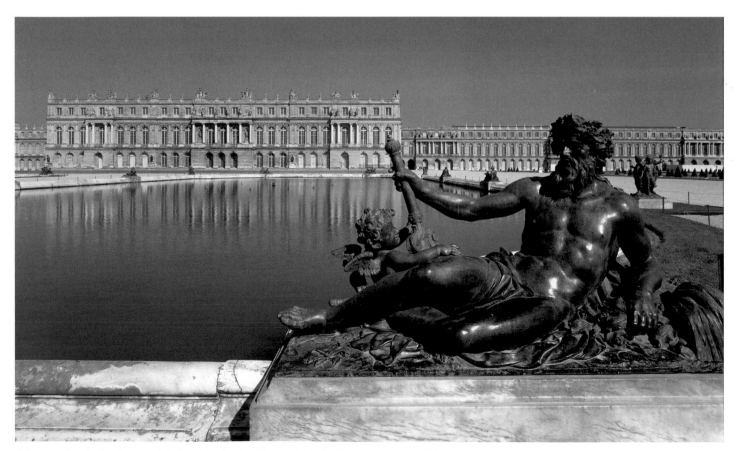

23-49 • Louis Le Vau and Jules Hardouin-Mansart GARDEN FAÇADE OF THE PALACE OF VERSAILLES
1678–1685. Foreground: Jean-Baptiste Tuby *Neptune*.

Watch a video about Versailles on myartslab.com

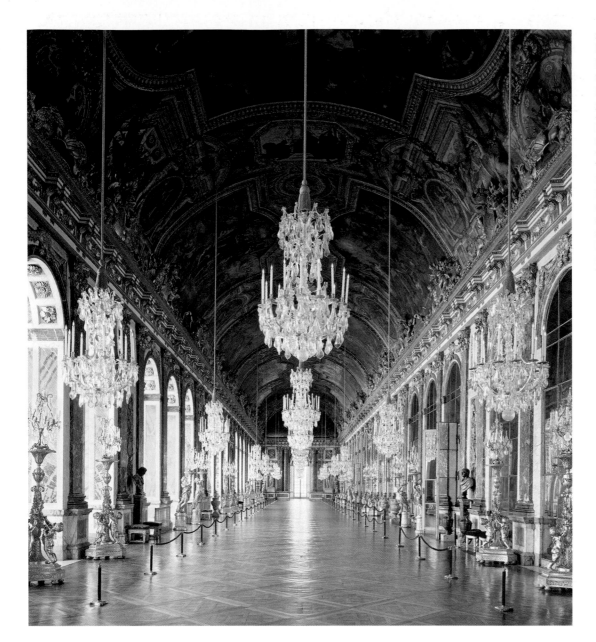

23-50 • Jules Hardouin-Mansart and Charles Le Brun HALL OF MIRRORS, PALACE OF VERSAILLES Begun 1678. Length approx. 240′ (73 m).

In the seventeenth century, mirrors and clear window glass were enormously expensive. To furnish the Hall of Mirrors, hundreds of glass panels of manageable size had to be assembled into the proper shape and attached to one another with glazing bars, which became part of the decorative pattern of the vast room.

of the Classical style of his compatriot Nicolas Poussin. As "first painter to the king" and director of the Royal Academy of Painting and Sculpture, Le Brun controlled art education and patronage from 1661/63 until his death in 1690. He tempered the warmly exuberant Baroque ceilings he had seen in Rome with Poussin's cool Classicism. The underlying theme for his design and decoration of Versailles was the glorification of the king as Apollo the sun god, with whom Louis identified. Louis XIV thought of the duties of kingship, including its pageantry, as a solemn performance, so it is most appropriate that Rigaud's portrait presents him on a raised, stagelike platform, with a theatrical curtain (see FIG. 23-48). Versailles became the splendid stage on which the king played the principal role in the grandiose drama of state.

PAINTING

Sixteenth-century French Mannerism began to give way in the 1620s to Classicism and the impact of Caravaggio, especially his tenebrism and compression of large-scale figures into the foreground. As the century progressed, the control of the Royal Academy and its encouragement of studies of the Classics and the surviving antiquities in Rome, guided French painting toward the Classicism propounded by Le Brun.

CARAVAGGIO'S INFLUENCE: GEORGES DE LA TOUR AND THE LE NAIN BROTHERS One of Caravaggio's most important followers in France, Georges de La Tour (1593–1652) received major royal and ducal commissions and became court painter to Louis XIII in 1639. La Tour may have traveled to Italy in 1614–1616, and in the 1620s he almost certainly visited the Netherlands, where Caravaggio's style was having an impact (see FIG. 23-30). Like Caravaggio, La Tour filled the foreground of his compositions with imposing figures, but in place of Caravaggio's focus on descriptive detail, La Tour's work revels in the dramatic effects of lighting, usually from sources within the paintings

Wealthy and aristocratic French landowners commissioned garden designers to transform their large properties into gardens extending over many acres. The challenge for garden designers was to unify diverse elements—buildings, pools, monuments, plantings, natural land formations—into a coherent whole. At Versailles, André Le Nôtre imposed order upon the vast expanses of palace gardens and park by using broad, straight avenues radiating from a series of round focal points (**FIG. 23–51**). He succeeded so thoroughly that his plan inspired generations of urban designers as well as landscape architects.

In Le Nôtre's hands, the palace terrain became an extraordinary work of art and a visual delight for its inhabitants. Neatly contained expanses of lawn and broad, straight vistas seemed to stretch to the horizon, while the formal gardens became an exercise in precise geometry. The gardens at Versailles are classically harmonious in their symmetrical, geometric design but Baroque in their vast size and extension into the surrounding countryside, where the gardens thickened into woods cut by straight avenues.

The most formal gardens lay nearest the palace, and plantings became progressively less elaborate and larger in scale as their distance from the palace increased. Broad, intersecting paths separated reflecting pools and planting beds, which are called embroidered **parterres** for their colorful patterns of flowers outlined with trimmed hedges. After the formal zone of parterres came lawns, large fountains on terraces, and trees planted in thickets to conceal features such as an open-air ballroom and a colonnade. Statues carved by at least 70 sculptors also adorned the park. A mile-long canal, crossed by a second canal nearly as large, marked the main axis of the garden. Fourteen waterwheels brought the water from the river to supply the canals and the park's 1,400 fountains. Only the fountains near the palace played all day; the others were turned on only when the king approached.

At the north of the secondary canal, a smaller pavilion-palace, the Trianon, was built in 1669. To satisfy the king's love of flowers year-round, the gardens of the Trianon were bedded out with blooming plants from the south, shipped in by the French navy. Even in midwinter, the king and his guests could stroll through a summer garden. The head gardener is said to have had nearly 2 million flowerpots at his disposal. In the eighteenth century, Louis XV added greenhouses and a botanical garden. The facilities of the fruit and vegetable garden that supplied the palace in 1677–1683 today house the National School of Horticulture.

23-51 • Louis Le Vau and André Le Nôtre PLAN OF THE GARDENS OF THE PALACE OF VERSAILLES Versailles, France. c. 1661–1785.

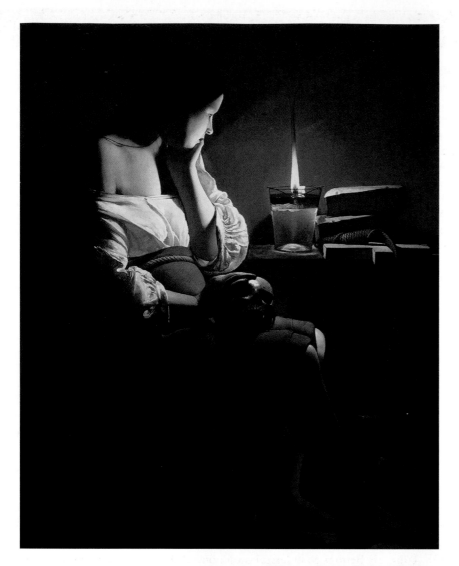

23-52 • Georges de La Tour **MARY MAGDALEN WITH THE SMOKING FLAME**
c. 1640. Oil on canvas, 46¼″ × 36⅛″
(117 × 91.8 cm). Los Angeles County Museum of Art.
Gift of the Ahmanson Foundation (M. 77.73)

themselves. Often, it seems, light is his real subject (see Introduction, "A Closer Look," page xxx FIG. B).

La Tour painted many images of Mary Magdalen. In **MARY MAGDALEN WITH THE SMOKING FLAME** (FIG. 23-52), as in many of his other paintings, the light emanates from an internal source, in this case the flame from an oil lamp. Its warm glow gently brushes over hand and skull—symbol of mortality—to establish the foreground. The compression of the figure into the front of the pictorial space lends a sense of intimacy to the saint's relationship with viewers, although the Magdalen is completely unaware of our presence. Light not only unifies the painting; its controlled character creates its somber mood. Mary Magdalen has put aside her rich clothing and jewels to meditate on the frailty and vanity of human life. Even the flickering light that rivets our attention on her meditative face and gesture is of limited duration.

This same feeling of timelessness, and a comparable interest in effects of light, characterize the

23-53 • Louis or Antoine Le Nain **A PEASANT FAMILY IN AN INTERIOR**
c. 1640. Oil on canvas, 44½″ × 62½″ (1.13 × 1.59 m). Musée du Louvre, Paris.

The members of the French Royal Academy of Painting and Sculpture considered ancient Classical art to be the standard by which contemporary art should be judged. By the 1680s, however, younger artists of the academy began to argue that modern art might equal, or might even surpass, the art of the ancients—a radical thought that sparked controversy.

A debate arose over the relative merits of drawing and color in painting. The conservatives argued that drawing was superior to color because drawing appealed to the mind while color appealed to the senses. They saw Nicolas Poussin as embodying perfectly the Classical principles of subject and design. But the young artists who admired the vivid colors of Titian, Veronese, and Rubens claimed that painting should deceive the eye, and since color achieves this deception more convincingly than drawing, application of color should be valued over drawing. Adherents of the two positions were called *poussinistes* (in honor of Poussin) and *rubénistes* (for Rubens).

The portrait painter and critic Roger de Piles (1635–1709) took up the cause of the *rubénistes* in a series of pamphlets. In *The Principles of Painting*, de Piles evaluated the most important painters on a scale of 0 to 20 in four categories. He gave no score higher than 72 (18 in each category), since no mortal artist could achieve perfection. Caravaggio received a 0 in expression and a 6 in drawing, while Michelangelo and Leonardo both got a 4 in color and Rembrandt a 6 in drawing.

Most of the painters examined here do not do very well. Raphael and Rubens get 65 points (A on our grading scale), Van Dyck comes close with 55 (C+). Poussin and Titian earn 53 and 51 (solid Cs), while Rembrandt slips by with 50 (C–). Leonardo da Vinci gets 49 (D), and Michelangelo and Dürer with 37 and Caravaggio with 28 are resounding failures in de Piles's view. Tastes change. Someday our own ideas may seem just as misguided as those of the academicians.

paintings of the Le Nain brothers, Antoine (c. 1588–1648), Louis (c. 1593–1648), and Mathieu (1607–1677). Although all three were working in Paris by about 1630 and were founding members of the Royal Academy of Painting and Sculpture in 1648, little else is known about their lives and careers. Because they collaborated closely with each other, art historians have only recently begun to sort out their individual styles. They are best known for their painting of genre scenes in which French peasants pause from honest labor for quiet family diversions. **A PEASANT FAMILY IN AN INTERIOR** (**FIG. 23-53**) of about 1640, probably by Louis Le Nain, is the largest, and one of the most lyrical, of these noble scenes of peasant life. Three generations of this family are gathered around a table. The adults acknowledge our presence—a spotlighted woman at left even seems to offer us some wine—whereas the children remain lost in their dreams or focused on their play. The casualness of costume and deportment is underlined by the foreground clutter of pets and kitchen equipment. It is only after we survey the frieze of figures illuminated around the table that the painting reveals one of its most extraordinary passages—a boy in the left background, warming himself in front of a fireplace and represented only as a dark silhouette from behind, edged by the soft golden firelight. Why the brothers chose to paint these peasant families, and who bought their paintings, are questions still unresolved.

THE CLASSICAL LANDSCAPE: POUSSIN AND CLAUDE LORRAIN French painters Nicolas Poussin (1594–1665) and Claude Gellée (called "Claude Lorrain" or simply "Claude," 1600–1682) pursued their careers in Italy although they usually worked for French patrons. They perfected the French ideal of the "Classical" landscape and profoundly influenced painters for the next two centuries. We refer to Poussin and Claude as

Classicists because they organized natural elements and figures into gently illuminated, idealized compositions. Both were influenced by Annibale Carracci and to some extent by Venetian painting, yet each evolved an unmistakably personal style that conveyed an entirely different mood from that of their sources and from each other.

Nicolas Poussin was born in Normandy but settled in Paris, where his initial career as a painter was unremarkable. He arrived in Rome, and the Barberini family became his foremost patrons. Bernini considered Poussin one of the greatest painters in Rome, and others clearly agreed. In 1639, Giovanni Maria Roscioli, secretary to Pope Urban VIII, commissioned from Poussin two large paintings showing the evangelists John and Matthew composing their texts within expansive landscapes dotted with Classical buildings and antique ruins (**FIGS. 23-54, 23-55**). The paintings were completed by October 1640, just before Poussin left for two years in Paris to work for Louis XIII. Perhaps they were the first installment of a set of four evangelists within landscapes, but only these two had been painted when the patron died in 1644.

These paintings epitomize and are among the earliest examples of a new style of rigorously ordered and highly idealized Classical landscapes with figures—an artistic theme and format created by Poussin that would have a long history in European painting. Although individually composed to create an ordered whole on its own, the paintings were designed as a pair. The large clumps of trees at the outside edges form "bookends" that bring lateral closure to the broad panorama that stretches across both canvases. Their unity is emphasized by the evangelists' postures, turned inward toward each other, and solidified at the lower inside corners where huge blocks of Classical masonry converge from both pictures as coordinated remains of the same ruined monument. A consistent perspective progression in both pictures moves

23-54 • Nicolas Poussin LANDSCAPE WITH ST. MATTHEW AND THE ANGEL
1639–1640. Oil on canvas, 39″ × 53⅛″ (99 × 135 cm). Staatliche Museen, Berlin.

from the picture plane back into the distance through a clearly defined foreground, middle ground, and background, illuminated by an even light with gentle shadows and highlights. In the middle distance, behind St. John, are a ruined temple and an obelisk; the round building in the distant city is Hadrian's Tomb, which Poussin knew from Rome. Precisely placed trees, hills, mountains, water, and even clouds take on a solidity of form that seems almost as structural as this architecture. The subject of Poussin's paintings is not the writing evangelists but the balance and order of nature.

When Claude Lorrain went to Rome in 1613, he first studied with Agostino Tassi, an assistant of Guercino and a specialist in architectural painting. Claude, however, preferred landscape. He sketched outdoors for days at a time, then returned to his studio to compose paintings. Claude was fascinated with light, and his works are often studies of the effect of the rising or setting sun on colors and the atmosphere. A favorite and much-imitated device was to place one or two large objects in the foreground—a tree, building, a figural group, or hill—past which the viewer's eye enters the scene and proceeds, often by diagonal paths, into the distance.

Claude used this compositional device to great effect in paintings such as **A PASTORAL LANDSCAPE** of the late 1640s (**FIG. 23-56**). Instead of balancing symmetrically placed elements in a statement of stable order, Claude leads his viewers actively into the painting in a continuing, zigzagging fashion. A conversing couple frames the composition at the right. Their gestures and the ambling of the cows they are tending lead our attention toward the left on a slightly rising diagonal, where a bridge and the traveler moving across it establish a middle ground. Across the bridge into the distance is a city, setting up a contrast between the warm, soft contours of the pastoral right foreground and the misty angularity of the fortified walls and blocks composing the distant fortress. More distant still are the hazy outlines of hills that seem to take this space into infinity. The picture evokes a city dweller's nostalgia and longing for the simpler and more sensuous life of the country, and it is easy to imagine the foreground shepherd extolling to his companion the superior virtues of their own life in contrast to that in the city, toward which he gestures to underline his point.

23–55 • Nicolas Poussin
LANDSCAPE WITH ST. JOHN ON PATMOS
1640. Oil on canvas, 39½″ × 53⅝″ (100.3 × 136.4 cm). The Art Institute of Chicago. A.A. Munger Collection (1930.500)

Read the document related to Nicolas Poussin on myartslab.com

23–56 • Claude Lorrain
A PASTORAL LANDSCAPE
c. 1648. Oil on copper, 15½″ × 21″ (39.3 × 53.3 cm). Yale University Art Gallery, New Haven, Connecticut. Leonard C. Hanna, Jr., B.A. 1913, Fund (1959.47)

23-57 • Inigo Jones **BANQUETING HOUSE, WHITEHALL PALACE**
London. 1619–1622.

ENGLAND

England and Scotland were joined in 1603 with the ascent to the English throne of James VI of Scotland, who reigned over Great Britain as James I (r. 1603–1625). James increased royal patronage of British artists, especially in literature and architecture. William Shakespeare wrote *Macbeth*, featuring the king's legendary ancestor Banquo, in tribute to the new royal family, and the play was performed at court in December 1606.

Although James's son Charles I was an important collector and patron of painting, religious and political tensions that erupted into civil war cost Charles his throne and his life in 1649. A succession of republican and monarchical rulers who alternately supported Protestantism or Catholicism followed, until the Catholic king James II was deposed in the Glorious Revolution of 1689 by his Protestant son-in-law and daughter, William and Mary. After Mary's death in 1694, William (the Dutch great-grandson of William of Orange, who had led the Netherlands' independence movement) ruled on his own until his death in 1702. He was succeeded by Mary's sister, Anne (r. 1702–1714).

ARCHITECTURE

In sculpture and painting, the English court favored foreign artists. The field of architecture, however, was dominated in the seventeenth century by the Englishmen Inigo Jones, Christopher Wren, and Nicholas Hawksmoor. They replaced the country's long-lived Gothic style with Classicism.

INIGO JONES In the early seventeenth century, Inigo Jones (1573–1652) introduced his version of Renaissance Classicism—based on the style of Italian architect Andrea Palladio—into England. Jones had studied Palladio's work in Venice, and he filled his copy of Palladio's *Four Books of Architecture*—still preserved—with notes. Appointed surveyor-general in 1615, Jones was commissioned to design the Queen's House in Greenwich and the Banqueting House for the royal palace of Whitehall.

The **BANQUETING HOUSE (FIG. 23-57)**, built in 1619–1622 to replace an earlier hall destroyed by fire, was used for court ceremonies and entertainments such as the popular masques—stylized dramas combining theater, music, and dance in spectacles by a balcony, with antechambers at each end. Ionic columns and pilasters suggest a colonnade but do not impinge on the ideal, double-cube space, which measures 55 feet in width by 110 feet in length by 55 feet in height. In 1630, Charles I commissioned Peter Paul Rubens—who was in England on a peace mission—to decorate the ceiling. Jones had divided the flat ceiling into nine compartments, for which Rubens painted canvases glorifying the reign of James I. Installed in 1635, the central oval shows the triumph of the Stuart dynasty with the king carried to heaven on clouds of glory. The large rectangular panel beyond it depicts the birth of the new nation, flanked by allegorical paintings of heroic strength and virtue overcoming vice. In the long paintings alongside the oval, *putti* holding the fruits of the earth symbolize the peace and prosperity of England and Scotland under Stuart rule. So proud was Charles of the result that, rather than allow the smoke of candles and torches to harm the ceiling decoration, he moved evening entertainments to an adjacent pavilion.

performed by professional actors, courtiers, and even members of the royal family itself. The west front, shown here, consisting of what appears to be two upper stories with superimposed Ionic and Composite orders raised over a plain basement level, exemplifies the understated elegance of Jones's interpretation of Palladian design. Pilasters flank the end bays, and engaged columns subtly emphasize the three bays at the center, a disposition repeated in the balustrade along the roofline. A rhythmic effect results from varying window treatments—triangular and segmental (semicircular) pediments on the first level, cornices with volute (scroll-form) brackets on the second. The sculpted garlands just below the roofline add an unexpected decorative touch.

Although the exterior suggests two stories, the interior of the Banqueting House (**FIG. 23-58**) is actually one large hall divided

CHRISTOPHER WREN After Jones's death, English architecture was dominated by Christopher Wren (1632–1723) who began his professional career in 1659 as a professor of astronomy. For Wren, architecture was a sideline until 1665, when he traveled to France to further his education. While there, he met with French architects and with Bernini, who was in Paris to consult on designs for the Louvre. Wren returned to England with architecture books, engravings, and a greatly increased admiration for French Classical Baroque design. In 1669, he was made surveyor-general, the position once held by Inigo Jones, and in 1673, he was knighted.

After the Great Fire of 1666 destroyed large parts of central London, Wren was continuously involved in rebuilding the city, including more than 50 churches. His major project from 1675

23-59 • Christopher Wren FAÇADE OF ST. PAUL'S CATHEDRAL, LONDON
Designed 1673, built 1675–1710.

Read the document related to Christopher Wren on myartslab.com

to 1710, was the rebuilding of **ST. PAUL'S CATHEDRAL** (**FIGS. 23-59, 23-60**). Attempts to salvage the burned-out Gothic church on the site failed, and a new cathedral was needed. Wren's famous second design for St. Paul's (which survives in the so-called "Great Model" of 1672–1673) was for a centrally planned building with a great dome in the manner of Bramante's original plan for St. Peter's. This was rejected, but Wren ultimately succeeded both in reconciling Reformation tastes for a basilica and the unity inherent in the use of a dome. St. Paul's has a long nave and equally long sanctuary articulated by small, domed bays. Semicircular, colonnaded porticos open into short transepts that compress themselves against the crossing, where the dome rises 633 feet

23-60 • SCHEMATIC DRAWING OF ST. PAUL'S CATHEDRAL

from ground level. Wren's dome has an interior masonry vault with an oculus and an exterior sheathing of lead-covered wood, but also has a brick cone rising from the inner oculus to support a tall lantern. The ingenuity of the design and engineering remind us that Wren had been a mathematician and professor of astronomy at Oxford. The columns surrounding the drum on the exterior recall Bramante's Tempietto in Rome (see FIG. 21-19), although Wren never went to Italy and knew Italian architecture only from books.

On the façade of St. Paul's (see FIG. 23-59), two levels of paired Corinthian columns support a carved pediment. The deep-set porticos and columned pavilions atop the towers create dramatic areas of light and shadow. Not only the huge size of the cathedral, but also its triumphant verticality, complexity of form, and *chiaroscuro* effects, make it a major monument of English architecture. Wren recognized the importance of the building. On the simple marble slab that forms his tomb in the crypt of the cathedral, he had engraved: "If you want to see his memorial, look around you."

THINK ABOUT IT

23.1 Discuss how Bernini and Caravaggio established the Baroque style in sculpture and painting respectively. Locate the defining traits of the period style in at least one work from the chapter by each of these artists.

23.2 Discuss the development of portraiture, still life, and genre painting in the Dutch Republic during the seventeenth century. What accounts for the increased importance of these subjects at this time?

23.3 Choose two paintings of monarchs in this chapter and explain how the artists who painted them embodied the ruler's prestige and power. Are the strategies of these painters different from those employed by painters of powerful people in the sixteenth century?

23.4 Determine how Poussin's landscapes depart from other stylistic currents at the time. What is meant by the term "Classicism" in relation to Poussin's style? Comment on its importance for the future of French art.

CROSSCURRENTS

Ch. 16
Closer Look,
page 483

FIG. 23–15

These two works visualize the same religious theme—the Last Judgment. But they are placed in different locations within their buildings, engaging different audiences in distinct ways. How do these works represent the cultural goals and stylistic systems of their time and place? Do they have anything other than their subject in common?

✓•—Study and review on myartslab.com

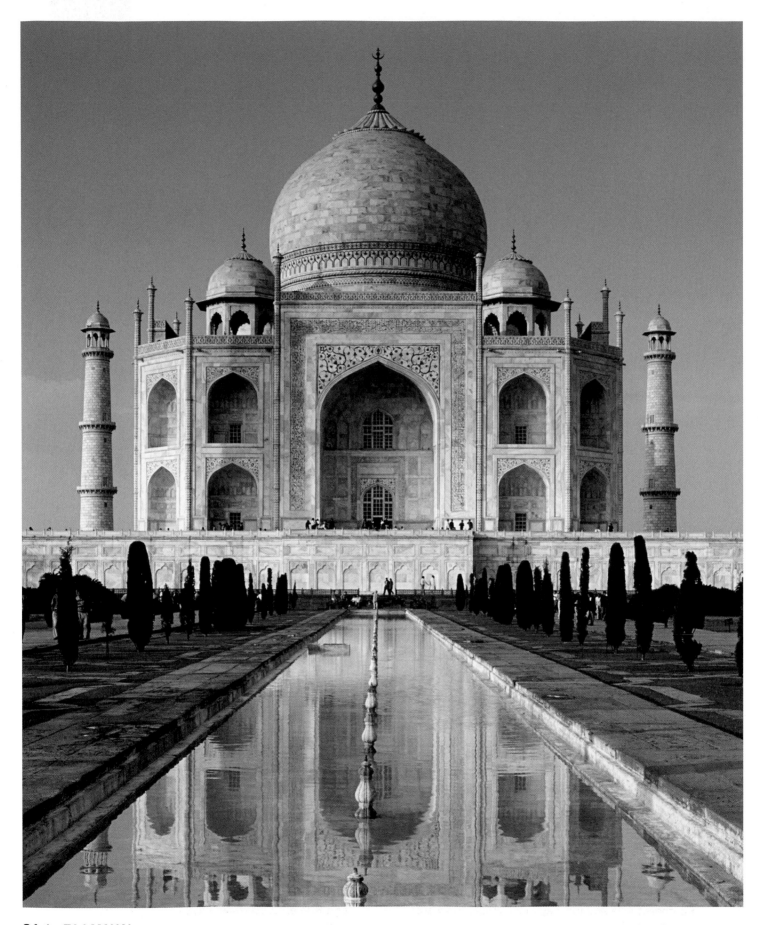

24-1 • TAJ MAHAL

Agra, India. Mughal period, reign of Shah Jahan, c. 1632–1648.

👁—**Watch** an architectural simulation about the Taj Mahal on myartslab.com

Art of South and Southeast Asia after 1200

Upon entering the gateway that today serves as the entrance to the great Taj Mahal complex, the visitor beholds the majestic white marble structure that is one of the world's best-known monuments. Its reflection shimmers in the pools of the garden meant to evoke a vision of paradise as described in the Qur'an. The building's façades are delicately inlaid with inscriptions designed by India's foremost calligrapher of the time, Amanat Khan, and floral arabesques in semiprecious stones—carnelian, agate, coral, turquoise, garnet, lapis, and jasper. Above, its luminous, white marble dome reflects each shift in light, flushing rose at dawn, dissolving in its own brilliance in the noonday sun. This extraordinary building, originally and appropriately called the Illuminated Tomb and only from the nineteenth century known as the **TAJ MAHAL** (**FIG. 24-1**), was built between 1632 and 1648 by the Mughal ruler Shah Jahan as a mausoleum for his favorite wife, Mumtaz Mahal, who died in childbirth, and likely as a tomb for himself.

Inside, the Taj Mahal invokes the *hasht behisht* ("eight paradises"), with the eight small chambers that ring the interior—one at each corner and one behind each *iwan*, a vaulted opening with an arched portal, that is a typical feature of eastern Islamic architecture. In two stories (for a total of 16 chambers), the rooms ring the octagonal central area, which rises the full two stories to a domed ceiling that is lower than the outer dome. In this central chamber, surrounded by a finely carved octagonal openwork marble screen, are the exquisite inlaid **cenotaphs** (funerary monuments) of Shah Jahan and his wife, whose actual tombs lie in the crypt below.

The Taj Mahal complex includes much more than the white marble tomb. On one side is a mosque, while opposite and very similar in appearance is a building that may have served as a rest house. The enormous garden, both in front of the building and in its continuation on the opposite side of the Jamuna River, lends a lush setting consistent with Islamic notions of paradise. Both the side buildings and the two parts of the garden provide a sense of perfect symmetry to the entire complex.

A dynasty of Central Asian origin, the Mughals were the most successful of the many Islamic groups that established themselves in India beginning in the twelfth century. Under their patronage, Persian and Central Asian influences mingled with older traditions of the South Asian subcontinent, adding yet another dimension to the already ancient and complex artistic heritage of India.

LEARN ABOUT IT

24.1 Consider how an artwork's scale and the choice of media relates to its intended function and audience.

24.2 Understand how exogenous influences from trade and conquest affected the art of South and Southeast Asia and the way those influences were shaped locally.

24.3 Recognize that similar-looking works of art, like religious icons or traditional architectural forms, can function differently in different contexts.

24.4 Understand how a work of art like the Taj Mahal or a Khmer Buddha can have both a personal and public meaning.

((•—**Listen** to the chapter audio on myartslab.com

MAP 24–1 • SOUTH AND SOUTHEAST ASIA

Throughout its history, the kingdoms comprising the Indian subcontinent engaged—sometimes peacefully, sometimes militarily—with neighboring and more distant people, contributing significantly to the development of its art.

SOUTH ASIA AFTER 1200

By 1200, India was already among the world's oldest civilizations (see "Foundations of Indian Culture," page 774). The art that survives from its earlier periods is almost exclusively sacred, most of it inspired by the three principal religions: Buddhism, Hinduism, and Jainism. These three religions remained a primary focus for Indian art, even as dynasties arriving from the northwest began to establish the new religious culture of Islam.

CHANGES IN RELIGION AND ART

After many centuries of prominence, Buddhism began to decline as a cultural force in India after the eighth century. As patronage diminished, many Indian Buddhist monks sought out more supportive communities in Southeast Asia for whom Buddhism remained an important religion. At the start of the twelfth century, Kyanzittha, the Burmese king of Bagan, who was known to have hosted Indian monks, actually sent crews to Buddhist centers in South Asia to repair the neglected monuments. By 1200, the remaining Buddhist enclaves in South Asia were concentrated in the northeast, in the region that had been ruled by the Pala dynasty (c. 750–1199). There, in great monastic universities that attracted monks from as far away as China, Korea, and Japan, a form of Buddhism known as Tantrism or Vajrayana was cultivated.

Over these same centuries, Hinduism quickly rose to new prominence, inspiring grand temples, sculpture, and poetry across the subcontinent. Jainism continued to prosper as its relatively small community of adherents grew in regional influence. And the new religion of Islam entered from the northwest, growing to have a profound influence on South Asian culture.

THE BODHISATTVA AVALOKITESHVARA The practices of Tantric Buddhism, which include techniques for visualizing deities, encourage the development of images with precise iconographic details such as the twelfth-century gilt-bronze sculpture

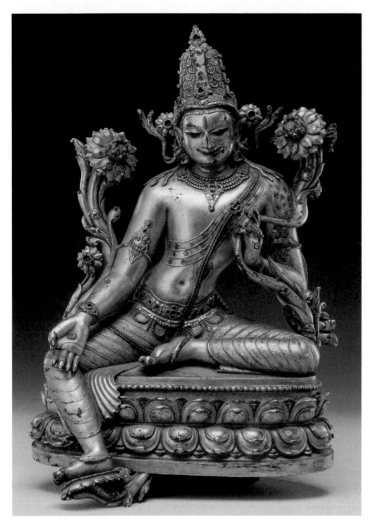

24-2 • THE BODHISATTVA AVALOKITESHVARA
From Kurkihar, Bihar. Pala dynasty, 12th century. Gilt-bronze, height 10″ (25.5 cm). Patna Museum, Patna.

of **THE BODHISATTVA AVALOKITESHVARA** in **FIGURE 24-2** from the site of Kurkihar in eastern India. Bodhisattvas are compassionate beings who are well advanced on the path to buddhahood (enlightenment) and who have vowed to help others achieve enlightenment. Avalokiteshvara, the bodhisattva of greatest compassion, who vowed to forgo buddhahood until all others become buddhas, became the most popular of these saintly beings in India and in East Asia.

Characteristic of bodhisattvas, Avalokiteshvara is distinguished in art by his princely garments, unlike a buddha, who wears monk's robes. Avalokiteshvara is specifically recognized by the lotus flower he holds and by the presence in his crown of his "parent" Buddha, in this case Amitabha, the Buddha of the Western Pure Land (a Buddhist paradise). Other marks of Avalokiteshvara's extraordinary status are the third eye (symbolizing his omniscience) and the wheel on his palm (an emblem of the Buddhist *dharma*). Avalokiteshvara is shown here in the relaxed pose known as the posture of "royal ease." One leg angles down; the other is drawn up onto the lotus seat.

With the fall of the Pala dynasty in the late twelfth century, the last centers of Buddhism in northern India collapsed, and most of the monks dispersed, mainly into Nepal and Tibet (**MAP 24-1**). From that time, they have remained the principal stronghold of Tantric Buddhist practice and its arts. The artistic style perfected under the Palas, however, came to influence international style throughout East and Southeast Asia.

LUNA VASAHI, MOUNT ABU The history of Jainism makes an interesting counterpoint to that of Buddhism. Although both are monastic traditions, the Jains never gained the widespread popularity of Buddhism but neither did they suffer a precipitous decline. The Jain religion traces its roots to a spiritual leader called Mahavira (c. 599–527 BCE), whom it regards as the last in a series of 24 saviors known as pathfinders (*tirthankaras*). Devotees seek through purification and moral action to become worthy of escaping the cycle of rebirth. Jain monks live a life of austerity, and even lay persons avoid killing any living creature. The Jain commitment to non-violence means that there are relatively few Jain kings in South Asian history, but this same commitment led many Jains to gravitate toward lucrative professions in banking and trade. It is from these ranks of merchants and ministers that some of the most important donors of Jain art come, as in the case of the Dilwara Temples erected on Mount Abu in Rajasthan, India. The modest exterior enclosure walls and relatively small size of the of the five Dilwara Temples do little to prepare the visitor for the lacelike splendor of the interior. Every inch of these spaces is filled with deeply cut relief carvings in white marble whose complicated details had to be produced through abrasion and rubbing rather than with a chisel. One of the most impressive of these temples, the Luna Vasahi, was dedicated to the 22nd Jain *tirthankara*, Neminatha, and was built in 1230 by two brothers, Tejpala and Vastupala, who served as ministers to the local ruler. They are known to have sponsored temples in at least two other locations. The structure has had to be repaired in places, the damage most likely caused by raids, but most of the delicate sculpture is still intact.

The main sanctuary is set in a courtyard surrounded by two columned arcades. These open to reveal the temple's most impressive architectural feature, the ornate dome that crowns the *mandapa* hall. This corbeled dome is made of concentric bands of sculpted stone capped with a meticulously carved pendant which hangs down from the apex. Surrounding this decorative element are images of 16 goddesses of wisdom, attached individually to the surface of the dome. This, in turn, is held aloft by eight pillars linked by undulating architraves (**FIG. 24-3**). Every surface is adorned with narrative scenes, animals, protective deities, and plant motifs. These riotous forms highlight the calm, unadorned image of the *tirthankara*, which looks out from the quietude of the sanctuary. The dramatic contrast speaks to the difference between the active world of constant rebirth and the steady peace of enlightenment.

The earliest civilization on the Indian subcontinent flourished toward the end of the third millennium BCE along the Indus River in present-day Pakistan. Remains of its expertly engineered brick cities have been uncovered, together with works of art that intriguingly suggest spiritual practices and reveal artistic traits known in later Indian culture.

The decline of the Indus civilization during the mid second millennium BCE coincides with the arrival from the northwest of a seminomadic people who spoke an Indo-European language and referred to themselves as Aryans. Over the next millennium they were influential in formulating the new civilization that gradually emerged. The most important Aryan contributions to this new civilization included the Sanskrit language and the sacred texts called the Vedas. The evolution of Vedic thought under the influence of indigenous Indian beliefs culminated in the mystical philosophical texts called the Upanishads, which took shape sometime after 800 BCE.

The Upanishads teach that the material world is illusory; only Brahman, the universal soul, is real and eternal. We—that is, our individual souls—are trapped in this illusion in a relentless cycle of birth, death, and rebirth. The ultimate goal of religious life is to liberate ourselves from this cycle and to unite our individual soul with Brahman.

Buddhism and Jainism are two of the many religions that developed in the wake of Upanishadic thought. Buddhism (see "Buddhism," page 301) is based on the teachings of Shakyamuni Buddha, who lived in central India about 500 BCE. Jainism was shaped slightly earlier by the followers of the spiritual leader Mahavira. Both religions acknowledged the cyclical nature of existence and taught a means of liberation from it, but they rejected the authority, rituals, and social strictures of Vedic religion. Whereas the Vedic religion was in the hands of a hereditary priestly class, Buddhist and Jain communities welcomed all members of society, which gave them great appeal. The Vedic tradition eventually evolved into the many sects now collectively known as Hinduism (see "Hinduism," page 309).

Through most of its history India was a mosaic of regional dynastic kingdoms, but from time to time empires emerged that unified large parts of the subcontinent. The first was that of the Maurya dynasty (c. 322–185 BCE), whose great king Ashoka patronized Buddhism. From this time Buddhist doctrines spread widely and its artistic traditions were established.

In the first century CE the Kushans, a Central Asian people, created an empire extending from present-day Afghanistan down into central India. Buddhism prospered under Kanishka, the most powerful Kushan king, and spread into Central Asia and to East Asia. At this time, under the new Kushan cultural and political climate, the image of the Buddha in art first appeared.

Later, under the Gupta dynasty (c. 320–550 CE) in northern India, Buddhist art and culture reached a high point. However, Gupta monarchs also patronized Hindu art, and from this time Hinduism grew to become the dominant Indian religious tradition, with its emphasis on the great gods Vishnu, Shiva, and the Goddess—all with multiple forms.

After the tenth century, numerous regional dynasties prevailed, some quite powerful and long-lasting. Hindu temples, in particular, developed monumental and complex forms that were rich in symbolism and ritual function, with each region of India producing its own variation.

24-3 • LUNA VASAHI, MANDAPA CEILING
Mount Abu, India. 1230.

TEMPLE AT MADURAI As Buddhism gradually declined, Hinduism grew in prominence. With the increasing popularity of Hindu sects came the rapid development of Hindu temples. Spurred by the ambitious building programs of wealthy rulers, well-formulated regional styles had evolved by about 900. The most spectacular structures of the era were monumental, with a complexity and grandeur of proportion rarely equaled even in later Indian art.

Emphasis on monumental temples gave way to the building of vast temple complexes and more moderately scaled, yet more richly ornamented, individual temples. These developments took place largely in the south of India, although some of the largest temples are in the north, for example, the Sun Temple at Konarak, built in the thirteenth century, and the Govind Deva Temple in Brindavan, built in the sixteenth century under the patronage of the Mughal emperor Akbar. The mightiest of the southern Indian kingdoms was Vijayanagar (c. 1336–1565), whose rulers successfully countered the potential incursions of neighboring dynasties, both Hindu and Muslim, for more than 200 years. Under the patronage of the Vijayanagar kings and their successors, the Nayaks, some of India's most spectacular Hindu architecture was created.

The enormous temple complex at Madurai, one of the capitals of the Nayaks, is an example of this fervent expression of Hindu faith. Founded around the thirteenth century, it is dedicated to the goddess Minakshi (the local name for Parvati, the consort of the god Shiva) and to Sundareshvara (the local name for Shiva himself). The temple complex stands in the center of the city and is the focus of Madurai life. At its heart are the two oldest shrines, one to Minakshi and the other to Sundareshvara. Successive additions over the centuries gradually expanded the complex around these small shrines and came to dominate the visual landscape. The most dramatic features of this and similar southern "temple cities" were the thousand-pillar halls, large ritual-bathing pools, and especially the entrance gateways (**gopuras**) that tower above the temple site and the surrounding city like modern skyscrapers (**FIG. 24–4**).

Gopuras proliferated as a temple city grew, necessitating new and bigger enclosing walls, and thus new gateways. Successive rulers, often seeking to outdo their predecessors, donated taller and taller *gopuras*. As a result, the tallest structures in temple cities are often at the periphery, rather than at the central temples, which are sometimes totally overwhelmed by the height of the surrounding structures. The temple complex at Madurai has 11 *gopuras*, the largest over 160 feet tall.

Formally, the *gopura* has its roots in the pyramidal tower characteristic of the seventh-century southern temple style. As the *gopura* evolved, it took on the graceful concave silhouette shown here. The exterior is embellished with thousands of sculpted figures, evoking a teeming world of gods and goddesses. Inside, stairs lead to the top for an extraordinary view.

QUTB MINAR Traders and merchants were probably the first to bring Islam to South Asia, but the backing of powerful

24-4 • OUTER GOPURA OF THE MINAKSHI-SUNDARESHVARA TEMPLE
Madurai, Tamil Nadu, south India. Nayak dynasty, mostly 13th to mid 17th century, with modern renovations.

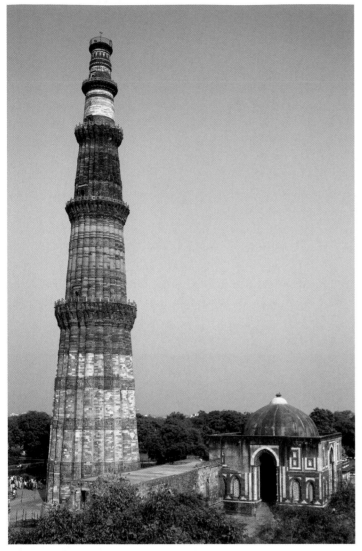

24-5 • QUTB MINAR
Quwwat ul-Islam Mosque, Mehrauli Archaeological Park, Delhi. 1211–1236.

Hindu religious structures from this location were reused in the construction of the mosque. By far the most visible element of this complex is the tower known as the **QUTB MINAR** (FIG. 24-5). This minaret was begun by Aibak and completed under his successor Iltutmish. It stands over 237 feet high and was among the tallest structures in South Asia at the time. It was constructed of sandstone in five segments, each of which is marked by the presence of a balcony that encircles the tower. The stories get smaller further up the tower and the final balcony rests on the top. Minarets are traditionally used to call Muslims to prayer, but this tower is too tall to serve that purpose easily and serves more clearly as an expression of power and political authority than as a functioning religious structure.

MUGHAL PERIOD

The Mughals, like many of the Delhi sultans, came from Central Asia. Muhammad Zahir-ud-Din, known as Babur ("Lion" or "Panther"), was the first Mughal emperor of India (r. 1526–30). He emphasized his Turkic heritage, though he had equally impressive Mongol ancestry. After some initial conquests in Central Asia, he amassed an empire stretching from Afghanistan to Delhi, which he conquered in 1526. Akbar (r. 1556–1605), the third ruler, extended Mughal control over most of north India, and under his two successors, Jahangir and Shah Jahan, northern India was generally unified by 1658. The Mughal Empire lasted until 1858, when the last Mughal emperor was deposed and exiled to Burma (Myanmar) by the British.

Mughal architects were heir to a 300-year-old tradition of Islamic building in India. The Delhi sultans who preceded them had great forts housing government and court buildings. Their architects had introduced two fundamental Islamic structures, the mosque and the tomb, along with construction based on the arch and the dome. (Earlier Indian architecture had been based primarily on post-and-lintel construction.) They had also drawn freely on Indian architecture, borrowing both decorative and structural elements to create a variety of hybrid styles, and had especially benefited from the centuries-old Indian virtuosity in stonecarving and masonry. The Mughals followed in this tradition, synthesizing Indian, Persian, and Central Asian elements for their forts, palaces, mosques, tombs, and cenotaphs (tombs or monuments to someone whose remains are actually somewhere else).

The third emperor, Akbar presided over a period of openness and expansion. His inclusive policies and tolerance toward religious difference did much to help solidify and stabilize his massive empire. A dynamic, humane, and just leader, Akbar enjoyed religious discourse and loved the arts, especially painting. He created an imperial atelier (workshop) of painters, which he placed under the direction of two artists from the Persian court. Learning from these two masters, the Indian painters of the atelier soon transformed Persian styles into the more vigorous, naturalistic styles that mark Mughal painting (see "Indian Painting on Paper," page 782).

political rulers, which helped to establish it across the region, did not occur until the eighth century, when Arab armies captured a small territory near the Indus River. Later, beginning around 1000, Turkic factions from Central Asia, relatively recent converts to Islam, began military campaigns into north India, at first purely for plunder, then seeking territorial control. From the thirteenth century various Turkic and Afghan dynasties ruled portions of the subcontinent from the northern city of Delhi. These sultanates, as they are known, constructed forts, mausoleums, monuments, and mosques.

The first Delhi Sultanate was founded in 1206 by Qutb-ud-din Aibak of the Slave dynasty, so named because Aibak had begun his life as a soldier-slave (*mamluk*) under the Ghorids. Although he did not reign long, he began construction of a large mosque adorned with a truly massive minaret. The mosque complex, called Quwwat ul-Islam (strength of Islam), was built over the citadel of Delhi's previous rulers and portions of the Jain and

FATEHPUR SIKRI Despite all this success Akbar was concerned about who would follow him on the throne. In desperation, he sought the advice of the Sufi mystic Shaikh Salim Chishti. This Muslim holy man foretold the birth of a prince, and when his prediction proved accurate, Akbar built a new capital near Chishti's home to commemorate and celebrate the event. Built primarily during Akbar's residence at the site from about 1572 to 1585, there are two major components to Fatehpur Sikri: a religious section including the Jami Mosque, which houses the tomb of Salim Chishti, and the administrative and residential section. Among the most extraordinary buildings in the administrative and residential section is the private audience hall or **DIWAN-I-KHAS** (FIG. 24-6). In the center of the hall is a tall pillar supporting a circular platform reached by four walkways. On this perch Akbar could sit in safety as he received his nobles and dispensed justice. The structure recalls, perhaps consciously, the pillars erected by Ashoka (see Chapter 10) to promulgate his law.

24-7 • AKBAR INSPECTING THE CONSTRUCTION OF FATEHPUR SIKRI

From the *Akbarnama*. c. 1590. Opaque watercolor on paper, 14¾″ × 10″ (37.5 × 25 cm). Victoria & Albert Museum, London. (I.S.2-1896 91/117)

Many of the painters in the Mughal imperial workshops are recorded in texts of the period. Based on those records and on signatures that occur on some paintings, the design of this work has been attributed to Tulsi Kalan (Tulsi the Elder), the painting to Bandi, and the portraits to Madhu Kalan (Madhu the Elder) or Madhu Khurd (Madhu the Younger).

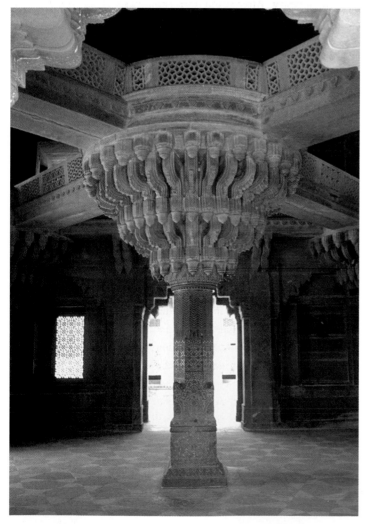

24-6 • DIWAN-I-KHAS (PRIVATE AUDIENCE HALL)
Fatehpur Sikri, India. 1570.

View the Closer Look for the Diwan-i-Khas (private audience hall) on myartslab.com

Unlike most Mughal emperors, Akbar did not write his own biography; instead he entrusted its creation to his vizier Abul Fazl. This text, the *Akbarnama*, details the actions and accomplishments of the emperor including the events leading to the construction of Fatehpur Sikri. Paintings commissioned to illustrate this event round out our understanding of Mughal building techniques and reveal Akbar's personal interest in the progress. Among the most fascinating illustrations in this manuscript are those that record Akbar's supervision of the construction of Fatehpur Sikri. One painting (FIG. 24-7) documents his inspection of the stonemasons and other craftsmakers. Akbar's love of painting set a royal precedent that his successors enthusiastically continued.

At first glance this painting of two rulers embracing seems to tell of a close bond of friendship between the men (**FIG. 24–8**). The presence of a lion and lamb lying peacefully together, an ancient symbol of harmony, also appears to bolster this interpretation. Indeed, the fact that the men are framed by the sun and moon while standing on a map of the world might imply that these bonds of trust and peace extend even to their respective states. Yet nothing could be further from the truth.

This painting was created in a moment of high tension between Shah Abbas and the Mughal throne. The trouble centered on Kandahar in Afghanistan. The prosperous city had been given to Shah Abbas's ancestor by the Mughal emperor Humayun, but later, in the time of Akbar, the Mughals took back control of the city. Shah Abbas then waited for a chance to reclaim it, believing it was his right to do so. When the Mughals were distracted by a war in Iran, he seized the opportunity and recaptured Kandahar in a swift assault. He immediately made conciliatory gestures to Jahangir, who was furious but unable to spare the military force needed to retake the city.

Another look at the painting reveals new details. Jahangir is depicted much larger than Shah Abbas, who appears to bow deferentially to the Mughal emperor. Jahangir's head is centered in the halo and he stands on the predatory lion, whose body spans a vast territory, including Shah Abbas's own holdings in Afghanistan and Iran. These details invert the initial impression conveyed by the subject, revealing a new meaning. The painting is a strong reminder of Mughal power and a potent warning against further expansion, but couched in the diplomatic language of reconciliation.

24-8 • Nadir al-Zaman (Abu'l Hasan)
JAHANGIR AND SHAH ABBAS
From the St. Petersburg Album. Mughal period, c. 1618. Opaque watercolor, gold and ink on paper, 9⅜″ × 6″ (23.8 × 15.4 cm). Freer Gallery of Art, Smithsonian Institution, Washington, DC. Purchase, F1945.9. Freer Gallery, Washington

24-9 • JAHANGIR AND PRINCE KHURRAM FEASTED BY NUR JAHAN
Mughal period, 1617. Paint and gold on paper, 9¹⁵⁄₁₆″ × 5⅝″ (25.2 × 14.3 cm). Freer Gallery of Art, Smithsonian Institution, Washington, DC. Gift of Charles Lang Freer (F1907.258)

PAINTING IN THE COURT OF JAHANGIR Jahangir (r. 1605–1627), Akbar's son and successor, was a connoisseur of painting; he had his own workshop, which he established even before he became emperor. His focus on detail was much greater than that of his father. In his memoirs, he claimed:

> My liking for painting and my practice in judging it have arrived at such a point that when any work is brought before me, either of deceased artists or of those of the present day, without their names being told me I say on the spur of the moment that it is the work of such and such a man, and if there be a picture containing many portraits, and each face be the work of a different master, I can discover which face is the work of each of them. And if any other person has put in the eye and eyebrow of a face, I can perceive whose work the original face is and who has painted the eye and eyebrows.

Portraits become a major art under Jahangir. We can only speculate on the target audience for the portrait Jahangir commissioned of himself with the Safavid-dynasty Persian ruler, Shah Abbas. A painting of such small size could not be publicly displayed and was, therefore, certainly not intended for Jahangir's subjects. But because we know that paintings were commonly conveyed by embassies from one kingdom to another, it may have been intended as a gift for Shah Abbas, one with a message of clear strength and superiority cloaked in the diplomatic language of cordiality (see "Painting of Jahangir and Shah Abbas," opposite).

Despite the proliferation of portrait painting, depictions of court women occur rarely in Mughal art due in part to the restricted access male painters had to the women's quarters. An important exception to this was Jahangir's favorite wife, the Empress Nur Jahan, of whom a few images exist. As Jahangir grew older he succumbed to addiction and illness. During this period, in which he was largely incapacitated, Nur Jahan ran the empire on his behalf, carrying his seal and issuing decrees in his name. Although she ruled in Jahangir's name, the images of her at court and the imperial coins that bore her name suggest her role was no secret.

The idyllic scene depicted in **FIGURE 24-9** portrays Nur Jahan serving food and drink to Jahangir and his son by another wife, Prince Khurram. Seated on ornate carpets the royal family members sit near a fountain as court women bring food and wave fans. This deceptively harmonious tableau is qualified by the verses in Persian surrounding the painting. These refer to Jahangir's displeasure over Khurram's attempts to take the throne, an outcome that Nur Jahan also wished to forestall. After Jahangir died, however, and Nur Jahan was confined to her palace, Khurram managed to seize the throne, taking the royal name Shah Jahan.

THE TAJ MAHAL Shah Jahan (r. 1628–58) achieved a number of military and political victories but he is best known as the patron of what is perhaps the most famous of all Indian Islamic structures, the Taj Mahal. Built between 1631 and 1648 on the banks of the Jamuna River, it was commissioned as a mausoleum for Mumtaz Mahal, the wife of Shah Jahan, who is believed to have taken a major part in overseeing its design and construction. Shah Jahan's personal motivations add a poignancy to this structure, but it must also be recalled that this was the first major architectural undertaking of Shah Jahan's reign. That the Taj Mahal effectively evokes both personal loss and imperial authority is perhaps its most remarkable strength.

As visitors enter through a monumental, hall-like gate, the tomb rises before them across a spacious garden set with long reflecting pools (see FIG. 24-1). Measuring some 1,000 by 1,900 feet, the enclosure is unobtrusively divided into quadrants planted with trees and flowers, and framed by broad walkways and stone inlaid in geometric patterns. In Shah Jahan's time, fruit trees and

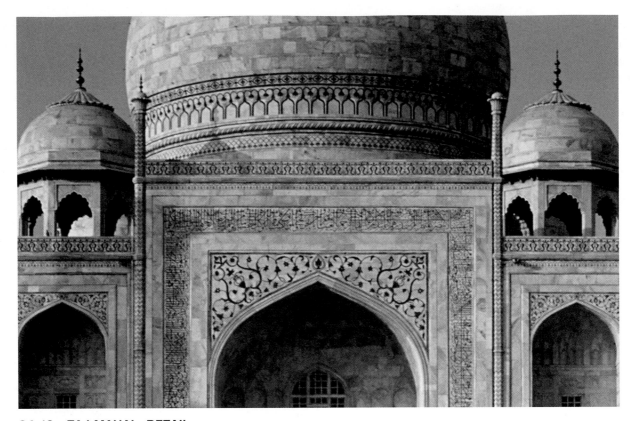

24-10 • TAJ MAHAL, DETAIL
Agra, India. Mughal period, reign of Shah Jahan, c. 1631–1648.

View the Closer Look for the Taj Mahal on myartslab.com

cypresses—symbolic of life and death, respectively—lined the walkways, and fountains played in the shallow pools. Collectively these features evoked paradise on earth.

Recent archaeology has revealed that the garden continues on the far bank of the Jamuna River. A garden filled with night-blooming plants and a large octagonal fountain provided a vantage point for viewing the Taj Mahal from across the river. Thus while the structure appears to visitors to be set at the end of a garden, it is in fact in the center of a four-part garden, a traditional Mughal tomb setting used for earlier tombs. The tomb is flanked by two smaller structures not visible in FIGURE 24-1, one a mosque and the other a hall designed to mirror it. Like the entrance hall, they are made mostly of red sandstone, rendering even more startling the full glory of the tomb's white marble, a material previously reserved for the tombs of saints and here implying an elevated religious stature for Shah Jahan and Mumtaz Mahal. The tomb is raised higher than these structures on its own marble platform emphasizing its importance. This aggrandizement of the tomb is further achieved by having the minarets flank the tomb rather than the mosque. The minarets' three levels correspond to those of the tomb, creating a bond between them. Crowning each minaret is a **chattri** (pavilion). Traditional embellishments of Indian palaces, *chattris* quickly passed into the vocabulary of Indian Islamic architecture, where they appear prominently. A lucid geometric symmetry pervades the tomb. It is basically square, but its **chamfered**

(sliced-off) corners create a subtle octagon. Measured to the base of the **finial** (the spire at the top), the tomb is almost exactly as tall as it is wide. Each façade is identical, with a central *iwan* flanked by two stories of smaller *iwans*. By creating voids in the façades, these *iwans* contribute to the building's sense of weightlessness. On the roof, four octagonal *chattris*, one at each corner, create a visual transition to the lofty, bulbous dome. Framed but not obscured by the *chattris*, the dome rises gracefully and is lifted higher by its drum than in earlier Mughal tombs, allowing the swelling curves and elegant lines of its surprisingly large form to emerge with perfect clarity.

The pristine surfaces of the Taj Mahal are embellished with utmost subtlety (**FIG. 24-10**). Even the sides of the platform on which the Taj Mahal stands are carved in relief with a **blind arcade** (decorative arches set into a wall) motif and carved relief panels of flowers. The portals are framed with verses from the Qur'an and inlaid in black marble, while the spandrels are decorated with floral arabesques inlaid in colored semiprecious stones, a technique known by its Italian name *pietra dura*. Not strong enough to detract from the overall purity of the white marble, the embellishments enliven the surfaces of this impressive yet delicate masterpiece.

RAJPUT PAINTING Outside the Mughal strongholds at Delhi and Agra, much of northern India was governed regionally by local princes, often descendants of the so-called Hindu Rajput warrior clans, who were allowed to keep their lands in return for allegiance to the Mughals. Like the Mughals, Rajput princes frequently supported painters at their courts, and in these settings a variety of strong, indigenous Indian painting styles were perpetuated. Rajput painting, more abstract than the Mughal style, included subjects like those treated by Mughal painters, royal portraits and court scenes, as well as indigenous subjects such as Hindu myths, love poetry, and Ragamala illustrations (illustrations of musical modes).

The Hindu devotional movement known as *bhakti*, which had done much to spread the faith in the south from around the seventh century, now experienced a revival in the north. As it had earlier in the south, *bhakti* inspired an outpouring of poetic literature, this time devoted especially to Krishna, the popular human incarnation of the god Vishnu. Most renowned is the *Gita Govinda*, a cycle of rhapsodic poems about the love between God and humans expressed metaphorically through the love between the young Krishna and the cowherd Radha.

The illustration here (**FIG. 24-11**) is from a manuscript of the *Gita Govinda* probably produced in present-day Rajasthan about 1525–1550. The blue god Krishna sits in dalliance with a group of cowherd women. Standing with her maid and consumed with love for Krishna, Radha peers through the trees, overcome by jealousy. Her feelings are indicated by the cool blue color behind her, while the crimson red behind the Krishna grouping suggests passion. The bold patterns of curving stalks and flowering vines express both the exuberance of springtime, when the story unfolds, and the heightened emotional tensions of the scene. Birds, trees, and flowers are as brilliant as fireworks against the black, hilly landscape edged in an undulating white line. All the figures are of a single type, with plump faces in profile and oversized eyes. Yet the resilient line of

24-11 • KRISHNA AND THE GOPIS
From the *Gita Govinda*, Rajasthan, India. Mughal period, c. 1525–1550. Gouache on paper, 4⅞″ × 7½″ (12.3 × 19 cm). Prince of Wales Museum, Mumbai.

The lyrical poem *Gita Govinda*, by the poet-saint Jayadeva, was probably written in eastern India during the latter half of the twelfth century. The episode illustrated here occurs early in the relationship of Radha and Krishna, which in the poem is a metaphor for the connection between humans and God. The poem traces the progress of their love through separation, reconciliation, and fulfillment.

Before the fourteenth century most painting in India had been on walls or palm leaves. With the introduction of paper, about the same time in India as in Europe, Indian artists adopted painting techniques from Persia and over the ensuing centuries produced jewel-toned works on paper.

Painters usually began their training early. As young apprentices, they learned to make brushes and grind pigments. Brushes were made from the curved hairs of a squirrel's tail, arranged to taper from a thick base to a single hair at the tip. Paint came from pigments of vegetables and minerals—lapis lazuli to make blue, malachite for pale green—that were ground to a paste with water, then bound with a solution of gum from the acacia plant. Paper was made by crushing fibers of cotton and jute to a pulp, pouring the mixture onto a woven mat, drying it, and then burnishing with a smooth piece of agate, often achieving a glossy finish.

First, the painter applied a thin wash of a chalk-based white, which sealed the surface of the paper while allowing the underlying sketch to show through. Next, outlines were filled with thick washes of brilliant, opaque, unmodulated color. When the colors were dry, the painting was laid face down on a smooth marble surface and burnished with a rounded agate stone, rubbing first up and down, then side to side. The indirect pressure against the marble polished the pigments to a high luster. Then outlines, details, and modeling—depending on the style—were added with a fine brush.

Sometimes certain details were purposely left until last, such as the eyes, which were said to bring the painting to life. Gold and raised details were applied when the painting was nearly finished. Gold paint, made from pulverized, 24-carat gold leaf bound with acacia gum, was applied with a brush and burnished to a high shine. Raised details such as the pearls of a necklace were made with thick, white, chalk-based paint, with each pearl a single droplet hardened into a tiny raised mound.

---

the drawing gives them life, and the variety of textile patterns provides some individuality. The intensity of the color and resolute flatness of the scene engage the viewer in the drama.

24-12 • HOUR OF COWDUST
From Punjab Hills, India. Mughal period, Kangra School, c. 1790. Gouache on paper, 14^{15}⁄$_{16}$″ × 12^9⁄$_{16}$″ (36 × 31.9 cm). Museum of Fine Arts, Boston. Denman W. Ross Collection (22.683)

Quite a different mood pervades **HOUR OF COWDUST**, a work from the Kangra School in the Punjab Hills, foothills of the Himalayas north of Delhi (**FIG. 24-12**). Painted around 1790, some 250 years later than the *Gita Govinda* illustration, it shows the influence of Mughal naturalism on the later schools of Indian painting. The theme is again Krishna. Wearing his peacock crown, garland of flowers, and yellow garment—all traditional iconography of Krishna-Vishnu—he returns to the village with his fellow cowherds and their cattle. All eyes are upon him as he plays his flute, said to enchant all who hear it. Women with water jugs on their heads turn to look; others lean from windows to watch and call out to him. We are drawn into this charming village scene by the diagonal movements of the cows as they surge through the gate and into the courtyard beyond. Pastel houses and walls create a sense of space, and in the distance we glimpse other villagers going about their work or peacefully sitting in their houses. A rim of dark trees softens the horizon, and an atmospheric sky completes the aura of enchanted naturalism. Again, all the figures are similar in type, this time with a perfection of proportion and a gentle, lyrical movement that complement the idealism of the setting.

BRITISH COLONIAL PERIOD AND THE INDEPENDENCE MOVEMENT

By the time *Hour of Cowdust* was painted, India's regional rulers, both Hindu and Muslim, had reasserted themselves, and the vast Mughal Empire had shrunk to a small area around Delhi. At the same time, however, a new power, Britain, was making itself felt, inaugurating a markedly different period in Indian history.

First under the mercantile interests of the British East India Company in the seventeenth and eighteenth centuries, and then under the direct control of the British government as a part of the British Empire in the nineteenth century, India was brought forcefully into contact with the West and its culture. The political

24-13 • Frederick Stevens VICTORIA TERMINUS
Mumbai, India. 1887.

concerns of the British Empire extended even to the arts. Over the course of the nineteenth century, the great cities of India, such as Calcutta (present-day Kolkata), Madras (Chennai), and Bombay (Mumbai), took on a European aspect as British architects built in the revivalist styles favored in England.

VICTORIA TERMINUS, MUMBAI The British insistence on utilizing European styles of architecture was at its most strident in the early years of colonial rule. Even after South Asia transitioned to direct control by the British Crown in 1858, a period known as the Raj, British architects were keen on emphasizing difference. Nowhere is this more visible than at the **VICTORIA TERMINUS** (now Chhatrapati Shivaji Terminus) in Mumbai (**FIG. 24-13**). This massive train station built in a Gothic Revival style was designed by architect Frederick William Stevens and opened in 1887, the year of Queen Victoria's Golden Jubilee. The building makes a few concessions to its South Asian setting, as with the inclusion of turretlike domes, but it is overwhelmingly a self-conscious statement of British imperial power. This pairing of cathedral architecture and train station celebrates ideas of British technology and authority. In place of the saints that might normally decorate a cathedral,

personifications of Progress, Commerce, Agriculture, and Science adorn the exterior. Originally, this structure was crowned by an image of Queen Victoria, which has subsequently been removed.

GATEWAY OF INDIA, MUMBAI Over time, the British reduced their insistence on promoting difference through their choice of architectural forms and began to appreciate aspects of indigenous style. Completed in 1924, the **GATEWAY OF INDIA** was built to welcome King George V on his visit to India (**FIG. 24-14**). The British constructed the monument in the form of a European triumphal arch, while embellishing it with architec-

**24-14 • George Wittet
GATEWAY OF INDIA**
Mumbai, India. 1924.

tural features drawn heavily from South Asian precedents. Stone screens, ornate brackets, pointed arches, and floral decorations were taken directly from earlier architectural practices in the subcontinent. This hybrid style, known as the Indo-Saracenic style, borrows techniques from the Hindu and Muslim architectural traditions of South Asia and became the preferred architectural style for British governmental buildings and elite private estates by the late nineteenth century, a few examples of which were built in England and in other parts of the empire. India won its independence in 1947 and the last British troops in South Asia departed through this gate a year later in 1948.

MOTHER INDIA Far prior to Britain's consolidation of imperial power in New Delhi a new spirit asserting Indian independence and pan-Asiatic solidarity was awakening. For example, working near Calcutta (Kolkata), the painter Abanindranath Tagore (1871–1951)—nephew of the poet Rabindranath Tagore (1861–1941), who went on to win the Nobel Prize for Literature in 1913—deliberately rejected the medium of oil painting and the academic realism of Western art. Like the Nihonga artists of Japan (see FIG. 26–18) with whom he was in contact, Tagore strove to create a style that reflected his ethnic origins. In **BHARAT MATA** (Mother India) he invents a nationalistic icon by using Hindu

Prior to the fourteenth century China dominated the international trade in ceramics, but with the rise of the Ming dynasty, China began to look inward, limiting and regulating most forms of international trade. The resulting scarcity of Chinese trade ceramics, sometimes called the "Ming gap," was an opportunity for the merchants and artists of Southeast Asia. Both the Burmese and Thai kingdoms produced ceramics, often inspired by stonewares and porcelains from China. Sukhothai potters, for example, made green-glazed and brown-glazed wares at the renowned kilns of Sawankhalok. But it was the potters of Vietnam who were most successful in meeting the international demand for porcelains. So many ceramics were exported from Vietnam that most of what remained to be found by archaeologists were the broken or discarded leftovers.

This changed with the excavation of a sunken ship laden with ceramics for export found 22 miles off the coast of Hoi An. This wreck brought to light over 250,000 ceramic works made by Vietnamese potters of the late fifteenth to early sixteenth century (FIG. 24–16). Painted in underglaze cobalt blue and further embellished with overglaze enamels, these wares were shipped throughout Southeast Asia and beyond, as far east as Japan and as far west as England and the Netherlands.

24–16 • GROUP OF VIETNAMESE CERAMICS FROM THE HOI AN HOARD
Late 15th to early 16th century. Porcelain with underglaze blue decoration; barbed-rim dishes: (left) diameter 14″ (35.1 cm); (right) diameter 13¼″ (34.7 cm). Phoenix Art Museum, Arizona. (2000.105–109)

symbols while also drawing upon the format and techniques of Mughal and Rajput painting (FIG. 24-15).

SOUTHEAST ASIA AFTER 1200

India's Buddhist and Hindu traditions found acceptance in Southeast Asia (discussed in Chapter 10), and were instrumental in validating newly rising kingdoms. These religions, Buddhism in particular, quickly found wide acceptance among the populace. Starting in the twelfth century, Islam, carried by Arab and Chinese traders, began to gain influence in the region as well. Religious ideas, however, were not the only sort of foreign influence at work in Southeast Asia. Throughout this time trade expanded and, as

demand for Southeast Asian goods rose abroad, colonial powers saw the region as an attractive target (see "Southeast Asian Ceramics," above). European, East Asian, and American economic and military interests had profound consequences on regional history, culture, and society.

BUDDHIST ART AND KINGSHIP

As Buddhism declined in the land of its origin, it continued to thrive in Southeast Asia, where it was shaped and developed in new ways. As it gained adherents among the population it, at times, became vital for rulers to align themselves with Buddhist ideas. Yet, in each case the individual incentives for espousing Buddhist ideas were as varied as the artistic forms they employed.

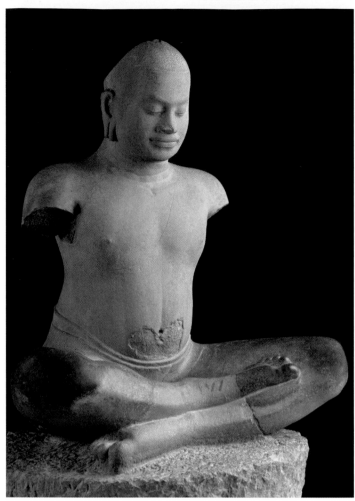

24–17 • SEATED BUDDHA
From Angkor Thom. Reign of Jayavarman VII, late 12th–early 13th century. Sandstone, 4′6″ (1.4 m). National Museum of Cambodia, Phnom Penh.

SEATED BUDDHA When Khmer king Jayavarman VII took his place on the throne of Angkor in 1181, it marked the end of a long struggle against internal rebellions and foreign invaders. Under his reign, he raised up the kingdom of Angkor in a final efflorescence, building more than any of his royal predecessors. In an unusual move, he elected to associate himself with the Buddha, rather than with a Hindu deity and in so doing adapted Buddhist ideas to the Khmer concept of the god-king or, in his case, the buddha-king (*buddharaja*). Before undertaking construction of his massive temple-mountain complex at Angkor Thom, he sought legitimacy for his claims of Buddhist authority by dedicating large temples to each of his parents in the guise of bodhisattvas. This process was taken to a logical conclusion by associating himself directly with the Buddha (as well as with the bodhisattva Lokeshvara).

Although Jayavarman VII's artists and architects produced a staggering number of spectacular sculptures and grand temples, few are as sublime as a simple sandstone Buddha image in the collection of the National Museum of Cambodia in Phnom Penh (**FIG. 24–17**). A few similar images exist and in each example the seated

Buddha displays similar physiognomic features. The consistency in these facial features has led scholars to believe that these works are in fact portraits of Jayavarman VII himself, seated serenely in the guise of the Buddha. Just as his ancestors had conceptually linked themselves with Hindu deities, Jayavarman VII represented himself as a Buddha with downturned meditative eyes, distended earlobes, hair pulled back into a topknot, and dressed in a simple garment. The authority of the king and Buddha are here expressed in a single understated, almost humble, image.

SHWEDAGON STUPA, MYANMAR In northern Burma, from the eleventh to the thirteenth century, rulers raised innumerable religious monuments—temples, monasteries, and stupas—in the Bagan Plain, following the scriptures of Theravada Buddhism. To the south arose the port city of Yangon (formerly known as Rangoon, called Dagon in antiquity). Established by Mon rulers before the eleventh century, Yangon is the site of the **SHWEDAGON STUPA** (**FIG. 24–18**), which enshrines relics of the four past Buddhas, including hair from Shakyamuni. The modern structures of Shwedagon ("Golden Dagon") rise from an ancient Mon core that was rebuilt and enlarged in the fourteenth century.

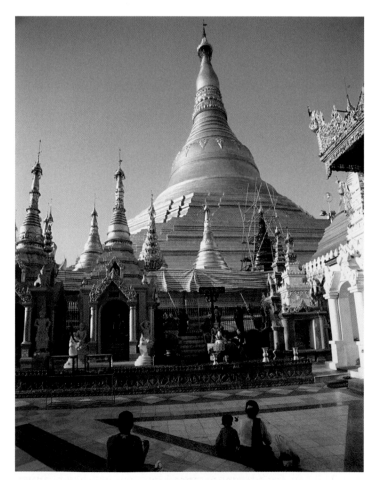

24–18 • SHWEDAGON STUPA (PAGODA)
Yangon, Myanmar. 15th century; construction at the site dates from at least the 14th century, with continuous replastering and redecoration to the present.

A CLOSER LOOK | The Sukhothai Buddha

From Wat Mahathat, now in Wat Benchamabophit, Bangkok, Thailand.
Bronze, 7'22" (2.2 m). Sukhothai period, 14th–15th century.

The graceful Buddhas of the Sukhothai period were at times further enhanced by a second Sukhothai innovation, images of the walking Buddha. Sukhothai Buddhas reveal not just the surface of the Buddha's form, but also suggest aspects of his character and life. Smooth skin is indicative of royal upbringing; long arms and broad shoulders mark someone born into a linage of warriors; and by not depicting his genitals the artists allude to his celibacy as an ascetic. Consider the following descriptions taken from Buddhist texts in relation to this example.

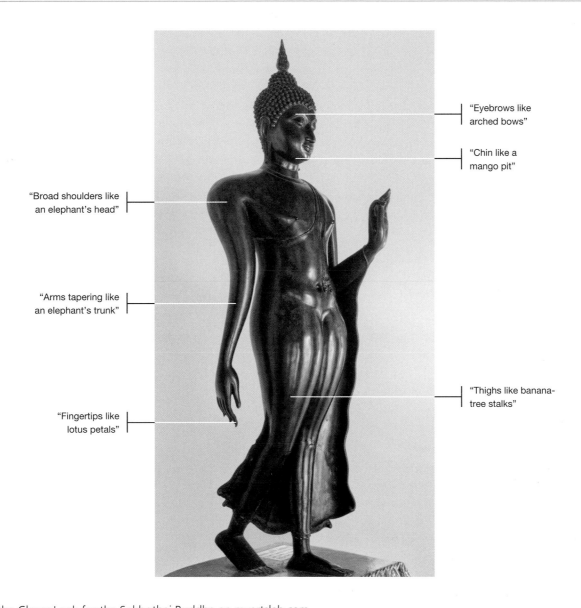

"Eyebrows like arched bows"

"Chin like a mango pit"

"Broad shoulders like an elephant's head"

"Arms tapering like an elephant's trunk"

"Thighs like banana-tree stalks"

"Fingertips like lotus petals"

 View the Closer Look for the Sukhothai Buddha on myartslab.com

In subsequent decades it underwent continual restoration and enhancement at the hands of pious Burmese kings and queens. The site continues to be a focus for lavish devotion and generosity. The bell-shaped spire is capped by a umbrellalike ornament (*hti*) adorned with a large diamond and the sides of the terraces are covered in sheets of gold plate. While most of this wealth was donated by royalty, over the centuries people from all walks of life have offered gold for its construction and maintenance. Images of the Buddha, and sometimes his footprints alone, provide focal points for devotion.

TEMPLE OF THE EMERALD BUDDHA, THAILAND The Dvaravati culture remained regionally dominant until Khmer invasions in the tenth century. During this turmoil a new ethnic group, the Thai, entered the scene from the north, gradually gaining control and adopting Buddhism, as well as some aspects of Hinduism, from the Mon. The first Thai kingdom, Sukhothai, was established in 1238 and flourished under the guidance of kings like the renowned Ram Khamhaeng, before falling to rival Thai states.

The Sukhothai period is praised as a formative time of innovation and creativity in Thai art. Among their creations, the artists of this period championed an elegant new style of Buddha image. With attenuated heads adorned with spirelike flames and draping, almost boneless, limbs, the Buddha images of this period are immediately recognizable. The otherworldly qualities of the Sukhothai Buddhas have led art historians to explore possible explanations for their distinctive features. One strong possibility is that they are, quite literally, poetry given tangible form (see "A Closer Look," page 787). The artists may have been working from descriptions found in the Indian Buddhist texts, which use evocative similes to describe the Buddha's beautiful appearance.

Despite its cultural importance, the kingdom of Sukhothai did not last long, giving way to a succession of dynasties. The capital was eventually moved south to Bangkok and under the rule of the Chakri king Rama I, construction began there on a grand new temple to house the Thais' most sacred Buddha image.

The Emerald Buddha ("emerald" refers to its color; it is actually made of jadeite) is featured in legends that place its creation in India under the direction of major Buddhist figures and trace its travels through great Buddhist nations of the past. These stories, although not grounded in historical evidence, suggest that the image has a special link to the world's foremost Buddhist kings, among whose lineage the Thai king is the most recent. The king himself ritually changes the image's golden garments three times a year. In one of these costumes the Emerald Buddha is dressed as a king, further strengthening the association between the Buddha and the state.

The temple complex that houses this sacred image is suitably spectacular (**FIG. 24–19**). The enclosure covers over 200 acres and contains hundreds of buildings, most of which are crowned by high pointed roofs tiled in vibrant orange and green. These colorful rooftops shade the walls and pillars whose surfaces are inset with intricate patterns of glass, gold leaf, and tile that shimmer in

24–19 • TEMPLE OF THE EMERALD BUDDHA (WAT PHRA KAEW)
Grand Palace Complex, Bangkok, Thailand. 1782, and greatly expanded in later centuries.

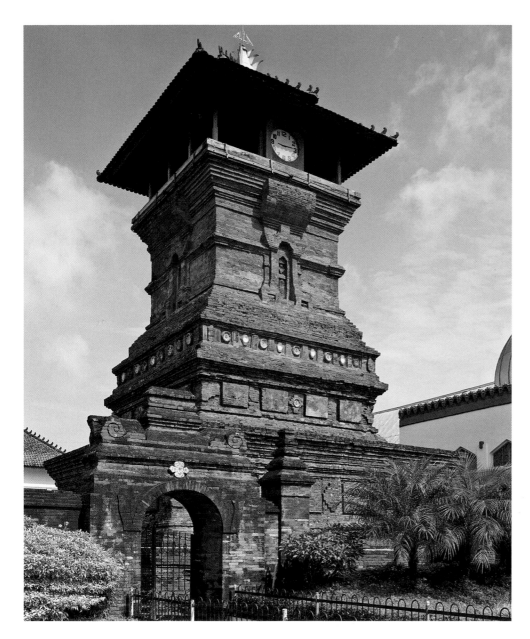

dedicated to one of Java's nine great saints. Although the mosque itself has been renovated, most of the towerlike **MINARET** still survives from the earliest phase of construction in 1549 (**FIG. 24-20**). Its brickwork and decorative niches are reminiscent of earlier Hindu shrine towers but this structure served to call Muslims to worship five times daily. In a traditional Javanese fashion, this was done with a large drum (*bedug*) along with the sung prayers typical in other parts of the world. The lower bands of the tower are decorated with inset porcelain plates imported from China, which add color to the exterior. The various indigenous and international influences that helped shape this tower speak to the remarkably cosmopolitan nature of sixteenth-century Java.

the intense sunlight. Although the core of this complex dates to 1782, it has been greatly expanded in later centuries and remains an important Thai religious and political center.

ISLAMIC ART IN SOUTHEAST ASIA

Muslim merchants played a major role in overseas trade and they frequently spent months at port waiting for the trade winds to change. Over time their faith, Islam, was accepted by local populations living in Malaysia and the island of Sumatra (Indonesia) around the Straits of Malacca. From there it spread across island Southeast Asia. Indonesia is today the world's most populous Muslim country.

KUDUS MOSQUE, INDONESIA Islamic monuments in Indonesia, like the earlier Hindu and Buddhist ones, draw from a rich and diverse repertoire of styles and motifs. One of the earliest examples of Islamic architecture in Java is the Kudus mosque,

THE MODERN PERIOD

Marked by both inspirational expressions of peaceful resistance and bloody warfare, the modern history of South and Southeast Asia has been a study in extremes. But as the turmoil of earlier decades fades across most of the region, many states have emerged as leaders in international commerce, technology, and finance. In an international age, they are capitalizing on the region's centuries-old tradition of bridging cultures and adapting new ideas. These qualities are seen clearly in the South and Southeast Asian art of the Modern period which blends the traditional with the new.

MODERN SOUTH ASIA

In the wake of World War II, the imperial powers of Europe began to shed their colonial domains. The attainment of self-rule had been five long decades in the making, when finally—chastened by the non-violent example of Mahatma Gandhi (1869–1948)—the British Empire relinquished its "Jewel in the Crown," which was

24–21 • Maqbool Fida Husain VEDIC
From the *Theorama* series, 1994. Limited
edition color print, 23½″ × 36″ (60 × 92 cm).

24–22 • PETRONAS TOWERS
Kuala Lumpur, Malaysia. 1998.

partitioned to form the modern nations of India, Pakistan, and (in 1972) Bangladesh. After independence in 1947, the exuberant young nations welcomed a modern, internationalist approach to art and architecture.

MAQBOOL FIDA HUSAIN One of India's most influential and prolific modern artists was M. F. Husain (1915–2011). Beginning his career in the 1940s, he embraced Modernism and used its techniques to express South Asian themes. He drew his subjects from diverse sources such as Hindu literature, historical events, and the natural world, as well as from the traditions of his Muslim upbringing. He was exceedingly productive and his range of subject matter at times drew controversy from religious groups who objected to his appropriation of religious imagery. These complaints led him reluctantly to spend the final years of his life in Qatar but he consistently returned to South Asian themes for his inspiration.

His simplified and schematic style can be seen in the *Theorama* series, which addresses nine of the world's major religions. Pictured here is **VEDIC** (**FIG. 24-21**), Hussain's tribute to Hinduism. Despite its abstraction, the figure of Krishna can be seen dancing on the serpent deity Kaliya, whose body merges with the story of the Churning of the Ocean of Milk (see **FIG. 10-41**). The event pivots on a triangular form with three faces reminiscent of the Shiva from Elephanta (see **FIG. 10-22**), and a goddess on elephant-back dispenses abundance in the form of coins or seeds falling from her outstretched hand. The composition is framed on the right by a seated ascetic whose head is a spoked wheel. This wheel may reference the spinning wheels whose use Gandhi advocated to break dependence on British textiles, but it also reaches back further into the South Asian past and evokes the wheel of *dharma*.

MODERN SOUTHEAST ASIA

The transition from colonial control varied greatly across Southeast Asia, due largely to the range of colonial powers in the region and their varying attitudes toward relinquishing control. Some nations, like Thailand, managed to avoid imperial domination entirely, whereas others fought long wars to establish their independence. In some cases, the power vacuum was filled by local regimes that brought new hardship, like the horrors perpetrated by the Khmer Rouge in Cambodia. The region has gradually achieved stability and growing prosperity as exemplified by its internationally recognized artwork and contemporary architecture.

THE PETRONAS TOWERS, MALAYSIA Dominating the skyline of Kuala Lumpur, Malaysia, are the **PETRONAS TOWERS** (**FIG. 24-22**), which from 1998 to 2004 were the tallest structures in the world. These paired skyscrapers, linked by a sky bridge at the 41st and 42nd floors, are built primarily of reinforced concrete surrounded by a casing of steel and glass. They were designed collaboratively by Argentine architect César Pelli and Filipino-Malaysian engineer Deejay Cerico, who drew inspiration in their designs from traditional Malaysian Islamic forms. The towers stand 1,242 feet tall and took seven years to build. Today the buildings house many business offices, a shopping mall, and the Malaysian Philharmonic Orchestra, and are characteristic of the new growth and development across the region.

THINK ABOUT IT

24.1 Consider the paintings *Jahangir and Shah Abbas* (FIG. 24–8) and *Mother India* (FIG. 24–15). What are the political messages and at whom were they directed? Who would have seen these works?

24.2 Analyze the form of the Gateway of India (FIG. 24–14) in relation to the ancient Roman form of the triumphal arch—see, for example, the Arch of Titus (FIG. 6–36). Explain what aspects are European and which derive from South Asian architecture.

24.3 The Emerald Buddha and the Seated Buddha from the reign of Jayavarman VII are both closely associated with royal power. Explain how each image lends authority to the king; emphasize both similarities and differences between the two examples.

24.4 Consider the Qutb Minar (FIG. 24–5) and Fatehpur Sikri. Do these structures reveal differences in the way each kingdom viewed itself in relation to wider Indian culture? If so, explain how. Can similar differences be seen when comparing the Victoria Terminus and the Gateway of India? Explain.

CROSSCURRENTS

FIG. 24–1

FIG. 24–20

Consider some of the ways that Islamic art and culture impacted South and Southeast Asia. Explain how the Taj Mahal and the Kudus mosque minaret are similar. In what ways do they differ from one another? What historical and cultural influences help account for those differences?

✔—**Study** and review on myartslab.com

石上苔羹水上洞瀑溪聲主瀑門
前千歲石聲兮流方天引飛气
入洞天

　　庚戌腊月晨写是幸幸甪室匠法
寫庚人詩意
　　　　　写目出之一石谷子暈

日照層崖暮
翠岡群神人
在溪岡尝堂
林汀岡永塘
幹溪見四伴
天上之六
丁子而題

**25-1 • Wang Hui A THOUSAND PEAKS
AND MYRIAD RAVINES**

Qing dynasty, 1693. Hanging scroll with ink on
paper, 8′2½″ × 3′4½″ (2.54 × 1.03 m). National
Palace Museum, Taibei, Taiwan, Republic of
China.

Read the document related to
A Thousand Peaks and Myriad Ravines
on myartslab.com

Chinese and Korean Art after 1279

A THOUSAND PEAKS AND MYRIAD RAVINES (FIG. 25-1), painted by Wang Hui (1632–1717) in 1693, exemplifies the subjects of Chinese landscape painting: mountains, rivers, waterfalls, trees, rocks, temples, pavilions, houses, bridges, boats, wandering scholars, fishers—familiar motifs from a tradition now many centuries old. On it, the artist has written:

> Moss and weeds cover the rocks and mist hovers over the water.
> The sound of dripping water is heard in front of the temple gate.
> Through a thousand peaks and myriad ravines the spring flows,
> And brings the flying flowers into the sacred caves.
> In the fourth month of the year 1693, in an inn in the capital, I painted this based on a Tang-dynasty poem in the manner of [the painters] Dong [Yuan] and Ju[ran].
>
> (Translation by Chu-tsing Li)

The inscription refers to the artist's inspiration—for the subject, found in the lines of a Tang-dynasty poem, and for the style, found in the paintings of tenth-century painters Dong Yuan and Juran. Wang Hui's art embodies the ideals of the scholar in imperial China.

China's scholar class was unique, the product of an examination system designed to recruit the finest minds in the country for government service. Instituted during the Tang dynasty (618–907) and based on even earlier traditions, the civil service examinations were excruciatingly difficult, but for the tiny percentage who passed at the highest level, the rewards were great—prestige, position, power, and wealth. Steeped in philosophy, literature, and history, China's scholars—often called *wenren* (literati)—shared a common outlook. Following Confucianism, they became officials to fulfill their obligation to the world; pulled by Daoism, they retreated from society in order to come to terms with nature and the universe—to create a garden, to write poetry, to paint.

During the Song dynasty (960–1279) the examinations were expanded and regularized. More than half of all government positions came to be filled by scholars. In the subsequent Yuan and Ming periods, the tradition of **literati painting** (a style that reflected the taste of the educated class) further developed. When the Yuan period of foreign rule came to an end, the new Ming ruling house revived the court traditions of the Song. The Ming became the model for the rulers of Korea's Joseon dynasty, under whose patronage these styles achieved a distinctive and austere beauty.

In the Qing era, China was again ruled by an outside group, this time the Manchus. While maintaining their traditional connections to Tibet and inner Asia through their patronage of Tibetan Buddhism, the Manchu rulers also embraced Chinese ideals, especially those of the literati. Practicing painting and calligraphy, composing poetry in Chinese, and collecting esteemed Chinese works of art, these rulers amassed the great palace collections that can now be seen in Beijing and Taibei.

LEARN ABOUT IT

25.1 Explore the literati style and its relationship to the scholarly life in later Chinese and Korean art.

25.2 Understand the development and significance of the theme of landscape in Chinese and Korean painting.

25.3 Assess the influence of court life and patronage on art in China and Korea.

25.4 Analyze and learn to characterize the emergence of expression beyond representation as a valued aspect of art in China and Korea, from the thirteenth century to the present.

(((•—[Listen to the chapter audio on myartslab.com

THE MONGOL INVASIONS

At the beginning of the thirteenth century the Mongols, a nomadic people from the steppes north of China, began to amass an empire. Led first by Genghiz Khan (c. 1162–1227), then by his sons and grandsons, they swept westward into central Europe and overran Islamic lands from Central Asia through present-day Iraq. To the east, they quickly captured northern China, and in 1279, led by Kublai Khan, they conquered southern China as well. Grandson of the mighty Genghiz, Kublai proclaimed himself emperor of China and founded the Yuan dynasty (1279–1368).

The Mongol invasions were traumatic; their effect on China was long-lasting. During the Song dynasty, China had grown increasingly introspective. Rejecting foreign ideas and influences, intellectuals had focused on defining the qualities that constituted true "Chinese-ness." They drew a clear distinction between their own people, whom they characterized as gentle, erudite, and sophisticated, and the "barbarians" outside China's borders, whom they regarded as crude, wild, and uncivilized. Now, faced with the reality of foreign occupation, China's inward gaze intensified in spiritual resistance. For centuries to come, long after the Mongols had gone, leading scholars continued to seek intellectually more challenging, philosophically more profound, and artistically more subtle expressions of all that could be identified as authentically Chinese (see "Foundations of Chinese Culture," opposite).

YUAN DYNASTY

The Mongols established their capital in the northern city now known as Beijing (MAP 25–1). The cultural centers of China,

MAP 25-1 • CHINA AND KOREA

The map shows the borders of both contemporary China and Korea. The colored areas indicate the historical extent of the Qing-dynasty empire (1644–1911), including its tributary states.

Chinese culture is distinguished by its long and continuous development. Between 6000 and 2000 BCE a variety of Neolithic cultures flourished across China. Through long interaction these cultures became increasingly similar and they eventually gave rise to the three Bronze Age dynastic states with which Chinese history traditionally begins: the Xia, the Shang (c. 1700–1100 BCE), and the Zhou (1100–221 BCE).

The Shang developed traditions of casting ritual vessels in bronze, working jade in ceremonial shapes, and writing consistently in scripts that directly evolved into the modern Chinese written language. Society was stratified, and the ruling group maintained its authority in part by claiming power as intermediaries between the human and spirit worlds. Under the Zhou a feudal society developed, with nobles related to the king ruling over numerous small states.

During the latter part of the Zhou dynasty, states began to vie for supremacy through intrigue and increasingly ruthless warfare. The collapse of social order profoundly influenced China's first philosophers, who largely concerned themselves with the pragmatic question of how to bring about a stable society.

In 221 BCE, rulers of the state of Qin triumphed over the remaining states, unifying China as an empire for the first time. The Qin created the mechanisms of China's centralized bureaucracy, but their rule was harsh and the dynasty was quickly overthrown. During the ensuing Han dynasty (206 BCE–220 CE), China at last knew peace and prosperity. Confucianism was made the official state ideology, in the process assuming the form and force of a religion. Developed from the thought of Confucius (551–479 BCE), one of the many philosophers of the Zhou, Confucianism is an ethical system for the management of society based on establishing correct relationships among people. Providing a counterweight was Daoism, which also came into its own during the Han dynasty. Based on the thought of Laozi, a possibly legendary contemporary of Confucius, and the philosopher Zhuangzi (369–286 BCE), Daoism is a view of life that seeks to harmonize the individual with the Dao, or Way, the process of the universe. Confucianism and Daoism have remained central to Chinese thought—the one addressing the public realm of duty and conformity, the other the private world of individualism and creativity.

Following the collapse of the Han dynasty, China experienced a centuries-long period of disunity (220–589 CE). Invaders from the north and west established numerous kingdoms and dynasties, while a series of six precarious Chinese dynasties held sway in the south. Buddhism, which had begun to spread over trade routes from India during the Han era, now flourished. The period also witnessed the economic and cultural development of the south (previous dynasties had ruled from the north).

China was reunited under the Sui dynasty (581–618 CE), which quickly fell to the Tang (618–907), one of the most successful dynasties in Chinese history. Strong and confident, Tang China fascinated and, in turn, was fascinated by the cultures around it. Caravans streamed across central Asia to the capital, Chang'an, then the largest city in the world. Japan and Korea sent thousands of students to study Chinese culture, and Buddhism reached the height of its influence before a period of persecution signaled the start of its decline.

The mood of the Song dynasty (960–1279) was quite different. The martial vigor of the Tang gave way to a culture of increasing refinement and sophistication, and Tang openness to foreign influences was replaced by a conscious cultivation of China's own traditions. In art, landscape painting emerged as the most esteemed genre, capable of expressing both philosophical and personal concerns. With the fall of the north to invaders in 1126, the Song court set up a new capital in the south, which became the cultural and economic center of the country.

however, remained the great cities of the south, where the Song court had been located for the previous 150 years. Combined with the tensions of Yuan rule, this separation of China's political and cultural centers created a new dynamic in the arts.

Throughout most of Chinese history, the imperial court had set the tone for artistic taste: Artisans attached to the court produced architecture, paintings, gardens, and objects of jade, lacquer, ceramics, and silk especially for imperial use. Over the centuries, painters and calligraphers gradually moved higher up the social scale, for these "arts of the brush" were often practiced by scholars and even emperors, whose high status reflected positively on whatever interested them. With the establishment of an imperial painting academy during the Song dynasty, painters finally achieved a status equal to that of court officials. For the literati, painting came to be grouped with calligraphy and poetry as the trio of accomplishments suited to members of the cultural elite.

But while the literati elevated the status of painting by virtue of practicing it, they also began to develop their own ideas of what painting should be. Not needing to earn an income from their art, they cultivated an amateur ideal in which personal expression counted for more than professional skill. They created for themselves a status as artists totally separate from and superior to professional painters, whose art they felt was inherently compromised, since it was done to please others, and impure, since it was tainted by money.

The conditions of Yuan rule now encouraged a clear distinction between court taste, ministered to by professional artists and artisans, and literati taste. The Yuan dynasty continued to see patronage of the arts as an imperial responsibility, commissioning buildings, murals, gardens, paintings, and decorative arts. Western visitors, such as the Italian Marco Polo, were mightily impressed by the magnificence of the Yuan court (see "Marco Polo," page 796). But scholars, profoundly alienated from the new government, took little notice of these accomplishments. Nor did Yuan rulers have much use for scholars, especially those from the south. The civil service examinations were abolished, and the highest government positions were bestowed, instead, on Mongols and their foreign allies. Scholars now tended to turn inward, to search for solutions of their own, and to try to express themselves in personal and symbolic terms.

China under Kublai Khan was one of four Mongol khanates that together extended west into present-day Iraq and through Russia to the borders of Poland and Hungary. For roughly a century, travelers moved freely across this vast expanse, making the era one of unprecedented cross-cultural exchange. Diplomats, missionaries, merchants, and adventurers flocked to the Yuan court, and Chinese envoys were dispatched to the West. The most celebrated European traveler of the time was a Venetian named Marco Polo (c. 1254–1324), whose descriptions of his travels were for several centuries the only firsthand account of China available in Europe.

Marco Polo was still in his teens when he set out for China in 1271. He traveled with his uncle and father, both merchants, bearing letters for Kublai Khan from Pope Gregory X. After a four-year journey the Polos arrived at last in Beijing. Marco became a favorite of the emperor and spent the next 17 years in his service, during which time he traveled extensively throughout China. He eventually returned home in 1295.

Imprisoned later during a war between Venice and Genoa, rival Italian city-states, Marco Polo passed the time by dictating an account of his experiences to a fellow prisoner. The resulting book, *A Description of the World*, has fascinated generations of readers with its depiction of prosperous and sophisticated lands in the East. Translated into many European languages, it was an important influence in stimulating further exploration. When Columbus set sail across the Atlantic in 1492, one of the places he hoped to find was a country Marco Polo called Zipangu—Japan.

ZHAO MENGFU Zhao Mengfu (1254–1322) was a descendant of the imperial line of Song. Unlike many scholars of his time, he eventually chose to serve the Yuan government and was made a high official. A distinguished painter, calligrapher, and poet, Zhao was especially known for his carefully rendered paintings of horses. But he also cultivated another manner, most famous in his landmark painting **AUTUMN COLORS ON THE QIAO AND HUA MOUNTAINS** (**FIG. 25-2**).

Zhao painted this work for a friend whose ancestors came from Jinan, the present-day capital of Shandong Province, and the painting supposedly depicts the landscape there. Yet the mountains and trees are not painted in the accomplished naturalism of Zhao's own time but rather in the archaic yet elegant manner of the earlier Tang dynasty (618–907). The Tang had ruled during a great era in Chinese history, when the country was both militarily strong and culturally vibrant. Through his painting Zhao evoked a nostalgia not only for his friend's distant homeland but also for China's distant past.

This educated taste for the "spirit of antiquity" became an important aspect of literati painting in later periods. Also typical of literati taste are the unassuming brushwork, the subtle colors sparingly used (many literati paintings forgo color altogether), the use of landscape to convey personal meaning, and even the intended audience—a close friend. The literati did not paint for public display but for each other. They favored small formats such as handscrolls, **hanging scrolls**, or **album** leaves (book pages), which could easily be shown to friends or shared at small gatherings (see "Formats of Chinese Painting," page 799).

NI ZAN Of the considerable number of Yuan painters who took up Zhao's ideas, several became models for later generations. One was Ni Zan (1301–1374), whose most famous surviving painting is **THE RONGXI STUDIO** (**FIG. 25-3**). Done entirely in ink, the painting depicts the lake region in Ni's home district. Mountains, rocks, trees, and a pavilion are sketched with a minimum of detail using a dry brush technique—a technique in which the brush is not fully loaded with ink but rather is about to run out, so that white paper "breathes" through the ragged strokes. The result is a painting with a light touch and a sense of simplicity and purity. Literati styles were believed to reflect an individual painter's personality, and Ni's spare, dry style became associated with a noble spirit. Many later painters adopted it or paid homage to it.

25-2 • Zhao Mengfu AUTUMN COLORS ON THE QIAO AND HUA MOUNTAINS
Yuan dynasty, 1296. Handscroll with ink and color on paper, 11¼″ × 3⅖″ (28.6 × 9.3 cm). National Palace Museum, Taibei, Taiwan, Republic of China.

25-3 • Ni Zan THE RONGXI STUDIO
Yuan dynasty, 1372. Hanging scroll with ink on paper, height 29⅜″ (74.6 cm). National Palace Museum, Taibei, Taiwan, Republic of China.

The idea that a painting is not an attempt to capture the visual appearance of nature nor to satisfy others but is executed freely and carelessly for the artist's own amusement is at the heart of the literati aesthetic. Ni Zan once wrote this comment on a painting: "What I call painting does not exceed the joy of careless sketching with a brush. I do not seek formal likeness but do it simply for my own amusement. Recently I was rambling about and came to a town. The people asked for my pictures, but wanted them exactly according to their own desires and to represent a specific occasion. [When I could not satisfy them,] they went away insulting, scolding, and cursing in every possible way. What a shame! But how can one scold a eunuch for not growing a beard?" (translated in Bush and Shih, p. 266).

Ni Zan's eccentric behavior became legendary in the history of Chinese art. In his early years he was one of the richest men in the region, the owner of a large estate. His pride and his aloofness from daily affairs often got him into trouble with the authorities. His cleanliness was notorious. In addition to washing himself several times daily, he also ordered his servants to wash the trees in his garden and to clean the furniture after his guests had left. He was said to be so unworldly that late in life he gave away most of his possessions and lived as a hermit in a boat, wandering on rivers and lakes.

Whether these stories are true or not, they were important elements of Ni's legacy to later painters, for Ni's life as well as his art served as a model. Literati painting was associated with a viewpoint concerning what constituted an appropriate life. The ideal, as embodied by Ni Zan and others, was a brilliantly gifted scholar whose spirit was too refined for the dusty world of government service and who thus preferred to live as a recluse, or as one who had retired after having become frustrated by a brief stint as an official.

MING DYNASTY

The founder of the next dynasty, the Ming (1368–1644), came from a family of poor uneducated peasants. As he rose through the ranks in the army, he enlisted the help of scholars to gain power and solidify his following. Once he had driven the Mongols from Beijing and firmly established himself as emperor, however, he grew to distrust intellectuals. His rule was despotic, even ruthless. Throughout the nearly 300 years of Ming rule, most emperors shared his attitude, so although the civil service examinations were reinstated, scholars remained alienated from the government they were trained to serve.

COURT AND PROFESSIONAL PAINTING

The contrast between the luxurious world of the court and the austere ideals of the literati continued through the Ming dynasty.

A typical example of Ming court taste is **HUNDREDS OF BIRDS ADMIRING THE PEACOCKS**, a large painting on silk by Yin Hong, an artist active during the late fifteenth and early sixteenth centuries (**FIG. 25-4**). A pupil of well-known courtiers, Yin most probably served in the court at Beijing. This painting is an example of the birds-and-flowers genre, which had been popular with artists of the Song academy. Here the subject takes on symbolic meaning, with the homage of the birds to the peacocks representing the homage of court officials to the imperial state. Although the style is faithful to Song academic models, the large format and pervasive attention to detail are traits of the Ming.

A related, yet bolder and less constrained, landscape style was also popular during this period. It is sometimes called the Zhe style since its roots were in Hangzhou, Zhejiang Province, where the Southern Song court had been located. A representative example

25-4 • Yin Hong HUNDREDS OF BIRDS ADMIRING THE PEACOCKS
Ming dynasty, late 15th–early 16th century. Hanging scroll with ink and color on silk, 7′10½″ × 6′5″ (2.4 × 1.96 m). The Cleveland Museum of Art. Purchase from the J.H. Wade Fund (1974.31)

25-5 • Dai Jin RETURNING HOME LATE FROM A SPRING OUTING
Ming dynasty. Hanging scroll with ink on silk, 5′6″ × 2′8¾″ (1.68 × 0.83 m). National Palace Museum, Taibei, Taiwan, Republic of China.

is **RETURNING HOME LATE FROM A SPRING OUTING** (**FIG. 25-5**), unsigned but attributed to Dai Jin (1388–1462). Zhe-style works such as this will become sources for Korean and Japanese artists such as An Gyeon (see **FIG. 25-18**) and Sesshu (see **FIG. 26-3**).

QIU YING A preeminent professional painter in the Ming period was Qiu Ying (1494–1552), who lived in Suzhou, a prosperous southern city. He inspired generations of imitators with

exceptional works, such as a long handscroll known as **SPRING DAWN IN THE HAN PALACE** (**FIG. 25-6**). The painting is based on Tang-dynasty depictions of women in the court of the Han dynasty (206 BCE–220 CE). While in the service of a well-known collector, Qiu Ying had the opportunity to study many Tang paintings, whose artists usually concentrated on the figures, set on blank backgrounds. Qiu's graceful and elegant figures—although modeled after those in Tang works—are situated within a

25-6 • Qiu Ying SECTION OF SPRING DAWN IN THE HAN PALACE
Ming dynasty, 1500–1550. Handscroll with ink and color on silk, 1′ × 18′13⁄16″ (0.3 × 5.7 m). National Palace Museum, Taibei, Taiwan, Republic of China.

With the exception of large wall paintings that typically decorated palaces, temples, and tombs, most Chinese paintings were created from ink and water-based colors on silk or paper. Finished works were generally mounted as handscrolls, hanging scrolls, or leaves in an album.

An album comprises a set of paintings of identical size mounted in a book. (A single painting from an album is called an album leaf.) The paintings in an album are usually related in subject, such as various views of a famous site or a series of scenes glimpsed on one trip.

Album-sized paintings might also be mounted as a handscroll, a horizontal format generally about 12 inches high and anywhere from a few feet to dozens of feet long. More typically, however, a handscroll would be a single continuous painting. Handscrolls were not meant to be displayed all at once, the way they are commonly presented today in museums. Rather, they were unrolled only occasionally, to be savored in much the same spirit as we might view a favorite film. Placing the scroll on a flat surface such as a table, a viewer would unroll it a foot or two at a time, moving gradually through the entire scroll from right to left, lingering over favorite details. The scroll was then rolled up and returned to its box until the next viewing.

Like handscrolls, hanging scrolls were not displayed permanently but were taken out for a limited time: a day, a week, a season. Unlike a handscroll, however, the painting on a hanging scroll was viewed as a whole—unrolled and hung on a wall, with the roller at the lower end acting as a weight to help the scroll hang flat. Although some hanging scrolls are quite large, they are still fundamentally intimate works, not intended for display in a public place.

Creating a scroll was a time-consuming and exacting process accomplished by a professional mounter. The painting was first backed with paper to strengthen it. Next, strips of paper-backed silk were pasted to the top, bottom, and sides, framing the painting on all four sides. Additional silk pieces were added to extend the scroll horizontally or vertically, depending on the format. The assembled scroll was then backed again with paper and fitted with a half-round dowel, or wooden rod, at the top of a hanging scroll or on the right end of a handscroll, with ribbons for hanging and tying, and with a wooden roller at the other end. Hanging scrolls were often fashioned from several patterns of silk, and a variety of piecing formats were developed and codified. On a handscroll, a painting was generally preceded by a panel giving the work's title and often followed by a long panel bearing colophons—inscriptions related to the work, such as poems in its praise or comments by its owners over the centuries. A scroll would be remounted periodically to better preserve it, and colophons and inscriptions would be preserved in each remounting. Seals added another layer of interest. A treasured scroll often bears not only the seal of its maker but also those of collectors and admirers through the centuries.

colophon panel   frontispiece

label

handscroll rolled for storage

handscroll

front   back

hanging scroll

carefully described setting of palace buildings. They engage in courtly pastimes, such as chess, music, calligraphy, and painting. With its antique subject matter, refined technique, brilliant color, and controlled composition, *Spring Dawn in the Han Palace* brought professional painting to another level (see a detail from this scroll in "A Closer Look," page 801).

DECORATIVE ARTS

Qiu Ying painted to satisfy his patrons in Suzhou. The cities of the south were becoming wealthy, and newly rich merchants collected paintings, antiques, and art objects. The court, too, was prosperous and lavishly funded the arts. In such a setting, the decorative arts thrived.

Marco Polo, it is said, was the one who named a new type of ceramic he found in China. Its translucent purity reminded him of the smooth whiteness of the cowry shell, *porcellana* in Italian. Porcelain is made from kaolin, an extremely refined white clay, and petuntse, a variety of the mineral feldspar. When properly combined and fired at a sufficiently high temperature (generally in the range of 1300° to 1400°C), the two materials fuse into a glasslike, translucent ceramic that is far stronger than it looks.

Porcelaneous stoneware, fired at lower temperatures, was known in China by the seventh century, but true porcelain was perfected during the Song dynasty. To create blue-and-white porcelain such as the flask in FIGURE 25–7, blue pigment was made from cobalt oxide, finely ground and mixed with water. The decoration was painted directly onto the unfired porcelain vessel, then a layer of clear glaze was applied over it. (In this technique, known as **underglaze** painting, the pattern is painted beneath the glaze.) After firing, the piece emerged from the kiln with a clear blue design set sharply against a snowy white background.

Entranced with the exquisite properties of porcelain, European potters tried for centuries to duplicate it. The technique was finally discovered in 1709 by Johann Friedrich Böttger in Dresden, Germany, who tried—but failed—to keep it a secret.

MING BLUE-AND-WHITE WARES Ming China became famous the world over for its exquisite ceramics, especially porcelain (see "The Secret of Porcelain," above). The imperial kilns in Jingdezhen, in Jiangxi Province, became the most renowned center for porcelain not only in China, but in all the world. Particularly noteworthy are the blue-and-white wares produced there during the ten-year reign of the ruler known as the Xuande Emperor (r. 1426–1435). The subtle shape, the refined yet vigor-ous decoration of dragons on the sea, and the flawless glazing of the **FLASK** in FIGURE 25–7 are representative of the high achievement of Ming ceramic artists.

ARCHITECTURE AND CITY PLANNING

Centuries of warfare and destruction have left very few early Chinese architectural monuments intact. The most important remaining example of traditional architecture is **THE FORBIDDEN CITY**, the imperial palace compound in Beijing, whose principal buildings were constructed during the Ming dynasty (FIG. 25–8).

THE FORBIDDEN CITY The basic plan of Beijing was the work of the Mongols, who laid out their capital city according to traditional Chinese principles. City planning had begun early in China—in the seventh century, in the case of Chang'an (present-day Xi'an), the capital of the Sui and Tang emperors. The walled city of Chang'an was organized on a rectangular grid, with evenly spaced streets that ran north–south and east–west. At the northern end stood a walled imperial complex.

25-7 • FLASK
Ming dynasty, 1426–1435. Porcelain with decoration painted in underglaze cobalt blue. Collection of the Palace Museum, Beijing.

Dragons have featured prominently in Chinese folklore from earliest times—Neolithic examples have been found painted on pottery and carved in jade. In Bronze Age China, dragons came to be associated with powerful and sudden manifestations of nature, such as wind, thunder, and lightning. At the same time, dragons became associated with superior beings such as virtuous rulers and sages. With the emergence of China's first firmly established empire during the Han dynasty, the dragon was appropriated as an imperial symbol, and it remained so throughout Chinese history. Dragon sightings were duly recorded and considered auspicious. Yet even the Son of Heaven could not monopolize the dragon. During the Tang and Song dynasties the practice arose of painting pictures of dragons to pray for rain, and for Chan (Zen) Buddhists, the dragon was a symbol of sudden enlightenment.

A CLOSER LOOK | *Spring Dawn in the Han Palace*

by Qiu Ying. Ming dynasty, 1500–1550. Section of a handscroll with ink and color on silk.
1' × 18'13⁄16" (0.3 × 5.7 m). National Palace Museum, Taibei, Taiwan, Republic of China.

Two ladies unwrap a *qin*, the zither or lute that was the most respected of musical instruments.

A seated lady plays the *pipa*, an instrument introduced from Central Asia during the Tang dynasty.

Antique vessels of bronze, lacquer, and porcelain adorn the room and suggest the ladies' refined taste.

A tray landscape featuring an eroded rock provides a sculptural counterpart to landscape (mountain-and-water) painting and suggests a place where immortals might dwell.

Two ladies dance together letting their sleeves and sashes swirl.

 View the Closer Look for *Spring Dawn in the Han Palace* on myartslab.com

Beijing, too, was developed as a walled, rectangular city with streets laid out in a grid. The palace enclosure occupied the center of the northern part of the city, which was reserved for the Mongols. Chinese lived in the southern third of the city. Later, Ming and Qing emperors preserved this division, with officials living in the northern or Inner City and commoners living in the southern or Outer City. The third Ming emperor, Yongle (ruled 1403–1424), rebuilt the Forbidden City as we see it today.

The approach was impressive. Visitors entered through the Meridian Gate, a monumental complex with perpendicular side wings (see FIG. 25–8). After passing through the Meridian Gate, visitors encountered a broad courtyard crossed by a bow-shaped waterway spanned by five arched marble bridges. At the opposite end of this courtyard is the Gate of Supreme Harmony, opening onto an even larger courtyard that houses three ceremonial halls raised on a broad platform. First is the Hall of Supreme Harmony, where, on the most important state occasions, the emperor sat on his throne, facing south. Beyond is the smaller Hall of Central Harmony, then the Hall of Protecting Harmony. Behind these vast ceremonial spaces, still on the central axis, is the inner court, again with a progression of three buildings, this time more intimate in scale. In its balance and symmetry the plan of the Forbidden City reflects ancient Chinese beliefs about the harmony of the universe, and it emphasizes the emperor's role as the Son of Heaven, whose duty was to maintain the cosmic order from his throne in the middle of the world.

25-8 • THE FORBIDDEN CITY
Now the Palace Museum, Beijing. Mostly Ming dynasty. View from the southwest.

✷⎯Explore the architectural panoramas of the Forbidden City on myartslab.com

THE LITERATI AESTHETIC

In the south, particularly in the district of Suzhou, literati painting, associated with the educated men who served the court as government officials, remained the dominant artistic trend. One of the major literati painters from the Ming period is Shen Zhou (1427–1509), who had no desire to enter government service and spent most of his life in Suzhou. He studied the Yuan painters avidly and tried to recapture their spirit in such works as *Poet on a Mountaintop* (see "*Poet on a Mountaintop*," opposite). Although the style of the painting recalls the freedom and simplicity of Ni Zan (see FIG. 25-3), the motif of a poet surveying the landscape from a mountain plateau is Shen's creation.

**LITERATI INFLUENCE ON FURNITURE, ARCHITEC-
TURE, AND GARDEN DESIGN** The taste of the literati also influenced the design of furniture, architecture, and especially gardens. Characteristic of Chinese furniture during the Ming period, the **ARMCHAIR** in **FIGURE 25-9** is constructed without the use of glue or nails. Instead, pieces fit together based on the

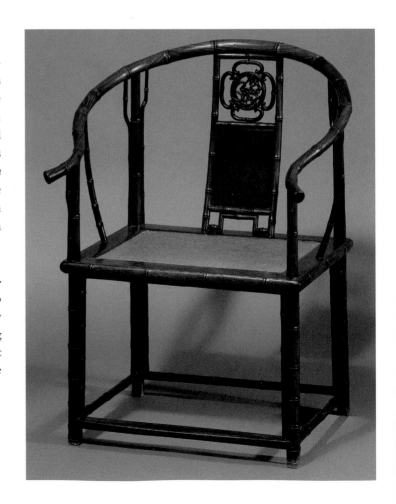

25-9 • ARMCHAIR
Ming dynasty, 16th–17th century. Huanghuali wood (hardwood), 39⅜″ × 27¼″ × 20″ (100 × 69.2 × 50.8 cm). Nelson-Atkins Museum of Art, Kansas City, Missouri. Purchase: William Rockhill Nelson Trust (46–78/1)

In earlier landscape paintings, human figures were typically shown dwarfed by the grandeur of nature. Travelers might be seen scuttling along a narrow path by a stream, while overhead towered mountains whose peaks conversed with the clouds and whose heights were inaccessible. In **FIGURE 25–10** the poet has climbed the mountain and dominates the landscape. Even the clouds are beneath him. Before his gaze, a poem hangs in the air, as though he were projecting his thoughts.

The poem, composed by Shen Zhou himself, and written in his distinctive hand, reads:

White clouds like a scarf enfold the mountain's
    waist;
Stone steps hang in space—a long, narrow
    path.
Alone, leaning on my cane, I gaze intently at
    the scene,
And feel like answering the murmuring brook
    with the music of my flute.

(Translation by Jonathan Chaves, *The Chinese Painter as Poet*, New York, 2000, p. 46.)

Shen Zhou composed the poem and wrote the inscription at the time he painted the album. The style of the calligraphy, like the style of the painting, is informal, relaxed, and straightforward—qualities that were believed to reflect the artist's character and personality.

The painting visualizes Ming philosophy, which held that the mind, not the physical world, was the basis for reality. With its tight synthesis of poetry, calligraphy, and painting, and with its harmony of mind and landscape, *Poet on a Mountaintop* represents the essence of Ming literati painting.

25–10 • Shen Zhou POET ON A MOUNTAINTOP
Leaf from an album of landscapes; painting mounted as part of a handscroll. Ming dynasty, c. 1500. Ink and color on paper, 15¼″ × 23¾″ (40 × 60.2 cm). The Nelson-Atkins Museum of Art, Kansas City, Missouri. Purchase: William Rockhill Nelson Trust (46-51/2)

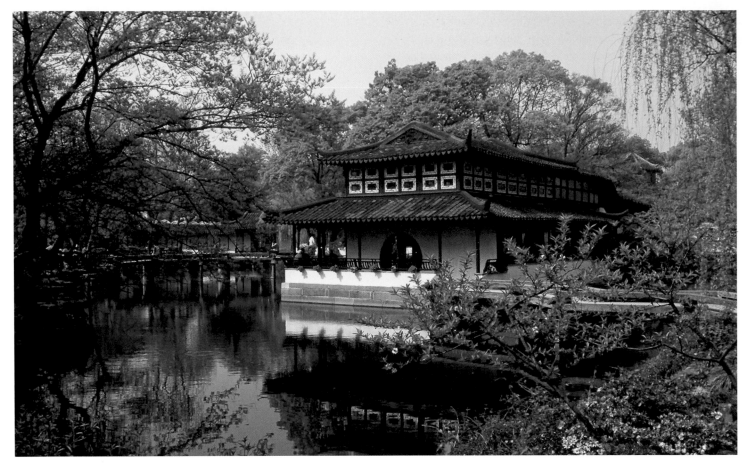

25-11 • GARDEN OF THE CESSATION OF OFFICIAL LIFE (ALSO KNOWN AS THE HUMBLE ADMINISTRATOR'S GARDEN)
Suzhou, Jiangsu. Ming dynasty, early 16th century.

Early in the sixteenth century, an official in Beijing, frustrated after serving in the capital for many years without promotion, returned home. Taking an ancient poem, "The Song of Leisurely Living," for his model, he began to build a garden. He called his retreat the Garden of the Cessation of Official Life to indicate that he had exchanged his career as a bureaucrat for a life of leisure. By leisure, he meant that he could now dedicate himself to calligraphy, poetry, and painting, the three arts dear to scholars in China.

principle of the mortise-and-tenon joint, in which a projecting element (tenon) on one piece fits snugly into a cavity (mortise) on another. Each piece of the chair is carved—not bent or twisted—and the joints are crafted with great precision. The patterns of the wood grain provide subtle interest, unconcealed by painting or other embellishment. The style, like that of Chinese architecture, is simple, clear, symmetrical, and balanced. The effect is formal and dignified but natural and simple—virtues central to the traditional Chinese view of proper human conduct as well.

The art of landscape gardening also flourished during the Ming dynasty, as many literati surrounded their homes with gardens. The most famous gardens were created in the southern cities of the Yangzi Delta, especially in Suzhou, including the largest surviving garden of the era—the **GARDEN OF THE CESSATION OF OFFICIAL LIFE (FIG. 25-11)**. Although modified and reconstructed many times since the sixteenth century, it still reflects many of the basic ideas of the original Ming owner. About one third of the garden is devoted to water through artificially created

brooks and ponds. The landscape is dotted with pavilions, kiosks, libraries, studios, and corridors—many with poetic names, such as Rain Listening Pavilion and Bridge of the Small Flying Rainbow.

DONG QICHANG, LITERATI THEORIST The ideas underlying literati painting found their most influential expression in the writings of Dong Qichang (1555–1636). This high official in the late Ming period embodied the literati tradition as poet, calligrapher, and painter. He developed a view of Chinese art history that divided painters into two opposing schools, northern and southern. The categorization is unrelated to the actual geographic home of the painters—a painter from the south might well be classed as northern—but reflects parallels Dong perceived with the northern and southern schools of Chan (Zen) Buddhism in China. The southern school of Chan, founded by the eccentric monk Huineng (638–713), was unorthodox, radical, and innovative; the northern Chan school was traditional and conservative. Similarly, Dong's two schools of painters represented progressive and conservative traditions. In Dong's view, the conservative northern school was dominated by professional painters whose academic, often decorative, style emphasized technical skill. In contrast, the progressive southern school preferred ink to color and free brushwork to meticulous detail. Its painters aimed for poetry and personal expression. In promoting this theory, Dong privileged literati painting, which he positioned as the culmination of the southern school, and this viewpoint fundamentally influenced the way the Chinese viewed their own tradition.

Dong Qichang summarized his views on the proper training for literati painters in the famous statement "Read ten thousand books and walk ten thousand miles." By this he meant that one must first study the works of the great masters, then follow "heaven and earth," the world of nature. Such study would prepare the way for greater self-expression through brush and ink, the goal of literati painting. Dong's views rested on an awareness that a painting of scenery and the actual scenery are two very different things. The excellence of a painting does not lie in its degree of resemblance to the natural world—that gap can never be bridged—but in its expressive power. In this view, the expressive language of painting is inherently abstract, rooted in the construction of its brushstrokes. For example, in a painting of a rock, the rock itself is not expressive; rather, the brushstrokes that suggest the rock are expressive.

With such thinking Dong brought painting close to the realm of calligraphy, which had long been considered the highest form of artistic expression in China. More than a thousand years before Dong's time, a body of critical terms and theories had evolved to discuss calligraphy in relation to the formal and expressive properties of brushwork and composition. Dong incorporated some of these terms—categories such as opening and closing, rising and falling, and void and solid—into the criticism of painting.

Dong's theories take visual form in his painting of **THE QINGBIAN MOUNTAINS** (**FIG. 25-12**). As documented in his own inscription, he based this painting on a work by the tenth-century artist Dong Yuan. Dong Qichang's style, however, is quite different from the styles of the masters he admired. Although there is some indication of foreground, middle ground, and distant mountains, the space is ambiguous, as if all the elements were compressed to the surface of the picture. With this flattening of space, the trees, rocks, and mountains become more readily legible as semiabstract forms made of brushstrokes.

Six trees arranged diagonally at lower right define the extreme foreground and announce themes that the rest of the painting repeats, varies, and develops. The left-most of these foreground trees, with its outstretched branches and full foliage, is echoed first in the shape of another tree just across the river and again in a tree farther up and to the left. The tallest tree of the foreground grouping anticipates the high peak that towers in the distance almost directly above it, while the forms of the smaller foreground trees, especially the one with the darkest leaves, are repeated in numerous variations across the painting. At the same time, the simple and ordinary-looking boulder in the foreground is transformed in the

25-12 • Dong Qichang THE QINGBIAN MOUNTAINS
Ming dynasty, 1617. Hanging scroll with ink on paper, 21′8″ × 7′4⅜″ (6.72 × 2.25 m). Cleveland Museum of Art. Leonard C. Hanna, Jr., Fund

conglomeration of rocks, ridges, hills, and mountains above. This double reading—both abstract and representational, on the surface and into space—parallels the work's dual nature as a painting of a landscape and an interpretation of a traditional landscape painting.

The influence of Dong Qichang on the development of Chinese painting of later periods cannot be overstated. Indeed, nearly all Chinese painters since the early seventeenth century have engaged with his ideas in one way or another.

QING DYNASTY

In 1644, when the armies of the Manchu people to the northeast of China marched into Beijing, many Chinese reacted as though their civilization had come to an end. Yet, the Manchus had already adopted many Chinese customs and institutions before their conquest. After gaining control of all of China, a process that took decades, they showed great respect for Chinese tradition. All the major artistic trends of the late Ming dynasty eventually continued into the Manchu, or Qing, dynasty (1644–1911).

ORTHODOX PAINTING

Literati painting had been established as the dominant tradition; it now became orthodox. Scholars followed Dong Qichang's recommendation, basing their approach on the study of past masters—especially Song and Yuan artists—and imitating antique styles as a way of expressing their own learning, technique, and taste.

The Qing emperors of the late seventeenth and eighteenth centuries were painters themselves. They collected literati painting,

25-13 • Yun Shouping AMARANTH
Leaf from an album of flowers, bamboo, fruits, and vegetables. 1633–1690. Album of 10 leaves; ink and color on paper; each leaf 10″ × 13″ (25.3 × 33.5 cm). Collection of Phoenix Art Museum, Arizona. Gift of Marilyn and Roy Papp

The leaf is inscribed by the artist: "Autumn garden abounds in beauty, playfully painted by Ouxiangguan (Yun Shouping)." (Translation by Momoko Soma Welch)

25-14 • Shitao
LANDSCAPE
Leaf from *An Album of Landscapes*. Qing dynasty, c. 1700. Ink and color on paper, 9½″ × 11″ (24.1 × 28 cm). Collection C.C. Wang family.

and their taste was shaped mainly by artists such as Wang Hui (see FIG. 25-1). Thus literati painting, long associated with reclusive scholars, ultimately became an academic style practiced at court. Imbued with values associated with scholarship and virtue, these paintings constituted the highest art form of the Qing court. The emperors also valued a style of bird-and-flower painting developed by Yun Shouping (1633–1690) that, like the orthodox style of land-scape painting, was embraced by literati painters, many of them court officials themselves. The style, most often seen in albums or fans, recalled aspects of Song- and Yuan-dynasty bird-and-flower painting, and artists cited their ancient models as a way to enrich both the meaning and the beauty of these small-format works. In a leaf from an album of flowers, bamboo, fruits and vegetables, which employs a variety of brush techniques (FIG. 25-13), Yun Shouping represents flowers of the autumn season.

INDIVIDUALIST PAINTING

The first few decades of Qing rule had been both traumatic and dangerous for those who were loyal—or worse, related—to the Ming. Some committed suicide, while others sought refuge in monasteries (e.g., Zhu Da, see Introduction, "A Closer Look," page xxxiv, FIG. B), or wandered the countryside. Among them were several painters who expressed their anger, defiance, frustra-tion, and melancholy in their art. They took Dong Qichang's idea

of painting as an expression of the artist's personal feelings very seriously and cultivated highly original styles. These painters have become known as the individualists.

SHITAO One of the individualists was Shitao (1642–1707), who was descended from the first Ming emperor and who took refuge in Buddhist temples when the dynasty fell. In his later life he brought his painting to the brink of abstraction in such works as **LANDSCAPE** (FIG. 25-14). A monk sits in a small hut, looking out onto mountains that seem to be in turmoil. Dots, used for centuries to indicate vegetation on rocks, here seem to have taken on a life of their own. The rocks also seem alive—as if about to swallow up the monk and his hut. Throughout his life Shitao continued to identify himself with the fallen Ming, and he felt that his secure world had turned to chaos with the Manchu conquest.

THE MODERN PERIOD

In the mid and late nineteenth century, China was shaken from centuries of complacency by a series of humiliating military defeats at the hands of Western powers and Japan. Only then did the gov-ernment finally realize that these new rivals were not like the Mon-gols of the thirteenth century. China was no longer at the center of the world, a civilized country surrounded by "barbarians."

Spiritual resistance was no longer sufficient to solve the problems brought on by change. New ideas from Japan and the West began to filter in, and the demand arose for political and cultural reforms. In 1911, the Qing dynasty was overthrown, ending 2,000 years of imperial rule, and China was reconceived as a republic.

During the first decades of the twentieth century Chinese artists traveled to Japan and to Europe to study Western art. Returning to China, many sought to introduce the ideas and techniques they had learned, and they explored ways to synthesize the Chinese and the Western traditions. After the establishment of the present-day Communist government in 1949, individual artistic freedom was curtailed as the arts were pressed into the service of the state and its vision of a new social order. After 1979, however, cultural attitudes began to relax, and Chinese painters again pursued their own paths.

WU GUANZHONG One artist who emerged during the 1980s as a leader in Chinese painting was Wu Guanzhong (1919–2010). Combining his French artistic training with his Chinese background, Wu Guanzhong developed a semiabstract style to depict scenes from the Chinese landscape. He made preliminary sketches on site. Then, back in his studio, he developed these sketches into free interpretations based on his feeling and vision. An example of his work, **PINE SPIRIT**, depicts a scene in the Huang (Yellow) Mountains (**FIG. 25-15**). The technique, with its sweeping gestures of paint, is clearly linked to Abstract Expressionism, an influential Western movement of the post–World War II years (Chapter 33); yet the painting also claims a place in the long tradition of Chinese landscape as exemplified by such masters as Shitao.

Like all aspects of Chinese society, Chinese art has felt the strong impact of Western influence, and the question remains whether Chinese artists will absorb Western ideas without losing their traditional identity. Interestingly, landscape remains an important subject, as it has been for more than a thousand years, and calligraphy continues to play a vital role. Using the techniques and methods of the West, some of China's artists have joined an international avant-garde (see, for example, Wenda Gu in Chapter 33, **FIG. 33-68**), while other painters still seek communion with nature through their ink brushstrokes as a means to come to terms with human life and the world.

ARTS OF KOREA: THE JOSEON DYNASTY TO THE MODERN ERA

In 1392, General Yi Seonggye (1335–1408) overthrew the Goryeo dynasty (918–1392), establishing the Joseon dynasty (1392–1910), sometimes called the Yi dynasty. He first maintained his capital at Gaeseong, the old Goryeo capital, but moved it to Seoul in 1394, where it remained through the end of the dynasty. The Joseon regime rejected Buddhism, espousing Neo-Confucianism as the state philosophy. Taking Ming-dynasty China as its model, the new government patterned its bureaucracy on that of the Ming

25-15 • Wu Guanzhong PINE SPIRIT
1984. Ink and color on paper, 2'3⅝" × 5'3½" (0.70 × 1.61 m). Spencer Museum of Art, The University of Kansas, Lawrence. Gift of the E. Rhodes and Leonard B. Carpenter Foundation (1991.0003)

emperors, even adopting as its own such outward symbols of Ming imperial authority as blue-and-white porcelain. The early Joseon era was a period of cultural refinement and scientific achievement, during which Koreans invented Han'geul (the Korean alphabet) and movable type, not to mention the rain gauge, astrolabe, celestial globe, sundial, and water clock.

JOSEON CERAMICS

Like their Silla and Goryeo forebears (see Chapter 11), Joseon potters excelled in the manufacture of ceramics, taking their cue from contemporaneous Chinese wares, but seldom copying them directly.

BUNCHEONG CERAMICS Descended from Goryeo celadons, Joseon-dynasty stonewares, known as *buncheong* wares, enjoyed widespread usage throughout the peninsula. Their decorative effect relies on the use of white slip that makes the humble stoneware resemble more expensive white porcelain. In fifteenth-century examples, the slip is often seen inlaid into repeating design elements stamped into the clay body.

Sixteenth-century *buncheong* wares are characteristically embellished with wonderfully fluid, calligraphic brushwork painted in iron-brown slip on a white slip ground. Most painted *buncheong* wares have stylized floral décor, but rare pieces, such as the charming **WINE BOTTLE** in **FIGURE 25-16**, feature pictorial decoration. In fresh, lively brushstrokes, a bird with outstretched wings grasps a fish that it has just caught in its talons; waves roll below, while two giant lotus blossoms frame the scene.

Japanese armies repeatedly invaded the Korean peninsula between 1592 and 1597, destroying many of the *buncheong* kilns, and essentially bringing ceramic production to a halt. Tradition holds that the Japanese took many *buncheong* potters home

with them to produce *buncheong*-style wares, which were greatly admired by connoisseurs of the tea ceremony. In fact, the spontaneity of Korean *buncheong* pottery has inspired Japanese ceramics to this day.

PAINTED PORCELAIN Korean potters produced porcelains with designs painted in underglaze cobalt blue as early as the fifteenth century, inspired by Chinese porcelains of the early Ming period (see FIG. 25-7). The Korean court dispatched artists from the royal painting academy to the porcelain kilns—located some 30 miles southeast of Seoul—to train porcelain painters. As a result, from the fifteenth century onward, the painting on the best Korean porcelains closely approximated that on paper and silk, unlike in China, where ceramic decoration followed a path of its own with little reference to painting traditions.

In another unique development, Korean porcelains from the sixteenth and seventeenth centuries often feature designs painted in underglaze iron-brown rather than the cobalt blue customary in Ming porcelain. Also uniquely Korean are porcelain jars with bulging shoulders, slender bases, and short, vertical necks, which appeared by the seventeenth century and came to be the most characteristic ceramic shapes in the later Joseon period. Painted in underglaze iron-brown, the seventeenth-century jar shown in **FIGURE 25-17** depicts a fruiting grape branch around its shoulder. In typical Korean fashion, the painting spreads over a surface unconstrained by borders, resulting in a balanced but asymmetrical design that incorporates the Korean taste for unornamented spaces.

JOSEON PAINTING

Korean secular painting came into its own during the Joseon dynasty. Continuing Goryeo traditions, early Joseon examples employ Chinese styles and formats, their range of subjects

25-16 • HORIZONTAL WINE BOTTLE WITH DECORATION OF A BIRD CARRYING A NEWLY CAUGHT FISH
Korea. Joseon dynasty, 16th century. Buncheong ware: light gray stoneware with decoration painted in iron-brown slip on a white slip ground, 6¹⁄₁₀″ × 9½″ (15.5 × 24.1 cm). Museum of Oriental Ceramics, Osaka, Japan. Gift of the Sumitomo Group (20773)

25-17 • BROAD-SHOULDERED JAR WITH DECORATION OF A FRUITING GRAPEVINE
Korea. Joseon dynasty, 17th century. Porcelain with decoration painted in underglaze iron-brown slip, height 22⅛" (53.8 cm). Ewha Women's University Museum, Seoul, Republic of Korea.

Korean potters learned to make porcelain during the Goryeo dynasty, probably as early as the eleventh or twelfth century, though few Goryeo examples remain today. For many centuries, only the Chinese and Koreans were able to produce porcelains.

expanding from botanical motifs to include landscapes, figures, and a variety of animals.

Painted in 1447 by An Gyeon (b. 1418), **DREAM JOURNEY TO THE PEACH BLOSSOM LAND** (FIG. 25-18) is the earliest extant and dated Joseon secular painting. It illustrates a fanciful tale by China's revered nature poet Tao Qian (365–427), and recounts a dream about chancing upon a utopia secluded from the world for centuries while meandering among the peach blossoms of spring.

As with their Goryeo forebears, the monumental mountains and vast, panoramic vistas of such fifteenth-century Korean paintings echo Northern Song painting styles. Chinese paintings of the Southern Song (1127–1279) and Ming periods (1368–1644) also influenced Korean painting of the fifteenth, sixteenth, and seventeenth centuries, though these styles never completely supplanted the imprint of the Northern Song masters.

THE SILHAK MOVEMENT In the eighteenth century, a truly Korean style emerged, inspired by the *silhak* ("practical learning") movement, which emphasized the study of things Korean in addition to the Chinese classics. The impact of the movement is exemplified by the painter Jeong Seon (1676–1759), who chose well-known Korean vistas as the subjects of his paintings, rather than the Chinese themes favored by earlier artists. Among Jeong Seon's paintings are numerous representations of the Diamond Mountains (Geumgang-san), a celebrated range of craggy peaks along Korea's east coast. Painted in 1734, the scroll reproduced in **FIGURE 25-19** aptly captures the Diamond Mountains' needlelike peaks. The subject is Korean, and so is the energetic spirit and the intensely personal style, with its crystalline mountains, distant clouds of delicate ink wash, and individualistic brushwork.

Among figure painters, Sin Yunbok (b. 1758) is an important exemplar of the *silhak* attitude. Active in the late eighteenth and early nineteenth centuries, Sin typically depicted aristocratic

25-18 • An Gyeon DREAM JOURNEY TO THE PEACH BLOSSOM LAND
Korea. Joseon dynasty, 1447. Handscroll with ink and light colors on silk, 15¼" × 41¾" (38.7 × 106.1 cm). Central Library, Tenri University, Tenri (near Nara), Japan.

金剛全圖
謙齋

萬二千峯皆骨山何人用
意寫真顏眾香浮
而抉赤外
積氣雄諧
世界
間
芙蓉口素
武半林松
柏倏玄圖從今脚
蜡頂今遍多似枕邊者不惜
甲寅
夏本

25-19 • Jeong Seon
PANORAMIC VIEW OF THE
DIAMOND MOUNTAINS
(GEUMGANG-SAN)
Korea. Joseon dynasty, 1734. Hanging
scroll with ink and colors on paper,
40⅝″ × 37″ (130.1 × 94 cm). Lee'um,
Samsung Museum, Seoul, Republic
of Korea.

figures in native Korean garb. The album leaf entitled **PICNIC AT THE LOTUS POND** (FIG. 25-20) represents a group of Korean gentlemen enjoying themselves in the countryside on an autumn day in the company of several *gisaeng* (female entertainers). The figures are recognizably Korean—the women with their full coiffures, short jackets, and generous skirts, and the men with their beards, white robes, and wide-brimmed hats woven of horsehair and coated with black lacquer. The stringed instrument played by the gentleman seated at lower right is a *gayageum* (Korean zither), the most hallowed of all Korean musical instruments.

MODERN KOREA

Long known as "the Hermit Kingdom," the Joseon dynasty pursued a policy of isolationism, closing its borders to most of the world, except China, until 1876. Japan's annexation of Korea in 1910 brought the Joseon dynasty to a close, but effectively prolonged the country's seclusion from the outside world. The legacy of self-imposed isolation compounded by colonial occupation (1910–1945)—not to mention the harsh circumstances imposed by World War II (1939–1945), followed by the even worse conditions of the Korean War (1950–1953)—impeded Korea's

25-20 • Sin Yunbok PICNIC AT THE LOTUS POND
Leaf from an album of genre scenes. Korea. Joseon dynasty, late 18th century. Album of 30 leaves; ink and
colors on paper, 11⅛″ × 13⅞″ (28.3 × 35.2 cm). Kansong Museum of Art, Seoul, Republic of Korea.

artistic and cultural development during the first half of the twentieth century.

A MODERNIST PAINTER FROM KOREA Despite these priva-
tions, some modern influences did reach Korea indirectly via China
and Japan, and beginning in the 1920s and 1930s a few Korean artists
experimented with contemporary Western styles, typically painting in the manner of Cézanne or Gauguin, but sometimes trying
abstract, nonrepresentational styles. Among these, Gim Hwangi
(1913–1974) was influenced by Constructivism and geometric
abstraction and would become one of twentieth-century Korea's
influential painters. Like many Korean artists after the Korean War,
Gim wanted to examine Western modernism at its source. He visited Paris in 1956 and then, from 1964 to 1974, lived and worked
in New York, where he produced his best-known works. His painting **5-IV-71** presents a large pair of circular radiating patterns composed of small dots and squares in tones of blue, black, and gray

(**FIG. 25-21**). While appearing wholly Western in style, medium,
concept, and even in the adoption of the date of the work's
creation as its title, *5-IV-71* also seems related to East Asia's venerable tradition of monochrome **ink painting**, while suggesting
a transcendence that seems Daoist or Buddhist in feeling. Given
that the artist was Korean, that he learned the Chinese classics
in his youth, that he studied art in Paris, and that he then worked
in New York, it is possible that his painting embodies all of the
above. Gim's painting illustrates the dilemma faced by many modern artists seeking to find a distinctive, personal style: whether to
paint in an updated version of a traditional style, in a wholly international style, in an international style with a distinctive local twist,
or in an eclectic, hybrid style that incorporates both native and
naturalized elements from diverse artistic traditions. By addressing these questions, Gim Hwangi blazed a trail for subsequent
Korean-born artists, such as the renowned video artist Nam June
Paik (1932–2006), whose work will be discussed in Chapter 33.

25–21 • Gim Hwangi 5-IV-71
Korea. 1971. Oil on canvas, 39½″ × 39½″ (100 × 100 cm). Whanki Museum, Seoul, Republic of Korea.

THINK ABOUT IT

25.1 Discuss the place of Dong Qichang's *The Qingbian Mountains* (FIG. 25–12) within the history of Chinese landscape painting, drawing specific comparisons with works that came before and after it.

25.2 Examine a work commissioned by the court at Beijing and distinguish which of its features are typical of court art.

25.3 Characterize the culture of the literati, including their values and their art patronage.

25.4 Theorize reasons for the emergence of individualist painting in China, using specific works to support your argument.

CROSSCURRENTS

FIG. 18–15

FIG. 25–10

Both of these expansive paintings use landscape, figures, and text, to create compositions that embody important ideas, values, and themes that are characteristic of two very different cultures. Discuss the meanings the artists embodied in these two works. How do they represent the aspirations of the artists who created them and the viewers who originally encountered them?

✓—[Study and review on myartslab.com

浮世美人寄花
山千代やゑ浦 山千代やゑ浦
八重桜
春の日に
匂ひを
ほろく
山偽の
さくら
ゆくゑ
八重
さく
ら

春信画

26-1 • Suzuki Harunobu THE FLOWERS OF BEAUTY IN THE FLOATING WORLD: MOTOURA AND YAEZAKURA OF THE MINAMI YAMASAKIYA
Edo period, 1769. Polychrome woodblock print on paper, 11⅜″ × 8½″ (28.9 × 21.8 cm). Chicago Art Institute.
Clarence Buckingham Collection (1925.2116)

👁—❚**Watch** a video about *ukiyo-e* techniques on myartslab.com

Japanese Art after 1333

Perched on a window seat, a young woman pauses from smoking her pipe while the girl at her side peers intently through a telescope at boats in the bay below (**FIG. 26-1**). The scene takes place in the city of Edo (now Tokyo) in the 1760s, during an era of peace and prosperity that had started some 150 years earlier when the Tokugawa shoguns unified the nation. Edo was then the largest city in the world, with over 1 million inhabitants: samurai-bureaucrats and working-class townspeople. The commoners possessed a vibrant culture centered in urban entertainment districts, where geisha and courtesans, such as the lady and her young trainee portrayed in this woodblock print, worked.

In the 1630s, the Tokugawa shogunate banned Japanese citizens from traveling abroad and restricted foreign access to the country. Nagasaki became Japan's sole international port, which only Koreans, Chinese, and Dutch could enter—and they could not travel freely in the country once there. The government did this to deter Christian missionaries and to assert authority over foreign powers. Not until 1853, when Commodore Matthew Perry of the United States forced Japan to open additional ports, did these policies change. Even so, foreign influences and products could not be prevented, as the tobacco pipe and telescope in this print testify.

The Japanese had first encountered Westerners—Portuguese traders—in the mid sixteenth century. The Dutch reached Japan by 1600 and brought tobacco and, soon after that, the telescope and other exotic optical devices— including spectacles and microscopes—and curious objects, including books, many illustrated. The Japanese eagerly welcomed these foreign goods and imitated foreign customs, which conferred an air of sophistication on the user. Looking through telescopes like the one in this print was a popular amusement of courtesans and their customers. It conveyed the sort of sexual overtones—because of the telescope's phallic shape—that characterized the ribald humor then in vogue. Novel Western optical devices, all readily available by the mid eighteenth century, offered a new way of seeing that affected the appearance of Japanese pictorial art. As in the early history of Japanese art, however, Chinese influence remained strong and now spread throughout the population as never before, due to new efforts to educate the broader populace in Chinese studies. In varying degrees, the intermingling of diverse native and foreign artistic traditions continued to shape the arts of Japan.

LEARN ABOUT IT

26.1 Survey and evaluate the variety of styles and modes of Japanese art after 1333 that develop in relation to Zen Buddhism.

26.2 Explore the principal themes and subjects portrayed in secular art during the Edo period, especially the popularized imagery featured in *ukiyo-e*.

26.3 Compare art created in Kyoto with art made in Edo during the Edo period and evaluate the relationship of these works to the very different cultural and social climates of the two cities.

26.4 Understand and learn to characterize the way imported artistic traditions, from Europe as well as Asia, interacted with traditional Japanese practices to create new forms of art in the modern period.

((•—[**Listen** to the chapter audio on myartslab.com

MUROMACHI PERIOD

By the year 1333, the history of Japanese art was already long and rich (see "Foundations of Japanese Culture," page 819). Very early, a particularly Japanese sensitivity to artistic production had emerged, including a love of natural materials, a fondness for representing elements of the natural world, and the cultivation of fine craft. Aesthetically, Japanese art manifested a taste for asymmetry, abstraction, boldness of expression, and humor—characteristics that will continue to distinguish Japanese art in its evolving history.

Late in the twelfth century, the authority of the emperor had been superseded by powerful and ambitious warriors (samurai) under the leadership of the shogun, the general-in-chief. But in 1333, Emperor Go-Daigo attempted to retake power. He failed and was forced into hiding in the mountains south of Kyoto where he set up a "southern court." Meanwhile, the shogunal family then in power, the Minamoto, was overthrown by warriors of the Ashikaga clan, who placed a rival to the upstart emperor on the throne in Kyoto, in a "northern court," and had him declare their clan head as shogun. They ruled the country from the Muromachi district in Kyoto, and finally vanquished the southern court emperors in 1392. The Muromachi period, also known as the Ashikaga era (1392–1573), formally began with this event.

The Muromachi period is marked by the ascendance of Zen Buddhism, introduced into Japan in the late twelfth century, whose austere ideals particularly appealed to the highly disciplined samurai. While Pure Land Buddhism, which had spread widely during the latter part of the Heian period (794–1185), remained popular, Zen (which means meditation) became the dominant cultural force in Japan among the ruling elite.

ZEN INK PAINTING

During the Muromachi period, the creation of brightly colored narrative handscrolls in traditional Japanese style continued, but monochrome painting in black ink and its diluted grays—which had just been introduced to Japan from the continent at the end of the Kamakura period (1185–1333)—reigned supreme. Muromachi ink painting was heavily influenced by the aesthetics of Zen, but unlike earlier Zen paintings that had concentrated on portrayals of important individuals associated with the Zen monastic tradition, many artists also began painting Chinese-style landscapes in ink. Traditionally, the monk-artist Shubun (active c. 1418–1463) is regarded as Japan's first great master of ink landscape painting. Unfortunately, no undisputed work of his survives. Two landscapes by Shubun's pupil Bunsei (active c. 1450–1460), however, do survive. The one reproduced in **FIGURE 26-2** is closely modeled on Korean ink landscape paintings that themselves copied Chinese models from the Ming period (such as **FIG. 25-5**). It contains a foreground consisting of a spit of rocky land with an overlapping series of motifs—a spiky pine tree, a craggy rock, a poet seated in a hermitage, and a brushwood fence surrounding a small garden of trees and bamboo. In the middle ground is open space—emptiness,

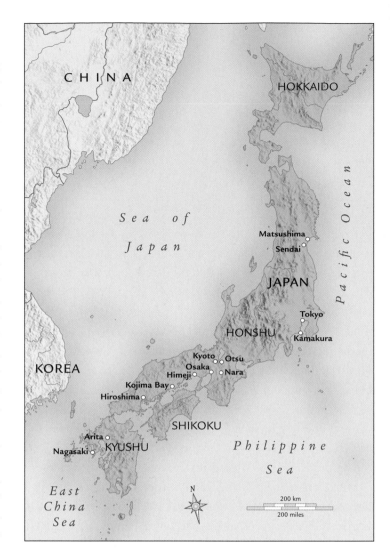

MAP 26-1 • JAPAN

Japan's wholehearted emulation of myriad aspects of Chinese culture began in the fifth century and was challenged by new influences from the West only in the mid nineteenth century after Western powers forced Japan to open its treaty ports to international trade.

the void. We are expected to "read" the unpainted expanse as water. Beyond the blank space, subtle tones of gray ink delineate a distant shore where fishing boats, a small hut, and two people stand. The two parts of the painting seem to echo each other across a deep expanse. The painting illustrates well the pure, lonely, and ultimately serene spirit of the poetic landscape tradition influenced by Zen.

SESSHU Another of Shubun's pupils, Sesshu (1420–1506), has come to be regarded as one of the greatest Japanese painters of all time. Although they completed training to become Zen monks, at the monastery, Shubun and his followers specialized in art rather than in religious ritual or teaching. This distinguished them from earlier Zen monk-painters for whom painting was but one facet of their lives. By Shubun's day, temples had formed their own professional painting ateliers in order to meet the large

26-2 • Bunsei LANDSCAPE
Muromachi period, mid 15th century. Hanging scroll with ink and light colors on paper, 28¾″ × 13″ (73.2 × 33 cm). Museum of Fine Arts, Boston. Special Chinese and Japanese Fund (05.203)

Japan, where he could concentrate on painting unencumbered by monastic duties and entanglements with the political elite. His new temple was under the patronage of a wealthy warrior clan that engaged in trade with China. Funded by them, he had the opportunity to visit China in 1467 on a diplomatic mission. He traveled extensively there for three years, viewing the scenery, stopping at Chan (the Chinese word for Zen) monasteries, and studying Chinese paintings by professional artists rather than those by contemporary literati masters.

When Sesshu returned from China, he remained in the provinces to avoid the turmoil in Kyoto, at that time devastated by civil warfare that would last for the next hundred years. Only a few paintings created prior to his sojourn in China have recently come to light. They are in a style closer to Shubun, and Sesshu signed them with another name. In contrast, the paintings he produced after his return demonstrate a conscious break artistically with the refined landscape style of his teacher. These masterful later paintings exhibit a bold, new spirit, evident in his **WINTER LANDSCAPE** (FIG. 26–3). A cliff descending from the mist seems to cut

26-3 • Sesshu WINTER LANDSCAPE
Muromachi period, c. 1470s. Hanging scroll with ink on paper, 18¼″ × 11½″ (46.3 × 29.3 cm). Collection of the Tokyo National Museum. National Treasure.

demand for paintings from warrior patrons. Sesshu trained as a Zen monk at Shokokuji, where Shubun had his studio. There, he worked in the painting atelier under Shubun for 20 years, before leaving Kyoto to head a small provincial Zen temple in western the composition in two parts. Sharp, jagged brushstrokes delineate a series of rocky hills, where a lone figure makes his way to a Zen monastery. Instead of a gradual recession into space, flat overlapping planes fracture the composition into crystalline facets. The white of the paper is left to indicate snow, while the sky is suggested by tones of gray. A few trees cling desperately to the rocky land. The harsh chill of winter is almost palpable.

THE ZEN DRY GARDEN

Zen monks led austere lives in their quest for the attainment of enlightenment. In addition to daily meditation, they engaged in manual labor to provide for themselves and maintain their temple properties. Many Zen temples constructed dry landscape courtyard gardens, not for strolling but for contemplative viewing. Cleaning and maintaining these gardens—pulling weeds, tweaking unruly shoots, and raking the gravel—was a kind of active meditation. It helped to keep their minds grounded.

The dry landscape gardens of Japan, *karesansui* ("dried-up mountains and water"), exist in perfect harmony with Zen Buddhism. The dry garden in front of the abbot's quarters in the Zen temple at Ryoanji is one of the most renowned Zen creations in Japan (**FIG. 26-4**). A flat rectangle of raked gravel, about 29 by 70 feet, surrounds 15 stones of different sizes in islands of moss.

The stones are set in asymmetrical groups of two, three, and five. Low, plaster-covered walls establish the garden's boundaries, but beyond the perimeter wall maple, pine, and cherry trees add color and texture to the scene. Called "borrowed scenery," these elements are a considered part of the design even though they grow outside the garden. This garden is celebrated for its severity and its emptiness.

Dry gardens began to be built in the fifteenth and sixteenth centuries in Japan. By the sixteenth century, Chinese landscape painting influenced the gardens' composition, and miniature clipped plants and beautiful stones were arranged to resemble famous paintings. Especially fine and unusual stones were coveted and even carried off as war booty, such was the cultural value of these seemingly mundane objects.

The Ryoanji garden's design, as we see it today, probably dates from the mid seventeenth century, at which point such stone and gravel gardens had become highly intellectualized, abstract reflections of nature. This garden has been interpreted as representing islands in the sea, or mountain peaks rising above the clouds, perhaps even a swimming tigress with her cubs, or constellations of stars and planets. All or none of these interpretations may be equally satisfying—or irrelevant—to a monk seeking clarity of mind through contemplation.

26-4 • ROCK GARDEN, RYOANJI, KYOTO
Muromachi period, c. 1480. Photographed spring 1993. UNESCO World Heritage Site, National Treasure.

The American composer John Cage once exclaimed that every stone at Ryoanji was in just the right place. He then said, "And every other place would also be just right." His remark is thoroughly Zen in spirit. There are many ways to experience Ryoanji. For example, we can imagine the rocks as having different visual "pulls" that relate them to one another. Yet there is also enough space between them to give each one a sense of self-sufficiency and permanence.

With the end of the last Ice Age roughly 15,000 years ago, rising sea levels submerged the lowlands connecting Japan to the Asian landmass, creating the chain of islands we know today as Japan (**MAP 26–1**). Not long afterward, early Paleolithic cultures gave way to a Neolithic culture known as Jomon (c. 11,000–400 BCE) after its characteristic cord-marked pottery. During the Jomon period, a sophisticated hunter-gatherer culture developed. Agriculture supplemented hunting and gathering by around 5000 BCE, and rice cultivation began some 4,000 years later.

A fully settled agricultural society emerged during the Yayoi period (c. 400 BCE–300 CE), accompanied by hierarchical social organization. As people learned to manufacture bronze and iron, use of those metals became widespread. Yayoi architecture, with its unpainted wood and thatched roofs, already showed the Japanese affinity for natural materials and clean lines, and the style of Yayoi granaries in particular persisted in the design of shrines in later centuries. The trend toward social organization continued during the Kofun period (c. 300–552 CE), an era characterized by the construction of large royal tombs, following the Korean practice. Veneration of leaders grew into the beginnings of the imperial system that has lasted to the present day.

The Asuka era (552–645 CE) began with a period of profound change as elements of Chinese civilization flooded into Japan, initially through the intermediary of Korea. The three most significant Chinese contributions to the developing Japanese culture were Buddhism (with its attendant art and architecture), a system of writing, and the structures of a centralized bureaucracy. The earliest extant Buddhist temple compound in Japan, Horyuji, which contains the oldest currently existing wooden buildings in the world, dates from this period.

The arrival of Buddhism also prompted some formalization of Shinto, the loose collection of indigenous Japanese beliefs and practices. Shinto is a religion that connects people to nature. Its rites are shamanistic and emphasize ceremonial purification. These include the invocation and appeasement of spirits, including those of the recently dead. Many Shinto deities are thought to inhabit various aspects of nature, such as particularly magnificent trees, rocks, and waterfalls, and living creatures such as deer. Shinto and Buddhism have in common an intense awareness of the transience of life, and as their goals are complementary—purification in the case of Shinto, enlightenment in the case of Buddhism—they have generally existed comfortably alongside each other to the present day.

The Nara period (645–794) takes its name from the location of Japan's first permanently established imperial capital. During this time the founding works of Japanese literature were compiled and Buddhism became the most important force in Japanese culture. Its influence at court grew so great that in 794 the emperor moved the capital from Nara to Heian-kyo (present-day Kyoto), far from powerful monasteries.

During the Heian period (794–1185) an extremely refined court culture thrived, embodied today in an exquisite legacy of poetry, calligraphy, and painting. An efficient method for writing the Japanese language was developed, and with it a woman at the court wrote Japan's most celebrated fictional story, which some describe as the world's first novel: *The Tale of Genji*. Esoteric Buddhism, as hierarchical and intricate as the aristocratic world of the court, became popular.

The end of the Heian period was marked by civil warfare as regional warrior (samurai) clans were drawn into the factional conflicts at court. Pure Land Buddhism, with its simple message of salvation, offered consolation to many in troubled times. In 1185, the Minamoto clan defeated their arch rivals, the Taira, and their leader, Minamoto Yoritomo, assumed the position of shogun (general-in-chief). While paying respect to the emperor, Minamoto Yoritomo took actual military and political power for himself, setting up his own capital in Kamakura. The Kamakura era (1185–1333) began a tradition of rule by shogun that lasted in various forms until 1868. It was also the time in which renewed contacts with China created the opportunity for Zen Buddhism, which was then flourishing in China (known there as Chan), to be introduced to Japan. By the end of the Kamakura period, numerous Zen monasteries had been founded in Kyoto and Kamakura, and Chinese and Japanese Chan/Zen monks were regularly visiting each other's countries.

MOMOYAMA PERIOD

The civil wars sweeping Japan laid bare the basic flaw in the Ashikaga system—samurai were primarily loyal to their own feudal lord (*daimyo*), rather than to the central government. Battles between feudal clans grew more frequent, and it became clear that only a warrior powerful and bold enough to unite the entire country could control Japan. As the Muromachi period drew to a close, three leaders emerged who would change the course of Japanese history.

The first of these leaders was Oda Nobunaga (1534–1582), who marched his army into Kyoto in 1568 and overthrew the reigning Ashikaga shogun in 1573, initiating a new age of Japanese politics. A ruthless warrior, Nobunaga went so far as to destroy a Buddhist monastery because the monks refused to join his forces. Yet he was also a patron of the most rarefied and refined arts. Having taken his own life to avoid succumbing to his enemies in the midst of a military campaign, Nobunaga was succeeded by one of his generals, Toyotomi Hideyoshi (1537–1598), who soon gained complete power in Japan. He, too, was a patron of the arts when not leading his army since he considered culture a vital adjunct to his rule. Hideyoshi, however, was overly ambitious. He believed he could conquer both Korea and China, and he wasted much of his resources on two ill-fated invasions. A stable and long-lasting military regime finally emerged soon after 1600 with the triumph of a third leader, Tokugawa Ieyasu (1543–1616), a former ally of Nobunaga who served as a senior retainer to Hideyoshi, and only asserted his power after Hideyoshi's death. But despite its turbulence, the era of Nobunaga and Hideyoshi, known as the Momoyama period (1573–1615), was one of the most creative eras in Japanese history.

Today the very word Momoyama conjures up images of bold warriors, luxurious palaces, screens shimmering with gold leaf, and, in contrast, rustic tea-ceremony ceramics. Europeans first made an impact in Japan at this time. After the arrival of a few wayward Portuguese explorers in 1543, traders and missionaries soon followed. It was only with the rise of Nobunaga, however, that Westerners were able to extend their activities beyond the ports of Kyushu, Japan's southernmost island. Nobunaga welcomed foreign traders, who brought him various products, the most influential of which were firearms.

ARCHITECTURE

European muskets and cannons quickly changed the nature of Japanese warfare and Japanese castle architecture. In the late sixteenth century, to protect castles from these new weapons, they became heavily fortified garrisons. Some were eventually lost to warfare or torn down by victorious enemies, and others have been extensively altered over the years. One of the most beautiful of the few that have survived intact is **HIMEJI**, not far from the city of Osaka (**FIG. 26-5**). Rising high on a hill above the plains, Himeji has been given the name White Heron. To reach the upper fortress, visitors must follow angular paths beneath steep walls, climbing from one area to the next past stone ramparts and through narrow fortified gates, all the while feeling as though lost in a maze, with no sense of direction or progress.

At the main building, a further climb up a series of narrow ladders leads to the uppermost chamber. There, the footsore visitor is rewarded with a stunning 360-degree view of the surrounding countryside.

DECORATIVE PAINTINGS FOR *SHOIN* ROOMS

Castles such as Himeji were sumptuously decorated, offering artists unprecedented opportunities to work on a grand scale. Interiors were divided into rooms by paper-covered sliding doors (**fusuma**), perfect canvases for large-scale murals. Free-standing folding screens (*byobu*) were also popular. Some had gold-leaf backgrounds, whose glistening surfaces not only reflected light back into the castle rooms but also displayed the wealth of the warrior leaders. Temples, too, commissioned large-scale paintings in these formats for grand reception rooms where the monks met with their wealthy warrior patrons (see "*Shoin* Design," opposite).

Daitokuji, a celebrated Zen monastery in Kyoto, has a number of subtemples for which Momoyama artists painted magnificent *fusuma*. The *fusuma* of one, the Jukoin, were painted by Kano Eitoku (1543–1590), one of the most brilliant painters from the hereditary lineage of professional artists known as the Kano school. Eitoku headed this school, which was founded by his grandfather. The Kano school painted for the highest-ranking warriors from

26-5 • HIMEJI CASTLE, HYOGO, NEAR OSAKA
Momoyama period, 1601–1609. UNESCO World Heritage Site, National Treasure.

The Japanese tea ceremony and *shoin*-style interior residential architecture are undoubtedly the most significant and most enduring expressions of Japanese taste to become established during the Momoyama period. **Shoin** combine a number of interior features in more-or-less standard ways, though no two rooms are ever the same. These features include wide verandas, walls divided by wooden posts, floors covered with woven straw *tatami* mats, recessed panels in ceilings, sometimes painted and sometimes covered with reed matting, several shallow alcoves for prescribed purposes, *fusuma* (paper-covered sliding doors), and **shoji** screens—wood frames covered with translucent rice paper. The *shoin* illustrated here was built in 1601 as a guest hall, called Kojoin, at the Buddhist temple of Onjoji near Kyoto.

The *shoin* is a formal room for receiving important upper-class guests. With some variations due to differences in status, these rooms were designed for buildings used by samurai, aristocrats, and even well-to-do commoners. They are found in various types of buildings: private residences; living quarters, guesthouses, and reception rooms at religious complexes (both Shinto shrines and Buddhist temples); and the finest houses of entertainment (such as seen in FIG. 26–1) where geisha and courtesans entertained important guests. The owner of the building or the most important guest would be seated in front of the main alcove (*tokonoma*), which would contain a hanging scroll, an arrangement of flowers, or a large painted screen. Alongside that alcove was another that featured staggered shelves, often for displaying precious objects. The veranda side of the room also contained a writing space fitted with a low writing desk.

The architectural harmony of a *shoin* is derived from standardization of its basic units, or modules. In Japanese carpentry, the common module of design and construction is the bay, reckoned as the distance from the center of one post to the center of another, which is governed in turn by the standard size of **tatami** floor mats. Although varying slightly from region to region, the size of a single *tatami* is about 3 by 6 feet. Room area in Japan is still expressed in terms of the number of *tatami* mats; for example, a room may be described as an eight-mat room.

shoji · veranda · writing alcove · *tokonoma* · *tatami* · staggered shelves · *fusuma*

26–6 • ARTIST'S RENDERING OF THE KOJOIN GUEST HOUSE AT ONJOJI
Otsu, Shiga prefecture. Momoyama period, 1601. National Treasure.

Watch an architectural simulation about *shoin* design on myartslab.com

the sixteenth century through 1868. They perfected a new style that combined the Muromachi ink-painting tradition with the brightly colored and decorative *yamato-e* style, developed during the Heian period (see Chapter 12). **FIGURE 26–7** shows two of the three walls of Fusuma panels at Jukoin painted by Eitoku when he was in his mid twenties. To the left, the subject is the familiar Kano school theme of cranes and pines, both symbols of long life; to the right is a great gnarled plum tree, symbol of spring. The trees are so massive they seem to extend far beyond the panels. An island rounding both walls of the far corner provides a focus for the outreaching trees. Ingeniously, it belongs to both compositions at the same time, thus uniting them into an organic whole. Eitoku's vigorous use of brush and ink, his powerfully jagged outlines, and his dramatic compositions recall the style of Sesshu, but the bold new sense of scale in his works is a defining characteristic of the Momoyama period.

26-7 • Kano Eitoku FUSUMA
Depicting pine and cranes (left) and plum tree (right) from the central room of the Jukoin, Daitokuji, Kyoto. Momoyama period, c. 1563–1573. *Fusuma* (sliding door panels) with ink and gold on paper, height 5′9⅛″ (1.76 m). National Treasure.

THE TEA CEREMONY

Japanese art is never one-sided. Along with castles and their opulent interior decoration, there was an equal interest during the Momoyama period in the quiet, the restrained, and the natural. This was expressed primarily through the tea ceremony.

The term "tea ceremony," a phrase now in common use, does not convey the full meaning of *chanoyu*, the Japanese ritual drinking of tea. There is no counterpart in Western culture. Tea had been introduced to Japan in the ninth century, when it was molded into cakes and boiled. However, the advent of Zen brought to Japan a different way of preparing tea, with the leaves ground into powder and then whisked in bowls with hot water. Zen monks used such tea as a mild stimulant to aid meditation. Others found it had medicinal properties.

SEN NO RIKYU The most famous tea master in Japanese history was Sen no Rikyu (1522–1591). He conceived of the tea ceremony as an intimate gathering in which a few people, often drawn from a variety of backgrounds—warriors, courtiers, wealthy merchants—would enter a small rustic room, drink tea carefully prepared in front of them by their host, and quietly discuss the tea utensils or a Zen scroll hanging on the wall. He largely established the aesthetic of modesty, refinement, and rusticity that permitted the tearoom to serve as a respite from the busy and sometimes violent world outside. A traditional tearoom combines simple elegance and rusticity. It is made of natural materials such as bamboo and wood, with mud walls, paper windows, and a floor covered with *tatami*. One tearoom that preserves Rikyu's design is named **TAIAN** (**FIG. 26-8**). Built in 1582, it has a tiny door (guests must crawl to enter) and miniature *tokonoma* (alcove) for displaying a Zen scroll or a simple flower arrangement. At first glance, the room seems symmetrical. But a longer look reveals the disposition of the *tatami* does not match the spacing of the *tokonoma*, providing a subtle undercurrent of irregularity. The walls seem scratched

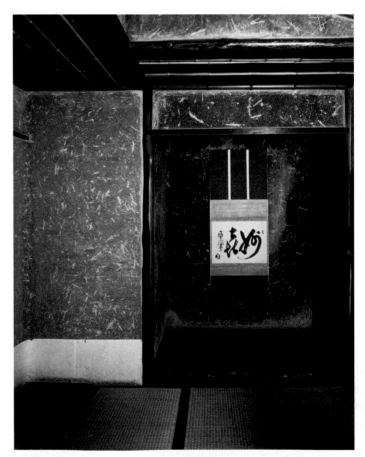

26-8 • Sen no Rikyu TAIAN TEAROOM
Myokian Temple, Kyoto. Momoyama period, 1582. National Treasure.

and worn with age, but the *tatami* are replaced frequently to keep them clean and fresh. The mood is quiet; the light is muted and diffused through three small paper windows. Above all, there is a sense of spatial clarity. Since nonessentials have been eliminated, there is nothing to distract from focused attention. This tearoom aesthetic became an important element in Japanese culture.

THE TEA BOWL Every utensil connected with tea, including the water jar, the kettle, the tea scoop, the whisk, the tea caddy, and, above all, the tea bowl, came to be appreciated for its aesthetic quality, and many works of art were created for use in *chanoyu*.

The age-old Japanese admiration for the natural and the asymmetrical found full expression in tea ceramics. Korean-style rice bowls made for peasants were suddenly considered the epitome of refined taste, and tea masters urged potters to mimic their imperfect shapes. But not every misshapen bowl would be admired. A rarified appreciation of beauty developed that took into consideration such factors as how well a tea bowl fitted into the hands, how subtly the shape and texture of the bowl appealed to the eye, and who had previously used and admired it. For this purpose, the inscribed storage box became almost as important as the ceramic that fitted within it, and if a bowl had been given a name by a leading tea master, it was especially treasured by later generations.

One of the finest surviving early **TEA BOWLS** (**FIG. 26-9**) is attributed to Chojiro (1516–1592), the founder of the Raku family of potters. Named *Yugure* ("Twilight") by tea master Sen no Sotan (1578–1658), a grandson of Rikyu, this bowl is an excellent example of red **raku** ware—a hand-built, low-fired ceramic of gritty red clay, developed especially for use in the tea ceremony. The effect created by the glaze-shaded red hue and lively surface texture evokes a gentle landscape, illuminated by the setting sun. With its small foot, straight sides, irregular shape, and crackled texture, this bowl exemplifies tea taste at the beginning of its development.

EDO PERIOD

When Tokugawa Ieyasu gained control of Japan, he forced the emperor to proclaim him shogun, a title neither Nobunaga nor Hideyoshi had held. His reign initiated the Edo period (1615–1868), named after the city that he founded (present-day Tokyo) as his capital. This period is alternatively known as the Tokugawa era. Under the rule of the Tokugawa family, peace and prosperity came at the price of a rigid and repressive bureaucracy. The problem of a potentially rebellious *daimyo* was solved by ordering all feudal lords to spend either half of each year, or every other year, in Edo, where their families were required to live. Zen Buddhism was supplanted as the prevailing intellectual force by a form of Neo-Confucianism, a philosophy formulated in Song-dynasty China that emphasized loyalty to the state, although the popularity of Buddhism among the commoner population surged at this time.

26-9 • Chojiro TEA BOWL, CALLED YUGURE ("TWILIGHT")
Momoyama period, late 16th century. Raku ware, height 3½″ (9 cm). The Gotoh Museum, Tokyo.

Connoisseurs developed a subtle vocabulary to discuss the aesthetics of tea. A favorite term was *sabi* ("loneliness"), which refers to the tranquility found when feeling alone. Other virtues were *wabi* ("poverty"), which suggests the artlessness of humble simplicity, and *shibui* ("bitter" or "astringent"), meaning elegant restraint. Tea bowls, such as this example, embody these aesthetics.

The shogunate officially divided Edo society into four classes. Samurai officials constituted the highest class, followed by farmers, artisans, and finally merchants. As time went on, however, merchants began to control the money supply, and in Japan's increasingly mercantile economy their accumulation of wealth soon exceeded that of the samurai, which helped, unofficially, to elevate their status. Reading and writing became widespread at all levels of society, and with literacy came intellectual curiosity and interest in the arts. All segments of the population—including samurai, merchants, townspeople, and rural peasants—were able to acquire art. A rich cultural atmosphere developed unlike anything Japan had experienced before, in which artists worked in a wide variety of styles that appealed to these different groups of consumers.

RINPA SCHOOL PAINTING

During the Edo period, Edo was the shogun's city while life in Kyoto took its cues from the resident emperor and his court. Kyoto was also home to wealthy merchants, artists, and craftsmakers who served the needs of the courtiers and shared their interest in refined pursuits, such as the tea ceremony, and also their appreciation of art styles that recalled those perfected by aristocratic artists in the Heian period. The most famous and original Kyoto painter who worked for this group of patrons was Tawaraya Sotatsu (active c. 1600–1640). Sotatsu is considered the first great painter of the Rinpa school, the modern name given to a group of artists whose art reinterpreted ancient courtly styles. These artists are grouped together because of their shared artistic interests;

This **LACQUER BOX** (**FIG. 26–10**) reflects collaborative artistic production and demonstrates the fluidity with which some Japanese artists were able to work in a variety of media. It was designed by the Rinpa-school painter Ogata Korin (1658–1716), who oversaw its execution, although he left the actual work to highly trained craftsmakers. He also frequently collaborated with his brother Kenzan, a celebrated potter. The upper tray housed writing implements, the larger bottom section stored paper (see "Inside a Writing Box," page 826). Korin's design sets a motif of irises and a plank bridge in a dramatic asymmetrical composition created from mother-of-pearl, silver, lead, and gold lacquer. The subject was one he frequently represented in painting because it was immensely popular with the educated Japanese of his day, who would have recognized the imagery as an allusion to a famous passage from the tenth-century Japanese literary classic *Tales of Ise*. A nobleman poet, having left his wife in the capital, pauses at a place called Eight Bridges, where a river branches into eight streams, each covered with a plank bridge. Irises are in full bloom, and his traveling companions urge the poet to write a *waka*—a five-line, 31-syllable poem—beginning each line with a syllable from the word for "iris": *Kakitsubata* (ka-ki-tsu-ba-ta; *ba* is the voiced form of *ha*, which here begins the penultimate line). The poet responds:

> **Ka**ragoromo
> **ki**tsutsu narenishi
> **tsu**ma shi areba
> **ha**rubaru kinuru
> **ta**bi o shi zo omou.
> When I remember
> my wife, fond and familiar
> as my courtly robe,
> I feel how far and distant
> my travels have taken me.
>
> (Translated by Stephen Addiss)

The poem in association with the scene became so famous that any image of a group of irises, with or without a plank bridge, immediately called the episode to mind.

Lacquer is derived in Asia from the sap of the lacquer tree, *Rhus verniciflua*, indigenous to China but very early in history also grown commercially throughout East Asia. It is gathered by tapping into a tree and letting the sap flow into a container, and it can be colored with vegetable or mineral dyes. Applied in thin coats to a surface of wood or leather, lacquer hardens into a glasslike protective coating that is waterproof, heat- and acid-resistant, and airtight. Its practical qualities made it ideal for storage containers, and vessels for food and drink. The creation of a piece of lacquer can take several years. First, the item is fashioned of wood and sanded smooth. Next, up to 30 layers of lacquer are thinly applied, each dried and polished before the next is brushed on.

Japanese craftsmakers exploited the decorative potential of lacquer to create expensive luxury items, such as this box, which was created when lacquer arts had been perfected. It features inlays of mother-of-pearl and precious metals in a style known as *makie* ("sprinkled design"), in which flaked or powdered gold or silver was embedded in a still-damp coat of lacquer.

26–10 • Ogata Korin EXTERIOR (A) AND VIEWS OF INTERIOR AND LID (B) OF A LACQUER BOX FOR WRITING IMPLEMENTS

Edo period, late 17th–early 18th century. Lacquer, lead, silver, and mother-of-pearl, 5⅝″ × 10¾″ × 7¾″ (14.2 × 27.4 × 19.7 cm). Tokyo National Museum, Tokyo. National Treasure.

26–11 • Tawaraya Sotatsu WAVES AT MATSUSHIMA
Edo period, 17th century. Pair of six-panel folding screens with ink, mineral colors, and gold leaf on paper; each screen 4′9⅞″ × 11′8½″ (1.52 × 3.56 m). Freer Gallery of Art, Smithsonian Institution, Washington, DC. Gift of Charles Lang Freer (F1906.231 & 232)

The six-panel screen format was a triumph of scale and practicality. Each panel consisted of a light wood frame surrounding a latticework interior covered with several layers of paper. Over this foundation was pasted a high-quality paper, silk, or gold-leaf ground, ready to be painted by the finest artists. Held together with ingenious paper hinges, a screen could be folded for storage or transportation, resulting in a mural-size painting light enough to be carried by a single person, ready to be displayed as needed.

they did not constitute a formal school, such as the Kano. Rinpa masters were not just painters, however: They sometimes collaborated with craftsmakers (see "Lacquer Box for Writing Implements," opposite).

One of Sotatsu's most famous pairs of screens probably depict the islands of Matsushima near the northern city of Sendai (**FIG.**

26–11). On the right screen (shown here on top), mountainous islands echo the swing and sweep of the waves, with stylized gold clouds reserved from the gold ground at upper left. On the left screen (here below) the gold clouds continue until they become a sand spit from which twisted pines grow. One branch to the left seems to stretch down toward a strange island in the lower

Writing boxes hold tools basic for both writing and painting: ink stick, ink stone, brushes, and paper—all beautiful objects in their own right.

Ink sticks are basically soot from burning wood or oil that is bound into a paste with resin and pressed into small stick-shaped or cake-shaped molds to harden.

Fresh ink is made for each writing or painting session by grinding the hard, dry ink stick in water against a fine-grained stone. A typical ink stone has a shallow well at one end sloping up to a grinding surface at the other. The artist fills the well with water from a waterpot. The ink stick, held vertically, is dipped into the well to pick up a small amount of water, then is rubbed in a circular motion firmly on the grinding surface. Grinding ink is viewed as a meditative task, time for collecting one's thoughts and concentrating on the painting or calligraphy ahead.

Brushes are made from animal hair set in simple bamboo or hollow-reed handles. Brushes taper to a fine point that responds sensitively to any shift in pressure. Although great painters and calligraphers do eventually develop their own styles of holding and using the brush, all begin by learning the basic position for writing. The brush is held vertically, grasped firmly between the thumb and first two fingers, with the fourth and fifth fingers often resting against the handle for more subtle control.

well

ink stick

ink stone

writing implements

brushes

left, composed of an organic, amoebalike form in gold surrounded by mottled ink. This mottled effect was a specialty of Rinpa school painters.

As one of the "three famous beautiful views of Japan," Matsushima was often depicted in art. Most painters showed from above the pine-covered islands that make the area famous. Sotatsu's genius was to portray them in an abbreviated manner and from a fresh vantage point, as though the viewer were passing the islands in a boat on the roiling waters. The artist's asymmetrical composition and his use of thick mineral colors in combination with soft, playful brushwork and sparkling gold leaf create the boldly decorative effect that is the hallmark of the Rinpa tradition.

NATURALISTIC PAINTING

NAGASAWA ROSETSU By the middle of the eighteenth century, the taste of wealthy Kyoto merchants had shifted, influencing the styles of artists who competed for their patronage. The public was enthralled with novel imagery captured in magnifying glasses, telescopes, and an optical device that enhanced the three-dimensional effects of Western-style perspective pictures. Schools of independent artists emerged in Kyoto to satisfy demands for naturalistic-style paintings that reflected this fascination. The most influential was founded by Maruyama Okyo, who had perfected methods to incorporate Western shading and perspective into a more native Japanese decorative style, creating a sense of volume new to East Asian painting, while still retaining a sense of familiarity.

Okyo's most famous pupil was Nagasawa Rosetsu (1754–1799), a painter of great natural talent who added his own boldness and humor to his master's tradition. Rosetsu delighted in surprising his viewers with odd juxtapositions and unusual compositions. One of his finest works is a pair of screens, the left one depicting a **BULL AND PUPPY** (FIG. 26–12). The bull is so immense that

26–12 • Nagasawa Rosetsu **BULL AND PUPPY**
Edo period, late 18th century. Left of a pair of six-panel screens with ink and gold wash on paper, 5'7¼" × 12'3" (1.70 × 3.75 m). Los Angeles County Museum of Art, California. Joe and Etsuko Price Collection (L.83.45.3a)

his mammoth body exceeds the borders of the screen, an effect undoubtedly influenced by new optical devices. The tiny puppy, white against the dark gray of the bull, helps to emphasize the bull's huge size through its contrasting smallness. The puppy's relaxed and informal pose, looking happily straight out at the viewer, gives this powerful painting a humorous touch that increases its charm. In the hands of a master such as Rosetsu, plebeian subject matter became simultaneously delightful and monumental.

LITERATI PAINTING

Because the city of Kyoto was far from the watchful eyes of the government in Edo, and the emperor resided there with his court, it enjoyed a degree of privilege and independence not found in any other Japanese city. These conditions allowed for the creation of art in the new Rinpa and naturalistic styles. They also encouraged the emergence of new schools of philosophy based on interpretations of Chinese Confucianism that disagreed with those taught at schools sponsored by Tokugawa shoguns. These new interpretations incorporated ideas from Chinese Daoism, which promoted cultivation of a person's uniqueness, thus encouraging artistic creativity. Kyoto's intellectuals, who admired Chinese culture, even created a new, more informal tea ceremony of their own, featuring steeped tea called *sencha* because it was the tea drunk by Ming-dynasty Chinese literati. They did this as political protest—by then *chanoyu* had become encumbered by rules and was closely associated with the repressive shogunate. Influenced by such new ideas, a Chinese manner of painting arose in the mid eighteenth century in emulation of literati painting. Artists who embraced this style—both professionals who painted for paying clients and amateurs who painted for their own enjoyment—quickly grew to number hundreds as its popularity spread throughout Japan along with increased interest in drinking *sencha*, as well as in other aspects of Chinese culture. These artists learned about Chinese literati painting not only from the paintings themselves, but also from woodblock-printed painting manuals imported from China, and also from Chinese emigrant monks and merchants who lived in Japan.

The best and most successful of these artists took Chinese literati painting models as starting points for their own original interpretations of literati themes. One of them was Ike Taiga (1723–1776), admired as much for his magnetic personality as for his art. He was born into a poor farming family near Kyoto and showed innate talent for painting at a young age. Moving to Kyoto in his teens, he became friends with Chinese scholars there, including those who promoted drinking *sencha*. Taiga became a leader in this group, attracting admirers who were enamored of both his quasi-amateurish painting style and his quest for spiritual self-cultivation. His character and personal style are seen in the scintillating, rhythmic layering of strokes used to define the mountains in his **VIEW OF KOJIMA BAY** (**FIG. 26-13**), which blends Chinese models, Japanese aesthetics, and personal brushwork. The gentle rounded forms of the mountains intentionally recall the work of famous Chinese literati painters, and Taiga utilizes a stock landscape composition that separates foreground and background mountains with a watery expanse (compare FIG. 26-2). However, he did not paint an imaginary Chinese landscape but a personal vision of an actual Japanese place that he had visited—Kojima Bay—as a document accompanying the painting explains. Still, in deference to his admiration for Chinese literati, Taiga places two figures clad in Chinese robes on the right, midway up the mountain.

26-13 • Ike Taiga VIEW OF KOJIMA BAY
Edo period, third quarter of 18th century. Hanging scroll with ink and color on silk, 39¼″ × 14⅝″ (99.7 × 37.6 cm). Hosomi Museum, Kyoto.

The production of woodblock prints combined the expertise of three individual specialists: the artist, the carver, and the printer. Coordinating and funding this collaborative endeavor was a publisher, who commissioned the project and distributed the prints to stores or itinerant vendors, who would sell them.

The artist designed and supplied the master drawing for the print, executing its outlines with brush and ink on tissue paper. Colors might be indicated, but more often they were understood or determined later. The drawing was passed on to the carver, who pasted it face down on a hardwood block—preferably cherrywood—so that the outlines were visible through the tissue paper in reverse. A light coating of oil might be brushed on to make the paper more transparent, allowing the drawing to stand out even more clearly. The carver then cut around the lines of the drawing with a sharp knife, always working in the same direction as the original brushstrokes. The rest of the block was then chiseled away, leaving only the outlines in relief. This block, which reproduced the master drawing, was called the **key block**. If the print was to be polychrome, involving multiple colors, prints made from the key block were in turn pasted face down on blocks that would be used as guides for the carver of the color blocks. Each color generally required a separate block, although both sides of a block might be used for economy.

Once the blocks were completed, the printer took over. Paper for printing was covered lightly with animal glue (gelatin), and before printing, the coated paper was lightly moistened so that it would take ink and color well. Water-based ink or color was brushed over the blocks, and the paper was placed on top and rubbed with a smooth, padded device called a *baren*, until the design was completely transferred. The key block was printed first, then the colors, one by one. Each block was carved with two small marks called **registration marks**, in exactly the same place in the margins, outside of the image area—an L in one corner, and a straight line in another. By aligning the paper with these marks before letting it fall over the block, the printer ensured that the colors would be placed correctly within the outlines. One of the most characteristic effects of later Japanese prints is a grading of color from dark to pale. This was achieved by wiping some of the color from the block before printing, or by moistening the block and then applying the color gradually with an unevenly loaded brush—a brush loaded on one side with full-strength color and on the other with diluted color.

26-14 • Toshusai Sharaku OTANI ONIJI IN THE ROLE OF YAKKO EDOBE
Edo period, 1794. Polychrome woodblock print with ink, colors, and white mica on paper, 15″ × 9⅞″ (38.1 × 25.1 cm). Metropolitan Museum of Art, New York. Henry L. Phillips Collection, Bequest of Henry L. Phillips, 1939 (JP2822)

👁—**Watch** a video about the woodblock printmaking process on myartslab.com

UKIYO-E: PICTURES OF THE FLOATING WORLD

Edo served as the shogun's capital as well as the center of a flourishing popular culture associated with tradespeople. Deeply Buddhist, commoners were acutely aware of the transience of life, symbolized, for example, by the cherry tree which blossoms so briefly. Putting a positive spin on this harsh realization, they sought to live by the mantra: Let's enjoy it to the full as long as it lasts. This they did to excess in the restaurants, theaters, bathhouses, and brothels of the city's pleasure quarters, named after the Buddhist phrase *ukiyo* ("floating world"). Every major city in Japan had these quarters, and most were licensed by the government. But those of Edo were the largest and most famous. The heroes of the floating world were not famous samurai or aristocratic poets. Instead, swashbuckling kabuki actors and beautiful courtesans were admired. These paragons of pleasure soon became immortalized in paintings and—because paintings were too expensive for common people—in woodblock prints known as **ukiyo-e** ("pictures of the floating world"; see "Japanese Woodblock Prints," above). Most prints were inexpensively produced by the hundreds and not considered serious fine art. Yet when first imported to Europe and America, they were immediately acclaimed and strongly influenced late nineteenth- and early twentieth-century Western art (see "Modern Artists and World Cultures: Japonisme," page 996).

HARUNOBU The first woodblock prints had no color, only black outlines. Soon artists were adding colors by hand, but to produce colored prints more rapidly they gradually devised a system to print colors using multiple blocks. The first artist to design prints that took advantage of this new technique, known as *nishiki-e* ("brocade pictures"), was Suzuki Harunobu (1724–1770), famous for his images of courtesans (see FIG. 26-1).

SHARAKU Toshusai Sharaku is one of the most mysterious, if today among the most admired, masters of *ukiyo-e*. He seems to have been active less than a year in 1794–1795, during which he produced 146 prints, of which all but ten are pictures of famous actors in a popular form of drama known as kabuki. He was renowned for half-length portraits that captured the dramatic intensity of noted performers outfitted in the costumes and makeup of the characters they played on stage. Much as people today buy posters of their favorite sports, music, or movie stars,

so, too, in the Edo period people clamored for images of their kabuki idols. The crossed eyes, craning neck, and stylized gestures of Sharaku's portrayal of actor **OTANI ONIJI** (FIG. 26-14) capture a frozen, tension-filled moment in an action-packed drama, precisely the sort of stylized intensity that was valued in kabuki performance.

HOKUSAI During the first half of the nineteenth century, pictures of famous sights of Japan grew immensely popular. The two most famous *ukiyo-e* printmakers, Utagawa Hiroshige (1797–1858; see "Modern Artists and World Cultures: Japonisme," page 996) and Katsushika Hokusai (1760–1849), specialized in this genre. Hiroshige's *Fifty-Three Stations of the Tokaido* and Hokusai's *Thirty-Six Views of Mount Fuji* became the most successful sets of graphic art the world has known. The woodblocks were printed, and printed again, until they wore out. They were then recarved, and still more copies were printed. This process continued for decades, and thousands of prints from the two series still survive.

THE GREAT WAVE (FIG. 26-15) is the most famous of the scenes from *Thirty-Six Views of Mount Fuji*. The great wave rears up like a dragon with claws of foam, ready to crash down on the

26-15 • Katsushika Hokusai THE GREAT WAVE
From *Thirty-Six Views of Mount Fuji*. Edo period, c. 1831. Polychrome woodblock print on paper, 9⅞″ × 14⅝″ (25 × 37.1 cm).
Honolulu Academy of Art. Gift of James A. Michener 1995 (HAA 13, 695)

Read the document related to Hokusai on myartslab.com

figures huddled in the boats below. Exactly at the point of imminent disaster, but far in the distance, rises Japan's most sacred peak, Mount Fuji, whose slopes, we suddenly realize, swing up like waves and whose snowy crown is like foam—comparisons the artist makes clear in the wave nearest us, caught just at the moment of greatest resemblance. In the late nineteenth century when Japonisme, or *japonism*, became the vogue in the West, Hokusai's art was greatly appreciated, even more so than it had been in Japan: The first book on the artist was published in France.

ZEN PAINTING: BUDDHIST ART FOR RURAL COMMONERS

Outside Japan's urban centers, art for commoners also flourished, much of it tied to their devotion to Buddhism. Deprived of the support of the samurai officials who now favored Confucianism, Buddhism nevertheless thrived during the Edo period through patronage from private individuals, many of them rural peasants. In the early eighteenth century, one of the great monks who preached in the countryside was the Zen master Hakuin Ekaku (1685–1769), born in a small village near Mount Fuji. After hearing a fire-and-brimstone sermon in his youth he resolved to become a monk and for years he traveled around Japan seeking out the strictest Zen teachers. He became the most important Zen master of the last 500 years, and composed many *koan* (questions posed to novices by Zen masters to guide their progression toward enlightenment during meditation), including the famous "What is the sound of one hand clapping?" He was also, in his later years, a self-taught painter and calligrapher, who freely gave away his scrolls to admirers—who included not only farmers but also artisans, merchants, and even samurai—as a way of spreading his religious message.

Hakuin's art differed from that of Muromachi period monk-painters like Bunsei and Sesshu (see FIGS. 26–2, 26–3). His work featured everyday Japanese subjects or Zen themes that conveyed his ideas in ways his humble followers could easily understand. He often painted Daruma (Bodhidharma in Sanskrit) (FIG. 26–16), the semilegendary Indian monk who founded Zen (see Chapter 12). Hundreds of Zen monks of the Edo period and later created simply brushed Zen ink paintings, largely within the standards that Hakuin had set.

CLOTH AND CERAMICS

The ingenuity and technical proficiency that contributed to the development of *ukiyo-e* came about because of Japan's long and distinguished history of what the Western tradition considers fine crafts production. Japanese artists had excelled in the design and production of textiles, ceramics, lacquer, woodwork, and metalwork for centuries, and in pre-modern Japan, unlike the West, no separate words distinguished fine arts (painting and sculpture) from "crafts." (The Japanese word for fine art and corresponding modern Japanese language words for various types of craft were not coined until 1872.) This was largely because professional Japanese artistic studios basically followed the same hereditary, hierarchical

structure, regardless of medium. A master artist directed all activity in a workshop of trainees, who gradually gained seniority through years of apprenticeship and innate talent. Sometimes, such as when a pupil was not chosen to succeed the master, he would leave to establish his own studio. Teamwork under masterful supervision was the approach to artistic production.

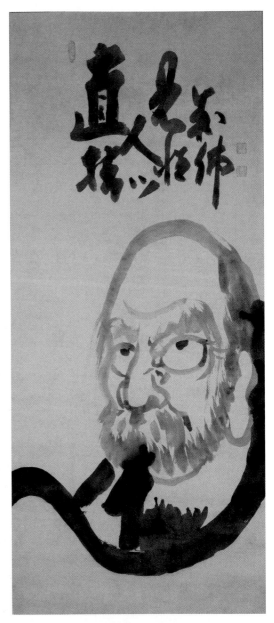

26–16 • Hakuin Ekaku GIANT DARUMA
Edo period, mid 18th century. Hanging scroll with ink on paper, 4′3½″ × 1′9¾″ (130.8 × 55.2 cm). Manyo'an Collection, New Orleans. (1973.2)

As a self-taught amateur painter, Hakuin's painting style is the very antithesis of that of consummate professionals, such as painters of the Kano or Rinpa schools. The appeal of his art lies in its artless charm, humor, and astonishing force. Here Hakuin has portrayed the wide-eyed Daruma during his nine years of meditation in front of a temple wall in China. Intensity, concentration, and spiritual depth are conveyed by a minimal number of broad, forceful brushstrokes. The inscription is the ultimate Zen message, attributed to Daruma himself: "Pointing directly to the human heart, see your own nature and become Buddha."

A CLOSER LOOK | Woman's *Kosode*

With design of bamboo fence and citrus tree (*tachibana*). Edo period, early 18th century.
White figured satin (*rinzu*), with embroidery (gold and silk thread) and stencil dyeing.
Length 62½″ (158.8 cm).
Philadelphia Museum of Art. Gift of Mr. and Mrs. Rodolphe Meyer de Schauensee, 1951

Embroidery with vermilion threads gives a vibrant tonality to this citrus fruit and other motifs throughout the design.

The white silk damask fabric from which this robe is constructed is woven with a key-fret pattern, most visible with reflected light as the robe shifts with the movement of the wearer.

Some of the leaves and citrus fruits are embroidered with radiant gold threads. In a few instances, the gold threads have become loose, revealing the written inscriptions that informed the embroiderer which kind of thread to use.

The decoration flows up the back of the robe in the form of an inverted "C," leaving an area of unornamented silk at middle left. This design is characteristic of an early 18th-century taste for asymmetry.

There is extensive use of the *kata-kanoko* technique, in which stencils were used to create dotted patterns with the application of resist paste and dipping and/or painting with dye. This imitated the elaborate tie-dying that had been popular in earlier robes but was now too time-consuming to meet a growing demand for garments.

  View the Closer Look for the woman's *kosode* on myartslab.com

KOSODE In the West, the robe most often known as a kimono has become as emblematic of Japanese culture as the "tea ceremony." These loose, unstructured garments, wrapping around the body and cinched with a sash, were the principal outer article of clothing for both men and women by the end of the fifteenth century. Robes with short sleeves were known as *kosode* ("small sleeves"). Because of the wear occasioned by their use, few *kosode* prior to the Edo period have survived, but the early examples that remain reveal the opulent tastes of affluent women at this time (see "A Closer Look," above). In this early eighteenth-century *kosode*, the curving branches of a citrus tree (the *tachibana*, native to Japan) emerge above a bamboo fence along the bottom of the robe to grow up its height and across its sleeves, creating an asymmetrical composition with an area of undecorated fabric concentrated at the center toward the left. The textile artists employed many techniques to create the rich interplay of textures and pictures on this gorgeous robe. The extensive use of stencil dyeing and embroidery associate this *kosode* with the tastes of wives of warriors during the early eighteenth century. The individual design elements and the principles of composition resemble those found in paintings and on ceramics during the Edo period, when the pattern books created for garment-makers disseminated motifs among artists working in a variety of media.

26-17 • PLATE WITH WISTERIA AND TRELLIS PATTERN
Edo period, 18th century. Nabeshima ware. Porcelain with underglaze blue decoration and overglaze enamels, diameter 12³⁄₁₆″ (31 cm). Kyushu National Museum, Japan. Important Cultural Property.

JAPANESE PORCELAIN While the history of ceramic production dates to the earliest days of Japanese civilization, production of glazed, high-fired stoneware ceramics proliferated in Japan only from the sixteenth century. The industry thrived in southern Japan, where, in the years following 1600, influxes of more highly skilled Korean potters helped native artisans learn new continental technologies that allowed them to manufacture porcelain for the first time. One town, Arita, became the center for the production of porcelain, created not only for domestic use but for export to the West. While tea ceremony aesthetics still favored rustic wares such as Chojiro's tea bowl (see FIG. 26–9), porcelain was more widely adopted for everyday use in response to a growing fashion for Chinese arts. Porcelains made in Arita are known by various names according to their dating and decorative schemes. The plate in **FIGURE 26-17** is an example of Nabeshima ware, produced in kilns that had been established in Arita by the Nabeshima samurai clan as early as 1628. Initially, ceramics from these kilns were reserved for family use or as gifts to the Tokugawa shogunate, but eventually Nabeshima ware was also acquired by other powerful noble families. The multicolor decorative motifs often juxtapose an organically irregular natural form (here a branch of flowering wisteria) and a more abstracted, stabilizing design drawn from the built environment (here a trellis on which the wisteria can grow). Contemporary textile designs—well known through the publication of pattern books that documented the latest fashion—frequently served as source material for the decoration of Nabeshima ware.

THE MODERN PERIOD

The tensions that resulted from Commodore Matthew Perry's forced opening of trade ports in Japan in 1853 precipitated the downfall of the Tokugawa shogunate. In 1868, the emperor was formally restored to power, an event known as the Meiji Restoration. The court soon moved from Kyoto to Edo, which was

26-18 • Yokoyama Taikan FLOATING LIGHTS
Meiji period, 1909. One of a pair of hanging scrolls with ink, colors, and gold on silk, 56½″ × 20½″ (143 × 52 cm). Museum of Modern Art, Ibaraki.

renamed Tokyo ("Eastern Capital"). After a period of intense industrialization in the first two decades after the Meiji Restoration, influential private individuals and government officials, sometimes working cooperatively, created new arts institutions including juried exhibitions, artists' associations, arts universities, and cultural heritage laws. These rekindled appreciation for the art of the past, encouraged perpetuation of artistic techniques threatened by adoption of Western ways, and stimulated new artistic production. Many of these arts institutions still exist today.

MEIJI-PERIOD NATIONALIST PAINTING

The Meiji period (1868–1912) marked a major change for Japan. Japanese society adopted various aspects of Western education, governmental systems, clothing, medicine, industrialization, and technology in efforts to modernize the nation. Teachers of sculpture and oil painting came from Italy, while adventurous Japanese artists traveled to Europe and America to study.

A MEIJI PAINTER Ernest Fenollosa (1853–1908), an American who had recently graduated from Harvard, traveled to Japan in 1878 to teach philosophy and political economy at Tokyo University. Within a few years, he and a former student, Okakura Kakuzo (1862–1913), began urging artists to study traditional Japanese arts rather than focusing exclusively on Western art styles and media, but to infuse these traditional practices with a modern sensibility. Yokoyama Taikan (1868–1958) subsequently developed his personal style within the Nihonga (modern Japanese painting) genre promoted by Okakura. Encouraged by Okakura, who had gone there before him, Taikan visited India in 1903. He embraced Okakura's ideals of pan-Asian cultural nationalism, expressed in the first line of Okakura's book, *Ideals of the East* (1903), with the words "Asia is One." This outlook later contributed to fueling Japan's imperialist ambitions. Taikan's **FLOATING LIGHTS** (**FIG. 26-18**) was inspired by a visit to Calcutta (Kolkata), where he observed women engaged in divination on the banks of the Ganges. The naturalism of their semitransparent robes and the gently rippling water reveal his indebtedness to Western art. In contrast, the lightly applied colors and gracefully composed branches with delicate, mottled brushwork defining the leaves, recall techniques of Rinpa-school artists.

JAPAN AFTER WORLD WAR II

In the aftermath of World War II (1941–1945), Japan was a shambles, her great cities ruined. Nevertheless, under the U.S.-led Allied Occupation (1946–1952), the Japanese people immediately began rebuilding, unified by a sense of national purpose. Within ten years, Japan established nascent automobile, electronics, and consumer goods industries. Rail travel, begun in 1872, expanded and improved significantly after the war, and by the time of the Tokyo Olympics in 1964, the capital had an extensive commuter rail system. Japan became the world leader in city-to-city high-speed rail transit with its new Shinkansen (bullet train). As the rest of the world came to know Japan, foreign interest in its arts focused especially on the country's still thriving "crafts" traditions. Not only were these a source of national pride and identity, the skills and attitudes they fostered also served as the basis for Japan's national revival.

TANGE KENZO The **HIROSHIMA PEACE MEMORIAL MUSEUM** and Park (**FIG. 25-19**) was one of the first monuments constructed after World War II. A memorial to those who perished on August 6, 1945, and an expression of prayers for world peace, it attests the spirit of the Japanese people at this difficult juncture in history. Tange Kenzo (1913–2005), who would

26-19 • Tange Kenzo HIROSHIMA PEACE MEMORIAL MUSEUM
Showa period, 1955. Main building (center) repaired in Heisei period, 1991. East building (right), the former Peace Memorial Hall, which first opened in 1955, was rebuilt in June 1994 and attached to the main building. Designated UNESCO World Heritage site in 1996.

Throughout the history of Japanese art, there has been a salient sensitivity toward the surface quality of things, for polish, for line, for exquisite facture and stylish articulation. This is certainly the case with an exquisite wooden box (**FIG. 26–20**) created in 2006 by Eri Sayoko (1945–2007). In 2002, the government had designated her a Living National Treasure for her accomplishment in the art of cut-gold leaf (*kirikane*), traditionally used to decorate Buddhist sculpture and paintings (as in FIG. 12–17). The National Treasure designation originated in Japanese laws of 1897 that were intended to safeguard the nation's artistic heritage at a time when art was being bought by Western collectors but suffering neglect at home. In 1955, the government added provisions to honor living individuals who excel in traditional craft techniques with the title Living National Treasure. This historic preservation system is the most complex of its type in the world.

Eri was the third person awarded the title for cut-gold-leaf decoration and the first woman. In its encouragement of traditional arts, the Living National Treasure system has greatly assisted women in gaining much-deserved recognition. In pre-modern Japan (encompassing the prehistoric era up to the start of the Meiji period in 1868), women mostly operated in the private sphere of the home where they created crafts for their own enjoyment or for devotional purposes. By the eighteenth century, this situation had begun to change, so that women could be poets, calligraphers, and painters; the wives or daughters of famous male artists gained the most recognition. Among the most famous was Gyokuran, wife of the literati painter Ike Taiga (see FIG. 26–13). However, the conservative nature of traditional Japanese crafts workshops meant women could not hold leadership positions in them, and until the postwar period they were seldom recognized for their achievements. Eri Sayoko flourished in the new climate, as one of the first women to work in the medium of cut-gold, which she took up via an unorthodox route.

Eri specialized in Japanese painting in high school and in design-dyeing in junior college. After marriage to a traditional Buddhist sculptor she started producing Buddhist paintings and began an apprenticeship with a master *kirikane* craftsmaker. She was so talented that after only three years she was able to exhibit her work professionally. Her art is informed by her deep study of the history of the technique, and her special sensitivity for color betrays her training in dyeing. Eri's elegant, functional objects, typified by this box, are infused with modern sensibilities, proving that adherence to a traditional technique can still result in artistic originality.

26–20 • Eri Sayoko ORNAMENTAL BOX: DANCING IN THE COSMOS
Heisei period, 2006. Wood with polychrome and cut gold, height 33⅞″ (86 cm), width 6½″ (16.5 cm), depth 6½″ (16.5 cm). Collection of Eri Kokei.

eventually become one of the masters of Modernist architecture, designed the complex after winning an open competition as a young, up-and-coming architect.

The building's design befits the solemnity of its context. Concrete piers raise its compact concrete form 20 feet off the ground. The wood formwork of the concrete recalls the wooden forms of traditional Japanese architecture, but the use of concrete as a building material was inspired by Le Corbusier's 1920s Modernist villas (see Chapter 32). Evenly spaced vertical concrete fins lining the façade afford light shade. They suggest both the regular spacing of elements present in modular *shoin* architecture (see "*Shoin* Design," page 821) and the values of Modernist architects who demanded a strict correlation between structure and form. In this commission Tange infuses Modernist tendencies and materials with a Japanese sense of interval and refinement, characteristics still seen in the work of younger contemporary Japanese architects active today.

FUKAMI SUEHARU Perhaps because the arts of tea ceremony and flower arrangement both require ceramic vessels, the Japanese have long had a particular affection for pottery. While some ceramicists continue to create *raku* tea bowls and other

26–21 • Fukami Sueharu SKY II
Heisei period, c. 1990. Celadon-glazed porcelain with wood base, 3″ × 44⅛″ × 9½″ (7.7 × 112.1 × 24.2 cm).
Helen Foresman Spencer Museum of Art, University of Kansas, Lawrence, Kansas. Museum purchase: R. Charles and
Mary Margaret Clevenger Fund (1992.0072)

traditional wares, others experiment with new styles and innovative techniques.

Fukami Sueharu (b. 1947) is among the most innovative clay artists in Japan today. Yet his art has roots in the past—in his case, in Chinese porcelains with pale bluish-green glazes (*seihakuji*). Even so, his forms and fabrication methods, typified by his **SKY II**, are ultramodern (**FIG. 26–21**). He created the piece using a slip casting technique, in which he injected liquid clay into a mold using a high-pressure compressor. Although he sometimes makes functional pieces, mainly cylinders that could hold flower arrangements, *Sky II* shows his mastery of pure form. The title suggests sources of this abstract sculptural shape: a wing or a blade of an aircraft slicing through the sky. The pale sky-blue glaze only enhances this allusion. The fusion here of traditions, media, techniques, and forms looks back to a distinguished artistic heritage, but the suave mastery of abstraction and the subtle evocation of thematic meaning point forward to a global art world, where Japanese artists are clearly taking their place.

THINK ABOUT IT

26.1 Discuss how the Japanese tea ceremony works and observe the role that art plays within it. Explore the unique aesthetics of the tearoom and artistic practices associated with the ceremony, making reference to at least one work from this chapter.

26.2 Chose one woodblock print discussed in this chapter and explain how its subject matter represents the culture of the "floating world" in Edo.

26.3 Reflect on the differences between the styles practiced by artists from the cities of Kyoto and Edo. How do these distinctions relate to the variations in the social status and cultural and intellectual interests of the residents of these two cities? How would you fit the lacquer box by a Rinpa-school artist from Kyoto (FIG. 26–10) and the *kosode* robe made in Edo (see "A Closer Look," page 831) into your discussion?

26.4 Chose one of the three Japanese works in this chapter dating from the period after World War II and evaluate the ways in which it draws from both traditional Japanese and foreign artistic practices. Is there a larger debt to tradition or to innovation?

CROSSCURRENTS

FIG. 23–51

FIG. 26–4

Garden design weaves its way through the history of art during most times and places. These two distinguished examples were produced for two very different architectural complexes and to serve very different populations. Assess the way these two gardens were used and discuss how their form is related to their function. How are they representative of their cultural contexts?

✔—[**Study** and review on myartslab.com

27-1 • Julia Jumbo **TWO GREY HILLS TAPESTRY WEAVING**
Navajo, 2003. Handspun wool, 36″ × 24½″ (91.2 × 62.1 cm). Wheelwright Museum of the American Indian, Santa Fe, New Mexico.

Art of the Americas after 1300

According to Navajo mythology, the universe itself is a weaving, its fibers spun by Spider Woman out of sacred cosmic materials. Spider Woman taught the art of weaving to Changing Woman (a Mother Earth figure), and she in turn taught it to Navajo women, who continue to keep this art vital, seeing its continuation as a sacred responsibility. Early Navajo blankets were composed of simple horizontal stripes, but over time weavers have introduced more intricate patterns, and today Navajo rugs are woven in numerous distinctive styles.

The tapestry weaving in **FIGURE 27–1** is designed in the Two Grey Hills style that developed during the early twentieth century around a trading post of that name in northwest New Mexico. Weavers who work in this style use the natural colors of undyed sheep's wool (only the black wool is sometimes dyed) to create dazzling geometric patterns. Julia Jumbo (1928–2007), who learned to weave as a child, used her weavings to support her family. She raised her own sheep, and carded and spun her wool by hand before incorporating it into painstakingly made textiles. Jumbo is renowned for the clarity of her designs and the technical perfection of her fine weave.

When the first Europeans arrived, the Western Hemisphere was already inhabited from the Arctic Circle to Tierra del Fuego by peoples with long histories and rich cultural traditions (**MAP 27–1**). After 1492, when Christopher Columbus and his companions first sailed to the New World, the arrival of Europeans completely altered the destiny of the Americas. In Mesoamerica and South America the break with the past was sudden and violent: two great empires—the Aztec in Mexico and the Inca in South America—that had risen to prominence in the fifteenth century were rapidly destroyed. In North America the change took place more gradually, but the outcome was much the same. In both North and South America, natives succumbed to European diseases to which they had no immunity, especially smallpox, leading to massive population loss and social disruption. Over the next 400 years, many Native Americans were displaced from their ancestral homelands, and many present-day Native American ethnic groupings were formed by combinations of various survivor groups.

Despite all the disruption, during the past century the indigenous arts of the Americas have undergone a re-evaluation that has renewed the conception of what constitutes "American art." Native artists like Julia Jumbo continue to revive and reimagine indigenous traditions, revisit traditional outlooks, and restate their ancient customs and ideas in new ways. After being pushed to the brink of extinction, Native American cultures are experiencing a revival in both North and South America, as Native Americans assert themselves politically and insist on the connections between their history and the land.

LEARN ABOUT IT

27.1 Explore the variety of styles, media, and techniques that characterize indigenous art and architecture across the Americas, both before and after contact with Europeans.

27.2 Recognize and understand the themes and symbols developed by Native American artists to express cultural, religious, and political ideas and values.

27.3 Explore how an understanding of the ritual and political use, as well as the practical function, of works are critical to interpreting their meaning in Native American arts.

27.4 Recognize and evaluate how indigenous arts have changed in the centuries since contact with Europeans.

((•—[Listen to the chapter audio on myartslab.com

THE AZTEC EMPIRE

In November 1519, the army of the Spanish soldier Hernán Cortés beheld for the first time the great Aztec capital of Tenochtitlan. The shimmering city, which seemed to be floating on the water, was built on an island in the middle of Lake Texcoco in the Valley of Mexico, and linked by broad causeways to the mainland. One of Cortés's companions later recalled the wonder the Spanish felt at that moment: "When we saw so many cities and villages built on the water and other great towns on dry land and that straight and level causeway going towards [Tenochtitlan], we were amazed … on account of the great towers and temples and buildings rising from the water, and all built of masonry. And some of our soldiers even asked whether the things that we saw were not a dream." (Bernal Díaz del Castillo, cited in Coe and Koontz 2005, p. 190.)

The Mexica people who lived in the remarkable city that Cortés found were then rulers of much of the land that later took their name, Mexico. Their rise to power had been recent and swift. Only 400 years earlier, according to their own legends, they had been a nomadic people living far north of the Valley of Mexico in a distant place called Aztlan. The term Aztec derives from the word Aztlan, and refers to all those living in Central Mexico who came from this mythical homeland, not just to the Mexica of Tenochtitlan.

The Mexica arrived in the Valley of Mexico in the thirteenth century. They eventually settled on an island in Lake Texcoco where they had seen an eagle perching on a prickly pear cactus (*nochtli*) growing out of a stone (*tetl*), a sign that their god Huitzilopochtli told them would mark the end of their wandering. They called the place Tenochtitlan. The city on the island was gradually expanded by reclaiming land from the lake, and serviced by a grid of artificial canals. In the fifteenth century, the Mexica—joined by allies in a triple alliance—began an aggressive campaign of

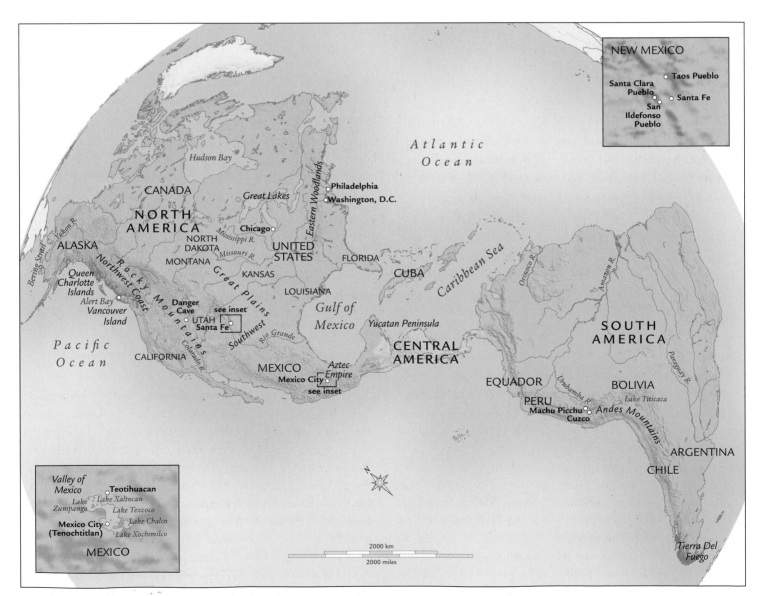

MAP 27-1 • THE AMERICAS AFTER 1300

Diverse cultures inhabited the Americas, each shaping a distinct artistic tradition.

expansion. The tribute they exacted from all over Mexico transformed Tenochtitlan into a glittering capital.

Aztec religion was based on a complex pantheon that combined Aztec deities with more ancient ones that had long been worshiped in Central Mexico. According to Aztec belief, the gods had created the current era, or sun, at the ancient city of Teotihuacan in the Valley of Mexico (see Chapter 13). The continued existence of the world depended on human actions, including rituals of blood-letting and human sacrifice. Many Mesoamerican peoples believed that the world had been created multiple times before the present era. But while most Mesoamericans believed that they were living in the fourth era, or sun, the Mexica asserted that they lived in the fifth sun, a new era that coincided with the Aztec Empire. The Calendar Stone (see "A Closer Look," page 841) boldly makes this claim, using the dates of the destructions of the four previous eras to form the glyph that names the fifth sun, 4 Motion. The end of each period of 52 years in the Meso-american calendar was a particularly dangerous time that required a special fire-lighting ritual.

TENOCHTITLAN

An Aztec scribe drew an idealized representation of the city of Tenochtitlan and its sacred ceremonial precinct (FIG. 27-2) for the Spanish viceroy in 1545. It forms the first page of the Codex Mendoza. An eagle perched on a prickly pear cactus growing out of a stone—the symbol of the city—fills the center of the page. Waterways divide the city into four quarters, and indicate the lake surrounding the city. Early leaders of Tenochtitlan are shown sitting in the four quadrants. The victorious warriors at the bottom of the page represent Aztec conquests, and a count of years surrounds the entire scene. This image combines historical narration with idealized cartography, showing the city in the middle of the lake at the moment of its founding.

At the center of Tenochtitlan was the sacred precinct, a walled enclosure that contained dozens of temples and other buildings. This area has been the site of intensive archaeological excavations in Mexico City since 1978, work that has greatly increased our understanding of this aspect of the Aztec city. The focal point of the sacred precinct was the Great Pyramid (or Templo Mayor), with paired temples on top: The one on the north was dedicated to Tlaloc, an ancient rain god with a history extending back to Teotihuacan, and the one on the south to Huitzilopochtli, the solar god of the newly arrived Mexica tribe (FIG. 27-3). During the winter rainy season the sun rose behind the temple of Tlaloc, and during the dry season it rose behind the temple of Huitzilopochtli. The double temple thus united two natural forces, sun and rain, or fire and water. During the spring and autumn equinoxes, the sun rose between the two temples.

27-2 • THE FOUNDING OF TENOCHTITLAN
Page from Codex Mendoza. Mexico. Aztec, 1545. Ink and color on paper, 12⅜″ × 8⁷⁄₁₆″ (31.5 × 21.5 cm). Bodleian Library, University of Oxford, England. MS. Arch Selden. A.1, fol. 2r

Two steep staircases led up the west face of the pyramid from the plaza in front. Sacrificial victims climbed these stairs to the temple of Huitzilopochtli, where priests threw them over a stone, quickly cut open their chests, and pulled out their still-throbbing hearts, a sacrifice that ensured the survival of the sun, the gods, and the Aztecs. The bodies were then rolled down the stairs and dismembered. Thousands of severed heads were said to have been kept on a skull rack in the plaza, represented in FIGURE 27-2 by the rack with a single skull to the right of the eagle. In addition to major works of Aztec sculpture, current excavations have uncovered a series of deep shafts containing multiple levels of offerings—precious objects as well as animals—and some believe that eventually human burials will be discovered, perhaps those of Aztec kings.

27–3 • RECONSTRUCTION OF THE GREAT PYRAMID (TEMPLO MAYOR) OF TENOCHTITLAN, c. 1500

SCULPTURE

Aztec sculpture was monumental, powerful, and often unsettling. A particularly striking example is an imposing statue of **COATLICUE**, mother of the Mexica god Huitzilopochtli (**FIG. 27–4**). Coatlicue means "she of the serpent skirt," and this broad-shouldered figure with clawed feet has a skirt of twisted snakes. The sculpture may allude to the moment of Huitzilopochtli's birth: When Coatlicue conceived Huitzilopochtli from a ball of down, her other children—the stars and the moon—jealously conspired to kill her. As they attacked, Huitzilopochtli emerged from his mother's body fully grown and armed, drove off his half-brothers, and destroyed his half-sister, the moon goddess Coyolxauhqui. Coatlicue, however, did not survive the encounter. In this sculpture, she has been decapitated and a pair of serpents, symbols of gushing blood, rise from her neck to form her head. Their eyes are her eyes; their fangs, her tusks. Around her stump of a neck hangs a necklace of human hands, hearts, and a dangling skull. Despite the surface intricacy, the statue's massive form creates an impression of

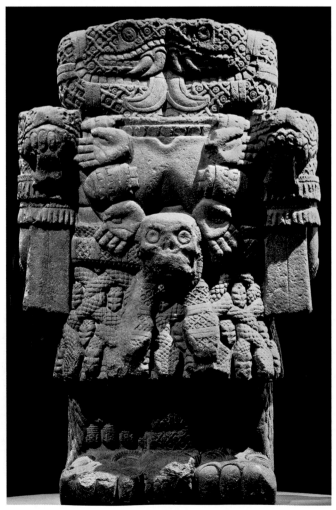

27–4 • THE GODDESS COATLICUE

Mexico. Aztec, c. 1500. Basalt, height 8′6″ (2.65 m). Museo Nacional de Antropología, Mexico City.

 View the Closer Look for *The Goddess Coatlicue* on myartslab.com

A CLOSER LOOK | Calendar Stone

Mexico. Aztec, c. 1500. Diameter 11′6¾″ (3.6 m).
Museo Nacional de Antropología, Mexico City.

According to Mexica belief, the gods created the world four times before the present era. These cartouches name the days on which the four previous suns were destroyed: 4 Jaguar, 4 Wind, 4 Rain, and 4 Water.

Together, these four calendrical glyphs and the face and claws of the central god combine to form the glyph for 4 Motion, the day on which the fifth sun will be destroyed by a giant earthquake.

This central face combines elements of the sun god as the night sun in the underworld with the clawed hands and flint tongue of earth gods, symbolizing the night sun and the hungry earth.

This band forms the Aztec symbol for the sun, a round disk with triangular projections denoting the sun's rays.

Two fire serpents encircle the outer part of the disk. Stylized flames rise off their backs. Their heads meet at the bottom, and human faces emerge from the mouths of the serpents.

This band contains the 20 day signs of the 260-day ritual calendar.

 View the Closer Look for the calendar stone on myartslab.com

---

solidity, and the entire sculpture leans forward, looming over the viewer. The colors with which it was originally painted would have heightened its dramatic impact.

FEATHERWORK

Indeed Aztec art was colorful. An idea of its iridescent splendor is captured in the **FEATHER HEADDRESS** (**FIG. 27-5**) said to have been given by the Aztec emperor Moctezuma to

27-5 • FEATHER HEADDRESS OF MOCTEZUMA
Mexico. Aztec, before 1519. Quetzal, blue cotinga, and other feathers and gold on a fiber frame, 45⅝″ × 68⅞″ (116 × 175 cm). Museo Nacional de Antropología, Mexico City, Mexico.

Cortés, and thought to be the one listed in the inventory of treasures Cortés shipped to Charles V, the Habsburg emperor in Spain, in 1519. Featherwork was one of the glories of Mesoamerican art, but very few of these extremely fragile artworks survive. The tropical feathers in this headdress exemplify the exotic tribute paid to the Aztecs; the long iridescent green feathers that make up most of the headdress are the exceedingly rare tail feathers of the quetzal bird—each male quetzal has only two such plumes. The feathers were gathered in small bunches, their quills reinforced with reed tubes, and then sewn to the frame in overlapping layers, the joins concealed by small gold plaques. Featherworkers were esteemed artists. After the Spanish invasion, they turned their exacting skills to "feather paintings" of Christian subjects.

MANUSCRIPTS

Aztec scribes also created brilliantly colored books: histories, maps, and divinatory almanacs. Instead of being bound on one side like European books, Mesoamerican books took the form of a screenfold, accordion-pleated so that each page was connected only to the two adjacent pages. This format allowed great flexibility: a book could be opened to show two pages, or unfolded to show six or eight pages simultaneously; different sections of the book could also be juxtaposed. A rare manuscript that survived the Spanish conquest provides a concise summary of Mesoamerican cosmology (**FIG. 27-6**). Mesoamerican peoples recognized five key directions: north, south, east, west, and center. At the center of the image is Xiuhtecuhtli, god of fire, time, and the calendar. Radiating from him are the four cardinal directions—each associated with a specific color, a deity, and a tree with a bird in its branches. The 260 dots that trace the eight-lobed path around the central figure refer to the 260-day Mesoamerican divinatory calendar; the 20 day signs of this calendar are also distributed throughout the image. By linking the 260-day calendar to the four directions, this image speaks eloquently of the unity of space and time in the Mesoamerican worldview.

The Aztec Empire was short-lived. Within two years of their arrival in Mexico, the Spanish conquistadors and their indigenous allies overran Tenochtitlan. They built their own capital, Mexico City, over its ruins and established their own cathedral on the site of Tenochtitlan's sacred precinct.

27-6 • A VIEW OF THE WORLD
Page from Codex Fejervary-Mayer. Mexico. Aztec or Mixtec, c. 1400–1519. Paint on animal hide, each page 6⅞″ × 6⅞″ (17.5 × 17.5 cm), total length 13′3″ (4.04 m). National Museums, Liverpool.

THE INCA EMPIRE

At the beginning of the sixteenth century the Inca Empire was one of the largest states in the world. It extended more than 2,600 miles along western South America, encompassing most of modern Peru, Ecuador, Bolivia, and northern Chile and reaching into present-day Argentina. Like the Aztec Empire, its rise was rapid and its destruction sudden.

The Incas called their empire the "Land of the Four Quarters." At its center was their capital, Cuzco, "the navel of the world," located high in the Andes Mountains. The Inca state began as one of many small competing kingdoms that emerged in the highlands. In the fifteenth century the Incas began to expand, suddenly and rapidly, and had subdued most of their vast domain—through conquest, alliance, and intimidation—by 1500.

To hold this linguistically and ethnically diverse empire together, the Inca ("Inca" refers to both the ruler and the people) relied on religion, an efficient bureaucracy, and various forms of labor taxation, in which the payment was a set amount of time spent performing tasks for the state. In return the state provided gifts through local leaders and sponsored lavish ritual entertainments. Men might cultivate state lands, serve in the army, or work periodically on public works projects—building roads and terracing hillsides, for example—while women wove cloth as tribute. No Andean civilization ever developed writing, but the Inca kept detailed accounts and historical records on knotted and colored cords (*quipu*).

To move their armies and speed transport and communication within the empire, the Incas built more than 23,000 miles of roads. These varied from 50-foot-wide thoroughfares to 3-foot-wide paths. Two main north–south roads, one along the coast and the other through the highlands, were linked by east–west roads. Travelers journeyed on foot, using llamas as pack animals. Stairways helped them negotiate steep mountain slopes, and rope suspension bridges allowed river gorge crossings. All along the roads, storehouses and lodgings—more than a thousand have been found—were spaced a day's journey apart. A relay system of runners could carry messages between Cuzco and the farthest reaches of the empire in about a week.

CUZCO

Cuzco, a capital of great splendor, was home to the Inca, ruler of the empire. Its urban plan was said to have been designed by the

ELEMENTS OF ARCHITECTURE | Inca Masonry

Working with the simplest of tools—mainly heavy stone hammers—and using no mortar, Inca builders created stonework of great refinement and durability: roads and bridges that linked the entire empire, terraces for growing crops, and structures both simple and elaborate. The effort expended on stone construction by the Inca was prodigious. Fine Inca masonry consisted of either rectangular blocks or irregular polygonal blocks (see FIG. 27-7). In both types, adjoining blocks were painstakingly shaped to fit tightly together without mortar. Their stone faces might be slightly beveled along their edges so that each block presented a "pillowed" shape expressing its identity, or walls might be smoothed into a continuous flowing surface in which the individual blocks form a seamless whole. At a few Inca sites, the stones used in construction were boulder-size: up to 27 feet tall. In Cuzco, and elsewhere in the Inca Empire, Inca masonry has survived earthquakes that have destroyed later structures.

At Machu Picchu (see FIGS. 27-7, 27-8), all buildings and terraces within its 3-square-mile extent were made of granite, the hard stone occurring at the site. Commoners' houses and some walls were constructed of irregular stones that were carefully fitted together, while fine polygonal or smoothed masonry distinguished palaces and temples.

polygonal-stone wall

smooth-surfaced wall

 Watch an architectural simulation about Inca masonry on myartslab.com

27-7 • INCA MASONRY, DETAIL OF A WALL AT MACHU PICCHU
Peru. Inca, 1450–1530.

27-8 • MACHU PICCHU
Peru. Inca, 1450–1530.

👁—|**Watch** a video about Machu Picchu on myartslab.com

Inca Pachacuti (r. 1438–1471) in the shape of a puma, its head the fortress of Sacsahuaman, and its belly the giant plaza at the center of town. The city was divided into upper and lower parts, reflecting the dual organization of Inca society. Cuzco was the symbolic as well as the political center of the Inca Empire: everyone had to carry a burden when entering the city, and gold, silver, or textiles brought into the city could not afterward be removed from it.

Cuzco was a showcase of the finest Inca masonry, some of which can still be seen in the present-day city (see "Inca Masonry," page 843). Architecture was a major expressive form for the Inca, the very shape of individually worked stones conveying a powerful aesthetic impact (**FIG. 27-7**). In contrast to the massive walls, Inca buildings had gabled, thatched roofs. Doors, windows, and niches were trapezoids, narrower at the top than the bottom.

MACHU PICCHU

MACHU PICCHU, one of the most spectacular archaeological sites in the world, provides an excellent example of Inca architectural planning (**FIG. 27-8**). At 9,000 feet above sea level, it straddles a ridge between two high peaks in the eastern slopes of the Andes and looks down on the Urubamba River. Stone buildings, today lacking only their thatched roofs, occupy terraces around central

27-9 • TUNIC

Peru. Inca, c. 1500. Camelid fiber and cotton, 35⅞" × 30" (91 × 76.5 cm). Dumbarton Oaks Research Library and Collections, Pre-Columbian Collection, Washington, DC.

plazas, and narrow agricultural terraces descend into the valley. The site, near the eastern limits of the empire, was the royal estate of the Inca ruler Pachacuti. The court might retire to this warmer, lower-altitude palace when the Cuzco winter became too harsh to enjoy. Important diplomatic negotiations and ceremonial feasts may also have taken place at this country retreat. The entire complex is designed with great sensitivity to its surroundings, with walls and plazas framing stupendous vistas of the surrounding landscape, and carefully selected stones echoing the shapes of the mountains beyond.

TEXTILES

The production of fine textiles was already an important art in the Andes by the third millennium BCE (see "Andean Textiles," page 397). Among the Incas, textiles of cotton and camelid fibers (from llama, vicuña, and alpaca) were an indication of wealth. One form of labor taxation required the manufacture of fibers and cloth, and textiles as well as agricultural products filled Inca storehouses. Cloth was deemed a fitting gift for the gods, so fine garments were draped around statues, and even burned as sacrificial offerings.

The patterns and designs on garments were not simply decorative; they carried symbolic messages, including indications of a person's ethnic identity and social rank. In the elaborate **TUNIC** in **FIGURE 27–9**, each square represents a miniature tunic with a different pattern and meaning. For example, tunics with checkerboard patterns were worn by military officers and royal escorts; the four-part motifs may refer to the empire as the

Land of the Four Quarters. While we may not be sure what was meant in every case, patterns and colors appear to have been standardized like uniforms in order to convey information at a glance. Perhaps an exquisite tunic such as this, containing patterns associated with multiple ranks and statuses, was woven as a royal garment.

METALWORK

When they arrived in Peru in 1532, the Spanish were far less interested in Inca cloth than in their vast quantities of gold and silver. The Inca valued objects made of gold and silver not for their precious metal, but because they saw in them symbols of the sun and the moon. They are said to have called gold the "sweat of the sun" and silver the "tears of the moon." On the other hand, the Spanish exploration of the New World was propelled by feverish tales of native treasure. Whatever gold and silver objects the Spanish could obtain were melted down to enrich their royal coffers. Only a few small figures buried as offerings, like the little **LLAMA** shown in **FIGURE 27–10**, escaped destruction. The llama was thought to have a special connection with the sun, with rain, and with fertility, and a llama was sacrificed to the sun every morning in Cuzco. In this small silver figurine, the essential character of a llama is rendered with a few well-chosen details, but in keeping with the value that Andeans placed on textiles the blanket on its back is carefully described.

THE AFTERMATH OF THE SPANISH CONQUEST

Native American populations in Mexico and Peru declined sharply after the conquest because of the exploitative policies of the conquerors and the ravages of smallpox and other European diseases against which the indigenous people had no immunity. This demographic collapse meant that the population of the Americas declined by as much as 90 percent in the century after contact with Europe. European missionaries suppressed local beliefs and practices and worked to spread Christianity throughout the Americas. Although increasing numbers of Europeans began to settle and dominate the land, the production of art did not end with the Spanish conquest. Traditional media, including fine weaving, continue to flourish to this day, transforming and remaining vital as indigenous peoples adjust to a changing world.

NORTH AMERICA

In America north of Mexico, from the upper reaches of Canada and Alaska to the southern tip of Florida, many different peoples with widely varying cultures coexisted. Here, the Europeans came less as military men seeking riches to plunder than as families seeking land to farm. Unlike the Spaniards, they found no large cities with urban populations to resist them. However, although they imagined that the lands they settled were an untended wilderness, in fact nearly all of North America was populated and possessed by indigenous peoples. Over the next 400 years, by means of violence, bribery, and treaties, the English colonies and, in turn, the United States displaced nearly all Native Americans from their ancestral homelands. For example, beginning in the 1830s and continuing through the nineteenth century, thousands of Native Americans (46,000 by 1938) were relocated from their ancestral homelands to newly assigned territory in present-day Oklahoma, a forced migration that became known as the Trail of Tears.

The indigenous art Euro-Americans encountered they viewed as a curiosity, not art. Native American works were small, portable, fragile, and impermanent—appreciated not for their aesthetic qualities, but collected as anthropological artifacts, curiosities, or souvenirs, often under coercive conditions. Today, Native peoples have begun to reclaim sacred objects and human remains that were forcibly taken from them, and museums are beginning to work with Native communities to present their art in respectful and culturally sensitive ways. Here, we will be able to look at art from only four North American cultural areas: the Eastern Woodlands, the Great Plains, the Northwest Coast, and the Southwest (**MAP 27–2**).

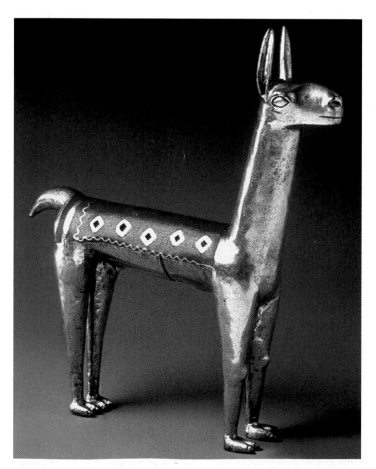

27–10 • LLAMA
From Bolivia or Peru, found near Lake Titicaca, Bolivia. Inca, 15th century. Cast silver with gold and cinnabar, 9″ × 8½″ × 1¾″ (22.9 × 21.6 × 4.4 cm). American Museum of Natural History, New York.

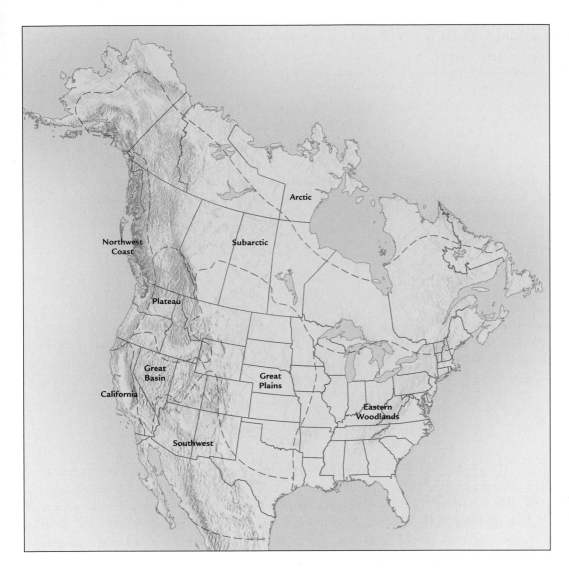

MAP 27-2 • NORTH AMERICAN CULTURAL AREAS
The varied geographic regions of North America supported diverse cultures adapted to their distinct environments.

THE EASTERN WOODLANDS

In the Eastern Woodlands, after the decline of the great Mississippian centers (see Chapter 13), most tribes lived in stable villages, and they combined hunting, gathering, and agriculture for their livelihood. In the sixteenth century, the Iroquois formed a powerful confederation of five northeastern Native American nations, which played a prominent military and political role until after the American Revolution. The Huron and Illinois also formed sizable confederacies.

In the seventeenth century, the arrival on the Atlantic coast of a few boatloads of Europeans seeking religious freedom, farmland, and a new life for themselves brought major changes. Trade with these settlers gave the Woodlands peoples access to things they valued, while on their part the colonists learned Native forms of agriculture, hunting, and fishing—skills they needed in order to survive. In turn, Native Americans traded furs for such useful items as metal tools, cookware, needles, and cloth, and they especially prized European glass beads and silver. These trade items largely replaced older materials, such as crystal, copper, and shell.

WAMPUM Woodlands peoples made belts and strings of cylindrical purple and white shell beads called wampum. The Iroquois and Delaware peoples used wampum to keep records (the purple and white patterns served as memory devices) and exchanged belts of wampum to conclude treaties (FIG. 27-12). Few actual wampum treaty belts have survived, so this one, said to commemorate an unwritten treaty when the land now comprising the state of Pennsylvania was ceded by the Delawares in 1682, is especially prized. The belt, with two figures of equal size holding hands, suggests the mutual respect enjoyed by the Delaware and Penn's Society of Friends (Quakers), a respect that later collapsed into land fraud and violence. In general, wampum strings and belts had the authority of legal agreement and also symbolized a moral and political order.

QUILLWORK Woodlands art focused on personal adornment—tattoos, body paint, elaborate dress—and fragile arts such as **quillwork**. Quillwork involved dyeing porcupine and bird quills with a variety of natural dyes, soaking the quills to soften them, and then working them into rectilinear, ornamental surface patterns

Basketry is the weaving of reeds, grasses, and other plant materials to form containers. In North America the earliest evidence of basketwork, found in Danger Cave, Utah, dates to as early as 8400 BCE. Over the subsequent centuries, Native American women, notably in California and the American Southwest, developed basketry into an art form that combined utility with great beauty.

There are three principal basket-making techniques: coiling, twining, and plaiting. **Coiling** involves sewing together a spiraling foundation of rods with some other material. **Twining** twists multiple elements around a vertical warp of rods. Plaiting weaves strips over and under each other.

The coiled basket shown here was made by a Pomo woman in California (**FIG. 27–11**). According to Pomo legend, the Earth was dark until their ancestral hero stole the sun and brought it to Earth in a basket. He hung the basket first just over the horizon, but, dissatisfied with the light it gave, he kept suspending it in different places across the dome of the sky. He repeats this process every day, which is why the sun moves across the sky from east to west. In the Pomo basket, the structure of coiled willow and bracken fern root produces a spiral surface into which the artist worked sparkling pieces of clam shell, trade beads, and soft tufts of woodpecker and quail feathers. The underlying basket, the glittering shells, and the soft, moving feathers make this an exquisite

container. Such baskets were treasured possessions, cremated with their owners at death.

27–11 • FEATHERED BASKET
California. Pomo culture, c. 1877. Willow, bulrush, fern, feather, shells, glass beads. Height 5½″ (14 cm), diameter 12″ (36.5 cm). The Philbrook Museum of Art, Inc., Tulsa, Oklahoma. Gift of Clark Field (1948.39.37)

on deerskin clothing and on birch-bark items like baskets and boxes. A Sioux legend recounts how a mythical ancestor, Doublewoman ("double" because she was both beautiful and ugly, benign and dangerous), appeared to a woman in a dream and taught her the art of quillwork. As the legend suggests, quillwork was a woman's art form, as was basketry (see "Basketry," above). The Sioux **BABY CARRIER** in **FIGURE 27-13** is richly decorated with symbols of protection and well-being, including bands of antelopes in profile and thunderbirds flying with their heads turned and tails outspread. The thunderbird was an especially

27-12 • WAMPUM BELT, TRADITIONALLY CALLED WILLIAM PENN'S TREATY WITH THE DELAWARE
1680s. Shell beads, 17⅜″ × 6⅛″ (44 × 15.5 cm). Royal Ontario Museum, Canada.

beneficent symbol, thought to be capable of protecting against both human and supernatural adversaries.

BEADWORK In spite of the use of shell beads in wampum, decorative beadwork did not become commonplace until after European contact. In the late eighteenth century, Native American artists began to acquire European colored-glass beads, and in the nineteenth century they favored the tiny seed beads from Venice and Bohemia. Early beadwork mimicked the patterns and colors of quillwork. In the nineteenth century it largely replaced quillwork and incorporated European designs. Among other sources of inspiration, Canadian nuns introduced the young women in their schools to embroidered European floral motifs, and Native embroiderers began to adapt these designs, as well as European needlework techniques and patterns from European garments, into their own work. Functional aspects of garments might be transformed into purely decorative motifs; for example, a pocket would be replaced by an area of beadwork shaped like a pocket. A **BANDOLIER BAG** from Kansas, made by a Delaware woman (**FIG. 27-14**), is covered with curvilinear plant motifs in contrast to the rectilinear patterns of traditional quillwork. White lines outline brilliant pink and blue leaf-shaped forms on both bag and shoulder straps, heightening the intensity of the colors, which alternate within repeated patterns, exemplifying the evolution of beadwork design and its adaptation to a changing world.

27-13 • BABY CARRIER
Upper Missouri River area. Eastern Sioux, 19th century. Wooden board, buckskin, porcupine quill, length 31″ (78.8 cm). Department of Anthropology, Smithsonian Institution Libraries, Washington, DC. Catalogue No. 7311

27-14 • BANDOLIER BAG
Kansas. Delaware people, c. 1860. Wool fabric, cotton fabric and thread, silk ribbon, and glass beads, 22″ × 17″ (56 × 43 cm); bag without strap, 8⅝″ × 7¾″ (22 × 19.7 cm). The Detroit Institute of Arts. Founders Society Purchase (81.216)

The very shape of this bandolier bag is adapted from European military uniforms.

THE GREAT PLAINS

Between the Eastern Woodlands region and the Rocky Mountains to the west lay an area of prairie grasslands called the Great Plains. On the Great Plains, two differing ways of life developed, one a relatively recent and short-lived (1700–1870) nomadic lifestyle—dependent on the region's great migrating herds of buffalo for food, clothing, and shelter—and the other, a much older sedentary and agricultural lifestyle. Horses, from wild herds descended from feral horses brought to America by Spanish explorers in the sixteenth and seventeenth centuries, made travel, and thus a nomadic way of life, easier for the dispossessed eastern groups that moved to the plains.

European settlers on the eastern seaboard put increasing pressure on the Eastern Woodlands peoples, seizing their farmlands and forcing them westward. Both Native Americans and backcountry settlers were living in loosely village-based, farming societies and thus were competing for the same resources. The resulting interaction of Eastern Woodlands artists with one another and with Plains artists led in some cases to the emergence of a new hybrid style, while other artists consciously fought to maintain their own traditional cultures.

PORTABLE ARCHITECTURE The nomadic Plains peoples hunted buffalo for food and hides from which they created clothing and a light, portable dwelling known as a tipi (formerly spelled teepee) (**FIG. 27-15**). The tipi was well adapted to withstand the strong and constant wind, the dust, and the violent storms of the prairies. The framework of a tipi consisted of a stable pyramidal frame of three or four long poles, filled out with about 20 additional poles, in a roughly oval plan. The framework was covered with hides specially prepared to make them flexible and waterproof—or, later, with canvas—to form a conical structure. Between 20 and 40 hides were used to make a tipi, depending on its size. An opening at the top served as the smoke hole for a central hearth. The tipi leaned slightly into the prevailing west wind while the flap-covered door and smoke hole faced east, away from the wind. An inner lining covered the lower part of the walls and the perimeter of the floor to protect the occupants from drafts.

Tipis were the property and responsibility of women, who set them up at new encampments and lowered them when the group moved on. Blackfoot women could set up their huge tipis in less than an hour. Women quilled, beaded, and embroidered tipi linings, as well as backrests, clothing, and equipment. The patterns with which tipis were decorated, like their proportions and colors, varied from nation to nation, family to family, and individual to individual. In general, the bottom was covered with traditional motifs and the center section held personal images. When disassembled and packed to be dragged by a horse to another location, the tipi served as a platform for transporting other possessions. The Sioux arranged their tipis in two half-circles—one for the sky people and one for the earth people—divided along an east–west axis. When the Blackfoot people gathered in the summer for their ceremonial Sun Dance, their encampment contained hundreds of tipis in a circle a mile in circumference.

PLAINS INDIAN PAINTING Plains men recorded their exploits in paintings on tipis and on buffalo-hide robes. The earliest documented painted buffalo-hide robe, presented to Lewis and Clark during their transcontinental expedition, illustrates a battle fought in 1797 by the Mandan (of what is now North Dakota) and their allies against the Sioux (**FIG. 27-16**). The painter, trying to capture the full extent of a conflict in which five nations took part, shows a party of warriors in 22 separate episodes. The party is led by a man with a pipe and an elaborate eagle-feather headdress, and the warriors are armed with bows and arrows, lances, clubs, and flintlock rifles. Details of equipment and emblems of rank—headdresses, sashes, shields, feathered lances, powder horns for the rifles—are depicted carefully. Horses are shown in profile with stick legs, C-shaped hooves, and either clipped or flowing manes.

The figures stand out clearly against the light-colored background of the buffalo hide. The painter pressed lines into the hide, then filled in the forms with black, red, green, yellow, and brown pigments. A strip of colored porcupine quills runs down the spine of the buffalo hide. The robe would have been worn draped over the shoulders of the powerful warrior whose deeds it commemorates. As the wearer moved, the painted horses and warriors would seem to come alive, transforming him into a living representation of his exploits.

Life on the Great Plains changed abruptly in 1869, when the transcontinental railway linking the east and west coasts of

27-15 • BLACKFOOT WOMEN RAISING A TIPI
Photographed c. 1900. Montana Historical Society Research Center.

27-16 • BATTLE SCENE, HIDE PAINTING
North Dakota. Mandan, 1797–1800. Tanned buffalo hide, dyed porcupine quills, and black, red, green, yellow, and brown pigment, 7'10" × 8'6" (2.44 × 2.65 m). Courtesy of the Peabody Museum of Archaeology and Ethnology, Harvard University. Peabody 99-12-10/53121

This robe, "collected" in 1804 by Meriwether Lewis and William Clark on their expedition into western lands acquired by the United States in the Louisiana Purchase, is the earliest documented example of Plains painting. It was one of a number of Native American artworks that Lewis and Clark sent to President Thomas Jefferson, who displayed the robe in the entrance hall of his home at Monticello, Virginia.

the United States was completed, providing easy access to Native American lands. Between 1871 and 1890, Euro-American hunters killed off most of the buffalo, and soon ranchers and then farmers moved into the Great Plains. The U.S. government forcibly moved the outnumbered and outgunned Native Americans to reservations, land considered worthless until the later discovery of oil and, in the case of the Black Hills, gold.

THE NORTHWEST COAST

From southern Alaska to northern California, the Pacific coast of North America is a region of unusually abundant resources. Its many rivers fill each year with salmon returning to spawn. Harvested and dried, the fish could sustain large populations throughout the year. The peoples of the Northwest Coast—among them the Tlingit, the Haida, and the Kwakwaka'wakw (formerly spelled

Kwakiutl)—exploited this abundance to develop a complex and distinctive way of life in which the arts played a central role.

ANIMAL IMAGERY Animals feature prominently in Northwest Coast art because each extended family group (clan) claimed descent from a mythic animal or animal-human ancestor, from whom the family derived its name and the right to use certain animals and spirits as totemic emblems, or crests. These emblems appear frequently in Northwest Coast art, notably in carved cedar house poles and the tall, free-standing mortuary poles erected to memorialize dead chiefs. Chiefs, who were males in the most direct line of descent from the mythic ancestor, validated their status and garnered prestige for themselves and their families by holding ritual feasts known as potlatches, during which they gave valuable gifts to the invited guests. Shamans, who were sometimes also chiefs, mediated between the human and spirit worlds. Some shamans were female, giving them unique access to certain aspects of the spiritual world.

Northwest Coast peoples lived in large, elaborately decorated communal houses made of massive timbers and thick planks. Carved and painted partition screens separated the chief's quarters from the rest of the house. The Tlingit screen illustrated in **FIGURE 27-17** came from the house of Chief Shakes of Wrangell (d. 1916), whose family crest was the grizzly bear. The image of a rearing grizzly painted on the screen is itself made up of smaller bears and bear heads that appear in its ears, eyes, nostrils, joints, paws, and body. The oval door opening is a symbolic vagina; passing through it re-enacts the birth of the family from its ancestral spirit.

TEXTILES Blankets and other textiles produced collaboratively by the men and women of the Chilkat Tlingit had great prestige among Northwest Coast peoples (**FIG. 27-18**). Men drew the patterns on boards, and women wove them into the blankets, using shredded cedar bark and mountain-goat wool. The weavers did not use looms; instead, they hung cedar warp threads from a rod and twined colored goat wool back and forth through them to make the pattern, which in this technique can be defined by curving lines. The ends of the warp form the fringe at the bottom of the blanket.

The popular design used here is known as the diving whale—the central panel shows the downward-facing whale(s), while the panels to the sides have been interpreted as this animal's body or seated ravens seen in profile. Characteristic of Northwest painting and weaving, the images are composed of two basic elements: the ovoid (a slightly bent rectangle with rounded corners) and the formline (a continuous, shape-defining line). Here, subtly swelling black formlines define gently curving ovoids and C shapes. When the blanket was worn, its two-dimensional shapes would have become three-dimensional, with the dramatic central figure curving over the wearer's back and the intricate side panels crossing over his shoulders and chest.

MASKS To call upon guardian spirits, many Native American cultures staged ritual dance ceremonies in which dancers wore complex costumes and striking carved and painted wooden masks. Among the most elaborate masks were those used by the Kwakwaka'wakw in the Winter Ceremony that initiated members into the shamanistic Hamatsa society (see "Hamatsa Masks," page 854). The dance re-enacted the taming of Hamatsa, a cannibal spirit, and his three attendant bird spirits. Magnificent carved and painted masks transformed the dancers into Hamatsa and the bird attendants, who searched for victims to eat. Strings allowed the dancers to manipulate the masks so that the beaks opened and snapped shut with spectacular effect. Isolated in museums as "art," the masks doubtless lose some of the shocking vivacity they have in performance; nevertheless their bold forms and color

27-17 • GRIZZLY BEAR HOUSE-PARTITION SCREEN
From the house of Chief Shakes of Wrangell, Canada. Tlingit people, c. 1840. Cedar, paint, and human hair, 15′ × 8′ (4.57 × 2.74 m). Denver Art Museum Collection. Native Arts acquisition funds (1951.315)

27–18 • CHILKAT BLANKET
Southeast Alaska. Tlingit people, c. 1850. Mountain-goat wool, yellow cedar bark, linen thread, approx. 55″ × 72″ (130 × 183 cm). Thaw Collection, Fenimore Art Museum, Cooperstown, New York.

schemes retain power and meaning that can be activated by the viewer's imagination.

THE SOUTHWEST

The Native American peoples of the southwestern United States include, among others, the Puebloans (sedentary village-dwelling groups) and the Navajo. The modern Puebloans are heirs of the Ancestral Puebloans (Anasazi) and Hohokam cultures (see Chapter 13). The Ancestral Puebloans built apartmentlike villages and cliff dwellings whose ruins are found throughout the Four Corners region of New Mexico, Colorado, Arizona, and Utah. The Navajo, who arrived in the region sometime between 1100 and 1500 CE, developed a semisedentary way of life based on agriculture and (after the introduction of sheep by the Spaniards) shepherding. Being among the very few Native American tribal groups whose reservations are located on their actual ancestral homelands, both groups have succeeded in maintaining the continuity of their traditions despite Euro-American pressure. Today, their arts reflect the adaptation of traditional forms to new technologies, new media, and the influences of the dominant American culture that surrounds them.

THE PUEBLOS Some Pueblo villages, like those of their ancient ancestors, consist of multi-storied dwellings made of adobe. One of these, **TAOS PUEBLO**, shown in **FIGURE 27-19** in a photograph taken in 1947 by the American photographer of the Southwest, Laura Gilpin (1891–1979), is located in north-central New Mexico. Continually occupied and modified for over 500 years, the up to five-story house blocks of Taos Pueblo provide flexible, communal dwellings. Ladders provide access to the upper stories and to insulated inner rooms, entered through holes in the ceiling. Two large house blocks are arrayed around a central plaza that opens toward the neighboring mountains, rising in a stepped

27-19 • Laura Gilpin **TAOS PUEBLO**
Taos, New Mexico. Photographed 1947. © 1979 Amon Carter Museum of American Art, Fort Worth, Texas. Bequest of the artist (P1979.208.698)

Laura Gilpin, photographer of the landscape, architecture, and people of the American Southwest, began her series on the Pueblos and Navajos in the 1930s. She published her work in four volumes of photographs between 1941 and 1968.

During the harsh winter season, when spirits are thought to be most powerful, many Northwest Coast peoples seek spiritual renewal through their ancient rituals—including the potlatch, or ceremonial gift giving, and the initiation of new members into the prestigious Hamatsa society. With snapping beaks and cries of "Hap! Hap! Hap!" ("Eat! Eat! Eat!"), Hamatsa, the people-eating spirit of the north, and his three assistants—horrible masked monster birds—begin their wild ritual dance. The dancing birds threaten and even attack the Kwakwaka'wakw people who gather for the Winter Ceremony.

In the Winter Ceremony, youths are captured, taught the Hamatsa lore and rituals, and then in a spectacular theater-dance performance are "tamed" and brought back into civilized life. All the members of the community, including singers, gather in the main room of the great house, which is divided by a painted screen (see FIG. 27–17). The audience members fully participate in the performance; in early times, they brought containers of blood so that when the bird-dancers attacked them, they could appear to bleed and have flesh torn away.

Whistles from behind the screen announce the arrival of the Hamatsa (danced by an initiate), who enters through the central hole in the screen in a flesh-craving frenzy. Wearing hemlock, a symbol of the spirit world, he crouches and dances wildly with outstretched arms as attendants try to control him. He disappears but returns again, now wearing red cedar and dancing upright. Finally tamed, a full member of society, he even dances with the women.

Then the masked bird-dancers appear—first Raven-of-the-North-End-of-the-World, then Crooked-Beak-of-the-End-of-the-World, and finally the untranslatable Huxshukw, who cracks open skulls with his beak and eats the brains of his victims. Snapping their beaks, these masters of illusion enter the room backward, their masks pointed up as though the birds are looking skyward. They move slowly counterclockwise around the floor. At each change in the music they crouch, snap their beaks, and let out their wild cries of "Hap! Hap! Hap!" Essential to the ritual dances are the huge carved and painted wooden masks, articulated and operated by strings worked by the dancers. Among the finest masks are those by Willie Seaweed (1873–1967), a Kwakwaka'wakw chief, whose brilliant colors and exuberantly decorative carving style determined the direction of twentieth-century Kwakwaka'wakw sculpture (FIG. 27–20).

The Canadian government, abetted by missionaries, outlawed the Winter Ceremony and potlatches in 1885, claiming the event was injurious to health, encouraged prostitution, endangered children's education, damaged the economy, and was cannibalistic. But the Kwakwaka'wakw refused to give up their "oldest and best" festival—one that spoke powerfully to them in many ways, establishing social rank and playing an important role in arranging marriages. By 1936, the government and the missionaries, who called the Kwakwaka'wakw "incorrigible," gave up. But not until 1951 could the Kwakwaka'wakw people gather openly for winter ceremonies, including the initiation rites of the Hamatsa society.

27–20 • Attributed to Willie Seaweed KWAKWAKA'WAKW BIRD MASK
Alert Bay, Vancouver Island, Canada. Prior to 1951. Cedar wood, cedar bark, feathers, and fiber, 10″ × 72″ × 15″ (25.4 × 183 × 38.1 cm). Collection of the Museum of Anthropology, Vancouver, Canada. (A6120)

The name "Seaweed" is an anglicization of the Kwakwaka'wakw name *Siwid*, meaning "Paddling Canoe," "Recipient of Paddling," or "Paddled To"—referring to a great chief to whose potlatches guests paddled from afar. Willie Seaweed was not only the chief of his clan, but a great orator, singer, and tribal historian who kept the tradition of the potlatch alive during years of government repression.

27-21 • Maria Montoya Martinez and Julian Martinez **BLACKWARE STORAGE JAR**
New Mexico. c. 1942. Ceramic, height 18¾″ (47.6 cm), diameter 22½″ (57.1 cm). Museum of Indian Arts and Culture/Laboratory of Anthropology, Museum of New Mexico, Santa Fe.

fashion to provide a series of roof terraces that can serve as viewing platforms. The plaza and roof terraces are centers of communal life and ceremony, as can be seen in Pablita Velarde's painting of the winter solstice celebrations (see FIG. 27-22).

CERAMICS Traditionally, pottery was women's art among Pueblo peoples. Wares were made by coiling and other hand-building techniques, and then fired at low temperature in wood fires. The best-known twentieth-century Pueblo potter was Maria Montoya Martinez (1887–1980) of San Ildefonso Pueblo in New Mexico. Inspired by prehistoric pottery that was unearthed at nearby archaeological excavations and by the then-fashionable Art Deco style, she and her husband, Julian Martinez (1885–1943), developed a distinctive **blackware** ceramic style notable for its elegant forms and subtle textures (**FIG. 27-21**). Maria Martinez made pots covered with a slip that was then burnished. Using additional slip, Julian Martinez painted the pots with designs that interpreted traditional Pueblo and Ancestral Puebloan imagery. After firing, the burnished ground became a lustrous black and the slip painting retained a matte surface. By the 1930s, production of blackware in San Ildefonso had become a communal enterprise. Family members and friends all worked making pots, and Maria Martinez signed all the pieces so that, in typical Pueblo communal solidarity, everyone profited from her fame within the art market.

THE SANTA FE INDIAN SCHOOL In the 1930s, Anglo-American art teachers and dealers worked with Native Americans of the Southwest to create a distinctive, stereotypical "Indian" style in several media—including jewelry, pottery, weaving, and painting—to appeal to tourists and collectors. A leader in this effort was Dorothy Dunn (1903–1991), who taught painting in the Santa Fe Indian School, an off-reservation government boarding school in New Mexico, from 1932 to 1937. Dunn inspired her students to create a painting style that combined the outline drawing and flat colors of folk art, the decorative qualities of Art Deco, and exotic "Indian" subject matter. She and her students formed the Studio School. Restrictive as the school was, Dunn's success made painting a viable occupation for young Native American artists.

Pablita Velarde (1918–2006), from Santa Clara Pueblo in New Mexico and a 1936 graduate of Dorothy Dunn's school, was only a teenager when one of her paintings was selected for exhibition at the Chicago World's Fair in 1933. Thereafter, Velarde documented Pueblo ways of life in a large series of murals for Bandelier National Monument, launching a long and successful career. In smaller works on paper, such as the one illustrated here, she continued this focus on Pueblo life. **KOSHARES OF TAOS** (**FIG. 27-22**) illustrates a moment during a ceremony celebrating the winter solstice when *koshares*, or clowns, take over the plaza from the Katsinas. Katsinas—the supernatural counterparts of animals, natural phenomena like clouds, and geological features like mountains—are central to traditional Pueblo religion. They manifest themselves in the human dancers who impersonate them during ceremonies throughout the year, as well as in the small figures known as Katsina dolls that are given to children as educational aids in learning to identify the masks. Velarde's painting combines bold, flat colors and a simplified decorative line with European perspective. Her paintings, with their Art Deco abstraction, helped establish the popular idea of the "Indian" style in art.

THE NAVAJOS While some Navajo arts, like sand painting, have deep traditional roots, others have developed over the centuries of European contact. Navajo weaving (see FIG. 27-1) depends on the

27–22 • Pablita Velarde KOSHARES OF TAOS
New Mexico. 1940s. Watercolor on paper, 13⅞" × 22⅜" (35.3 × 56.9 cm). Philbrook Museum of Art, Tulsa, Oklahoma.
Museum Purchase (1947.37)

wool of sheep introduced by the Spaniards, and the designs and colors of Navajo blankets continue to evolve today in response to tourism and changing aesthetics. Similarly, jewelry made of turquoise and silver did not become an important Navajo art form until the mid nineteenth century. Traditionally, Navajo arts had strict gender divisions: women wove cloth, and men worked metal.

Sand painting, a traditional Navajo art, is the exclusive province of men. Sand paintings are made to the accompaniment of chants by shaman-singers in the course of healing and blessing ceremonies, and they have great sacred significance. The Night Chant, sung toward the end of the ceremony, signals the restoration of inner harmony and balance:

In beauty (happily) I walk.
With beauty before me I walk.
With beauty behind me I walk.
With beauty below me I walk.
With beauty all around me I walk.
It is finished (again) in beauty.
It is finished in beauty.

Navajo sand paintings depict mythic heroes and events; and as ritual art, they follow prescribed rules and patterns that ensure their power. To make them, the singer dribbles pulverized colored stones, pollen, flowers, and other natural colors over a hide or sand ground. The rituals are intended to cure by restoring harmony to the world. The paintings are not meant to be seen by the public and certainly not to be displayed in museums. They are meant to be destroyed by nightfall of the day on which they are made.

In 1919, a respected shaman-singer named Hosteen Klah (1867–1937) began to incorporate sand-painting images into weaving, breaking with the traditional prohibitions. Many Navajos took offense at Klah both for recording the sacred images and for doing so in what was traditionally a woman's art form. Klah had learned to weave from his mother and sister. The Navajo traditionally recognize at least three genders; Hosteen Klah was a *nadle*, or Navajo third-gender. Hence, he could learn both female and male arts; that is, he was trained both to weave and to heal. Hosteen Klah was not breaking artistic barriers in a conventional sense, but rather exemplifying the complexities of the traditional Navajo gender system. Klah's work was ultimately accepted because of his great skill and prestige.

The **WHIRLING LOG CEREMONY** sand painting, woven into tapestry (**FIG. 27-23**), depicts part of the Navajo creation myth. The Holy People create the earth's surface and divide it into four parts. They create humans, and bring forth corn, beans, squash, and tobacco—the four sacred plants. A male–female pair

ART AND ITS CONTEXTS | Craft or Art?

In many cultures, the distinction between "fine art" and "craft" does not exist. The traditional Western academic hierarchy of materials—in which marble, bronze, oil, and fresco are valued more than ceramic, glass, and watercolor—and the equally artificial hierarchy of subjects—in which history painting, including religious history, stands supreme—are irrelevant to non-Western art, and to much art produced in the West before the modern era.

The indigenous peoples of the Americas did not produce objects as works of art to be displayed in museums. In their eyes all pieces were utilitarian objects, adorned in ways necessary for their intended purposes. A work was valued for its effectiveness and for the role it played in society. Some, like a Sioux baby carrier (see FIG. 27–13), enrich mundane life with their aesthetic qualities. Others, such as Pomo baskets (see "Basketry," page 848), commemorate important events. The function of an Inca tunic may have been to identify or confer status on its owner or user through its material value or symbolic associations. And as with art in all cultures, many pieces had great spiritual or magical power. Such works of art cannot be fully comprehended or appreciated when they are seen only on pedestals or encased in glass boxes in museums or galleries. They must be imagined, or better yet seen, as acting in their societies. How powerfully might our minds and emotions be engaged if we saw Kwakwaka'wakw masks (see FIG. 27–20) functioning in religious drama, changing not only the outward appearance, but also the very essence of the individual.

At the beginning of the twentieth century, European and American artists broke away from the academic bias that extolled the Classical heritage of Greece and Rome. They found new inspiration in the art—or craft, if you will—of many different non-European cultures. Artists explored a new freedom to use absolutely any material or technique that effectively challenged outmoded assumptions and opened the way for a free and unfettered delight in, and an interest in understanding, Native American art as well as the art of other non-Western cultures. The more recent twentieth- and twenty-first-century conception of art as a multimedia adventure has helped validate works of art once seen only in ethnographic collections. Today, objects once called "primitive" are recognized as great works of art and acknowledged to be an essential dimension of a twenty-first-century worldview. The line between "art" and "craft" seems more artificial and less relevant than ever before.

---

of humans and one of the sacred plants stand in each of the four quarters, defined by the central cross. The four Holy People (the elongated figures) surround the image, and the guardian figure of Rainbow Maiden frames the scene on three sides. Like all Navajo artists, Hosteen Klah hoped that the excellence of the work would make it pleasing to the spirits. Recently, shaman-singers have made permanent sand paintings on boards for sale, but they usually introduce slight errors in them to render the paintings ceremonially harmless.

A NEW BEGINNING

While Native American art has long been displayed in anthropology and natural history museums, today the art of indigenous peoples is finally achieving full recognition by the art establishment (see "Craft or Art?" above). The Institute of American Indian Arts (IAIA), founded in 1962 in Santa Fe and attended by Native American students from all over North America, supports Native American aspirations in the arts today just as Dorothy Dunn's Studio School did in the 1930s. Staffed by Native American artists, the school encourages the incorporation of indigenous ideals in the arts without creating an official "style." As alumni achieved distinction and the IAIA museum in Santa Fe established a reputation for excellence, the institute has led Native American art into the mainstream of contemporary art (see Chapter 33).

To cite just one example, contemporary Native American artist Jaune Quick-to-See Smith (b. 1940) borrowed a well-known image by Leonardo da Vinci for **THE RED MEAN** (FIG. 27-24). She describes the work as a self-portrait, and indeed the center of the work has a bumper sticker that reads "Made in the U.S.A." above an identification number. The central figure quotes Leonardo's *Vitruvian Man* (see "The Vitruvian Man," page 639), but the message here is autobiographical. Leonardo inscribed the human form within perfect geometric shapes to emphasize the perfection

27-23 • Hosteen Klah WHIRLING LOG CEREMONY
Sand painting; tapestry by Mrs. Sam Manuelito. Navajo, c. 1925. Wool, 5′5″ × 5′10″ (1.69 × 1.82 m). Heard Museum, Phoenix, Arizona.

of the human body, while Smith put her silhouette inside the red X that signifies nuclear radiation. This image alludes both to the uranium mines found on some Indian reservations and to the fact that many have become temporary repositories for nuclear waste. The image's background is a collage of Native American tribal newspapers. Her self-portrait thus includes her ethnic identity and life on the reservation as well as allusions to the history of Western art.

Other artists, such as Canadian Haida artist Bill Reid (1920–1998), have sought to sustain and revitalize traditional art in their work. Trained as a woodcarver, painter, and jeweler, Reid revived the art of carving totem poles and dugout canoes in the Haida homeland of Haida Gwaii—"Islands of the People"—known on maps today as the Queen Charlotte Islands. Late in life he began to create large-scale sculptures in bronze. With their black patina, these works recall traditional Haida carvings in shiny black argillite.

Reid's imposing **THE SPIRIT OF HAIDA GWAII** now stands outside the Canadian Embassy in Washington, DC (**FIG. 27-25**). This sculpture, which Reid viewed as a metaphor for modern Canada's multicultural society, depicts a boatload of figures from the natural and mythic worlds struggling to paddle forward. The dominant figure is a shaman in a spruce-root basket hat and Chilkat blanket holding a speaker's pole. On the prow, the place reserved for the chief in a war canoe, sits the Bear. He faces backward rather than forward, and is bitten by an Eagle, with formline-patterned wings. The Eagle, in turn, is bitten by the Seawolf. The Eagle and the Seawolf, together with the man behind them, nevertheless continue paddling. At the stern, steering the canoe, is the Raven, the trickster in Haida mythology. The Raven is assisted by Mousewoman, the traditional guide and escort of humans in the spirit realms. According to Reid, the work represents a "mythological and environmental lifeboat," where "the entire family of living things … whatever their differences, … are paddling together in one boat, headed in one direction" (Bringhurst, 1991).

THE NATIONAL MUSEUM OF THE AMERICAN INDIAN In September 2004, the National Museum of the American Indian finally opened on the Mall in Washington, DC, directly below Capitol Hill and across from the National Gallery of Art. Inspired by the colors, textures, and forms of the American Southwest, the museum building establishes a new presence for Native Americans on the Mall (**FIG. 27-26**). Symbolizing the

27-25 • Bill Reid **THE SPIRIT OF HAIDA GWAII**
Haida, 1991. Bronze, approx. 13′ × 20′ (4 × 6 m). Canadian Embassy, Washington, DC.

27–26 • NATIONAL MUSEUM OF THE AMERICAN INDIAN
The Smithsonian Institution, Washington, DC. Opened September, 2004. Architectural design: GBQC in association with Douglas Cardinal (Blackfoot). Architectural consultants: Johnpaul Jones (Cherokee-Choctaw) and Ramona Sakiestewa (Hopi). Landscape consultant: Donna House (Navajo-Oneida), ethno-botanist.

Native relationship to the environment, the museum is surrounded by boulders ("Grandfather Rocks"), water, and plantings that recall the varied landscapes of North America, including wetlands, meadows, forest, and traditional cropland with corn, squash, and tomatoes. The entrance to the museum on the east side faces the morning sun and recalls the orientation of prairie tipis. Inside the building a Sun Marker of stained glass in the south wall throws its dagger of light across the vast atrium as the day progresses. Once again the great spirits of earth and sky take form in a creation of the art of the Americas.

THINK ABOUT IT

27.1 Distinguish characteristic styles and techniques developed by two Native American cultures—one in the north, and one in the south—and discuss their realization in one specific work from each culture.

27.2 Explain how symbols and themes are used in FIGURE 27–6 to articulate the Aztec worldview.

27.3 Choose a work of art in this chapter that is best understood in connection with its use in religious or political ritual. Discuss its meaning in relation to its ceremonial context. How can such works be displayed in museums in such a way that viewers will be able to understand this critical aspect of their meaning?

27.4 Evaluate the ways in which two Native North American works from this chapter exhibit influence from European culture.

CROSSCURRENTS

FIG. 21–6   FIG. 27–24

As is frequently the case in the history of art, artist Jaune Quick-to-See Smith has drawn, in *The Red Mean: Self-Portrait*, on a famous work of art from the past—in this case Leonardo da Vinci's *Vitruvian Man*. Discuss how grasping the meaning of Smith's work depends on the viewer's understanding of Leonardo's drawing. Does thinking about the comparison change the way you understand the earlier work?

 Study and review on myartslab.com

28–1 • THE BARUNGA STATEMENT
Various artists from Arnhem Land and central Australia. 1988. Ochers on composition board with collage of printed text on paper, 48″ × 47¼″ (122 × 120 cm). Reproduced with permission of the Northern and Central Land Councils.

Art of Pacific Cultures

In 1788, when Captain James Cook arrived in Australia, it was home to at least 300,000 Indigenous Australians, whose ancestors had arrived 50,000 years earlier, and who spoke over 250 languages. For 40,000 years the Indigenous Australians had been creating rock art and were the oldest continuous culture in the world. Nevertheless, Cook claimed Australia for Britain as a *terra nullius*, a land that belonged to no one. Within a few decades, European diseases had killed 50 percent of Indigenous Australians. Colonization and the arrival of missionaries would change their lives forever.

Two hundred years later, Indigenous Australians presented what is now known as **THE BARUNGA STATEMENT** (**FIG. 28-1**) to the then prime minister Bob Hawke. It was inspired by the Yirrkala Bark Petitions, which 25 years earlier had gained national attention when indigenous land rights claims were presented to the government on traditional bark paintings from Arnhem Land in the Northern Territory. The Barunga Statement placed its call for broader Aboriginal rights in text on paper collaged onto composition board decorated with two different styles of indigenous painting: one from Arnhem Land (on the left; see also FIG. 28-3) and the other from Australia's Central Desert area (on the right; see also "A Closer Look," page 878). Painted in natural ochers,

the cross hatching (*rarrk*) and zigzag patterns from the north contrast with the more fluid curved lines and dots that fill the central desert painting. In both, the artists used a dazzling array of symbols to retell stories about the adventures of ancestral beings.

In 1992, the Australian High Court rejected Cook's *terra nullius* argument and granted land rights to Indigenous Australians. When no treaty between the national government and Indigenous Australians followed, Galarrwuy Yunupingu, an indigenous leader, asked for the Barunga Statement back so that he could bury it. Today, however, it still hangs in Parliament and the struggle for full rights for Indigenous Australians continues.

Throughout the Pacific, contact with the West has had a significant impact on indigenous cultures, though to different degrees. In New Zealand, for example, the Treaty of Waitangi (1840) recognized Maori ownership of land and gave Maori the rights of British subjects, establishing early on a different political dynamic. Nonetheless, although numerous issues remain there, as well as in other parts of the region, Pacific islanders continue to use the arts to express and preserve their own rich and distinctive cultural identities.

LEARN ABOUT IT

28.1 Recognize how the availability of raw materials affects artistic choices and styles throughout the Pacific.

28.2 Examine the role the human body plays as a subject and medium in Pacific art.

28.3 Investigate ways that ancestor rituals influence the art in different Pacific cultures.

28.4 Assess the impact of Western contact on art in the Pacific.

((•—[**Listen** to the chapter audio on myartslab.com

THE PEOPLING OF THE PACIFIC

On a map with the Pacific Ocean as its center, only the peripheries of the great landmasses of Asia and the Americas appear. Nearly one-third of the earth's surface is taken up by this vast watery expanse. Europeans arriving in Oceania in the late eighteenth and early nineteenth centuries noted four distinct but connected cultural-geographic areas: Australia, Melanesia, Micronesia, and Polynesia (**MAP 28–1**). Australia includes the continent, as well as the island of Tasmania to the southeast. Melanesia ("black islands," a reference to the dark skin color of its inhabitants) includes New Guinea and the string of islands that extends eastward from it as far as Fiji and New Caledonia. Micronesia ("small islands"), to the north of Melanesia, is a region of small islands and coral atolls. Polynesia ("many islands") is scattered over a huge, triangular region defined by New Zealand in the south, Rapa Nui (Easter Island) in the east, and the Hawaiian islands to the north. The last region on earth to be inhabited by humans, Polynesia covers some 7.7 million square miles, of which fewer than 130,000 square miles are dry land—and most of that is New Zealand. With the exception of temperate New Zealand, with its marked seasons and snowcapped mountains, Oceania is in the tropics, that is, between the tropic of Cancer in the north and the tropic of Capricorn to the south.

Australia, Tasmania, and New Guinea formed a single continent during the last Ice Age, which began some 2.5 million years ago. About 50,000 years ago, when the sea level was about 330 feet lower than it is today, people moved to this continent from Southeast Asia, making at least part of the journey over open water. Around 27,000 years ago, humans were settled on the large islands north and east of New Guinea as far south as San Cristobal, but they ventured no farther for another 25,000 years. By about 4000 BCE—possibly as early as 7000 BCE—the people of Melanesia were raising pigs and cultivating taro, a plant with edible rootstocks. As the glaciers melted, the sea level rose, flooding low-lying coastal land. By around 4000 BCE a 70-mile-wide waterway, now called the Torres Strait, separated New Guinea from Australia, whose indigenous people continued their hunting and gathering way of life into the twentieth century.

The settling of the rest of the islands of Melanesia and the westernmost islands of Polynesia—Samoa and Tonga—coincided with the spread of the Lapita culture, named for a site in New Caledonia. The Lapita people were Austronesian speakers who probably migrated from Taiwan to Melanesia about 6,000 years ago. They spread throughout the islands of Melanesia, beginning around 1500 BCE. They were farmers and fisherfolk who cultivated taro and yams, and brought with them dogs, pigs, and chickens, animals that these colonizers needed for food. They also carried with them the distinctive ceramics whose remnants today enable us to trace the extent of their travels. Lapita potters produced dishes, platters, bowls, and jars. Sometimes they covered their wares with a red slip, and they often decorated them with bands of incised and stamped patterns—dots, lines, and hatching—that may also have been used on bark cloth and in tattoos. Most of the decoration was geometric, but some was figurative. The human face that appears in the example in **FIGURE 28-2** is among the earliest representations of a human being, one of the most important subjects in Oceanic art. The Lapita people were skilled shipbuilders and navigators and engaged in inter-island trade. Over time the Lapita culture lost its widespread cohesion and evolved into various local forms. Its end is generally dated to the early centuries of the Common Era.

Polynesian culture emerged in the eastern Lapita region on the islands forming Tonga and Samoa. Just prior to the beginning of the first millennium CE, daring Polynesian seafarers, probably in double-hulled sailing canoes, began settling the scattered islands of Far Oceania and eastern Micronesia. Voyaging over open water, sometimes for thousands of miles, they reached Hawaii and Rapa Nui after about 500 CE and settled New Zealand around 800/900–1200 CE.

While this history of migrations across Melanesia to Polynesia and Micronesia allowed for cross-cultural borrowings, there are distinctions between these areas and within the regions as well. The islands that make up Micronesia, Melanesia, and Polynesia include both low-lying coral atolls and the tall tops of volcanic mountains that rise from the ocean floor. Raw materials available to residents of these islands vary greatly, and islander art and architecture utilize these materials in different ways. The soil of volcanic islands can be very rich, supporting densely populated settlements with a local diversity of plants and animals. On the other hand, the poorer soil of coral atolls cannot support large populations. In a like manner, whereas volcanic islands provide good stone for tools and building (as at Nan Madol, see FIG. 28–10), coral is sharp but not particularly

28-2 • FRAGMENTS OF A LARGE LAPITA JAR
From Venumbo Reef, Santa Cruz Island, Solomon Islands. c. 1200–1100 BCE. Clay, height of human face motif approx. 1½" (4 cm).

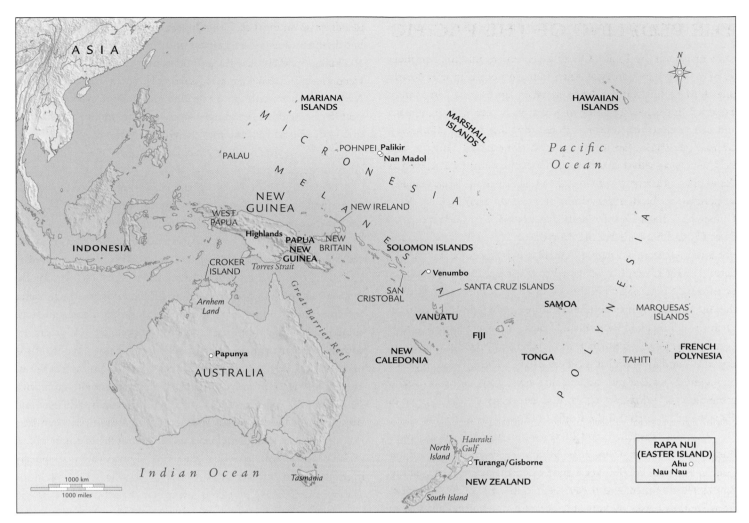

MAP 28–1 • PACIFIC CULTURAL-GEOGRAPHIC REGIONS
The Pacific cultures are spread over four vast areas: Australia, Melanesia, Micronesia, and Polynesia.

hard, and the strongest tools on a coral atoll are often those made from giant clam shells. Generally, the diversity of both plants and animals decreases from west to east among the Pacific islands.

The arts of this vast and diverse region display an enormous variety that is closely linked to each community's ritual and religious life. In this context, the visual arts were often just one strand in a rich weave that also included music, dance, and oral literature.

AUSTRALIA

Until European settlers disrupted their way of life, the hunter-gatherers of Australia were closely attuned to the environments in which they lived. Their only modification of the landscape was regular controlled burning of the underbrush, which encouraged new plant life and attracted animals. Their intimate knowledge of plants, animals, and water sources enabled them to survive and thrive in a wide range of challenging environments.

Indigenous Australian life is intimately connected with the concept of the Dreamtime, or the Dreaming. Not to be confused

with our notions of sleep and dreams, the Dreaming refers to the period before humans existed. (The term, a translation from Arrente, one of the more than 250 languages spoken in Australia when Europeans arrived, was first used in the late nineteenth century in an attempt to understand the indigenous worldview.) According to this complex belief system, the world began as a flat, featureless place. Ancestral Spirit Beings emerged from the earth or arrived from the sea, taking many different forms. The Spirit Beings had numerous adventures, and in crossing the continent, they created all of its physical features: mountains, sand hills, creeks, and water holes. They also brought about the existence of animals, plants, and humans and created the ceremonies and sacred objects needed to ensure that they themselves were remembered, a system sometimes referred to as Aboriginal Laws. The Spirit Beings eventually returned to the earth or became literally one of its features. Thus, they are identified with specific places, which are honored as sacred sites. Indigenous Australians who practice this traditional religion believe that they are descended from the Spirit Beings and associate themselves with particular places related to the ancestors' stories and transformations.

Knowledge of the Dreaming stories, and of the objects related to them, is sacred and secret. Multiple levels of meaning are learned over a lifetime and restricted to those properly trained and initiated to know each level. As a result, an outsider's understanding of the stories and related art (objects and motifs) is strictly limited to what is allowed to be public. Some stories are shared by many tribes across great distances, while others are specific to one area. Men and women have their own stories, women's often associated with food and food gathering.

Since the Dreaming has never ceased, the power of the ancestral Spirit Beings still exists. Indigenous Australians have developed a rich artistic life to relive the stories of the ancestors and transmit knowledge about them to subsequent generations. Ceremonial art forms include paintings on rock and bark, sand drawings, and ground sculptures. Sacred objects, songs, and dances are used to renew the supernatural powers of the ancestors in ceremonial meetings, called corroborees. In **FIGURE 28-3**, Western Arnhem Land artist Jimmy Midjaw Midjaw depicts such a meeting held by a group of Mimi, spirits who live in the narrow spaces between rocks by day and come out at night. Specific to this area, they taught humans how to hunt and cook animals, as well as to dance, sing, and play instruments in ceremonies. Tall, thin, humanlike figures, often in motion, they were painted in ancient rock shelters, and since at least the late nineteenth century, on eucalyptus bark.

Bark paintings are found throughout northern Australia, where numerous regional styles exist. In Western Arnhem Land, the background is usually a monochromatic red ocher wash, with figures in white, black, and red pigments. In the 1950s and 1960s, Midjaw Midjaw was part of a prolific group of artists on Minjilang (Croker Island) that became well known through the anthropologists and collectors working in the area.

MELANESIA

Since they usually rely at least partially on agriculture for survival, the inhabitants of Melanesia live in permanent settlements, many of which feature spaces set aside for ritual use. Social position and status are not inherited or determined by birth, but are achieved by the accumulation of wealth (often in the form of pigs), by the demonstration of leadership, and, often, by participation in men's societies. Much ceremony is related to rituals associated with these societies, including initiation into different levels or grades. Other important rituals facilitate relationships with the deceased and with supernatural forces. Melanesian art is often bold and dazzling. Masking and body decoration, often as part of ceremonial performances, are important, though often ephemeral. Men are prominent in the sculptural and masking traditions; women play significant roles as audience and are also known for their skill in making bark cloth, woven baskets, pottery, and other aesthetically pleasing objects.

28-3 • Jimmy Midjaw Midjaw **THREE DANCERS AND TWO MUSICIANS: CORROBOREE OF MIMI, SPIRITS OF THE ROCKS**
Minjilang (Croker Island), West Arnhem Land, Australia. Mid 20th century. Natural pigments on eucalyptus bark, 23″ × 35″ (59 × 89 cm). Musée du Quai Branly, Paris, France. (MNAO 64.9.103)

NEW GUINEA

New Guinea, the largest island in the Pacific (and, at 1,500 miles long and 1,000 miles wide, the second-largest island in the world), is today divided between two countries. Its eastern half is part of the modern nation of Papua New Guinea; the western half is West Papua, a province of present-day Indonesia. Located near the equator and with mountains that rise to 16,000 feet, the island affords its inhabitants a variety of environments, from coastal mangrove marshes to grasslands, from dense rainforests to swampy river valleys. The population is equally diverse, with coastal fishermen, riverine hunters, slash-and-burn agriculturalists, and more stable farmers in the highlands. Between New Guinea itself and the smaller neighboring islands, more than 700 languages have been identified.

THE *KORAMBO* OR CEREMONIAL HOUSE OF THE ABELAM OF PAPUA NEW GUINEA The Abelam, who live in the foothills of the mountains on the north side of the Sepik River in Papua New Guinea, raise pigs and cultivate yams, taro, bananas, and sago palms. In traditional Abelam society, people live in

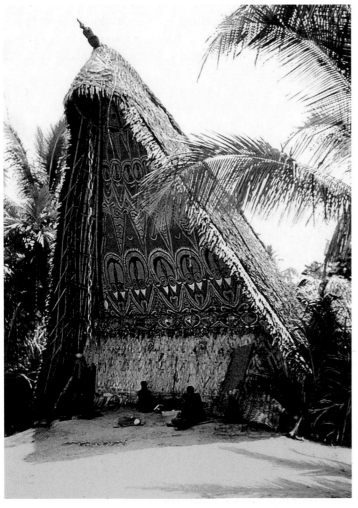

28-4 • EXTERIOR OF KORAMBO (HAUS TAMBARAN)
Kinbangwa village, Sepik River, Papua New Guinea. Abelam, 20th century.

extended families or clans in hamlets. Wealth among the Abelam is measured in pigs, but men gain status from participation in a yam cult that has a central place in Abelam society. The yams that are the focus of this cult—some of which reach an extraordinary 12 feet in length—are associated with clan ancestors and the potency of their growers. Village leaders renew their relationship with the forces of nature as represented by yams during the Long Yam Festival, which is held at harvest time and involves processions, masked figures, singing, and the ritual exchange of the finest yams.

An Abelam hamlet includes sleeping houses, cooking houses, storehouses for yams, a central space for rituals, and a ceremonial or spirit house, the **korambo** (*haus tambaran* in Pidgin). In this ceremonial structure reserved for the men of the village, the objects associated with the yam cult and with clan identity are kept hidden from women and uninitiated boys. Men of the clan gather in the *korambo* to organize rituals, especially initiation rites, and to conduct community business. The prestige of a hamlet is linked to the quality of its *korambo* and the size of its yams. Constructed on a frame of poles and rafters and roofed with split cane and thatch, *korambo* are built with a triangular floor plan, the side walls meeting at the back of the building. The elaborately decorated façade consists of three parts, beginning at the bottom: a woven mat, a painted and carved wooden lintel, and painted sago bark panels (**FIG. 28-4**). In this example, built about 1961, red, white, and black faces of spirits (*nggwal*) appear on the façade's bark panels, and the figure at the top is said to represent a female flying witch. This last figure is associated with the feminine power of the house itself. The projecting pole at the top of the *korambo* is the only male element of the architecture, and is said to be the penis of the house. The small door at the lower right is a female element, a womb; entering and exiting the house is the symbolic equivalent to death and rebirth. The Abelam believe the paint itself has magical qualities. Regular, ritual repainting revitalizes the images and ensures their continued potency.

Every stage in the construction of a *korambo* is accompanied by ceremonies, which are held in the early morning while women and boys are still asleep. The completion of the façade of a house is celebrated with a ceremony called *mindja*, which includes all-night dancing, and which may continue for six months, until the roof is completely thatched. Women participate in these inaugural ceremonies and are allowed to enter the new house, which afterward is ritually cleansed and closed to them.

BILUM—CONTEMPORARY NET BAGS OF HIGHLAND NEW GUINEA Women's arts in Papua New Guinea tend to be less spectacular and more subtle than men's, but nonetheless significant. Both functionally and symbolically, they contribute to a balance between male and female roles in society. **Bilum**, for example, are netted bags made mainly by women throughout the central highlands of New Guinea (**FIG. 28-5**). Looped from a single long thread spun on the thigh, *bilum* are very strong and, as

28-5 • WOMEN WEARING NET BAGS (BILUM)
Wahgi Valley, Western Highlands Province, Papua New Guinea. 1990.

loosely woven work bags, are used to carry items from vegetables to beer. The bones of a deceased man may be stored in a special *bilum* in a village's men's house (which is similar in function to the Abelam *korambo* in FIGURE 28-4), while his widow wears his personal bag as a sign of mourning. Women wear decorative *bilum*, into which marsupial fur is often incorporated, as adornment, exchange them as gifts, and use them to carry babies.

Bilum are rich metaphorical symbols. Among the women of the Wahgi tribe, who live in the Wahgi Valley of the central highlands, seen in FIGURE 28-5, the term *bilum* may be used as a synonym for womb and bride, and they are also associated with ideas of female attractiveness; depending on how they are worn, they can indicate whether a girl is eligible for marriage.

In the past, *bilum* were made from natural fibers, most commonly the inner bark of a ficus plant. Today, while the technique for making them remains unchanged, a wide array of colorful contemporary fibers, including nylon and acrylic yarn, are used, and new designs incorporating complicated patterns and words are constantly appearing. *Bilum* are now made by women throughout Papua New Guinea, not just in the highlands. They are sold

commercially in markets and towns, and have become one of the country's national symbols.

SPIRIT POLES OF THE ASMAT OF WEST PAPUA The Asmat, who live along rivers in the coastal swamp forests of the southwest coast, were known in the past as warriors and head-hunters. In Asmat culture, trees are identified with human beings, their fruit with human heads. Fruit-eating birds were thus the equivalent of headhunters, and were often represented in war and mortuary arts, along with the praying mantis, whose female bites off the head of the male during mating. In the past, the Asmat believed that death was always caused by an enemy, either by direct killing or through magic, and that it required revenge, usually in the form of taking an enemy's head, to appease the spirit of the person who had died and thus maintain balance between hostile groups.

Believing that the spirit of the dead person remained in the village, the Asmat erected elaborately sculpted memorial poles (**FIG. 28-6**), known as *bisj* (pronounced bish), which embodied the spirits of the ancestors and paid tribute to them. Placed in front of special houses belonging to the village's men's society, *bisj* poles are generally carved from mangrove trees, although some in a museum in Leiden recently have been identified as wild nutmeg wood. The felling of a tree is a ritual act in which a group of men attack the tree as if it were an enemy. The figures on the poles represent the dead individuals who are to be avenged; small figures represent dead children. The bent pose of the figures associates them with the praying mantis. The large, lacy phalluses emerging from the figures at the top of the poles are carved from the projecting roots of the tree and symbolize male fertility, while the surface decoration suggests body ornamentation. The poles faced the river to ensure that the spirits of the dead would travel to the realm of the ancestors (*safan*), which lay beyond the sea. The *bisj* pole also served symbolically as the dugout canoe that would take the spirit of the deceased down the river to *safan*.

By carving *bisj* poles (usually for several deceased at the same time) and organizing a *bisj* feast, relatives publicly indicated their responsibility to avenge their dead in a headhunting raid. As part of the ceremonies, mock battles were held, the men boasting of their bravery, the women cheering them on. After the ceremonies, the poles were left in the swamp to deteriorate and transfer their supernatural power back to nature. Today, Asmat continue to carve *bisj* poles and use them in funerary ceremonies, although they stopped headhunting in the 1970s. Poles are also made to sell to outsiders.

NEW IRELAND

MALAGAN DISPLAY OF NEW IRELAND New Ireland is one of the large eastern islands of the nation of Papua New Guinea. The northern people on the island still practice a complex set of death and commemorative rites known as *malagan* (pronounced malang-gan), which can take place as much as two years after a person's death. In the past, clan leaders rose to prominence primarily through *malagan* ceremonies that honored their wives' recently deceased family members. The greater the *malagan* ceremony, the greater prominence the clan leader had achieved.

Malagan also include rites to initiate young men and women into adulthood. After several months' training in seclusion in a ritual enclosure, they are presented to the public and given carved and

28-6 • ASMAT ANCESTRAL SPIRIT POLES (BISJ)
Buepis village, Fajit River, West Papua Province, Indonesia. c. 1960. Wood, paint, palm leaves, and fiber, height approx. 18′ (5.48 m).

28-7 • MALAGAN DISPLAY
Medina village, New Ireland, Papua New Guinea. c. 1930. Height 6'10⅝" (2.1 m), width 11'5¾" (3.5 m).
Museum für Völkerkunde, Basel, Switzerland.

painted figures. The combined funerary and initiation ceremonies include feasts, masked dances, and the creation of a special house to display elaborately carved and painted sculptures (**FIG. 28-7**) that honor the dead. The display house illustrated, which dates to the early 1930s, is more than 14 feet wide and honors 12 deceased individuals. The carvings are large (the first on the left is nearly 6 feet in height) and take the form of horizontal friezes, standing figures, and poles containing several figures. They are visually complex, with tensions created between solids and voids, and between the two-dimensional painted patterns on three-dimensional sculptural forms. Such displays are kept secret until their unveiling at the climax of festivities. After the ceremonies they are no longer considered ritually "active" and are destroyed or, since the late nineteenth century, sold to outsiders. *Malagan* figures are still being carved in association with continuing ceremonies.

NEW BRITAIN

TUBUAN MASK OF NEW BRITAIN In the Papua New Guinea province of New Britain—including the Duke of York Islands—Tubuan masks represent the Tolai male secret society, which has different levels or grades of increasing knowledge and power, and wields both spiritual and social control, especially during the three months of ceremonies known as the "Time of the Tubuan." Though initiation to the society is the main purpose of the ceremonies, the men of the village, who have achieved power through the accumulation of wealth, and in the past through bravery in war, use this period to call up the spirits represented by the

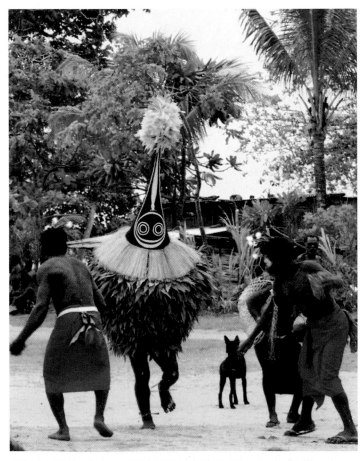

28-8 • TUBUAN MASK BEING DANCED
Tolai people, Duke of York Islands, New Britain, Papua New Guinea.
c. 1990. Cloth, paint, fiber, and feathers.

masks, who have the authority to settle disputes, stop fights, punish lawbreakers, and force the payment of debts. Political power and authority are underscored and enhanced by their appearance. In the past they had the power of life and death.

The masks represent both female and male spirits, though all the masks are danced by men. Local stories say women originally owned the masks and that men stole them. The **TUBUAN MASK** (**FIG. 28–8**) represents the Mother, who gives birth to her children, the Duk Duk masks, representing the new initiates into the society. With the appearance, first of the Mother masks, then of the Duk Duk masks, the initiates return to the village from the bush, where they have undergone intensive preparation to enter the society. The Tubuan mask has a distinctive, tall conical shape and prominent eyes formed by concentric white circles. The green leaf skirt is a very sacred part of the mask, which is itself made from painted bark cloth, various fibers, and feathers. Black feathers on top indicate a more powerful spirit than white feathers.

MICRONESIA

The majority of Micronesia's islands are small, low-lying coral atolls, but in the western region several are volcanic in origin. The eastern islands are more closely related culturally to Polynesia, while those in the west show connections to Melanesia, especially in the men's houses found on Palau and Yap. The atolls—circular coral reefs surrounding lagoons where islands once stood—have a limited range of materials for creating objects of any kind. Micronesians are known especially for their navigational skills and their fine canoes. They also create textiles from banana and coconut fibers, bowls from turtle shells, and abstract human figures from wood, which is scarce. As in other parts of the Pacific, tattooing and performative arts remain central to life.

WAPEPE **NAVIGATION CHART** Sailors from the Marshall Islands relied on celestial navigation—using the sun and moon and stars—as well as a detailed understanding of the ocean currents and trade winds to travel from one island to another. To teach navigation to younger generations, elders traditionally used stick charts (*wapepe* or *mattang*)—maps that showed land, but also the path from one island to the next, the water sailors would cross during their voyage.

In common use until the 1950s, stick charts (**FIG. 28–9**) were schematic diagrams of the prevailing ocean currents and the characteristic wave patterns encountered between islands. Currents are represented by sticks held together by coconut fibers; attached shells mark islands along the route. The arrangement of sticks around a shell indicates a zone of distinctive waves shaped by the effect of an island deflecting the prevailing wind. Such refracted waves enable a navigator to sense the proximity of land without being able to see it, and to discern the least difficult course for making landfall. Although *wapepe* are primarily functional, their combination of clarity, simplicity, and abstraction has an aesthetic impact.

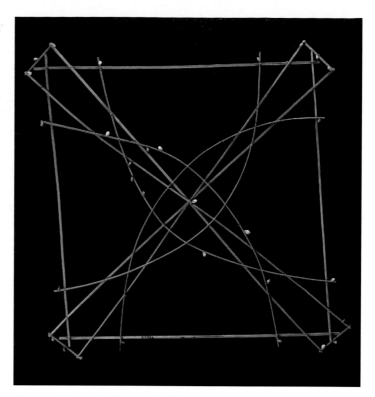

28-9 • WAPEPE NAVIGATION CHART
Marshall Islands. 19th century. Sticks, coconut fiber, and shells, 29½″ × 29½″ (75 × 75 cm). Peabody Essex Museum, Salem.

NAN MADOL The basalt cliffs of the island of Pohnpei provided the building material for one of the largest and most remarkable stone architectural complexes in Oceania. Nan Madol, on its southeast coast, consists of 92 artificial islands set within a network of canals covering about 170 acres (**MAP 28-2**). Seawalls and breakwaters 15 feet high and 35 feet thick protect the area from the ocean. When it was populated, openings in the breakwaters gave canoes access to the ocean and allowed seawater to flow in and out with the tides, flushing clean the canals. While other similar complexes have been identified in Micronesia, Nan Madol is the largest and most impressive, reflecting the importance of the kings who ruled from the site. The artificial islands and the buildings atop them were constructed between the early thirteenth century and the dynasty's political decline in the seventeenth. The site had already been abandoned by the time Europeans discovered it in the nineteenth century.

Nan Madol was an administrative and ceremonial center for powerful kings, who commanded a local labor force to construct this monumental city of as many as 1,000 people. Both the buildings and the underlying islands are built of massive masonry set in alternating layers of log-shaped stones and boulders of prismatic basalt. The largest of the artificial islets is more than 100 yards long, and one basalt cornerstone alone is estimated to weigh about 50 tons. The stone logs were split from the cliffs by alternately heating the stone and dousing it with water. Most of the islands are oriented northeast–southwest, receiving the benefit of the cooling prevailing winds.

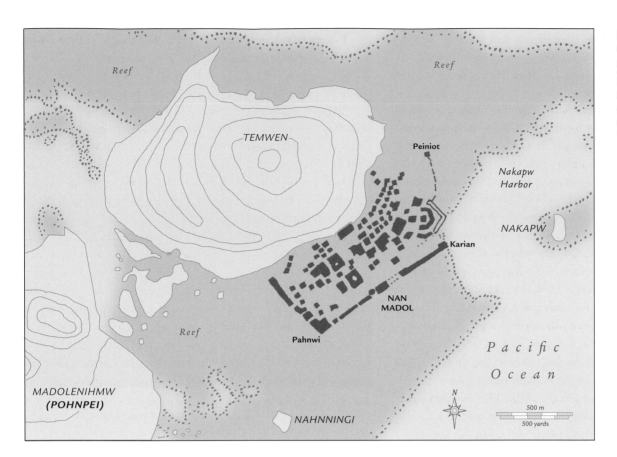

MAP 28-2 • THE COMPLEX OF NAN MADOL

Pohnpei, Federated States of Micronesia. c. 1200/1300– c. 1500/1600.

The walls of the **ROYAL MORTUARY COMPOUND**, which once dominated the northeast side of Nan Madol (**FIG. 28-10**), rise in subtle upward and outward curves to a height of 25 feet. To achieve the sweeping, rising lines, the builders increased the number of stones in the header courses (those with the ends of the stones laid facing out along the wall) relative to the stretcher courses (those with the lengths of the stones laid parallel to the wall) as they came to the corners and entryways. The plan of the structure consists of progressively higher rectangles within rectangles—the outer walls leading by steps up to interior walls that lead up to a central courtyard with a small, cubical tomb.

POLYNESIA

The settlers of the far-flung islands of Polynesia developed distinctive cultural traditions but also retained linguistic and cultural affinities that reflect their common origin. Traditional Polynesian society was generally far more stratified than Melanesian society: A person's genealogy, tracing his or her descent from an ancestral god, determined his or her place in society. First-born children of the hereditary elite were considered the most sacred because they inherited more spiritual power (*mana*) at their birth. *Mana* could

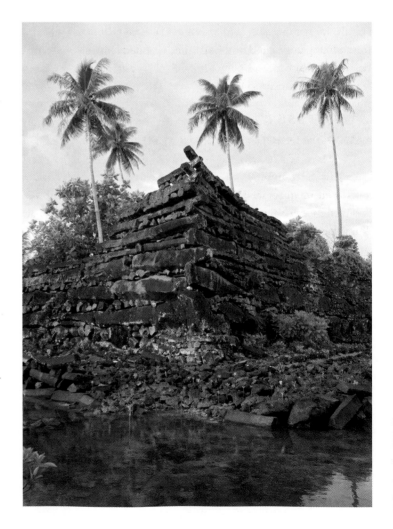

28-10 • ROYAL MORTUARY COMPOUND, NAN MADOL
Pohnpei, Federated States of Micronesia. Basalt blocks, wall height up to 25' (7.62 m).

be gained through leadership, courage, or skill, but it could be lost because of failure in warfare. It was protected by strict laws of conduct called *tapu*, a word that came into the English language as "taboo."

All of the arts in Polynesia were sacred, and their creation was a sacred act. Master artists were also ritual specialists. Objects were crafted from a variety of materials, some of which, like jadeite in New Zealand, were considered spiritually powerful. Some objects were practical, such as canoes, fishhooks, and weapons; others indicated the status and rank of the society's elite. Objects had their own *mana*, which could increase or decrease depending on how successful they were in performing their functions. Quality and beauty were important. Objects were made to endure, and many were handed down as heirlooms from generation to generation. In addition, the human body itself was the canvas for the art of tattoo (*tatau* in several Polynesian languages).

Polynesian religions included many levels of gods, from creator gods and semidivine hero-gods (such as Maui, who appears in the stories of many of the Polynesian cultures) to natural forces, but the most important were ancestors, who became gods at their death. Since they remained influential in daily life, they had to be honored and placated, and their help was sought for important projects and in times of trouble. Throughout much of Polynesia, figures in human form—often generically called *tiki*—were carved in stone, wood, and in some places, including the Marquesas Islands, human bone. These statues represented the ancestors and were often placed on sacred ritual sites attended by ritual specialists (see FIG. 28-13) or, as in New Zealand, incorporated into meeting houses (see "Te-Hau-ki-Turanga," page 872).

MARQUESAS ISLANDS

TATTOO IN THE MARQUESAS ISLANDS The art of tattoo was widespread and ancient in Oceania. Tattoo chisels made of bone have been found in Lapita sites. They are quite similar to the tools used to decorate Lapita pottery, suggesting some symbolic connection between the marking of both pottery and human skin. The Polynesians, descendants of the Lapita people, brought tattooing with them as they migrated throughout the Pacific, and as they became isolated from each other over time, distinctive styles evolved. Spirals became a hallmark of the Maori facial tattoo (*moko*), and rows of triangles became prominent in Hawaiian designs.

The people of the Marquesas Islands—an archipelago about 900 miles northeast of Tahiti—were the most extensively tattooed of all Polynesians. The process of tattooing involves shedding blood, the most *tapu* (sacred) substance in Polynesia. In the Marquesas, the process for a young man of high social rank began around age 18; by age 30 he would be fully tattooed. Because of the sacredness and prestige of the process, some men continued to be tattooed until their skin was completely covered and the designs disappeared. Marquesan women were also tattooed, usually on the hands, ankles, lips, and behind the ears.

Tattooing was painful and expensive. Though women could be tattooed with little ceremony in their own homes, in the case of both men and women of high rank, special houses were built for the occasion. The master tattooer and his assistants had to be fed and paid, and at the end of the session a special feast was held to display the new tattoos. Each design had a name and a meaning. Tattooing marked passages in people's lives and their social positions; it commemorated special events or accomplishments. Some tattoos denoted particular men's societies or eating groups. Especially for men, tattoos demonstrated courage and were essential to their sexual attractiveness to women.

Tattooing was forbidden in the nineteenth century by French colonial administrators and Catholic missionaries, and it died out in the Marquesas. Beginning in the 1970s, however, there was a resurgence of the art throughout the Pacific, and in 1980 **TEVE TUPUHIA** became the first Marquesan in modern times to be fully tattooed (**FIG. 28-11**). He went to Samoa—the only place in Polynesia where the traditional art form continued—to be tattooed by master Samoan artist Lese I'io. The process took six weeks and cost $35,000. Teve based his tattoo designs on drawings made by George Langsdorff, a German naturalist who visited

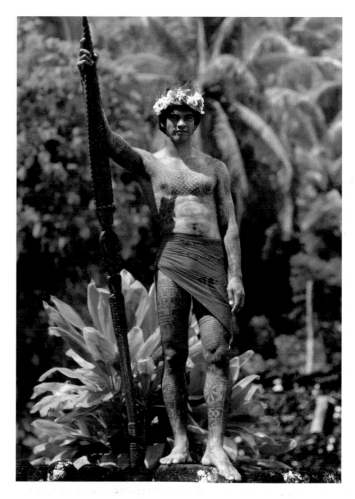

28-11 • TEVE TUPUHIA
Marquesan man tattooed in 1980 by Samoan Lese I'io.

New Zealand was settled sometime after 800 CE by intrepid seafaring Polynesians now known as the Maori. As part of the process of adapting their Polynesian culture to the temperate New Zealand environment, they began to build wooden-frame homes, the largest of which, the chief's house, evolved after Western contact into the meeting house (*whare nui*). The meeting house stands on an open plaza (*marae*), a sacred place where a Maori tribe (*iwi*) or subtribe (*hapu*) still today greets visitors, discusses important issues, and mourns the dead. In it, tribal history and genealogy are recorded and preserved. Created by the master carver Raharuhi Rukupo and his 18 named assistants in the early 1840s, **TE-HAU-KI-TURANGA** is the oldest existing,

fully decorated meeting house in New Zealand (**FIG. 28–12**). Built by Rukupo as a memorial to his elder brother, its name refers to the region of New Zealand where it was made—Turanga, today Gisborne and its region, on the northeast coast of North Island—and has been translated as "The Breezes of Turanga" or "The Spirit of Turanga."

In this area of New Zealand, the meeting house symbolizes the tribe's founding ancestor, for whom it is often named. The ridgepole is the backbone, the rafters are the ribs, and the slanting bargeboards—the boards attached to the projecting end of the gable—are the outstretched enfolding arms. The face appears in the gable mask. Relief figures of ancestors cover the support poles,

wall planks, and the lower ends of the rafters. The ancestors, in effect, support the house. They were thought to take an active interest in community affairs and to participate in the discussions held in the meeting house. Rukupo, an important political and religious leader as well as a master carver, included an unusual naturalistic portrait of himself among them.

Painted curvilinear patterns (**kowhaiwhai**) decorate the rafters in white on a red and black background. The **koru** pattern, a curling stalk with a bulb at the end that resembles the young tree fern, dominates the design system. Lattice panels (**tukutuku**) made by women fill the spaces between the wall planks. Because ritual prohibitions, or taboos, prevented

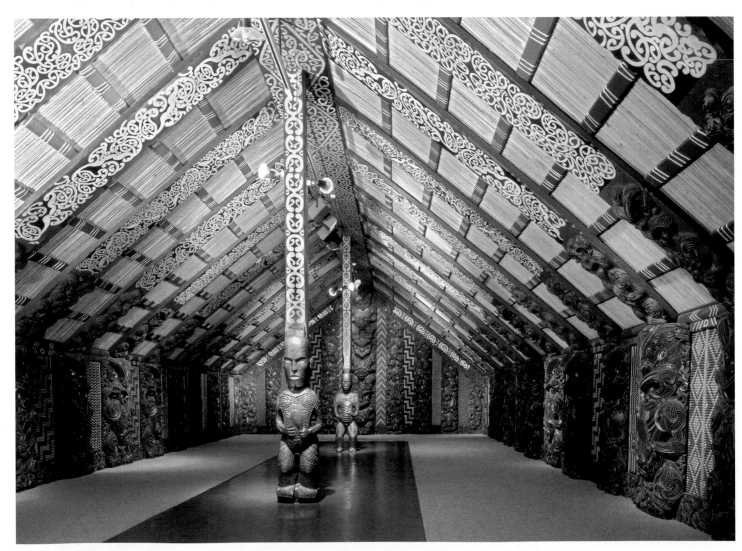

28-12 • Raharuhi Rukupo, master carver **TE-HAU-KI-TURANGA (MAORI MEETING HOUSE)**
Gisborne/Turanga, New Zealand; built and owned by the Rongowhakaata people of Turanga. 1842–1843, restored in 1935. Wood, shell, grass, flax, and pigments. Museum of New Zealand/Te Papa Tongarewa, Wellington. (Neg. B18358)

women from entering the meeting house, they worked from the outside and wove the panels from the back. They created the black, white, and orange patterns from grass, flax, and flat slats. Each pattern has a symbolic meaning: chevrons representing the teeth of the sea monster Taniwha, steps the stairs of heaven climbed by the hero-god Tawhaki, and diamonds the flounder.

When Captain Cook arrived in New Zealand in the second half of the eighteenth century, each tribe and geographical region had its own style. A storehouse doorway from the Ngäti Päoa tribe (FIG. 28–13), who lived in the Hauraki Gulf area to the west of Turanga, dates to this period of time (or earlier) and shows the soft, shallow surface carving resulting from the use of stone tools. In comparison, a house panel (**poupou**) from Te-Hau-ki-Turanga (**FIG. 28–14**), carved with steel tools, shows the deeply cut, very precisely detailed surface carving characteristic of that time.

As is typical throughout Polynesia (see FIG. 28–16), the figures face frontally and have large heads with open eyes. The Hauraki Gulf figure has both hands placed on its stomach and represents a male ancestor, while the Te-Hau-ki-Turanga figure is a female ancestor nursing a child. In both, a small figure, representing their descendants, stands between their legs.

Considered a national treasure by the Maori, this meeting house was restored in 1935 by Maori artists who knew the old, traditional methods; it is now preserved at the Museum of New Zealand/Te Papa Tongarewa in Wellington and considered *taonga* (cultural treasure).

28–13 • CARVED FIGURE FROM STOREHOUSE DOORWAY
Ngäti Päoa, Hauraki Gulf, New Zealand. 1500–1800. Wood, height 33⅞″ (86 cm). Museum of New Zealand/Te Papa Tongarewa, Wellington.

28–14 • POUPOU (PANEL)
From Te-Hau-ki-Turanga. Wood and red pigment, height 4′7″ (140 cm). Museum of New Zealand/Te Papa Tongarewa, Wellington.

interior side wall

Parts of the meeting house

front

interior rear wall

the Marquesas in 1804 as part of a Russian scientific expedition. Today, Marquesan-style tattoo designs are seen throughout French Polynesia.

HAWAII

FEATHER CLOAK FROM HAWAII The Hawaiian islanders had one of the most highly stratified of all Polynesian societies, with valleys and whole islands ruled by high chiefs. Soon after contact with the West, the entire archipelago was unified for the first time under the rule of Kamehameha I (r. 1810–1819), who assumed the title of king in the European manner.

Among the members of the Hawaiian elite, feathered capes and cloaks were emblems of high social status. A full-length cloak made with thousands of red and yellow feathers (**FIG. 28-15**), was reserved for the highest ranks of the elite men and called an *'ahu 'ula* ("red cloak")—the color red is associated with high status and rank throughout Polynesia. Often given as gifts to important visitors to Hawaii, this particular cloak was presented in 1843 to Commodore Lawrence Kearny, commander of the USS *Constellation*, by King Kamehameha III (r. 1825–1854).

Draped over the wearer's shoulders, such a cloak creates a sensuously textured and colored abstract design, which in this example joins to create matching patterns of paired crescents on front and back. The cloak's foundation consisted of coconut fiber netting onto which were tied bundles of feathers—part of an annual tribute paid to the king by his subjects. The red, and especially the yellow feathers, were highly prized and came from several species of birds including the *i'iwi, apapane, 'o'o,* and *mamo* (which is now extinct). In some cases, each bird yielded only seven or eight feathers, making the collecting of feathers very labor-intensive and increasing the value of the cloaks.

Cloaks were so closely associated with the spiritual power (*mana*) of the elite person that they could be made only by specialists trained in both the complicated technique of manufacture and the rituals attending their fabrication. Surrounded by protective objects, they created the cloak while reciting the chief's genealogy to imbue it with the power of his ancestors. As a result, the cloaks were seen as protective of the wearer, while also proclaiming his elite status and political and economic power.

Feathers were used for decorating not just cloaks, but also helmets, capes, blankets, and garlands (*leis*), all of which conferred status and prestige. The annual tribute paid to the king by his subjects included feathers, and tall feather pompons (*kahili*) mounted on long slender sticks were symbols of royalty. Even the effigies of gods that Hawaiian warriors carried into battle were made of light, basketlike structures covered with feathers.

MONUMENTAL MOAI ON RAPA NUI

Rapa Nui (Easter Island) is the most isolated inhabited locale in Oceania, located 2,300 miles west of the coast of South America and 1,200 miles from Pitcairn Island, the nearest Polynesian outpost. Three volcanoes, one at each corner, make up the small triangular island. Originally known to its native inhabitants as Te Pito o te Henúa (Navel of the World) and now known as Rapa Nui, it was named Easter Island by Captain Jacob Roggeveen, the Dutch explorer who first landed there on Easter Sunday in 1722. Rapa Nui became part of Chile in 1888.

MONUMENTAL MOAI Rapa Nui is the site of Polynesia's most impressive stone sculpture. Though many imaginative theories have been posited regarding the origins of its statues—from space aliens to Native Americans—they are most definitely part of an established Polynesian tradition. Sacred religious sites (*marae*) with stone altar platforms (*ahu*) are common throughout Polynesia. On

28-15 • FEATHER CLOAK, KNOWN AS THE KEARNY CLOAK
Hawaii. c. 1843. Red, yellow, and black feathers, olona cordage, and netting, length 55¾" (143 cm). Bishop Museum, Honolulu.

King Kamehameha III (r. 1825–1854) presented this cloak to Commodore Lawrence Kearny, commander of the frigate USS *Constellation*.

Rapa Nui the Polynesians who arrived at the island in canoes between 800 and 1200 CE built most of the *ahu* near the coast, parallel to the shore, and began to erect stone figures on them, perhaps as memorials to deceased chiefs or ancestors. Nearly 1,000 of these figures, called **moai**, have been found on the island, including some 400 unfinished ones in the quarry at Rano Raraku where they were being carved. The statues themselves are made from yellowish-brown volcanic tuff. On their heads, *pukao* (topknots of hair) were rendered in red scoria, another volcanic stone. When the statues were in place, the insertion of white coral and stone "opened" the eyes. In 1978, several figures on Ahu Nau Nau (**FIG. 28–16**) were restored to their original condition. These are about 36 feet tall, but *moai* range in size from much smaller to a 65-foot statue that is still in the quarry, where the sculptures were produced before being transported up to 11 miles to the sites of the *anu*. A recent theory proposes that the completed *moai* were "walked" from the quarry to the *anu* as handlers rocked them from side to side using attached ropes. The fragmentary remains of statues, which line the road away from the quarry, indicate that not all *moai* completed the journey.

Like other Polynesian statues, the *moai* face frontally. Their large heads have deep-set eyes under a prominent brow ridge; a long, concave, pointed nose; a small mouth with pursed lips; and an angular chin. The extremely elongated earlobes have parallel engraved lines that suggest ear ornaments. The figures have schematically indicated breastbones and pectorals, and small arms with hands pressed close to the sides. Since their bodies emerge from the ground at just below waist level, they have no legs.

The island's indigenous population, which has been estimated at 3,000 people when the Dutch arrived in 1722, was nearly eradicated in 1877 when Peruvian slave traders precipitated an epidemic of smallpox and tuberculosis that left only 110 inhabitants alive. Today, a vibrant population of some 5,000 people is known especially for its energetic and athletic dance performances and thrives primarily on tourism.

SAMOA

***TAPA (SIAPO)* IN SAMOA** As they migrated across the Pacific, Polynesians brought with them the production of bark cloth. Known by various names throughout the Pacific, most commonly

28-16 • MOAI ANCESTOR FIGURES
Ahu Nau Nau, Rapa Nui (Easter Island). c. ?1000–1500 CE, restored 1978. Volcanic stone (tufa), average height approx. 36′ (11 m).

👁 **Watch** a video about Easter Island on myartslab.com

as **tapa**, in Samoa bark cloth is called **siapo**. It is usually made by women, although sometimes men help obtain the bark or decorate the completed cloth. In Samoa, *siapo* is made by stripping the inner bark from branches of the paper mulberry tree (banyan and breadfruit are sometimes used in other archipelagos). The bark is beaten with a wooden mallet, then folded over and beaten again, to various degrees of softness. Larger pieces can be made by building up the cloth in a process of felting or using natural pastes as glue. The heavy wooden mallets used for beating the cloth are often incised with complex patterns, which leave impressions like watermarks in the cloth, viewable when held up to the light.

Plain and decorated *tapa* of various thicknesses and qualities was used throughout Polynesia for clothing, sails, mats, and ceremonial purposes, including wrapping the dead. *Tapa* was also used to cover wooden or wicker frames to make human effigies in the Marquesas and Rapa Nui, serving a purpose we still do not completely understand. In western Polynesia (Samoa and Tonga), very large pieces, 7–10 feet across and hundreds of feet long, were traditionally given in ceremonial exchanges of valuables and as gifts. Along with fine mats, *siapo* is still sometimes given on important ceremonial occasions. And *tapa* was widely used for clothing. Samoan men and women wore large pieces of *siapo* as wraparound skirts (*lavalava*) (see FIG. 28–19). Special chiefs, called talking chiefs, who spoke on behalf of the highest-ranking chief in the village council, wore special *tapa* skirts called *siapo vala* (**FIG. 28–17**).

Distinctive design styles for *tapa* evolved across the Pacific, even when the cloth used was essentially the same from one island to the next. It could be dyed bright yellow with turmeric

28–17 • TAPA (SIAPO VALA)
Samoa. 20th century. 58⅝″ × 57″ (149 × 145 cm). Auckland Museum, New Zealand. (AM 46892)

or brown with dyes made from nuts. It could also be exposed to smoke to turn it black or darker brown. Today, contemporary fabric paint is often used. Decorative designs were made through a variety of means from freehand painting to printing with tiny bamboo stamps, or using stencils, as is done in Fiji. This Samoan *siapo vala* has designs that were produced by first placing the cloth over a wooden design tablet, an **upeti**, and then rubbing pigment over the cloth to pick up the carved pattern. Subsequently, this lighter rubbed pattern was overpainted by hand. The result is a boldly patterned, symmetrical design.

RECENT ART IN OCEANIA

In the late 1960s and early 1970s, a cultural resurgence swept across the Pacific. Growing independence and autonomy throughout the region, the model of civil rights and other movements in the United States, and dramatic increases in tourism, among other factors, brought a new awareness of the importance of indigenous cultures. Many of them had been fundamentally changed, if not nearly destroyed, by colonial rule and missionary efforts to eradicate local customs and beliefs.

FESTIVAL OF PACIFIC ARTS

In the early 1970s, the South Pacific Commission conceived the idea of an arts festival that would promote traditional song and dance. The first Festival of Pacific Arts was held in 1972 in Fiji; subsequent festivals, held every four years, have been hosted by New Zealand, Papua New Guinea, Tahiti, Australia, Cook Islands, Samoa, New Caledonia, Palau, and American Samoa.

Musicians from the highlands of Papua New Guinea (**FIG. 28–18**) were among the more than 2,000 participants from 27 countries at the tenth festival at Pago Pago, American Samoa, in 2008. Carrying traditional drums, they wore elaborate headdresses topped with bird of paradise feathers and neck ornaments made from kina shells, a once valuable medium of exchange in New Guinea.

In the 36 years since their founding, the festivals have had an enormous impact on the arts. Many Pacific cultures now have their own festivals; in the Marquesas Islands one is held every four years. In an age of globalization and the Internet, festivals are one of the main ways in which young people become involved in, and learn about, their culture and heritage. However, the festivals are not without controversy: Some people are critical of an increasing level of professionalism and commercialism.

CENTRAL DESERT PAINTING

In Australia, indigenous artists have adopted canvas and acrylic paint for rendering imagery traditionally associated with more ephemeral media like body and sand drawing. Sand drawing is an ancient ritual art form that involves creating large colored designs on bare earth. Made with red and yellow ochers, seeds, and feathers arranged on the ground in symbolic patterns, they are used to

28-18 • MUSICIANS FROM PAPUA NEW GUINEA AT THE FESTIVAL OF PACIFIC ARTS
Pago Pago, American Samoa, 2008.

convey tribal knowledge to initiates. In 1971, several indigenous Pintubi men who were trained and initiated in sacred knowledge, and were living in government-controlled Papunya Tula in the Central Desert of Australia, were encouraged by non-indigenous art teacher Geoffrey Bardon to transform their ephemeral art into a painted mural on the school wall. The success of the public mural encouraged community elders to allow others to try their hand at painting. In Utopia, a neighboring community, it was the women who began painting in 1988 after success in tie-dyeing with fabrics. Art galleries, originally located in Alice Springs, spread the art form, and "dot paintings" were a worldwide phenomenon by the late 1980s. Paintings also became an economic mainstay for many Aboriginal groups in the central and western Australia desert. Although they are creating work for sale, the artists can paint only stories to which they have rights, and must be careful to depict only what a non-initiated person is allowed to know.

Clifford Possum Tjapaltjarri (c. 1932–2002), a founder of the Papunya Tula Artists Cooperative in 1972, gained an international reputation after a 1988 exhibition of his paintings. He worked with his canvases on the floor, as in traditional sand painting, using ancient patterns and colors, principally red and yellow, as well as touches of blue. The superimposed layers of concentric circles and undulating lines and dots in a painting like *Man's Love Story* (see "A Closer Look," page 878) create an effect of shifting colors and lights that was highly valued in a global art world.

The painting seems entirely abstract, but it actually conveys a narrative involving two mythical ancestors. One of these ancestors—represented by the white U shape on the left, seated in front of a water hole with an ants' nest indicated by concentric circles—came to Papunya in search of honey ants. His digging stick lies to his right, and white sugary leaves lie to his left. The straight white "journey line" represents his trek from the west. The second ancestor—represented by the brown-and-white U-shaped form—came from the east, leaving footprints, and sat down by another water hole nearby. He began to spin a hair string on a spindle (the form leaning toward the upper right of the painting) but was distracted by thoughts of the woman he loved, who belonged to a kinship group into which he could not marry. When she approached, he let his hair string blow away (represented by the brown flecks below him) and lost all his work. Four women (the dotted U shapes) came at night and surrounded the camp to guard the lovers. Rich symbolism also fills other areas of the painting: the white footprints are those of another ancestral figure following a woman, and the wavy line at the top is the path of yet another ancestor. The black, dotted oval area indicates the site where young men were taught this story. The long horizontal bars are mirages, while the wiggly shapes represent caterpillars, a source of food. Possum Tjapaltjarri painted numerous variations of this Dreaming story.

The painting is effectively a map showing the ancestors' journeys. To begin the work Possum Tjapaltjarri first painted the

A CLOSER LOOK | *Man's Love Story*

by Clifford Possum Tjapaltjarri. 1978. Synthetic polymer paint on canvas.
6'11¾" × 8'4¼" (2.15 × 2.57 m). Art Gallery of South Australia, Adelaide.
Visual Arts Board of the Australia Council Contemporary Art Purchase Grant, 1980

Designs may have multiple meanings. A circle can represent a water hole or ant hole, as here, but also a hole where the ancestral Spirit Beings exited and entered the earth, a person as viewed from above, or a campfire.

Honey ants are a sweet delicacy. A digging stick is used to open up the nest, exposing the ant colony so that the ants can be removed and eaten.

Hair is spun into string using a spindle that is rotated across the thigh. The string is surprisingly strong and was used for utilitarian and ceremonial purposes, depending on the region.

Synthetic polymer, or acrylic, paint replaces the earth-toned ochers used in the original sand paintings that provide the model for paintings such as this.

Women are important figures in the Dreaming stories and are represented in several places in this painting. Indigenous women artists paint their own stories, too, which usually center on food and food gathering.

The dots are made using a stick with a round, flat end that is dipped into the paint. Several people can work at the same time to fill in dotted areas.

 View the Closer Look for *Man's Love Story* on myartslab.com

---

landscape features and the impressions left on the earth by the figures—their tracks, direction lines, and the U-shaped marks they left when sitting. Then, working carefully, dot by dot, he captured the vast expanse and shimmering light of the arid landscape. The painting's resemblance to modern Western painting styles such as Abstract Expressionism, gestural painting, pointillism, or color field painting (see Chapter 32) is accidental. Possum Tjapaltjarri's work is rooted in the mythic narratives of the Dreaming. He and other contemporary artists working in both age-old and new media continue to create arts that express the deepest meanings of their culture.

SHIGEYUKI KIHARA

Many contemporary Pacific artists live in urban settings, were trained at colleges and universities, and create artworks in modern media that deal with a range of political issues, including the colonial legacy, discrimination, misappropriation, cultural identity, and land rights. Shigeyuki Kihara is a multimedia and performance artist of Samoan and Japanese descent who lives in New Zealand. In **ULUGALI'I SAMOA: SAMOAN COUPLE** (**FIG. 28–19**), she explores issues of culture, identity, stereotypes, authenticity, representation, and gender roles through a reappropriation of nineteenth- and early twentieth-century colonial photographs. Made in studio settings, colonial photographs were often turned into postcards depicting Pacific island men and women, both alone and in couples, the women as bare-breasted and sexualized "dusky maidens" and the men as emasculated "noble savages." Kihara confronts these stereotyped images of the South Seas in carefully restaged, sepia-toned photographs that, through ironic twists, also directly challenge the viewer's understanding of gender and gender roles.

In this photograph of a male and female couple both figures are clothed as they might have been in the nineteenth century, wearing large pieces of Samoan bark cloth (see FIG. 28-17), and holding traditional Samoan status objects—a plaited fan and a fly-whisk. Kihara herself poses as the native woman, but has also superimposed her own face, with wig and mustache, onto the body of the male figure. *Ulugali'i Samoa: Samoan Couple* is part of a series of photographs called "Fa'a fafine: In a Manner of a Woman." *Fa'a fafine* is the Samoan term for a biological male who lives as a woman, the "third gender" socially accepted historically throughout much of Polynesia (as in the Americas, see FIG. 27-23). Kihara is, herself, *fa'a fafine*, a transgender woman who lives and identifies in that gender role. In this photograph and the others in the series, she blurs stereotyped notions of who or what is male or female, original or copy, reality or perception. This work was part of the exhibition "Shigeyuki Kihara: Living Photographs," the first solo exhibition by a Samoan in the Metropolitan Museum of Art in New York. Her work and that of other urban artists draws on the richness of Pacific cultures while addressing global issues of the twenty-first century.

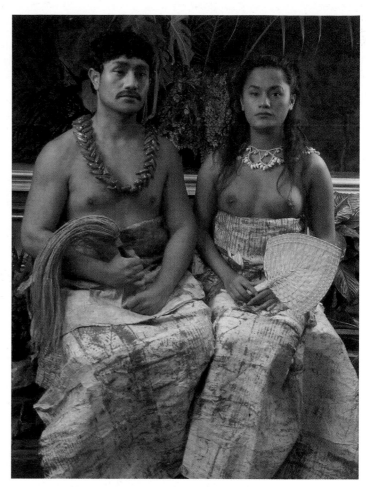

28-19 • Shigeyuki Kihara ULUGALI'I SAMOA: SAMOAN COUPLE
2004–2005. C-type photograph, edition 5, 31½″ × 23⅜″ (80 × 60 cm). Metropolitan Museum of Art, New York. Gift of Shigeyuki Kihara, 2009

THINK ABOUT IT

28.1 Explain how differences in environment, including available resources, affect the nature of the visual arts in the Pacific. Include architectural forms and body adornment in your answer.

28.2 How is the human body adorned and/or depicted in art across the Pacific? How do these adornments and depictions define or enhance status, authority, and gender roles?

28.3 Assess the importance of ancestors and the different ways in which ancestors are engaged, honored, or invoked through various Pacific art forms. Focus your answer on two works from two different cultural and geographic settings.

28.4 Discuss the impact of contact with Western society on the arts and cultures of the peoples of the Pacific. How are contemporary indigenous artists throughout the Pacific addressing the issues of their own time and place?

CROSSCURRENTS

FIG. 27–9   FIG. 28–17

The production of fabric was an important aspect of the culture of both Peru and Samoa. Although there are compelling similarities in the designs of these two cloths, their style, media, and their context of production are distinct in significant ways. Discuss these differences and how they relate to the cultural values and distinctive environments of the artists who made them and the societies that valued them.

✓•—|**Study** and review on myartslab.com

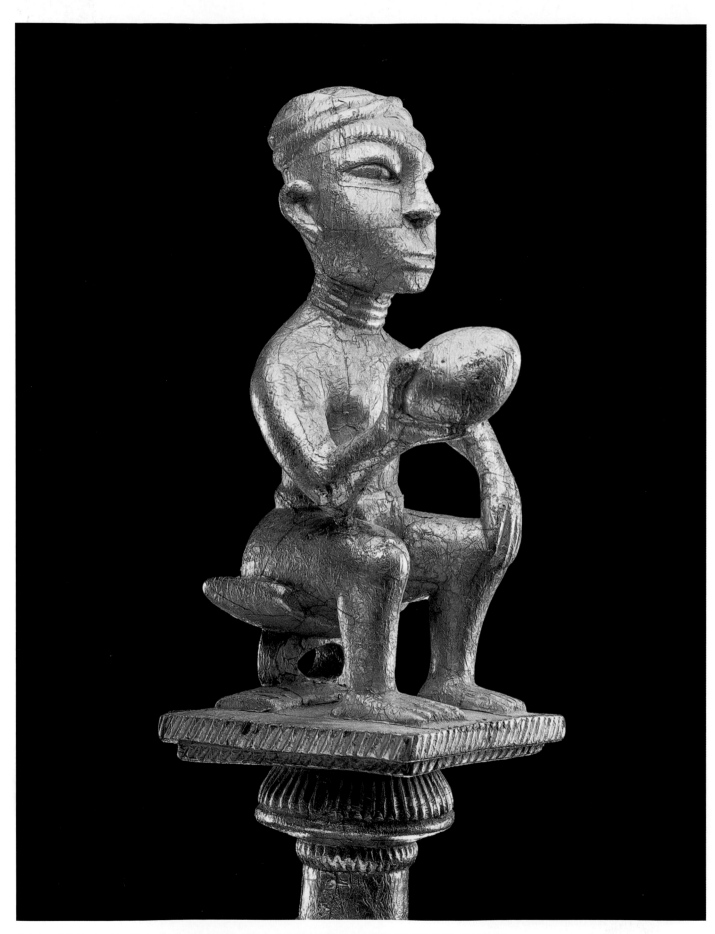

29-1 • Attributed to Kojo Bonsu **FINIAL OF A SPEAKER'S STAFF (OKYEAME POMA)**
Ghana. Ashanti culture, 1960s–1970s. Wood and gold, height 11¼″ (28.57 cm).
Gold of Africa Barbier-Mueller Museum.

Art of Africa in the Modern Era

Political power is like an egg, says an Ashanti proverb. Grasp it too tightly and it will shatter in your hand; hold it too loosely and it will slip from your fingers. Whenever the *okyeame* (spokesman) for one twentieth-century Ashanti ruler was conferring with that ruler or communicating the ruler's words to others, he held a staff with this symbolic caution on the use and abuse of power prominently displayed on the gold-leaf-covered finial (**FIG. 29–1**). Since about 1900 these advisors have carried staffs of office such as the one pictured here. The carved figure at the top illustrates a story that may have multiple meanings when told by a witty owner. This staff was probably carved in the 1960s or 1970s by Kojo Bonsu. The son of Osei Bonsu (1900–1976), a famous carver, Kojo Bonsu lives in the Ashanti city of Kumasi and continues to carve prolifically.

A staff or scepter is a nearly universal symbol of authority and leadership. Today in many colleges and universities a ceremonial mace is still carried by the leader of an academic procession, and it is often placed in front of the speaker's lectern, as a symbol of the speaker's authority. The Ashanti spokesmen who carry their image-topped staffs are part of this widespread tradition.

Since the fifteenth century, when the first Europeans explored Africa, objects such as this staff have been shipped back to Western collections and museums, where they were initially enjoyed as marvelous curiosities, and later catalogued as ethnographic artifacts of "primitive cultures." Toward the end of the nineteenth century, however, changes in Western thinking about African culture gradually led more and more people to appreciate the inherent aesthetic qualities of these unfamiliar objects and at last to embrace them fully as art. In recent years the appreciation of traditional African arts has been further enhanced through the exploration of their meaning from the point of view of the people who made and first experienced them.

If we are to understand African art such as this staff on its own terms, we must envision it out of the glass case of the museum where we usually encounter it, and playing its vital role in a human community. Indeed, this is true of any work of art produced anywhere in the world. When we recognize in an artwork the true expression of values and beliefs, our imaginations can allow us to cross a bridge to understanding.

LEARN ABOUT IT

29.1 Explore the variety of styles, media, and techniques used by artists across Africa during the nineteenth and twentieth centuries.

29.2 Understand the themes and symbols used in African societal rituals of leadership, initiation, divination, and death.

29.3 Evaluate the role of masquerade in African rites of passage such as initiation and funeral rituals.

29.4 Examine the relationship of African arts to the colonial experience.

((•— **Listen** to the chapter audio on myartslab.com

TRADITIONAL AND CONTEMPORARY AFRICA

The second-largest continent in the world, Africa is a land of enormous diversity (MAP 29–1). Geographically, it ranges from vast deserts to tropical rainforest, from flat grasslands to spectacular mountains and dramatic rift valleys. Cultural diversity in Africa is equally impressive. More than 1,000 African languages have been identified and grouped into five major linguistic families. Various languages represent unique cultures, with their own history, customs, and art forms.

Before the nineteenth century, the most important outside influence to pervade Africa had been the religious culture of Islam, which spread gradually and largely peacefully through much of west Africa and along the east African coast (see "Foundations of African Cultures," page 885). The modern era, in contrast, begins with the European exploration during the nineteenth century and subsequent colonization of the African continent, developments that brought traditional African societies into sudden and traumatic

contact with the "modern" world that Europe had largely created.

European ships first visited sub-Saharan Africa in the fifteenth century. For the next several hundred years, however, European contact with Africa was almost entirely limited to coastal areas, where trade, including the tragic slave trade, was carried out. Between the sixteenth and nineteenth centuries, over 10 million slaves were taken from Africa to colonies in North and South America and the Caribbean islands. Countries that participated in the Atlantic slave trade included Great Britain, Portugal, France, Spain, Denmark, Holland, and the United States.

During the nineteenth century, as the slave trade was gradually eliminated, European explorers began to investigate the unmapped African interior in earnest. They were soon followed by Christian missionaries, whose reports excited popular interest in the continent. Drawn by the potential wealth of Africa's natural resources, European governments began to seek territorial concessions from African rulers. Diplomacy soon gave way to force, and toward the end of the century competition among rival European powers fueled the so-called Scramble for Africa, during which England, France, Germany, Belgium, Italy, Spain, and Portugal raced to lay claim to whatever part of the continent they could. By 1914 virtually all of Africa had fallen under colonial rule.

Public and private collections of African art grew rapidly in size during this period. This was due not only to geographic exploration and colonial expansion, but also to the development of anthropology as a field of study. Artifacts from various African cultures became instruments through which university professors and museum curators could explain human development in purely evolutionary terms. Museums and collectors competed with one another to collect everywhere and as quickly as possible, believing that "traditional" African cultures were being rapidly altered by the colonial experience. As territory was subsumed under European control, vast quantities of art objects flowed into European city, state, and national collections.

Objects also entered Western collections through conflict. For example, when a British expedition headed by the newly appointed Acting Council-General, James Phillips, embarked on a mission to discuss the trade agreement with the *oba* of Benin City, he was told he could not meet with the king because he was engaged in an important annual ceremony honoring his ancestors. Phillips refused to postpone his visit and the expedition was attacked, without the king's knowledge, by a group headed by two chiefs; all but two expedition members were killed. A punitive expedition was launched in

29-2 • MEMBERS OF THE BRITISH PUNITIVE EXPEDITION IN THE BENIN PALACE IN 1897 WITH OBJECTS FROM THE ROYAL TREASURY

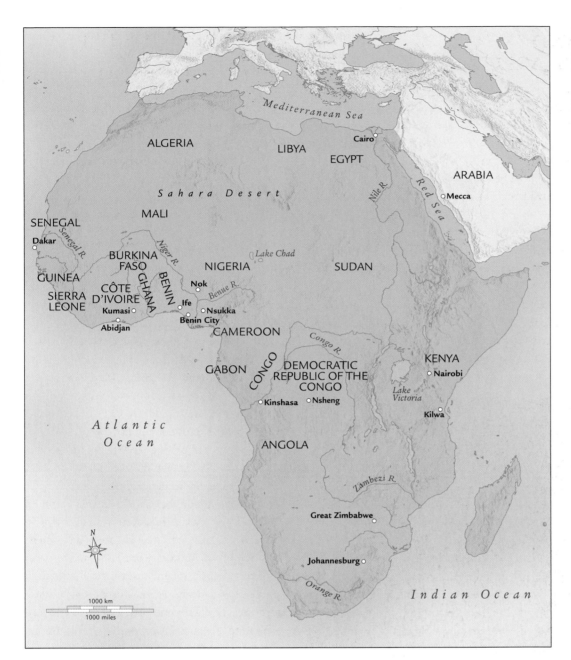

MAP 29-1 • PRESENT-DAY AFRICA

The vast continent of Africa is home to over 50 countries and innumerable cultures.

1897 by the British (**FIG. 29-2**) which resulted the destruction of much of the town, including the palace, and the seizing of over 2,000 antiquities—nearly the entire store of artifacts from the royal palace. The king was deposed and sent into exile, and his successor only assumed the throne in 1914. The antiquities were taken to Europe and auctioned to defray the costs of the expedition and provide pensions for those who had been ambushed or their survivors. These objects are now dispersed in museums and private collections throughout the world.

Changes in Western thinking about art gradually led people to appreciate the aesthetic qualities of African "artifacts" and finally to embrace them fully as art. The earliest collections of African art were, for the most part, acquired by museums of natural history or ethnography, which exhibited the works as curious artifacts of "primitive" cultures. By the latter half of the twentieth century, art museums, both in Africa and in the West, began to collect African

art seriously and methodically. Today, these collections afford us a rich sampling of African art created for the most part in the nineteenth and twentieth centuries.

In the years following World War I, nationalistic movements resisting European incursion arose across Africa. Their leaders generally did not advocate a return to earlier forms of political organization but rather demanded the transformation of colonial divisions into modern nation-states governed by Africans. From the 1950s through the mid 1970s, one colony after another gained its independence, and the present-day map of Africa took shape. Today, the continent is composed of over 50 independent countries.

While African societies were profoundly disrupted during the colonial period, numerous tribal or ethnic-based societies persist, both within and across contemporary political borders, and art continues to play a vital role in the spiritual and social life of the community. This chapter explores African art in light of how

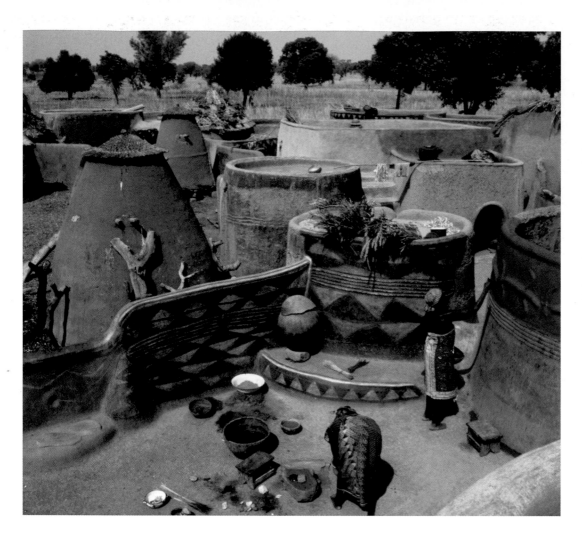

Among the Nankani people, creating living areas is a cooperative but gender-specific project. Men build the structures, women decorate the surfaces. The structures are also gendered. The round dwellings shown here are women's houses located in an interior courtyard; men occupy rectangular flat-roofed houses. The bisected lozenge design on the dwelling to the left is called *zalanga*, the name for the braided sling that holds a woman's gourds and most treasured possessions.

it addresses some of the fundamental concerns of human existence. Works of art are often directly related to the commemoration of significant rites of passage such as procreation and birth, initiation to adulthood, socialization in adult life, and death. While political leaders throughout the world use art to express their authority and status, in Africa community leaders are thought to connect the living community with the spirit world. In this regard, African art often especially idealizes the spirits of community leaders and deceased persons, who are expected to mediate between the temporal and supernatural worlds to help achieve well-being both for themselves and for the entire community. In these contexts, art is often intended to help mediate aid and support from a supernatural world of ancestors and other spirit forces. These concerns—rather than geographical region or time frame—form the backdrop against which we look at artworks in this chapter, as African art can be more fully understood within contexts of production and use.

Generally, the full meaning of traditional works of art can only be realized in the context of their use. For instance, when masked dancers perform within a specific ceremonial event, the mask itself—which we generally see isolated as an artwork in a museum—is only one part of a temporal process that most fully reveals its meaning in performance.

DOMESTIC ARCHITECTURE

Shelter is a basic human concern, yet, as we have seen, different cultures approach its design and construction in different ways, ways that often help us understand cultural values and priorities. The farming communities of the Nankani people in the border area between Burkina Faso and Ghana, in west Africa, have developed a distinctive painted architecture. The earthen buildings of their walled compounds are low and single-storied, with either conical roofs or flat roofs that form terraces. Each compound is surrounded by a defensive wall with a single entrance on the west side. Each building inside the enclosure is arranged so that it has a direct view of the entrance. Some buildings are used only by men, others only by women. For example, Nankani men are in charge of the ancestral shrine near the entrance of the compound, the corral for cattle, and the granary; they have rectangular houses. The inner courtyards, outdoor kitchen, and round houses are women's areas (**FIG. 29-3**). Men build the compound; women paint the buildings inside and out.

The women decorate the walls with horizontal molded ridges called *yidoor* ("rows in a cultivated field") and long eye ("long life"), to express good wishes for the family. They paint the walls with rectangles and squares divided diagonally to create triangular patterns that contrast with the curvature of the walls. The painted

Africa was the site of one of the great civilizations of the ancient world: Egypt developed along the fertile banks of the Nile River during the fourth millennium BCE and endured for 3,000 years. Egypt's rise coincided with the emergence of the Sahara—now the largest desert in the world—from the formerly lush grasslands of northern Africa. Some of the oldest-known African art, images inscribed and painted in the mountains of the central Sahara beginning around 8000 BCE, bear witness to this gradual transformation and how it affected the lives of the pastoral peoples who once lived in the region.

As the grassland dried up, its populations migrated in search of pasture and arable land. Many probably made their way to the Sudan, the broad band of savanna south of the Sahara. During the sixth century BCE, knowledge of iron smelting spread across the Sudan, enabling larger and more complex societies to emerge, including the ironworking Nok culture, which arose in present-day Nigeria around 500 BCE and lasted until about 200 CE. Terra-cotta figures created by Nok artists are the earliest-known sculpture from sub-Saharan Africa.

Farther south, in present-day Nigeria, a remarkable culture developed in the city of Ife, which rose to prominence around 800 CE. There, from roughly 1000 to 1400, a tradition of naturalistic sculpture in bronze and terra cotta flourished. Ife was, and remains, the sacred city of the Yoruba people. According to legend, Ife artists brought the techniques of bronze casting to the kingdom of Benin, and from 1170 to the present century, Benin artists in the service of the court created numerous works in bronze, at first in the naturalistic style of Ife, then in an increasingly stylized and elaborate manner.

With the Arab conquest of North Africa during the seventh and eighth centuries, Islamic travelers and merchants became regular visitors to the Sudan. Largely through their writings, we know of the powerful west African empires of Ghana and Mali, which flourished successively from the fourth through the sixteenth centuries along the great bend in the Niger River. Both grew wealthy by controlling the flow of African gold and forest products into the lucrative trans-Sahara trade. The city of Jenné, in Mali, served not only as a commercial hub but also as a prominent center of Islam.

Meanwhile, since before the Common Era, peoples along the coast of east Africa had participated in a maritime trade network that ringed the Indian Ocean and extended east to the islands of Indonesia. Over time, trading centers arose along the coastline, settled by Arab, Persian, and Indian merchants as well as Africans. By the thirteenth century these settlements were important port cities, and a new language, Swahili, had developed from the longtime mingling of Arabic with local African languages. Peoples of the interior organized extensive trade networks to funnel goods to these ports. From 1000 to 1500 many of these interior routes were controlled by the Shona people from Great Zimbabwe. The extensive stone palace compound there stood in the center of a city of 10,000 people at its height. Numerous cities and kingdoms, often of great wealth and opulence, greeted the astonished eyes of the first European visitors to Africa at the end of the fifteenth century.

---

patterns are called braided sling, broken pottery, broken gourd, and sometimes, since the triangular motifs can be seen as pointing up or down, they are called filed teeth. The same geometric motifs are used on pottery and baskets, and for scarification of the skin. When people decorate themselves, their homes, and their possessions with the same patterns, art serves to enhance cultural identity.

CHILDREN AND THE CONTINUITY OF LIFE

Among the most fundamental of human concerns is the continuation of life from one generation to the next. In some African societies children are especially important: Not only do they represent the future of the family and the community, but they also provide a form of "social security," guaranteeing that parents will have someone to care for them when they are old.

In the often harsh and unpredictable climates of Africa, human life can be fragile. In some areas half of all infants die before the age of 5, and the average life expectancy may be as low as 40 years. In these areas women bear many children in hopes that at least a few will survive into adulthood, and failure to have children is a disaster for a wife, her husband, and her husband's lineage. Women who have had difficulty bearing children appeal for help with special offerings or prayers, often involving the use of art.

YORUBA TWIN FIGURES The Yoruba people of southwestern Nigeria have one of the highest rates of twin births in the world. The birth of twins is a joyful occasion, yet it is troubling as well, for twins are more delicate than single babies, and one or both may well die. Many African peoples believe that a dead child continues its life in a spirit world and that the parents' care and affection may reach it there, often through the medium of art. When a Yoruba twin dies, parents often consult a diviner, a specialist in ritual and spiritual practices, who may tell them that an image of a twin (*ere ibeji*) must be carved to serve as a dwelling place for the deceased twin's spirit (**FIG. 29–4**).

When the image is finished, the mother brings the artist gifts. Then, carrying the figure as she would a living child, she dances home accompanied by the singing of neighborhood women. She places the figure in a shrine in her bedroom and lavishes care upon it, feeding it, dressing it with beautiful textiles and jewelry, anointing it with cosmetic oils. The Yoruba believe that the spirit of a dead twin, thus honored, is appeased and will look with favor on the surviving family members.

The twins here are female. They may be the work of the Yoruba artist Akiode, who died in 1936. Like most objects that Africans produce to encourage the birth and growth of children, the figures emphasize health and well-being. They have beautiful, glossy surfaces to suggest that they are well fed, as well as marks of

29-4 • TWIN FIGURES (ERE IBEJI)
Nigeria. Yoruba culture, 20th century. Wood, height 7⅞″ (20 cm). The University of Iowa Museum of Art, Iowa City. The Stanley Collection (x1986.489 and x1986.488)

As with other African sculpture, patterns of use result in particular signs of wear. The facial features of *ere ibeji* are often worn down or even obliterated by repeated feedings and washings. Camwood powder applied as a cosmetic builds to a thick crust in areas that are rarely handled, and the blue indigo dye regularly applied to the hair eventually builds to a thin layer of color.

adulthood, such as elaborate hairstyles and scarification patterns, that will one day be achieved. They represent hope for the future, for survival, and for prosperity.

CHILDREN, ART, AND PERFORMANCE In sub-Saharan Africa, as elsewhere, children from an early age are intensely interested in adult roles and activities, including art making and the performative arts. In many societies a child's link to a particular artistic or craft activity is fixed. For example, in Africa, wood carving is universally a male-dominated activity, while women are most often involved in pottery production, and individual children may be apprenticed to a wood carver or potter according to their gender. But, even beyond such formal apprenticeships, children are especially interested in the festive activities of community life, such as masquerade. While mask making and masquerade performance are usually controlled by adult associations, children are given space at the edges of events to experiment with their home-made masks and costumes. Yoruba masquerades such as Gelede or Egungun are often organized so that children perform first (**FIG.**

29-5). Some families even purchase or make elaborate costuming for their children in a similar style to that worn by adults. Adults view these early forays into masquerade as a training ground. As children perform, they are encouraged and gently corrected from the sidelines by family members. The Yoruba of Nigeria, especially, place a significant value on the training of children in adult performance and aesthetic forms, and children are encouraged to perform from an early age.

INITIATION

In contemporary North America, initiation into the adult world is extended over several years and punctuated by numerous rites, such as being confirmed in a religion, earning a driver's license, and graduating from high school. These steps all involve acquiring the knowledge society deems appropriate and accepting the corresponding responsibilities. In other cultures, initiation can take other forms. The acquisition of knowledge can be supplemented

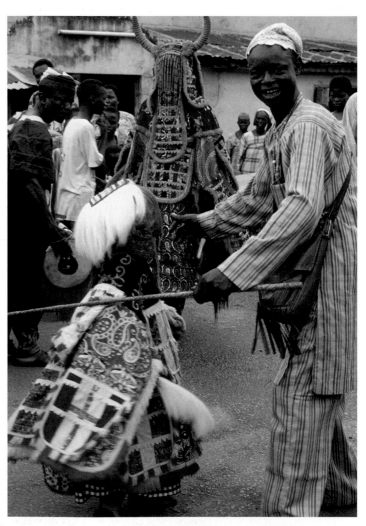

29-5 • ELDER GUIDING SMALL BOY IN EGUNGUN PERFORMANCE WHILE ADULT EGUNGUN PERFORMER LOOKS ON
Nigeria. Yoruba culture, 1986. National Museum of African Art, Smithsonian Institution, Washington, DC. Eliot Elisofon Photographic Archive, Henry John Drewal and Margaret Thompson Drewal Collection (1992-028-02691)

by trials of endurance to prove that candidates are equal to the responsibilities of adult life.

MASKS OF BWA INITIATION The Bwa people of central Burkina Faso initiate young men and women into adulthood following the onset of puberty. The initiates are first separated from younger playmates by being "kidnapped" by older relatives, though their disappearance is explained in the community by saying that they have been devoured by wild beasts. The initiates remove their clothing and sleep on the ground without blankets. Isolated from the community, they are instructed about the world of nature spirits and about the masks that represent them. They learn of the spirit each mask represents, and they memorize the story of each spirit's encounter with the founding ancestors of the clan. They also learn how to construct costumes from hemp to be worn with the masks, and they learn the songs and instruments that accompany the masks in performance. Only boys wear each mask in turn and learn the dance steps that express the character and personality each mask represents. Returning to the community, the initiates display their new knowledge in a public ceremony. Each boy performs with one of the masks, while the girls sing the accompanying songs. At the end of the mask ceremony the young men and young women rejoin their families as adults, ready to marry, to start farms, and to begin families of their own.

Most Bwa masks depict spirits that have taken an animal form, such as crocodile, hyena, hawk, or serpent. Others represent spirits in human form. Among the most spectacular masks, however, are those that represent spirits that have taken neither human nor animal form. Crowned with tall, narrow planks (**FIG. 29-6**), these masks are covered in abstract patterns that are easily recognized by the initiated. The white crescent at the top represents the quarter moon, under which the initiation is held. The white triangles below represent bull roarers—sacred sound-makers that are swung around the head on a long cord to recreate spirit voices. The large central X represents the scar that every initiated Bwa bears as a mark of devotion. The horizontal zigzags at the bottom represent the path of the ancestors and symbolize adherence to ancestral ways. That the path is difficult to follow is clearly conveyed. The curving red hook that projects in front of the face is said to represent the beak of the hornbill, a bird associated with the supernatural world and believed to be an intermediary between the living and the dead. The mask thus proudly announces the initiate's passage to adulthood while encoding secrets of initiation in abstract symbols of proper moral conduct.

29-6 • FIVE MASKS IN PERFORMANCE
Dossi, Burkina Faso. Bwa culture, 1984. Wood, mineral pigments, and fiber, height approx. 7′ (2.13 m).

The Bwa have been making and using such masks since well before Burkina Faso achieved its independence in 1960. We might assume their use is centuries old, but in this case, the masks are a comparatively recent innovation. The elders of the Bwa family who own these masks state that they, like all Bwa, once followed the cult of the spirit of Do, who is represented by masks made of leaves. In the last quarter of the nineteenth century, the Bwa were the targets of slave raiders from the north and east. Their response to this new danger was to acquire wooden masks from their neighbors, for such masks seemed a more effective and powerful way of communicating with spirits who could help them. Thus, faced with a new form of adversity, the Bwa sought a new tradition to cope with it.

👁 **Watch** a video of the Bwa masks in a performance on myartslab.com

INITIATION TO WOMANHOOD IN WEST AFRICA
Among the Mende, Temne, Vai, and Kpelle peoples of Sierra Leone, the initiation of girls into adulthood is organized by a society of older women called Sande or Bondo. The initiation culminates with a ritual bath in a river, after which the initiated return to the village. At the ceremony, the Sande women wear black gloves and stockings, black costumes of shredded raffia fibers that cover the entire body, and black masks called *nowo* or *sowei* (**FIG. 29-7**).

With its glossy black surface, high forehead, elaborately plaited hairstyle decorated with combs, and refined facial features, the mask represents ideal female beauty. The mask is worn by a senior member of the women's Sande society whose responsibility it is to prepare Sande girls for their adult roles in society, including marriage and child rearing. The meanings of the mask are complex. It has been related to the chrysalis of a certain African butterfly, with the creases at the base of the mask representing its body segments. Thus, the young woman entering adulthood is like a butterfly emerging from its cocoon. The comparison extends even further, for just as the butterfly feeds on the toxic sap of

the milkweed to make itself poisonous to predatory birds, so the medicinal powers of the Sande society are believed to protect the young women from danger. The creases may additionally refer to the concentric waves that radiate outward as the initiate emerges from the river to take her place as a member of the adult community.

***BWAMI* ASSOCIATION AMONG THE LEGA** A ceremony of initiation may also accompany the achievement of other types of membership. Among the Lega people, who live in the dense forests between the headwaters of the Congo River and the great lakes of east Africa, the political system is based on a voluntary association called *bwami*, which comprises six levels or grades. Some 80 percent of Lega men belong to *bwami*, and all aspire to the highest grade. Women can also belong to *bwami*, although not at a higher grade than their husbands.

Promotion from one grade of *bwami* to the next takes many years. It is based not only on a candidate's character but also on his or her ability to pay the initiation fees, which increase dramatically with each grade. No candidate for any level of *bwami* can pay the fees without assistance and must enlist the help of relatives to provide the necessary payment, which may include cowrie shells, goats, wild game, palm oil, clothing, and trade goods. Thus, the ambition to move from one level of *bwami* to the next encourages a harmonious community, for all must stay on good terms with other members of the community if they are to advance.

Bwami initiations into advanced grades are held in the plaza at the center of the community in the presence of all members.

29-8 • BWAMI MASK (LUKWAKONGO)
Democratic Republic of Congo. 20th century. Wood, plant fiber, and pigment, height 22¾″ (57.5 cm). Fowler Museum of Cultural History, University of California in Los Angeles.

Dances and songs are performed, and the values and ideals of the appropriate grade are explained through proverbs and sayings. These standards are illustrated by natural or crafted objects, which are presented to the initiate as signs of membership. At the highest two levels of *bwami*, such objects include exquisitely made small masks and sculpted figures.

The mask in **FIGURE 29-8** is associated with *yananio*, the second-highest grade of *bwami*. Typical of Lega masks, the head is fashioned as an oval into which is carved a concave, heart-shaped face with narrow, raised features. The masks are often colored white with clay and fitted with a long beard made of plant fibers. Too small to cover the face, they are displayed in other ways—held in the palm of a hand, for example, or attached to a thigh. Each means of display recalls a different value or saying, so that one mask may convey a variety of meanings. Generally, the masks symbolize continuity between the ancestors and the living community and are thought to be direct links to deceased relatives and past members of *bwami*.

***KIKAKU* OF THE NKANU PEOPLES** During the late nineteenth and early twentieth century, Nkanu peoples residing in the Democratic Republic of Congo and Angola celebrated the completion of coming-of-age initiation rites (*nkanda*) by creating brightly painted figurative sculpture and decorated wall panels adorned with human and animal figures, displayed in a *kikaku*—a three-sided roofed enclosure built at a crossroads near the initiation campground. These displays reinforced the values taught during *nkanda* and announced to the community that initiation was coming to a close—that their children would soon be home.

The *kikaku* resembled a stage. Wall panels were carved, painted, and attached to its back and sides, and sculpted figures were placed in front of the wall panels on the floor of the structure. The *kikaku* wall panels were brightly colored with symbolically charged patterns that conveyed specific meanings associated with the initiation ritual (**FIG. 29-9**). European colonial officials were a favorite subject. Their depictions were considered "portraits" of specific individuals, included distinguishing characteristics such as costume and hairstyle—often ridiculing officials who were despised for their cruelty or because of their dalliances with Nkanu women. These caricatures became a means of confronting colonial domination without openly attacking colonial officials, which would have undoubtedly led to severe repercussions.

The wall panels here depict a central colonial administrator flanked by two figures representing Congolese men who served in the Force Publique, the Belgian colonial military force. One soldier wears an ammunition belt, while the other assumes the awkward stance of an initiate, required to balance on one leg. Both the stance and the painted patterns on the panels symbolize the virility and procreative capacity of the initiate upon the successful completion of *nkanda*. After the initiation sequence, the *kikaku* and its contents were left to decay. A few individual pieces—but no entire *kikaku*—have been acquired by Western museums.

29-9 • INITIATION WALL PANELS
Democratic Republic of Congo. Nkanu peoples, Kimvula region, early 20th century. Wood, pigment, height 33⅜″ (84.8 cm).
National Museum of African Art, Smithsonian Institution, Washington, DC. Museum purchase (99-2-1)

THE SPIRIT WORLD

While African religious beliefs have been influenced by Christianity and Islam for hundreds of years, many African peoples still rely on local customs and belief systems to find the answers to universal human problems. Why does one child fall ill and die while another remains healthy? Why does one year bring rain and a bountiful crop, while the next brings drought and famine? People everywhere confront these fundamental and troubling questions. In many African belief systems, a supreme creator god is not thought to be fundamentally involved in the daily lives of humans. Instead, numerous subordinate spirit forces are believed to be ever-present and involved in human affairs. For instance, such spirits may inhabit agricultural fields, the river that provides fish, the forest that is home to game, or the land that must be cleared in order to build a new village. Families, too, may acknowledge the existence of ancestral spirits. These spirits control success and failure in life, and if a proper relationship is not maintained with them, harm in the form of illness or misfortune can befall an individual, a family, or an entire community.

***NKISI NKONDE* OF THE KONGO** To communicate with these all-important spirits, many African societies rely on a specialist, such as a diviner who serves as a link between the supernatural and human worlds, opening the lines of communication through such techniques as prayer, sacrifice, offerings, ritual performance, and divination. Sometimes art plays a role in the diviner's dealings with the spirit world, giving visible identity and personality to what is imaginary and intangible (see "Divination Among the Chokwe," page 893). *Minkisi* (the plural of *Nkisi*, a Kikongo word meaning "container") are objects harnessing spirit forces or powers, and were made by the Kongo and Songye peoples of the Democratic Republic of Congo, primarily during the nineteenth and early to mid twentieth centuries, to alleviate illness, protect vulnerable individuals, and bring success in hunting, trade, and other endeavors. The more specialized *Nkisi Nkonde* object served a divinatory and judicial function to seek out wrongdoers and punish them for their misdeeds (see "A Closer Look," page 894). A *Nkisi Nkonde* began as an unadorned wooden figure, often in human or animal form. It was commissioned by a diviner or chief on behalf of his society if it had encountered some adversity. The diviner prescribed medicinal ingredients (*bilongo*) from the plant, animal, and mineral worlds, which activated the object with potent earthly and supernatural powers. A *Nkisi Nkonde* served an important public function as an impartial arbiter of justice in smaller villages where European colonial rule had removed local judicial authorities to the capital cities. Two warring rural communities, for example, might agree to end their conflict by swearing an oath of peace and then driving a nail into the *Nkisi Nkonde* to seal the agreement. Should either party break the oath, it was believed that the *Nkisi Nkonde* would avenge the wronged party by meting out an appropriate punishment to the offender.

29-10 • SPIRIT SPOUSE (BLOLO BLA)
Ivory Coast. Baule culture, early–mid 20th century. Wood, glass beads, gold hollow beads, plant fiber, white pigment, encrustation, height 19¼″ (48.9 cm). National Museum of African Art, Smithsonian Institution, Washington, DC. Museum purchase (85-15-2)

SPIRIT SPOUSE OF THE BAULE Some African peoples conceive of the spirit world as a parallel realm in which spirits may have families, live in villages, attend markets, and possess personalities, complete with faults and virtues. The Baule people in the Ivory Coast believe that each of us lived in the spirit world before we were born. While there, we had a spirit spouse, whom we left behind when we entered this life. A person who has difficulty assuming his or her gender-specific role as an adult Baule—a man who has not married or achieved his expected status in life, for example, or a woman who has not borne children—may dream of his or her spirit spouse.

For such a person, the diviner may prescribe the carving of an image of the **SPIRIT SPOUSE** (**FIG. 29-10**)—a *blolo bla* (otherworld wife) for a man, or a *blolo bian* (otherworld husband) for a woman. The figures display the most admired and desirable marks of beauty so that the spirit spouses may be encouraged to enter and inhabit them. Spirit spouse figures are broadly naturalistic, with swelling, fully rounded musculature and careful attention to details of hairstyle, jewelry, and scarification patterns. They may be carved standing in a quiet, dignified pose or seated on a stool. The owner keeps the figure in his or her room, dressing it in beautiful textiles and jewelry, washing it, anointing it with oil, feeding it, and caressing it. Over time, the surface of the figure softens as it takes on a glossy sheen indicating the attention it has been given. The Baule hope that by caring for and pleasing his or her spirit spouse a balance may be restored that will free the individual's human life to unfold smoothly.

YORUBA DIVINATION While spirit beings are often portrayed in African art, major deities are generally considered to be far removed from the everyday lives of humans and are thus rarely depicted. Such is the case with Olodumare, the creator god of the Yoruba people of Nigeria.

The Yoruba have a sizable pantheon of lesser, but still important, gods (*orisha*). Two *orisha* are principal mediators: Orunmila who represents certainty, fate, order, and equilibrium; and his counterpart Eshu who represents uncertainty, disorder, and chance. Commonly represented in art, Eshu is a capricious and mischievous trickster who loves nothing better than to disrupt things that appear to be going well. The opposing forces of order and disorder are mediated through the agency of a diviner (*babalawo*) who employs a divination board (*opon ifa*) and its paraphernalia to reveal the causes of a client's problems (**FIG. 29-11**). The divination board is sprinkled with a white wood dust and the *orisha* Orunmila and Eshu are called to the divination by tapping the board with a special tapper. The *babalawo* throws 16 palm nuts and after each toss records the way the palm nuts have landed in the white wood dust on the divination board. Each configuration of the palm nuts relates to particular verses from a complex oral tradition also known as Ifa. As the selected verses are recited by the diviner, the client relates the verses to his or her own particular problems or concerns.

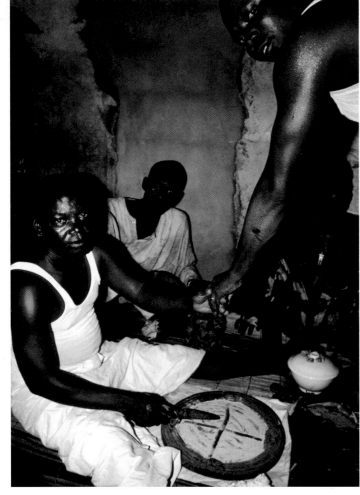

29-11 • IFA DIVINATION SESSION
Yoruba culture, Nigeria, 1982. National Museum of African Art, Smithsonian Institution, Washington, DC. Henry John Drewal and Margaret Thompson Drewal Collection (EEPA 1992-028-02016)

Eshu's image often appears on divination objects and in shrines employed by his worshipers. His image always appears at the top of the divination board, while other images along the edge of the board relate symbolically to the world of Ifa divination. Eshu is associated with two eternal sources of human conflict—sex and money—and is usually portrayed with a long hairstyle: The Yoruba consider long hair to represent excess libidinous energy and unrestrained sexuality. Figures of Eshu are usually adorned with long strands of cowrie shells, a traditional African currency. Shrines to him are erected wherever there is the potential for encounters that lead to conflict, especially at crossroads, in markets, or in front of banks. Eshu's followers hope their offerings will persuade the god to spare them the pitfalls he places in front of others.

LEADERSHIP

As in societies throughout the world, art in Africa is used to identify those who hold power, to validate their right to their authority as representatives of the family or community, and to communicate the rules for moral behavior that must be obeyed by all members of the society. This chapter opened with one example—a gold-and-wood spokesman's staff (see FIG. 29-1) from the culture of the Ashanti of Ghana, in west Africa. The Ashanti greatly admire fine language—one of their adages is, "We speak to the wise man in proverbs, not in plain speech"—and consequently their governing system includes the special post of spokesman to the ruler.

The Ashanti use gold not only for objects, such as the staff, that are reserved for the use of rulers, but also for jewelry, as do other peoples of the region. But for the Ashanti, who live in the middle of the richest goldfields of west Africa, gold was long a major source of power; for centuries they traded it, first via intermediaries across the Sahara to the Mediterranean world, then later directly to Europeans on the west African coast.

KENTE CLOTH The Ashanti are also renowned for the beauty of their woven textiles (**kente**) (**FIG. 29-13**). Weaving was introduced in Ghana sometime during the seventeenth century from neighboring regions of west Africa. Ashanti weavers—traditionally men—work on small, light, horizontal looms that produce long, narrow strips of cloth that are subsequently sewn together to form large rectangles of finished *kente* cloth. Weavers begin by laying out the long warp threads in brightly colored stripes. Today the threads are likely to be rayon. Formerly, however, they were cotton and later silk, which the Ashanti first procured in the seventeenth century by unraveling silk cloth obtained through European trade. Weft threads are woven through the warp to produce complex patterns. The example shown belongs to a type known as *faprenu*, with a dense double weave consisting of twice as many weft threads as warp threads.

Kente cloth was originally associated with royalty and produced under royal control. A man wore a single piece, about 6–7 feet by 12–13 feet, wrapped like a toga, with no belt and the right shoulder bare. Women wore two pieces—a skirt and a shawl. Even though its use is now more widespread, *kente* cloth is primarily reserved for festive attire worn at special occasions. The pattern in FIGURE 29-13 is known as *Oyokoman Adweneasa*, characterized by wide gold and green stripes set on deep red grounds. *Oyokoman* refers to the powerful Oyoka clan, and *Adweneasa* means "my skill is exhausted," a reference to the way the artist has woven elaborate patterns into every available area to the very edge of the fabric, until running out of space.

THE KUBA *NYIM* The Kuba people of the Democratic Republic of Congo also relate art and leadership. At the pinnacle of the political hierarchy sits the Kuba paramount ruler (*nyim*) whose residence was located approximately in the center of the Kuba region. The current *nyim* can trace his predecessors back to the founding of the kingdom in the seventeenth century. At the installation of a new monarch, a new capital city (*Nsheng*) is built that includes the residence of the *nyim* and his wives and children, as well as areas for other governmental functions, all surrounded by a high palisade.

Chokwe peoples of the Democratic Republic of Congo and Angola consult diviners (*nganga*) about problems such as death, illness, impotence, sterility, and theft. As the mediator between this world and the supernatural, the diviner's role is to ascertain the true meaning and underlying cause of an affliction or misfortune, and whether it is due to a conflict with human protagonists or with spirit forces. The diviner's ability to uncover the cause of a client's problems comes through the agency of powerful spirit forces and the efficacy of divinatory paraphernalia. A Chokwe *nganga*, utilizing a rattle to call the spirits to the divination, begins to shake a shallow covered basket (*ngombo ya kuse*kula) (**FIG. 29–12**) containing a variety of natural objects including small antelope horns, seeds, and minerals. The basket also contains a number of carved wooden objects representing humans (in various symbolic poses), animals, and other objects such as small models of masks and masked figures. The objects in the basket are tossed about as the basket is shaken and when finished the cover is removed to reveal the arrangement of the objects as they came to rest inside. The *nganga* interprets the results of multiple tosses to disclose the underlying cause of the client's problem and suggests what steps need to be taken to remedy the situation.

29-12 • DIVINATION BASKET (NGOMBO)
Democratic Republic of Congo and Angola. Chokwe peoples, mid 19th–early 20th century. Plant fiber, seed, stone, horn, shell, bone, metal, feather, and camwood, depth 12¹⁄₁₆″ (30.7 cm). National Museum of African Art, Smithsonian Institution, Washington, DC. Museum purchase (86-12-17.1)

29-13 • KENTE CLOTH
Ghana. Ashanti culture, c. 1980. Rayon, 10′3½″ × 7′1½″ (3.14 × 2.17 m). Fowler Museum of Cultural History, University of California in Los Angeles.

Power Figure (*Nkisi Nkonde*).
From the Democratic Republic of Congo. Kongo culture, 19th century. Wood, nails, pins, blades, and other materials, height 44″ (111.7 cm). The Field Museum, Chicago.

The *bilongo* (medicinal ingredients) may be placed on the head of the figure, thought to be an especially appropriate site to communicate with spirit forces.

Clients drive a nail, blade, or other pointed object into the figure to capture the *Nkonde*'s attention and prick it into action. The large number of objects driven into this *Nkonde* suggests that its powers were both formidable and efficacious.

This *Nkonde* stands in a pose called *pakalala*, a stance of alertness like that of a wrestler challenging an opponent. Other *Nkonde* figures hold a knife or spear in an upraised hand, ready to strike or attack.

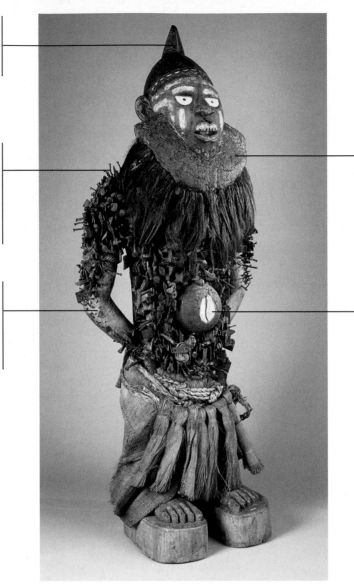

Bilongo may also be suspended in a packet from the figure's neck or waist or even placed into the figure's beard. The beard is associated with the powers that come with age and seniority.

Additional *bilongo* are inserted into a body cavity such as the figure's belly, as this is thought to be the seat of a person's life or soul. The term *mooyo* means both "belly" and "life."

 View the Closer Look for the Kongo *Nkisi Nkonde* on myartslab.com

Powerful individuals often lavish elaborate surface decoration on objects that belong to them to indicate their rank and prestige within the political and social hierarchy. In Kuba culture this happens with geometric decoration—woven on the walls of royal buildings (**FIG. 29-14**) and intricately carved on wooden drums, boxes, and other objects. It is also seen on the lavishly embroidered textiles for men and women and on regalia such as headdresses and jewelry that serve as prestige and festive attire for celebratory occasions. An eagle feather chief (*kum apoong*) displays sumptuous adornment at his investiture. Each element of regalia signifies a prerogative of an individual's titled position relative to the position of others within a complicated system of titleholding. Naturally the most extravagant adornment is worn by the paramount ruler, as can be seen in a photograph of the Kuba *nyim* taken in 1971 (**FIG. 29-15**). Textile display is also an essential aspect of funeral rituals where textiles are worn at celebratory dances and displayed on the body of the deceased. The textiles are subsequently buried in the deceased's grave, where the Kuba believe an individual remains for a period of time before being reborn.

29-14 • DECORATED BUILDING (SLEEPING ROOM FOR NYIM) IN THE ROYAL COMPOUND OF THE KUBA NYIM
Nsheng, Democratic Republic of Congo. 1980.

👁 Watch an architectural simulation about Kuba woven decoration on walls on myartslab.com

YORUBA PALACE ART The kings of the Yoruba people of Nigeria also manifested their authority and power through the large palaces in which they lived. In a typical palace plan, the principal rooms opened onto a veranda with elaborately carved posts facing a courtyard (**FIG. 29-16**). Elaborate carving also covered the palace doors. Among the most important Yoruba artists of the early twentieth century was Olowe of Ise (d. 1938), who carved doors and veranda posts for the rulers of the Ekiti-Yoruba kingdoms in southwestern Nigeria.

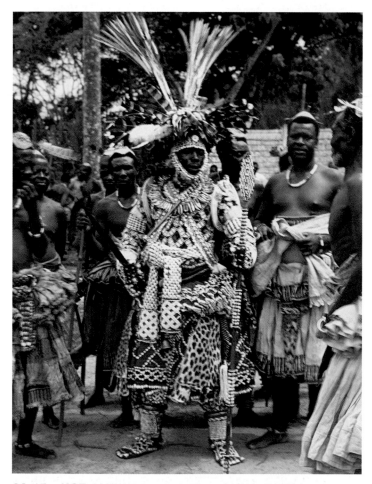

29-15 • KOT AMBWEEK IN CEREMONIAL DRESS
Democratic Republic of Congo. Photograph 1971. National Museum of African Art, Smithsonian Institution, Washington, DC. (EEPA EECL 2145)

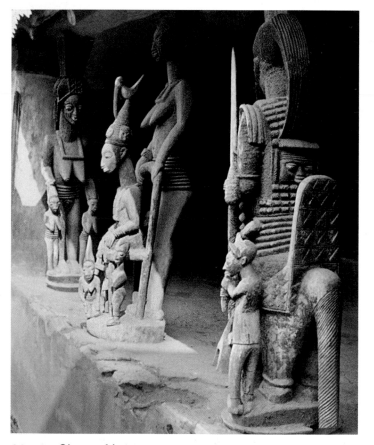

29-16 • Olowe of Ise **VERANDA POSTS INSTALLED IN THE COURTYARD OF THE PALACE OF THE OGAGA OF IKERE**
Nigeria. Yoruba culture, c. 1910–1914. Wood and pigment. Photograph 1964.

📖 **Read** the document related to Olowe of Ise on myartslab.com

The Kuba people of the Democratic Republic of Congo perform funerary masquerades to honor deceased members of the men's initiation society and high-ranking individuals who belonged to the community council of elders.

In the southern Kuba region, funeral rites for initiated men are often accompanied by the appearance of one or more masquerade figures on the day of interment of the deceased. On these occasions, initiation society members and family and friends of the deceased celebrate the departed's life while mourning his death. In part, funeral rites are elaborate because of the belief that the spirit of the recently deceased (*mwendu*) may bring harm to his family or community if his achievements and status in life are not acknowledged at the funeral. The *mwendu* may be angered for a variety of reasons. Perhaps outstanding debts were not paid and money or other goods were kept back by a family member. Or the deceased had asked for something to be buried with him and this request was not honored. Disrespect is most often shown if the deceased is not given a proper burial, one equal to his rank in life. For an initiated man, a funeral masquerade is mandatory in this region, and members of the community-based men's initiation society show their solidarity with the deceased and his spirit by performing a masquerade at his funeral.

Among the most spectacular masquerades performed in the Kuba region is that of *Ngady mwaash*—the name means literally "female mask" (**FIG. 29–17**). The mask is carved from wood, and attached to a framework covered with cloth and decorated with beads and shells that forms the top, sides, and back of the head.

Wooden ears, carved separately, are attached to the sides of the head. The face of the mask presents an exuberant blend of bold geometric patterns composed of contrasting areas of triangles and parallel lines. A triangular-shaped hat, identical to that worn by female diviners, is attached to the mask. The hat signifies that *Ngady mwaash* is invested with the power of nature spirits (*ngesh*) to whom Kuba diviners attribute their extraordinary powers.

The costume for *Ngady mwaash* is composed of a shirt and leggings made from animal hide or cloth, often extensively decorated with painted black-and-white triangles. Small wooden dowels attached to the front of the shirt represent breasts. Although wearing a woman's long embroidered skirt under a short decorated skirt affixed with a belt, *Ngady mwaash* is always performed by a man. Costume accessories include strands of beaded and shell-laden bandoliers that crisscross the chest and decorated arm- and legbands. The mask, costume, and accessories, as well as the fly-whisk that *Ngady mwaash* carries, represent wealth and high status.

29–17 • NGADY MWAASH MASK
Democratic Republic of Congo. Kuba peoples, late 19th–mid 20th century. Wood, pigment, glass beads, cowrie shells, fabric, and thread, height 12½″ (31.8 cm). The Art Institute of Chicago. (1982.1505)

29-18 • BWOOM MASKED DANCER AT THE FUNERAL OF AN INITIATED MAN
Democratic Republic of Congo. Southern Kuba peoples, 1982.

The funeral masquerade performance is held near the residence of the man who has died, just prior to burial. The perimeter of the dance ground is lined with family, friends, and onlookers who have come to bid a final farewell to the deceased and witness the performance. *Ngady mwaash* takes turns performing with another masked figure designated as male, such as the masked figure *Bwoom*.

The individual character or persona of male and female masked figures is fully realized during performance. *Bwoom*, who carries a short sword, exudes power and restrained aggression. The dancer employs lunging movements and quick short jabs with his sword, causing onlookers to suspect that he may suddenly lose control and harm someone. This feeling of apprehension is a constituent part of the performance style of *Bwoom*, and is a principal reason why community members look forward to masquerade with such anticipation. In contrast, the performance style of *Ngady mwaash* is decidedly nonthreatening, with graceful movements as the dancer's body, legs, arms, and hands move in fluid gestures. The differences in the performance styles of male and female masquerade figures parallel the difference in the dance styles of men and women in Kuba culture. The men's initiation society, which organizes funeral masquerades, expresses its control and dominance of ritual affairs in part through the contrasting performance styles of *Bwoom* and *Ngady mwaash* (**FIGS. 29-18, 29-19**).

29-19 • NGADY MWAASH MASKED DANCER AT THE FUNERAL OF AN INITIATED MAN
Democratic Republic of Congo. Southern Kuba peoples, 1982.

29-20 • Olowe of Ise PALACE DOOR
From the palace at Ise, Nigeria, Yoruba culture, c. 1904–1910. Wood and pigment, height 81½″ × width 34⅝″ × depth 6¼″ (207 × 88 × 15.9 cm). National Museum of African Art, Smithsonian Institution, Washington, DC. Gift of Dr. and Mrs Robert Kuhn (88-13-1)

figures. The relief is so high that the figures' upper portions are actually carved in the round. The energetic movement of the figures is set against an underlying decorative pattern. The entire surface of the doors was originally painted, but only traces of the original colors remain.

This door panel commemorates the *arinjale* (king) of Ise's reception of Major W.R. Reeve-Tucker, the first British traveling commissioner for the province, and his entourage. A separate door panel, in a private collection, presents the European entourage. In the second register of this panel, the *arinjale* appears on horseback wearing a conical crown and accompanied by court messengers. Other registers contain other members of the court—royal wives lifting their breasts (a gesture of generosity and affection performed by elder women), men carrying kegs of gunpowder, royal guards, and priests. The bottom register portrays a human sacrifice, with birds pecking at the corpse, and the two rows of heads on the left side of the panel may represent either ancestors of the *arinjale* or enemies taken in battle.

Olowe seems to have worked from the early 1900s until his death in 1938. Although he was famous throughout Yorubaland and called upon by patrons as distant as 60 miles from his home, few records of his activities remain, and only one European, Philip Allison, wrote of meeting him and watching him work. Allison described Olowe carving the iron-hard African oak "as easily as [he would] a calabash [gourd]."

DEATH AND ANCESTORS

In the view of many African peoples, death is not an end but a transition—the leaving behind of one phase of life and the beginning of another. Just as ceremonies mark the initiation of young men and women into the community of adults, so too they mark the initiation of the newly dead into the community of spirits. Like the rites of initiation into adulthood, death begins with a separation from the community, in this case the community of the living. A period of isolation and trial follows, during which the newly dead spirit may, for example, journey to the land of ancestors. Finally, the deceased is reintegrated into a community, this time the community of ancestral spirits. The living who preserve the memory of the deceased may appeal to his or her spirit to intercede on their behalf with nature spirits or to prevent the spirits of the dead from using their powers to harm (see "Kuba Funerary Mask," page 896).

Olowe carved the door panel for the royal palace at Ise (**FIG. 29-20**) as an asymmetrical composition, combining narrative and symbolic scenes in horizontal rectangular panels. Tall figures with bodies in profile turn their heads outward to confront the viewer. Their long necks and elaborate hairstyles make them appear even taller, unlike typical Yoruba sculpture which uses short, static

DOGON FUNERARY *DAMA* Among the Dogon people of Mali, in west Africa, a collective funeral rite called *dama*, is held every 12 to 13 years (**FIG. 29-21**). During *dama*, a variety of different masks perform to the sound of gunfire to drive the souls of the deceased from the village. Among the most common masks to perform is the *kanaga*, whose rectangular face supports a superstructure of planks that depict a woman, bird, or lizard with splayed legs.

For a deceased man, men from the community later engage in a mock battle on the roof of his home and participate in ritual hunts; for a deceased woman, the women of the community smash her cooking vessels on the threshold of her home. These portions of *dama* are reminders of human activities the deceased will no longer engage in. The *dama* may last as long as six days and include the performance of hundreds of masks. Because a *dama* is so costly, it is performed for several deceased elders at the same time. However, in certain Dogon communities frequented by tourists, *dama* performances have become more frequent as new masked characters are invented, including masks representing tourists holding wooden cameras or anthropologists holding notebooks in their hands. Dogon mask-makers produce additional masks that are offered for sale to tourists at the conclusion of the performance.

FANG ANCESTOR GUARDIAN The Fang, along with other peoples who live near the Atlantic coast from southern Cameroon through Rio Muni and into Gabon, shared a number of similar institutions and beliefs in which the skulls, bones, and relics of ancestors who had performed great deeds during their lifetimes were collected after burial and placed in a cylindrical bark container (*nsek-bieri*), which was preserved by the family. Deeds thus honored included victory in warfare, killing an elephant, being the first to trade with Europeans, bearing an especially large number of children, or founding a particular lineage or community. The bones and relics of deceased family members were thought to have special powers that could be drawn upon to aid the living with problems that confronted or threatened the family. Before colonial officials banned many ritual practices, ancestral spirits

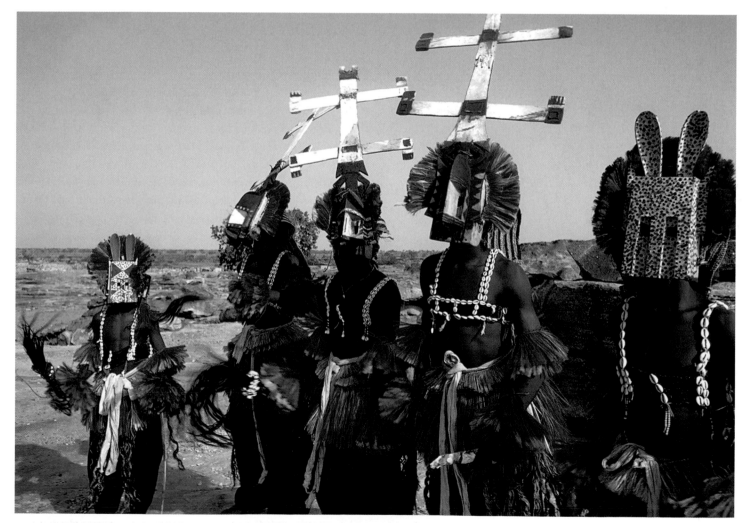

29-21 • KANAGA AND RABBIT MASQUERADE FIGURES AT DAMA
Mali. Dogon culture, 1959. National Museum of African Art, Smithsonian Institution, Washington, DC. (EEPA 3502)

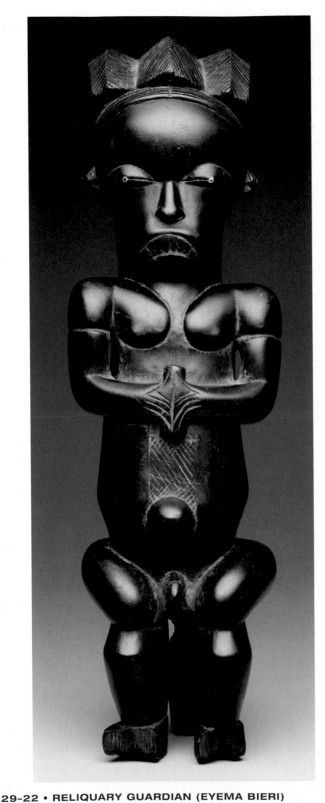

29-22 • RELIQUARY GUARDIAN (EYEMA BIERI)
Gabon. Fang people, Mvai group, mid–late 19th century. Wood, metal, and shell, height 21¼″ (53.97 cm). Dallas Museum of Art. The Eugene and Margaret McDermott Art Fund, Inc. (2000.3.MCD)

One authority on Fang culture suggests that *bieri* aim to achieve a balance between the opposing forces of chaos and order, male and female, pure and impure, powerful and weak. The Fang value an attitude of quiet composure, of reflection and tranquility—qualities embodied in the symmetry of the *bieri*, which communicates the calm and wisdom of the ancestor while also instilling awe and fear in those not initiated into the Fang religion.

represented by the reliquaries were regularly consulted on problems with fertility—failure in conceiving and bringing to term children—or with hunting and farming, or before embarking on a commercial venture.

As a point of focus for mediation between the ancestors and the living, the Fang placed a wooden sculpture called an *eyema bieri* on top of the container holding the relics. These sculptures functioned as points of contact for ancestral support and veneration and also as guardians to protect the relics from malevolent spirit forces (**FIG. 29-22**).

Bieri were carved in a number of different forms and styles. Some are large heads with long necks that are secured into the lid of the container, which represents the ancestral body. Other *bieri* were created as full figures with carefully arranged hairstyles, fully rounded torsos, and heavily muscled legs and arms. Here, the figure's firmly set jaw and powerfully built, muscular body exudes a sense of authority and confidence. These powerfully realized sculptures were often enhanced by the frequent application of cleansing and purifying palm oil over an extended period of time, producing a rich, glossy black surface that may literally exude oil.

CONTEMPORARY ART

The photographs of rituals and ceremonies in this chapter show ways in which African traditional arts have continued during the modern era. All of the photographs are somewhat dated, yet even today performances are staged in which the traditional types of masks appear. But Africa is ever-changing, and, as new experiences pose new challenges and offer new opportunities, African art moves with the times.

Perhaps the most obvious modern development in African art has been the adaptation of new materials to traditional forms. Some Yoruba, for example, have used photographs and children's brightly colored, imported plastic dolls in place of the traditional *ere ibeji*, images of twins, shown in FIGURE 29-4. The Guro people of Ivory Coast continue to commission delicate masks dressed with costly textiles and other materials, but they enliven them with brilliantly colored oil-based enamel paints. The Baule create brightly painted versions of spirit-spouse figures dressed as businessmen or soccer players.

Throughout the colonial period and especially during the years following World War II, many African artists trained in the techniques of European art. In the postcolonial era, numerous African artists have studied in Europe and the United States, and many have become internationally renowned through exhibitions of their work in galleries and museums around the world. Yet the diversity of influences on contemporary Africa makes it impossible to render a homogeneous view of what constitutes contemporary African art. As the art historian and curator Salah Hassan writes: "The development of a modern idiom in African art is closely linked to modern Africa's search for identity. Most contemporary works have apparent ties to traditional African folklore, belief

29-23 • Seydou Keïta UNTITLED
1952–1955. Gelatin-silver print, 24″ × 20″ (61 × 50.8 cm). Edition of ten.

Seydou Keïta said about his work, "It's easy to take a photo, but what really made a difference was that I always knew how to find the right position, and I never was wrong. Their head slightly turned, a serious face, the position of the hands … I was capable of making someone look really good. The photos were always very good. That's why I always say that it's a real art."

he specialized as a portraitist, taking unidealized and engaging photographs of the proud people of this newly independent nation. He was among the first to portray his own nation and people as prosperous and urban rather than objectified as ethnographic subjects, as seen in magazines such as *National Geographic*. In the image shown here (**FIG. 29-23**), the sitters occupy a visually luxurious space but are not confined by it. The heavy, strong patterns of the wife's clothing contrast with the stark white worn by her husband and child. Keïta's elegant composition monumentalizes individuals whose power and pride are communicated through their commanding poses and relaxed gestures. The sitters look out of the photograph with disarming frankness, inviting and returning our gaze, demanding that we see them as real people, as equals, with identities as multivalent and as complex as our own. While Keïta made his photographs for domestic consumption (his studio archive comprised over 10,000 negatives), he was "discovered" by the Western art world during the 1990s and is frequently exhibited in Europe and the United States.

EL ANATSUI OF GHANA The complex, multimedia work of El Anatsui affirms Africa's rich legacy with unexpected materials. Born in Ghana in 1944, Anatsui studied art in Kumasi where he took course work he describes as predominantly Western in orientation, while Ghana's own rich legacy was ignored. Following his own inclinations, he began to study Ghanaian surface design traditions as produced by Ewe and Ashanti textile artists. In 1975, Anatsui took a position in the Fine Arts Department of the University of Nigeria at Nsukka. There he found a like-minded spirit in Uche Okeke, who was intensely interested in revitalizing *uli*, an important Igbo surface design system. Anatsui began to create what would become a large body of work inspired by *uli* and other graphic systems using tools such as chain saws and blowtorches. More recently, while still concerned with the survival and transmission of inherited traditions, Anatsui began to appropriate cast-off objects he found in and around Nsukka, including broken and discarded mortars, large coconut graters, liquor-bottle caps, and aluminum labels from whiskey bottles to create revelatory art forms in a variety of media. These include immense wall sculptures that fold and undulate like textiles but are made from metal sewn together with copper wire (**FIG. 29-24**).

Although he lives in Nigeria, El Anatsui, like many contemporary African artists, also participates in international art events—including workshops, symposia, biennial exhibitions, and art festivals that dramatically invigorate our global visual culture. On the other hand, many other African artists have moved

systems and imagery. The only way to interpret or understand these works is in the light of the dual experience of colonialism and assimilation into Western culture in Africa. They reflect the search for a new identity."

SEYDOU KEÏTA OF MALI Photography was among earliest modern art media to be embraced broadly in Africa, and Seydou Keïta (c. 1921–2001) has become one of the best-known photographers. Trained as a carpenter, Keïta's interest in photography was serendipitously sparked by his uncle's gift of a Kodak Brownie Flash camera in 1935, and after using this unassuming equipment to hone his craft, he acquired a large-format camera and in 1948 opened his own studio in his hometown of Bamako, Mali. There

29-24 • El Anatsui
FLAG FOR A NEW WORLD POWER
2004. Found aluminum and copper wire, 16'4" × 14'9" (5 × 4.5 m). Private collection.

permanently to major European and American cities, which offer them increased opportunities for exposure to art dealers, museum curators, art critics, and the expanding base of public and private collectors of African contemporary art.

AFRICAN ARTISTS IN DIASPORA While many African artists are primarily influenced by their own culture and traditions, others—especially some who no longer live on the continent—seem entirely removed from African stylistic influences and yet still express the search for a new African identity in revelatory ways. Their experiences of movement, accommodation, and change often become important elements in their art making and form an additional basis for the interpretation of their work.

Julie Mehretu (**FIG. 29-25**) is an eminent example of this kind of artist. Born in Ethiopia in 1970, but having lived in Senegal and the United States, and now in New York City, Mehretu makes intensely energetic large-scale paintings and wall drawings. Her works speak not only to her own history of movement and change, but also to the transnational movement of myriad others uprooted by choice or by force as they create new identities in this increasingly turbulent period of globalization and change.

The underpinnings of her intricately layered canvases are architectural plans of airports, passenger terminals, and other places where people congregate and pass through during their lives. Layered and at times obscuring these architectural elements is an immense inventory of signs and markings influenced by cartography, weather maps, Japanese and Chinese calligraphy, tattooing, graffiti, and various stylized forms suggesting smoke and explosions borrowed from cartoons, comic books, and anime. The ambiguous reading of the paintings as either implosion and chaos or explosion and regeneration gives the works visual and conceptual complexity. Mehretu explains that she is not interested in

29-25 • Julie Mehretu DISPERSION
2002. Ink and acrylic on canvas, 90″ × 144″ (228.6 × 365.8 cm). Collection of Nicolas and Jeanne Greenberg Rohatyn, New York.

👁—▕**Watch** a video about Julie Mehretu on myartslab.com

describing or mapping specific locations but "in the multi-faceted layers of place, space, and time that impact the formation of personal and communal identity." Mehretu's concerns echo those of other contemporary African artists whose identification with the continent becomes increasingly complex as they move from Africa and enter a global arena.

THINK ABOUT IT

29.1 Compare the representation of the human figure in FIGURES 29–10 and 29–22. How could the differences in style be related to the function of these two works and their origin in distinct cultures?

29.2 Explain the use of art during African divination rituals and discuss one work from the chapter that is used in the practice.

29.3 Explain the role of masquerade in African art by analyzing the rite-of-passage ceremony of the Bwa culture in Burkina Faso.

29.4 Analyze the initiation wall panels shown in FIGURE 29–9 and discuss how the artist addresses the experience of colonialism.

CROSSCURRENTS

FIG. 28–19

FIG. 29–23

How do these two photographers from Samoa and Mali—whose work has received attention and acclaim within a contemporary global art world—address the specific concerns of their own cultural situation and at the same time evoke concerns shared by people around the world?

✓•—▕**Study** and review on myartslab.com

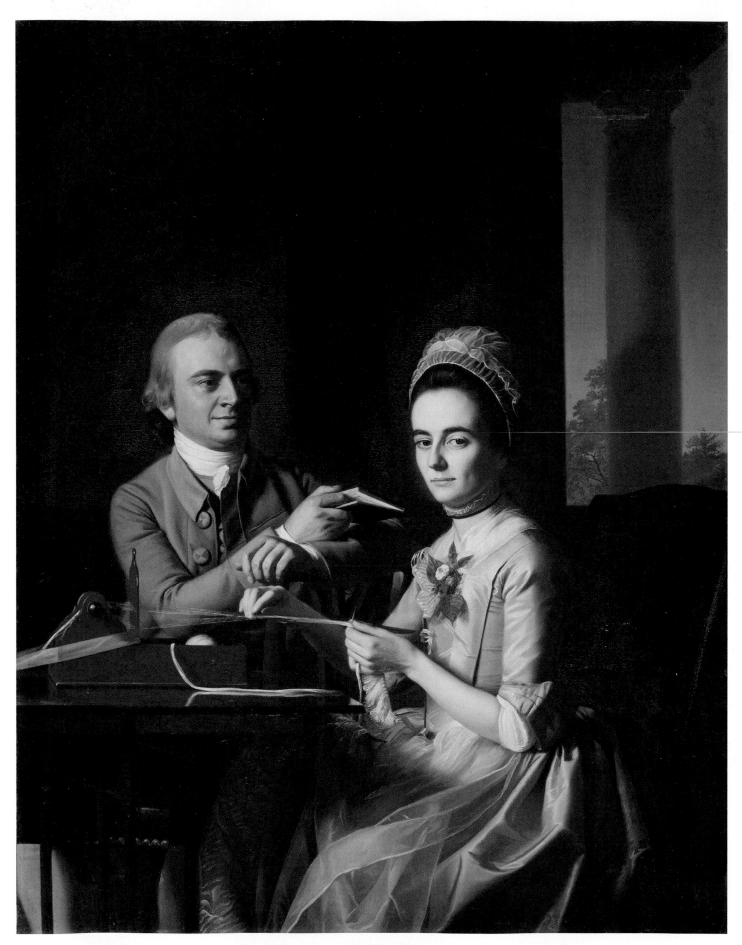

30-1 • John Singleton Copley **THOMAS MIFFLIN AND SARAH MORRIS (MR. AND MRS. MIFFLIN)**
1773. Oil on canvas, 61⅝″ × 48″ (156.5 × 121.9 cm). Philadelphia Museum of Art.

Eighteenth- and Early Nineteenth-Century Art in Europe and North America

John Singleton Copley (1738–1815) painted this double portrait of Thomas Mifflin and his wife, Sarah Morris (**FIG. 30–1**), in 1773, when the Philadelphia couple was visiting Boston for a family funeral. This was the same year when American colonists protested against the British tax on tea by staging the Boston Tea Party—seizing British tea and tossing it into Boston harbor. The painting must have hung in the couple's Philadelphia home when Thomas Mifflin, a prominent merchant and politician, and other leading representatives of the colonies negotiated a strategy for the impending break with Britain at the First Continental Congress. Indeed, the painting proclaims the couple's identity as American patriots, committed to the cause of independence.

Sarah—not her famous husband—is the center of attention. She sits in the foreground, wearing a stylish silk dress decorated with expensive laces, a finely wrought lace cap atop her smoothly coiffed head. She is certainly rich and elegant, but she wears no jewelry except for a modest choker. In fact, rather uncharacteristically for a woman of her social status, she is shown with her sleeves rolled up, working silk threads on the large wooden frame that sits on her polished table. Her work is domestic and pragmatic, not the kind of activity we expect to see highlighted in a large and expensive formal portrait, but it was included here for important political reasons. Sarah is weaving a type of decorative silk fringe that would have been imported from England in the past. By

portraying her involved in this work, Copley demonstrates her commitment both to her home as a good and industrious wife, and also to the revolutionary cause as a woman without pretension who can manage well without British imported goods. Meeting the viewer's gaze with confidence and intelligence, she is clearly a full partner with her patriot husband in the important work of resisting British colonial power. He is content to sit in the background of this picture, interrupting his reading to look admiringly at his beloved Sarah.

John Singleton Copley was, by 1773, Boston's preeminent portrait painter and a wealthy man. His reputation stood on his remarkable ability to represent the upper strata of society in a clear, sharp, precise painting style that seemed to reveal not only every detail of his sitter's physical appearance and personality, but also the gorgeous satins, silks and laces of the women's dresses and the expensive polished furniture that were the signs of his patrons' wealth and status. Although his father-in-law was the Boston representative of the East India Company (whose tea was dumped into the harbor), Copley was sympathetic to the revolutionary cause and, in fact, tried unsuccessfully to mediate the crisis in Boston. This portrait of Sarah Morris and Thomas Mifflin was painted when Copley himself was ambivalent about the political future of the colonies—he would flee the unsettled climate of the colonies the following year to begin a second career in London—but his sitters reveal only their own sober commitment to the cause.

LEARN ABOUT IT

30.1 Investigate the origins and understand the characteristics of the stylistic movements art historians label Rococo, Neoclassicism, and Romanticism.

30.2 Explore the many subjects of Romanticism, from the sublime in nature to the cruelty of the slave trade, with a common interest in emotion and feeling.

30.3 Trace the relationships between the complex mix of artistic styles in this period and the complex political climate of Europe and America.

30.4 Discover Neoclassicism's relationship with Enlightenment values and its roots in the study of Classical antiquity in Rome.

((•—**Listen** to the chapter audio on myartslab.com

INDUSTRIAL, INTELLECTUAL, AND POLITICAL REVOLUTIONS

The American War of Independence was just one of many revolutions to shake the established order during the eighteenth and early nineteenth centuries. This was an age of radical change in society, thought, and politics, and while these transformations were felt especially in England, France, and the United States, they had consequences throughout the West and, eventually, the world.

The transformations of this period were informed by a new way of thinking that had its roots in the scientific revolution of the previous century (see "Science and the Changing World-view," page 756). In England, John Locke (1632–1704) argued that reasonable and rational thought should supplant superstition, and Isaac Newton (1643–1727) insisted upon empirical observation, rational evaluation, and logical consideration in mathematics and science. In 1702, Bernard de Fontenelle (1657–1757), a French popularizer of scientific innovation, wrote that he anticipated "a century which will become more enlightened day by day, so that all previous centuries will be lost in darkness by comparison." Over the course of the eighteenth century, this emphasis on thought "enlightened" by reason was applied to political and moral philosophy as well as science. Enlightenment thinking is marked by a conviction that humans are not superstitious beings ruled by God or the aristocracy, and that all men (some thinkers also included women) should have equal rights and opportunities for "life, liberty, and the pursuit of happiness." Most Enlightenment philosophers believed that, when freed of past religious and political shackles, men and women could and would act rationally and morally. The role of the state was to protect and facilitate these rights, and when the state failed, the moral solution was to change it. Both the American Revolution of 1776 and the French Revolution of 1789 were justified on this basis.

The eighteenth century was also a period of economic and social transformation, set in motion by the Industrial Revolution. In the Europe of 1700, wealth and power belonged to the aristocracy, who owned the land and controlled the lives of poor tenant farmers. The Industrial Revolution eventually replaced the land-based power of the aristocracy with the financial power of capitalists, who were able to use new sources of energy to mechanize manufacturing and greatly increase the quantity and profitability of saleable goods. Factory work lured the poor away from the

MAP 30–1 • EUROPE AND NORTH AMERICA IN THE EIGHTEENTH CENTURY

During the 18th century, three major artistic styles—Rococo, Neoclassicism, and Romanticism—flourished in Europe and North America.

countryside to the cities with the promise of wages and greater independence. The conditions that urban workers endured, however, were dreadful, both at their grueling factory jobs and in their overcrowded and unsanitary neighborhoods. These conditions would sow the seeds of dissent and revolution in several European countries in the mid nineteenth century. Industrialization also produced a large middle class that both bought and sold the new goods made in factories.

By the early nineteenth century, the aristocracy was weak and ineffectual in many nations, and virtually eliminated in France. Upper-middle-class industrialists and merchants dominated European commerce, industry, and politics, and their beliefs and customs defined social norms. At the same time, the idealism of the Enlightenment had eroded, particularly in France in the wake of the Revolution, when the new republican form of government "by the people" brought chaos and bloodshed rather than order and stability. A new intellectual trend, known as Romanticism, started as a literary movement in the 1790s and served as a counterpoint to Enlightenment rationalism. It critiqued the idea that the world was knowable and ruled by reason alone. The central premise of Romanticism was that an exploration of emotions, the imagination, and intuition—areas of the mind not addressed by Enlightenment philosophy—could lead to a more nuanced understanding of the world. Rather than one supplanting the other, Romanticism and Enlightenment thought coexisted as different parts of a complex cultural whole.

30-2 • Germain Boffrand **SALON DE LA PRINCESSE, HÔTEL DE SOUBISE**
Paris. Begun 1732.

ROCOCO

In the modern age, the shift from art produced at the behest of individual or institutional patrons—the monarchy, aristocracy, Church, as well as wealthy merchants—to art produced as a commodity on sale to the industrial rich and even the emerging middle classes had its roots in the Rococo when the court culture of Versailles was replaced by the salon culture of Paris. The term Rococo combines the Italian word *barocco* (an irregularly shaped pearl, possibly the source of the word "baroque") and the French *rocaille* (a popular form of garden or interior ornamentation using shells and pebbles) to describe the refined and fanciful style that became fashionable in parts of Europe during the eighteenth century. The Rococo developed in France around 1715, when the duc d'Orléans, regent for the boy-king Louis XV (r. 1715–1774), moved his home and the French court from Versailles to Paris. The movement spread quickly across Europe (**MAP 30–1**).

ROCOCO SALONS

The French court was happy to escape its confinement in the rural palace of Versailles and relocate to Paris. There courtiers built elegant town houses (in French, *hôtels*), whose social rooms may have been smaller than at Versailles, but were no less lavishly decorated. These became the center of social life for aristocrats who cultivated witty exchanges, elegant manners, and a playfully luxurious life

specifically dedicated to pleasure, leisure, and sensuality that frequently masked social insecurity and ambivalence. **Salons**, as the rooms and the events held in them were known, were intimate, fashionable, and intellectual gatherings, often including splendid entertainments that mimicked in miniature the rituals of the Versailles court. The salons were hosted on a weekly basis by accomplished, educated women of the upper class including Mesdames de Staël, de La Fayette, de Sévigné, and du Châtelet.

The Rococo style cannot be fully appreciated through single objects, but is evident everywhere in the salons, with their profusely decorated walls and ceilings bursting with exquisite three-dimensional embellishments in gold, silver, and brilliant white paint; their intimate, sensual paintings hung among the rich ornament; and their elaborate crystal chandeliers, mirrored walls, and delicate decorated furniture and tabletop sculptures. When these Parisian salons were lit by candles, they must have glittered with light reflected and refracted by the gorgeous surfaces. The rooms were no doubt also enlivened by the energy of aristocrats, fancifully dressed in a profusion of pastel blues, yellows, greens, and pinks to complement the light, bright details of the Rococo architecture, paintings, and sculptures around them.

The **SALON DE LA PRINCESSE** in the Hôtel de Soubise (**FIG. 30–2**), designed by Germain Boffrand (1667–1754), was the

30–3 • Jean-Antoine Watteau THE SIGNBOARD OF GERSAINT
c. 1721. Oil on canvas, 5′4″ × 10′1″ (1.62 × 3.06 m). Stiftung Preussische Schlössen und Gärten Berlin-Brandenburg, Schloss Charlottenburg.

Watteau painted this signboard for the Paris art gallery of Edmé-François Gersaint, a dealer who introduced to France the English idea of selling paintings by catalog. The systematic listing of works for sale gave the name of the artist and the title, the medium, and the dimensions of each work of art. The shop depicted on the signboard, however, is not Gersaint's but a gallery created from Watteau's imagination and visited by typically elegant and cultivated patrons. The sign was so admired that Gersaint sold it only 15 days after it was installed. Later it was cut down the middle, and each half was framed separately, which resulted in the loss of some canvas along the sides of each section. The painting was restored and its two halves reunited only in the twentieth century.

Read the document related to Jean-Antoine Watteau on myartslab.com

setting for such intimate gatherings of the Parisian aristocracy in the years prior to the French Revolution. Its delicacy and lightness are typical of French Rococo salon design of the 1730s, with architectural elements rendered in sculpted stucco, including arabesques (characterized by flowing lines and swirling shapes), S-shapes, C-shapes, reverse C-shapes, volutes, and naturalistic plant forms. Intricate polished surfaces included carved wood panels called *boiseries* and inlaid wood designs on furniture and floors. The glitter of silver and gold against white and pastel shades and the visual confusion of mirror reflections all enhanced this Rococo interior.

ROCOCO PAINTING AND SCULPTURE

The paintings and sculpture that decorated Rococo salons and other elegant spaces were instrumental in creating their atmosphere of sensuality and luxury. Pictorial themes were often taken from Classical love stories, and both pictures and sculpted ornament were typically filled with playful *putti*, lush foliage, and fluffy clouds. The paintings of Jean-Antoine Watteau, François Boucher, and Jean-Honoré Fragonard and the tabletop sculpture of Claude Michel, known as Clodion, were highly coveted in salon culture.

WATTEAU Jean-Antoine Watteau (1684–1721) has been seen as the originator, and for some the greatest practitioner, of the French Rococo style in painting. Born in the provincial town of Valenciennes, Watteau came to Paris around 1702, where he studied Rubens's paintings for Marie de' Medici (see FIG. 23-27), then displayed in the Luxembourg Palace, and the paintings and drawings of sixteenth-century Venetians such as Giorgione and Titian (see FIGS. 21-24, 21-25), which he saw in a Parisian private collection. Incorporating the fluent brushwork and rich colors of such works from the past, Watteau perfected a graceful personal style that embodied the spirit of his own time.

Watteau painted for the new urban aristocrats who frequently purchased paintings for their homes through art dealers in the city.

The signboard he painted for the art dealer Edmé-François Gersaint (**FIG. 30-3**) shows the interior of one of these shops—an art gallery filled with paintings from the Venetian and Netherlandish schools that Watteau admired. Indeed, the glowing satins and silks of the women's gowns pay homage to artists such as Gerard ter Borch (see **FIG. 23-41**). The visitors to the gallery are elegant ladies and gentlemen, at ease in these surroundings and apparently knowledgeable about painting; they create an atmosphere of aristocratic sophistication. At the left, a woman in shimmering pink satin steps across the threshold, ignoring her companion's outstretched hand, to watch the two porters packing. While one porter holds a mirror, the other carefully lowers into the wooden case a portrait of Louis XIV, which may be a reference to the name of Gersaint's shop, *Au Grand Monarque* ("At the Sign of the Great King"). It also suggests the passage of time, for Louis had died six years earlier.

Other elements in the work also suggest transience. On the left, the clock directly above the king's portrait, surmounted by an allegorical figure of Fame and sheltering a pair of lovers, is a **memento mori**, a reminder of mortality, suggesting that both love and fame are subject to the ravages of time. Well-established *vanitas* emblems are the easily destroyed straw (in the foreground)

and the young woman gazing into the mirror (set next to a vanity case on the counter)—mirrors and images of young women looking at their reflections had been familiar symbols of the fragility of human life since the Baroque period. Notably, the two gentlemen at the end of the counter also appear to gaze at the mirror, and are thus also implicated in the *vanitas* theme. Watteau, who died from tuberculosis before he was 40, produced this painting during his last illness. Gersaint later wrote that Watteau had completed the painting in eight days, working only in the mornings because of his failing health. When the *Signboard* was installed, it was greeted with almost universal admiration; Gersaint sold it within a month.

In **PILGRIMAGE TO THE ISLAND OF CYTHERA** (**FIG. 30-4**), painted four years earlier, Watteau portrayed an imagined vision of the idyllic and sensual life of Rococo aristocrats, but with the same undertone of melancholy that hints at the fleeting quality of human happiness. This is a dream world in which beautifully dressed and elegantly posed couples, accompanied by *putti*, conclude the romantic trysts of their day on Cythera, the island sacred to Venus, the goddess of love, whose garlanded statue appears at the extreme right. The lovers, dressed in exquisite satins, silks, and velvets, gather in the verdant landscape. Such idyllic and wistfully melancholic visions of aristocratic leisure charmed

30-4 • Jean-Antoine Watteau PILGRIMAGE TO THE ISLAND OF CYTHERA
1717. Oil on canvas, 4′3″ × 6′4½″ (1.3 × 1.9 m). Musée du Louvre, Paris.

**30–5 • François Boucher
GIRL RECLINING:
LOUISE O'MURPHY**
1751. Oil on canvas, 28¾″ ×
23¼″ (73 × 59 cm).
Wallraf-Richartz Museum,
Cologne.

both early eighteenth-century Paris and most of Europe. Watteau painted *Pilgrimage to the Island of Cythera* in 1717 as his official examination canvas for admission to membership of the French Royal Academy of Painting and Sculpture (see "Academies and Academy Exhibitions," page 926). Although there was no academic category to cover the painting, the academicians were so impressed by the canvas that they created a new category, the **fête galante**, or elegant outdoor entertainment, to describe this genre.

BOUCHER The artist most closely associated with Parisian Rococo painting after Watteau's death is François Boucher (1703–1770). The son of a minor painter, Boucher in 1723 entered the workshop of an engraver where he was hired to reproduce Watteau's paintings for a collector, laying the groundwork for the future direction of his career.

After studying in Rome from 1727 to 1731 at the academy founded there by the French Royal Academy of Painting and Sculpture, Boucher settled in Paris and became an academician. Soon his life and career were intimately bound up with two women. The first was his artistically talented wife, Marie-Jeanne Buseau, who was her husband's frequent model as well as his studio assistant. The other was Louis XV's mistress, Madame de Pompadour, who became his major patron and supporter. Pompadour was an amateur artist herself and took lessons in printmaking from Boucher. After he received his first royal commission in 1735, Boucher worked almost continuously on the decorations for the

royal residences at Versailles and Fontainebleau. In 1755, he was made chief inspector at the Gobelins tapestry manufactory, and provided designs for it as well as for the Sèvres porcelain and Beauvais tapestry manufactories. All these workshops produced both furnishings for the king and wares for sale on the open market by merchants such as Gersaint. Indeed, Boucher operated in a much more commercial market than artists in the previous century.

In 1765, Boucher became First Painter to the King. In this role he painted several portraits of Louis XV, scenes of daily life and mythological pictures, and a series of erotic works for private enjoyment, often depicting the adventures of Venus. The subject of one such painting—**GIRL RECLINING: LOUISE O'MURPHY** (**FIG. 30–5**)—however, is hardly mythological. The teenage Louise O'Murphy, who would soon be one of the mistresses of Louis XV, appears provocatively pink and completely naked, sprawled across a day bed on her stomach, looking out of the painting and completely unaware of our presence. Her satiny clothing is crushed beneath her, and her spread legs sink into a pillow; braids and a blue ribbon decorate her hair, while a fallen pink rose is highlighted on the floor. Louise's plump buttocks are displayed enticingly at the very center of the painting, leaving little doubt about the painting's subject. In contrast to Watteau's *fête galante*, in which imaginary aristocrats and *putti* frolic decorously in idyllic settings, the overtly sensual woman shown here is clearly human, a known contemporary personality, and presented to us a very real Rococo room.

FRAGONARD Another noteworthy master of French Rococo painting, Jean-Honoré Fragonard (1732–1806), studied with Boucher, who encouraged him to enter the competition for the Prix de Rome, the three- to five-year scholarship awarded to the top students graduating from the art school of the French Royal Academy of Painting and Sculpture. Fragonard won the prize in 1752 and spent the years 1756 to 1761 in Italy; however, it was not until 1765 that he was finally accepted as a member of the Academy. He catered to the tastes of an aristocratic clientele, and, as a decorator of interiors, began to fill the vacuum left by Boucher's death in 1770.

Fragonard's **THE SWING** (FIG. **30-6**) of 1767 was originally commissioned from painter Gabriel-François Doyen, although the identity of the patron is unknown. Doyen described the subject he

30-6 • Jean-Honoré Fragonard THE SWING
1767. Oil on canvas, 2′8⅝″ × 2′2″ (82.9 × 66 cm). The Wallace Collection, London.

was asked to paint as sensually explicit, and he refused the commission, giving it to Fragonard, who created a small jewel of a painting. A pretty young woman is suspended on a swing, her movement created by an elderly bishop obscured by the shadow of the bushes on the right, who pulls her with a rope. On the left, the girl's blushing lover hides in the bushes, swooning with anticipation. As the swing approaches, he is rewarded with an unobstructed view up her skirt, lifted on his behalf by an extended leg. The young man reaches out toward her with his hat as if to make a mockingly useless attempt to conceal the view, while she glances down, seductively tossing one of her shoes toward him. The playful abandon of the lovers, the complicity of the sculpture of Cupid on the left, his shushing gesture assuring that he will not tell, the *putti* with a dolphin beneath the swing who seem to urge the young woman on, and the poor duped bishop to the right, all work together to create an image that bursts with anticipation and desire, but also maintains a robust sense of humor.

CLODION In the last quarter of the eighteenth century, Rococo largely fell out of favor in France, its style and subject matter attacked for being frivolous at best and immoral at worst. One sculptor who clung onto the style almost until the French Revolution, however, was Claude Michel, known as Clodion (1738–1814). Most of his work consisted of playful, erotic tabletop sculpture, mainly in unpainted terra cotta. Typical of his Rococo designs is the terra-cotta model he submitted to win a 1784 royal commission for a large monument to **THE INVENTION OF THE BALLOON** (**FIG. 30-7**). In the eighteenth-century, hot-air balloons were elaborately decorated with painted Rococo scenes, gold braid, and tassels. Clodion's balloon, circled with bands of ornament, rises from a columnar launching pad belching billowing clouds of smoke, assisted at the left by a puffing wind god with butterfly wings and heralded at the right by a trumpeting Victory. Some *putti* stoke the fire basket, providing the hot air that allows the balloon to ascend, while others gather reeds for fuel and carry them up to feed the fire.

ROCOCO CHURCH DECORATION

The beginning of the Rococo coincided with the waning importance of the Church as a major patron of art in northern Europe. Although churches continued to be built and decorated, the dominance of both the Church and the hereditary aristocracy as patrons diminished significantly. The Rococo proved, however, to be a powerful vehicle for spiritual experience. Several important churches were built in the style, showing how visual appearance can be tailored to a variety of social meanings. One of the most opulent Rococo churches is dedicated to the Vierzehnheiligen (the "Fourteen Auxiliary Saints" or "Holy Helpers") and designed by Johann Balthasar Neumann (1687–1753). Constructed in Bavaria between 1743 and 1772, the plan (**FIG. 30-8**), based on six interpenetrating oval spaces of varying sizes around a vaulted ovoid center, recalls that of Borromini's Baroque church of San Carlo alle Quattro Fontane in Rome (see **FIG. 23-6B**). But the effect here is airy lightness. In the nave (**FIG. 30-9**), the Rococo love of undulating surfaces with overlays of decoration creates a visionary world where surfaces scarcely exist. Instead, the viewer is surrounded by clusters of pilasters and engaged columns interspersed with two levels of arched openings to the side aisles, and large clerestory

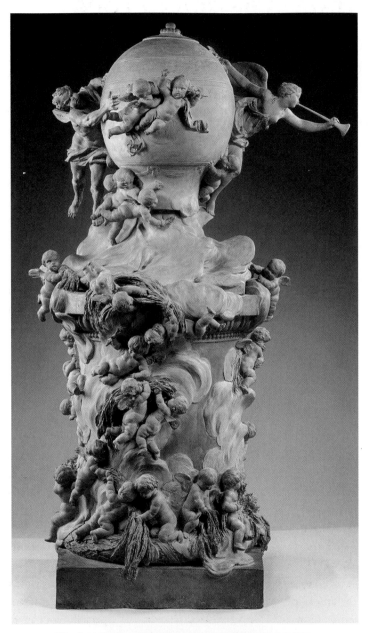

30-7 • Clodion THE INVENTION OF THE BALLOON
1784. Terra-cotta model for a monument, height 43½″ (110.5 cm). Metropolitan Museum of Art, New York. Rogers Fund and Frederick R. Harris Gift, 1944 (44.21a b)

Clodion had a long career as a sculptor in the exuberant Rococo manner seen in this work commemorating the 1783 invention of the hot-air balloon. During the austere revolutionary period of the First Republic (1792–1795), he became one of the few Rococo artists to adopt successfully the more acceptable Neoclassical manner. In 1806, he was commissioned by Napoleon to provide the relief sculpture for two Paris monuments, the Vendôme Column and the Carrousel Arch near the Louvre.

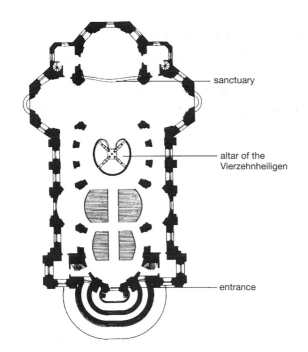

30-8 • PLAN OF THE CHURCH OF THE VIERZEHNHEILIGEN
Near Bamberg, Bavaria, Germany. c. 1743.

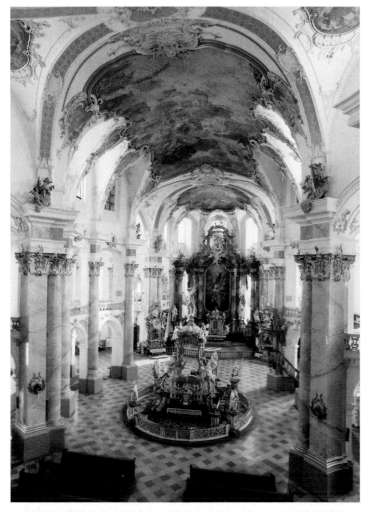

30-9 • Johann Balthasar Neumann INTERIOR, CHURCH OF THE VIERZEHNHEILIGEN
Near Bamberg, Bavaria, Germany. 1743–1772.

windows illuminating the gold and white of the interior. The foliage of the fanciful capitals is repeated in arabesques, wreaths, and the ornamented frames of irregular panels lining the vault. An ebullient sense of spiritual uplift is achieved by the complete integration of architecture and decoration.

ITALY: THE GRAND TOUR AND NEOCLASSICISM

From the late 1600s until well into the nineteenth century, the education of a wealthy young northern European or American gentleman—few women were considered worthy of such education—was completed on the **Grand Tour**, an extended visit to the major cultural sites of southern Europe. Accompanied by a tutor and an entourage of servants, the Grand Tourist began in Paris, moved on to southern France to visit a number of well-preserved Roman buildings and monuments there, then headed to Venice, Florence, Naples, and Rome. As the repository of the Classical and Renaissance pasts, Italy was the focus of the Grand Tour.

Italy, and Rome in particular, was also the primary destination for artists and scholars interested in the Classical past. In addition to the ancient architecture and sculpture throughout Rome, the nearby sites of Pompeii and Herculaneum offered sensational new material for study and speculation (see Chapter 6). In the mid eighteenth century, archaeologists began the systematic excavation of these two prosperous Roman towns, buried by a sudden volcanic eruption in 79 CE.

The artists and intellectuals who found inspiration in the Classical past were instrumental in the development of Neoclassicism, which was both a way of viewing the world and an influential movement in the visual arts. Neoclassicism (*neo* means "new") sought to present Classical ideals and subject matter in a style derived from Classical Greek and Roman sources. Neoclassical paintings reflect the crystalline forms, tight compositions, and shallow space of ancient relief sculpture. Because the ancient world was considered the font from which British and European democracy, secular government, and civilized thought and action flowed, its art was viewed as the embodiment of timeless civic and moral lessons. Neoclassical paintings and sculptures were frequently painted for and displayed in public places in order to inspire patriotism, nationalism, and courage. Neoclassicism was especially popular in Britain, America, and France as a visual expression of the state and political stability.

GRAND TOUR PORTRAITS AND VIEWS

Artists in Italy benefited not only from their access to authentic works of antiquity, but also from the steady stream of wealthy art collectors on the Grand Tour. Tourists visited the studios of important Italian artists in order to view and purchase works that could be brought home and displayed as evidence of their cultural travels.

CARRIERA Wealthy European visitors to Italy frequently sat for portraits by Italian artists. Rosalba Carriera (1675–1757), the leading portraitist in Venice in the first half of the eighteenth century, worked mainly in pastel, a medium better suited than slow-drying oil to accommodate sitters whose time in the city was limited. **Pastel** is a fast and versatile medium: Pastel crayons, made of pulverized pigment bound to a chalk base by weak gum water, can be used to sketch quickly and spontaneously, or they can be rubbed and blended on the surface of paper to produce a shiny and highly finished surface.

Carriera began her career designing lace patterns and painting miniature portraits on the ivory lids of snuffboxes before she graduated to pastel portraits. Her portraits were so widely admired that she was awarded honorary membership of Rome's Academy of St. Luke in 1705, and was later admitted to the academies in Bologna and Florence. In 1720, she traveled to Paris, where she made a pastel portrait of the young Louis XV and was elected to the French Royal Academy of Painting and Sculpture, despite the 1706 rule forbidding the further admission of women. Returning to Italy in 1721, she established herself in Venice as a portraitist

30-11 • Canaletto THE DOGE'S PALACE AND THE RIVA DEGLI SCHIAVONI
Late 1730s. Oil on canvas, 24⅛″ × 39¼″ (61.3 × 99.8 cm). National Gallery, London.
Wynn Ellis Bequest 1876 (NG 940)

30–12 • Giovanni Battista Piranesi VIEW OF THE PANTHEON, ROME

From the *Views of Rome* series, first printed in 1756. Etching, 18⁹⁄₁₆″ × 27⅛″ (47.2 × 69.7 cm). Kupferstich-Kabinett, Staatliche Museen, Berlin.

of handsome young men such as the British aristocrat **CHARLES SACKVILLE, 2ND DUKE OF DORSET** (**FIG. 30-10**).

CANALETTO A painted city view was by far the most prized souvenir of a stay in Venice. Two kinds of views were produced in Venice: the **capriccio** ("caprice," plural *capricci*), an imaginary landscape or cityscape in which the artist mixed actual structures, such as famous ruins, with imaginary ones to create attractive compositions; and the **veduta** ("view," plural *vedute*), a more naturalistic rendering of famous views and buildings, well-known tourist attractions, and local color in the form of tiny figures of the Venetian people and visiting tourists. *Vedute* often encompassed panoramic views of famous landmarks, as in **THE DOGE'S PALACE AND THE RIVA DEGLI SCHIAVONI** (**FIG. 30-11**) by the Venetian artist Giovanni Antonio Canal, called Canaletto (1697–1768). It was thought that Canaletto used the camera obscura (see page 968) to render his *vedute* with exact topographical accuracy, but his drawings show that he seems to have worked freehand. In fact, his views are rarely topographically accurate; more often than not, they are composite images, so skillfully composed that we want to believe that Canaletto's *vedute* are "real." He painted and sold so many to British visitors that his dealer sent him to London from 1746 to 1755 to paint views of the English capital city for his British clients, who included several important aristocrats as well as King George III.

PIRANESI The city of Rome was also captured in *vedute* for the pleasure of tourists and armchair travelers, notably by Giovanni Battista Piranesi (1720–1778). Trained in Venice as an architect, he moved to Rome in 1740 and studied etching, eventually establishing a publishing house and becoming one of the century's most successful printmakers. Piranesi produced a large series of *vedute* of ancient Roman monuments, whose ruined, deteriorating condition made them even more interesting for his customers. His **VIEW OF THE PANTHEON** (**FIG. 30-12**) is informed by a careful study of this great work of ancient Roman architecture, which seems even more monumental in relation to the dramatic clouds that frame it and the lively, small figures who surround it on the ground, admiring its grandeur from all directions.

NEOCLASSICISM IN ROME

The intellectuals and artists who came to study and work in Rome often formed communities with a shared interest in Neoclassical ideals. A British coterie, for example, included Angelica Kauffmann (see **FIG. 30-26**), Benjamin West (see **FIG. 30-28**), and Gavin Hamilton (1723–1798), all of whom contributed to early Neoclassicism, and there were similar gatherings of artists from France and Germany. One of the most influential communities formed at the Villa Albani on the outskirts of Rome, under the sponsorship of Cardinal Alessandro Albani (1692–1779).

Cardinal Albani built his villa in 1760–1761 specifically to house and display his vast collection of antique sculpture, sarcophagi, intaglios (objects in which the designs are carved into the surface), cameos, and ceramics, and it became one of the most important stops on the Grand Tour. The villa was more than a museum: It was also a place to buy art and artifacts. Albani sold

30-13 • Anton Raphael Mengs PARNASSUS
Ceiling fresco in the Villa Albani, Rome. 1761.

items to artists and tourists alike, to help satisfy the growing craze for antiquities; unfortunately, many were faked or heavily restored by artisans in the cardinal's employ.

In 1758, Albani hired Johann Joachim Winckelmann (1717–1768), the leading theoretician of Neoclassicism, as his secretary and librarian. The Prussian-born Winckelmann had become an expert on Classical art while working in Dresden, where the French Rococo style that he deplored was still fashionable. In 1755, he published a pamphlet, *Thoughts on the Imitation of Greek Works in Painting and Sculpture*, in which he attacked the Rococo as decadent, arguing that modern artists could only claim their status as legitimate artists by imitating Greek art. Shortly after relocating to Rome to work for Albani, Winckelmann published a second influential treatise, *The History of Ancient Art (1764)*, often considered the beginning of modern art-historical study. Here Winckelmann analyzed the history of art for the first time as a succession of period styles, an approach which later became the norm for art history books (including this one).

MENGS Winckelmann's closest friend and colleague in Rome was a fellow German, the painter Anton Raphael Mengs (1728–1779). In 1761, Cardinal Albani commissioned Mengs to paint the ceiling of the great gallery in his new villa. To our eyes Mengs's **PARNASSUS** ceiling (**FIG. 30-13**) may seem stilted, but it is nevertheless significant as the first full expression of Neoclassicism in painting. The scene is taken from Classical mythology. Mount Parnassus in cen-

tral Greece was where the ancients believed Apollo (god of poetry, music, and the arts) and the nine Muses (female personifications of artistic inspiration) resided. Mengs depicted Apollo—practically nude and holding a lyre and olive branch to represent artistic accomplishment—standing at the compositional center, his pose copied from the famous *Apollo Belvedere* in the Vatican collection, one of Winckelmann's favorite Greek statues. Around Apollo are the Muses and their mother, Mnemosyne (Memory, leaning on a Doric column). Mengs arranged his figures in a roughly symmetrical, pyramidal composition parallel to the picture plane, like the relief sculpture he had studied at Herculaneum. Winckelmann praised this work, claiming that it captured the "noble simplicity and calm grandeur" of ancient Greek sculpture. Shortly after its completion, Mengs left for Spain, where he served as court painter until 1777, bringing Neoclassical ideas with him. Other artists from Rome carried the style elsewhere in Europe.

CANOVA The theories of the Albani–Winckelmann circle were applied most vigorously by sculptors in Rome, who remained committed to Neoclassicism for almost 100 years. The leading Neoclassical sculptor of the late eighteenth and early nineteenth centuries was Antonio Canova (1757–1822). Born near Venice into a family of stonemasons, he settled in Rome in 1781, where he adopted the Neoclassical style under the guidance of the Scottish painter Gavin Hamilton and quickly became the most sought-after European sculptor of the period.

30-14 • Antonio Canova **PAULINE BORGHESE AS VENUS**
1808. Marble, length 6'7" (2.18 m). Galleria Borghese, Rome.

Canova specialized in two types of sculpture: grand public monuments for Europe's leaders, and eroticized mythological subjects for the pleasure of private collectors. His **PAULINE BORGHESE AS VENUS** (**FIG. 30-14**) falls into the latter category, although it was commissioned by one of the most powerful rulers of Europe in the later eighteenth century, Emperor Napoleon of France (1769–1821). This is actually a portrait of Napoleon's sister, Pauline, whom the emperor had arranged to marry Prince Camillo Borghese, a member of the famous Roman Borghese family. But Pauline wished to be portrayed as Venus. She is shown seminude, reclining on a divan, holding the golden apple given to Venus by Paris, prince of Troy, as a sign that she was the fairest of the three major goddesses. The marble renderings of cushions and drapery seem almost real, while the glistening white marble flesh evokes the sensuality seen in Hellenistic sculpture, especially in contrast to the precise linearity of the gray, white, and gold piece of furniture that serves as a base. Pauline's husband was displeased with the sculpture, which seemed to confirm rumors about his wife's questionable behavior, and installed Canova's work in a private room in the Villa Borghese, where it remains today.

NEOCLASSICISM AND EARLY ROMANTICISM IN BRITAIN

British tourists and artists in Italy became leading supporters of early Neoclassicism, partly because of the early burgeoning taste for revival styles at home, but the Classical revival in Britain had a slightly different focus from what we saw in Rome. While Roman Neoclassicism looked to the past in order to revive a sense of moral and civic virtue, many later eighteenth-century British artists harnessed the concept of civic virtue to patriotism to create more Romantic works of art dedicated specifically to the British nation. It is in British art and literature that we find the beginnings of Romanticism.

Like Neoclassicism, Romanticism describes not only a style but also an attitude: It celebrates the individual and the subjective, while Neoclassicism celebrates the universal and the rational. Romanticism takes its name and many of its themes from the "romances"—novellas, stories, and poems written in Romance (Latin-derived) languages. The term "Romantic" suggests something fantastic or novelistic, perhaps set in a remote time or place, infused by a poetic melancholy, occasionally inciting terror or horror. One of the best examples of early Romanticism in literature is *The Sorrows of Young Werther* (1774) by Johann Wolfgang von Goethe (1749–1832), in which a sensitive, outcast young man fails at love and kills himself. This is a story about a troubled individual who loses his way; it does not recall ancient virtues or civic responsibility.

Neoclassicism and Romanticism existed side by side in the later eighteenth and early nineteenth centuries—two ways of looking at the world, serving distinct purposes in society. Neoclassicism tended to be a more public art form, and Romanticism more individual and private. Sometimes Neoclassicism even functioned within Romanticism. Distinctions were not always clear.

THE CLASSICAL REVIVAL IN ARCHITECTURE AND DESIGN

Ancient Greece and Rome provided impeccable pedigrees for eighteenth-century British buildings, utensils, poetry, and even clothing fashions. Women donned white muslin gowns and men curled their hair forward in imitation of Classical statues. In the 1720s, a group of professional architects and wealthy amateurs in Britain, led by a Scot, Colen Campbell (1676–1729), stood against what they viewed as the immoral extravagance of the Italian Baroque. They advocated a return to the austerity and simplicity of the Classically inspired architecture of Andrea Palladio, and his country houses in particular.

CHISWICK HOUSE Designed in 1724 by its owner, Richard Boyle, the third Earl of Burlington (1695–1753), **CHISWICK HOUSE** (**FIG. 30-15**) is a fine example of British Neo-Palladianism. In visiting Palladio's country houses in Italy, Burlington was particularly struck by the Villa Rotonda (see **FIGS. 21-45, 21-46**), which inspired his design for Chiswick House. The plan shares the bilateral symmetry of Palladio's villa, although its central core is octagonal rather than round and there are only two entrances. The

30-15 • Richard Boyle (Lord Burlington) PLAN (A) AND EXTERIOR VIEW (B) OF CHISWICK HOUSE
West London, England. 1724–1729. Interior decoration (1726–1729) and new gardens (1730–1740) by William Kent.

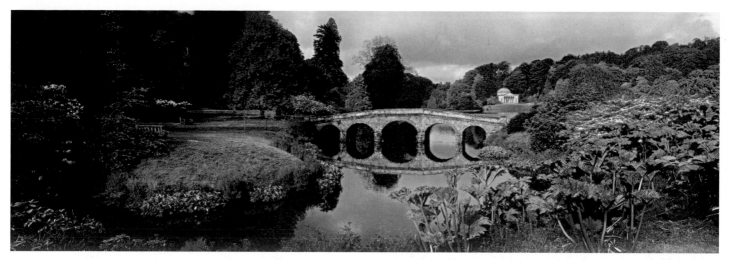

30-16 • Henry Flitcroft and Henry Hoare **THE PARK AT STOURHEAD**
Wiltshire, England. Laid out 1743, executed 1744–1765, with continuing additions.

main entrance, flanked here by matching staircases, is a Roman temple front, an imposing entrance for the earl. Chiswick's elevation is characteristically Palladian, with a main floor resting on a basement, and tall, rectangular windows with triangular pediments. The few, crisp details seem perfectly suited to the refined proportions of the whole. The result is a lucid evocation of Palladio's design.

When in Rome, Burlington persuaded the English expatriate William Kent (1685–1748) to return to London as his collaborator. Kent designed Chiswick's surprisingly ornate interior as well as its grounds, the latter in a style that became known throughout Europe as the English landscape garden. Kent's garden abandoned the regularity and rigid formality of Baroque gardens (see "Garden Design," page 761). It featured winding paths, a lake with a cascade, irregular plantings of shrubs, and other effects that imitated the appearance of a natural rural landscape. In fact, it was carefully designed and manicured.

STOURHEAD Following Kent's lead at Chiswick, landscape architecture flourished in England in the hands of such designers as Lancelot ("Capability") Brown (1716–1783) and Henry Flitcroft (1697–1769). In the 1740s, the banker Henry Hoare began redesigning the grounds of his estate at Stourhead in Wiltshire (**FIG. 30-16**) with the assistance of Flitcroft, a protégé of Burlington. The resulting gardens at Stourhead carried Kent's ideas for the English garden much further. Stourhead is a perfect example of the English **picturesque** garden. Its conception and views intentionally mimic the compositional devices of "pictures" by French landscape painter Claude Lorrain (see **FIG. 23-56**), whose paintings were popular in England. The picturesque view illustrated here shows a garden designed with "counterfeit neglect," intentionally contrived to look natural and unkempt. The small lake is crossed by a rustic bridge, while in the background we see a "folly," a miniature version of the Pantheon in Rome. The park is punctu-

ated by other Classically inspired temples, copies of antique statues, artificial grottoes, a rural cottage, a Chinese bridge, a Gothic spire, and even a Turkish tent. The result is a delightful mixture of styles and cultures that combines aspects of both the Neoclassical and the Romantic. Inside the house, Hoare commissioned Mengs to paint *The Meeting of Antony and Cleopatra*, a blended work that chooses from Classical history a Romanticized subject.

WEDGWOOD The interiors of country houses like Chiswick and Stourhead were designed partly as settings for the art collections of British aristocrats, which included antiquities as well as a range of Neoclassical paintings, sculpture, and decorative wares (see "A Closer Look," page 921). The most successful producer of Neoclassical decorative art was Josiah Wedgwood (1730–1795). In 1769, near his native village of Burslem, he opened a pottery factory called Etruria after the ancient Etruscan civilization in central Italy known for its pottery. His production-line shop had several divisions, each with its own kilns and employing workers trained in diverse specialties. A talented chemist, in the mid 1770s Wedgwood perfected a fine-grained, unglazed, colored pottery which he called **jasperware**. His most popular jasperware featured white figures against a blue ground, as in **THE APOTHEOSIS OF HOMER** jar (**FIG. 30-17**). The low-relief decoration was designed by the sculptor John Flaxman, Jr. (1755–1826), who worked for Wedgwood from 1775 to 1787. Flaxman based this scene on a book illustration portraying a particular Greek vessel in the collection of William Hamilton (1730–1803), a leading collector of antiquities and one of Wedgwood's major patrons. Flaxman simplified the original design to accommodate both the popular and idealized notion of ancient Greek art and the demands of mass production.

The socially conscious Wedgwood, informed by Enlightenment thinking, established a village for his employees and showed concern for their well-being. He was also active in the international

30-17 • (left) Josiah Wedgwood **THE APOTHEOSIS OF HOMER**
Made at the Wedgwood Etruria factory, Staffordshire, England. 1790–1795. White jasperware body with a mid-blue dip and white relief, height 18″ (45.7 cm). Relief of The Apotheosis of Homer adapted from a plaque by John Flaxman, Jr., 1778. Trustees of the Wedgwood Museum, Barlaston, Staffordshire, England.

30-18 • (above) William Hackwood for Josiah Wedgwood
"AM I NOT A MAN AND A BROTHER?"
1787. Black-and-white jasperware, 1⅜″ × 1⅜″ (3.5 × 3.5 cm).
Trustees of the Wedgwood Museum, Barlaston, Staffordshire, England.

30-19 • Horace Walpole and others **STRAWBERRY HILL**
Twickenham, England. 1749–1776.

Elizabeth Morley: George III toddy ladle, 1802; Alice and George Burrows: George III snuffbox, 1802; Elizabeth Cooke: George III salver, 1767; Ann and Peter Bateman: George III goblet, 1797; Hester Bateman: George III double beaker, 1790

National Museum of Women in the Arts, Washington, DC. Silver collection assembled by Nancy Valentine. Purchased with funds donated by Mr. and Mrs. Oliver Grace and family

All of the objects shown here bear the marks of silver shops run either wholly or partly by women, who played a significant role in the production of silver during the Georgian period—the years from 1714 to 1830, when Great Britain was ruled by four successive kings named George.

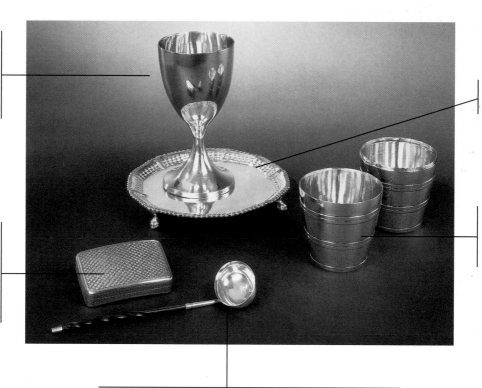

This goblet was used for drinking punch, a potent alcoholic beverage enjoyed by British high society. The gilded interior protected the silver from the acid in alcoholic drinks.

The filled goblets would have been served on a flat salver.

This box contained snuff, a pulverized tobacco inhaled by both men and women of the upper class. This snuffbox has curved sides for easy insertion into the pocket of a gentleman's tight-fitting trousers.

These "double beaker" cups are also for drinking punch. The smaller size made them convenient for use when traveling.

This ladle was used to pour punch from a bowl into a goblet. Its twisted whalebone handle floats, making it easy to retrieve from the bowl.

 View the Closer Look for Georgian silver on myartslab.com

---

effort to halt the African slave trade and abolish slavery. In an attempt to publicize the abolitionist cause, he commissioned the sculptor William Hackwood (c. 1757–1839) to design an emblem for the British Committee to Abolish the Slave Trade, formed in 1787. Hackwood created a small medallion of black-and-white jasperware, with a cameo likeness of an African man kneeling in chains, and the legend **"AM I NOT A MAN AND A BROTHER?"** (**FIG. 30–18**). Wedgwood sent copies of the medallion to Benjamin Franklin, the president of the Philadelphia Abolition Society, and to others in the abolitionist movement. The image was so compelling that the women's suffrage movement in the United States later used it to represent a woman in chains with the motto "Am I Not a Woman and a Sister?"

THE GOTHIC REVIVAL IN ARCHITECTURE AND DESIGN

The Gothic Revival emerged alongside Neoclassicism in Britain in the mid eighteenth century and spread to several other nations after 1800. An early advocate of the Gothic Revival was the conservative politician and author Horace Walpole (1717–1797), who in 1764 published *The Castle of Otranto*, widely regarded as the first Gothic novel. This tale of mysterious and supernatural happenings, set in the Middle Ages, almost single-handedly launched a fashion for the Gothic. In 1749, Walpole began to remodel his country house, **STRAWBERRY HILL**, transforming it into the kind of Gothic castle that he described in his fiction (**FIG. 30–19**). Working with several friends and architects, over the next 30 years he added decorative crenellations (alternating higher and lower sections along the top of a wall), tracery windows, and turrets, to create a fanciful Gothic castle. The interior, too, was redesigned according to Walpole's interpretation of the British historical past. In the **PICTURE GALLERY** (**FIG. 30-20**), he drew on engravings of medieval architecture from antiquarian books in his library. The gallery ceiling is modeled on that of the Chapel of Henry VII at Westminster, but transformed to suit Walpole's taste. For example, the strawberry design on the fan vaults would not have appeared in medieval architecture.

TRENDS IN BRITISH PAINTING

In the mid eighteenth century, portraits remained popular in British painting among those with the means to commission them. But a taste was also developing for other subjects, such as moralizing satire and caricature, ancient and modern history, scenes from British literature, and the actual British landscape and its people. Whatever their subject matter, many of the paintings and prints created in Britain reflected Romantic sensibilities and Enlightenment values, including an interest in social change, an embrace of natural beauty, and an enthusiasm for science and technology.

THE SATIRIC SPIRIT The industrialization of Britain created a large and affluent middle class with the disposable income to purchase smaller and less formal paintings such as landscapes and genre scenes, as well as prints. Relatively inexpensive printed versions of paintings could also be sold to large numbers of people. William Hogarth (1697–1764) capitalized on this new market for

art and was largely responsible for reviving the British print industry in the eighteenth century.

Trained as a portrait painter, Hogarth believed art should contribute to the improvement of society. He worked within the flourishing culture of satire in Britain directed at a variety of political and social targets, illustrating works by John Gay, a writer whose 1728 play *The Beggar's Opera* portrayed all classes as corrupt, but caricatured aristocrats in particular as feckless. In about 1730, Hogarth began illustrating moralizing tales of his own invention in sequences of four to six paintings, which he then produced in sets of mass-produced prints, enabling him to both maximize his profits and reach as many people as possible.

Between 1743 and 1745, Hogarth produced his *Marriage à la Mode* suite, inspired by Joseph Addison's 1712 essay in the *Spectator* promoting the concept of marriage based on love rather than on aristocratic machinations. In his series of paintings and later prints, Hogarth portrays the sordid story and sad end of an arranged marriage between the children of an impoverished aristocrat and a social-climbing member of the newly wealthy merchant class. In the opening scene of the series, **THE MARRIAGE CONTRACT** (**FIG. 30-21**), the cast of characters is assembled to legalize the union. At the right of the painting sits Lord Squanderfield, raising his gout-ridden right foot on a footstool as he points to his lengthy family tree (with a few wilted branches), which goes all the way back to medieval knights, as if to say that the pile of money in front of him on the table is not payment enough for the marriage contract he is being asked to sign. Young Squanderfield, a fop and a simpleton, sits on the far left, admiring himself in the

30-21 • William Hogarth THE MARRIAGE CONTRACT
From *Marriage à la Mode*, 1743–1745. Oil on canvas, 27½″ × 35¾″ (69.9 × 90.8 cm). National Gallery, London.

mirror and ignoring his future wife as he takes a pinch of snuff. His neck is already showing signs of syphilis. The unhappy bride-to-be is extravagantly dressed but rather plain, and her wedding ring is threaded through a handkerchief to wipe away her tears. In the center, her father, the uncultured but wealthy merchant in the brash red coat, leans forward to study Lord Squanderfield's pedigree, an empty sack of money at his feet. The other men are lawyers, including the slippery Silvertongue, who is sharpening the quill that will seal the young couple's fate. The next five scenes of this sad tale describe the progressively disastrous results of such a union, culminating in murder and suicide.

Hogarth hoped to create a distinctively British style of art, free of obscure mythological references and encouraging the self-improvement in viewers that would lead to social progress. His contempt for the decadent tastes of the aristocracy can be seen in the comic detail of the paintings hanging on Lord Squanderfield's walls. Hogarth wanted to entertain and amuse his audiences, but at the same time his acerbic wit lays open the tensions of class and wealth so prevalent in the Britain of his day. Hogarth's work became so popular that in 1745 he was able to give up portraiture, which he considered a deplorable form of vanity.

PORTRAITURE Sir Joshua Reynolds (1723–1792) was a generation younger than Hogarth, and represented the mainstream of British art at the end of the century. After studying Renaissance art in Italy, Reynolds settled in London in 1753, where he worked vigorously to educate artists and patrons to appreciate Classically inspired history painting. In 1768, he was appointed the first president of the Royal Academy (see "Academies and Academy Exhibitions," page 926). His *Fifteen Discourses to the Royal Academy* (1769–1790) set out his theories on art in great detail. He argued that artists should follow rules derived from studying the great masters of the past, especially those who worked in the Classical tradition; he claimed that the ideal image communicated universal truths, and that artists should avoid representations based solely on observation, as these paintings merely communicated base reality.

Reynolds was able to combine his own taste for history painting with his patrons' desire for images of themselves by developing a type of historical or mythological portraiture that he called the **Grand Manner**. **LADY SARAH BUNBURY SACRIFICING TO THE GRACES** (**FIG. 30–22**) is a good example. The large scale of the canvas suggests that it is a history painting, and its details evoke a Classical setting. Framed by a monumental Classical pier and

30-22 • Joshua Reynolds LADY SARAH BUNBURY SACRIFICING TO THE GRACES

1765. Oil on canvas, 7′10″ × 5′ (2.42 × 1.53 m). The Art Institute of Chicago. Mr. and Mrs. W. W. Kimball Collection, 1922.4468

Lady Sarah Bunbury was one of the great beauties of her era. A few years before this portrait was painted, she turned down a proposal of marriage from George III.

Read the document related to Joshua Reynolds on myartslab.com

residences. Reynolds's Grand Manner portraits were widely celebrated, and his London studio was abuzz with sitters, patrons, and assistants. But Reynolds experimented with his paints, so many of his canvases have faded badly.

A counterpoint to Reynolds's style of portraiture is found in the art of Thomas Gainsborough (1727–1788). Gainsborough later set up a studio in Bath, a resort frequented by the rich and fashionable, and catered to his clients' tastes for the informal poses and natural landscapes introduced to England by Van Dyck in the 1620s (see FIG. 23–28). Gainsborough's early, unfinished **ROBERT ANDREWS AND FRANCES CARTER** (FIG. **30–23**), painted soon after their wedding in 1748, shows the wealthy young rural landowner and his wife posed on the grounds of their estate, with the Sudbury River and the hills of Suffolk in the background. The youthful Frances Carter sits stiffly on a decorative seat, the shimmering satin of her fine dress arranged around her, while her husband appears more relaxed, his hunting rifle tucked casually under his arm and his favorite dog at his side. The couple's good care of the land is revealed as well: The neat rows of grain stocks and stubble in the foreground show Robert Andrews's use of the seed drill and plant husbandry. Sheep and horses graze in separate fields. The significance of this painting lies in the natural pose of the couple, the depictions of their land and the pride they take in it and the wealth and power it provides, and the artist's emphasis on nature as the source of bounty and beauty.

THE ROMANCE OF SCIENCE In the English Midlands, artist Joseph Wright of Derby (1734–1797) shows an Enlightenment fascination with the drama and romance of science in his depiction of **AN EXPERIMENT ON A BIRD IN THE AIR-PUMP** (FIG. **30–24**). Wright set up his studio during the first wave of the Industrial Revolution, and many of his patrons were self-made wealthy industrial entrepreneurs. He belonged to the Lunar Society, a group of industrialists (including Wedgwood), merchants, traders, and progressive aristocrats who met monthly in or near Birmingham to exchange ideas about science and technology. As part of the society's attempts to popularize science, Wright painted a series of "entertaining" scenes of scientific experiments.

The second half of the eighteenth century was an age of rapid technological change (see "Iron as a Building Material," page 928), and the development of the air-pump was among the

arch, and dressed in a classicizing costume, Lady Sarah plays the part of a Roman priestess making a sacrifice to the Three Graces, personifications of female beauty. Portraits such as this were intended for the public rooms, halls, and stairways of aristocratic

30-23 • Thomas Gainsborough **ROBERT ANDREWS AND FRANCES CARTER (MR. AND MRS. ANDREWS)**
c. 1748–1750. Oil on canvas, 27½″ × 47″ (69.7 × 119.3 cm). National Gallery, London.

Gainsborough was engaged to paint this couple's portrait shortly after the 20-year-old Robert Andrews married 16-year-old Frances Carter in November 1748. An area of painting in Frances's lap has been left unfinished, perhaps anticipating the later addition of a child for her to hold.

30-24 • Joseph Wright of Derby **AN EXPERIMENT ON A BIRD IN THE AIR-PUMP** 1768. Oil on canvas, 6′ × 8′ (1.82 × 2.43 m). National Gallery, London.

During the seventeenth century, the French government founded a number of **academies** for the support and instruction of students in literature, painting and sculpture, music and dance, and architecture. In 1664, the French Royal Academy of Painting and Sculpture in Paris began to mount occasional exhibitions of members' recent work. This exhibition came to be known as the Salon because it was held in the Salon Carré in the Palace of the Louvre. As of 1737, the Salon was held every other year, with a jury of members selecting the works to be shown.

History paintings (based on historical, mythological, or biblical narratives and generally conveying a high moral or intellectual idea) were accorded highest place in the Academy's hierarchy of genres, followed by historical portraiture, landscape painting, various other forms of portraiture, genre painting, and still life. The Salon shows were the only public art exhibitions of importance in Paris, so they were highly influential in establishing officially approved styles and in molding public taste; they also consolidated the Academy's control over the production of art.

In recognition of Rome's importance as a training ground for aspiring history painters, the French Royal Academy of Painting and Sculpture opened a French Academy in Rome in 1666. A competitive "Prix de Rome," or Rome Prize, enabled the winners to study in Rome for three to five years. A similar prize was established by the French Royal Academy of Architecture in 1720. Many Western cultural capitals emulated the French academic model: Academies were established in Berlin in 1696, Dresden in 1705, London in 1768 (**FIG. 30–25**), Boston in 1780, Mexico City in 1785, and New York in 1802.

Although there were several women members of the European academies of art before the eighteenth century, their inclusion amounted to little more than an honorary recognition of their achievements. In France, Louis XIV proclaimed in his founding address to the French Royal Academy that its purpose was to reward all worthy artists "without regard to the difference of sex," but this resolve was not put into practice. Only seven women gained the title of "Academician" between 1648 and 1706, after which the Academy was closed to women. Nevertheless, four more women were admitted by 1770; however, the men, worried that women would become "too numerous," limited the total number of female members to four. Young women were neither admitted to the French Academy School nor allowed to compete for Academy prizes, both of which were required for professional success. They fared even worse at London's Royal Academy. The Swiss painters Mary Moser and Angelica Kauffmann were both founding members in 1768, but no other women were elected until 1922, and then only as associates.

30–25 • Johann Zoffany **ACADEMICIANS OF THE ROYAL ACADEMY**
1771–1772. Oil on canvas, 47½″ × 59½″ (120.6 × 151.2 cm). The Royal Collection, Windsor Castle, England.

Zoffany's group portrait of members of the London Royal Academy reveals how mainstream artists were taught in the 1770s. The painting shows artists, all men, setting up a life-drawing class and engaging in lively conversation. The studio is decorated with the academy's study collection of Classical statues and plaster copies. Propriety prohibited the presence of women in life-drawing studios, so Zoffany includes Royal Academicians Mary Moser and Angelica Kauffmann in portraits on the wall on the right.

many scientific innovations of the time. Although primarily used to study the properties of gas, it was also widely used in dramatic public demonstrations of scientific principles. In the experiment shown here, air was pumped out of the large glass vessel above the scientist's head until the bird inside collapsed from lack of oxygen. Before the animal died, air was reintroduced by a simple mechanism at the top. Wright depicts the exciting moment before air is reintroduced. Dramatically lit from below by a single light source on the table, the scientist peers out of the picture and gestures like a magician about to perform a trick. By delaying the reintroduction of air, the scientist has created considerable suspense. The three men on the left watch the experiment with great interest, while the young girls on the right have a more emotional response to the proceedings. Near the window at upper right—through which a full moon shines (an allusion to the "Lunar" Society)—a boy stands ready to lower a cage when the bird revives. Science, the painting suggests, holds the potential for wonder, excitement, and discovery about matters of life and death.

HISTORY PAINTING By the time it was adapted to Neoclassicism, history painting had long been considered the highest form of art. The Swiss history painter Angelica Kauffmann (1741–1807), trained in Italy and one of the greatest exponents of early Neoclassicism, arrived in London in 1766 to great acclaim, inspiring British artists to paint Classical history paintings and British patrons to buy them. She was welcomed immediately

30-26 • Angelica Kauffmann CORNELIA POINTING TO HER CHILDREN AS HER TREASURES
c. 1785. Oil on canvas, 40″ × 50″ (101.6 × 127 cm). Virginia Museum of Fine Arts, Richmond, Virginia.
The Adolph D. and Wilkins C. Williams Fund

into Joshua Reynolds's inner circle; in 1768 she was one of only two women artists named among the founding members of the Royal Academy (see "Academies and Academy Exhibitions," opposite).

Already accepting portrait commissions at age 15, Kauffmann painted Winckelmann's portrait in Rome, became an ardent practitioner of Neoclassicism, and was elected to the Roman Academy of St. Luke. Most eighteenth-century women artists specialized in the "lower" painting genres of portraiture or still life, but Kauffmann boldly embarked on an independent career as a history painter. In London, where she lived from 1766 to 1781, she produced numerous history paintings, many of them with subjects drawn from Classical antiquity. After her return to Italy, Kauffmann painted **CORNELIA POINTING TO HER CHILDREN AS HER TREASURES** (FIG. 30-26) for an English patron. The scene

in the painting took place in the second century BCE, during the republican era of Rome. A woman visitor shows Cornelia her jewels and then asks to see those of her hostess. In response, Cornelia shows off her daughter and two sons, saying: "These are my most precious jewels." Cornelia exemplifies the "good mother," a popular theme among some later eighteenth-century patrons who preferred Classical subjects that taught metaphorical lessons of civic and moral virtue. The value of her maternal dedication is emphasized by the fact that her sons, Tiberius and Gaius Gracchus, grew up to be political reformers. Kauffmann's composition is severe and Classical, but she softens the image with warm, subdued lighting and with the tranquil grace of her figures.

Kauffmann's devotion to Neoclassical history painting emerged during her friendship with American-born Benjamin West (1738–1820) in Rome. West studied in Philadelphia before he left for

In 1779, Abraham Darby III built a bridge over the Severn River (**FIG. 30–27**) at Coalbrookdale in Shropshire, England, a town typical of industrial England, with factories and workers' housing filling the valley. Built primarily for function, the bridge demonstrated a need for newer, better transportation routes for moving industrial goods. Its importance lies in the fact that it is probably the first large-scale example of the use of structural metal in bridge building, in which iron struts replace the heavy, hand-cut stone voussoirs of earlier bridges. Five pairs of cast-iron, semicircular arches form a strong, economical 100-foot span.

In functional architecture such as this, the available technology, the properties of the material, and the requirements of engineering in large part determine form, often producing an unintended new aesthetic. Here, the use of metal made possible the light, open, skeletal structure sought by builders since the twelfth century. Cast iron was quickly adopted for the construction of such engineering wonders as the soaring train stations of the nineteenth century, leading ultimately to such marvels as the Eiffel Tower (see **FIG. 31–1**).

30-27 • Abraham Darby III
SEVERN RIVER BRIDGE
Coalbrookdale, England. 1779.

 View a simulation about cast-iron structures on myartslab.com

Rome in 1759, where he met Winckelmann and became a student of Mengs. In 1763, he moved permanently to London, where he specialized in Neoclassical history painting. In 1768, along with Kauffmann and Reynolds, he became a founding member of the Royal Academy.

Two years later, West shocked Reynolds and his other academic friends with his painting **THE DEATH OF GENERAL WOLFE** (**FIG. 30-28**), which seemed to break completely with Neoclassicism and academic history painting. West argued that history painting was not dependent on dressing figures in Classical costume; in fact, it could represent a contemporary subject as long as the grand themes and elevated message remained intact. Thus, West's painting, and the genre it spawned, came to be known as "modern history" painting. At first, George III and Joshua Reynolds were appalled, but modern history pieces had too strong an attraction for both British collectors and the British public. The king eventually commissioned one of the four replicas of the painting.

West's painting glorifies the British general James Wolfe, who died in 1759 in a British victory over the French for the control of Quebec during the Seven Years War (1756–1763). West depicted Wolfe in his red uniform expiring in the arms of his comrades under a cloud-swept sky. In fact, Wolfe actually died at the base of a tree, surrounded by two or three attendants, but the laws of artistic decorum demanded a much nobler scene. Thus, though West's painting seems naturalistic, it is not an objective document, nor was it intended to be. West employs the Grand Manner that Reynolds proposed in his *Discourses*, celebrating the valor of the fallen hero, the loyalty of the British soldiers, and the justice of their cause. To indicate the North American setting, West also included at the left a Native American warrior who contemplates the fallen Wolfe. This was another fiction, since the Native Americans in this battle fought on the side of the French, but his presence here establishes the North American site of the event. The dramatic illumination increases the emotional intensity of the scene, as do the poses of Wolfe's attendants, arranged to suggest a Lamentation

30-28 • Benjamin West THE DEATH OF GENERAL WOLFE
1770. Oil on canvas, 4'11½" × 7' (1.51 × 2.14 m). National Gallery of Canada, Ottawa. Transfer from the Canadian War Memorials, 1921. Gift of the 2nd Duke of Westminster, Eaton Hall, Cheshire, 1918

The famous actor David Garrick was so moved by this painting that he enacted an impromptu interpretation of the dying Wolfe in front of the work when it was exhibited at the Royal Academy.

over the dead Christ. Extending the analogy, the British flag above Wolfe replaces the Christian cross. Just as Christ died for humanity, Wolfe sacrificed himself for the good of the nation. The brilliant color, emotional intensity, and moralizing message made this image extremely popular with the British public. It was translated into a print and received the widest circulation of any image in Britain up to that time.

ROMANTIC PAINTING The emotional drama of West's painting helped launch Romanticism in Britain. Among its early practitioners was John Henry Fuseli (1741–1825), who arrived in London from his native Switzerland in 1764. Trained in theology, philosophy, and the Neoclassical aesthetics of Winckelmann (whose writings he translated into English), Fuseli quickly became a member of London's intellectual elite. Joshua Reynolds encouraged Fuseli to become an artist, and in 1770 he left England to study in Rome, where he spent most of the next eight years.

His encounter with the sometimes tortured and expressive aspects of both Roman sculpture and Michelangelo's painting led him not to Neoclassicism but to develop his own powerfully expressive style. In his work, Fuseli drew more heavily on the passion of some Roman art, and later that of Michelangelo, than on the ancient Greek art admired by Winckelmann.

Back in London, Fuseli established himself as a history painter, but he specialized in dramatic subjects drawn from Homer, Dante, Shakespeare, and Milton. His interest in the dark recesses of the human mind led him to paint supernatural and irrational subjects. In **THE NIGHTMARE** (FIG. 30-29), he depicts a sleeping woman sprawled across a divan with her head thrown back, oppressed by a gruesome incubus (or *mara*, an evil spirit) crouching on her pelvis in an erotic dream. According to legend, the incubus was believed to feed by stealing women and having sex with them. In the background a horse with wild, phosphorescent eyes thrusts its head into the room through a curtain. The image communicates fear

30-29 • John Henry Fuseli THE NIGHTMARE
1781. Oil on canvas, 39¾″ × 49½″ (101 × 127 cm). The Detroit Institute of Arts.
Founders Society purchase with Mr. and Mrs. Bert L. Smokler and Mr. and Mrs. Lawrence A. Fleischmann funds

Fuseli was not popular with the English critics. One writer said that his 1780 entry in the London Royal Academy exhibition "ought to be destroyed," and Horace Walpole called another painting in 1785 "shockingly mad, mad, mad, madder than ever." Even after achieving the highest official acknowledgment of his talents, Fuseli was called "the Wild Swiss" and "Painter to the Devil." But the public appreciated his work, and *The Nightmare*, exhibited at the Royal Academy in 1782, was repeated in at least three more versions and its imagery was disseminated through prints published by commercial engravers. One of these prints would later hang in the office of the Austrian psychoanalyst Sigmund Freud, who believed that dreams were manifestations of the dreamer's repressed desires.

of the unknown and unknowable, and sexuality without restraint. The painting was exhibited at the Royal Academy in 1782, and although not well received by Fuseli's peers, it clearly struck a chord with the public. He painted at least four versions of this subject and prints of it had a wide circulation.

Fuseli's friend William Blake (1757–1827), a highly original poet, painter, and printmaker, was also inspired by the dramatic aspect of Michelangelo's art. Trained as an engraver, he enrolled briefly at the Royal Academy, where he quickly rejected the teachings of Reynolds, believing that rules hinder rather than aid

creativity. He became a lifelong advocate of probing the unfettered imagination. For Blake, the imagination provided access to the higher realm of the spirit while reason was confined to the lower world of matter.

Blake was interested in probing the nature of good and evil, developing an idiosyncratic form of Christian belief that drew on elements from the Bible, Greek mythology, and British legend. His "prophetic books," designed and printed in the mid 1790s, brought together painting and poetry to explore themes of spiritual crisis and redemption. Thematically related to the prophetic

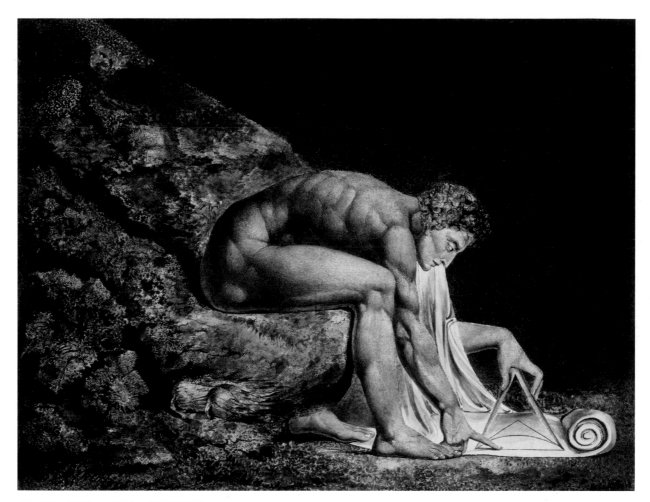

30-30 • William Blake NEWTON
1795–c. 1805. Color print finished in ink and watercolor, 18⅛″ × 23⅝″ (46 × 60 cm). Tate, London.

books are an independent series of 12 large color prints that he executed mostly in 1795. These include the large print of **NEWTON** (**FIG. 30-30**), the epitome of eighteenth-century rationalism, heroically naked in a cave, obsessed with reducing the universe to a mathematical drawing with his compasses in an image that recalls medieval representations of God the Creator, designing the world.

John Singleton Copley, whose portrait of Sarah Morris and Thomas Mifflin opened this chapter (see FIG. **30-1**), moved from Boston to London after the Revolutionary War, never to return to his native land. In London, he established himself as a portraitist and painter of modern history in the vein of fellow American expatriate Benjamin West. Copley's most distinctive modern history painting was **WATSON AND THE SHARK** (**FIG. 30-31**), commissioned by Brook Watson, a wealthy London merchant and Tory politician, in 1778. Copley's painting dramatizes an episode of 1749, in which the 14-year-old Watson was attacked by a shark while swimming in Havana Harbor, and lost part of his right leg before being rescued by his comrades. Copley's pyramidal composition is made up of figures in a boat and the hapless Watson in the water with a highly imaginary shark set against the backdrop of the harbor. Several of the figures were inspired by Classical sources, but the scene portrayed is anything but Classical. In the

foreground, the ferocious shark lunges toward the helpless, naked Watson, while at the prow of the rescue boat a man raises his harpoon to attack the predator. At the left, two of Watson's shipmates strain to reach him while others in the boat look on in alarm. An African man, standing at the apex of the painting, holds a rope that curls over Watson's extended right arm, connecting him to the boat.

Some scholars have read the African figure as a servant waiting to hand the rope to his white master, but his inclusion has also been interpreted in more overtly political terms. The shark attack on Watson in Havana Harbor occurred while he was working in the transatlantic shipping trade, one aspect of which involved the shipment of slaves from Africa to the West Indies. At the time when Watson commissioned this painting, debate was raging in the British Parliament over the interconnected issues of the Americans' recent Declaration of Independence and the slave trade. Several Tories, including Watson, opposed American independence, highlighting the hypocrisy of American calls for freedom from the British crown while the colonists continued to deny freedom to African slaves. Indeed, during the Revolutionary War the British offered freedom to every runaway American slave who joined the British army or navy.

30-31 • John Singleton Copley WATSON AND THE SHARK
1778. Oil on canvas, 5'10¾" × 7'6½" (1.82 × 2.29 m). National Gallery of Art, Washington, DC. Ferdinand Lammot Belin Fund

Copley's painting, its subject doubtless dictated by Watson, may therefore indicate Watson's sympathy for American slaves; or the figure may be included simply to indicate that the event took place in Havana, much as the inclusion of a Native American in West's painting of the death of Wolfe (see FIG. 30–28) sites that picture. Copley was one of the first artists in the capital to exhibit his modern history paintings in public places around London, making money by charging admission fees and advertising his large paintings for sale. His extraordinary images and exhibitions took advantage of the spectacular displays of early nineteenth-century London's Phantasmagoria (a sensational magic lantern display with smoke, mirrors, lights, and gauze "ghosts"), panoramas, dioramas, and the Eidophusikon (a miniature theater with special effects).

LATER EIGHTEENTH-CENTURY ART IN FRANCE

In late eighteenth-century France, the Rococo was replaced by Enlightenment ideas and by the gathering storm clouds of revolution. French art moved increasingly toward Neoclassicism as French architects held closer to Roman proportions and sensibility, while

painters and sculptors increasingly embraced didactic presentations in sober, Classical style.

ARCHITECTURE

French architects of the late eighteenth century generally considered Classicism not one of many alternative artistic styles but as the single, true style. Winckelmann's argument that "imitation of the ancients" was the key to good taste was taken to heart in France. The leading French Neoclassical architect was Jacques-Germain Soufflot (1713–1780), whose church of Sainte-Geneviève, known today as the **PANTHÉON** (FIG. 30–32), is the most typical Neoclassical building in Paris. In it, Soufflot attempted to integrate three traditions: the Roman architecture he had seen on two trips to Italy; French and English Baroque Classicism; and the Palladian style being revived at the time in England. The façade of the Panthéon, with its huge portico, is modeled on the proportions of ancient Roman temples. The dome, on the other hand, was inspired by seventeenth-century architecture, including Sir Christopher Wren's St. Paul's Cathedral in London (see FIG. 23–60), while the radical geometry of its central-plan layout (FIG. 30–33) owes as much to Burlington's Neo-Palladian Chiswick House (see FIG.

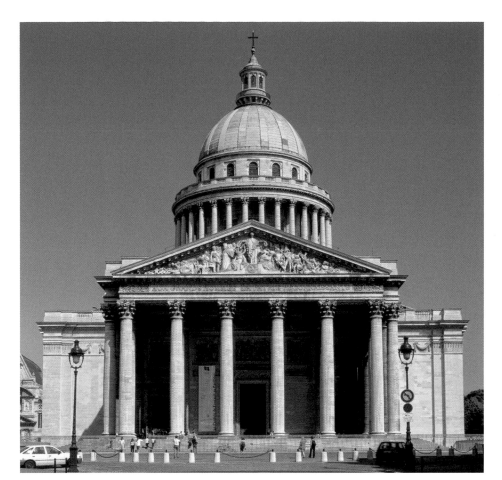

This building has an interesting history. Before it was completed, the revolutionary government in control of Paris confiscated all religious properties to raise desperately needed public funds. Instead of selling Sainte-Geneviève, however, they voted in 1791 to make it the Temple of Fame for the burial of Heroes of Liberty. Under Napoleon I (r. 1799–1814), the building was resanctified as a Catholic church and was again used as such under King Louis-Philippe (r. 1830–1848) and Napoleon III (r. 1852–1870). Then it was permanently designated a nondenominational lay temple. In 1851, the building was used as a physics laboratory. Here the French physicist Jean-Bernard Foucault suspended his now-famous pendulum in the interior of the high crossing dome, and by measuring the path of the pendulum's swing proved his theory that the Earth rotated on its axis in a counterclockwise motion. In 1995, the ashes of Marie Curie, who had won the Nobel Prize for Chemistry in 1911, were moved into this "memorial to the great men of France," making her the first woman to be enshrined there.

**30-33 • CUTAWAY
ILLUSTRATION OF
THE PANTHÉON**

✳ **Explore** the architectural panoramas of the Panthéon on myartslab.com

30–15) as it does to Christian tradition. The Panthéon, however, is not simply the sum of its parts. Its rational, ordered plan is constructed with rectangles, squares, and circles, while its relatively plain surfaces communicate severity and powerful simplicity.

PAINTING AND SCULPTURE

While French painters such as Boucher, Fragonard, and their followers continued to work in the Rococo style in the later decades of the eighteenth century, a strong reaction against the Rococo had set in by the 1760s. A leading detractor of the Rococo was Denis Diderot (1713–1784), whose 32-volume compendium of knowledge and skill, the *Encyclopédie* (produced in collaboration with Jean le Rond d'Alembert, 1717–1783) served as an archive of Enlightenment thought in France. In 1759, Diderot began to write reviews of the official Salon for a periodic newsletter for wealthy subscribers, and he is generally considered to be the founder of modern art criticism. Diderot believed that it was art's proper function to "inspire virtue and purify manners," a function that the Rococo was not designed to fulfill.

CHARDIN Diderot greatly admired Jean-Siméon Chardin (1699–1779), an artist who as early as the 1730s began to create moralizing pictures in the tradition of seventeenth-century Dutch genre painting by focusing on carefully structured but touching scenes of everyday middle-class life. **THE GOVERNESS** (FIG. **30-34**), for instance, shows a finely dressed boy with books under his arm, addressed by his governess as she prepares to brush his tricorne (three-cornered hat). Scattered on the floor are a racquet, a shuttlecock, and playing cards, the childish pleasures that the boy leaves behind as he prepares to go to his studies and, ultimately, to a life of responsible adulthood. The work suggests the benevolent exercise of authority and willing submission to it, both seen as critical to proper political as well as familial life.

GREUZE Diderot reserved his highest praise for Jean-Baptiste Greuze (1725–1805), and his own plays of the late 1750s served as a source of inspiration for Greuze's painting. Diderot expanded the traditional range of theatrical works in Paris from mostly tragedy and comedy to include the *drame bourgeois* (middle-class drama) and "middle tragedy" (later called the "melodrama"), both of which communicated moral and civic lessons through simple, clear stories of ordinary life. Greuze's domestic genre paintings, such as **THE VILLAGE BRIDE** (FIG. **30-35**), were visual counterparts to Diderot's *drame bourgeois* and "middle tragedy." In this painting, Greuze presents the action on a shallow, stagelike space under a dramatic spotlight. An elderly father reaches out to his affectionate family as he hands the dowry for his daughter to his new son-in-law; a notary records the event. The young couple tentatively link their arms, while the bride is embraced within her family by her mother and sister. What a contrast to the simmering deception and self-serving objectives highlighted in Hogarth's marriage contract (see FIG. 30-21). Greuze's painting seeks to demonstrate that virtue and poverty can coexist. This kind of highly emotional, theatrical, and moralizing genre scene was widely praised in Greuze's time, offering a counterpoint to early Neoclassical history painting in France.

VIGÉE-LEBRUN While Greuze painted scenes of the poor and middle class, Marie-Louise-Élisabeth Vigée-Lebrun (1755–1842) became famous as Queen Marie Antoinette's

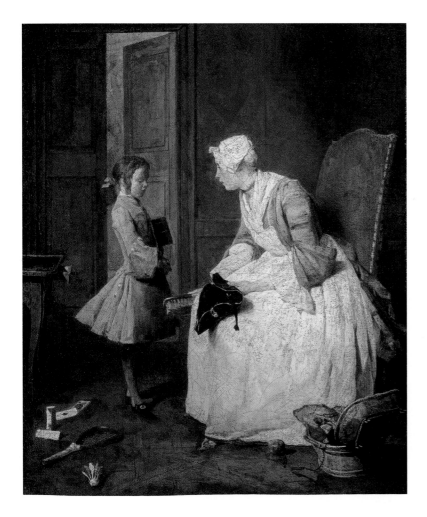

30-34 • Jean-Siméon Chardin THE GOVERNESS
1739. Oil on canvas, 18⅛″ × 14¾″ (46 × 37.5 cm). National Gallery of Canada, Ottawa. Purchase, 1956

Chardin was one of the first French artists to treat the lives of women and children with sympathy and to portray the dignity of women's work in his images of young mothers, governesses, and kitchen maids. Shown at the Salon of 1739, *The Governess* was praised by contemporary critics, one of whom noted "the graciousness, sweetness, and restraint that the governess maintains in her discipline of the young man about his dirtiness, disorder, and neglect; his attention, shame, and remorse; all are expressed with great simplicity."

favorite portrait painter. Vigée-Lebrun was also notable for her election into the French Royal Academy of Painting and Sculpture, which then made only four places available to women. In 1787, she painted **MARIE ANTOINETTE WITH HER CHILDREN** (FIG. 30–36). Drawing on the theme of the "good mother" seen earlier in Angelica Kauffmann's Neoclassical painting of Cornelia (see FIG. 30–26), Vigée-Lebrun portrays the queen as a kindly, stabilizing mother, a flagrant work of royal propaganda aimed at counteracting public perceptions of her as selfish, extravagant, and immoral. The queen maintains her appropriately regal pose, but her children are depicted more sympathetically. The princess leans affectionately against her mother's arm and the little dauphin—heir to a throne he

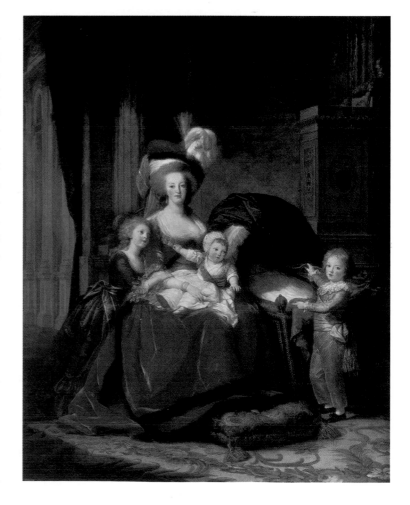

30–36 • Marie-Louise-Élisabeth Vigée-Lebrun **PORTRAIT OF MARIE ANTOINETTE WITH HER CHILDREN**
1787. Oil on canvas, 9′1½″ × 7′5⅝″ (2.75 × 2.15 m). Musée National du Château de Versailles.

As the favorite painter to the queen, Vigée-Lebrun escaped from Paris with her daughter on the eve of the Revolution of 1789 and fled to Rome. After a very successful self-exile working in Italy, Austria, Russia, and England, the artist finally resettled in Paris in 1805 and again became popular with Parisian art patrons. Over her long career, she painted about 800 portraits in a vibrant style that changed very little over the decades.

would never inherit—poignantly points to the empty cradle of a recently deceased sibling. The image alludes to the allegory of Abundance and is intended to signify peace and prosperity for France under the reign of Marie Antoinette's husband, Louis XVI, who came to the throne in 1774 but would be executed, along with the queen, in 1793.

DAVID The most important French Neoclassical painter of the era was Jacques-Louis David (1748–1825), who dominated French art for over 20 years during the French Revolution and the subsequent reign of Napoleon. In 1774, he won the Prix de Rome and spent six years in that city, studying antique sculpture and learning the principles of Neoclassicism. After his return to Paris, he produced a series of severely plain Neoclassical paintings extolling the antique virtues of stoicism, masculinity, and patriotism.

Perhaps the most significant of these works was the **OATH OF THE HORATII** (**FIG. 30-37**) of 1784–1785. A royal commission that David returned to Rome to paint, the work reflects the taste and values of Louis XVI, who, along with his minister of the arts, Count d'Angiviller, was sympathetic to the Enlightenment. Like Diderot, d'Angiviller and the king believed that art should improve public morals. One of d'Angiviller's first official acts was to ban indecent nudity from the Salon of 1775 and commission a series of didactic history paintings. The commission for David's *Oath of the Horatii* in 1784 was part of that general program.

The subject of the painting was inspired by the drama *Horace*, written by the great French playwright Pierre Corneille (1606–1684), which was in turn based on ancient Roman historical texts. The patriotic oath-taking incident David depicted, however, is not taken directly from these sources and was apparently the artist's

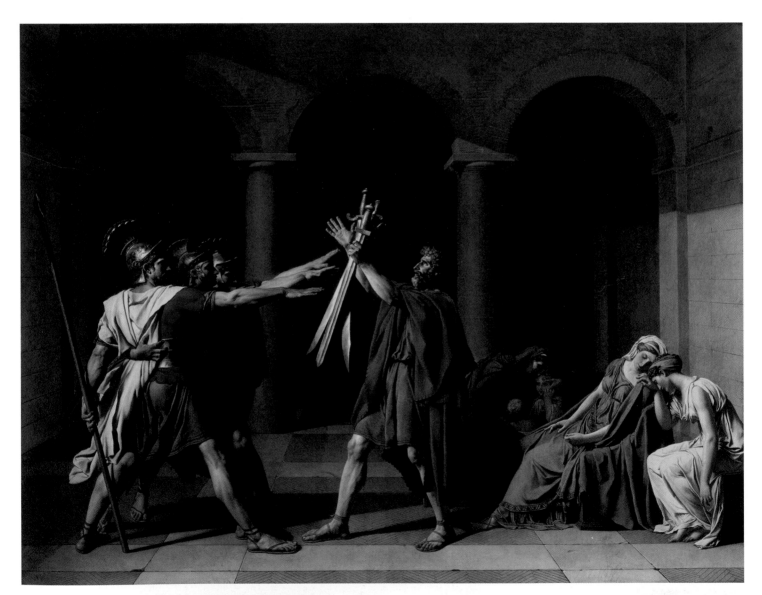

30-37 • Jacques-Louis David **OATH OF THE HORATII**
1784–1785. Oil on canvas, 10′8¼″ × 14′ (3.26 × 4.27 m). Musée du Louvre, Paris.

Read the document related to Jacques-Louis David on myartslab.com own invention. The story is set in the seventh century BCE, at a time when Rome and its rival, Alba, a neighboring city-state, agreed to settle a border dispute and avert a war by holding a battle to the death between the three sons of Horace (the Horatii), representing Rome, and the three Curatii, representing Alba. In David's painting, the Horatii stand with arms outstretched toward their father, who reaches toward them with the swords on which they pledge to fight and die for Rome. The power gestures of the young men's outstretched hands almost pushes their father back. In contrast to the upright, tensed, muscular angularity of the men, the group of swooning women and frightened children are limp. They weep for the lives of both the Horatii and the Curatii. Sabina (in the center) is a sister of the Curatii, and also married to one of the Horatii; Camilla (at the far right) is sister to the Horatii and engaged to one of the Curatii. David's composition, which separates the men from the women and children spatially by the use of framing background arches, dramatically contrasts the young men's stoic and willing self-sacrifice with the women's emotional collapse.

The moving intensity of this history painting pushed French academic rules on decorum to their limit. Originally a royal commission, it quickly and ironically became an emblem of the 1789 French Revolution since its message of patriotism and sacrifice for the greater good effectively captured the mood of the leaders of the new French Republic established in 1792. As the revolutionaries abolished the monarchy and titles of nobility, took education out of the hands of the Church, and wrote a declaration of human rights, David joined the leftist Jacobin party.

In 1793, David painted the death of the Jacobin supporter, Jean-Paul Marat (**FIG. 30-38**). A radical journalist, Marat lived simply among the packing cases that he used as furniture, writing pamphlets urging the abolition of aristocratic privilege. Because he suffered from a painful skin ailment, he would often write while sitting in a medicinal bath. Charlotte Corday, a supporter of an opposition party, held Marat partly responsible for the 1792 riots in which hundreds of political prisoners judged sympathetic to the king were killed, and in retribution she stabbed Marat as he sat in his bath. David avoids the potential for sensationalism in the subject by portraying not the violent event but its tragic aftermath—the dead Marat slumped in his bathtub, his right hand still holding a quill pen, while his left hand grasps the letter that Corday used to gain access to his home. The simple wooden block beside the bath, which Marat used as a desk, is inscribed with the names of both Marat and the painter's in a dedicatory inscription—"to Marat, David." It almost serves as the martyr's tombstone.

David's painting is a tightly composed, powerfully stark image. The background is blank, adding to the quiet mood and timeless feeling of the picture, just as the very different background of the

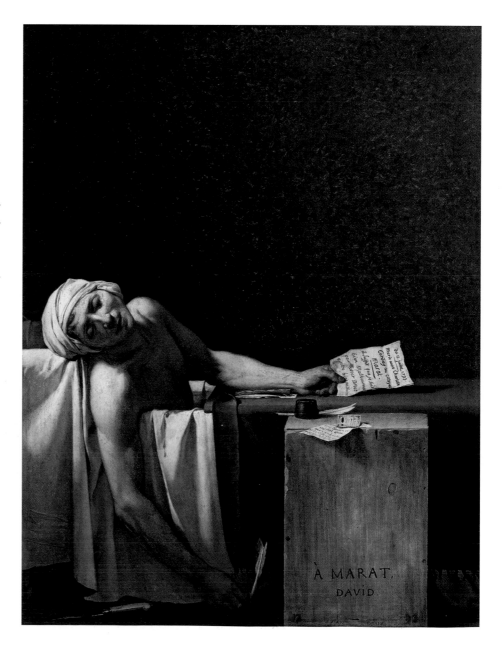

30-38 • Jacques-Louis David
DEATH OF MARAT
1793. Oil on canvas, 5′5″ × 4′2½″ (1.65 × 1.28 m). © Royal Museums of Fine Arts of Belgium, Brussels.

Oath of the Horatii also added to its drama. The color of Marat's pale body coordinates with the bloodstained sheets on which he lies, creating compact shape that is framed by the dark background and green blanket draped over the bathtub. David manages to transform an ugly, brutal event into an elegiac statement of somber eloquence. Marat's pose, which echoes Michelangelo's Vatican *Pietà* (see FIG. 21-9), implies that, like Christ, Marat was a martyr for the people.

The French Revolution eventually degenerated into mob rule in 1793–1794 as Jacobin leaders orchestrated the ruthless execution of thousands of their opponents in what became known as the Reign of Terror. David, as a Jacobin, was elected a deputy to the National Convention and served a two-week term as president, during which time he signed several arrest warrants. When the Jacobins lost power in 1794, he was twice imprisoned, albeit under lenient conditions that allowed him to continue to paint. He later emerged as a supporter of Napoleon and re-established his career at the height of Napoleon's ascendancy.

GIRODET-TRIOSON David was a charismatic and influential teacher who trained most of the major French painters of the 1790s and early 1800s, including Anne-Louis Girodet-Trioson (1767–1824). His **POR-TRAIT OF JEAN-BAPTISTE BELLEY** (**FIG. 30-39**) combines the restrained color and tight composition of David with a relaxed elegance that makes the subject more accessible to the viewer. And like many of David's works, this portrait was political. The Senegal-born Belley (1747?–1805) was a former slave who was sent to Paris as a representative to the French Convention by the colony of Saint-Domingue (now Haiti). The Haitian Revolution of 1791, in which African slaves overturned the French colonial power, resulted in the first republic to be ruled by freed African slaves. In 1794, Belley led the successful legislative campaign to abolish slavery in the colonies and to grant full citizenship to people of African descent. In the portrait, Belley leans casually on the pedestal of a bust of the abbot Guillaume Raynal (1711–1796), the French philosopher whose 1770 book condemned slavery and paved the way for such legislation, making the portrait a tribute to both Belley and Raynal. Napoleon re-established slavery in the Caribbean islands in 1801, but the revolt continued until 1804, when Haiti finally achieved full independence.

LABILLE-GUIARD Also reflecting the revolutionary spirit of the age, the painter Adélaïde Labille-Guiard (1749–1803) championed the rights of women artists. Elected to the French Royal Academy of Painting and Sculpture in the same year as Vigée-Lebrun, Labille-Guiard asserted her worthiness for this honor in a **SELF-PORTRAIT WITH TWO PUPILS** that she submitted to the Salon of 1785 (**FIG. 30-40**). The painting was a response to sexist rumors that her work, and that of Vigée-Lebrun, had actually been painted by men. In a witty role reversal, the only male in this monumental painting of the artist at her easel is her father, shown in a bust behind her canvas, as her muse, a role usually played by women. While the self-portrait flatters the painter, it also portrays Labille-Guiard as a force to be reckoned with, a woman who engages our gaze uncompromisingly, and whose students are serious and intent on their study. In the year following the French Revolution, Labille-Guiard successfully petitioned the French Academy of Painting and Sculpture to end the restriction that lim-

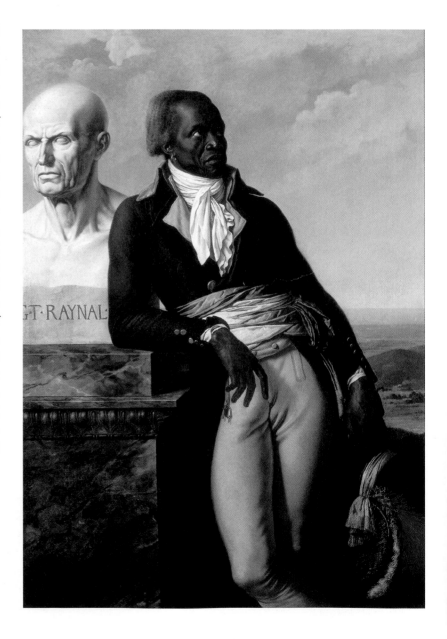

30-39 • Anne-Louis Girodet-Trioson **PORTRAIT OF JEAN-BAPTISTE BELLEY**
1797. Oil on canvas, 5′2½″ × 3′8½″ (1.59 × 1.13 m). Musée National du Château de Versailles.

30–40 • Adélaïde Labille-Guiard SELF-PORTRAIT WITH TWO PUPILS
1785. Oil on canvas, 6′11″ × 4′11½″ (2.11 × 1.51 m). Metropolitan Museum of Art, New York.
Gift of Julia A. Berwind, 1953 (53.225.5)

ited its membership to four women. The reform was later reversed by the revolutionary government as it became more authoritarian.

HOUDON The French Neoclassical sculptor Jean-Antoine Houdon (1741–1828), who studied in Italy between 1764 and 1768 after winning the Prix de Rome, imbued the Classical style with a new sense of realism. He carved busts and full-length statues of a number of the important figures of his time, including Diderot, Voltaire, Jean-Jacques Rousseau, Catherine the Great, Thomas Jefferson, Benjamin Franklin, Lafayette (a Revolutionary hero), and Napoleon, and his studio produced a steady supply of replicas, much in demand because of the cult of great men promoted by Enlightenment thinkers to provide models of virtue and patriotism. On the basis of his bust of Benjamin Franklin, Houdon was commissioned by the Virginia State Legislature to make a portrait of its native son **GEORGE WASHINGTON** to be installed in the Neoclassical Virginia state capitol building designed by Jefferson. In 1785, Houdon traveled to the United States to make a cast of Washington's features and create a bust in plaster, returning to Paris to execute the life-size marble figure (FIG. 30–41). The sculpture represents Washington in the Classical manner but dressed in contemporary clothes, much as Benjamin West had

30–41 • Jean-Antoine Houdon GEORGE WASHINGTON
1788–1792. Marble, height 6′2″ (1.9 m). State Capitol, Richmond, Virginia.

The plow share behind Washington alludes to Cincinnatus, a Roman soldier of the fifth century BCE who was appointed dictator and dispatched to defeat the Aequi, who had besieged a Roman army. After the victory, Cincinnatus resigned the dictatorship and returned to his farm. Washington's contemporaries compared him with Cincinnatus because, after leading the Americans to victory over the British, he resigned his commission and went back to farming rather than seeking political power. Just below Washington's waistcoat hangs the badge of the Society of the Cincinnati, founded in 1783 by the officers of the disbanding Continental Army who were returning to their peacetime occupations. Washington lived in retirement at his Mount Vernon, Virginia, plantation for five years before his 1789 election as the first president of the United States.

represented General Wolfe (see FIG. 30–28). Houdon imbues the portrait with Classical ideals of dignity, honor, and civic responsibility. Washington wears the uniform of a general, the rank he held in the Revolutionary War, but he also rests his left hand on a Roman *fasces*, a bundle of 13 rods (representing the 13 colonies) tied together with an axe face, that served as a Roman symbol of authority. Attached to the *fasces* are both a sword of war and a plowshare of peace. Significantly, Houdon's Washington does not touch the sword.

ART IN SPAIN AND SPANISH AMERICA

In the first half of the eighteenth century, Philip V (r. 1700–1746) marginalized the Spanish art world by awarding most royal commissions to foreign artists. German painter Mengs introduced Neoclassicism into Spain with his work for Charles III (r. 1759–1788), but Spanish artists did not embrace Neoclassicism the way they had Baroque during the previous century. At the end of the eighteenth century, however, the Spanish court appointed one of the greatest Spanish artists of the period as court painter: Francisco Goya y Lucientes (1746–1828).

Since the sixteenth century, the Spanish had commissioned art in the distant lands of their American colonies. During the eighteenth century this colonial art and architecture remained rooted in the enduring traditions of the Spanish Baroque intermingled with the artistic traditions of native peoples, joining the symbolism and the artistic vocabulary of two distinct cultures into a new art in Mexico and the American Southwest.

PORTRAITURE AND PROTEST IN SPAIN: GOYA

Goya was introduced to the Spanish royal workshop in 1774, when he produced tapestry cartoons under the direction of Mengs. He painted for Charles III and served as court painter to Charles IV (r. 1788–1808), but he also belonged to an intellectual circle that embraced the ideals of the French Revolution, and his work began subtly to criticize the court in which he served.

Charles IV, threatened by the possibility of similar social upheaval in Spain, reinstituted the Inquisition soon after the French Revolution, halted reform, and even prohibited the entry of French books into Spain. Goya responded to this new situation by creating a series of prints aimed at the ordinary people, with whom he identified. The theme of *Los Caprichos* (*The Caprices*, a folio of 80 etchings produced between 1796 and 1798) is that reason ignored is a sleeping monster. In the print entitled **THE SLEEP OF REASON PRODUCES MONSTERS** (FIG. 30–42), the slumbering personification of Reason is haunted by a menagerie of demonic-looking owls, bats, and a cat that are let loose when Reason sleeps. Other *Caprichos* enumerate the follies of Spanish society that Goya and his circle considered equally monstrous. His implicit goal with this series was to incite action, to alert the Spanish people

30-42 • Francisco Goya THE SLEEP OF REASON PRODUCES MONSTERS

No. 43 from *Los Caprichos* (*The Caprices*). 1796–1798; published 1799. Etching and aquatint, 8½″ × 6″ (21.6 × 15.2 cm). Courtesy of the Hispanic Society of America, New York.

After printing about 300 sets of this series, Goya offered them for sale in 1799. He withdrew them two days later without explanation. Historians believe that he was probably warned by the Church that if he did not do so he might have to appear before the Inquisition because of the unflattering portrayal of the Church in some of the etchings. In 1803, Goya donated the plates to the Royal Printing Office.

View the Closer Look for *The Sleep of Reason Produces Monsters* on myartslab.com

to the errors of their foolish ways, and to reawaken them to reason. He tried to market his etchings as Hogarth had done in England, but his work aroused controversy and was brought to the attention of his royal patrons. To deflect additional trouble, Goya presented the metal plates of the series to the king, suggesting that the images were not intentionally critical of the monarchy. He was torn between his position as a court painter who owed allegiance to the king and his passionate desire for a more open Spain.

His large portrait of the **FAMILY OF CHARLES IV** (**FIG. 30-43**) reveals some of Goya's ambivalence. He clearly wanted his patron to connect this portrait to an earlier Spanish royal portrait,

30-43 • Francisco Goya FAMILY OF CHARLES IV
1800. Oil on canvas, 9′2″ × 11′ (2.79 × 3.36 m). Museo del Prado, Madrid.

30–44 • Francisco Goya THIRD OF MAY, 1808
1814–1815. Oil on canvas, 8′9″ × 13′4″ (2.67 × 4.06 m). Museo del Prado, Madrid.

Las Meninas by Velázquez (see FIG. 23–21), thereby raising his own status as well as that of the king. Like Velázquez, Goya includes himself in the painting, to the left behind the easel. The king and queen appear at the center of this large family portrait, surrounded by their immediate family. The figures are formal and stiff. Much has been written about how Goya seems to show his patrons as faintly ridiculous here. Some seem bored; the somewhat dazed king, chest full of medals, stands before a relative who looks distractedly out of the painting (perhaps the face was added at the last minute); the double-chinned queen gazes obliquely toward the viewer (at that time she was having an open affair with the prime minister); their eldest daughter, to the left, stares into space; and another, older relative behind seems almost surprised to be there. One French art critic even described the painting as resembling "The corner baker and his family after they have won the lottery." Yet the royal family was apparently satisfied with Goya's depiction. At a time when the authority of the Spanish aristocracy was

crumbling, this complex representation of conflicted emotions, aspirations, and responsibilities may have struck a chord with them. Some viewers who first saw it may have thought its candid representations were refreshingly modern.

In 1808, Napoleon launched a campaign to conquer Spain and would eventually place his brother, Joseph Bonaparte (1768–1844), on the Spanish throne. At first many Spanish citizens, Goya included, welcomed the French, who brought political reform, including a new, more liberal constitution. But on May 2, 1808, a rumor spread through Madrid that the French planned to kill the royal family. The populace rose up against the French and a day of bloody street fighting ensued, followed by mass arrests. Hundreds were herded into a convent and then executed by a French firing squad before dawn on May 3rd. In Goya's impassioned memorial to that slaughter (FIG. 30–44), the violent gestures of the defenseless rebels and the mechanical efficiency of the tight row of executioners in the firing squad create a nightmarish tableau. A spotlighted victim in a brilliant white shirt confronts his faceless killers with outstretched arms recalling the crucified Christ, an image of searing pathos. This painting is not a cool, didactic representation of civic sacrifice like David's Neoclassical *Oath of the Horatii* (see FIG. 30-37). It is an image of blind terror and desperate fear, the essence of Romanticism—the sensational current event, the loose brushwork, the lifelike poses, the unbalanced composition, and the dramatic lighting. There is no moral here, only hopeless rage. When asked why he painted such a brutal scene, Goya responded: "To warn men never to do it again."

Soon after, the Spanish monarchy was restored. Ferdinand VII (r. 1808, 1814–1833) once again reinstated the Inquisition and abolished the new constitution. In 1815, Goya was called before the Inquisition and charged with obscenity for an earlier painting of a female nude. He was acquitted and retired to his home outside Madrid, where he vented his anger at the world in a series of nightmarish "black paintings" rendered directly on the walls, and then spent the last four years of his life in France.

THE ART OF THE AMERICAS UNDER SPAIN

The sixteenth-century Spanish conquest of Central and South America led to the suppression of indigenous religions. Temples were demolished and replaced with Roman Catholic churches, while Franciscan, Dominican, and Augustinian friars worked to convert the indigenous populations. Some missionaries were so appalled by the conquerors' brutal treatment of the native peoples that they petitioned the Spanish king to help improve conditions.

In the course of the Mesoamericans' forced conversion to Roman Catholicism, Christian symbolism became inextricably mixed with the symbolism of indigenous religious beliefs. An example of such blending can be seen in colonial **atrial crosses**, carved early on by indigenous sculptors. Missionaries placed these crosses in church atriums, where converts gathered for education in Christianity. The sixteenth-century **ATRIAL CROSS** now in the Basilica of Guadalupe near Mexico City (FIG. 30-45) is richly carved in the low relief of native sculptural traditions and interweaves images from Christian and native religions into a dense and rich symbolic whole. The Christian images were probably copied from the illustrated books and Bibles of the missionaries. Visible here are the Arms of Christ (the "weapons" that Christ used to defeat the devil; the holy face, placed where his head would appear on a crucifix; the crown of thorns, draped around the cross bar; and the holy shroud, wrapped around the cross's arms. Winged angel heads and pomegranates surround the inscription at the top as symbols of regeneration. While the cross represents the redemption of humanity in Christianity, it symbolizes the tree of life in Mesoamerican religions. The blood that sprays out where the nails pierce the hands and feet of Christ are a reference to his sacrifice, and such representations of sacrificial blood were common in indigenous religious art.

Images of the Virgin Mary also took on a Mesoamerican inflection after she was believed to have appeared in Mexico. In

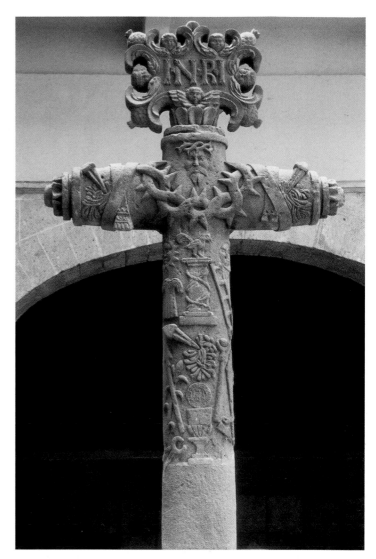

30-45 • ATRIAL CROSS
Before 1556. Stone, height 11'3" (3.45 m). Chapel of the Indians, Basilica of Guadalupe, Mexico City.

one such case, in 1531, a Mexican peasant named Juan Diego claimed that the Virgin Mary visited him to tell him in his native Nahuatl language to build a church on a hill where an Aztec goddess had once been worshiped, subsequently causing flowers to bloom so that Juan Diego could show them to the archbishop as proof of his vision. When Juan Diego opened his bundle of flowers, the cloak he had used to wrap them is said to have borne the image of a Mexican Mary, presented in a composition used in Europe to portray the Virgin of the Immaculate Conception, popular in Spain (see FIG. 23-22). The site of Juan Diego's vision was renamed Guadalupe after Our Lady of Guadalupe in Spain, and it became a venerated pilgrimage center. In 1754, pope Benedict XIV declared the **VIRGIN OF GUADALUPE**, as depicted here in a 1779 work by Sebastian Salcedo, the patron saint of the Americas (FIG. 30-46).

Spanish colonial builders sought to replicate the architecture of their native country in the Americas. One of the finest examples is the **MISSION SAN XAVIER DEL BAC**, in the American

30-46 • Sebastian Salcedo VIRGIN OF GUADALUPE

1779. Oil on panel and copper, 25″ × 19″ (63.5 × 48.3 cm). Denver Art Museum.

Funds contributed by Mr. and Mrs. George G. Anderman and an anonymous donor (1976.56)

At the bottom right is the female personification of New Spain (Mexico) and at the left is Pope Benedict XIV (pontificate 1740–1758), who in 1754 declared the Virgin of Guadalupe to be the patroness of the Americas. Between the figures, the sanctuary of Guadalupe in Mexico can be seen in the distance. The four small scenes circling the Virgin represent the story of Juan Diego, and at the top three scenes depict Mary's miracles. The six figures above the Virgin represent Hebrew Bible prophets and patriarchs and New Testament apostles and saints.

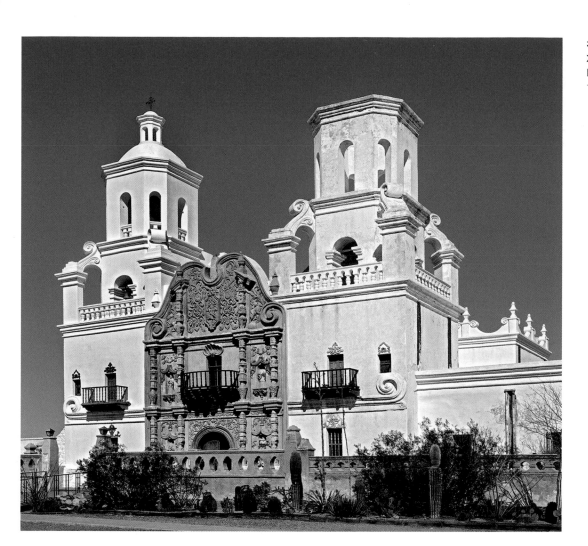

Southwest near Tucson, Arizona (**FIG. 30-47**). In 1700, the Jesuit priest Eusebio Kino (1644–1711) began laying the foundations for San Xavier del Bac using stone quarried locally by people of the Pima nation. The Pima had already laid out the desert site with irrigation ditches, so, as Father Kino wrote in his reports, there would be running water in every room and workshop of the new mission. In 1768, before construction began, the site was turned over to the Franciscans as part of a larger change in Spanish policy toward the Jesuits. Father Kino's vision was eventually realized by the Spanish Franciscan Juan Bautista Velderrain, who arrived at the mission site in 1776.

This huge church, 99 feet long with a domed crossing and flanking bell towers, is unusual for the area because it was built of bricks and mortar rather than adobe, which is made from earth and straw. The basic structure was finished by the time of Velderrain's death in 1790, and the exterior decoration was completed by his successor in 1797. The façade of San Xavier is not a copy of Spanish architecture, although the focus of visual attention on the central entrance to the church and the style of the decoration are consistent with the Spanish Baroque decoration. Since the mission was dedicated to Francis Xavier, his statue once stood at the top of the portal decoration, and there are still four female saints,

tentatively identified as Lucy, Cecilia, Barbara, and Catherine of Siena, in the niches. Hidden in the sculpted mass is one humorous element: a cat confronting a mouse, which inspired a local Pima saying: "When the cat catches the mouse, the end of the world will come" (cited in Chinn and McCarty, p. 12).

EARLY NINETEENTH-CENTURY ART: NEOCLASSICISM AND ROMANTICISM

Neoclassicism and Romanticism existed side by side well into the nineteenth century in European and American art. In fact, Neoclassicism survived in both architecture and sculpture beyond the middle of the century, as patrons and artists continued to use it to promote the virtues of democracy and republicanism. The longevity of Neoclassicism was also due in part to its embrace by art academies, where training was grounded in the study of antique sculpture and the work of Classical artists, such as Raphael. The Neoclassical vision of art as the embodiment of universal standards of taste and beauty complemented the academy's idea of itself as a repository of venerable tradition in fast-changing times.

Romanticism, whose roots in eighteenth-century Britain we have already seen (pages 929–932), took a variety of forms in the early nineteenth century. The common connecting thread continued to be an emphasis on emotional expressiveness and the unique experiences and tastes of the individual. Romantic paintings continued to explore dramatic subject matter taken from literature, current events, the natural world, or the artist's own imagination, with the goal of stimulating the viewer's sentiments and feelings.

DEVELOPMENTS IN FRANCE

Paris increasingly established itself as a major artistic center during the nineteenth century. Between 1800 and 1830, the French academy system was the arbiter of artistic success in Paris. The École des Beaux-Arts attracted students from all over Europe and the Americas, as did the **ateliers** (studios) of Parisian academic artists who offered private instruction. Artists competed fiercely for a spot in the Paris Salon, the annual exhibition that gradually opened to those who were not academy members. At the beginning of the nineteenth century there was a deep division between the *poussinistes* and *rubénistes* (see "Grading the Old Masters," page 763). The *poussinistes* argued that line, as used in the work of Poussin (see FIGS. 23-54, 23-55), created fundamental artistic structure and should be the basis of all painting. The *rubénistes* argued that essential structure could be achieved more eloquently through a sophisticated use of rich, warm color, as exemplified by the paintings of Rubens (see FIG. 23-27). Similarly, the relative value of the **esquisse**, a preliminary sketch for a much larger work, was hotly debated. Some claimed that it was simply a tool for the larger, finished work, while others began to argue that the fast, impulsive expression of imagination captured in the *esquisse* made the finished painting seem dull and flat by comparison. This emphasis on expressiveness blossoms in Romanticism between 1815 and 1830.

THE GRAND MANNER PAINTINGS OF DAVID AND GROS With the rise of Napoleon Bonaparte, Jacques-Louis David re-established his dominant position in French painting. David saw in Napoleon the best hope for realizing France's Enlightenment-oriented political goals, and Napoleon saw in David a tested propagandist for revolutionary values. As Napoleon gained power and extended his rule across Europe, reforming law codes and abolishing aristocratic privilege, he commissioned David and his students to document his deeds.

In 1800, four years before Napoleon became emperor, David already glorifies him in **NAPOLEON CROSSING THE SAINT-BERNARD** (or *Bonaparte Crossing the Alps*) (FIG. 30-48). Napoleon is represented in the Grand Manner, and David used artistic license to imagine how Napoleon might have appeared as he led his troops over the Alps into Italy. Framed by a broad shock of red drapery, he exhorts his troops to follow as he charges uphill on his powerful rearing horse.

His horse's flying mane and wild eyes, coordinated with the swirl of his cape, convey energy, impulse, and power, backed up by the heavy guns and troops in the background. When Napoleon fell from power in 1814, David went into exile in Brussels, where he died in 1825.

Antoine-Jean Gros (1771–1835) began working in David's studio as a teenager and eventually vied with his master for commissions from Napoleon. Gros traveled with Napoleon in Italy in 1797 and later became an official chronicler of his military campaigns. His painting **NAPOLEON IN THE PLAGUE HOUSE AT JAFFA** (FIG. 30-49), like David's portrait, represents an actual event in the Grand Manner. During Napoleon's campaign against the Ottoman Turks in 1799, bubonic plague broke out among his troops. To quiet fears and forestall panic among his soldiers, Napoleon decided to visit the sick and dying, who were housed in a converted mosque in the town of Jaffa (now in Israel but then part of the Ottoman Empire). The format of Gros's painting— a shallow stage with a series of pointed arches framing the main

30-48 • Jacques-Louis David NAPOLEON CROSSING THE SAINT-BERNARD
1800–1801. Oil on canvas, 8′11″ × 7′7″ (2.7 × 2.3 m). Versailles, Châteaux de Versailles et de Trianon.

David flattered Napoleon by reminding the viewer of two other great generals from history who had led armies across the Alps—Charlemagne and Hannibal—by inscribing the names of all three on the rock at lower left.

30–49 • Antoine-Jean Gros NAPOLEON IN THE PLAGUE HOUSE AT JAFFA
1804. Oil on canvas, 17'5" × 23'7" (5.32 × 7.2 m). Musée du Louvre, Paris.

The huddled figures to the left were based on those around the mouth of hell in Michelangelo's *Last Judgment* (see FIG. 21–38).

protagonists—recalls David's *Oath of the Horatii* (see FIG. 30–37). But Gros's painting is quite different from that of his teacher. His color is more vibrant and his brushwork more spontaneous. The overall effect is Romantic, not simply because of the dramatic lighting and the wealth of details, both exotic and horrific, but also because the main action is meant to incite veneration of Napoleon the man more than republican sentiments in general. At the center of the painting, surrounded by a small group of soldiers and a doctor who keep a cautious distance from the contagious patients or hold handkerchiefs to their noses to block their stench, a heroic and fearless Napoleon reaches his bared hand toward the sores of one of the victims in a pose that was meant to evoke Christ healing the sick with his touch.

GÉRICAULT The life of Théodore Géricault (1791–1824), a major proponent of French Romanticism, was cut short by his untimely death at age 32, but his brief career had a large impact on the early nineteenth-century Parisian art world. After a short stay in Rome in 1816–1817, where he discovered the art of Michelangelo, Géricault returned to Paris determined to paint a great modern history painting. He chose for his subject the scandalous and sensational shipwreck of the *"Medusa"* (FIG. 30–50; see *"The Raft of the 'Medusa',"* page 948). In 1816, this French ship bound for Senegal, ran aground close to its destination. Its captain, an incompetent aristocrat commissioned by the newly restored monarchy of Louis XVIII, reserved all six lifeboats for himself, his officers, and several government representatives. The remaining 152 passengers were set adrift on a makeshift raft. When those on the raft were rescued 13 days later, just 15 had survived, some only by eating human flesh. Since the captain had been a political appointee, the press used the horrific story to indict the monarchy for this and other atrocities in French-ruled Senegal. The moment in the story that Géricault chose to depict is one fraught with emotion, as the survivors on the raft experience both the fear that

Théodore Géricault's monumental *The Raft of the "Medusa"* (FIG. 30–50) fits the definition of a history painting in that it is a large (16 by 23 feet), multi-figured composition that represents an event in history. It may not qualify, however, on the basis of its function—to expose incompetence and a willful disregard for human life rather than to ennoble, educate, or remind viewers of their civic responsibility. The hero of this painting is also an unusual choice for a history painting; he is not an emperor or a king, nor even an intellectual, but Jean Charles, a black man from French Senegal who showed endurance and emotional fortitude in the face of extreme peril.

Géricault's painting speaks powerfully through a composition that is arranged in a pyramid of bodies. The diagonal axis that begins in the lower left extends upward to the waving figure of Jean Charles; a complementary diagonal beginning with the dead man in the lower right extends through the mast and billowing sail, directing our attention to a huge wave. The painting captures the moment between the hope of rescue and the despair that the distant ship has not seen the survivors. The figures are emotionally suspended between hope of salvation and fear of imminent death. Significantly, the "hopeful" diagonal in Géricault's painting terminates in the vigorous figure of Jean Charles. By placing him at the top of the pyramid of survivors and giving him the power to save his comrades by signaling to the rescue ship, Géricault suggests metaphorically that freedom is often dependent on the most oppressed members of society.

Géricault prepared his painting carefully, using each of the prescribed steps for history painting in the French academic system. The work was the culmination of extensive study and experimentation. An early pen drawing (*The Sighting of the "Argus,"* FIG. 30–51) depicts the survivors' hopeful response to the appearance of the rescue ship on the horizon at the extreme left. Their excitement is in contrast to the mournful scene of a man grieving over a dead youth on the right side of the raft. The drawing is quick, spontaneous and bursting with energy, like the *esquisse*. A later pen-and-wash drawing (FIG. 30–52) reverses the composition, creates greater unity among the figures, and establishes the modeling of their bodies through light and shade. This is primarily a study of light and shade. Other studies would have focused on further analyses of the composition, arrangement of figures, and overall color scheme. The drawings look ahead to the final composition of the *The Raft of the "Medusa,"* but both still lack the figure of Jean Charles at the apex of the painting and

30–50 • Théodore Géricault THE RAFT OF THE "MEDUSA"
1818–1819. Oil on canvas, 16'1" × 23'6" (4.9 × 7.16 m). Musée du Louvre, Paris.

the dead and dying figures at the extreme left and lower right, which fill out the composition's base.

Géricault also made separate studies of many of the figures, as well as of actual corpses, severed heads, and dissected limbs (FIG. 30–53) supplied to him by friends who worked at a nearby hospital. For several months, according to Géricault's biographer, "his studio was a kind of morgue. He kept cadavers there until they were half-decomposed, and insisted on working in this charnel-house atmosphere…" However, he did not use cadavers for any specific figures in The Raft of the "Medusa." Rather, he traced the outline of his final composition onto its large canvas, and then painted each body directly from a living model, gradually building up his composition figure by figure. He drew from corpses and body parts in his studio to make sure that he understood the nature of death and its impact on the human form.

Indeed, Géricault did not describe the actual physical condition of the survivors on the raft: exhausted, emaciated, sunburned, and close to death. Instead, following the dictates of the Grand Manner, he gave his men athletic bodies and vigorous poses, evoking the work of Michelangelo and Rubens (Chapters 21 and 23). He did this to generalize and ennoble his subject, elevating it above the particulars of a specific shipwreck in the hope that it would speak to more fundamental human conflicts: humanity against nature, hope against despair, and life against death.

30–51 • Théodore Géricault THE SIGHTING OF THE "ARGUS" (TOP)
1818. Pen and ink on paper, 13¾″ × 16⅛″ (34.9 × 41 cm). Musée des Beaux-Arts, Lille.

30–52 • Théodore Géricault THE SIGHTING OF THE "ARGUS" (MIDDLE)
1818. Pen and ink, sepia wash on paper, 8⅛″ × 11¼″ (20.6 × 28.6 cm). Musée des Beaux-Arts, Rouen.

30–53 • Théodore Géricault STUDY OF HANDS AND FEET (BOTTOM)
1818–1819. Oil on canvas, 20½″ × 25³⁄₁₈″ (52 × 64 cm). Musée Fabre, Montpellier.

 View the Closer Look feature for The Raft of the "Medusa" on myartslab.com the distant ship might pass them by and the hope that they will be rescued.

Géricault exhibited *The Raft of the "Medusa"* at the 1819 Salon, where it caused considerable controversy. Most contemporary French critics and royalists interpreted the painting as a political jibe at the king, on whose good grace many academicians depended, while independent liberals praised Géricault's attempt to expose corruption. The debate raised the question of the point at which a painting crosses the line between art and political advocacy. Although it was intended to shock and horrify rather than to edify and ennoble, the painting conforms to academy rules in every other way. The crown refused to buy it, so Géricault exhibited *The Raft of the "Medusa"* commercially on a two-year tour of Ireland and England; the London exhibition alone attracted more than 50,000 paying visitors.

DELACROIX The French novelist Stendhal characterized the Romantic spirit when he wrote, "Romanticism in all the arts is what represents the men of today and not the men of those remote, heroic times which probably never existed anyway." Eugène Delacroix (1798–1863), the most important Romantic painter in Paris after Géricault's untimely death, depicted contemporary heroes and victims engaged in the violent struggles of the times. In 1830, he created what has become his masterpiece, **LIBERTY LEADING THE PEOPLE: JULY 28, 1830** (FIG. 30–54), a painting that encapsulated the history of France after the fall of Napoleon. When Napoleon was defeated in 1815, the victorious neighboring nations reimposed the French monarchy under Louis XVIII (r. 1815–1824), brother of Louis XVI. The king's power was limited by a constitution and a parliament, but the government became more conservative as years passed, undoing many

30-54 • Eugène Delacroix LIBERTY LEADING THE PEOPLE: JULY 28, 1830
1830. Oil on canvas, 8′6½″ × 10′8″ (2.6 × 3.25 m). Musée du Louvre, Paris.

revolutionary reforms. Louis's younger brother and successor, Charles X (r. 1824–1830), reinstated press censorship, returned education to the control of the Catholic Church, and limited voting rights. These actions triggered a large-scale uprising in the streets of Paris. Over the course of three days in July 1830, the Bourbon monarchical line was overthrown and Louis-Philippe d'Orléans (r. 1830–1848), replaced his more moderate cousin Charles X, promising to abide by a new constitution. This period in French history is known as the "July Monarchy."

In his large modern history painting Delacroix memorialized the July 1830 revolution just a few months after it took place. Though it records aspects of the actual event, it also departs from the facts in ways that further the intended message. Delacroix's revolutionaries are a motley crew of students, artisans, day laborers, and even children and top-hatted intellectuals. They stumble forward through the smoke of battle, crossing a barricade of refuse and dead bodies. The towers of Notre-Dame loom through the smoke and haze of the background. This much of the work is plausibly accurate. Their leader, however, is an energetic, allegorical figure of Liberty, personified by a gigantic, muscular, half-naked woman charging across the barricade with the revolutionary flag in one hand and a bayoneted rifle in the other. Delacroix has placed a Classical allegorical figure within the battle itself, outfitted with a contemporary weapon and Phrygian cap—the ancient symbol for a freed slave that was worn by the insurgents. He presents the event as an emotionally charged moment just before the ultimate sacrifice, as the revolutionaries charge the barricades to near-certain death. This dramatic example of Romantic painting is full of passion, turmoil, and danger—part real and part dream.

RUDE Artists working for the July Monarchy increasingly used the more dramatic subjects and styles of Romanticism to represent the 1830 revolution, just as Neoclassical principles had been used to represent the previous one. Early in the July Monarchy, the minister of the interior decided, as an act of national reconciliation, to complete the triumphal arch on the Champs-Élysées in Paris begun by Napoleon in 1806. François Rude (1784–1855) received the commission for a sculpture to decorate the main arcade with a scene that commemorated the volunteer army that had halted a Prussian invasion in 1792–1793. Beneath

30-55 • François Rude **DEPARTURE OF THE VOLUNTEERS OF 1792 (THE MARSEILLAISE)**
Arc de Triomphe, Place de l'Étoile, Paris. 1833–1836. Limestone, height approx. 42′ (12.8 m).

the urgent exhortations of the winged figure of Liberty, the volunteers surge forward, some nude, others in Classical armor (**FIG. 30-55**). Despite these Classical details, the overall impact of this sculpture is Romantic. The crowded, excited group stirred patriotism in Paris, and the sculpture quickly became known simply as the *Marseillaise*, the name of the French national anthem written in 1792, the same year as the action depicted.

30-56 • Jean-Auguste-Dominique Ingres LARGE ODALISQUE
1814. Oil on canvas, approx. 35″ × 64″ (88.9 × 162.5 cm). Musée du Louvre, Paris.

During Napoleon's campaigns against the British in North Africa, the French discovered the exotic Near East. Upper-middle-class European men were particularly attracted to the institution of the harem, partly as a reaction against the egalitarian demands of women of their own class that had been unleashed by the French Revolution.

INGRES Jean-Auguste-Dominique Ingres (1780–1867), perhaps David's most famous student, served as director of the French Academy in Rome between 1835 and 1841. As a teacher and theorist, Ingres became one of the most influential artists of his time. His paintings offer another variant on the Romantic and Neoclassical, combining the precise drawing, formal idealization, Classical composition, and graceful lyricism of Raphael (see FIG. 21-7) with an interest in creating sensual and erotically charged images that appeal to viewers' emotions.

Although Ingres fervently desired to be accepted as a history painter, it was his paintings of female nudes as orientalizing fantasies and his sultry portraits of aristocratic women that made him famous. He painted numerous versions of the **odalisque**, an exoticized version of a female slave or harem concubine. In his **LARGE ODALISQUE** (FIG. 30-56), the woman's cool gaze is leveled directly at her master, while she twists her reclined naked body in a sinuous, snakelike, concealing pose of calculated eroticism. The saturated cool blues of the couch and the curtain at the right set off the effect of her cool, pale skin and blue eyes, while the tight angularity of the crumpled sheets accentuates the the languid, sensual contours of her body. She is a male fantasy of a "white" slave. The exotic details of her headdress

and the brush of the peacock fan against her thigh only intensify her sensuality. Ingres's commitment to academic line and formal structure was grounded in his Neoclassical training, but his fluid, attenuated female nudes speak more strongly of the Romantic tradition.

Although Ingres complained that making portraits was a "considerable waste of time," his skill in rendering physical likeness with scintillating clarity and in mimicking in paint the material qualities of clothing, hairstyles, and jewelry was unparalleled. He painted many life-size and highly polished portraits, but he also produced—usually in just a day—exquisite, small portrait drawings that are extraordinarily fresh and lively. The charming **PORTRAIT OF MADAME DÉSIRÉ RAOUL-ROCHETTE** (FIG. 30-57) is a flattering yet credible representation of the relaxed and elegant sitter. Her gloved right hand draws to Madame Raoul-Rochette's social status; fine kid gloves were worn only by members of the European upper class, who did not work with their hands. And her ungloved left hand reveals her marital status with a wedding band. Ingres renders her shiny taffeta dress, with its fashionably high waist and puffed sleeves, with deft economy and swift spontaneity, using subdued marks that suggest rather than describe the fabric. A a result, emphasis rests on the sitter's refined face and

30–57 • Jean-Auguste-Dominique Ingres PORTRAIT OF MADAME DÉSIRÉ RAOUL-ROCHETTE

1830. Graphite on paper, 12⅝" × 9½" (32.2 × 24.1 cm). Cleveland Museum of Art, Ohio.

Purchase from the J. H. Wade Fund (1927.437)

Madame Raoul-Rochette (1790–1878), née Antoinette-Claude Houdon, was the youngest daughter of the famous Neoclassical sculptor Jean-Antoine Houdon (see FIG. 30–41). In 1810, at age 20, she married Désiré Raoul-Rochette, a noted archaeologist, who later became the secretary of the Académie des Beaux-Arts (Academy of Fine Arts, founded in 1816 to replace the French Royal Academy of Painting and Sculpture) and a close friend of Ingres. Ingres's drawing of Madame Raoul-Rochette is inscribed to her husband ("Ingres to his friend and colleague, Mr. Raoul-Rochette"), whose portrait Ingres also drew around the same time.

elaborate coiffure, which Ingres has drawn precisely and modeled with subtle evocations of light and shade.

DAUMIER Honoré Daumier (1808–1879) came to Paris from Marseille in 1816. He studied drawing at the Académie Suisse, but he learned the technique of **lithography** (see "Lithography," page 954) as assistant to the printmaker Bélaird. Daumier published his first lithograph in 1829, at age 21, in the weekly satirical magazine *La Silhouette*. In the wake of the 1830 revolution in Paris, Daumier began supplying pictures to *La Caricature*, an anti-monarchist, pro-republican magazine, and the equally partisan *Le Charivari*, the first daily newspaper illustrated with lithographs. His 1834 lithograph, calling attention to the atrocities on **RUE TRANSNONAIN** (FIG. 30–58), was part of a series of large prints sold by subscription to raise money for *Le Charivari*'s legal defense fund and thus further freedom

30–58 • Honoré Daumier RUE TRANSNONAIN, LE 15 AVRIL 1834

1834. Lithograph, 11" × 17⅜" (28 × 44 cm). Bibliothèque Nationale, Paris.

Lithography, invented in the mid 1790s, is based on the natural antagonism between oil and water. The artist draws on a flat surface—traditionally, fine-grained stone (*lithos* is Greek for stone)—with a greasy, crayonlike instrument. The stone's surface is first wiped with water and then with an oil-based ink. The ink adheres to the greasy areas but not to the damp ones. After a series of such steps, a sheet of paper is laid face down on the inked stone, pressed together with a scraper, and then rolled through a flatbed press. This transfers ink from stone to paper, thus making lithography (like relief and intaglio) a direct method of creating a printed image. Unlike earlier processes, however, grease-based lithography enables the artist to capture the subtleties of drawing with crayon and a liquid mixture called *tusche*. Francisco Goya, Théodore Géricault, Eugène Delacroix, Honoré Daumier, and Henri de Toulouse-Lautrec used the medium to great effect.

Daumier is probably the greatest exponent of lithography in the nineteenth century. The technique was widely used in France for fine-art prints and to illustrate popular magazines and even newspapers. By the 1830s, the print trade in France had exploded. Artists could use lithography to produce their own prints without the cumbersome, expensive, and time-consuming intermediary of the engraver. Daumier's picture of **THE PRINT LOVERS** (FIG. 30–59) shows three men who have fixed their attention on the folio of prints in front of them, despite being surrounded by works of art packed tightly on the wall behind them. By the end of the nineteenth century, inexpensive prints were in every house and owned by people at every level of society.

30–59 • Honoré Daumier **THE PRINT LOVERS**
c. 1863–1865. Watercolor, black pencil, black ink, gray wash, 10⅛" × 12⅛" (25.8 × 30.7 cm). Musée du Louvre, Paris.

scraper   paper   inked stone   moving base

diagram of the lithographic process

◉ **Watch** a video about the process of lithography on myartslab.com

of the press. A government guard had been shot and killed on the rue Transnonain—only a few blocks from Daumier's home—during a demonstration by workers, and in response, the riot squad killed everyone in the building where they believed the marksman was hiding. Daumier shows the bloody aftermath of the event: an innocent family disturbed from their sleep and then murdered. The wife lies in the shadows to the left, her husband in the center of the room, and an elderly man to the right. It takes a few minutes for viewers to realize that under the central figure's back there are also the bloody head and arms of a murdered child. Daumier was known for his biting caricatures and social commentary in print form, but this image is one of his most powerful.

ROMANTIC LANDSCAPE PAINTING

The Romantics saw nature as ever-changing, unpredictable, and uncontrollable, and they saw in it an analogy to equally unpredictable and changeable human moods and emotions. They found nature awesome, fascinating, powerful, domestic, and delightful, and landscape painting became an important visual theme in Romantic art.

CONSTABLE John Constable (1776–1837), the son of a successful miller, claimed that the quiet domestic landscape of his youth in southern England had made him a painter before he ever picked up a paintbrush. Although he was trained at the

Royal Academy, he was equally influenced by the seventeenth-century Dutch landscape-painting tradition (see FIG. 23–44). After moving to London in 1816, he dedicated himself to painting monumental views of the agricultural landscape (known as "six-footers"), which he considered as important as history painting. Constable's commitment to contemporary English subjects was so strong that he opposed the establishment of the English National Gallery of Art in 1832 on the grounds that it might distract painters by enticing them to paint foreign or ancient themes in unnatural styles.

THE HAY WAIN (FIG. 30–60) of 1821 shows a quiet, slow-moving scene from Constable's England. It has the fresh color and sense of visual exactitude that persuades viewers to believe that it must have been painted directly from nature. But although Constable made numerous drawings and small-scale color studies for his open-air paintings, the final works were carefully constructed images produced in the studio. His paintings are very large even for landscape themes of historic importance, never mind views derived from the local countryside. *The Hay Wain* represents England as Constable imagined it had been for centuries—comfortable,

rural, and idyllic. Even the carefully rendered and meteorologically correct details of the sky seem natural. The painting is, however, deeply nostalgic, harking back to an agrarian past that was fast disappearing in industrializing England.

TURNER Joseph Mallord William Turner (1775–1851) is often paired with Constable. The two were English landscape painters of roughly the same period, but Turner's career followed a different path. He entered the Royal Academy in 1789, was elected a full academician at the unusually young age of 27, and later became a professor at the Royal Academy Schools. By the late 1790s, he was exhibiting large-scale oil paintings of grand natural scenes and historical subjects, in which he sought to capture the **sublime**, a concept defined by philosopher Edmund Burke (1729–1797). According to Burke, when we witness something that instills fascination mixed with fear, or when we stand in the presence of something far larger than ourselves, our feelings transcend those we encounter in normal life. Such savage grandeur strikes awe and terror into the heart of the viewer, but there is no real danger. Because the sublime is experienced vicariously, it is

30–60 • John Constable THE HAY WAIN
1821. Oil on canvas, 51¼″ × 73″ (130.2 × 185.4 cm). National Gallery, London. Gift of Henry Vaughan, 1886

Read the document related to John Constable on myartslab.com

30-61 • Joseph Mallord William Turner **SNOWSTORM: HANNIBAL AND HIS ARMY CROSSING THE ALPS**

1812. Oil on canvas, 4'9″ × 7'9″ (1.46 × 2.39 m). Tate, London.

30-62 • Joseph Mallord William Turner **THE BURNING OF THE HOUSES OF LORDS AND COMMONS, 16TH OCTOBER 1834**
Oil on canvas, 36¼″ × 48½″ (92.1 × 123.2 cm). Philadelphia Museum of Art. The John Howard McFadden Collection, 1928

thrilling and exciting rather than threatening, and it often evokes the transcendent power of God. Turner translated this concept of the sublime into powerful paintings of turbulence in the natural world and the urban environment.

His **SNOWSTORM: HANNIBAL AND HIS ARMY CROSSING THE ALPS** (FIG. 30–61) of 1812 epitomizes Romanticism's view of the awesomeness of nature. An enormous vortex of wind, mist, and snow masks the sun and threatens to annihilate the soldiers marching below it. Barely discernible in the distance is the figure of Hannibal, mounted on an elephant to lead his troops through the Alps toward their encounter with the Roman army in 218 BCE. Turner probably meant his painting as an allegory of the Napoleonic Wars. Napoleon himself had crossed the Alps, an event celebrated by David in his laudatory portrait (see FIG. 30–48). But while David's painting, which Turner saw in Paris in 1802, conceived Napoleon as a powerful figure, commanding not only his troops but nature itself, Turner reduced Hannibal to a speck on the horizon, threatened with his troops by natural disaster, as if foretelling their eventual defeat.

Closer to home, Turner based another dramatic and thrilling work on the tragic fire that severely damaged London's historic Parliament building. Blazing color and light dominate **THE BURNING OF THE HOUSES OF LORDS AND COMMONS, 16TH OCTOBER 1834** (FIG. 30–62), and we are not the only ones transfixed by the sight of a magnificent conflagration here. The foreground of the painting shows the south bank of the Thames packed with spectators. This fire was a national tragedy; these buildings had witnessed some of the most important events in English history. Turner himself was witness to the scene and hurriedly made watercolor sketches on site; within a few months he had the large painting ready for exhibition. The painting's true theme is the brilliant light and color that spirals across the canvas in the explosive energy of loose brushwork, explaining why Turner was called "the painter of light."

COLE Thomas Cole (1801–1848) was one of the first great professional landscape painters in the United States. Cole emigrated from England at age 17 and by 1820 was working as an itinerant portrait painter. With the help of a patron, he traveled in Europe between 1829 and 1832, and upon his return to the United States he settled in New York and became a successful landscape painter. He frequently worked from observation when making sketches for his paintings. In fact, his self-portrait is tucked into the foreground of **THE OXBOW** (FIG. 30–63), where he stands turning back to look at us while pausing from his work. He is executing an oil sketch on a portable easel, but like most landscape painters of his generation, he produced his large finished works in the studio during the winter months.

Cole painted this work in the mid 1830s for exhibition at the National Academy of Design in New York. He considered it one of his "view" paintings because it represents a specific place and time. Although most of his other view paintings were small, this one is monumentally large, probably because it was created for exhibition at the National Academy. Its scale allows for a sweeping view of a spectacular oxbow bend in the Connecticut River from

30-63 • Thomas Cole THE OXBOW
1836. Oil on canvas, 51½″ × 76″ (1.31 × 1.94 m). Metropolitan Museum of Art, New York. Gift of Mrs. Russell Sage, 1908 (08.228)

 View the Closer Look for *The Oxbow* on myartslab.com

30–64 • Caspar David Friedrich **ABBEY IN AN OAK FOREST** 1809–1810. Oil on canvas, 44″ × 68½″ (111.8 × 174 cm). Nationalgalerie, Berlin.

the top of Mount Holyoke in western Massachusetts. Cole wrote that the American landscape lacked the historic monuments that made European landscape interesting; there were no castles on the Hudson River of the kind found on the Rhine, and there were no ancient monuments in America of the kind found in Rome. On the other hand, he argued, America's natural wonders, such as this oxbow, should be viewed as America's natural "antiquities." The painting's title tells us that Cole depicts an actual spot, but, like other landscape painters who wished to impart a larger message about the course of history in their work, he composed the scene to stress the landscape's grandeur and significance, exaggerating the steepness of the mountain and setting the scene below a dramatic sky. Along a great sweeping arc produced by the dark clouds and the edge of the mountain, he contrasts the two sides of the American landscape: its dense, stormy wilderness and its congenial, pastoral valleys with settlements. The fading storm seems to suggest that the land is bountiful and ready to yield its fruits to civilization.

FRIEDRICH In Germany, the Romantic landscape painter Caspar David Friedrich (1774–1840) conceived landscape as a vehicle through which to achieve spiritual revelation. As a young man, he had been influenced by the writings and teachings of Gotthard Kosegarten, a local Lutheran pastor and poet who taught that the divine was visible through a deep personal connection with nature. Kosegarten argued that just as God's book was the Bible, the landscape was God's "Book of Nature." Friedrich studied at the Copenhagen Academy before settling in Dresden, where the poet Johann Wolfgang von Goethe encouraged him to make landscape the principal subject of his art. He sketched from nature but painted in the studio, synthesizing his sketches with his memories of and feelings about nature. Through the

foggy atmosphere of **ABBEY IN AN OAK FOREST** (FIG. 30-64), a funeral procession of monks in the lower foreground is barely visible through the gloom that seems to be settling heavily down on the snow-covered world of human habitation. Most prominent are the boldly silhouetted trunks and bare branches of a grove of oak trees, and nestled among them the ruin of a Gothic wall, a formal juxtaposition that creates a natural cathedral from this cold and mysterious landscape.

GOTHIC AND NEOCLASSICAL STYLES IN EARLY NINETEENTH-CENTURY ARCHITECTURE

A mixture of Neoclassicism and Romanticism motivated architects in the early nineteenth century, many of whom worked in either mode, depending on the task at hand. Neoclassicism in architecture often imbued secular public buildings with a sense of grandeur and timelessness, while Romanticism evoked, for instance, the Gothic past with its associations of spirituality and community.

GOTHIC ARCHITECTURE The British claimed the Gothic as part of their patrimony and erected many Gothic Revival buildings during the nineteenth century, prominent among them the new **HOUSES OF PARLIAMENT** (FIG. 30-65). After Westminster Palace burned in 1834, in the fire so memorably painted by Turner (see FIG. 30-62), the British government announced a competition for a new building to be designed in the English Perpendicular Gothic style, harmonizing with the neighboring thirteenth-century church of Westminster Abbey where English monarchs are crowned.

30-65 • Charles Barry and Augustus Welby Northmore Pugin **HOUSES OF PARLIAMENT, LONDON**
1836–1860. Royal Commission on the Historical Monuments of England, London.

Pugin published two influential books in 1836 and 1841, in which he argued that the Gothic style of Westminster Abbey was the embodiment of true English genius. In his view, the Greek and Roman Classical orders were stone replications of earlier wooden forms and therefore fell short of the true principles of stone construction.

Charles Barry (1795–1860) and Augustus Welby Northmore Pugin (1812–1852) won the commission. Barry devised the essentially Classical plan of the new building, whose symmetry suggests the balance of powers within the British parliamentary system, while Pugin designed the intricate Gothic decoration. The leading advocate of Gothic architecture at this time, Pugin published *Contrasts* in 1836, in which he compared the troubled modern era of materialism and mechanization unfavorably with the Middle Ages, which he represented as an idyllic epoch of deep spirituality and satisfying handcraft. For Pugin, Gothic was not a style but a principle, like Classicism. The Gothic, he insisted, embodied two "great rules" of architecture: "first, that there should be no features about a building which are not necessary for convenience, construction or propriety; second, that all ornament should consist of enrichment of the essential structure of the building."

Most Gothic Revival buildings of this period, however, were churches, principally either Roman Catholic or Anglican (Episcopalian in the United States). The British-born American architect Richard Upjohn (1802–1878) designed many of the most important American examples, including **TRINITY CHURCH** in New York (**FIG. 30-66**). With its tall spire, long nave, and squared-off chancel, Trinity church quotes the early fourteenth-century British Gothic style particularly admired by Anglicans and Episcopalians. Every detail is rendered with historical accuracy, but the vaults are plaster, not masonry. The stained-glass windows above the altar were among the earliest of their kind in the United States.

NEOCLASSICAL ARCHITECTURE In several European capitals in the early nineteenth century, the Neoclassical designs of national museums positioned these buildings as both temples of culture and expressions of nationalism. Perhaps the most significant was the **ALTES MUSEUM** (Old Museum) in Berlin, designed in 1822 by Karl Friedrich Schinkel (1781–1841) and built between 1824 and 1830 (**FIG. 30-67**). Commissioned to display the royal art collection, the building was built directly across from the Baroque royal palace on an island in the Spree River in the heart of Berlin. The museum's imposing façade consists of

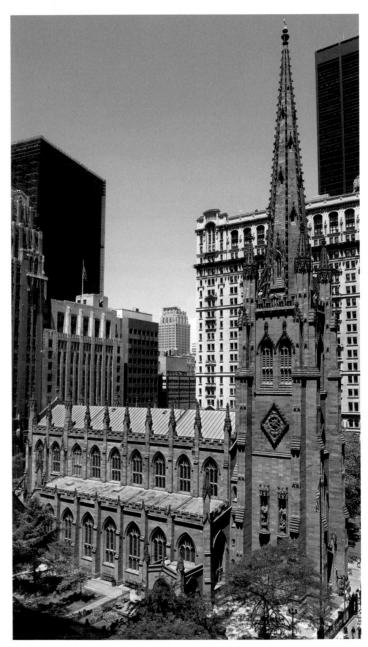

30-66 • Richard Upjohn **TRINITY CHURCH, NEW YORK CITY**
1839–1846.

30-67 • Karl Friedrich Schinkel **ALTES MUSEUM, BERLIN** 1822–1830.

a screen of 18 Ionic columns raised on a platform with a central staircase. Attentive to the problem of lighting artworks on both the ground and the upper floors, Schinkel created interior courtyards on either side of a central rotunda. Tall windows on the museum's outer walls provide natural illumination, and partition walls perpendicular to the windows eliminate glare on the varnished surfaces of the paintings on display.

Neoclassical style was also popular for large public buildings in the United States, perhaps most significantly and symbolically in the U.S. Capitol, in Washington, DC, initially designed in 1792 by William Thornton (1759–1828), an amateur architect. His monumental plan featured a large dome over a temple front flanked by two wings to accommodate the House of Representatives and the Senate. In 1803, President Thomas Jefferson (1743–1826), also an amateur architect, hired a British-trained professional, Benjamin Henry Latrobe (1764–1820), to oversee the actual construction of the Capitol. Latrobe modified Thornton's design by adding a grand staircase and Corinthian colonnade on the east front (**FIG. 30-68**). After the British gutted the building in the war of 1812, Latrobe repaired the wings and designed a higher dome. Seeking new symbolic forms for the nation within the traditional Classical vocabulary, he also created a variation on the Corinthian order for the interior by substituting indigenous crops such as corn and tobacco for the Corinthian order's acanthus leaves. In 1817, he resigned his

30-68 • Benjamin Henry Latrobe **U.S. CAPITOL, WASHINGTON, DC**
c. 1808. Engraving by T. Sutherland, 1825. New York Public Library. I.N. Phelps Stokes Collection, Myriam and Ira Wallach Division of Art, Prints, and Photographs

30–69 • Thomas Jefferson MONTICELLO
Charlottesville, Virginia. 1769–1782, 1796–1809.

👁—Watch a video about Monticello on myartslab.com

post. The reconstruction was completed under Charles Bulfinch (1763–1844), and another major renovation, resulting in a much larger dome, began in 1850.

Thomas Jefferson's graceful designs for the mountaintop home he called **MONTICELLO** (Italian for "little mountain") near Charlottesville, Virginia, employ Neoclassical architecture in a private setting (**FIG. 30–69**). Jefferson began the first phase of construction (1769–1782) when Virginia was still a British colony, using the English Palladian style (see Chiswick House, FIG. 30–15). By 1796, however, he had become disenchanted with both the English and their architecture, and had come to admire French architecture while serving as the American minister in Paris. He then embarked upon a second building campaign at Monticello (1796–1809), enlarging the house and redesigning its brick and wood exterior so that its two stories appeared from the outside as one large story, in the manner then fashionable in Paris. The modern worlds of England, France, and America, as well as the ancient worlds of Greece and Rome, come together in this residence. In the second half of the nineteenth century, cultural borrowings would take on an even broader global scope.

THINK ABOUT IT

30.1 Summarize some of the key stylistic traits of French Rococo art and architecture, and explain how these traits relate to the social context of salon life. Then analyze one Rococo work from the chapter and explain how it is typical of the period style.

30.2 Explain why artists as visually diverse as Delacroix and Friedrich can be classified under the category of Romanticism. How useful is "Romanticism" as a classifying term?

30.3 How did the political climate during Francisco Goya's life affect his art? Focus your answer on a discussion of *Third of May, 1808* (FIG. 30–44).

30.4 Discuss the relationship of the Enlightenment interest in archaeology with the new movement of Neoclassicism in the eighteenth century.

CROSSCURRENTS

FIG. 19–1   FIG. 30–1

Double portraits of couples are common in the history of European art. Assess the ways in which these two examples portray the nature of the marital relationship of these men and women. How do the portrayals represent the social structures and concerns of the cultural situations in which the couples lived?

✔—Study and review on myartslab.com

31-1 • Gustave Eiffel **EIFFEL TOWER, PARIS**
1887–1889. Photographed in March 1889. Height 984′ (300 m).

Mid- to Late Nineteenth-Century Art in Europe and the United States

The world-famous **EIFFEL TOWER** (FIG. 31–1) is a proud reminder of the nineteenth-century French belief in the progress and ultimate perfectibility of civilization through science and technology. Structural engineer Gustave Eiffel (1832–1923) designed and constructed the tower to serve as a monumental approach to the 1889 Universal Exposition in Paris. When completed, it stood 984 feet tall and was the tallest structure in the world, taller than the Egyptian pyramids or Gothic cathedrals. The Eiffel Tower was the main attraction of the Universal Exposition, one of more than 20 such international fairs staged throughout Europe and the United States in the second half of the nineteenth century. These events showcased and compared international industry, science, and the applied, decorative, and fine arts. An object of pride for the French nation, the Eiffel Tower was intended to demonstrate France's superior engineering, technological and industrial knowledge, and power. Although originally conceived as a temporary structure, it still stands today.

The initial response to the Eiffel Tower was mixed. In 1887, a group of 47 writers, musicians, and artists wrote to *Le Temps* protesting "the erection … of the useless and monstrous Eiffel Tower," which they described as "a black and gigantic factory chimney." Gustave Eiffel, however, said, "I believe the tower will have its own beauty," and that it "will show that [the French] are not simply an amusing people, but also the country of engineers." Indeed, when completed, the Eiffel Tower quickly became an international symbol of advanced thought and modernity among artists, and was admired by the public as a wondrous spectacle. Today it is the symbol of Paris itself.

The tower was one of the city's most photographed structures in 1889, its immensity dwarfing the tiny buildings below. Thousands of tourists to the Exposition bought souvenir photographs taken by professional and commercial photographers. This one, from late March 1889, shows the tower still under construction but almost complete. A close look at the bottom two tiers with the fairgrounds below betrays evidence of rapid last-minute construction in preparation for the May 6th opening.

LEARN ABOUT IT

31.1 Understand and evaluate the role played by academic art and architecture, as well as the emergence of various movements that arose in opposition to its principles, in the late nineteenth century.

31.2 Investigate the interest in subjects drawn from modern life, as well as the development of new symbolic themes, in Realist, Impressionist, and Post-Impressionist art.

31.3 Analyze the ways in which the movement toward realism in art reflected the social and political concerns of the nineteenth century.

31.4 Examine the early experiments that led to the emergence of photography as a new art form.

(((•—[**Listen** to the chapter audio on myartslab.com

EUROPE AND THE UNITED STATES IN THE MID TO LATE NINETEENTH CENTURY

The technological, economic, and social transformations initiated by the Industrial Revolution intensified during the nineteenth century. Increasing demands for coal and iron necessitated improvements in mining, metallurgy, and transportation. Likewise, the development of the locomotive and steamship facilitated the shipment of raw materials and merchandise, made passenger travel easier, and encouraged the growth of cities (MAP 31–1). These changes also set in motion a vast population migration, as the rural poor moved to cities to find work in factories, mines, and mechanical manufacturing. Industrialists and entrepreneurs enjoyed new levels of wealth and prosperity in this system, but conditions for workers—many of them women and children—were often abysmal. Although new government regulations led to some improvements, socialist movements condemned the exploitation of workers by capitalist factory owners and advocated communal or state ownership of the means of production and distribution.

In 1848, workers' revolts broke out in several European capitals. In that year also, Karl Marx and Friedrich Engels published the *Communist Manifesto*, which predicted the violent overthrow of the bourgeoisie (middle class) by the proletariat (working class), the abolition of private property, and the creation of a classless society. At the same time, the Americans Lucretia Mott and Elizabeth Cady Stanton organized the country's first women's rights convention, in Seneca Falls, New York. They called for the equality of women and men before the law, property rights for married women, the acceptance of women into institutions of higher education, the admission of women to all trades and professions, equal pay for equal work, and women's suffrage.

The nineteenth century also witnessed the rise of imperialism. In order to create new markets for their products and to secure access to cheap raw materials and cheap labor, European nations established numerous new colonies by dividing up most of Africa and nearly a third of Asia. Colonial rule frequently suppressed indigenous cultures while exploiting the colonies for the economic development of the European colonial powers.

Scientific discoveries led to the invention of the telegraph, telephone, and radio. By the end of the nineteenth century, electricity powered lighting, motors, trams, and railroads in most European and American cities. Developments in chemistry created many new products, such as aspirin, disinfectants, photographic chemicals, and more effective explosives. The new material of steel, an alloy of iron and carbon, was lighter, harder, and more malleable than iron, and replaced it in heavy construction and transportation. In medicine and public health, Louis Pasteur's purification of beverages through heat (pasteurization) and the development of vaccines, sterilization, and antiseptics led to a dramatic decline in mortality rates all over the Western world.

Some scientific discoveries challenged traditional religious beliefs and affected social philosophy. Geologists concluded that the Earth was far older than the estimated 6,000 years sometimes claimed by biblical literalists. In 1859, Charles Darwin proposed that life evolved gradually through natural selection. Religious conservatives attacked Darwin's account, which seemed to deny divine creation and even the existence of God. Some of his more extreme supporters, however, suggested that the "survival of the fittest" had advanced the human race, with certain types of people—particularly the Anglo-Saxon upper classes—achieving the pinnacle of social evolution. "Social Darwinism" provided a rationalization for the poor conditions of the working class and a justification for colonizing the "underdeveloped" parts of the world.

Industrialists, merchants, professionals, the middle classes, some governments, and national academies of art became new sources of patronage in the arts. Large annual exhibitions in European and American cultural centers took on increasing importance as a means for artists to show their work, win prizes, attract buyers, and gain commissions. Cheap illustrated newspapers and magazines published art criticism that influenced the reception and production of art, both making and breaking artistic careers, and commercial art dealers emerged as important brokers of taste.

The second half of the nineteenth century saw vast changes in how art was conceptualized and created. Some artists became committed political or social activists as industrialization and social unrest continued, while others retreated into their own imagination. Some responded to the ways in which photography transformed vision and perception, many setting themselves up as photographers, while other artists emulated the new medium's clarity in their own work. Still others investigated the difference between photography's detailed but superficial description of visual reality and a deeper, more human reality as a source of inspiration, and others explored the artistic potential of photography's sometimes visually unbalanced compositions, its tendency to compress the illusion of depth and assert its flatness, its sharp framing and abrupt cropping of aspects of the broader world, its lack of an even focus across the picture plane or sometimes the reverse, or even the inability of early photography to "see" red and green equally, causing blank areas of white and black in a photograph. By the end of the century, while many artists were still exploring the reliability of observed reality, others were venturing ever farther into the realm of abstraction.

FRENCH ACADEMIC ARCHITECTURE AND ART

The Académie des Beaux-Arts (founded in 1816 to replace the disbanded Royal Academy of Painting and Sculpture) and its official art school, the École des Beaux-Arts, continued to exert a powerful influence over the visual arts in France during the nineteenth century. Academic artists controlled the Salon juries, and major public commissions routinely went to academic architects,

MAP 31–1 • EUROPE AND THE UNITED STATES IN THE NINETEENTH CENTURY

In the nineteenth century, Europe and the United States became increasingly industrialized and many European nations established colonial possessions around the world. Paris was firmly established as the center of the Western art world.

painters, and sculptors. It was to Paris that artists and architects from Europe and the United States came to study the conventions of academic art.

Academic art and architecture frequently depended upon motifs drawn from historic models—a practice called **historicism**. Elaborating on earlier Neoclassical and Romantic revivals, historicist art and architecture encompassed the sweep of history. Historicists often combined allusions to several different historical periods in a single work. Some academic artists catered to the public taste for exotic sights with Orientalist paintings (see "Orientalism," page 968). These works also combined disparate elements, borrowing from Egyptian, Turkish, and Indian cultures to create an imaginary Middle Eastern world.

ACADEMIC ARCHITECTURE

In 1848, after rioting over living conditions erupted in French cities, Napoleon III (r. as emperor 1852–1870) launched sweeping new reforms. The riots had devastated Paris's central neighborhoods, and Georges-Eugène Haussmann (1809–1891) was engaged to redraw the street grid and rebuild the city. Haussmann imposed a new rational plan of broad avenues, parks, and open public places upon the medieval heart of Paris. He demolished entire neighborhoods, erasing networks of narrow, winding, medieval streets and summarily evicting the poor from their slums. Then he replaced what he had destroyed with grand new buildings erected along wide, straight, tree-lined avenues that were more suitable for horse-drawn carriages and strolling pedestrians.

The **OPÉRA** (**FIG. 31-2**), a new city opera house designed by Charles Garnier (1825–1898) and still a major Parisian landmark, was built at an intersection of Haussmann's grand avenues. Accessible from many directions, the Opéra was designed with transportation and vehicular traffic in mind, and with a modern cast-iron internal frame; yet in other respects it is a masterpiece of historicism derived mostly from the Baroque style, revived here to recall an earlier period of greatness in France. The massive façade, featuring a row of paired columns over an arcade, was intended to recall the seventeenth-century wing of the Louvre, an association meant to assert the continuity of the French nation and to flatter Napoleon III by comparing him favorably with Louis XIV. The building's primary function—as a place of entertainment for the

31-2 • Charles Garnier
OPÉRA, PARIS
1861–1874.

31-3 • GRAND STAIRCASE, OPÉRA

Explore the architectural panoramas of the interior of the
Opéra, Paris on myartslab.com

emperor, his entourage, and the high echelons of French society—accounts for its luxurious detail. The interior, described as a "temple of pleasure," was even more opulent, with neo-Baroque sculptural groupings, heavy gilded decoration, and a lavish mix of expensive, polychromed materials. More spectacular than the performance on stage was that on the grand, sweeping Baroque staircase (**FIG. 31-3**), where members of the Paris elite displayed themselves. As Garnier said, the purpose of the Opéra was to fulfill the human desire to hear, to see, and to be seen.

ACADEMIC PAINTING AND SCULPTURE

The taste that dominated painting and sculpture in the Académie des Beaux-Arts by the mid nineteenth century is well represented by **THE BIRTH OF VENUS** by Alexandre Cabanel (1823–1889), one of the leading academic artists of the time (**FIG. 31-4**). After studying with an academic master, Cabanel won the Prix de Rome in 1845, and garnered top honors at the Salon three times in the 1860s and 1870s. In his version of this popular mythological subject (compare **FIG. 20-40**), Venus floats above the waves, as flying *putti* playfully herald her arrival with conch shells. Cabanel's mastery of anatomy, flesh tones, and the rippling sea derives from his academic training and technical virtuosity. But the image also carries a strong erotic charge, in the languid limbs, arched back, and diverted eyes of Venus. This combination of mythological pedigree and sexual allure proved irresistible to Napoleon III, who bought *The Birth of Venus* for his private collection.

Although academic and avant-garde art are often seen as polar opposites, the relationship was more complex. Some academic artists

31–4 • Alexandre Cabanel THE BIRTH OF VENUS
1863. Oil on canvas, 52″ × 90″ (1.35 × 2.29 m). Musée d'Orsay, Paris.

experimented while maintaining academic conventions, while avant-garde artists held many academic practices in high esteem and sought academic approval. The academic artist Jean-Baptiste Carpeaux (1827–1875) illustrates the kind of experimentation that took place even within the academy. Carpeaux, who had studied at the École des Beaux-Arts under the Romantic sculptor François Rude (see FIG. 30–55), was commissioned to carve a large sculptural group for the façade of Garnier's Opéra. His work, **THE DANCE** (**FIG. 31–5**), shows a winged male personification of Dance leaping up joyfully in the midst of a compact group of mostly nude female dancers, an image of uninhibited Dionysian revelry. Like Cabanel's *Birth of Venus*, the work imbues a mythological subject with an erotic charge.

Unlike Cabanel's figures, Carpeaux's were not smooth and generalized in a Neoclassical manner, and this drew criticism from some academicians. The arrangement of his sculptural group also seemed too spontaneous, the facial expressions of the figures too vivid, their musculature too exact, their bone structure and proportions too much of this world, rather than reflections of an ideal one. Carpeaux's work signaled a new direction in academic art, responding to the values of a new generation of patrons from the industrial and merchant classes. These practical new collectors were less interested in art that idealized than in art that brought the ideal down to earth.

31–5 • Jean-Baptiste Carpeaux THE DANCE
1867–1868. Plaster, height approx. 15′ (4.6 m).
Musée d'Orsay, Paris.

In **THE SNAKE CHARMER** (FIG. 31–6), French academic painter Jean-León Gérôme (1824–1904) luxuriates in the nineteenth-century fantasy of the Middle East—a characteristic example of **Orientalism**. A young boy, entirely naked, handles a python, while an older man behind him plays a fipple flute, and a huddled audience sits within the background shadows in a blue-tiled room decorated with calligraphic patterns. Gérôme paints the scene with photographic clarity and scrupulous attention to detail, leading us to think that it is an accurate representation of a specific event and locale. Gérôme traveled to the Middle East several times, and was praised by critics of the 1855 Salon for his ethnographic accuracy, but his *Snake Charmer* is a complete fiction, mixing Egyptian, Turkish, and Indian cultures together in a fantastized pastiche.

Orientalism, the European fascination with Middle Eastern cultures, dates to Napoleon's 1798 invasion of Egypt and his rampant looting of Egyptian objects for the Louvre Museum, which he opened in 1804, and the 24-volume *Description de l'Egypte* (1809–1822), recording Egyptian people, lands, and culture that followed. In the 1840s and 1850s, British, French, and Italian photographers established studios at major tourist sites in the Middle East in order to provide photographs for visitors and armchair tourists at home, thus fueling a popular interest in the region.

The scholar Edward Said has described Orientalism, characterizing both academic and avant-garde art in the nineteenth century, as the colonial gaze upon the colonized Orient (the Middle East rather than Asia), seen by the colonizer as something to possess, as a "primitive" or "exotic" playground for the "civilized" European visitor. "Native" men become savage and despotic, and "native" women—and here boys—are sensuously described and sexually available.

31-6 • Jean-Léon Gérôme **THE SNAKE CHARMER** c. 1870. Oil on canvas, 33″ × 48⅛″ (83.8 × 122.1 cm). Clark Art Institute, Williamstown, MA. Acquired by Sterling and Francine Clark, 1942. (1955.51)

EARLY PHOTOGRAPHY IN EUROPE AND THE UNITED STATES

The nineteenth-century desire to record the faces of the new mercantile elite, their achievements and possessions, and even the imperial possessions of nations, found expression in photography. Since the late Renaissance, artists and others had sought a mechanical method for drawing from nature. One early device was the camera obscura (Latin, meaning "dark chamber"), which consists of a darkened room or box with a lens through which light passes, projecting an upside-down image of the scene onto the opposite wall (or box side), which an artist can then trace. By the nineteenth century, a small, portable camera obscura or even lighter *camera lucida* had become standard equipment for artists. Photography developed as a way to fix—that is, to make permanent—the images produced by a camera obscura (later called a "camera") on light-sensitive material.

Photography had no single "inventor." Several individuals worked on the technique simultaneously, each contributing some part to a process that emerged over many years. Around 1830, a handful of experimenters understood ways to "record" the image, but the last step, "stopping" or "fixing" that image so that further exposure to light would not further darken the image, proved more challenging.

In France, while experimenting with ways to duplicate his paintings, Louis-Jacques-Mandé Daguerre (1787–1851) discovered that a plate coated with light-sensitive chemicals and exposed to light for 20 to 30 minutes would reveal a "latent image" when then exposed to mercury vapors. By 1837, he had developed a method of fixing his image by bathing the plate in a solution of salt, and he vastly improved the process by using the chemical hyposulphate of soda (known as "hypo") as suggested by Sir John Frederick Herschel (1792–1871). The final image was negative, but when viewed upon a highly polished silver plate it appeared positive. The resulting picture could not be duplicated easily and was very fragile, but its quality was remarkably precise. In Daguerre's photograph of his studio tabletop (**FIG. 31–7**), the details are exquisite (though impossible to see in reproduction, even using today's technology) and the composition mimics the conventions of still-life painting. Daguerre, after he patented and announced his new technology, produced an early type of photograph called a **daguerreotype**, in August 1839.

Even before Daguerre announced his photographic technique in France, the American artist Samuel Morse (1791–1872) traveled to Paris to negotiate exchanging information about his own invention, the telegraph, for information about Daguerre's photography. Morse introduced the daguerreotype process to America within weeks of Daguerre's announcement, and by 1841 had reduced exposure times enough to take portrait photographs (**FIG. 31–8**).

At the same time in England, Henry Fox Talbot (1800–1877), a wealthy amateur, made negative copies of engravings, lace, and plants by placing them on paper soaked in silver chloride and

31-8 • DAGUERREOTYPE OF SAMUEL FINLEY BREESE MORSE
c. 1845. Sixth plate daguerreotype, 2¾″ × 3¼″ (7 × 8.3 cm). The Daguerreotype Collection of the Library of Congress, Washington, DC.

exposing them to light. He also found that the negative image on paper could be exposed again on top of another piece of paper to create a positive image, thus discovering the negative-positive process that became the basis of photographic printing. Talbot's negative could be used more than once, so he could produce a number of positive images inexpensively. But the **calotype**, as he later called it, produced a soft, fuzzy image. When he heard of Daguerre's announcement, Talbot rushed to make his own announcement and patent his process. The term for these processes—photography, derived from the Greek for "drawing with light"—was coined by Herschel.

The emerging technology of photography was quickly put to use in making visual records for contemporary audiences and future generations. Early on, however, photographers also experimented with the expressive possibilities of the new medium and worked to create striking compositions. Between 1844 and 1846, Talbot published a book in six parts entitled *The Pencil of Nature*, illustrated entirely with salt-paper prints made from calotype negatives. Most of the photographs were of idyllic rural scenery or carefully arranged still lifes; they were presented as works of art rather than documents of a precisely observed reality. Talbot realized that the imprecision of his process could not compete with the commercial potential of the daguerreotype, and so rather than trying to do so, he chose to view photography in visual and artistic terms. In

31-7 • Louis-Jacques-Mandé Daguerre THE ARTIST'S STUDIO
1837. Daguerreotype, 6½″ × 8½″ (16.5 × 21.6 cm). Société Française de Photographie, Paris.

31-9 • Henry Fox Talbot THE OPEN DOOR
1843. Salt-paper print from a calotype negative, 5⅝″ × 7¹¹⁄₁₆″ (14.3 × 19.5 cm). Science Museum, London. Fox Talbot Collection

THE OPEN DOOR (FIG. 31-9), for example, shadows create a repeating pattern of diagonal lines that contrast with the rectlinear lines of the architecture. And it conveys meaning, expressing nostalgia for a rural way of life that was fast disappearing in industrial England.

In 1851, Frederick Scott Archer, a British sculptor and photographer, took a major step in the development of early photography. Archer found that silver nitrate would adhere to glass if it was mixed with collodion, a combination of guncotton, ether, and alcohol used in medicinal bandages. When wet, this collodion–silver nitrate mixture needed only a few seconds' exposure to light to create an image. The result was a glass negative, from which countless positive proofs with great tonal subtleties could be made.

American photographers used this newly refined process to document the momentous events of the Civil War (1861–1865) in artfully composed pictures. Alexander Gardner (1821–1882)

was a "camera operator" for Mathew Brady (1822–1896) at the beginning of the conflict, and, working with his assistant Timothy O'Sullivan (c. 1840–1882), he made war photographs that were widely distributed. **THE HOME OF THE REBEL SHARPSHOOTER** (FIG. 31-10) was taken after the Battle of Gettysburg in July 1863. The technical difficulties were considerable. Wet-plate technology required that the glass plate used to make the negative be coated with a sticky substance holding the light-sensitive chemicals. If the plate dried, the photograph could not be taken, and if dust contaminated the plate, the image would be ruined. Since long exposure times made action photographs impossible, early war photographs were taken in camp or in the aftermath of battle. Gardner's image seems to show a rebel sharpshooter who has been killed in his look-out. But this rock formation was in the middle of the battlefield, and had neither the height nor the view needed for a sharpshooter. In fact, the photographers dragged the dead body to the site and posed it; the rifle propped against the wall was theirs. The staging of this photograph raises questions about visual fact and fiction. Like a painting, a photograph is composed to create a picture, but photography promises a kind of factuality that we do not expect from painting. Interestingly, the manipulation

31-10 • Alexander Gardner
THE HOME OF THE REBEL SHARPSHOOTER: BATTLEFIELD AT GETTYSBURG
1863. Albumen print, 7″ × 9″ (18 × 23 cm). Library of Congress, Washington, DC.

A camera is essentially a lightproof box with a hole, called an aperture, which is usually adjustable in size and regulates the amount of light that strikes the film. The aperture is covered with a lens, to focus the image on the film, and a shutter, a hinged flap that opens for a controlled amount of time in order to regulate the length of time the film is exposed to light—usually a small fraction of a second. Modern cameras with viewfinders and small single-lens reflex cameras are generally used at eye level, permitting the photographer to see virtually the same image that will be captured on film.

In modern black-and-white chemical photography, silver halide crystals (silver combined with iodine, chlorine, or other halogens) are suspended in a gelatin base to make an emulsion that coats the film; in early photography, before the invention of plastic, a glass plate was coated with a variety of emulsions. When the shutter is open, light reflected off objects enters the camera and strikes the film, exposing it. Pale objects reflect more light than dark ones. The silver in the emulsion collects most densely where it is exposed to the most light, producing a "negative" image on the film. Later, when the film is placed in a chemical bath (developed), the silver deposits turn black, as if tarnishing. The more light the film receives, the denser the black tone created. A positive image is created from a negative in the darkroom, where the film negative is placed over a sheet of paper that, like the film, has also been treated to make it light-sensitive. Light is then directed through the negative onto the paper to create a positive image. Multiple positive prints can be generated from a single negative.

Today this chemical process has been largely replaced by digital photography, which records images as digital information files that can be manipulated on computers rather than in darkrooms. The exploitation of the artistic potential of this new photographic medium is a major preoccupation of contemporary artists.

of this photograph did not concern nineteenth-century viewers, who understood clearly photography's inability to record the visual world without bias.

One of the most creative early photographers was Julia Margaret Cameron (1815–1879), who received her first camera as a gift from her daughters when she was 49. Her principal subjects were the great men and women of British arts, letters, and sciences, many of whom had long been family friends. Cameron's approach was experimental and radical. Like many of her portraits, that of the famous British historian **THOMAS CARLYLE** is deliberately slightly out of focus (**FIG. 31-11**): Cameron consciously rejected the sharp focus of commercial portrait photography, which she felt accentuated the merely physical attributes and neglected the inner character of the subject. By blurring the details, she sought to call attention to the light that suffused her subjects and to their thoughtful expressions. In her autobiography, Cameron said: "When I have had such men before my camera my whole soul has endeavoured to do its duty towards them in recording faithfully the greatness of the inner as well as the features of the outer man."

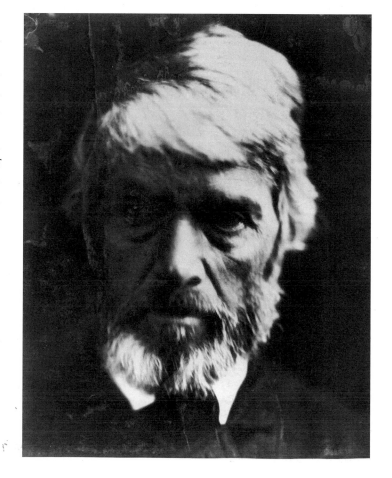

31-11 • Julia Margaret Cameron PORTRAIT OF THOMAS CARLYLE
1867. Silver print, 10″ × 8″ (25.4 × 20.3 cm). The Royal Photographic Society, Collection at National Museum of Photography, Film, and Television, England.

REALISM AND THE AVANT-GARDE

In reaction to the rigidity of academic training, some French artists began to consider themselves members of an **avant-garde**, meaning "advance guard" or "vanguard." The term was coined by the French military during the Napoleonic era to designate the forward units of an advancing army that scouted territory that the main force would soon occupy. Avant-garde artists saw themselves as working in advance of an increasingly bourgeois society. The term was first mentioned in connection with art around 1825 in the political programs of French utopian socialists. Henri de Saint-Simon (1760–1825) suggested that in order to transform modern industrialized society into an ideal state, it would be necessary to gather together an avant-garde of intellectuals, scientists, and artists to lead France into the future.

In 1831, the architect Eugène Viollet-le-Duc applied the term to the artists of Paris in the aftermath of the revolution of 1830. Viollet-le-Duc vehemently opposed the French academic system of architectural training. His concept of the avant-garde called for a small elite of independent radical thinkers, artists, and architects to break away from the Académie des Beaux-Arts and the norms of society in order to forge new thoughts, ideas, and ways of looking at the world and art. He foresaw that this life would require the sacrifice of artists' reputations and reduce sales of their work. Most avant-garde artists were neither as radical nor as extreme as Viollet-le-Duc, and, as we have seen, the relationship between the Académie des Beaux-Arts and the avant-garde was complex. Nonetheless, the idea was embraced by a number of artists who have come to characterize the period.

REALISM AND REVOLUTION

In the modern world of Paris at mid-century—a world plagued by violence, social unrest, overcrowding, and poverty—the grand, abstract themes of academic art seemed irrelevant to those thinkers who would come to represent the avant-garde. Rising food prices, high unemployment, political disenfranchisement, and government inaction ignited in a popular rebellion known as the Revolution of 1848, led by a coalition of socialists, anarchists, and workers. It brought an end to the July Monarchy and established the Second Republic (1848–1852). Conflicts among the reformers, however, led to another uprising, in which more than 10,000 of the working poor were killed or injured in their struggle against the new government's forces. Against this social and political backdrop a new intellectual movement, known as Realism, originated in the novels of Émile Zola, Charles Dickens, Honoré de Balzac, and others who wrote about the real lives of the urban lower classes. What art historians have labeled Realism is less of a style than a commitment to paint the modern world honestly, without turning away from the brutal truths of life for all people, poor as well as privileged.

COURBET Gustave Courbet (1819–1877) was one of the first artists to call himself "avant-garde" or "Realist." A big, blustery man, he was, in his own words, "not only a Socialist but a democrat and a Republican: in a word, a supporter of the whole Revolution." Born and raised near the Swiss border in the French town of Ornans, he moved to Paris in 1839. The street fighting in Paris in 1848 radicalized him and became a catalyst for two large canvases that have come to be regarded as the defining works of Realism.

Painted in 1849, the first of these, **THE STONE BREAKERS** (**FIG. 31-12**), depicts a young boy and an old man crushing rock

31-12 • Gustave Courbet THE STONE BREAKERS 1849. Oil on canvas, 5'3" × 8'6" (1.6 × 2.59 m). Formerly Gemäldegalerie, Dresden; destroyed in World War II.

to produce the gravel used for roadbeds. Stone breakers represent the disenfranchised peasants on whose backs modern life was being built. The younger figure strains to lift a large basket of rocks to the side of the road, dressed in tattered shirt and trousers, but wearing modern work boots. His older companion, seemingly broken by the lowly work, pounds the rocks as he kneels, wearing the more traditional clothing of a peasant, including wooden clogs. The boy thus seems to represent a grim future, while the man signifies an increasingly obsolete rural past. Both are conspicuously faceless. Courbet recorded his inspiration for this painting:

> [N]ear Maisières [in the vicinity of Ornans], I stopped to consider two men breaking stones on the highway. It's rare to meet the most complete expression of poverty, so an idea for a picture came to me on the spot. I made an appointment with them at my studio for the next day … . On the one side is an old man, seventy … . On the other side is a young fellow … in his filthy tattered shirt … . Alas, in labor such as this, one's life begins that way, and it ends the same way.

Two things are clear from this description: Courbet set out to make a political statement, and he invited the men back to his studio so that he could study them more carefully, following academic practice.

By rendering labor on the scale of a history painting—the canvas is over 5 × 8 feet—Courbet intended to provoke. In academic art, monumental canvases were reserved for heroic subjects, but Courbet asserts that peasant laborers should be venerated as heroes. Bypassing the highly finished style and inspiring message of history painting, he signifies the brutality of modern life in his rough use of paint and choice of dull, dark colors, awkward poses, and stilted composition. The scene feels realistically gloomy and degrading. In 1865, his friend, the anarchist philosopher Pierre-Joseph Proudhon (1809–1865), described *The Stone Breakers* as the first socialist picture ever painted, "an irony of our industrial civilization, which continually invents wonderful machines to perform all kinds of labor … yet is unable to liberate man from the most backbreaking toil." Courbet himself described the work as a portrayal of "injustice."

Courbet began to paint **A BURIAL AT ORNANS** (**FIG. 31-13**) immediately after *The Stone Breakers* and exhibited the two paintings together at the 1850–1851 Salon. This is a vast painting, measuring roughly 10 by 21 feet, and depicts a rural burial life-size. A crush of people line up in rows across the length of the picture. The gravedigger kneels over the gaping hole in the ground, placed front and center, and flanked by a bored altar boy and a distracted dog; to the left, clergy dressed in red seem indifferent and bored; while to the right, the huddle of rural mourners—Courbet's

31-13 • Gustave Courbet A BURIAL AT ORNANS
1849. Oil on canvas, 10′3½″ × 21′9″ (3.1 × 6.6 m). Musée d'Orsay, Paris.

A Burial at Ornans was inspired by the 1848 funeral of Courbet's maternal grandfather, Jean-Antoine Oudot, a veteran of the French Revolution of 1789. The painting is not meant as a record of that particular funeral, however, since Oudot is shown alive in profile at the extreme left of the canvas, his image adapted by Courbet from an earlier portrait. The two men to the right of the open grave, dressed not in contemporary but in late eighteenth-century clothing, are also revolutionaries of Oudot's generation. Their proximity to the grave suggests that one of their peers is being buried. Perhaps Courbet's picture links the revolutions of 1789 and 1848, both of which sought to advance the cause of democracy in France.

heroes of modern life—weep in genuine grief. Although painted on a scale befitting the funeral of a hero, Courbet's depiction has none of the idealization of traditional history painting; instead, it captures the awkward, blundering numbness of a real funeral and emphasizes its brutal, physical reality. When shown at the Salon, the painting was attacked by critics who objected to the elevation of a provincial funeral to this heroic scale, to Courbet's disrespect for the rules of academic composition, and even to the lack of any suggestion of the afterlife. Courbet had submitted his work to the Salon knowing that it would be denounced; he wanted to challenge the prescribed subjects, style, and finish of academic painting, to establish his position in the avant-garde, and to create controversy. At the cancellation of the 1854 Salon, and the rejection of some of his works by the International Exposition of 1855, Courbet constructed a temporary building on rented land near the fair's Pavilion of Art and installed a show of his own works that he called the "Pavilion of Realism," boldly asserting his independence from the Salon. Many artists after him would follow in his footsteps.

MILLET Similar accusations of political radicalism were leveled against Jean-François Millet (1814–1875). This artist grew up on a farm and, despite living and working in Paris between 1837 and 1848, he never felt comfortable with urban life. A state commission (with stipend), awarded for his part in the 1848 revolution, allowed him to move to the village of Barbizon, just south of Paris, where he painted the hardships and simple pleasures of the rural poor.

Among his best-known works is **THE GLEANERS** (FIG. **31-14**), which shows three women gathering stray grain from the ground after harvest. Despite its soothing, warm colors, the scene is one of extreme poverty. Gleaning was a form of relief offered to the rural poor by landowners, although it required hours of backbreaking work to collect enough wheat to make a single loaf of bread. Two women bend over to reach the tiny stalks of grain remaining on the ground, while a third straightens to ease her back. When Millet exhibited the painting in 1857, critics noted its implicit social criticism and described the work as "Realist." Millet denied the accusations, but his paintings contradict him.

31-14 • Jean-François Millet THE GLEANERS
1857. Oil on canvas, 33″ × 44″ (83.8 × 111.8 cm). Musée d'Orsay, Paris.

31-15 • Jean-Baptiste-Camille Corot FIRST LEAVES, NEAR MANTES
c. 1855. Oil on canvas, 13⅜″ × 18⅛″ (34 × 46 cm). Carnegie Museum of Art, Pittsburgh, Pennsylvania.

COROT The landscape paintings of Jean–Baptiste-Camille Corot (1796–1875) take a more romantic and less political approach to depicting rural life. After painting historical landscapes early in his career, Corot steadily moved toward more "naturalistic" and intimate scenes of rural France. **FIRST LEAVES, NEAR MANTES** (**FIG. 31-15**) depicts a scene infused with the soft mist of early spring in the woods. Corot's feathery brushwork representing the soft, new foliage contrasts with the stark, vertical tree trunks and branches, and, together with the fresh green of the new undergrowth, creates the lyrical mood of a clear spring day. A man and woman pause to talk on the road winding from left to right through the painting, while a woman labors in the woods at the lower right. Corot invites us to imagine ourselves in the picture and feel the crisp, bright air. These images of peaceful country life held great appeal for Parisians who had experienced the chaos of the 1848 revolution and who lived in an increasingly crowded, noisy, and fast-paced metropolis.

BONHEUR Rosa Bonheur (1822–1899) was one of the most popular French painters of farm life. Her success in what was then a male domain owed much to the socialist convictions of her parents, who belonged to a radical utopian sect—founded by the Comte de Saint-Simon (1760–1825)—that believed not only in the equality of women but also in a future female Messiah. Bonheur's father, a drawing teacher, provided most of her artistic training.

Bonheur dedicated herself to accurate depictions of modern draft animals, which were becoming increasingly obsolete as technology and industrialization transformed farming. She studied her subjects intensely by reading zoology books and making detailed studies in stockyards and slaughterhouses. In fact, to gain access to these all-male preserves, she had to obtain police permission to dress in men's clothing. Her professional breakthrough came at the Salon of 1848, where she showed eight paintings and won a first-class medal. **THE HORSE FAIR** (**FIG. 31-16**),

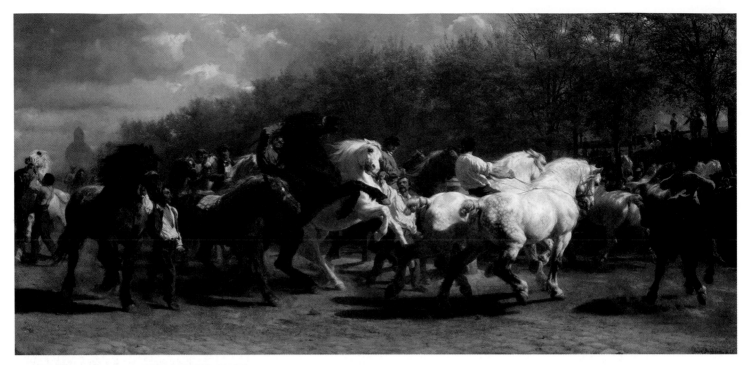

31–16 • Rosa Bonheur **THE HORSE FAIR**
1853–1855. Oil on canvas, 8′1¼″ × 16′7½″ (2.45 × 5.07 m). Metropolitan Museum of Art, New York.

[▣] **Read** the document related to Rosa Bonheur on myartslab.com

painted in 1853, was based on a horse market near Salpêtrière, but was also partly inspired by the Parthenon marbles in London and by the art of Géricault. The scene shows grooms displaying splendid Percheron horses, some walking obediently in their circle, others rearing up, not yet quite broken. Some have interpreted the painting as a commentary on the lack of rights for women in the 1850s, but it was not read that way at the time. Although unusually monumental for a painting of farm animals, it was highly praised at the 1848 Salon. When the painting later toured throughout Britain and the United States, members of the public paid to see it, and it was widely disseminated in print form on both sides of the Atlantic. In 1887, Cornelius Vanderbilt purchased it for the new Metropolitan Museum of Art in New York. Bonheur became so famous working within the Salon system that in 1865 she received France's highest award, membership in the Legion of Honor, becoming the first woman to be awarded its Grand Cross.

MANET: "THE PAINTER OF MODERN LIFE"

Along with the concept of the avant-garde, the idea of "modernity" also shaped art in France at this time. The experience of modern life—of constant change and renewal—was linked to the dynamic nature of the city. The themes of the modern city and of political engagement with modern life in an industrialized world are key to understanding the development of painting and literature in France in the second half of the nineteenth century.

In his 1863 essay "The Painter of Modern Life," poet Charles Baudelaire argued that, in order to speak for their time and place, artists' work had to be infused with the idea of modernity. He

called for artists to be painters of contemporary manners and "of the passing moment and of all the suggestions of eternity that it contains," using both modern urban subjects and new approaches to seeing and representing the visual world. This break with the past was critical in order to comprehend and comment on the present. Especially after the invention of photography, art was expected to offer new ways of representing reality. One artist who rose to Baudelaire's challenge was the French painter Édouard Manet (1832–1883).

LE DÉJEUNER SUR L'HERBE At mid-century, the Académie des Beaux-Arts increasingly opened Salon exhibitions to non-academic artists, resulting in a surge in the number of works submitted, and inevitably rejected by, the Salon jury. In 1863, the jury turned down nearly 3,000 works. A storm of protest erupted, prompting Emperor Napoleon III to order an exhibition of the rejected work called the *Salon des Refusés* ("Salon of the Rejected Ones"). Featured in it was Manet's painting **LE DÉJEUNER SUR L'HERBE (THE LUNCHEON ON THE GRASS)** (FIG. **31-17**). A well-born Parisian who had studied in the early 1850s with the independent artist Thomas Couture (1815–1879), Manet had by the early 1860s developed a strong commitment to Realism and modernity, largely as a result of his friendship with Baudelaire. *Le Déjeuner sur l'Herbe* scandalized contemporary viewers all the way up to Napoleon III himself, provoking a critical avalanche that mixed shock with bewilderment. Ironically, the resulting *succès de scandale* ("success from scandal") helped establish Manet's career as a radical, avant-garde, modern artist.

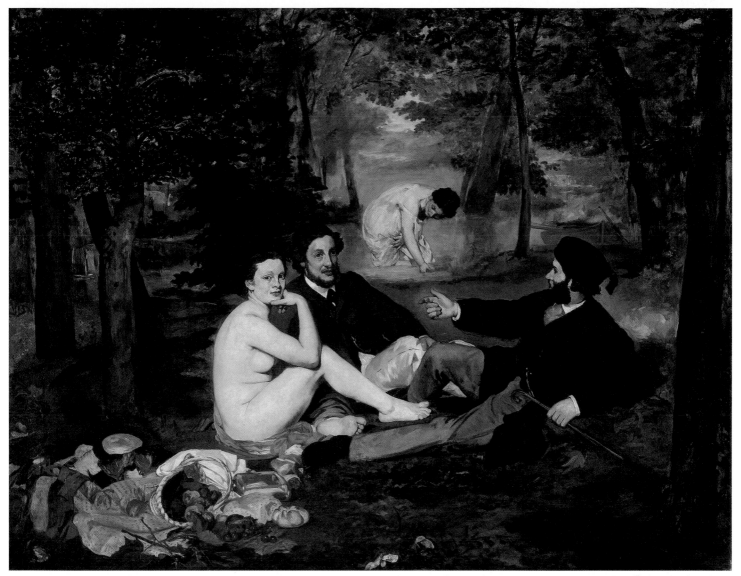

31–17 • Édouard Manet LE DÉJEUNER SUR L'HERBE (THE LUNCHEON ON THE GRASS)
1863. Oil on canvas, 7′ × 8′8″ (2.13 × 2.64 m). Musée d'Orsay, Paris.

The most scandalous aspect of the painting was the "immorality" of Manet's theme: a suburban picnic featuring two fully dressed bourgeois gentlemen seated alongside a completely naked woman, with another scantily dressed woman in the background. Manet's scandalized audience assumed that these women were prostitutes, and the men their customers. Equally shocking were its references to important works of art of the past, which Académie des Beaux-Arts artists were expected to make, combined with its crude, unvarnished modernity. In contrast, one of the paintings that gathered most renown at the official Salon in that year was Alexandre Cabanel's *Birth of Venus* (see FIG. 31-4), which, because it presented nudity in a conventionally acceptable, Classical environment and mythological context, was favorably reviewed and quickly entered the collection of Napoleon III.

Manet apparently conceived of *Le Déjeuner sur l'Herbe* as a modern version of a Venetian Renaissance painting in the Louvre, *The Pastoral Concert*, then believed to be by Giorgione but now

attributed to both Titian and Giorgione or to Titian exclusively (see FIG. 21-25). Manet's composition also refers to a Marcantonio Raimondi engraving of Raphael's *The Judgment of Paris*—itself based on Classical reliefs of river gods and nymphs. Manet's modern interpretation of the scene, however, combined with his modern style, was intentionally provocative. Presenting the seamier side of city life under a flimsy guise of Classical art only underlined Manet's subversiveness. And the stark lighting and sharp outlining of his nude, the cool colors, the flat, cutout quality of his figures, who seem as if they are silhouetted cut-outs set against a painted backdrop, were unsettling to viewers accustomed to the traditional use of controlled gradations of shadows to model smoothly rounded forms nestled into logically mapped spaces.

OLYMPIA Shortly after completing *Le Déjeuner sur l'Herbe*, Manet painted **OLYMPIA** (FIG. 31-18), its title alluding to a socially

Just as contemporary artists can distribute photographic reproductions of their work, in the nineteenth century, artists used engraving or etching to reproduce their work for distribution to a larger audience.

Works of art that won prizes or created controversy were often engraved for reproduction by specialists in printmaking, and the prints sold at bookstores or magazine stands. J. M. W. Turner hired a team of engravers to capture the delicate tonal shadings of his works. An engraved copper plate could be printed upward of 100 times before the repeated pressing took its toll on image quality. In the later nineteenth century, artists increasingly used steel engraving, wood engraving, and lithography for printing. Those more durable surfaces could print up to 10,000 copies of an image without much loss of quality, though only a few artists experienced such demand.

One of the canniest self-marketers of the century was Alexandre Cabanel. After Napoleon III bought *The Birth of Venus* (see FIG. 31–4), the artist sold the reproduction rights to the art dealer Adolphe Goupil, who in turn hired other artists to create at least two smaller-scale copies of the work. After the original artist had approved the copies and signed them, the dealer used these as models for engravers who cut the steel plates. The dealer then sold the smaller painted copies.

ambitious prostitute of the same name in a novel and play by Alexandre Dumas the Younger. Like *Le Déjeuner sur l'Herbe*, Manet's *Olympia* was based on a Venetian Renaissance source, Titian's "*Venus*" *of Urbino* (see FIG. 21–28), which Manet had earlier copied in Florence. At first, his painting appears to pay homage to Titian's in its subject matter (at that time believed to be a Venetian courtesan) and composition, but Manet made his modern counterpart the very antithesis of Titian's reclining nude. Titian's female is curvaceous and softly rounded; Manet's is angular and flattened. Titian's colors are warm and rich; Manet's are cold and harsh, like a photograph; Titian's "Venus" looks coyly at the male spectator, Manet's Olympia appears coldly indifferent. And instead of looking up at us, Olympia gazes down at us, indicating that she is in the position of power and that we are subordinate,

31–18 • Édouard Manet OLYMPIA
1863. Oil on canvas, 4'3" × 6'2¼" (1.31 × 1.91 m). Musée d'Orsay, Paris.

31-19 • Édouard Manet A BAR AT THE FOLIES-BERGÈRE
1881–1882. Oil on canvas. 37¾″ × 51¼″ (95.9 × 130 cm). The Samuel Courtauld Trust, The Courtauld Gallery, London. (P.1934.SC.234)

View the Closer Look for *A Bar at the Folies-Bergère* on myartslab.com

akin to the black servant at the foot of the bed who brings her a bouquet of flowers. Our relationship with Olympia is underscored by the reaction of her cat, which—unlike the sleeping dog in the Titian—arches its back at us. In reversing the Titian, Manet overturns the entire tradition of the accommodating female nude. Not surprisingly, conservative critics vilified *Olympia* when it was exhibited at the Salon of 1865.

Manet generally submitted his work to every Salon, but when several were rejected in 1867, he did as Courbet had done in 1855: He asserted his independence by renting a hall nearby and staging his own show. This made Manet the unofficial leader of a group of progressive artists and writers who gathered at the Café Guerbois in the Montmartre district of Paris. Among the artists who frequented the café were Degas, Monet, Pissarro, and Renoir, all of whom would soon exhibit together as the Impressionists and follow Manet's lead in challenging academic conventions.

LATER WORKS Manet worked closely with all these artists and frequently painted themes similar to those favored by the Impressionists, but always retaining his previous dedication to the portrayal of modern urban life. In his last major painting, **A BAR AT THE FOLIES-BERGÈRE** (FIG. 31-19), he maintains his focus on the complex theme of gender and class relations in modern urban life. Here a hard-working young girl serves drinks at a bar in the famous nightclub that offered circuses, musicals, and vaudeville acts (note the legs of a trapeze artist in the upper left corner). She has an unfashionably ruddy face and hands scrubbed raw. In the glittering light created by the electric bulbs and mirrors of the café-concert she seems stiff and distant, certainly self-absorbed, perhaps even depressed, refusing to meet the gaze of her client. The barmaid is at once detached from the scene and part of it, one of the many items among the still life of liquor bottles, tangerines, and flowers, on display for purchase. This image is about sexualized looking and the barmaid's uneasy reflection in the mirror, which seems to acknowledge that both her class and gender expose her to visual and even sexual consumption.

RESPONSES TO REALISM BEYOND FRANCE

Artists of other nations embraced their own forms of realism in the period after 1850 as the social effects of urbanization and industrialization began to be felt in their countries. While these artists did not label themselves as "Realists" like their contemporaries in France, they did share an interest in presenting unflinching looks at grim reality that exposed the difficult lives of the working poor and the complexities of urban life.

REALISM IN RUSSIA: THE WANDERERS In Russia, a variant on French Realism developed in relation to a new concern for the peasantry. In 1861, the tsar abolished serfdom, emancipating Russia's peasants from the virtual slavery they had endured on the large estates of the aristocracy. Two years later, a group of painters inspired by the emancipation declared allegiance both to the peasant cause and to freedom from the St. Petersburg Academy of Art, which had controlled Russian art since 1754. Reacting against what they considered the escapist aesthetics of the academy, the members of the group dedicated themselves to a socially useful realism. Committed to bringing art to the people in traveling exhibitions, they called themselves "The Wanderers." By the late 1870s, members of the group, like their counterparts in music and literature, had also joined a nationalist movement to reassert what they considered to be an authentic Russian culture rooted in the traditions of the peasantry, rejecting the Western European customs that had long predominated among the Russian aristocracy.

Ilya Repin (1844–1930), who attended the St. Petersburg Academy and won a scholarship to study in Paris, joined the Wanderers in 1878 after his return to Russia. He painted a series of works illustrating the social injustices then prevailing in his homeland, including **BARGEHAULERS ON THE VOLGA** (FIG. 31-20), which features a wretched group of peasants condemned to the brutal work of pulling ships up the Volga River. To heighten our sympathy for these workers, Repin placed a youth in the center of the group, a young man who will soon be as worn out as his companions unless something is done to rescue him. This painting was a call to action.

REALISM IN THE UNITED STATES: A CONTINUING TRADITION Though it was not a term used in the United States, realism—often with a political edge—was an unbroken tradition stretching back to Colonial portrait painters (see FIG. 30-1) and continuing in the pioneering work of photographers during the civil war (see FIG. 31-10). There were several kinds of realism in later nineteenth-century American art. Thomas Eakins (1844–1916), for instance, made a series of uncompromising paintings that were criticized for their controversial subject matter. Born in Philadelphia, Eakins trained at the Pennsylvania Academy of the Fine Arts, but since he thought the training in anatomy lacked rigor, he supplemented his studies at the Jefferson Medical College nearby. He later enrolled at the École des Beaux-Arts in Paris and then spent six months in Spain, where he encountered the profound realism of Baroque artists such as Jusepe de Ribera and Diego Velázquez (see FIGS. 23-17, 23-19). After he returned to Philadelphia in 1870, Eakins specialized in frank portraits and scenes of

31-20 • Ilya Repin BARGEHAULERS ON THE VOLGA
1870–1873. Oil on canvas, 4'3¾" × 9'3" (1.3 × 2.81 m). State Russian Museum, St. Petersburg.

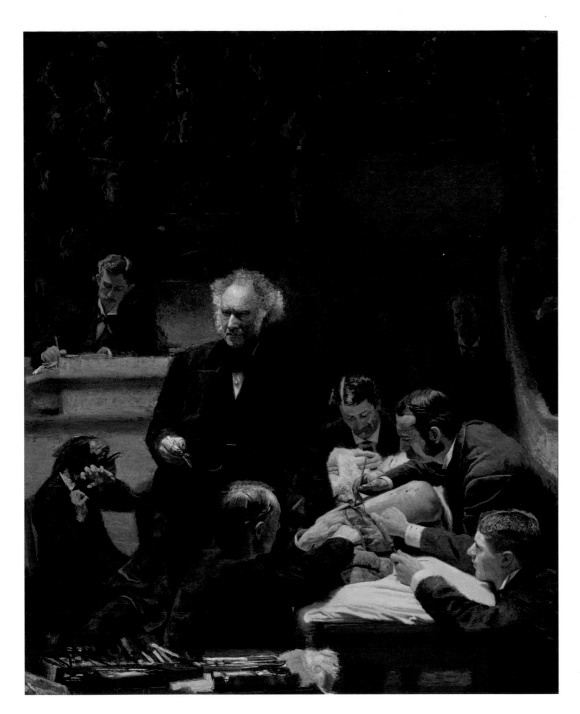

**31–21 • Thomas Eakins
THE GROSS CLINIC**
1875. Oil on canvas, 8′ × 6′5″
(2.44 × 1.98 m). Philadelphia
Museum of Art, Pennsylvania.
Gift of the Alumni Association to
Jefferson Medical College in 1878
and purchased by the Pennsylvania
Academy of the Fine Arts and the
Philadelphia Museum of Art in 2007

Eakins, who taught anatomy
and figure drawing at the
Pennsylvania Academy of the
Fine Arts, disapproved of the
academic technique of drawing
from plaster casts. In 1879, he
said, "At best, they are only
imitations, and an imitation of an
imitation cannot have so much
life as an imitation of nature
itself." He added, "The Greeks
did not study the antique … the
draped figures in the Parthenon
pediment were modeled from life,
undoubtedly."

everyday life whose lack of conventional charm generated little popular interest. But he was a charismatic teacher, and was soon appointed director of the Pennsylvania Academy.

THE GROSS CLINIC (FIG. 31–21) was one of Eakins's most controversial paintings. Although created specifically for the 1876 Philadelphia Centennial Exhibition, it was rejected for the fine-art exhibition—the jury did not consider surgery a fit subject for art—and relegated to the scientific and medical display. The monumental painting shows Dr. Samuel David Gross performing an operation that he pioneered in the surgical amphitheater of Jefferson Medical College, as he pauses to lecture to medical students taking notes in the background—as well as to Eakins himself, whose self-portrait appears along the painting's right edge. A woman at left, presumably a relative of the patient, cringes in horror at the bloody spectacle. At this time, surgeons were regarded with fear, especially teaching surgeons who frequently thought of the poor as objects on which to practice. But Eakins portrays Gross as a heroic figure, spotlighted by beams of light on his forehead and bloodied right hand with glinting scalpel. Principal illumination, however, is reserved for the patient, presented here not as an entire body but a dehumanized jumble of thigh, buttock, socked feet, and bunches of cloth. In conceiving this portrait, Eakins must have had Rembrandt's famous Baroque painting of Dr. Tulp in mind (see FIG. 23–34), and the American painter's use of light seems to point to a similar homage to scientific achievement—amid the darkness of ignorance and fear, modern science is the light of knowledge

31-22 • Winslow Homer THE LIFE LINE
1884. Oil on canvas, 28¾″ × 44⅝″ (73 × 113.3 cm). Philadelphia Museum of Art, Pennsylvania.
The George W. Elkins Collection, 1924

In the early sketches for this work, the man's face was visible. The decision to cover it focuses attention on the victim, and also on the true hero, the mechanical apparatus known as the "breeches buoy."

and the source of progress. The procedure showcased here, in fact, was a surgical innovation that allowed Dr. Gross to save a patient's leg that heretofore would have been routinely amputated.

Winslow Homer (1836–1910) also developed into a realist painter. Born in Boston, he began his career as a 21-year-old free-lance illustrator for popular periodicals such as *Harper's Weekly*, which sent him to cover the Civil War in 1862. In 1867, after a ten-month sojourn in France, Homer returned to paint nostalgic visions of the rural scenes that had figured in his magazine illustrations, but following a sojourn during 1881–1882 in a tiny English fishing village on the rugged North Sea coast, Homer developed a commitment to depicting the working poor. Moved by the hard lives and strength of character of the people he encountered in England, he set aside idyllic subjects for themes of heroic struggle against natural adversity. In England, he had been particularly impressed by the "breeches buoy," a mechanical apparatus used for rescues at sea. During the summer of 1883, he made sketches of one imported by the lifesaving crew in Atlantic City, New Jersey. The following year he painted **THE LIFE LINE** (FIG. **31-22**), which depicts a coastguard saving a shipwrecked woman

with the use of a breeches buoy—a testament not simply to valor but also to human ingenuity.

The sculptor Edmonia Lewis (1845–c. 1911) was born in New York State to a Chippewa mother and an African-American father, orphaned at the age of 4, and raised by her mother's family. As a teenager, with the help of abolitionists, she attended Oberlin College, the first college in the United States to grant degrees to women, and then moved to Boston. Her highly successful busts and medallions of abolitionist leaders and Civil War heroes financed her move to Rome in 1867, where she was welcomed into the sculptural circle of American expatriate artist Harriet Hosmer (1830–1908) and used Neoclassical style to address modern, realist concerns. Galvanized by the struggle of recently freed slaves for equality, Lewis created **FOREVER FREE** (FIG. **31-23**) in 1867 as a memorial to the Emancipation Proclamation (1862–1863). A diminutive woman kneels in prayerful gratitude beside the looming figure of her male companion, who boosts himself up on the ball that once bound his ankle and raises his broken shackles in a gesture of triumphant liberation. Lewis's enthusiasm outran her financial realities; she had to borrow money to pay for the marble for this work. She shipped it from Rome back to Boston hoping that a subscription drive among abolitionists would redeem her loan. The effort was only partially successful, but her steady income from the sale of commemorative medallions eventually paid it off.

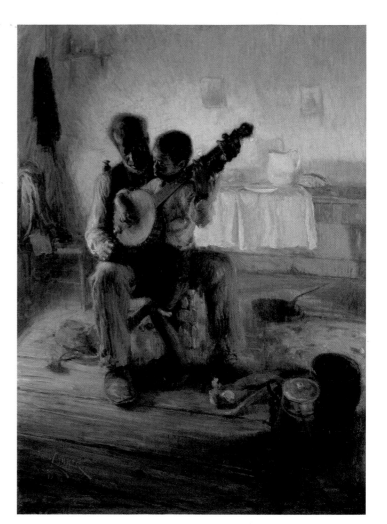

31-24 • Henry Ossawa Tanner THE BANJO LESSON
1893. Oil on canvas, 49″ × 35½″ (124.4 × 90 cm). Hampton University Museum, Virginia.

31-23 • Edmonia Lewis FOREVER FREE
1867. Marble, 41¼″ × 22″ × 17″ (104.8 × 55 × 43.2 cm). Howard University Gallery of Art, Washington, DC.

This sculpture not only celebrates emancipation, but also subtly reflects white attitudes toward women and people of color. Lewis's female is less racialized and more submissive than her male counterpart to align her with the contemporary ideal of womanhood and make her more appealing to white audiences.

Among Eakins's students at the Pennsylvania Academy of the Fine Arts were women and African-Americans, groups often excluded from art schools. One of the star pupils was Henry Ossawa Tanner (1859–1937), who became the most successful African-American painter of the late nineteenth and early twentieth centuries. The son of a bishop in the African Methodist Episcopal Church, Tanner grew up in Philadelphia, and after studying at the academy, he initially worked as a photographer and drawing teacher in Atlanta. In 1891, to further his academic training, he moved to Paris, where his painting received favorable critical attention. In the early 1890s, he painted scenes from African-American and rural French life that combined Eakins's realism with the delicate brushwork he encountered in France. With strongly felt, humanizing images like **THE BANJO LESSON** (**FIG. 31-24**), he sought to counter caricatures of African-American life created by other artists. An elderly man is teaching a young boy seated on his lap, and as their seriousness and concentration connect them, their poverty seems to fade. The use of the banjo here is especially significant since it had become identified with images of minstrels—just the sort of derogatory caricatures that Tanner sought to replace with his sympathetic genre scenes focused on the intimate interactions that brought dignity and pride to family life. After a trip to Palestine in 1897, Tanner turned to religious subjects, believing that Bible stories could illustrate the struggles and hopes of contemporary African-Americans.

DEVELOPMENTS IN BRITAIN Britain also encountered social and political upheaval at the middle of the nineteenth century. The depression of the "hungry forties," the Irish Potato Famine, and the Chartist Riots threatened social stability in England. Mid-century British artists painted scenes of religious, medieval, or moral exemplars using a tight realistic style that was quite different from both French and American Realism.

In 1848, seven young London artists formed the Pre-Raphaelite Brotherhood in response to what they considered the misguided practices of contemporary British art. Instead of the "Raphaelesque" conventions taught at the Royal Academy, the Pre-Raphaelites looked back to the Middle Ages and early Renaissance (before Raphael) for a beauty and spirituality that they found lacking in their own time. They believed this earlier art was more moralistic and "real."

Dante Gabriel Rossetti (1828–1882) was a leading member of the Pre-Raphaelite Brotherhood. His painting **LA PIA DE' TOLOMEI** (**FIG. 31-25**) illustrates a scene from Dante's *Purgatory* in which La Pia (the Pious One), wrongly accused of infidelity and imprisoned by her husband in a castle, is dying. The rosary and prayer book at her side refer to her piety, while the sundial and ravens suggest the passage of time and her impending death. La Pia's continuing love for her husband is represented by his letters, which lie under her prayer book. The luxuriant fig leaves that surround her are traditionally associated with shame, and they seem to suck her into themselves. They have no source in Dante, but had personal relevance for Rossetti: Jane Burden, his model for this and many other paintings, was the wife of his friend William Morris, but she had also become Rossetti's lover. By fingering her wedding ring, La Pia/Jane suggests that she is a captive not of her husband but of her marriage, evoking Rossetti's own unhappy situation.

Other British artists drew inspiration from the medieval past as a panacea for modern life in London. William Morris (1834–1896) worked briefly as a painter under the influence of the Pre-Raphaelites before turning his attention to interior design and decoration. Morris's interest in crafts developed in the context of a

31-25 • Dante Gabriel Rossetti LA PIA DE' TOLOMEI

1868–1869. Oil on canvas, 41½" × 47½" (105.4 × 119.4 cm). Spencer Museum of Art, The University of Kansas. (1956.0031)

The massive gilded frame Rossetti designed for La Pia de' Tolomei features simple moldings on either side of broad, sloping boards, embellished with a few large roundels. The title of the painting is inscribed above the paired roundels at the lower center. On either side of them appear four lines from Dante's Purgatory spoken by the spirit of La Pia, in Italian at the left and in Rossetti's English translation at the right: "Remember me who am La Pia,—me / From Siena sprung and by Maremma dead. / This in his inmost heart well knoweth he/With whose fair jewel I was ringed and wed."

This is a partial transcript of Whistler's testimony at the libel trial that he initiated against the art critic John Ruskin. Whistler's responses often provoked laughter, and the judge at one point threatened to clear the courtroom.

Q: What is your definition of a Nocturne?

A: I have, perhaps, meant rather to indicate an artistic interest alone in the work, divesting the picture from any outside sort of interest which might have been otherwise attached to it. It is an arrangement of line, form, and color first ... The *Nocturne in Black and Gold* [see FIG. 31–27] is a night piece, and represents the fireworks at Cremorne.

Q: Not a view of Cremorne?

A: If it were called a view of Cremorne, it would certainly bring about nothing but disappointment on the part of beholders. It is an artistic arrangement. It was marked 200 guineas ...

Q: I suppose you are willing to admit that your pictures exhibit some eccentricities; you have been told that over and over again?

A: Yes, very often.

Q: You send them to the gallery to invite the admiration of the public?

A: That would be such a vast absurdity on my part that I don't think I could.

Q: Did it take you much time to paint the *Nocturne in Black and Gold*? How soon did you knock it off?

A: I knocked it off in possibly a couple of days; one day to do the work, and another to finish it.

Q: And that was the labor for which you asked 200 guineas?

A: No, it was for the knowledge gained through a lifetime.

The judge ruled in Whistler's favor; Ruskin had indeed libeled him. But he awarded Whistler damages of only one farthing. Since in those days the person who brought the suit had to pay all the court costs, the case ended up bankrupting the artist.

---

widespread reaction against the shoddy design of industrially produced goods. Unable to find satisfactory furnishings for his new home after his marriage in 1859, Morris designed and constructed them himself, with the help of friends, later founding a decorating firm to produce a full range of medieval-inspired objects. Although many of the furnishings offered by Morris & Company were expensive, one-of-a-kind items, others, such as the rush-seated chair illustrated here (**FIG. 31-26**), were inexpensive and simple, intended as a handcrafted alternative to machine-made furniture. Concerned with creating a "total" environment, Morris and his colleagues designed not only furniture but also stained glass, tiles, wallpaper, and fabrics, such as the "Peacock and Dragon" curtain seen in the background of FIGURE 31–26.

Morris inspired what became known as the Arts and Crafts Movement. He rebelled against the idea that art was a highly specialized product made for a small elite, and he hoped to usher in a new era of art for the people. He said in lectures: "I do not want art for a few, any more than education for a few, or freedom for a

31-26 • FOREGROUND: Philip Webb SINGLE CHAIR FROM THE SUSSEX RANGE

In production from c. 1865. Ebonized wood with rush seat, 33″ × 16½″ × 14″ (83.8 × 42 × 35.6 cm).

BACKGROUND: William Morris "PEACOCK AND DRAGON" CURTAIN

1878. Handloomed jacquard-woven woolen twill, 12′10½″ × 11′5⅝″ (3.96 × 3.53 m). Chair and curtain manufactured by Morris & Company. The William Morris Gallery, London Borough of Waltham Forest.

Morris and his principal furniture designer, Philip Webb (1831–1915), adapted the Sussex range from traditional rush-seated chairs of the Sussex region. The handwoven curtain in the background is typical of Morris's fabric designs in its use of flat patterning that affirms the two-dimensional character of the textile medium. The pattern's prolific organic motifs and soothing blue and green hues—the decorative counterpart to those of naturalistic landscape painting—were meant to provide relief from the stresses of modern urban existence.

31-27 • James Abbott McNeill Whistler NOCTURNE IN BLACK AND GOLD, THE FALLING ROCKET
1875. Oil on panel, 23¾" × 18⅜" (60.2 × 46.7 cm). Detroit Institute of Arts, Detroit, Michigan. Gift of Dexter M. Ferry Jr. (46.309)

Read the document related to James Abbott McNeill Whistler's *Nocturne in Black and Gold, The Falling Rocket* on myartslab.com

few." A socialist, Morris opposed mass production and the deadening impact of factory life on the industrial worker. He argued that when laborers made handcrafted objects, they derived satisfaction from being involved in the entire process of creation and thus produced honest and beautiful things.

The American expatriate James Abbott McNeill Whistler (1834–1903) also focused his attention on the rooms and walls where art was hung, but he did so to satisfy elitist tastes for beauty as its own reward. He also became embroiled in several artistic controversies that laid the groundwork for abstraction in the next century. After flunking out of West Point in the early 1850s, Whistler studied art in Paris, where he was briefly influenced by Courbet's Realism; the two artists painted several seascapes

together. Whistler settled in London in 1859, after which his art began to take on a more "decorative" quality that he called "aesthetic" and which increasingly diverged from observed reality. He believed that the arrangement of a room (or a painting) could be aesthetically pleasing in itself, without reference to the outside world. He occasionally designed exhibition rooms for his art, with the aim of creating a total harmony of objects and space.

Whistler's ideas about art were revolutionary. He was among the first artists to conceive of his paintings as abstractions from rather than representations of observed reality, and he was among the first to collect Japanese art, fascinated by what he perceived as "decorative" line, color, and shape, although he understood little about its meaning or intent. By the middle of the 1860s, Whistler began to entitle his works "Symphonies" and "Arrangements," suggesting that their themes resided in their compositions rather than their subject matter. He painted several landscapes with the musical title "Nocturne," and when he exhibited some of these in 1877, he drew the scorn of England's leading art critic, John Ruskin (1819–1900), a supporter of the Pre-Raphaelites and their moralistic intentions. Decrying Whistler's work as carelessly lacking in finish and purpose, Ruskin's review asked how an artist could "demand 200 guineas for flinging a pot of paint in the public's face."

The most controversial painting in Whistler's 1877 exhibition was **NOCTURNE IN BLACK AND GOLD, THE FALLING ROCKET** (**FIG. 31-27**), and Ruskin's objections to it precipitated one of the most notorious court dramas in art history. Painted in restricted tonalities, at first glance the work appears completely abstract. In fact, the painting is a night scene depicting a fireworks show over a lake at Cremorne Gardens in London, with viewers vaguely discernible along the lake's edge in the foreground. Whistler took the term Nocturne from the titles of piano compositions by Frederic Chopin, hoping to evoke an association between the abstract qualities of art and music. After reading Ruskin's review, Whistler sued the critic for libel (see "Art on Trial in 1877," page 985). He deliberately turned the courtroom into a public forum, both to defend and to advertise his art. On the witness stand, he maintained that art has no higher purpose than creating visual delight and denied the need for paintings to have "subject matter." While Whistler never made a completely abstract painting, his theories were integral to the development of abstract art in the next century.

IMPRESSIONISM

The generation of French painters maturing around 1870 continued to paint modern urban subjects, but their perspective differed from that of Manet and the Realists. Instead of challenging social commentary, these younger artists painted pretty pictures of the upper middle class at leisure in the countryside and in the city, and although several members of this group painted rural scenes, their point of view tended to be that of a city person on holiday. They also began to paint not in the studio, but **en plein air** (outdoors, "in the open air"), in an effort to record directly the fleeting effects of light and atmosphere by applying flat expanses of pure color directly onto the canvas. *Plein-air* painting was greatly facilitated by the invention in 1841 of collapsible metal tubes for oil paint that artists could conveniently pack and take with them. Eschewing the tedium of the academic program for painting, with its elaborate prepatory drawings and underpainting, prelude to laborious work in the studio, the Impressionists sought instead to capture the play of light quickly, before it changed.

In April 1874, a group of these artists—including Paul Cézanne, Edgar Degas, Claude Monet, Berthe Morisot, Camille Pissarro, and Pierre-Auguste Renoir—exhibited together in Paris under the title of the Société Anonyme des Artistes Peintres, Sculpteurs, Graveurs, etc. (Anonymous Corporation of Artist-Painters, Sculptors, Engravers, etc.). Pissarro organized the group along the lines advocated by anarchists such as Proudhon, who urged citizens to band together into self-supporting grass-roots organizations, rather than relying on state-sanctioned institutions. Pissarro envisioned the Société as a mutual aid group for artists who opposed the state-funded Salons. While the Impressionists are the most famous of its members today, at the time the group included artists working in several styles. All 30 participants agreed not to submit anything that year to the Salon, which had in the past often rejected their work. This was a declaration of independence from the Académie and a bid to gain the public's attention directly.

While their exhibition received some positive reviews, one critic, Louis Leroy, writing in the satirical journal *Charivari*, seized upon the title of Claude Monet's painting *Impression: Sunrise* (see **FIG. 31-28**), and dubbed the entire exhibition "impressionist." Leroy was ridiculing the fast, open brushstrokes and unfinished look of some of the paintings, but Monet and his colleagues embraced the term because it aptly described their aim of rendering the instantaneous impression and fleeting moment in paint. Seven more Impressionist exhibitions were held between 1876 and 1886, with the membership of the group varying slightly on each occasion; only Pissarro participated in all eight shows. The relative success of these exhibitions prompted other artists to organize their own alternatives to the Salon, and by 1900 the independent exhibition and gallery system had all but eradicated the French academic Salon system. Its centuries-old stranglehold on determining and controlling artistic "standards" was effectively ended.

LANDSCAPE AND LEISURE

Claude Monet (1840–1926) was a leading exponent of Impressionism. Born in Paris but raised in the port city of Le Havre, he trained briefly with an academic teacher but soon established his own studio. His friend Charles-François Daubigny urged him to "be faithful to his impression" and suggested that he create a floating studio on a boat and paint *en plein air*. Like other Impressionists, Monet's focus was the creation of a modern painting style, not the production of biting social commentary. Initially, the Impressionists celebrated the semirural pleasures of outings to the suburbs afforded to the middle class by the Paris train system. Few early works depict locations far from Paris; most feature the Parisians at leisure—walking, boating, and visiting the fashionable new parks within the city or just outside of town.

In the summer of 1870, the Franco-Prussian War broke out and Monet fled to London, where he spent time with Pissarro and his future art dealer, Paul Durand-Ruel. The disastrous loss of the major industrial regions of Alsace and Lorraine to Prussia at the end of the war devastated the French economy. In Paris, for two months between March and May 1871, workers rose up and established the Commune, a working-class city government, the suppression of which led to an estimated 20,000 dead and 7,500 imprisoned. The horror rocked Paris. Courbet was imprisoned for a short time and, in artists' circles, the fear of being branded as an

31-28 • Claude Monet
IMPRESSION: SUNRISE
1872. Oil on canvas, 19″ ×
24⅜″ (48 × 63 cm). Musée
Marmottan, Paris.

☐─┤**Read** the
document related
to Claude Monet
on myartslab.com

enemy of the state sent a chill through everyone. After 1871, overt political commentary in French art diminished even more, and the challenge of the avant-garde was expressed increasingly as an insular stylistic rebellion.

In 1873, just after returning to Paris, Monet painted **IMPRESSION: SUNRISE** (**FIG. 31-28**), a view of the sun rising in the morning fog over the harbor at his home town of Le Havre. The painting is rendered almost entirely of strokes of color (Leroy sneeringly called them "tongue-lickings"). The foreground is ambiguous and the horizon line disappears among the shimmering shapes of steamships and docks in the background, clouded by a thick atmosphere of mist. Monet registers the intensity and shifting forms of a first sketch and presents it as the final work of art. He records the ephemeral play of reflected light and color and its effect on the eye, rather than describing the physical substance of forms and the spatial volumes they occupy. The American painter Lilla Cabot Perry, who befriended Monet in his later years, recalled him telling her:

> When you go out to paint, try to forget what objects you
> have before you—a tree, a house, a field, or whatever.
> Merely think, Here is a little square of blue, here an oblong
> of pink, here a streak of yellow, and paint it just as it looks
> to you, the exact color and shape, until it gives your own
> naive impression of the scene before you.

31-29 • Claude Monet **ROUEN CATHEDRAL: THE PORTAL (IN SUN)**
1894. Oil on canvas, 39¼″ × 26″ (99.7 × 66 cm). Metropolitan Museum of Art, New York.

31–30 • Camille Pissarro WOODED LANDSCAPE AT L'HERMITAGE, PONTOISE
1878. Oil on canvas, 18⁵⁄₁₆″ × 22¹⁄₁₆″ (46.5 × 56 cm). Nelson-Atkins Museum of Art, Kansas City, Missouri.
Gift of Dr. and Mrs. Nicholas S. Pickard

Monet continued to explore personal impressions of light and color during a long career that extended well into the twentieth century. Beginning in the 1880s and 1890s he focused his vision even more intently, exploring a limited number of outdoor subjects through several series of paintings: haystacks, poplar trees silhouetted against the sky, and the façade of Rouen Cathedral (**FIG. 31–29**). He painted the cathedral not as an expression of personal religious conviction, but because of his fascination with the way light played across its undulating stone surface, changing its appearance constantly as the lighting changed throughout the day. He painted more than 30 canvases of the Rouen façade, begun from direct observation of the cathedral from a second-story window across the street and finished later in his studio at nearby Giverny. In these paintings, Monet continued his Impressionist

pursuit of capturing the fleeting effects of light and atmosphere, but his extensive reworking of the paintings in his studio produced pictures that were more carefully orchestrated and laboriously executed that his earlier, more spontaneous, **plein air** works.

Monet's friend and fellow artist Camille Pissarro (1830–1903) offered a new Impressionist image of the landscape, painting scenes where the urban meets the rural. At times he portrayed the rural landscape on its own, but he often shows urban visitors to the countryside and small towns or factories embedded in the land as the city encroaches upon them. Born in the Dutch West Indies to French parents and raised near Paris, Pissarro studied art in Paris during the 1850s and early 1860s. In 1870, while he and Monet lived in London, Pissarro had already espoused the principles that would later blossom in Impressionism. The two artists worked

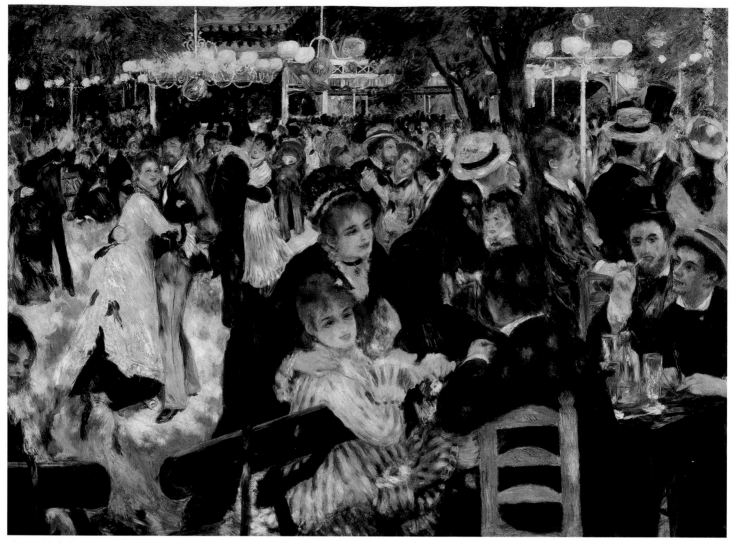

31-31 • Pierre-Auguste Renoir MOULIN DE LA GALETTE
1876. Oil on canvas, 4′3½″ × 5′9″ (1.31 × 1.75 m). Musée d'Orsay, Paris.

together in England, trying to capture what Pissarro described as "*plein air* light and fugitive effects" by lightening color intensity and hue, and loosening brushstrokes.

Following his return to France, Pissarro settled in Pontoise, a small, hilly village northwest of Paris where he worked for most of the 1870s in an Impressionist style, using high-keyed color and short brushstrokes to capture fleeting qualities of light and atmosphere. In the late 1870s, his painting became more visually complex with darkened colors. In his **WOODED LANDSCAPE AT L'HERMITAGE, PONTOISE** (**FIG. 31-30**), for instance, a foreground composition of trees screens the view of a rural path and village behind, flattening space and partly masking the figure at the lower right. Pissarro applies his paint thickly here, with a multitude of short, multi-directional brushstrokes.

In contrast, Impressionist painter Pierre-Auguste Renoir (1841–1919) focused most of his attention not on landscapes but on figures, producing mostly images of the middle class at leisure. When he met Monet at the École des Beaux-Arts in 1862, he was already working as a figure painter. Monet encouraged him

to lighten his palette and to paint outdoors, and by the mid 1870s Renoir was combining a spontaneous handling of natural light with animated figural compositions. In **MOULIN DE LA GALETTE** (**FIG. 31-31**), for example, Renoir depicts a convivial crowd relaxing on a Sunday afternoon at an old-fashioned dance hall—the Moulin de la Galette (the "Pancake Mill"), in the Montmartre section of Paris, which opened its outdoor courtyard during good weather. Renoir glamorizes the working-class clientele by placing his attractive bourgeois artist friends and their models among them, striking poses of relaxed congeniality, smiling, dancing, and chatting. He underscores the innocence of their flirtations by including children in the painting in the lower left, while emphasizing the ease of social relations through the relaxed informality of the scene. The overall mood is knit together by the dappled sunlight falling through the trees and Renoir's soft brushwork weaving blues and purples through the crowd and around the canvas. This naïve image of a carefree life of innocent leisure—a kind of bourgeois paradise removed from the real world—encapsulates Renoir's idea of the essence of art: "For me a picture should be

31–32 • Berthe Morisot SUMMER'S DAY
1879. Oil on canvas, 17¹³⁄₁₆″ × 29⁵⁄₁₆″ (45.7 × 75.2 cm). National Gallery, London. Lane Bequest, 1917

a pleasant thing, joyful and pretty—yes pretty! There are quite enough unpleasant things in life without the need for us to manufacture more."

Impressionist artist Berthe Morisot (1841–1895) defied societal conventions to become a professional painter. Morisot and her sister, Edma, copied paintings in the Louvre and studied with several teachers, including Corot, in the late 1850s and early 1860s. The sisters exhibited their art in the five Salons between 1864 and 1868, the year they met Manet. In 1869, Edma married and gave up painting to devote herself to domestic duties, but Berthe continued painting, even after her 1874 marriage to Manet's brother, Eugène, and the birth of their daughter in 1879. Morisot sent nine paintings to the first exhibition of the Impressionists in 1874 and showed her work in all but one of their subsequent shows.

As a respectable bourgeois lady, Berthe Morisot was not free to prowl the city looking for modern subjects, so she concentrated on depictions of women's lives, a subject she knew well. In the 1870s, she painted in an increasingly fluid and painterly style, flattening her picture plane and making her brushwork more prominent. In **SUMMER'S DAY** (**FIG. 31-32**), Morisot shows two elegant young ladies enjoying an outing on the lake of the fashionable Bois du Boulogne. First shown in the fifth Impressionist exhibition in 1880, the painting exemplifies the emphasis on formal features in Impressionist painting—the brushstrokes and the colors are as much its subject as the figures themselves.

MODERN LIFE

Subjects from urban life also attracted Edgar Degas (1834–1917), although his paintings are closer to Realism in their intensely frank portrayals that often suggest social commentary. Instead of painting outdoors, Degas composed his pictures in the studio from working drawings and photographs. His rigorous academic training at the École des Beaux-Arts in the mid 1850s and his three years in Italy studying the Old Masters blossomed in paintings characterized by complex compositional structure and striking representational clarity. In many respects his themes and style were closer to Manet's than to the Impressionists.

After a period of painting psychologically probing portraits of friends and relatives, during the 1870s, Degas began painting the modern life of Paris, especially its venues of entertainment and spectacle—the racetrack, the music hall, and the opera, usually focusing on the entertainers rather than on the bourgeois audience. He was especially drawn to the ballet in the 1870s and 1880s, at a time when it was in decline. Degas did not draw or paint actual dancers in rehearsal; rather, he hired dancers, often very young "ballet rats" (as he called them), to come to his studio to pose for him. **THE REHEARSAL ON STAGE** (**FIG. 31-33**), for example, is a contrived scene, calculated to delight the eye but also to refocus the mind on the stern realities of modern life. Several of the dancers look bored or exhausted; others stretch, perhaps to mitigate the toll this physical work took on their bodies. In the right

31–33 • Edgar Degas THE REHEARSAL ON STAGE

c. 1874. Pastel over brush-and-ink drawing on thin, cream-colored wove paper, laid on bristol board, mounted on canvas, 21⅜″ × 28¾″ (54.3 × 73 cm). Metropolitan Museum of Art, New York. Bequest of Mrs. H. O. Havemeyer Collection, Gift of Horace Havemeyer, 1929 (29.160.26)

31–34 • Edgar Degas THE TUB

1886. Pastel on cardboard, 23⅝″ × 32⅝″ (60 × 83 cm). Musée d'Orsay, Paris.

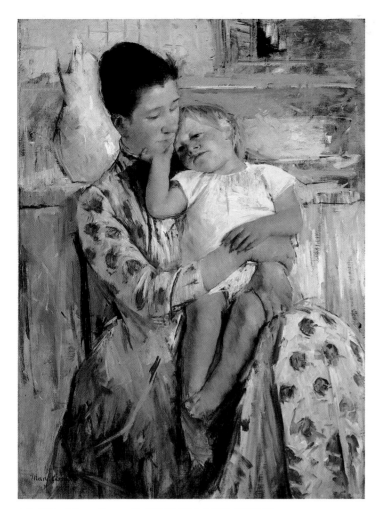

31–35 • Mary Cassatt MOTHER AND CHILD
c. 1890. Oil on canvas, 35½″ × 25⅜″ (90.2 × 64.5 cm). Wichita Art Museum, Kansas.

separate pictures: at the left the compactly posed woman, balanced precariously on the steep floor of a receding interior space, and juxtaposed next to it on the right, a tipped-up table with a still life of objects associated with bathing. But when coordinated, they establish the viewer's elevated, domineering vantage point. The dramatic, flattened juxtaposition, as well as the compression and cropping of the close frame, are further examples of the impact of Japanese prints and photography on Degas's art.

Another artist who exhibited with the Impressionists but whose art soon diverged from them in both style and technique—conditioned in part by her contact with Degas—was American expatriate Mary Cassatt (1844–1926). Born near Pittsburgh to a well-to-do family and raised in the cosmopolitan world of Philadelphia, she studied at the Pennsylvania Academy of the Fine Arts between 1861 and 1865, then moved to Paris for further academic training and lived there for most of the rest of her life. The realism of the figure paintings she exhibited at the Salons of the early and mid 1870s attracted the attention of Degas, who invited her to participate in the fourth Impressionist exhibition in 1879. Although she, like Degas, remained a studio painter and printmaker, her distaste for what she called the "tyranny" of the Salon jury system made her one of the group's staunchest supporters.

Cassatt focused her paintings on the world she knew best: the domestic and social life of bourgeois women. She is known for extraordinarily sensitive representations of women with children, which, like the genre paintings of fellow expatriate Henry Ossawa Tanner (see FIG. 31-24), sought to counteract the clichéd stereotypes of her age. In **MOTHER AND CHILD** from about 1890 (**FIG. 31-35**), she uses a contrast between the loosely painted, Impressionist treatment of clothing and setting and the solidly modeled forms of faces and hands to rivet our attention on the tender connection between mother and child at bedtime, right after a bath. The drowsy face and flushed cheeks of the child and the weighty limbs have a natural quality, even though the space occupied by the figures seems flattened. Because the structured composition and familiar subject recall much earlier portrayals of the Virgin and Child, Cassatt elevates this small vignette of modern private life into a homage to motherhood and a dialogue with the history of art.

Gustave Caillebotte (1848–1894), another friend of Degas, was instrumental in organizing several Impressionist exhibitions and used his wealth to purchase the work of his friends, amassing a large collection of paintings. He studied with an academic teacher privately and qualified for the École des Beaux-Arts, but never attended. Caillebotte was fascinated by the regularized, radiating streets of Haussmann's Paris (see FIG. 31-2), and his subjects and compositions often represent life along the boulevards. **PARIS STREET, RAINY DAY** (FIG. 31-36) has an unconventional, almost telescopic, asymmetrical composition with a tipped perspective. The broad, wet streets create the subject of this painting, with anonymous, huddled Parisians mostly pushed to the periphery, their shiny umbrellas as prominent as their silhouetted bodies.

background slouch two well-dressed, middle-aged men, each probably a "protector" of one of the dancers. Because ballerinas generally came from lower-class families and exhibited their scantily clad bodies in public—something that "respectable" bourgeois women did not do—they were widely assumed to be sexually available, and they often attracted the attentions of wealthy men willing to support them in exchange for sexual favors.

The composition is set in a raked space, as if viewed from a box close to the stage. The abrupt foreshortening is emphasized by the dark scrolls of the double basses that jut up from the lower left. The angular viewpoint from above may derive from Japanese prints, which Degas collected, while the seemingly arbitrary cropping of figures on the left suggests photography, which he also practiced.

Whereas Degas's ballet paintings highlight informal moments associated with public performance, his later images of bathing women are furtive glimpses of intimate moments drawn from private life, usually rendered in the medium of pastel, which only heightens their sense of immediacy. **THE TUB** of 1886 (**FIG. 31-34**) represents a crouching woman, perched within a small tub, washing her neck with a sponge. Initially, this may seem to be two

31-36 • Gustave Caillebotte PARIS STREET, RAINY DAY
1877. Oil on canvas, 83½″ × 108¾″ (212.2 × 276.2 cm). The Art Institute of Chicago. Charles H. and Mary F.S. Worcester Collection (1964.336)

Only the connected couple strolling toward us is fully realized and personalized. Squeezed between the lamppost and the saturated red and green of a shopfront, they stand within an internally framed rectangular composition, capped by the strong horizontal of the two juxtaposed umbrellas.

THE LATE NINETEENTH CENTURY

The Realists and Impressionists continued to create art until the end of the century, but by the mid 1880s they had relinquished their dominance to a younger generation of innovative artists. This period seems less unified, less directed, and less restricted geographically. Artists increasingly defined the avant-garde in terms of visual experimentation, developing new visual languages more appropriate to newly formulated messages.

These artists included French Post-Impressionists, who reinterpreted art as an expression of an interior world of the imagination or imposed a new scientific rigor on representations of the world around them; late nineteenth-century French sculptors, who studied the passionate physicality of the human form; Symbolist artists, who retreated into fantastical and sometimes horrifying worlds of the imagination; Art Nouveau artists, who rejected the rational order of the industrial world to create images and designs ruled by the writhing, moving asymmetrical shapes of growing plants; and even landscape architects, who recast the urban cityscape into a rambling natural landscape.

POST-IMPRESSIONISM

The English critic Roger Fry coined the term "Post-Impressionism" in 1910 to describe a diverse group of painters whose work he had collected for an exhibition. He acknowledged that these artists did not share a unified approach to art, but they all used Impressionism as a springboard for developing their individual styles.

SEURAT Georges Seurat (1859–1891), who was born in Paris and trained at the École des Beaux-Arts, sought to "correct" Impressionism, which he found too intellectually shallow and too improvisational. He preferred the clarity of structure he saw in Classical relief sculpture, and the seemingly systematic but actually quite emotive use of color suggested by optics and color theory. He was particularly interested in the "law of the simultaneous contrast of colors" formulated by Michel-Eugène Chevreul in the 1820s. Chevreul observed that adjacent objects not only cast reflections of their own color onto their neighbors, but also create the effect of their **complementary color**. Thus, when a blue object is set next to a yellow one, the eye will detect in the blue object a trace of purple, the complement of yellow, and in the yellow object a trace of orange, the complement of blue.

Seurat's goal was to find ways to create such retinal vibrations that enlivened the painted surface, using distinctive short, multidirectional strokes of almost pure color, in what came to be known as "Divisionism" or "Pointillism." In theory, these juxtaposed small strokes of color would merge in the viewer's eye to produce the impression of other colors. When perceived from a certain distance they would appear more luminous and intense than the same colors seen separately, while on close inspection Seurat's strokes and colors would remain distinct and separate.

Seurat's monumental painting **A SUNDAY AFTERNOON ON THE ISLAND OF LA GRANDE JATTE** (FIG. 31–37) was first exhibited at the eighth and final Impressionist exhibition in 1886. The theme of weekend leisure is typically Impressionist, but the

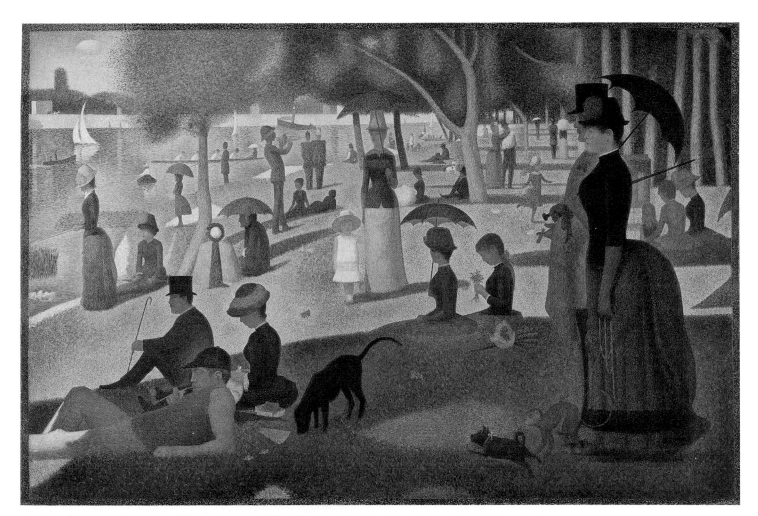

31–37 • Georges Seurat A SUNDAY AFTERNOON ON THE ISLAND OF LA GRANDE JATTE
1884–1886. Oil on canvas, 6′9½″ × 10′1¼″ (207 × 308 cm). The Art Institute of Chicago. Helen Birch Bartlett Memorial Collection (1926.22)

There was a social hierarchy in Parisian parks in the late nineteenth century; the Bois du Boulogne (see FIG. 31–32) was an upper-middle-class park in an area of grand avenues, whereas the Grande Jatte faced a lower-class industrial area across the river, and was easily accessible by train. The figures represent a range of "types" that would have been easily recognizable to the nineteenth-century viewer, such as the middle-class strolling man and his companion to the right, usually identified as a *boulevardier* (or citified dandy) and a *cocotte* (a single woman of the demi-monde), or the working-class *canotier* (oarsman) to the left.

View the Closer Look for *A Sunday Afternoon on the Island of La Grande Jatte* on myartslab.com

Deeply affected by recently imported examples of Japanese art and prints, which he appreciated for their "exotic" visual effects, Vincent van Gogh painted **JAPONAISERIE: FLOWERING PLUM TREE** (FIG. 31–39) in 1887. After a lengthy isolation, Japan was opened to Western trade and diplomacy in 1853, and in 1855 trade agreements permitted the regular exchange of goods. Among the first Japanese art objects to come to Paris was a sketchbook entitled *Manga* by Hokusai (1760–1849), which was eagerly passed around by Parisian artists. Several of them began to collect Japanese objects; the 1867 Paris International Exposition mounted the first show of Japanese prints in Europe; and immediately thereafter, Japanese lacquers, fans, bronzes, hanging scrolls, kimonos, ceramics, illustrated books, and *ukiyo-e* (prints of the "floating world," the realm of geishas and popular entertainment) began to appear for sale in specialty shops, art galleries, and even some department stores in Paris. The French obsession with Japan reached such a level by 1872 that the art critic Philippe Burty named the phenomenon **Japonisme**.

Vincent van Gogh admired the design and handcrafted quality of Japanese prints, which he both owned and copied. His *Japonaiserie: Flowering Plum Tree* is largely copied from Hiroshige's woodblock print *Plum Orchard, Kameido* (FIG. 31–38). Van Gogh places the same flattened tree with its asymmetrical branches, thin, shooting twigs, and tiny blossoms in his foreground; the same smaller trees in the middle ground; and the same railing in the background, behind which can be seen several figures and a small hut. Van Gogh has also appropriated Hiroshige's color scheme and flattened picture plane, as well as his banners of text. But he also made significant changes in his adaptation. He flattened the scene more extremely than Hiroshige. His grass is a uniform blanket of green, the gray trees with hard black outlines are flat and undifferentiated, and it is not clear whether

the yellow blossoms are in front of or behind the thickly painted red sky. Van Gogh also frames his painting with bold, orange borders containing pseudo-Japanese characters, executed crudely as if to accentuate the "primitiveness" of the image and its source. Van Gogh knew little about Japanese culture

and less about the Japanese painting or printmaking tradition. He used the Hiroshige print as a prompt in order to conjure up what he saw as a simpler, more "primitive" culture than his own, at a time when other artists, like Paul Gauguin, traveled the world in search of "primitive" cultures to inspire their art.

31-38 • Hiroshige PLUM ORCHARD, KAMEIDO
No. 30 from *One Hundred Famous Views of Edo*. 1857. Woodblock print, 13¼″ × 8⅝″ (33.6 × 22.6 cm). Brooklyn Museum, New York. Gift of Anna Ferris (30.1478.30)

31–39 • Vincent van Gogh JAPONAISERIE: FLOWERING PLUM TREE
1887. Oil on canvas, 21½″ × 18″ (54.6 × 45.7 cm). Vincent van Gogh Museum, Amsterdam.

rigorous technique, the stiff formality of the figures, and the highly calculated geometry of the composition produce a solemn effect quite at odds with the casual naturalism of Impressionism. Seurat painted the entire canvas using only 11 colors in three values. When viewed from a distance of about 9 feet, the painting reads as figures in a park rendered in many colors and tones; but when viewed from a distance of 3 feet, the individual marks of color become more salient, while the forms dissolve into abstraction.

From its first appearance, the painting has been the subject of a number of conflicting interpretations. Contemporary accounts of the island indicate that on Sundays—the newly designated official day off for French working families to spend time together—it was noisy, littered, and chaotic. By painting the island the way he did,

Seurat may have intended to represent an ideal image of working-class and middle-class life and leisure—a model of how tranquil the island, and perhaps life, *should* be in this fantasy of a harmonious blending of the classes. But some art historians see Seurat satirizing here the sterile habits and rigid attitudes of the growing Parisian middle class, not to mention their domineering presence within this working-class preserve. Or is he simply engaged in an intellectual exercise on the nature of form and color in works of art?

VAN GOGH Among the most famous Post-Impressionist artists is the Dutch painter Vincent van Gogh (1853–1890), who transformed his artistic sources into a highly expressive personal style. The oldest son of a Protestant minister, Van Gogh worked

31–40 • Vincent van Gogh THE STARRY NIGHT
1889. Oil on canvas, 28¾″ × 36¼″ (73 × 93 cm). Museum of Modern Art, New York.
Acquired through the Lillie P. Bliss Bequest (472.1941)

View the Closer Look for *The Starry Night* on myartslab.com as an art dealer, a teacher, and an evangelist before deciding in 1880 to become an artist. After brief periods of study in Brussels, The Hague, and Antwerp, in 1886 he moved to Paris, where he encountered the Parisian avant-garde. Van Gogh adapted Seurat's Pointillism by applying brilliantly colored paint in multi-directional strokes of impasto (thick applications of paint) to give his pictures a turbulent emotional energy and a palpable surface texture.

Van Gogh was a socialist who believed that modern life, with its constant social change and focus on progress and success, alienated people from one other and from themselves (see "Modern Artists and World Cultures: Japonisme," page 996). His own paintings are efforts to communicate his emotional state by establishing a direct connection between artist and viewer, thereby overcoming the emotional barrenness of modern society. In a prolific output over only ten years, he produced paintings that contributed significantly to the later emergence of Expressionism, in which the intensity of an artist's emotional state will override any desire for fidelity to the actual appearance of things. Van Gogh described his working method in a letter to his brother:

> I should like to paint the portrait of an artist friend who dreams great dreams, who works as the nightingale sings, because it is his nature. This man will be fair-haired. I should like to put my appreciation, the love I have for him, into the picture. So I will paint him as he is, as faithfully as I can—to begin with. But that is not the end of the picture. To finish it, I shall be an obstinate colorist. I shall exaggerate the fairness of the hair, arrive at tones of orange, chrome, pale yellow. Behind the head—instead of painting the ordinary wall of the shabby apartment, I shall paint infinity, I shall do a simple background of the richest, most intense blue that I can contrive, and by this simple combination, the shining fair head against this rich blue background, I shall obtain a mysterious effect, like a star in the deep blue sky.

One of the most famous examples of Van Gogh's approach is **THE STARRY NIGHT** (**FIG. 31-40**), painted near the asylum of Saint-Rémy, from careful observation and the artist's imagination. Above the quiet town, the sky pulsates with celestial rhythms and blazes with exploding stars. Contemplating life and death in a letter, Van Gogh wrote: "Just as we take the train to get to Tarascon or Rouen, we take death to reach a star." This idea is rendered visible here by the cypress tree, a traditional symbol of both death and eternal life, which rises dramatically to link the terrestrial and celestial realms. The brightest star in the sky is actually a planet, Venus, which is associated with love. It is possible that the picture's extraordinary energy also expresses Van Gogh's euphoric hope of gaining in death the love that had eluded him in life. The painting is a riot of brushwork, as rail-like strokes of intense color writhe across its surface. Van Gogh's brushwork is immediate, expressive, and intense, clearly more a record of what he felt than what he saw. During the last year and a half of his life, he experienced repeated psychological crises that lasted for days or weeks. While they were raging, he wanted to hurt himself, heard loud noises in his head, and could not paint. The stress and burden of these attacks led him to the asylum where he painted *The Starry Night*, and eventually to suicide in July 1890.

GAUGUIN In painting from imagination more than from nature in *The Starry Night*, Van Gogh may have been following the advice of his close friend Paul Gauguin (1848–1903), who once counseled another artist: "Don't paint from nature too much. Art is an abstraction. Derive this abstraction from nature while dreaming before it, and think more of the creation that will result." Born in Paris to a Peruvian mother and a radical French journalist father, Gauguin lived in Peru until age 7. During the 1870s and early 1880s, he enjoyed a comfortable bourgeois life as a stockbroker, painting in his spare time under the tutelage of Pissarro. Between 1880 and 1886, he exhibited in the final four Impressionist exhibitions. In 1883, he lost his job during a stock market crash, and three years later he abandoned his wife and five children to pursue a full-time painting career. Gauguin knew firsthand the business culture of his time and came to despise it. Believing that escape to a more "primitive" place would bring with it the simpler pleasures of preindustrial life, Gauguin lived for extended periods in the French province of Brittany between 1886 and 1891, traveled to Panama and Martinique in 1887, spent two months in Arles with Van Gogh in 1888, and then in 1891 sailed for Tahiti, a French colony in the South Pacific. After a final sojourn in France in 1893–1895, Gauguin returned to French Polynesia, where he died in 1903.

Gauguin's art was inspired by sources as varied as medieval stained glass, folk art, and Japanese prints; he sought to paint in a "primitive" way, employing the so-called "decorative" qualities of folk art, such as brilliantly colored flat shapes, anti-naturalist color, and bold, black outlines. Gauguin called his style "synthetism," because he believed it synthesized observation and the artist's feelings in an abstracted application of line, shape, space, and color.

MAHANA NO ATUA (*Day of the God*) (see "A Closer Look," page 1000) is very much a product of such synthesis. Despite its Tahitian subject, it was painted in France during Gauguin's brief return visit after two years in the South Pacific. He had gone to Tahiti hoping to find an unspoiled, preindustrial paradise, imagining the Tahitians to be childlike and close to nature. What he discovered was a thoroughly colonized country whose native culture was rapidly disappearing under the pressures of Westernization. In paintings such as this, however, Gauguin chose to ignore this reality and depict instead the Edenic ideal of his own imagination.

SYMBOLISM

Symbolism was an international movement in art and literature championed by a loose affiliation of artists who addressed the irrational fears, desires, and impulses of the human mind in their work. A fascination with the dark recesses of the psyche emerged over the last decades of the nineteenth century, encompassing

A CLOSER LOOK | *Mahana no atua (Day of the God)*

by Paul Gauguin. 1894. Oil on canvas. 27⅜" × 35⅝" (69.5 × 90.5 cm).
The Art Institute of Chicago. Helen Birch Bartlett Memorial Collection (1926.198)

Gauguin divided the painting into three horizontal zones, increasingly abstract from top to bottom. The upper zone, painted in the most lifelike manner, centers on the statue of a god set in a beach landscape populated by Tahitians.

As was his practice in many of his Tahitian paintings, Gauguin did not base this sculpted idol on a statue he saw in Tahiti, but rather on pictures he owned of the Buddhist temple complex at Borobudur (see FIG. 10–34).

This middle zone contains three figures posed on an unnaturalistically pink beach. The green, arched form behind the central woman links her visually to the idol immediately above her.

The central female bather dips her feet in the water and looks coyly out at viewers, while, on either side of her, two androgynous figures recline in fetuslike postures. Their poses perhaps symbolize—left to right—birth, life, and death.

Filling the bottom third of the painting is a striking pool of water, abstracted into a dazzling array of bright colors and arranged in a puzzlelike pattern of flat, curvilinear shapes. The left half of this pool seems rooted in natural description, evoking spatial recession. But on the right it becomes flatter and more stylized.

By reflecting a strange and unexpected reality exactly where we expect to see a mirror image of the familiar world, this magic pool seems the perfect symbol of Gauguin's desire to evoke "the mysterious centers of thought." His aim was symbolic rather than descriptive works of art.

 View the Closer Look for *Mahana no atua (Day of the God)* on myartslab.com

photographic and scientific examinations of the nature of insanity, as well as a popular interest in the spirit world of mediums. Some Symbolist artists sought escape from modern life in irrational worlds of unrestrained emotion as described by authors such as Edgar Allan Poe (1809–1849), whose terrifying stories of the supernatural were popular across Europe. It is hardly coincidental that Sigmund Freud (1856–1939), who compared artistic creation to the process of dreaming, wrote his pioneering *The Interpretation of Dreams* (1900) during this period.

The Symbolists rejected the value placed on rationalism and material progress in modern Western culture, choosing instead to explore the irrational realms of emotion, imagination, and spirituality. They sought a deeper and more mysterious reality beyond everyday life, which they conveyed through strange and ambiguous subject matter and stylized forms that suggest hidden and elusive meanings. They often compared their works to dreams.

Symbolism in painting closely paralleled a similar movement among poets and writers. For example, Joris-Karl Huysmans's novel *À Rebours (Against the Grain)*, published in 1884, has a single character, an aristocrat named Des Esseintes, who locked himself away from the world because "Imagination could easily be substituted for the vulgar realities of things." Claiming that nature was irrelevant, Des Esseintes mused: "Nature has had her day" and "wearied aesthetes" should take refuge in artworks "steeped in ancient dreams or antique corruptions, far removed from the manner of our present day."

MOREAU A visionlike atmosphere pervades the later work of Gustave Moreau (1826–1898), an academic artist whom the Symbolists regarded as a precursor. They particularly admired Moreau's renditions of the biblical Salomé, the young Judaean princess who, at the instigation of her mother, Herodias, performed an erotic dance before her stepfather, Herod, and demanded as reward the head of John the Baptist (Mark 6:21–28). In **THE APPARITION** (**FIG. 31–41**), exhibited at the Salon of 1876, the seductive Salomé confronts a vision of the saint's severed head, which hovers open-eyed in midair, dripping blood and radiating holy light. Moreau depicted this sensual and macabre scene and its exotic setting in meticulous detail, with touches of jewel-like color to create an atmosphere of voluptuous decadence that amplifies Salomé's role as *femme fatale* who uses her sensuality to destroy her male victim.

The Symbolists, like many smaller groups of artists in the late nineteenth century, staged independent art exhibitions, but unlike the Impressionists,

31–41 • Gustave Moreau THE APPARITION
1874–1876. Watercolor on paper, 41⁵⁄₁₆″ × 28³⁄₁₆″ (106 × 72.2 cm). Musée du Louvre, Paris.

31–42 • Edvard Munch THE SCREAM
?1910. Tempera and oil on unprimed canvas, 33″ × 26″ (83.5 × 66 cm). Munch Museum, Oslo.

who hired halls, printed programs, and charged a small admission fee for their exhibitions, the Symbolists mounted modest shows with little expectation of public interest. During the 1889 Universal Exposition, for example, they hung a few works in a café close to the fairgrounds, with the result that the exhibition went almost unnoticed by the press.

MUNCH Symbolism originated in France but had a profound impact on the avant-garde in other countries, where it frequently took on Expressionist tendencies. In Norway, Edvard Munch (1863–1944) produced a body of work that shows the terrifying workings of an anguished mind. **THE SCREAM** (**FIG. 31–42**) is the stuff of nightmares and horror movies; its harsh swirling colors and lines direct us wildly around the painting, but bring us right back to the haunting human head at the center and the echoes of its haunting scream, sensed visually. Munch described how the painting began: "One evening I was walking along a path; the city was on one side, and the fjord below. I was tired and ill … . I sensed a shriek passing through nature … . I painted this picture, painted the clouds as actual blood."

31-43 • James Ensor **THE INTRIGUE**
1890. Oil on canvas, 35½″ × 59″ (90.3 × 150 cm). Koninklijk Museum voor Schone Kunsten, Antwerp.

31-44 • Auguste Rodin **THE BURGHERS OF CALAIS**
1884–1889. Bronze, 6′10½″ × 7′11″ × 6′6″ (2.1 × 2.4 × 2 m). Hirshhorn Museum and Sculpture Garden, Smithsonian Institution, Washington, DC. Gift of Joseph H. Hirshhorn, 1966

Rodin's relocation of public sculpture from a high pedestal to a low base will lead, in the twentieth century, to the elimination of the pedestal itself and to the presentation of sculpture in the "real" space of the viewer.

ENSOR The Belgian painter and printmaker James Ensor (1860–1949) studied for four years at the Brussels Academy, but spent the rest of his life in the nearby coastal resort town of Ostend, where he produced equally terrifying paintings, also combining Symbolist and Expressionist tendencies. **THE INTRIGUE** (**FIG. 31-43**) shows a tightly packed group of agitated people, pushed toward the viewer into the foreground. Masks—modeled on the grotesque papier-mâché masks Ensor's family sold for the pre-Lenten carnival—conceal their faces, giving them a disturbing, mindless, menacing quality. Ensor's acidic colors and ener-getic handling of the painted surface only increase the viewers' anxiety.

FRENCH SCULPTURE

A defiance of conventional expectations and an interest in emotional expressiveness also characterize the work of late nineteenth-century Europe's most successful and influential sculptor, Auguste Rodin (1840–1917). Born in Paris, Rodin failed on three occasions to gain entrance to the École des Beaux-Arts and consequently spent the first 20 years of his career as an assistant to other sculptors and decorators. After a trip to Italy in 1875, where he saw the sculpture of Donatello and Michelangelo, Rodin developed a style of vigorously modeled figures in unconventional, even awkward poses, which was simultaneously scorned by academic critics and admired by the general public.

Rodin's status as a major sculptor was confirmed in 1884, when he won a competition to create **THE BURGHERS OF CALAIS** (**FIG. 31-44**), for the city of Calais, commemorating a local event from the Hundred Years' War. In 1347, Edward III of England offered to spare the besieged city if six leading citizens (burghers)—dressed only in sackcloth with rope halters and carrying the keys to the city—surrendered themselves to him for execution. Though it is unknown to them at this point, the king would be so impressed by their courage, that he would spare them.

The Calais commissioners were pleased neither with Rodin's conception of the event nor with his plan to display the figures on a low base, almost at street level, to suggest to viewers that ordinary people like themselves were capable of noble acts. Instead of calm, idealized heroes, Rodin presented ordinary-looking men in various attitudes of resignation and despair. He exaggerated their facial expressions, lengthened their arms, greatly enlarged their hands and feet, and swathed them in heavy fabric, showing not only how they may have looked but also how they must have felt as they forced themselves to take one difficult step after another. Rodin's willingness to stylize the human body for expressive purposes opened the way for subsequent sculptural abstractions.

Camille Claudel (1864–1943), who was Rodin's assistant while he worked on *The Burghers of Calais*, had already studied sculpture formally before joining Rodin's studio. She soon became his mistress, and their often-stormy relationship lasted 15 years. Most often remembered for her dramatic life story,

31-45 • Camille Claudel **THE WALTZ**
1892–1905. Bronze, height 9⅞″ (25 cm). Neue Pinakothek, Munich.

French composer Claude Debussy, a close friend of Claudel, displayed a cast of this sculpture on his piano. Debussy acknowledged the influence of art and literature on his musical innovations.

Claudel enjoyed independent professional success but suffered a breakdown that sent her to a mental hospital for the last 30 years of her life.

One of Claudel's most celebrated works is **THE WALTZ** (**FIG. 31-45**), produced in several versions and sizes between 1892 and 1905. The sculpture depicts a dancing couple, both nude, although the woman's lower body is covered with long, flowing drapery, a concession she made after an inspector from the Ministry of Fine Arts declared their sensuality unacceptable, recommending that her state commission for a marble version of the work be revoked. The subject of the waltz alone was controversial at this time because of the close contact demanded of dancers. Claudel added enough drapery to regain the commission, but she never finished it. She did, however, cast the modified *version* in bronze as a tabletop sculpture, in which the spiral flow of the cloth creates the illusion of rapturous movement as the embracing dancers twirl through space.

ART NOUVEAU

The swirling mass of drapery in Claudel's *The Waltz* has a stylistic affinity with Art Nouveau (French for "new art"), a movement launched in the early 1890s that permeated all aspects of European design for more than a decade. Art Nouveau embraced the use of modern industrial materials but rejected the functional aesthetic of works such as the Eiffel Tower (see FIG. 31-1) that showcased exposed structure as architectural design. Art Nouveau artists and architects drew particular inspiration from nature, especially from vines, snakes, flowers, and winged insects, whose delicate and sinuous forms were consistent with the graceful and attenuated aesthetic principles of the movement. The goal was to harmonize all aspects of design into an integrated whole, as found in nature itself.

HORTA The artist most responsible for developing the Art Nouveau style in architecture was the Belgian Victor Horta (1861–

1947). After academic training in Ghent and Brussels, Horta worked in the office of a Neoclassical architect in Brussels for six years before opening his own practice in 1890. In 1892, he received his first important commission, a private residence in Brussels for a Professor Tassel. The result, especially the house's entry hall and staircase (**FIG. 31-46**), was strikingly original. The ironwork, wall decoration, and floor tiles were all designed in an intricate series of long, graceful curves. Although Horta's sources are still debated, he was apparently impressed by the stylized linear designs of the English Arts and Crafts Movement of the 1880s. His concern for integrating the various arts into a more unified whole, like his reliance on sinuous decorative line, derived in part from English reformers such as William Morris.

GAUDÍ The application of graceful linearity to all aspects of design, evident in the entry hall of the Tassel House, began a vogue that spread across Europe. In Spain, where the style was called *Modernismo*, the major practitioner was the Catalan architect Antonio Gaudí i Cornet (1852–1926). Gaudí integrated natural forms into the design of buildings and parks that are still revolutionary in their dynamic freedom of line.

In 1904, the wealthy industrialist Josep Batlló commissioned Gaudí to design a private residence to surpass the lavish houses of other prominent families in Barcelona. Gaudí convinced his patron to retain the underlying structure of an existing building, but transform its façade and interior spaces. Gaudí's façade (**FIG. 31-47**) is a dreamlike fantasy of undulating sandstone sculptures and multicolored glass and tile surfaces, imaginatively mixing the Islamic, Gothic, and Baroque visual traditions of Barcelona. The gaping lower-story windows are the source of the building's nickname, the "house of yawns," while the use of what look like giant human tibias for upright supports led others to call it the "house of bones." The roof resembles a recumbent dragon with overlapping tiles as scales. A fanciful turret surfaces at its edge, recalling the sword of St. George—patron of Catalunya—plunged into the back of his legendary foe. Gaudí's highly personal alternative to academic historicism and modern industrialization in urban

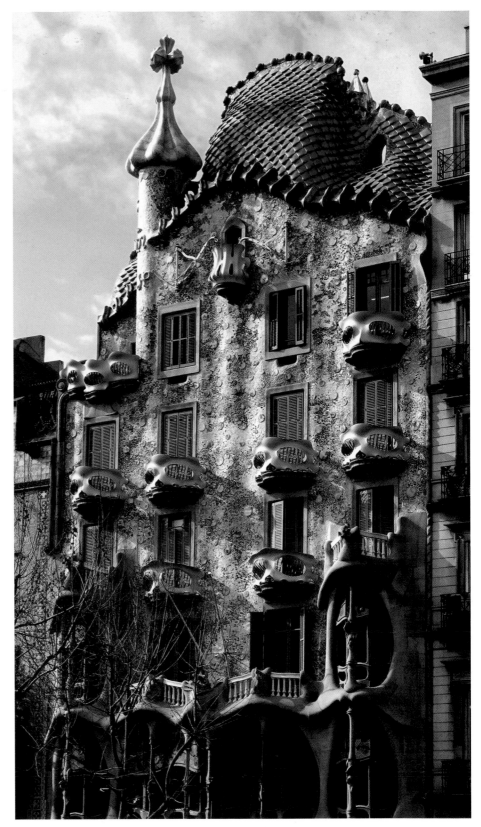

31-47 • Antonio Gaudí CASA BATLLÒ, BARCELONA
43 Passeig de Gracia. 1900–1907.

buildings such as this reflects his affinity with Iberian traditions as well as his concern to provide imaginative surroundings to enrich the lives of city dwellers.

31-48 • Hector Guimard **DESK**
c. 1899 (remodeled after 1909). Olive wood with ash panels, 28¾″ × 47¾″ (73 × 121 cm). Museum of Modern Art, New York. Gift of Madame Hector Guimard

GUIMARD The leading French practitioner of Art Nouveau was Hector Guimard (1867–1942), who embraced the movement after meeting Horta in 1895. Guimard is most famous for his designs of entrances to the Paris Métro (subway) at the turn of the century, but he devoted much of his career to interior design and furnishings, such as this **DESK** that he made for himself (**FIG. 31-48**). Instead of a static and stable object, Guimard handcrafted an asymmetrical, organic entity that seems to undulate and grow around the person who sits at its workspace.

TOULOUSE-LAUTREC Henri de Toulouse-Lautrec (1864–1901) suffered from a genetic disorder that stunted his growth and left him physically disabled. Born into an aristocratic family in southern France, he moved to Paris in 1882, where his private academic training was transformed when he discovered the work of Degas. He also discovered Montmartre, the entertainment district of Paris that housed the most bohemian of the avant-garde artists. From the late 1880s, Toulouse-Lautrec dedicated himself to depicting the nightlife of Montmartre—the cafés, theaters, dance halls, and brothels that he himself frequented.

Between 1891 and 1901, Toulouse-Lautrec designed roughly 30 lithographic posters for Montmartre's more famous nightspots, advertising their most popular entertainers. One features the notoriously limber dancer **JANE AVRIL** performing the infamous can-can (**FIG. 31-49**). Toulouse-Lautrec places Avril on a stage that zooms into the background. The hand and face of a double-bass player, part of his instrument, and pages of music frame the poster in the extreme foreground at lower right—a bold foreshortening that recalls the compositions of Degas (see FIG. 31-33).

31-49 • Henri de Toulouse-Lautrec **JANE AVRIL**
1893. Lithograph, 50½″ × 37″ (129 × 94 cm). San Diego Museum of Art. Gift of the Baldwin M. Baldwin Foundation (1987.32)

But Toulouse-Lautrec's image emphasizes Avril's sexuality in order to draw in the crowds, while Degas's pictures coax visual beauty from frank Realism. Toulouse-Lautrec outlines his forms, flattens his space, and suppresses modeling to accommodate the cheap colored lithographic printing technique he used, but the resulting emphasis on bold silhouettes and curving lines is distinctively Art Nouveau.

THE BEGINNINGS OF MODERNISM

The history of late nineteenth-century architecture reflects a dilemma faced by the industrial city, caught between the classicizing tradition of the Beaux-Arts academic style and the materials, construction methods, and new aesthetic of industry. The École des Beaux-Arts, although marginalized by the end of the century by new trends in painting, came into its own as the training ground for European and American architects after 1880, while industrialization in places like Chicago simultaneously demanded new ways of thinking about tall and large buildings.

At the same time, Paul Cézanne, late in his life, altered the course of avant-garde painting by returning to an intense visual study of the world around him, scrutinizing it like a specimen on a dissecting table and urging younger artists to consider new ways of creating artistic meaning. In 1906, the year Cézanne died, a retrospective exhibition of his life's work in Paris revealed his methods to the next generation of artists, who would be the creators of Modernism.

EUROPEAN ARCHITECTURE: TECHNOLOGY AND STRUCTURE

The pace of life speeded up considerably over the course of the nineteenth century. Industrialization allowed people to manufacture more, consume more, travel more, and do more, in greater numbers than before. Industrialization caused urbanization, which in turn demanded more industrialization. A belief in the perfectibility of society spawned more than 20 international fairs celebrating innovations in industry and technology. One of the first of these took place in London in 1851. The Great Exhibition of the Industry of All Nations was mounted by the British to display their industrial might, assert their right to empire, and quell lingering public unrest after the 1848 revolutions elsewhere in Europe. The centerpiece of the Great Exhibition, the Crystal Palace, introduced new modern building techniques and aesthetics.

THE CRYSTAL PALACE The revolutionary construction of **THE CRYSTAL PALACE** (**FIG. 31-50**), created by Joseph Paxton (1803–1865), featured a structural skeleton of cast iron that held iron-framed glass panes measuring 49 by 30 inches, the largest size that could be mass-produced at the time.

31-50 • Joseph Paxton THE CRYSTAL PALACE
London. 1850–1851. Iron, glass, and wood. (Print of the Great Exhibition of 1851; printed and published by Dickinson Brothers, London, 1854.)

Prefabricated wooden ribs and bars supported the panes. The triple-tiered edifice was the largest space ever enclosed up to that time—1,851 feet long, covering more than 18 acres, and providing almost a million square feet of exhibition space. The central vaulted transept—based on the design for new cast-iron train stations—rose 108 feet to accommodate a row of the elm trees dear to Prince Albert, the husband of Queen Victoria (r. 1837–1901). By the end of the exhibition, 6 million people had visited it, most agreeing that the Crystal Palace was a technological marvel. Even so, most architects and critics, still wedded to Neoclassicism and Romanticism, considered it a work of engineering rather than legitimate architecture because the novelty of its iron and glass frame overshadowed its Gothic Revival style.

BIBLIOTHÈQUE NATIONALE Henri Labrouste (1801–1875)—trained as an architect at the École des Beaux-Arts, where he also taught—had a radical desire to fuse the École's historicizing approach to architecture with the technical innovations of industrial engineering. Although reluctant to push his ideas at the École, he pursued them in his architecture. The **READING ROOM** of the Bibliothèque Nationale (**FIG. 31-51**) is an example of this fusion. A series of domes form the ceiling—faced with bright white ceramic tiles, crowned with glass-covered oculi that light the reading room, and supported on thin iron arches and columns that open the space visually. The mixture of historical allusions in the classical detailing, combined with the vast open space made possible by industrial materials, is thoroughly modern.

31-51 • Henri Labrouste **READING ROOM, BIBLIOTHÈQUE NATIONALE, PARIS**
1862–1868.

THE CHICAGO SCHOOL

In the United States, up until this time, as in Europe, major architectural projects were expected to embody Beaux-Arts historicism. But the modern city required new building types for industry, transportation, commerce, storage, and habitation—types that would accommodate more people and more activities in urban areas where land prices were skyrocketing. Chicago was a case in point. As the transportation hub for grain, livestock, and other produce headed from the rural Midwest to the cities of the east and west coasts, Chicago became a populous, wealthy city by the 1890s. As new department stores, commercial facilities, and office buildings were designed, primarily with practical needs in mind, Chicago also became the cradle for a novel way of thinking about urban design and construction, in which function gave birth to architectural form.

WORLD'S COLUMBIAN EXPOSITION Richard Morris Hunt (1827–1895) was the first American to study architecture at the École des Beaux-Arts in Paris. Extraordinarily skilled in Beaux-Arts historicism and determined to raise the standards of American architecture, he built in every accepted style, including Gothic, French Classicist, and Italian Renaissance. After the Civil War, Hunt built many lavish mansions for a growing class of wealthy eastern industrialists and financiers, emulating aristocratic European models.

Late in his career, Hunt supervised the design of the 1893 World's Columbian Exposition in Chicago, commemorating the 400th anniversary of Christopher Columbus's arrival in the Americas. Rather than focus on engineering wonders as in previous fairs (although the exhibition included the first ferris wheel), the Chicago planning board decided to build "permanent buildings—a dream city." To create a sense of unity among these buildings (which were, in fact temporary, constructed from a mixture of plaster and fibrous materials, rather than masonry), a single style for the fair was settled upon—the Classical style, alluding to ancient Greece and republican Rome to reflect America's pride in its own democratic institutions as well as its emergence as a world power. A photograph of Hunt's **COURT OF HONOR** (**FIG. 31-52**) shows the Beaux-Arts style of the so-called "White City."

The World's Columbian Exposition was intended to be a model of the ideal American city—clean, spacious, carefully planned, and Classically styled—in contrast to the soot and overcrowding of most unplanned American cities. Frederick Law Olmsted, the designer of New York City's Central Park (see "The City Park," page 1010), was responsible for the exhibition's landscape design. He converted the marshy lakefront into a series of lagoons, canals, ponds, and islands, some laid out formally, as in the White City, and others informally, as in the "Midway," containing the busy conglomerate of pavilions representing "less civilized" nations. Between these two parts stood the ferris wheel, which provided a spectacular view of the fair and the city. After the fair, most of its buildings were demolished, but Olmsted's landscaping has remained.

RICHARDSON The second American architect to study at the École des Beaux-Arts was Henry Hobson Richardson (1838–1886). Born in Louisiana and educated at Harvard and Tulane, Richardson returned from Paris in 1865 to settle in New York. He designed architecture in a variety of revival styles but is most

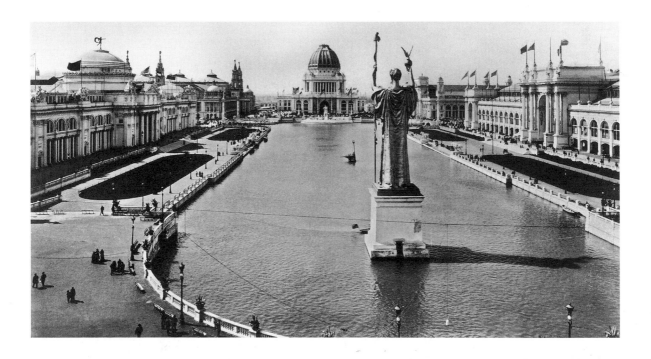

31-52 • Richard Morris Hunt COURT OF HONOR, WORLD'S COLUMBIAN EXPOSITION, CHICAGO
1893. View from the east.

Parks originated during the second millennium BCE in China as enclosed hunting reserves for kings and the nobility. In Europe, from the Middle Ages to the eighteenth century, they remained private recreation grounds for the privileged. The first urban park intended for the public was in Munich, Germany. Laid out by Friedrich Ludwig von Sckell in 1789–1795 in the picturesque style of an English landscape garden (see FIG. 30–16), the park contained irregular lakes, gently sloping hills, broad meadows, and paths meandering through wooded areas.

The crowding and pollution of cities during the Industrial Revolution prompted the creation of large public parks whose green open spaces would help purify the air and provide city dwellers of all classes with a place for healthy recreation. Numerous municipal parks were built in Britain during the 1830s and 1840s and in Paris during the 1850s and 1860s, when Georges-Eugène Haussmann redesigned the former royal hunting forests of the Bois de Boulogne and the Bois de Vincennes in the English style favored by Emperor Napoleon III.

In American cities before 1857, the only public outdoor spaces were small squares found between certain intersections, or larger gardens, such as the Boston Public Garden, neither of which filled the growing need for varied recreational facilities in the city. For a time, landscaped suburban cemeteries in the picturesque style were popular sites for strolling, picnicking, and even horse racing—an incongruous set of uses that strikingly demonstrated the need for more urban parks.

The rapid growth of Manhattan in the nineteenth century spurred civic leaders to set aside parkland while open space still existed. The city purchased an 843-acre tract in the center of the island and in 1857 announced a competition for its design as Central Park. The competition required that designs include a parade ground, playgrounds, a site for an

exhibition or concert hall, sites for a fountain and for a viewing tower, a flower garden, a pond for ice skating, and four east–west cross-streets so that the park would not interfere with the city's vehicular traffic. The latter condition was pivotal to the winning design, drawn up by architect Calvert Vaux (1824–1895) and park superintendent Frederick Law Olmsted (1822–1903), which sank the crosstown roads in trenches hidden below the surface of the park and designed separate routes for carriages, horseback riders, and pedestrians (FIG. 31–53).

Believing that the "park of any great city [should be] an antithesis to its bustling, paved, rectangular, walled-in streets," Olmsted and Vaux designed picturesque landscaping in the English tradition, with the irregularities of topography and planting used as positive design elements. Except for a few formal elements, such as the tree-lined mall that leads to the Classically designed Bethesda Terrace and Fountain, the park is remarkably informal and naturalistic. Where the land was low, Olmstead and Vaux further depressed it, installing drainage tiles and carving out ponds and meadows. They planted clumps of trees to contrast with open spaces, and exposed natural outcroppings of schist to provide dramatic, rocky scenery. They arranged walking trails, bridle paths, and carriage drives through the park with a series of changing vistas. Intentionally appealing were the views from the apartment houses of the wealthy on the streets surrounding the park. An existing reservoir divided the park into two sections. Olmsted and Vaux developed the southern half more completely and located most of the sporting facilities and amenities there, while leaving the northern half more like a nature reserve. Largely complete by the end of the Civil War, Central Park was widely considered a triumph, launching a movement to build similar parks in cities across the United States.

31-53 • Frederick Law Olmsted and Calvert Vaux MAP OF CENTRAL PARK, NEW YORK CITY
Revised and extended park layout as shown in a map of 1873.

👁️—⃝ **Watch** an architectural simulation about the city park on myartslab.com

famous for a robust, rusticated style known as Richardsonian Romanesque. In 1885, he designed the **MARSHALL FIELD WHOLESALE STORE** in Chicago (FIG. **31-54**), drawing on the

design and scale of Italian Renaissance palaces such as the Palazzo Medici-Riccardi in Florence (see FIG. 20–7). Although the block-like, rough stone facing, the arched windows, and the decorated cornice all evoke historical architectural antecedents, Richardson's eclecticism resulted in a readily identifiable personal style.

Plain and sturdy, Richardson's building was a revelation to the young architects of Chicago, then engaged in rebuilding the city after the disastrous fire of 1871. About the same time, new technology for producing steel—a strong, cheap alloy of iron—created new structural opportunities for architects. William Le Baron Jenney (1832–1907) built the first steel-skeleton building in Chicago; his lead was quickly followed by younger architects in what was known as the Chicago School. The rapidly rising cost of urban land made tall buildings desirable; structural steel and the electric elevator (developed during the 1880s) made them possible.

SULLIVAN Equipped with new structural materials and improved passenger elevators, driven by new economic considerations, and inspired by Richardson's developments beyond Beaux-Arts historicism, the Chicago School architects produced not only a new style of architecture but a new kind of building—the skyscraper. An early example is Louis Sullivan's **WAINWRIGHT BUILDING** in St. Louis, Missouri (**FIG. 31-55**). The Boston-born Sullivan (1856–1924) studied for a year at the Massachusetts Institute of Technology (MIT), home of the United States' first formal architecture program, and for an equally brief period at the École des Beaux-Arts in Paris, where he developed a distaste for historicism. He settled in Chicago in 1875, partly because of the building boom there that had followed the fire of 1871. In 1883 he entered into a partnership with the Danish-born engineer Dankmar Adler (1844–1900).

Sullivan's first major skyscraper, the Wainwright Building, has a U-shaped plan that provides an interior light-well for the illumination of inside offices. The ground floor, designed to house shops, has wide plate-glass windows for the display of merchandise. The second story, or mezzanine, also features large windows for the illumination of the shop offices. Above the mezzanine rise seven identical floors of offices, lit by rectangular windows. An attic story houses the building's mechanical plant and utilities. A richly decorated foliate frieze in terra-cotta relief crowns the building, punctuated by bull's-eye windows and capped by a thick cornice slab.

The Wainwright Building's outward appearance clearly articulates three different levels of function: shops at the bottom, offices in the middle, and mechanical utilities at the top. It illustrates Sullivan's stated architectural philosophy: "Form ever

31-55 • Louis Sullivan WAINWRIGHT BUILDING, ST. LOUIS
Missouri. 1890–1891.

View the Closer Look for the Wainwright Building on myartslab.com

follows function." This idea was adopted as a credo by Modernist architects, who used it to justify removal of all surface decoration from buildings. Sullivan designed the Wainwright Building for function, but he also created an expressive building. The thick corner piers, for example, are not structurally necessary—since an internal steel-frame skeleton supports the building—but they emphasize its vertical thrust. The thinner piers between the office windows, which rise uninterrupted from the third story to the attic, echo and reinforce its spring and verticality. As Sullivan put it, a tall office building "must be every inch a proud and soaring thing, rising in sheer exultation."

In the Wainwright Building that exultation culminates in the rich vegetative ornament that swirls around the crown of the building, serving a decorative function like that of the foliated capital of a Corinthian column. The tripartite structure of the building itself suggests the Classical column with its base, shaft, and capital, reflecting the lingering influence of Classical design principles. Only in the twentieth century would Modern architects reject tradition entirely to create an architectural aesthetic that was stripped of applied decoration.

CÉZANNE

No artist had a greater impact on the next generation of Modern painters than Paul Cézanne (1839–1906). The son of a prosperous banker in the southern French city of Aix-en-Provence, Cézanne studied art first in Aix and then in Paris, where he participated in the circle of Realist artists around Manet. His early pictures, somber in color and coarsely painted, often depicted Romantic themes of drama and violence, and were consistently rejected by the Salon.

In the early 1870s, under the influence of Pissarro, Cézanne changed his style. He adopted a bright palette and broken brushwork, and began painting landscapes. Like the Impressionists, with whom he exhibited in 1874 and 1877, Cézanne dedicated himself to the study of what he called the "sensations" of nature. Unlike the Impressionists, however, he did not seek to capture transitory effects of light and atmosphere; instead, he created highly structured paintings through

31–56 • Paul Cézanne MONT SAINTE-VICTOIRE

c. 1885–1887. Oil on canvas, 25½″ × 32″ (64.8 × 92.3 cm). Courtauld Gallery, London. © Samuel Courtauld Trust. (P.1934.SC.55)

👁—**Watch** a video about Paul Cézanne's *Mont Sainte-Victoire* on myartslab.com

a methodical application of color that merged drawing and modeling into a single process. His professed aim was to "make of Impressionism something solid and durable, like the art of the museums."

Cézanne's dedicated pursuit of this goal is evident in his repeated paintings of **MONT SAINTE-VICTOIRE**, a mountain close to his home in Aix, which he depicted in hundreds of drawings and about 30 oil paintings between the 1880s and his death in 1906. The painting in **FIGURE 31-56** presents the mountain rising above the Arc Valley, which is dotted with buildings and trees, and crossed at the far right by a railroad viaduct. Framing the scene to the left is an evergreen tree, which echoes the contours of the mountains, creating visual harmony between the two principal elements of the composition. The even light, still atmosphere, and absence of human activity create the sensation of timeless stillness.

Cézanne's handling of paint is deliberate and controlled. His brushstrokes, which vary from short, parallel hatchings, to light lines, to broader swaths of flat color, weave together the elements of the painting into a unified but flattened visual space. The surface design vies with the pictorial effect of receding space, generating tension between the illusion of three dimensions within the picture and the physical reality of its two-dimensional surface. Recession into depth is suggested by the tree in the foreground—a *repoussoir* (French for "something that pushes back") that helps draw the eye into the valley—and by the transition from the saturated hues in the foreground to the lighter values in the background, creating an effect of atmospheric perspective. But recession into depth is challenged by other more intense colors in both the foreground and background, and by the tree branches in the sky, which follow the contours of the mountain, avoiding overlapping and subtly suggesting that the two are on the same plane. Photographs of this scene show that Cézanne created a composition in accordance with a harmony that he felt the scene demanded, rather than reproducing in detail the landscape itself. His commitment to the painting as a work of art, which he called "something other than reality"—not a representation of nature but "a construction

31-57 • Paul Cézanne STILL LIFE WITH BASKET OF APPLES
1880–1894. Oil on canvas, 24⅜" × 31" (62.5 × 79.5 cm). The Art Institute of Chicago. Helen Birch Bartlett Memorial Collection (1926.252)

after nature"—was a crucial step toward the modern art of the next century.

Spatial ambiguities of a different sort appear in Cézanne's later still lifes, in which many of the objects may seem at first glance to be incorrectly drawn. In **STILL LIFE WITH BASKET OF APPLES** (**FIG. 31-57**), for example, the right side of the table is higher than the left, the wine bottle has two distinct silhouettes, and the pastries on the table next to it tilt upward toward the viewer, while we seem to see the apples head-on. Such shifting viewpoints are not evidence of incompetence; they derive from Cézanne's willful rejection of the rules of traditional perspective. Although scientific linear perspective mandates that the eye of the artist (and hence the viewer) occupy a fixed point relative to the scene (see Renaissance Perspective," page 610), Cézanne presents the objects in his still lifes from a variety of different positions just as we might move around or turn our heads to take everything in. The composition as a whole, assembled from multiple sightings, is consequently complex and dynamic. Instead of faithfully reproducing static objects from a stable vantage point, Cézanne recreated, or reconstructed, our viewing experiences through time and space.

Cézanne enjoyed little professional success until the last years of his life, when his paintings became more complex internally and more detached from observed reality. **THE LARGE BATHERS** (**FIG. 31-58**), probably begun in the last year of his life and left unfinished, was the largest canvas he ever painted. It returns in several ways to the academic conventions of history painting as a monumental, multi-figured composition of nude figures in a landscape setting that suggests a mythological theme. The bodies cluster in two pyramidal groups at left and right, beneath a canopy of trees that opens in the middle onto a triangular expanse of water, landscape, and sky. The figures assume statuesque, often Classical poses and seem to exist outside recognizable time and space. Using a restricted palette of blues, greens, ochers, and roses, laid down over a white ground, Cézanne suffused the picture with a cool light that emphasizes the scene's remoteness from everyday life. Despite its unfinished state, *The Large Bathers* brings nineteenth-century painting full circle by reviving the Arcadian landscape, a much earlier category of academic painting, while opening a new window on some radical rethinking about the fundamental practice and purpose of art.

31-58 • Paul Cézanne THE LARGE BATHERS
1906. Oil on canvas, 6'10" × 8'2" (2.08 × 2.49 m). Philadelphia Museum of Art. The W.P. Wilstach Collection

THINK ABOUT IT

31.1 Discuss the interests and goals of French academic painters and sculptors and explain how their work differed from other art of the same time and place, such as that of the Realists and Impressionists.

31.2 Discuss the innovative content of Impressionist paintings, and explain how it differs from that of traditional European paintings by focusing on one specific work discussed in the chapter.

31.3 Discuss Gustave Courbet's Realism in works such as *The Stone Breakers* (FIG. 31–12) and *A Burial at Ornans* (FIG. 31–13) in relation to the social and political issues of mid-century France.

31.4 Explain how the photographic process works and evaluate the roles played by Louis-Jacques-Mandé Daguerre and Henry Fox Talbot in the emergence of this medium.

CROSSCURRENTS

FIG. 21–28

FIG. 31–18

European artists often refer to or seek inspiration in works of art from the past when creating works that address the concerns of their own present. This is certainly the case with Manet, whose painting of *Olympia* recalls aspects of the composition and subject of Titian's *"Venus" of Urbino*. But the messages of these two works are very different. Analyze the meanings of these paintings. Do they express the concerns of artist, patron, society, or some mixture of the three?

✔—[**Study** and review on myartslab.com

32–1 • Pablo Picasso MA JOLIE

1911–1912. Oil on canvas, 39⅜″ × 25¾″ (100 × 65.4 cm). Museum of Modern Art, New York.

Acquired through the Lillie P. Bliss Bequest (176.1945)

Modern Art in Europe and the Americas, 1900–1950

Pablo Picasso was a towering presence at the center of the Parisian art world throughout much of the twentieth century, continually transforming the forms, meanings, and conceptual frameworks of his art as his style and themes developed in relation to the many factors at play in the world around him. Early in the century in his great Cubist work **MA JOLIE** (**FIG. 32-1**) of 1911–1912, Picasso challenged his viewers to think about the very nature of communication through painting. Remnants of the subjects Picasso worked from are evident throughout, but any attempt to reconstruct the "subject"—a woman with a stringed instrument—poses difficulties for the viewer. *Ma Jolie* ("My Pretty One") is in some sense a portrait, though hardly a traditional one. Picasso makes us work to see and to understand the figure. We can discover several things about Ma Jolie from the painting; we can see parts of her head, her shoulders, and the curve of her body, a hand or a foot. But in Paris in 1911, "Ma Jolie" was also the title of a popular song, so the inclusion of writing and a musical staff in the painting may also suggest other meanings. Our first impulse might be to wonder what exactly is pictured on the canvas. To that question, Picasso provided the sarcastic answer, "It's My Pretty One!"

On the other hand, it might be argued that the human subject provided only the raw material for a formal, abstract arrangement. A subtle tension between order and disorder is maintained throughout this painting. For example, the shifting effect of the surface—a delicately patterned texture of grays and browns—is unified through the use of short, horizontal brushstrokes. Similarly, with the linear elements, strict horizontals and verticals dominate, although curves and angles break up their regularity. The combination of horizontal brushwork and right angles firmly establishes a grid that effectively counteracts the surface flux. Moreover, the repetition of certain diagonals and the relative lack of details in the upper left and upper right create a pyramidal shape reminiscent of Classical systems of compositional stability (see **FIG. 21-5**). Thus, what at first may seem a chaotic composition of lines and muted colors turns out to be a carefully organized design. For many, the aesthetic satisfaction of such a work depends on the way chaos seems to resolve itself into order.

In 1923, Picasso said, "Cubism is no different from any other school of painting. The same principles and the same elements are common to all. The fact that for a long time Cubism has not been understood … means nothing. I do not read English, [but] this does not mean that the English language does not exist, and why should I blame anyone … but myself if I cannot understand [it]?"

LEARN ABOUT IT

32.1 Assess the impact of Cubism on abstract art in the early twentieth century and explore how and why Abstract Expressionism transformed painting after 1940.

32.2 Examine the different ways that artists in the Modern period responded directly or indirectly to the violence of war.

32.3 Determine the political and economic impact of the Great Depression on interwar European and American art.

32.4 Investigate how Dada and Surrealism changed the form, content, and concept of art.

((•—[**Listen** to the chapter audio on myartslab.com

EUROPE AND AMERICA IN THE EARLY TWENTIETH CENTURY

At the beginning of the twentieth century, the fragile idea that "civilization" would inexorably continue to progress began to fissure and finally cracked in an orgy of violence during World War I. Beginning in August 1914, the war initially pitted the Allies (Britain, France, and Russia) against the Central Powers (Germany and the Austro-Hungarian Empire) and the Ottoman Empire. The United States eventually entered the war on the side of Britain and France in 1917, helping to guarantee victory for the Allies the following year.

World War I transformed almost every aspect of Western society—including politics, economics, and culture (**MAP 32–1**). The war was fought with twentieth-century technology but nineteenth-century strategies. Trench warfare and the Maxim gun caused the deaths of millions of soldiers and the horrible maiming of as many again. Europe lost an entire generation of young men; whole societies were shattered. Europeans began to question the nineteenth-century imperial social and political order that had precipitated this carnage and foreshadowed a change in the character of warfare itself. Future wars would be fought over ideology rather than—as in the nineteenth century—territory.

In the first half of the twentieth century, three very different political ideologies struggled for world supremacy: communism (as in the U.S.S.R. and China), fascism (as in Italy and Germany), and liberal-democratic capitalism (as in North America, Britain, and Western Europe). The October 1917 Russian Revolution led to the Russian Civil War and the eventual triumph of the Bolshevik ("Majority") Communist Party led by Vladimir Lenin (1870–1924), as well as to the founding of the U.S.S.R. in 1922. After Lenin's death and an internal power struggle, Joseph Stalin (1878–1953) emerged as leader of the U.S.S.R. Under Stalin, the U.S.S.R. annexed several neighboring states, suffered through the Great Purge of the 1930s, and lost tens of millions during the war against Nazi Germany.

Fascism first took firm root in Italy in October 1922 when Benito Mussolini (1883–1945) came to power. In Germany, meanwhile, the postwar democratic Weimar Republic collapsed under a combination of rampant hyperinflation and the enmity between communists, socialists, centrists, Christian Democrats, and fascists. By the time of the 1932 parliamentary election, Germany's political and economic deterioration had paved the way for a Nazi Party victory and the chancellorship of its leader, Adolf Hitler (1889–1945). Fascism was not limited to Germany and Italy—it was widespread throughout Central and Eastern Europe and on the Iberian peninsula, where General Francisco Franco (1892–1975) emerged victorious from the Spanish Civil War.

The economic impact of World War I was global. Although the United States emerged from it as the leading economic power in the world, hyperinflation in Germany during the 1920s, the repudiation of German war debt under the Versailles Treaty, and the United States Stock Market Crash of 1929 plunged the Western world into a Great Depression that exacerbated political hostility between the major European countries, served as an incubator for fascism and communism in Europe, and tore apart the social and political fabric of Britain and America. In the United States, President Franklin D. Roosevelt (1882–1945, president 1933–1945) created the New Deal programs in 1933 to stimulate the economy with government spending, and France and Britain took their first steps toward the modern welfare state. But ultimately only the military build-up of World War II would end the Great Depression. The war lasted from 1939 to 1945, and the human carnage it caused to both soldiers and civilians, particularly in German concentration camps, raised difficult questions about the very nature of our humanity.

Changes in scientific knowledge were also dramatic. Albert Einstein's publication of his Special Theory of Relativity in 1905 had shaken the foundations of Newtonian physics; they collapsed with the subsequent development of quantum theory by Niels Bohr, Werner Heisenberg, and Max Planck. These developments in physics also unlocked the Pandora's box of nuclear energy, first opened when the British split the atom in 1919, and unleashed on the world when America dropped nuclear bombs on Japan in 1945.

The early twentieth century also witnessed a multitude of innovations in technology and manufacturing: the first powered flight (1903); the mass manufacture of automobiles (1909); the first public radio broadcast (1920); the electrification of most of Western Europe and North America (1920s); and the development of both television (1926) and the jet engine (1937), to mention only a few. Technology led both to better medicines for prolonging life and to more efficient warfare, which shortened it. Information about the outside world became ever more accessible with the advent of radio, television, and film. Where the visual culture of the nineteenth century was based on paper, that of the early twentieth century was centered in photographs and films.

Just as quantum physics fundamentally altered our understanding of the physical world, developments in psychology transformed our conception of the workings of the mind, and consequently how we view ourselves. In 1900, Austrian psychiatrist Sigmund Freud published *The Interpretation of Dreams*, which posited that our behavior is often motivated not only by reason, but by powerful forces that work below our level of awareness. The human unconscious, as he described it, includes strong urges for love and power that must be managed if society is to remain peaceful and whole. For Freud, we are always attempting to strike a balance between our rational and irrational sides, often erring on one side or the other. Also in 1900, Russian scientist Ivan Pavlov began feeding dogs just after ringing a bell. Soon the dogs salivated not at the sight of food but at the sound of the bell. The discovery that these "conditioned responses" also exist in humans showed that if we manage external stimuli we can control people's appetites. Political leaders of all stripes soon exploited this realization.

MAP 32-1 • EUROPE, THE AMERICAS, AND NORTH AFRICA, 1900–1950

Thus the first half of the twentieth century was a time of exciting new theories and technologies, as well as increased access of ordinary people to consumer items, but it was also a time of cataclysmic social, economic, and political change, and a time when millions died in wars and concentration camps. These changes, whether for the better or for the worse, shaped the art of the early twentieth century.

EARLY MODERN ART IN EUROPE

Modern artists explored myriad new ways of seeing their world. Few read academic physics or psychology texts, but they lived in a world that was being transformed by such fields, along with so many other technological advances. Modern art was frequently subversive and intellectually demanding, and it was often visually, socially, and politically radical. It seems as if every movement in early twentieth-century art chose or acquired a distinctive label and wrote a manifesto or statement of intent, leading this to be described later as the age of "isms."

Yet most Modern art was still bound to the idea that works of art, regardless of how they challenged vision and thought, were still precious objects—primarily pictures or sculptures. But a few artistic movements—notably Dada and some elements of

Surrealism, both of them prompted by the horrors of World War I—challenged this idea. Their preoccupations built the foundation for much art after 1950.

THE FAUVES: WILD BEASTS OF COLOR

The Salon system still operated in France, but the ranks of artists dissatisfied with its conservative precepts were swelling. In 1903, a group of malcontents, including André Derain (1880–1954), Henri Matisse (1869–1954), Georges Rouault (1871–1958), and Albert Marquet (1875–1947), organized the alternative exhibition known as the Salon d'Automne (Autumn Salon), so named to distinguish it from the official Salon that took place every spring. The Autumn Salon, which continued until after World War I, promised juries more open to avant-garde art, and the first major Modern movement of the twentieth century made its debut in this Salon's disorderly halls. Paintings by Derain, Matisse, and Maurice de Vlaminck (1876–1958) exhibited in 1905 were filled with such explosive colors and blunt brushwork that the critic Louis Vauxcelles described the young painters as *fauves* ("wild beasts"), the French term by which they soon became known. These artists took the French tradition of color and strong brushwork to new heights of intensity and expressive power, and entirely rethought the picture's surface.

Among the first major Fauve works were paintings that Derain and Matisse made in 1905 in the French Mediterranean port town of Collioure. In **MOUNTAINS AT COLLIOURE** (FIG. 32-2), Derain used short, broad strokes of pure pigment, juxtaposing the complementary colors of blue and orange together—as in the mountain range—or red and green together—as in the trees—to intensify the hue of each. He chose a range of semi-naturalistic colors—the grass and the trees are green, the trunks are close to brown. This is recognizable as a landscape, but it is also a self-conscious exercise in painting. The uniform brightness of the colors undermines any effect of atmospheric perspective. As a consequence, viewers remain aware that they are looking at a flat canvas covered with paint, not an illusionistic rendering of the natural world. This tension between image and painting, along with the explosive effect of the color, generates a visual energy that positively pulses from the painting. Derain described his colors as "sticks of dynamite," and his stark juxtapositions of complementary hues as "deliberate disharmonies."

Matisse was equally interested in "deliberate disharmonies." His **THE WOMAN WITH THE HAT** (FIG. 32-3) proved particularly controversial at the 1905 Autumn Salon because of its thick swatches of crude, seemingly arbitrary, nonnaturalistic color and its broad and blunt brushwork—the sitter, an otherwise conventional subject for a portrait, has thick green stripes across her brow and down her nose. The uproar did not stop siblings Gertrude and Leo

32-3 • Henri Matisse THE WOMAN WITH THE HAT
1905. Oil on canvas, 31¾″ × 23½″ (80.6 × 59.7 cm). San Francisco Museum of Modern Art. Bequest of Elise S. Haas

32-4 • Henri Matisse **LE BONHEUR DE VIVRE (THE JOY OF LIFE)**
1905–1906. Oil on canvas, 5′8½″ × 7′9¾″ (1.74 × 2.38 m). The Barnes Foundation, Merion, Pennsylvania. (BF 719)

Stein, among the most important American patrons of avant-garde art at this time, from purchasing the work in 1905.

The same year, Matisse also began painting **LE BONHEUR DE VIVRE (THE JOY OF LIFE)** (**FIG. 32-4**), a large pastoral landscape depicting a golden age—a reclining nude in the foreground plays pan pipes, another piper herds goats in the right mid-ground, lovers embrace in the foreground while others frolic in dance in the background. Like Cézanne's *The Large Bathers* painted in the same year (see FIG. 31-58), *The Joy of Life* is academic in scale and theme, but avant-garde in most other respects—notably in the way the figures appear "flattened" and in the distortion of the spatial relations between them. Matisse emphasized expressive color, drawing on folk-art traditions in his use of unmodeled forms and bold outlines. In the past, artists might express feeling through the figures' poses or facial expressions, but now, he wrote, "The whole arrangement of my picture is expressive. The place occupied by figures or objects, the empty spaces around them, the proportions, everything plays a part … . The chief aim of color should be to serve expression as well as possible."

PICASSO, "PRIMITIVISM," AND THE COMING OF CUBISM

Of all Modern art "isms" created before World War I, Cubism was probably the most influential. The joint invention of Pablo Picasso (1881–1973) and Georges Braque (1882–1963)—who worked side by side in Paris, the undisputed capital of the art world before 1950—Cubism proved a fruitful launching pad for both artists, allowing them to comment on modern life and investigate the ways in which artists perceive and represent the world around them.

PICASSO'S EARLY ART Born in Málaga, Spain, Picasso was an artistic child prodigy. During his teenage years at the National Academy in Madrid, he painted highly polished works that presaged a conservative artistic career, but his restless temperament led him to Barcelona in 1899, where he involved himself in avant-garde circles. In 1900, he first traveled to Paris, and in 1904 he moved there and would live in France for the rest of his life. During this early period Picasso painted urban outcasts in weary

32-5 • Pablo Picasso FAMILY OF SALTIMBANQUES
1905. Oil on canvas, 6'11¾" × 7'6⅜" (2.1 × 2.3 m). National Gallery of Art, Washington, DC. Chester Dale Collection (1963.10.190)

poses using a coldly expressive blue palette that led art historians to label this his Blue Period. These paintings seem motivated by Picasso's political sensitivity to those he considered victims of modern capitalist society, which eventually led him to join the Communist Party.

In 1904–1905, Picasso joined a larger group of Paris-based avant-garde artists and became fascinated with the subject of *saltimbanques* (traveling acrobats). He rarely painted these entertainers performing, however, focusing instead on the hardships of their existence on the margins of society. In **FAMILY OF SALTIMBANQUES (FIG. 32-5)**, a painting from his Rose Period (so called because of the introduction of that color into his palette), five *saltimbanques* stand in weary silence to the left, while a sixth, a woman, sits in curious isolation on the right. All seem psychologically withdrawn, as uncommunicative as the empty landscape they occupy. By 1905, Picasso began to sell these works to a number of important collectors.

Around 1906, Picasso became one of the first artists in Paris to appropriate images from African art in his paintings, inspired by an encounter with "primitive" art and art beyond the Western tradition that would prove decisive in the development of his

art. In 1906, the Louvre installed a newly acquired collection of sculpture from the Iberian peninsula (present-day Spain and Portugal) dating from the sixth and fifth centuries BCE, but it was an exhibition of African masks that he saw around the same time that really changed the way Picasso thought about art. The exact date of this encounter is not known, but it might have occurred at the Musée d'Éthnographie du Trocadéro (now the Musée du Quai Branly) which opened to the public in 1882, or at the Musée Permanent des Colonies (now the Musée National des Arts d'Afrique et d'Océanie), or in any number of Parisian shops that sold "primitive" objects, mostly brought back from French colonies in Africa. Picasso greatly admired the expressive power and formal strangeness of African masks, and since African art was relatively inexpensive, he also bought several pieces and kept them in his studio.

The term **primitivism**, as applied to the widespread tendency among Modern artists to scour the art of other cultures beyond the Western tradition for inspiration, is not benignly descriptive; it carries modern European perceptions of relative cultural superiority and inferiority. The inherent assumption is that Western culture is superior, more civilized, more developed, and more complex than other cultures, which are less civilized, less developed, and simpler. It could be argued that, just as colonizing nations exploited "primitive" lands in the nineteenth century for their raw materials and labor to increase their own wealth and power, so Western artists exploited the visual cultures of "primitive" nations merely to amplify ideas about themselves. Many early Modern artists thus represented other cultures and appropriated their art without understanding—without really caring to understand—how those cultures actually functioned or how their art was used. This was the case with Picasso.

His contact with African art had a huge impact on **LES DEMOISELLES D'AVIGNON (THE YOUNG LADIES OF AVIGNON)** (**FIG. 32-6**), one of the most radical and complex paintings of the twentieth century. Picasso deliberately sends mixed messages in this work, beginning with the title: Avignon was the seat of a papal court in the fourteenth century, so it may mean that these figures are young ladies of the court. On the other hand, "*demoiselle*" was also a euphemism for prostitute and "Avignon" was the name of a red-light district in Barcelona, forming the most common interpretation of the scene. The work's boldness resides not only in its subject matter, but also its size. Picasso may have undertaken such a large (nearly 8 feet square) painting in 1907 to compete with both Matisse—who exhibited *The Joy of Life* in the 1906 Salon—and Cézanne—whose *Large Bathers* was shown the same year. Like Matisse and Cézanne, Picasso revives and renegotiates the ideas of large-scale academic history painting, making use of the traditional subject of nude women shown in an interior space. There are other echoes of the Western tradition in the handling of the figures. The two in the center display themselves to the viewer like Venus rising from the sea (see FIGS. 20–40, 31–4), while that to the left takes a rigid pose with a striding stance, recalling a Greek kouros (see FIG. 5–18), and the one seated on the right might suggest the pose of Manet's *Le Déjeuner sur l'Herbe* (see FIG. 31–17). But not all visual references point to the Western tradition. Iberian sources stand behind the faces of the three leftmost figures, with their flattened features and wide, almond-shaped eyes. The mask-like faces of the two figures at right emulate African art.

Picasso has created an unsettling picture from these sources. The women are shielded by masks, flattened and fractured into sharp angular shapes. The space they inhabit is incoherent and convulsive. The central pair raise their arms in a conventional gesture of accessibility but contradict it with their hard, piercing gazes and tight mouths that create what one art historian has called "a tidal wave of aggression." Even the fruit displayed in the foreground, symbols of female sexuality, seems brittle and dangerous. The women, Picasso suggests, are not the gentle and passive creatures that men would like them to be. This viewpoint contradicts an enduring tradition, prevalent at least since the Renaissance, of portraying sexual availability in the female nude, just as strongly as Picasso's treatment of space shatters the reliance on orderly perspective, equally standard since the Renaissance.

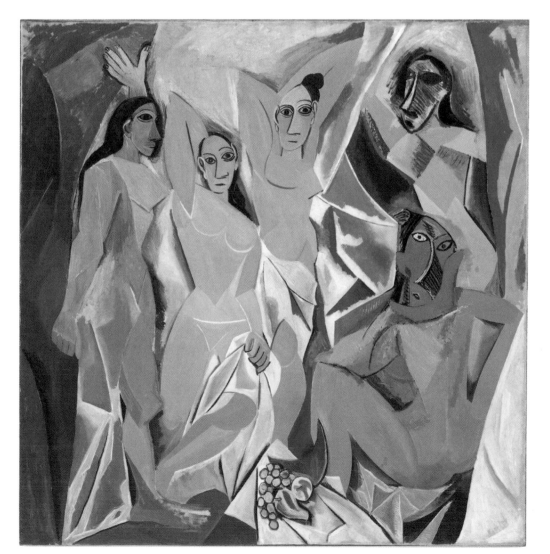

32-6 • Pablo Picasso LES DEMOISELLES D'AVIGNON (THE YOUNG LADIES OF AVIGNON)
1907. Oil on canvas, 8′ × 7′8″ (2.43 × 2.33 m). Museum of Modern Art, New York. Acquired through the Lillie P. Bliss Bequest (333.1939)

 View the Closer Look for *Les Demoiselles d'Avignon* on myartslab.com

32-7 • Georges Braque VIOLIN AND PALETTE
1909–1910. Oil on canvas, 36⅛″ × 16⅞″ (91.8 × 42.9 cm). Solomon R. Guggenheim Museum, New York. (54.1412)

Most of Picasso's friends were shocked by his new work. Matisse, for example, accused Picasso of making a joke of Modern art and threatened to break off their friendship. But one artist, Georges Braque, enthusiastically embraced Picasso's radical ideas—he saw in *Les Demoiselles d'Avignon* a potential for new visual experiments. In 1907–1908, Picasso and Braque began a close working relationship that lasted until the latter went to war in 1914. Together, they developed Picasso's formal innovations by flattening pictorial space, by incorporating multiple perspectives within a single picture, and by fracturing form, all features these artists had admired in Cézanne's late paintings. According to Braque, "We were like two mountain climbers roped together."

ANALYTIC CUBISM Braque, a year younger than Picasso, was born near Le Havre, France, where he trained as a decorator. In 1900, he moved to Paris and began painting brightly colored Fauvist landscapes, but it was the 1906 Cézanne retrospective and Picasso's *Demoiselles* in 1907 that established his future course by sharpening his interest in altered form and compressed space. In his landscapes after 1908, he reduced nature's complexity to its essential colors and elemental geometric shapes, but the Autumn Salon rejected his work. Matisse dismissively referred to Braque's "little cubes," and the critic Louis Vauxcelles picked up the phrase, claiming that Braque "reduced everything to cubes," thereby giving birth to the art-historical label of Cubism.

Braque's 1908–1909 **VIOLIN AND PALETTE (FIG. 32-7)** shows the kind of relatively small-scale still-life paintings that the two artists created during their initial collaborative experimentation as they moved together toward the gradual abstraction of recognizable subject matter and space. The still-life items here are not arranged in a measured progression from foreground to background depth, but push close to the picture plane, confined to a shallow space. Braque knits the various elements—a violin, an artist's palette, and some sheet music—together into a single shifting surface of forms and colors. In some areas of the painting, these formal elements have lost not only their natural spatial relations but their coherent shapes as well. Where representational motifs remain—the violin, for example—Braque fragmented them to facilitate their integration into the compositional whole.

Picasso's 1910 Cubist **PORTRAIT OF DANIEL-HENRY KAHNWEILER (FIG. 32-8)** depicts the artist's first and most important art dealer in Paris, who saved many artists from destitution by buying their early works. Kahnweiler (1884–1979) was an early champion of Picasso's art and one of the first to recognize the significance of *Les Demoiselles*. His impressive stable of artists included—in

32-8 • Pablo Picasso PORTRAIT OF DANIEL-HENRY KAHNWEILER
1910. Oil on canvas, 39½″ × 28⅝″ (100.6 × 72.8 cm). The Art Institute of Chicago. Gift of Mrs. Gilbert W. Chapman in memory of Charles B. Goodspeed

addition to Picasso—Braque, André Derain, Fernand Léger, and Juan Gris. Since he was German, Kahnweiler fled France for Switzerland during World War I, while the French government confiscated all his possessions, including his stock of paintings, which was sold by the state at auction after the war. Being Jewish, he was forced into hiding during World War II.

Braque's and Picasso's paintings of 1909 and 1910 initiated what is known as Analytic Cubism because of the way the artists broke objects into parts as if to analyze them. In works of 1911 and early 1912, such as Picasso's *Ma Jolie* (see FIG. 32-1), they begin to take a somewhat different approach to the breaking up of forms, in which they did not simply fracture objects visually, but picked them apart and rearranged their components. Thus, Analytic Cubism begins to resemble the actual process of perception, during which we examine objects from various points of view and reassemble our glances into a whole object in our brain. Only Picasso and Braque reassembled their shattered subjects not according to the process of perception but conforming to principles of artistic composition, to communicate meaning rather than to represent

observed reality. For example, remnants of the subject are evident throughout Picasso's *Ma Jolie*, but any attempt to reconstruct from them the image of a woman with a stringed instrument would be misguided since the subject provided only the raw material for a formal composition. *Ma Jolie* is not a representation of a woman, a place, or an event; it is simply a painting.

SYNTHETIC CUBISM Works such as *Ma Jolie* brought Picasso and Braque to the brink of complete abstraction, but in the spring of 1912 they pulled back and began to create works that suggested more clearly discernible subjects. Neither artist wanted to break the link to reality; Picasso said that there was no such thing as completely abstract art, because "You have to start somewhere." This second major phase of Cubism is known as Synthetic Cubism because of the way the artists created complex compositions by combining and transforming individual elements, as in a chemical synthesis. Picasso's **LA BOUTEILLE DE SUZE (BOTTLE OF SUZE)** (FIG. 32-9), like many of the works he and Braque created from 1912 to 1914, is a **collage** (from the French *coller*, meaning "to glue"), a work composed of separate elements pasted

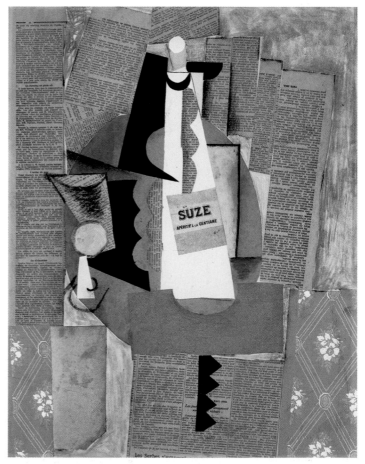

32-9 • Pablo Picasso LA BOUTEILLE DE SUZE (BOTTLE OF SUZE)
1912. Pasted paper, gouache, and charcoal, 25¾″ × 19¾″ (65.4 × 50.2 cm). Mildred Lane Kemper Art Museum, Washington University in St. Louis. University purchase, Kende Sale Fund, 1946

together. At the center, assembled newsprint and construction paper suggest a tray or round table supporting a glass and a bottle of liquor with an actual label. Around this arrangement Picasso pasted larger pieces of newspaper and wallpaper.

As in earlier Cubism, Picasso offers multiple perspectives. We see the top of the blue table, tilted to face us, and simultaneously the side of the glass. The bottle stands on the table, its label facing us, while we can also see the round profile of its opening, as well as the top of the cork that plugs it. The elements together evoke not only a place—a bar—but also an activity—the viewer alone with a newspaper, enjoying a quiet drink. The newspaper clippings glued to this picture, however, disrupt the quiet mood. They address the First Balkan War of 1912–1913, which contributed to the outbreak of World War I. Did Picasso want to underline the disorder in his art by comparing it with the disorder building in the world around him, or was he warning his viewers not to sit blindly and sip Suze while political events threatened to shatter the peaceful pleasures this work evokes? Or is this simply a painting?

Picasso employed collage three-dimensionally to produce Synthetic Cubist sculpture, such as **MANDOLIN AND CLARINET** (FIG. 32-10). Composed of wood scraps, the sculpture suggests the Cubist subject of two musical instruments, here shown at right angles to each other. Sculpture had traditionally been either carved, modeled, or cast. Picasso's sculptural collage was a new idea and introduced **assemblage**, giving sculptors the option not only of carving or modeling but also of constructing their works by assembling found objects and unconventional materials. Another of Picasso's innovations was his introduction of space into the interior of the sculpture, created by gaps and holes. Since this sculpture creates volume by using both forms and spaces, rather than mass alone, Picasso has challenged the traditional conception of sculpture as a condensed solid form surrounded by space.

32–10 • Pablo Picasso MANDOLIN AND CLARINET
1913. Construction of painted wood with pencil marks, 25⅝″ × 14⅛″ × 9″ (58 × 36 × 23 cm). Musée Picasso, Paris.

THE BRIDGE AND PRIMITIVISM

At the same time as Picasso and Braque were transforming painting in Paris, a group of radical German artists came together in Dresden as Die Brücke (The Bridge), taking their name from a passage in Friedrich Nietzsche's *Thus Spake Zarathustra* (1883) which describes contemporary humanity's potential as a "bridge" to a more perfect humanity in the future. Formed in 1905, The Bridge included architecture students Fritz Bleyl (1880–1966), Erich Heckel (1883–1970), Ernst Ludwig Kirchner (1880–1938), and Karl Schmidt-Rottluff (1884–1976). Other German and northern European artists later joined the group, which continued until 1913. These artists hoped The Bridge would be a gathering place for "all revolutionary and surging elements" who opposed Germany's "pale, overbred, and decadent" society.

Drawing on northern visual prototypes, such as Van Gogh or Munch, and adopting traditional northern media such as woodcuts, these artists created intense, brutal, expressionistic images of alienation and anxiety in response to Germany's rapid and intensive urbanization. Not surprisingly, among their favorite motifs were the natural world and the nude body—nudism was also a growing

32–11 • Erich Heckel STANDING CHILD
1910. Color woodcut, 14¾″ × 10¾″ (37.5 × 27.5 cm).
Los Angeles County Museum of Art.

in 1900, but he never painted as he was taught. Nolde regularly visited Parisian ethnographic museums to study the art of Africa and Oceania, which impressed him with the radical and forceful visual presence of the human figure, especially in masks. His painting **MASKS** (**FIG. 32-12**) of 1911 seems to derive both from what he saw in Paris, as well as the masquerades familiar to him from European carnivals (see **FIG. 31-43**). By merging these traditions, Nolde transforms his African and Oceanic sources into a European nightmare full of horror and implicit violence. The gaping mouths and hollow eyes of the hideously colored and roughly drawn masks taunt viewers, appearing to advance from the picture plane into their space. Nolde also uses the juxtaposition of complementaries to intensify his colors and the painting's emotionality. Nolde stopped frequenting The Bridge's studio in 1907 but remained friendly with the group's members. On the eve of World War I, Nolde accompanied a German scientific expedition to New Guinea, explaining that what attracted him to the "native art" of Pacific cultures was their "primitivism," their "absolute originality, the intense and often grotesque expression of power and life in very simple forms."

During the summers, members of The Bridge returned to nature, visiting remote areas of northern Germany, but in 1911 they moved to Berlin—perhaps preferring to imagine rather than actually live the natural life. Their images of cities, especially Berlin,

cultural trend in Germany in those years, as city dwellers forsook the city to reconnect with nature. Erich Heckel's three-color woodcut print **STANDING CHILD** (**FIG. 32-11**) of 1910 presents a strikingly stylized but powerfully expressive image of a naked girl—whose flesh is the reserved color of the paper itself—isolated against a spare background landscape created from broad areas of pure black, green, and red. She stares straight out at the viewer with an incipient, but already confident, sexuality that becomes more unsettling when we learn that this girl was the 12-year old Fränzi Fehrmann, a favorite of Brücke artists who, with her siblings, modeled to provide financial support for her widowed mother.

Although not part of the original Bridge group, Emil Nolde (1867–1956) joined in 1906 and quickly became its most committed member. Originally trained in industrial design, Nolde studied academic painting privately in Paris for a few months

32–12 • Emil Nolde MASKS
1911. Oil on canvas, 28¾″ × 30½″ (73.03 × 77.47 cm). The Nelson-Atkins Museum, Kansas City, Missouri. Gift of the Friends of Art (54-90)

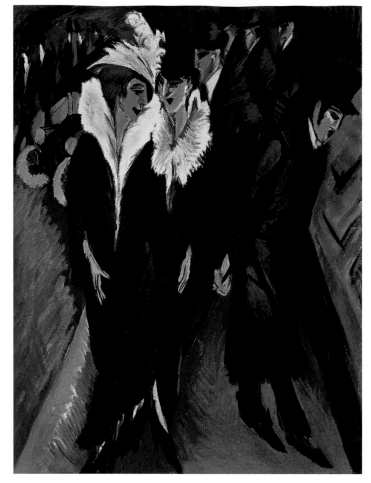

32–13 • Ernst Ludwig Kirchner STREET, BERLIN
1913. Oil on canvas, 47½″ × 35⅞″ (120.6 × 91 cm). Museum of Modern Art, New York. Purchase (274.39)

 View the Closer Look for *Street, Berlin* on myartslab.com

INDEPENDENT EXPRESSIONISTS

Beyond the members of The Bridge, many other artists in Germany and Austria worked Expressionistically before World War I. For example, Käthe Kollwitz (1867–1945) used her art to further working-class causes and pursue social change. She perferred printmaking because its affordability gave it the potential to reach a wide audience. Between 1902 and 1908, she produced a series of seven etchings showing the sixteenth-century German Peasants' War. **THE OUTBREAK** (FIG. 32-14), a lesson in the power of group action, portrays the ugly fury of the peasants as they charge forward armed only with their tools, bent on revenge against their oppressors for years of abuse. The faces of the two figures at the front of the charge are particularly grotesque, while the leader, Black Anna—whom Kollwitz modeled on herself—signals the attack with a fierce gesture, her arms silhouetted against the sky. Behind her, the crowded and chaotic mass of workers wielding farm tools forms a passionate picture of political revolt.

Like Kollwitz, Paula Modersohn-Becker (1876–1907) studied at the Berlin School of Art for Women. In 1898, she moved to Worpswede, an artists' retreat in rural northern Germany. Dissatisfied with the Worpswede artists' naturalistic approach to rural life, after 1900 she made four trips to Paris to view recent developments in Post-Impressionist painting. Although obviously informed by the "primitivizing" tendencies of other artists such as Gauguin (see "A Closer Look," page 1000) toward women at the time, her **SELF-PORTRAIT WITH AN AMBER NECKLACE** (FIG. 32-15) subverts those same tendencies. The monumentalized image of Modersohn-Becker seems at home within nature, surrounded by plants, holding and wearing flowers. She looks out of the canvas directly at us, calmly returning our gaze and establishing

are powerfully critical of urban existence. In Ernst Ludwig Kirchner's **STREET, BERLIN** (FIG. 32-13), two prostitutes—their profession advertised by their large feathered hats and fur-trimmed coats—strut past well-dressed bourgeois men whom they view as potential clients. They seem to have deliberately embarrassed the man to their left, smirking as he hurriedly refocuses his attention on the shop window to the right. The figures are artificial and dehumanized, with masklike faces and stiff gestures. Their bodies crowd together, but they are psychologically distant. The harsh biting colors, tilted perspective, and brutal brushstrokes make this a disturbing Expressionistic image of urban degeneracy and alienation.

32–14 • Käthe Kollwitz THE OUTBREAK
From the *Peasants' War* series. 1903. Etching, 20″ × 23⅓″ (50.7 × 59.2 cm). Kupferstichkabinett, Staatliche Museen zu Berlin.

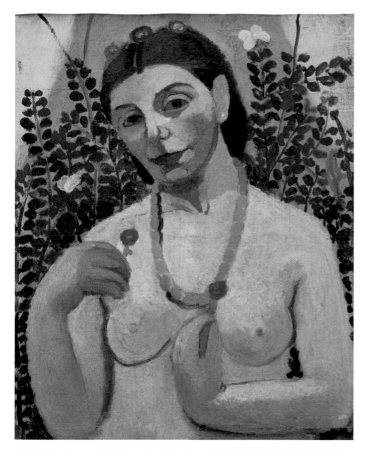

32–15 • Paula Modersohn-Becker **SELF-PORTRAIT WITH AN AMBER NECKLACE**
1906. Oil on canvas, 24″ × 19¾″ (61 × 50 cm). Öffentliche Kunstsammlung Basel.

32–16 • Egon Schiele **SELF-PORTRAIT NUDE**
1911. Gouache and pencil on paper, 20¼″ × 13¾″ (51.4 × 35 cm). Metropolitan Museum of Art, New York. Bequest of Scofield Thayer, 1982 (1984.433.298)

a comfortable human connection. While painted in the manner of other Modernists, her tender self-portrait reveals an artist of strong independent ideas and a woman of sharp intelligence.

In contrast, the 1911 **SELF-PORTRAIT NUDE** (**FIG. 32-16**) of Austrian artist Egon Schiele (1890–1918) challenges viewers with his physical and psychological torment. The impact of Schiele's father's death from untreated syphilis when the artist was just 14, led him to conflate suffering with sexuality throughout his life. In many drawings and watercolors, Schiele portrays women in demeaning, sexually explicit poses that emphasize their animal nature, and in numerous self-portraits, the artist turns the same harsh gaze upon himself, revealing deep ambivalence toward sexuality and the body. In this self-portrait he stares wildly at us with anguish, his emaciated body stretched and displayed in a halo of harsh light, lacking both hands and genitals. Some have interpreted this representational mutilation in Freudian fashion as the artist's symbolic self-punishment for indulgence in masturbation, then commonly believed to lead to insanity.

SPIRITUALISM OF THE BLUE RIDER

Formed in Munich by the Russian artist Vassily Kandinsky (1866–1944) and the German artist Franz Marc (1880–1916), Der Blaue

Reiter ("The Blue Rider") was named for a popular image of a blue knight, the St. George on the city emblem of Moscow. Just as St. George had been a spiritual leader in society, so The Blue Rider aspired to offer spiritual leadership in the arts. Its first exhibition was held in December 1911 and included the work of 14 artists working in a wide range of styles, from realism to radical abstraction.

By 1911, Marc was mostly painting animals rather than humans, rendering them in big, bold forms painted in almost-primary colors. He felt animals were more "primitive" and thus purer than humans, enjoying a more spiritual relationship with nature. In **THE LARGE BLUE HORSES** (**FIG. 32-17**), the animals—blue, in an allusion to St. George and symbolizing natural spirituality—merge into a homogeneous whole. Their sweeping contours reflect the harmony of their collective existence and echo the curved lines of the hills behind them, suggesting that they live in harmony with their surroundings.

32-18 • Vassily Kandinsky IMPROVISATION 28 (SECOND VERSION)
1912. Oil on canvas, 43⅞″ × 63⅞″ (111.4 × 162.2 cm). Solomon R. Guggenheim Museum, New York. Solomon R. Guggenheim Founding Collection (37.239)

Read the document related to Vassily Kandinsky on myartslab.com

Born into a wealthy Moscow family, Kandinsky initially trained as a lawyer, but after visiting exhibitions of Modern art in Germany and taking private art lessons, he abandoned his legal career, moved to Munich, and established himself as an artist.

Kandinsky may have been a synesthete—someone who "hears" colors and "sees" sound. His art is clearly that of an artist for whom sound and color were inextricably linked. His early study of the work of Whistler (see FIG. 31–27) convinced him that the arts of painting and music were related—just as a composer organizes sound, so a painter organizes color and form. Kandinsky's musical interests led him to contact with Austrian composer Arnold Schoenberg, who around 1910 introduced a momentous change in musical history. Since antiquity, Western music had been based on the arrangement of notes into scales, or modes (such as today's common major and minor), chosen by composers for expressive reasons. Each note in any given scale had a role to play, and these roles operated in a clear hierarchy that served to reinforce what became known as the "tonal center," a kind of home base or place of repose in the musical composition. Schoenberg eliminated the tonal center and treated all tones equally, denying the listener any place of repose and prolonging the expressive tension of his music indefinitely. Kandinsky wondered, if music can exist without a tonal center, can painting exist without subject matter?

Kandinsky was thus one of the first artists to investigate the theoretical possibility of purely abstract painting. Like Whistler, he gave his works musical titles, such as "Composition" and "Improvisation," and aspired to make paintings that responded to his own inner state and would be entirely autonomous, making no reference to the visible world. In 1912, he painted a series of works, including **IMPROVISATION 28** (**FIG. 32–18**), that he claimed represented the first truly abstract art. In these works, colors leap and dance, expressing a variety of emotions. For Kandinsky, painting was a utopian spiritual force. He saw art's traditional focus on accurate rendering of the physical world as a misguided materialistic quest, and he hoped that his paintings would lead humanity toward a deeper awareness of spirituality and the inner world. Rather than searching for correspondence between the painting and the world where none is intended, the artist asks us to look at the painting as if we were hearing a symphony, responding instinctively and spontaneously to this or that passage, and then to the total experience. Kandinsky further explained the musical analogy in his book *Concerning the Spiritual in Art*: "Color directly influences the soul. Color is the keyboard, the eyes are the hammers, the soul is the piano with many strings. The artist is the hand that plays, touching one key or another purposively, to cause vibrations in the soul."

EXTENSIONS OF CUBISM

As Cubist paintings emerged from the studios of Braque and Picasso, it was clear to the art world that they had altered the artistic discourse irrevocably. Cubism's way of viewing the world resonated with artists all over Europe, in Russia, and even in the United States. These artists interpreted Cubism in personal ways, significantly broadening and extending its visual message beyond the ideas and objects of Picasso and Braque.

FRANCE Robert Delaunay (1885–1941) and his wife, the Ukrainian-born Sonia Delaunay (1885–1979, born Sonia Stern and adopted by her uncle in 1890 as Sonia Terk; sometimes known as Sonia Delaunay-Terk), took the relatively monochromatic and static forms of Cubism in a new direction. Fauvist color inflected Delaunay's early work; his deep interest in communicating spirituality through color led him to participate in Blue Rider exhibitions. In 1910, he began to fuse his interest in color with Cubism to create paintings celebrating the modern city and modern technology. In **HOMAGE TO BLÉRIOT** (**FIG. 32–19**), Delaunay pays tribute to Louis Blériot—the French pilot who in 1909 became the first person to fly across the English Channel—by portraying his airplane flying over the Eiffel Tower, the Parisian symbol of modernity. The brightly colored circular forms that fill the rest of the canvas suggest the movement of the airplane's propeller, a blazing sun in the sky, and the great rose window of the Cathedral

32–19 • Robert Delaunay **HOMAGE TO BLÉRIOT**
1914. Watercolor on paper, 31″ × 26″ (78 × 67 cm). Musée d'Art Moderne de la Ville de Paris. Donation of Henry-Thomas, 1976

of Notre-Dame, representing Delaunay's ideas of "progressive" science and spirituality. This painting's fractured colors also suggest the fast-moving parts of modern machinery.

The critic Guillaume Apollinaire labeled the art of both Robert and Sonia Delaunay "Orphism" after Orpheus, the legendary Greek poet whose lute playing charmed wild beasts, thus implying that their art had similar power. They preferred the term "simultaneity," a concept based on Michel-Eugène Chevreul's law of the simultaneous contrast of colors that proposed collapsing spatial distance and temporal sequence into the simultaneous "here and now" to create a harmonic unity out of the disharmonious world. They envisioned a simultaneity that combined the modern world of airplanes, telephones, and automobiles with spirituality.

Sonia Delaunay produced Orphist paintings with Robert, but she also designed fabric and clothing on her own. She created new patterns similar to Cubist paintings that she called Simultaneous Dresses and exhibited a line of inexpensive ready-to-wear garments with bold geometric designs at the important 1925 International

32-20 • Sonia Delaunay **CLOTHES AND CUSTOMIZED CITROËN B-12 (EXPO 1925 MANNEQUINS AVEC AUTO)** From *Maison de la Mode*. 1925.

32-21 • Fernand Léger **THREE WOMEN**
1921. Oil on canvas, 6′1½″ × 8′3″ (1.84 × 2.52 m). Museum of Modern Art, New York. Mrs. Simon Guggenheim Fund

Exposition of Modern Decorative and Industrial Arts, decorating a Citroën sports car to match one of her ensembles for the exhibition (**FIG. 32-20**). She saw the sports car as an expression of the new automobile age, because like her clothing, this car was produced inexpensively for a mass market and because the small three-seater was designed specifically to appeal to the newly independent woman of the time, Delaunay's clientele base. Sadly, there are only black-and-white photographs of these designs.

Technology also fascinated Fernand Léger (1881–1955), who painted a more static but brilliantly colored version of Cubism based on machine forms. **THREE WOMEN** (**FIG. 32-21**) is a Purist, machine-age version of the French academic subject of the reclining nude. Purism was developed in Paris by Le Corbusier (b. Charles-Édouard Jeanneret, 1887–1965) and Amédée Ozenfant in a 1925 book, *The Foundation of Modern Art*, that argued for a return to clear, ordered forms and ideas to express the efficient clarity of the machine age. In Léger's painting, the women's bodies are constructed from large machinelike shapes arranged in an asymmetrical geometric grid that evokes both cool Classicism and an arrangement of plumbing parts. The women are dehumanized, with identical, bland, round faces; they seem to be assembled from standard, interchangeable parts. The exuberant colors and patterns that surround them suggest an orderly industrial society in which everything has its place.

ITALY In Italy, Cubism developed into Futurism, with its emphasis on portraying technology and a sense of speed. In 1908, Italy was a state in crisis Huge disparities of wealth separated the north from the south; four-fifths of the country was illiterate; poverty and near-starvation were rampant; and as many as 50,000 people had recently died in one of the nation's worst earthquakes. On February 20, 1909, Milanese poet and editor Filippo Tommaso Marinetti (1876–1944) published "Foundation and Manifesto of Futurism" on the front page of the Parisian newspaper *Le Figaro*. He attacked everything old, dull, and "feminine," and proposed to shake Italy free of its past by embracing an exhilarating, "masculine," "futuristic," and even dangerous world based on the thrill, speed, energy, and power of modern urban life.

In April 1911, a group of Milanese artists followed Marinetti's manifesto with the "Technical Manifesto of Futurist Painting," in which they demanded that "all subjects previously used must be swept aside in order to express our whirling life of steel, of pride, of fever, and of speed." Some of these artists traveled to Paris for a Futurist exhibition in 1912, after which they used the visual forms of Cubism to express in art their love of machines, speed, and war.

32-22 • Gino Severini ARMORED TRAIN IN ACTION
1915. Oil on canvas, 45⅝″ × 34⅞″ (115.8 × 88.5 cm). Museum of Modern Art, New York. Gift of Richard S. Zeisler (287.86)

Gino Severini (1883–1966) signed the "Technical Manifesto" while living in Paris, where he served as an intermediary between the Italian-based Futurists and the French avant-garde. Perhaps more than other Futurists, Severini embraced the concept of war as a social cleansing agent. In **ARMORED TRAIN IN ACTION** (**FIG. 32-22**) of 1915—probably based on a photograph of a Belgian armored car on a train going over a bridge—Severini uses the jagged forms and splintered overlapping surfaces of Cubism to describe a tumultuous scene of smoke, violence, and cannon blasts issuing from the speeding train as seen from a dizzying and disorienting viewpoint.

In 1912, Umberto Boccioni (1882–1916) argued for a Futurist "sculpture of environment," in which form should explode in a violent burst of motion from the closed and solid mass into the surrounding space. In **UNIQUE FORMS OF CONTINUITY IN SPACE** (**FIG. 32-23**), Boccioni portrays a figure striding powerfully through space, like the ancient *Nike (Victory) of Samothrace* (see

32-23 • Umberto Boccioni UNIQUE FORMS OF CONTINUITY IN SPACE
1913. Bronze, 43⅞" × 34⅞" × 15¾" (111 × 89 × 40 cm). Museum of Modern Art,
New York. Acquired through the Lillie P. Bliss Bequest (231.1948)

📖 Read the document related to Futurism on myartslab.com

forms like an analytical Cubist force. Goncharova turned to mixtures of Russian folk art and Modern abstraction in costumes and sets she designed for Sergei Diaghilev's Ballets Russes stagings, including *Le Coq d'or* (1914), *Night on Bald Mountain* (1923), and the revival of Stravinsky's *Firebird* (1926).

After 1915, Kazimir Malevich (1878–1935) emerged as the leader of the Moscow avant-garde. According to his later reminiscences, "in the year 1913, in my desperate attempt to free art from the burden of the object, I took refuge in the square form and exhibited a picture which consisted of nothing more than a black square on a white field." *The Black Square* was one of the backdrops for Mikhail Matiushin's Russian futurist opera, *Victory Over the Sun*. At the "Last Futurist Exhibition of Paintings: 0.10," held in St. Petersburg in the winter of 1915–1916 Malevich exhibited 39 works of art, consisting of flat, geometric shapes collaged together in a style he termed Suprematism, defined as "the supremacy of pure feeling

FIG. 5-65), with muscular forms like wings flying out energetically behind it. Many of Boccioni's sculptures made use of unconventional materials; this sculpture was actually made of plaster and only cast in bronze after the artist's death. In keeping with his Futurist ideals, Boccioni celebrated Italy's entry into World War I by enlisting. He was killed in combat.

RUSSIA By 1900, Russian artists and art collectors in the cosmopolitan cities of St. Petersburg and later Moscow had begun to embrace avant-garde art, making trips to Paris to see it. Russian artists also drew on Futurist tendencies to celebrate technology and the aesthetic of speed. In 1912, Russian Futurist artists, also known as Cubo-Futurists—claiming to have emerged independently of Italian Futurism—began to move increasingly toward abstraction.

ELECTRIC LIGHT (FIG. 32-24), painted in 1913 by Natalia Goncharova (1881–1962), shows the brightly artificial light from a new electric lamp fracturing and dissolving its surrounding

32-24 • Natalia Goncharova ELECTRIC LIGHT
1913. Oil on canvas, 41½" × 32" (105.5 × 81.3 cm). Musée National d'Art Moderne, Centre National d'Art et de Culture Georges Pompidou.

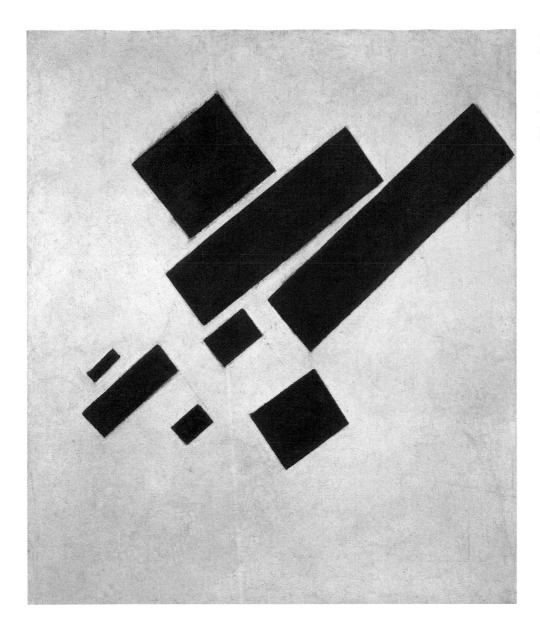

32–25 • Kazimir Malevich
SUPREMATIST PAINTING
(EIGHT RED RECTANGLES)
1915. Oil on canvas, 22½″ × 18⅞″
(57 × 48 cm). Stedelijk Museum,
Amsterdam.

Read the document
related to Kazimir Malevich
on myartslab.com

32–26 • Vladimir Tatlin CORNER COUNTER-RELIEF
1915. Mixed media, 31½″ × 59″ × 29½″ (80 × 150 × 75 cm).
Present whereabouts unknown.

in creative art." One of these works, **SUPREMATIST PAINTING
(EIGHT RED RECTANGLES)** (**FIG. 32-25**), arranges eight red
rectangles, set diagonally on a white ground—a pure abstraction.

At the same time Vladimir Tatlin (1885–1953) began to
construct entirely abstract sculptures that he entitled **CORNER
COUNTER-RELIEFS** (**FIG. 32-26**). He created these sculptures
from various nonprecious, nonart materials such as metal, glass,
wood, plaster, and wire. Although his move away from a conception of free-standing sculpture formed from traditional materials may have been inspired by a visit to Picasso's studio (see **FIG.**
32-10), Tatlin created his new formal and conceptual language for
sculpture by actively using open and negative space, eliminating
sculpture's reliance on mass and monumentality, and producing
fragile and physically unstable objects that hung in the corners of
rooms—the space formerly reserved for religious icons. In effect,
Tatlin intended these "Counter-Reliefs" to be modern abstract
replacements of the icons of the Russian Orthodox faith.

32–27 • Constantin Brancusi THE NEWBORN
1915. Marble, 5¾″ × 8¼″ × 5⅞″ (14.6 × 21 × 14.8 cm). Philadelphia Museum of Art. Louise and Walter Arensberg Collection. (195.134.10)

TOWARD ABSTRACTION IN TRADITIONAL SCULPTURE

It is clear that sculpture underwent a revolution as profound as that of painting in the years prior to World War I. Perhaps Picasso's creation of three-dimensional works from diverse materials, assembled and hung on a wall rather than placed on pedestals—an idea developed in Russia by Tatlin—was the most radical innovation, but not all change involved new materials and display contexts. The Romanian artist Constantin Brancusi (1876–1957), who settled in Paris in 1904 and working in Rodin's studio by 1907, became immediately captivated by the "primitive" art on display in the city. He admired the semiabstracted forms of much art beyond the Western tradition, believing that the artists who made such art succeeded in capturing the "essence" of their subject. In Brancusi's search for a sculptural essence he, like Picasso, rejected superficial realism. Brancusi wrote, "What is real is not the external form but the essence of things. Starting from this truth it is impossible for anyone to express anything essentially real by imitating its exterior surface."

For Brancusi, the egg symbolized the potential for birth, growth, and development—the "essence" of life contained in a perfect, organic, abstract ovoid. In **THE NEWBORN** (FIG. 32–27) of 1915, he conflates its shape with the disembodied head of a human infant to suggest the essence of humanity at the moment of birth. In his 1924 **TORSO OF A YOUNG MAN** (FIG. 32–28), Brancusi distills the figure's torso and upper legs into three essential

32–28 • Constantin Brancusi TORSO OF A YOUNG MAN
1924. Bronze on stone and wood bases; combined figure and bases 40⅜″ × 20″ × 18¼″ (102.4 × 50.5 × 46.1 cm). Hirshhorn Museum and Sculpture Garden, Smithsonian Institution, Washington, DC.

and highly polished metal cylinders. Although its machine-like regularity might recall the works of Léger or the Futurists, this bold abstraction carries a Classical gravity and stillness, especially when perched atop the elemental earthiness of the impressive pedestal Brancusi created for it in wood and stone.

DADA: QUESTIONING ART ITSELF

When the Great War broke out in August 1914, most European leaders thought it would be over by Christmas. Both sides reassured their citizens that the efficiency of their armies and bravery of their soldiers would ensure a speedy resolution, that the political status quo would resume. These hopes proved illusory. World War I was the most brutal and costly in human history up to this time. On the Western Front in 1916 alone, Germany lost 850,000 soldiers, France 700,000, and Great Britain 400,000. The conflict settled into a vicious stalemate on all fronts as each side deployed new killing technologies, such as improved machine guns, flame throwers, fighter aircraft, and poison gas. On the home front, governments exerted control over industry and labor to manage the war effort, and ordinary people were forced to endure food rationing, propaganda attacks, and shameless war profiteering.

Horror at the enormity of the carnage arose on many fronts. One of the first artistic movements to address the slaughter and the moral questions it posed was Dada—a transnational movement with distinct local manifestations that arose almost simultaneously in Zürich, New York, Paris, and Berlin. If Modern art until that time questioned the traditions of art, Dada went further to question the concept of art itself. Witnessing how thoughtlessly life was discarded in the trenches, Dada mocked the senselessness of rational thought and even the foundations of modern society. It embraced a "mocking iconoclasm," even in its name, which has no real or fixed meaning. *Dada* is baby talk in German; in French it means "hobbyhorse"; in Romanian and Russian, "yes, yes"; in the Kru African dialect, "the tail of a sacred cow." Dada artists annihilated the conventional understanding of art as something precious, replacing it with a strange and irrational art about ideas and actions rather than about objects.

HUGO BALL AND THE CABARET VOLTAIRE Dada's opening moment was probably the first performance of poet Hugo Ball's poem "Karawane" at the Cabaret Voltaire. Ball (1886–1927) and his companion, Emmy Hennings (d. 1949), a nightclub singer, moved from Germany to neutral Switzerland when World War I broke out and opened the Cabaret Voltaire in Zürich on February 5, 1916. Cabaret Voltaire was based loosely on the bohemian artists' cafés of prewar Berlin and Munich, and its mad irrational world became a meeting place for exiled avant-garde writers and artists of various nationalities who shared Ball's and Hennings's disgust for the war.

It was here that Ball solemnly recited one of his sound poems, **"KARAWANE"** (FIG. 32-29), wearing a strange costume, with his legs and body encased in blue cardboard tubes and

32-29 • HUGO BALL RECITING THE SOUND POEM "KARAWANE"
Photographed at the Cabaret Voltaire, Zürich. 1916.

a white-and-blue "witch doctor's hat," as he called it, on his head. He also wore a huge, gold-painted cardboard cape that flapped when he moved his arms and lobsterlike cardboard hands or claws. The text of Ball's poem—included in the photograph documenting the event—consists of a string of nonsensical sounds, renouncing "the language devastated and made impossible by journalism," and mocking traditional poetry. He self-consciously abandoned the rationality of adulthood and created a new, and wholly incomprehensible private language of random sounds that seemed to mimic baby talk.

MARCEL DUCHAMP Although not formally a member of the movement, Marcel Duchamp (1887–1968) created some of Dada's most complex and challenging works. He also took Dada to New York when he crossed the Atlantic in 1915 to escape the war in Europe. In Paris in 1912, Duchamp had experimented with Cubism, painting *Nude Descending a Staircase No. 2*, one of the most controversial works to be included later in the Armory Show (see page 1041). But by the time Duchamp arrived in the

32–30 • Marcel Duchamp FOUNTAIN
1917. Porcelain plumbing fixture and enamel paint. Photograph by Alfred Stieglitz. Philadelphia Museum of Art, Pennsylvania. Louise and Walter Arensberg Collection (1998-74-1)

Stieglitz's photograph is the only known image of Duchamp's original *Fountain*, which mysteriously disappeared after it was rejected by the jury of the American Society of Independent Artists exhibition. In 1950, Duchamp produced several replicas of the lost original simply by buying more urinals and signing them "R. Mutt/1917." One of these replicas sold at auction in 1999 for $1.76 million, setting a record for a work by Duchamp.

👁⃞ **Watch** a video about Marcel Duchamp on myartslab.com

United States, he had discarded painting, which he claimed had become for him a mindless activity, and had devised the Dada genre that he termed the **readymade**, in which he transformed ordinary, often manufactured objects into works of art.

Duchamp was warmly welcomed into the American art world. The American Society of Independent Artists invited him to become a founding member, and he chaired the hanging committee for its first annual "Forum" exhibition in 1917. The show advertised itself as unjuried—any work of art submitted with the entry fee of $6 would be hung. Yet, in Dada fashion, Duchamp spent almost two years devising a work of art that would be shocking and offensive enough to be rejected, thus commenting on the contemporary process of art making and its exhibition. His anonymous submission was a common porcelain urinal that he purchased from a plumber, which he turned on one side so that it was no longer functional and signed "R. Mutt" in a play on the name of the urinal's manufacturer, J. L. Mott Iron Works. It was indeed rejected.

FOUNTAIN (**FIG. 32-30**) remains one of the most controversial works of art of the twentieth century. *It* is transgressive. It incites laughter, anger, embarrassment, and disgust, by openly referring to private bathroom activities, to human carnality and vulnerability. In it Duchamp questions the very essence of what constitutes a work of art. How much can be stripped away before the essence of art disappears? Since Whistler's famous court case (see "Art on Trial in 1877," page 985), most avant-garde artists agreed that a work of art need be neither descriptive nor well-crafted but, before 1917, none would have argued, as Duchamp does in this piece, that "art" was primarily conceptual. For centuries, perhaps millennia, artists had regularly employed studio assistants to craft parts, if not all, of the art objects that they designed. On one level, Duchamp updated that practice into modern terms by arguing that art objects might not only be crafted (in part) by others, but that the objects of art could actually be mass-produced

32–31 • Marcel Duchamp L.H.O.O.Q.
1919. Pencil on reproduction of Leonardo da Vinci's *Mona Lisa*, 7¾" × 4¾" (19.7 × 12.1 cm). Philadelphia Museum of Art, Pennsylvania. Louise and Walter Arensberg Collection

for the artist by industry. In a clever twist of logic, Duchamp simultaneously creates a commentary on consumption and on the irrationality of the modern age by arguing that the "readymade" work of art, as a manufactured object, simply bypasses the craft tradition, qualifying as a work of art through human conceptualization rather than by human facture.

When *Fountain* was rejected, as Duchamp anticipated it would be, the artist resigned from the Society of Independent Artists in mock horror, and published an unsigned editorial in a Dada journal detailing what he described as the scandal of the R. Mutt case. He wrote: "The only works of art America has given are her plumbing and bridges," adding, "Whether Mr. Mutt with his own hands made the fountain or not has no importance. He CHOSE it. He took an ordinary article of life, placed it so that its useful significance disappeared under the new title and point of view—created a new thought for that object."

After Duchamp returned to Paris, he challenged the French art world with a work that he entitled **L.H.O.O.Q.** (**FIG. 32-31**) and described as a "modified readymade." In 1911, a Louvre employee had stolen Leonardo's famous *Mona Lisa* (see FIG. 21-5), believing it should be returned to Italy. It took two years to recover it. While missing, however, the *Mona Lisa* became even more famous and was widely and badly reproduced on postcards and posters, and in advertising. In his work, Duchamp chose to comment on the nature of fame and on the degraded image of the *Mona Lisa* by purchasing a cheap postcard reproduction and drawing a mustache and beard on her famously enigmatic face. In doing so he turned a sacred cultural artifact into an object of crude ridicule. The letters that he scrawled across the bottom of the card, "L.H.O.O.Q.," when read aloud sound phonetically similar to the French slang phrase *elle a chaud au cul*, politely translated as "she's hot for it," thus adding a crude sexual innuendo to the already cheapened image. Like *Fountain*, this work challenges preconceived notions about what constitutes art and introduces ridicule and crude bodily functions as viable artistic content. As one of Dada's founders said: "Dada was born of disgust."

Duchamp made only a few readymades. In fact, he created very little art at all after about 1922, when he devoted himself almost entirely to chess. When asked about his occupation, he described himself as a "retired artist," but his early twentieth-century radical ideas about art continue to exert influence, especially since around 1960.

BERLIN DADA Early in 1917, Hugo Ball and the Romanian-born poet Tristan Tzara (1896–1963) organized the Galerie Dada in Zürich. Tzara also edited the magazine *Dada*, which quickly attracted the attention of like-minded artists and writers in several European capitals and in the United States. The movement spread farther when expatriate members of Hugo Ball's circle in Switzerland returned to their homelands after the war. Richard Huelsenbeck (1892–1974), for instance, took Dada to Germany, where he helped found the Club Dada in Berlin in April 1918.

32-32 • Kurt Schwitters MERZBILD 5B (PICTURE-RED-HEART-CHURCH)
April 26, 1919. Collage, tempera, and crayon on cardboard, 32⅞″ × 23¾″ (83.4 × 60.3 cm). Solomon R. Guggenheim Museum, New York. (52.1325)

Dada pursued a slightly different agenda and took on different forms in each of its major centers. One distinctive feature of Berlin Dada was its agitprop agenda. Compared to the more literary forms of Dada elsewhere, Berlin Dada also produced an unusually large amount of visual art—especially collage and **photomontage** (photographic collage).

Kurt Schwitters (1887–1948), for instance, who met Huelsenbeck and other Dadaists in 1919, used discarded rail tickets, postage stamps, ration coupons, beer labels, and other street detritus to create visual poetry. Schwitters termed his two- and three-dimensional works of art, made out of the wasted ephemera of the industrial world, *Merzbilder* (German for "refuse picture"). In these works Schwitters combines fragments of newspaper and other printed material with drawn or painted images. He wrote that garbage demanded equal rights with painting. In **MERZBILD 5B (FIG. 32-32)**, Schwitters's collage includes printed fragments from the street with newspaper scraps to comment on the postwar disorder of defeated Germany. One fragment describes the brutal overthrow of the short-lived socialist republic in Bremen.

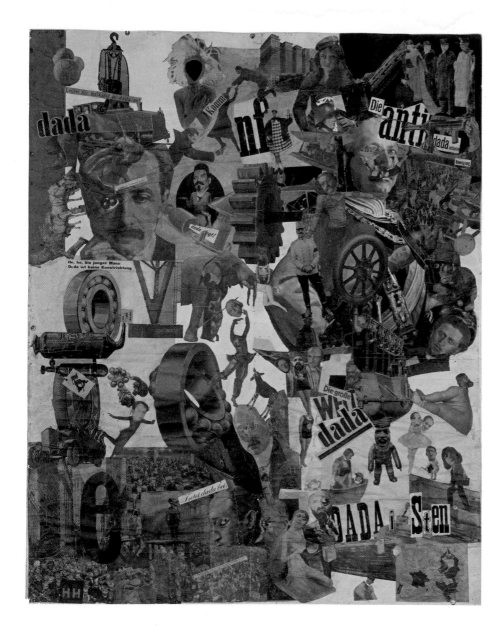

Hannah Höch (1889–1978) produced even more pointed political photomontages. Between 1916 and 1926, she worked for Verlag, Berlin's largest publishing house, designing decorative patterns and writing articles on crafts for a women's magazine. Höch considered herself part of the women's movement in the 1920s. She disapproved of contemporary mass-media representations of women and had to fight for her place as the sole woman among the Berlin Dada group, one of whom described her contribution disparagingly as merely conjuring up beer and sandwiches. In **CUT WITH THE DADA KITCHEN KNIFE THROUGH THE LAST WEIMAR BEER-BELLY CULTURAL EPOCH IN GERMANY** (FIG. 32-33), Höch combines images and words from the popular press, political posters, and photographs to create a complex and angry critique of the Weimar Republic in 1919. She shows women physically cutting apart the beer-bloated German establishment in this photomontage and includes portraits of androgynous Dada characters, such as herself and several other Berlin Dada

artists, along with Marx and Lenin. It is tempting to wonder which side she really thinks her fellow Dadaists stand on.

MODERNIST TENDENCIES IN AMERICA

When avant-garde Modern art was first widely exhibited in the United States, it received a cool welcome. While some American artists did work in abstract or Modern ways, most preferred to work in a more naturalistic manner, at least until around 1915.

STIEGLITZ AND THE "291" GALLERY

The chief proponent of European Modernism in the United States was the photographer Alfred Stieglitz (1864–1946), who in the years before World War I organized several small exhibitions featuring the art of major Modernists at a tiny gallery at 291 Fifth

Avenue, known simply as 291. Stieglitz, like Kahnweiler in Paris, supported many of the early American Modernist artists in New York. As a photographer himself, he sought to establish the legitimacy of photography as a fine art with these exhibitions.

Born in New Jersey to a wealthy German immigrant family, Stieglitz studied photography in the 1880s at the Technische Hochschule in Berlin, quickly recognizing photography's artistic potential. In 1890, he began to photograph New York City street scenes. He promoted his views through an organization called the Photo-Secession, founded in 1902, and two years later opened the 291 gallery. By 1910, this gallery had become a focal point for both photographers and painters, with Stieglitz giving shows (sometimes their first) to artists such as Arthur Dove, John Marin, and Georgia O'Keeffe, and bringing to America the art of European artists such as Kandinsky, Braque, Cézanne, and Rodin.

In his own photographs, Stieglitz tried to compose poetic images of romanticized urban scenes. In **THE FLATIRON BUILDING** (**FIG. 32-34**), the tree trunk to the right is echoed by branches in the grove farther back, and in the wedge-shaped Flatiron Building to the rear. The entire scene is suffused with a misty wintery atmosphere, which the artist created by manipulating his viewpoint, exposure, and possibly both the negative and positive images. Ironically, Stieglitz softens and romanticizes the Flatiron Building, one of New York's earliest skyscrapers and a symbol of the city's modernity. The magazine *Camera Work*, a high-quality photographic publication that Stieglitz edited, and which published this photograph in photogravure form in 1903, also featured numerous photogravures of American and European Modernist art as well as some important American Modern art criticism.

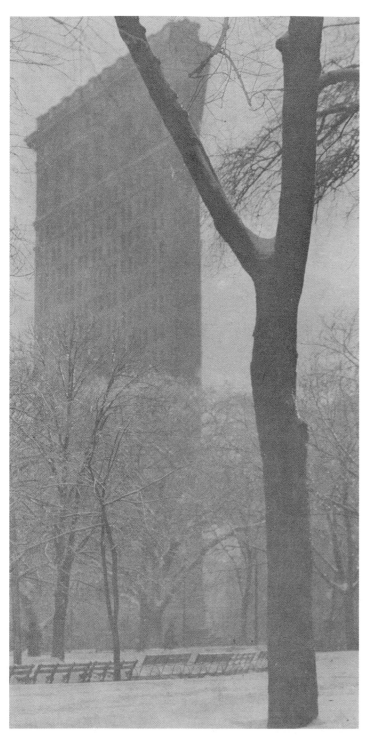

32-34 • Alfred Stieglitz THE FLATIRON BUILDING, NEW YORK
1903. Photogravure, 6¹¹⁄₁₆″ × 3⁵⁄₁₆″ (17 × 8.4 cm) mounted. Metropolitan Museum of Art, New York. Gift of J.B. Neumann, 1958 (58.577.37)

THE ARMORY SHOW AND HOME-GROWN MODERNISM

In 1913, Modernist art arrived in New York en masse with an enormous exhibition held in the drill hall of the 69th Regiment Armory on Lexington Avenue between 25th and 26th Streets. Walt Kuhn (1877–1949) and Arthur B. Davies (1862–1928) were the principal organizers of the "Armory Show," which featured more than 1,600 works, a quarter of them by European artists. Most of the art, even the Modernist art, was well received and sold well, but the art of a few European Modernists, including Matisse and Duchamp in particular, caused a public outcry, in which they were described as "cousins to the anarchists." When selected works from the exhibition traveled on to Chicago, a few faculty and some students of the School of the Art Institute even hanged Matisse in effigy, while civic leaders called for a morals commission to investigate the show. Yet the exhibition consolidated American Modernist art and inspired its artists, who subsequently found more enthusiastic collectors and exhibition venues.

One of the most significant early American Modernists was Arthur Dove (1880–1946). Dove studied the work of the Fauves in Europe in 1907–1909, and he even exhibited at the Autumn Salon. After returning home, he began painting abstract nature studies about the same time as Kandinsky, although each was unaware of the other. Dove's **NATURE SYMBOLIZED NO. 2** (**FIG. 32-35**) is one of a remarkable series of small works that reveals his beliefs about the spiritual power of nature. But while Kandinsky's art focuses on an inner vision of nature, Dove abstract paintings reflect his deeply felt experience of the landscape itself, saying that

A CLOSER LOOK | *Portrait of a German Officer*

by Marsden Hartley. 1914. Oil on canvas, 68¼″ × 41⅜″ (1.78 × 1.05 m).
Metropolitan Museum of Art, New York. The Alfred Stieglitz Collection, 1949 (49.70.42)

Symbolic references to Freyburg include epaulettes, lance tips, and the Iron Cross he was awarded the day before he was killed.

The black-and-white checkerboard patterns represent Freyburg's love of chess.

Freyburg's regiment number ("4") is shown at the center of the abstracted chest along with a red cursive "E," which stands for "Edmund" (Hartley's given name). This places Hartley over Freyburg's heart.

The blue-and-white diamond pattern comes from the Bavarian flag; the red, white, and black bands constitute the flag of the German Empire, adopted in 1871; and the black-and-white stripes are those of the historic flag of Prussia.

The funereal black background heightens the intensity of the foreground colors.

Hartley identifies his subject with his initials ("Kv.F") in gold on red.

The young man's age ("24") is noted in gold on blue.

While living in Berlin in 1914, Hartley fell in love with a young Prussian lieutenant, Karl von Freyburg, whom Hartley described as "in every way a perfect being—physically, spiritually, and mentally." Freyburg's death in World War I devastated Hartley, who memorialized his fallen lover in this symbolic portrait.

 View the Closer Look for *Portrait of a German Officer* on myartslab.com

32-35 • Arthur Dove NATURE SYMBOLIZED NO. 2
c. 1911. Pastel on paper, 18″ × 21⅝″ (45.8 × 55 cm). The Art Institute of Chicago. Alfred Stieglitz Collection (1949.533)

he had "no [artistic] background except perhaps the woods, running streams, hunting, fishing, camping, the sky." Dove supported himself by farming in rural Connecticut, but he exhibited his art in New York and was both well received by and well connected to the New York art community.

Another pioneer of American Modernism who exhibited at the Armory Show was Marsden Hartley (1877–1943), who was also a regular exhibitor at the 291 gallery. Between 1912 and 1915, Hartley lived mostly abroad, first in Paris, where he discovered Cubism, then in Berlin, where he began to paint colorful Expressionistic art. Around 1914, however, Hartley developed a powerfully original and intense style of his own in *Portrait of a German Officer* (see "A Closer Look," opposite), a tightly arranged composition of boldly colored shapes and patterns, interspersed with numbers, letters, and fragments of German military imagery that symbolically memorialize Hartley's fallen lover, a tragic victim of the war.

Stieglitz "discovered" Georgia O'Keeffe (1887–1986)—born in rural Wisconsin, and already studying and teaching art between 1905 and 1915—when a New York friend showed him some of her charcoal drawings. Stieglitz's reported response: "At last, a woman on paper!" In 1916, he included O'Keeffe's work in a group show at 291 and mounted her first solo exhibition the following year. O'Keeffe moved to New York in 1918 and married Stieglitz in 1924. In 1925, she began to paint New York skyscrapers, which were acclaimed at the time as embodiments of American inventiveness and energy. But paintings such as **CITY NIGHT** (**FIG. 32-36**) are not unambiguous celebrations of lofty buildings. She portrays the skyscrapers from a low vantage point so that they appear to loom ominously over the viewer; their dark tonalities,

32-36 • Georgia O'Keeffe CITY NIGHT
1926. Oil on canvas, 48″ × 30″ (123 × 76.9 cm). Minneapolis Institute of Arts. Gift of funds from the Regis Corporation, Mr. and Mrs. W. John Driscoll, the Beim Foundation, the Larsen Fund (80.28)

stark forms, and exaggerated perspective produce a sense of menace that also appears in the art of other American Modernists.

In 1925, O'Keeffe also began to exhibit a series of close-up paintings of flowers that have become her best-known subjects. In **RED CANNA** (**FIG. 32-37**), O'Keeffe brings the heart of the heavy sensual flower to the front and center of the picture plane, revealing its tender inner forms and soft, delicate surfaces. By painting the flower's hidden organic energy rather than the way it actually looks to a distant viewer, she creates from it a new abstract beauty, distilling the pure vigor of the plant's life force. Critics described O'Keeffe's flower paintings as elementally feminine and vaginal, and Stieglitz did little to dissuade viewers from this reading of O'Keeffe's art. In fact, he promoted it, in spite of O'Keeffe's strenuous objections to this critical caricature and its implicit pigeonholing of her as a "woman artist." In 1929, O'Keeffe began

32-37 • Georgia O'Keeffe RED CANNA
1924. Oil on canvas mounted on Masonite, 36″ × 29⅞″ (91.44 × 75.88 cm). Collection of the University of Arizona Museum of Art, Tucson. Gift of Oliver James (1950.1.4)

32-38 • Edward Weston SUCCULENT
1930. Gelatin-silver print, 7½″ × 9½″ (19.1 × 24 cm). Collection Center for Creative Photography © 1981 Arizona Board of Regents.

spending summers in New Mexico and moved there permanently in the 1940s, dedicating her art to evocative representations of the local landscape and culture.

California artist Edward Weston (1886–1958) followed in O'Keeffe's footsteps with a series of experimental photographs begun in the late 1920s that emphasize the abstract patterns of plants by zooming in to extract them from their natural context. During a trip to New York in 1922, Weston had met O'Keeffe, as well as fellow photographers Stieglitz and Paul Strand (1890–1976), both kindred spirits in his own journey to claim photography as a legitimate medium of high art, capable of abstraction as well as documentation. In **SUCCULENT** (FIG. **32-38**), Weston used straightforward camera work without any manipulation in the darkroom to portray his subject with startlingly crisp detail, well captured on his large-format glass negative. He argued that although the camera sees more than the human eye, the quality of the photographic image rests solely on the artistic choices made by the photographer.

EARLY MODERN ARCHITECTURE

New industrial materials and engineering innovations enabled twentieth-century architects to create tall buildings of unprecedented height that vastly increased the usable space in structures built on scarce and valuable city lots. At the same time that Modern artists in Europe rejected the decorative in painting and sculpture, American architects increasingly embraced the plain geometric shapes and undecorated surfaces of skyscraper architecture.

EUROPEAN MODERNISM

In Europe, a stripped-down and severely geometric style of Modern architecture developed, partly in reaction to the natural organic lines of Art Nouveau. In Vienna, Adolf Loos (1870–1933), one of the pioneers of European architectural Modernism, insisted in his 1913 essay "Ornament and Crime" that "The evolution of a culture is synonymous with the removal of ornament from utilitarian objects." For Loos, ornament was a sign of cultural degeneracy. Thus his **STEINER HOUSE** (FIG. **32-39**) is a stucco-covered, reinforced concrete construction without decorative embellishment. The rectangular windows, for instance, are completely plain, and they were arranged only in relation to the functional demands of interior spaces. Loos argued that the only purpose of

32-39 • Adolf Loos STEINER HOUSE, VIENNA
1910.

a building's interior was to provide protection from the elements.

The most important French Modern architect was Le Corbusier, who established several important precepts that influenced architects for the next half-century. His **VILLA SAVOYE** (**FIG. 32-40**), a private home outside Paris, became an icon of the International Style (see "The International Style," page 1057) and reflects his Purist ideals in its geometric design and avoidance of ornamentation. It is also one of the best expressions of Le Corbusier's **domino construction** system, first elaborated in 1914, in which slabs of ferroconcrete (concrete reinforced with steel bars) rest on six free-standing steel posts, placed at the positions of the six dots on a domino playing piece. Over the next decade Le Corbusier further explored the possibilities of the domino system and in 1926 published "The Five Points of a New Architecture," in which he proposed raising houses above the ground on pilotis (free-standing posts); using flat roofs as terraces; using movable partition walls slotted between supports on the interior and **curtain walls** (nonload-bearing

32-40 • Le Corbusier VILLA SAVOYE, POISSY-SUR-SEINE
France. 1929–1930.

✳ **Explore** the architectural panoramas of the Villa Savoye on myartslab.com walls) on the exterior to allow greater design flexibility; and using ribbon windows (windows that run the length of the wall). These became common features of Modern architecture. Le Corbusier described the Villa Savoye as "a machine for living in," meaning that it was designed as rationally and functionally as an automobile or a machine. After World War I—like his fellow Modern architects—Le Corbusier also developed designs for mass-produced standardized housing to help rebuild Europe's destroyed infrastructure.

AMERICAN MODERNISM

CONNECTION TO THE LAND Frank Lloyd Wright (1867–1959) was not only America's most important Modern architect, he was also one of the most influential architects in the world during the early twentieth century. After briefly studying engineering at the University of Wisconsin, Wright apprenticed to a Chicago architect, then spent five years with the firm of Dankmar Adler and Louis Sullivan (see FIG. 31–55), advancing to the post of chief drafter. In 1893, Wright established his own office, specializing in domestic architecture. Around 1900, he and several other architects in the Oak Park suburb of Chicago—together known as the Prairie School—began to design low, horizontal houses with flat roofs and heavy overhangs that echoed the flat plains of the prairie in the Midwest.

The **FREDERICK C. ROBIE HOUSE** (**FIG. 32–41**) is one of Wright's early **Prairie Style** masterpieces. A central chimney, above a fireplace that radiated heat throughout the house in the bitter Chicago winter, forms the center of the sprawling design.

Low, flat overhanging roofs—dramatically cantilevered on both sides of the chimney—shade against the summer sun, and open porches provide places to sleep outside in cool summer nights. Low bands of windows—many with stained glass—surround the house, creating a colored screen between the interior and the outside world, while also inviting those inside to look through the windows into the garden beyond.

The main story is one long space divided into living and dining areas by a free-standing fireplace. There are no dividing walls. Wright had visited the Japanese exhibit at the 1893 Chicago World's Fair and was deeply influenced by the aesthetics of Japanese architecture, particularly its sense of space and screenlike windows (see "*Shoin* Design," page 821). Wright's homes frequently featured built-in closets and bookcases, and he hid heating and lighting fixtures when possible. He also designed and arranged the furniture for his interiors (**FIG. 32–42**). Here, machine-cut components create the chairs' modern geometric designs, while their high backs huddle around the table to form the intimate effect of a room within a room. Wright integrated lights and flower holders into the posts closest to the table's corners so that there would no need for lights or flowers on the table.

Wright had an uneasy relationship with European Modernist architecture; he was uninterested in the machine aesthetic of Le Corbusier. Although he routinely used new building materials such as ferroconcrete, plate glass, and steel, he sought to maintain a natural sensibility, connecting his buildings to their sites by using brick and local wood or stone. **FALLINGWATER** (**FIG. 32–43**) in rural Pennsylvania is a prime example of this practice. It is also

32–41 • Frank Lloyd Wright FREDERICK C. ROBIE HOUSE, CHICAGO
1906–1909. Chicago History Museum. (HB-19312A2)

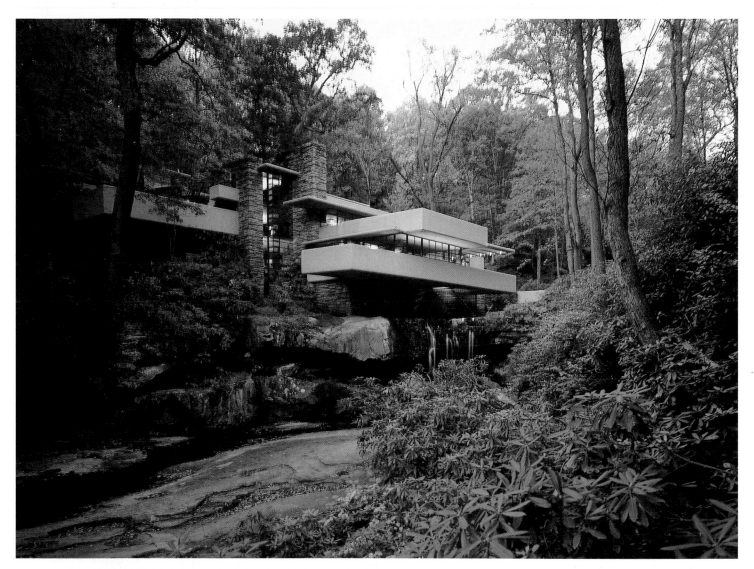

32–43 • Frank Lloyd Wright **FALLINGWATER (EDGAR KAUFMANN HOUSE), MILL RUN**
Pennsylvania. 1937.

✳──**Explore** the architectural panoramas of Fallingwater on myartslab.com

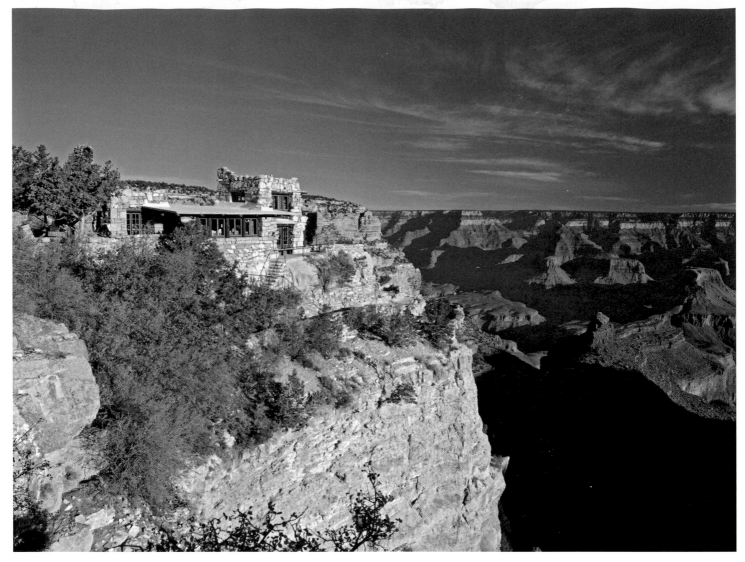

32-44 • Mary Colter LOOKOUT STUDIO, GRAND CANYON NATIONAL PARK
Arizona. 1914. Grand Canyon National Park Museum Collection.

the most famous expression of Wright's conviction that buildings should not simply sit *on* the landscape but coordinate *with* it.

Fallingwater was commissioned by Edgar Kaufmann, a Pittsburgh department-store owner, to replace a family summer cottage on the site of a waterfall and a pool where his children played. To Kaufmann's surprise, Wright decided to build the new house right into the cliff and over the pool, allowing the waterfall to flow around and under the house. A large boulder where the family had sunbathed in the summers was used for the central hearthstone of the fireplace. In a dramatic move that engineers questioned (with reason, as subsequent history has shown), Wright used cantilevers to extend a series of broad concrete terraces out from the cliff to parallel the great slabs of natural rock below. Poured concrete forms the terraces, but Wright painted the material a soft earth tone. Long bands of windows and glass doors offer spectacular views, uniting woods, water, and house. Such houses do not simply testify to the ideal of living in harmony with nature; they declare war on the modern city. When asked what could

be done to improve city architecture, Wright responded: "Tear it down."

Mary Colter (1869–1958) expressed an even stronger connection to the landscape in her architecture. Born in Pittsburgh and educated at the California School of Design in San Francisco, she spent much of her career as architect and decorator for the Fred Harvey Company, a firm in the Southwest that catered to the tourist trade. Colter was an avid student of Native American arts, and her buildings quoted liberally from Puebloan traditions, notably in the use of exposed logs for structural supports. She designed several visitor facilities at Grand Canyon National Park, of which **LOOKOUT STUDIO** (**FIG. 32-44**) is the most dramatic. Built on the edge of the canyon's south rim, the building's foundation is in natural rock, and its walls are built from local stone. The roofline is deliberately irregular to echo the surrounding canyon wall. The only concession to modernity is a liberal use of glass windows and a smooth cement floor. Colter's designs for hotels and railroad stations throughout the region helped establish the distinctive Southwest style.

The development of the skyscraper design and aesthetic depended on several things: The use of metal beams and girders for the structural-support skeleton; the separation of the building-support structure from the enclosing wall layer (the cladding); the use of fireproof materials and measures; the use of elevators; and the overall integration of plumbing, central heating, artificial lighting, and ventilation systems. The first generation of skyscrapers, built between about 1880 and 1900, were concentrated in the Midwest, chiefly in Chicago and St. Louis (see FIG. 31–55). Second-generation skyscrapers, mostly with over 20 stories, date from after 1895 and are found more frequently in New York. The first tall buildings were free-standing towers, sometimes with a base, such as the Woolworth Building of 1911–1913 (see FIG. 32–45). New York City's Building Zone Resolution of 1916 introduced mandatory setbacks—decreases in girth as the building rose—to ensure light and ventilation to adjacent sites. Built in 1931, the 1,250-foot setback form of the Empire State Building, diagrammed here, has a streamlined design. The Art Deco exterior cladding (see inset below) conceals the structural elements and mechanisms such as elevators that make its great height possible. The Empire State Building was the tallest building in the world when it was built and its distinctive profile ensures that it remains one of the most recognizable even today.

elevator shafts (layer two)

stairwells (layer one)

masonry wall

girder

cladding

heat source

concrete slab flooring

beam

setbacks

skyscraper

👁 **Watch** an architectural simulation about skyscraper construction on myartslab.com

THE AMERICAN SKYSCRAPER After 1900, New York City assumed a lead over Chicago in the development of the skyscraper, whose soaring height was made possible by the use of the steel-frame skeleton for structural support (see "The Skyscraper," above). New York clients, however, rejected the more utilitarian Chicago style of Louis Sullivan and others, preferring the historicizing approach then still popular on the east coast. The **WOOL-** WORTH BUILDING (FIG. 32–45) of 1911–1913, designed by the Minnesota-based firm of Cass Gilbert (1859–1934), was the world's tallest building at 792 feet and 55 floors when first completed. Its Gothic-style external details, inspired by the soaring towers of late medieval churches, gave the building a strong visual personality. Because of its Gothic style, Gilbert called it his "Cathedral of Commerce."

ART BETWEEN THE WARS IN EUROPE

World War I had a devastating effect on Europe's artists and architects. Many responded to the destruction and loss of a generation of young men by criticizing the European tradition, while others concentrated on rebuilding. Either way, much of the art created between 1919 and 1939 addressed directly the needs and concerns of society in turmoil or transition.

UTILITARIAN ART FORMS IN RUSSIA

In the 1917 Russian Revolution, the radical socialist Bolsheviks overthrew the tsar, withdrew Russia from the world war, and turned inward to fight a civil war that lasted until 1920 and led to the establishment of the U.S.S.R. (Union of Soviet Socialist Republics). Most Russian avant-garde artists enthusiastically supported the Bolsheviks, who initially supported them.

CONSTRUCTIVISM The case of Aleksandr Rodchenko (1891–1956) is fairly representative. An early associate of Malevich (see FIG. 32-25), Rodchenko used drafting tools to make abstract drawings. He exhibited as a Suprematist in 1921 when he showed three large, flat, monochromatic panels painted red, yellow, and blue, which he titled *Last Painting* (now lost). After this, he renounced painting as a basically selfish activity and condemned self-expression as weak, unproductive, and socially irresponsible. Also in 1921, Rodchenko helped to establish the Constructivists, a post-revolutionary group of artists dedicated not to expressing themselves but to working collectively for the good of the state. They described themselves as workers who literally "constructed" art for the people. After 1921, Rodchenko worked as a photographer producing posters, books, textiles, and theater sets to promote communism.

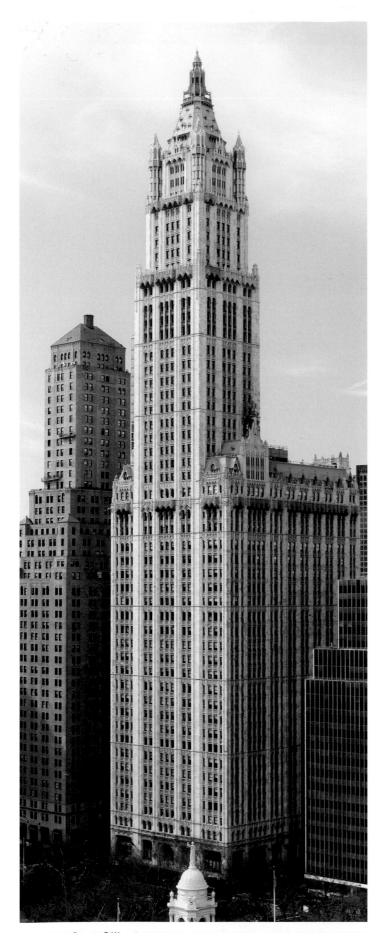

32-45 • Cass Gilbert **WOOLWORTH BUILDING, NEW YORK**
1911–1913.

32-46 • Aleksandr Rodchenko **WORKERS' CLUB**
Exhibited at the International Exposition of Modern Decorative and Industrial Arts, Paris. 1925. Art © Estate of Aleksandr Rodchenko/RAO, Moscow/VAGA, New York

32-47 • El Lissitzky PROUN SPACE
Created for the Great Berlin Art Exhibition. 1923, reconstruction 1971. Collection Van Abbemuseum, Eindhoven, The Netherlands.

In 1925, Rodchenko designed a model **WORKERS' CLUB** for the Soviet Pavilion at the Paris International Exposition of Modern Decorative and Industrial Arts (**FIG. 32-46**). Rodchenko emphasized ease of use and simplicity of construction; he made the furniture of wood because Soviet industry was best equipped for mass production in wood. The high, straight backs of the chairs were meant to promote a physical and moral posture of uprightness among the workers.

Another artist active in early Soviet Russia was El Lissitzky (1890–1941). After the Revolution, he taught architecture and graphic arts at the Vitebsk School of Fine Arts where Malevich also taught. By 1919, Lissitzky was both teaching and using a Constructivist vocabulary for propaganda posters and for artworks he called Prouns (pronounced "pro-oon"), thought to be an acronym for the Russian *proekt utverzhdenya novogo* ("project for the affirmation of the new"). Although most Prouns were paintings or prints, there were a few early examples of **installation art** (**FIG. 32-47**)—artworks created for a specific site, arranged to create a total environment. Lissitzky rejected painting as too personal and imprecise, preferring to "construct" Prouns for the collective using the less personal instruments of mechanical drawing. Like many other Soviet artists of the late 1920s, Lissitzky also turned to more socially engaged projects such as architectural design, typography, photography, and photomontage for publication.

SOCIALIST REALISM In the mid 1920s, Soviet artists increasingly rejected abstraction in favor of a more universally accessible, and thus more politically useful, Socialist Realism that was ultimately established as official Soviet art. Many of Russia's pioneering Modernists and Constructivists, including Rodchenko,

DE STIJL IN THE NETHERLANDS

In the Netherlands after World War I, abstraction took a different turn from that in the U.S.S.R. The Dutch artist Piet Mondrian (1872–1944) encountered Cubism on a trip to Paris in 1912, where he began to abstract animals, trees, and landscapes, searching for their "essential" form. After his return to the Netherlands, he met Theo van Doesburg (1883–1931) who, in 1917, started a magazine named *De Stijl* (*The Style*) that became a focal point for Dutch artists, architects, and designers after the war. Writing in the magazine, Van Doesburg argued that beauty took two distinct forms: sensual or subjective beauty, and a higher, rational, and universal beauty. He challenged De Stijl (note the term translates as "*The* Style" rather than "*A* Style") artists to aspire to universal beauty. Mondrian sought to accomplish this by eliminating everything sensual or subjective from his paintings, but he also followed M.H.J. Schoenmaekers's ideas about Theosophy, as expressed in his 1915 book *New Image of the World*. Schoenmaekers argued that an inner visual construction of nature consisted of a balance between opposing forces, such as heat and cold, male and female, order and disorder, and that artists might represent this inner construction in abstract paintings by using only horizontal and vertical lines and primary colors.

Mondrian's later paintings are visual embodiments of both Schoenmaekers's theory and De Stijl's artistic ideas. In **COMPOSITION WITH YELLOW, RED, AND BLUE** (**FIG. 32–49**), for example, Mondrian uses the three primary colors (red, yellow, and blue), three neutrals (white, gray, and black), and a grid of horizontal and vertical lines in his search for the essence of higher beauty and the balance of forces. Mondrian's opposing lines and colors balance a harmony of opposites that he called a "dynamic equilibrium" and which he achieved by carefully plotting an arrangement of colors, shapes, and visual weights grouped asymmetrically around the edges of a canvas, with the center acting as a blank white fulcrum. Mondrian hoped that De Stijl would have applications in the real world by creating an entirely new visual environment for living, designed according to the rules of a "universal beauty" that, when perfectly balanced, would bring equilibrium and purity to the world. Mondrian said that he hoped to be the world's last artist, because, while art brought humanity to everyday life, when "universal beauty" infused all aspects of life, there would no longer be a need for art.

The architect and designer Gerrit Rietveld (1888–1964) applied Mondrian's principles of dynamic equilibrium and De Stijl's aesthetic theories to architecture and created one of the most important examples of the International Style (see "The International Style," page 1057). Interlocking gray and white planes of varying sizes, combined with horizontal and vertical accents in primary colors and black, create the radically asymmetrical exterior of the **SCHRÖDER HOUSE** in Utrecht (**FIG. 32–50**). Inside, the **"RED-BLUE" CHAIR** (**FIG. 32–51**) echoes this same arrangement. Sliding partitions allow modifications in the interior spaces used for sleeping, working, and entertaining. The patron of the house, Truus

32-48 • Vera Mukhina WORKER AND COLLECTIVE FARM WOMAN
Sculpture for the Soviet Pavilion, Paris Universal Exposition. 1937. Stainless steel, height approx. 78′ (23.8 m).

made the change willingly because they were already committed to the national cause, but others, who refused to change, were fired from public positions and lost public support.

The move to Socialist Realism was led by the Association of Artists of Revolutionary Russia (AKhRR), founded in 1922 to depict Russian workers, peasants, revolutionary activists, and the Red Army. AKhRR sought to document the history of the U.S.S.R. by promoting its leaders and goals. Artists were commissioned to create public paintings and sculptures as well as posters for mass distribution; their subjects were heroic or inspirational people and themes, and their style was an easily readable realism.

Vera Mukhina (1889–1953) was a member of AKhRR and is best known for her 78-foot-tall stainless-steel sculpture of a **WORKER AND COLLECTIVE FARM WOMAN** (**FIG. 32–48**) made for the Soviet Pavilion at the Paris Universal Exposition of 1937. The sculpture shows a powerfully built male factory worker and an equally powerful female farm laborer, with hammer and sickle held high in the air, the same two tools that appeared on the Soviet flag. The figures stand as equals, partners in their common cause, striding purposefully into the future with determined faces, their windblown clothing billowing behind them.

32-49 • Piet Mondrian
COMPOSITION WITH YELLOW, RED, AND BLUE
1927. Oil on canvas, 14⅞″ × 13¾″ (37.8 × 34.9 cm). The Menil Collection, Houston.
© 2012 Mondrian/Holtzman Trust c/o HCR International USA

32-50 • Gerrit Rietveld
SCHRÖDER HOUSE, UTRECHT
The Netherlands. 1925.

32-51 • Gerrit Rietveld INTERIOR, SCHRÖDER HOUSE, WITH "RED-BLUE" CHAIR
1925.

Schröder-Schröder, wanted a home that suggested an elegant austerity, with basic necessities sleekly integrated into a balanced and restrained whole.

THE BAUHAUS IN GERMANY

In Germany, the creators of the Bauhaus ("House of Building"), which had been founded by Walter Gropius (1883–1969) in Weimar in 1919, found the strict geometric shapes and lines of Purism (see FIG. 32-40) and De Stijl too rigid and argued that a true German architecture and design should emerge organically. Gropius brought together German architects, designers, and craftsmakers at the Bauhaus, where their collective creative energy could be harnessed to create an integrated system of design and production based on German traditions and styles. Gropius believed that he could revive the spirit of collaboration of the medieval building guilds (*Bauhütten*) that had erected Germany's cathedrals.

Although Gropius's "Bauhaus Manifesto" of 1919 declared that "the ultimate goal of all artistic activity is the building," the Bauhaus offered no formal training in architecture until 1927. Gropius only allowed his students to begin architectural training after they completed a mandatory foundation course and received full training in design and

32-52 • Walter Gropius BAUHAUS BUILDING, DESSAU
Anhalt, Germany. 1925–1926. View from northwest.

32-53 • Marianne Brandt COFFEE AND TEA SERVICE
1924. Silver and ebony, with Plexiglas cover for sugar bowl. Tray, 13″ × 20¼″ (33 × 51.5 cm). Bauhaus Archiv, Berlin.

crafts in the Bauhaus workshops. These included pottery, metalwork, textiles, stained glass, furniture, wood carving, and wall paintings. In 1922, Gropius also added a new emphasis on industrial design and the next year hired the Hungarian-born László Moholy-Nagy (1895–1946) to reorient the workshops toward more functional design suitable for mass production.

In 1925, when the Bauhaus moved to Dessau, Gropius designed its new building. Although the structure openly acknowledges its reinforced concrete, steel, and glass materials, there is also a balanced asymmetry to its three large cubic areas that was intended to convey the dynamism of modern life (**FIG. 32-52**). A glass-panel wall wraps around two sides of the workshop wing of the building to provide natural light for the workshops inside, while a parapet below demonstrates how modern engineering methods could create light, airy spaces. Both Moholy-Nagy and Gropius left the Bauhaus in 1928. The school eventually moved to Berlin in 1932, but lasted only one more year before the new German chancellor, Adolf Hitler, forced its closure (see "Suppression of the Avant-Garde in Nazi Germany," page 1056). Hitler opposed Modern art on two grounds. First, he believed it was cosmopolitan rather than nationalistic; second, he erroneously maintained that it was overly influenced by Jews.

Marianne Brandt's (1893–1983) elegant **COFFEE AND TEA SERVICE** (**FIG. 32-53**)—a prototype hand-crafted in silver for mass production in cheaper metals—is an example of the collaboration between design and industry at the Bauhaus. After the Bauhaus moved to Dessau, Brandt also designed lighting fixtures and table lamps for mass production, earning much-needed revenue for the school. After the departure of Moholy-Nagy and Gropius, Brandt took over the metal workshop for a year before she too left, in 1929. As a woman in the otherwise all-male metal workshop, Brandt made an exceptional contribution to the Bauhaus.

Although the Bauhaus claimed that women were admitted on an equal basis with men, Gropius opposed their education as architects and channeled them into what he considered the more gender-appropriate workshops of pottery and textiles. Berlin-born Anni Albers (b. Annelise Fleischmann, 1899–1994) arrived at the school in 1922 and married the Bauhaus graduate and professor Josef Albers (1888–1976) in 1925. Obliged to enter the textiles workshop rather than the painting studio, Anni Albers made "pictorial" weavings and wall hangings (**FIG. 32-54**) that were so innovative that they actually replaced paintings on the walls of several modern buildings. Her decentralized, rectilinear designs make reference to the aesthetics of De Stijl, but differ in their open

32-54 • Anni Albers WALL HANGING
1926. Silk, three-ply weave, 5′11⁵⁄₁₆″ × 3′11⁵⁄₈″ (1.83 × 1.22 m). Harvard Art Museums/Busch-Reisinger Museum, Association Fund.

In the 1930s, the avant-garde was increasingly disparaged by Hitler and the rising Nazi Party. This led to a concerted effort to suppress it. One of the principal targets was the Bauhaus. Through much of the 1920s, important artists such as Paul Klee, Vassily Kandinsky, Josef Albers, and Ludwig Mies van der Rohe taught classes there, but they struggled against an increasingly hostile and reactionary political climate. As early as 1924, conservatives accused the Bauhaus of being not only educationally unsound but also politically subversive. To avoid having the school shut down by the opposition, Gropius moved it to Dessau in 1925, at the invitation of Dessau's liberal mayor, but he left office soon after the relocation and his successors faced increasing political pressure to close the school as it was a prime center of Modernist practice. The Bauhaus moved again in 1932, this time to Berlin.

After Adolf Hitler came to power in 1933, the Nazi Party mounted an even more aggressive campaign against Modern art. In his youth Hitler had been a mediocre landscape painter, and he developed an intense hatred of the avant-garde. During the first year of his regime, the Bauhaus was forced to close permanently. A number of the artists, designers, and architects who had been on its faculty—including Albers, Gropius, and Mies—fled to the United States.

The Nazis also attacked German Expressionist artists, whose often-intense depictions of German politics and the economic crisis after the war criticized the state and whose frequent caricatures of German facial features and body types undermined Nazi attempts to redraw Germans as idealized Aryans. Expressionist and avant-garde art was removed from museums and confiscated, and artists were forbidden to buy paint or canvas and were subjected to public intimidation.

In 1937, the Nazi leadership organized an exhibition of what they termed "Degenerate Art" in an attempt to ridicule the banned Modern art and erase its makers. The Nazis described avant-garde Modernism as sick and degenerate, presenting the confiscated paintings and sculptures as specimens of pathology and scrawling slogans and derisive commentaries on the walls of the exhibition (**FIG. 32–55**). Ironically, in Munich as many as 2 million people viewed the four-month exhibition of 650 paintings, sculptures, prints, and books confiscated from German museums and artists, and another 1 million visitors saw it on its three-year tour of German cities.

Large numbers of confiscated works destined for destruction were actually looted by Nazi officials and sold in Switzerland in exchange for foreign currency. The ownership of much of the surviving art is still in question. Many artists fled to neighboring countries or the United States, but some, like Ernst Ludwig Kirchner, whose *Street, Berlin* (see FIG. 32–13) appeared in the "Degenerate Art" exhibition, were driven to suicide by their loss. Even the work of artists sympathetic to the Nazi position was not safe. The works of Emil Nolde (see FIG. 32–12), who joined the Nazi Party in 1932, were also confiscated.

32–55 • THE DADA WALL IN ROOM 3 OF THE "DEGENERATE ART" ("ENTARTETE KUNST") EXHIBITION
Munich. 1937. Art © Estate of George Grosz/Licensed by VAGA, New York, NY.

After World War I, increased communication among Modern architects led to the development of a common formal language, transcending national boundaries, which came to be known as the International Style. The first concentrated manifestation of the movement was in 1927 at the Deutscher Werkbund's Weissenhofsiedlung exhibition in Stuttgart, Germany, directed by Ludwig Mies van der Rohe (1886–1969), an architect who, like Gropius, was associated with the Bauhaus in Germany. The purpose of this semipermanent show was to present a range of model homes that used new technologies and made no reference to historical styles. The buildings featured flat roofs, plain walls, off-center openings, and rectilinear designs by Mies, Gropius, Le Corbusier, and others.

The term "International Style" gained currency as a result of a 1932 exhibition at the Museum of Modern Art in New York, "The International Style: Architecture Since 1922," organized by architectural historian Henry-Russell Hitchcock and architect and curator Philip Johnson. Hitchcock and Johnson identified three fundamental principles of the style.

The first was "the conception of architecture as volume rather than mass." The use of a structural skeleton of steel and ferroconcrete made it possible to eliminate loadbearing walls on both the exterior and the interior. As a result, buildings could be wrapped in skins of glass, metal, or masonry, creating the effect of enclosed space (volume) rather than dense material (mass). Interiors featured open, free-flowing plans providing maximum flexibility in the organization of space.

The second was "regularity rather than symmetry as the chief means of ordering design." Regular distribution of structural supports and the use of standard building parts promoted rectangular regularity rather than the balanced axial symmetry of Classical architecture. The avoidance of Classical balance also encouraged an asymmetrical disposition of the building's components, including doors and windows.

The third was the rejection of "arbitrary applied decoration." The new architecture depended on the intrinsic elegance of its materials and the formal arrangement of its elements to produce harmonious aesthetic effects. The most extreme International Style buildings would be unadorned glass boxs.

According to Hitchcock and Johnson, the International Style originated in the Netherlands (De Stijl), France (Purism), and Germany (Bauhaus). After the 1932, it spread to the United States. The conceptual clarity of the International Style allowed it to remain vital until the 1970s, especially in the United States, where many of its original European architects, such as Mies and Gropius, who had escaped Hitler and the rise of Nazism in Germany in the 1930s, practiced.

---

acknowledgment of the natural process of weaving. Albers's goal was "to let threads be articulate … and find a form for themselves to no other end than their own orchestration."

SURREALISM AND THE MIND

In France during the early 1930s, a group of artists and writers took a very different approach to Modernism in a revolt against logic and reason. Embracing irrational, disorderly, aberrant, and even violent social interventions, Surrealism emerged initially as an off-shoot of Dada born from the mind of poet André Breton (1896–1966). Breton trained in medicine and psychiatry and served in a neurological hospital during World War I where he used Freudian analysis on shell-shocked soldiers. By 1924, Breton, still drawn to the vagaries of the human mind, published the "Manifesto of Surrealism," reflecting Freud's conception of the human mind as a battleground where the irrational forces of the unconscious wage a constant war against the rational, orderly, and oppressive forces of the conscious. Breton sought to explore humanity's most base, irrational, and forbidden sexual desires, secret fantasies, and violent instincts by freeing the conscious mind from reason. As Breton wrote in 1934, "we still live under the rule of logic." To escape this restraint, he and other Surrealists developed strategies to liberate the unconscious using dream analysis, free association, automatic writing, word games, and hypnotic trances. Surrealists studied acts of "criminal madness" and the "female mind" in particular, believing the latter to be weaker and more irrational than the male mind. The only way to improve the war-sick society of the 1920s, Breton thought, was to discover the more intense "surreality" that transcended rational constraint.

AUTOMATISM Surrealist artists employed a variety of techniques, including **automatism**—releasing the subconscious to create the work of art without rational intervention in order to produce surprising new juxtapositions of imagery and forms. Max Ernst (1891–1976), a self-taught German artist who collaborated in Cologne Dada and later joined Breton's circle in Paris, developed the automatist technique of **frottage** in 1925. First he rubbed a pencil or crayon over a piece of paper placed on a textured surface and allowed the resulting image to stimulate his imagination, discovering within it fantastic creatures, plants, and landscapes that he articulated more clearly with additional drawing. In painting, Ernst called this new technique **grattage**, with which he scraped layers of paint over a canvas laid on a textured surface, and then "revealed" the imagery he saw in the paint with additional painting. THE HORDE (FIG. 32-56) of 1927 shows a nightmarish scene of monsters advancing against an unseen force. Surely the horrors of World War I that Ernst had experienced firsthand in the German army lie behind such frightening images.

UNEXPECTED JUXTAPOSITIONS The paintings of Salvador Dalí (1904–1989) include more recognizable figures and forms, but they also reveal the visual wonders of a subconscious mind run wild. Dalí trained at the San Fernando Academy of Fine Arts in Madrid, where he mastered the traditional methods of illusion-

32-56 • Max Ernst THE HORDE
1927. Oil on canvas, 44⅞" × 57½" (114 × 146.1 cm).
Stedelijk Museum, Amsterdam.

istic representation, and traveled to Paris in 1928, where he met the Surrealists. Dalí's contribution to Surrealist theory was the "paranoid-critical method," in which he cultivated the paranoid's ability to misread, mangle, and misconstrue ordinary appearances, thus liberating himself from the shackles of conventional rational thought. Then he painted what he had imagined.

Dalí's paintings focus on a few key themes: sexuality, violence, and putrefaction. In the **BIRTH OF LIQUID DESIRES** (**FIG. 32-57**), we see a large yellow **biomorphic** form (an organic shape resembling a living organism)–looking like a monster's face, a painter's palette, or a woman's body—that serves as the backdrop for four figures. A woman in white embraces a hermaphroditic figure who stands with one foot in a bowl that is being filled with liquid by a third figure, partially hidden, while a fourth figure enters a cavernous hole to the left. A thick black cloud above the scene poses a question: "Consign: to waste the total slate?" Dalí claimed that he simply painted what his paranoid-critical mind had conjured up in his nightmares. Dalí's images are thus, as Breton advocated, "the true process of thought, free from the exercise of reason and from any aesthetic or moral purpose." They defy rational interpretation although they trigger fear, anxiety, and even regression in our empathetic minds.

Dalí's strangely compelling art also draws on the Surrealist interest in unexpected juxtapositions of disparate realities. Surrealists argued that by juxtaposing several disparate ordinary objects in strange new contexts artists could create uncanny surrealities. One of the most disturbingly exquisite and mockingly humorous examples is **OBJECT (LUNCHEON IN FUR)** (**FIG. 32-58**), by the Swiss artist Meret Oppenheim (1913–1985). Oppenheim was one of the few women invited to participate in the Surrealist movement. Surrealists generally treated women as their muses or as objects of

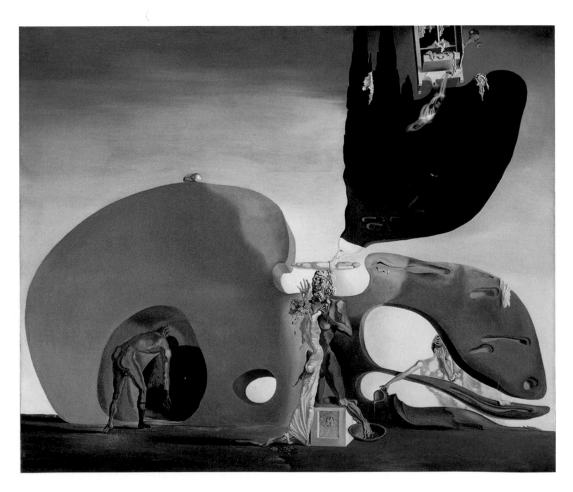

**32-57 • Salvador Dalí
BIRTH OF LIQUID DESIRES**
1931–1932. Oil and collage on canvas, 37⅞" × 44¼" (96.1 × 112.3 cm). The Solomon R. Guggenheim Foundation. Peggy Guggenheim Collection, Venice 1976 (76.2553 PG 100)

32-58 • Meret Oppenheim **OBJECT (LUNCHEON IN FUR)**

1936. Fur-covered cup, diameter 4⅜″ (10.9 cm); fur-covered saucer, diameter 9⅜″ (23.7 cm); fur-covered spoon, length 8″ (20.2 cm); overall height, 2⅞″ (7.3 cm). Museum of Modern Art, New York.

View the Closer Look for *Object* on myartslab.com

study, but not their equals: Picasso even claimed to have "given" Oppenheim the idea for this sculpture. *Object* consists of an actual cup, saucer, and spoon covered with the fur of a Chinese gazelle (chosen for its resemblance in texture to pubic hair). It transposes two objects (a tea setting and gazelle fur) from their ordinary reality, recontextualizes them in an irrational new surreality, and transforms them into an uncanny object that is simultaneously desirable and deeply disturbing.

BIOMORPHIC ABSTRACTION The Catalan artist Joan Miró (1893–1983) exhibited regularly with the Surrealists but never formally joined the movement. Miró's biomorphic abstraction is also intended to free the mind from rationality, but in a more benign manner. His **COMPOSITION** (**FIG. 32-59**) of 1933 is populated by curving biomorphic primal or mythic shapes that seem arranged by chance, emerging from the artist's mind uncensored, like doodles, to dance gleefully around the canvas. The Surrealists

32-59 • Joan Miró **COMPOSITION**

1933. Oil on canvas, 51¼″ × 63½″ (130.2 × 161.3 cm). Wadsworth Athenaeum, Hartford, Connecticut.

used the free association of doodling to relax the conscious mind so that images could bubble up from the unconscious. Miró reportedly first doodled on his canvases, then painted the revealed shapes and forms. His images do seem to take shape before our eyes, but their identity is always in flux. Miró was also fascinated by children's art, which he thought of as spontaneous and expressive and, although he was a well-trained artist himself, he said that he wished he could learn to paint with the freedom of a child.

UNIT ONE IN ENGLAND

In 1933, the English artists Barbara Hepworth (1903–1975), Henry Moore (1898–1986), and Paul Nash (1889–1946), along with the poet and critic Herbert Read (1893–1968), founded Unit One. Although short-lived, this group promoted the use of hand-crafted, Surrealist-influenced biomorphic forms in sculpture, brought new energy to British art in the 1930s, and exerted a lasting impact on British sculpture.

Hepworth studied at the Leeds School of Art. She punctuated her exquisitely crafted sculptures with holes so that air and light could pass through them. **FORMS IN ECHELON** (FIG. 32-60) consists of two biomorphic shapes carved in highly polished wood. Hepworth hoped that viewers would allow their eyes to play around with these organic forms, letting viewer imagination generate changing associations and meanings.

Moore also carved punctured sculptural abstractions, although his works were more obviously based on the human form. He also studied at the Leeds School of Art and then at the Royal College of Art in London. The African, Oceanic, and Pre-Columbian sculpture that he saw at the British Museum, however, had a more powerful impact on his developing aesthetic than his academic training. He felt that artists beyond the Western tradition showed a greater respect for the inherent qualities of materials such as stone or wood than their Western counterparts.

The reclining female nude is the dominant theme of Moore's art. The massive simplified body in **RECUMBENT FIGURE** (FIG. 32-61) refers to the *chacmool*, a reclining human form in Toltec and Maya art (see FIG. 13–14). Moore's sculptures also reveal his special sensitivity to the inherent qualities of his stone, which he sought out in remote quarries, always insisting that each of his works be labeled with the specific kind of stone he had used. While certain aspects of the human body are clearly described in this sculpture—the head, breasts, supporting elbow, and raised knee—other parts seem to flow together into an undulating mass suggestive of a hilly landscape. The cavity at the center inverts our expectations about the solid and void. In 1937, Moore wrote: "A hole can itself have as much shape-meaning as a solid mass."

MODERN ART IN THE AMERICAS BETWEEN THE WARS

A need for a national visual identity emerged in American art between the wars, but since the United States was a large, diverse nation with multiple "identities," attempts to consolidate the fiction of a single, essentially male, Anglo-Saxon national profile only heightened the visibility of the creative and experimental works of art by African Americans, immigrants, women, and others.

THE HARLEM RENAISSANCE

In the 1930s, hundreds of thousands of African Americans migrated from the rural, mostly agricultural American South to the urban, industrialized North to escape racial oppression and find greater social and economic opportunities. This Great Migration prompted the formation of the nationwide New Negro movement and the Harlem Renaissance in New York, which called for greater social and political activism among African Americans.

Harlem's wealthy middle-class African-American community produced some of the nation's most talented artists of the 1920s and 1930s, such as the jazz musician Duke Ellington, the novelist Jean Toomer, and the poet Langston Hughes. The movement's

32-60 • Barbara Hepworth FORMS IN ECHELON
1938. Wood, 42½″ × 23⅔″ × 28″ (108 × 60 × 71 cm). Tate, London. Presented by the artist 1964 © Bowness, Hepworth Estate.

Read the document related to Barbara Hepworth on myartslab.com

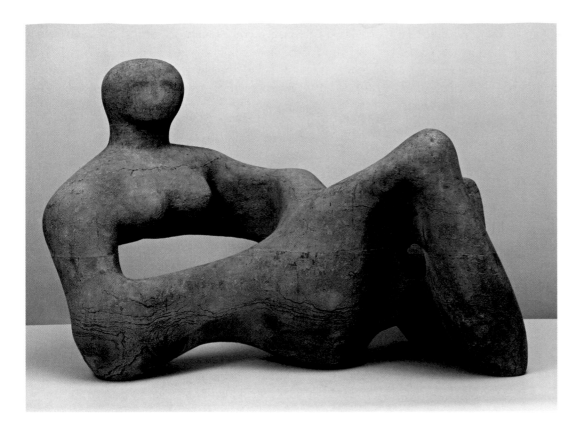

Moore created this work to fulfill a commission from Russian-born British architect Serge Chermayeff, who installed it on the terrace of his modern home on the Downs.

intellectual leader was Alain Locke (1886–1954), a critic and philosophy professor who argued that black artists should seek their artistic roots in the traditional arts of Africa rather than assimilate within mainstream American or European artistic traditions.

James Van Der Zee (1886–1983), a studio photographer who took carefully crafted portraits of the Harlem upper-middle classes, opened his studio in 1916, working both as a news reporter and a society photographer. **COUPLE WEARING RACCOON COATS**

WITH A CADILLAC (**FIG. 32-62**) captures a wealthy man and woman posing with their new car in 1932, at the height of the Great Depression. The photograph reveals the glamor of Harlem, then the center of African-American cultural life.

The painter Aaron Douglas (1898–1979), from Topeka, Kansas, moved to New York City in 1925. He developed a collaged silhouette style that owes much to African art and had a lasting impact on later African-American artists (see **FIG. 33-73**). He painted

32-62 • James Van Der Zee **COUPLE WEARING RACCOON COATS WITH A CADILLAC, TAKEN ON WEST 127TH STREET, HARLEM, NEW YORK**
1932. Gelatin-silver print.

In January 1937, as the Spanish Civil War between the Republicans and the Nationalists began to escalate, the Spanish artist Pablo Picasso, who was then living in Paris, was commissioned to make a large painting for the Spanish Pavilion of the 1938 Paris Exposition, a direct descendant of the nineteenth-century World's Fairs that resulted in the Crystal Palace and the Eiffel Tower. The 1938 Spanish Pavilion was the first Spanish national pavilion at any World's Fair.

As Picasso pondered what he might create for the exposition, on April 26, 1937, Nationalist-supporting German bombers attacked the town of Guernica in the Basque region of Spain, killing and wounding 1,600 civilians. The cold-blooded, calculating nature of the inhuman attack on Guernica shocked Europe. For more than three hours, 25 bombers dropped 100,000 pounds of explosives on the town, while more than 20 fighter planes strafed anyone caught in the streets trying to flee destroyed or burning buildings. Fires burned in Guernica for three days. By the end, one-third of the town's population was killed or wounded and 75 percent of its buildings had been destroyed (**FIG. 32–63**). The attack seemed to serve no military purpose, other than to allow Franco's Nationalist forces to terrorize civilian populations, but the true horror only emerged with the revelation that the German commander had planned the massacre merely as a "training mission" for the German air force. The horrified Picasso now had his subject for the Fair.

On May 1, 1 million protesters marched in Paris, and the following day Picasso made his first preliminary sketches for his visual response to this atrocity. Picasso had been trained in the traditions of academic painting, and he planned **GUERNICA** (**FIG. 32–64**) as an monumental history painting detailing the historic, and ignoble, events of the attack. He made several preliminary sketches (*esquisses*) to develop the composition, colors, during ten days of intensive planning, before moving on to canvas. He worked at the painting itself—changing figures, altering colors, and developing his themes—for another month.

Guernica is a complex painting, layered with meaning. Picasso rarely used specific or obvious symbolism in his art, preferring to let individual viewers interpret specific details themselves. What is beyond question,

32–63 • RUINS OF GUERNICA, SPAIN April 1937.

however, is that *Guernica* is a scene of brutality, chaos, terror, and suffering. Painted in black, white, and dark blue, the image resonates with anguish. It freezes figures in mid-movement in stark black and white as if caught by the flashbulb of a reporter's camera.

32–64 • Pablo Picasso GUERNICA 1937. Oil on canvas, 11'6" × 25'8" (3.5 × 7.8 m). Museo Nacional Centro de Arte Reina Sofía, Madrid. On permanent loan from the Museo del Prado, Madrid.

Many of the collected subjects are clearly identifiable: an expressionistically reconfigured head of a bull in the upper left, a screeching wounded horse in the center, broken human forms scattered across the expanse, a giant light bulb suggesting an all-seeing eye at the top, a lamp below it, and smoke and fire visible beyond the destroyed room in which the disjointed action takes place. These images have inspired a variety of interpretations. Some have seen in the bull and horse, symbols of Nationalist and Republican forces, variously identified with one or the other. The light bulb, javelin, dagger, lamp, and bird have also been assigned specific meanings. Picasso, however, refused to acknowledge any particular significance to any of these seeming symbols. *Guernica*, he claimed, is about the massacred victims of this atrocity—beyond that, its meaning remains fluid.

Guernica appeared in the Spanish Pavilion along with other works of art supporting the Republican cause, including works by painter Joan Miró, sculptor Alexander Calder, filmmaker Luis Buñuel, and others. Because Picasso refused to allow *Guernica* to be shown in Spain under the regime of Nationalist leader General Franco, it hung in the Museum of Modern Art in New York for years, finally traveling to Spain for installation in the Reina Sofía in Madrid only in 1981, six years after Franco's death. Since 1985, a tapestry copy of *Guernica* has hung as a powerful reminder of the brutal human cost of unrestrained warfare in the headquarters of the United Nations in New York.

32-65 • Aaron Douglas ASPECTS OF NEGRO LIFE: FROM SLAVERY THROUGH RECONSTRUCTION
1934. Oil on canvas, 5′ × 11′7″ (1.5 × 3.5 m). Schomburg Center for Research in Black Culture, New York Public Library. Art © Heirs of Aaron Douglas/Licensed by VAGA, New York, NY

ASPECTS OF NEGRO LIFE: FROM SLAVERY THROUGH RECONSTRUCTION (**FIG. 32-65**) for the Harlem branch of the New York Public Library under the sponsorship of the Depression-era Public Works of Art Project. To the right, slaves are celebrating the 1863 Emancipation Proclamation of 1863, from which radiate concentric circles of light. At the center, an orator gestures dramatically, pointing to the United States Capitol in the background, as if to urge all African Americans, some of whom are still picking cotton in the foreground, to exercise their right to vote. To the left, Union soldiers leave the South after Reconstruction, while Ku Klux Klan members, hooded and on horseback, charge in, reminding viewers that the fight for civil rights has only just begun.

The career of sculptor Augusta Savage (1892–1962) reflects the myriad difficulties faced by African Americans in the art world. Savage studied at Cooper Union in New York, but her 1923 application to study in Europe was turned down because of her race. In a letter of protest, she wrote: "Democracy is a strange thing. My brother was good enough to be accepted in one of the regiments that saw service in France during the war, but it seems his sister is not good enough to be a guest of the country for which he fought." Finally, in 1930, Savage was able to study in Paris. On her return to the United States, she sculpted portraits of several African-American leaders, including Marcus Garvey and W.E.B.

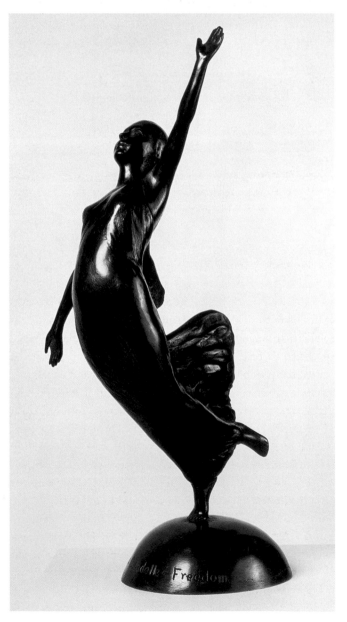

32-66 • Augusta Savage LA CITADELLE: FREEDOM
1930. Bronze, 14½″ × 7″ × 6″ (35.6 × 17.8 × 15.2 cm). Howard University Gallery of Art, Washington, DC.

32-67 • Jacob Lawrence **THE MIGRATION SERIES, PANEL NO. 1: DURING WORLD WAR I THERE WAS A GREAT MIGRATION NORTH BY SOUTHERN AFRICAN AMERICANS**
1940–1941. Tempera on masonite, 12″ × 18″ (30.5 × 45.7 cm). The Phillips Collection, Washington, DC.

DuBois. Inspired by the story of the Haitian Revolution in 1791 following the Slave Revolt (see FIG. 30-39), she portrayed a female figure of freedom in **LA CITADELLE: FREEDOM** (**FIG. 32-66**), raising her hand to the sky and balancing on the toes of one foot while she flies through the air. La Citadelle was the castle residence of one of Haiti's first leaders of African heritage. For Savage, it represented the possibility and promise of freedom and equality.

Savage established a small private art school in Harlem and received Federal funds under the Works Progress Administration (see "Federal Patronage for American Art During the Depression," page 1066) to transform it into the Harlem Community Art Center. Hundreds of these centers were eventually established all over the country, but Savage's became an unofficial salon for Harlem artists, poets, composers, dancers, and historians.

One of the best-known artists to emerge from the Harlem Community Art Center was Jacob Lawrence (1917–2000). Lawrence's early works often depict African-American history in several series of small narrative paintings, each accompanied by a text. His themes include the history of Harlem and the lives of Haitian revolutionary leader Toussaint L'Ouverture and American abolitionist John Brown. Lawrence created his most expansive

series in 1940–1941. Entitled **THE MIGRATION SERIES**, 60 panels chronicle the Great Migration, a journey that had brought Lawrence's own parents from South Carolina to Atlantic City, New Jersey. In the first panel (**FIG. 32-67**), African-American migrants stream through the doors of a Southern train station on their way to Chicago, New York, or St. Louis. Lawrence's boldly abstracted silhouette style, with its flat bright shapes and colors, draws consciously and directly—like that of Douglas—on African visual sources. Lawrence later illustrated books by Harlem Renaissance authors.

RURAL AMERICA

In the 1930s, other artists, known collectively as the Regionalists, developed Midwestern themes. In 1931, at the height of the Depression, Grant Wood (1891–1942), who later taught at the University of Iowa, painted **AMERICAN GOTHIC** (**FIG. 32-69**), which was purchased by the Art Institute of Chicago and established Wood's national fame. This picture embodied all that was good and bad about the heartland in the 1930s. Wood portrays an aging father standing with his unmarried daughter in front of their Gothic Revival framed house. Even for the time their clothes are

In the early 1930s, during the Great Depression, President Franklin D. Roosevelt's New Deal established a series of programs to provide relief for the unemployed and to revive the nation's economy, including several initiatives to create work for American artists. The 1933 Public Works of Art Project (PWAP) lasted only five months but supplied employment to 4,000 artists, who produced more than 15,000 works. The Treasury Department established a Section of Painting and Sculpture in October 1934, which survived until 1943, commissioning murals and sculptures for public buildings. The Federal Art Project (FAP) of the Works Progress Administration (WPA), which ran from 1935 to 1943, succeeded the PWAP and was the most important work-relief agency of the Depression era. By 1943, it had employed more than 6 million workers in programs that included, in addition to the FAP, the Federal Theater Project and the Federal Writers' Project. About 10,000 artists participated in the FAP, producing a staggering 108,000 paintings, 18,000 sculptures, 2,500 murals, and thousands of prints, photographs, and posters, all of which became public property. Many of the murals and sculptures, commissioned for public buildings such as train stations, schools, hospitals, and post offices, survive today, but most easel paintings were later sold as "plumber's canvas" and destroyed.

To build public support for Federal assistance in rural America, the Resettlement Agency (RA) and Farm Security Administration (FSA) hired photographers to document the effects of the Depression across the country in photographs available to this day, copyright-free, to any newspaper, magazine, or publisher. San Francisco-based Dorothea Lange (1895–1965), an RA/FSA photographer between 1935 and 1939, documented the plight of migrant farm laborers who fled the Dust Bowl conditions of the Great Plains and then flooded California looking for work.

MIGRANT MOTHER, NIPOMO, CALIFORNIA (FIG. 32–68) shows Florence Owens Thompson, a 32-year-old mother of seven children, a representative of the poverty suffered by thousands of migrant workers in California. Lange carefully constructed her photograph to tug at the heartstrings. She zooms in very close to the subject focusing on the mother's worn expression and apparent resolve. The composition may remind viewers of the images of the Virgin Mary holding the Child Jesus (see FIG. 21–7), or perhaps sorrowful scenes in which she contemplates his loss (see FIG. 21–9). Lange chose to eliminate from this photograph the makeshift tent in which the family is camped, the dirty dishes on a battered trunk, trash strewn around the campsite, and, most significant, Thompson's teenage daughter—all documented in her other photographs of the same scene. Lange decided to focus here on the purity and moral worth of her subject, for whom she sought Federal aid; she could not allude to the fact that Thompson had been a teenage mother, or even that she was Cherokee. Migrant Mother (then unidentified by name) became the "poster child" of the Great Depression, and her powerfully sad, distant gaze still resonates with audiences today, demonstrating the propaganda power of the visual image.

During the Depression, the FAP paid a generous average salary of about $20 a week (a salesclerk at Woolworth's earned only about $11) for painters and sculptors to devote themselves full time to art. New York City's painters, in particular, developed a group identity, meeting in the bars and coffeehouses of Greenwich Village to discuss art. The FAP thus provided the financial grounds on which New York artists built a sense of community—a community that would produce the Abstract Expressionists, and that allowed New York to supersede Paris as the center of the world of Modern art.

32-68 • Dorothea Lange MIGRANT MOTHER, NIPOMO, CALIFORNIA

February 1936. Gelatin-silver print. Library of Congress, Washington, DC.

In 1960, Lange described the experience of taking this photograph: "I saw and approached the hungry and desperate mother, as if drawn by a magnet. I do not remember how I explained my presence or my camera to her, but I do remember she asked me no questions. I made five exposures, working closer and closer from the same direction. I did not ask her name or her history. She told me her age, that she was thirty-two. She said that they had been living on frozen vegetables from the surrounding fields, and birds that the children killed. She had just sold the tires from her car to buy food. There she sat in that lean-to tent with her children huddled around her, and seemed to know that my pictures might help her, and so she helped me. There was a sort of equality about it. (*Popular Photography*, Feb. 1960)

32-69 • Grant Wood AMERICAN GOTHIC
1930. Oil on beaverboard, 29⅞″ × 24⅞″ (74.3 × 62.4 cm). The
Art Institute of Chicago. Friends of American Art Collection, 1930.934.
Art © Figge Art Museum, successors to the Estate of Nan Wood
Graham/Licensed by VAGA, New York, NY

CANADA

In the nineteenth century, Canadian artists, like their counterparts in the United States, began to assert independence from European art by painting Canada's great untamed wilderness. A number of Canadians, however, used the academic realism they learned in Paris to paint figurative subjects, while others painted the Canadian landscape through the lens of Impressionism.

LANDSCAPE AND IDENTITY In the early 1910s, a young group of Toronto artists, many of whom worked for the same commercial art firm, began to sketch together, adopting the rugged landscape of the Canadian north as an expression of national identity.

A key figure in this movement was Tom Thomson (1877–1917), who, as of 1912, spent the warm months of each year in Algonquin Provincial Park, a large forest reserve 180 miles north of Toronto. He made numerous small, swiftly painted, oil-on-board sketches as the basis for the full-size paintings that he executed in his studio during the winter. A sketch made in the spring of 1916 led to **THE JACK PINE** (**FIG. 32-70**). This tightly organized composition features a stylized pine tree rising from a rocky foreground and silhouetted against a luminous background of lake and sky,

old-fashioned. Wood's dentist and his sister Nan—wearing a home-made ricrac-edged apron and Wood's mother's cameo—posed for the painting; the building was modeled on an actual, modest small-town home in Eldon, Iowa. The daughter's long sad face echoes her father's—she is unmarried and likely to stay that way. In 1931, husbands were hard to come by in the Midwest because many young men had fled the farms for jobs in Chicago. With its tightly painted descriptive detail, this painting is a homage to the Flemish Renaissance painters that Wood admired.

32-70 • Tom Thomson THE JACK PINE
1916–1917. Oil on canvas, 49⅞″ × 54½″ (127.9 × 139.8 cm).
National Gallery of Canada, Ottawa, Ontario. Purchase, 1918

horizontally divided by cold blue hills. The hauntingly beautiful painting's reverential mood—suggesting a divine presence in the lonely northern landscape—has made it an icon of Canadian national art.

NATIVE AMERICAN INFLUENCE Born in Victoria, British Columbia, the West Coast artist Emily Carr (1871–1945) studied art in San Francisco, England, and Paris. On a 1907 trip to Alaska she encountered the monumental carved poles of Northwest Coast Native peoples and resolved to document these "real art treasures of a passing race." Over the next 23 years, Carr visited more than 30 sites across British Columbia, making drawings and watercolors as a basis for oil paintings. After a commercially unsuccessful exhibition of her Native subjects, Carr returned to Victoria in 1913, opened a boarding house, and painted very little for the next 15 years. In 1927, however, she was invited to participate in an exhibition of West Coast art at the National Gallery of Canada. On her trip east for the show's opening, Carr met members of the Group of Seven, which had been established in 1920 by some of Tom Thomson's former colleagues. They rekindled her interest in painting.

With the Group of Seven, Carr developed a dramatic and powerfully sculptural style full of dark, brooding energy. **BIG RAVEN** (**FIG. 32-71**), painted in 1931 from a 1912 watercolor, shows an abandoned village in the Queen Charlotte Islands where Carr found a carved raven on a pole, the surviving member of a pair that originally marked a mortuary house. In her autobiography Carr described the raven as "old and rotting," but in the painting she shows it as strong and majestic, thrusting dynamically above the swirling vegetation, a symbol of enduring spiritual power and national pride.

MEXICO

The Mexican Revolution of 1910 overthrew the 35-year dictatorship of General Porfirio Díaz and inititated ten years of political instability. In 1920, reformist president Álvaro Obregón restored political order, and the leaders of his new government—as in the U.S.S.R.—engaged artists in the service of the people and state. Several Mexican artists received government commissions to decorate public buildings with murals celebrating the history, life, and work of the Mexican people. These artists painted in a naturalistic style because the new government believed abstract art was incomprehensible to the public at large.

Diego Rivera (1886–1957) was prominent in the Mexican mural movement that developed from these commissions. He enrolled in Mexico City's Academia de San Carlos at age 11, and from 1911 to 1919, he lived in Paris where he met Picasso and David Siqueiros (1896–1974), another Mexican muralist. Both Rivera and Siqueiros sought to create a revolutionary art in the service of the people in their public murals. In 1920–1921, Rivera traveled to Italy to study Renaissance frescoes, and he also visited ancient Mexican sites to study indigenous mural paintings. In 1945,

32–72 • Diego Rivera
**THE GREAT CITY
OF TENOCHTITLAN
(DETAIL)**
Mural in patio corridor,
National Palace, Mexico
City. 1945. Fresco, 16′1¾″ ×
31′10¼″ (4.92 × 9.71 m).

Watch a video
about Diego Rivera's
fresco technique
on myartslab.com

he painted **THE GREAT CITY OF TENOCH-
TITLAN** (**FIG. 32-72**) as part of a mural cycle
that used stylized forms and brilliant local
colors to portray the history of Mexico in the
National Palace in Mexico City. Rivera also
painted murals in the United States.

The art of Frida Kahlo (1907–1954) is
more personal. André Breton claimed Kahlo
as a natural Surrealist, although she herself
said: "I never painted dreams. I painted my
own reality." That reality included her mixed
heritage, born of a German father and Mexican mother. In a double self-portrait—**THE
TWO FRIDAS** (**FIG. 32-73**)—Kahlo presents
an identity split into two ethnic selves: the
European one, in a Victorian dress; and the
Mexican one, wearing traditional Mexican
clothing. The painting also reflects her stormy
relationship with Diego Rivera, whom she
married in 1929 but was divorcing in 1939

32-73 • Frida Kahlo THE TWO FRIDAS
1939. Oil on canvas, 5′8½″ × 5′8½″ (1.74 ×
1.74 m). Museo de Arte Moderno, Instituto
Nacional de Bellas Artes, Mexico City.

32-74 • Tarsila do Amaral ABAPORÚ (THE ONE WHO EATS)
1928. Oil on canvas, 34" × 29" (86.4 × 73.7 cm). Museo de Arte Latinoamericano, Buenos Aires. Courtesy of Guilherme Augusto do Amaral/Malba-Coleccion Constantini, Buenos Aires.

while painting this picture. She told an art historian at the time that the Mexican image was the Frida whom Diego loved, and the European image was the Frida he did not. The two Fridas join hands and the artery running between them begins at a miniature portrait of Rivera as a boy held by the Mexican Frida, travels through the exposed hearts of both Fridas, and ends in the lap of the Europeanized Frida, who attempts without success to stem the flow of blood. Kahlo had suffered a broken pelvis in an accident at age 17, and she endured a lifetime of surgical interventions. This work alludes to her constant pain, as well as to the Aztec custom of human sacrifice by heart removal.

BRAZIL

Elsewhere in Latin America, art was often dominated by the academic tradition in the nineteenth century. Several nations had thriving academies and large art communities; artists traveled in significant numbers to study in Paris. By 1914, artists in many Latin American countries adopted their own versions of Impressionism to paint national themes. After the war, artists who studied abroad also brought home ideas drawn from Modern art and the European avant-garde which they translated into a specifically Latin American vision. For instance, in 1922, as Brazil marked the centenary of

its independence from Portugal, the avant-garde in São Paulo celebrated with Modern Art Week, an event Brazilian artists used to declare their artistic independence from Europe. Modern Art Week brought avant-garde poets, dancers, and musicians as well as visual artists to São Paulo and took on a distinctly confrontational character. Poets derided their elders in poetry, dancers enacted modern versions of traditional dances, and composer Hector Villa-Lobos (1887–1959) appeared on stage in a bathrobe and slippers to play new music based on Afro-Brazilian rhythms.

In 1928, the São Paulo poet Oswald de Andrade, one of Modern Art Week's organizers, wrote the *Anthropophagic Manifesto* proposing a tongue-in-cheek, if radical, solution to Brazil's seeming dependence on European culture. He suggested that Brazilians imitate the ancient Brazilians' response to Portuguese explorers arriving on their shore—eat them. He mockingly described this relationship as anthropophagic or cannibalistic and proposed that Brazilians gobble up European culture, digest it, let it strengthen their Brazilianness, and then get rid of it.

The painter who most closely embodies this irreverent attitude is Tarsila do Amaral (1887–1974), a daughter of the coffee-planting aristocracy who studied in Europe with Fernand Léger (see FIG.

32-75 • Amelia Peláez MARPACÍFICO (HIBISCUS)
1943. Oil on canvas, 45½" × 35" (115.6 × 88.9 cm). Art Museum of the Americas, Washington, DC. Gift of IBM

32-21), among others. Her painting **ABAPORÚ (THE ONE WHO EATS)** (**FIG. 32-74**) shows an appreciation of the art of Léger and Brancusi (see FIGS. 32-21, 32-28), which Tarsila collected. But she also inserted several "tropical" clichés—the abstracted forms of a cactus and a lemon-slice sun. The subject is Andrade's irreverent cannibal, sitting in a caricatured Brazilian landscape, as if to say: If Brazilians are caricatured abroad as cannibals, then let us act like cannibals. As Andrade wrote in one of his manifestos: "Carnival in Rio is the religious outpouring of our race. Richard Wagner yields to the samba. Barbaric but ours. We have a dual heritage: The jungle and the school."

CUBA

Cuba's 1920s avant-garde was one of the most interdisciplinary, consisting of anthropologists, poets, composers, and even a few scientists, who gathered in Havana and called themselves "The Minority." They issued a manifesto in 1927 repudiating government corruption, "Yankee imperialism," and dictatorship on any continent. "Minority" artists, they urged, should pursue a new, popular, Modern art rooted in Cuban soil.

Amelia Peláez (1896–1968) left Cuba for Paris shortly after this manifesto was issued. When she returned home, she joined the anthropologist Lydia Cabrera to study Cuban popular and folk arts. Her paintings focus on the woman's realm—the domestic interior—and national identity, as in **MARPACÍFICO (HIBISCUS)** (**FIG. 32-75**). Her visual language is Cubist, as seen in the flattened overlapping forms and compressed pictorial space, but it shows recognizable objects—a mirror, a tabletop, and local hibiscus flowers—whose heavy black outlines and pure color reflected the flat, fan-shaped stained-glass windows that decorate many Cuban homes.

POSTWAR ART IN EUROPE AND THE AMERICAS

The horrors of World War II surpassed even those of World War I. The human loss was almost too profound and grotesque to comprehend. Between loss of life in action, those killed in work camps and death camps (concentration camps), those lost to starvation, and those lost in the bombing of civilian targets, more than 30 million people died and a further estimated 40 million people were displaced. The unimaginable horror of the concentration camps and the awful impact of the dropping of nuclear bombs shook humanity to its core. Winston Churchill described the extent of the catastrophe: "What is Europe now? A rubble heap, a charnel house, a breeding ground of pestilence and hate."

FIGURAL RESPONSES AND *ART INFORMEL* IN EUROPE

Most European artists in the immediate postwar period tried to use their art to come to terms with what they had experienced, many debating about how best to do this. Some worked figuratively while others painted abstractions.

In England, Francis Bacon (1909–1992) captured in his canvases the horrors that haunted him. Bacon was self-taught and produced very few pictures until the 1940s. He served as an air-raid warden during World War II and saw the bloody impact of the bombing of civilians in London firsthand. In **HEAD SURROUNDED BY SIDES OF BEEF** (**FIG. 32-76**), Bacon presents the imperious Pope Innocent X, reduced to an anguished and insubstantial man, howling in a black void, as two bloody sides of beef enclose him in a claustrophobic box that contains his frightful screams and amplifies his terror. The painting was directly inspired by Diego Velázquez's 1650 portrait of Pope Innocent X and by Rembrandt's paintings of dripping meat. Bacon wrote of his art: "I hope to make the best human cry in painting … to remake the violence of reality itself."

One of the most distinctive postwar European art movements was *Art Informel* ("formless art"), which was also called *tachisme*

32-76 • Francis Bacon HEAD SURROUNDED BY SIDES OF BEEF 1954. Oil on canvas, 50¾″ × 48″ (129 × 122 cm). The Art Institute of Chicago. Harriott A. Fox Fund (1956.1201)

32-77 • Wols (Wolfgang Schulze) PAINTING
1944–1945. Oil on canvas, 31⅞″ × 32″ (81 × 81.1 cm). Museum of Modern Art, New York. Gift of D. and J. de Menil Fund (29.1956)

and self-discovery to his art. He studied at the National Academy in Havana, moved to Paris, where he knew both Picasso and the Surrealists, and was forced to return to Cuba when the Nazis invaded France. He found himself on the same ship as the Surrealist leader André Breton; Lam disembarked at Havana, while Breton traveled on to New York. Once home, Lam explored his African-Cuban heritage in the company of anthropologist Lydia Cabrera and novelist Alejo Carpentier, and his work from the late 1940s reflects African-Cuban art, the polytheistic spirituality imagery of *santería*. The jagged, semi-abstracted forms of **ZAMBE-ZIA, ZAMBEZIA** (**FIG. 32-78**) recall European Modernism, but their source is in *santería* religious ritual; the central figure is a composite *santería* deity. "Zambezia" was the early colonial name for Zimbabwe in southeastern Africa, at this time a British colonial possession known as Rhodesia. Much earlier, Zambezia had been a source for slaves who were brought to Cuba. Lam said of his art: "I wanted with all my heart to paint the drama of my country … . In this way I could act as a Trojan horse spewing forth hallucinating figures with the power to surprise, to disturb the dreams of the exploiters."

In Buenos Aires, two groups of avant-garde artists formed immediately after the war—Arte Concreto-Invención and Madí, even though Argentina's fascist leader Juan Perón (1895–1974)

(*tache* is French for "spot" or "stain"). *Art Informel* was promoted by French critic Michel Tapié (1909–1987) who suggested that art should express an authentic concept of postwar humanity through simple, honest marks.

The informal leader of *Art Informel* was Wolfgang Schulze, called Wols (1913–1951), who lived through the dislocation and devastation experienced by millions in Europe in the 1930s and 1940s. Born in Germany, Wols left his homeland in protest when Hitler came to power, first settling in Paris, where he worked as a photographer for *Vogue* and *Harper's Bazaar.* When the Germans occupied France, he fled to Spain but was arrested, stripped of his passport, and deported to spend the rest of the war as a stateless person in a refugee camp in southern France. When the war ended, Wols returned to Paris and resumed painting, producing passionate pictures by applying paint with whatever came to hand, scraping his heavy surfaces with a knife and allowing the paint to drip and run. **PAINTING** (**FIG. 32-77**) represents a disease-ridden and violent world in which the semiabstracted forms resemble either infected cells or dark, muddy bacterial growths. Wols was temporarily supported by the French philosopher and novelist Jean-Paul Sartre, but died of food poisoning in 1951.

EXPERIMENTS IN LATIN AMERICA

In Cuba, the abstract and Surrealist paintings of Wifredo Lam (1902–1980) embody the violence and anguish of his country's struggle against colonialism. Lam was of mixed Chinese, Spanish, and African heritage and brought issues of identity

32-78 • Wifredo Lam ZAMBEZIA, ZAMBEZIA
1950. Oil on canvas, 49⅝″ × 43⅝″ (125 × 110 cm). Solomon R. Guggenheim Museum, New York. Gift, Mr. Joseph Cantor, 1974 (74.2095)

32-79 • Joaquín Torres-García ABSTRACT ART IN FIVE TONES AND COMPLEMENTARIES 1943. Oil on board mounted on panel, 20½″ × 26⅝″ (52.1 × 67 cm). Albright Knox Art Gallery, Buffalo, NY. Gift of Mr. and Mrs. Armand J. Castellani, 1979

disliked Modern art profoundly. The best-known Latin American artist of the time was the Uruguayan Joaquín Torres-García (1874–1949), who established the "School of the South" in Montevideo, Uruguay's capital. Torres-García had spent 43 years in Europe before returning home after the war, but his art was deeply rooted in the indigenous art of the Inca (e.g., see FIG. 27–9), believing ancient Uruguayan culture to be a fertile soil in which to grow a new national and cultural visual identity. In **ABSTRACT ART IN FIVE TONES AND COMPLEMENTARIES** (FIG. 32–79), Torres-García fuses European ideas of abstraction and Modernism with Inca imagery and masonry patterns in a style that he named Constructive Universalism.

ABSTRACT EXPRESSIONISM IN NEW YORK

The United States recovered from World War II more quickly than Europe. Its territory was spared the ravages of war and the trauma it felt was limited to those Americans who saw action in Europe or the Pacific, to European refugees to the United States, and to Japanese-American citizens who had been interned. While the European art world took decades to recover and Paris lost its artistic vibrancy, New York, as the art historian Serge Guilbault wrote, "Stole the Idea of Modern Art."

THE CENTER SHIFTS TO NEW YORK Many leading European artists and writers escaped to the United States during World War II. By 1941, André Breton, Salvador Dalí, Fernand Léger,

Piet Mondrian, and Max Ernst were all living in New York, where they altered the character and artistic concerns of the art scene. American artists were most deeply affected by the work of the European Surrealist artists in New York, but ultimately Abstract Expressionist artists developed their own uniquely American artistic identities by drawing from, but radically reimagining, European and American Modernism.

The term "Abstract Expressionism" describes the art of a fairly wide range of artists in New York in the 1940s and early 1950s. It was not a formally organized movement but rather a loosely affiliated group of artists who worked in the city and were bound by a common purpose: to express their profound social alienation after World War II and to make new art that was both moral and universal.

The influential **Formalist** (concerning form over content) critic Clement Greenberg urged the Abstract Expressionists to consider their paintings "autonomous" and completely self-referential objects. The best paintings, he argued, made no reference to the outside world, but had their own internal narrative and order. Abstract Expressionism was also deeply influenced by the theories of the Swiss psychoanalyst Carl Jung (1875–1961), who described a collective unconscious of universal archetypes shared by all humans. The Abstract Expressionists aspired to create heroic and sublime worlds in paint inhabited by universal symbolic forms. As the 1940s progressed, the symbolic content of their paintings became increasingly personal and abstract. Some sought in "primitive," mythic imagery and archaic, archetypal, and primal

**32-80 • Arshile Gorky
GARDEN IN SOCHI**
c. 1943. Oil on canvas, 31″ ×
39″ (78.7 × 99.1 cm). Museum
of Modern Art, New York.
Acquired through the Lillie P. Bliss
Bequest (492.1969)

symbolism a connection among all people through the collective unconscious; several used biomorphic forms or developed an individual symbolic language in their paintings; all made passionate and expressive statements on large canvases. The Abstract Expressionists felt destined to make a major mark on art history, convinced that they had the power to transform the world with their art.

Though their paintings project a personal vision, the Abstract Expressionists shared a commitment to four major projects: (1) an interest in the tradition of painting, but a desire to rebel against it and to recalibrate the ideas of European Modernism; (2) a desire to treat the act of painting on canvas as a self-contained expressive exercise; (3) a mining of Jungian visual archetypes to communicate universal ideas in paint; and, (4) the ambition to paint sublime art on a heroic scale. Critic Harold Rosenberg divided Abstract Expressionism into two major categories—"**Action painting**" and "Color Field painting"—but the Abstract Expressionists disliked these terms, arguing, with good reason, that they were too simplistic. As general typologies, however, the terms remain useful.

THE FORMATIVE PHASE Arshile Gorky (1904–1948) was older than the other Abstract Expressionists, but his ideas and images resonated deeply with them. Gorky was born in Armenia and fled with surviving family members to the United States in 1920 during the Ottoman Turkish genocide of the Armenian people. His mother died soon after her escape, leaving Gorky mostly alone. The trauma of this loss fills his paintings. He threads

idyllic images of his childhood home and garden through Surrealist and Jungian ideas about the collective unconscious to create visual memorials to the people and places he has lost.

A series of paintings in the early 1940s called **GARDEN IN SOCHI** (**FIG. 32-80**) transform Gorky's memories of his father's garden in Khorkom, Armenia, into a mythical dreamscape. According to the artist, this garden was known locally as the Garden of Wish Fulfillment because it contained both a rock upon which village women, his mother included, rubbed their bared breasts when making a wish, as well as a "Holy Tree" to which people tied strips of clothing. In this painting, the mythical garden floats on a dense white ground. Forms, shapes, and colors coalesce into a bare-breasted woman to the left, the Holy Tree to the center, strips of clothing, and "the beautiful Armenian slippers" that Gorky and his father wore in Khorkom. The painting suggests vital life forces, an ancient connection to the earth, and Gorky's vision of a lost world that exists only in his memory.

JACKSON POLLOCK AND ACTION PAINTING Jackson Pollock (1912–1956) is the most famous Abstract Expressionist painter. Born in Wyoming. Pollock moved to New York in 1930. By all accounts, he was self-destructive from an early age, developing a drinking problem by age 16, reading Jung by 22, institutionalized for psychiatric problems and alcohol abuse at 26. Friends described two Pollocks—one shy and sober, the other obnoxious and drunk. When he entered Jungian psychotherapy in 1939,

32-81 • Jackson Pollock AUTUMN RHYTHM (NUMBER 30)
1950. Oil on canvas, 8'9" × 17'3" (2.66 × 5.25 m). Metropolitan Museum of Art, New York. George A. Hearn Fund, 1957 (57.92)

Read the document related to Jackson Pollock on myartslab.com

he already knew Jung's theory that visual images had the ability to tap into the primordial consciousness of viewers. Pollock remained free of alcohol for most of the 1940s, the period when he was supported emotionally by Lee Krasner. This was when he created his most celebrated works.

Pollock's first solo exhibition was in 1943 at Peggy Guggenheim's gallery. He was propelled into stardom by the critic Clement Greenberg, who, by 1947, described Pollock as "the most powerful painter in North America." Pollock pushed beyond the Surrealist strategy of automatic painting by placing unstretched, raw canvas on the floor, and throwing, dripping, and dribbling paint onto it to create abstract networks of overlapping lines as it fell. In 1950, *Time* magazine described Pollock as "Jack the Dripper," and two years later, Rosenberg coined the term "Action painting" for Pollock's painting process in an essay, "The American Action Painters." Rosenberg described the development and purpose of Action painting as follows: "At a certain moment the canvas began to appear to one American painter after another as an arena in which to act—rather than a space in which to reproduce, redesign, analyze, or 'express' an object, actual or imagined."

In 1950, while Pollock painted **AUTUMN RHYTHM (NUMBER 30)** (**FIG. 32-81**), Hans Namuth filmed him (**FIG. 32-82**). Pollock worked in a renovated barn, where he could reach into the laid canvas from all four sides. The German expatriate artist Hans Hofmann (1880–1966) had poured and dripped paint before Pollock, but Pollock's unrestrained gestures transformed the idea of painting itself by moving around and within the canvas, dripping and scoring commercial-grade enamel paint (rather than specialist artist's paint) onto it using sticks and trowels. Some have described Pollock's urgent arcs and whorls of paint as chaotic, but he saw them as labyrinths that led viewers along complex paths and into an organic calligraphic web of natural and biomorphic forms. Pollock's compositions lack hierarchical arrangement, contain multiple moving focal points, and deny perspectival space. Yet, as the paint travels around the canvas, it never escapes the edges. There is a top and a bottom. Like a coiled spring, the self-contained painting bursts with anxious energy, ready to explode at any moment.

Autumn Rhythm is heroic in scale, almost 9 feet tall by over 17 feet wide. It engulfs the viewer's entire field of vision. According to Lee Krasner, Pollock was a "jazz addict" who spent many hours listening to the explosively improvised bebop of Charlie Parker and Dizzy Gillespie. His interests extended to Native American art, which he associated with his western roots and which enjoyed widespread coverage in popular and art magazines in the 1930s. Pollock was particularly intrigued by the images and processes of Navajo sand painters who demonstrated their work at the Natural History Museum in New York. Of course, he also drew on Jung's theories of the collective unconscious. But Pollock was more than the sum of his influences. His paintings communicate on a grand, Modern, primal level. In a radio interview, he said that he was creating for "the age of the airplane, the atom bomb, and the radio."

OTHER ACTION PAINTERS Lee Krasner (1908–1984) studied in New York with Hans Hofmann and produced fully nonrepresentational paintings with all-over compositions several years before Pollock. She moved in with Pollock in 1942 and virtually stopped painting in order to take care of him. When they moved to Long Island in 1945, she set up a small studio in a guest bedroom, where she produced small, tight, gestural paintings. After Pollock's death in an automobile crash in 1956, however, Krasner took over his studio and produced a series of large, dazzling gestural paintings that marked her re-emergence into the mainstream art world. Works such as **THE SEASONS** (FIG. 32-83) feature bold, sweeping curves that express not only a new sense of liberation but also her powerful identification with the forces of nature in bursting, rounded forms and springlike colors. Krasner said that "Painting, for me, when it really 'happens' is as miraculous as any natural phenomenon."

In contrast, Willem de Kooning (1904–1997) wrote that "Art never seems to make me peaceful or pure," and remarked "I work out of doubt." An 1926 immigrant from the Netherlands who settled in New York, de Kooning made connections with several Modern artists, including Elaine Marie Fried, whom he married. His paintings were highly structured and controlled, guided by careful under-drawings. Although his gestural strokes appear spontaneous, they are, in fact, the result of hours of experiment and failure. De Kooning painted strokes, scraped them off, and repeated the process until the exact effect he wanted emerged. In 1953, he shocked the art world by moving away from pure abstraction with a series of figurative paintings of women. **WOMAN I** (FIG. 32-84) took the artist two years to complete, and de Kooning's wife Elaine estimated

32-82 • Hans Namuth JACKSON POLLOCK
1950. Courtesy Center for Creative Photography, University of Arizona.
© 1991 Hans Namuth Estate.

👁 **Watch** a video of Jackson Pollock painting on myartslab.com

32-83 • Lee Krasner THE SEASONS
1957. Oil on canvas, 7'8¾" × 16'11¾" (2.36 × 5.18 m). Whitney Museum of American Art, New York.
Purchased with funds from Frances and Sydney Lewis (by exchange), the Mrs. Percy Uris Purchase Fund, and the Painting and Sculpture Committee (87.7)

32–84 • Willem de Kooning WOMAN I
1950–1952. Oil on canvas, 75⅞″ × 58″ (192.7 × 147.3 cm). Museum of Modern Art, New York.

that he scraped and repainted it about 200 times. The portrayal of the woman seems at once grotesque and rapacious; the image is hostile, sexist, and powerfully sexual, full of implied violence and intense passion. De Kooning described his paintings in this series as images of great fertility goddesses like those he saw in prehistoric statuettes (see FIGS. 1–7, 1–8), or as a composite of stereotypes taken from the media and film.

A second generation of Abstract Expressionist painters assembled in the Greenwich Village neighborhood of New York during the 1950s, forming a close-knit community that organized discussion groups to share their ideas, and cooperative galleries to exhibit their work. Prominent among them was Joan Mitchell (1925–1992) who moved to New York after studying first at Smith College and then at the Art Institute in her native Chicago. After a decade in New York, painting energetic but lyrical abstract paintings that show the impact of Gorky and de Kooning in particular, she moved permanently to France in 1959, where she continued to develop her abstract style of painting, untouched by the new developments of Pop art that transformed the New York scene during the 1960s. Mitchell painted in a personal adaptation of Abstract Expressionism, visualizing her own memories of natural and urban landscapes and how they affected her. In **LADYBUG** (**FIG. 32–85**), she created energetic but controlled rhythms with gestural brushstrokes and set the lyrical complexity of her

32–85 • Joan Mitchell LADYBUG
1957. Oil on canvas, 6′7⅞″ × 9′ (1.98 × 2.74 m). Museum of Modern Art, New York. © Estate of Joan Mitchell. Purchase (385.1961)

32–86 • Jean-Paul Riopelle KNIGHT WATCH
1953. Oil on canvas, 38″ × 76⅝″ (96.6 × 194.8 cm). National Gallery of Canada, Ottawa, Ontario.

32–87 • Helen Frankenthaler MOUNTAINS AND SEA
1952. Oil and charcoal on canvas, 7′2¾″ × 9′8¼″ (2.2 × 2.95 m). Helen Frankenthaler Foundation, Inc., on loan to the National Gallery of Art, Washington, DC.

distinctive palette against a neutral ground in a seeming nod to the figure and field relationship of traditional painting. She said, "The freedom in my work is quite controlled. I don't close my eyes and hope for the best."

Abstract Expressionism spread quickly to Canada. In his native Montreal, the French Canadian painter Jean-Paul Riopelle (1923–2002) worked with Les Automatistes, a group of artists using the Surrealist technique of automatism to create abstract paintings. In 1947, Riopelle moved to Paris and, in the early 1950s, in paintings such as **KNIGHT WATCH** (**FIG. 32-86**), he began to squeeze paint directly onto canvas before spreading it with a palette knife to create bright swatches of color traversed by networks of spidery lines.

Helen Frankenthaler (b. 1928) visited Pollock's studio in 1951 and began to create a more lyrical version of Action painting that had a significant impact on later artists. Like Pollock, she worked on the floor, but she poured paint onto unprimed canvas in thin washes so that it soaked into the fabric rather than sitting on its surface. Frankenthaler described her process as starting with an aesthetic question or image, which evolved as the self-expressive act of painting took over—"I will sometimes start a picture feeling, What will happen if I work with three blues … ? And very often midway through the picture I have to change the basis of the experience. Or I add and add to the canvas … . When I say gesture, my gesture, I mean what my mark is. I think there is something now that I am still working out in paint; it is a struggle for me to both discard and retain what is gestural and personal." In **MOUNTAINS AND SEA** (**FIG. 32-87**), Frankenthaler poured several diluted colors onto the canvas and outlined selected forms in charcoal. The result reminded her of the coast of Nova Scotia where she frequently went to sketch.

32-88 • Mark Rothko
LAVENDER AND MULBERRY
1959. Oil on paper mounted on fiberboard, 37¾″ × 24¾″ (95.9 × 62.8 cm). Hirshhorn Museum and Sculpture Garden, Smithsonian Institution, Washington, DC.
Gift of Joseph H. Hirshhorn 1966

COLOR FIELD PAINTING New York School artists used abstract means to express various kinds of emotional states, not all of them as urgent or improvisatory as those of the Action painters. The Color Field painters moved in a different direction, painting large, flat areas of color to evoke more transcendent, contemplative moods in paint.

Mark Rothko (1903–1970) had very little formal art training, but by 1940 he was already producing paintings that were deeply influenced by the European Surrealists and by Jung's archetypal imagery. By the mid 1940s, Rothko began to paint very large canvases with rectangular shapes arranged in a vertical format in which he allowed his colors to bleed into one another. Paintings such as **LAVENDER AND MULBERRY** (**FIG. 32–88**) or *Magenta, Black, Green, on Orange (No. 3/No. 13)* (see **FIG. Intro–1**), are not simply arrangements of flat geometric shapes on a canvas, nor are they atmospheric, archetypical landscapes. Rothko thought of his shapes as fundamental "ideas" expressed in rectangular form, unmediated by a recognizable subject, which sit in front of a painted field (hence the name "Color Field painting"). He preferred to show his paintings together in series or rows, illuminated indirectly to evoke moods of transcendental meditation.

Barnett Newman (1905–1970) also addressed modern humanity's existential condition in very large canvases, some painted mostly in a single brilliant, color, torn or split by thin jagged lines in another color that he called "zips." Newman claimed his art was about "[t]he self, terrible and constant." **VIR HEROICUS SUBLIMIS** (Latin for "Man, Heroic and Sublime") (**FIG. 32–89**) shows how Newman's total concentration on a single color focuses his meaning. The broad field of red does not describe any form; it presents an absolute state of sublime redness across a vast, heroic canvas, interrupted only by the dangerous zips of other colors that threaten, like a tragic human flaw, to unbalance it. Newman wrote: "The present painter is concerned not with his own feelings or with the mystery of his own personality but with the penetration into the world mystery. His imagination is therefore attempting to dig into metaphysical secrets. To that extent his art is concerned with the sublime."

SCULPTURE OF THE NEW YORK SCHOOL Sculpture tended to resist the kind of instantaneous gestural processes developed by artists such as Pollock, although some sculptors managed to communicate both abstractly and Expressionistically in three dimensions. David Smith (1906–1965) learned to weld and rivet while working at an automobile plant in Indiana. He trained as a painter, but became a sculptor after seeing reproductions of welded metal sculptures by artists such as Picasso. Smith avoided the precious materials of traditional sculpture and created works out of standard industrial materials. After World War II, Smith began to weld horizontally formatted, open-form sculptures that were like drawings in space. The forms of the vertical **CUBI** series (**FIG. 32–90**) were actually determined by standardized, precut sizes of stainless-steel sheets. In photographs they sometimes look coldly industrial, but when observed outdoors as Smith intended, their highly burnished surfaces show the gestural marks of the sculptor's tools upon them, and reflect and refract the sun in different ways depending on the time of day, weather conditions, and distance from which they are viewed. Vaguely anthropomorphic like giant totemic figures, the sculptures are surprisingly organic when seen at close range.

32–89 • Barnett Newman VIR HEROICUS SUBLIMIS
1950–1951. Oil on canvas, 95⅜" × 213¼" (242 × 541.7 cm). Museum of Modern Art, New York. Gift of Mr. and Mrs. Ben Heller

32-90 • David Smith CUBI

Cubi series shown installed at Bolton Landing, New York, in 1965. *Cubi XVIII* (left), 1964. Stainless steel, 9'8" (2.94 m).
Museum of Fine Arts, Boston. *Cubi XVII* (center), 1963. Stainless steel, 9'2" (2.79 m). Dallas Museum of Fine Arts, Dallas.
Cubi XIX (right), 1964. Stainless steel, 9'5⅝" (2.88 m). Tate, London. Art © Estate of David Smith/Licensed by VAGA, New
York, NY.

THINK ABOUT IT

32.1 Discuss the goals and interests of the painters
associated with Abstract Expressionism. Characterize the
role played by Surrealism and other early twentieth-century
avant-garde art movements in the formation of this new
direction in Modern art.

32.2 Explain the impact of the two World Wars on the visual
arts in Europe and North America. Use two works—one
European and one American—as the focus of your
discussion.

32.3 Summarize the events of the Great Depression and
discuss its impact on American art.

32.4 Explain how both Dada and Surrealism changed the
form, content, and concept of art. Which two works of art
discussed in the chapter would you choose to represent
these two movements? Why?

CROSSCURRENTS

FIG. 30–44

FIG. 32–64

Throughout the history of art, artists have
created eloquent and moving expressions
of the horrific violence of war and political
oppression. Discuss the political circumstances that led to the creation of these two
examples, and assess how they relate to the
styles of these two artists and their time. Who
was the audience for these works?

✓●—|**Study** and review on myartslab.com

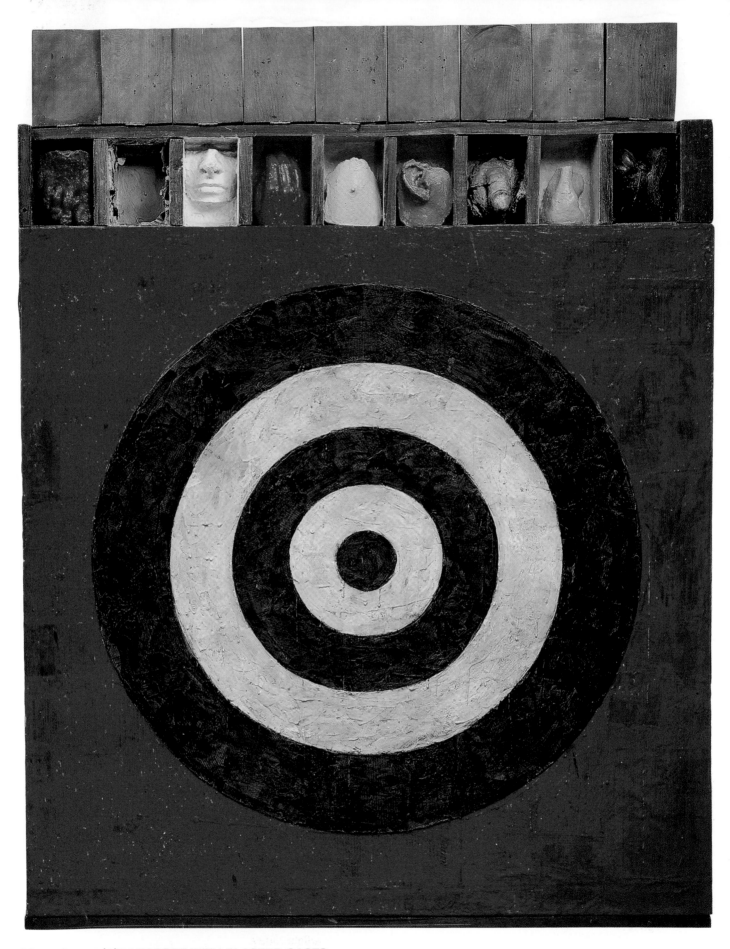

33–1 • Jasper Johns TARGET WITH PLASTER CASTS
1955. Encaustic and collage on canvas with objects, 51″ × 44″ (129.5 × 111.8 cm). Collection Mr. and Mrs. Leo Castelli.
Art © Jasper Johns/Licensed by VAGA, New York, NY.

The International Scene since 1950

In the early 1950s, a new generation of artists in New York challenged the artistic assumptions of the previous generation of Abstract Expressionists. They believed that art should be firmly anchored in real life. Two artists in particular, Jasper Johns and Robert Rauschenberg, questioned the goals of the New York School as defined by Clement Greenberg's version of Formalism: that art should be autonomous and internally coherent (deeply meaningful but abstract, with the act of painting as its subject, and with an all-over composition); that it should avoid the taint of popular culture and be exhibited in the isolated "white cube" of the gallery space; and that artists should be vigilantly self-critical. In **TARGET WITH PLASTER CASTS** (**FIG. 33–1**), Johns not only stretches formalism to its limits; he actually mocks it.

This work is neither a painting nor a sculpture but both. The arrangement of casts of body parts in recessed spaces across the top parodies the nonhierarchical manner of Abstract Expressionism, while the target pictured below is the very embodiment of hierarchy. The target's flatness of suggests an all-over composition, but targets always have a central focus. And neither the target nor the casts are abstractions; both actually refer to popular culture and the world around Johns. The target also raises thorny questions about the nature of representation: Is this a painting of a target or is it an actual target? The meaning of this work is fluid and unfixed—it contains recognizable body parts and a recognizable object (a target) but the purpose of their inclusion is unclear. Unlike Abstract Expressionist paintings, Johns's art is emotionally cool and highly cerebral. Like many artists of his generation, Johns reintroduces readily recognizable, real-world images and objects that he strategically recontextualized, in order to question the form, appearance, content, and meaning of art. Thus, like much art after 1950, Johns's art is as intellectual as it is visual.

Johns and Rauschenberg were critical figures in the New York art world and beyond. They expanded the intellectual bases of Abstract Expressionism, cooled its passion and intensity, and made art that connected to and was inspired by the vastly expanded visual culture of postwar America. They also prefigured the next generation's interest in introducing popular culture into art, its investigation of the conceptual foundations of art, its expanded understanding of the use of nontraditional materials in art, and its exploration of the performative possibilities of art.

LEARN ABOUT IT

33.1 Understand the "dematerialization" of the object since 1950 and account for its return after 1980.

33.2 Assess the ways in which artists since 1950 have introduced popular culture into the world of "high art."

33.3 Examine the engagement of artists since 1950 with social, political, cultural, and/or religious issues.

33.4 Explore the growing globalism of the contemporary art world and the ways it has created new opportunities, strategies, and subjects for artists today.

((•—**Listen** to the chapter audio on myartslab.com

THE WORLD SINCE THE 1950s

The United States and the U.S.S.R. emerged from World War II as the world's most powerful nations. The Soviet occupation and sponsorship of communist governments in several Central and Eastern European states, and the emergence of the People's Republic of China in 1949 compelled the United States to attempt to contain the further expansion of Soviet power and communism into American spheres of influence, particularly in Western Europe, Japan, and Latin America. This precipitated a "Cold War" and what Winston Churchill described as the descending of an "Iron Curtain" across Europe (MAP 33-1). The United States initially provided both financial and political support to states sympathetic to American interests, but then resorted to military force, most notably in Korea (1950–1953) and then Vietnam (1954–1975). Europe lost most of its imperial holdings by the early 1960s, often after protracted guerrilla wars of the kind that the French experienced in Vietnam and Algeria. The British granted India independence in 1946 and by 1971 had withdrawn from "East of Suez."

During the Cold War, the United States and the U.S.S.R. amassed large nuclear arsenals, eventually adopting a strategy of mutually assured destruction, which was supposed to deter nuclear war by threatening to destroy the civilian population on both sides. The Cold War effectively ended with the fall of the Berlin Wall in October 1989. When the Soviet Union dissolved in 1992, the United States emerged as the world's unchallenged superpower.

The United Nations, sponsored by American power, was established in 1945 to provide collective security and legitimacy to the Anglo-American design for a new postwar world order. It eventually emerged as a forum for the sovereign recognition of the governments of the many newly independent states in Asia and Africa after the war. Despite the UN mandate to intervene in conflicts between states, however, its efforts to maintain global peace have proven inadequate in the face of ethnic and religious conflicts that have erupted around the world in regions such as the Indian subcontinent, central and eastern Africa, the Balkans, and the Middle East. The terrorist attacks on the World Trade Center and the Pentagon on September 11, 2001, exacerbated many preexisting racial, ethnic, and religious conflicts, and led to both civil wars and wars between states, most notably in the recent and controversial American-led wars in Afghanistan and Iraq.

THE ART WORLD SINCE THE 1950s

Since 1950, artists have faced fundamental questions: What is art? Do works of art have to be objects? Can art be purely idea? Is it some combination of idea and object? Artists of this period reconceptualized and reimagined art, producing radically new forms, content, ideas, and agendas. They have used art to address increasingly divisive and complex social and political questions for which there is no clear right or wrong answer. They have raised questions about gender, race, ethnicity, sexual orientation, religion, class, death, colonialism, terrorism, violence against the less powerful, and resistance to power. Their art has not sought to edify us by showing moral exemplars (as in Neoclassicism); rather it has challenged us to question our own morality, behavior, and complacency. Much of this art is difficult to look at and to understand; we are frequently assaulted and accused by it. It is rarely pretty. But today's art holds a mirror to contemporary life, revealing things that we might not see or hear in any other context, and it forces us to confront ourselves in that mirror. We may not like recent art initially, but once we learn something about it, we will discover that, at its best, it has the power, like all great art, to affect us deeply—to engage us in challenging conversation.

THE EXPANDING ART WORLD

The generation of artists who began to make art in the 1950s increasingly addressed the real world, acknowledging its fragmentation, its relativism, and its messy relation to popular culture. Assemblage and collage broke apart the physical forms and the meanings of art along with the distinction between painting and sculpture, and high and low art. Pop artists investigated the power of advertising and explored a newly visible domestic world. Photographers showed us aspects of the world around us that we had not seen, or had chosen not to see, before.

ASSEMBLAGE

One new artistic path developed in the second half of the twentieth century was assemblage—combining disparate elements to construct a work of art. By 1950, Louise Nevelson (1899–1988) had already developed an Analytic Cubist-inspired version of assemblage. Prowling the streets of downtown Manhattan, she collected discarded packing boxes in which she would carefully arrange chair legs, broom handles, cabinet doors, spindles, and other wooden refuse. She painted these assemblages matte black to obscure the identity of the individual elements, to integrate them formally, and to provide an air of detached mystery. After stacking several of these boxes together against a studio wall, Nevelson realized that the accumulated effect was more powerful than viewing them individually and began creating monumental wall assemblages such as SKY CATHEDRAL (FIG. 32-2) of 1958. What she particularly liked about the new schema was the way it could transform an ordinary space just as the prosaic elements she worked with had themselves been transformed into a work of art. To add a further poetic dimension, Nevelson first displayed *Sky Cathedral* bathed in soft blue light, recalling moonlight.

Like Nevelson, visual artists Jasper Johns (b. 1930) and Robert Rauschenberg (1925–2008), and composer John Cage (1912–1992), consciously introduced the world around them (rather than representations of it) into their art and music, creating distinct sorts of assemblage. Cage, who taught for a time at Black Mountain College near Asheville, North Carolina, explored the idea of

MAP 33–1 • THE WORLD SINCE 1950

International sites in the contemporary art world in the Americas, Europe, and Africa.

creating music that incorporated the ambient noises of the world around him. In 1952, Cage "composed" *4′33″* (4 minutes 33 seconds). At the premiere in Woodstock, New York, the pianist came on stage, sat silently at the piano for 4 minutes and 33 seconds, and then closed the keyboard to signal the end of the work. The sounds of the work consisted of noise made by audience members as they rustled, shuffled, whispered, and coughed for four minutes and 33 seconds. Thus, the composition differs each time it is performed, gathering a new set of sounds and meanings in every new location and with every new audience, open to multiple interpretations. Similarly, Johns and Rauschenberg in their assemblages brought or "assembled" disparate found objects and images to create visual works of art with equally open-ended and multiple meanings.

33–2 • Louise Nevelson SKY CATHEDRAL
1958. Assemblage of wood construction painted black, 11′3½″ × 10′¼″ × 18″ (3.44 × 3.05 × 0.46 m). The Museum of Modern Art, New York.

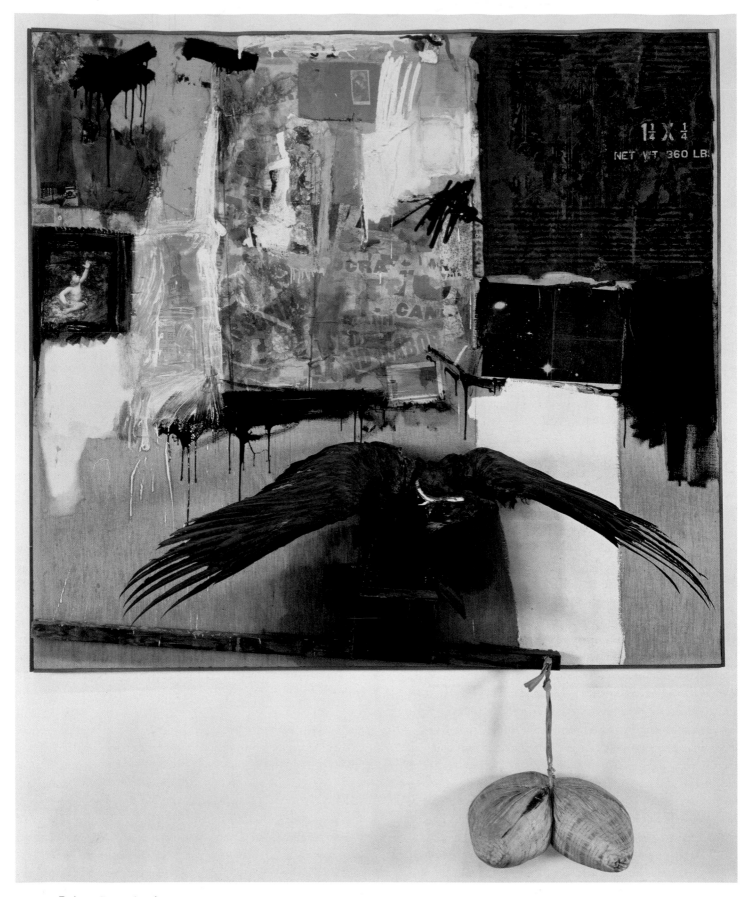

33-3 • Robert Rauschenberg CANYON
1959. Oil, pencil, paper, metal, photograph, fabric, wood on canvas, plus buttons, mirror, stuffed eagle, pillow tied with cord, and paint tube, 81¾″ × 70″ × 24″ (2.08 × 1.78 × 0.61 m). Sonnabend Collection. Art © Estate of Robert Rauschenberg/Licensed by VAGA, New York, NY. (RR-00016)

Rauschenberg grew up in Texas and moved to New York to paint in 1947. He attended Black Mountain College where he studied with Cage and de Kooning (see FIG. 32-84), exploring ways to "work in the gap between art and life." In 1951, he exhibited a series of brightly lit blank white paintings in which the shadows cast by viewers on the canvases became the content of the work, a clear visual parallel to Cage's *4'33"* of the following year. Between 1955 and 1960, Rauschenberg made a series of objects that he called **combines**—combinations of painting and sculpture using nontraditional art materials. **CANYON (FIG. 33-3)** incorporates an assortment of old family photographs, public imagery (the Statue of Liberty), fragments of political posters (in the center), and various objects salvaged from the trash (the flattened steel drum at upper right), or purchased, and projecting three-dimensional forms such as a stuffed eagle (donated by a friend) perched on a box and a dirty pillow tied with cord and suspended from a piece of wood. The rich disorder, enhanced by the seemingly sloppy application of paint, challenges viewers to make sense of what they see. Since he meant his work to be open to various readings, Rauschenberg assembled material that each viewer might interpret differently. Cheerfully accepting the chaos and unpredictability of modern urban experience, he sought its metaphorical representation in art. "I only consider myself successful," he said, "when I do something that resembles the lack of order I sense."

When the Museum of Modern Art organized an exhibition titled "The Art of Assemblage" in 1961, Rauschenberg was one of two major American artists included in the show; the other was his fellow southerner, close friend, and at times lover, Jasper Johns. Inspired by the example of Marcel Duchamp (see FIG. 32-30), Johns produced controlled, cerebral, and puzzling works during the 1950s that addressed directly issues raised in contemporary art. *Target with Plaster Casts* (see FIG. 33-1)—neither a painting nor a sculpture but both—probes a psychological dimension that may stem from the artist's own anxieties and fears. The casts above the target fragment a human body without any sense of the organic whole, rendering them as blank and empty as the target itself. The viewer can complete the process of depersonalization by closing some, or just a few, of the hinged flaps over the closetlike boxes that contain the casts, obliterating all or a selective part of the human presence. The juxtaposition of fragmented and partially hidden body parts with the sharply defined target takes on richer meaning in the context of Johns's position as a gay artist in the restrictive, often paranoid, climate of Cold War America. Steadfastly silent but boldly present, in this painting personal identity remains elusive, selectively masked, removed from the center, and safely off target.

Johns, Cage, and Rauschenberg collaborated on several theatrical events that extended the idea of the assemblage into temporal space in the late 1950s and early 1960s. Cage composed music while Johns and Rauschenberg designed sets and sometimes actually performed. They worked with the Merce Cunningham Dance Company, which specialized in creating dance based on everyday actions such as waiting for a bus or reading a newspaper. Prior to these events, none of the participants informed the others what they were planning to do, so the performances became legendary for their unpredictability.

HAPPENINGS AND PERFORMANCE ART

In the 1950s and 1960s, several artists, arguing that the artistic process was as important as the finished object, began to replace the traditional materials of art with the actions, movements, and gestures of their own bodies. These events were termed **Happenings** by Allan Kaprow, but the more common term is **Performance art**. Performance art owes a debt to Pollock (see FIG. 32-82)—whose physical enactment of the act of painting resulted in a work of art in its own right—and to Cage, Johns, and Rauschenberg, who relied on spontaneous and unpredictable actions to provide a new set of variables for each of their events. Performance art tears down the barrier that has traditionally existed between the viewer and the work of art as it literally comes to life and actively invades the viewers' space, both physically and intellectually. Performance art is often radical, and assaultive. It exists in the moment and, although often photographed or filmed, is ephemeral.

THE GUTAI GROUP Some of the earliest postwar performances took place in Japan. In 1954, several Japanese artists formed the Gutai (meaning "embodiment") group to "pursue the possibilities of pure and creative activity with great energy." In Gutai performances, the act of creating itself was the artwork. Gutai organized outdoor installations (art installed in a specific place for which it was made) theatrical events, and dramatic performances. At the second Gutai Exhibition in 1956, Shozo Shimamoto (b. 1928) performed **HURLING COLORS (FIG. 33-4)** by smashing bottles of paint against a canvas on the floor. He pushed Pollock's gestural painting technique to the point where the work of art resided in the performance of painting, not in the object produced. In fact, Gutai artists regularly destroyed the physical products they created at the end of each performance.

KAPROW In 1958, Allan Kaprow (1927–2006), another student of John Cage, began to create environments and, in 1959, Happenings. **YARD (FIG. 33-5)** was staged in 1961 within the walled garden space behind the Martha Jackson Gallery in Manhattan. Kaprow filled the space with used tires, tar paper, and barrels, and asked viewers to walk though it, to experience the smell and physicality of the rubber and tar firsthand, recontextualized (removed from one context to another to create a new meaning) in the art gallery space. Kaprow later described how gallery audiences—more formally dressed then than they would be today, especially the women, who wore dresses and heels—experienced aspects of the urban environment in unfamiliar and unanticipated ways as they tumbled in and over the tires.

KLEIN In Europe, Performance art occurred as part of the activities of the New Realism movement, a term coined by art critic Pierre Restany. Restany argued that the age of painting ended with the New York School and *Art Informel* and art would now take its form from the real world. He wrote: "The passionate adventure of the real, perceived in itself .... The New Realists consider the world a painting: a large, fundamental work of which they appropriate fragments."

The French artist Yves Klein (1928–1962) first staged his *Anthropometries of the Blue Period* in 1960, when he directed three female models covered in blue paint as they pressed their naked bodies against large sheets of paper to the musical accompaniment of a 20-piece orchestra playing a single note. The performance was clearly a satirical commentary on the perceived pretentiousness of Pollock's action painting, of which Klein wrote: "I dislike artists who empty themselves into their paintings. They spit out every rotten complexity as if relieving themselves." He offered instead a sensuous and diverting display, leading to a work created without even touching it himself.

Klein is perhaps best known for the 1960 **LEAP INTO THE VOID** (**FIG. 33-6**), a manipulated photograph showing the artist leaping from a wall into the street, arms outstretched with apparently nothing but the pavement below him. Klein originally published the photograph to support his mock claim that he could undertake lunar travel unaided, and published it again in a pamphlet denouncing NASA's bid to land a man on the moon as arrogant and foolish. Klein argued that his works were visible only as imprints, in this case his imprint on the pavement.

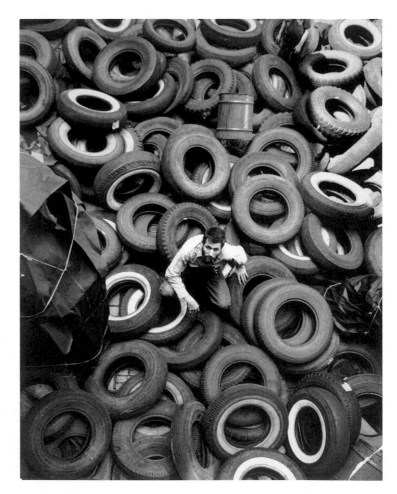

33-5 • Allan Kaprow **YARD** 1961. View of tires in court of Martha Jackson Gallery, New York, 1961.

33-6 • Yves Klein LEAP INTO THE VOID
1960. Photograph by Harry Shunk of a performance by Yves Klein at Rue Gentil-Bernard, Fontenay-aux-Roses, October 1960. Gelatin-silver print, 10³⁄₁₆″ × 7⅞″ (25.9 × 20 cm).

SCHNEEMANN Many early Performance artists were women, whose bodies had been the object of the male gaze in art for centuries. Performance art enabled women to control how their bodies were viewed and to look back and even challenge their audience. One of the most important early examples is **MEAT JOY** (**FIG. 33-7**) by Carolee Schneemann (b. 1939), a radical feminist performance, first enacted by Jean-Jacques Lebel and the Kinetic Group Theater at the Festival de la Libre Expression in Paris, and a second time in New York, where it was filmed and photographed. Eight men and women first undressed one another, then danced, rolled on the floor ecstatically, and played with a mixture of raw fish, raw sausages, partially plucked raw and bloody chickens, wet paint, and scraps of paper. Schneemann wanted both performers and audience to smell, taste, and feel the body and its fluids. Critics described the piece variously as an erotic rite and a visceral celebration of flesh and blood. It countered the expectation that a work of art was something to be examined in the cool unemotional space of an art gallery with the viewer in control. The audience must have squirmed as control was wrenched away by the performers.

PHOTOGRAPHY

Photography was an important tool for documenting Performance art in the 1950s and 1960s, but it was also an important medium in its own right. Although the 1955 "Family of Man" exhibition of photographs at the Museum of Modern Art, New York, curated by Edward Steichen, presented a world at peace and in harmony,

33-7 • Carolee Schneemann MEAT JOY
1964. Gelatin-silver print. A photograph by Tony Ray-Jones, taken at a Performance art piece or happening by Carolee Schneeman, performed in Judson Memorial Church in November 1964.

33-8 • Robert Frank
TROLLEY, NEW ORLEANS
1955. Gelatin-silver print, 9″ ×
13″ (23 × 33 cm). The Art Institute
of Chicago. © Robert Frank,
from *The Americans*; courtesy
Pace/MacGill Gallery, New York.
Photography Gallery Fund (1961.943)

and illustrated magazines such as *Life* projected an image of modern life as comfortable, suburban, white, and domestic, other photographers emphasized an alternative view of American society.

FRANK Robert Frank (b. 1924), a Swiss photographer who emigrated to the United States in the 1940s, took gritty social portraits, trying to capture some of the disharmony that Johns and Rauschenberg presented in their art. In 1948, frustrated by the pressure and banality of news and fashion assignments, Frank abandoned his freelance work with magazines such as *Life* and *Vogue* and traveled to Peru and Bolivia. Four years later, he took

a series of photographs documenting the lives of Welsh coalminers, and he received a Guggenheim Fellowship in 1955 to travel around America photographing the "social landscape." Frank took more than 28,000 photographs that year, from which he chose 83 to publish in a book. The images were so raw, grim, and full of biting social commentary, however, that at first he could not find a publisher in the United States and instead published the book in France under the title *Les Américains* (1958). *The Americans* finally appeared in the United States the following year with an introduction by Jack Kerouac, a writer of the new Beat generation who criticized mainstream American values. In **TROLLEY, NEW**

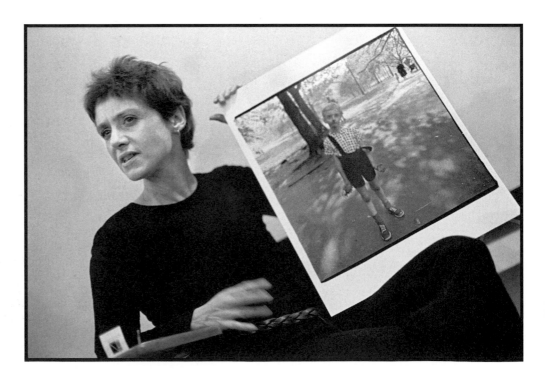

33-9 • Diane Arbus photographed
in 1970 holding **CHILD WITH
A TOY HAND GRENADE IN
CENTRAL PARK, NEW YORK**
1962. Gelatin-silver print.

ORLEANS (FIG. 33–8), stiff, smartly dressed white passengers sit in the front of the street car, while more casually posed African Americans sit in the back, as required by law in the 1950s. The composition of the image, in which the rectangular symmetry of the windows frames and isolates the figures, underscores visually both racial segregation and urban alienation, while the ghostly reflections on the closed windows along the top could almost be photographs themselves.

ARBUS Diane Arbus (1923–1971), even more than Frank, rejected the dictates of elegant art photography, partly because of her experience as a fashion photographer—she and her husband, Allan Arbus, had been *Seventeen* magazine's favorite cover photographers in the 1950s—but mostly because she did not want formal niceties to distract viewers from her riveting, often disturbing subjects (FIG. 33–9). Arbus moved beyond the boundaries of what had been acceptable artistic subject matter, photographing nudists, people with physical deformities, or others on the fringes of society. Since she usually allowed her subjects—like this disheveled and menacing child—to sense the presence of the camera, they confront the viewer directly, challenging the safe distance between us and what we view. "I really believe there are things that nobody would see," she said, "unless I photographed them."

POP ART

In the late 1950s, several artists began to focus attention on the mid-century explosion in visual culture, fueled by the growing presence of mass media and the growing disposable income of the postwar generation. Pop art originated in Britain, but its primary development was in the United States during the early 1960s, at a time when individual and mass identity was increasingly determined by how people looked and dressed, as well as by what they displayed and consumed. Homes, automobiles, and the visible display of objects—both within the home and on the person—reflected life as it was portrayed on television, in films, and in print advertising. Pop artists critiqued the superficiality of popular culture's fiction of the perfect home and perfect person.

HAMILTON In the 1950s, while the British government maintained that the country's postwar recovery depended on sustained consumption, an interdisciplinary collection of artists, architects, photographers, and writers came together as the Independent Group in London in order to discuss the place of art in this consumer society, periodically exhibiting at the Institute of Contemporary Arts. One of its members, Richard Hamilton (1922–2011), argued that modern mass visual culture was fast replacing traditional art for the general public, that movies, television, and advertising, not high art, defined standards of beauty. Society's idols were no longer politicians or military heroes but international movie stars; social status was increasingly measured by the number of one's possessions. To create a visual expression of this disharmonious world of excessive consumption, Hamilton created collages composed of images drawn from advertising. In **JUST WHAT IS IT THAT MAKES TODAY'S HOMES SO DIFFERENT, SO APPEALING?** (FIG. 33–10) from 1956, Hamilton critiques marketing strategies by imitating them. The title parodies an

33–10 • Richard Hamilton **JUST WHAT IS IT THAT MAKES TODAY'S HOMES SO DIFFERENT, SO APPEALING?**
1956. Collage, 10¼″ × 9¾″ (26 × 24.7 cm). Kunsthalle Tübingen, Collection Zundel.

Watch a podcast about Richard Hamilton's work on myartslab.com advertising slogan, while the collage itself shows two figures named Adam and Eve in a domestic setting. Like the biblical forebears, these figures are almost naked, but the "temptations" to which they have succumbed are those of consumer culture. Adam is a bodybuilder and Eve a pin-up girl. In an attempt to recreate their lost Garden of Eden, the first couple has filled their home with all the best new products: a television, a tape recorder, a vacuum cleaner, modern furniture. Displayed on the wall is not "high art" but a poster advertising a romance novel, hung next to a portrait of John Ruskin, the critic who accused the painter Whistler of destroying art (see "Art on Trial in 1877," page 985). Adam holds a huge, suggestively placed Tootsie Pop, which the English critic Lawrence Alloway cited when he described this work as "Pop art," thus naming the broader movement. Like assemblages in the United States, Hamilton's collage comments on the visual overload of the 1950s and on culture's inability to differentiate between important and trivial images or between the advertising world and the real one. In 1968, Hamilton designed the cover for the Beatles's *White Album*, devoid of any images at all.

WARHOL By 1960, several American artists, like the earlier British Pop artists, began to incorporate images from popular mass culture into their art. Unlike their British counterparts, however, they developed a slicker Pop art style using the mass-production techniques of advertising to give their works a flat, commercial feel that would erase the presence of the hand of the artist, consciously defying Abstract Expressionism's emphasis on individual artistic practice. American Pop art both imitated and critiqued 1960s popular culture, often including images of newly independent women and their ambivalent relationship to domesticity. The emotional tone of Pop art was more ironic, camp, and cynical than the irreverent but serious stance of artists such as Johns and Rauschenberg. As Pop art flourished in the United States, Andy Warhol (1928–1987), artistic giant and playful heir to Duchamp's challenging ideas about the nature of art and its production, emerged as the dominant figure.

Warhol created an immense body of work between 1960 and his death in 1987, including prints, paintings, sculptures, and films. He published *Interview* magazine and managed The Velvet Underground, a radical and hugely influential rock band. Since he trained as a commercial artist, Warhol knew advertising culture well, and by 1962, he was incorporating images from American mass-media advertising in his art. He took as subjects popular consumer items such as Campbell's Soup cans and Coca-Cola bottles, reproducing them with the cheap industrial print method of **silkscreen** (in which a fine mesh silk screen is used as a printing stencil), as well as in paintings and sculptures.

In 1964, in his first sculptural project, Warhol hired carpenters to create plywood boxes identical in size and shape to the cardboard cartons used to ship boxes of Brillo soap pads to supermarkets. By silkscreening onto these boxes the logos and texts that appeared on the actual cartons, the artist created what were essentially useless replicas of commercial packaging (**FIG. 33-11**). Stacking the fabricated boxes in piles, Warhol transformed the interior space of the Stable Gallery in New York into what looked like a grocery stockroom, simultaneously pointing to the commercial foundation of the art gallery system and critiquing the nature of art in a maneuver that aped Duchamp's 1917 transformation of a commercial urinal into *Fountain* (see FIG. 32-30), although in 1964 Warhol even abandoned the artifice of signature and date.

Warhol argued that whereas past art demanded thought and understanding, advertising and celebrity culture demanded only immediate attention, very quickly becoming uninteresting and boring. In keeping with this position, he suggested that art should be like movie stars, interesting for 15 minutes. In 1962, movie star Marilyn Monroe died suddenly, an apparent suicide. Warhol's **MARILYN DIPTYCH** (**FIG. 33-12**) is one of a series of silkscreens that Warhol made immediately after the actress's death. He memorializes the screen image of Monroe, using a famous publicity photograph transferred directly onto silkscreen, thus rendering it flat and bland so that Monroe's signature features—her bleach-blond hair, her ruby lips, and her sultry blue-shadowed eyes—stand out as a caricature of the actress. The face portrayed is not that of Norma Jeane (Monroe's real name) but of Monroe the celluloid sex symbol as made over by the movie industry. Warhol made multiple prints from this screen, aided—as in the creation of the

33-11 • Andy Warhol BRILLO SOAP PADS BOX
1964. Silkscreen print on painted wood, 17″ × 17″ × 14″ (43.2 × 43.2 × 35.6 cm). Collection of The Andy Warhol Museum, Pittsburgh.

Watch a video about the silkscreen process on myartslab.com

33-12 • Andy Warhol MARILYN DIPTYCH
1962. Oil, acrylic, and silkscreen on enamel on canvas, two panels, each 6'10″ × 4'9″ (2.05 × 1.44 m). Tate, London.

Brillo boxes—by a host of assistants working with assembly-line efficiency. In 1965, Warhol ironically named his studio "The Factory," further mocking the commercial aspect of his art by suggesting he was only in it for the profit.

The *Marilyn Diptych*, however, has deeper undertones. The diptych format carries religious connotations (see "Altars and Altarpieces," page 566), perhaps implying that Monroe was a martyred saint or goddess in the pantheon of departed movie stars. In another print, Warhol surrounded her head with the gold background used in Orthodox religious icons. Additionally, the flat and undifferentiated Monroes on the colored left side of the diptych contrast with those in black and white on the right side, which fade progressively as they are printed and reprinted without reinking the screen until all that remains of the original portrait is the ghostly image of a disappearing person.

Warhol was one of the first artists to exploit the realization that while the mass media—television in particular—seem to bring us closer to the world, they actually allow us to observe the world only as detached voyeurs, not real participants. We become desensitized to death and disaster by the constant repetition of images on television, which we are able literally to switch off at any time. Warhol's art, especially in the *Marilyn Diptych*, is like television—the presentation is superficial and bland, uses seemingly mindless repetition, and inures us to the full impact of the tragic moment of death. Warhol, known for his quotable phrases, once said: "I am a deeply superficial person." But the seeming superficiality of his art is deeply intellectual.

RUSCHA In 1962, Andy Warhol's first solo show as a Pop artist—the exhibition of his 32 paintings of Campbell's Soup cans—took place not in New York, but in the Ferus Gallery in Los Angeles. By that time, a group of younger artists—some still in college—had already developed a West Coast version of Pop art in an environment famously saturated with fanciful commercial imagery and the glamorous artifice of the movie industry. Prominent among these artists was Ed Ruscha (b. 1937)—born in Omaha, Nebraska, raised in Oklahoma City, and settled in Los Angeles by 1956. Like Warhol, he challenged the hierarchies

33-13 • Ed Ruscha **STANDARD STATION, AMARILLO, TEXAS**
1963. Oil on canvas, 5′5″ × 10′ (1.65 × 3 m). Hood Museum of Art, Dartmouth College, Hanover, NH. Gift of James Meeker, Class of 1958

of fine art by portraying the products and bastions of American commerce, with a special concentration on signage in advertising. His monumental 1963 painting **STANDARD STATION, AMARILLO, TEXAS** (**FIG. 33-13**) is based on an image in a 1962 book of his 26 black-and-white photographs of gas stations along Route 66 between Oklahoma City and Los Angeles, a roadside culture he knew well from his travels on this highway. But in the painting, Ruscha pushes the image beyond representation to flattened abstraction and dramatic stylization, academic linear perspective and saturated pure color. Also in 1962, Ruscha's work appeared in a group show at the Pasadena Museum of Art—one of the first exhibitions of Pop art in America. It also included the paintings of East Coast artists Andy Warhol and Roy Lichtenstein.

LICHTENSTEIN Roy Lichtenstein (1923–1997) also investigated the various ways that popular imagery resonated with high art, imitating the format of comic books in his critique of mass-market visual culture. In 1961, while teaching at Rutgers University with Allan Kaprow (see FIG. 33-5), Lichtenstein began to make paintings based on panels from war and romance comic books. He tightened and clarified the source images to focus on significant emotions or actions,

33-14 • Roy Lichtenstein **OH, JEFF ... I LOVE YOU, TOO ... BUT ...**
1964. Oil and magna on canvas, 48″ × 48″ (122 × 122 cm).
Private collection.

simultaneously representing and parodying the flat, superficial ways in which a comic book communicates with its readers. The heavy black outlines, flat primary colors, and **Benday dots** used in commercial printing imitate the character of cartoons. **OH, JEFF ... I LOVE YOU, TOO ... BUT ...** (**FIG. 33-14**) compresses a popular romance storyline involving a crisis that temporarily threatens a love relationship into a single frame. But Lichtenstein plays ironic games by pitting illusion against reality; we know that comic books are unrealistically melodramatic, yet he presents this overblown episode vividly, almost reverently, enshrined in a work of high art.

OLDENBURG Like Warhol and Lichtenstein, Swedish-born artist Claes Oldenburg (b. 1929) created ironic critiques of consumer culture, in his case in the form of sculptures. Oldenburg foregrounds humor in his large-scale public projects, such as **LIPSTICK (ASCENDING) ON CATERPILLAR TRACKS** (**FIG. 33-15**), made

for his *alma mater*, Yale University. A group of graduate students from the Yale School of Architecture invited him to create this monument to the "Second American Revolution" of the late 1960s, a period marked by student demonstrations against the Vietnam War. Oldenburg mounted a giant lipstick tube on top of steel tracks taken from a Caterpillar tractor. Visually the sculpture suggests both the warlike aggression of a mobile missile launcher and the phallic eroticism of lipstick, perhaps in a play on the popular slogan of the time, "make love, not war." The lipstick was to have included a suggestive balloonlike vinyl tip that could be pumped up with air and then left to deflate slowly, but the pump was never installed and the drooping tip, vulnerable to vandalism, was quickly replaced with a metal one. The lipstick monument was installed provocatively on a campus plaza in front of both a war memorial and the president's office. Not surprisingly, Yale asked Oldenburg to remove it. In 1974, however, he reworked the sculpture in the more permanent materials of fiberglass, aluminum, and steel and donated it to Yale, where it was placed in the courtyard of Morse College.

THE DEMATERIALIZATION OF THE ART OBJECT

In the same decade when Pop artists critiqued the visual world of popular culture, other artists questioned the role, purpose, and relevance of the art object in contemporary culture. Their restlessness parallels the social upheaval that marked the era of the mid-1960s and early 1970s. During this period, the youth of Europe and America questioned the authority and rights of the state with civil rights movements, massive rallies against the draft and the Vietnam War, environmentalist and feminist movements, and the Paris revolts of 1968. Women artists made their presence felt in large numbers, and increasingly artists made art meant to be viewed outside the gallery system. The decade ended with a move toward noncommodifiable and "dematerialized" art.

MINIMALISM

Minimalism, which dominated the New York scene in the late 1960s, sought the dematerialization of the art object. In the mid-1960s, a group of articulate young sculptors, including Donald Judd (1928–1994), Robert Morris (b. 1931), and Carl Andre (b. 1935), proposed what was variously called ABC Art, Primary Structures, or Minimalism. They produced slab- or boxlike sculptures, frequently fabricated for them from industrial materials such as Plexiglas, fluorescent lighting, steel, and mirrors, totally rejecting the gesture and emotion invested in the handcrafted object, as well as the traditional materials of sculpture. Judd and Morris described their theories eloquently in the journal *Artforum*, by asking viewers to comprehend their art objects as united wholes without a focal point, allowing the energy of the work and the viewers' interest to be dissipated throughout the object in a kind of entropy.

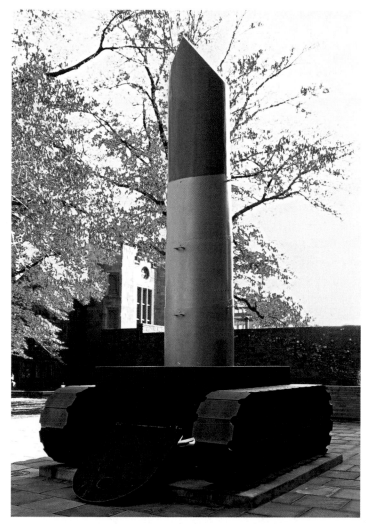

33-15 • Claes Oldenburg LIPSTICK (ASCENDING) ON CATERPILLAR TRACKS
1969, reworked 1974. Painted steel body, aluminum tube, and fiberglass tip, 21′ × 19′5½″ × 10′11″ (6.70 × 5.94 × 3.33 m). Yale University Art Gallery, New Haven, Connecticut. © Claes Oldenburg, Coosje van Bruggen.

33-17 • Robert Morris UNTITLED (MIRROR CUBE)
1965–1971. Mirror, plate glass, and wood, 36″ × 36″ × 36″ (91.4 × 91.4 × 91.4 cm). Tate, London.

33-16 • Donald Judd UNTITLED
1969. Galvanized iron and Plexiglas, 10 units, each 6″ × 27⅛″ × 24″ (15.24 × 68.8 × 60.96 cm), overall 120″ × 27⅛″ × 24″ (3.05 × 0.69 × 0.61 m). Albright-Knox Art Gallery, Buffalo, NY. Art © Judd Foundation. Licensed by VAGA, New York, NY.

JUDD In 1965, Donald Judd argued in an *Artforum* article entitled "Specific Objects" that Minimalism should consist of real or "specific" objects. He chose mathematically constructed impersonal shapes arranged without hierarchy, legible as complete forms in a single glance, occupying real space, having neither a base below nor a glass case around them. **UNTITLED** of 1969 (**FIG. 33-16**)

consists of 10 identical rectangular units fabricated from galvanized iron and tinted Plexiglas, hung in a vertical row on the gallery wall. The arrangement avoids allusion to any imagined subject allowing the objects to be aggressively themselves. Judd offers viewers clear, self-contained visual facts, setting the conceptual clarity and physical perfection of his art against the messy complexity of the real world.

MORRIS By the early 1970s, Robert Morris chose to explore the banal and uninteresting by making simple, unitary objects. **UNTITLED (MIRROR CUBE)** (**FIG. 33-17**) groups four wooden cubes created from industrial mirror glass. They literally reflect and deflect any attempt to discover interest *in* the boxes themselves, which hold no meaning within their form. There is no point of focus; instead the boxes reflect the world around them. The artfulness of this piece lies almost entirely in the artistic concept behind it—interrogating the purposes and goals of the artist. The artists' manifestos worked hand-in-hand with actual objects to communicate the ideas of Minimalism. Viewers had to work hard to learn how to read, understand, and appreciate the art itself.

Minimalism had many critics. The formalist Michael Fried, for instance, wrote that Minimal objects suffered from "objecthood," that they held no more interest than nonart objects. He also criticized Minimalism for its "theatricality." In his view, Minimalism, like Pop art, demanded viewers' immediate attention but could not hold that attention long, therefore becoming very boring very quickly.

CONCEPTUAL AND PERFORMANCE ART

The logical extension of the Minimalist move away from the handcrafted art object was Conceptual art. Unlike Duchamp and Dada artists earlier in the century, who argued that the idea *is* the work of art, Conceptual artists argue that "idea" and "form" are separable in art. Thus, for Conceptual artists, at times a physical object is an appropriate vehicle for a work of art, at other times a performance is more appropriate, and at still other times a conceptual manifestation, sometimes in the form of written or spoken instructions, is most appropriate. Conceptual art literally "dematerialized" the art object by suggesting that the catalyst for a work of art is a concept, and the means by which the concept is communicated can vary. Conceptual works of art usually leave behind some visual trace, in the form of a set of instructions, writing on a chalkboard, a performance, photographs, or a piece of film, and in some cases even objects. Conceptual art is theoretically driven and noncommodifiable because it leaves behind no precious object for purchase, although collectors and many museums now collect the remaining "trace" objects.

BEUYS Some of the most radical Conceptual art came out of Europe, and that of Joseph Beuys (1921–1986) was perhaps the most significant. He served as a fighter pilot in the German Luftwaffe during World War II, when he claimed to have been shot down over the Crimea and saved by Tartars who wrapped him in animal fat and felt. There is no evidence that this actually occurred, although something traumatic clearly happened to Beuys during the war. As an artist, he developed a mysterious shamanistic persona, and created a repertoire of significant materials and objects that he used symbolically and performatively in his art in an attempt to explain the inexplicable to audiences. Beuys's symbolism was deeply personal and difficult for others to grasp. His art centered on the desire to communicate and the complexities of that process.

In **HOW TO EXPLAIN PICTURES TO A DEAD HARE** (**FIG. 33-18**), Beuys initially sat on a chair in a gallery surrounded by his own drawings, his head coated in honey and covered by a mask of gold leaf. In his lap he cradled a dead hare to which he muttered incomprehensibly. His left foot rested on felt, suggesting spiritual warmth, while his right foot rested on steel, symbolizing cold hard reason. He carried the hare's corpse around the gallery for several hours, quietly explaining his pictures, reasoning that he had as much chance of communicating fully with the dead hare as with another person thus performing the problems inherent in the normal communication. Beuys said: "Even a dead animal preserves more powers of intuition than some human beings."

KOSUTH Joseph Kosuth (b. 1945) abandoned painting in 1965 to examine the intersection between language and vision, abstract idea and concrete imagery. His early work was indebted to Duchamp, semiotic theory, and the linguistic philosophy of Ludwig Wittgenstein (1889–1951). Kosuth's art is not about beauty, but the imperfect possibilities of communication, either visual or verbal. **ONE AND THREE CHAIRS** (**FIG. 33-19**) is a visual

33-18 • Joseph Beuys HOW TO EXPLAIN PICTURES TO A DEAD HARE
1965. Photograph of performance.

33-19 • Joseph Kosuth ONE AND THREE CHAIRS
1965. Wooden folding chair, photograph of chair, and photographic enlargement of dictionary definition of chair; chair, 32⅜″ × 14⅞″ × 20⅞″ (82.2 × 37.8 × 53 cm); photo panel, 36″ × 24⅛″ (91.4 × 61.3 cm); text panel 24⅛″ × 24½″ (61.3 × 62.2 cm). Museum of Modern Art, New York. Larry Aldrich Foundation Fund (383.1970 a–c)

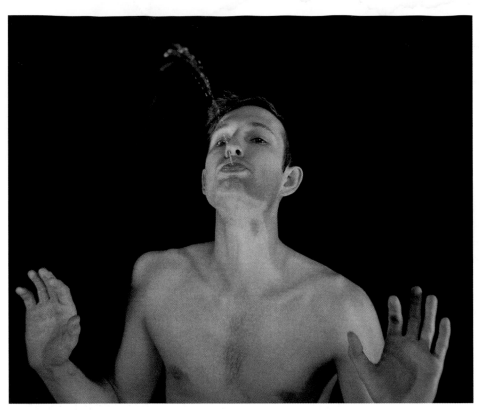

33-20 • Bruce Nauman SELF-PORTRAIT AS A FOUNTAIN
1966–1967. Color photograph, 19¾″ × 23¾″ (50.1 × 60.3 cm). Courtesy Leo Castelli Gallery, New York.

33-21 • Eva Hesse NO TITLE
1969–1970. Latex over rope, string, and wire; two strands, dimensions variable. Whitney Museum of American Art, New York. Purchase, with funds from Eli and Edythe L. Broad, the Mrs. Percy Uris Purchase Fund, and the Painting and Sculpture Committee (88.17 a–b)

Read the document related to Eva Hesse on myartslab.com

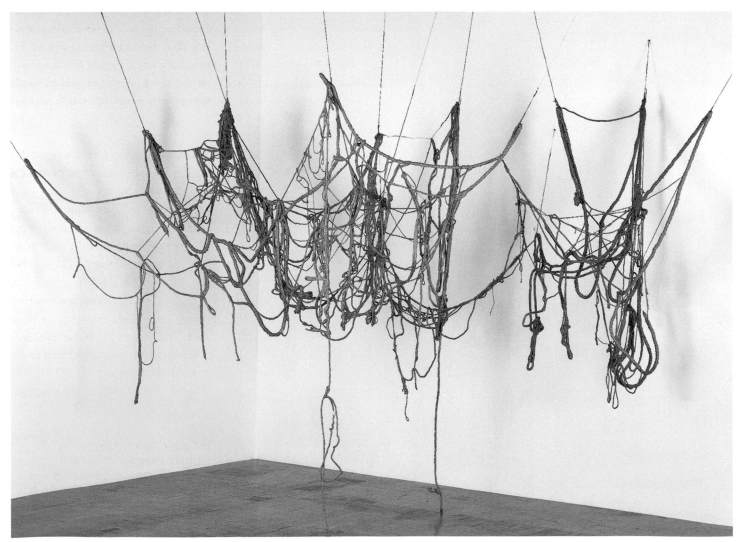

rendition of semiotic theory. In this installation there is an actual chair, a photograph of a chair, and a dictionary definition of "chair"—that is an object, an imperfect visual representation or idea of the object, and a verbal abstraction of the object. The title indicates that we can read this work as one chair represented three different ways or as three different chairs. Either way, Kosuth demonstrates the impossibility of precise representation and communication of an idea, leaving us to ponder the question: Which is the "real" chair?

NAUMAN In 1966–1967, the California-based artist Bruce Nauman (b. 1941) made a series of 11 color photographs based on wordplay and visual puns in which he cleverly complicated the problem of communication. In **SELF-PORTRAIT AS A FOUNTAIN** (**FIG. 33-20**), for example, the bare-chested artist tips his head back and spurts water into the air, thereby showing us that he is a fountain, or perhaps the *Fountain*, the title of Duchamp's infamous urinal (see FIG. 32-30). Nauman, like Kosuth, leaves us with the question: Which is the "real" fountain? Is it our abstracted idea of a fountain alluded to in the title (conceptual), Nauman's claim to be a fountain (visual), or could it be his sly reference to Duchamp's *Fountain* (art-historical)?

PROCESS ART

By the early 1970s, it was evident that Minimalism and Conceptualism had boxed art into an impossible absolutist corner—their reductivist approaches seemed too elitist, too detached from a society that was being torn apart by social and political conflict. Some artists refused to eliminate personal meaning from their work, and in opposition to Minimalism they explored the physicality, personality, even the sensuality of the process of making art.

HESSE Eva Hesse (1936–1970), for instance, infused her elegantly crafted art with personal history and meaning. She was born in Hamburg and narrowly escaped the Nazi Holocaust, moving to New York with her family in 1939. After graduating from the Yale School of Art in 1959, she painted dark Expressionistic self-portraits, but in 1964 she began to make abstract sculpture that adapted the vocabulary of Minimalism to her own, more self-expressive purpose. She wrote: "For me art and life are inseparable. If I can name the content [of my art] … it's the total absurdity of life." **NO TITLE** (**FIG. 33-21**) is about instability; it takes on a different size and shape each time it is installed. The work consists of several skeins of rope dipped in latex, knotted and tangled, and then hung from wires attached to the gallery ceiling. It is fragile and evocative, sensuous and delicate. Hesse embraced the instability, irrationality, and emotive power of art, reflecting her own life and emotions in the work. Her last pieces, made before her premature death from cancer, are heartbreaking.

WINSOR Jackie Winsor's (b. 1941) elegant and moving **BURNT PIECE** (**FIG. 33-22**), constructed from wire mesh, cement, and burnt wood, which Winsor worked intensively, also subverts the boxlike shapes of Minimalist sculpture. The detail is really only visible on the inside, within a closed, private, and secretive place. The woodwork refers to Winsor's childhood in Newfoundland, where her father was employed in the house-building trade.

33-22 • Jackie Winsor
BURNT PIECE
1977–1978. Cement, burnt wood, and wire mesh, 36″ × 36″ × 36″ (91.4 × 91.4 × 91.4 cm). © Jackie Winsor. Courtesy Paula Cooper Gallery, New York. Museum of Modern Art, Gift of Agnes Gund (90.1991)

Judy Chicago's **THE DINNER PARTY** (**FIG. 33-23**) is a large, complex, mixed-media installation dedicated to hundreds of women and women artists rescued from anonymity by early feminist artists and historians. It took five years of collaborative effort to make, and it drew on the assistance of hundreds of female and several male volunteers working as ceramists, needleworkers, and china painters. *The Dinner Party* includes a large, triangular table, each side stretching 48 feet; Chicago conceived of the equilateral triangle as a symbol of both the feminine and the equalized world sought by feminism. The table rests on a triangular platform of 2,300 triangular porcelain tiles comprising the "Heritage Floor" that bears the names of 999 notable women from myth, legend, and history. Along each side of the table are 13 place settings representing famous women—13 being the number of men at the Last Supper as well

as the number of witches in a coven. The 39 women thus honored by individual place settings include the mythical, including the goddess Ishtar and an Amazon, and historical personages such as the Egyptian queen Hatshepsut, the Roman scholar Hypatia, the medieval French queen Eleanor of Aquitaine, the author Christine de Pizan (see page 533), the Italian Renaissance noblewoman Isabella d'Este (see page 660), the Italian Baroque painter Artemisia Gentileschi (see FIG. 23-13), the eighteenth-century English feminist writer Mary Wollstonecraft, the nineteenth-century American abolitionist Sojourner Truth, and the twentieth-century American painter Georgia O'Keeffe (setting shown here).

Each larger-than-life place setting includes a 14-inch-wide painted porcelain plate, ceramic flatware, a ceramic chalice with a gold interior, and an embroidered napkin, sitting upon an elaborately ornamented woven and stitched

runner, with techniques and motifs appropriate to the time and place in which each woman lived. Most of the plates feature abstract designs based on female genitalia because, as Chicago said, "that is all [these women] had in common … . They were from different periods, classes, ethnicities, geographies, experiences, but what kept them within the same confined historical space" was their biological sex. The empty plates represent the fact that they "had been swallowed up and obscured by history instead of being recognized and honored."

The prominent place accorded to china painting and needlework in *The Dinner Party* both celebrates traditional women's crafts and argues for their place in the pantheon of "high art," while at the same time informing the viewer about some of the unrecognized contributions that women have made to history.

33-23 • Judy Chicago THE DINNER PARTY
1974–1979. Overall installation view. White tile floor inscribed in gold with 999 women's names; triangular table with painted porcelain, sculpted porcelain plates, and needlework, each side 48′ × 42′ × 3′ (14.6 × 12.8 × 1 m). Brooklyn Museum of Art, New York. Gift of the Elizabeth A. Sackler Foundation (2002.10)

Georgia O'Keeffe
Place setting, detail of *The Dinner Party.*

FEMINISM AND ART

The idea of feminist art developed alongside the women's liberation movement of the 1960s as a challenge to one of the major unspoken conventions of art history: that great art could only be made by men. Since the 1960s, there have been three waves of feminist art and art history.

A major aim of first-generation feminism artists was increased recognition for the accomplishment of women artists, both past and present. As feminists examined the history of art, they found that women had contributed to most of the movements of Western art but were almost never mentioned in histories of art. Art historians began to salvage the histories of as many women artists as possible, instating them in the "canon," and arguing that they were as accomplished and important as the male artists already enshrined within it. Early feminists also attacked the traditional Western hierarchy that placed "the fine arts" (painting, sculpture, architecture) at a level of achievement higher than "the crafts" (ceramics, textiles, jewelry making). Since most craft media have been historically dominated by women, favoring art over craft tends to relegate women's achievements to second-class status. Thus early feminist art tended to embrace craft media (see Introduction, page xxix). Meanwhile, early feminist artists represented the physicality and sexuality of the female body as defined by women rather than as it appeared in male fantasies. This early feminist art was essentialist; it focused on women's bodies and defined gender in biological terms.

The second wave of feminist art defined gender in more relativist terms. In 1971, Linda Nochlin wrote a groundbreaking essay entitled "Why Have There Been No Great Women Artists?" in which she argued that many women artists in history cannot be described as "great" if the only standard of judgment for "great" art is a masculine canon. Nochlin argued that art institutions had systematically denied women access to art education and opportunities available to men throughout history, thereby making competition on male terms impossible. Thus, the terms of the canon must be challenged and the art system changed so that women can compete on their own terms. Second-wave feminist artists deconstructed the canon by which art was currently judged and called for a re-evaluation of the place of so-called feminine arts, such as ceramics, textiles, jewelry making, and miniature painting. In 1972 and 1973, Laura Mulvey and John Berger also challenged how women are looked at (gazed upon) by men in life and in art.

Third-wave feminist art emerged in the 1990s. This latest generation of artists has addressed an expanded range of issues surrounding the discrimination against or denigration of women, including such hybrid concerns such as gender and class, gender and race, violence against women, postcolonialism, transgenderism, transnationalism, and eco-feminism. In the process they have explored the many strategies that women employ to navigate life.

CHICAGO AND SCHAPIRO Born Judy Cohen, Judy Chicago (b. 1939) adopted the name of the city of her birth in

33-24 • Miriam Schapiro PERSONAL APPEARANCE #3
1973. Acrylic and fabric on canvas, 60″ × 50″ (152.4 × 127 cm).
Private collection.

order to free herself from "all names imposed upon her through male social dominance." In the late 1960s, she began making abstracted images of female genitalia to challenge the male-dominated art world and to validate the female body and experience. In 1970, she established a feminist studio art course at Fresno State College (now California State University, Fresno) and the next year moved to Los Angeles to join the painter Miriam Schapiro (b. 1923) in establishing a Feminist Art Program at the new California Institute of the Arts (CalArts). At this time she also began to create *The Dinner Party*, one of the largest and best-known feminist artworks of the 1970s (see "*The Dinner Party*," opposite).

In 1971–1972, Chicago, Schapiro, and 21 of their female students created *Womanhouse*, a collaborative art environment located in a run-down Hollywood mansion which the artists renovated and filled with feminist installations. In collaboration with Sherry Brody, Schapiro also created *Dollhouse*, a mixed-media construction of several miniature rooms adorned with richly patterned fabrics. She subsequently began to incorporate pieces of fabric into her acrylic paintings, developing a type of work she called femmage (from "female" and "collage"). Schapiro's femmages, such as **PERSONAL APPEARANCE #3** (**FIG. 33-24**), celebrate traditional women's crafts with a formal and emotional richness that was meant to counter the Minimalist aesthetic of the 1960s that she considered typically male. Schapiro later returned to New York to lead the Pattern and Decoration movement, a group of both female and male artists who merged the aesthetics of abstraction with ornamental motifs derived from women's craft, folk art, and art beyond the Western tradition in a nonhierarchical manner.

MENDIETA Ana Mendieta (1948–1985) was born in Cuba but sent to Iowa in 1961 as part of "Operation Peter Pan," which relocated 14,000 unaccompanied Cuban children after the 1959 revolution that brought Fidel Castro and communism to power in Cuba. Mendieta never fully recovered from the trauma of her removal. A sense of personal dislocation haunted her, and a desire to leave her bodily imprint on the earth drove Mendieta to use ritualistic actions in performances that connected her to the earth. She was inspired by both *santería*, the African-Cuban religion (see FIG. 32-78), and the work of Beuys (see FIG. 33-18). Mendi-

33-25 • Ana Mendieta UNTITLED, FROM THE TREE OF LIFE SERIES
1977. Color photograph, 20″ × 13¼″ (50.8 × 33.7 cm). © Estate of Ana Mendieta Collection.

eta produced more than 200 body works called "Silhouettes" in which she "planted" herself in the earth, and she recorded these performances in photographs and on film. The **TREE OF LIFE** series (FIG. 33-25) was created in Iowa, where she studied and lived. This photograph shows Mendieta with arms upraised like an earth goddess, pressed against a tree and covered in mud, as if to invite the tree to absorb her and connect her to her "maternal source." Like many of Mendieta's other works, this piece celebrates the notion that women have a deeper identification than men with nature.

EARTHWORKS AND SITE-SPECIFIC SCULPTURE

In the early 1970s, as Process artists reintroduced the handcrafted into art, another group of artists began working with the earth itself, using it as a medium to manipulate, craft, and change. Using the land as their canvas, Earth artists made art outdoors, frequently manipulating raw materials found at the site to create **earthworks** that are usually **site-specific** (designed for a specific location). Some of these artists created vast sculptures that altered the landscape permanently, while others made ambitious temporary works. Some Earth art appeared in remote locations, directly accessible to only a few people, while other examples are available to many. Earth art, like Performance and Conceptual art, is often intended to be noncommodifiable but is frequently recorded in photographs and on film, with the result that these images become collectable objects rather than the work itself. Earth art should not be confused with Environmental art. The former uses the land (or city) as a place on which to make art, whereas the latter seeks to draw attention to an imperiled natural environment.

SMITHSON Robert Smithson (1938–1973) sought to illustrate what he called the "ongoing dialectic" in nature between the constructive forces that build and shape form, and the destructive forces that destroy it. **SPIRAL JETTY** (FIG. 33-26) of 1970, a 1,500-foot stone and earth platform spiraling into the Great Salt Lake in Utah, reflects these ideas. To Smithson, the salty water and algae of the lake suggested both the primordial ocean where life began and a dead sea that killed it. The abandoned oil rigs dotting the lake's shore brought to mind dinosaur skeletons and the remains of vanished civilizations. Smithson used the spiral because it is an archetypal shape that appears in nature—from galaxies to seashells—and has been used in human art for millennia. Unlike Modernist squares and circles, it is a "dialectical" shape, that opens and closes, curls and uncurls endlessly, suggesting growth and decay, creation and destruction, or in Smithson's words, the perpetural "coming and going of things." He ordered that no maintenance be done on *Spiral Jetty* so that the work would be governed by the natural elements over time. It is now covered with crystallized salt but remains visible, as can be seen on Google Earth.

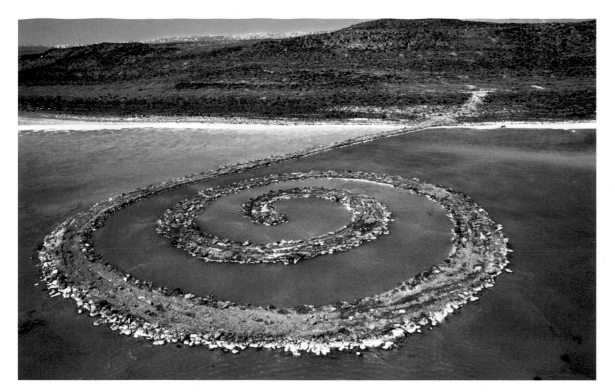

33-26 • Robert Smithson **SPIRAL JETTY**
1969–1970. Mud, precipitated salt crystals, rocks, and water, length 1,500′ × width 15′ (457 × 4.5 m). Great Salt Lake, Utah. Art © Estate of Robert Smithson/ Licensed by VAGA, New York, NY.

Smithson incorporated one of the few living organisms found in the otherwise dead lake into his work: an alga that turns a reddish color under certain conditions. *Spiral Jetty* is one vehicle wide: To create the work, earth was hauled out into the lake in a huge land-moving truck.

CHRISTO AND JEANNE-CLAUDE The most visible site-specific artists in America were Christo Javacheff (b. 1935) and Jeanne-Claude de Guillebon (1935–2009), who embarked on vast projects (both rural and urban) that sometimes took many years of planning to realize. In 1958, Christo emigrated from Bulgaria to Paris, where he met Jeanne-Claude; they moved to New York together in 1964. Their work was political and interventionist, frequently commenting on capitalism and consumer culture by wrapping or packaging buildings or large swatches of land in fabric: They "wrapped" the Reichstag in Berlin and 1 million square feet of Australian coastline, for instance. In each case the process of planning and battling bureaucracies was part of the art, frequently taking years to complete. By contrast, the wrapping itself usually took only a few weeks and the completed project was in place for even less time. Christo and Jeanne-Claude funded each new project from the sale of books, Christo's original artworks (like drawings and collages), and other ephemera relating to the preceding projects.

In February 2005, Christo and Jeanne-Claude installed **THE GATES, CENTRAL PARK, NEW YORK, 1979–2005** (**FIG. 33-27**), a project that took 26 years to realize, during which time the artists battled their way through various New York bureaucracies, meeting many obstacles and making changes to the work along the way. They finally installed 7,503 saffron-colored nylon panels on "gates" along 23 miles of pathway in Central Park. The brightly colored flapping panels enlivened the frigid February landscape and were an enormous public success. The installation lasted for only 16 days.

33-27 • Christo and Jeanne-Claude **THE GATES, CENTRAL PARK, NEW YORK**
1979–2005. Shown here during its installation in 2005.

ARCHITECTURE: MID-CENTURY MODERNISM TO POSTMODERNISM

The International Style, with its plainly visible structure and rejection of historicism, dominated new urban construction in much of the world after World War II, which meant that the utopian and revolutionary aspects of Modernist architecture settled into a form that largely came to stand for corporate power and wealth. Several major European International Style architects, such as Walter Gropius (see FIG. 32–52), migrated to the United States and assumed important positions in architecture schools, where they trained several generations of like-minded architects.

MID-CENTURY MODERNIST ARCHITECTURE

Ludwig Mies van der Rohe (1886–1969) created the most extreme examples of postwar International Style buildings (see "The International Style," page 1057). A former Bauhaus teacher and a refugee from Nazi Germany, Mies designed the rectilinear glass towers that came to personify postwar capitalism. The crisp, clean lines of the **SEAGRAM BUILDING** in New York City (**FIG. 33-28**), designed with Philip Johnson, epitomize the standardization and impersonality that became synonymous with modern corporations. Such buildings, with their efficient construction methods and use of materials, allowed architects to pack an immense amount of office space into a building on a very small lot; it was also economical to construct. Although criticized for building relatively unadorned glass boxes, Mies advocated: "Less is more." He did, however, use nonfunctional, decorative bronze beams on the outside of the Seagram Building to echo the functional beams inside and give the façade a sleek, rich, and dignified appearance.

Although the pared-down, rectilinear forms of the International Style dominated the urban skyline, other architects departed from its impersonal principles so that, even in commercial architecture, expressive designs using new structural techniques and more materials also appeared. For instance, the **TRANS WORLD AIRLINES (TWA) TERMINAL** (**FIG. 33-29**) at John F. Kennedy Airport in New York City, by the Finnish-born American architect Eero Saarinen (1910–1961), dramatically breaks out of the box. Saarinen sought to evoke the thrill and glamor of air travel by giving the TWA Terminal's roof two broad winglike canopies of reinforced concrete that suggest a huge bird about to take flight. The interior consists of large, open, dramatically flowing spaces. Saarinen designed each detail of the interior—from ticket counters to telephone booths—to complement his gull-winged shell.

33-28 • Ludwig Mies van der Rohe and Philip Johnson
SEAGRAM BUILDING, NEW YORK
1954–1958.

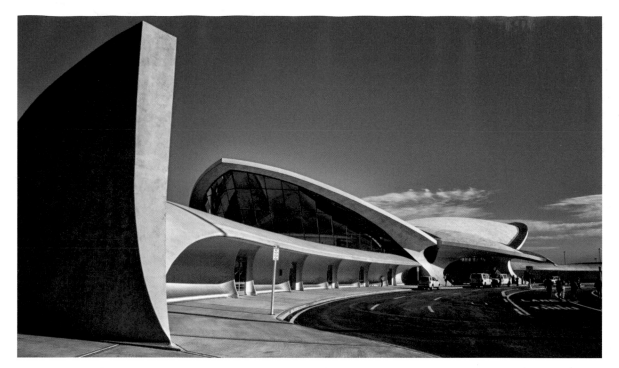

33-29 • Eero Saarinen **TRANS WORLD AIRLINES (TWA) TERMINAL, JOHN F. KENNEDY AIRPORT, NEW YORK**
1956–1962.

Frank Lloyd Wright (see FIGS. 32–41, 32–42, 32–43) transformed museum architecture with the **GUGGENHEIM MUSEUM** (**FIG. 33-30**) in New York, designed as a sculptural work of art in its own right. The Guggenheim was created to house Solomon Guggenheim's personal collection of Modern art and, like the TWA Terminal, took on an organic shape, in this case a spiral. The museum's galleries spiral downward from a glass ceiling, wrapping themselves around a spectacular five-story atrium. Wright intended visitors to begin by taking the elevator to the top floor and then walk down the sloping and increasingly

33-30 • Frank Lloyd Wright
SOLOMON R. GUGGENHEIM MUSEUM, NEW YORK
1943–1959.

The large building behind the museum is a later addition, designed in 1992 by Gwathmey Siegel and Associates.

widening ramp, enjoying paintings along the way. Today, the interior maintains the intended intimacy of a "living room," despite alterations by the museum's first directors. Wright wanted the building to contrast with skyscrapers like the Seagram Building and become a Manhattan landmark—indeed, it remains one of the twentieth century's most distinctive museum spaces.

POSTMODERN ARCHITECTURE

In the 1970s, architects began to move away from the sleek glass-and-steel boxes of the International Style and reintroduce quotations from past styles into their designs. Architectural historians trace the origins of this new Postmodern style to the work of Jane Jacobs (1916–2006), who wrote *The Death and Life of Great American Cities* (1961), as well as to Philadelphia architect Robert Venturi (b. 1925), who rejected the abstract purity of the International Style by incorporating elements drawn from vernacular (meaning popular, common, or ordinary) sources into his designs.

Venturi parodied Mies van der Rohe's aphorism, "Less is more," with his own—"Less is a bore." He accused Mies and other Modernist architects of ignoring human needs in their quest for uniformity, purity, and abstraction, and challenged Postmodernism to address the complex, contradictory, and heterogeneous mixture of "high" and "low" architecture that comprised the modern city. Venturi encouraged new architecture to embrace eclecticism, and

he reintroduced references to past architectural styles into his own designs, and began to apply decoration to his buildings.

While writing his treatise on Postmodernism—*Complexity and Contradiction in Architecture* (1966)—Venturi designed a house for his mother (FIG. 33-31) that put many of his new ideas into practice. The shape of the façade returns to the traditional Western "house" shape that Modernists (see FIGS. 32-39, 32-40, 32-50) had rejected because of its clichéd historical associations. Venturi's vocabulary of triangles and squares is arranged in a playful asymmetry that skews the staid harmonies of Modernist design, while the curved moldings are a purely decorative flourish—heretical in the strict tenets of the International Style. But the most disruptive element of the façade is the deep cleavage over the door, which opens to reveal a mysterious upper wall and chimney top. The interior is also complex and contradictory. The irregular floor plan, including an odd stairway leading up to the second floor, is further complicated by irregular ceiling levels that are partially covered by a barrel vault.

In the 1970s, Postmodern ideas were also applied to commercial architecture. One of the first examples was the **AT&T CORPORATE HEADQUARTERS** (now the Sony Building) in New York City (FIG. 33-32) by Philip Johnson (1906–2005). This elegant, granite-clad skyscraper has 36 oversized stories, making it as tall as the average 60-story building. It mimics its International

33-31 • Robert Venturi FAÇADE (A) AND PLAN (B), VANNA VENTURI HOUSE, CHESTNUT HILL
Philadelphia, Pennsylvania. 1961–1964.

33-32 • Philip Johnson and John Burgee MODEL OF THE AT&T CORPORATE HEADQUARTERS, NEW YORK 1978–1983.

Style neighbors with its smooth uncluttered skin, while its Classical window groupings set between vertical piers also echo nearby skyscrapers from much earlier in the century. But the overall profile of the building bears a whimsical resemblance to the shape of a Chippendale highboy, an eighteenth-century chest of drawers with a long-legged base and angled top—Johnson seems to have intended a pun on the terms "highboy" and "high-rise." The round notch at the top of the building as well as the rounded entryway at its base suggest the coin slot and coin return of an old pay telephone in a clever reference to Johnson's patron, the AT&T telephone company.

POSTMODERNISM

Scholars disagree about the exact date when the theories of Postmodernism—developing in the 1970s—filtered through the Western art world, but most agree that it took place sometime in the early 1980s. By then, Modern ideas of art as absolute, ideal, pure, or perfect, and of the artist as a serious, single-minded individual who held her/himself above and apart from society, were beginning to seem both arrogant and foolhardy to younger artists.

Rather than a style, Postmodernism is perhaps better thought of as a strategy for making art. Its manifestations are many and varied. Postmodern artists reject the seriousness of Modernism, creating visually interesting, messy, sometimes contrary, and often political images that mock the rules of Modern art. They "appropriate" or take images wholesale from both "high art" and "popular" sources, repositioning and recontextualizing them, making them partially their own, twisting and changing their meanings. Postmodern artists create new images and new meanings out of the old, welcoming oddity, contradiction, and eccentricity, seriously questioning the idea of "originality."

Just as Modern art heralded an industrial, technological society, the advent of Postmodern art heralded a post-industrial, advanced capitalist society based on communication and information, and demanding a flexible population that embraces difference and change. Postmodern art reflects the **pluralism** (social and cultural diversity) of our globalized society, in which the only real constant is change and the only thing we have in common is difference. Postmodern art also embraces the vast visual culture of the 1980s, the age of personal computers, video cameras, cable television, and an emerging Internet culture; it harnesses images from this infinitely mutable world in which it is difficult to know what is real and what is not. As Andy Warhol observed presciently some time before, "I don't know where the artificial stops and the real starts."

PAINTING

Neo-Expressionism, one of the first international expressions of Postmodernism, was launched by two highly visible exhibitions in London ("A New Spirit") and Berlin ("Zeitgeist") in the early 1980s. Included in these exhibitions were large-scale figural paintings that recovered the luxury of the painted surface. Neo-Expressionism was almost exclusively a male movement: "A New Spirit" featured the art of 38 male artists and "Zeitgeist" featured the art of one female and 43 male artists.

KIEFER The German Neo-Expressionist Anselm Kiefer (b. 1945), born in the final weeks of World War II, both pays homage to and critiques the art of the German Expressionists of the 1930s, which was banned by the Nazis (see "Suppression of the Avant-Garde in Nazi Germany," page 1056). In the burned and barren landscape of **HEATH OF THE BRANDENBURG MARCH** (**FIG. 33-33**) from 1974 Kiefer grapples with his country's Nazi past, building on the

33–33 • Anselm Kiefer HEATH OF THE BRANDENBURG MARCH
1974. Oil, acrylic, and shellac on burlap, 3′10½″ × 8′4″ (1.18 × 2.54 m). Collection Van Abbemuseum, Eindhoven, The Netherlands © Anselm Kiefer.

ideas of his teacher Beuys. Instead of simply documenting Nazism in this painting, Kiefer juxtaposes the devastating physical impact of the war on the Brandenburg Heath (near Berlin) with Nazi history by scrawling the first words of the Nazi marching song "Märkische Heide, märkische Sand" across the road in the foreground, both quoting from the past and critiquing it.

BASQUIAT In the United States, the tragically short-lived Jean-Michel Basquiat (1960–1988) painted Neo-Expressionist canvases that grew out of graffiti art. The Brooklyn-born Basquiat was raised in middle-class comfort but rebelled by quitting high school and leaving home to become a street artist. For three years he covered the walls of lower Manhattan with short and witty philosophical texts signed with the tag "SAMO©." In 1980, Basquiat participated in the highly publicized "Times Square Show" which showcased the raw and aggressive styles of subway and graffiti artists. Basquiat said he wanted to make "paintings that look as if they were

33–34 • Jean-Michel Basquiat HORN PLAYERS
1983. Acrylic and oil paintstick on canvas, three panels, overall 8′ × 6′5″ (2.44 × 1.91 m). Broad Art Foundation, Santa Monica, California.

33-35 • Gerhard Richter MAN SHOT DOWN (1) ERSCHOSSENER (1) FROM OCTOBER 18, 1977
1988. Oil on canvas, 39½″ × 55¼″ (100 × 140 cm). Museum of Modern Art, New York. © Gerhard Richter 2012. The Sidney and Harriet Janis Collection, gift of Philip Johnson, and acquired through the Lillie P. Bliss Bequest (all by exchange); Enid A. Haupt Fund; Nina and Gordon Bunshaft Bequest Fund; and gift of Emily Rauh Pulitzer (169.1995.g.)

made by a child," but in reality his work is a sophisticated mix of appropriated imagery from Modern art combined with blunt references to race and the street.

The strongly emotional **HORN PLAYERS** (**FIG. 33-34**) of 1983 portrays legendary jazz musicians Charlie Parker (upper left) and Dizzy Gillespie (center right) using urgent paint application and hurried lettering to convey Basquiat's dedication to jazz and his passionate determination to foreground African-American subjects in an unsentimental way. He said: "Black people are never portrayed realistically, not even portrayed, in Modern art, and I'm glad to do that." He died from a heroin overdose at age 27.

RICHTER Neo-Expressionism was only one of the many forms taken by Postmodern painting. German artist Gerhard Richter (b. 1932), for example, rejected the idea of adopting a single personal style, arguing that each painting's content should determine its form. In 1988, he created a series of paintings, including **MAN SHOT DOWN (1) ERSCHOSSENER (1) FROM OCTOBER 18, 1977** (**FIG. 33-35**) that featured life-size painted copies of grainy black-and-white newspaper photographs of the bodies of three members of the terrorist group Red Army Faction (commonly known as the Baader-Meinhof Gang), who were found dead in their prison cells in 1977, probably by suicide. They had been imprisoned for the kidnap and murder of Hans Martin Schleyer, president of the powerful German Federation of Industries. Richter simultaneously critiques the single-minded pursuit of a political ideologue willing to die for an idea, the powerful role of the mass media in creating meaning with images, and the value of the hand of the artist, even when, as in this case, it is almost invisible.

POSTMODERNISM AND GENDER

In 1982, critic Craig Owens argued that Postmodernism represents a crisis in normal cultural authority because of the way it questions the fictive homogeneity of Modernism. Moreover, since photography, which had never been fully integrated into the fine art canon, was perhaps the perfect medium for appropriating images, Owens argued that photography might also be the ideal medium for Postmodernism. Feminism had already challenged the "patriarchy" (the masculine control of power in society), and Owens characterized Modernism as patriarchal, authoritative, single-minded, and driven by the quest for originality and artistic mastery. He therefore argued that feminists and photographers were better positioned to create outstanding Postmodern art than the mostly male Neo-Expressionist painters. Postmodernism, feminism, and photography all forced viewers to confront difference; all challenged the authority of the canon; none particularly valued originality or individual artistic mastery. In keeping with this, many women artists used Postmodern strategies to create feminist art (see "The Guerrilla Girls," page 1110).

SHERMAN In 1977, Cindy Sherman (b. 1954) began work on her "Untitled Film Stills" series that exemplifies Postmodern strategies of looking. These black-and-white photographs eerily resemble publicity stills from the early 1960s, but they are actually contemporary photographs of Sherman herself in which she poses, appropriately made-up, in settings that seem to quote from the well-known plots of old movies. In **UNTITLED FILM STILL #21** (**FIG. 33-36**), for instance, she appears as a small-town "girl" recently arrived in the big city to find work. Other photographs from the series show her variously as a Southern belle, a hard-working housewife, and a teenager waiting by the phone for a call.

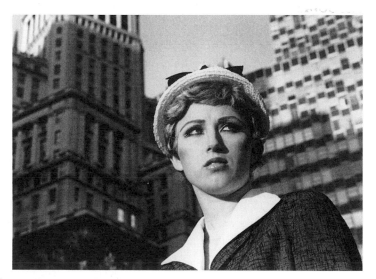

33-36 • Cindy Sherman UNTITLED FILM STILL #21
1978. Black-and-white photograph, 8″ × 10″ (20.3 × 25.4 cm). Courtesy of the artist and Metro Pictures, New York.

👁 **Watch** a video about Cindy Sherman on myartslab.com

In 1984, the Museum of Modern Art mounted "An International Survey of Painting and Sculpture," an exhibition that supposedly displayed the most important art of the time, yet of the 169 (mostly white) artists included in the exhibition, only 13 were women. By way of a rejoinder to this and several other such exhibitions, the following year the radical feminist group the Guerrilla Girls was founded in New York to function, they said, as "the conscience of the art world." Its members wear gorilla masks to hide their identity and to prevent personal reprisals; they call themselves "girls" as a play on the demeaning term "girl" as applied to women. Each Guerrilla Girl takes as a pseudonym the name of a famous dead woman artist. They have declared that the new "f" word is feminism.

Their mandate is to reveal gender and racial inequities in the art world, to demonstrate against discrimination, and to fight for the rights of women and artists of color. The Guerrilla Girls use the strategies of guerrilla warfare—they act covertly and strike anonymously at the heart of their enemy. They compile statistics on discrimination in the art world, produce sharp, witty, sophisticated posters that draw on the best advertising theory, and paste these posters at night on walls in the art districts of New York, close to offending galleries and museums. The posters are highly visible, damning, and very funny, and they have made a difference.

One of their most famous posters features a variation on Ingres's *Large Odalisque* (see FIG. 30–56) and the words "Do women have to be naked to get into the Met. Museum?" As the poster explains, 85 percent of the nudes on display in the Metropolitan Museum at the time (1989) were women, while less than 5 percent of art in the museum was by women. Sadly, the Guerrilla Girls repeated their survey in 2005 and found that there were even fewer women artists (3 percent), but, as they said, at least there were more naked men!

THE ADVANTAGES OF BEING A WOMAN ARTIST (FIG. 33–37) delivers a clever, ironic, and sadly accurate list of the "benefits" of being a woman artist. Today's Guerrilla Girls have broadened their reach to address larger issues of race and political discrimination in the world. They have made significant differences in the art world, if not yet at the Met.

THE ADVANTAGES OF BEING A WOMAN ARTIST:

Working without the pressure of success
Not having to be in shows with men
Having an escape from the art world in your 4 free-lance jobs
Knowing your career might pick up after you're eighty
Being reassured that whatever kind of art you make it will be labeled feminine
Not being stuck in a tenured teaching position
Seeing your ideas live on in the work of others
Having the opportunity to choose between career and motherhood
Not having to choke on those big cigars or paint in Italian suits
Having more time to work when your mate dumps you for someone younger
Being included in revised versions of art history
Not having to undergo the embarrassment of being called a genius
Getting your picture in the art magazines wearing a gorilla suit

A PUBLIC SERVICE MESSAGE FROM **GUERRILLA GIRLS** CONSCIENCE OF THE ART WORLD

33–37 • Guerrilla Girls THE ADVANTAGES OF BEING A WOMAN ARTIST
1988. Offset print, 17″ × 22″ (43.2 × 55.9 cm).
Collection of the artists. © Guerrilla Girls.

Critics have discussed these images in terms of second-wave feminism since they question the culturally constructed roles played by women in society, and since they critique the male gaze. In each, Sherman is both the photographer and the photographed. By assuming both roles, she complicates the relationship between the person looking and the person being observed, and she subverts the way in which photographs of women communicate stereotypes.

KRUGER Barbara Kruger (b. 1945) makes an even stronger point about how women are observed in **UNTITLED (YOUR GAZE HITS THE SIDE OF MY FACE)** (FIG. 33–38). Kruger began her career as a designer for *Mademoiselle* magazine before using photography to make art. Her signature style is a combination of black-and-white photographic images with the red three-color printing used in cheap advertising. Kruger appropriates the visual

33–38 • Barbara Kruger UNTITLED (YOUR GAZE HITS THE SIDE OF MY FACE)
1981. Photograph, red painted frame, 55″ × 41″ (140 × 104 cm).
Mary Boone Gallery, New York. © Barbara Kruger.

View the Closer Look for
Tar Beach on myartslab.com

character of advertising—its layout style, and its characteristic use of slogans—to suggest and subvert the advertising image. Here she personalizes the relationship between viewer and viewed—the person who looks (the spectator) and the person who is looked at (the subject)—by addressing viewers directly with the personal pronoun "you." The spectator is active, while subject is passive. Usually the person who looks holds the power of the "gaze," implicitly subjugating the person being looked at. But if the person being looked at returns, rejects, or deflects the gaze, the traditional power relationship is upset. That is what happens in Kruger's image, where the observer ("you") is blocked by the subject, who declares that "your gaze" is deflecting by "the side of my face." Kruger's art is subversive and interventionist; she has distributed it on posters, on T-shirts, even on pencils and pens.

POSTMODERNISM AND RACE OR ETHNICITY

Other artists have likewise used Postmodern strategies to draw attention to racial and ethnic difference, advocating for change and exploring how race and gender combine to silence artists.

RINGGOLD Faith Ringgold (b. 1930) draws on the tradition of African-American quilt making combined with the heritage of African textiles to paint significant statements about race in America. In the early 1970s, Ringgold began to introduce traditional women's crafts into her art, painting on soft fabrics rather than on stretched canvases and framing her paintings with decorative quilted borders. Ringgold's mother, Willi Posey, a fashion designer and dressmaker, made the quilted borders until her death in 1981, after which Ringgold began to do the quilting herself. In 1977, Ringgold started writing her autobiography (*We Flew Over the Bridge: The Memoirs of Faith Ringgold*, 1995) but, unable to find a publisher, decided to sew her stories into quilts instead—what she termed "story quilting."

Animated by a feminist sensibility, Ringgold's story quilts are narrated by women and usually address women's issues. In **TAR BEACH** (**FIG. 33–39**), the narrator is 8-year-old Cassie Louise Lightfoot—although the story is actually based on Ringgold's own memories of growing up in Harlem. "Tar Beach" refers to the roof of the apartment building in which Ringgold's family lived. They

33-40 • Lorna Simpson
STEREO STYLES
1988. Ten black-and-white
Polaroid prints and ten
engraved plastic plaques,
5′4″ × 9′8″ (1.63 × 2.95 m)
overall. Private collection.

slept there on hot summer nights, and Ringgold describes it as a magical place. Cassie and her brother lie on a blanket while their parents and neighbors play cards. She dreams that she can fly and that she can possess everything over which she passes. Cassie is shown flying over the George Washington Bridge, claiming it for herself; over a new union-constructed building, claiming it for her father who, as an African-American construction worker, was not allowed to join the union; and over an ice-cream factory, claiming for her mother "ice cream every night for dessert." Cassie's fantasy is charming, but it reminds viewers of the real social and economic prejudices that African Americans have faced in America's past and present.

SIMPSON In **STEREO STYLES** (**FIG. 33–40**), Lorna Simpson (b. 1960) arranges in a double row ten Polaroid images of African-American women photographed from behind. Each wears a different hairstyle, described variously and ironically as "Daring," "Sensible," "Severe," "Long and Silky," "Boyish," "Ageless," "Silly," "Magnetic," "Country Fresh," and "Sweet." Simpson frequently photographs African-American women with their faces turned away to suggest that they are seen only in terms of their bodies or, in this case, of their African-American hair styles. Her images ask us to consider how African-American women are stereotyped and to contemplate the role that hair plays as an indicator of race, gender, and class in society.

33-41 • Judith F. Baca THE DIVISION OF THE BARRIOS (DETAIL FROM THE GREAT WALL OF LOS ANGELES)
1976–1983 (section shown painted summer 1983). Acrylic on cast concrete, height 13′ (4 m), overall length of mural approx. 2,500′ (762 m). San Fernando Valley Tujunga Wash, Van Nuys, California. © SPARC.

33-42 • Kerry James Marshall MANY MANSIONS
1994. Acrylic on paper mounted on canvas, 114¼″ × 135⅛″ (290 × 343 cm). The Art Institute of Chicago. Max V. Kohnstamm Fund (1995.147)

👁 Watch a video about Kerry James Marshall on myartslab.com

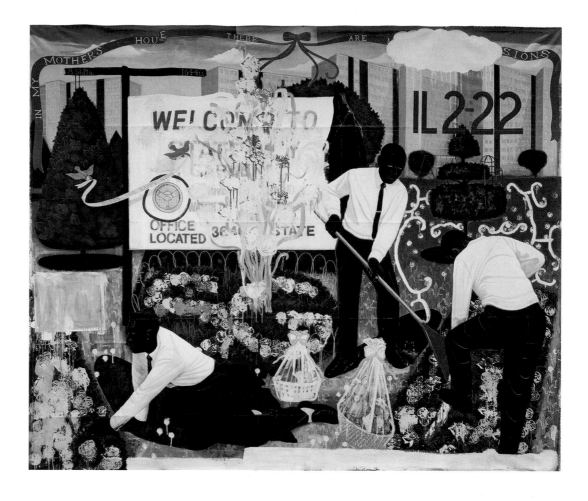

BACA Judith F. Baca (b. 1946) pays tribute to her Mexican-American heritage in *The Great Wall of Los Angeles*—begun in 1976 and extending almost 2,500 feet along a flood drainage canal—which looks back to the Mexican mural movement to recount the history of California as seen through Mexican-, African-, and Japanese-American eyes. This detail, **THE DIVISION OF THE BARRIOS** (**FIG. 33–41**), depicts the residents of a Mexican-American neighborhood protesting futilely against the division of their neighborhood by a new freeway. Other scenes include the deportation of Mexican-American citizens during the Great Depression and the internment of Japanese-American citizens during World War II. Like Judy Chicago's *Dinner Party* (see **FIG. 33–23**), Baca's *The Great Wall of Los Angeles* was a collaborative effort involving many professional artists and hundreds of young people.

MARSHALL MANY MANSIONS (**FIG. 33–42**) by African-American painter Kerry James Marshall (b. 1955) is a wry, ironic commentary on race, class, and poverty in American society. The work refers to Stateway Gardens, Chicago, one of the largest and worst-maintained housing projects in America. The scandalously inadequate conditions were the subject of much debate prior to its demolition in 2007. Marshall shows an unrealistically idyllic attempt by three African-American men—impossibly well dressed for gardening—to create an equally impossibly tidy garden that includes manicured topiary in the background and flowerbeds in the foreground. The painting includes a number of biting details, including the statement "In my mother's house there are many mansions," which both changes the gender of the biblical quotation (John 14:2) and comments on the disrepair of the projects by labeling them, ironically, "mansions." Adding irony on top of irony, two cute cartoon bluebirds with a baby-blue ribbon fly into the scene like the birds that bring the fairy godmother's gifts to Cinderella in rags in the Disney film, while two Easter baskets neatly wrapped in plastic sit in the garden. Marshall based the off-center triangular composition of this large painting on Géricault's *The Raft of the "Medusa"* (see **FIG. 30–50**). He told an television interviewer from PBS, "That whole genre of history painting, that grand narrative style of painting, was something that I really wanted to position my work in relation to."

LUNA James Luna (b. 1950) asks us to confront Native American stereotypes in **THE ARTIFACT PIECE** (**FIG. 33–43**), first staged in 1987 in a hall dedicated to a traditional ethnographic exhibition at the Museum of Man in San Diego. Luna lay, almost naked, in a glass display case filled with sand embedded with artifacts from his life, including his favorite music and books, and personal legal papers. Museum-style labels pointed to marks and scars on his body that he had acquired while drinking or fighting, or in accidents. In this way, Luna literally turned his living body and his life into an ethnographic object for people to ogle, assess, and judge. By physically objectifying himself, he challenges our prejudices, stereotypes, and assumptions about Native Americans in general and about him specifically.

SCULPTURE

In the 1980s, several sculptors became embroiled in controversies over the nature and purpose of sculpture itself. Following in the footsteps of Andy Warhol (see FIG. 33-11), some of their works challenged sculptural orthodoxy by introducing images and objects appropriated from popular and mass culture, while others raised questions about the rights of sculptors to create deliberately confrontational or offensive works, especially when fulfilling government commissions for site-specific sculptures in the public domain.

KOONS Jeff Koons (b. 1955)—self-publicist and critical celebrant of the superficial, consumption-crazy suburban society of the 1980s—has enshrined as art such household objects as vacuum cleaners, inflatable bunny rabbits, topiary puppy dogs, and porcelain pornography, all with sly references to Duchamp (see FIG. 32-30). **PINK PANTHER** (FIG. **33-44**) shows a cheesy centerfold pin-up's unsettling embrace of the cuddly cartoon figure. At more than 3 feet tall, this slick and glossy work is almost life-size, made from porcelain, a material more commonly used for knick-knacks than sculpture. The flat pastel colors recall Warhol's Marilyn Monroe portraits (see FIG. 33-12). Koons's unsettlingly bland and pretty work invites, even welcomes, critical disapproval, embracing kitschy lower-middle-class consumer culture without seeming to critique it, openly materialistic and straightforwardly shallow.

SERRA Richard Serra (b. 1939) studied sculpture at the University of California at Berkeley and at Santa Barbara, and at Yale. In his early works, he draped vulcanized rubber in different

33-44 • Jeff Koons **PINK PANTHER**
1988. Porcelain, ed. 1/3. 41″ × 20½″ × 19″ (104.1 × 52.1 × 48.3 cm). Collection Museum of Contemporary Art, Chicago. © Jeff Koons.

👁 **Watch** a video about Jeff Koons on myartslab.com

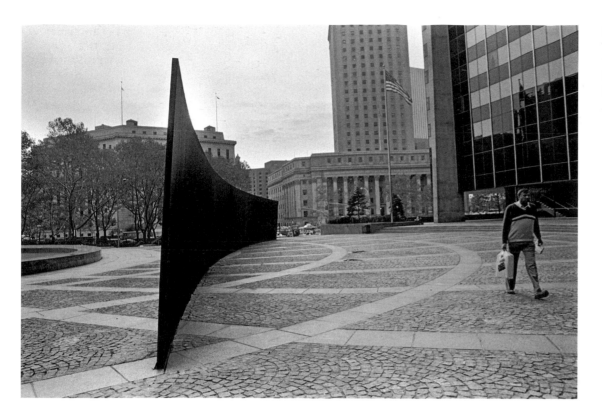

33–45 • Richard Serra
TILTED ARC
1981–1989. Jacob K. Javitz
Federal Plaza, New York.
Steel. Destroyed.

arrangements and threw molten lead against gallery walls, but in the early 1970s, he began making the sculptures from very large steel plates for which he is now (in)famous. In 1981, he won a commission from the General Services Administration (GSA) to create a sculpture, **TILTED ARC** (**FIG. 33-45**), for the banal plaza in front of the Javitz Federal Building in New York. The GSA approved plans for the proposed work, but once installed, the sculpture, a long curved Cor-Ten steel wall 120 feet long, 12 feet tall, and 2½ inches thick, bisected the plaza, completely changing it as a public space and making it impossible to hold concerts or performances. Even casual use by those who worked in the building was made difficult. Over time *Tilted Arc* rusted and was soon covered in graffiti and pigeon droppings. Public outrage against it became so intense that in 1986 Serra's sculpture was removed to a Brooklyn parking lot, an action that incited further furor, this time among artists and critics. Serra argued that moving the site-specific piece had destroyed it; he filed a lawsuit claiming censorship, but the Federal district court found no legal merit in his case.

Tilted Arc raised several important questions about the rights and responsibilities of artists, as well as the obligations of those who commission public works of art. Clearly Serra's sculpture had intentionally changed (for some spoiled) Javitz Plaza. In court, the artist did not attempt to defend his work on aesthetic grounds, but to claim the right to create the piece as planned and approved. This well-publicized legal case precipitated changes in the commissioning of public sculpture. Today neighborhood groups and local officials meet with artists well in advance of public commissions. Important questions, however, remain unresolved. Does the institution of such public safeguards lead to better public sculpture?

Or do they merely guarantee that it will be bland, inoffensive, and decorative?

LIN Maya Lin (b. 1959) was an architecture student at Yale University in 1981 when a jury of architects, landscape architects, and sculptors awarded her the commission for the **VIETNAM VETER-ANS MEMORIAL** (**FIG. 33-46**) near the Mall in Washington, DC. Lin (one of 2,573 who submitted design proposals) envisioned a simple and dramatic memorial cut into the ground in a V-shape. Two highly polished black granite slabs reach out from deep in the earth at the center. Each of these arms is 247 feet long, and they meet at a 130-degree angle where the slabs are 10 feet tall. The names of 58,272 American soldiers killed or declared missing in action during the Vietnam War are listed chronologically, in the order they died or were lost, beginning in 1956 at the shallowest point to the left and climaxing in 1968 at the tallest part of the sculpture, representing the year of highest casualties. Since the polished granite reflects the faces of visitors, they read the names of the dead and missing with their own faces superimposed over them. The memorial, commissioned by Vietnam Veterans for Vietnam Veterans, serves both to commemorate the dead and missing and to provide a place where survivors can confront their own loss. This sculpture is one of the best-known works of public art in the United States and has transformed the way the nation mourns its war dead. Visiting it is a powerful and profound experience.

Yet, when it was first commissioned, the Vietnam Veterans Memorial was the subject of intense debate. It was described as a "black gash in the Mall," its color contrasting with the pervasive

33-46 • Maya Lin **VIETNAM VETERANS MEMORIAL, WASHINGTON, DC**
1981–1983.

white marble of the surrounding memorials. Lin was accused of creating a monument of shame, one critic going so far as to claim that black was the universal color of "shame, sorrow, and degradation in all races, all societies." Opposition to the sculpture was so intense in some quarters that, in 1983, the Vietnam Veterans Memorial Fund commissioned a second, naturalistic sculpture showing three soldiers from Georgia-born artist Frederick Hart (1943–1999), placed 120 feet from the wall; in 1993, Texas sculptor Glenda Goodacre (b. 1939) created a comparable sculpture of three nurses, added 300 feet to the south to memorialize the contribution of women during the war.

ART, ACTIVISM, AND CONTROVERSY: THE NINETIES

The passage from the 1980s to the 1990s was marked by what is commonly referred to as the "Culture Wars" (see "Controversies Over Public Funding for the Arts," page 1118), a confrontation between artists and public officials in America over freedom of

speech and public funding for the arts, particularly with regard to the right to make art that might be considered offensive or obscene by others. At the same time many artists who had previously worked on the periphery of society and established art institutions began to claim center stage by making aggressive images about identity and unequal treatment on the grounds of gender, sexual orientation, race, or class. Many of these artists worked with particular passion and urgency as they or their friends and partners died from AIDS. The 1990s also saw the beginning of the digital age, when a new interest in the mutability of photography and film opened imaginative new vistas for artists.

THE CULTURE WARS

In the early 1990s, several previously marginalized younger artists achieved fame by producing narrative images deliberately intended to disrupt, provoke, and offend viewers (see "Controversies over Public Funding of the Arts," page 1118). In the United States, Andres Serrano defamed an image of the Christian crucifix while Robert Mapplethorpe confronted audiences with openly gay sexuality. In the United Kingdom, Damien Hirst defiled the mortal

Puryear spent a year with the Peace Corps in Sierra Leone, working with African carpenters to learn their woodworking methods and skills. Note the gentle and beautifully irregular hand-finishing at the mouth of the sculpture and in the binding of its tail.

Puryear, who studied furniture making with James Krenov, maintains the highest craft standards. Notice the radiating grain on the inside of the horn, the spiraling grain on its tail, and the exquisite quality of the joints.

The clarity, abstract nature, and monumental scale (it is 5½ feet tall) of the sculpture seem to refer to Minimalism, but evidence of the human hand in the crafting of the piece, as in the wobble in the line of the bell, suggests something closer to Process art.

The twisting tail suggests the empty shell of a strange animal or plant. Although it is lying passively at the moment, it looks as if it could flex quickly (note the jointing) to deliver a deadly sting.

The bell shape evokes many forms, such as a musical horn, an old-fashioned gramophone horn, a flower's bell, or a cornucopia (horn of plenty).

Puryear wants viewers to see ghosts of resemblances in his allusive sculpture. Perhaps most obviously, *Plenty's Boast* suggests a cornucopia, filled with the fruits of harvest and symbolizing abundance. But the cone is empty, implying an "empty boast"—a phrase suggested by the title.

 View the Closer Look for *Plenty's Boast* on myartslab.com

Should public money help pay for art that some taxpayers believe to be offensive and indecent? This question started a political battle in 1989–1990 after controversial works of art by Robert Mapplethorpe (1946–1989) and Andres Serrano (b. 1950) went on public display in exhibitions funded in part by the National Endowment for the Arts (NEA), an agency of the Federal government. The ensuing debate pitted artists and museum administrators against political and religious figures in what is now referred to as the "Culture Wars."

Serrano's *Piss Christ* (see FIG. 33–48) was at the center of the debate. Serrano did not use public money directly to create this work, but the Southeastern Center for Contemporary Art (SECCA), which exhibited *Piss Christ* in a group exhibition, was a recipient of NEA funds. The Reverend Donald Wildmon, leader of the American Family Association, described *Piss Christ* as "hate-filled, bigoted, anti-Christian, and obscene," and told his many followers to flood Congress and the NEA with letters protesting the misuse of public funds. Several high-profile conservative Republican politicians swiftly joined his attack.

At the same time, the traveling exhibition "The Perfect Moment," a retrospective of the work of photographer Mapplethorpe, who had recently died from AIDS, was canceled by the Corcoran Gallery of Art in Washington, DC, for fear that the show's content might cause offense or threaten the museum's government funding. "The Perfect Moment" had been organized by the Institute of Contemporary Art (ICA) in Philadelphia, was NEA-funded, and included several homoerotic and sadomasochistic images, including very provocative self-portraits of the artist. When it was shown in Cincinnati, the museum director was arrested. Additionally, in 1990 amid a flurry of debate, the NEA rescinded the grants awarded to four artists—who became known as the "NEA Four" (Karen Finley, John Fleck, Holly Hughes, and Tim Miller)—because they made lesbian, gay, or radical feminist art. Congress slashed NEA funding by $45,000: the sum of Serrano's $15,000 SECCA grant, plus the ICA's $30,000 grant for the Mapplethorpe show. The NEA Four sued and won back their grants in 1993, but a so-called "obscenity clause" was added to NEA regulations requiring jurors to consider the "general standards of decency and respect for the diverse beliefs and values of the American public" when making awards.

During the next five years, the NEA was largely restructured by the Republican-controlled House of Representatives, some of whose members wanted to eliminate the agency altogether. In 1996, Congress reduced the NEA's budget by 40 percent.

Controversies over public funding continued, however. In 1999, the Brooklyn Museum of Art exhibited "Sensation: Young British Artists from the Saatchi Collection," causing another major controversy over public funding and offensive art. The Brooklyn Museum kept the show open in direct defiance of a threat from Mayor Rudolph Giuliani to eliminate city funding and evict the museum from its city-owned building if it persisted in showing art that he considered "sick" and "disgusting." Giuliani and Catholic leaders took particular offense at Chris Ofili's **THE HOLY VIRGIN MARY** (FIG. 33–47). When the Brooklyn Museum of Art still refused to cancel the show, Giuliani withheld the city's monthly maintenance payment to the museum of $497,554 and filed a suit in the state court to revoke its lease. In response, the museum filed for an injunction against Giuliani's actions on the grounds that they violated the First Amendment, and the United States District Court for the Eastern District of New York eventually barred Giuliani from punishing or retaliating against the museum in any way for mounting the exhibition. Guiliani had argued that Ofili's art fostered religious intolerance, but the court ruled that the government has "no legitimate interest in protecting any or all religions from views distasteful to them," adding that taxpayers "subsidize all manner of views with which they do not agree" and even those "they abhor."

33-47 • Chris Ofili THE HOLY VIRGIN MARY
1996. Acrylic, oil paint, polyester resin, paper collage, glitter, map pins, and elephant dung on linen, 7'11" × 5'11⁵⁄₁₆" (2.44 × 1.83 m). MONA, Museum of Old and New Art, Hobart, Tasmania, Australia © Chris Ofili.

remains of domestic animals while Chris Ofili created a racially and culturally hybrid Christian Madonna. The resulting social and political backlash triggered the Culture Wars.

SERRANO In 1987, Andres Serrano (b. 1950) created **PISS CHRIST** (**FIG. 33–48**). Like other artists of the time, Serrano's art explores social taboos in deliberately confrontational and offensive ways. His art dances between the luxuriously beautiful and the abject. His photographs of the homeless, Ku Klux Klansmen, suicides, and murder victims have proven so difficult for some viewers that they have inspired vandalism. *Piss Christ* is an almost 2-foot-high, brilliantly colored Cibachrome print of a Christian crucifix which the artist submerged in a Plexiglas box filled with his own urine. Serrano, who was raised a strict Catholic, has argued that this image is about confronting the physicality of the death of the body of Christ, sometimes too easily forgotten, and that it critiques the commercialization of Christ's image in the media, which is why it is also so provocative and offensive to others.

HIRST In London in the 1980s, a group of Young British Artists (YBAs) banded together to exhibit their work, led informally by Damien Hirst (b. 1965). In 1995, the Walker Art Center in Minneapolis mounted an exhibition entitled "Brilliant," featuring 22 British artists, many of whom used nontraditional materials and images in their art, had working-class backgrounds or sympathies, or had an adversarial relationship with mainstream society. Two years later, the London Royal Academy featured many of the same artists in "Sensation," an exhibition of art from the Charles Saatchi Collection, which consolidated the reputation of many YBAs. When the show traveled to the Brooklyn Museum in 1999, however, it was considered so offensive that the mayor of New York threatened to close the museum if it was not removed.

Damien Hirst is one of the most outrageous of the original YBAs and his most outrageous work of art may be *For the Love of God* (2007), a diamond-encrusted human skull with an asking price of $100m. His art probes the physical reality of death and the impossibility of imagining our own death, and he frequently uses dead animals in his work. In **MOTHER AND CHILD (DIVIDED)** (**FIG. 33–49**) he has bisected vertically and longitudinally the bodies of a cow and her calf and displayed them in glass display cases filled with formaldehyde solution. This sculpture resembles the kind of display that viewers might see in a natural history museum—but with some significant differences. The cases are arranged so that viewers can walk not only around them, but also see between them. On the outside, these animals retain an amazingly lifelike look (even their eyelashes and individual hairs are visible) within the formaldehyde solution, but once we see the cleavages in their bones, muscles, organs, and flesh on the inside, the actuality of their death is overwhelming. Taking into account that in the 1990s British cattle were being slaughtered daily in an attempt to stop the spread of the terrifying BSE (Mad Cow Disease), *Mother and Child (Divided)* creates a feeling of being caught between life and death, between mother and child, between scientific presentation and, as in Serrano's work, a set of barely suppressed and disturbingly powerful emotions.

OFILI The art of Nigerian-British artist Chris Ofili (b. 1968) provided the focal point for criticism of the 1999 "Sensation" exhibition at the Brooklyn Museum. Ofili exhibited *The Holy Virgin Mary* (see **FIG. 33–47**), a glittering painting of a stylized African Madonna which includes among its myriad media elephant dung and

33–48 • Andres Serrano PISS CHRIST
1989. Cibachrome print mounted on Plexiglas, 23½″ × 16″ (59.7 × 40.6 cm).

33-49 • Damien Hirst **MOTHER AND CHILD (DIVIDED), EXHIBITION COPY 2007 (ORIGINAL 1993)**
2007. Glass, painted stainless steel, silicone, acrylic, monofilament, stainless steel, cow, calf, and formaldehyde solution, two tanks at 82⅓″ × 126⅞″ × 43″ (209 × 322 × 109 cm), two tanks at 45″ × 66½″ × 24⅝″ (114 × 169 × 62.5 cm). © 2012 Damien Hirst and Science Ltd. All rights reserved/ DACS,London/ARS, NY. Photographed by Prudence Cuming Associates.

small found photographs of women's buttocks. Ofili, who spent a year in Zimbabwe studying the use of materials in art, explained that many African nations have a tradition of using found or salvaged objects and materials in both popular and high art. Ofili's painting is a contemporary bicultural reinvention of the Western Madonna tradition, and its use of elephant dung intends to reinforce this black Madonna's connection to the art and religion of Zimbabwe and to represent her fertility. Then-mayor of New York Rudolph Giuliani and his allies, however, considered the picture so shocking and sacrilegious that they ordered it removed immediately or the exhibition closed. Giuliani maintained that "There's nothing in the First Amendment that supports horrible and disgusting projects!"

ACTIVIST ART

The Culture Wars were fueled by a significant increase in Activist art during the 1990s. AIDS decimated the younger art scene in New York's East Village and triggered a global health crisis by mid decade. Increasingly, anger over the agony of those dying from, and losing friends and lovers to, AIDS, combined with government inaction, spilled over into art. Thus the 1990s opened with angry art about the body, AIDS, and identity, as well as with continued clamoring for acknowledgment of the discrimination faced by people of different races, ethnicities, classes, and sexual orientations. The Culture Wars were, in many ways, about artists searching for a place in the world while so many were fading from it.

GONZALEZ-TORRES In the mid-1980s, the spread of the human immunodeficiency virus (HIV), the underlying cause of AIDS, had begun to reap its deadly harvest within the gay community. Felix Gonzalez-Torres (1957–1996) created "**UNTITLED**" **(LOVERBOY)** (FIG. 33-50) in 1990 as his long-time partner Ross Laycock was dying from AIDS. The piece is deceptively simple: a stack of pale blue paper sat on the gallery floor and

33-50 • Felix Gonzalez-Torres **"UNTITLED" (LOVERBOY)**
1990. Blue paper, endless supply, 7½″ (at ideal height) × 29″ × 23″ (19.1 × 73.7 × 58.4 cm). Installation view of *Felix Gonzalez-Torres* at Andrea Rosen Gallery, New York, 1990.

visitors followed instructions by taking a sheet as they walked by. As time passed, the stack of paper gradually diminished, the disappearance of which could be understood as a touching allegory of the slowly disappearing body of Gonzalez-Torres's partner. The artist said: "I wanted to make something that would disappear completely." There is a poignant directness to this work. Gonzalez-Torres himself died of AIDS in 1996.

WOJNAROWICZ David Wojnarowicz (1955–1992) railed against death before he too died from AIDS in 1992. In 1987, Wojnarowicz's lover, photographer Peter Hujar died from AIDS and Wojnarowicz himself was diagnosed as HIV-positive. In response, he began to make forcefully aggressive art about the fear and confusion of watching a loved one die while facing one's own death. In **UNTITLED (HANDS)** (FIG. 33-51), Wojnarowicz photographed, in black and white, two bandaged hands outstretched as if in a begging gesture. Superimposed is a text in angry red type taken from Wojnarowicz's book *Memories That Smell Like Gasoline*, in which he describes how he is hollowing out from the inside and becoming invisible as he dies. Parts of Wojnarowicz's book were reprinted in the catalog of an exhibition, "Witnesses Against Our Vanishing," which featured art by and about artists with AIDS and which became a flashpoint in the Culture Wars.

33–51 • David Wojnarowicz "UNTITLED (HANDS)"
1992. Silver print with silkscreened text, 38″ × 26″ (96.5 × 66.0 cm).
Courtesy of the estate of David Wojnarowicz and PPOW Gallery, New York.

SMITH In sculpture of the early 1990s, the physicality of the human body reasserted itself as a site for the discourse on AIDS. The sculptor Kiki Smith (b. 1954), who lost a sister to AIDS, explores the body, bodily functions, and the loss of physical control that the dying experience in works such as the 1990 **UNTITLED** (FIG. 33-52). This disturbing sculpture shows two life-size naked figures, female and male, made from flesh-colored painted beeswax and hanging passively, but not quite lifelessly, side by side about a foot above the ground. Milk drips from the woman's breasts and semen drips down the man's leg, as if both have lost control of bodily functions that were once a source of vitality and pleasure. There is a profound sense of loss, but also of release. Smith has written that since our society abhors the reality of bodily functions, we strive to conceal and control them, making our loss of control as death nears humiliating and frightening. This sculpture asks us to consider bodily control—both our own sense of control and the control that others exert on our body as we die—and suggests that relinquishing it may be as liberating as it is devastating.

WODICZKO Some artists took their art beyond the gallery, not only advocating social change but working to make a tangible difference within society. In the late 1980s, Polish-born Canadian artist Krzysztof Wodiczko (b. 1943) created the **HOMELESS VEHICLE** (FIG. 33-53), designed in collaboration with the homeless in New York as "an instrument for survival for urban nomads." Wodiczko wanted to draw attention to the problem of homelessness in New York, one of the richest cities in

33–53 • Krzysztof
Wodiczko **HOMELESS
VEHICLE**
1988–1989. Aluminum and
mixed media. Variant 3 of
4, pictured at Trump Tower,
New York. © Krzysztof
Wodiczko.

👁 **Watch** a video
about Krzysztof
Wodiczko on
myartslab.com

33-54 • Rachel Whiteread HOUSE
1993. Corner of Grove and Roman Roads, London. 1993. Concrete. Destroyed 1994. Commissioned by Artangel. Received the Turner Prize, Tate Britain, London. © Rachel Whiteread. Photo: Sue Omerod. Courtesy of the artist, Luhring Augustine, New York, and Gagosian Gallery.

the richest country in the world. But he did not want simply to illustrate homelessness or evoke pity. Rather, he wanted to dramatize homelessness by making it visible while at the same time actually helping the homeless. The Homeless Vehicle is a modified and "upgraded" version of the shopping cart that so many homeless people use to carry around their worldly possessions. Wodiczko designed the cart with a waterproof and relatively safe sleeping pod, a series of baskets underneath in which to store belongings, and a brightly colored flag to indicate approach. The homeless who were lucky enough to get a vehicle were pleased with the way it worked, but the New York city authorities felt that the carts made the homeless too visible. They disappeared quickly.

WHITEREAD The British sculptor Rachel Whiteread (b. 1963) made her reputation as a YBA by casting the inverse of everyday objects such as a bathtub or worn mattress to reveal the ghostliness of their absence. In 1993, she turned her attention to the invisibility of the urban poor with her largest and most controversial work, **HOUSE** (**FIG. 33-54**). For this project, Whiteread cast in concrete the inner space of an entire three-story terraced house, one of a row in London's East End slated for demolition by developers, who effectively erased the last vestiges of a community that had pulled together heroically during the Blitz in World War II. *House* is about how memories are contained in places and times, and how easily they can be destroyed. As the other houses around it were demolished, Whiteread sprayed concrete on the inner walls of "her house" to make a cast of the space within it. Then she dismantled the house itself. The white concrete left behind outlined a ghostly trace of the space within the house that had once been someone's home. The publicity surrounding Whiteread's *House* brought to the fore several critical issues in British society—including homelessness, the costs and benefits of urban renewal, and the social position of the working class—by articulating controversial concerns in ways that are impossible using other means of communication. Whiteread intended *House* to make a political statement about "the state of housing in England; the ludicrous policy of knocking down homes like this and building badly designed tower blocks which themselves have to be knocked down after 20 years."

33-55 • Shirin Neshat REBELLIOUS SILENCE
1994. Black-and-white RC print and ink (photograph by C. Preston),
11″ × 14″ (27.9 × 35.6 cm). Barbara Gladstone Gallery, New York.

POSTCOLONIAL DISCOURSE

With increasing migration and the expansion of global communications and economies, questions of personal, political, cultural, and national identity also emerged in the 1990s. Postcolonial artists began to address issues of contested identity and the identity struggle of postcolonial peoples, and to investigate the dissonance produced by transnational (mis)communication between colonizers and the postcolonized. Many of these artists, such as Shirin Neshat and Rasheed Araeen, speak with unfamiliar but forthright and significant new artistic voices.

NESHAT In **REBELLIOUS SILENCE** (**FIG. 33-55**) from her 1994 "Women of Allah" series of photographs, Shirin Neshat (b. 1957) explores how Iranian women are stereotyped in the West, claiming that their Islamic identities are more varied and complex than

is frequently perceived. Each of Neshat's "Women of Allah" photographs portrays both a part of an Iranian woman's body—such as her hands or her feet—overwritten with Farsi text and a weapon. In *Rebellious Silence*, the woman wears the traditional chador but her face is exposed, overwritten with calligraphy and bisected by a rifle barrel. Both calligraphy and rifle seem to protect her from the viewer, but they also create a sense of incomprehensibility or foreignness that prompts us to try to categorize her. Likewise, although the woman wears a chador, she looks directly and defiantly out of the photograph at us, meeting and returning our gaze. She challenges us to acknowledge her as an individual—in this case a strong and beautiful woman—but simultaneously and paradoxically prompts us to see her as a stereotypical Iranian woman in a chador. Neshat confronts our prejudices while also raising questions about the position of women in contemporary Iran.

ARAEEN Pakistani artist Rasheed Araeen (b. 1935) lives in London, where he founded the journal *Black Phoenix* in 1978 (renamed *Third Text* in 1989), a leading journal on postcolonial art, culture, and ethnicity. Araeen's 1985–1986 **GREEN PAINTING IV** (**FIG. 33-56**) of nine equal-sized panels, the central five containing photographs of the head of a young bull with garlands around its neck, prepared for ritual sacrifice and framed above and below by Urdu text. The remaining four panels are uniformly green—the primary color in the Pakistani flag, an important color in Islam, and a color that Araeen associates with youthful rawness and flexibility, as in a green twig. Yet the central panels also form a cross. Araeen has said that his pictures are not just superimpositions of Western and Pakistani cultures, that they address "cutting and rupturing" and investigate postcolonial dissonance and miscommunication. He argues that when someone British or American recognizes the cross in his art, for instance, they almost invariably read Pakistani culture through a Christian lens, thereby distorting, misinterpreting, and stereotyping the "other." Araeen's art calls for a more nuanced understanding of cultures on their own terms and according to their own visual languages.

SEARLE Berni Searle's (b. 1964) art explores her South African identity in the wake of Apartheid. In the **COLOR ME** series (**FIG. 33-57**), she photographs her head and torso coated with powdered pigment that changes her skin color from red to yellow to brown to white. Searle invites us to recognize that race and identity are not as simple as skin pigmentation, that superficial or skin-deep characteristics do not define a person. The fragility and impermanence of the pigmentation also underscore the instability of stereotypes and the complexity of real identity.

33-57 • Berni Searle **UNTITLED, FROM COLOR ME SERIES**
1998. Michael Stevenson Gallery, Cape Town. © Berni Searle.

HIGH TECH AND DECONSTRUCTIVIST ARCHITECTURE

Computer-aided design (CAD) programs with 3-D graphics transformed architecture and architectural practice in the 1980s and 1990s. These new tools enabled architects to design structures virtually, to calculate engineering stresses faster and more precisely, to experiment with advanced building technologies and materials, and to imagine new ways of composing a building's mass.

HIGH TECH ARCHITECTURE High Tech architects broke out of the restrictive shape of the Modernist "glass box" (see FIG. 33-28) to experiment with dramatically designed engineering marvels. These buildings are characterized by a spectacular use of new technologies, materials, equipment, and components, and frequently by their visible display of service systems such as heating and power.

The **HONG KONG & SHANGHAI BANK** (FIG. 33-58) by British architect Norman Foster (b. 1935) is among the most spectacular examples of High Tech architecture. Foster was invited to spare no expense in designing this futuristic 47-story skyscraper. The load-bearing steel skeleton, composed of giant masts and girders, is on the exterior. The individual stories hang from it, making possible the uninterrupted rows of windows that fill the building with natural light. In addition, the banking hall in the lower part of the building has a ten-story atrium space that is flooded with daylight refracted into it by motorized "sunscoops" at the top of the structure that track the sun's rays and channel them into the building. The sole concession Foster makes to tradition in this design is his placement of two bronze lions taken from the bank's previous headquarters flanking the public entrance. Touching the lions before entering the bank is believed to bring good luck.

DECONSTRUCTIVIST ARCHITECTURE Deconstructivist architecture, more theory-based than High Tech, emerged in the early 1990s. Deconstructivist architects deliberately disturb traditional architectural assumptions about harmony, unity, and stability to create "decentered," skewed, and distorted designs. The aesthetic of Russian Suprematists and Constructivists (see FIG. 32-26) is an influence, as are the principles of Deconstruction as developed by French philosopher Jacques Derrida (1930–2004). Derridean Deconstruction asserts written texts possesses no single, intrinsic meaning, that meaning is always "intertextual," a product of one text's relationship to other texts. Meaning is always "decentered," "dispersed," or "diffused" through an infinite web of "signs," which themselves have unstable meanings. Deconstructivist architecture is likewise "intertextual," in that it plays with meaning by mixing diverse architectural features, forms, and contexts, and it is "decentered" in its diffusion as well as in its perceived instability of both meaning and form.

A good example of Deconstructivist architecture is the **VITRA FIRE STATION** in Weil-am-Rhein, Germany (**FIG. 33-59**), designed by Baghdad-born architect Zaha Hadid (b. 1950), who studied in London and established her practice there in 1979. Formally influenced by the paintings of Kasimir Malevich (see FIG. 32-25), the Vitra Fire Station features reinforced concrete walls that lean into one another, meet at unexpected angles, and jut out dramatically into space, denying a sense of visual unity or structural coherence, but creating a feeling of immediacy, speed, and dynamism appropriate to the building's function.

The Toronto-born, California-based Frank O. Gehry (b. 1929) also creates unstable and Deconstructivist building masses and curved winglike shapes that extend far beyond the building's mass. One of his most spectacular designs is the **GUGGENHEIM MUSEUM** in Bilbao, Spain (**FIG. 33-60**). In the 1990s, the designing of art museums became more and more spectacular as they increasingly came to define the visual landscape of cities. Gehry developed his asymmetrical design using a CATIA CAD program that enabled him to create a powerfully organic, sculptural structure. The complex steel skeleton is covered by a thin skin of silvery titanium that shimmers gold or silver depending on the time of day and the weather conditions. From the north the building resembles a living organism, while from other angles it looks like a giant ship, a reference to the industry on which Bilbao has traditionally depended, thereby identifying the museum with the city. Despite

33-58 • Norman Foster HONG KONG & SHANGHAI BANK, HONG KONG
1986.

👁 **Watch** an architectural simulation about the steel skeleton of the Hong Kong and Shanghai Bank Corporation Limited building on myartslab.com

33-59 • Zaha Hadid **VITRA FIRE STATION, WEIL-AM-RHEIN**
Germany. 1989–1993.

33-60 • Frank O. Gehry **GUGGENHEIM MUSEUM, BILBAO**
Spain. 1993–1997. Sculpture of a spider in the foreground: Louise Bourgeois (1911–2010), *Maman*, 1999.

the sculptural beauty of the museum, however, the interior is a notoriously difficult space in which to display art, a characteristic this building shares with Frank Lloyd Wright's spiraling design of the New York Guggenheim (see FIG. 33-30), a notable forebear of Gehry's explorations of the bold sculptural potential of architecture.

VIDEO AND FILM

In the last decades of the twentieth century, the rapid development and increasingly widespread availability of hand-held video cameras created a new medium for artists. Video artists rejected traditional forms and meanings to make art that was deliberately nonprecious, often using the video image to address the place and prevalence of television in our culture. Today Video art is even more prevalent because of the explosion in digital and visual imagery. In fact, most contemporary Video art is digitally produced, while innovations in projecting video and DVD images on large screens (or on any surface) have transformed how and where Video art is projected and, to a certain extent, its subjects.

PAIK One of the pioneers of Video art was the Korean-born Nam June Paik (1931–2006), who composed experimental music in the late 1950s and early 1960s under the influence of John Cage. He began working with modified television sets in 1963, and making Video art in 1965, the same year that Sony released the first portable video camera. Paik predicted that just "as collage technique replaced oil paint, the cathode ray [television] tube will replace the canvas." Later, he worked with live, recorded, and computer-generated images displayed on video monitors of varying sizes, which he often combined into works of art such as **ELECTRONIC SUPERHIGHWAY: CONTINENTAL U.S.** (FIG. 33-61), a work created for the Holly Solomon Gallery in New York. This featured a neon outline map of the continental United States set against a wall of dozens of computer-controlled video monitors displaying rapidly changing soundtracked images reflecting each state's culture and history; Alaska and Hawaii were on the side walls. The work addresses the prevalence and the power of the mixed messages transmitted by television. The monitor for New York State projected a closed-circuit live video feed of gallery visitors, who were thus transformed from passive spectators into active participants in the piece as the monitor constructed their media identity in front of them as they watched.

VIOLA In 1996, the California video artist Bill Viola (b. 1951) created **THE CROSSING** (FIG. 33-62), which consists of a double projection of two brilliantly colored videos on opposite sides of a 16-foot screen. On one side, Viola projects a video loop of a silhouetted man who slowly emerges from the background to fill the entire screen. As he begins, a drop of water starts to fall, growing in size as the man moves forward slowly until at last a deluge washes him away. The soundtrack meanwhile goes from a small dripping noise to a torrential roar. On the reverse screen, a similar scenario unfolds, except this time the man appears in the background with tiny flames licking at his feet and eventually growing into a wild conflagration that finally engulfs him as

33-61 • Nam June Paik **ELECTRONIC SUPERHIGHWAY: CONTINENTAL U.S.** 1995. Forty-seven-channel closed-circuit video installation with 313 monitors, neon, steel structure, color, and sound, approx. 15′ × 32′ × 4′ (4.57 × 9.75 × 1.2 m). The Smithsonian American Art Museum, Washington, DC. © Estate of Nam June Paik. Gift of the artist

33-62 • Bill Viola THE CROSSING

1996. Two channels of color video projections from opposite sides of a large dark gallery onto two back-to-back screens suspended from the ceiling and mounted on the floor; four channels of amplified stereo sound, four speakers. Height 16′ (4.88 m).

the sound of the fire grows in intensity. But Viola is interested in the way that vision informs perception. In fact there is only one soundtrack—we simply perceive it differently according to which video we are watching. Viola's video is profoundly sensory but also meditative; its elemental symbolism is informed by Viola's spirituality and intense study of world religions.

GLOBALISM: INTO THE NEW MILLENNIUM

In the last decade, the growth in international art exhibitions and art fairs has created new opportunities for artists, dealers, and collectors to meet and network in ways that, until quite recently, would have been considered impossible, or unproductive. Until recently, the only truly international fora for new art were the Venice Biennale (established in 1903 and held every two years) and Documenta, in Kassel, West Germany (established in 1955 and held roughly every five years). Today there are at least 30 international biennial exhibitions around the world, as well as many more vast international art fairs: Art Basel in Switzerland, Art Basel Miami in Miami Beach, the Frieze Art Fair in London, the

Armory Show in New York, and the Fiore Internationale d'Art Contemporain (FIAC) in Paris, to mention just a few. At the same time, the Internet has allowed quick and easy visual access to art globally. We can find information on practically any exhibited art, and much that is not exhibited, in our homes on our laptops. This new globalism has forced artists to question how their own identities and those of others are formed, and to realize that neither identity nor art is as simple or as univalent as it might have seemed as recently as in the 1990s.

Art in the new millennium seems to be heading in several directions simultaneously, constantly shifting and recalibrating new perspectives and concerns as part of an increasingly complicated global discourse. The art of our own times may be the most difficult to classify and analyze, but it has increasingly focused on global issues, raising questions about national identities; ethnic and racial identities; colonial and postcolonial identities; human rights; global economic, political, and natural environments; the widening divide between the rich and poor, more powerful and less powerful, nations of the world; and technological change in every aspect of our lives. Today's artists are actively engaged in society at many levels and their art frequently reflects their ambition to be agents of change or stability in troubling and uncentered times.

ART AND TECHNOLOGY

SCULPTURE IN NEW MEDIA Dale Chihuly (b. 1941) has produced major public sculptures in glass for 30 years, but his creations are as fresh today as they were in 1975. Chihuly's sculptures are both technologically innovative and experimental. **THE SUN** (FIG. 33-63), a multi-part blown-glass sculpture using the latest glassmaking techniques, shows Chihuly's profound interest in natural forms and global energies. The sun bursts forth in a multitude of twisting, wriggling, spiraling forms as if the unremittingly intense light of Phoenix has taken physical shape and come to life. Brilliantly liquid, visually thrilling, and accessible, this sculpture suggests a deeper connection with nature, inviting contemplation, meditation, and an awareness of global environmentalism.

DIGITAL PHOTOGRAPHY SINCE 2000 From the beginning, photography has been a malleable and mutable medium. Even in the nineteenth century, photographs were manipulated to create fictional imagery out of what appeared to be a factual visual record. It is often difficult and time-consuming to manipulate a chemical-mechanical process, however, and it was only with the development of digital technology that manipulation became a fast, easy, and standard way to create photographic images.

The Canadian artist Jeff Wall (b. 1946) uses multiple digital photographs and elaborate stage sets to create large, complex, photographic narratives that he considers analogous to the history paintings of the nineteenth century, and which he exhibits as gloriously colored transparencies mounted in light boxes—a format frequently used in modern advertising in public places.

Wall creates his photographs like a movie director, carefully designing the sets and posing his actors. He takes multiple photographs that he then combines digitally to create one final transparency. **AFTER "INVISIBLE MAN" BY RALPH ELLISON, THE PREFACE** (FIG. 33-64) is an elaborate composition for which Wall spent 18 months designing and constructing the sets and three weeks actually taking photographs. The image illustrates a passage from Ralph Ellison's 1951 novel about an African-American man's search for fulfillment that ends in disillusionment and retreat. Wall shows us the cellar room, "warm and full of light," to which Ellison's character retreats and which is heated and lit by 1,369 light bulbs powered by electricity stolen from the power company. For Ellison, these lights only illuminate the sad truth of the character's existence.

INSTALLATION ART Tony Oursler's 2009 exhibition at Metro Pictures raises issues about how average Americans constructs their identities in the digital age. The installation included several oversized sculptural versions of things that we cannot seem to live without today: an enormous cellphone entitled **MULTIPLEXED** (FIG. 33-65), a giant five-dollar bill, a "forest of smoldering cigarettes," an arrangement of oversized self-help books, and a Genie bottle containing a video

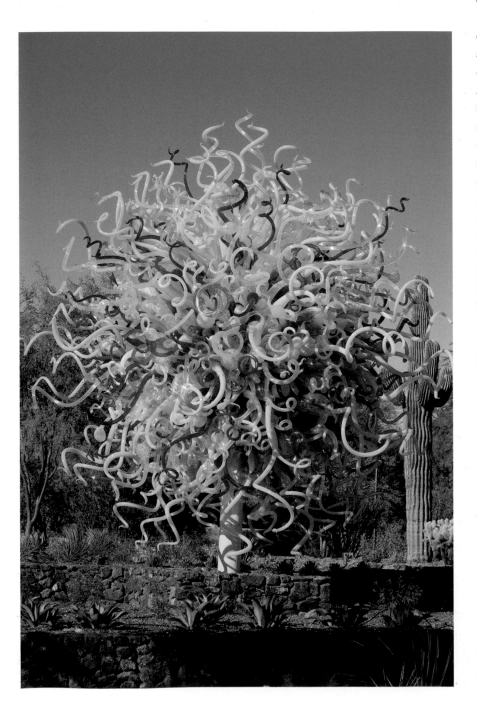

33-63 • Dale Chihuly THE SUN
2008. Desert Botanical Garden, Phoenix, Arizona. Installed November 22, 2008–May 31, 2009.

33-64 • Jeff Wall AFTER "INVISIBLE MAN" BY RALPH ELLISON, THE PREFACE
1999–2001. Transparency in lightbox, 68½″ × 98⅝″ (174 × 250.5 cm).

Read the document related to Jeff Wall on myartslab.com

of the artist himself. Oursler's exhibition is a clever updating of Pop art's critique of consumer society, making sly references to Warhol, Oldenburg, and even Lichtenstein (see FIGS. 33–11, 33–15, 33–14). Objects come to life by means of superimposed animated video projections that make the cigarettes seem to burn, "Abe" Lincoln to pull faces, Oursler himself to try to escape his bottle, and the cellphone (in this illustration) to spew forth, as the press release states, "disjointed snippets of conversations." Oursler's

33-65 • Tony Oursler
MULTIPLEXED
2008. Fiberglass, 37″ × 33″ × 17″ (94 × 83.8 × 43.2 cm). Metro Pictures. (MP 574)

art asks us to consider how the world of technology, constantly bombarding us with objects and images, creates an intense visual overload that frames our concept of identity.

ART AND IDENTITIES

The artists featured in this final section investigate their individual and group identities—a growing and ever-more complex concern in the new millennium—in a wide range of ways, breaking down traditional distinctions between medium and message in the process, and dissolving boundaries to create art that is as interesting, exciting, difficult, and confusing as the world itself is today.

BARNEY Between 1994 and 2002, Matthew Barney (b. 1967) created an already legendary series of films entitled *The Cremaster Cycle* in which he developed an arcane sexual mythology. The concept of gender mutability dominates the narrative, which questions gender assignation and roles throughout. The cremaster

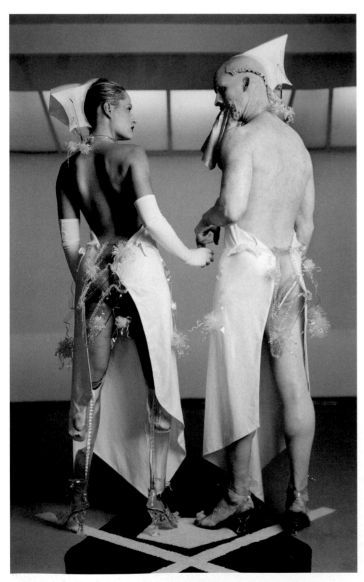

33-66 • Matthew Barney CREMASTER 3: MAHABYN
2002. 46½″ × 54″ × 1½″ (118 × 137 × 3.8 cm). © Matthew Barney.

muscle, for which the series is named, controls the ascent and descent of the testes, usually in response to changes in temperature but also in response to fear or sexual arousal. It also determines sexual differentiation in the human embryo. Barney uses a diagrammatic representation of the cremaster muscle as his visual emblem throughout the series.

Each film has its own complex narrative and catalog of multilayered symbols. *Cremaster 3* (2002) describes the construction of the Chrysler Building in New York and features Richard Serra (see FIG. 33-45) as the architect. The New York Guggenheim Museum's rotunda (see FIG. 33-30) is the setting for one segment of the film. Barney, playing Serra's apprentice, dressed in a peach-colored kilt and gagged, must accomplish a series of tasks to assert his supremacy over Serra. As in a video game, Barney scales the walls of the Guggenheim rotunda to complete a task on each level before gaining enlightenment. Along the way he encounters a series of challenges—a line of Rockettes dressed as Masonic lambs, warring punk-rock bands, a leopard woman (played by Aimee Mullins), and finally Serra. The settings and costumes are lavish, and the epic plot is complex and interconnected. In **MAHABYN** (FIG. 33-66), Barney and the leopard woman transform into Masons by donning modified Masonic costume. The entire filmic cycle addresses the crisis of identity experienced by white, middle-class, heterosexual male artists in America during an era seemingly dominated by identity politics.

BEECROFT Vanessa Beecroft, an Italian artist who now lives in Los Angeles, also set her **VB35** (FIG. 33-67) in the Guggenheim Museum's rotunda and also uses performance to examine gender roles, although she explores perceptions of the female body and femininity. Unlike Barney, Beecroft does not appear in her work, although many of her performances refer obliquely to her own battle with anorexia. In *vb35*—she numbers her performances; this is her 35th piece—she questions both the nature of today's distorted concept of feminine beauty and the prevalence of voyeuristic looking. Beecroft hired 15 professional fashion models—each fashionably thin, tall, and white—and directed them to stand in a loose group, facing forward. Ten wore high heels and designer bikinis, while five wore nothing but high heels. As they stood staring blankly ahead, the audience observed them from the foyer or the ramp of the museum, thus acquiescing in the gaze that objectified them. The performance was "invitation only," so the atmosphere was charged with exclusivity, but Beecroft complicated this piece by heightening the tension in two ways. First, the group of professional models whose business it is to be looked at commanded the museum; and second, the audience was instructed to behave in very precise ways—they were not allowed to make eye contact with or speak to the models, or in any way invade their physical or emotional space. This strategy cleverly inverted the normal relationship between looker and looked-at. A sexual charge filled the air, but ironically the models claimed control. Viewers found that they felt intimidated and discomfited, as though they had been caught in the act of looking illicitly. As one critic put it: "we found ourselves confronted by the cool authority of the art's nakedness, and we had no role to play … so we drifted and loitered."

GU Wenda Gu (b. 1955) dedicates his art to bringing people together. Trained in traditional ink painting at China's National Academy of Fine Arts, he emigrated to the United States in 1987 and began an ongoing global project entitled "United Nations Series" in 1992. Each "monument" in this series is made from human hair collected from barbershops and hair salons worldwide, which Gu presses into bricks or weaves into carpets and curtains covered with ideograms of his own invention. **CHINA MONUMENT: TEMPLE OF HEAVEN** (**FIG. 33-68**) contains hair from many different nations and blended scripts based on Chinese, English, Hindi, and Arabic characters that "evoke the

33-68 • Wenda
Gu **CHINA**
MONUMENT:
TEMPLE OF
HEAVEN
1998. Installation with
screens of human
hair, wooden chairs
and tables, and video.
Commissioned by the
Asia Society. Permanent
collection of the Hong
Kong Museum of Art ©
Wenda Gu.

33-69 • David Hammons UNTITLED 2004. Nylon, 6′ × 10′ (1.82 × 3 m). Studio Museum, Harlem. Gift of the artist (04.2.19)

limitations of human knowledge." Gu also creates "national" monuments—examples have been installed in Poland, Israel, and Taiwan, among other places—made from hair collected in, and addressing issues specific to, that particular country. The "transnational" monuments from the "United Nations Series," on the other hand, address more global themes, using hair blended from several different countries to suggest a "brave new racial identity" for the new millennium.

HAMMONS A socially minded artist strongly committed to working in the public realm, David Hammons (b. 1943) is an outspoken critic of the gallery system in America, lamenting the lack of challenging content and representation of African Americans in exhibitions. He has described the art world as being "like Novocain. It used to wake you up but now it puts you to sleep." Hammons argues that only art that intervenes in and transacts with society is uncontaminated by commerce and capable of jolting people awake. In **UNTITLED** (FIG. 33-69), the artist creates a witty, poignant, and biting satire on the still-ambiguous place of African Americans in American society. Hammons originally created this flag in 1990 for the Studio Museum in Harlem, in response to a controversy concerning the flying of the Confederate flag on public buildings in some states. It has since been installed in several other museums, including the Museum of Modern Art in New York in 2000. The colors in Hammons's flag are those of the Pan-African or Universal Negro Improvement Association and African Communities League flag, which was created in 1920 by African Americans to symbolize the "Rights of Negro Peoples of the World." The red stands for the blood that unites all people

of African descent and that was spilled in the quest for liberation; the black stands for the symbolic nation of black people; and the green stands for the verdant lands of Africa.

SHONIBARE Yinka Shonibare (b. 1962), a British-Nigerian artist based in London, uses his art to examine how identity is constructed and perceived through the twists and turns of colonial history, as well as through class, race, and self-perception. **HOW TO BLOW UP TWO HEADS AT ONCE (LADIES)** (FIG. 33-70) is a life-size sculpture of two headless women whose skin color, and thus on a superficial level whose race, is indeterminate. Although the figures have women's bodies, they seem to have masculine hands. They face off against one another, striking dueling poses with nineteenth-century flintlock pistols pointed at each other's absent heads. They wear what appear to be nineteenth-century costumes, but their brightly colored dresses are made of a Dutch wax fabric that is usually associated with West African nations. The complexities of the history of the fabric, and the way that Shonibare uses it, give us some idea of the multiple and eliding meanings in this sculpture. This brilliantly colored and patterned fabric, worn by millions of Africans today, originally came from Indonesia, imported and copied by Dutch colonists in Africa and manufactured in bulk in cotton mills in Manchester, England, then exported to West Africa, where it was copied, modified, transformed, and now possessed. Ironically, Shonibare buys the fabric for his sculptures at London's Brixton market. His work, although witty and ironic, is also acerbic as it uncovers the tangled web of forces that construct identity and challenges our perceptions about race, postcolonialism, property, ownership, violence, and class.

**33-70 • Yinka Shonibare
HOW TO BLOW UP
TWO HEADS AT ONCE
(LADIES)**
2006. Two fiberglass
mannequins, two prop guns,
Dutch, wax printed cotton
textile, shoes, leather riding
boots, plinth, 93½″ × 63″ × 48″
(237 × 160 × 122 cm). Museum
purchase with funds provided by
Wellesley College Friends of Art
(2007.124.1-2)

👁 **Watch** a video about
Yinka Shonibare
on myartslab.com

SIERRA Santiago Sierra (b. 1966), a Spanish artist living in Mexico City, also addresses race, ethnicity, and the capitalist exploitation of the poor in his interventionist artworks. At the 49th Venice Biennale in 2001, Sierra offered a visible commentary on the luxurious indulgence and elitist atmosphere of the exhibition, where both poverty and racial tension were invisible. Sierra paid 133 non-European men to dye their naturally black hair blond and to make themselves visible around Venice for the duration of the exhibition (**FIG. 33-71**). The shocking sight of white hair on dark-skinned men made them very visible, catapulting a group of individuals who normally melt into the background of society to front and center, persistent reminders not only of their presence but their relative poverty—the only reason their hair was blond was because they needed the money.

WILSON In the 1990s, artists increasingly critiqued the constructed narratives of traditional museum exhibitions. The

**33-71 • Santiago Sierra 133 PEOPLE PAID TO HAVE THEIR
HAIR DYED BLOND**
2001. Arsenale, 49th Venice Biennale

Sierra paid 133 non-European men to dye their hair blond. In the
exhibition, he presented video footage of the dyeing process.

33-72 • Fred Wilson CHANDELIER MORI
2003. United States Pavilion, 50th Venice Biennale. © Fred Wilson, courtesy The Pace Gallery.

museum was acknowledged as a place where curators, by making decisions about what works to show and how to arrange them, create art history rather than revealing it and, in the process, frequently reveal their own prejudices. Installation artist Fred Wilson (b. 1954) is best known for *Mining the Museum* (1992), an interventionist piece in which he inverted and subverted the Baltimore Historical Society's collection. Wilson "mined" the museum's storerooms and discovered that, while the objects exhibited were mostly about white history, there were numerous objects relating to African-American history in storage. He "inserted" many of these into the main museum display, including disturbing objects used to restrain African-American slaves, thereby upsetting and reshaping the story told in the original exhibition.

In 2003, Wilson represented the United States at the Venice Biennale with *Speak of Me As I Am*, a multi-part installation that focused on the history of Africans in Venice. This included several black sculptures made with Murano glass, a kind of glass made in Venice for centuries, set in a black-and-white tiled room with "graffiti" on the walls consisting of excerpts from African-American slave narratives and a video installation of Shakespeare's *Othello* being screened backwards. The title of the work, *Speak of Me As I Am*, is taken from words spoken by Othello, the "Moor," in Shakespeare's play. **CHANDELIER MORI** (FIG. 33-72), a part of Wilson's installation, is also made from Murano glass but, unlike the brilliantly glittering Venetian glass chandeliers seen around the city, this one emphasizes blackness. Wilson's title suggests the *memento mori* or *vanitas* painting that reminds viewers that death comes to all of us, drawing attention to the fact that the commerce of Venice was built on the back of African labor and at the cost of African lives.

WALKER Kara Walker (b. 1969) makes some of the most challenging and provocative art made in America today, hitting raw nerves, shocking and horrifying viewers. She cuts large-scale silhouettes of figures out of black construction paper, waxing them to the walls of galleries, and illuminating them with projected light. In **DARKYTOWN REBELLION** (FIG. 33-73), she shows a slave revolt and massacre by covering the walls of the gallery with her black-silhouetted figures to tell an unfolding tale of horror. The room swirls with beautifully colored white, black, pink, green, blue, and yellow projected lights and shadows that dance on the walls. As we walk around the space looking at the figures, we step in front of the projector, casting our own shadows on the walls, placing us uncomfortably close to or actually within the narrative itself. Walker's stories are drawn variously from slave narratives, minstrel shows, advertising memorabilia, and even from Harlequin romance novels, blending fiction and fact to evoke a history of oppression and terrible violence. And she does not balk at portraying unpleasant or painful bodily functions, such as defecation, vomiting, and childbirth. Walker's characters are black and white stereotypes, even caricatures. She contrasts the tight, cramped features of her white people with the stereotypical black features of her African Americans. She even refers to some of her characters as "nigger wenches" or "pickaninnies."

Walker plays on white fears of miscegenation and insecurities about racial purity. She pushes so far over the border of the acceptable that visiting one of her installations can be an uncomfortable and disruptive experience. Her figures disturb us intensely because of what they make us do. As silhouettes, they are all black, which means that we cannot identify their race by skin color. In order to read the narrative, however, we need to differentiate the characters by looking for other visual markers of race, making us draw upon an entire history of ugly stereotypes in the process. We are forced to examine the figures for thin or big lips, flat or frizzy hair, elegant or raggedy clothes. In this way Walker catches us in racist acts, making clear that she is speaking to us personally, not to some theoretical racist, and that racism is neither theoretical nor a thing of the past. As Walker has said: "It's interesting that as soon as you start telling the story of racism you start reliving it."

Walker shows us that identity is not nearly as clear-cut in the early twenty-first century as we would like to think. We are all complicated beings, constantly negotiating and renegotiating our place in the world, changing and reinventing ourselves. Kara Walker's art is not pleasant, but it changes us by altering our perception of the world. It reminds us that the works of visual artists—past, present, and future—has the power to reveal things about the time and place in which they were created, but also about the world we now inhabit, in ways that are beyond the reach of any other form of communication. If this broad and long survey of the history of art has had a single unifying theme, it is that.

33-73 • Kara Walker DARKYTOWN REBELLION
2001. Cut paper and projection on wall, 14′ × 37′ (4.3 × 11.3 m) overall. Collection Musée d'Art Moderne Grand-Duc Jean, Mudam Luxembourg. © Kara Walker.

THINK ABOUT IT

33.1 Write about the importance of the dematerialized object in the art of postwar United States. Then discuss how representational art regained importance in later years, particularly after 1980, and explain the new forms taken by such representation.

33.2 Discuss the emergence of Pop art in the 1950s and 1960s and characterize the new subjects favored by Pop artists. Explain how and why Pop reacted to Abstract Expressionism.

33.3 Analyze how contemporary American artists have used their art to address the social and political issues surrounding race. Select and discuss the work of at least two artists from the chapter.

33.4 Explain how globalism has transformed the visual arts and discuss how artists use contemporary strategies to speak to issues in their local cultures.

CROSSCURRENTS

FIG. 32–43

FIG. 33–31

Distinguished twentieth-century architects have designed private homes as well as large, commercial, religious, or public buildings. Discuss the circumstances that led to the creation of these two famous houses. How do these works fit into the careers of their architects and also engage with the larger concerns of architectural design at the moment when they were built? How is their physical context related to their design?

✓●─ **Study** and review on myartslab.com

Glossary

abacus (p. 108) The flat slab at the top of a **capital**, directly under the **entablature**.

abbey church (p. 239) An abbey is a monastic religious community headed by an abbot or abbess. An abbey church often has an especially large **choir** to provide space for the monks or nuns.

absolute dating (p. 12) A method, especially in archaeology, of assigning a precise historical date at which, or span of years during which, an object was made. Based on known and recorded events in the region, as well as technically extracted physical evidence (such as carbon-14 disintegration). See also **radiometric dating**, **relative dating**.

abstract (p. 7) Of art that does not attempt to describe the appearance of visible forms but rather to transform them into stylized patterns or to alter them in conformity to ideals.

academy (p. 926) An institution established for the training of artists. Academies date from the Renaissance and after; they were particularly powerful, state-run institutions in the seventeenth and eighteenth centuries. In general, academies replaced **guild**s as the venues where students learned the craft of art and were educated in art theory. Academies helped the recognition of artists as trained specialists, rather than craftsmakers, and promoted their social status. An academician is an academy-trained artist.

acanthus (p. 110) A Mediterranean plant whose leaves are reproduced in Classical architectural ornament used on **molding**s, **frieze**s, and **capital**s.

acroterion (*pl.* acroteria) (p. 110) An ornament at the corner or peak of a roof.

Action painting (p. 1074) Using broad gestures to drip or pour paint onto a pictorial surface. Associated with mid-twentieth-century American Abstract Expressionists, such as Jackson Pollock.

adobe (p. 399) Sun-baked blocks made of clay mixed with straw. Also: buildings made with this material.

aedicula (p. 609) A decorative architectural frame, usually found around a niche, door, or window. An aedicula is made up of a **pediment** and **entablature** supported by **column**s or **pilaster**s.

aerial perspective (p. 626) See under **perspective**.

agora (p. 137) An open space in a Greek town used as a central gathering place or market. Compare **forum**.

aisle (p. 225) Passage or open corridor of a church, hall, or other building that parallels the main space, usually on both sides, and is delineated by a row, or **arcade**, of **column**s or **pier**s. Called side aisles when they flank the **nave** of a church.

akropolis (p. 128) The citadel of an ancient Greek city, located at its highest point and housing temples, a treasury, and sometimes a royal palace. The most famous is the Akropolis in Athens.

album (p. 796) A book consisting of a series of paintings or prints (album leaves) mounted into book form.

allegory (p. 627) In a work of art, an image (or images) that symbolizes an idea, concept, or principle, often moral or religious.

alloy (p. 23) A mixture of metals; different metals melted together.

altarpiece (p. xlii) A painted or carved panel or ensemble of panels placed at the back of or behind and above an altar. Contains religious imagery (often specific to the place of worship for which it was made) that viewers can look at during liturgical ceremonies (especially the **Eucharist**) or personal devotions.

amalaka (p. 302) In Hindu architecture, the circular or square-shaped element on top of a spire (**shikhara**), often crowned with a **finial**, symbolizing the cosmos.

ambulatory (p. 224) The passage (walkway) around the **apse** in a church, especially a **basilica**, or around the central space in a **central-plan building**.

amphora (*pl.* amphorae) (p. 101) An ancient Greek or Roman jar for storing oil or wine, with an egg-shaped body and two curved handles.

animal style or **interlace** (p. 433) Decoration made of interwoven animals or serpents, often found in early medieval Northern European art.

ankh (p. 51) A looped cross signifying life, used by ancient Egyptians.

appropriation (p. xxx) The practice of some Postmodern artists of adopting images in their entirety from other works of art or from visual culture for use in their own art. The act of recontextualizing the appropriated image allows the artist to critique both it and the time and place in which it was created.

apse (p. 192) A large semicircular or polygonal (and usually **vaulted**) recess on an end wall of a building. In a Christian church, it often contains the altar. "Apsidal" is the adjective describing the condition of having such a space.

arabesque (p. 267) European term for a type of linear surface decoration based on foliage and calligraphic forms, thought by Europeans to be typical of Islamic art and usually characterized by flowing lines and swirling shapes.

arcade (p. 170) A series of **arch**es, carried by **column**s or **pier**s and supporting a common wall or **lintel**. In a **blind arcade**, the arches and supports are **engaged** and have a purely decorative function.

arch (p. 95) In architecture, a curved structural element that spans an open space. Built from wedge-shaped stone blocks called **voussoir**s placed together and held at the top by a trapezoidal **keystone**. It forms an effective space-spanning and weight-bearing unit, but requires **buttress**es at each side to contain the outward **thrust** caused by the weight of the structure. *Corbeled arch*: an arch or **vault** formed by **course**s of stones, each of which projects beyond the lower course until the space is enclosed; usually finished with a **capstone**. *Horseshoe arch*: an arch of more than a half-circle; typical of western Islamic architecture. *Round arch*: an arch that displaces most of its weight, or downward thrust along its curving sides, transmitting that weight to adjacent supporting uprights (door or window **jamb**s, **column**s, or **pier**s). *Ogival arch*: a sharply pointed arch created by S-curves. *Relieving arch*: an arch built into a heavy wall just above a **post-and-lintel** structure (such as a gate, door, or window) to help support the wall above by transferring the load to the side walls. *Transverse arch*: an arch that connects the wall **pier**s on both sides of an interior space, up and over a stone **vault**.

Archaic smile (p. 114) The curved lips of an ancient Greek statues in the period c. 600–480 BCE, usually interpreted as a way of animating facial features.

architrave (p. 107) The bottom element in an **entablature**, beneath the **frieze** and the **cornice**.

archivolt (p. 478) A band of **molding** framing an **arch**, or a series of stone blocks that form an arch resting directly on flanking **column**s or **pier**s.

ashlar (p. 99) A highly finished, precisely cut block of stone. When laid in even **course**s, ashlar masonry creates a uniform face with fine joints. Often used as a facing on the visible exterior of a building, especially as a veneer for the **façade**. Also called **dressed stone**.

assemblage (p. 1026) Artwork created by gathering and manipulating two- and/or three-dimensional found objects.

astragal (p. 110) A thin convex decorative **molding**, often found on a Classical **entablature**, and usually decorated with a continuous row of beadlike circles.

atelier (p. 946) The studio or workshop of a master artist or craftsmaker, often including junior associates and apprentices.

atmospheric perspective (p. 183) See under **perspective**.

atrial cross (p. 943) A cross placed in the **atrium** of a church. In Colonial America, used to mark a gathering and teaching place.

atrium (p. 158) An unroofed interior courtyard or room in a Roman house, sometimes having a pool or garden, sometimes surrounded by **column**s. Also: the open courtyard in front of a Christian church; or an entrance area in modern architecture.

automatism (p. 1057) A technique in which artists abandon the usual intellectual control over their brushes or pencils to allow the subconscious to create the artwork without rational interference.

avant-garde (p. 972) Term derived from the French military word meaning "before the group," or "vanguard." Avant-garde denotes those artists or concepts of a strikingly new, experimental, or radical nature for their time.

axis (p. xxxiv) In pictures, an implied line around which elements are composed or arranged. In buildings, a dominant line around which parts of the structure are organized and along which human movement or attention is concentrated.

axis mundi (p. 300) A concept of an "axis of the world," which marks sacred sites and denotes a link between the human and celestial realms. For example, in Buddhist art, the axis mundi can be marked by monumental free-standing decorative pillars.

baldachin (p. 472) A canopy (whether suspended from the ceiling, projecting from a wall, or supported by columns) placed over an honorific or sacred space such as a throne or church altar.

bar tracery (p. 510) See under **tracery**.

barbarian (p. 149) A term used by the ancient Greeks and Romans to label all foreigners outside their cultural orbit (e.g., Celts, Goths, Vikings). The word derives from an imitation of what the "barblings" of their language sounded like to those who could not understand it.

barrel vault (p. 187) See under **vault**.

bas-relief (p. 325) Another term for low relief ("bas" is the French word for "low"). See under **relief sculpture**.

basilica (p. 191) A large rectangular building. Often built with a **clerestory**, side **aisles** separated from the center **nave** by **colonnades**, and an **apse** at one or both ends. Originally Roman centers for administration, later adapted to Christian church use.

bay (p. 170) A unit of space defined by architectural elements such as **columns**, **piers**, and walls.

beehive tomb (p. 98) A **corbel-vaulted** tomb, conical in shape like a beehive, and covered by an earthen mound.

Benday dots (p. 1095) In modern printing and typesetting, the individual dots that, together with many others, make up lettering and images. Often machine- or computer-generated, the dots are very small and closely spaced to give the effect of density and richness of tone.

bilum (p. 865) Netted bags made mainly by women throughout the central highlands of New Guinea. The bags can be used for everyday purposes or even to carry the bones of the recently deceased as a sign of mourning.

biomorphic (p. 1058) Denoting the biologically or organically inspired shapes and forms that were routinely included in abstracted Modern art in the early twentieth century.

black-figure (p. 105) A technique of ancient Greek **ceramic** decoration in which black figures are painted on a red clay ground. Compare **red-figure**.

blackware (p. 855) A **ceramic** technique that produces pottery with a primarily black surface with **matte** and glossy patterns on the surface.

blind arcade (p. 780) See under **arcade**.

bodhisattva (p. 311) In Buddhism, a being who has attained enlightenment but chooses to remain in this world in order to help others advance spiritually. Also defined as a potential Buddha.

Book of Hours (p. 549) A prayer book for private use, containing a calendar, services for the canonical hours, and sometimes special prayers.

boss (p. 556) A decorative knoblike element that can be found in many places, e.g. at the intersection of a Gothic **rib vault** or as a buttonlike projection on metalwork.

bracket, bracketing (p. 341) An architectural element that projects from a wall to support a horizontal part of a building, such as beams or the eaves of a roof.

buon fresco (p. 87) See under **fresco**.

burin (p. 592) A metal instrument used in **engraving** to cut lines into the metal plate. The sharp end of the burin is trimmed to give a diamond-shaped cutting point, while the other end is finished with a wooden handle that fits into the engraver's palm.

buttress, buttressing (p. 170) A projecting support built against an external wall, usually to counteract the lateral **thrust** of a **vault** or **arch** within. In Gothic church architecture, a **flying buttress** is an arched bridge above the **aisle** roof that extends from the upper **nave** wall, where the lateral thrust of the main vault is greatest, down to a solid **pier**.

cairn (p. 17) A pile of stones or earth and stones that served both as a prehistoric burial site and as a marker for underground tombs.

calligraphy (p. 275) Handwriting as an art form.

calyx krater (p. 119) See under **krater**.

calotype (p. 969) The first photographic process utilizing negatives and paper positives; invented by William Henry Fox Talbot in the late 1830s.

came (*pl.* **cames**) (p. 501) A lead strip used in the making of leaded or **stained-glass** windows. Cames have an indented groove on the sides into which individual pieces of glass are fitted to make the overall design.

cameo (p. 172) Gemstone, clay, glass, or shell having layers of color, carved in low relief (see under **relief sculpture**) to create an image and ground of different colors.

camera obscura (p. 750) An early cameralike device used in the Renaissance and later for recording images from the real world. It consists of a dark box (or room) with a hole in one side (sometimes fitted with a lens). The camera obscura operates when bright light shines through the hole, casting an upside-down image of an object outside onto the inside wall of the box.

canon of proportions (p. 64) A set of ideal mathematical ratios in art based on measurements, as in the proportional relationships between the basic elements of the human body.

canopic jar (p. 53) In ancient Egyptian culture, a special jar used to store the major organs of a body before embalming.

capital (p. 110) The sculpted block that tops a **column**. According to the **conventions** of the orders, capitals include different decorative elements (see **order**). A *historiated* capital is one displaying a figural composition and/or narrative scenes.

capriccio (*pl.* *capricci*) (p. 915) A painting or print of a fantastic, imaginary landscape, usually with architecture.

capstone (p. 17) The final, topmost stone in a **corbeled arch** or **vault**, which joins the sides and completes the structure.

cartoon (p. 501) A full-scale drawing of a design that will be executed in another **medium**, such as wall painting, **tapestry**, or **stained glass**.

cartouche (p. 187) A frame for a **hieroglyphic** inscription formed by a rope design surrounding an oval space. Used to signify a sacred or honored name. Also: in architecture, a decorative device or plaque, usually with a plain center used for inscriptions or epitaphs.

caryatid (p. 107) A sculpture of a draped female figure acting as a **column** supporting an **entablature**.

cassone (*pl.* *cassoni*) (p. 616) An Italian dowry chest often highly decorated with carvings, paintings, inlaid designs, and gilt embellishments.

catacomb (p. 215) An underground cemetery consisting of tunnels on different levels, having niches for urns and **sarcophagi** and often incorporating rooms (**cubicula**).

cathedral (p. 220) The principal Christian church in a diocese, the bishop's administrative center and housing his throne (*cathedra*).

celadon (p. 358) A high-fired, transparent **glaze** of pale bluish-green hue whose principal coloring agent is an oxide of iron. In China and Korea, such glazes were typically applied over a pale gray **stoneware** body, though Chinese potters sometimes applied them over **porcelain** bodies during the Ming (1368–1644) and Qing (1644–1911) dynasties. Chinese potters invented celadon glazes and initiated the continuous production of celadon-glazed wares as early as the third century CE.

cella (p. 108) The principal interior room at the center of a Greek or Roman temple within which the cult statue was usually housed. Also called the **naos**.

celt (p. 383) A smooth, oblong stone or metal object, shaped like an axe-head.

cenotaph (p. 771) A funerary monument commemorating an individual or group buried elsewhere.

centering (p. 170) A temporary structure that supports a masonry **arch**, **vault**, or **dome** during construction until the mortar is fully dried and the masonry is self-sustaining.

central-plan building (p. 225) Any structure designed with a primary central space surrounded by symmetrical areas on each side, e.g., a **rotunda**.

ceramics (p. 20) A general term covering all types of wares made from fired clay.

chacmool (p. 396) In Maya sculpture, a half-reclining figure probably representing an offering bearer.

chaitya (p. 305) A type of Buddhist temple found in India. Built in the form of a hall or **basilica**, a *chaitya* hall is highly decorated with sculpture and usually is carved from a cave or natural rock location. It houses a sacred shrine or **stupa** for worship.

chamfer (p. 780) The slanted surface produced when an angle is trimmed or beveled, common in building and metalwork.

chasing (p. 432) Ornamentation made on metal by incising or hammering the surface.

château (*pl.* **châteaux**) (p. 693) A French country house or residential castle. A *château fort* is a military castle incorporating defensive works such as towers and battlements.

chattri (p. 780) In Indian architecture, a decorative pavilion with an umbrella-shaped **dome**.

chevron (p. 357) A decorative or heraldic motif of repeated Vs; a zigzag pattern.

chiaroscuro (p. 636) An Italian word designating the contrast of dark and light in a painting, drawing, or print. *Chiaroscuro* creates spatial depth and volumetric forms through gradations in the intensity of light and shadow.

choir (p. 225) The part of a church reserved for the clergy, monks, or nuns, either between the **transept** crossing and the **apse** or extending farther into the **nave**; separated from the rest of the church by screens or walls and fitted with stalls (seats).

cista (*pl.* **cistae**) (p. 157) Cylindrical containers used in antiquity by wealthy women as a case for toiletry articles such as a mirror.

clerestory (p. 57) In a **basilica**, the topmost zone of a wall with windows, extending above the **aisle** roofs. Provides direct light into the **nave**.

cloisonné (p. 257) An **enameling** technique in which artists affix wires or strips to a metal surface to delineate designs and create compartments (*cloisons*) that they subsequently fill with enamel.

cloister (p. 448) An enclosed space, open to the sky, especially within a monastery, surrounded by an **arcade**d walkway, often having a fountain and garden. Since the most important monastic buildings (e.g., dormitory, refectory, church) open off the cloister, it represents the center of the monastic world.

codex (*pl.* **codices**) (p. 245) A book, or a group of **manuscript** pages (folios), held together by stitching or other binding along one edge.

coffer (p. 197) A recessed decorative panel used to decorate ceilings or **vaults**. The use of coffers is called coffering.

coiling (p. 848) A technique in basketry. In coiled baskets a spiraling coil, braid, or rope of material is held in place by stitching or interweaving to create a permanent shape.

collage (p. 1025) A composition made of cut and pasted scraps of materials, sometimes with lines or forms added by the artist.

colonnade (p. 69) A row of **columns**, supporting a straight **lintel** (as in a **porch** or **portico**) or a series of **arches** (an **arcade**).

colophon (p. 438) The data placed at the end of a book listing the book's author, publisher, illuminator, and other information related to its production. In East Asian **handscrolls**, the inscriptions which follow the painting are also called colophons.

column (p. 110) An architectural element used for support and/or decoration. Consists of a rounded or polygonal vertical **shaft** placed on a **base** and topped by a decorative **capital**. In Classical architecture, columns are built in accordance with the rules of one of the architectural **order**s. They can be free-standing or attached to a background wall (**engaged**).

combine (p. 1087) Combination of painting and sculpture using nontraditional art materials.

complementary color (p. 995) The primary and secondary colors across from each other on the color wheel (red and green, blue and orange, yellow and purple). When juxtaposed, the intensity of both colors increases. When mixed together, they negate each other to make a neutral gray-brown.

Composite order (p. 161) See under **order**.

composite pose or **image** (p. 10) Combining different viewpoints within a single representation.

composition (p. xxxi) The overall arrangement, organizing design, or structure of a work of art.

conch (p. 236) A halfdome.

connoisseur (p. 289) A French word meaning "an expert," and signifying the study and evaluation of art based primarily on formal, visual, and stylistic analysis. A connoisseur studies the style and technique of an object to assess its relative quality and identify its maker through visual comparison with other works of secure authorship. See also **Formalism**.

continuous narrative (p. 245) See under **narrative image**.

contrapposto (p. 120) Italian term meaning "set against," used to describe the Classical convention of representing human figures with opposing alternations of tension and relaxation on either side of a central **axis** to imbue figures with a sense of the potential for movement.

convention (p. 31) A traditional way of representing forms.

corbel, corbeling (p. 19) An early roofing and arching technique in which each **course** of stone projects slightly beyond the previous layer (a corbel) until the uppermost corbels meet; see also under **arch**. Also: **bracket**s that project from a wall.

corbeled vault (p. 99) See under **vault**.

Corinthian order (p. 108) See under **order**.

cornice (p. 110) The uppermost section of a Classical **entablature**. More generally, a horizontally projecting element found at the top of a building wall or **pedestal**. A *raking cornice* is formed by the junction of two slanted cornices, most often found in **pediment**s.

course (p. 99) A horizontal layer of stone used in building.

crenellation, crenellated (p. 44) Alternating high and low sections of a wall, giving a notched appearance and creating permanent defensive shields on top of fortified buildings.

crocket (p. 587) A stylized leaf used as decoration along the outer angle of spires, pinnacles, gables, and around **capital**s in Gothic architecture.

cruciform (p. 228) Of anything that is cross-shaped, as in the cruciform plan of a church.

cubiculum (*pl.* **cubicula**) (p. 220) A small private room for burials in a **catacomb**.

cuneiform (p. 28) An early form of writing with wedge-shaped marks impressed into wet clay with a **stylus**, primarily used by ancient Mesopotamians.

curtain wall (p. 1045) A wall in a building that does not support any of the weight of the structure.

cyclopean (p. 93) A method of construction using huge blocks of rough-hewn stone. Any large-scale, monumental building project that impresses by sheer size. Named after the Cyclopes (sing. Cyclops), one-eyed giants of legendary strength in Greek myths.

cylinder seal (p. 35) A small cylindrical stone decorated with **incised** patterns. When rolled across soft clay or wax, the resulting raised pattern or design served in Mesopotamian and Indus Valley cultures as an identifying signature.

dado (*pl.* **dadoes**) (p. 161) The lower part of a wall, differentiated in some way (by a **molding** or different coloring or paneling) from the upper section.

daguerreotype (p. 969) An early photographic process that makes a positive print on a light-sensitized copperplate; invented and marketed in 1839 by Louis-Jacques-Mandé Daguerre.

dendrochronology (p. xxxviii) The dating of wood based on the patterns of the tree's growth rings.

dentils (p. 110) A row of projecting rectangular blocks forming a **molding** or running beneath a **cornice** in Classical architecture.

desert varnish (p. 406) A naturally occurring coating that turns rock faces into dark surfaces. Artists would draw images by scraping through the dark surface and revealing the color of the underlying rock. Extensively used in southwest North America.

diptych (p. 212) Two panels of equal size (usually decorated with paintings or reliefs) hinged together.

dogu (p. 362) Small human figurines made in Japan during the Jomon period. Shaped from clay, the figures have exaggerated expressions and are in contorted poses. They were probably used in religious rituals.

dolmen (p. 17) A prehistoric structure made up of two or more large upright stones supporting a large, flat, horizontal slab or slabs.

dome (p. 187) A rounded **vault**, usually over a circular space. Consists of curved masonry and can vary in shape from hemispherical to bulbous to ovoidal. May use a supporting vertical wall (**drum**), from which the vault springs, and may be crowned by an open space (**oculus**) and/or an exterior **lantern**. When a dome is built over a square space, an intermediate element is required to make the transition to a circular drum. There are two systems. A dome on **pendentives** incorporates arched, sloping intermediate sections of wall that carry the weight and **thrust** of the dome to heavily **buttress**ed supporting **pier**s. A dome on **squinch**es uses an arch built into the wall (squinch) in the upper corners of the space to carry the weight of the dome across the corners of the square space below. A halfdome or **conch** may cover a semicircular space.

domino construction (p. 1045) System of building construction introduced by the architect Le Corbusier in which reinforced concrete floor slabs are floated on six free-standing posts placed as if at the positions of the six dots on a domino playing piece.

Doric order (p. 108) See **order**.

dressed stone (p. 84) Another term for **ashlar**.

drillwork (p. 188) The technique of using a drill for the creation of certain effects in sculpture.

drum (p. 110) The circular wall that supports a **dome**. Also: a segment of the circular **shaft** of a **column**.

drypoint (p. 748) An **intaglio** printmaking process by which a metal (usually copper) plate is directly inscribed with a pointed instrument (**stylus**). The resulting design of scratched lines is inked, wiped, and printed. Also: the print made by this process.

earthenware (p. 20) A low-fired, opaque **ceramic** ware, employing humble clays that are naturally heat-resistant and remain porous after firing unless **glaze**d. Earthenware occurs in a range of earth-toned colors, from white and tan to gray and black, with tan predominating.

earthwork (p. 1102) Usually very large-scale, outdoor artwork that is produced by altering the natural environment.

echinus (p. 110) A cushionlike circular element found below the **abacus** of a Doric **capital**. Also: a similarly shaped **molding** (usually with egg-and-dart motifs) underneath the **volutes** of an Ionic capital.

electronic spin resonance (p. 12) Method that uses magnetic field and microwave irradiation to date material such as tooth enamel and its surrounding soil.

elevation (p. 108) The arrangement, proportions, and details of any vertical side or face of a building. Also: an architectural drawing showing an exterior or interior wall of a building.

embroidery (p. 397) Stitches applied in a decorative pattern on top of an already-woven fabric ground.

en plein air (p. 987) French term (meaning "in the open air") describing the Impressionist practice of painting outdoors so artists could have direct access to the fleeting effects of light and atmosphere while working.

enamel (p. 255) Powdered, then molten, glass applied to a metal surface, and used by artists to create designs. After firing, the glass forms an opaque or transparent substance that fuses to the metal background. Also: an object created by the enameling technique. See also *cloisonné*.

encaustic (p. 246) A painting **medium** using pigments mixed with hot wax.

engaged (p. 171) Of an architectural feature, usually a **column**, attached to a wall.

engraving (p. 592) An **intaglio** printmaking process of inscribing an image, design, or letters onto a metal or wood surface from which a print is made. An engraving is usually drawn with a sharp implement (**burin**) directly onto the surface of the plate. Also: the print made from this process.

entablature (p. 107) In the Classical **order**s, the horizontal elements above the **column**s and **capital**s. The entablature consists of, from bottom to top, an **architrave**, a **frieze**, and a **cornice**.

entasis (p. 108) A slight swelling of the **shaft** of a Greek **column**. The optical illusion of entasis makes the column appear from afar to be straight.

esquisse (p. 946) French for "sketch." A quickly executed drawing or painting conveying the overall idea for a finished painting.

etching (p. 748) An **intaglio** printmaking process in which a metal plate is coated with acid-resistant resin and then inscribed with a **stylus** in a design, revealing the plate below. The plate is then immersed in acid, and the exposed metal of the design is eaten away by the acid. The resin is removed, leaving the design etched permanently into the metal and the plate ready to be inked, wiped, and printed.

Eucharist (p. 220) The central rite of the Christian Church, from the Greek word for "thanksgiving." Also known as the Mass or Holy Communion, it reenacts Christ's sacrifice on the cross and commemorates the Last Supper. According to traditional Catholic Christian belief, consecrated bread and wine become the body and blood of Christ; in Protestant belief, bread and wine symbolize the body and blood.

exedra (*pl.* **exedrae**) (p. 197) In architecture, a semicircular niche. On a small scale, often used as decoration, whereas larger exedrae can form interior spaces (such as an **apse**).

expressionism (p. 149) Artistic styles in which aspects of works of art are exaggerated to evoke subjective emotions rather than to portray objective reality or elicit a rational response.

façade (p. 52) The face or front wall of a building.

faience (p. 88) Type of **ceramic** covered with colorful, opaque glazes that form a smooth, impermeable surface. First developed in ancient Egypt.

fang ding (p. 334) A square or rectangular bronze vessel with four legs. The *fang ding* was used for ritual offerings in ancient China during the Shang dynasty.

fête galante (p. 910) A subject in painting depicting well-dressed people at leisure in a park or country setting. It is most often associated with eighteenth-century French Rococo painting.

filigree (p. 90) Delicate, lacelike ornamental work.

fillet (p. 110) The flat ridge between the carved-out **flutes** of a **column shaft**.

finial (p. 780) A knoblike architectural decoration usually found at the top point of a spire, pinnacle, canopy, or gable. Also found on furniture. Also the ornamental top of a staff.

flutes (p. 110) In architecture, evenly spaced, rounded parallel vertical grooves incised on **shafts** of **column**s or on columnar elements such as **pilaster**s.

flying buttress (p. 503) See under **buttress**.

flying gallop (p. 88) A non-naturalistic pose in which animals are depicted hovering above the ground with legs fully extended backwards and forwards to signify that they are running.

foreshortening (p. xxxiii) The illusion created on a flat surface by which figures and objects appear to recede or project sharply into space. Accomplished according to the rules of **perspective**.

formal analysis (p. xxxi) An exploration of the visual character that artists bring to their works through the expressive use of elements such as line, form, color, and light, and through its overall structure or composition.

Formalism (p. 1073) An approach to the understanding, appreciation, and valuation of art based almost solely on considerations of form. The Formalist's approach tends to regard an artwork as independent of its time and place of making.

forum (p. 176) A Roman town center; site of temples and administrative buildings and used as a market or gathering area for the citizens.

fresco (p. 81) A painting technique in which water-based pigments are applied to a plaster surface. If the plaster is painted when wet, the color is absorbed by the plaster, becoming a permanent part of the wall (*buon fresco*). *Fresco secco* is created by painting on dried plaster, and the color may eventually flake off. Murals made by both these techniques are called frescos.

frieze (p. 107) The middle element of an **entablature**, between the **architrave** and the **cornice**. Usually decorated with sculpture, painting, or **molding**s. Also: any continuous flat band with **relief sculpture** or painted decoration.

frottage (p. 1057) A design produced by laying a piece of paper over a textured surface and rubbing with charcoal or other soft **medium**.

fusuma (p. 820) Sliding doors covered with paper, used in traditional Japanese construction. *Fusuma* are often highly decorated with paintings and colored backgrounds.

gallery (p. 236) A roofed passageway with one or both of its long sides open to the air. In church architecture, the story found above the side **aisle**s of a church or across the width at the end of the **nave** or **transept**s, usually open to and overlooking the area below. Also: a building or hall in which art is displayed or sold.

garbhagriha (p. 302) From the Sanskrit word meaning "womb chamber," a small room or shrine in a Hindu temple containing a holy image.

genre painting (p. 714) A term used to loosely categorize paintings depicting scenes of everyday life, including (among others) domestic interiors, parties, inn scenes, and street scenes.

geoglyph (p. 399) Earthen design on a colossal scale, often created in a landscape as if to be seen from an aerial viewpoint.

gesso (p. 546) A ground made from glue, gypsum, and/or chalk, used as the ground of a wood panel or the priming layer of a canvas. Provides a smooth surface for painting.

gilding (p. 90) The application of paper-thin gold leaf or gold pigment to an object made from another **medium** (for example, a sculpture or painting). Usually used as a decorative finishing detail.

giornata (*pl.* **giornate**) (p. 539) Adopted from the Italian term meaning "a day's work," a *giornata* is the section of a **fresco** plastered and painted in a single day.

glazing (p. 600) In **ceramics**, an outermost layer of vitreous liquid (**glaze**) that, upon firing, renders the ware waterproof and forms a decorative surface. In painting, a technique used with oil **media** in which a transparent layer of paint (glaze) is laid over another, usually lighter, painted or glazed area. In architecture, the process of filling openings in a building with windows of clear or **stained glass**.

gold leaf (p. 47) Paper-thin sheets of hammered gold that are used in **gilding**. In some cases (such as Byzantine **icon**s), also used as a ground for paintings.

gopura (p. 775) The towering gateway to an Indian Hindu temple complex.

Grand Manner (p. 923) An elevated style of painting popular in the eighteenth century in which the artist looked to the ancients and to the Renaissance for inspiration; for portraits as well as history painting, the artist would adopt the poses, compositions, and attitudes of Renaissance and antique models.

Grand Tour (p. 913) Popular during the eighteenth and nineteenth centuries, an extended tour of cultural sites in France and Italy intended to finish the education of a young upper-class person primarily from Britain or North America.

granulation (p. 90) A technique of decoration in which metal granules, or tiny metal balls, are fused onto a metal surface.

graphic arts (p. 698) A term referring to those arts that are drawn or printed and that utilize paper as the primary support.

grattage (p. 1057) A pattern created by scraping off layers of paint from a canvas laid over a textured surface. Compare **frottage**.

grid (p. 65) A system of regularly spaced horizontally and vertically crossed lines that gives regularity to an architectural plan or in the composition of a work of art. Also: in painting, a grid is used to allow designs to be enlarged or transferred easily.

grisaille (p. 540) A style of monochromatic painting in shades of gray. Also: a painting made in this style.

groin vault (p. 187) See under **vault**.

grozing (p. 501) Chipping away at the edges of a piece of glass to achieve the precise shape needed for inclusion in the composition of a **stained-glass** window.

guild (p. 419) An association of artists or craftsmakers. Medieval and Renaissance guilds had great economic power, as they controlled the marketing of their members' products and provided economic protection, political solidarity, and training in the craft to its members. The painters' guild was usually dedicated to St. Luke, their patron saint.

hall church (p. 521) A church with **nave** and **aisle**s of the same height, giving the impression of a large, open hall.

halo (p. 215) A circle of light that surrounds and frames the heads of emperors and holy figures to signify their power and/or sanctity. Also known as a nimbus.

handscroll (p. 343) A long, narrow, horizontal painting or text (or combination thereof) common in Chinese and Japanese art and of a size intended for individual use. A handscroll is stored wrapped tightly around a wooden pin and is unrolled for viewing or reading.

hanging scroll (p. 796) In Chinese and Japanese art, a vertical painting or text mounted within sections of silk. At the top is a semicircular rod; at the bottom is a round dowel. Hanging scrolls are kept rolled and tied except for special occasions, when they are hung for display, contemplation, or commemoration.

haniwa (p. 362) Pottery forms, including cylinders, buildings, and human figures, that were placed on top of Japanese tombs or burial mounds during the Kofun period (300–552 CE).

Happening (p. 1087) An art form developed by Allan Kaprow in the 1960s, incorporating performance, theater, and visual images. A Happening was organized without a specific narrative or intent; with audience participation, the event proceeded according to chance and individual improvisation.

hemicycle (p. 512) A semicircular interior space or structure.

henge (p. 17) A circular area enclosed by stones or wood posts set up by Neolithic peoples. It is usually bounded by a ditch and raised embankment.

hierarchic scale (p. 27) The use of differences in size to indicate relative importance. For example, with human figures, the larger the figure, the greater her or his importance.

hieratic (p. 484) Highly stylized, severe, and detached, often in relation to a strict religious tradition.

hieroglyph (p. 52) Picture writing; words and ideas rendered in the form of pictorial symbols.

high relief (p. 307) See under **relief sculpture**.

historiated capital (p. 484) See under **capital**.

historicism (p. 965) The strong consciousness of and attention to the institutions, themes, styles, and forms of the past, made accessible by historical research, textual study, and archaeology.

history paintings (p. 926) Paintings based on historical, mythological, or biblical narratives. Once considered the noblest form of art, history paintings generally convey a high moral or intellectual idea and are often painted in a grand pictorial style.

horizon line (p. 569) A horizontal "line" formed by the implied meeting point of earth and sky. In **linear perspective**, the **vanishing point** or points are located on this "line."

horseshoe arch (p. 272) See under **arch**.

hue (p. 77) Pure color. The saturation or intensity of the hue depends on the purity of the color. Its value depends on its lightness or darkness.

hydria (p. 139) A large ancient Greek or Roman jar with three handles (horizontal ones at both sides and one vertical at the back), used for storing water.

hypostyle hall (p. 66) A large interior room characterized by many closely spaced **column**s that support its roof.

icon (p. 246) An image representing a sacred figure or event in the Byzantine (later the Orthodox) Church. Icons are venerated by the faithful, who believe their prayers are transmitted through them to God.

iconic image (p. 215) A picture that expresses or embodies an intangible concept or idea.

iconoclasm (p. 248) The banning and/or destruction of images, especially **icon**s and religious art. Iconoclasm in eighth- and ninth-century Byzantium and sixteenth- and seventeenth-century Protestant territories arose from differing beliefs about the power, meaning, function, and purpose of imagery in religion.

iconography (p. xxxv) Identifying and studying the subject matter and **conventional** symbols in works of art.

iconology (p. xxxvii) Interpreting works of art as embodiments of cultural situation by placing them within broad social, political, religious, and intellectual contexts.

iconophile (p. 247) From the Greek for "lover of images." In periods of **iconoclasm**, iconophiles advocate the continued use of sacred images.

idealization (p. 134) A process in art through which artists strive to make their forms and figures attain perfection, based on pervading cultural values and/or their own personal ideals.

illumination (p. 431) A painting on paper or parchment used as an illustration and/or decoration in a **manuscript** or **album**. Usually richly colored, often supplemented by gold and other precious materials. The artists are referred to as illuminators. Also: the technique of decorating manuscripts with such paintings.

impasto (p. 749) Thick applications of pigment that give a painting a palpable surface texture.

impluvium (p. 178) A pool under a roof opening that collected rainwater in the **atrium** of a Roman house.

impost block (p. 170) A block of masonry imposed between the top of a **pier** or above the **capital** of a **column** in order to provide extra support at the springing of an **arch**.

incising (p. 118) A technique in which a design or inscription is cut into a hard surface with a sharp instrument. Such a surface is said to be incised.

ink painting (p. 812) A monochromatic style of painting developed in China, using black ink with gray washes.

inlay (p. 30) To set pieces of a material or materials into a surface to form a design. Also: material used in or decoration formed by this technique.

installation, installation art (p. 1051) Contemporary art created for a specific site, especially a gallery or outdoor area, that creates a complete and controlled environment.

intaglio (p. 592) A technique in which the design is carved out of the surface of an object, such as an engraved seal stone. In the **graphic arts**, intaglio includes **engraving**, **etching**, and **drypoint**—all processes in which ink transfers to paper from incised, ink-filled lines cut into a metal plate.

intarsia (p. 618) Technique of **inlay** decoration using variously colored woods.

intuitive perspective (p. 182) See under **perspective**.

Ionic order (p. 107) See under **order**.

iwan (p. 277) In Islamic architecture, a large, vaulted chamber with a monumental arched opening on one side.

jamb (p. 478) In architecture, the vertical element found on both sides of an opening in a wall, and supporting an **arch** or **lintel**.

Japonisme (p. 996) A style in French and American nineteenth-century art that was highly influenced by Japanese art, especially prints.

jasperware (p. 919) A fine-grained, unglazed, white **ceramic** developed in the eighteenth century by Josiah Wedgwood, often with raised designs remaining white above a background surface colored by metallic oxides.

Jataka tales (p. 303) In Buddhism, stories associated with the previous lives of Shakyamuni, the historical Buddha.

joggled voussoirs (p. 268) Interlocking **voussoirs** in an **arch** or **lintel**, often of contrasting materials for colorful effect.

joined-block sculpture (p. 373) Large-scale wooden sculpture constructed by a method developed in Japan. The entire work is made from smaller hollow blocks, each individually carved, and assembled when complete. The joined-block technique allowed production of larger sculpture, as the multiple joints alleviate the problems of drying and cracking found with sculpture carved from a single block.

kantharos (p. 117) A type of ancient Greek goblet with two large handles and a wide mouth.

keep (p. 477) The innermost and strongest structure or central tower of a medieval castle, sometimes used as living quarters, as well as for defense. Also called a donjon.

kente (p. 892) A woven cloth made by the Ashanti peoples of West Africa. *Kente* cloth is woven in long, narrow pieces featuring complex and colorful patterns, which are then sewn together.

key block (p. 828) The master block in the production of a colored **woodblock print**, which requires different blocks for each color. The key block is a flat piece of wood upon which the outlines for the entire design of the print were first drawn on its surface and then all but these outlines were carved away with a knife. These outlines serve as a guide for the accurate **registration** or alignment of the other blocks needed to add colors to specific parts of a print.

keystone (p. 170) The topmost **voussoir** at the center of an **arch**, and the last block to be placed. The pressure of this block holds the arch together. Often of a larger size and/or decorated.

kiln (p. 20) An oven designed to produce enough heat for the baking, or firing, of clay, for the melting of the glass used in **enamel** work, and for the fixing of vitreous paint on **stained glass**.

kiva (p. 405) A subterranean, circular room used as a ceremonial center in some Native American cultures.

kondo (p. 366) The main hall inside a Japanese Buddhist temple where the images of Buddha are housed.

korambo (p. 865) A ceremonial or spirit house in Pacific cultures, reserved for the men of a village and used as a meeting place as well as to hide religious artifacts from the uninitiated.

kore (*pl.* **kourai**) (p. 114) An Archaic Greek statue of a young woman.

koru (p. 872) A design depicting a curling stalk with a bulb at the end that resembles a young tree fern; often found in Maori art.

kouros (*pl.* **kouroi**) (p. 114) An Archaic Greek statue of a young man or boy.

kowhaiwhai (p. 872) Painted curvilinear patterns often found in Maori art.

krater (p. 99) An ancient Greek vessel for mixing wine and water, with many subtypes that each have a distinctive shape. *Calyx krater*: a bell-shaped vessel with handles near the base that resembles a flower calyx. *Volute krater*: a krater with handles shaped like scrolls.

Kufic (p. 275) An ornamental, angular Arabic script.

kylix (p. 120) A shallow ancient Greek cup, used for drinking, with a wide mouth and small handles near the rim.

lacquer (p. 824) A type of hard, glossy surface varnish, originally developed for use on objects in East Asian cultures, made from the sap of the Asian sumac or from shellac, a resinous secretion from the lac insect. Lacquer can be layered and manipulated or combined with pigments and other materials for various decorative effects.

lakshana (p. 306) The 32 marks of the historical Buddha. The *lakshana* include, among others, the Buddha's golden body, his long arms, the wheel impressed on his palms and the soles of his feet, and his elongated earlobes.

lamassu (p. 42) Supernatural guardian-protector of ancient Near Eastern palaces and throne rooms, often represented sculpturally as a combination of the bearded head of a man, powerful body of a lion or bull, wings of an eagle, and the horned headdress of a god, usually possessing five legs.

lancet (p. 505) A tall, narrow window crowned by a sharply pointed arch, typically found in Gothic architecture.

lantern (p. 464) A turretlike structure situated on a roof, vault, or dome, with windows that allow light into the space below.

lekythos (*pl.* **lekythoi**) (p. 141) A slim ancient Greek oil vase with one handle and a narrow mouth.

linear perspective (p. 595) See under **perspective**.

linga shrine (p. 315) A place of worship centered on an object or representation in the form of a phallus (the lingam), which symbolizes the power of the Hindu god Shiva.

lintel (p. 18) A horizontal element of any material carried by two or more vertical supports to form an opening.

literati painting (p. 793) A style of painting that reflects the taste of the educated class of East Asian intellectuals and scholars. Characteristics include an appreciation for the antique, small scale, and an intimate connection between maker and audience.

lithography (p. 953) Process of making a print (lithograph) from a design drawn on a flat stone block with greasy crayon. Ink is applied to the wet stone and adheres only to the greasy areas of the design.

loggia (p. 534) Italian term for a **gallery**. Often used as a corridor between buildings or around a courtyard, a loggia usually features an **arcade** or **colonnade**.

longitudinal-plan building (p. 225) Any structure designed with a rectangular shape and a longitudinal axis. In a cross-shaped building, the main arm of the building would be longer than any arms that cross it. For example, a **basilica**.

lost-wax casting (p. 36) A method of casting metal, such as bronze. A wax mold is covered with clay and plaster, then fired, thus melting the wax and leaving a hollow form. Molten metal is then poured into the hollow space and slowly cooled. When the hardened clay and plaster exterior shell is removed, a solid metal form remains to be smoothed and polished.

low relief (p. 40) See under **relief sculpture**.

lunette (p. 221) A semicircular wall area, framed by an **arch** over a door or window. Can be either plain or decorated.

lusterware (p. 277) Pottery decorated with metallic **glaze**s.

madrasa (p. 277) An Islamic institution of higher learning, where teaching is focused on theology and law.

maenad (p. 104) In ancient Greece, a female devotee of the wine god Dionysos who participated in orgiastic rituals. Often depicted with swirling drapery to indicate wild movement or dance. Also called a Bacchante, after Bacchus, the Roman equivalent of Dionysos.

majolica (p. 573) Pottery painted with a tin **glaze** that, when fired, gives a lustrous and colorful surface.

mandala (p. 302) An image of the cosmos represented by an arrangement of circles or concentric geometric shapes containing diagrams or images. Used for meditation and contemplation by Buddhists.

mandapa (p. 302) In a Hindu temple, an open hall dedicated to ritual worship.

mandorla (p. 479) Light encircling, or emanating from, the entire figure of a sacred person.

manuscript (p. 244) A hand-written book or document.

maqsura (p. 272) An enclosure in a Muslim **mosque**, near the *mihrab*, designated for dignitaries.

martyrium (*pl.* **martyria**) (p. 238) A church, chapel, or shrine built over the grave of a Christian martyr.

mastaba (p. 53) A flat-topped, one-story structure with slanted walls built over an ancient Egyptian underground tomb.

matte (p. 573) Of a smooth surface that is without shine or luster.

mausoleum (p. 175) A monumental building used as a tomb. Named after the tomb of King Mausolos erected at Halikarnassos around 350 BCE.

medallion (p. 222) Any round ornament or decoration. Also: a large medal.

medium (*pl.* **media**) (p. xxxi) The material from which a work of art is made.

megalith (*adj.* **megalithic**) (p. 16) A large stone used in some prehistoric architecture.

megaron (p. 93) The main hall of a Mycenaean palace or grand house.

memento mori (p. 909) From Latin for "remember that you must die." An object, such as a skull or extinguished candle, typically found in a *vanitas* image, symbolizing the transience of life.

menorah (p. 186) A Jewish lampstand with seven or nine branches; the nine-branched menorah is used during the celebration of Hanukkah. Representations of the seven-branched menorah, once used in the Temple of Jerusalem, became a symbol of Judaism.

metope (p. 110) The carved or painted rectangular panel between the **triglyph**s of a Doric **frieze**.

mihrab (p. 265) A recess or niche that distinguishes the wall oriented toward Mecca (*qibla*) in a **mosque**.

millefiori (p. 434) A glassmaking technique in which rods of differently colored glass are fused in a long bundle that is subsequently sliced to produce disks or beads with small-scale, multicolor patterns. The term derives from the Italian for "a thousand flowers."

minaret (p. 274) A tower on or near a **mosque** from which Muslims are called to prayer five times a day.

minbar (p. 265) A high platform or pulpit in a **mosque**.

miniature (p. 245) Anything small. In painting, miniatures may be illustrations within **album**s or **manuscript**s or intimate portraits.

mirador (p. 280) In Spanish and Islamic palace architecture, a very large window or room with windows, and sometimes balconies, providing views to interior courtyards or the exterior landscape.

mithuna (p. 305) The amorous male and female couples in Buddhist sculpture, usually found at the entrance to a sacred building. The *mithuna* symbolizes the harmony and fertility of life.

moai (p. 875) Statues found in Polynesia, carved from tufa, a yellowish brown volcanic stone, and depicting the human form. Nearly 1,000 of these statues have been found on the island of Rapa Nui but their significance has been a matter of speculation.

modeling (p. xxxi) In painting, the process of creating the illusion of three-dimensionality on a two-dimensional surface by use of light and shade. In sculpture, the process of molding a three-dimensional form out of a malleable substance.

module (p. 346) A segment or portion of a repeated design. Also: a basic building block.

molding (p. 319) A shaped or sculpted strip with varying contours and patterns. Used as decoration on architecture, furniture, frames, and other objects.

mortise-and-tenon (p. 18) A method of joining two elements. A projecting pin (tenon) on one element fits snugly into a hole designed for it (mortise) on the other.

mosaic (p. 145) Image formed by arranging small colored stone or glass pieces (**tesserae**) and affixing them to a hard, stable surface.

mosque (p. 265) A building used for communal Islamic worship.

Mozarabic (p. 439) Of an eclectic style practiced in Christian medieval Spain when much of the Iberian peninsula was ruled by Islamic dynasties.

mudra (p. 307) A symbolic hand gesture in Buddhist art that denotes certain behaviors, actions, or feelings.

mullion (p. 510) A slender straight or curving bar that divides a window into subsidiary sections to create **tracery**.

muqarna (p. 280) In Islamic architecture, one of the nichelike components, often stacked in tiers to mark the transition between flat and rounded surfaces and often found on the **vault** of a **dome**.

naos (p. 236) The principal room in a temple or church. In ancient architecture, the **cella**. In a Byzantine church, the **nave** and **sanctuary**.

narrative image (p. 215) A picture that recounts an event drawn from a story, either factual (e.g. biographical) or fictional. In **continuous narrative**, multiple scenes from the same story appear within a single compositional frame.

narthex (p. 220) The vestibule or entrance porch of a church.

nave (p. 191) The central space of a church, two or three stories high and usually flanked by **aisle**s.

necropolis (p. 53) A large cemetery or burial area; literally a "city of the dead."

nemes headdress (p. 51) The royal headdress of ancient Egypt.

niello (p. 90) A metal technique in which a black sulfur **alloy** is rubbed into fine lines engraved into metal (usually gold or silver). When heated, the alloy becomes fused with the surrounding metal and provides contrasting detail.

oculus (*pl.* **oculi**) (p. 187) In architecture, a circular opening. Usually found either as windows or at the apex of a **dome**. When at the top of a dome, an oculus is either open to the sky or covered by a decorative exterior **lantern**.

odalisque (p. 952) Turkish word for "harem slave girl" or "concubine."

oil painting (p. 575) Any painting executed with pigments suspended in a **medium** of oil. Oil paint has particular properties that allow for greater ease of working: among others, a slow drying time (which allows for corrections), and a great range of relative opaqueness of paint layers (which permits a high degree of detail and luminescence).

oinochoe (p. 126) An ancient Greek jug used for wine.

olpe (p. 105) Any ancient Greek vessel without a spout.

one-point perspective (p. 259) See under **perspective**.

orant (p. 220) Of a standing figure represented praying with outstretched and upraised arms.

oratory (p. 228) A small chapel.

order (p. 110) A system of proportions in Classical architecture that includes every aspect of the building's plan, elevation, and decorative system. *Composite*: a combination of the Ionic and the Corinthian orders. The **capital** combines **acanthus** leaves with **volute** scrolls. *Corinthian*: the most ornate of the orders, the Corinthian includes a **base**, a **fluted column shaft** with a capital elaborately decorated with acanthus leaf carvings. Its **entablature** consists of an **architrave** decorated with **molding**s, a **frieze** often containing **relief sculpture**, and a **cornice** with **dentils**. *Doric*: the column shaft of the Doric order can be fluted or smooth-surfaced and has no base. The Doric capital consists of an undecorated **echinus** and **abacus**. The Doric entablature has a plain architrave, a frieze with **metope**s and **triglyph**s, and a simple cornice. *Ionic*: the column of the Ionic order has a base, a fluted shaft, and a capital decorated with volutes. The Ionic entablature consists of an architrave of three panels and moldings,

a **frieze** usually containing sculpted relief ornament, and a **cornice** with dentils. *Tuscan*: a variation of Doric characterized by a smooth-surfaced column shaft with a base, a plain architrave, and an undecorated frieze. *Colossal* or *giant*: any of the above built on a large scale, rising through two or more stories in height and often raised from the ground on a **pedestal**.

Orientalism (p. 968) A fascination with Middle Eastern cultures that inspired eclectic nineteenth-century European fantasies of exotic life that often formed the subject of paintings.

orthogonal (p. 138) Any line running back into the represented space of a picture perpendicular to the imagined **picture plane**. In **linear perspective**, all orthogonals converge at a single **vanishing point** in the picture and are the basis for a **grid** that maps out the internal space of the image. An orthogonal plan is any plan for a building or city that is based exclusively on right angles, such as the grid plan of many major cities.

pagoda (p. 347) An East Asian **reliquary** tower built with successively smaller, repeated stories. Each story is usually marked by an elaborate projecting roof.

painterly (p. 253) A style of painting which emphasizes the techniques and surface effects of brushwork (also color, light, and shade).

palace complex (p. 41) A group of buildings used for living and governing by a ruler and his or her supporters, usually fortified.

palazzo (p. 602) Italian term for palace, used for any large urban dwelling.

palette (p. 183) A hand-held support used by artists for arranging colors and mixing paint during the process of painting. Also: the choice of a range of colors used by an artist in a particular work, as typical of his or her style. In ancient Egypt, a flat stone used to grind and prepare makeup.

panel painting (p. xliii) Any painting executed on a wood support, usually planed to provide a smooth surface. A panel can consist of several boards joined together.

parchment (p. 245) A writing surface made from treated skins of animals. Very fine parchment is known as **vellum**.

parterre (p. 761) An ornamental, highly regimented flowerbed; especially as an element of the ornate gardens of a seventeenth-century palace or **château**.

passage grave (p. 17) A prehistoric tomb under a **cairn**, reached by a long, narrow, slab-lined access passageway or passageways.

pastel (p. 914) Dry pigment, chalk, and gum in stick or crayon form. Also: a work of art made with pastels.

pedestal (p. 107) A platform or base supporting a sculpture or other monument. Also: the block found below the base of a Classical **column** (or **colonnade**), serving to raise the entire element off the ground.

pediment (p. 107) A triangular gable found over major architectural elements such as Classical Greek **portico**s, windows, or doors. Formed by an **entablature** and the ends of a sloping roof or a raking **cornice**. A similar architectural element is often used decoratively above a door or window, sometimes with a curved upper **molding**. A *broken pediment* is a variation on the traditional pediment, with an open space at the center of the topmost angle and/or the horizontal cornice.

pendant (also **pendent**) (p. 640) One of a pair of artworks meant to be seen in relation to each other as a set.

pendentive (p. 236) The concave triangular section of a **vault** that forms the transition between a square or polygonal space and the circular base of a **dome**.

Performance art (p. 1087) A contemporary artwork based on a live, sometimes theatrical performance by the artist.

peristyle (p. 66) In Greek architecture, a surrounding **colonnade**. A peristyle building is surrounded on the exterior by a colonnade. Also: a peristyle court is an open colonnaded courtyard, often having a pool and garden.

perspective (p. xxix) A system for representing three-dimensional space on a two-dimensional surface. *Atmospheric* or *aerial perspective*: a method of rendering the effect of spatial distance by subtle variations in color and clarity of representation. *Intuitive perspective*: a method of giving the impression of recession by visual instinct, not by the use of an overall system or program. *Oblique perspective*: an intuitive spatial system in which a building or room is placed with one corner in the **picture plane**, and the other parts of the structure recede to an imaginary **vanishing point** on its other side. Oblique perspective is not a comprehensive, mathematical system. *One-point* and multiple-point perspective (also called linear, scientific, or mathematical perspective): a method of creating the illusion of three-dimensional space on a two-dimensional surface by delineating a **horizon line** and multiple **orthogonal** lines. These recede to meet at one or more points on the horizon (vanishing point), giving the appearance of spatial depth. Called scientific or mathematical because its use requires some knowledge of geometry and mathematics, as well as optics. *Reverse perspective*: a Byzantine perspective theory in which the orthogonals or rays of sight do not converge on a vanishing point in the picture, but are thought to originate in the viewer's eye in front of the picture. Thus, in reverse perspective the image is constructed with orthogonals that diverge, giving a slightly tipped aspect to objects.

photomontage (p. 1039) A photographic work created from many smaller photographs arranged (and often overlapping) in a composition, which is then rephotographed.

pictograph (p. 337) A highly stylized depiction serving as a symbol for a person or object. Also: a type of writing utilizing such symbols.

picture plane (p. 575) The theoretical plane corresponding with the actual surface of a painting, separating the spatial world evoked in the painting from the spatial world occupied by the viewer.

picturesque (p. 919) Of the taste for the familiar, the pleasant, and the agreeable, popular in the eighteenth and nineteenth centuries in Europe. Originally used to describe the "picturelike" qualities of some landscape scenes. When contrasted with the **sublime**, the picturesque stood for the interesting but ordinary domestic landscape.

piece-mold casting (p. 334) A casting technique in which the mold consists of several sections that are connected during the pouring of molten metal, usually bronze. After the cast form has hardened, the pieces of the mold are disassembled, leaving the completed object.

pier (p. 270) A masonry support made up of many stones, or rubble and concrete (in contrast to a column **shaft** which is formed from a single stone or a series of **drums**), often square or rectangular in plan, and capable of carrying very heavy architectural loads.

pietà (p. 230) A devotional subject in Christian religious art. After the Crucifixion the body of Jesus was laid across the lap of his grieving mother, Mary. When other mourners are present, the subject is called the Lamentation.

pietra serena (p. 602) A gray Tuscan sandstone used in Florentine architecture.

pilaster (p. 158) An **engaged** columnlike element that is rectangular in format and used for decoration in architecture.

pilgrimage church (p. 239) A church that attracts visitors wishing to venerate **relic**s as well as attend religious services.

pinnacle (p. 503) In Gothic architecture, a steep pyramid decorating the top of another element such as a **buttress**. Also: the highest point.

plate tracery (p. 505) See under **tracery**.

plein air (p. 989) See under *en plein air*.

plinth (p. 161) The slablike base or **pedestal** of a **column**, statue, wall, building, or piece of furniture.

pluralism (p. 1107) A social structure or goal that allows members of diverse ethnic, racial, or other groups to exist peacefully within the society while continuing to practice the customs of their own divergent cultures. Also: an adjective describing the state of having a variety of valid contemporary styles available at the same time to artists.

podium (p. 138) A raised platform that acts as the foundation for a building, or as a platform for a speaker.

poesia (*pl.* **poesie**) (p. 656) Italian Renaissance paintings based on Classical themes, often with erotic overtones, notably in the mid-sixteenth-century works of the Venetian painter Titian.

polychromy (p. 524) Multicolored decoration applied to any part of a building, sculpture, or piece of furniture. This can be accomplished with paint or by the use of multicolored materials.

polyptych (p. 566) An **altarpiece** constructed from multiple panels, sometimes with hinges to allow for movable wings.

porcelain (p. 20) A type of extremely hard and fine white **ceramic** first made by Chinese potters in the eighth century CE. Made from a mixture of kaolin and petuntse, porcelain is fired at a very high temperature, and the final product has a translucent surface.

porch (p. 108) The covered entrance on the exterior of a building. With a row of **column**s or **colonnade**, also called a **portico**.

portal (p. 40) A grand entrance, door, or gate, usually to an important public building, and often decorated with sculpture.

portico (p. 63) In architecture, a projecting roof or porch supported by **column**s, often marking an entrance. See also **porch**.

post-and-lintel (p. 19) An architectural system of construction with two or more vertical elements (posts) supporting a horizontal element (**lintel**).

potassium-argon dating (p. 12) Archaeological method of **radiometric dating** that measures the decay of a radioactive potassium isotope into a stable isotope of argon, and inert gas.

potsherd (p. 20) A broken piece of **ceramic** ware.

poupou (p. 873) In Pacific cultures, a house panel, often carved with designs.

Prairie Style (p. 1046) Style developed by a group of Midwestern architects who worked together using the aesthetic of the prairie and indigenous prairie plants for landscape design to create mostly domestic homes and small public buildings.

predella (p. 550) The base of an **altarpiece**, often decorated with small scenes that are related in subject to that of the main panel or panels.

primitivism (p. 1022) The borrowing of subjects or forms, usually from non-European or prehistoric sources by Western artists, in an attempt to infuse their work with the expressive qualities they attributed to other cultures, especially colonized cultures.

pronaos (p. 108) The enclosed vestibule of a Greek or Roman temple, found in front of the **cella** and marked by a row of **column**s at the entrance.

proscenium (p. 148) The stage of an ancient Greek or Roman theater. In a modern theater, the area of the stage in front of the curtain. Also: the framing **arch** that separates a stage from the audience.

psalter (p. 256) In Jewish and Christian scripture, a book of the Psalms (songs) attributed to King David.

psykter (p. 126) An ancient Greek vessel with an extended base to allow it to float in a larger **krater**; used to chill wine.

putto (*pl.* **putti**) (p. 224) A plump, naked little boy, often winged. In Classical art, called a cupid; in Christian art, a cherub.

pylon (p. 66) A massive gateway formed by a pair of tapering walls of oblong shape. Erected by ancient Egyptians to mark the entrance to a temple complex.

qibla (p. 274) The **mosque** wall oriented toward Mecca; indicated by the *mihrab*.

quatrefoil (p. 508) A four-lobed decorative pattern common in Gothic art and architecture.

quillwork (p. 847) A Native American technique in which the quills of porcupines and bird feathers are dyed and attached to materials in patterns.

radiometric dating (p. 12) Archaeological method of **absolute dating** by measuring the degree to which radioactive materials have degenerated over time. For dating organic (plant or animal) materials, one radiometric method measures a carbon isotope called radiocarbon, or carbon-14.

raigo (p. 378) A painted image that depicts the Amida Buddha and other Buddhist deities welcoming the soul of a dying believer to paradise.

raku (p. 823) A type of **ceramic** made by hand, coated with a thick, dark **glaze**, and fired at a low heat. The resulting vessels are irregularly shaped and glazed and are highly prized for use in the Japanese tea ceremony.

readymade (p. 1038) An object from popular or material culture presented without further manipulation as an artwork by the artist.

red-figure (p. 119) A technique of ancient Greek **ceramic** decoration characterized by red clay-colored figures on a black background. The figures are reserved against a painted ground and details are drawn, not engraved; compare **black-figure**.

register (p. 30) A device used in systems of spatial definition. In painting, a register indicates the use of differing groundlines to differentiate layers of space within an image. In **relief sculpture**, the placement of self-contained bands of reliefs in a vertical arrangement.

registration marks (p. 828) In Japanese **woodblock prints**, two marks carved on the blocks to indicate proper alignment of the paper during the printing process. In multicolor printing, which used a separate block for each color, these marks were essential for achieving the proper position or registration of the colors.

relative dating (p. 12) Archaeological process of determining relative chronological relationships among excavated objects. Compare **absolute dating**.

relic (p. 239) Venerated object or body part associated with a holy figure, such as a saint, and usually housed in a **reliquary**.

relief sculpture (p. 5) A three-dimensional image or design whose flat background surface is carved away to a certain depth, setting off the figure. Called *high* or *low (bas-) relief* depending upon the extent of projection of the image from the background. Called *sunken relief* when the image is carved below the original surface of the background, which is not cut away.

reliquary (p. 366) A container, often elaborate and made of precious materials, used as a repository for sacred relics.

repoussé (p. 90) A technique of pushing or hammering metal from the back to create a protruding image. Elaborate reliefs are created by pressing or hammering metal sheets against carved wooden forms.

rhyton (p. 88) A vessel in the shape of a figure or an animal, used for drinking or pouring liquids on special occasions.

rib vault (p. 499) See under **vault**.

ridgepole (p. 16) A longitudinal timber at the apex of a roof that supports the upper ends of the rafters.

roof comb (p. 392) In a Maya building, a masonry wall along the apex of a roof that is built above the level of the roof proper. Roof combs support the highly decorated false **façade**s that rise above the height of the building at the front.

rose window (p. 505) A round window, often filled with stained glass set into tracery patterns in the form of wheel spokes, found in the **façade**s of the **nave**s and **transept**s of large Gothic churches.

rosette (p. 105) A round or oval ornament resembling a rose.

rotunda (p. 195) Any building (or part thereof) constructed in a circular (or sometimes polygonal) shape, usually producing a large open space crowned by a **dome**.

round arch (p. 170) See under **arch**.

roundel (p. 158) Any ornamental element with a circular format, often placed as a decoration on the exterior of a building.

rune stone (p. 442) In early medieval northern Europe, a stone used as a commemorative monument and carved or inscribed with runes, a writing system used by early Germanic peoples.

rustication (p. 602) In architecture, the rough, irregular, and unfinished effect deliberately given to the exterior facing of a stone edifice. Rusticated stones are often large and used for decorative emphasis around doors or windows, or across the entire lower floors of a building.

sacra conversazione (p. 630) Italian for "holy conversation." Refers to a type of religious painting developed in fifteenth-century Florence in which a central image of the Virgin and Child is flanked by standing saints of comparable size who stand within the same spatial setting and often acknowledge each other's presence.

salon (p. 907) A large room for entertaining guests or a periodic social or intellectual gathering, often of prominent people, held in such a room. Also: a hall or **gallery** for exhibiting works of art.

sanctuary (p. 102) A sacred or holy enclosure used for worship. In ancient Greece and Rome, consisted of one or more temples and an altar. In Christian architecture, the space around the altar in a church called the chancel or presbytery.

sarcophagus (*pl.* **sarcophagi**) (p. 49) A stone coffin. Often rectangular and decorated with **relief sculpture**.

scarab (p. 51) In ancient Egypt, a stylized dung beetle associated with the sun and the god Amun.

scarification (p. 409) Ornamental decoration applied to the surface of the body by cutting the skin for cultural and/or aesthetic reasons.

school of artists or **painting** (p. 285) An art-historical term describing a group of artists, usually working at the same time and sharing similar styles, influences, and ideals. The artists in a particular school may not necessarily be directly associated with one another, unlike those in a workshop or **atelier**.

scriptorium (*pl.* **scriptoria**) (p. 244) A room in a monastery for writing or copying **manuscripts**.

scroll painting (p. 347) A painting executed on a flexible support with rollers at each end. The rollers permit the horizontal scroll to be unrolled as it is studied or the vertical scroll to be hung for contemplation or decoration.

sculpture in the round (p. 5) Three-dimensional sculpture that is carved free of any background or block. Compare **relief sculpture**.

serdab (p. 53) In ancient Egyptian tombs, the small room in which the *ka* statue was placed.

sfumato (p. 636) Italian term meaning "smoky," soft, and mellow. In painting, the effect of haze in an image. Resembling the color of the atmosphere at dusk, *sfumato* gives a smoky effect.

sgraffito (p. 604) Decoration made by incising or cutting away a surface layer of material to reveal a different color beneath.

shaft (p. 110) The main vertical section of a **column** between the **capital** and the base, usually circular in cross section.

shaft grave (p. 97) A deep pit used for burial.

shikhara (p. 302) In the architecture of northern India, a conical (or pyramidal) spire found atop a Hindu temple and often crowned with an *amalaka*.

shoin (p. 821) A term used to describe the various features found in the most formal room of upper-class Japanese residential architecture.

shoji (p. 821) A standing Japanese screen covered in translucent rice paper and used in interiors.

siapo (p. 876) A type of **tapa** cloth found in Samoa and still used as an important gift for ceremonial occasions.

silkscreen printing (p. 1092) A technique of printing in which paint or ink is pressed through a stencil and specially prepared cloth to reproduce a design in multiple copies.

sinopia (*pl. sinopie*) (p. 539) Italian word taken from Sinope, the ancient city in Asia Minor that was famous for its red-brick pigment. In **fresco** paintings, a full-sized, preliminary sketch done in this color on the first rough coat of plaster or *arriccio*.

site-specific (p. 1102) Of a work commissioned and/or designed for a particular location.

slip (p. 118) A mixture of clay and water applied to a **ceramic** object as a final decorative coat. Also: a solution that binds different parts of a vessel together, such as the handle and the main body.

spandrel (p. 170) The area of wall adjoining the exterior curve of an **arch** between its **springing** and the **keystone**, or the area between two arches, as in an **arcade**.

spolia (p. 471) Fragments of older architecture or sculpture reused in a secondary context. Latin for "hide stripped from an animal."

springing (p. 170) The point at which the curve of an **arch** or **vault** meets with and rises from its support.

squinch (p. 238) An **arch** or **lintel** built across the upper corners of a square space, allowing a circular or polygonal **dome** to be securely set above the walls.

stained glass (p. 287) Glass stained with color while molten, using metallic oxides. Stained glass is most often used in windows, for which small pieces of different colors are precisely cut and assembled into a design, held together by lead **cames**. Additional details may be added with vitreous paint.

stave church (p. 443) A Scandinavian wooden structure with four huge timbers (staves) at its core.

stele (*pl.* **stelai**), also **stela** (*pl.* **stelae**) (p. 27) A stone slab placed vertically and decorated with inscriptions or reliefs. Used as a grave marker or commemorative monument.

stereobate (p. 110) In Classical architecture, the foundation upon which a temple stands.

still life (*pl.* **still lifes**) (p. xxxvii) A type of painting that has as its subject inanimate objects (such as food and dishes) or fruit and flowers taken out of their natural contexts.

stoa (p. 107) In Greek architecture, a long roofed walkway, usually having **columns** on one long side and a wall on the other.

stoneware (p. 20) A high-fired, vitrified, but opaque **ceramic** ware that is fired in the range of 1,100 to 1,200 degrees Celsius. At that temperature, particles of silica in the clay bodies fuse together so that the finished vessels are impervious to liquids, even without glaze. Stoneware pieces are glazed to enhance their aesthetic appeal and to aid in keeping them clean. Stoneware occurs in a range of earth-toned colors, from white and tan to gray and black, with light gray predominating. Chinese potters were the first in the world to produce stoneware, which they were able to make as early as the Shang dynasty.

stringcourse (p. 503) A continuous horizontal band, such as a **molding**, decorating the face of a wall.

stucco (p. 72) A mixture of lime, sand, and other ingredients made into a material that can easily be molded or modeled. When dry, it produces a durable surface used for covering walls or for architectural sculpture and decoration.

stupa (p. 302) In Buddhist architecture, a bell-shaped or pyramidal religious monument, made of piled earth or stone, and containing sacred **relics**.

style (p. xxxviii) A particular manner, form, or character of representation, construction, or expression that is typical of an individual artist or of a certain place or period.

stylobate (p. 110) In Classical architecture, the stone foundation on which a temple **colonnade** stands.

stylus (p. 28) An instrument with a pointed end (used for writing and printmaking), which makes a delicate line or scratch. Also: a special writing tool for **cuneiform** writing with one pointed end and one triangular.

sublime (p. 955) Of a concept, thing, or state of greatness or vastness with high spiritual, moral, intellectual, or emotional value; or something awe-inspiring. The sublime was a goal to which many nineteenth-century artists aspired in their artworks.

sunken relief (p. 71) See under **relief sculpture**.

symposium (p. 119) An elite gathering of wealthy and powerful men in ancient Greece that focused principally on wine, music, poetry, conversation, games, and love making.

syncretism (p. 220) A process whereby artists assimilate and combine images and ideas from different cultural traditions, beliefs, and practices, giving them new meanings.

taotie (p. 334) A mask with a dragon or animal-like face common as a decorative motif in Chinese art.

tapa (p. 876) A type of cloth used for various purposes in Pacific cultures, made from tree bark stripped and beaten, and often bearing subtle designs from the mallets used to work the bark.

tapestry (p. 292) Multicolored decorative weaving to be hung on a wall or placed on furniture. Pictorial or decorative motifs are woven directly into the supporting fabric, completely concealing it.

tatami (p. 821) Mats of woven straw used in Japanese houses as a floor covering.

temenos (p. 108) An enclosed sacred area reserved for worship in ancient Greece.

tempera (p. 141) A painting **medium** made by blending egg yolks with water, pigments, and occasionally other materials, such as glue.

tenebrism (p. 723) The use of strong *chiaroscuro* and artificially illuminated areas to create a dramatic contrast of light and dark in a painting.

terra cotta (p. 114) A **medium** made from clay fired over a low heat and sometimes left unglazed. Also: the orange-brown color typical of this medium.

tessera (*pl.* **tesserae**) (p. 145) A small piece of stone, glass, or other object that is pieced together with many others to create a **mosaic**.

thatch (p. 16) Plant material such as reeds or straw tied over a framework of poles to make a roof, shelter, or small building.

thermo-luminescence dating (p. 12) A method of **radiometric** **dating** that measures the irradiation of the crystal structure of material such as flint or pottery and the soil in which it is found, determined by luminescence produced when a sample is heated.

tholos (p. 98) A small, round building. Sometimes built underground, e.g. as a Mycenaean tomb.

thrust (p. 170) The outward pressure caused by the weight of a **vault** and supported by **buttressing**. See also under **arch**.

tondo (*pl.* **tondi**) (p. 126) A painting or **relief sculpture** of circular shape.

torana (p. 302) In Indian architecture, an ornamented gateway arch in a temple, usually leading to the **stupa**.

torc (p. 149) A circular neck ring worn by Celtic warriors.

toron (p. 422) In West African **mosque** architecture, the wooden beams that project from the walls. Torons are used as support for the scaffolding erected annually for the replastering of the building.

tracery (p. 503) Stonework or woodwork forming a pattern in the open space of windows or applied to wall surfaces. In *plate tracery*, a series of openings are cut through the wall. In *bar tracery*, **mullions** divide the space into segments to form decorative patterns.

transept (p. 225) The arm of a **cruciform** church perpendicular to the **nave**. The point where the nave and transept intersect is called the crossing. Beyond the crossing lies the **sanctuary**, whether **apse**, **choir**, or **chevet**.

transverse arch (p. 463) See under **arch**.

trefoil (p. 298) An ornamental design made up of three rounded lobes placed adjacent to one another.

triforium (p. 505) The element of the interior elevation of a church found directly below the **clerestory** and consisting of a series of arched openings in front of a passageway within the thickness of the wall.

triglyph (p. 110) Rectangular block between the **metope**s of a Doric **frieze**. Identified by the three carved vertical grooves, which approximate the appearance of the end of wooden beams.

triptych (p. 566) An artwork made up of three panels. The panels may be hinged together in such a way that the side segments (wings) fold over the central area.

trompe l'oeil (p. 618) A manner of representation in which artists faithfully describe the appearance of natural space and forms with the express intention of fooling the eye of the viewer, who may be convinced momentarily that the subject actually exists as three-dimensional reality.

trumeau (p. 478) A **column**, **pier**, or post found at the center of a large **portal** or doorway, supporting the **lintel**.

tugra (p. 288) A calligraphic imperial monogram used in Ottoman courts.

tukutuku (p. 872) Lattice panels created by women from the Maori culture and used in architecture.

Tuscan order (p. 158) See under **order**.

twining (p. 848) A basketry technique in which short rods are sewn together vertically. The panels are then joined together to form a container or other object.

tympanum (p. 478) In medieval and later architecture, the area over a door enclosed by an **arch** and a **lintel**, often decorated with sculpture or mosaic.

ukiyo-e (p. 828) A Japanese term for a type of popular art that was favored from the sixteenth century, particularly in the form of color **woodblock print**s. *Ukiyo-e* prints often depicted the world of the common people in Japan, such as courtesans and actors, as well as landscapes and myths.

undercutting (p. 212) A technique in sculpture by which the material is cut back under the edges so that the remaining form projects strongly forward, casting deep shadows.

underglaze (p. 800) Color or decoration applied to a **ceramic** piece before glazing.

upeti (p. 876) In Pacific cultures, a carved wooden design tablet, used to create patterns in cloth by dragging the fabric across it.

uranium-thorium dating (p. 12) Technique used to date prehistoric cave paintings by measuring the decay of uranium into thorium in the deposits of calcium carbinate that cover the surfaces of cave walls, to determine the minimum age of the paintings under the crust.

urna (p. 306) In Buddhist art, the curl of hair on the forehead that is a characteristic mark of a buddha. The *urna* is a symbol of divine wisdom.

ushnisha (p. 306) In Asian art, a round turban or tiara symbolizing royalty and, when worn by a buddha, enlightenment.

vanishing point (p. 610) In a **perspective** system, the point on the **horizon line** at which **orthogonals** meet. A complex system can have multiple vanishing points.

vanitas (p. xxxviii) An image, especially popular in Europe during the seventeenth century, in which all the objects symbolize the transience of life. *Vanitas* paintings are usually of **still lifes** or genre subjects.

vault (p. 17) An arched masonry structure that spans an interior space. *Barrel* or *tunnel vault*: an elongated or continuous semicircular vault, shaped like a half-cylinder. *Corbeled vault*: a vault made by projecting **course**s of stone; see also under **corbel**. *Groin* or *cross vault*: a vault created by the intersection of two barrel vaults of equal size which creates four side compartments of identical size and shape. *Quadrant vault*: a half-barrel vault. *Rib vault*: a groin vault with ribs (extra masonry) demarcating the junctions. Ribs may function to reinforce the groins or may be purely decorative.

veduta (*pl.* **vedute**) (p. 915) Italian for "vista" or "view." Paintings, drawings, or prints, often of expansive city scenes or of harbors.

vellum (p. 245) A fine animal skin prepared for writing and painting. See also **parchment**.

verism (p. 168) Style in which artists concern themselves with describing the exterior likeness of an object or person, usually by rendering its visible details in a finely executed, meticulous manner.

vihara (p. 305) From the Sanskrit term meaning "for wanderers." A *vihara* is, in general, a Buddhist monastery in India. It also signifies monks' cells and gathering places in such a monastery.

volute (p. 110) A spiral scroll, as seen on an Ionic **capital**.

votive figure (p. 31) An image created as a devotional offering to a deity.

voussoir (p. 170) Wedge-shaped stone block used to build an **arch**. The topmost voussoir is called a **keystone**. See also **joggled voussoirs**.

warp (p. 292) The vertical threads in a weaver's loom. Warp threads make up a fixed framework that provides the structure for the entire piece of cloth, and are thus often thicker than **weft** threads.

wattle and daub (p. 16) A wall construction method combining upright branches, woven with twigs (wattles) and plastered or filled with clay or mud (daub).

weft (p. 292) The horizontal threads in a woven piece of cloth. Weft threads are woven at right angles to and through the **warp** threads to make up the bulk of the decorative pattern. In carpets, the weft is often completely covered or formed by the rows of trimmed knots that form the carpet's soft surface.

westwork (p. 446) The monumental, west-facing entrance section of a Carolingian, Ottonian, or Romanesque church. The exterior consists of multiple stories between two towers; the interior includes an entrance vestibule, a chapel, and a series of **galleries** overlooking the **nave**.

white-ground (p. 141) A type of ancient Greek pottery in which the background color of the object was painted with a **slip** that turns white in the firing process. Figures and details were added by painting on or incising into this slip. White-ground wares were popular in the Classical period as funerary objects.

woodblock print (p. 591) A print made from one or more carved wooden blocks. In Japan, woodblock prints were made using multiple blocks carved in relief, usually with a block for each color in the finished print. See also **woodcut**.

woodcut (p. 592) A type of print made by carving a design into a wooden block. The ink is applied to the block with a roller. As the ink touches only on the surface areas and lines remaining between the carved-away parts of the block, it is these areas that make the print when paper is pressed against the inked block, leaving the carved-away parts of the design to appear blank. Also: the process by which the woodcut is made.

yaksha, yakshi (p. 301) The male (*yaksha*) and female (*yakshi*) nature spirits that act as agents of the Hindu gods. Their sculpted images are often found on Hindu temples and other sacred places, particularly at the entrances.

yamato-e (p. 374) A native style of Japanese painting developed during the twelfth and thirteenth centuries, distinguished from Japanese painting styles that emulate Chinese traditions.

ziggurat (p. 28) In ancient Mesopotamia, a tall stepped tower of earthen materials, often supporting a shrine.

Bibliography

Susan V. Craig, updated by **Carrie L. McDade**

This bibliography is composed of books in English that are suggested "further reading" titles. Most are available in good libraries, whether college, university, or public. Recently published works have been emphasized so that the research information would be current. There are three classifications of listings: general surveys and art history reference tools, including journals and Internet directories; surveys of large periods that encompass multiple chapters (ancient art in the Western tradition, European medieval art, European Renaissance through eighteenth-century art, modern art in the West, Asian art, and African and Oceanic art, and art of the Americas); and books for individual Chapters 1 through 33.

General Art History Surveys and Reference Tools

Adams, Laurie Schneider. *Art Across Time*. 4th ed. New York: McGraw-Hill, 2011.

Barnet, Sylvan. *A Short Guide to Writing about Art*. 10th ed. Upper Saddle River, NJ: Pearson/Prentice Hall, 2010.

Bony, Anne. *Design: History, Main Trends, Main Figures*. Edinburgh: Chambers, 2005.

Boström, Antonia. *Encyclopedia of Sculpture*. 3 vols. New York: Fitzroy Dearborn, 2004.

Broude, Norma, and Mary D. Garrard, eds. *Feminism and Art History: Questioning the Litany*. Icon Editions. New York: Harper & Row, 1982.

Chadwick, Whitney. *Women, Art, and Society*. 4th ed. New York: Thames & Hudson, 2007.

Chilvers, Ian, ed. *The Oxford Dictionary of Art*. 4th ed. New York: Oxford Univ. Press, 2009.

Curl, James Stevens. *A Dictionary of Architecture and Landscape Architecture*. 2nd ed. Oxford: Oxford Univ. Press, 2006.

Davies, Penelope J.E., et al. *Janson's History of Art: The Western Tradition*. 8th ed. Upper Saddle River, NJ: Prentice Hall, 2010.

The Dictionary of Art. Ed. Jane Turner. 34 vols. New York: Grove's Dictionaries, 1996.

Frank, Patrick, Duane Preble, and Sarah Preble. *Prebles' Artforms*. 10th ed. Upper Saddle River, NJ: Pearson/Prentice Hall, 2011.

Gaze, Delia, ed. *Dictionary of Women Artists*. 2 vols. London: Fitzroy Dearborn, 1997.

Griffiths, Antony. *Prints and Printmaking: An Introduction to the History and Techniques*. 2nd ed. London: British Museum Press, 1996.

Hadden, Peggy. *The Quotable Artist*. New York: Allworth Press, 2002.

Hall, James. *Dictionary of Subjects and Symbols in Art*. 2nd ed. Boulder, CO: Westview Press, 2008.

Holt, Elizabeth Gilmore, ed. *A Documentary History of Art*. 3 vols. New Haven: Yale Univ. Press, 1986.

Honour, Hugh, and John Fleming. *The Visual Arts: A History*. 7th ed. rev. Upper Saddle River, NJ: Pearson/Prentice Hall, 2010.

Johnson, Paul. *Art: A New History*. New York: HarperCollins, 2003.

Kemp, Martin, ed. *The Oxford History of Western Art*. Oxford: Oxford Univ. Press, 2000.

Kleiner, Fred S. *Gardner's Art through the Ages*. Enhanced 13th ed. Belmont, CA: Thomson/Wadsworth, 2011.

Kostof, Spiro. *A History of Architecture: Settings and Rituals*. 2nd ed. Revised Greg Castillo. New York: Oxford Univ. Press, 1995.

Mackenzie, Lynn. *Non-Western Art: A Brief Guide*. 2nd ed. Upper Saddle River, NJ: Pearson/Prentice Hall, 2001.

Marmor, Max, and Alex Ross, eds. *Guide to the Literature of Art History 2*. Chicago: American Library Association, 2005.

Onians, John, ed. *Atlas of World Art*. New York: Oxford Univ. Press, 2004.

Sayre, Henry M. *Writing about Art*. 6th ed. Upper Saddle River, NJ: Pearson/Prentice Hall, 2009.

Sed-Rajna, Gabrielle. *Jewish Art*. Trans. Sara Friedman and Mira Reich. New York: Abrams, 1997.

Slatkin, Wendy. *Women Artists in History: From Antiquity to the Present*. 4th ed. Upper Saddle River, NJ: Pearson/Prentice Hall, 2001.

Sutton, Ian. *Western Architecture: From Ancient Greece to the Present*. World of Art. New York: Thames & Hudson, 1999.

Trachtenberg, Marvin, and Isabelle Hyman. *Architecture, from Prehistory to Postmodernity*. 2nd ed. Upper Saddle River, NJ: Pearson/Prentice Hall, 2002.

Watkin, David. *A History of Western Architecture*. 4th ed. New York: Watson-Guptill, 2005.

Art History Journals: A Select List of Current Titles

African Arts. Quarterly. Los Angeles: Univ. of California at Los Angeles, James S. Coleman African Studies Center, 1967–.

American Art: The Journal of the Smithsonian American Art Museum. 3/year. Chicago: Univ. of Chicago Press, 1987–.

American Indian Art Magazine. Quarterly. Scottsdale, AZ: American Indian Art Inc., 1975–.

American Journal of Archaeology. Quarterly. Boston: Archaeological Institute of America, 1885–.

Antiquity: A Periodical of Archaeology. Quarterly. Cambridge: Antiquity Publications Ltd., 1927–.

Apollo: The International Magazine of the Arts. Monthly. London: Apollo Magazine Ltd., 1925–.

Architectural History. Annually. Farnham, UK: Society of Architectural Historians of Great Britain, 1958–.

Archives of American Art Journal. Quarterly. Washington, DC: Archives of American Art, Smithsonian Institution, 1960–.

Archives of Asian Art. Annually. New York: Asia Society, 1945–.

Ars Orientalis: The Arts of Asia, Southeast Asia, and Islam. Annually. Ann Arbor: Univ. of Michigan Dept. of Art History, 1954–.

Art Bulletin. Quarterly. New York: College Art Association, 1913–.

Art History: Journal of the Association of Art Historians. 5/year. Oxford: Blackwell Publishing Ltd., 1978–.

Art in America. Monthly. New York: Brant Publications Inc., 1913–.

Art Journal. Quarterly. New York: College Art Association, 1960–.

Art Nexus. Quarterly. Bogota, Colombia: Arte en Colombia Ltda, 1976–.

Art Papers Magazine. Bimonthly. Atlanta: Atlanta Art Papers Inc., 1976–.

Artforum International. 10/year. New York: Artforum International Magazine Inc., 1962–.

Artnews. 11/year. New York: Artnews LLC, 1902–.

Bulletin of the Metropolitan Museum of Art. Quarterly. New York: Metropolitan Museum of Art, 1905–.

Burlington Magazine. Monthly. London: Burlington Magazine Publications Ltd., 1903–.

Dumbarton Oaks Papers. Annually. Locust Valley, NY: J.J. Augustin Inc., 1940–.

Flash Art International. Bimonthly. Trevi, Italy: Giancarlo Politi Editore, 1980–.

Gesta. Semiannually. New York: International Center of Medieval Art, 1963–.

History of Photography. Quarterly. Abingdon, UK: Taylor & Francis Ltd., 1976–.

International Review of African American Art. Quarterly. Hampton, VA: International Review of African American Art, 1976–.

Journal of Design History. Quarterly. Oxford: Oxford Univ. Press, 1988–.

Journal of Egyptian Archaeology. Annually. London: Egypt Exploration Society, 1914–.

Journal of Hellenic Studies. Annually. London: Society for the Promotion of Hellenic Studies, 1880–.

Journal of Roman Archaeology. Annually. Portsmouth, RI: Journal of Roman Archaeology LLC, 1988–.

Journal of the Society of Architectural Historians. Quarterly. Chicago: Society of Architectural Historians, 1940–.

Journal of the Warburg and Courtauld Institutes. Annually. London: Warburg Institute, 1937–.

Leonardo: Art, Science, and Technology. 6/year. Cambridge, MA: MIT Press, 1968–.

Marg. Quarterly. Mumbai, India: Scientific Publishers, 1946–.

Master Drawings. Quarterly. New York: Master Drawings Association, 1963–.

October. Cambridge, MA: MIT Press, 1976–.

Oxford Art Journal. 3/year. Oxford: Oxford Univ. Press, 1978–.

Parkett. 3/year. Zürich, Switzerland: Parkett Verlag AG, 1984–.

Print Quarterly. Quarterly. London: Print Quarterly Publications, 1984–.

Simiolus: Netherlands Quarterly for the History of Art. Quarterly. Apeldoorn, Netherlands: Stichting voor Nederlandse Kunsthistorische Publicaties, 1966–.

Woman's Art Journal. Semiannually. Philadelphia: Old City Publishing Inc., 1980–.

Internet Directories for Art History Information: A Selected List

ARCHITECTURE AND BUILDING,
http://www.library.unlv.edu/arch/rsrce/webresources/
A directory of architecture websites collected by Jeanne Brown at the Univ. of Nevada at Las Vegas. Topical lists include architecture, building and construction, design, history, housing, planning, preservation, and landscape architecture. Most entries include a brief annotation and the last date the link was accessed by the compiler.

ART HISTORY RESOURCES ON THE WEB,
http://witcombe.sbc.edu/ARTHLinks.html
Authored by Professor Christopher L.C.E. Witcombe of Sweet Briar College in Virginia, since 1995, the site includes an impressive number of links for various art-historical eras as well as links to research resources, museums, and galleries. The content is frequently updated.

ART IN FLUX: A DIRECTORY OF RESOURCES FOR RESEARCH IN CONTEMPORARY ART,
http://www.boisestate.edu/art/artinflux/intro.html
Cheryl K. Shurtleff of Boise State Univ. in Idaho has authored this directory, which includes sites selected according to their relevance to the study of national or international contemporary art and artists. The subsections include artists, museums, theory, reference, and links.

ARTCYCLOPEDIA: THE GUIDE TO GREAT ART ON THE INTERNET,
http://www.artcyclopedia.com
With more than 2,100 art sites and 75,000 links, this is one of the most comprehensive Web directories for artists and art topics. The primary search is by artist's name but access is also available by title of artwork, artistic movement, museums and galleries, nationality, period, and medium.

MOTHER OF ALL ART AND ART HISTORY LINKS PAGES,
http://umich.edu/~motherha
Maintained by the Dept. of the History of Art at the Univ. of Michigan, this directory covers art history departments, art museums, fine arts schools and departments, as well as links to research resources. Each entry includes annotations.

VOICE OF THE SHUTTLE,
http://vos.ucsb.edu
Sponsored by Univ. of California, Santa Barbara, this directory includes more than 70 pages of links to humanities and humanities-related resources on the Internet. The structured guide includes specific subsections on architecture, on art (modern and contemporary), and on art history. Links usually include a one-sentence explanation and the resource is frequently updated with new information.

ARTBABBLE,
http://www.artbabble.org/
An online community created by staff at the Indianapolis Museum of Art to showcase art-based video content, including interviews with artists and curators, original documentaries, and art installation videos. Partners and contributors to the project include Art21, Los Angeles County Museum of Art, The Museum of Modern Art, The New York Public Library, San Francisco Museum of Modern Art, and Smithsonian American Art Museum.

YAHOO! ARTS>ART HISTORY,
http://dir.yahoo.com/Arts/Art_History/
Another extensive directory of art links organized into subdivisions with one of the most extensive being "Periods and Movements." Links include the name of the site as well as a few words of explanation.

Ancient Art in the Western Tradition, General

Amiet, Pierre. *Art in the Ancient World: A Handbook of Styles and Forms.* New York: Rizzoli, 1981.
Beard, Mary, and John Henderson. *Classical Art: From Greece to Rome.* Oxford History of Art. Oxford: Oxford Univ. Press, 2001.
Boardman, John. *Oxford History of Classical Art.* New York: Oxford Univ. Press, 2001.
Chitham, Robert. *The Classical Orders of Architecture.* 2nd ed. Boston: Elsevier/Architectural Press, 2005.
Ehrich, Robert W., ed. *Chronologies in Old World Archaeology.* 3rd ed. 2 vols. Chicago: Univ. of Chicago Press, 1992.
Gerster, Georg. *The Past from Above: Aerial Photographs of Archaeological Sites.* Ed. Charlotte Trümpler. Trans. Stewart Spencer. Los Angeles: J. Paul Getty Museum, 2005.
Groenewegen-Frankfort, H.A., and Bernard Ashmole. *Art of the Ancient World: Painting, Pottery, Sculpture, Architecture from Egypt, Mesopotamia, Crete, Greece, and Rome.* Library of Art History. Upper Saddle River, NJ: Prentice Hall, 1972.
Haywood, John. *The Penguin Historical Atlas of Ancient Civilizations.* New York: Penguin, 2005.
Milleker, Elizabeth J., ed. *The Year One: Art of the Ancient World East and West.* New York: Metropolitan Museum of Art, 2000.
Nagle, D. Brendan. *The Ancient World: A Social and Cultural History.* 7th ed. Upper Saddle River, NJ: Pearson/Prentice Hall, 2010.
Saggs, H.W.F. *Civilization before Greece and Rome.* New Haven: Yale Univ. Press, 1989.
Smith, William Stevenson. *Interconnections in the Ancient Near East: A Study of the Relationships between the Arts of Egypt, the Aegean, and Western Asia.* New Haven: Yale Univ. Press, 1965.
Tadgell, Christopher. *Imperial Form: From Achaemenid Iran to Augustan Rome.* New York: Whitney Library of Design, 1998.
———. *Origins: Egypt, West Asia, and the Aegean.* New York: Whitney Library of Design, 1998.
Trigger, Bruce G. *Understanding Early Civilizations: A Comparative Study.* New York: Cambridge Univ. Press, 2003.
Woodford, Susan. *The Art of Greece and Rome.* 2nd ed. New York: Cambridge Univ. Press, 2004.

European Medieval Art, General

Backman, Clifford R. *The Worlds of Medieval Europe.* 2nd ed. New York: Oxford Univ. Press, 2009.
Bennett, Adelaide Louise, et al. *Medieval Mastery: Book Illumination from Charlemagne to Charles the Bold: 800–1475.* Trans. Lee Preedy and Greta Arblaster-Holmer. Turnhout: Brepols, 2002.
Benton, Janetta R. *Art of the Middle Ages.* World of Art. New York: Thames & Hudson, 2002.
Binski, Paul. *Painters.* Medieval Craftsmen. London: British Museum Press, 1991.
Brown, Sarah, and David O'Connor. *Glass-painters.* Medieval Craftsmen. London: British Museum Press, 1991.

Calkins, Robert G. *Medieval Architecture in Western Europe: From A.D. 300 to 1500.* New York: Oxford Univ. Press, 1998.
Cherry, John F. *Goldsmiths.* Medieval Craftsmen. London: British Museum Press, 1992.
Clark, William W. *The Medieval Cathedrals.* Westport, CT: Greenwood Press, 2006.
Coldstream, Nicola. *Masons and Sculptors.* Medieval Craftsmen. London: British Museum Press, 1991.
———. *Medieval Architecture.* Oxford History of Art. Oxford: Oxford Univ. Press, 2002.
De Hamel, Christopher. *Scribes and Illuminators.* Medieval Craftsmen. London: British Museum Press, 1992.
Duby, Georges. *Art and Society in the Middle Ages.* Trans. Jean Birrell. Malden, MA: Blackwell, 2000.
Fossier, Robert, ed. *The Cambridge Illustrated History of the Middle Ages.* Trans. Janet Sondheimer and Sarah Hanbury Tenison. 3 vols. Cambridge: Cambridge Univ. Press, 1986–97.
Hürlimann, Martin, and Jean Bony. *French Cathedrals.* Rev. & enlarged ed. London: Thames & Hudson, 1967.
Jotischky, Andrew, and Caroline Susan Hull. *The Penguin Historical Atlas of the Medieval World.* New York: Penguin, 2005.
Kenyon, John. *Medieval Fortifications.* Leicester: Leicester Univ. Press, 1990.
Pfaffenbichler, Matthias. *Armourers.* Medieval Craftsmen. London: British Museum Press, 1992.
Rebold Benton, Janetta. *Art of the Middle Ages.* World of Art. New York: Thames & Hudson, 2002.
Rudolph, Conrad, ed. *A Companion to Medieval Art.* Blackwell Companions to Art History. Oxford: Blackwell, 2006.
Sekules, Veronica. *Medieval Art.* Oxford History of Art. New York: Oxford Univ. Press, 2001.
Snyder, James, Henry Luttikhuizen, and Dorothy Verkerk. *Art of the Middle Ages.* 2nd ed. Upper Saddle River, NJ: Pearson/Prentice Hall, 2006.
Staniland, Kay. *Embroiderers.* Medieval Craftsmen. London: British Museum Press, 1991.
Stokstad, Marilyn. *Medieval Art.* 2nd ed. Boulder, CO: Westview Press, 2004.
———. *Medieval Castles.* Greenwood Guides to Historic Events of the Medieval World. Westport, CT: Greenwood Press, 2005.

European Renaissance through Eighteenth-Century Art, General

Black, C.F., et al. *Cultural Atlas of the Renaissance.* New York: Prentice Hall, 1993.
Blunt, Anthony. *Art and Architecture in France, 1500–1700.* 5th ed. Revised Richard Beresford. Pelican History of Art. New Haven: Yale Univ. Press, 1999.
Brown, Jonathan. *Painting in Spain: 1500–1700.* Pelican History of Art. New Haven: Yale Univ. Press, 1998.
Cole, Bruce. *Studies in the History of Italian Art, 1250–1550.* London: Pindar Press, 1996.
Graham-Dixon, Andrew. *Renaissance.* Berkeley: Univ. of California Press, 1999.
Harbison, Craig. *The Mirror of the Artist: Northern Renaissance Art in Its Historical Context.* Perspectives. New York: Abrams, 1995.
Harris, Ann Sutherland. *Seventeenth-Century Art & Architecture.* 2nd ed. Upper Saddle River, NJ: Pearson/Prentice Hall, 2008.
Harrison, Charles, Paul Wood, and Jason Gaiger. *Art in Theory 1648–1815: An Anthology of Changing Ideas.* Oxford: Blackwell, 2000.
Hartt, Frederick, and David G. Wilkins. *History of Italian Renaissance Art: Painting, Sculpture, Architecture.* 7th ed. Upper Saddle River, NJ: Pearson/Prentice Hall, 2011.
Jestaz, Bertrand. *The Art of the Renaissance.* Trans. I. Mark Paris. New York: Abrams, 1994.
Minor, Vernon Hyde. *Baroque & Rococo: Art & Culture.* New York: Abrams, 1999.
Paoletti, John T., and Gary M. Radke. *Art in Renaissance Italy.* 3rd ed. Upper Saddle River, NJ: Pearson/Prentice Hall, 2005.
Smith, Jeffrey Chipps. *The Northern Renaissance.* Art & Ideas. London and New York: Phaidon Press, 2004.
Stechow, Wolfgang. *Northern Renaissance, 1400–1600: Sources and Documents.* Upper Saddle River, NJ: Pearson/Prentice Hall, 1966.
Summerson, John. *Architecture in Britain, 1530–1830.* 9th ed. Pelican History of Art. New Haven: Yale Univ. Press, 1993.

Waterhouse, Ellis K. *Painting in Britain, 1530–1790.* 5th ed. Pelican History of Art. New Haven: Yale Univ. Press, 1994.
Whinney, Margaret Dickens. *Sculpture in Britain: 1530–1830.* 2nd ed. Revised John Physick. Pelican History of Art. London: Penguin, 1988.

Modern Art in the West, General

Arnason, H.H., and Elizabeth C. Mansfield. *History of Modern Art: Painting, Sculpture, Architecture, Photography.* 6th ed. Upper Saddle River, NJ: Pearson/Prentice Hall, 2009.
Ballantyne, Andrew, ed. *Architectures: Modernism and After.* New Interventions in Art History, 3. Malden, MA: Blackwell, 2004.
Barnitz, Jacqueline. *Twentieth-Century Art of Latin America.* Austin: Univ. of Texas Press, 2001.
Bjelajac, David. *American Art: A Cultural History.* Rev. and expanded ed. Upper Saddle River, NJ: Pearson/Prentice Hall, 2005.
Bowness, Alan. *Modern European Art.* World of Art. New York: Thames & Hudson, 1995.
Brettell, Richard R. *Modern Art, 1851–1929: Capitalism and Representation.* Oxford History of Art. Oxford: Oxford Univ. Press, 1999.
Chipp, Herschel B. *Theories of Modern Art: A Source Book by Artists and Critics.* California Studies in the History of Art, 11. Berkeley: Univ. of California Press, 1984.
Clarke, Graham. *The Photograph.* Oxford History of Art. Oxford: Oxford Univ. Press, 1997.
Craven, David. *Art and Revolution in Latin America, 1910–1990.* New Haven: Yale Univ. Press, 2002.
Craven, Wayne. *American Art: History and Culture.* 2nd ed. Boston: McGraw-Hill, 2003.
Doordan, Dennis P. *Twentieth-Century Architecture.* New York: Abrams, 2002.
Doss, Erika. *Twentieth-Century American Art.* Oxford History of Art. Oxford: Oxford Univ. Press, 2002.
Edwards, Steve, and Paul Wood, eds. *Art of the Avant-Gardes.* Art of the 20th Century. New Haven: Yale Univ. Press, 2004.
Foster, Hal, et al. *Art Since 1900: Modernism, Antimodernism, Postmodernism.* New York: Thames & Hudson, 2004.
Gaiger, Jason, ed. *Frameworks for Modern Art.* Art of the 20th Century. New Haven: Yale Univ. Press, 2003.
———, and Paul Wood, eds. *Art of the Twentieth Century: A Reader.* New Haven: Yale Univ. Press, 2003.
Hamilton, George Heard. *Painting and Sculpture in Europe, 1880–1940.* 6th ed. Pelican History of Art. New Haven: Yale Univ. Press, 1993.
Hammacher, A.M. *Modern Sculpture: Tradition and Innovation.* Enl. ed. New York: Abrams, 1988.
Harris, Ann Sutherland, and Linda Nochlin. *Women Artists: 1550–1950.* Los Angeles: Los Angeles County Museum of Art, 1976.
Harrison, Charles, and Paul Wood, eds. *Art in Theory: 1900–2000: An Anthology of Changing Ideas.* 2nd ed. Malden, MA: Blackwell, 2003.
Hunter, Sam, John Jacobus, and Daniel Wheeler. *Modern Art: Painting, Sculpture, Architecture, Photography.* 3rd rev. & exp. ed. Upper Saddle River, NJ: Pearson/Prentice Hall, 2004.
Krauss, Rosalind E. *Passages in Modern Sculpture.* Cambridge, MA: MIT Press, 1977.
Mancini, JoAnne Marie. *Pre-Modernism: Art-World Change and American Culture from the Civil War to the Armory Show.* Princeton, NJ: Princeton Univ. Press, 2005.
Marien, Mary Warner. *Photography: A Cultural History.* 3rd ed. Upper Saddle River, NJ: Pearson/Prentice Hall, 2011.
Meecham, Pam, and Julie Sheldon. *Modern Art: A Critical Introduction.* 2nd ed. New York: Routledge, 2005.
Newlands, Anne. *Canadian Art: From Its Beginnings to 2000.* Willowdale, Ont.: Firefly Books, 2000.
Phaidon Atlas of Contemporary World Architecture. London: Phaidon Press, 2004.
Powell, Richard J. *Black Art: A Cultural History.* World of Art. 2nd ed. New York: Thames & Hudson, 2003.
Rosenblum, Naomi. *A World History of Photography.* 4th ed. New York: Abbeville Press, 2007.
Ruhrberg, Karl. *Art of the 20th Century.* Ed. Ingo F. Walther. 2 vols. New York: Taschen, 1998.
Scully, Vincent Joseph. *Modern Architecture and Other Essays.* Princeton, NJ: Princeton Univ. Press, 2003.
Stiles, Kristine, and Peter Selz. *Theories and Documents of Contemporary Art: A Sourcebook of Artists' Writings.* California Studies in the History of Art, 35. Berkeley: Univ. of California Press, 1996.

Tafuri, Manfredo. *Modern Architecture*. History of World Architecture. 2 vols. New York: Electa/Rizzoli, 1986.

Upton, Dell. *Architecture in the United States*. Oxford History of Art. Oxford: Oxford Univ. Press, 1998.

Wood, Paul, ed. *Varieties of Modernism*. Art of the 20th Century. New Haven: Yale Univ. Press, 2004.

Woodham, Jonathan M. *Twentieth-Century Design*. Oxford History of Art. Oxford: Oxford Univ. Press, 1997.

Asian Art, General

Addiss, Stephen, Gerald Groemer, and J. Thomas Rimer, eds. *Traditional Japanese Arts and Culture: An Illustrated Sourcebook*. Honolulu: Univ. of Hawai'i Press, 2006.

Barnhart, Richard M. *Three Thousand Years of Chinese Painting*. New Haven: Yale Univ. Press, 1997.

Blunden, Caroline, and Mark Elvin. *Cultural Atlas of China*. 2nd ed. New York: Checkmark Books, 1998.

Brown, Kerry, ed. *Sikh Art and Literature*. New York: Routledge in collaboration with the Sikh Foundation, 1999.

Chang, Léon Long-Yien, and Peter Miller. *Four Thousand Years of Chinese Calligraphy*. Chicago: Univ. of Chicago Press, 1990.

Chang, Yang-mo. *Arts of Korea*. Ed. Judith G. Smith. New York: Metropolitan Museum of Art, 1998.

Clark, John. *Modern Asian Art*. Honolulu: Univ. of Hawai'i Press, 1998.

Clunas, Craig. *Art in China*. 2nd ed. Oxford History of Art. Oxford: Oxford Univ. Press, 2009.

Coaldrake, William H. *Architecture and Authority in Japan*. London: Routledge, 1996.

Collcutt, Martin, Marius Jansen, and Isao Kumakura. *Cultural Atlas of Japan*. New York: Facts on File, 1988.

Craven, Roy C. *Indian Art: A Concise History*. Rev. ed. World of Art. New York: Thames & Hudson, 1997.

Dehejia, Vidya. *Indian Art*. Art & Ideas. London: Phaidon Press, 1997.

Fisher, Robert E. *Buddhist Art and Architecture*. World of Art. New York: Thames & Hudson, 1993.

Fu, Xinian. *Chinese Architecture*. Ed. & exp., Nancy S. Steinhardt. New Haven: Yale Univ. Press, 2002.

Hearn, Maxwell K., and Judith G. Smith, eds. *Arts of the Sung and Yüan: Papers Prepared for an International Symposium*. New York: Dept. of Asian Art, Metropolitan Museum of Art, 1996.

Heibonsha Survey of Japanese Art. 31 vols. New York: Weatherhill, 1972–80.

Hertz, Betti-Sue. *Past in Reverse: Contemporary Art of East Asia*. San Diego: San Diego Museum of Art, 2004.

Japanese Arts Library. 15 vols. New York: Kodansha International, 1977–87.

Kerlogue, Fiona. *Arts of Southeast Asia*. World of Art. New York: Thames & Hudson, 2004.

Khanna, Balraj, and George Michell. *Human and Divine: 2000 Years of Indian Sculpture*. London: Hayward Gallery, 2000.

Lee, Sherman E. *A History of Far Eastern Art*. 5th ed. Ed. Naomi Noble Richards. New York: Abrams, 1994.

———. *China, 5000 Years: Innovation and Transformation in the Arts*. New York: Solomon R. Guggenheim Museum, 1998.

Liu, Cary Y., and Dora C.Y. Ching, eds. *Arts of the Sung and Yüan: Ritual, Ethnicity, and Style in Painting*. Princeton, NJ: Art Museum, Princeton Univ., 1999.

McArthur, Meher. *The Arts of Asia: Materials, Techniques, Styles*. New York: Thames & Hudson, 2005.

———. *Reading Buddhist Art: An Illustrated Guide to Buddhist Signs and Symbols*. New York: Thames & Hudson, 2002.

Mason, Penelope. *History of Japanese Art*. 2nd ed. Upper Saddle River, NJ: Pearson/Prentice Hall, 2005.

Michell, George. *Hindu Art and Architecture*. World of Art. London: Thames & Hudson, 2000.

———. *The Penguin Guide to the Monuments of India*. 2 vols. New York: Viking, 1989.

Mitter, Partha. *Indian Art*. Oxford History of Art. Oxford: Oxford Univ. Press, 2001.

Murase, Miyeko. *Bridge of Dreams: The Mary Griggs Burke Collection of Japanese Art*. New York: Metropolitan Museum of Art, 2000.

Nickel, Lukas, ed. *Return of the Buddha: The Qingzhou Discoveries*. London: Royal Academy of Arts, 2002.

Pak, Youngsook, and Roderick Whitfield. *Buddhist Sculpture*. Handbook of Korean Art. London: Laurence King Publishing, 2003.

Sullivan, Michael. *The Arts of China*. 5th ed., rev. & exp. Berkeley: Univ. of California Press, 2008.

Thorp, Robert L., and Richard Ellis Vinograd. *Chinese Art & Culture*. New York: Abrams, 2001.

Topsfield, Andrew, ed. *In the Realm of Gods and Kings: Arts of India*. London: Philip Wilson, 2004.

Tucker, Jonathan. *The Silk Road: Art and History*. Chicago: Art Media Resources, 2003.

Tregear, Mary. *Chinese Art*. Rev. ed. World of Art. New York: Thames & Hudson, 1997.

Vainker, S.J. *Chinese Pottery and Porcelain: From Prehistory to the Present*. New York: Braziller, 1991.

African and Oceanic Art and Art of the Americas, General

Anderson, Richard L., and Karen L. Field, eds. *Art in Small-Scale Societies: Contemporary Readings*. Upper Saddle River, NJ: Pearson/Prentice Hall, 1993.

Bacquart, Jean-Baptiste. *The Tribal Arts of Africa*. New York: Thames & Hudson, 1998.

Bassani, Ezio, ed. *Arts of Africa: 7000 Years of African Art*. Milan: Skira, 2005.

Benson, Elizabeth P. *Retratos: 2,000 Years of Latin American Portraits*. San Antonio, TX: San Antonio Museum of Art, 2004.

Berlo, Janet Catherine, and Lee Anne Wilson. *Arts of Africa, Oceania, and the Americas: Selected Readings*. Upper Saddle River, NJ: Prentice Hall, 1993.

Calloway, Colin G. *First Peoples: A Documentary Survey of American Indian History*. 3rd ed. Boston: Bedford/St. Martin's, 2008.

Coote, Jeremy, and Anthony Shelton, eds. *Anthropology, Art, and Aesthetics*. New York: Oxford Univ. Press, 1992.

Drewal, Henry, and John Pemberton III. *Yoruba: Nine Centuries of African Art and Thought*. New York: Center for African Art, 1989.

Evans, Susan Toby. *Ancient Mexico & Central America: Archaeology and Culture History*. 2nd ed. New York: Thames & Hudson, 2008.

———, and David L. Webster, eds. *Archaeology of Ancient Mexico and Central America: An Encyclopedia*. New York: Garland, 2001.

———, and Joanne Pillsbury, eds. *Palaces of the Ancient New World: A Symposium at Dumbarton Oaks, 10th and 11th October, 1998*. Washington, DC: Dumbarton Oaks Research Library and Collection, 2004.

Geoffroy-Schneiter, Bérénice. *Tribal Arts*. New York: Vendome Press, 2000.

Hiller, Susan, ed. & compiled. *The Myth of Primitivism: Perspectives on Art*. London: Routledge, 1991.

Mack, John, ed. *Africa, Arts and Cultures*. London: British Museum Press, 2000.

Mexico: Splendors of Thirty Centuries. New York: Metropolitan Museum of Art, 1990.

Nunley, John W., and Cara McCarty. *Masks: Faces of Culture*. New York: Abrams in assoc. with the Saint Louis Art Museum, 1999.

Perani, Judith, and Fred T. Smith. *The Visual Arts of Africa: Gender, Power, and Life Cycle Rituals*. Upper Saddle River, NJ: Pearson/Prentice Hall, 1998.

Phillips, Tom, ed. *Africa: The Art of a Continent*. New York: Prestel, 1995.

Price, Sally. *Primitive Art in Civilized Places*. 2nd ed. Chicago: Univ. of Chicago Press, 2001.

Rabineau, Phyllis. *Feather Arts: Beauty, Wealth, and Spirit from Five Continents*. Chicago: Field Museum of Natural History, 1979.

Schuster, Carl, and Edmund Carpenter. *Patterns that Connect: Social Symbolism in Ancient & Tribal Art*. New York: Abrams, 1996.

Scott, John F. *Latin American Art: Ancient to Modern*. Gainesville: Univ. Press of Florida, 1999.

Stepan, Peter. *Africa*. Trans. John Gabriel and Elizabeth Schwaiger. London: Prestel, 2001.

Visonà, Monica Blackmun, et al. *A History of Art in Africa*. 2nd ed. Upper Saddle River, NJ: Pearson/Prentice Hall, 2008.

Introduction

Acton, Mary. *Learning to Look at Paintings*. 2nd ed. New York: Routledge, 2009.

Arnold, Dana. *Art History: A Very Short Introduction*. Oxford and New York: Oxford Univ. Press, 2004.

Baxandall, Michael. *Patterns of Intention: On the Historical Explanation of Pictures*. New Haven: Yale Univ. Press, 1985.

Clearwater, Bonnie. *The Rothko Book*. London: Tate Publishing, 2006.

Decoteau, Pamela Hibbs. *Clara Peeters, 1594–ca.1640 and the Development of Still-Life Painting in Northern Europe*. Lingen: Luca Verlag, 1992.

Geertz, Clifford. "Art as a Cultural System." *Modern Language Notes* 91 (1976): 1473–1499.

Hochstrasser, Julie Berger. *Still Life and Trade in the Dutch Golden Age*. New Haven: Yale Univ. Press, 2007.

Holstein, Jonathan. *The Pieced Quilt: An American Design Tradition*. New York: Galahad Books, 1973.

Jolly, Penny Howell. "Rogier van der Weyden's Escorial and Philadelphia Crucifixions and Their Relation to Fra Angelico at San Marco." *Oud Holland* 95 (1981): 113–126.

Mainardi, Patricia. "Quilts: The Great American Art." *The Feminist Art Journal* 2/1 (1973): 1, 18–23.

Miller, Angela L., et al. *American Encounters: Art, History, and Cultural Identity*. Upper Saddle River, NJ: Pearson/Prentice Hall, 2008.

Minor, Vernon Hyde. *Art History's History*. Upper Saddle River, NJ: Pearson/Prentice Hall, 2001.

Nelson, Robert S., and Richard Shiff, eds. *Critical Terms for Art History*. 2nd ed. Chicago: Univ. of Chicago Press, 2003.

Panofsky, Erwin. *Studies in Iconology: Humanistic Themes in the Art of the Renaissance*. New York: Oxford Univ. Press, 1939.

———. *Meaning in the Visual Arts*. Phoenix ed. Chicago: Univ. of Chicago Press, 1982.

Preziosi, Donald, ed. *The Art of Art History: A Critical Anthology*. 2nd ed. Oxford and New York: Oxford Univ. Press, 2009.

Rothko, Mark. *Writings on Art*. Ed. Miguel López-Remiro. New Haven: Yale Univ. Press, 2006.

———. *The Artist's Reality: Philosophies of Art*. Ed. Christopher Rothko. New Haven: Yale Univ. Press, 2004.

Schapiro, Meyer. "The Apples of Cézanne: An Essay on the Meaning of Still Life." *Art News Annual* 34 (1968): 34–53. Reprinted in *Modern Art 19th & 20th Centuries: Selected Papers 2*, London: Chatto & Windus, 1978.

Sowers, Robert. *Rethinking the Forms of Visual Expression*. Berkeley: Univ. of California Press, 1990.

Taylor, Joshua. *Learning to Look: A Handbook for the Visual Arts*. 2nd ed. Chicago: Chicago Univ. Press, 1981.

Tucker, Mark. "Rogier van der Weyden's 'Philadelphia Crucifixion.'" *Burlington Magazine* 139 (1997): 676–683.

Wang, Fangyu, et al., eds. *Master of the Lotus Garden: The Life and Art of Bada Shanren (1626–1705)*. New Haven: Yale Univ. Press, 1990.

Chapter 1 Prehistoric Art

Aujoulat, Norbert. *Lascaux: Movement, Space, and Time*. New York: Abrams, 2005.

Bahn, Paul G. *The Cambridge Illustrated History of Prehistoric Art*. Cambridge Illustrated History. Cambridge: Cambridge Univ. Press, 1998.

Bataille, Georges. *The Cradle of Humanity: Prehistoric Art and Culture*. Ed. Stuart Kendall. Trans. Michelle Kendall and Stuart Kendall. New York: Zone Books, 2005.

Berghaus, Gunter. *New Perspectives on Prehistoric Art*. Westport, CT: Praeger, 2004.

Chippindale, Christopher. *Stonehenge Complete*. 3rd ed. New York: Thames & Hudson, 2004.

Clottes, Jean. *Chauvet Cave: The Art of Earliest Times*. Salt Lake City: Univ. of Utah Press, 2003.

———. *World Rock Art*. Trans. Guy Bennett. Los Angeles: Getty Conservation Institute, 2002.

———, and J. David Lewis-Williams. *The Shamans of Prehistory: Trance and Magic in the Painted Caves*. Trans. Sophie Hawkes. New York: Abrams, 1998.

Connah, Graham. *African Civilizations: An Archaeological Perspective*. 2nd ed. Cambridge: Cambridge Univ. Press, 2001.

Coulson, David, and Alec Campbell. *African Rock Art: Painting and Engravings on Stone*. New York: Abrams, 2001.

Cunliffe, Barry W., ed. *The Oxford Illustrated History of Prehistoric Europe*. New York: Oxford Univ. Press, 2001.

Forte, Maurizio, and Alberto Siliotti. *Virtual Archaeology: Re-Creating Ancient Worlds*. New York: Abrams, 1997.

Freeman, Leslie G. *Altamira Revisited and Other Essays on Early Art*. Chicago: Institute for Prehistoric Investigation, 1987.

Garlake, Peter S. *The Hunter's Vision: The Prehistoric Art of Zimbabwe*. Seattle: Univ. of Washington Press, 1995.

Gowlett, John A.J. *Ascent to Civilization: The Archaeology of Early Humans*. 2nd ed. New York: McGraw-Hill, 1993.

Guthrie, R. Dale. *The Nature of Paleolithic Art*. Chicago: Univ. of Chicago Press, 2005.

Jope, E.M. *Early Celtic Art in the British Isles.* 2 vols. New York: Oxford Univ. Press, 2000.

Kenrick, Douglas M. *Jomon of Japan: The World's Oldest Pottery.* New York: Kegan Paul, 1995.

Leakey, Richard E., and Roger Lewin. *Origins Reconsidered: In Search of What Makes Us Human.* New York: Doubleday, 1992.

Le Quellec, Jean-Loïc. *Rock Art in Africa: Mythology and Legend.* Trans. Paul Bahn. Paris: Flammarion, 2004.

Leroi-Gourhan, André. *The Dawn of European Art: An Introduction to Paleolithic Cave Painting.* Trans. Sara Champion. Cambridge: Cambridge Univ. Press, 1982.

Lewis-Williams, J. David. *The Mind in the Cave: Consciousness and the Origins of Art.* New York: Thames & Hudson, 2002.

O'Kelly, Michael J. *Newgrange: Archaeology, Art, and Legend.* New Aspects of Antiquity. London: Thames & Hudson, 1982.

Price, T. Douglas. *Images of the Past.* 5th ed. Boston: McGraw-Hill, 2008.

Renfrew, Colin, ed. *The Megalithic Monuments of Western Europe.* London: Thames & Hudson, 1983.

Sandars, N.K. *Prehistoric Art in Europe.* 2nd ed. Pelican History of Art. New Haven: Yale Univ. Press, 1992.

Sura Ramos, Pedro A. *The Cave of Altamira.* Gen. Ed. Antonio Beltran. New York: Abrams, 1999.

Sieveking, Ann. *The Cave Artists.* Ancient People and Places, vol. 93. London: Thames & Hudson, 1979.

White, Randall. *Prehistoric Art: The Symbolic Journey of Mankind.* New York: Abrams, 2003.

Chapter 2 Art of the Ancient Near East

Akurgal, Ekrem. *Ancient Civilizations and Ruins of Turkey: From Prehistoric Times until the End of the Roman Empire.* 5th ed. London: Kegan Paul, 2002.

Aruz, Joan, et al., eds. *Beyond Babylon: Art, Trade, and Diplomacy in the Second Millennium B.C.* New Haven: Yale Univ. Press, and Metropolitan Museum of Art, 2008.

———, ed. *Art of the First Cities: The Third Millennium B.C. from the Mediterranean to the Indus.* New York: Metropolitan Museum of Art, 2003.

Bahrani, Zainab. *The Graven Image: Representation in Babylonia and Assyria.* Archaeology, Culture, and Society Series. Philadelphia: Univ. of Pennsylvania Press, 2003.

Boardman, John. *Persia and the West: An Archaeological Investigation of the Genesis of Achaemenid Art.* London: Thames & Hudson, 2000.

Bottero, Jean. *Everyday Life in Ancient Mesopotamia.* Trans. Antonia Nevill. Baltimore, MD: Johns Hopkins Univ. Press, 2001.

Charvat, Petr. *Mesopotamia before History.* Rev. & updated ed. New York: Routledge, 2002.

Crawford, Harriet. *Sumer and the Sumerians.* 2nd ed. New York: Cambridge Univ. Press, 2004.

Curtis, John, and Nigel Tallis, eds. *Forgotten Empire: The World of Ancient Persia.* Berkeley: Univ. of California Press, 2005.

Ferrier, R.W., ed. *The Arts of Persia.* New Haven: Yale Univ. Press, 1989.

Frankfort, Henri. *The Art and Architecture of the Ancient Orient.* 5th ed. Pelican History of Art. New Haven: Yale Univ. Press, 1996.

Haywood, John. *Ancient Civilizations of the Near East and Mediterranean.* London: Cassell, 1997.

Meyers, Eric M., ed. *The Oxford Encyclopedia of Archaeology in the Near East.* 5 vols. New York: Oxford Univ. Press, 1997.

Moorey, P.R.S. *Idols of the People: Miniature Images of Clay in the Ancient Near East.* The Schweich Lectures of the British Academy, 2001. New York: Oxford Univ. Press, 2003.

Polk, Milbry, and Angela M.H. Schuster. *The Looting of the Iraq Museum, Baghdad: The Lost Legacy of Ancient Mesopotamia.* New York: Abrams, 2005.

Reade, Julian. *Assyrian Sculpture.* Cambridge, MA: Harvard Univ. Press, 1999.

Roaf, Michael. *Cultural Atlas of Mesopotamia and the Ancient Near East.* New York: Facts on File, 1990.

Roux, Georges. *Ancient Iraq.* 3rd ed. London: Penguin, 1992.

Winter, Irene. "Sex, Rhetoric, and the Public Monument: The Alluring Body of the Male Ruler." In *Sexuality in Ancient Art,* eds Natalie Kampen and Bettina A. Bergmann. Cambridge: Cambridge Univ. Press, 1996: 11–26.

Zettler, Richard L., and Lee Horne, ed. *Treasures from the Royal Tombs of Ur.* Philadelphia: Univ. of Pennsylvania, Museum of Archaeology and Anthropology, 1998.

Chapter 3 Art of Ancient Egypt

Arnold, Dieter. *Temples of the Last Pharaohs.* New York: Oxford Univ. Press, 1999.

Baines, John, and Jaromír Málek. *Cultural Atlas of Ancient Egypt.* Rev. ed. New York: Facts on File, 2000.

Brier, Bob. *Egyptian Mummies: Unraveling the Secrets of an Ancient Art.* New York: Morrow, 1994.

Egyptian Art in the Age of the Pyramids. New York: Metropolitan Museum of Art, 1999.

The Egyptian Book of the Dead: The Book of Going Forth by Day: Being the Papyrus of Ani (Royal Scribe of the Divine Offerings). 2nd rev. ed. Trans. Raymond O. Faulkner. San Francisco: Chronicle, 2008.

Freed, Rita E., Sue D'Auria, and Yvonne J. Markowitz. *Pharaohs of the Sun: Akhenaten, Nefertiti, Tutankhamen.* Boston: Museum of Fine Arts in assoc. with Bulfinch Press/Little, Brown, 1999.

Hawass, Zahi A. *Tutankhamun and the Golden Age of the Pharaohs.* Washington, DC: National Geographic, 2005.

Johnson, Paul. *The Civilization of Ancient Egypt.* Updated ed. New York: HarperCollins, 1999.

Kozloff, Arielle P. *Egypt's Dazzling Sun: Amenhotep III and His World.* Cleveland: Cleveland Museum of Art, 1992.

Lehner, Mark. *The Complete Pyramids.* New York: Thames & Hudson, 2008.

Love Songs of the New Kingdom. Trans. John L. Foster. New York: Scribner, 1974; Austin: Univ. of Texas Press, 1992.

Málek, Jaromir. *Egypt: 4,000 Years of Art.* London: Phaidon Press, 2003.

Pemberton, Delia. *Ancient Egypt.* Architectural Guides for Travelers. San Francisco: Chronicle, 1992.

Robins, Gay. *The Art of Ancient Egypt.* Rev. ed. Cambridge, MA: Harvard Univ. Press, 2008.

Roehrig, Catharine H., Renee Dreyfus, and Cathleen A. Keller. *Hatshepsut, from Queen to Pharaoh.* New York: Metropolitan Museum of Art, 2005.

Russmann, Edna R. *Egyptian Sculpture: Cairo and Luxor.* Austin: Univ. of Texas Press, 1989.

Smith, Craig B. *How the Great Pyramid Was Built.* Washington, DC: Smithsonian Books, 2004.

Smith, William Stevenson. *The Art and Architecture of Ancient Egypt.* 3rd ed. Revised William Kelly Simpson. Pelican History of Art. New Haven: Yale Univ. Press, 1998.

Strouhal, Eugen. *Life of the Ancient Egyptians.* Trans. Deryck Viney. Norman: Univ. of Oklahoma Press, 1992.

Strudwick, Nigel, and Helen Strudwick. *Thebes in Egypt: A Guide to the Tombs and Temples of Ancient Luxor.* Ithaca, NY: Cornell Univ. Press, 1999.

Thomas, Thelma K. *Late Antique Egyptian Funerary Sculpture: Images for this World and for the Next.* Princeton, NJ: Princeton Univ. Press, 2000.

Tiradritti, Francesco. *Ancient Egypt: Art, Architecture and History.* Trans. Phil Goddard. London: British Museum Press, 2002.

The Treasures of Ancient Egypt: From the Egyptian Museum in Cairo. New York: Rizzoli, 2003.

Wilkinson, Richard H. *The Complete Temples of Ancient Egypt.* New York: Thames & Hudson, 2000.

———. *Reading Egyptian Art: A Hieroglyphic Guide to Ancient Egyptian Painting and Sculpture.* London: Thames & Hudson, 1992.

Winstone, H.V.F. *Howard Carter and the Discovery of the Tomb of Tutankhamen.* Rev. ed. Manchester: Barzan, 2006.

Ziegler, Cristiane, ed. *The Pharaohs.* New York: Rizzoli, 2002.

Zivie-Coche, Christiane. *Sphinx: History of a Monument.* Trans. David Lorton. Ithaca, NY: Cornell Univ. Press, 2002.

Chapter 4 Art of the Ancient Aegean

Castleden, Rodney. *The Knossos Labyrinth: A New View of the "Palace of Minos" at Knossos.* London: Routledge, 1990.

———. *Mycenaeans.* New York: Routledge, 2005.

Demargne, Pierre. *The Birth of Greek Art.* Trans. Stuart Gilbert and James Emmons. Arts of Mankind, vol. 6. New York: Golden, 1964.

Doumas, Christos. *The Wall-Paintings of Thera.* 2nd ed. Trans. Alex Doumas. Athens: Kapon Editions, 1999.

Fitton, J. Lesley. *Cycladic Art.* 2nd ed. London: British Museum Press, 1999.

Getz-Gentle, Pat. *Personal Styles in Early Cycladic Sculpture.* Madison: Univ. of Wisconsin Press, 2001.

Hamilakis, Yannis. ed. *Labyrinth Revisited: Rethinking "Minoan" Archaeology.* Oxford: Oxbow, 2002.

Hendrix, Elizabeth. "Painted Ladies of the Early Bronze Age," *The Metropolitan Museum of Art Bulletin* New Series, 55/3 (Winter 1997–1998): 4–15.

Higgins, Reynold A. *Minoan and Mycenean Art.* New. ed. World of Art. New York: Thames & Hudson, 1997.

Hitchcock, Louise. *Minoan Architecture: A Contextual Analysis.* Studies in Mediterranean Archaeology and Literature, Pocket-Book, 155. Jonsered: P. Åstroms Förlag, 2000.

Hoffman, Gail L. "Painted Ladies: Early Cycladic II Mourning Figures?" *American Journal of Archaeology* 106/4 (October 2002): 525–550.

Immerwahr, Sara Anderson. *Aegean Painting in the Bronze Age.* University Park: Pennsylvania State Univ. Press, 1990.

Preziosi, Donald, and Louise Hitchcock. *Aegean Art and Architecture.* Oxford History of Art. Oxford: Oxford Univ. Press, 1999.

Shelmerdine, Cynthia W., ed. *The Cambridge Companion to the Aegean Bronze Age.* New York: Cambridge Univ. Press, 2008.

Strasser, Thomas F. "Location and Perspective in the Theran Flotilla Fresco," *Journal of Mediterranean Archaeology* 23/1 (2010): 3–26.

Chapter 5 Art of Ancient Greece

Barletta, Barbara A. *The Origins of the Greek Architectural Orders.* New York: Cambridge Univ. Press, 2001.

Beard, Mary. *The Parthenon.* Cambridge, MA: Harvard Univ. Press, 2003.

Belozerskaya, Marina, and Kenneth D.S. Lapatin. *Ancient Greece: Art, Architecture, and History.* Los Angeles: J. Paul Getty Museum, 2004.

Boardman, John. *Early Greek Vase Painting: 11th–6th Centuries B.C.: A Handbook.* World of Art. London: Thames & Hudson, 1998.

———. *Greek Sculpture: The Archaic Period: A Handbook.* World of Art. London: Thames & Hudson, 1991.

———. *Greek Sculpture: The Classical Period: A Handbook.* London: Thames & Hudson, 1985.

———. *Greek Sculpture: The Late Classical Period and Sculpture in Colonies and Overseas.* World of Art. New York: Thames & Hudson, 1995.

———. *The History of Greek Vases: Potters, Painters, and Pictures.* New York: Thames & Hudson, 2001.

Burn, Lucilla. *Hellenistic Art: From Alexander the Great to Augustus.* Los Angeles: J. Paul Getty Museum, 2004.

Clark, Andrew J., Maya Elston, and Mary Louise Hart. *Understanding Greek Vases: A Guide to Terms, Styles, and Techniques.* Los Angeles: J. Paul Getty Museum, 2002.

De Grummond, Nancy T. and Brunilde S. Ridgway. *From Pergamon to Sperlonga: Sculpture in Context.* Berkeley: Univ. of California Press, 2000.

Donohue, A.A. *Greek Sculpture and the Problem of Description.* New York: Cambridge Univ. Press, 2005.

Fullerton, Mark D. *Greek Art.* Cambridge: Cambridge Univ. Press, 2000.

Hard, Robin. *The Routledge Handbook of Greek Mythology: Based on H.J. Rose's "Handbook of Greek Mythology."* 7th ed. London: Routledge, 2008.

Hurwit, Jeffrey M. *The Acropolis in the Age of Pericles.* New York: Cambridge Univ. Press, 2004.

Karakasi, Katerina. *Archaic Korai.* Los Angeles: J. Paul Getty Museum, 2003.

Lawrence, A.W. *Greek Architecture.* 5th ed. Revised R.A. Tomlinson. Pelican History of Art. New Haven: Yale Univ. Press, 1996.

Martin, Roland. *Greek Architecture: Architecture of Crete, Greece, and the Greek World.* History of World Architecture. New York: Electa/Rizzoli, 1988.

Neils, Jenifer. *The British Museum Concise Introduction to Ancient Greece.* Ann Arbor: Univ. of Michigan, 2008.

Osborne, Robin. *Archaic and Classical Greek Art.* Oxford History of Art. Oxford: Oxford Univ. Press, 1998.

Palagia, Olga, ed. *Greek Sculpture: Function, Materials, and Techniques in the Archaic and Classical Periods.* New York: Cambridge Univ. Press, 2006.

———, and J.J. Pollitt, eds. *Personal Styles in Greek Sculpture.* Yale Classical Studies, vol. 30. Cambridge: Cambridge Univ. Press, 1996.

Pedley, John Griffiths. *Greek Art and Archaeology.* 5th ed. Upper Saddle River, NJ: Pearson/Prentice Hall, 2012.

Pollitt, J.J. *Art and Experience in Classical Greece.* Cambridge: Cambridge Univ. Press, 1972; reprinted 1999.

———. *The Art of Ancient Greece: Sources and Documents.* 2nd ed. rev. Cambridge: Cambridge Univ. Press, 2001.

Ridgway, Brunilde Sismondo. *The Archaic Style in Greek Sculpture.* 2nd ed. Chicago: Ares, 1993.

———. *Fifth Century Styles in Greek Sculpture.* Princeton, NJ: Princeton Univ. Press, 1981.

——. *Fourth Century Styles in Greek Sculpture.* Wisconsin Studies in Classics. Madison: Univ. of Wisconsin Press, 1997.

——. *Hellenistic Sculpture 1: The Styles of ca. 331–200 B.C.* Wisconsin Studies in Classics. Madison: Univ. of Wisconsin Press, 1990.

Stafford, Emma J. *Life, Myth, and Art in Ancient Greece.* Los Angeles: J. Paul Getty Museum, 2004.

Stewart, Andrew F. *Greek Sculpture: An Exploration.* 2 vols. New Haven: Yale Univ. Press, 1990.

Whitley, James. *The Archaeology of Ancient Greece.* New York: Cambridge Univ. Press, 2001.

Chapter 6 Etruscan and Roman Art

Bianchi Bandinelli, Ranuccio. *Rome: The Centre of Power: Roman Art to A.D. 200.* Trans. Peter Green. Arts of Mankind, 15. London: Thames & Hudson, 1971.

——. *Rome: The Late Empire: Roman Art A.D. 200–400.* Trans. Peter Green. Arts of Mankind, 17. New York: Braziller, 1971.

Borrelli, Federica. *The Etruscans: Art, Architecture, and History.* Ed. Stefano Peccatori and Stefano Zuffi. Trans. Thomas Michael Hartmann. Los Angeles: J. Paul Getty Museum, 2004.

Brendel, Otto J. *Prolegomena to the Study of Roman Art.* New Haven: Yale Univ. Press, 1979.

——. *Etruscan Art.* 2nd ed. Pelican History of Art. New Haven: Yale Univ. Press, 1995.

Conlin, Diane Atnally. *The Artists of the Ara Pacis: The Process of Hellenization in Roman Relief Sculpture.* Studies in the History of Greece & Rome. Chapel Hill: Univ. of North Carolina Press, 1997.

Cornell, Tim, and John Matthews. *Atlas of the Roman World.* New York: Facts on File, 1982.

D'Ambra, Eve. *Roman Art.* Cambridge: Cambridge Univ. Press, 1998.

Elsner, Jas. *Imperial Rome and Christian Triumph: The Art of the Roman Empire A.D. 100–450.* Oxford History of Art. Oxford: Oxford Univ. Press, 1998.

Gabucci, Ada. *Ancient Rome: Art, Architecture, and History.* Eds. Stefano Peccatori and Stephano Zuffi. Trans. T.M. Hartman. Los Angeles: J. Paul Getty Museum, 2002.

Haynes, Sybille. *Etruscan Civilization: A Cultural History.* Los Angeles: J. Paul Getty Museum, 2000.

Holloway, R. Ross. *Constantine & Rome.* New Haven: Yale Univ. Press, 2004.

Kleiner, Fred. S. *A History of Roman Art.* Belmont, CA: Thomson/Wadsworth, 2007.

MacDonald, William L. *The Architecture of the Roman Empire: An Introductory Study.* Rev. ed. 2 vols. Yale Publications in the History of Art, 17, 35. New Haven: Yale Univ. Press, 1982.

——. *The Pantheon: Design, Meaning, and Progeny.* New foreword by John Pinto. Cambridge, MA: Harvard Univ. Press, 2002.

Mattusch, Carol C. *Pompeii and the Roman Villa: Art and Culture around the Bay of Naples.* Washington, DC: National Gallery of Art, 2008.

Mazzoleni, Donatella. *Domus: Wall Painting in the Roman House.* Los Angeles: J. Paul Getty Museum, 2004.

Packer, James E. *The Forum of Trajan in Rome: A Study of the Monuments in Brief.* Berkeley: Univ. of California Press, 2001.

Pollitt, J.J. *The Art of Rome, c. 753 B.C.–337 A.D.: Sources and Documents.* Upper Saddle River, NJ: Pearson/Prentice Hall, 1966.

Polybius. *The Histories.* Trans. W.R. Paton. 6 vols. Loeb Classical Library. Cambridge, MA: Harvard Univ. Press, 2000.

Ramage, Nancy H., and Andrew Ramage. *Roman Art: Romulus to Constantine.* 5th ed. Upper Saddle River, NJ: Pearson/Prentice Hall, 2009.

Spivey, Nigel. *Etruscan Art.* World of Art. New York: Thames & Hudson, 1997.

Stamper, John W. *The Architecture of Roman Temples: The Republic to the Middle Empire.* New York: Cambridge Univ. Press, 2005.

Stewart, Peter. *Statues in Roman Society: Representation and Response.* Oxford Studies in Ancient Culture and Representation. New York: Oxford Univ. Press, 2003.

Strong, Donald. *Roman Art.* 2nd ed. rev. & annotated. Ed. Roger Ling. Pelican History of Art. New Haven: Yale Univ. Press, 1995.

Ward-Perkins, J.B. *Roman Architecture.* History of World Architecture. New York: Electa/Rizzoli, 1988.

——. *Roman Imperial Architecture.* Pelican History of Art. New Haven: Yale Univ. Press, 1981.

Wilson Jones, Mark. *Principles of Roman Architecture.* New Haven: Yale Univ. Press, 2000.

Chapter 7 Jewish and Early Christian Art

Age of Spirituality: Late Antique and Early Christian Art, Third to Seventh Century. New York: Metropolitan Museum of Art, 1979.

Beckwith, John. *Early Christian and Byzantine Art.* 2nd ed. Pelican History of Art. New Haven: Yale Univ. Press, 1986.

Bleiberg, Edward, ed. *Tree of Paradise: Jewish Mosaics from the Roman Empire.* Brooklyn: Brooklyn Museum, 2005.

Cioffarelli, Ada. *Guide to the Catacombs of Rome and Its Surroundings.* Rome: Bonsignori, 2000.

Fine, Steven. *Art and Judaism in the Greco–Roman World: Toward a New Jewish Archaeology.* New York: Cambridge Univ. Press, 2005.

Hachlili, Rachel. *Ancient Mosaic Pavements: Themes, Issues, and Trends.* Leiden: Brill, 2009.

Jensen, Robin Margaret. *Understanding Early Christian Art.* New York: Routledge, 2000.

Krautheimer, Richard, and Slobodan Curcic. *Early Christian and Byzantine Architecture.* 4th ed. Pelican History of Art. New Haven: Yale Univ. Press, 1992.

Levine, Lee I., and Zeev Weiss, eds. *From Dura to Sepphoris: Studies in Jewish Art and Society in Late Antiquity.* Journal of Roman Archaeology: Supplementary Series, no. 40. Portsmouth, RI: Journal of Roman Archaeology, 2000.

Lowden, John. *Early Christian and Byzantine Art.* Art & Ideas. London: Phaidon Press, 1997.

Mathews, Thomas F. *The Clash of Gods: A Reinterpretation of Early Christian Art.* Rev. ed. Princeton, NJ: Princeton Univ. Press, 1999.

Olin, Margaret. *The Nation without Art: Examining Modern Discourses on Jewish Art.* Lincoln: Univ. of Nebraska Press, 2001.

Olsson, Birger, and Magnus Zetterholm, eds. *The Ancient Synagogue from Its Origins until 200 C.E.: Papers Presented at an International Conference at Lund University, October 14–17, 2001.* Coniectanea Biblica: New Testament Series, 39. Stockholm: Almqvist & Wiksell International, 2003.

Rutgers, Leonard V. *Subterranean Rome: In Search of the Roots of Christianity in the Catacombs of the Eternal City.* Leuven: Peeters, 2000.

Sed-Rajna, Gabrielle. *Jewish Art.* Trans. Sara Friedman and Mira Reich. New York: Abrams, 1997.

Spier, Jeffrey, ed. *Picturing the Bible: The Earliest Christian Art.* New Haven: Yale Univ. Press, 2007.

Tadgell, Christopher. *Imperial Space: Rome, Constantinople and the Early Church.* New York: Whitney Library of Design, 1998.

Webb, Matilda. *The Churches and Catacombs of Early Christian Rome: A Comprehensive Guide.* Brighton, UK: Sussex Academic Press, 2001.

Weitzmann, Kurt. *Late Antique and Early Christian Book Illumination.* New York: Braziller, 1977.

Wharton, Annabel Jane. *Refiguring the Post-Classical City: Dura Europos, Jerash, Jerusalem and Ravenna.* Cambridge: Cambridge Univ. Press, 1995.

White, L. Michael. *The Social Origins of Christian Architecture.* 2 vols. Baltimore, MD: Johns Hopkins Univ. Press, 1990.

Chapter 8 Byzantine Art

Beckwith, John. *Early Christian and Byzantine Art.* 2nd ed. Pelican History of Art. New Haven: Yale Univ. Press, 1986.

Cormack, Robin. *Byzantine Art.* Oxford: Oxford Univ. Press, 2000.

——, and Maria Vassilaki, eds. *Byzantium, 330–1453.* London: Royal Academy of Arts, 2008.

Cutler, Anthony. *The Hand of the Master: Craftsmanship, Ivory, and Society in Byzantium 9th–11th Centuries.* Princeton, NJ: Princeton Univ. Press, 1994.

Durand, Jannic. *Byzantine Art.* Paris: Terrail, 1999.

Eastmond, Antony, and Liz James, eds. *Icon and Word: The Power of Images in Byzantium: Studies Presented to Robin Cormack.* Burlington, VT: Ashgate, 2003.

Evans, Helen C., ed. *Byzantium: Faith and Power (1261–1557).* New York: Metropolitan Museum of Art, 2004.

——, and William D. Wixom, eds. *The Glory of Byzantium: Art and Culture of the Middle Byzantine era, A.D. 843–1261.* New York: Abrams, 1997.

Freely, John. *Byzantine Monuments of Istanbul.* Cambridge & New York: Cambridge Univ. Press, 2004.

Gerstel, Sharon, and Robert Nelson. *Approaching the Holy Mountain: Art and Liturgy at St. Catherine's Monastery in the Sinai.* Turnhout: Brepols, 2010.

Grabar, André. *Byzantine Painting: Historical and Critical Study.* Trans. Stuart Gilbert. New York: Rizzoli, 1979.

Kitzinger, Ernst. *The Art of Byzantium and the Medieval West: Selected Studies.* Ed. W. Eugene Kleinbauer. Bloomington: Indiana Univ. Press, 1976.

——. *Byzantine Art in the Making: Main Lines of Stylistic Development in Mediterranean Art, 3rd–7th Century.* Cambridge, MA: Harvard Univ. Press, 1977.

Kleinbauer, W. Eugene. *Hagia Sophia.* London: Scala, 2004.

Krautheimer, Richard, and Slobodan Curcic. *Early Christian and Byzantine Architecture.* 4th ed. Pelican History of Art. New Haven: Yale Univ. Press, 1992.

Lowden, John. *Early Christian and Byzantine Art.* Art & Ideas. London: Phaidon Press, 1997.

Maguire, Henry. *The Icons of Their Bodies: Saints and Their Images in Byzantium.* Princeton, NJ: Princeton Univ. Press, 1996.

Mainstone, Rowland J. *Hagia Sophia: Architecture, Structure and Liturgy of Justinian's Great Church.* 2nd ed. New York: Thames & Hudson, 2001.

Mango, Cyril. *Art of the Byzantine Empire, 312–1453: Sources and Documents.* Upper Saddle River, NJ: Pearson/Prentice Hall, 1972.

Mathews, Thomas F. *Byzantium: From Antiquity to the Renaissance.* Perspectives. New York: Abrams, 1998.

Ousterhout, Robert. *Master Builders of Byzantium.* Princeton, NJ: Princeton Univ. Press, 1999.

Pentcheva, Bissera. *The Sensual Icon: Space, Ritual, and the Senses in Byzantium.* University Park: Pennsylvania State Univ. Press, 2010.

Procopius, with an English translation by H.B. Dewing. 7 vols. Loeb Classical Library. Cambridge, MA: Harvard Univ. Press, 1940.

Rodley, Lyn. *Byzantine Art and Architecture: An Introduction.* Cambridge: Cambridge Univ. Press, 1994.

Weitzmann, Kurt. *Place of Book Illumination in Byzantine Art.* Princeton, NJ: Art Museum, Princeton Univ., 1975.

Chapter 9 Islamic Art

Al-Faruqi, Isma'il R., and Lois Ibsen Al-Faruqi. *Cultural Atlas of Islam.* New York: Macmillan, 1986.

Atil, Esin. *The Age of Sultan Suleyman the Magnificent.* Washington, DC: National Gallery of Art, 1987.

Baker, Patricia L. *Islam and the Religious Arts.* London: Continuum, 2004.

Barry, Michael A. *Figurative Art in Medieval Islam and the Riddle of Bihzâd of Herât (1465–1535).* Paris: Flammarion, 2004.

Blair, Sheila S., and Jonathan Bloom. *The Art and Architecture of Islam 1250–1800.* Pelican History of Art. New Haven: Yale Univ. Press, 1995.

Dodds, Jerrilynn D., ed. *Al-Andalus: The Art of Islamic Spain.* New York: Metropolitan Museum of Art, 1992.

Ecker, Heather. *Caliphs and Kings: The Art and Influence of Islamic Spain.* Washington, DC: Arthur M. Sackler Gallery, 2004.

Ettinghausen, Richard, Oleg Grabar, and Marilyn Jenkins-Madina. *Islamic Art and Architecture, 650–1250.* 2nd ed. Pelican History of Art. New Haven: Yale Univ. Press, 2001.

Frishman, Martin, and Hasan-Uddin Khan. *The Mosque: History, Architectural Development and Regional Diversity.* London: Thames & Hudson, 1994.

Grabar, Oleg. *The Formation of Islamic Art.* Rev. and enl. New Haven: Yale Univ. Press, 1987.

——. *The Great Mosque of Isfahan.* New York: New York Univ. Press, 1990.

——. *Islamic Visual Culture, 1100–1800.* Burlington, VT: Ashgate, 2006.

——. *Mostly Miniatures: An Introduction to Persian Painting.* Princeton, NJ: Princeton Univ. Press, 2000.

——, Mohammad Al-Asad, Abeer Audeh, and Said Nuseibeh. *The Shape of the Holy: Early Islamic Jerusalem.* Princeton, NJ: Princeton Univ. Press, 1996.

Hillenbrand, Robert. *Islamic Art and Architecture.* World of Art. London: Thames & Hudson, 1999.

Irwin, Robert. *The Alhambra.* Cambridge, MA: Harvard Univ. Press, 2004.

Khalili, Nasser D. *Visions of Splendour in Islamic Art and Culture.* London: Worth Press, 2008.

Komaroff, Linda, and Stefano Carboni, eds. *The Legacy of Genghis Khan: Courtly Art and Culture in Western Asia, 1256–1353.* New York: Metropolitan Museum of Art, 2002.

Lentz, Thomas W., and Glenn D. Lowry. *Timur and the Princely Vision: Persian Art and Culture in the Fifteenth Century.* Los Angeles: Los Angeles County Museum of Art, 1989.

Necipolu, Gülru. *The Age of Sinan: Architectural Culture in the Ottoman Empire.* Princeton, NJ: Princeton Univ. Press, 2005.

Petruccioli, Attilio, and Khalil K. Pirani, eds. *Understanding Islamic Architecture.* New York: Routledge Curzon, 2002.

Roxburgh, David J., ed. *Turks: A Journey of a Thousand Years, 600–1600.* London: Royal Academy of Arts, 2005.

Sims, Eleanor, B.I. Marshak, and Ernst J. Grube. *Peerless Images: Persian Painting and Its Sources.* New Haven: Yale Univ. Press, 2002.

Stanley, Tim, Mariam Rosser-Owen, and Stephen Vernoit. *Palace and Mosque: Islamic Art from the Middle East.* London: V&A Publications, 2004.

Stierlin, Henri. *Islamic Art and Architecture.* New York: Thames & Hudson, 2002.

Tadgell, Christopher. *Four Caliphates: The Formation and Development of the Islamic Tradition.* London: Ellipsis, 1998.

Ward, R.M. *Islamic Metalwork.* New York: Thames & Hudson, 1993.

Watson, Oliver. *Ceramics from Islamic Lands.* New York: Thames & Hudson in assoc. with the al-Sabah Collection, Dar al-Athar al-Islamiyyah, Kuwait National Museum, 2004.

Chapter 10 Art of South and Southeast Asia before 1200

Atherton, Cynthia Packert. *The Sculpture of Early Medieval Rajasthan.* Studies in Asian Art and Archaeology, vol. 21. New York: Brill, 1997.

Behl, Benoy K. *The Ajanta Caves: Artistic Wonder of Ancient Buddhist India.* New York: Abrams, 1998.

Behrendt, Kurt A. *The Buddhist Architecture of Gandhara.* Handbook of Oriental Studies: Section Two: India, vol. 17. Boston: Brill, 2004.

Chakrabarti, Dilip K. *India, an Archaeological History: Palaeolithic Beginnings to Early Historic Foundations.* 2nd ed. New York: Oxford Univ. Press, 2009.

Craven, Roy C. *Indian Art: A Concise History.* Rev. ed. World of Art. New York: Thames & Hudson, 1997.

Dehejia, Vidya. *Art of the Imperial Cholas.* New York: Columbia Univ. Press, 1990.

———. *The Sensuous and the Sacred: Chola Bronzes from South India.* New York: American Federation of Arts, 2002.

Dessai, Vishakha N., and Darielle Mason, eds. *Gods, Guardians, and Lovers: Temple Sculptures from North India, A.D. 700–1200.* New York: Asia Society Galleries, 1993.

Dhavalikar, Madhukar Keshav. *Ellora.* New York: Oxford Univ. Press, 2003.

Girard-Geslan, Maud. *Art of Southeast Asia.* Trans. J.A. Underwood. New York: Abrams, Inc., 1998.

Heller, Amy. *Early Himalayan Art.* Oxford: Ashmolean Museum, 2008.

Huntington, Susan L. *The Art of Ancient India: Buddhist, Hindu, Jain.* New York: Weatherhill, 1985.

———. *Leaves from the Bodhi Tree: The Art of Pala India (8th–12th Centuries) and Its International Legacy.* Dayton, OH: Dayton Art Institute, 1990.

Hutt, Michael. *Nepal: A Guide to the Art and Architecture of the Kathmandu Valley.* Boston: Shambhala, 1995.

Knox, Robert. *Amaravati: Buddhist Sculpture from the Great Stupa.* London: British Museum Press, 1992.

Khanna, Sucharita. *Dancing Divinities in Indian Art: 8th–12th Century A.D.* Delhi: Sharada Pub. House, 1999.

Kramrisch, Stella. *The Art of Nepal.* New York: Abrams, 1964.

———. *The Presence of Siva.* Princeton, NJ: Princeton Univ. Press, 1981.

Meister, Michael, ed. *Encyclopedia of Indian Temple Architecture.* 2 vols. in 7. Philadelphia: Univ. of Pennsylvania Press, 1983.

Michell, George. *Elephanta.* Bombay: India Book House, 2002.

———. *Hindu Art and Architecture.* World of Art. London: Thames & Hudson, 2000.

Mitter, Partha. *Indian Art.* Oxford History of Art. Oxford: Oxford Univ. Press, 2001.

Neumayer, Erwin. *Lines on Stone: The Prehistoric Rock Art of India.* New Delhi: Manohar, 1993.

Pal, Pratapaditya, ed. *The Ideal Image: The Gupta Sculptural Tradition and Its Influence.* New York: Asia Society, 1978.

Poster, Amy G. *From Indian Earth: 4,000 Years of Terracotta Art.* Brooklyn, NY: Brooklyn Museum, 1986.

Skelton, Robert, and Mark Francis. *Arts of Bengal: The Heritage of Bangladesh and Eastern India.* London: Whitechapel Art Gallery, 1979.

Stierlin, Henri. *Hindu India: From Khajuraho to the Temple City of Madurai.* Taschen's World Architecture. New York: Taschen, 1998.

Tadgell, Christopher. *India and South-East Asia: The Buddhist and Hindu Tradition.* New York: Whitney Library of Design, 1998.

Williams, Joanna G. *Art of Gupta India, Empire and Province.* Princeton, NJ: Princeton Univ. Press, 1982.

Chapter 11 Chinese and Korean Art before 1279

Ciarla, Roberto, ed. *The Eternal Army: The Terracotta Soldiers of the First Chinese Emperor.* Vercelli: White Star, 2005.

Fong, Wen, ed. *Beyond Representation: Chinese Painting and Calligraphy, 8th–14th Century.* Princeton Monographs in Art and Archaeology, 48. New York: Metropolitan Museum of Art, 1992.

Fraser, Sarah Elizabeth. *Performing the Visual: The Practice of Buddhist Wall Painting in China and Central Asia, 618–960.* Stanford, CA: Stanford Univ. Press, 2004.

James, Jean M. *A Guide to the Tomb and Shrine Art of the Han Dynasty 206 B.C.–A.D. 220.* Chinese Studies, 2. Lewiston, NY: Mellen Press, 1996.

Karetzky, Patricia Eichenbaum. *Court Art of the Tang.* Lanham, MD: Univ. Press of America, 1996.

Kim, Kumja Paik. *Goryeo Dynasty: Korea's Age of Enlightenment, 918–1392.* San Francisco: Asian Art Museum—Chong-Moon Lee Center for Asian Art and Culture in cooperation with the National Museum of Korea and the Nara National Museum, 2003.

Li, Jian, ed. *The Glory of the Silk Road: Art from Ancient China.* Dayton, OH: Dayton Art Institute, 2003.

Little, Stephen, and Shawn Eichman. *Taoism and the Arts of China.* Chicago: Art Institute of Chicago, 2000.

Liu, Cary Y., Dora C.Y. Ching, and Judith G. Smith, eds. *Character & Context in Chinese Calligraphy.* Princeton, NJ: Art Museum, Princeton Univ., 1999.

Luo, Zhewen. *Ancient Pagodas in China.* Beijing, China: Foreign Languages Press, 1994.

Ma, Chengyuan. *Ancient Chinese Bronzes.* Ed. Hsio-Yen Shih. Hong Kong: Oxford Univ. Press, 1986.

Murck, Alfreda. *Poetry and Painting in Song China: The Subtle Art of Dissent.* Harvard-Yenching Institute Monograph Series. Cambridge, MA: Harvard Univ. Asia Center for the Harvard-Yenching Institute, 2000.

Ortiz, Valérie Malenfer. *Dreaming the Southern Song Landscape: The Power of Illusion in Chinese Painting.* Studies in Asian Art and Archaeology, vol. 22. Boston: Brill, 1999.

Paludan, Ann. *Chinese Tomb Figurines.* Hong Kong: Oxford Univ. Press, 1994.

Portal, Jane. *Korea: Art and Archaeology.* New York: Thames & Hudson, 2000.

Rawson, Jessica. *Mysteries of Ancient China: New Discoveries from the Early Dynasties.* London: British Museum Press, 1996.

Rhie, Marylin M. *Early Buddhist Art of China and Central Asia.* 2 vols in 3. Handbuch der Orientalistik. Vierte Abteilung; China, 12. Leiden: Brill, 1999.

Scarpari, Maurizio. *Splendours of Ancient China.* London: Thames & Hudson, 2000.

So, Jenny F. ed. *Noble Riders from Pines and Deserts: The Artistic Legacy of the Qidan.* Hong Kong: Art Museum, Chinese Univ. of Hong Kong, 2004.

Sturman, Peter Charles. *Mi Fu: Style and the Art of Calligraphy in Northern Song.* New Haven: Yale Univ. Press, 1997.

Wang, Eugene Y. *Shaping the Lotus Sutra: Buddhist Visual Culture in Medieval China.* Seattle: Univ. of Washington Press, 2005.

Watson, William. *The Arts of China to A.D. 900.* Pelican History of Art. New Haven: Yale Univ. Press, 1995.

———. *The Arts of China 900–1620.* Pelican History of Art. Reissue ed. 2003. New Haven: Yale Univ. Press, 2000.

Watt, James C.Y. *China: Dawn of a Golden Age, 200–750 A.D.* New York: Metropolitan Museum of Art, 2004.

Whitfield, Susan, and Ursula Sims-Williams, eds. *The Silk Road: Trade, Travel, War and Faith.* Chicago: Serindia Publications, 2004.

Wu Hung. *Monumentality in Early Chinese Art and Architecture.* Stanford, CA: Stanford Univ. Press, 1995.

Yang, Xiaoneng, ed. *The Golden Age of Chinese Archaeology: Celebrated Discoveries from the People's Republic of China.* Washington, DC: National Gallery of Art, 1999.

Chapter 12 Japanese Art before 1333

Cunningham, Michael R. *Buddhist Treasures from Nara.* Cleveland: Cleveland Museum of Art, 1998.

Harris, Victor, ed. *Shinto: The Sacred Art of Ancient Japan.* London: British Museum Press, 2001.

Izutsu, Shinryu, and Shoryu Omori. *Sacred Treasures of Mount Koya: The Art of Japanese Shingon Buddhism.* Honolulu: Koyasan Reihokan Museum, 2002.

Kurata, Bunsaku. *Horyu-ji, Temple of the Exalted Law: Early Buddhist Art from Japan.* New York: Japan Society, 1981.

Levine, Gregory P.A., and Yukio Lippit. *Awakenings: Zen Figure Painting in Medieval Japan.* New York: Japan Society, 2007.

McCallum, Donald F. *The Four Great Temples: Buddhist Archaeology, Architecture, and Icons of Seventh-Century Japan.* Honolulu: Univ. of Hawai'i Press, 2009.

Mino, Yutaka. *The Great Eastern Temple: Treasures of Japanese Buddhist Art from Todai-ji.* Chicago: Art Institute of Chicago, 1986.

Mizoguchi, Koji. *An Archaeological History of Japan: 30,000 B.C. to A.D. 700.* Philadelphia: Univ. of Pennsylvania Press, 2002.

Murase, Miyeko. *The Tale of Genji: Legends and Paintings.* New York: Braziller, 2001.

Nishiwara, Kyotaro, and Emily J. Sano. *The Great Age of Japanese Buddhist Sculpture, A.D. 60–1300.* Fort Worth, TX: Kimbell Art Museum, 1982.

Pearson, Richard J. *Ancient Japan.* Washington, DC: Arthur M. Sackler Gallery, 1992.

Ten Grotenhuis, Elizabeth. *Japanese Mandalas: Representations of Sacred Geography.* Honolulu: Univ. of Hawai'i Press, 1999.

Washizuka, Hiromitsu, Park Youngbok, and Kang Woo-bang. *Transmitting the Forms of Divinity: Early Buddhist Art from Korea and Japan.* Ed. Naomi Noble Richard. New York: Japan Society, 2003.

Wong, Dorothy C., and Eric M. Field, eds. *Horyuji Reconsidered.* Newcastle: Cambridge Scholars, 2008.

Chapter 13 Art of the Americas before 1300

Benson, Elizabeth P., and Beatriz de la Fuente. *Olmec Art of Ancient Mexico.* Washington, DC: National Gallery of Art, 1996.

Berrin, Kathleen, ed. *Feathered Serpents and Flowering Trees: Reconstructing the Murals of Teotihuacan.* San Francisco: Fine Arts Museums of San Francisco, 1988.

Brody, J.J. *Anasazi and Pueblo Painting.* Albuquerque: Univ. of New Mexico Press, 1991.

Burger, Richard L. *Chavin and the Origins of Andean Civilization.* New York: Thames & Hudson, 1992.

Clark, John E., and Mary E. Pye, eds. *Olmec Art and Archaeology in Mesoamerica.* Studies in the History of Art, 58: Symposium Papers, 35. Washington, DC: National Gallery of Art, 2000.

Clayton, Lawrence A., Vernon J. Knight, and Edward Moore, eds. *The De Soto Chronicles: The Expedition of Hernando de Soto to North America, 1539–1543.* 2 vols. Tuscaloosa: Univ. of Alabama Press, 1993.

Coe, Michael D. and Rex Koontz. *Mexico: From the Olmecs to the Aztecs.* 5th ed. New York: Thames & Hudson, 2005.

———. *Breaking the Maya Code.* Rev. ed. New York: Thames & Hudson, 1999.

Donnan, Christopher. *Moche Portraits from Ancient Peru.* Austin: Univ. of Texas Press, 2003.

Fagan, Brian M. *Chaco Canyon: Archaeologists Explore the Lives of an Ancient Society.* New York: Oxford Univ. Press, 2005.

Hall, Robert L. *An Archaeology of the Soul: North American Indian Belief and Ritual.* Urbana: Univ. of Illinois Press, 1997.

Heyden, Doris, and Paul Gendrop. *Pre-Columbian Architecture of Mesoamerica.* Trans. Judith Stanton. History of World Architecture. New York: Electa/Rizzoli, 1988.

Korp, Maureen. *The Sacred Geography of the American Mound Builders.* Native American Studies. Lewiston, NY: Mellen Press, 1990.

Kubler, George. *The Art and Architecture of Ancient America: The Mexican, Maya, and Andean Peoples.* 3rd ed. with updated bib. Pelican History of Art. New Haven: Yale Univ. Press, 1993.

Labbé, Armand J. *Shamans, Gods, and Mythic Beasts: Colombian Gold and Ceramics in Antiquity.* New York: American Federation of Arts, 1998.

LeBlanc, Steven A. *Painted by a Distant Hand: Mimbres Pottery from the American Southwest.* Cambridge, MA: Peabody Museum Press, 2004.

Loendorf, Lawrence L., Christopher Chippindale, and David S. Whitley, eds. *Discovering North American Rock Art*. Tucson: Univ. of Arizona Press, 2005.

Martin, Simon, and Nikolai Grube. *Chronicle of the Maya Kings and Queens: Deciphering the Dynasties of the Ancient Maya*. 2nd ed. New York: Thames & Hudson, 2008.

Miller, Mary Ellen. *The Art of Mesoamerica: From Olmec to Aztec*. 4th ed. World of Art. London: Thames & Hudson, 2006.

———. *Maya Art and Architecture*. World of Art. London: Thames & Hudson, 1999.

———, and Simon Martin. *Courtly Art of the Ancient Maya*. San Francisco: Fine Arts Museums of San Francisco, 2004.

———, and Karl Taube. *The Gods and Symbols of Ancient Mexico and the Maya: An Illustrated Dictionary of Mesoamerican Religion*. London: Thames & Hudson, 1993.

Milner, George R. *The Moundbuilders: Ancient Peoples of Eastern North America*. Ancient Peoples and Places, 110. London: Thames & Hudson, 2004.

Noble, David Grant. *In Search of Chaco: New Approaches to an Archaeological Enigma*. Santa Fe, NM: School of American Research Press, 2004.

O'Connor, Mallory McCane. *Lost Cities of the Ancient Southeast*. Gainesville: Univ. Press of Florida, 1995.

Pasztory, Esther. *Teotihuacan: An Experiment in Living*. Norman: Univ. of Oklahoma Press, 1997.

Pillsbury, Joanne, ed. *Moche Art and Archaeology in Ancient Peru*. Studies in the History of Art: Center for Advanced Study in the Visual Arts, 63: Symposium Papers, 40. Washington, DC: National Gallery of Art, 2001.

Power, Susan C. *Early Art of the Southeastern Indians: Feathered Serpents & Winged Beings*. Athens: Univ. of Georgia Press, 2004.

Rohn, Arthur H., and William M. Ferguson. *Puebloan Ruins of the Southwest*. Albuquerque: Univ. of New Mexico Press, 2006.

Sharer, Robert J., and Loa P. Traxler. *The Ancient Maya*. 6th ed. Stanford, CA: Stanford Univ. Press, 2006.

Stierlin, Henri. *The Maya: Palaces and Pyramids of the Rainforest*. Cologne: Taschen, 2001.

Stone-Miller, Rebecca. *Art of the Andes: From Chavin to Inca*. 2nd ed. World of Art. New York: Thames & Hudson, 2002.

———. *To Weave for the Sun: Ancient Andean Textiles*. New York: Thames & Hudson 1994.

Townsend, Richard F., and Robert V. Sharp, eds. *Hero, Hawk, and Open Hand: American Indian Art of the Ancient Midwest and South*. Chicago: Art Institute of Chicago, 2004.

Von Hagen, Adriana, and Craig Morris. *The Cities of the Ancient Andes*. New York: Thames & Hudson, 1998.

Chapter 14 Early African Art

Ben-Amos, Paula. *The Art of Benin*. Rev. ed. Washington, DC: Smithsonian Institution Press, 1995.

Berzock, Kathleen Bickford. *Benin: Royal Arts of a West African Kingdom*. Chicago: Art Institute of Chicago, 2008.

Blier, Suzanne Preston. *The Royal Arts of Africa: The Majesty of Form*. Perspectives. New York: Abrams, 1998.

Cole, Herbert M. *Igbo Arts: Community and Cosmos*. Los Angeles: Fowler Museum of Cultural History, Univ. of California, 1984.

Connah, Graham. *African Civilizations: An Archaeological Perspective*, 2nd ed. New York: Cambridge Univ. Press, 2001.

———. *Forgotten Africa: An Introduction to Its Archaeology*. New York: Routledge, 2004.

Darish, Patricia J. "Memorial Head of an Oba: Ancestral Time in Benin Culture." In *Tempus Fugit, Time Flies*. Ed. Jan Schall. Kansas City, MO: Nelson-Atkins Museum of Art, 2000: 290–297.

Eyo, Ekpo, and Frank Willett. *Treasures of Ancient Nigeria*. Ed. Rollyn O. Kirchbaum. New York: Knopf, 1980.

Garlake, Peter S. *Early Art and Architecture of Africa*. Oxford History of Art. Oxford: Oxford Univ. Press, 2002.

Grunne, Bernard de. *The Birth of Art in Africa: Nok Statuary in Nigeria*. Paris: A. Biro, 1998.

Huffman, Thomas N. *Symbols in Stone: Unravelling the Mystery of Great Zimbabwe*. Johannesburg: Witwatersrand Univ. Press, 1987.

LaViolette, Adria Jean. *Ethno-Archaeology in Jenné, Mali: Craft and Status among Smiths, Potters, and Masons*. Oxford: Archaeopress, 2000.

M'Bow, Babacar, and Osemwegie Ebohon. *Benin, a Kingdom in Bronze: The Royal Court Art*. Ft. Lauderdale, FL: African American Research Library and Cultural Center, Broward County Library, 2005.

Phillipson, D.W. *African Archaeology*. 3rd ed. Cambridge World Archaeology. New York: Cambridge Univ. Press, 2005.

Schädler, Karl-Ferdinand. *Earth and Ore: 2500 Years of African Art in Terra-Cotta and Metal*. Trans. Geoffrey P. Burwell. Munich: Panterra, 1997.

Chapter 15 Early Medieval Art in Europe

Alexander, J.J.G. *Medieval Illuminators and Their Methods of Work*. New ed. New Haven: Yale Univ. Press, 1994.

The Art of Medieval Spain, A.D. 500–1200. New York: Metropolitan Museum of Art, 1993.

Backhouse, Janet, D.H. Turner, and Leslie Webster, eds. *The Golden Age of Anglo-Saxon Art, 966–1066*. Bloomington: Indiana Univ. Press, 1984.

Bandmann, Günter. *Early Medieval Architecture as Bearer of Meaning*. New York: Columbia Univ. Press, 2005.

Brown, Michelle P. *The Lindisfarne Gospels: Society, Spirituality and the Scribe*. Toronto: Univ. of Toronto Press, 2003.

Calkins, Robert G. *Illuminated Books of the Middle Ages*. Ithaca, NY: Cornell Univ. Press, 1983.

Carver, Martin. *Sutton Hoo: A Seventh-Century Princely Burial Ground and Its Context*. London: British Museum Press, 2005.

Davis-Weyer, Caecilia. *Early Medieval Art, 300–1150: Sources and Documents*. Upper Saddle River, NJ: Pearson/Prentice Hall, 1971.

Diebold, William J. *Word and Image: An Introduction to Early Medieval Art*. Boulder, CO: Westview Press, 2000.

Dodwell, C.R. *Pictorial Arts of the West, 800–1200*. Pelican History of Art. New Haven: Yale Univ. Press, 1993.

Farr, Carol. *The Book of Kells: Its Function and Audience*. London: British Library, 1997.

Fitzhugh, William W., and Elisabeth I. Ward, eds. *Vikings: The North Atlantic Saga*. Washington, DC: Smithsonian Institution Press, 2000.

Harbison, Peter. *The Golden Age of Irish Art: The Medieval Achievement, 600–1200*. London: Thames & Hudson, 1999.

Henderson, George. *From Durrow to Kells: The Insular Gospel-Books, 650–800*. London: Thames & Hudson, 1987.

Horn, Walter W., and Ernest Born. *Plan of Saint Gall: A Study of the Architecture and Economy of and Life in a Paradigmatic Carolingian Monastery*. California Studies in the History of Art, 19. 3 vols. Berkeley: Univ. of California Press, 1979.

Lasko, Peter. *Ars Sacra, 800–1200*. 2nd ed. Pelican History of Art. New Haven: Yale Univ. Press, 1994.

McClendon, Charles B. *The Origins of Medieval Architecture: Building in Europe, A.D. 600–900*. New Haven: Yale Univ. Press, 2005.

Mayr-Harting, Henry. *Ottonian Book Illumination: An Historical Study*. 2nd rev. ed. 2 vols. London: Harvey Miller, 1999.

Mentré, Mireille. *Illuminated Manuscripts of Medieval Spain*. New York: Thames & Hudson, 1996.

Nees, Lawrence. *Early Medieval Art*. Oxford History of Art. Oxford: Oxford Univ. Press, 2002.

Richardson, Hilary, and John Scarry. *An Introduction to Irish High Crosses*. Dublin: Mercier, 1990.

Schapiro, Meyer. *Language of Forms: Lectures on Insular Manuscript Art*. Ed. Jane Rosenthal. New York: Pierpont Morgan Library, 2006.

Stalley, R.A. *Early Medieval Architecture*. Oxford History of Art. Oxford: Oxford Univ. Press, 1999.

Wickham, Chris. *Framing the Early Middle Ages: Europe and the Mediterranean 400–800*. New York: Oxford Univ. Press, 2005.

Williams, John. *Early Spanish Manuscript Illumination*. New York: Braziller, 1977.

Wilson, David M. *Anglo-Saxon Art: From the Seventh Century to the Norman Conquest*. London: Thames & Hudson, 1984.

———, and Ole Klindt-Jensen. *Viking Art*. 2nd ed. Minneapolis: Univ. of Minnesota Press, 1980.

Chapter 16 Romanesque Art

Barral i Altet, Xavier. *The Romanesque: Towns, Cathedrals and Monasteries*. Taschen's World Architecture. New York: Taschen, 1998.

The Book of Sainte Foy. Ed. and trans. Pamela Sheingorn. Philadelphia: Univ. of Pennsylvania Press, 1995.

Cahn, Walter. *Romanesque Manuscripts: The Twelfth Century*. 2nd ed. 2 vols. A Survey of Manuscripts Illuminated in France. London: Harvey Miller, 1996.

Caviness, Madeline H. "Hildegard as Designer of the Illustrations to her Works." In *Hildegard of Bingen: The*

Context of her Thought and Art. Ed. Charles Burnett and Peter Dronke. London: Warburg Institute, 1998: 29–63.

Davis-Weyer, Caecilia. *Early Medieval Art, 300–1150. Sources and Documents*. Upper Saddle River, NJ: Pearson/Prentice Hall, 1971.

Dimier, Anselme. *Stones Laid before the Lord: A History of Monastic Architecture*. Trans. Gilchrist Lavigne. Cistercian Studies Series, no. 152. Kalamazoo, MI: Cistercian Publications, 1999.

Fergusson, Peter. *Architecture of Solitude: Cistercian Abbeys in Twelfth-Century England*. Princeton, NJ: Princeton Univ. Press, 1984.

Forsyth, Ilene H. *The Throne of Wisdom: Wood Sculptures of the Madonna in Romanesque France*. Princeton, NJ: Princeton Univ. Press, 1972.

Gaud, Henri, and Jean-François Leroux-Dhuys. *Cistercian Abbeys: History and Architecture*. Cologne: Könemann, 1998.

Gerson, Paula, ed. *The Pilgrim's Guide to Santiago de Compostela: A Critical Edition*. 2 vols. London: Harvey Miller, 1998.

Grivot, Denis, and George Zarnecki. *Gislebertus: Sculptor of Autun*. New York: Orion Press, 1961.

Hearn, M. F. *Romanesque Sculpture: The Revival of Monumental Stone Sculptures in the Eleventh and Twelfth Centuries*. Ithaca, NY: Cornell Univ. Press, 1981.

Hicks, Carola. *The Bayeux Tapestry: The Life Story of a Masterpiece*. London: Chatto & Windus, 2006.

Holt, Elizabeth Gilmore, ed. *A Documentary History of Art*. 2 vols. Princeton, NJ: Princeton Univ. Press, 1982–86.

Hourihane, Colum, ed. *Romanesque Art and Thought in the Twelfth Century: Essays in Honor of Walter Cahn*. The Index of Christian Art Occasional Papers 10. University Park, PA: Penn State Press, 2008.

Kubach, Hans E. *Romanesque Architecture*. History of World Architecture. New York: Electa/Rizzoli, 1988.

Minne-Sève, Viviane, and Hervé Kergall. *Romanesque and Gothic France: Architecture and Sculpture*. Trans. Jack Hawkes and Lory Frankel. New York: Abrams, 2000.

Newman, Barbara. *Sister of Wisdom: St. Hildegard's Theology of the Feminine*. 2nd ed. Berkeley: Univ. of California Press, 1997.

Rudolph, Conrad. *The "Things of Greater Importance": Bernard of Clairvaux's Apologia and the Medieval Attitude Toward Art*. Philadelphia: Univ. of Pennsylvania Press, 1990.

Schapiro, Meyer. *Romanesque Art: Selected Papers*. New York: George Braziller, 1977.

———. *The Romanesque Sculpture of Moissac*. New York: Braziller, 1985.

———. *Romanesque Architectural Sculpture: The Charles Eliot Norton Lectures*. Ed. Linda Seidel. Chicago: Univ. of Chicago Press, 2006.

Seidel, Linda. *Legends in Limestone: Lazarus, Gislebertus, and the Cathedral of Autun*. Chicago: Univ. of Chicago Press, 1999.

Sundell, Michael G. *Mosaics in the Eternal City*. Tempe: Arizona Center for Medieval and Renaissance Studies, 2007.

Swanson, R.N. *The Twelfth-Century Renaissance*. Manchester: Manchester Univ. Press, 1999.

Theophilus. *On Divers Arts: The Foremost Medieval Treatise on Painting, Glassmaking, and Metalwork*. Trans. John G. Hawthorne and Cyril Stanley Smith. New York: Dover, 1979.

Toman, Rolf, ed. *Romanesque: Architecture, Sculpture, Painting*. Trans. Fiona Hulse and Ian Macmillan. Cologne: Könemann, 1997.

Wilson, David M. *The Bayeux Tapestry: The Complete Tapestry in Color*. London: Thames & Hudson and New York: Knopf, 2004.

Zarnecki, George, Janet Holt, and Tristram Holland, eds. *English Romanesque Art, 1066–1200*. London: Weidenfeld and Nicolson, 1984.

Chapter 17 Gothic Art of the Twelfth and Thirteenth Centuries

Barnes, Carl F. *The Portfolio of Villard de Honnecourt: A New Critical Edition and Color Facsimile*. Burlington, VT: Ashgate, 2009.

Binding, Günther. *High Gothic: The Age of the Great Cathedrals*. Taschen's World Architecture. London: Taschen, 1999.

Binski, Paul. *Becket's Crown: Art and Imagination in Gothic England, 1170–1300*. New Haven: Yale Univ. Press, 2004.

Bony, Jean. *French Gothic Architecture of the 12th and 13th Centuries*. California Studies in the History of Art, 20. Berkeley: Univ. of California Press, 1983.

Camille, Michael. *Gothic Art: Glorious Visions*. Perspectives. New York: Abrams, 1996.

Coldstream, Nicola. *Masons and Sculptors*. Toronto & Buffalo, NY: Univ. of Toronto Press, 1991.

Crosby, Sumner M. *The Royal Abbey of Saint-Denis from Its Beginnings to the Death of Suger, 475–1151*. Yale Publications in the History of Art, 37. New Haven: Yale Univ. Press, 1987.

Erlande-Brandenburg, Alain. *Gothic Art*. Trans. I. Mark Paris. New York: Abrams, 1989.

Frankl, Paul. *Gothic Architecture*. Revised Paul Crossley. Pelican History of Art. New Haven: Yale Univ. Press, 2000.

Frisch, Teresa G. *Gothic Art, 1140–c.1450: Sources and Documents*. Upper Saddle River, NJ: Pearson/Prentice Hall, 1971.

Grodecki, Louis, and Catherine Brisac. *Gothic Stained Glass, 1200–1300*. Ithaca, NY: Cornell Univ. Press, 1985.

Jordan, Alyce A. *Visualizing Kingship in the Windows of the Sainte-Chapelle*. Turnhout: Brepols, 2002.

Moskowitz, Anita Fiderer. *Nicola & Giovanni Pisano: The Pulpits: Pious Devotion, Pious Diversion*. London: Harvey Miller, 2005.

Nussbaum, Norbert. *German Gothic Church Architecture*. Trans. Scott Kleager. New Haven: Yale Univ. Press, 2000.

Panofsky, Erwin. *Abbot Suger on the Abbey Church of St.-Denis and Its Art Treasures*. 2nd ed. Ed. Gerda Panofsky-Soergel. Princeton, NJ: Princeton Univ. Press, 1979.

Parry, Stan. *Great Gothic Cathedrals of France*. New York: Viking Studio, 2001.

Sauerländer, Willibald. *Gothic Sculpture in France, 1140–1270*. Trans. Janet Sandheimer. London: Thames & Hudson, 1972.

Scott, Robert A. *The Gothic Enterprise: A Guide to Understanding the Medieval Cathedral*. Berkeley: Univ. of California Press, 2003.

Simson, Otto Georg von. *The Gothic Cathedral: Origins of Gothic Architecture and the Medieval Concept of Order*. 3rd ed. exp. Bollingen Series. Princeton, NJ: Princeton Univ. Press, 1988.

Suckale, Robert, and Matthias Weniger. *Painting of the Gothic Era*. Ed. Ingo F. Walther. New York: Taschen, 1999.

Williamson, Paul. *Gothic Sculpture, 1140–1300*. Pelican History of Art. New Haven: Yale Univ. Press, 1995.

Chapter 18 Fourteenth-Century Art in Europe

Alexander, Jonathan, and Paul Binski, eds. *Age of Chivalry: Art in Plantagenet England, 1200–1400*. London: Royal Academy of Arts, 1987.

Backhouse, Janet. *Illumination from Books of Hours*. London: British Library, 2004.

Boehm, Barbara Drake, and Jiří Fajt, eds. *Prague: The Crown of Bohemia, 1347–1437*. New York: Metropolitan Museum of Art, 2005.

Bony, Jean. *The English Decorated Style: Gothic Architecture Transformed, 1250–1350*. The Wrightsman Lecture, 10. Oxford: Phaidon Press, 1979.

Cennini, Cennino. *The Craftsman's Handbook "Il libro dell'arte."* Trans. D.V. Thompson, Jr. New York: Dover, 1960.

Derbes, Anne, and Mark Sandona, eds. *The Cambridge Companion to Giotto*. Cambridge and New York: Cambridge Univ. Press, 2003.

Fajt, Jiří, ed. *Magister Theodoricus, Court Painter to Emperor Charles IV: The Pictorial Decoration of the Shrines at Karlstejn Castle*. Prague: National Gallery, 1998.

Holt, Elizabeth Gilmore, ed. *A Documentary History of Art*. 2 vols. Princeton, NJ: Princeton Univ. Press, 1982–86.

Ladis, Andrew. ed, *The Arena Chapel and the Genius of Giotto: Padua*. Giotto and the World of Early Italian Art, 2. New York: Garland, 1998.

Meiss, Millard. *Painting in Florence and Siena after the Black Death: The Arts, Religion, and Society in the Mid-Fourteenth Century*. 2nd ed. Princeton, NJ: Princeton Univ. Press, 1978.

Moskowitz, Anita Fiderer. *Italian Gothic Sculpture: c. 1250–c. 1400*. New York: Cambridge Univ. Press, 2001.

Norman, Diana, ed. *Siena, Florence, and Padua: Art, Society, and Religion 1280–1400*. 2 vols. New Haven: Yale Univ. Press, 1995.

Poeschke, Joachim. *Italian Frescoes, the Age of Giotto, 1280–1400*. New York: Abbeville Press, 2005.

Schleif, Corine. "St. Hedwig's Personal Ivory Madonna: Women's Agency and the Powers of Possessing Portable Figures." In *The Four Modes of Seeing: Approaches to Medieval Imagery in Honor of Madeline Harrison Caviness*. Eds. Evelyn Staudinger Lane, Elizabeth Carson Paston,

and Ellen M. Shortell. Farnham, Surrey: Ashgate, 2009: 282–403.

Vasari, Giorgio. *The Lives of the Artists*. Trans. Julia Conaway Bondanella and Peter Bondanella. Oxford World's Classics. New York: Oxford Univ. Press, 2008.

Welch, Evelyn S. *Art in Renaissance Italy, 1350–1500*. New ed. Oxford History of Art. Oxford: Oxford Univ. Press, 2000.

White, John. *Art and Architecture in Italy, 1250 to 1400*. 3rd ed. Pelican History of Art. Harmondsworth, UK: Penguin, 1993.

Wieck, Roger S. *Time Sanctified: The Book of Hours in Medieval Art and Life*. 2nd ed. New York: Braziller, 2001.

Chapter 19 Fifteenth-Century Art in Northern Europe

Art from the Court of Burgundy: The Patronage of Philip the Bold and John the Fearless 1364–1419. Dijon: Musée des Beaux-Arts and Cleveland: Cleveland Museum of Art, 2004.

Baxandall, Michael. *The Limewood Sculptors of Renaissance Germany*. New Haven: Yale Univ. Press, 1980.

Blum, Shirley. *Early Netherlandish Triptychs: A Study in Patronage*. California Studies in the History of Art, 13. Berkeley: Univ. of California Press, 1969.

Borchert, Till-Holger. *Age of Van Eyck: The Mediterranean World and Early Netherlandish Painting, 1430–1530*. New York: Thames & Hudson, 2002.

Campbell, Lorne. *The Fifteenth-Century Netherlandish Schools* (National Gallery Catalogues). London: National Gallery, 1998.

Cavallo, Adolph S. *The Unicorn Tapestries at the Metropolitan Museum of Art*. New York: Metropolitan Museum of Art, 1998.

Chastel, Andrè. *French Art: The Renaissance, 1430–1620*. Paris: Flammarion, 1995.

Dhanens, Elisabeth. *Van Eyck: The Ghent Altarpiece*. New York: Viking Press, 1973.

Füssel, Stephan. *Gutenberg and the Impact of Printing*. Trans. Douglas Martin. Burlington, VT: Ashgate, 2005.

Koster, Margaret L. "The Arnolfini Double Portrait: A Simple Solution." *Apollo* 157 (September 2003): 3–14.

Lane, Barbara G. *The Altar and the Altarpiece: Sacramental Themes in Early Netherlandish Painting*. New York: Harper & Row, 1984.

Marks, Richard, and Paul Williamson, eds. *Gothic: Art for England 1400–1547*. London: V&A Publications, 2003.

Meiss, Millard. *French Painting in the Time of Jean de Berry: The Limbourgs and their Contemporaries*. 2 vols. New York: Braziller, 1974.

Müller, Theodor. *Sculpture in the Netherlands, Germany, France, and Spain: 1400–1500*. Trans. Elaine and William Robson Scott. Pelican History of Art. Harmondsworth, UK: Penguin, 1966.

Pächt, Otto. *Early Netherlandish Painting: From Rogier van der Weyden to Gerard David*. Ed. Monika Rosenauer. Trans. David Britt. London: Harvey Miller, 1997.

———. *Van Eyck and the Founders of Early Netherlandish Painting*. London: Miller, 1994.

Panofsky, Erwin. *Early Netherlandish Painting, Its Origins and Character*. 2 vols. Cambridge, MA: Harvard Univ. Press, 1966.

Parshall, Peter W., and Rainer Schoch. *Origins of European Printmaking: Fifteenth-Century Woodcuts and their Public*. Washington, DC: National Gallery of Art, 2005.

Plummer, John. *The Last Flowering: French Painting in Manuscripts, 1420–1530, from American Collections*. New York: Pierpont Morgan Library, 1982.

Seidel, Linda. *Jan van Eyck's Arnolfini Portrait: Stories of an Icon*. New York: Cambridge Univ. Press, 1993.

Smith, Jeffrey Chipps. *The Northern Renaissance*. London and New York: Phaidon Press, 2004.

Snyder, James. *Northern Renaissance Art: Painting, Sculpture, the Graphic Arts from 1350 to 1575*. 2nd ed. rev. Larry Silver and Henry Luttikhuizen. Upper Saddle River, NJ: Prentice Hall, 2005.

Vos, Dirk de. *The Flemish Primitives: The Masterpieces*. Princeton, NJ: Princeton Univ. Press, 2002.

Zuffi, Stefano. *European Art of the Fifteenth Century*. Trans. Brian D. Phillips. Art through the Centuries. Los Angeles: J. Paul Getty Museum, 2005.

Chapter 20 Renaissance Art in Fifteenth-Century Italy

Adams, Laurie Schneider. *Italian Renaissance Art*. Boulder, CO: Westview Press, 2001.

Ahl, Diane Cole, ed. *The Cambridge Companion to Masaccio*. New York: Cambridge Univ. Press, 2002.

Ames-Lewis, Francis. *Drawing in Early Renaissance Italy*. 2nd ed. New Haven: Yale Univ. Press, 2000.

———. *The Intellectual Life of the Early Renaissance Artist*. New Haven: Yale Univ. Press, 2000.

Baxandall, Michael. *Painting and Experience in Fifteenth-Century Italy: A Primer in the Social History of Pictorial Style*. 2nd ed. Oxford: Oxford Univ. Press, 1988.

Boskovits, Miklós. *Italian Paintings of the Fifteenth Century*. The Collections of the National Gallery of Art. Washington, DC: National Gallery of Art, 2003.

Botticelli and Filippino: Passion and Grace in Fifteenth-Century Florentine Painting. Milan: Skira, 2004.

Brown, Patricia Fortini. *Art and Life in Renaissance Venice*. Perspectives. New York: Abrams, 1997. Reissue ed. Upper Saddle River, NJ: Pearson/Prentice Hall, 2006.

Brucker, Gene. *Florence: The Golden Age, 1138–1737*. Berkeley: Univ. of California Press, 1998.

Christiansen, Keith, Laurence B. Kanter, and Carl Brandon Strehlke. *Painting in Renaissance Siena, 1420–1500*. New York: Metropolitan Museum of Art, 1988.

Gilbert, Creighton, ed. *Italian Art, 1400–1500: Sources and Documents*. Evanston, IL: Northwestern Univ. Press, 1992.

Heydenreich, Ludwig Heinrich. *Architecture in Italy, 1400–1500*. Revised Paul Davies. Pelican History of Art. New Haven: Yale Univ. Press, 1996.

Hind, Arthur M. *An Introduction to a History of Woodcut*. New York: Dover, 1963.

Hyman, Timothy. *Sienese Painting: The Art of a City-Republic (1278–1477)*. World of Art. New York: Thames & Hudson, 2003.

King, Ross. *Brunelleschi's Dome: How a Renaissance Genius Reinvented Architecture*. New York: Walker, 2000.

Lavin, Marilyn Aronberg, ed. *Piero della Francesca and his Legacy*. Studies in the History of Art, 48: Symposium Papers, 28. Washington, DC: National Gallery of Art, 1995.

Pächt, Otto. *Venetian Painting in the 15th Century: Jacopo, Gentile and Giovanni Bellini and Andrea Mantegna*. Ed. Margareta Vyoral-Tschapka and Michael Pächt. Trans. Fiona Elliott. London: Harvey Miller, 2003.

Paoletti, John T., and Gary M. Radke. *Art in Renaissance Italy*. 4th ed. Upper Saddle River, NJ: Pearson/Prentice Hall, 2012.

Partridge, Loren W. *The Art of Renaissance Rome, 1400–1600*. 2nd ed. Upper Saddle River, NJ: Pearson/Prentice Hall, 2006.

———. *Art of Renaissance Florence, 1400–1600*. Berkeley: Univ. of California Press, 2009.

de Pisan, Christine. *The Book of the City of Ladies*. Trans. Rosalind Brown-Grant. London: Penguin Books, 1999.

Poeschke, Joachim. *Donatello and His World: Sculpture of the Italian Renaissance*. Trans. Russell Stockman. New York: Abrams, 1993.

Pope-Hennessy, John. *Italian Renaissance Sculpture*. 4th ed. London: Phaidon Press, 1996.

Radke, Gary M., ed. *The Gates of Paradise: Lorenzo Ghiberti's Masterpiece*. New Haven: Yale Univ. Press, 2007.

Randolph, Adrian W.B., *Engaging Symbols: Gender, Politics, and Public Art in Fifteenth-Century Florence*. New Haven: Yale Univ. Press, 2002.

Troncelliti, Latifah. *The Two Parallel Realities of Alberti and Cennini: The Power of Writing and the Visual Arts in the Italian Quattrocento*. Studies in Italian Literature, vol. 14. Lewiston, NY: Mellen Press, 2004.

Turner, Richard. *Renaissance Florence: The Invention of a New Art*. Perspectives. New York: Abrams, 1997. Reissue ed. Upper Saddle River, NJ: Pearson/Prentice Hall, 2006.

Vasari, Giorgio. *The Lives of the Artists*. Trans. Julia Conaway Bondanella and Peter Bondanella. Oxford World's Classics. New York: Oxford Univ. Press, 2008.

Verdon, Timothy, and John Henderson, eds. *Christianity and the Renaissance: Image and Religious Imagination in the Quattrocento*. Syracuse, NY: Syracuse Univ. Press, 1990.

Walker, Paul Robert. *The Feud that Sparked the Renaissance: How Brunelleschi and Ghiberti Changed the Art World*. New York: William Morrow, 2002.

Welch, Evelyn S. *Art and Society in Italy, 1350–1500*. Oxford History of Art. Oxford: Oxford Univ. Press, 1997.

Chapter 21 Sixteenth-Century Art in Italy

Acidini Luchinat, Cristina, et al. *The Medici, Michelangelo, & the Art of Late Renaissance Florence*. New Haven: Yale Univ. Press, 2002.

Bambach, Carmen. *Drawing and Painting in the Italian Renaissance Workshop: Theory and Practice, 1330–1600*. Cambridge: Cambridge Univ. Press, 1999.

Barriault, Anne B., ed. *Reading Vasari*. London: Philip Wilson in assoc. with the Georgia Museum of Art, 2005.

Brambilla Barcilon, Pinin. *Leonardo: The Last Supper*. Chicago: Univ. of Chicago Press, 2001.

Brown, Patricia Fortini. *Art and Life in Renaissance Venice*. Perspectives. New York: Abrams, 1997.

Cellini, Benvenuto. *Autobiography*. Rev. ed. Trans. George Bull. Penguin Classics. New York: Penguin, 1998.

Chelazzi Dini, Giulietta, Alessandro Angelini, and Bernardina Sani. *Sienese Painting: From Duccio to the Birth of the Baroque*. New York: Abrams, 1998.

Cole, Alison. *Virtue and Magnificence: Art of the Italian Renaissance Courts*. Perspectives. New York: Abrams, 1995. Reissue ed. as *Art of the Italian Courts*. Upper Saddle River, NJ: Pearson/Prentice Hall, 2006.

Franklin, David, ed. *Leonardo da Vinci, Michelangelo, and the Renaissance in Florence*. Ottawa: National Gallery of Canada in assoc. with Yale Univ. Press, 2005.

Freedberg, S.J. *Painting in Italy, 1500 to 1600*. 3rd ed. Pelican History of Art. New Haven: Yale Univ. Press, 1993.

Goffen, Rona. *Renaissance Rivals: Michelangelo, Leonardo, Raphael, Titian*. New Haven: Yale Univ. Press, 2002.

———. *Titian's Venus of Urbino*. Masterpieces of Western Painting. Cambridge: Cambridge Univ. Press, 1997.

———. *Titian's Women*. New Haven: Yale Univ. Press, 1997.

Hall, Marcia B. *After Raphael: Painting in Central Italy in the Sixteenth Century*. New York: Cambridge Univ. Press, 1999.

———, ed. *The Cambridge Companion to Raphael*. New York: Cambridge Univ. Press, 2005.

Hollingsworth, Mary. *Patronage in Sixteenth Century Italy*. London: John Murray, 1996.

Hopkins, Andrew. *Italian Architecture: From Michelangelo to Borromini*. World of Art. New York: Thames & Hudson, 2002.

Hughes, Anthony. *Michelangelo*. Art & Ideas. London: Phaidon Press, 1997.

Huse, Norbert, and Wolfgang Wolters. *Art of Renaissance Venice: Architecture, Sculpture, and Painting, 1460–1590*. Trans. Edmund Jephcott. Chicago: Univ. of Chicago Press, 1990.

Joannides, Paul. *Titian to 1518: The Assumption of Genius*. New Haven: Yale Univ. Press, 2001.

Klein, Robert, and Henri Zerner. *Italian Art, 1500–1600: Sources and Documents*. Upper Saddle River, NJ: Pearson/Prentice Hall, 1966.

Kliemann, Julian-Matthias, and Michael Rohlmann. *Italian Frescoes: High Renaissance and Mannerism, 1510–1600*. Trans. Steven Lindberg. New York: Abbeville Press, 2004.

Landau, David, and Peter Parshall. *The Renaissance Print: 1470–1550*. New Haven: Yale Univ. Press, 1994.

Lieberman, Ralph. *Renaissance Architecture in Venice, 1450–1540*. New York: Abbeville Press, 1982.

Lotz, Wolfgang. *Architecture in Italy, 1500–1600*. Revised Deborah Howard. Pelican History of Art. New Haven: Yale Univ. Press, 1995.

Meilman, Patricia, ed. *The Cambridge Companion to Titian*. New York: Cambridge Univ. Press, 2004.

Mitrovic, Branko. *Learning from Palladio*. New York: Norton, 2004.

Murray, Linda. *The High Renaissance and Mannerism: Italy, the North and Spain, 1500–1600*. World of Art. London: Thames & Hudson, 1995.

Partridge, Loren W. *The Art of Renaissance Rome, 1400–1600*. 2nd ed. Upper Saddle River, NJ: Pearson/Prentice Hall, 2006.

———. *Art of Renaissance Florence, 1400–1600*. Berkeley: Univ. of California Press, 2009.

———. *Michelangelo, the Last Judgment: A Glorious Restoration*. New York: Abrams, 1997.

Pilliod, Elizabeth. *Pontormo, Bronzino, Allori: A Genealogy of Florentine Art*. New Haven: Yale Univ. Press, 2001.

Pope-Hennessy, John. *Italian High Renaissance and Baroque Sculpture*. 4th ed. London: Phaidon Press, 1996.

Rosand, David. *Painting in Cinquecento Venice: Titian, Veronese, Tintoretto*. Rev. ed. Cambridge: Cambridge Univ. Press, 1997.

Rowe, Colin, and Leon Satkowski. *Italian Architecture of the 16th Century*. New York: Princeton Architectural Press, 2002.

Rowland, Ingrid D. *The Culture of the High Renaissance: Ancients and Moderns in Sixteenth Century Rome*. Cambridge: Cambridge Univ. Press, 1998.

Shearman, John. *Mannerism*. Harmondsworth, UK: Penguin, 1967. Reissue ed. New York: Penguin, 1990.

Vasari, Giorgio. *The Lives of the Artists*. Trans. Julia Conaway Bondanella and Peter Bondanella. Oxford World's Classics. New York: Oxford Univ. Press, 2008.

Verheyen, Egon. *The Paintings in the Studiolo of Isabella d'Este at Mantua*. Monographs on Archaeology and Fine Arts, 23. New York: New York Univ. Press, 1971.

Williams, Robert. *Art, Theory, and Culture in Sixteenth-Century Italy: From Techne to Metateche*. Cambridge: Cambridge Univ. Press, 1997.

Chapter 22 Sixteenth-Century Art in Northern Europe and the Iberian Peninsula

Bartrum, Giulia. *Albrecht Dürer and his Legacy: The Graphic Work of a Renaissance Artist*. London: British Museum Press, 2002.

———. *German Renaissance Prints 1490–1550*. London: British Museum Press, 1995.

Brown, Jonathan. *Painting in Spain, 1500–1700*. Pelican History of Art. New Haven: Yale Univ. Press, 1998.

Buck, Stephanie, and Jochen Sander. *Hans Holbein the Younger: Painter at the Court of Henry VIII*. Trans. Rachel Esner and Beverley Jackson. New York: Thames & Hudson, 2004.

Chapuis, Julien. *Tilman Riemenschneider: Master Sculptor of the Late Middle Ages*. Washington, DC: National Gallery of Art, 1999.

Davies, David, and John H. Elliott. *El Greco*. London: National Gallery, 2003.

Dixon, Laurinda. *Bosch*. Art & Ideas. New York: Phaidon Press, 2003.

Foister, Susan. *Holbein and England*. New Haven: Published for Paul Mellon Centre for Studies in British Art by Yale Univ. Press, 2004.

Hayum, Andrée. *The Isenheim Altarpiece: God's Medicine and the Painter's Vision*. Princeton Essays on the Arts, 18. Princeton, NJ: Princeton Univ. Press, 1989.

Hearn, Karen, ed. *Dynasties: Painting in Tudor and Jacobean England, 1530–1630*. New York: Rizzoli, 1996.

Koerner, Joseph Leo. *The Reformation of the Image*. Chicago: Univ. of Chicago Press, 2004.

Kubler, George. *Building the Escorial*. Princeton, NJ: Princeton Univ. Press, 1982.

Nash, Susie. *Northern Renaissance Art*. Oxford History of Art. New York: Oxford Univ. Press, 2008.

Price, David Hotchkiss. *Albrecht Dürer's Renaissance: Humanism, Reformation, and the Art of Faith*. Studies in Medieval and Early Modern Civilization. Ann Arbor: Univ. of Michigan Press, 2003.

Roberts-Jones, Philippe, and Françoise Roberts-Jones. *Pieter Bruegel*. New York: Abrams, 2002.

Smith, Jeffrey Chipps. *Nuremberg, a Renaissance City, 1500–1618*. Austin: Huntington Art Gallery, Univ. of Texas, 1983.

———. *German Sculpture of the Later Renaissance, c.1520–1580: Art in an Age of Uncertainty*. Princeton, NJ: Princeton Univ. Press, 1994.

———. *The Northern Renaissance*. London and New York: Phaidon Press, 2004.

Snyder, James. *Northern Renaissance Art: Painting, Sculpture, the Graphic Arts from 1350 to 1575*. 2nd ed. rev. Larry Silver and Henry Luttikhuizen. Upper Saddle River, NJ: Pearson/Prentice Hall, 2005.

Strong, Roy C. *Artists of the Tudor Court: The Portrait Miniature Rediscovered, 1520–1620*. London: V&A Publications, 1983.

Zerner, Henri. *Renaissance Art in France: The Invention of Classicism*. Paris: Flammarion, 2003.

Zorach, Rebecca. *Blood, Milk, Ink, Gold: Abundance and Excess in the French Renaissance*. Chicago: Univ. of Chicago Press, 2005.

Chapter 23 Seventeenth-Century Art in Europe

Adams, Laurie Schneider. *Key Monuments of the Baroque*. Boulder, CO: Westview Press, 2000.

Allen, Christopher. *French Painting in the Golden Age*. World of Art. New York: Thames & Hudson, 2003.

Alpers, Svetlana. *The Art of Describing: Dutch Art in the Seventeenth Century*. Chicago: Chicago Univ. Press, 1983.

———. *The Making of Rubens*. New Haven: Yale Univ. Press, 1995.

Blankert, Albert. *Rembrandt: A Genius and His Impact*. Melbourne: National Gallery of Victoria, 1997.

Boucher, Bruce. *Italian Baroque Sculpture*. World of Art. New York: Thames & Hudson, 1998.

Brown, Beverly Louise, ed. *The Genius of Rome, 1592–1623*. London: Royal Academy of Arts, 2001.

Brown, Jonathan. *Painting in Spain, 1500–1700*. Pelican History of Art. New Haven: Yale Univ. Press, 1998.

———, and Carmen Garrido. *Velásquez: The Technique of Genius*. New Haven: Yale Univ. Press, 1998.

Careri, Giovanni. *Baroques*. Tran. Alexandra Bonfante-Warren. Princeton: Princeton Univ. Press, 2003.

Chapman, H. Perry. *Rembrandt's Self-Portraits: A Study in 17th-Century Identity*. Princeton: Princeton Univ. Press, 1990.

Chong, Alan, and Wouter Kloek. *Still-Life Paintings from the Netherlands, 1550–1720*. Zwolle: Waanders, 1999.

Enggass, Robert, and Jonathan Brown. *Italian and Spanish Art, 1600–1750: Sources and Documents*. 2nd ed. Evanston, IL: Northwestern Univ. Press, 1992.

Franklin, David, and Sebastian Schütze. *Caravaggio and his Followers in Rome*. New Haven: Yale Univ. Press, 2011.

Frantis, Wayne E., ed. *The Cambridge Companion to Vermeer*. Cambridge: Cambridge Univ. Press, 2001.

———. *Dutch Seventeenth-Century Genre Painting: Its Stylistic and Thematic Evolution*. New Haven: Yale Univ. Press, 2004.

Harbison, Robert. *Reflections on Baroque*. Chicago: Univ. of Chicago Press, 2000.

Keazor, Henry. *Nicolas Poussin, 1594–1665*. Cologne & London: Taschen, 2007.

Kiers, Judikje, and Fieke Tissink. *Golden Age of Dutch Art: Painting, Sculpture, Decorative Art*. London: Thames & Hudson, 2000.

Lagerlöf, Margaretha Rossholm. *Ideal Landscape: Annibale Carracci, Nicolas Poussin, and Claude Lorrain*. New Haven: Yale Univ. Press, 1990.

McPhee, Sarah. *Bernini and the Bell Towers: Architecture and Politics at the Vatican*. New Haven: Yale Univ. Press, 2002.

Millon, Henry A., ed. *The Triumph of the Baroque: Architecture in Europe, 1600–1750*. 2nd ed. rev. New York: Rizzoli, 1999.

Morrissey, Jake. *The Genius in the Design: Bernini, Borromini, and the Rivalry that Transformed Rome*. New York: William Morrow, 2005.

Puttfarken, Thomas. *Roger de Piles' Theory of Art*. New Haven: Yale Univ. Press, 1985.

Rand, Richard. *Claude Lorrain, the Painter as Draftsman: Drawings from the British Museum*. New Haven: Yale Univ. Press; Williamstown, MA: Clark Art Institute, 2006.

Slive, Seymour. *Dutch Painting 1600–1800*. Pelican History of Art. New Haven: Yale Univ. Press, 1995.

Summerson, John. *Inigo Jones*. New Haven: Published for the Paul Mellon Centre for Studies in British Art by Yale Univ. Press, 2000.

Tomlinson, Janis. *From El Greco to Goya: Painting in Spain, 1561–1828*. Perspectives. New York: Abrams, 1997.

Vlieghe, Hans. *Flemish Art and Architecture, 1585–1700*. Pelican History of Art. Reissue ed. 2004. New Haven: Yale Univ. Press, 1998.

Walker, Stefanie, and Frederick Hammond, eds. *Life and the Arts in the Baroque Palaces of Rome: Ambiente Barocco*. New Haven: Yale Univ. Press; for the Bard Graduate Center for Studies in the Decorative Arts, New York, 1999.

Wheelock Jr., Arthur K. *Flemish Paintings of the Seventeenth Century*. Washington, DC: National Gallery of Art, 2005.

Wittkower, Rudolf. *Art and Architecture in Italy, 1600–1750*. 3 vols. 6th ed. Revised Joseph Connors and Jennifer Montague. Pelican History of Art. New Haven: Yale Univ. Press, 1999.

Zega, Andrew, and Bernd H. Dams. *Palaces of the Sun King: Versailles, Trianon, Marly: The Châteaux of Louis XIV*. New York: Rizzoli, 2002.

Chapter 24 Art of South and Southeast Asia after 1200

Asher, Catherine B. *Architecture of Mughal India*. New York: Cambridge Univ. Press, 1992.

Beach, Milo Cleveland. *Mughal and Rajput Painting*. New York: Cambridge Univ. Press, 1992.

Guy, John, and Deborah Swallow, eds. *Arts of India, 1550–1900*. London: V&A Publications, 1990.

Khanna, Balraj, and Aziz Kurtha. *Art of Modern India*. London: Thames & Hudson, 1998.

Koch, Ebba. *Mughal Art and Imperial Ideology: Collected Essays*. New Delhi: Oxford Univ. Press, 2001.

Love Song of the Dark Lord: Jayadeva's Gitagovinda. Trans. Barbara Stoler Miller. New York: Columbia Univ. Press, 1977.

Michell, George. *Hindu Art and Architecture.* World of Art. London: Thames & Hudson, 2000.

Moynihan, Elizabeth B., ed. *The Moonlight Garden: New Discoveries at the Taj Mahal.* Asian Art & Culture. Washington, DC: Arthur M. Sackler Gallery, 2000.

Nou, Jean-Louis. *Taj Mahal.* Text by Amina Okada and M.C. Joshi. New York: Abbeville Press, 1993.

Pal, Pratapaditya. *Court Paintings of India, 16th–19th Centuries.* New York: Navin Kumar, 1983.

———. *The Peaceful Liberators: Jain Art from India.* New York: Thames & Hudson, 1994.

Rossi, Barbara. *From the Ocean of Painting: India's Popular Paintings, 1589 to the Present.* New York: Oxford Univ. Press, 1998.

Schimmel, Annemarie. *The Empire of the Great Mughals: History, Art and Culture.* Ed. Burzine K. Waghmar. Trans. Corinne Attwood. London: Reaktion Books, 2004.

Stronge, Susan. *Painting for the Mughal Emperor: The Art of the Book, 1560–1660.* London: V&A Publications, 2002.

Tillotson, G.H.R. *Mughal India.* Architectural Guides for Travelers. San Francisco: Chronicle Books, 1990.

———. *The Tradition of Indian Architecture: Continuity, Controversy, and Change since 1850.* New Haven: Yale Univ. Press, 1989.

Verma, Som Prakash. *Painting the Mughal Experience.* New York: Oxford Univ. Press, 2005.

Welch, Stuart Cary. *The Emperors' Album: Images of Mughal India.* New York: Metropolitan Museum of Art, 1987.

———. *India: Art and Culture 1300–1900.* New York: Metropolitan Museum of Art, 1985.

Chapter 25 Chinese and Korean Art after 1279

Andrews, Julia Frances, and Kuiyi Shen. *A Century in Crisis: Modernity and Tradition in the Art of Twentieth-Century China.* New York: Solomon R. Guggenheim Museum, 1998.

Barnhart, Richard M. *Painters of the Great Ming: The Imperial Court and the Zhe School.* Dallas: Dallas Museum of Art, 1993.

Barrass, Gordon S. *The Art of Calligraphy in Modern China.* London: British Museum Press, 2002.

Berger, Patricia Ann. *Empire of Emptiness: Buddhist Art and Political Authority in Qing China.* Honolulu: Univ. of Hawai'i Press, 2003.

Bickford, Maggie. *Ink Plum: The Making of a Chinese Scholar-Painting.* New York: Cambridge Univ. Press, 1996.

Billeter, Jean François. *The Chinese Art of Writing.* New York: Skira/Rizzoli, 1990.

Bush, Susan, and Hsio-yen Shih, eds. *Early Chinese Texts on Painting.* Cambridge, MA: Harvard Univ. Press, 1985.

Cahill, James. *The Distant Mountains: Chinese Painting in the Late Ming Dynasty, 1580–1644.* New York: Weatherhill, 1982.

———. *Hills Beyond a River: Chinese Painting of the Y'uan Dynasty, 1279–1368.* New York: Weatherhill, 1976.

———. *Parting at the Shore: Chinese Painting of the Early and Middle Ming Dynasty 1368–1580.* New York: Weatherhill, 1978.

Chaves, Jonathan (trans.). *The Chinese Painter as Poet.* New York: Art Media Resources, 2000.

Chung, Anita. *Drawing Boundaries: Architectural Images in Qing China.* Honolulu: Univ. of Hawai'i Press, 2004.

Clunas, Craig. *Pictures and Visuality in Early Modern China.* Princeton, NJ: Princeton Univ. Press, 1997.

Fang, Jing Pei. *Treasures of the Chinese Scholar: Form, Function, and Symbolism.* Ed. J. May Lee Barrett. New York: Weatherhill, 1997.

Fong, Wen C. *Between Two Cultures: Late-Nineteenth- and Twentieth-Century Chinese Paintings from the Robert H. Ellsworth Collection in the Metropolitan Museum of Art.* New York: Metropolitan Museum of Art, 2001.

Hearn, Maxwell K., and Judith G. Smith, eds. *Chinese Art: Modern Expressions.* New York: Dept. of Asian Art, Metropolitan Museum of Art, 2001.

Ho, Chuimei, and Bennet Bronson. *Splendors of China's Forbidden City: The Glorious Reign of Emperor Qianlong.* Chicago: Field Museum, 2004.

Ho, Wai-kam, ed. *The Century of Tung Ch'i-Ch'ang, 1555–1636.* 2 vols. Kansas City, MO: Nelson-Atkins Museum of Art, 1992.

Kim, Hongnam. *The Life of a Patron: Zhou Lianggong (1612–1672) and the Painters of Seventeenth-Century China.* New York: China Institute in America, 1996.

Knapp, Ronald G. *China's Vernacular Architecture: House Form and Culture.* Honolulu: Univ. of Hawai'i Press, 1989.

Lee, Sherman, and Wai-Kam Ho. *Chinese Art Under the Mongols: The Y'uan Dynasty, 1279–1368.* Cleveland: Cleveland Museum of Art, 1968.

Lim, Lucy, ed. *Wu Guanzhong: A Contemporary Chinese Artist.* San Francisco: Chinese Culture Foundation, 1989.

Moss, Paul. *Escape from the Dusty World: Chinese Paintings and Literati Works of Art.* London: Sydney L. Moss, 1999.

Ng, So Kam. *Brushstrokes: Styles and Techniques of Chinese Painting.* San Francisco: Asian Art Museum of San Francisco, 1993.

The Poetry [of] Ink: The Korean Literati Tradition, 1392–1910. Paris: Réunion des Musées Nationaux: Musée National des Arts Asiatiques Guimet, 2005.

Smith, Karen. *Nine Lives: The Birth of Avant-Garde Art in New China.* Zürich: Scalo, 2006.

Till, Barry. *The Manchu Era (1644–1912), Arts of China's Last Imperial Dynasty.* Victoria, BC: Art Gallery of Greater Victoria, 2004.

Vainker, S.J. *Chinese Pottery and Porcelain: From Prehistory to the Present.* London: British Museum Press, 1991.

Watson, William. *The Arts of China 900–1620.* Pelican History of Art. New Haven: Yale Univ. Press, 2000.

Weidner, Marsha Smith. *Views from Jade Terrace: Chinese Women Artists, 1300–1912.* Indianapolis, IN: Indianapolis Museum of Art, 1988.

Xinian, Fu, et al. *Chinese Architecture.* Ed. Nancy S. Steinhardt. New Haven: Yale Univ. Press, 2002.

Chapter 26 Japanese Art after 1333

Addiss, Stephen. *The Art of Zen: Painting and Calligraphy by Japanese Monks, 1600–1925.* New York: Abrams, 1989.

Berthier, François. *Reading Zen in the Rocks: The Japanese Dry Landscape Garden.* Trans. & essay Graham Parkes. Chicago: Univ. of Chicago Press, 2000.

Calza, Gian Carlo. *Ukiyo-e.* New York: Phaidon Press, 2005.

Graham, Patricia J. *Faith and Power in Japanese Buddhist Art, 1600–2005.* Honolulu: Univ. of Hawai'i Press, 2007.

———. *Tea of the Sages: The Art of Sencha.* Honolulu: Univ. of Hawai'i Press, 1998.

Guth, Christine. *Art of Edo Japan: The Artist and the City 1615–1868.* Perspectives. New York: Abrams, 1996.

Hickman, Money L. *Japan's Golden Age: Momoyama.* New Haven: Yale Univ. Press, 1996.

Kobayashi, Tadashi, and Lisa Rotondo-McCord. *An Enduring Vision: 17th to 20th Century Japanese Painting from the Gitter-Yelen Collection.* New Orleans: New Orleans Museum of Art, 2003.

Lillehoji, Elizabeth, ed. *Critical Perspectives on Classicism in Japanese Painting, 1600–1700.* Honolulu: Univ. of Hawai'i Press, 2004.

McKelway, Matthew P. *Traditions Unbound: Groundbreaking Painters of Eighteenth-Century Kyoto.* San Francisco: Asian Art Museum–Chong-Moon Lee Center, 2005.

Meech, Julia, and Jane Oliver. *Designed for Pleasure: The World of Edo Japan in Prints and Paintings, 1680–1860.* Seattle: Univ. of Washington Press in association with the Asia Society and Japanese Art Society of America, New York, 2008.

Miyajima, Shin'ichi and Sato Yasuhiro. *Japanese Ink Painting.* Ed. George Kuwayama. Los Angeles: Los Angeles County Museum of Art, 1985.

Munroe, Alexandra. *Japanese Art after 1945: Scream Against the Sky.* New York: Abrams, 1994.

Murase, Miyeko, ed. *Turning Point: Oribe and the Arts of Sixteenth-Century Japan.* New York: Metropolitan Museum of Art, 2003.

Newland, Amy Reigle, ed. *The Hotei Encyclopedia of Japanese Woodblock Prints.* 2 vols. Amsterdam: Hotei Publishing, 2005.

Ohki, Sadako. *Tea Culture of Japan.* New Haven: Yale Univ. Press, 2009.

Rousmaniere, Nicole, ed. *Crafting Beauty in Modern Japan: Celebrating Fifty Years of the Japan Traditional Art Crafts Exhibition.* Seattle: Univ. of Washington Press, 2007.

Screech, Timon. *The Lens Within the Heart: The Western Scientific Gaze and Popular Imagery in Later Edo Japan.* 2nd ed. Honolulu: Univ. of Hawai'i Press, 2002.

Singer, Robert T., and John T. Carpenter. *Edo, Art in Japan 1615–1868.* Washington, DC: National Gallery of Art, 1998.

Chapter 27 Art of the Americas after 1300

Bauer, Brian S. *Ancient Cuzco: Heartland of the Inca.* Joe R. and Teresa Lozano Long Series in Latin American and Latino Art and Culture. Austin: Univ. of Texas Press, 2004.

Berlo, Janet Catherine, and Ruth B. Phillips. *Native North American Art.* Oxford History of Art. Oxford: Oxford Univ. Press, 1998.

Bringhurst, Robert. *The Black Canoe: Bill Reid and the Spirit of Haida Gwaii.* Seattle: Univ. of Washington Press, 1991.

Burger, Richard L., and Lucy C. Salazar, eds. *Machu Picchu: Unveiling the Mystery of the Incas.* New Haven: Yale Univ. Press, 2004.

Coe, Michael D. and Rex Koontz. *Mexico: From the Olmecs to the Aztecs.* 5th ed. New York: Thames & Hudson, 2005.

Fields, Virginia M., and Victor Zamudio-Taylor. *The Road to Aztlan: Art from a Mythic Homeland.* Los Angeles: Los Angeles County Museum of Art, 2001.

Griffin-Pierce, Trudy. *Earth is my Mother, Sky is my Father: Space, Time, and Astronomy in Navajo Sandpainting.* Albuquerque: Univ. of New Mexico Press, 1992.

Jonaitis, Aldona. *Art of the Northwest Coast.* Seattle: Univ. of Washington Press, 2006.

Kaufman, Alice, and Christopher Selser. *The Navajo Weaving Tradition: 1650 to the Present.* New York: Dutton, 1985.

Macnair, Peter L., Robert Joseph, and Bruce Grenville. *Down from the Shimmering Sky: Masks of the Northwest Coast.* Vancouver: Douglas & McIntyre, 1998.

Matos Moctezuma, Eduardo, and Felipe R. Solís Olguín. *Aztecs.* London: Royal Academy of Arts, 2002.

Matthews, Washington. "The Night Chant: A Navaho Ceremony." In *Memoirs of the American Museum of Natural History,* vol. 6. New York, 1902.

Moseley, Michael E. *The Incas and Their Ancestors: The Archaeology of Peru.* Rev. ed. London: Thames & Hudson, 2001.

Nabokov, Peter, and Robert Easton. *Native American Architecture.* New York: Oxford Univ. Press, 1989.

Pasztory, Esther. *Aztec Art.* Norman: Univ. of Oklahoma Press, 2000.

Rushing III, W. Jackson, ed. *Native American Art in the Twentieth Century: Makers, Meanings, Histories.* New York: Routledge, 1999.

Shaw, George Everett. *Art of the Ancestors: Antique North American Indian Art.* Aspen, CO: Aspen Art Museum, 2004.

Taylor, Colin F. *Buckskin & Buffalo: The Artistry of the Plains Indians.* New York: Rizzoli, 1998.

Townsend, Richard F., ed. *The Aztecs.* 2nd rev. ed. Ancient Peoples and Places. London: Thames & Hudson, 2000.

Trimble, Stephen. *Talking with the Clay: The Art of Pueblo Pottery in the 21st Century.* 20th anniversary rev ed. Santa Fe, NM: School for Advanced Research Press, 2007.

Wood, Nancy C. *Taos Pueblo.* New York: Knopf, 1989.

Chapter 28 Art of Pacific Cultures

Caruana, Wally. *Aboriginal Art.* 2nd ed. World of Art. New York: Thames & Hudson, 2003.

Craig, Barry, Bernie Kernot, and Christopher Anderson, eds. *Art and Performance in Oceania.* Honolulu: Univ. of Hawai'i Press, 1999.

D'Alleva, Anne. *Arts of the Pacific Islands.* Perspectives. New York: Abrams, 1998.

Herle, Anita, et al. *Pacific Art: Persistence, Change, and Meaning.* Honolulu: Univ. of Hawai'i Press, 2002.

Kaeppler, Adrienne Lois, Christian Kaufmann, and Douglas Newton. *Oceanic Art.* Trans. Nora Scott and Sabine Bouladon. New York: Abrams, 1997.

Kirch, Patrick Vinton. *The Lapita Peoples: Ancestors of the Oceanic World.* The Peoples of South-East Asia and the Pacific. Cambridge, MA: Blackwell, 1997.

Kjellgren, Eric. *Splendid Isolation: Art of Easter Island.* New York: Metropolitan Museum of Art, 2001.

———, and Carol Ivory. *Adorning the World: Art of the Marquesas Islands.* New Haven: Yale Univ. Press in assoc. with the Metropolitan Museum of Art, 2005.

Küchler, Susanne, and Graeme Were. *Pacific Pattern.* London: Thames & Hudson, 2005.

Lilley, Ian, ed. *Archaeology of Oceania: Australia and the Pacific Islands.* Malden, MA: Blackwell, 2006.

McCulloch, Susan. *Contemporary Aboriginal Art: A Guide to the Rebirth of an Ancient Culture.* Rev. ed. Crows Nest, NSW, Australia: Allen & Unwin, 2001.

Moore, Albert C. *Arts in the Religions of the Pacific: Symbols of Life.* Religion and the Arts Series. New York: Pinter, 1995.

Morphy, Howard. *Aboriginal Art.* London: Phaidon Press, 1998.

Morwood, M.J. *Visions from the Past: The Archaeology of Australian Aboriginal Art.* Washington, DC: Smithsonian Institution Press, 2002.

Neich, Roger, and Mick Pendergrast. *Traditional Tapa Textiles of the Pacific*. London: Thames & Hudson, 1997.

Newton, Douglas, ed. *Arts of the South Seas: Island Southeast Asia, Melanesia, Polynesia, Micronesia; The Collections of the Musée Barbier-Mueller*. Trans. David Radzinowicz Howell. New York: Prestel, 1999.

Rainbird, Paul. *The Archaeology of Micronesia*. Cambridge World Archaeology. New York: Cambridge Univ. Press, 2004.

Smidt, Dirk, ed. *Asmat Art: Woodcarvings of Southwest New Guinea*. New York: George Braziller in assoc. with Rijksmuseum voor Volkenkunde, Leiden, 1993.

Starzecka, D. C., ed. *Maori Art and Culture*. London: British Museum Press, 1996.

Taylor, Luke. *Seeing the Inside: Bark Painting in Western Arnhem Land*. Oxford Studies in Social and Cultural Anthropology. New York: Oxford Univ. Press, 1996.

Thomas, Nicholas. *Oceanic Art*. World of Art. New York: Thames & Hudson, 1995.

———, Anna Cole, and Bronwen Douglas, eds. *Tattoo: Bodies, Art, and Exchange in the Pacific and the West*. Durham, NC: Duke Univ. Press, 2005.

Chapter 29 Art of Africa in the Modern Era

Anatsui, El. *El Anatsui Gawu*. Llandudno, Wales, UK: Oriel Mostyn Gallery, 2003.

Astonishment and Power. Washington, DC: National Museum of African Art, Smithsonian Institution Press, 1993.

Beckwith, Carol, and Angela Fisher. *African Ceremonies*. 2 vols. New York: Abrams, 1999.

Binkley, David A. "Avatar of Power: Southern Kuba Masquerade Figures in a Funerary Context." *Africa— Journal of the International African Institute* 57/1 (1987): 75–97.

Cameron, Elisabeth L. *Art of the Lega*. Los Angeles: UCLA Fowler Museum of Cultural History, 2001.

Cole, Herbert M., ed. *I Am Not Myself: The Art of African Masquerade*. Los Angeles: Fowler Museum of Cultural History, Univ. of California, 1985.

———. *Icons: Ideals and Power in the Art of Africa*. Washington, DC: National Museum of African Art, Smithsonian Institution Press, 1989.

A Fiction of Authenticity: Contemporary Africa Abroad. St. Louis, MO: Contemporary Art Museum St. Louis, 2003.

Fogle, Douglas, and Olukemi Ilesanmi. *Julie Mehretu: Drawing into Painting*. Minneapolis, MN: Walker Art Center, 2003.

Gillow, John. *African Textiles*. San Francisco: Chronicle Books, 2003.

Graham, Gilbert. *Dogon Sculpture: Symbols of a Mythical Universe*. Brookville, NY: Hillwood Art Museum, Long Island Univ., C. W. Post Campus, 1997.

Hess, Janet Berry. *Art and Architecture in Postcolonial Africa*. Jefferson, NC: McFarland, 2006.

Jordán, Manuel, ed. *Chokwe! Art and Initiation Among the Chokwe and Related Peoples*. Munich: Prestel, 1998.

Kasfir, Sidney Littlefield. *Contemporary African Art*. World of Art. London: Thames & Hudson, 2000.

Morris, James, and Suzanne Preston Blier. *Butabu: Adobe Architecture of West Africa*. New York: Princeton Architectural Press, 2004.

Oguibe, Olu, and Okwui Enwezor. *Reading the Contemporary: African Art from Theory to the Marketplace*. Cambridge, MA: MIT Press, 1999.

Pemberton III, John, ed. *Insight and Artistry in African Divination*. Washington, DC: Smithsonian Institution Press, 2000.

Perrois, Louis, and Marta Sierra Delage. *The Art of Equatorial Guinea: The Fang Tribes*. New York: Rizzoli, 1990.

Picton, John, et al. *El Anatsui: A Sculpted History of Africa*. London: Saffron Books in conjunction with the October Gallery, 1998.

Roberts, Mary Nooter, and Allen F. Roberts, eds. *Memory: Luba Art and the Making of History*. New York: Museum for African Art, 1996.

Roy, Christopher D. *Art of the Upper Volta Rivers*. Meudon, France: Chaffin, 1987.

Stepan, Peter. *Spirits Speak: A Celebration of African Masks*. Munich: Prestel, 2005.

Van Damme, Annemieke. *Spectacular Display: The Art of Nkanu Initiation Rituals*. Washington, DC: National Museum of African Art, Smithsonian Institution Press, 2001.

Vogel, Susan Mullin. *Baule: African Art, Western Eyes*. New Haven: Yale Univ. Press, 1997.

Chapter 30 Eighteenth- and Early Nineteenth-Century Art in Europe and North America

Bailey, Colin B., Philip Conisbee, and Thomas W. Gaehtgens. *The Age of Watteau, Chardin, and Fragonard: Masterpieces of French Genre Painting*. New Haven: Yale Univ. Press in assoc. with the National Gallery of Canada, Ottawa, 2003.

Boime, Albert. *Art in an Age of Bonapartism, 1800–1815*. Chicago: Univ. of Chicago Press, 1990.

———. *Art in an Age of Counterrevolution, 1815–1848*. Chicago: Univ. of Chicago Press, 2004.

———. *Art in an Age of Revolution, 1750–1800*. Chicago: Univ. of Chicago Press, 1987.

Bowron, Edgar Peters, and Joseph J. Rishel, eds. *Art in Rome in the Eighteenth Century*. London: Merrell in association with Philadelphia Museum of Art, 2000.

Brown, David Blayney. *Romanticism*. London: Phaidon Press, 2001.

Chinn, Celestine, and Kieran McCarty. *Bac: Where the Waters Gather*. Univ. of Arizona: Mission San Xavier Del Bac, 1977.

Craske, Matthew. *Art in Europe, 1700–1830: A History of the Visual Arts in an Era of Unprecedented Urban Economic Growth*. Oxford History of Art. Oxford: Oxford Univ. Press, 1997.

Denis, Rafael Cardoso, and Colin Trodd, eds. *Art and the Academy in the Nineteenth Century*. New Brunswick, NJ: Rutgers Univ. Press, 2000.

Goodman, Elise, ed. *Art and Culture in the Eighteenth Century: New Dimensions and Multiple Perspectives*. Studies in Eighteenth-Century Art and Culture. Newark: Univ. of Delaware Press, 2001.

Hofmann, Werner. *Goya: To Every Story There Belongs Another*. New York: Thames & Hudson, 2003.

Irwin, David G. *Neoclassicism*. Art & Ideas. London: Phaidon Press, 1997.

Jarrassé, Dominique. *18th-Century French Painting*. Trans. Murray Wyllie. Paris: Terrail, 1999.

Kalnein, Wend von. *Architecture in France in the Eighteenth Century*. Trans. David Britt. Pelican History of Art. New Haven: Yale Univ. Press, 1995.

Levey, Michael. *Painting in Eighteenth-Century Venice*. 3rd ed. New Haven: Yale Univ. Press, 1994.

Lewis, Michael J. *The Gothic Revival*. World of Art. New York: Thames & Hudson, 2002.

Lovell, Margaretta M. *Art in a Season of Revolution: Painters, Artisans, and Patrons in Early America*. Early American Studies. Philadelphia: Univ. of Pennsylvania Press, 2005.

Monneret, Sophie. *David and Neo-Classicism*. Trans. Chris Miller and Peter Snowdon. Paris: Terrail, 1999.

Natter, Tobias, ed. *Angelica Kauffman: A Woman of Immense Talent*. Ostfildern: Hatje Cantz, 2007.

Porterfield, Todd, and Susan L. Siegfried. *Staging Empire: Napoleon, Ingres, and David*. University Park: Pennsylvania State Univ. Press, 2006.

Poulet, Anne L. *Jean-Antoine Houdon: Sculptor of the Enlightenment*. Washington, DC: National Gallery of Art, 2003.

Summerson, John. *Architecture of the Eighteenth Century*. World of Art. New York: Thames & Hudson, 1986.

Wilton, Andrew, and Ilaria Bignamini, eds. *Grand Tour: The Lure of Italy in the Eighteenth Century*. London: Tate Gallery, 1996.

Chapter 31 Mid- to Late Nineteenth-Century Art in Europe and the United States

Adams, Steven. *The Barbizon School and the Origins of Impressionism*. London: Phaidon Press, 1994.

Bajac, Quentin. *The Invention of Photography*. Discoveries. New York: Abrams, 2002.

Barger, M. Susan, and William B. White. *The Daguerreotype: Nineteenth-Century Technology and Modern Science*. Washington, DC: Smithsonian Institution Press, 1991.

Benjamin, Roger. *Orientalist Aesthetics: Art, Colonialism, and French North Africa, 1880–1930*. Berkeley: Univ. of California Press, 2003.

Bergdoll, Barry. *European Architecture, 1750–1890*. Oxford History of Art. Oxford: Oxford Univ. Press, 2000.

Blühm, Andreas, and Louise Lippincott. *Light!: The Industrial Age 1750–1900: Art & Science, Technology & Society*. New York: Thames & Hudson, 2001.

Boime, Albert, *The Academy and French Painting in the Nineteenth Century*. 2nd ed. New Haven: Yale Univ. Press, 1986.

Butler, Ruth, and Suzanne G. Lindsay. *European Sculpture of the Nineteenth Century*. Washington, DC: National Gallery of Art, 2000.

Callen, Anthea. *The Art of Impressionism: Painting Technique & the Making of Modernity*. New Haven: Yale Univ. Press, 2000.

Chu, Petra ten-Doesschate. *Nineteenth Century European Art*. 3rd. ed. Upper Saddle River, NJ: Pearson/Prentice Hall, 2012.

Clark, T. J. *The Painting of Modern Life: Paris in the Art of Manet and His Followers*. Rev. ed. London: Thames & Hudson, 1999.

Conrads, Margaret C. *Winslow Homer and the Critics: Forging a National Art in the 1870s*. Princeton, NJ: Princeton Univ. Press in assoc. with the Nelson-Atkins Museum of Art, 2001.

Denis, Rafael Cardoso, and Colin Trodd. *Art and the Academy in the Nineteenth Century*. New Brunswick, NJ: Rutgers Univ. Press, 2000.

Eisenman, Stephen F. *Nineteenth Century Art: A Critical History*. 3rd ed. New York: Thames & Hudson, 2007.

Eitner, Lorenz. *Nineteenth Century European Painting: David to Cezanne*. Rev. ed. Boulder, CO: Westview Press, 2002.

Frazier, Nancy. *Louis Sullivan and the Chicago School*. New York: Knickerbocker Press, 1998.

Fried, Michael. *Manet's Modernism, or, The Face of Painting in the 1860s*. Chicago: Univ. of Chicago Press, 1996.

Gerdts, William H. *American Impressionism*. 2nd ed. New York: Abbeville Press, 2001.

Greenhalgh, Paul, ed. *Art Nouveau, 1890–1914*. London: V&A Publications, 2000.

Grigsby, Darcy Grimaldo. *Extremities: Painting Empire in Post-Revolutionary France*. New Haven: Yale Univ. Press, 2002.

Groseclose, Barbara. *Nineteenth-Century American Art*. Oxford History of Art. Oxford: Oxford Univ. Press, 2000.

Harrison, Charles, Paul Wood, and Jason Gaiger. *Art in Theory 1815–1900: An Anthology of Changing Ideas*. Oxford: Blackwell, 1998.

Herrmann, Luke. *Nineteenth Century British Painting*. London: Giles de la Mare, 2000.

Hirsh, Sharon L. *Symbolism and Modern Urban Society*. New York: Cambridge Univ. Press, 2004.

Kaplan, Wendy. *The Arts & Crafts Movement in Europe & America: Design for the Modern World*. New York: Thames & Hudson in assoc. with the Los Angeles County Museum of Art, 2004.

Kendall, Richard. *Degas: Beyond Impressionism*. London: National Gallery, 1996.

Lambourne, Lionel. *Japonisme: Cultural Crossings between Japan and the West*. New York: Phaidon Press, 2005.

Lemoine, Bertrand. *Architecture in France, 1800–1900*. Trans. Alexandra Bonfante-Warren. New York: Abrams, 1998.

Lewis, Mary Tompkins, ed.. *Critical Readings in Impressionism and Post-Impressionism: An Anthology*. Berkeley: Univ. of California Press, 2007.

Lochnan, Katharine Jordan. *Turner Whistler Monet*. London: Tate Publishing in assoc. with the Art Gallery of Ontario, 2004.

Miller, Angela L., et al. *American Encounters: Art, History, and Cultural Identity*. Upper Saddle River, NJ: Pearson/Prentice Hall, 2008.

Noon, Patrick J. *Crossing the Channel: British and French Painting in the Age of Romanticism*. London: Tate Publishing, 2003.

Pissarro, Joachim. *Pioneering Modern Painting: Cézanne & Pissarro 1865–1885*. New York: Museum of Modern Art, 2005.

Rodner, William S. *J.M.W. Turner: Romantic Painter of the Industrial Revolution*. Berkeley: Univ. of California Press, 1997.

Rosenblum, Robert, and H.W. Janson. *19th Century Art*. Rev. & updated ed. Upper Saddle River, NJ: Pearson/Prentice Hall, 2005.

Rubin, James H. *Impressionism*. Art & Ideas. London: Phaidon Press, 1999.

Rybczynski, Witold. *A Clearing in the Distance: Frederick Law Olmsted and America in the Nineteenth Century*. New York: Scribner, 1999.

Smith, Paul. *Seurat and the Avant-Garde*. New Haven: Yale Univ. Press, 1997.

Thomson, Belinda. *Impressionism: Origins, Practice, Reception*. World of Art. New York: Thames & Hudson, 2000.

Twyman, Michael. *Breaking the Mould: The First Hundred Years of Lithography*. The Panizzi Lectures, 2000. London: British Library, 2001.

Vaughan, William, and Francoise Cachin. *Arts of the 19th Century*. 2 vols. New York: Abrams, 1998.

Werner, Marcia. *Pre-Raphaelite Painting and Nineteenth-Century Realism.* New York: Cambridge Univ. Press, 2005.

Zemel, Carol M. *Van Gogh's Progress: Utopia, Modernity, and Late-Nineteenth-Century Art.* California Studies in the History of Art, 36. Berkeley: Univ. of California Press, 1997.

Chapter 32 Modern Art in Europe and the Americas, 1900–1950

Ades, Dawn, comp. *Art and Power: Europe under the Dictators, 1930–45.* Stuttgart, Germany: Oktagon in assoc. with Hayward Gallery, 1995.

Antliff, Mark, and Patricia Leighten. *Cubism and Culture.* World of Art. London: Thames & Hudson, 2001.

Bailey, David A. *Rhapsodies in Black: Art of the Harlem Renaissance.* London: Hayward Gallery, 1997.

Balken, Debra Bricker. *Debating American Modernism: Stieglitz, Duchamp, and the New York Avant-Garde.* New York: American Federation of Arts, 2003.

Barron, Stephanie, ed. *Degenerate Art: The Fate of the Avant-Garde in Nazi Germany.* Los Angeles: Los Angeles County Museum of Art, 1991.

———, and Wolf-Dieter Dube, eds. *German Expressionism: Art and Society.* New York: Rizzoli, 1997.

Bochner, Jay. *An American Lens: Scenes from Alfred Stieglitz's New York Secession.* Cambridge, MA: MIT Press, 2005.

Bohn, Willard. *The Rise of Surrealism: Cubism, Dada, and the Pursuit of the Marvelous.* Albany: State Univ. of New York Press, 2002.

Bowlt, John E., and Evgeniia Petrova, eds. *Painting Revolution: Kandinsky, Malevich and the Russian Avant-Garde.* Bethesda, MD: Foundation for International Arts and Education, 2000.

Bown, Matthew Cullerne. *Socialist Realist Painting.* New Haven: Yale Univ. Press, 1998.

Brown, Milton W. *Story of the Armory Show.* 2nd ed. New York: Abbeville Press, 1988.

Chassey, Eric de, ed. *American Art: 1908–1947, from Winslow Homer to Jackson Pollock.* Trans. Jane McDonald. Paris: Réunion des Musées Nationaux, 2001.

Corn, Wanda M. *The Great American Thing: Modern Art and National Identity, 1915–1935.* Berkeley: Univ. of California Press, 1999.

Curtis, Penelope. *Sculpture 1900–1945: After Rodin.* Oxford History of Art. Oxford: Oxford Univ. Press, 1999.

Dachy, Marc. *Dada: The Revolt of Art.* Trans. Liz Nash. New York: Abrams, 2006.

Elger, Dietmar. *Expressionism: A Revolution in German Art.* Ed. Ingo F. Walther. Trans. Hugh Beyer. New York: Taschen, 1998.

Fer, Briony. *On Abstract Art.* New Haven: Yale Univ. Press, 1997.

Fletcher, Valerie J. *Crosscurrents of Modernism: Four Latin American Pioneers: Diego Rivera, Joaquín Torres-García, Wifredo Lam, Matta.* Washington, DC: Hirshhorn Museum and Sculpture Garden in assoc. with the Smithsonian Institution Press, 1992.

Folgarait, Leonard. *Mural Painting and Social Revolution in Mexico, 1920–1940: Art of the New Order.* New York: Cambridge Univ. Press, 1998.

Forgács, Eva. *The Bauhaus Idea and Bauhaus Politics.* Trans. John Bátki. New York: Central European Univ. Press, 1995.

Frampton, Kenneth. *Modern Architecture: A Critical History.* 4th ed. World of Art. London: Thames & Hudson, 2007.

Gooding, Mel. *Abstract Art.* Movements in Modern Art. Cambridge: Cambridge Univ. Press, 2001.

Grant, Kim. *Surrealism and the Visual Arts: Theory and Reception.* New York: Cambridge Univ. Press, 2005.

Green, Christopher. *Art in France: 1900–1940.* Pelican History of Art. New Haven: Yale Univ. Press, 2000.

Harris, Jonathan. *Federal Art and National Culture: The Politics of Identity in New Deal America.* Cambridge Studies in American Visual Culture. New York: Cambridge Univ. Press, 1995.

Harrison, Charles, Francis Frascina, and Gill Perry. *Primitivism, Cubism, Abstraction: The Early Twentieth Century.* New Haven: Yale Univ. Press, 1993.

Haskell, Barbara. *The American Century: Art & Culture, 1900–1950.* New York: Whitney Museum of American Art, 1999.

Herskovic, Marika, ed. *American Abstract Expressionism of the 1950s: An Illustrated Survey: With Artists' Statements, Artwork and Biographies.* New York: New York School Press, 2003.

Hill, Charles C. *The Group of Seven: Art for a Nation.* Ottawa: National Gallery of Canada, 1995.

James-Chakraborty, Kathleen, ed. *Bauhaus Culture: From Weimar to the Cold War.* Minneapolis: Univ. of Minnesota Press, 2006.

Karmel, Pepe. *Picasso and the Invention of Cubism.* New Haven: Yale Univ. Press, 2003.

Lista, Giovanni. *Futurism.* Trans. Susan Wise. Paris: Terrail, 2001.

Lucie-Smith, Edward. *Latin American Art of the 20th Century.* 2nd ed. World of Art. London: Thames & Hudson, 2005.

McCarter, Robert, ed. *On and by Frank Lloyd Wright: A Primer of Architectural Principles.* New York: Phaidon Press, 2005.

Moudry, Roberta, ed. *The American Skyscraper: Cultural Histories.* New York: Cambridge Univ. Press, 2005.

Rickey, George. *Constructivism: Origins and Evolution.* Rev. ed. New York: Braziller, 1995.

Taylor, Brandon. *Collage: The Making of Modern Art.* London: Thames & Hudson, 2004.

Weston, Richard. *Modernism.* London: Phaidon Press, 1996.

White, Michael. *De Stijl and Dutch Modernism.* Critical Perspectives in Art History. New York: Manchester Univ. Press, 2003.

Whitfield, Sarah. *Fauvism.* World of Art. New York: Thames & Hudson, 1996.

Whitford, Frank. *The Bauhaus: Masters and Students by Themselves.* Woodstock, NY: Overlook Press, 1993.

Zurier, Rebecca, Robert W. Snyder, and Virginia M. Mecklenburg. *Metropolitan Lives: The Ashcan Artists and Their New York.* Washington, DC: National Museum of American Art, 1995.

Chapter 33 The International Scene since 1950

Alberro, Alexander, and Blake Stimson, eds. *Conceptual Art: A Critical Anthology.* Cambridge, MA: MIT Press, 1999.

Archer, Michael. *Art Since 1960.* 2nd ed. World of Art. New York: Thames & Hudson, 2002.

Atkins. Robert. *Artspeak: A Guide to Contemporary Ideas, Movements, and Buzzwords.* 2nd ed. New York: Abbeville Press, 1997.

Ault, Julie. *Art Matters: How the Culture Wars Changed America.* Ed, Brian Wallis, Marianne Weems, and Philip Yenawine. New York: New York Univ. Press, 1999.

Battcock, Gregory. *Minimal Art: A Critical Anthology.* Berkeley: Univ. of California Press, 1995.

Beardsley, John. *Earthworks and Beyond: Contemporary Art in the Landscape.* 4th ed. ebook. New York: Abbeville Press, 2006.

Bird, Jon, and Michael Newman, eds. *Rewriting Conceptual Art.* Critical Views. London: Reaktion Books, 1999.

Bishop, Claire. *Installation Art: A Critical History.* New York: Routledge, 2005.

Blais, Joline, and Jon Ippolito. *At the Edge of Art.* London: Thames & Hudson, 2006.

Buchloh, Benjamin H.D. *Neo-Avantgarde and Culture Industry: Essays on European and American Art from 1955 to 1975.* Cambridge, MA: MIT Press, 2000.

Carleback, Michael L. *American Photojournalism Comes of Age.* Washington, DC: Smithsonian Institution Press, 1997.

Causey, Andrew. *Sculpture Since 1945.* Oxford History of Art. Oxford: Oxford Univ. Press, 1998.

Corris, Michael, ed. *Conceptual Art: Theory, Myth, and Practice.* New York: Cambridge Univ. Press, 2004.

De Oliveira, Nicolas, Nicola Oxley, and Michael Petry. *Installation Art in the New Millennium: The Empire of the Senses.* New York: Thames & Hudson, 2003.

De Salvo, Donna, ed. *Open Systems: Rethinking Art c.1970.* London: Tate Gallery, 2005.

Fabozzi, Paul F. *Artists, Critics, Context: Readings In and Around American Art Since 1945.* Upper Saddle River, NJ: Pearson/Prentice Hall, 2002.

Fineberg, Jonathan. *Art Since 1940: Strategies of Being.* 3rd ed. Upper Saddle River, NJ: Pearson/Prentice Hall, 2011.

Flood, Richard, and Frances Morris. *Zero to Infinity: Arte Povera, 1962–1972.* Minneapolis, MN: Walker Art Center, 2001.

Fried, Michael. "Art and Objecthood." *Artforum* 5 (June 1967): 12–23.

Goldberg, RoseLee. *Performance Art: From Futurism to the Present.* Rev. and exp. ed. World of Art. London: Thames & Hudson, 2001.

Goldstein, Ann. *A Minimal Future? Art as Object 1958–1968.* Los Angeles: Museum of Contemporary Art, 2004.

Grande, John K. *Art Nature Dialogues: Interviews with Environmental Artists.* Albany: State Univ. of New York Press, 2004.

Grosenick, Uta, ed. *Women Artists in the 20th and 21st Century.* New York: Taschen, 2001.

———, and Burkhard Riemschneider, eds. *Art at the Turn of the Millennium.* New York: Taschen, 1999.

Grunenberg, Christoph, ed. *Summer of Love: Art of the Psychedelic Era.* London: Tate Gallery, 2005.

Hitchcock, Henry Russell, and Philip Johnson. *The International Style.* New York: Norton, 1995.

Hopkins, David. *After Modern Art: 1945–2000.* Oxford History of Art. Oxford: Oxford Univ. Press, 2000.

Jencks, Charles. *The New Paradigm in Architecture: The Language of Post-Modernism.* New Haven: Yale Univ. Press, 2002.

Jodidio, Philip. *New Forms: Architecture in the 1990s.* Taschen's World Architecture. New York: Taschen, 2001.

Johnson, Deborah, and Wendy Oliver, eds. *Women Making Art: Women in the Visual, Literary, and Performing Arts Since 1960.* Eruptions, vol. 7. New York: Peter Lang, 2001.

Jones, Caroline A. *Machine in the Studio: Constructing the Postwar American Artist.* Chicago: Univ. of Chicago Press, 1996.

Joselit, David. *American Art Since 1945.* World of Art. London: Thames & Hudson, 2003.

Legault, Réjean, and Sarah Williams Goldhagen, eds. *Anxious Modernisms: Experimentation in Postwar Architectural Culture.* Montréal: Canadian Centre for Architecture, 2000.

Lucie-Smith, Edward. *Movements in Art Since 1945.* New ed. World of Art. London: Thames & Hudson, 2001.

Madoff, Steven Henry, ed. *Pop Art: A Critical History.* The Documents of Twentieth-Century Art. Berkeley: Univ. of California Press, 1997.

Moos, David, ed. *The Shape of Colour: Excursions in Colour Field Art, 1950–2005.* Toronto: Art Gallery of Ontario, 2005.

Nochlin, Linda. "Why Have There Been No Great Women Artists?" *Art News* 69 (January 1972): 22–39.

Owens, Craig. "The Discourse of Others: Feminists and Postmodernism." In *The Anti-Aesthetic: Essays on Postmodern Culture,* ed. Hal Foster. Seattle: Bay Press, 1983: 57–82.

Paul, Christiane. *Digital Art.* 2nd ed. World of Art. London: Thames & Hudson, 2008.

Phillips, Lisa. *The American Century: Art and Culture, 1950–2000.* New York: Whitney Museum of American Art, 1999.

Pop Art: Contemporary Perspectives. Princeton, NJ: Princeton Univ. Art Museum, 2007.

Ratcliff, Carter. *The Fate of a Gesture: Jackson Pollock and Postwar American Art.* New York: Farrar, Straus, Giroux, 1996.

Reckitt, Helena, ed. *Art and Feminism.* Themes and Movements. London: Phaidon Press, 2001.

Robertson, Jean, and Craig McDaniel. *Themes of Contemporary Art: Visual Art after 1980.* 2nd ed. New York: Oxford Univ. Press, 2009.

Robinson, Hilary, ed. *Feminism-Art-Theory: An Anthology, 1968–2000.* Malden, MA: Blackwell, 2001.

Rorimer, Anne. *New Art in the 60s and 70s: Redefining Reality.* New York: Thames & Hudson, 2004.

Rush, Michael. *New Media in Late 20th-Century Art.* 2nd ed. World of Art. London: Thames & Hudson, 2005.

———. *Video Art.* 2nd ed. London: Thames & Hudson, 2007.

Sandler, Irving. *Art of the Postmodern Era: From the Late 1960s to the Early 1990s.* New York: Icon Editions, 1996.

Shohat, Ella. *Talking Visions: Multicultural Feminism in a Transnational Age.* Documentary Sources in Contemporary Art, vol. 5. New York: New Museum of Contemporary Art, 1998.

Smith, Terry. *Contemporary Art: World Currents.* Upper Saddle River, NJ: Pearson/Prentice Hall, 2011.

Stiles, Kristine, and Peter Selz. *Theories and Documents of Contemporary Art: A Sourcebook of Artists' Writings.* California Studies in the History of Art, 35. Berkeley: Univ. of California, 1996.

Sylvester, David. *About Modern Art.* 2nd ed. New Haven: Yale Univ. Press, 2001.

Varnedoe, Kirk, Paola Antonelli, and Joshua Siegel, eds. *Modern Contemporary: Art Since 1980 at MoMA.* Rev. ed. New York: Museum of Modern Art, 2004.

Waldman, Diane. *Collage, Assemblage, and the Found Object.* New York: Abrams, 1992.

Weintraub, Linda, Arthur Danto, and Thomas McEvilley. *Art on the Edge and Over: Searching for Art's Meaning in Contemporary Society, 1970s–1990s.* Litchfield, CT: Art Insights, 1996.

Credits

Chapter 33

Index

Figures in *italics* refer to illustrations and captions

A